P9-AGA-293

Index of County Maps

DIANE ALPERT

Historic Spots in California

Historic Spots in
CALIFORNIA

THIRD EDITION

By

Mildred Brooke Hoover

Hero Eugene Rensch

Ethel Grace Rensch

Revised by William N. Abeloe

Stanford University Press
Stanford, California
1966

Photograph credits: pp. 60, 74 bottom, 149, 159, 178, 188, 221, 235, 242, 252, 299, 336, 399 bottom, 417, 486, 493, 510 bottom, 538, 559, 574 top, by James D. McClure; p. 72 top, courtesy Frances Turner McBeth; pp. 75, 540, by Nancy Donovan; pp. 93, 94, courtesy Raymund F. Wood; p. 96, courtesy L. W. Wigmore; p. 136, by Ralph Powell, courtesy Leona K. Buckner; p. 145, courtesy Lassen County Historical Society; pp. 172, 173, courtesy Nathan C. Sweet; pp. 202, 209, 210, 473, 477, by J. T. Abeloe; pp. 515, 521, courtesy Wood Young.

All photographs not otherwise credited are by William N. Abeloe.

Historic Spots in California was originally published in three volumes: *The Southern Counties* (1932), by H. E. and E. G. Rensch; *Valley and Sierra Counties* (1933), by H. E. and E. G. Rensch and Mildred Brooke Hoover; and *Counties of the Coast Range* (1937), by Mildred Brooke Hoover. A revised edition, in one volume, was published in 1948. The present edition, with new maps and photographs, and with a text extensively revised and expanded by William N. Abeloe, was first published in 1966.

Stanford University Press
Stanford, California

Copyright 1932 by the Board of Trustees of the Leland Stanford Junior University. Copyright renewed 1960 by H. E. Rensch and E. G. Rensch. Copyright 1933 by the Board of Trustees of the Leland Stanford Junior University. Copyright renewed 1961 by H. E. Rensch, E. G. Rensch, and Mildred Brooke Hoover Willis. Copyright 1937 by the Board of Trustees of the Leland Stanford Junior University. Copyright renewed 1965 by Mildred Brooke Hoover Willis. Copyright © 1948 and 1966 by the Board of Trustees of the Leland Stanford Junior University.

Printed in the United States of America
L.C. 66-17562

Preface to the Third Edition

"THE PURPOSE of this work is threefold: to create interest in the local history of California among its citizens, both juvenile and adult; to make knowledge of the historic spots of the different localities available to tourists; and to arouse a state-wide interest in the preservation of those vanishing historic landmarks which still survive." With these words, written in 1932, Hero Eugene Rensch and Ethel Grace Rensch began their Preface to *The Southern Counties,* the first volume of the original edition of *Historic Spots in California.*

The second book, *Valley and Sierra Counties,* appeared the following year, with Mildred Brooke Hoover joining Mr. and Mrs. Rensch as co-author. In 1937 the series was completed with the publication of *Counties of the Coast Range,* written by Mrs. Hoover. The entire series was sponsored by the California State Conference of the National Society, Daughters of the American Revolution. It was a pioneer work and holds a unique place in California bibliography.

Shortly after World War II, Stanford University Press placed *Historic Spots in California* in the capable hands of Ruth Teiser, and in 1948, the first year of California's three-year centennial celebration, a new one-volume revised edition was published, retaining the original three geographic divisions. This second edition went through five printings.

Since 1948 tremendous changes have occurred in California. The population has grown steadily; by 1963 it surpassed that of New York, making California the nation's most populous state. New cities have arisen; old ones have been transformed; vast rural areas have become urbanized; creeks and rivers have been dammed and whole canyons and valleys filled with water for agricultural and domestic use; a network of freeways is being built from Oregon to Mexico and from the Sierra to the sea. All this, of course, is a part of California's historic pattern of progress, but much of it, unfortunately and not always inevitably, has been accomplished at the expense of the tangible evidence of California's historic past.

Other changes have been wrought by the less controllable factors of weather, fire, and deterioration. Thus it is that descriptions of landmarks and their locations, as given by the authors in the 1930's, or even as revised in 1948, are in many cases no longer accurate.

In 1962 Stanford University Press engaged me to prepare this thoroughly revised edition—a task approached with humility, for I had used the previous editions in research and travel for over fifteen years and had found them invaluable. In their original Preface Mr. and Mrs. Rensch expressed the desire "that the usefulness of the work may justify a future edition in which any inaccuracies may be corrected, more spots may be included, and the story of others rounded out." It is hoped that the second edition, and now the third, fulfill to some extent their wish.

The purpose of this revision remains the same as that of the authors in their original work: to stimulate the interest of Californians in the rich history of their native or adopted state; to guide travelers to the places where this history was made; and to call attention to the need for immediate action to preserve the rapidly disappearing landmarks of California's heritage. Although an attempt has been made to eliminate errors and anachronisms from the text, there are undoubtedly some points that require further clarification, and, to this end, the words of the first Preface are reiterated here: "Corrections and suggestions from all interested persons will be most cordially welcomed."

The lucid Introduction by the late scholar Robert Glass Cleland, first published in *The Southern Counties* in 1932, has been reprinted in all subsequent volumes and is retained here. In this edition, however, the 58 counties are presented alphabetically rather than geographically. Within each chapter the material is organized, as before, in a roughly chronological order: prehistoric times, the early explorations, the Spanish, Mexican, and pioneer American eras, and finally more recent times. A separate map is provided for each county, and there are a number of detailed maps of areas having large concentrations of historic places. The latest system of highway numbering has been followed on the maps and in the text.

The text is illustrated by over 200 photographs. Although some of the more familiar places are shown, most of the photographs were chosen with a view to helping the searcher identify lesser-known or unmarked historic buildings. Several landmarks pictured here have seldom, if ever, been portrayed before in standard historical works. A number of photographs used in this edition first appeared in James D. McClure's *California Landmarks*, published by Stanford University Press in 1948 as a companion volume to the second edition of *Historic Spots in California*.

In most cases landmarks no longer in existence have been noted as such and retained in the text; some of them are even pictured to help the reader re-create the former scene. By way of compensation for their loss, however, many historical places not previously described in the book have been included in the present edition. Among these are a number of outstanding landmarks associated with the growth and development of California during the first half of the twentieth century. There are, of course, many other such places that could have been added, but a choice among them must await the mature judgment of future historians. An effort has also been made to point out significant examples of historic preservation and restoration, particularly those which stand as proof that progress and urban redevelopment need not always mean the destruction of the worthwhile things of past generations.

This is the first book, apart from the official State and Federal publications, to include all of the registered State and National Historic Landmarks in California. The State program was just getting under way at the time of the first edition; now there are over 800 landmarks officially recognized. State Registered Landmarks are identified in the text by number, e.g., Saratoga *(SRL 435)*. Numbers were assigned in the order the applications were approved and do not reflect the relative importance of the landmarks. Some of the State Landmarks, in fact, are of little more than local significance; in recent years, however, criteria have been tightened, and only landmarks of statewide importance are now eligible for this distinction. At press time, the State Parks Commission was about to inaugurate still another program, the registration of "points of historical interest," in order to give due recognition to places of more localized importance. The Registry of National Historic Landmarks is of recent origin, having been begun by the Department of the Interior's National Park Service in 1960. About 40 California spots have so far been judged to be of nationwide significance.

It will be noted that the extent of the old Spanish and Mexican land grants is given sometimes in square leagues, sometimes in acres. In most cases, measurement in leagues is to be understood as the size of the rancho when granted, whereas measurement in acres (rounded off to the nearest whole number) indicates the size as determined by later United States survey and patent. A square league is approximately 4,439 acres, a linear league 2.63 miles. A vara is a Spanish yard, approximately 33 inches.

Most of the landmarks included in these pages were personally visited, their existence verified, their present condition recorded, and their locations clearly described. Many of California's finest historical buildings are privately owned and occupied—perhaps the best assurance of their continued preservation. The inclusion in this book of exact locations is not to be interpreted as permission or encouragement to invade private property. Most owners of old landmarks welcome visits from serious students of California history, especially if prior arrangements are made; but disregard for ordinary courtesy and the rights of others has led in some instances to locked gates and permissions denied, and at least once to the destruction of historic buildings by their owner.

The fruits of recent scholarship and research have, where available, been incorporated into the revision. One instance of this is the correction by Alan K. Brown of the material on the Portolá expeditions, on the basis of his studies of the documentary evidence, as outlined in his article "The Various Journals of Juan Crespí," *The Americas*, XXI, No. 4 (April 1965), 375–98. Statements concerning the establishment and operation of post offices have been checked against Walter N. Frickstad's *A Century of California Post Offices* (Oakland: Philatelic Research Society, 1955).

Credit for source material is given in the bibliographies to be found at the end of each county-chapter, and permission to quote is thereby acknowledged. These lists will also prove helpful to the reader who wishes to do further research in specific areas or background reading for a trip. The names of historians and others who helped the authors and the earlier reviser in their work will be found in previous editions. Some of these persons extended similar courtesies to me.

Grateful acknowledgment is given to the Most Reverend Floyd L. Begin, Bishop of Oakland, to the Right Reverend Monsignors Pearse P. Donovan and Robert J. Cullen, and to the Reverend John P. Quinn for permitting me to undertake this work in addition to my duties as a priest of the Diocese of Oakland.

Special thanks are due to Ruth Teiser, reviser of the 1948 edition, for making available the file of correspondence and notes gathered by her at that time. Some of the most important corrections in the book, carried over from that edition, are the result of her extensive research, particularly regarding the dates and sizes of the old Spanish and Mexican land grants.

It is impossible to acknowledge individually the many persons who have assisted with this revision: historians, librarians, newspaper and chamber-of-commerce personnel, owners and occupants of historic properties, elder citizens and descendants of pioneer families, readers who have submitted corrections over the years. To all of these, sincere thanks are extended. The cooperation of officers and members of the following county historical societies is especially appreciated: Alameda, Amador, Butte, Calaveras, Colusi, Contra Costa, Del Norte, El Dorado, Fresno, Humboldt, Kern, Kings, Lake, Lassen, Madera, Marin, Mariposa, Mendocino, Monterey, Napa, Orange, Placer, Sacramento, San Benito, San Bernardino, San Joaquin, San Luis Obispo, San Mateo, Solano, Sonoma, Trinity, Tulare, Tuolumne, Ventura, and Yolo. A similar debt of gratitude is owed to the historical societies of Hayward Area, La Puente Valley, Pajaro Valley, San Diego, Santa Barbara, Santa Cruz, Shasta, and Sonoma Valley; the Pioneer Historical Society of Riverside; the Eastern California Museum in Independence; the Cultural Heritage Board, Department of Municipal Art, City of Los Angeles; the Redevelopment Agency of the City of Sacramento; the Sacramento and San Jose Historic Landmarks Commissions; and the Conference of California Historical Societies.

Among the librarians assisting with the work were those of Amador County, Imperial County, Marin County, Merced County, Orange County, Yolo County, and Marysville. The kindness of the staffs of the Bancroft Library (University of California, Berkeley) and the Oakland Public Library is appreciated. Peter T. Conmy and Frances Buxton of the latter institution were especially helpful.

Allen W. Welts, State Park Historian, made available the files of State Registered Landmarks in Sacramento, as did Charles S. Pope the files of the Historic American Buildings Survey in San Francisco. Officers of the National Park Service in Washington, D.C., and San Francisco provided information on National Historic Landmarks. The county maps for all counties but San Francisco are reproduced by permission of the California State Automobile Association, Copyright owner.

To the following historians must go a major share of the credit for the revision of the chapters on their respective counties. Much of the material written and contributed by them has been incorporated *verbatim* in the text. Raymund F. Wood, Fresno County; L. W. Wigmore, Glenn County; the late M. J. Dowd, Imperial County; Dorothy C. Cragen, Inyo County; Richard C. Bailey, Kern County; Henry Mauldin, Lake County; Albert Shumate, M.D., San Francisco County; Alan K. Brown, San Mateo County; Wood Young, Solano County; and Rosemary H. Todd, Tehama County. Special research in Lassen, Modoc, and Sacramento counties was done by W. N. Davis, Jr., Historian of the California State Archives, and in Contra Costa County by Stephen Petersen. Unusual help was also given by Robert H. Power of Nut Tree, Ralph L. Milliken of Los Banos, Thomas Workman Temple II of San Gabriel, Mayo Hayes O'Donnell of Monterey, Ruth Paulding of Arroyo Grande, Rudolph A. Bagdons of Santa Maria, Callista Martin Dake and Margaret Koch of Glenwood, Jeanne Thurlow Miller of Santa Rosa, and J. H. Morrison of Ventura. To Clyde Arbuckle and Rosalind Boring of San Jose—deep appreciation of their guidance and encouragement in the field of California history for almost twenty years.

A special acknowledgment is due to my student secretaries at Bishop O'Dowd High School in Oakland, who were very helpful with typing and correspondence in the earlier stages of the work.

Finally, to my brother, J. T. Abeloe, go thanks for some of the best photographs, much of the research in ten counties, and almost all of the difficult and wearisome driving.

REV. WILLIAM N. ABELOE

Lafayette, California
August 9, 1966

Contents

Introduction

by ROBERT GLASS CLELAND

THE REIGN of the Emperor Charles the Fifth (1516–56) was the period of Spain's ascendancy and splendor. In Europe no nation held so dominant a place, and in the New World the amazing energy and rashness of the Spanish adventurers were bringing about the conquest of a continent and the development of one of the greatest empires the world has ever known.

As an incident in this dramatic era of exploration and conquest, on June 27, 1542, Juan Rodríguez Cabrillo, a "navigator of great courage and honor and a thorough seaman," set sail from the tiny port of Navidad on the west coast of Mexico to explore the unknown sea which stretched into the dim mists of the northwest and to find if possible the fabled Strait of Anian which all men supposed at that time joined the waters of the "South Sea" to those of the Atlantic.

On this voyage Cabrillo and his companion, Ferrelo, in two tiny ships, the *San Salvador* and the *Victoria,* sailed the full length of the California coast and for the first time made known to Europeans the characteristics and vast extent of the land which stretched away to the north above the peninsula of Lower California. Cabrillo himself did not live to return to Mexico but died from an injury he had received on the island of San Miguel, where it is supposed the body of this heroic seaman lies buried beneath the drifting sand.

But the region discovered by Cabrillo was not colonized by Spain during the reign of Charles. In 1579 a navigator even more renowned than Cabrillo appeared on the California coast. This was the Englishman, Sir Francis Drake, "master thief of the unknown world," who, having freighted the *Golden Hind* with looted treasure almost to the water's edge, sailed beyond the reach of Spanish vengeance and found refuge "in a convenient and fit harbor," supposed by most authorities to have been the present Drake's Bay, on the northern California coast. Upon leaving this port to complete his famous voyage "around the whole globe of the earth," Drake claimed the land for England, called it New Albion, and set up on the shore a "fair great poste" to which was fastened a brass plate and "a piece of sixpence current English monie" bearing the arms and picture of the Queen, as evidence of his visit and his claim.

A generation after Drake, Sebastián Vizcaíno, a man of an unusually varied and adventurous career, sailed from the port of Navidad to follow the route first taken by Cabrillo. Entering nearly all the ports of California, including that of Monterey, but missing for some mysterious reason the magnificent harbor of San Francisco, Vizcaíno carefully charted and named the prominent landmarks of the California coast. Many of these, it is true, had long before been named by Cabrillo, but, probably in ignorance of this, Vizcaíno gave no heed to the work of his heroic predecessor and today most of the names along the coast from San Diego to Monterey are those of Vizcaíno's choosing.

Following the voyage of Vizcaíno, more than 160 years went by before California became again the subject of definite concern to the Spanish Crown. Then, primarily because of the fear of the advance of England to the Pacific following the Seven Years' War and the no less tangible danger of the Russian progress down the northwest coast from Alaska, the Spanish Crown awoke to the necessity of occupying Alta California or of forfeiting the control of New Spain. At that time a genuinely great king, Charles III, was on the throne and was fortunately able to find agents peculiarly fitted for the task of carrying out the colonization program. In the person of José de Gálvez, whom he appointed visitor-general of New Spain, Charles possessed an official capable of organizing and infusing with his own dynamic energy the California enterprise; and from the Franciscan Order he obtained the spiritual enthusiasm and leadership necessary for its success. Under the direction of Gálvez, four colonizing expeditions, two by sea and two by land, were sent to California in 1769. The commander in chief of the entire force was Don Gaspar de Portolá, a Spanish soldier of the old school, courageous, determined, jealous of his prerogatives, and unswervingly loyal to the instructions laid upon him; and in charge of the spiritual phase of the expeditions was the heroic and saintly Father Junípero Serra.

The expeditions which came by sea suffered fearfully from scurvy and many of their number died. The two overland companies reached San Diego without serious difficulty, and established there a tiny settlement, the fate of which, however, was for many months in gravest doubt. Despite this discouraging outlook, Portolá determined to carry out his instructions to open an overland route to the port of Monterey which Vizcaíno had so enthusiastically described more than a century and a half before. The members of his expedition suffered extremely from hardship, sickness, and lack of food; and, to make matters even worse, when Portolá came to the port of Monterey he failed to recognize it and continued his journey northward until his way was barred by the waters of the hitherto undiscovered San Francisco Bay. Failing utterly to appreciate the significance of this discovery, the expedition, discouraged, disheartened, and suffering continually from lack of food, retraced its steps to San Diego.

The condition of the Spanish settlement at this port was now extremely critical. Portolá, however, had no intention of abandoning the province, but on the contrary set about the organization of a second company to renew the search for Monterey; and in this determination to maintain the ground already won in California, Serra and his companions joined with even fiercer zeal. Portolá's second expedition succeeded where his first had failed, and, as a result, the long-desired settlement was founded at Monterey. With the control of this port and of San Diego definitely established, the Spanish hold on California was assured. Further explorations were carried out along the coast, other settlements were established at strategic points, and in 1775–76 Juan Bautista de Anza, one of the noblest figures in early California history, led a company of colonists overland from Sonora by way of the Gila River and the Colorado Desert to San Gabriel and thence to Monterey. From this time on the development of California proceeded as it had in other border provinces of New Spain. In such regions three institutions had long since proved their value in the subjugation of the wilderness and the control of the frontier; these were the presidio or military fortress, the pueblo or town, and the missions of the various monastic orders. All three of these institutions played a definite part in the development of Spanish California.

Presidios were founded at the four strategic ports of San Diego, Santa Barbara, Monterey, and San Francisco. Pueblos, where colonists from Mexico were settled, were established at Los Angeles, Branciforte, and San José. And the Franciscan missions, which the Crown looked upon not only as a means of spreading the faith but also as most effective agencies for civilizing and governing the Indians, were erected at more or less regular intervals, about a day's journey apart, from San Diego to Sonoma. The name most commonly spoken of in connection with the foundation and early development of these missions is that of Father Junípero Serra, whom some would almost call the patron saint of California. With Serra's name, however, should also be associated those of his companions, Palou, Crespí, and Lasuén, men of lesser fame but no less genuine heroism and devotion.

The years which followed the settlement of California by the Spaniards constitute the romantic period in the history of the state. Life was simple, unhurried, picturesque. Almost the sole industry of the province was cattle-raising, and since a limitless empire lay at hand the landholdings, first of the missions and later of the ranchos, were of princely size. Because of the congenial nature of the climate and the fertility of the virgin soil, grass grew abundantly and the herds of cattle running wild on the ranges multiplied to an amazing degree. These herds furnished both a large part of the food supply of the population and almost their only commercial products. Some grain, however, was raised for local consumption both by the missions and to a lesser degree on the ranchos, and for the same purpose there were also gardens and orchards.

The industrial life of the province was exceedingly primitive. Handicrafts were taught at the missions, and some of these in the course of time developed into small industrial centers where the Indians were trained as blacksmiths, workers in leather, soap-makers, weavers of the coarser grades of cloth, and artisans in other lines. The women in their turn were taught to cook and sew, and even the children were trained in the simpler household tasks. The development of some such industrial life was an absolute necessity, since the province, shut off from Mexico by hundreds of miles of almost impassable mountain and desert wilderness and by an almost equally perilous ocean voyage, was thrown almost wholly on its own resources and compelled to become self-sustaining.

An event of major consequence in this period of California history was the so-called secularization of the missions in 1833–34. This measure, which resulted in the downfall of the missions and the scattering of the Indian populations gathered about them, is scarcely defensible from the humanitarian or the economic point of view. Politically, however, it was merely in keeping with the general policy of the Spanish Crown that the missions should be disestablished as soon as the region had ceased to exhibit its frontier character; and thus, while the consequences were most unfortunate, from the standpoint both of the Indians and of the Church, the measure was not in theory at least so revolutionary as at first it might appear.

So long as Spain retained control of her provinces in the New World the political life of California ran for the most part an uneventful course. The province was governed, in accordance with the uniform policy of Spain in her control of the frontier, almost entirely by officials dependent upon the viceroy, and revolutions were practically unknown; but after the establishment of the independence of Mexico, California began to experience something of the same unrest which so continually characterized the central government. Revolutions were particularly numerous between 1835 and the outbreak of the Mexican War. In part these were a protest of the Californians against officials sent from Mexico to rule the province and in part they were merely sectional rivalries between the north and south or factional contests between the California leaders for the control of the government. In most instances these uprisings were individually of no great consequence in the life of the people or in the history of the province, but their cumulative effect was unfortunate, particularly in their influence upon the attitude of the Californians toward the sovereignty of Mexico.

It was hardly to be expected that a territory so vast and so rich in undeveloped resources as California should remain indefinitely under control of a weak and turbulent government. Mexico, torn by almost constant civil war, virtually bankrupt, and wretchedly weak from a military standpoint, was in no position to retain her hold on a province so distant, so difficult to defend, and so inviting to other nations. Indeed, very early in the nineteenth century the United States had begun to manifest an interest in the possibilities of California and a concern in her destiny. The factors which in the succeeding decades developed this interest to the point where the annexation of California became both an ambition and a necessity on the part of the United States are of definite historic significance. First came the commercial intercourse of New England with California, when through the activities of the "merchant adventurers" from Boston, Salem, and other New England ports a trade in the skins of the sea otter and the fur seal was carried on between the long reaches of the California coast and the Chinese Empire. Somewhat later New England whalers on their long voyages to the strange corners of the North and South Pacific frequently resorted to California ports for recuperation and fresh supplies. Through the visits of these New England seamen the people of the Atlantic seaboard thus became acquainted with the riches and defenseless condition of California and developed an interest in her destiny.

The interest aroused in California by these early American contacts was further increased and given new direction by the advent of the Russians in California and the establishment of the Russian colony at Bodega Bay, north of San Francisco, about the time of the War of 1812. This venture, which was rightly regarded by the American government not merely as an attempt at the economic control of northern California by the subjects of the Czar but also as a direct threat of political domination over the entire province, played a major role in the enunciation of the Monroe Doctrine in 1823, and directed the official attention of our government to the ultimate fate of the great bay of San Francisco and of the vast region stretching along the Pacific, west of the Rocky Mountains.

Shortly after 1820, also, the hide and tallow trade was opened between California and New England. For two decades and a half this trade constituted the chief feature of the economic life of California and in a very definite way identified still further the interests of New England with those of the distant Mexican province on the Pacific. The extent and characteristic features of this trade were afterward made familiar to the whole United States by Dana's classic, *Two Years Before the Mast.*

Another factor which led to the further development of the relation of the United States with California in these early years was the opening of the overland trails and the discovery of the routes across the mountains by the restless feet of the fur traders. These men, who played so large a part in the development of the West and whose adventurous activities shaped the whole destiny of the American nation, began to appear in California prior to 1830. The leader of the first overland expedition to California was Jedediah Strong Smith, who came with a party of 15 ragged and semi-lawless followers from the vicinity of Salt Lake by way of the Colorado, the Mojave, and El Cajón Pass to the Mission of San Gabriel in the fall of 1826. Smith, one of the greatest explorers in the annals of Western America, an outstanding contributor to the history of California and the true pathfinder of the Sierra, was followed almost immediately by others of his adventurous kind. Space does not permit a detailed account of these fur-trading explorations, which disclosed the passes to California and made it possible for the settlers of the Missouri and Mississippi valleys to cross the mountains into California and take possession of the new land. To every student of California history, however, the names and exploits of the Patties, Joseph Walker, Ewing Young, and Kit Carson are familiar.

The coming of these fur traders prepared the way for the advance of overland emigration from the Mississippi Valley to California during the next decade. The first of these overland trains, in which John Bidwell was the outstanding figure, followed the Platte River trail from Missouri to Salt Lake and thence crossed the unexplored desert to the Humboldt River. Eventually the party, by this time in dire extremity from fatigue and lack of provisions, found its desperate way across the Sierra through the Sonora Pass into the valley of the San Joaquin, and its members later established homes in various parts of California.

The Bidwell party was the predecessor of numerous kindred expeditions of settlers from the Mississippi Valley into California prior to the outbreak of the Mexican War. Some of these came by way of Oregon, some by way of the Humboldt and Truckee rivers, some by way of the Owens Valley, and others by way of the old Spanish trail from Santa Fe. The exploring activities of John C. Frémont also belong to this period, but lack of space prevents a detailed discussion of the genuinely great contribution this scientist-adventurer made to California history. To this period also belongs the greatest of the misfortunes of the Western trails—the tragedy of the Donner party.

With the opening of the routes to California and the advent of American explorers and settlers the people and government of the United States became definitely interested in securing this fair province on the Pacific. Conditions in California contributed also very largely to the growing feeling in the United States that the territory must become an American possession or pass into the hands of Great Britain or one of the other more powerful European nations. Mexico, as already indicated, was utterly unable to control the province, and the military defenses of California were ridiculously weak. Dissatisfaction was everywhere in evidence and revolution was resorted to on the slightest provocation. It was accordingly universally recognized that the actual control of California had all but slipped from the hands of Mexico and that the province would become either an independent state, a protectorate of one of the European nations, or a part of the United States.

At this juncture the Mexican War gave to President Polk, one of the most ardent of the expansionist presidents of the United States, an opportunity to realize his publicly expressed ambition to secure possession of California. At least two of Polk's predecessors had sought to purchase the territory from Mexico, and on one occasion, supposing that war had actually been declared between Mexico and the United States, Commodore Thomas ap Catesby Jones, an American commander, had taken possession for a few hours of the port of Monterey. The American consul and confidential agent of President Polk at Monterey, Thomas O. Larkin, had also been exceedingly active in promoting the interests of the United States in California a few years prior to the outbreak of hostilities and was deliberately setting on foot a movement among the people of California to declare their independence of Mexico and to unite with the United States. Polk himself had likewise sought to secure California by peaceful means; but these had failed, and the President, apparently convinced that California was about to pass to England, seized the opportunity of the Mexican War to establish American control over the long-desired province.

The actual military conquest of California which followed the declaration of war between Mexico and the United States must be summed up very briefly. As a prelude to the formal conquest came the highly dramatic incident of the Bear Flag Revolt. In this uprising a group of settlers in the Sacramento Valley and John C. Frémont's company of explorers sought to overthrow the California officials and set up an independent government. The movement, however, had only entered its initial stages when it was learned that the United States and Mexico were formally at war and that the American commander, Sloat, had officially taken possession of Monterey. From this beginning the sovereignty of the United States was rapidly and almost without bloodshed extended over the greater part of California. But before long, unfortunately, the smoldering hostility of the Californians flared up into armed resistance and the real struggle for the control of California thereupon began.

In this contest the most significant engagements were those of Rancho Domínguez, Natividad, San Pasqual, San Gabriel River, and La Mesa. The outstanding commanders of the American forces were Kearny, Stockton, and Frémont. So far as the Californians were concerned, the war was fought almost wholly by irregular mounted bands whose mobility, courage, and horsemanship to some degree made up for their lack of military equipment and regular training.

The close of hostilities came on January 13, 1847, when Andrés Pico, the leader of the last of the California detachments, entered into a formal agreement with John C. Frémont to acknowledge the sovereignty of the United States. This agreement, known as the Cahuenga Capitulations, for all practical purposes marked the close of the long period of Spanish-Mexican rule in California. The formal transfer of the territory to the United States did not take place until the Treaty of Guadalupe Hidalgo on February 2, 1848.

By a singular twist of fate, only a few days prior to the signing of this treaty a few particles of gold had been discovered by James W. Marshall in the tailrace of a sawmill which he was constructing for John A. Sutter on the South Fork of the American River in the Sierra Nevada foothills. It is no exaggeration to say that this chance discovery by a man of no more than ordinary ability or fame changed both the destiny of California and the whole course of American history as well.

With almost incredible rapidity the news of Marshall's find spread throughout the world, and within a few months the "Great Migration" was in progress. The story of the adventures, hardships, and heroism of those who joined in this rush and of the picturesque life which grew out of this mingling together of the adventurous spirits from the world's four quarters constitutes perhaps the most vivid chapter in the history of California or of any other American state.

It was hardly to be expected that the political, social, and economic institutions which function satisfactorily in a normal society could immediately adapt themselves to the unprecedented and turbulent conditions which prevailed in California in the first years of the gold rush. It is therefore a tribute to the native aptitude of the Anglo-Saxon citizen for self-government that even in the midst of such chaotic conditions he was able through his own initiative to devise ways and means of furnishing reasonable safeguards of life and property and to insure some stability for society.

In 1850, despite the obstacles imposed by the question of slavery and the long-drawn-out contest in the American Congress over the Compromise of 1850, California was formally admitted as a state of the Union. A regularly organized government then began to function, and conditions within the state gradually assumed more normal characteristics. Society, however, was as yet by no means fully stabilized, and for fully another decade "Vigilante" movements from time to time sprang up in San Francisco, Los Angeles, and other sections of the state.

By 1855 gold-mining in California had definitely declined and agriculture was coming to take its place. But to make possible the new economic development of the state it was necessary first of all to provide adequate transportation facilities. Within the state this development of transportation was at first largely by means of stagecoaches and freight wagons. Lines were opened between San Francisco, Stockton, Sacramento, Los Angeles, and other important centers. Later the great Butterfield Line was operated between St. Louis, El Paso, Los Angeles, and San Francisco. Later still came the Pony Express. But it was not until 1869 that the Central Pacific Railway, built by Stanford, Crocker, Hopkins, and Huntington, united with the Union Pacific to give California its needed transcontinental rail connection with the rest of the United States.

With the coming of the railways California entered upon its present-day development, and with the history of that development it is not necessary here to deal. Looking on toward the future one's imagination is scarcely bold enough to visualize the destiny which awaits California. Looking to the past one sees a history, fascinating, romantic, inseparably a part of the great drama of international affairs and of the development of the United States, made inspiring by the heroic figures which move across its pages, and touched everywhere by elements of true greatness. To identify and preserve the landmarks where so many of the stirring episodes of this history occurred is assuredly to render a notable service to the state. For this service we acknowledge our obligation and offer our lasting appreciation to the Daughters of the American Revolution.

Alameda County

ALAMEDA COUNTY was created in 1853 from portions of Contra Costa and Santa Clara counties. The county seat was originally at Alvarado. It was moved officially to San Leandro in 1856, but since 1873 it has been at Oakland.

The primary meaning of the word *alameda* is "a place where poplar trees grow" and it is derived from *alamo,* meaning "poplar" or "cottonwood." The county doubtless received its name from El Arroyo de la Alameda (Alameda Creek), which, when first discovered, was lined as it is now with willow and silver-barked sycamore trees, giving it the appearance of an *alameda* or road lined with trees.

Brushy Peak

Brushy (Brusha) Peak is a remarkable natural formation eight miles northeast of Livermore. The front of it forms a conspicuous brush-clad eminence, rising high above the surrounding hills. Beyond lies a beautiful valley in which a group of immense rocks, now weatherbeaten and full of caves formed by the action of wind and weather, appears like an ancient ruined city. Like many another rocky outcropping situated in remote places in California, this place is said by tradition to have been one of the hideouts of Joaquín Murieta.

The Emeryville Shell Mound

Since the 1850's, says W. Egbert Schenck, "a number of artificial shellmounds scattered along the shoreline of San Francisco Bay . . . excited the curiosity of the incoming white settlers." As early as the 1870's "collections were being made of the aboriginal relics found on their surfaces or turned out by the plow."

The shell mounds of this area were first studied scientifically in the spring of 1902 by Dr. John C. Merriam and Dr. Max Uhle of the University of California. They made careful excavations on the site of the Emeryville mound and published methodical considerations of the evidence obtained. N. C. Nelson in 1908 completed a survey of the entire San Francisco Bay region, in which he located, numbered, and mapped nearly 425 shell heaps, analyzing them in detail and publishing a summary of his observations and conclusions. Field work was made possible by the generous support of Mrs. Phoebe A. Hearst, through the Department of Anthropology of the University of California, and was carried on by graduate students under the direct supervision of Professor Merriam.

Practically none of these ancient relics of a prehistoric people remain intact today. Encroaching tides, steam shovels and bulldozers leveling grounds for factory sites, city streets and modern residences, the farmer's plow or his search for fertilizer, all these and other factors have entered into the gradual but final demolition of the fascinating monuments of a vanished race. All that remain for us are one tablet of commemoration, a few monographs written by scholars, and many museum collections, sometimes widely separated from their original geographical locations.

In the Nelson survey the site of the Emeryville mound is designated as No. 329 and shows one large and two small "mounds" or cones "still present" and two larger ones "disappeared." Schenck explains that these several cones were not "a number of isolated 'mounds' but of a single, widespread, perhaps rather thin mass of mound material from which there arose a number of cones of the same material."

"The first people who came to the site," writes Schenck, "camped just above the shoreline, possibly on little hummocks at the edge of the marsh. As shell-fish were obtained, the shells were thrown aside, and these with the by-products of daily life increased the camp ground and gradually crept out into the marsh. . . . As the shell area increased, subsequent people utilized it because it was drier, placing camps, perhaps, over what had previously been marsh. . . . This shell area grew until it covered some hundreds of thousands of square feet marked by several cones."

The mound was situated on the eastern shore of San Francisco Bay almost due east of the Golden Gate. It lay on the western side of the old Peralta grant, or that part of Rancho San Antonio apportioned to Vicente Peralta by his father Don Luís María Peralta. This section became known later as Emeryville, now an incorporated town lying between the cities of Oakland and Berkeley. The shell mound *(SRL 335)* was located between the bay and the Southern Pacific Railroad tracks. Shellmound Street identifies the site.

The mound was located at a point that was favorable for use as a camping ground by prehistoric peoples. Lying on the narrow, alluvial plain that stretches from north to south along the Contra Costa ("opposite coast") between the foothills and the bay, it was bordered on the north by open, almost treeless plains, and on the south by "a willow thicket some 20 acres in extent. . . . Farther south . . . the thicket merged into a marsh extending about one and a half miles along the shore and gradually increasing in width until at its southern end it was three-quarters of a mile wide." Beyond the marshes stretched a mile of rolling, oak-studded fields, the Encinal de Temescal.

Temescal Creek held a very important relation to the ancient mound in prehistoric times. The creek itself supplied fresh water to the nomadic peoples who visited its banks, and the abundant shellfish beds at its mouth supplied food, while the quiet reaches of the bay were full of sea otter, hunted perhaps in balsa rafts. Waterfowl filled the marshes, and deer were plentiful in the willow thicket and the oak grove to the south, as were acorns, seeds, and other vegetable foods, as is indicated by the numerous mortars found in the vicinity. The willow thickets too supplied ample firewood.

To this favored spot groups of primitive peoples came yearly from the surrounding country, perhaps from long distances. They may have spent six months out of each year at this site, fishing and hunting, drying and pounding the shellfish for future food supplies, and taking the otter skins for clothing.

Although there may be older mounds in the bay region and although no certainty can be attached to any estimate of when human beings first camped at the spot, scientists compute that the maximum age of the Emeryville mound is about 1,000 years. Likewise there is no certain evidence as to the time when the place was last used as a rendezvous for nomadic tribes. Schenck says that it was apparently unoccupied when Fages passed that way in 1772, for no mention is made of it in the chronicles of that expedition. Anza, in 1776, and Gabriel Moraga, in the early 1800's, also failed to mention having seen Indians in the Oakland-Berkeley neighborhood, although they did note their presence both to the south and to the north. Yet even if these early explorers did not see Indians there, and even though there were no fogs concealing their whereabouts, it is very possible that the oak groves of which Father Crespí wrote, together with the willow thickets near the mouth of Temescal Creek, may have formed an effectual screen behind which the Indians at the Emeryville mound were encamped when the first white travelers passed that way.

Vicente Peralta erected his adobe dwelling not far from Temescal Creek and about one and a half miles east of the Emeryville mound about 1836. At the mouth of the creek was the Temescal embarcadero, and the ancient mound was a landmark familiar to travelers along the old creek road during those early days.

In 1857 the Peralta grant was surveyed and mapped by Julius Kellersberger, and in 1859 Edward Wiard purchased that portion of it on which the mound stood. Maps of that date show buildings on both the eastern and the western cones, but in 1871 Wiard leveled a part of the eastern cone and laid out the mile race track which became noted as the Oakland Trotting Park. On the western cone in 1876 he opened the Shellmound Park, a holiday resort and picnic grounds long popular among pleasure seekers of the entire bay area. In 1879 the park was leased to Captain Ludwig Siebe, who held the lease until the destruction of the mound in 1924. In the meantime James Mee had acquired the property from Wiard in 1887 and had passed it on to the Mee Estate in 1906.

The Emeryville shell mound, in the old amusement-park days, was a picturesque landmark. On its low, truncated summit were a circle of trees, some windmills, and the round dance pavilion surrounded by a high cypress hedge. A historical atlas dated 1878 shows this mound with the residence of J. S. Emery in the foreground.

The Emeryville mound was leveled in 1924 in order to convert the area into a factory site. John Hubert Mee, president of the Mee Estate, made known his intentions and permitted the University of California to use the land as desired, while Captain Siebe, proprietor of the Shellmound Park, rendered every assistance possible in the work of excavation. The mound was razed by steam shovel; careful observations were made and collections were taken during the process. After the leveling operations were completed, controlled excavations of its lower levels were made by hand, excavations made possible by the generous financial patronage of P. E. Bowles of Oakland.

During the entire period extensive and intensive observations were made, and many skeletal and artifact materials were collected. The pile was found to be composed principally of shells—mostly clams, mussels, and oysters, with a plentiful mixture of cockleshells. Certain other kinds, found only in rare quantities, had been treated in the manner of possessions. Besides human burials, the accumulation disclosed the skeletal remains of birds, quadrupeds, sea mammals, and fish. Many of these bone remains were placed in the Museum of Vertebrate Zoology at the University of California.

The Lincoln Park Shell Mound

One shell mound of the 425 mapped by Nelson in 1906–8 has been memorialized. The site of this mound, located in the city of Alameda and now covered by modern streets and residences, extended over three acres of ground bounded by what are now Central Avenue, Court Street, Johnson Avenue, and Lover's Lane, the last a double row of trees back of the house at 2854 Santa Clara Avenue. The mound was removed by the city authorities in the summer of 1908, and the earth, combined with tons of mussel shells, was used for the making of roads on Bay Farm Island.

The lower levels of this ground were examined by Captain W. A. Clark, who, working the ground carefully with a hand trowel, was able to save a number of fine relics. These were placed in the Alameda Public Library, where they are still on display.

A stone monument bearing a bronze tablet was placed in Lincoln Park near the site of the old Indian mound. The inscription reads: "One thousand feet due west was a prehistoric mound, 400 feet long, 150 feet wide, 14 feet high. The remains of 450 Indians, with stone implements and shell ornaments, were found when the mound was opened in 1908. Erected by Copa de Oro Chapter, D.A.R., 1914."

Other Indian Sites

From Albany in the north to Mowry's Landing in the south, there were at least 20 shell mounds scattered along the bayshore in Alameda County at the time they were catalogued and mapped by

Nelson in 1906–8. Among these there were, besides the famous Emeryville and Lincoln Park mounds, others at the mouth of El Cerrito Creek, at the mouth of Strawberry Creek, at the eastern end of the San Antonio estuary in East Oakland, at the mouth of Alameda Creek near Alvarado, at Centerville, and at Mowry's Landing west of Irvington.

"It is not to be supposed," writes N. C. Nelson in speaking of the survey of the San Francisco Bay shellmounds, "that this figure 425 exhausts the evidence of aboriginal occupation to be found within the given territorial limits, because the shellmounds are confined to a narrow belt around the open waters of the bay and grade off landwards into earth mounds of a more or less artificial character.... According to reports ... earth mounds and 'old Indian rancherias' are situated on the banks of the Alameda Creek ... above the alluvial plain in the foothills; and ... sites of this character could be found in great numbers by following up any other minor streams. As it is, several more or less obliterated camp and village sites of late and ancient date are definitely known in the region, some of them even on the university campus in Berkeley; and the publication of news items relating to discoveries here and there of relics and skeletal material is no uncommon occurrence."

The sites mentioned on the campus of the University of California are located west of Sather Gate on the south bank of Strawberry Creek just west of the Life Science Building.

At the curve of Indian Rock Avenue where it meets the south end of San Diego Road in North Berkeley, a huge, irregular rock mass looms above the drive. From its level summit there is a commanding view of the valley and of the bay beyond. At the base of the main boulder are a number of smaller rocks in which are deeply worn holes or mortars where the Indian women once ground the nutritious acorn for meal. Gnarled buckeyes and green bays encircle this ancient monument of a primitive people, and at the foot the City of Berkeley has planted a garden, creating of the spot a tiny public park, known as the Mortar Rock Park. A few hundred feet lower down on Indian Rock Avenue at the head of San Mateo Road is Indian Rock Park, another prehistoric landmark set among small live oak and tall eucalyptus trees.

In Indian Gulch (now Trestle Glen) in Oakland, there is a level spot where an Indian village once stood. It was originally called Indian Gulch because Indians still lived there when the first white people came to that region. Nothing remains today as a reminder of the Indians, and Trestle Glen, which extends northeast from Lake Merritt, is now filled with fine residences. The narrow, winding canyon, still shaded by immense live oaks and other trees, is today made accessible by Trestle Glen Road, off Lakeshore Avenue.

Temescal

Temescal, a name of Aztec origin meaning "sweat house," was brought to California by the Franciscan Fathers. A. L. Kroeber describes the *temescal* thus:

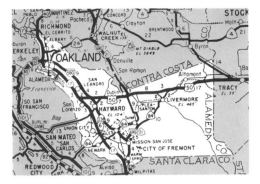

"From the outside its appearance is that of a small mound. The ground has been excavated to the depth of a foot or a foot and a half, over a space of about twelve by seven or eight feet. In the center of this area two heavy posts are set up three or four feet apart. These are connected at the top by a log laid in their forks. Upon this log, and in the two forks, are laid some fifty or more logs and sticks of various dimensions, their ends sloping down to the edge of the excavation. It is probable that brush covers these timbers. The whole is thoroughly covered with earth. There is no smoke hole. The entrance is on one of the long sides, directly facing the space between the two center posts, and only a few feet from them. The fireplace is between the entrance and the posts. It is just possible to stand upright in the center of the house. In Northern California, the so-called sweathouse is of larger dimensions, and was preeminently a ceremonial or assembly chamber."

Dr. L. H. Bunnell, in his history of his discovery of the Yosemite Valley, notes some interesting details of the use of the sweat house. "It ... was used as a curative for disease, and as a convenience for cleansing the skin, when necessity demanded it.... I have seen a half-dozen or more enter one of these rudely constructed sweathouses through the small aperture left for the purpose. Hot stones are taken in, the aperture is closed until suffocation would seem impending, when they would crawl out, reeking with perspiration, and with a shout, spring like acrobats into the cold waters of the stream. As a remedial agent for disease, the same course is pursued."

Through what is now a busy part of Oakland, Temescal Creek wandered down from the Piedmont hills to San Francisco Bay. When white men first came to this section of the country, it is said that they found an old Indian sweat house on the arroyo and that because of this circumstance they named it Temescal Creek. W. E. Schenck, however, believes that the name may have arisen, not from the presence of a native Indian village and sweat house, but because the Indian retainers on the Peralta rancho doubtless set up a *temescal* on the bank of the creek near their cabins. The Vicente Peralta adobe was built about two blocks north of the point where the present Telegraph Avenue crosses the creek. Around this nucleus the settlement of Temescal grew up. The name first appears on the Kellersberger survey map of 1857 as "Temesconta," which, Schenck says, "may or may not be Temescal."

Temescal Creek flowed about 450 feet southeast of the center of the Emeryville shell mound and discharged into the bay some 800 feet southwest of the center of the mound. The creek seems to have been the determining physiographical feature of the region in prehistoric as well as in pioneer times, tending to focus population by its supply of fresh water as well as of food. For hundreds of years before the coming of the white man, it had been a favorite camping and hunting ground for nomadic tribes of Indians. "Within the memory of men living nearby," wrote Schenck in 1926, "it has had salmon runs. And Mr. P. E. Bowles informs me that in the early 1880's it was a favorite resort for amateur fishermen. The marshy overflow of the stream near the bay, formed excellent coverts for game among its luxuriant plant growth."

With the coming of the Spaniards to the Contra Costa, Mission San José was settled, and later the great ranchos of San Antonio, San Leandro, San Pablo, San Lorenzo, and others were granted. Gradually embarcaderos sprang up along the eastern shore of the bay. Among others the Temescal landing at the mouth of Temescal Creek near the old Emeryville shell mound became a landing place for occasional parties from San Francisco. The path of the old Temescal Creek road, over which the Spaniards once passed on foot or on horseback or in creaking *carretas*, doubtless followed the general course of the creek as far east as Telegraph Avenue and beyond.

Land now covered with immense factories, paved streets, and miles of closely set homes and gardens was still a wilderness during those early years. Only a few adobe houses stood many miles apart on the vast ranchos, and these were joined merely by horse paths or by narrow dirt roads which amounted to little more than trails through the brush. Over all that fertile plain "giants of a thousand years' growth remained undisturbed by the woodsman's axe. . . . The songs of birds and the bellowing of the Spanish bull almost alone disturbed the air. . . . Wild cattle roamed at large in thousands; wild oats covered the hills"; and wild mustard, each spring, colored the entire countryside with tangled, golden thickets taller than a man.

The age of the native Californian lasted from 1833 to 1846. This was the time when the missions were breaking up, the presidios were practically deserted, and land could be had almost for the asking. The owners of the great landed estates or ranchos lived a simple, carefree life, idyllic in many respects in spite of the crudities and hardships occasioned by frontier conditions.

During this period, visitors to the Contra Costa, landing in boats at the mouth of Temescal Creek, continued to the ranchos or to the mission by way of the Vicente Peralta adobe one and one-half miles inland. All who came were sure to be hospitably entertained. From there they would proceed close to the foothills to Antonio Peralta's adobe near what is now Fruitvale, and thence to Ignacio Peralta's on the bank of San Leandro Creek. The next stop was the Estudillo rancho on the south side of the creek, and from there

they went to Guillermo Castro's adobe at the site of the present town of Hayward. Here roads led east to Amador's and Livermore's ranchos and south to Mission San José.

The old Temescal Creek road no longer exists, and the free flow of the stream was stopped in 1866, when it was dammed up in the hills to form the reservoir still known as Lake Temescal. At that time it furnished the principal water supply for several thousand inhabitants. The course of the arroyo itself is still plainly indicated in some places by a winding lane of native oak, willow, bay, elder, buckeye, and cottonwood trees.

Beginning at the bay, where the land has been filled in and occupied by factories, the stream bed is mostly invisible. Leaving San Pablo Avenue, the creek runs between 48th and 47th streets on the south and 53d and 52d streets on the north. Its course is marked at first by a sparse growth of willow and elderberry trees, and farther on by elm, eucalyptus, acacia, and other exotic trees. Through this section, the arroyo forms the northern boundary of Emeryville.

East of Shattuck Avenue the pursuit becomes interesting, for there the old watercourse, sometimes entirely lost sight of and again appearing in unexpected places, proceeds through one of the busiest parts of Oakland. Now it passes under paved streets, and again houses are built directly over it. The channel disappears under Telegraph Avenue between 50th and 51st streets, where it runs beneath a shopping center. From there it tends eastward along a well-defined line of trees paralleled by Claremont Avenue and Chabot Road.

As one approaches the hills, the trees bordering the arroyo become thicker and larger. Especially attractive bits, in which giant oaks predominate, may be seen at the end of Arbor Avenue, off Hudson, and on Ivanhoe Road just south of Chabot Road, in one of Oakland's finest residential districts. The main branch of Temescal Creek continues south of Chabot Road to Lake Temescal, while the north branch crosses Claremont Avenue. From there it proceeds eastward, paralleling Claremont Avenue as far as Hotel Claremont. Beyond is Fish Canyon, in which the north fork has its origin.

The Grove–Shafter Freeway, to be constructed in the late 1960's, will follow the bed of Temescal Creek in some places, and a number of the finest old trees will be lost.

Ortega First to See the "Contra Costa"

While he was encamped on San Francisquito Creek (on the San Mateo–Santa Clara county line), after his historic discovery of the great Bay of San Francisco, Gaspar de Portolá sent a reconnoitering party under the command of José Francisco de Ortega to find a land route up the eastern shore of the newly discovered bay to Point Reyes (in Marin County) and Cermeño's harbor, to a place which was to be called San Francisco and on which was to be founded the mission dedicated to St. Francis.

Passing around the southern end of San Francisco Bay, Ortega and his men forded the Guadalupe River (in Santa Clara County). From there, writes Fray Juan Crespí, chronicler and chaplain to Portolá, "they went forward on the other side of the estuary eight or ten leagues, but there was still a long distance for them to go. At this distance of ten leagues, they came upon another very large stream with a very strong current, and its bed was also wooded and its course was through a great plain which was also quite well wooded." They must have gone as far north as Niles or farther, says Bolton, and the second "very large stream" with wooded arroyo was doubtless Alameda Creek, from which the county takes its name.

On the evening of November 10, 1769, "the explorers returned, very sad, and no longer believing in the reports of the heathen, which they confessed they had not understood. They said that all the territory which they had examined to the northeast and north was impassable because of the scarcity of pasture and especially because of the ferocity and ill-temper of the heathen, who received them angrily and tried to stop their passage. They said also that they had seen another estuary [San Pablo Bay] of equal magnitude and extent with the one we had in sight and with which it communicated, but that in order to go round it one would have to travel many leagues ... and that the mountains were rough and difficult."

The austere aspect of what the Spaniards came to call the Contra Costa ("coast opposite" San Francisco) on that November day two centuries ago put dismay into the hearts of Portolá's weary, half-starved soldiers. They had gone far enough north to sight the Bay of San Pablo, but the view had only made further passage seem an impossible undertaking. Already disheartened because the long-sought port of Monterey had not been found, they voted unanimously to return to the Point of Pines (in Monterey County).

Fages, Trail Blazer of the Contra Costa

Alameda County was again penetrated by white men in the autumn of 1770, when Pedro Fages, one of Portolá's men left by him in command at Monterey, decided on his own initiative to make another attempt to reach Point Reyes by land. It was on this trip that Fages opened the first inland route from Monterey to the future site of San Jose. From there he continued over the trail opened the year before as far as Niles and on to a point "seven leagues beyond the point reached by Ortega."

During this time the party had, says Bolton, "skirted the Contra Costa for two days.... From the Berkeley hills they looked west through the Golden Gate and to the north they beheld San Pablo Bay cutting across their route to Point Reyes."

Fages made a second attempt in the spring of 1772 to reach Cermeño's bay. Accompanied by Fray Juan Crespí, "six Catalonian volunteers, six leather-jackets, a muleteer, and an Indian servant," he followed the trail that he had opened more than a year before. Northwest to the region of Hayward the party retraced the ground already twice covered by Ortega and Fages. To the Berkeley hills they were on Fages' old trail. Thereafter they were pathbreakers once more.

Crespí, missionary and chronicler of the expedition, wrote on Wednesday, March 25: "On this day of the Incarnation, after Mass had been said, we set out ... in the direction of the north–northwest. At the start we travelled about a league from the estuary at the foot of a bare mountain range, and after travelling a short distance we were three leagues from the estuary. All the land is level, black, and very well covered with good grass, mallows, and other herbs.... We passed five villages of heathen, which are all on the banks of the arroyos with running water.... We halted on the bank of a large arroyo close to the mountains skirting the broad plain. The bed of the arroyo is very full of alders, cottonwoods, and willows."

Their route, like that of the long line of travelers who were to follow in their steps, lay close to the hills, and camp was made at San Lorenzo Creek, called San Salvador de Horta by Crespí.

Advancing as far as the site of Fruitvale on March 26, they pitched camp near the point where Mills College is now located. During the day they had had their first view of elk, which Crespí thought were buffalo but which the soldiers called mule deer. Five arroyos of running water had been crossed, their banks green with alder, cottonwood, live oak, and bay trees. At the end of five leagues, Fages and his men saw the Alameda peninsula, now an island, and the intervening *encinal* or live-oak groves. "The site," wrote Crespí, "is very suitable for a good settlement ... on account of the proximity of the forest.... This place was called Arroyo del Bosque" —probably Fruitvale Creek.

From here the march, as described by Bolton, crossed country now covered by crowded cities, then only a pleasant wilderness: "On the 27th they turned inland to round the estuary and the adjacent marshes, and emerged from the hills near the site of Lake Merritt. Near the Technical High School Father Crespí made his observations of the Golden Gate. The islands which he describes in the gate are Alcatraz Island, Goat Island (Yerba Buena), and Angel Island. The arroyo where they camped, a league north of the point of observation, was probably Strawberry Creek, and the campsite near the western side of the campus of the University of California. On the 28th they continued past the sites of Berkeley and Albany to eastern Richmond" in Contra Costa County.

The first stop made in Alameda County on the return trip was made on April 1 at a place west of Pleasanton in front of the Hacienda del Pozo de Verona, the country home of Phoebe Apperson Hearst, now the Castlewood Country Club. On April 2 "they descended Arroyo de la Laguna, crossing it near Suñol. Leaving Suñol Valley [Santa Coleta] they crossed Alameda Creek, ascended Mission Pass, re-entered the valley of San Francisco Bay, and continued past the head of the bay at a point near Milpitas."

"This historic journey," says Bolton, "had more

than merely exploratory significance. It was a decisive factor in determining the location of San Francisco. Cermeño's Bay on Point Reyes had been predestined for that honor ... but the new-found bay and its affluents stood in the way. It was now concluded that communication with Point Reyes must be maintained by water ... and ... that the proposed settlement might be planted south of the Golden Gate, in reach from Monterey by land, and on the shore of the superb new harbor. The Fages-Crespí expedition marks a distinct step forward, both in discovery and in choice of a site for San Francisco."

Anza Follows the Contra Costa Trail

After he had explored the sites for the presidio and the mission to be established at the port of San Francisco, Captain Juan Bautista de Anza, accompanied by Lieutenant José Moraga, his second in command, and by Father Pedro Font, master chronicler and chaplain of the second overland expedition from Sonora to California, passed around the southern extremity of San Francisco Bay into Alameda County. With 11 soldiers, six muleteers, and servants, Anza and his companions were on their way to "explore the Río Grande de San Francisco, that is, Carquinez Strait and the waters above it."

On the frosty Sunday morning of March 31, 1776, after Father Font had said Mass, the travelers left their camp on the Guadalupe and, meeting with a network of sloughs and marshes along Coyote Creek, where it runs west, were forced to twist their way about for three leagues until they emerged on higher ground at the foot of the hills. From this point forward, the line of march followed "far away from the water ... through very level country, green and flower-covered all the way to the estuary, but with no other timber or firewood than that afforded by the trees in the arroyos which we encountered, which were five."

Font's map showed that the line of march was now close to the hills all the way, and Bolton identifies it as the route passing by way of the Arroyo de la Encarnación, probably Scott Creek, and from there "northeastward past Warm Springs, Irvington, and the Lagoon (the 'somewhat salty' lagoon mentioned by Font). The Arroyo 'about half way on the road' was apparently Alameda Creek," with its "very deep pools ... many sycamores, cottonwoods, and some live oaks and other trees." It was here that a band of about 30 armed but peaceful Indians ran out to greet them with the weird chorus of "Au, au, au, au," which seemed to Father Font "like something infernal."

Passing three arroyos and two deserted Indian villages, Anza and his men crossed the fifth stream, the San Lorenzo, near which they pitched their tents. Here they met a lone Indian, much frightened by the sudden apparition of strange beings. This is the last mention of Indians until Wildcat and San Pablo creeks were reached in Contra Costa County.

"All day," Font wrote that evening, "the com-mander and I have been in doubt as to whether the island at the end of the estuary which I mapped yesterday is really an island or not." "The supposed island," says Bolton, "was Coyote Hills. ... The other long island mentioned was Richmond Peninsula, likewise not an island. With a nearer view Font's conclusion was more accurate."

Mass was said in a thick and "very damp" fog on Monday, April 1, and a small army of long-billed mosquitoes pursued the travelers as they left the Arroyo de la Harina.

Continuing along the foothills, the route was much the same as that followed by the Foothill Boulevard of today. Professor Bolton has identified and sketched the way for us:

"The arroyo where they saw the bears was San Leandro Creek. Two leagues beyond they crossed the creek at Mills College. Just beyond they climbed the hill and from there Font drew the sketch of the Oakland Estuary and oak-covered Alameda Peninsula, now Alameda Island. ... Descending the hill they crossed Arroyo del Bosque, a stream in eastern Fruitvale. Continuing north-west they crossed the site of Oakland. It was from Berkeley that Font sighted through Lime Point and Point Bonita to determine the trend of the north shore of the Golden Gate. It was in Berkeley, too, that the elk were chased, 'at the Arroyo de la Bocana' of Crespí, a place of 'very little water' and 'a small growth of trees.' Farther down this arroyo there was 'a grove or growth of not very large timber.'" This was what is now known as Strawberry Creek.

Leaving the stream and its brushy coverts behind them, the explorers passed over a level plain and low hills into Contra Costa County. Following Suisun Bay as far as Antioch, they turned south on April 4. After a weary struggle with treacherous tulares and the blinding, wind-driven ash of burned tules, they proceeded some six leagues "along the general course of the Old River." At a point just south of Bethany, "perhaps near Lammersville School," Anza decided to give up his attempt to approach the Sierra Nevada, on account of the seemingly limitless and impassable tulares which intervened, and to return to Monterey.

Continuing south, the party entered the Lomas de las Tuzas, evidently by Midway Valley. Ascending Patterson Grade to the vicinity of the pass, they looked down into Livermore Valley (Santa Coleta) and "descried in the distance the range of redwoods [Sierra de Pinabetes] on San Francisco Peninsula." Bolton writes in this connection, "Mr. R. S. Sweet, keeper of Beacon no. 32, near the Pass, tells me that on clear days he can see the Coast Range on the San Francisco Peninsula."

"Continuing southeast along the northeastern edge of Crane Ridge for seven or eight miles, about to the San Joaquin County line, they climbed to the top of Crane Ridge, perhaps up Sulphur Springs Canyon, reaching the summit west of Eagle Mountain. Continuing south they descended to Arroyo Mocho, striking it about at

Callahan Gulch, some two miles north of the Santa Clara County line."

The Founding of Mission San José

"In 1794," writes Bancroft, "the eastern shores of San Francisco Bay were almost a tierra incognita to the Spaniards." For nearly 20 years after the coming of Anza in 1776, there is no record of any exploring expedition until 1795, when Sergeant Pedro Amador visited the southern part of Alameda County some time before June. In his report, acknowledged by Governor Borica on June 2, 1795, Amador used the name of Alameda, the first known official use of that designation. The Alameda was again visited in November 1795, when, in accordance with the governor's orders, Hermenegildo Sal and Father Antonio Danti set out from Monterey to search for suitable mission sites.

"Having arrived at Santa Clara on the 21st," says Bancroft, "they were joined by Alférez Raimundo Carrillo, and started the next day to examine the Alameda previously explored by Amador, whose diary they had. The river of the Alameda was also called by Danti, Río de San Clemente. The explorers continued their journey up to a point . . . nearly or quite to the site of the modern Oakland, perhaps, and then turned backwards discovering some important salt-marshes, and finally erected a cross at the spot somewhat south of the Alameda and called San Francisco Solano, arriving at Santa Clara . . . on the 25th of November."

And thus the preliminary explorations were made and the site was chosen for the location of Mission San José. In the year 1797 Corporal Alejandro Miranda and five men were detailed to act as protectors for the new adventure, and on June 9 the troops under Amador, accompanied by Father Fermín Francisco de Lasuén, set out for the spot called by the natives Oroysom in the valley of San José. The following day a temporary chapel or enramada was erected, and on June 11, Trinity Sunday, Padre Presidente Lasuén "raised and blessed the cross. In a shelter of boughs he celebrated holy Mass."

Five days after the founding, temporary buildings constructed of native timbers and thatched with grass were begun, and on June 28 Fathers Isidoro Barcenilla and Agustín Merino arrived to take charge of the new mission. Barcenilla served until April 1802, when Father Luís Gil y Taboada succeeded him, and Merino was replaced in 1799 by Father José Antonio Uría. Luís María Peralta succeeded Miranda in command of the mission guard in 1798.

Of the various fathers who served Mission San José, Narciso Durán, a native of Catalonia, who came to California from Mexico in 1806, was the most prominent. He went at once to Mission San José and, with Father Buenaventura Fortuni, in June 1806 began his long ministry, which continued until 1833, when he moved to Santa Barbara. Father Fortuni left the mission in 1825, and from then on Father Durán served alone, being also Padre Presidente of the missions during the

years 1825 to 1827, and again from 1831 to 1838, and from 1844 to 1846. He was *comisario prefecto* from 1837 to 1843. Father Durán, one of the most prominent friars in Alta California, was especially noted for his earnest and successful missionary work. Throughout the troubled years of secularization, he managed the affairs of the mission with marked ability, retaining the esteem of most of his adversaries as well as the love of the people of all classes. An accomplished musician, he taught the Indians how to read music and trained an orchestra of 30 Indians, with flutes, violins, trumpets, and drums.

The German explorer Georg Heinrich von Langsdorff, who came to California on the Russian ship *Nadeshda* in 1806, visited Mission San José early in May. Coming down San Francisco Bay in an Aleut bidarka, he was the first foreigner to tread the southeastern bay shores. He received a warm reception from Father Pedro de la Cueva, then in charge at the mission, and a great Indian dance was given for his benefit. Since he was particularly interested in the manners and customs of the natives, he devoted much space to them in his narrative of the expedition.

Langsdorff also wrote enthusiastically of the orchards and gardens of Mission San José:

"The quantity of corn in the granaries far exceeded my expectations . . . and a proportionate quantity of maize, barley, pease, beans, and other grain. The kitchen garden is extremely well laid out, and kept in very good order; the soil is everywhere rich and fertile, and yields ample returns. . . . A small rivulet runs through the garden, which preserves a constant moisture. . . . The situation of the establishment is admirably chosen, and according to the universal opinion the mission will in a few years be the richest and best in New California."

Langsdorff's prophecy was fulfilled to a large degree, for Mission San José grew and prospered throughout the years of its service, before the inevitable decadence following the secularization at last set in about 1841. Bancroft pictures this growth with the following graphic statistics:

"By the end of 1797 there were 33 converts, and in 1800 the number had increased to 286, the baptisms having been 364. . . . Meanwhile the large stock came to number 367, and there were 1,600 sheep and goats. Crops in 1800 were about 1,500 bushels, chiefly wheat."

Ten years later the number of neophytes had increased to 545. There were 1,806 people at the mission in 1824, when it was excelled only by Mission San Luís Rey in population, and in the number of baptisms San José greatly exceeded any other mission. It also stood fourth on the list in regard to the number of cattle and sheep raised, as well as in the average production of grain crops.

The highest population attained at Mission San José was 1,877 people in 1831; the number fell to 1,400 in 1834, and to 580 in 1840. However, this mission for the entire decade of the 1830's maintained a remarkable record and was probably the most prosperous of all the California missions both before and after secularization, which was effected between 1826 and 1837. Crops were good, and the livestock increased steadily. Engelhardt gives the last available official report (1832) as 12,000 cattle, 13,000 sheep, and 13,000 horses.

On April 22, 1809, Padre Presidente Estévan Tápis came to hold the vigil of St. Joseph and to bless the adobe just completed at the mission. On the following day, Father Tápis delivered the sermon, while Father Felipe Arroyo de la Cuesta, from Mission San Juan Bautista, said Mass in the presence of the officers, the other priests, and many people who had come from the neighboring Pueblo de San José (in Santa Clara County).

"Three different structures," writes Halley, "have at various times been placed on the site of the present church, owing to destruction and injury by earthquakes. The last of these occurred on the 21st of October, 1868. . . . The injured building was subsequently removed, and a wooden structure put up in its place."

When Durán left for Santa Barbara in 1833, his place at Mission San José was taken by Padre José María de Jesús Gonzalez Rubio, who remained to the end of the decade. San José was the last mission but one to be secularized. In November 1836 the property was turned over to José de Jesús Vallejo, *comisionado,* and the transfer was completed in December. Vallejo remained in charge until April 1840, when he was succeeded by José María Amador. Temporal management of twelve missions, including San José, was restored to the padres on March 29, 1843, but on May 5, 1846, Mission San José was finally sold by Governor Pío Pico to Andrés Pico and J. B. Alvarado for $12,000.

Most of the mission lands finally fell into the hands of strangers. The greater part of the estate of Mission San José was secured by E. L. Beard, who, according to Halley, still resided at the mission in 1876 and who possessed one of the loveliest places in the state. The Beard homestead at Mission San José was later owned by Juan Gallegos and is now the motherhouse and novitiate of the Sisters of the Holy Family.

Not only was Mission San José a center for the social life of the ranchos on the east side of San Francisco Bay during the 1830's and 1840's, but it was also a stopping place for expeditions sent against the Indians, who continually threatened the peace of the mission. During 1849 and 1850 it provided a wayside station for those Argonauts who used the land route from San Francisco to the mines by way of Mission Pass and Livermore. At this time Henry C. Smith, a member of Frémont's California Battalion in 1846, had a trading post in the old adobe mission building.

Of Mission San José *(SRL 334)* only a part of the living quarters remains today. In 1916, the Native Sons and Daughters of the Golden West began work to preserve and restore this building, and a roof was put over the whole structure in order to prevent the winter rains from washing away the adobe walls. Further restoration was accomplished in 1950.

Beside the present steepled St. Joseph's Church, built soon after the earthquake of 1868, is the old cemetery, shadowy under Monterey cypress trees, where members of old Spanish families are buried. The garden of the Dominican Sisters' convent is a profusion of old-fashioned flowers, and in the corner to the north is a life-sized statue of St. Dominic. The cemetery of the sisters, with its background of cypress and olive trees, is hedged in at the northwest corner of the garden. Each grave is marked by a trim white cross.

About a mile west of Mission San José on Washington Boulevard is the Ohlone burial ground. Here on a grassy knoll a granite monument marks the place where "sleep four thousand of the Ohlone tribe who helped the padres build this Mission San José." On January 6, 1965, Bishop Floyd L. Begin of the Diocese of Oakland presented the old cemetery to the American Indian Historical Society for restoration.

Although it is located nowhere near the Guadalupe River, Mission San José is often referred to as "San José de Guadalupe." Guadalupe was not a part of its original title, and was probably acquired somehow through association with the Pueblo de San José de Guadalupe, now the city of San Jose.

On January 24, 1956, the old community of Mission San José became part of the city of Fremont, at almost 100 square miles one of the largest municipalities in the state in area. The other four unincorporated towns that joined with the old mission town to form the new city were Centerville, Irvington, Niles, and Warm Springs.

Mission Pass, an Old Spanish Trail

Mission Pass, the starting point of an old Spanish and pioneer American trail, cuts through the Mount Hamilton Range just northeast of Mission San José. The winding Highway 21 long followed the route approximately, but now it has been straightened and widened into a freeway and taken into the Interstate Highway System as part of Route 680.

Crossing over the lower hills, the old trail dropped down into Suñol Valley, where it went in two directions. One branch skirted the western edge of Livermore Valley along the Arroyo de la Laguna and proceeded up the Amador and San Ramon valleys to the site of Concord, and from there on to the San Joaquin Valley. The other branch, the more traveled route, went straight across Livermore Valley through the hills into the San Joaquin.

In 1772 Pedro Fages and Father Juan Crespí came over the first of these trails by way of Concord on their return from the north, after having discovered the mouth of the San Joaquin River. Although the route is being replaced by a freeway, it may still be followed very closely by driving Foothill Road and its northern extensions, San Ramon Valley Boulevard and Danville Boulevard. The age of this scenic old road is demonstrated by the fact that it passes two adobes of the Mexican period, the old town of Dublin, and a number of homes from the pioneer American period.

Many expeditions after Fages' went through this same pass, among them the one led by

Gabriel Moraga that opened up the Sacramento Valley region. Various expeditions against the Indians, made by Moraga, Vallejo, and others, started from the mission through this pass. The first overland Argonauts from San Francisco to the mining regions also went by way of Mission San José and Mission Pass.

Jedediah Strong Smith, a Prisoner at Mission San José

In the month of May 1827, while Father Narciso Durán was in charge of Mission San José, Jedediah Strong Smith, the great American pathfinder, wrote a letter to the padre. Durán was suspicious of the strangers. Four hundred of the neophytes had run away from the mission on May 15 and 16, and the fur hunters were unjustly suspected of having been the instigators of the desertion.

Unsuccessful in his attempts to cross the Sierra Nevada, far from home, and low on all supplies, including food and clothing, Smith addressed to Durán a letter dated May 19, in which he made a frank statement of his purpose and condition, concluding with the words: "I am, Reverend Father, your strange, but real friend and Christian brother, J. S. Smith." Father Durán did not read the letter but forwarded it to Monterey for translation.

After his historic passage of the Sierra Nevada late in October, Smith, with three of his men and some Indian guides, proceeded from his camp on the Stanislaus River to Mission San José, where he hoped to procure the supplies needed for his journey out of California. Father Durán, however, was still on the defensive, and the unwelcome strangers were put in the guardhouse.

A visit from Captain J. B. R. Cooper, an influential citizen of Monterey, greatly relieved the uncertainty of the situation, since he offered to aid Smith in every way within his power. However, the pathfinder was detained at the mission for 12 or 14 days before receiving a letter from the governor and a guard to escort him to the capital. At Monterey, on November 12, Cooper signed a bond in favor of Smith.

Smith returned to Mission San José on November 24, and for two weeks he and his men were busy preparing for the journey out of California —rounding up their horses, drying meat, repairing their guns, and baling the goods allowed them by Governor Echeandía's orders. On Sundays and holy days they attended services at the mission and there listened to the father address his people in Latin or in Spanish. Smith makes special note in his journal of the music, which, he says, "consisted of 12 or 15 violins, 5 base vials and one flute."

Having obtained permission from Father Durán, Smith removed his company on December 24 "to a sheep farm belonging to the mission called St. Lorenzo [San Lorenzo], where there was plenty of grass and a pen in which I could shut up my horses and mules."

Impatient at continued delays and fearing further obstacles to an immediate departure, Smith finally "settled off with the father under pretence of moving to better grass," and on December 30, in rain and mud, the band began its march northward, not by way of Bodega and Fort Ross, as officially planned, but through Mission Pass across the Livermore Valley to the Old River branch of the San Joaquin (sometimes called the Pescador by the Spanish), and from there up the Sacramento Valley as far as Tehama, where Smith blazed a new trail out of California through Trinity, Humboldt, and Del Norte counties.

Rancho San Antonio

The present cities of Oakland, Alameda, Berkeley, Albany, Emeryville, Piedmont, and a part of San Leandro are located on what was once Rancho San Antonio (SRL 246). This vast estate extended five leagues along the eastern shore of San Francisco Bay, from San Leandro Creek on the south to El Cerrito Creek, now the boundary line of Alameda and Contra Costa counties, on the north. It comprised all of the land lying between the bay on the west and the crest of the Contra Costa hills on the east, a total of about ten square leagues.

On August 3, 1820, Pablo Vicente de Solá, the last Spanish governor of Alta California, ordered the grant of Rancho San Antonio to be made to Luís María Peralta, and on August 16 Peralta was given juridical possession of it. He was thereby rewarded for his loyalty, dedication, and service beyond the call of duty in almost 40 years in the army, and for the valuable assistance he rendered in the establishment of the missions of Santa Cruz and San José. A native of Tubac, Sonora (now in Arizona), Peralta was baptized on August 31, 1759. He came to California with the Anza expedition in 1775–76, and enlisted in military service about five years later. He was in command of the guard at Mission San José from 1798 to 1800, and from 1807 to 1822 he was comisionado of the Pueblo de San José. On February 23, 1784, he married María Loreto Alviso, to whom were born 17 children, of which four sons and five daughters lived to adulthood. Don Luís never made his home on Rancho San Antonio but maintained his residence in San José, where part of his adobe dwelling still stands at the rear of 184 West St. John Street.

Rancho San Antonio was occupied by the four living sons of Don Luís—Hermenegildo Ignacio, José Domingo, Antonio María, and José Vicente —and the original adobe home was located in what is now the Fruitvale district of East Oakland. There in the 1820's the first permanent settlement, after Mission San José, on the east side of San Francisco Bay was erected, and there for a number of years the four brothers stayed whenever they visited the rancho.

The site of this adobe is at 2511 34th Avenue at the northwest corner of Paxton Avenue, one block east of Coolidge Avenue (formerly Peralta Avenue), near the north bank of Peralta Creek. This first adobe was torn down in 1897. Some of the adobe bricks were used to construct a small house in Dimond Park in East Oakland. This building, overshadowed by the gigantic gnarled branches of an evergreen oak (Quercus agrifolia), was used for years by the Boy Scouts, but was finally destroyed by fire. Part of the adobe construction was saved, however, and incorporated into the present building under the old oak. A few of the bricks from the original Peralta adobe were also used in a home built by a descendant of Ignacio Peralta at 384 West Estudillo Avenue in San Leandro, where they may be seen today near the front entrance.

Soon each of the Peralta brothers began to build his own adobe on the section of the rancho later apportioned to him. To these homes they brought their wives, and there they reared their children. Their surroundings and mode of living were truly patriarchal. Thousands of horned cattle grazed among the oak trees. Sometimes Don Luís Peralta's former companions in arms from the Presidio de San Francisco would cross in small boats to participate in rodeos and to enjoy the festivities of the Contra Costa. To the north (in Contra Costa County) the Castros held Rancho San Pablo, while to the south there were the Estudillos, the Higueras, the José de Jesús Vallejos, and the Guillermo Castros, all living on vast estates of their own before 1842.

The legal division of the lands of Rancho San Antonio took place in August 1842. At this time, Don Luís Peralta came up from San José to divide the estate among his four sons. As they rode over the land together, the father parceled it out among them, marking out the boundaries by natural objects. It was divided, as nearly as possible, into four equal parts, each running from the bay to the hills. The total area was over 43,000 acres.

Ignacio, the oldest, was given the southern end of the grant, bordering on the north bank of San Leandro Creek. Domingo was given the northern end, where the cities of Berkeley and Albany now stand. Antonio received what is now East Oakland (where the original house stood) and the Encinal de San Antonio (now the city of Alameda). And to Vicente fell the Encinal de Temescal, the portion that is now occupied by Central and North Oakland, Piedmont, and Emeryville.

To the south of the original adobe (on the present 34th Avenue) Antonio Peralta built a second adobe in 1840, and also an eight-foot wall enclosing an area of about three acres. Two additional structures were erected that year on the same plat, one of which was a guest house located on the southwest corner of the enclosure. Extensive additions were made to the guest house in 1851. All of these houses, except the first one built in the 1820's, were leveled in 1870. In that year Antonio built a frame structure on Paxton Avenue about halfway between Coolidge and 34th avenues.

Professor J. N. Bowman of Berkeley relocated the sites of Antonio Peralta's buildings, and determined the bounds of the old enclosure. The southern end of the three-acre plot is intersected by Paxton Avenue, and 34th Avenue cuts across the eastern side. In 1897, Don Antonio's frame house was moved to the southwest corner of Paxton and 34th avenues, where it still stands.

Ignacio erected his first house on the north bank of San Leandro Creek about 1835, after his term as alcalde of San José. The site is at the end

Last Home of Antonio María Peralta, Oakland

of 105th Avenue, near the Nimitz Freeway. In later years, this was called the Francisco House, because Ignacio's son, Francisco Peralta, lived there. A short distance east of this house, Ignacio built a second adobe in 1842. These adobes disappeared in the late 1870's.

About 1860 William P. Toler built a brick house (SRL 285), said to be the first in Alameda County, for Ignacio Peralta, his father-in-law. It is now the Alta Mira Club House and stands at Lafayette and Leo avenues in San Leandro, one block west of East 14th Street. A few magnolia trees remain from the garden that once lined the drive from the old road (now East 14th Street) to the house.

The Domingo adobe was built in 1841 on the site of what is now 1304 Albina Avenue in Berkeley, just off Hopkins Street and on the south bank of Codornices ("quail") Creek. This adobe remained standing until the 1860's. Domingo constructed a frame dwelling about 1851 on a lot east of 1505 Hopkins Street. This house was moved in 1876 to Sacramento Street between Rose and Cedar streets but was razed in August 1933.

The first adobe house of Vicente Peralta was erected in 1836 in that part of Oakland known as Temescal. The site is east of Telegraph Avenue at the rear of 5527 Vicente Street between 55th and 56th streets. The second adobe was built south of the first and back of 486 55th Street in 1847–48. These adobes were leveled during the 1880's. A frame structure, built at 5511–21 Vicente Street in 1867, was moved in 1892 to 5275 Claremont Avenue, one block south of the adobe sites and near the north bank of Temescal Creek, but was destroyed by fire in June 1932.

A section of the old camino of Rancho San Antonio (SRL 299) that led from Temescal south to San Leandro, San Lorenzo, and Mission San José was long distinguishable in the area of Moss and Santa Clara avenues. When, about 1870, Edward P. Flint from Boston purchased a large tract of land here, the ruts made by the old wheels were plainly discernible along the rear of what is now 60 Santa Clara Avenue. From Harrison Street to Grand Avenue, Santa Clara Avenue follows approximately the route of the old Mexican road. In strange contrast, the MacArthur Freeway passes a stone's throw from the site of the ancient road.

The pleasant years of the 1830's and early 1840's on the old ranchos of the Contra Costa were but a brief episode in the history of California. Anglo-Saxons began to visit the region as early as 1846, and the Peraltas soon found that their fertile lands were the envy of these shrewd newcomers, who saw that they could be made valuable for other than pastoral purposes. In 1850, when the greater portion of the territorial patrimony of Domingo and Vicente Peralta was sold, the first encroachment upon Rancho San Antonio was made. Don Luís Peralta, grantee of the original princely estate, died on August 25, 1851, on or about his 92nd birthday, having lived to realize that what he had given to his sons was one of the most valuable tracts of land in California and that it was gradually melting away

Ignacio Peralta Brick House, San Leandro

before their eyes. The immense value of the grant, the claim that his daughters were entitled to a share of it, the alleged insanity of the father when he made his will, all gave rise to complicated litigation, which, says Bancroft, can hardly be regarded as ended in 1885.

The great rancho and the four Peralta homes are jointly commemorated by a bronze tablet set in a boulder and placed in Lakeside Park in Oakland by 11 bay region chapters of the Daughters of the American Revolution. The spot is just above the municipal boathouse on the northern shore of Lake Merritt.

Rancho San Ramón

José María Amador, the first white settler of Murray Township, arrived there, tradition has it, before 1830. He brought with him a rich heritage of ingenuity and industry from his father Pedro Amador, that fine old Mexican soldier who had come to California with Portolá in 1769. Don José, himself a soldier, had been born in San Francisco in 1794, and had served as a private in the San Francisco Company from 1810 to 1827, being stationed in the Escolta at Sonoma from 1824 to 1827. He took part in the expedition of Luís Argüello to the Sacramento Valley in 1821 and went with Gabriel Moraga to Fort Ross and Bodega that same year. After his discharge in 1827 he was mayordomo at Mission San José, and on January 22, 1834, and August 14, 1835, he was granted more than four square leagues of the rancho later known as San Ramón, the greater part of which lay in Contra Costa County.

The Californians were not without native manufacturers, and they did not rely entirely upon the sale of hides and tallow. Amador was one of the first manufacturers and farmers in Alameda County, herding vast numbers of cattle over his broad, unfenced acres and making leather, soap, saddles, harness, blankets, shoes, and even wagons in the adobe workshops on his rancho with the aid of Mexican labor. At one time 300 to 400 horses, 13,000 to 14,000 head of cattle, and 3,000 to 4,000 sheep grazed on his lands. In 1848 the lure of gold drew Amador, with thousands of others, to the Mother Lode country. Assisted by a number of Indians, according to Hittell, he mined in the county that was later named after him.

The site of the two-story adobe that Amador

erected at his home is on the northwest corner of San Ramon Road and Dublin Boulevard at Dublin. It stood north of the spring still visible under the weeping-willow trees. Robert Livermore helped Amador to build another adobe, and Amador reciprocated by assisting Livermore at his Rancho Las Positas, located to the east.

Natural landmarks usually designated the boundary lines between the early Spanish and Mexican land grants, although later surveys often varied from the original, less scientific ones; the first surveys that marked out the confines of Rancho San Ramón may still be identified. To the west, the Pita Navaga ("knife point"), a sharp knob above the summit of Bulmer Hill Grade, indicated the division line between Rancho San Ramón and Rancho San Lorenzo. It is mentioned frequently in early deeds. The southern boundary was another natural feature, a large oak tree in the small gulch running up the hillside opposite the old Fallon house on Foothill Road. This tree once bore the marks of early surveyors, who used it as a landmark from which the boundary line between ranchos San Ramón and Santa Rita was drawn.

Becoming financially involved, Amador gradually sold portions of his estate to various newcomers. Michael Murray and Jeremiah Fallon, natives of Ireland, who had come west together in 1846 and who had settled temporarily at Mission San José, bought sections of the Amador holdings south of the present Dublin Boulevard (the old Stockton road) before 1852. Murray Township, organized in June 1853, was named for Michael Murray, the first county supervisor from the district.

The old one-story Murray house, built in the 1850's, still stands on the west side of San Ramon Road just south of Dublin Boulevard, beside the later two-story Green residence. The Murray house is about 100 yards west of its original location. The floor and siding of this interesting landmark were of pine shipped around the Horn, while the redwood joists were cut at Redwood City and shipped from there.

Michael Murray sold his house and lands in 1862 to John Green, a man who became prominent in local affairs and who was a leading businessman of the district during the 1870's and 1880's. Green, a native of Ireland, was a druggist by trade. He had come west at the urging of his brother, who was a physician at San Antonio (East Oakland). John Green did not like the drug business, however, and longed for land of his own. In 1857 he packed his goods into an oxcart, crossed the hills east of Hayward, and stopped in the vicinity of the present old Dublin schoolhouse. This well-watered, wooded spot appealed to him, and he decided to set up his tent there. No sooner had the newcomer started to unload his wagon than Michael Murray arrived, informing him that he was squatting on land already owned and occupied. The property in question was under dispute at that time, since both Murray and James Witt Dougherty claimed to have purchased it from Amador. Murray, therefore, invited Green to drive down and locate on the

ranch on which he was living, and Green accepted.

During the earthquake of 1868, a deep fissure in the earth two feet wide passed just west of the original site of the old Murray house, and the wells at this location dried up. Prospecting for springs west of the fault, Green found water and moved to that spot, where the house still stands. The dwelling was enlarged in 1870, and in 1890 a two-story structure was erected beside the smaller one. The earthquake of 1906 caused the tall brick chimney of the newer house to collapse and to crash through the roof and the floor of the pioneer structure. In the process of repairing the floor, each of the old boards was found to bear the stamp of a Boston company. In 1966, the old Murray house and the big Green house next door were vacant shells, awaiting the hand of man— demolition or, hopefully, restoration.

A regular town plat was never laid out at Dublin. The place just grew. The old Amador Valley road to Suñol passed just east of the present Green house. Deep mire during the winter rains made it almost impassable, and its course was rerouted to higher ground to the west. The decided jog in the road as it runs at present is explained by this change.

John Green led an active and useful life. He was not only storekeeper, postmaster, and supervisor for Murray Township, but also a large-scale rancher, who owned lands both at Dublin and in the Livermore mountains to the east. The settlement of Greenville, four miles east of Livermore at the entrance to Altamont Pass, was named for him, since he started the first store there. In spite of full days, Green spent his evenings studying law, especially the land-tenure laws pertaining to the Spanish and Mexican land grants. He had learned Spanish during his apprenticeship to a New York drug firm which had trade relations with South American countries. Thus it was natural that Green became a friend and adviser to the native Californians of the Amador and Livermore valleys, and the old ranchers often drove to Dublin to discuss their increasingly complex land problems with their good Irish neighbors.

Less than a mile south of Dublin, at 6035 Foothill Road, is located the Jeremiah Fallon house also built in the 1850's. Its timbers were hand hewn from the San Antonio redwoods back of Oakland, but, like the Murray house, its floor and siding were brought around the Horn. The original location of the house was on the lowlands to the east, where the road skirted the base of the hills instead of following the slopes, as the present road does. The old house has been somewhat remodeled.

During the year 1852, James Witt Dougherty, a native of Mississippi who had come to California in 1849, acquired Amador's two-story adobe when he purchased the greater portion of the rancho, the bulk of which lay north of the Stockton road. Dougherty lived in the old Amador adobe until it was damaged by the severe earthquake of 1861. A rude dwelling of resawed siding was then put up south of the spring, and a por tion of this old house, added to and altered from time to time, stood well into the 1960's.

About the Amador adobes a town gradually grew up, generally known until 1860 as Amador's or Amador Valley. The post office which was established there then was called Dougherty's Station. The portion of the settlement south of the Stockton road, however, was called Dublin. It is said that Dougherty first called it that when a traveler asked him the name of the community. Dougherty replied that the post office was called Dougherty's Station but that, since there were so many Irish living south of the road, they might as well call that part Dublin. The name stuck, but the post office was not called Dublin until the present office, a branch of the Pleasanton post office, was established on September 16, 1963. The original post office at Dublin was opened as Dougherty's Station on February 15, 1860, shortened to Dougherty on January 18, 1896, and discontinued on February 29, 1908.

The first business house in Dublin (then Amador's) was the two-story Amador adobe, which served as a wayside station until its destruction in the 1860's. Meanwhile, the Amador Valley Hotel, built in 1858 by Tom Donlon, was becoming popular, with Pete Donlon as proprietor. It stood on the southwest corner of San Ramon Road and Dublin Boulevard until 1914, when it was destroyed by fire.

The oldest business house still standing in Dublin is the John Green store, built in 1864 on the south side of Dublin Boulevard west of San Ramon Road. The two-story structure has retained its original shape, but gray stucco covers the old resawed siding. A wall at the back alone retains its original appearance.

The little white church and neat cemetery mark Dublin as a spot of historic interest. Set apart from the noise and hurry of the great highway that passes near the town, St. Raymond's Church, though fallen into disrepair, still keeps the charm of other days. Built in 1859 and dedicated on April 22, 1860, it was the first church in the township. Land for the church and the adjoining Catholic cemetery was donated by Michael Murray and Jeremiah Fallon, both of whom are buried there. The first interment, in 1859, was Tom Donlon, who was killed in an accident during construction of the church. The street on which the church stands is called Donlon Way. The nonsectarian portion of the cemetery was given by James W. Dougherty.

The old church gradually fell out of use and began to crumble, although the cemeteries were always maintained by descendants of the pioneers and burials continued there. St. Raymond's Church, a prey to fire and vandalism, seemed destined to fall eventually under the wrecker's hammer, but in February 1966 Bishop Floyd L. Begin of the Diocese of Oakland presented it to the Amador-Livermore Valley Historical Society for restoration. It is the oldest extant Catholic church building in the diocese (which comprises Alameda and Contra Costa counties), since the one remaining adobe building of Mission San José served as living quarters rather than church.

St. Raymond's Church, Dublin

It is fitting that old St. Raymond's will continue to stand as a memorial to the devout Irish pioneers who built it.

When Highway 50, which long passed through Dublin, was rerouted around the town, businesses closed and the old settlement began to fade away. Then new life was injected when the burgeoning subdivision of San Ramon Village was opened nearby. With the establishment of a post office, the entire area has begun to take on the name of Dublin, and there are plans to incorporate it as a city under that name. The population in 1966 was over 13,000. Dublin is one of the most historic towns in Alameda County, and it is to be hoped that the old section will be preserved. Now that the church has been saved, similar measures might well be taken to maintain the Green store and the old Fallon, Murray, and Green homes.

Rancho Agua Caliente

Warm Springs, a small settlement that is now part of the city of Fremont, is located on what was once Rancho Agua Caliente. This rancho was granted to Fulgencio Higuera on April 4, 1839, having been released by its earlier grantee, Antonio Suñol. About two miles south of Mission San José on Mission Boulevard is the area in which the homes of the Higuera family stood.

The hot springs at this point were first frequented by the Indians. To these springs later came the señores and señoras of the 1840's, bringing their linen for their Indian retainers to wash and holding their annual rodeos in the vicinity.

The portion of the rancho that includes the springs was purchased by Clemente Columbet in

1850, and buildings for a resort were erected. From this time until the earthquake of 1868, Warm Springs was one of the gayest and most fashionable watering places in the state. Persons of wealth and leisure as well as invalids from many places came to enjoy the benefits of the hot sulphur water.

Columbet moved a house all the way from San José to serve as a hotel at the springs. In 1858 he leased the place to Alexander Beaty, who maintained its reputation for grand festivities. Another hotel was built in 1869 by A. A. Cohen, but it was never used as such. Governor Leland Stanford purchased the estate about the same time and had it planted to orchards and vineyards. His brother Josiah, and later Josiah's son, Josiah W. Stanford, resided in Cohen's hotel. It was owned for a time by the Sisters of the Holy Names and used as a summer villa, but now it is a resort. The Stanford winery (SRL 642) is now operated by Weibel Vineyards, which uses some of the original brick buildings. It is located just east of Mission Boulevard on Stanford Avenue. The old wooden hotel stands beyond the winery at the end of the road.

South of and adjacent to the old hotel property is a ranch on which stands an old adobe owned for many years by Arthur Curtner, son of the pioneer Henry Curtner. It is traditionally associated with Abelardo Higuera, but there is evidence that it was actually the residence of Juan Crisóstomo Galindo. The old adobe, of one story and a half with very thick walls and partitions, is fast crumbling into ruin. Part of it is used as a storehouse and garage, but the roof that once protected it has deteriorated greatly. The location in the lower foothills commands a magnificent view of San Francisco Bay and the Santa Clara Valley. On the chance that the ranch might become a residential development in the growing city of Fremont, plans have been drafted for the preservation of the old adobe in a park at the site. The adobe stands slightly over a mile east of Mission Boulevard via Curtner Road and its private extension.

Rancho Las Positas

A young English sailor named Robert Livermore appeared in California in January 1822, a deserter from the trading ship Colonel Young. For a time, he worked at various places in California, gaining the good will of the Spanish settlers wherever he went. Soon after 1830 he came to Rancho Los Tularcitos (mostly in northeastern Santa Clara County), where he married Josefa Higuera as early as 1834.

Before 1837, the year in which Philip Leget Edwards passed through Alameda and Contra Costa counties on his way to the San Joaquin River with his herd of wild Mexican long-horned cattle, Robert Livermore had already established himself on Rancho Las Positas in what was later called Livermore Valley. He and William Gulnac had occupied a house on the land as early as 1835. In July 1834, Gulnac had petitioned the governor for Rancho Las Positas, but before the grant was made he turned over his rights to Livermore and José Noriega. On April 10, 1839, Governor Juan B. Alvarado granted the land to them. It consisted of two square leagues, or about 8,800 acres. Livermore later bought Noriega's interest.

Robert Livermore became a naturalized citizen of Alta California in 1844, and about the year 1846 he purchased Rancho Cañada de los Vaqueros, mostly in Contra Costa County but skirting the northern portion of Livermore Valley. The two ranchos were later confirmed to him, and Livermore became a wealthy man. The rancho was soon well stocked with cattle, but Livermore was more interested in horticulture and viticulture than he was in cows or sheep. After the fathers of Mission San José, he was the first man to plant a vineyard and an orchard of pears and olives in this section of California.

One of the first dwellings on Rancho Las Positas was an adobe erected by Livermore, assisted by José María Amador, his nearest white neighbor in the valley. Amador did not forget that Livermore had volunteered aid to him in a like situation several years before. At times, too, Indians so harassed Livermore and his family that he had to take refuge with Amador.

This friendly house, with its honest, hospitable host, became a popular stopping place for travelers on the Stockton road. In March 1850 when Nathaniel Greene Patterson (a member of the California Battalion in 1846–47 and a gold seeker of 1848) hired the adobe for a hotel, it became the first place of public entertainment in the valley. This house, which stood near the source of Las Positas Creek at a point about one and one-half miles north of the center of Livermore, was partly in ruins by 1876 and was later torn down.

Livermore built a large frame dwelling near the adobe in 1849, the first wooden building in Livermore Valley. A part of the original structure, the timbers of which had been shipped around the Horn, stood until the 1950's. On Junction Avenue, the western approach to Livermore from the freeway, is a monument in honor of Robert Livermore (SRL 241). An arrow on top of the monument points to Livermore's homesite, perhaps one-third of a mile to the north. On the present ranch there remain only some old trees and a few boards at the site of Livermore's frame house.

The first house to be erected within the present city limits of Livermore was built by Alphonso Ladd, who came to California from New Orleans in 1850. The following year he settled with his wife near the Suñol adobe, then the only white habitation in Suñol Valley. A few years later he took up 160 acres of government land in the Livermore Extension, and in 1855 he built a hotel on the Stockton road at the site of what was to become known as Laddville, a forerunner of Livermore. The Ladd Hotel, a frame structure built of lumber hauled across the hills from Mowry's Landing, was very prosperous during the late 1850's and the 1860's and was nearly always full. It was destroyed by fire in 1876.

The tracks of the Central Pacific Railroad were laid through Livermore Valley in the summer of 1869, and in August the first train passed through althought the entire line was not yet opened. The railroad station had been located about half a mile west of Laddville, and there William M. Mendenhall, who had come to California in 1846, had the town of Livermore surveyed on October 1, 1869. It was incorporated on April 30, 1876.

The Collegiate Institute, later called Livermore College, was founded by the Presbyterians at Livermore in 1870. The building has been destroyed by fire. For several years it was used as a sanatorium by J. W. Robertson, who sold it to John McGlinchey for use as a private residence. The site is at 1615 College Avenue.

The Livermore Valley has become well known for its vineyards. Two of the old wineries still in operation are the Cresta Blanca Winery *(SRL 586)*, founded in 1882 and located south of town on Arroyo Road, and Concannon Vineyards *(SRL 641)*, established the following year on Tesla Road southeast of Livermore.

Rancho San Leandro

José Joaquín Estudillo, the first white settler in Eden Township, petitioned for a grant of the land known as the Arroyo de San Leandro on January 8, 1837, "with the object of securing subsistence for and supporting a large family, consisting of his wife and ten children, after having been in the military service for a period of seventeen years, four months and seven days." The title was given in 1839 but the document was lost, and Estudillo had lived on his land for "the long term of five years, five months and several days" before he again secured his grant on October 16, 1842. It was well that he did so, for Guillermo Castro, his neighbor on Rancho San Lorenzo, also desired the lands of San Leandro, but Estudillo's long period of actual tenure won the battle for possession.

José Joaquín, son of José María Estudillo and brother of José Antonio Estudillo of San Diego, was born at the Presidio of Monterey on May 5, 1800. A member of one of the best of the old Californian families, he held several positions of honor in the military service and in the government in his own right. William Heath Davis, a son-in-law of Estudillo, said that José Joaquín moved to San Leandro early in the year 1836, after he had first obtained a written permit from Governor Alvarado to occupy the land. He brought with him 300 heifers, by which he increased his herd until, on his death in San Francisco on June 7, 1852, he left to his heirs about 3,000 head of cattle. His specialty and pride was "white cattle," because he said their color enabled him "to see his stock at a great distance."

Squatters first encroached upon Rancho San Leandro in 1851, when Americans began to settle there against the wishes of the legal owner. The intruders first made their appearance on the banks of San Lorenzo Creek, at a place subsequently known as Squattersville, now San Lorenzo. They soon overran the rancho, but Estudillo, "an educated, intelligent, and up-right man," with the aid of his sons and sons-in-law consistently "opposed the evildoers in seizing the land. At times . . . there was a tendency . . . towards a bloody affray. But among them [that is, the squatters], there were conservative counsel-

lors and prudent squatters, who invariably prevailed on the rougher class to avoid bloodshed." A malicious element among them, however, did much damage, shooting and wounding horses and cattle under cover of darkness, and fencing Estudillo's stock away from the creek. During "all these turbulent times [1851–54] the members of the family were in constant fear of their personal safety."

Through the instrumentality of John B. Ward and William Heath Davis, the squatters were finally brought to terms. Some of the property was deeded to an alien, Clement Boyreau, in order to bring the case into the federal courts. Judges Ogden Hoffman and Matthew Hall McAllister rendered a decision in favor of the Estudillo family. As a result the squatters took leases from the family pending the final decision of the United States Supreme Court, and eventually they purchased the land from the original owners.

The town of San Leandro was founded for the sole specific purpose of housing the seat of Alameda County. In 1854 the two sons-in-law, Ward and Davis, submitted a plan to José Joaquín's widow, Juana Martínez de Estudillo, and her children for laying out a town. The family gave land for county buildings and reserved 200 acres for the town, which was surveyed early in 1855. A popular election on December 30, 1854, brought the county seat to San Leandro from Alvarado. "The family mansion," says Davis, "was surrendered to the county for a temporary court house." It was damaged in 1855 by fire, probably set by an incendiary who wished the county seat to be returned to Alvarado. The election of 1854 was declared invalid, since it had not been authorized by the state legislature, and the center of justice went back to Alvarado. By action of the legislature, however, it was again in San Leandro in 1856, where it remained until 1873, when it was moved to Brooklyn, now a part of East Oakland and by that time annexed to the city of Oakland.

The first adobe dwelling built by José Joaquín Estudillo, about 1836–37, was located near the south bank of San Leandro Creek, roughly opposite the home of Ignacio Peralta. It was a little more than a mile west of the present center of San Leandro, possibly near Cleveland School, in the general vicinity of the Nimitz Freeway overpass across the creek.

Some ten or more years later Estudillo moved to what is now the block bounded by West Estudillo Avenue (formerly Ward Street), San Leandro Boulevard (formerly Estudillo Street), and Davis and Carpentier streets. There he erected a second home, possibly occupied by the spring of 1850. A wooden house, thought to be substantially the same as this second home, stood on that block until about 1947–48, when it was razed for construction of the priests' residence of St. Leander's Church. It is difficult to determine how much, if any, of this house was originally constructed of adobe; undoubtedly it required major repairs after the fire of 1855 (while it was temporary courthouse) and the earthquake of 1868. It was a two-story structure of 14 rooms, graced with balconies and surrounded by magnificent trees. The lower floor was below ground level, and a stairway at the entrance (1291 Carpentier Street) led directly to the second or main floor. The site of this house *(SRL 279)* was marked on the West Estudillo Avenue side on June 7, 1964, coincidentally the 112th anniversary of the death of José Joaquín Estudillo. The dedication was a part of the festivities celebrating the centennial of St. Leander's Parish; the present church (1957) and rectory (1948) stand on the site of the old home. The Estudillo family gave the land for the original St. Leander's Church, built in 1864 directly opposite the present church, where the primary school now stands. The venerable Gothic structure was razed in August 1957.

A permanent brick courthouse of two stories was erected in 1856–57 in the central part of the block bounded by West Estudillo Avenue, Carpentier, Davis, and Clarke streets. The main entrance was on Clarke Street, some distance back from the street. It collapsed in the earthquake of 1868, but was repaired and used until the county seat was transferred in 1873. In 1881 it became the first convent and school of St. Leander's Parish. Later a three-story wooden building was built around it, and it stood until 1926, when it was replaced by the present convent and school, constructed on either side of it.

Until 1929 the Estudillo House, a frame structure erected by the family in 1855 as a hotel, still stood in San Leandro at the corner of Davis Street and Washington Avenue. A beautiful patio, where a mammoth grapevine, orange and lemon trees, and bright flowers grew in profusion, gave it the atmosphere and charm of long ago. Modern progress has removed this historic landmark; its place on the old plaza is taken by the Godchaux Building.

María de Jesús Estudillo married William Heath Davis at Mission Dolores in 1847. After her father's death in 1852, she inherited the portion of Rancho San Leandro near the original homesite. The street that now runs west from San Leandro to the bay and crosses what was once the Davis ranch bears the name of its former owner, Davis Street.

At San Lorenzo (the one-time Squattersville) the old San Lorenzo Hotel stood until about 1950 at the northeast corner of Hesperian and Lewelling boulevards. It was erected in 1854 by Charles Crane, one of three brothers who came to California from New York in 1850. The place was used as a stage station on the old valley road from San Jose to Oakland. Emerson T. Crane, a brother of Charles, had a ranch on the northwest corner. The third brother, Addison Moses Crane, was the first judge of Alameda County. Another early hotel still stands on Hesperian Boulevard at the San Lorenzo Creek bridge. The pioneer cemetery at Hesperian and College Street has been restored.

Rancho El Valle de San José

The mission fathers early recognized the advantages of the fertile Arroyo Valle and pastured their herds among the great sycamores there. For many years after Mission San José was secularized, mission Indians still lived around Pleasanton. The original name of the locality was Alisal, from *aliso* meaning "alder tree," so called because of the many large alders lining the bed of the arroyo.

Rancho El Valle de San José was granted to four relatives, Antonio María Pico, his brothers-in-law Agustín Bernal and Juan Pablo Bernal, and his sister-in-law María Dolores Bernal de Suñol, on February 23 and April 10, 1839. It was patented in 1865 to Agustín and Juan Pablo Bernal and Antonio María Suñol.

Antonio María Pico, son of José Dolores Pico, was born in Monterey in 1808. He held various public and military offices throughout his career. He was stationed at San José from 1833 to 1839 and took part in the revolt against Micheltorena in the years 1844 and 1845. After having been a member of the Constitutional Convention, he was appointed by President Lincoln as registrar of the United States land office at Los Angeles in 1861. He was a grantee of Rancho Pescadero (San Joaquin County) in 1843 and co-purchaser of the San Rafael Mission estate in 1846. Don Antonio married Pilar Bernal and sold his fourth of Rancho El Valle de San José to Juan P. Bernal.

Antonio María Suñol, a native of Spain who had come to California as a sailor on the French ship *Bordelais,* from which he deserted in 1818, married María Dolores Bernal. He lived at the Pueblo de San José and never took up residence on Rancho El Valle de San José. A man of "excellent reputation," he held a few public offices but was mainly a stock raiser and trader. He was owner of the Rancho Los Coches in Santa Clara County after 1847 and purchaser of San Rafael Mission in 1846 with Pico.

The son of the same name, Antonio Suñol, had an adobe on the rancho in the pleasant valley of the sycamores and alder trees, where he lived in the late 1840's and early 1850's. The site of this adobe is near the Water Temple of the San Francisco water system, which stands near the intersection of three old valley roads, one from Suñol, another from Pleasanton, and a third through Mission Pass. The Suñol adobe was later owned by Charles Hadsell.

The Bernals, Agustín and Juan P., sons of Joaquín Bernal, were presidio soldiers who had served at San Francisco and San José. Agustín Bernal was in 1853 a claimant for Rancho Santa Teresa in Santa Clara County, of which his father had been grantee in 1834. In April 1850 Agustín moved to his section of Rancho El Valle de San José and erected an adobe home near the foothills at the western rim of the broad Livermore Valley. The picturesque adobe still stands in excellent condition in a beautiful ranch setting west of Pleasanton on the west side of Foothill Road, about a mile south of the Alviso adobe of Rancho Santa Rita. In September 1852 Juan P. Bernal, settling near Alisal, constructed an adobe dwelling, no longer standing, on the north bank of Arroyo Valle.

The Bernals were good business managers. Consequently, they were able to secure their large holdings from the aggressive encroachments of foreigners and to maintain possession of the original grant better than most of the native families.

The next settler in the vicinity of Pleasanton was John W. Kottinger, a native of Austria who came to California in 1849 and who married a daughter of Juan P. Bernal in 1850. Late in 1852 Kottinger went to live at Rancho El Valle de San José, and in that year he built at Alisal, later Pleasanton, an adobe and frame dwelling house on the south bank of Arroyo Valle opposite Bernal's residence. Kottinger was one of the founders of the town of Pleasanton and the first man to start a store there. His plat lay just south of Arroyo Valle and was surveyed in 1867 and 1869. Kottinger's house was torn down in 1930, but the old barn, also of adobe, still stands at the rear of the residence at 218 Ray Street.

Joshua Ayres Neal, a seaman and a native of New Hampshire who shipped to California on board a sailing vessel in March 1847, came to Livermore Valley in 1850, when he obtained the position of overseer for Robert Livermore. Afterward, by marrying a daughter of Agustín Bernal, he acquired 530 acres in the immediate vicinity of Pleasanton. Neal had his portion of the town surveyed by a Mr. Duerr in 1868.

On Rancho El Valle de San José, not far from the Agustín Bernal adobe, stands the beautiful mansion built by Phoebe Apperson Hearst, wife of Senator George Hearst and mother of the publisher William Randolph Hearst. Begun soon after her husband's death in 1891, Hacienda del Pozo de Verona was her home until her death in 1919. It is now the Castlewood Country Club.

Rancho Potrero de los Cerritos

The present community of Alvarado is on what was once a part of the Rancho Potrero de los Cerritos, granted to Agustín Alviso and Tomás Pacheco on March 21, 1844. Agustín Alviso, son of Ygnacio Alviso, was mayordomo of Mission San José from 1840 to 1841. He was a prosperous ranchero, locally well known, who married María Antonia Pacheco in 1830. Tomás Pacheco was a soldier of the San Francisco Company from 1826 to 1832 and later held various offices at the Pueblo San José from 1834 to 1843.

The old Alviso adobe was so badly damaged in the earthquake of 1868 that Agustín Alviso would not let his wife and children live in it. A frame house, no longer standing, was erected on the site of the adobe soon after the earthquake. In 1934, when the foundations of the building were being repaired, adobe bricks were uncovered. The adobe, and later the frame house, stood on the northeast bank of the Sanjón (Zanjón) de los Alisos, just south of Newark Boulevard at a point about two-tenths of a mile east of its junction with Jarvis Avenue.

The site of Tomás Pacheco's adobe is south of Decoto on the south bank of Alameda Creek and on the west side of Decoto Road, which is the northern continuation of Jarvis Avenue.

In 1850 John M. Horner purchased from A. Alviso 110 acres in the tract that had been the mission grazing lands. At once he plotted a townsite covering the whole of his purchase; the first lots were sold on September 9, 1850. The town of Union City was a success; it drew the trade of Mission San José from the more southerly sloughs and also provided a more direct outlet for the area east of the hills.

Henry C. Smith bought 465 acres from A. Alviso and T. Pacheco on December 27, 1850. Smith had the town of New Haven laid out "at the upper embarcadero just across the boundary line from Horner's Union City.... The first lots were sold March 18, 1851."

"These communities," writes J. N. Bowman, "became rivals of San Francisco. In this neighborhood, grain, vegetable and fruit ranching were proven feasible in California for Americans; flour and sugar factories were later erected, and people and investors were even attracted from San Francisco."

Because of the success of Union City and New Haven, "two San Francisco lawyers, Strode and Jones, bought 750 acres from A. Alviso on September 30, 1852, and a new town was planned that winter," being adjacent to the two older ones to the south and west. The new town was named for the former Mexican governor, Juan Bautista Alvarado.

"In March and part of April, 1853, there were three towns." Meanwhile on March 15, "Henry C. Smith introduced his bill in the State Legislature, then meeting at Benicia, creating the new county of Alameda from parts of Contra Costa and Santa Clara Counties and designating New Haven as the county seat and Alvarado as the seat of justice.... The new county officials met in the upper story of Smith's store in New Haven; but the first minutes of their meeting are dated April 11, 1853, in Alvarado," thus indicating that, "by this date, New Haven had discarded its old name and taken that of the neighboring town without taking the town itself."

The site of the New Haven embarcadero and of the building used as a county courthouse (SRL 503) is on the west side of the old highway through Alvarado. A service station now occupies the spot. About half a mile due west was the Union City embarcadero. Long after Smith's store and courthouse had disappeared, his old home, built in 1852, still stood at the head of Vallejo Street. It is gone now, but other wooden buildings of early date can be found on the streets of the old town. Northeast of Alvarado on Dyer Street is the site of the nation's first successful beet sugar factory (SRL 768), established in 1870 by E. H. Dyer. The property is now occupied by the Holly Sugar Company.

The pioneer name of Union City was restored to the area in 1958, when Alvarado and Decoto combined to incorporate as a city.

Rancho San Lorenzo

There were two divisions of Rancho San Lorenzo. That portion on which the towns of Hayward and Castro Valley are located was granted to Guillermo Castro on February 23, 1841, by Governor Juan B. Alvarado, and on October 25,

1843, by Governor Manuel Micheltorena. The portion west of Hayward and south of San Lorenzo Creek was granted to Francisco Soto on October 10, 1842, and February 20, 1844.

Guillermo Castro's adobe house was located on Mission Boulevard between C and D streets, on the site of the present city hall in Hayward. Its sandstone foundations were uncovered when excavations for the city hall were being made. Among the buildings damaged at Hayward in the earthquake of 1868 was this old adobe. Its roof was then covered with flat tile. Soto's adobe house was located less than half a mile south of Castro's on the south bank of Ward Creek and on the southwest side of Mission Boulevard, opposite the tennis courts of the Hayward Memorial Park.

Guillermo Castro married Luisa Peralta, and Francisco Soto married Barbara Castro, Guillermo's sister. Since Soto died before 1852, his wife and children were claimants for the rancho that year. Castro lived for many years.

One of the first Americans to come to Rancho San Lorenzo was William Hayward from Massachusetts. In the fall of 1851 he pitched his tent in Palomares Canyon under the impression that it was government land and that he would obtain there a homestead of 160 acres. Before long, however, he was visited by Guillermo Castro, who informed him that he was a trespasser. However, an agreement was made between Castro and Hayward so that the latter remained, and the relations between the two men continued to be most friendly.

Hayward soon removed his tent to the location of the hotel that later became famous as a resort. This site is on the hill north of A Street and east of Mission Boulevard. The hotel was destroyed by fire in 1923. In 1854 Castro laid out the plat of the town he called San Lorenzo but which instead took the name Haywards, later Hayward. William Hayward's monument in Lone Tree Cemetery, on Fairview Avenue, contains a bust of the pioneer.

The relations of Castro with another American, Faxon D. Atherton, illustrate how shrewd Yankees often bested native Californians. Atherton loaned money to Castro from time to time so that he might gamble. When the latter was unable to repay, Atherton took possession of a piece of land. And so it went until Castro lost all of his vast acreage. Finally, Castro and all of his family except a daughter and one son, Luís Castro, later surveyor of Alameda County, moved to South America.

On Mission Boulevard long stood the Villa Hotel, known in the 1860's as the American Exchange and in the 1870's as the Oakes Hotel. Tony Oakes, the proprietor, who wrote and sang his own songs, published a little booklet of songs in 1878 called *Tony Oakes' Songster*. A landmark still standing is the Odd Fellows Hall on B Street, built in 1868.

The Hayward fire department possesses a very interesting old hand-drawn, hand-pumped fire engine used in Hayward during the 1870's. It was in San Francisco as early as 1854 and was used in fighting fire at Stockton in the 1860's.

Several large old ranch homes still stand in the Hayward area. Outstanding among these is the beautiful Victorian mansion of William Meek at Hampton and Boston roads in San Lorenzo. Meek was one of California's pioneer orchardists. He came West prior to the gold rush, bringing to Oregon, on one trip, a wagonload of grafted trees. There, with Henderson and John Lewelling, he entered the nursery business, which they later moved to Alameda County. By 1866 he had clear title to 2,010 acres, most of which had originally belonged to the Soto portion of Rancho San Lorenzo. Much of this he planted to almond, cherry, and plum orchards. Meek was generous with his time and talent in public service. He was a member of the first board of trustees of Mills College and served four terms as an Alameda County supervisor. His home, surrounded by magnificent trees and gardens, was built in the late 1860's. Destruction of the estate was threatened in 1963, when it was sold to a subdivider for an apartment project. Efforts of citizens and groups, including the Hayward Area Historical Society, however, led to its purchase by the Hayward Area Recreational District for development as a park and museum. The old mansion and grounds will soon be once again one of the showplaces of the East Bay.

Another old home built about the same time is the former residence of Cornelius Mohr, still owned by the family, at 24985 Hesperian Boulevard in Mount Eden. Here, as at the Meek home, the old carriage house also stands. Most of the Mohr ranch is now the campus of Chabot College. The California State College at Hayward, east of Mission Boulevard, is built on what was once the ranch of Timm Hauschildt. Beyond lived Ahapius Honcharenko, Ukrainian patriot and Orthodox priest, from the 1870's until his death in 1916. He published the *Alaska Herald-Svoboda,* a bilingual newspaper, and translated the Constitution of the United States for the Russian-speaking people of Alaska. "Ukraina," the Honcharenko estate, is still a privately owned ranch.

In 1866 Josiah Grover Brickell gave the land for the first public school in Castro Valley (*SRL 776*). The site is now Redwood School, on Redwood Road between James and Alma avenues.

Rancho Arroyo de la Alameda

Rancho Arroyo de la Alameda, taking its name from the stream that flows for many miles through the open plains that drain to the bay, was granted to José de Jesús Vallejo on August 8, 1842. It consisted of 17,705 acres of fertile valley land. Don José, one of 13 children of Ignacio Vallejo, a Spanish soldier of Alta California, was an elder brother of General Mariano G. Vallejo. He himself was active in military and governmental affairs from 1818 to 1847; among other offices he was *comisionado* and administrator at Mission San José from 1836 to 1840 and military commander at the Pueblo de San José from 1841 to 1842. In 1850 he was appointed postmaster at Mission San José, where his mansion stood just west of the highway and opposite the mission.

Affairs on the rancho were left primarily in the hands of overseers, and an expensive flour mill, erected about 1850, became the most famous asset of the estate.

Where the tree-lined Alameda issues from Niles Canyon and passes into the plain that slopes away to the bay, the old settlement of Vallejo Mills, now known as Niles, grew up in the 1850's. Historic landmarks still may be found in the neighborhood. Stone foundations of a second flour mill (*SRL 46*), erected here by Vallejo in 1856, remain in a Fremont city park at the northeast corner of Mission Boulevard and Niles Canyon Road. A mile up the canyon the stone aqueduct, which he built to conduct water to the mill, still parallels the road for some distance. The site of one of the several adobes built by Vallejo for his overseers is located at the entrance of the canyon.

Perhaps the most picturesque reminder of adobe days in this vicinity is the little building in the gardens of the California Nursery Company northwest of Niles off Niles Boulevard. The California Nursery, founded in 1865, has played an important part in the development of the fruit industry and home beautification in California. This adobe, the first of the Vallejo adobes built in the vicinity, has been restored as a guest house.

The town of Niles, now part of the city of Fremont, was named in 1869 for Judge Addison C. Niles, an executive of the Central Pacific Railroad. Here, for several years ending in 1916, was located one of the first motion picture studios in the West. The Essanay Company ("S" for Spoor, "A" for Anderson) had been founded in Chicago by George K. Spoor and Gilbert M. "Broncho Billy" Anderson. The latter decided to move his base of operations to California and selected Niles as a suitable location. He made the first pictures at Niles in a barn, still standing at the rear of 37467 Second Street, but soon built a block long, story-and-a-half studio at Niles Boulevard and G Street. It has been razed, but the site is marked. Anderson starred himself in "Westerns," frequently using rugged Niles Canyon as a setting. Other actors who pioneered at Niles included Charles Chaplin, Ben Turpin, and Wallace Beery. Here Chaplin made his great film *The Tramp*. Some of the cottages built by the company along Second Street behind the main studio are still standing and occupied.

On Rancho Ex-Mission San José, adjoining the Vallejo grant, a building containing one adobe wall, of solid pounded earth, stood until the 1960's. It was located on the southwest side of Fremont Boulevard, a short distance southeast of Mowry Avenue. The early history of this building is uncertain, but in the American period the area was the ranch of Joshua Chadbourne, who came to California from Maine in 1853. The site has been developed as a shopping center, but the picturesque Victorian carriage house of the Chadbournes has been retained in a small park by the City of Fremont.

The site of the old Washington College, founded in 1871, is on the hill at the northeast corner of Washington Boulevard and Driscoll Road in

José de Jesús Vallejo Adobe, Niles

Irvington (formerly Washington Corners). It was established as a nonsectarian institution by certain pioneers interested in education, including E. L. Beard, Henry Curtner, and the Rev. W. F. B. Lynch, who intended making it a school of science and industrial arts. The Rev. S. S. Harmon, a pioneer missionary, was principal of the school until 1880, when he established a school of his own in Berkeley. In 1883 Washington College was taken over by the Christian Church, and after 1894 it ceased to exist as a college, although a private school was located there for a number of years, last known as the Anderson Military Academy. A 22-room house, built about 1889, remains on the property, surrounded by many of the old trees. It now serves as the private residence of Mr. and Mrs. C. F. Giles. Washington College was typical of the many rural colleges of early California.

Rancho Santa Rita

Rancho Santa Rita once skirted the western edge of the broad Livermore Valley and adjoined Rancho El Valle de San José to the east. It was granted to José Dolores Pacheco on April 10, 1839, and included more than 8,800 acres of excellent grazing land. Pacheco was often mentioned in the local annals of San José, where he held a number of public offices during the years 1838 to 1843 and again in 1846. He died in 1852.

Samuel and J. West Martin purchased about 5,000 acres of Rancho Santa Rita in 1854; there were enough cattle included in the sale to provide the purchase money.

The little adobe (*SRL 510*) which still stands beneath a giant oak tree at what is now the Meadow Lark Dairy was built about 1844 or 1845, possibly by Francisco Solano Alviso, who came to Rancho Santa Rita as mayordomo in 1844. The adobe is three and three-tenths miles south of Dublin on the east side of the old hill road from Dublin to Suñol.

Oakland

Oakland is known both as a city of homes and as a great manufacturing center of the West. Its site was an untended area on the San Antonio rancho of the Peraltas until after the gold rush to California in 1848–49.

Three men who separately had sailed around the Horn were responsible for the beginnings of

Francisco Solano Alviso Adobe,
near Pleasanton

the town, which was incorporated as Oakland in 1852, and changed its status from town to city two years later. These men were Edson Adams, Andrew Moon, and Horace W. Carpentier, an attorney, who after service in the California Militia was known as General Carpentier.

After a short time in the goldfields, the three determined to settle and lay out a town on the eastern shore of San Francisco Bay. There, on May 16, 1850, they landed at what is now the foot of Broadway in Oakland and built a cabin on Vicente Peralta's property. Later, after Peralta threatened to eject them, they each leased 160 acres from him. A line through the center of Carpentier's area passed through what is now Broadway. On either side of him the other two men staked out similar tracts, Adams to the east and Moon to the west. It was long before titles to the property were cleared.

Julius Kellersberger was employed to lay out the town for these three owners. The plat included the area now bounded by First, 14th, Market, and Fallon streets. Wide streets were planned, and the widest, 110 feet, was called Main Street, later Broadway. Sponsored by Carpentier, who had been made a member of the state legislature, a bill was approved by that body in 1852 to incorporate the town of Oakland.

Because adequate shipping facilities were necessary at once, the trustees of the town granted to Carpentier the right to all the waterfront of the town, where he was to build three wharves. Oakland Harbor now has over 27 miles of deepwater frontage and about five miles of channel dredged to a depth of 30 feet in the estuary.

Lake Merritt, containing 160 acres of water, is unique in that it is a wild-fowl sanctuary in the middle of a large city. It was named in honor of Samuel B. Merritt, a graduate of the medical department of Bowdoin College, who died in 1890. Dr. Merritt served as councilman and was chosen mayor in 1868. He furthered many projects favorable to the development of the young city. Merritt Hospital was founded by his fortune.

San Antonio Slough used to spread over a large region at the head of the San Antonio Estuary. Into it flowed salt tides from San Francisco Bay as well as several creeks carrying the fresh-water drainage from the outlying foothills of the Coast Range. Dr. Merritt was instrumental in having

a dam built to impound these waters—the first step in the formation of Lake Merritt as it is today, a salt-water lake with a broad causeway and a movable floodgate. His report as mayor in 1869 includes these words: "A dam has been constructed near the Oakland bridge at a cost of at least $20,000, converting the arm of San Antonio Creek north of the bridge into a beautiful lake." Lake Merritt was set aside by the state in 1869 as a wild-fowl refuge and is the oldest one in the United States. In 1909 the City of Oakland completed acquisition of the entire lake frontage and began to develop Lakeside Park. Organized feeding of birds began in 1915, and in 1926 banding of ducks was inaugurated. The Lake Merritt Refuge has been registered as a National Historic Landmark by the Department of the Interior.

The original city of Oakland lay on the west side of San Antonio Slough. Several men had settled there before the arrival of Adams, Moon, and Carpentier in May 1850. The first, in the winter of 1849, was Moses Chase. He was followed by the Patten brothers, Robert, William, and Edward, in February 1850. These four men turned their attention to the east side of the slough and leased land there from Antonio Peralta. They laid out the town of Clinton on a tract of 480 acres in 1853, and in the same year a bridge was built across the slough to connect Clinton with Oakland. The area included in Clinton lay, approximately, between Eighth and 24th streets and Lake Merritt and 14th Avenue, which was then a small creek. On the other side of this creek the town of San Antonio was surveyed on a tract of 200 acres in 1854. A flurry of excitement over a small gold discovery passed through the San Antonio region in 1856; hundreds of claims were staked out, but not enough gold was found to warrant continued enthusiasm.

By 1856 Clinton and San Antonio constituted a single town called Brooklyn. In 1870 Brooklyn was incorporated and two years later it was annexed to the city of Oakland. For some time it had been under consideration as a possible county seat to replace San Leandro, where the courthouse had been devastated by earthquake in 1868. In 1873 the people of Alameda County voted to move the seat of government to Oakland, and the site chosen was in what had been Brooklyn. The old wooden courthouse still stands at 1952 East 14th Street, and behind it, at 1417 20th Avenue, is the building, partly of brick, that housed the hall of records and the jail. Clinton Square, San Antonio Park, and Brooklyn Avenue in East Oakland commemorate these early towns. The home of Moses Chase stood until July 1948 at 404 East Eighth Street.

In 1874 it was decided to move the county offices to a downtown location. When Julius Kellersberger mapped the town in 1853, he had set aside two squares, Washington and Franklin, for a civic center. They were used instead as parks until the City of Oakland gave them to the County of Alameda for the new county buildings. The courthouse was opened in 1875 on Washington Square (bounded by Broadway, Fourth, Fifth, and Washington streets), and the hall of records about a year later on Franklin Square (bounded by Broadway, Fourth, Fifth, and Franklin streets). The old courthouse stood until 1950 and the hall of records until 1964. The county buildings are now located near Lake Merritt.

On November 8, 1869, the first train to arrive in Oakland over the newly completed transcontinental railroad pulled up to the station on Seventh Street. A salute of 37 guns was fired and a grand celebration was held at which notables addressed the enthusiastic citizens. The old depot, now remodeled, still stands at 464 Seventh Street between Broadway and Washington Street. Actually, Oakland had been preceded by Alameda as the western terminal about two months earlier. While construction of the line continued, a temporary connection had been made with the San Francisco, Alameda, San Leandro and Haywards Railroad (opened in 1865), and the first transcontinental train arrived in Alameda on September 6, 1869. The terminal (SRL 440), where festivities took place on that day, was located at the wharf at the foot of Pacific Avenue in Alameda, now the site of the turning basin of the U.S. Naval Air Station, about two-thirds of a mile west of the junction of Pacific Avenue and Main Street.

St. Mary's Catholic Church, at Eighth and Jefferson streets, was established as a mission in 1853 and a parish in 1858. The foundations of the present building were laid in 1868 and it was dedicated in 1872. The wooden structure has undergone much remodeling through the years, including a partial brick facing. St. James' Episcopal Church (SRL 694), at 12th Avenue and Foothill Boulevard, was founded in 1858. The structure built the following year still stands next to the present church and is now used as a social hall.

The former Galindo Hotel, built in 1877 and named for one of California's first families, stands at the southwest corner of Eighth and Franklin streets in an area that has been called "the outstanding concentration of commercial Victorian structures in the West." Downtown Oakland is to undergo a major redevelopment program within a few years, and there are plans to renovate and retain this historic section.

A number of interesting old homes are still to be seen in Oakland. The gabled house of J. Mora Moss, built in 1864, stands in Mosswood Park at Broadway and MacArthur Boulevard. The 24-room home of James deFremery, a native of Holland, was erected in 1868 and is preserved in DeFremery Park at 18th and Adeline streets. The home of John and James Treadwell, owners of the Tesla coal mine in eastern Alameda County, stands on the campus of the California College of Arts and Crafts at 5212 Broadway. The former residence of George C. Pardee is located at 672 11th Street. Pardee was a physician, mayor of Oakland from 1893 to 1895, and governor of California from 1903 to 1907. The house was built by his father in 1868. The Oakland Public Museum, at 1426 Lakeside Drive, was built in the mid-1870's as the home of William Camron, who married Alice Marsh, the daughter of Dr. John Marsh, famed pioneer of Contra Costa County. It was

later owned by Josiah Stanford. Oakland is currently building a four-block, $7 million museum complex nearby, but it is to be hoped that this beautiful old home will always be preserved as a landmark. The new museum is scheduled to open in March 1968.

Of the later homes, one of the most interesting is the Southern Colonial mansion of Alex Dunsmuir, east of the MacArthur Freeway and south of Knowland State Park, near the San Leandro boundary. Built in the late 1890's, it is now a conference center for the City of Oakland. Perhaps the most distinguished former citizen of Oakland is Earl Warren, Chief Justice of the United States Supreme Court. He was deputy city attorney in 1919–20, deputy district attorney of Alameda County in 1920–25, and district attorney from 1925 to 1939. Thereupon he became attorney general of California, a post he held until 1943, when he became governor. He was chief executive of the state until 1953, when he received his present appointment. Warren's home in Oakland, which he still uses as his permanent address, is at 88 Vernon Street, now owned by the Roman Catholic Diocese of Oakland.

The large and famous Claremont Hotel, where the cities of Oakland and Berkeley meet, was begun in 1906–7, but construction was interrupted several times. It was finally opened in 1915. The picturesque half-timbered Key Route Inn stood at Broadway and 22d Street from about 1906 until 1932. The man behind the Key System, originally known as the San Francisco, Oakland and San Jose Railroad, was the borax magnate Francis M. "Borax" Smith. The Key System has now been superseded by the Alameda–Contra Costa Transit.

The Oakland Free Library was established in 1878, with Ina Coolbrith, later California's poet laureate, as the first librarian. Other literary celebrities have lived in Oakland. Francis Bret Harte arrived in California on the Brother Jonathan in 1854 and came across the bay on the ferryboat Clinton. He had come with his sister Margaret to live with their stepfather, Colonel Andrew Williams, who in 1857 became the fourth mayor of Oakland. In the stories "The Devotion of Henriquez" and "Chu-chu" later written by Harte, he refers to Oakland as "Encinal." The home in which Harte lived at Fifth and Clay streets no longer stands, but several other old houses on Fifth Street between Jefferson and Clay have been organized into a distinctive shopping center and named in his honor the "Bret Harte Boardwalk." This interesting example of historical preservation was opened in September 1962.

John and Flora London lived at several different addresses in Oakland, as well as in Alameda and other places in the Bay Area. Their famous son Jack London, born in San Francisco, received most of his education in Oakland and much of his encouragement and literary guidance from Ina Coolbrith, the Oakland librarian. In 1893, upon his return to Oakland from his first ocean voyage, Jack London entered the prize-winning manuscript, "The Typhoon off the Coast of Japan," in the contest managed by the San Francisco Morning Call. He lived with his first wife, whom he married in 1900, at 1130 East 15th Street, and the following year they moved to a house of the Italian-villa type, the former home of the sculptor Felix Peano, at First Avenue and East 12th Street on the shore of Lake Merritt. Scenes from the windows of this house, which looked toward the bridge at Eighth Street, are described in his *Martin Eden*. While he wrote *The Call of the Wild* he was living with his family in a bungalow between Oakland and Scenic avenues in Piedmont. The most familiar Oakland landmark associated with Jack London is the old First and Last Chance Saloon at 50 Webster Street, where he spent many hours. Nearby, the foot of Broadway has been developed as Jack London Square, an area of fine restaurants.

The Hights, situated on the wooded hills overlooking San Francisco Bay and the Golden Gate, is above Dimond Canyon on Joaquin Miller Road. This was the estate of Joaquin Miller (Cincinnatus Heine Miller), "Poet of the Sierra," and is now a public park belonging to the City of Oakland. Miller spent many years of his life on this estate. He wrote most of his poems in the quaint building he called "The Abbey" *(SRL 107)*. Here, too, are several unique stone monuments erected by his hands, among them the "Sanctuary to Memory," the "Funeral Pyre," the "Tower to Robert Browning," and the "Tower to General John C. Frémont." This last monument was placed on the spot where Frémont, who named the Golden Gate, is said to have stood when he first saw the San Francisco Bay opening out into the Pacific. Joaquin Miller's first book of poetry, *Songs of the Sierras,* was published in 1871. His home has been registered as a National Historic Landmark by the Department of the Interior.

In June 1888 Robert Louis Stevenson returned to California with his family after eight years' absence. He had come to prepare for the trip to the South Seas, of which he had dreamed since boyhood and toward which Charles Warren Stoddard, his California author friend, had so greatly influenced him. Dr. Samuel Merritt's schooner yacht *Casco,* chartered by Stevenson, was anchored in the Oakland Estuary, about 100 yards north of the Webster Street bridge, and Stevenson spent several weeks there fitting her out. Part of that time he berthed aboard the trim little vessel which was to carry him on his romantic voyage to the islands of the Pacific.

The poet Edwin Markham called Oakland home from 1892 to 1899. After his most famous poem, "The Man with the Hoe," was published in 1899, he and his wife and son moved to New York.

Dr. Cyrus Mills and his wife conducted the Benicia Seminary in Benicia from 1865 to 1871. Then they moved to what is now East Oakland, where they hoped to make their school the Mount Holyoke of the Pacific. To Mills Seminary, Seminary Avenue and the Seminary district owe their names. In 1885 the name of the school was changed to Mills College. It is now the leading girls' college west of the Mississippi and holds high rank throughout the country.

St. Mary's College, founded in San Francisco in 1863, moved to Oakland in 1889. The large building at Broadway and Hawthorne Avenue became affectionately known as "the old brickpile." It no longer stands, but the site *(SRL 676)* has been marked by a small tablet on the structure at 3093 Broadway. In 1928 the college moved from Oakland to its present campus at Moraga.

The University of California

The University of California, now one of the largest and best equipped universities in the world, was established by the state legislature in 1868. Its forerunner, the College of California, began in 1853 in Oakland as the Contra Costa Academy. It had been founded by the Rev. Henry Durant, a Yale graduate, and the Rev. Samuel H. Willey, and was sponsored by the Association of Congregational and Presbyterian Churches, organized by missionaries sent to California by the American Home Missionary Society. The first location was at the corner of Broadway and Fifth Street, but eventually it settled on the four blocks bounded by 12th, 14th, Franklin, and Harrison streets. Many stores and office buildings now occupy the old campus *(SRL 45)*.

In 1855 the academy was incorporated as a college, and in 1860 instruction on the college level was offered. A site in Berkeley was purchased, to which it was planned to move the college. In 1867 the trustees offered to donate the Berkeley campus and other assets to the state if the state would establish a university there, with a college of letters as a nucleus for other departments. The offer was accepted, and the University of California was chartered on March 23, 1868. It became thus not merely a mechanical and agricultural school, as had been strongly advocated, but a real university formed around a liberal arts college. The old buildings on the campus in Oakland were used until 1873, when the first new buildings were completed on the Berkeley campus. One of these first structures, South Hall, still stands, a picturesque red brick building at the rear of Wheeler Hall near Sather Gate.

At the La Loma entrance to the Berkeley campus is the historic Founders' Rock. Standing on this rock on April 6, 1860, the founders of the University of California (then trustees of the College of California) dedicated it forever to learning. On Charter Day in 1896, the Class of 1896 marked it with a marble tablet.

The Hearst Memorial Mining Building, a granite structure near the La Loma entrance to the campus, was built by Mrs. Phoebe Apperson Hearst in 1907 in memory of her husband, Senator George Hearst, who came to California as a miner in 1850. George Hearst was one of the most celebrated miners throughout the West. He had mining interests not only in California but also in Nevada, Colorado, Utah, and Idaho. Among other important projects, he developed the famous Comstock Lode in Nevada. In 1886 he became United States Senator. After his death in 1891 his wife distributed his wealth among various philanthropies, making especially large gifts to the University of California.

The Le Conte Oak stands among other large live oaks at the western side of the university campus and is dedicated to the memory of John and Joseph Le Conte, the two brothers who did so much for higher education and scientific learning in California. The tree is marked with a bronze tablet.

Sather Tower was erected in 1914 in honor of Peder Sather, a prominent San Francisco banker, philanthropist, and trustee of the College of California, by his widow. Sather gave much money toward the establishing and building of the university. Sather Tower is a beautiful campanile with a carillon which is played three times daily and on special occasions. It is a landmark in the bay region, being visible for miles in all directions.

The Bancroft Library, one of the most valuable collections of books and materials on the history of California, is located in the library annex, built in 1949 on the site of old North Hall, one of the original buildings of 1873. The nucleus of the collection is the personal library of the great historian Hubert Howe Bancroft.

The University of California has been the scene of some of the most notable discoveries in the field of atomic physics and chemistry. Here Ernest O. Lawrence invented the cyclotron. In Room 307 of Gilman Hall, on the night of February 23–24, 1941, the man-made element plutonium was first identified by Professors Joseph W. Kennedy, Glenn T. Seaborg, and Arthur C. Wahl. No. 94 on the periodic table, plutonium is used in nuclear reactors and in atomic explosives. The small laboratory where this history-making discovery took place has been registered as a National Historic Landmark by the Department of the Interior.

Berkeley

Dr. Samuel H. Willey came in 1849 as one of the first four commissioned Protestant missionaries to California. He became a leader in pioneer religious and educational work and was one of the founders of the College of California in Oakland and also of Berkeley, the college town. The old Willey house, located on Dwight Way east of College Avenue, was built in 1865, the first town house in Berkeley. In this house the name of Berkeley was first discussed as being appropriate for the new college town. Bishop George Berkeley, renowned English philosopher and seer of the westward march of civilization, was the author of the poem including the line "Westward the course of empire takes its way," which prompted the use of his name for this new educational center of the West. In the home of Dr. Willey also was formed the first city government of Berkeley. The city thus owes its existence to the College of California, and the prime promoters of the University were also the builders of the town. The site of the old Willey house is now occupied by an apartment house, "The Bishop Berkeley," at 2709 Dwight Way.

SOURCES

Abeloe, William N. St. Leander's 1864–1964. St. Leander's Church, San Leandro, 1964.

Adams, Edson F. Oakland's Early History. Tribune Publishing Co., Oakland, 1932.

Akers, Toma Elizabeth. "Mexican Ranchos in the Vicinity of Mission San José." Master's thesis in history, University of California, Berkeley, 1931.

Bancroft, Hubert Howe. "California," of the series History of the Pacific States of North America. Vols. 18–24. The History Co., San Francisco, 1884–90.

Bolton, Herbert Eugene. Fray Juan Crespi, Missionary Explorer on the Pacific Coast, 1769–1774. University of California Press, Berkeley, 1927.

——, ed. Font's Complete Diary, A Chronicle of the Founding of San Francisco. Translation from the original Spanish manuscript. University of California Press, Berkeley, 1933.

—— Historical Memoirs of New California by Fray Francisco Palou, O.F.M. University of California Press, Berkeley, 1926.

Bowman, J. N. "The Early Peraltas of Rancho San Antonio." Ms., 1932.

—— "The Sites of the Peralta Dwellings on Rancho San Antonio." Ms., 1932.

—— "New Haven and the Two Alvarados," California Historical Society Quarterly, XII, No. 2 (1933), 173–75.

—— "The Peraltas and Their Houses," California Historical Society Quarterly, XXX, No. 3 (September 1951), 217–31.

—— and G. W. Hendry. "Spanish and Mexican Houses in the Nine Bay Counties." Ms., Bancroft Library, University of California, Berkeley; State Library, Sacramento, 1942.

Bunnell, Lafayette Houghton. Discovery of the Yosemite. Fleming H. Revell, Chicago, 1880.

The California Missions, a Pictorial History. By the editorial staff of Sunset Books. Lane Book Co., Menlo Park, 1964.

Conmy, Peter Thomas. The Beginnings of Oakland, California, A.U.C. Oakland Public Library, Oakland, 1961.

Cummings, G. A., and E. S. Pladwell. Oakland, a History. Grant D. Miller, Oakland, 1942.

Davis, William Heath. Seventy-five Years in California, ed. Douglas S. Watson. John Howell, San Francisco, 1929.

De Nier, Flora Loretta. "Robert Livermore and the Development of Livermore Valley to 1860." Master's thesis in history, University of California, Berkeley, 1926.

De Vere, Daisy Williamson. The Story of Rancho San Antonio. Privately published, Oakland, 1924.

Elder, David Paul. The Old Spanish Missions of California. Paul Elder & Co., San Francisco, 1913.

Engelhardt, Charles Anthony (Zephyrin). The Missions and Missionaries of California. 4 vols. San Francisco, 1908–15.

Farquhar, Francis P., ed. Up and Down California in 1860–1864, The Journal of William H. Brewer. University of California Press, Berkeley, 1949.

Faulkner, William B. Faulkner's Handbook and Directory of Murray Township, Alameda County. Livermore, 1886.

Ferrier, William Warren. Origin and Development of the University of California. Sather Gate Book Shop, Berkeley, 1930.

—— The Story of the Naming of Berkeley. Pamphlet in the Berkeley City Library.

Gillogly, Mrs. Lydia L. "Report" (on the Lincoln Park Shell Mound) in Alameda Times-Star, February 11, 1935.

Halley, William. The Centennial Year Book of Alameda County, California. William Halley, Oakland, 1876.

Historical Atlas of Alameda County, California. Thompson & West, Oakland, 1878.

History of Washington Township, Alameda County. Compiled and published by the Country Club, the Woman's Club of Washington Township. 3d ed. 1965.

Jones, William Carey. History of the University of California, 1868–1895. Frank H. Dukesmith, San Francisco, 1895.

Kroeber, A. L. "California Place Names of Indian Origin," University of California Publications in American Archaeology and Ethnology, XII, No. 2 (1916–17).

Langsdorff, G. H. von. Narrative of the Rezanoff Voyage. T. C. Russell, San Francisco, 1927.

Loud, L. L. "The Stege Mounds at Richmond, California," University of California Publications in American Archaeology and Ethnology, XVII, No. 6 (1924).

Luciw, Wasyl, and Theodore Luciw. Ahapius Honcharenko, "Alaska Man." Slavia Library, Toronto, 1963.

McCarthy, Francis Florence. The History of Mission San José, California, 1797–1835, ed. Raymund F. Wood. Academy Library Guild, Fresno, 1958.

McGinty, Ruth Mary. "Spanish and Mexican Ranchos in the San Francisco Bay Region: San Antonio, San Pablo, and San Leandro." Master's thesis in history, University of California, Berkeley, 1920.

Morrish, K. B. "Our Urbanized Wildfowl," *Westways*, XLV, No. 6 (June 1953), 6–7.

Nelson, N. C. "Shellmounds of the San Francisco Bay Region," *University of California Publications in American Archaeology and Ethnology*, VII, No. 4 (1909).

Older, Mrs. Fremont. *California Missions and Their Romances*. Coward-McCann, New York, 1938.

Peterson, Martin S. *Joaquin Miller: Literary Frontiersman*. Stanford University Press, Stanford, 1937.

Rider, Fremont, ed. *Rider's California; a Guide Book for Travelers*. Macmillan, New York, 1925.

Sanchez, Nellie Van de Grift. *Spanish and Indian Place Names of California*. A. M. Robertson, San Francisco, 1922.

Sandoval, John S. Articles in *Hayward Daily Review*, 1964.

Schenk, William Egbert. "The Emeryville Shellmound," *University of California Publications in American Archaeology and Ethnology*, XXIII, No. 3 (1926).

Stuart, Reginald R. *San Leandro, a History*. First Methodist Church, San Leandro, 1951.

——— and Grace D. Stuart. *Corridor Country. An Interpretive History of the Amador-Livermore Valley, the Spanish-Mexican Period*. Amador-Livermore Valley Historical Society, Livermore, 1966.

Sullivan, Maurice S. *The Travels of Jedediah Strong Smith, a Documentary Outline Including the Journal of the Great American Pathfinder*. The Fine Arts Press, Santa Ana, 1934.

Tays, George, ed. *Historical Sites and Landmarks of Alameda County, California*. Published under auspices of W.P.A. Alameda County Library, Oakland, 1938.

Uhle, Max. "The Emeryville Shellmound," *University of California Publications in American Archaeology and Ethnology*, VII, No. 1 (1907).

Ware, E. B. *History of the Disciples of Christ in California*. F. W. Cooke, Healdsburg, 1916.

Willey, Samuel Hopkins. *A History of the College of California*. Samuel Carson & Co., San Francisco, 1887.

Wood, Harry O., Maxwell W. Allen, and N. H. Heck. *Destructive and Near Destructive Earthquakes in California and Western Nevada, 1769–1933*. Coast and Geodetic Survey, Special Publication No. 191. U.S. Printing Office, Washington, D.C., 1934.

Wood, M. W. *History of Alameda County*. Pacific Press, Oakland, 1883.

Alpine County

ALPINE COUNTY (named for its similarity to the alpine country in Europe) was created March 16, 1864, from parts of El Dorado, Calaveras, Tuolumne, Mono, and Amador counties. The county seat was at first located at Silver Mountain but was transferred to Markleeville in 1875. Until 1863 Alpine County was thought to be a part of Nevada, to which it is more closely united geographically. Even today most of its social and economic ties are with Nevada.

Frémont's Crossing of the Sierra

Among the few government explorers who came to the Pacific Coast before the Mexican War was John C. Frémont. In his company were French trappers familiar with the Western trails, but Kit

Carson, almost as famous as his noted leader, was the chief guide.

Fired by a desire to see Klamath Lake, Mary's Lake, and the fabled Buenaventura River, Frémont left Oregon for St. Louis in November 1843. Following a circuitous route through Oregon and western Nevada, he finally reached the Carson River. By this time supplies had become greatly depleted, and with his horses and mules in no condition to negotiate the rough Rockies Frémont made the bold decision to find a pass through the Sierra into California.

Perhaps no part of the entire journey was more difficult than that through the rugged region that is now Alpine County. The trail necessarily followed along the ridges, where the wind had cleared away a little of the snow and sometimes exposed grass and brush on which the half-starved animals could feed. Because of the difficulty of beating a path through the deep snows, the party had to make camp every few miles. On February 2 or 3 a halt was made at a spot one and one-half miles northeast of Markleeville, near the confluence of Markleeville Creek and the East Fork of the Carson River, and, on the following night, camp was made near Grover's Hot Springs, five miles farther west.

On February 6, Frémont had his first view of the great Sacramento Valley lying in the dim distance far below him. From the top of a high peak Kit Carson, who had gone to California with Ewing Young 15 years before, recognized the low mountains of the Coast Range 100 miles to the west. "Spots of prairie," as well as "a dark line which . . . was imagined to be the course of the river," were vaguely distinguishable in the "snow-less valley."

Again, on the 14th, in company with Charles Preuss, Frémont climbed to the summit of another peak, generally assumed to have been Stevens Peak, although Red Mountain may have been the peak in question. From this height Frémont beheld a great sheet of crystal-clear water which his first map designated merely as the Mountain Lake, but which he later named Lake Bonpland, after Aimé Jacques Alexandre Bonpland (1773–1859), noted French botanist and companion of Baron von Humboldt. Early maps (1853–62) designated it as Lake Bigler. Millions know it today as Lake Tahoe.

At last on February 20 they reached the summit of what was later known as Kit Carson Pass, at an elevation of about 8,600 feet. Here on the 21st Frémont and his companions looked out across the magnificent panorama of snowy ridges and towering peaks interspersed with deep canyons, and far in the distance they beheld "a shining line of water directing its course towards another, a broader and larger sheet." These water courses Frémont believed to be "the Sacramento and the Bay of San Francisco." Crossing the divide between West Carson Canyon and the American River, Kit Carson led the way through the pass that now bears his name.

At the summit a bronze memorial plate (SRL 315) commemorates this heroic passage of the Sierra, giving special honor to the brave scout who led the way. Placed by the Native Sons of the Golden West, August 7, 1921, it bears the inscription:

"On this spot, which marks the summit of the Kit Carson Pass, stood what was known as the Kit Carson Tree on which the famous scout, Kit Carson, inscribed his name in 1844 when he guided the then Captain John C. Frémont, head of a government exploring expedition, over the Sierra Nevada....Above is a replica of the original inscription cut from the tree...and now in Sutter's Fort, Sacramento."

The label on the stump in the museum states that the pine tree on which the name was carved was felled and this portion cut out on September 5, 1888, and sent to the California State Mining Bureau, which later sent it to Sutter's Fort Historical Museum.

Thus was the first passage of the Sierra in midwinter accomplished, a feat then considered almost impossible. Later, the Kit Carson Emigrant Trail went by way of the Kit Carson Pass, and became one of the most popular routes followed by early pioneers. Today thousands of vacationists and lovers of historic and romantic places follow a modern highway over the old trail. On this Highway 88, three miles west of Carson Pass, a monument has been erected at the point where the old emigrant road of 1848 (SRL 661) swung down across a meadow now covered by Caples Lake (Twin Lakes).

Just a quarter of a mile east of the summit of Carson Pass are some large rocks on which a party of pioneers in 1849 inscribed their names and the emblem of the Independent Order of Odd Fellows. Some of the names are still legible. In 1941 the Grand Lodge of California, I.O.O.F., placed a plaque nearby and dedicated the spot as a memorial to the pioneer Odd Fellows (SRL 378).

"Snow-Shoe" Thompson

For 20 years — from 1856 to 1876 — John A. Thompson (Thomson), known as "Snow-Shoe" Thompson, braved the winter storms of the High Sierra to deliver the United States mail to early pioneers, in the days before railways. "Penetrating the mountains to isolated camps, rescuing the lost, and giving succor to those in need along the way," he was truly a "pioneer hero of the Sierra." On one occasion he rescued from certain death James Sisson, who had lain for 12 days in a deserted cabin in Lake Valley. When Sisson was found, both his feet were frozen and he had been four days without fire, his only food being a little flour. Thompson traveled all night through deep snow in order to bring aid from Genoa, Nevada. When the rescue was at last accomplished, it was found necessary to amputate Sisson's feet, and Thompson went all the way to Sacramento and back in order to obtain the anesthetic for the operation.

"Snow-Shoe" Thompson was a "man of splendid physique. . . . Within his breast lived and burned the spirit of the old Vikings. It was this inherited spirit of his daring ancestors that impelled him to embark on difficult and dangerous enterprises." Yet he was never reckless, and it was his knowledge of the mountains, as well as his assurance and strength, that enabled him successfully to defy the wild storms of the Sierra winters.

Early in January 1856, while still on his ranch at Putah Creek, Thompson read in the papers of the difficulties experienced in getting the mails across the summit of the Sierra Nevada in winter. He made himself a pair of "snow skates," or skis, such as he had used in Norway when a boy, and began the arduous and heroic work that he carried on for 20 years. His first trip was made in January 1856, from Placerville to Carson Valley, Nevada, a distance of 90 miles over the old emigrant road on which Placerville was the principal town. Not only was Thompson "the father of all the race of snowshoers in the Sierra Nevada," but he was also the forerunner of the stagecoach and the locomotive across the High Sierra. No matter how wild the mountain storms, he never failed to come through, usually on time.

During that entire period of 20 years Thompson lived in Diamond Valley on a ranch located at the head of Carson Valley, just across the line in California. This was near Woodfords, and Thompson was taken from that point to the deep snow line by sleigh or saddle horse. He had two general routes. One went from Woodfords to Placerville, following approximately the course of the present state highway along the West Carson River to a point near the mouth of Horse Thief Canyon, four and one-half miles from Woodfords. There, he bore directly west in the direction of Thompson Peak. The other route was from Woodfords to Murphys, by way of Indian Valley and sometimes by way of the Border

Ruffian Pass and Blue Lakes. On a few occasions he took the trail through Ebbetts Pass, stopping at Silver Mountain. These three routes to Murphys converged in Hermit Valley.

"Snow-Shoe" Thompson died at his ranch on May 15, 1876, and lies buried at Genoa, Nevada. A pair of skis are carved on his marble tombstone. A monument was placed near the site of his home in Diamond Valley by E Clampus Vitus, a social organization of historians, in 1956.

Alpine Highways

The entire surface of Alpine County is elevated and rugged and the view is grandly picturesque on every side. The western summit of the Sierra Nevada constitutes the western boundary of the county, which covers the eastern slope of the range as well as the outlying peak known as Silver Mountain. A road, said to have been the first surveyed route over the High Sierra, was constructed as early as 1857, from Hermit Valley to Hope Valley by way of Twin Lakes Pass. Hope Valley was named by members of the Mormon Battalion on their return to Salt Lake City in the summer of 1848. The emigrant trail through Ebbetts Pass (SRL 318) to Angels Camp was opened up in the early 1850's, but no road went that way until 1864, when, as a result of the opening up of the Comstock Lode in Nevada, a toll road was completed under the name of the Carson Valley and Big Tree Road. It was over this trail, in September 1861, that a little group of Bactrian camels from the Gobi Desert, Mongolia, was driven from San Francisco to Nevada, where they were used for transportation purposes in the mines.

Four branches of the present state highway system cross Alpine County, following, at least in part, the general course of old roads: one from Lake Tahoe by way of Meyers, Luther Pass, Hope Valley, and Carson Canyon; a second from Jackson over the Kit Carson Pass via Silver Lake; a third over the Big Tree or Ebbetts Pass Road from Angels Camp through Hermit and Pacific valleys; and the fourth, and most recent (1954), from the Ebbetts Pass Road southeast of Markleeville, through the site of the old town of Monitor, and thence, by new construction, over Monitor Pass to Highway 395. Over these scenic highways, historic in their many associations with the past, hundreds of vacationists each year find their way into the recreation grounds of Alpine County.

Alpine Ghost Cities

Silver Mountain, founded as Köngsberg (Konigsberg) in 1858 by Scandinavian miners, existed until 1886. The county seat was located there from 1864 to 1875. A ghost of Alpine's once thriving silver camps, its existence is marked today only by the crumbling walls of the old stone jail, the first in the county, near the site of the old courthouse. Silver Mountain is located on the Ebbetts Pass Road a few miles southwest of its junction with the Monitor Pass Road—a junction that was once the location of the town of Mt. Bullion or Bulliona. En route to the jail ruins at Silver Mountain a tall brick chimney is passed. This was part of the ore reduction plant of "Lord" Chalmers, an Englishman who came to Alpine County in 1867. Here, on Silver Creek, also stands his home, called the Chalmers Mansion. This picturesque frame house still contains some of the elegant furnishings of the past.

Of Silver King, located on the headwaters of the East Carson River west of Highway 395, only a little wreckage of old buildings remains to mark the site. Diamond Hill on the Ebbetts Pass state highway, and Mogul, four miles north of Monitor, are only lingering memories, little evidence aside from mining scars remaining to indicate the sites where they once stood. Monitor, flourishing from 1858 to 1886 and entirely deserted by 1893, showed some return to activity (under the name of Loope) from 1898 to 1911, when it was again deserted until 1930, at which time there was a brief revival of mining during the depression.

Although silver predominates in the Alpine region, in large low-grade ledges gold is encountered in nearly every mineralized district. "Uncle Billy Rogers' " Copper Mine, situated in Hope Valley in the northwest angle of the county, is said to have been the first deposit (1855) of this ore ever opened in California or anywhere on the Pacific Coast, a considerable development here antedating the Comstock discovery by several years.

Woodfords

In 1847 Sam Brannan, on his way to Salt Lake City, stopped at the present site of Woodfords and left two men to establish an outpost—the first white settlement in this area. The project was abandoned, but other settlers arrived at what had come to be called Brannan Springs. Daniel Woodford, who came in 1849, erected a hotel, the first building of any permanence. About 1851 a man named Cary built a sawmill, and the growing town soon became known as Cary's (Carey's) Mills, a name that yielded officially to Woodfords in 1869. Cary built a house, still standing but now generally called the Wade house, in 1852-53, from lumber milled at his own establishment. During the initial five weeks of its operation in 1860, the Pony Express was routed through Woodfords and maintained a remount station (SRL 805) at Cary's barn, the site of which is across the road from the present Woodfords store.

Markleeville

The tiny town of Markleeville, with fewer than 100 residents, is California's smallest county seat and the seat of its least populous county. The picturesque settlement had its beginning in the cabin of Jacob J. Marklee, who settled there in 1861, only to be shot and killed during a quarrel two years later. On the site of his dwelling (SRL 240) stands Alpine County's beautiful little courthouse, built of native stone in 1928.

By 1864 Markleeville had a population of over 2,500, but in 1875, when it succeeded Silver Mountain as the county seat, the entire county could boast only a few more than 1,200. Such was the effect of the decline of silver mining. Al-

Chalmers Mansion and Chimney, Silver Creek

though a fire about 1886 destroyed much of Mark-leeville, it still displays a few interesting old buildings. The tall Alpine Hotel was originally built in Silver Mountain as the Fisk Hotel and was moved to its present location in 1885. On a side street stands the old wooden jail, still displaying the iron cells moved to it in 1875 from the stone jail whose ruins can yet be seen at Silver Mountain. On a hill above Markleeville the old Webster School remains as another relic of a more prosperous past. It was built in 1882 by volunteer labor and was used until 1929.

SOURCES

Alpine Heritage. Souvenir booklet prepared by the Centennial Book Committee, Alpine County, 1964.

Cleland, Robert Glass. *Pathfinders,* of the series *California,* ed. John Russell McCarthy. Powell Publishing Co., Los Angeles, 1929.

Coy, Owen Cochran. *The Great Trek,* of the series *Cali-*

Former Jail, Markleeville

fornia, ed. John Russell McCarthy. Powell Publishing Co., Los Angeles, 1929.

"Crossing the Sierras," *Hutchings' Illustrated California Magazine,* I, No. 8 (February 1857), 349–52.

Dellenbaugh, Frederick S. *Frémont and '49.* Putnam, New York and London, 1914.

Farquhar, Francis P., "Frémont in the Sierra Nevada," *Sierra Club Bulletin,* XV, No. 1 (February 1930), 74–95.

Frémont, John C. *The Exploring Expedition to the Rocky Mountains, Oregon and California.* George H. Derby & Co., Buffalo, 1849.

Frémont, Brevet Captain J. C. *Report of the Exploring Expedition to the Rocky Mountains in the Year 1842 and to Oregon and North California in the Years 1843–44.* Washington, D.C., 1845.

James, George Wharton. *Heroes of California.* Little, Brown, Boston, 1910.

Quille, Dan de (William Wright). "Snow-Shoe Thompson," *Overland Monthly,* VIII, No. 46 (October 1886), 419–35.

Tyler, Sergeant Daniel. *A Concise History of the Mormon Battalion in the Mexican War, 1846–1847.* Privately published, Salt Lake City, 1881.

White, Chester Lee. "Surmounting the Sierras, the Campaign for a Wagon Road," *Quarterly of the California Historical Society,* VII, No. 1 (March 1928), 3–19.

Old Webster School, Markleeville

Amador County

AMADOR COUNTY (named in honor of José María Amador, who was a miner in that region in 1848, and was previously mayordomo of Mission San José) was created in 1854 and Jackson was made the county seat. Amador County is in the center of the Mother Lode district in the Sierra Nevada. Its southern border is the Mokelumne River, while on the north is the Cosumnes River, both linked inseparably with the "days of '49."

Kit Carson Emigrant Trail

One branch of the old emigrant trail went through Jackson, its general direction being that of a later stage road to Virginia City, Nevada, and that of the present Highway 88. On this trail, near the El Dorado–Amador county line, the Tragedy Springs massacre occurred on June 27, 1848, while members of the Mormon Battalion were returning to Utah. Three scouts of the party were killed at the springs by Indians. An account of the tragedy and the names of the scouts were carved on a tree at the spot. The tree has been removed, but the carved section is preserved in the museum at Sutter's Fort. The site was marked by the Native Sons of the Golden West on their Landmarking Pilgrimage in 1921.

Near Tragedy Springs, a monument indicates where the emigrant road *(SRL 662)* crosses the present Highway 88. Less than two miles west of this point, beside the highway, is the "Maiden's Grave" *(SRL 28)*, the last resting place of one of many emigrants who did not have the stamina to complete the long trek.

Kirkwood's log stage station and inn *(SRL 40)*, built in 1864 by Zack Kirkwood, still stands on Highway 88, eight miles northeast of Tragedy Springs. As sturdy as the day it was built, the place serves as a bar and restaurant. The old fireplace is one of its interesting features. When Alpine County was formed from Amador County, the division left the barn and milk house belonging to the Kirkwoods in Alpine, while the Alpine–El Dorado–Amador line went directly through the barroom of the inn. The post office, known as Roundtop from the mountain nearby, was also housed in the log cabin. The addition to the original cabin was made about 1880.

Gold Bars of the Mokelumne

Possibly the first gold found in Amador County was discovered somewhere along the Mokelumne River, in the spring of 1848, by Captain Charles M. Weber, founder of the city of Stockton. During the summer of the same year, within two months' time, a company of eight men, headed by James P. Martin, took out several thousand dollars' worth of gold each. In the autumn Colonel J. D. Stevenson came to the river with a mining expedition composed of about one hundred of his own men recently mustered out of the army. Perhaps the first code of mining laws to be drawn up in California was made by the Colonel for the benefit of his men while encamped along the Mokelumne River bars.

Thousands of eager miners from all over the world flocked to the gulches and rivers of the Sierra in 1849, and during the first years of the 1850's they continued to swarm up and down the rivers, building small cities overnight at all of the rich river bars. Within the two decades that followed, an almost unbelievable change took place. A historian writing in 1881 described the transformation even then evident to one walking along the banks of the Mokelumne River. Hardly could one realize, he said, "that the stillness, broken only by the murmur of the water, was ever otherwise." Today, scarcely a fragment remains of the numerous cabins where "the miner fried his flapjacks or dried his wet clothing after a day's toil under a broiling sun in the ice-cold water."

Of all the camps along the Mokelumne, the tide of trade and gold flowed most abundantly at Big Bar *(SRL 41)*. One of the old inns, Gardella's, still stands, at the Amador end of the bridge where the present highway from Jackson to Mokelumne Hill crosses the river. On the Calaveras side of the river was Kelton's inn. After the placers on the bars had been depleted, the center of trade moved across the river to the top of Mokelumne Hill, where the town of that name is still located. But the rushing river and the rugged canyon still recall vividly that lively era when hordes of miners thronged the alluring reaches of Big Bar.

A ferry, known as the Whale Boat Ferry, was established at Big Bar in 1850. It was superseded, in 1852 or 1853, by a toll bridge, which was swept away by the flood of 1862. Subsequently rebuilt, the bridge at this point has been

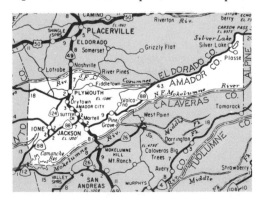

Gardella's, Big Bar

free for years, being on the state highway and maintained by the state.

In the 1920's there was a brief lode mining revival at Middle Bar (*SRL 36*), two miles below Big Bar. The old homesteads, however, were soon purchased by the East Bay Municipal Utility District which built the Pardee Dam across the Mokelumne River six miles below Middle Bar. This district was formed when 11 bay cities joined forces to secure water and power, and selected the Mokelumne River as the source of the purest and best water. Ex-Governor George Pardee was president of the company when the dam was completed in 1930. This region, where hundreds of busy miners with pans or cradles once washed the gold from the river, is now covered with water. The old lode mines included the Big Tunnel or Mammoth, the Hardenburg, the Marlette, and the St. Julian or Caminetti, successors of the earlier placers and all big producers in the past.

Below Middle Bar were James and French bars, once teeming with life and activity. Miners of 1849 and 1850 often took out several thousand dollars a day at these places. The flimsy dwellings of canvas or boards where they lived for a brief time, as well as the beautiful orchards and vineyards cultivated by the industrious citizens of French Bar, have vanished.

Lancha Plana

Farther down the river, in the southwestern part of the county, many mining camps centered about Lancha Plana, among them being Poverty Bar (Calaveras County), Winter's Bar, Oregon Bar, and Put's Bar. This area is now inundated by the Camanche Reservoir of the East Bay Municipal Utility District. Lancha Plana ("flatboat"), just across the river from the exceedingly rich gravels of Poverty Bar, came into existence as the mooring place for the flatboat ferry, which carried miners from the north side of the river across to Poverty Bar and the mines of Calaveras County. Lancha Plana (*SRL 30*) reached the height of its prosperity after 1856, when hill and bluff mining were bringing greater returns than mining in the river ever had brought. It became a place of carousing and merrymaking, where such desperadoes as the notorious Sam Brown frequently appeared.

Camp Opry, at the base of the hills not far from Lancha Plana, was a lively place in 1857, outdoing its neighbor in crime; for while Lancha Plana had many substantial citizens to hold its wilder element in check, Camp Opry was especially marked as the resort of desperadoes of various nationalities. The notorious bandit Joaquín Murieta is said to have been a frequent visitor. It is also said that the graveyard nearby was filled mostly with the victims of whiskey.

As a result of the copper excitement in the early 1860's the ephemeral mining camps of Copper Center and Townerville (or "Hotel de Twelve") arose in the vicinity of Camp Opry.

The Boston House, a combination store and inn, stood about four miles north of Lancha Plana on an old stage road to Jackson. A heap of stones marks the site today, but the road is still used as a shortcut from Ione to Pardee Dam.

Buena Vista ("beautiful view") was the name applied to a settlement about six miles north of Lancha Plana, as well as to a mountain and a valley in the vicinity. The valley, located where Jackson Creek leaves the mountains, was mainly agricultural, but some mining was carried on in the surrounding hills. The old store at the intersection of the Pardee-Ione Road and the Jackson Valley Road still serves the public well in its "new" location. It was originally built in Lancha Plana by William Cook. When the miners moved away to richer fields, the Chinese came to scavenge through the tailings. The only virgin territory was under Cook's store. The owner wanted to move his business to thriving Buena Vista, and the Chinese wanted to mine the old site. So a bargain was struck. The Chinese were to move the building in exchange for the untouched claim beneath it. Thereupon, an army of Chinese spent several weeks taking down the building stone by stone and rebuilding it six miles away. There at the crossroads it has been standing for over a century.

Butte City

The Ginocchio Store (*SRL 39*), on Highway 49 about one and one-half miles south of Jackson, is all that remains of what was once Butte City, a thriving mining camp in the Mother Lode country in the 1850's. As early as 1854 Xavier Benoist had a store and bakery in this building. For a time Butte City, located at the south side of Butte Basin, a section rich in auriferous deposits, rivaled Jackson. Today the spot is typical of the many ghost towns that are reminiscent of California's early mining activity: a roofless stone house standing mutely beside the highway in the midst of open fields where once a thousand miners' cabins stood; on the hill a lonely graveyard where forgotten miners lie buried. Above, Butte Peak, a high, conical mountain visible for many miles in all directions, stands sentinel.

Drytown

At Drytown (*SRL 31*), a mining camp on Dry Creek nine miles north of Jackson, mining for gold was first begun in the spring of 1848. It was not unusual, in 1849, in the surrounding gulches to wash as much as $100 in gold from a single pan. The names of these gulches—Blood Gulch,

Murderer's Gulch, Rattlesnake Gulch—indicate that, although there were no doubt plenty of steady, industrious miners at Drytown, there were also desperate characters who left their mark. The town prospered until 1857, when fire swept the place. It never recovered from this disaster, for gold was already becoming worked out there. Several old buildings still stand in Drytown, including an old stone and brick store still in use, and the Town Hall now the home of a little-theater group.

Lower Ranchería

Mining at Lower Ranchería, two miles east of Drytown, began in 1848. A mixed population, in which Mexicans and Chileans predominated, gathered there to the number of five or six hundred. Sombreros, serapes, knives, horses, and jingling spurs were strikingly in evidence at all gatherings. On the night of August 6, 1855, a series of robberies and murders were perpetrated by a gang of 12 desperate Mexican horsemen. As a result of this tragedy, the miners arose en masse and demanded that every Mexican be disarmed and driven from the region. Calmer counsels prevailed, but not until much injustice had been done.

Only the scars of early mining activities indicate the presence of this once busy camp, where once "the very ground seemed accursed for the crimes it had witnessed." To reach Lower Ranchería, turn off Highway 49 at the end of the main street of Amador City. After traveling half a mile, turn left on a road by a stone wall, and proceed one mile through the hills to the ford of Ranchería Creek. On a hill to the right, about one-quarter of a mile from the road, a monument marks the mass grave of the Diman family killed in the massacre.

Volcano

Volcano (SRL 29) is located at the bottom of a deep cup in the mountains, hence its name. In the early mining days it claimed a population of 5,000 people, and was famous for its "many saloons, dance halls, and churches." Such is the tradition that persists to this day.

Volcano's population has dwindled considerably since the 1850's, and its isolation, together with the weirdness of the gray rocks washed out by the miners of long ago, make it a veritable "Sleepy Hollow" of the West. Almost one looks for goblins among the ghost rocks, or for a headless horseman to come galloping down the steep wooded mountain road.

This was a very rich hydraulic mining district in early days, a million dollars in gold having been taken out of one mine alone, which was worked for over 30 years. Some gold is still found in the region, but activity of another sort is more evident, since many summer homes are being built in the surrounding hills.

The visitor of today may see the following historic places in Volcano: the stone brewery, built in 1856; the Lavezzo building; the old St. George Hotel building; the Masonic Temple, a two-story, stone building with a balcony, still in use; and others. Down to 1856 drinking water came from the spring in a rock on which the Masonic Hall was built. In this hall there are tintypes and

St. George Hotel, Volcano

daguerreotypes of pioneer members of the order, some of whom later became noted in the state. The old hostelry, which boasts three stories with broad balconies, is one of the most picturesque landmarks of the southern mining towns. On display near the Masonic Hall is "Old Abe," the cannon used by the Volcano Blues, a regiment of crack sharpshooters who saved California gold for the Union and thereby helped to win the Civil War for the North.

Volcano is about 12 miles northeast of Jackson, and about three miles from Pine Grove, to the north of Highway 88. Not far from Volcano, to the north and east, are the sites of other mining towns, among them Russell's Hill, Fort John, Aqueduct City, Plattsburg, Contreras, Upper Ranchería, Ashland, Grizzly Hill, Whiskey Slide, Spanish Gulch, Hunt's Gulch, and Wheeler Springs. Fort John in 1850 rivaled Volcano in importance, the first church and school in Amador County having been established there this early.

Other landmarks near Volcano include a huge Indian community mortar rock (now a State Monument), about halfway between Pine Grove and Volcano, and the site of the earliest known amateur astronomical observatory in California (SRL 715), built in 1860, on Shake Ridge Road four miles north of Volcano.

Cosumnes Mining Camps

In the northern part of Amador County numerous mining camps were once located on the Cosumnes River and its branches, the entire region being the setting for many scenes of mining life. Some of these camps have long since vanished, only scarred hills and an occasional chimney marking the spots where miners once toiled or where their crude cabins stood. Other camps remain today as mountain hamlets, while a few are marked only by an aging, historic building.

The richest location in the district was situated on the river bar at the main forks of the Cosumnes, and was called by the Indian name Yeomet. Several stores and a somewhat pretentious hotel were standing there in 1853, but the miners gradually took over the town, one building after another giving way to the diggings, until nothing was left except the old toll bridge. Another bar along the river on the Amador County side was Cape Cod Bar.

On the stage road to Sacramento, four or five miles south of Yeomet, was Plymouth, whose history is largely bound up with the quartz lodes of the region. The town was kept busy into the 1940's by the Plymouth Consolidated Mines. Between these two camps was Enterprise, also a quartz center. On the south side of Plymouth's main street, between the bank and the old Roos Building, is a brick structure (SRL 470) built in 1857 and at one time used as the office and commissary of the consolidated mining company. At the southwest end of the flat on which Plymouth is located was the hamlet of Pokerville, or Puckerville, at the site of which a unique building remains. Its side walls are of local fieldstone, but the front and back are of brick, which is also

Building at the Site of Pokerville, in Plymouth

used around the corners in a series of zigzag steps. A brick front was a status symbol among the early settlers.

A few miles east of Plymouth is the picturesque settlement of Fiddletown (SRL 35), immortalized in Bret Harte's story "An Episode of Fiddletown." It was first settled in 1849 by a party of Missourians. "They are always fiddling," said an old Missouri patriarch; "call it Fiddletown." And Fiddletown it was until 1878, when the name was changed to Oleta. The change was made by the state legislature, at the instance, it is said, of Judge Purinton, a prominent citizen who on frequent business trips to Sacramento and San Francisco had been greatly embarrassed at being known as "the man from Fiddletown." Through the efforts of the Committee on Historic Landmarks of the California Historical Society, the old name of Fiddletown was restored in 1932. One of the old-time buildings still to be seen in the town is the well-preserved Purinton home. The several brick structures remaining were built of brick fired locally. The present Community Hall was built in 1870 as the Schallhorne Blacksmith and Wagon Shop. A Chinese rammed-earth house is of particular interest.

In the 1850's and early 1860's Fiddletown was the trading center for a number of rich mining camps—American Flat and American Hill, French Flat, Loafer Flat, Lone Hill, and others. The entire region, including the ridge between Suckertown (now Bridgeport) and Slate Creek, forms a part of extensive ancient river deposits.

Central House, a popular stage station which stood on the road between Plymouth and Drytown at the present junction of Highways 16 and 49, was built of timbers brought around the Horn. Another much-frequented hostelry on this route was at Willow Springs, a few miles west of Drytown on the way to Sacramento. Forest Home, Arkansas Creek, and Yankee Hill were neighboring camps farther west. A beautiful old stone inn built in the late 1850's stood at Forest Home for many years, but now even the palm trees that once guarded it have disappeared.

The region about Fiddletown and Plymouth is now a prosperous dry-farming community, growing grapes, walnuts, pears, and various farm products. Shenandoah Valley, north of Plymouth, has been a rich farming section since the early

1850's, and descendants of pioneer settlers still occupy many of the old homesteads. The D'Agostini Winery (SRL 762), eight miles northeast of Plymouth, was founded in 1856. Its old stone cellar is still in use.

Sutter Creek

Sutter Creek (SRL 322) was named after John A. Sutter, the first white man to come to that region in 1846, and the first to mine the locality in 1848. There was little activity at Sutter Creek until 1851, when quartz gold was discovered. Quartz mining was a very hazardous occupation in the early days. The art of timbering the shafts and tunnels was not understood and many cave-ins resulted. The capital outlay, too, was so great and the profits were so uncertain that many men were ruined financially by the venture. Alvinza Hayward stands preeminent as the man who emerged victorious. Buying out several mines, ultimately, in the face of great odds, he made them produce millions. The Central Eureka, discovered in 1869, and at one time part of the Hayward holdings, continued production even after most of the mines were closed down by World War II. The shaft reached almost the 5,000-foot level and the mine produced about $17 million in gold. The Old Eureka Mine, once owned by Hetty Green, the peculiar old financial wizard, was first opened in 1852. It is located at the foot of the great sweeping curve of the highway going north into Sutter Creek.

In the late 1850's Leland Stanford, later governor of California and founder of Stanford University, financed the Lincoln Mine, between Sutter Creek and Amador City, for Robert Downs, maintaining a controlling interest in it during the years from 1859 to 1872. The returns proved so rich that Stanford, then a Sacramento businessman and merchant, was greatly aided in the building of the Central Pacific Railroad.

Sutter Creek is still a thriving town, with several deep, though inactive, quartz mines nearby. Among buildings of historic interest are the Masonic Hall and the Alvinza Hayward Office Building. Educational and religious activities thrived here from the beginning, making it distinctive as a moral center in the midst of the wilder mining camps of the region. The Methodist church, dating from 1863, is still in use.

Amador City

Amador City, located on Amador Creek three miles north of Sutter Creek, where it intercepts the Mother Lode ledge, had its beginning as a mining center in 1848. But the placers were never very rich, and, like Sutter Creek, the history of Amador City has been connected chiefly with quartz mining. The first quartz discovery in Amador County was made there in February 1851 by Davidson, a Baptist preacher. Since three other ministers were associated with him, the mine was called the "Ministers' Claim." A little later the vein was discovered on the north side of the creek, and became known as the "Original Amador Mine."

The Keystone Mine at Amador was the result of the consolidation of the Original Amador with the Spring Hill, Granite State, and Walnut Hill mines in 1857. But the enterprise was not a success until the discovery of the Bonanza in 1869, when the first month's crushing paid $40,000. This high production continued until well into the 1880's. The Keystone has been closed down since early in this century, but there are those who believe that millions of dollars in gold still lie hidden within the earth thereabouts and that Amador City may yet renew its old-time activity. A beautiful brick building, the office and residence of former superintendents, still stands in good repair and is used as a distinctive motel with period furnishings.

Jackson

Jackson, county seat of Amador County, is rich in old buildings reminiscent of the mining days of the 1850's. Built largely of stone, with massive doors, iron-shuttered windows, and balconied upper stories, they speak eloquently of the days of Indians and robbers and gold.

The presence of these old iron-barred stores lingers like a memory along the narrow winding street. The fact that the population is a mixture of Italian, Serbian, Slavonian, and Mexican, with descendants of pioneer Americans, gives the place an Old World atmosphere with echoes from the "days of '49." Most of the stone and brick buildings on Main and Court streets were constructed immediately after a disastrous fire that destroyed the town in 1862. The Independent Order of Odd Fellows Hall, of red brick, is one of the tallest three-story buildings ever built. The Wells Fargo office was located here. The A. C. Brown house, now the County Museum, was built of brick in the early 1860's. The entire block, including wrought-iron fences, a Victorian carriage house, and the two-story residence itself, is maintained in excellent condition. Located at 113–115 Main Street is the Pioneer Hall (SRL 34), where the Native Daughters of the Golden West were organized in 1886. Jackson's most picturesque building is the little white Serbian Orthodox Church of St. Sava, which stands at the end of town. It was built as late, however, as the mid-1890's. The Louisiana House or National Hotel, much altered through the years, has now been restored. The New York Ranch near Jackson, the site of the Hangman's Tree on the main street of the town, and other historic sites and landmarks complete the association of the present with the past.

Jackson was named by early miners in honor of Colonel Jackson, an energetic leader of the town during the first few years of its history. The location had previously been known as Botilleas Spring (Bottle Spring) because of the large piles of bottles that had collected there as early as 1848, travelers being accustomed to stop and camp on the road from Sacramento to the Mokelumne River mines.

The diggings in the immediate vicinity of the town were not rich, but, being the logical center for a large mining area and a convenient stopping place on the road from Sacramento to the southern mines, Jackson grew and prospered in the early 1850's. The richest location in the neighborhood was below the forks of Jackson Creek, where a few prospectors took out as much as $500 a day.

The flats and gulches in the vicinity of Tunnel Hill, one and a half miles south of Jackson, at Scottsville, were also good producers, as was the hill itself. A number of tunnels sunk into its sides gave rise to the name. This tremendously rich deposit was worked to bedrock, but the scarred hills are now grass grown and serve as pasturelands.

At Jackson Gate (SRL 118), one mile north of town, was another rich gravel digging. A deep, narrow fissure in the rocks through which the creek flows gave the place its name. There is an old store here, Chichizola's since 1850. Ohio Hill and Squaw Gulch nearby were also very rich producers. During a winter's work at the former place, the operators of one mine took out from forty to fifty thousand dollars, while Madame Pantaloons, a woman dressed as a man and doing a man's work, accumulated a hundred thousand dollars and then sold her claim for twenty thousand more.

Quartz mining continued to bring prosperity to Jackson after other forms of mining had ceased to be remunerative. Several deep quartz veins in the hills above the town were worked until World War II. The famous Argonaut and Kennedy mines (SRL 786), among the deepest in the world, are located here. The Argonaut, discovered in the early 1850's, experienced many failures as well as successes, but operated continuously from 1893 to 1942 and reached a vertical depth of 5,570 feet. Here, in August 1922, 47 miners lost their lives, trapped by fire in the mine in the lower levels. The total production of this mine has been estimated at over $25 million. The Argonaut can be located many miles away by its lofty water tower.

Across Highway 49 from the Argonaut is the Kennedy, opened prior to 1870. It, too, had its ups and downs, vast sums being expended with little returns. Later, however, it became a record producer, yielding a total estimated $45 million in gold. In this century modern equipment was installed, including a second hoist at the 4,600-foot level of its vertical shaft, which reached an ultimate depth of 5,912 feet before mining was stopped. A half-mile east of the Kennedy Mine are several huge tailing wheels, used to raise the tailings, or mill waste, to the summit of a small hill, beyond which lay the disposal dump. Although built only in 1902, these wheels are among the most photographed landmarks in the Mother Lode country. They are now included in a county park reached from North Main Street.

The Oneida, one and a half miles northeast of Jackson, was located in 1851 by a party of men from the central part of New York. The history of the mine has shown from the first an erratic production record.

North and east of Jackson, remnants of several smaller mining camps may still be found among the hills. Clinton (SRL 37), eight miles east of Jackson, with its historic Catholic church built

in 1877 and still in good repair though unattended, is now surrounded by small ranches. A number of miners were attracted to the vicinity in the 1850's after water had been brought in by means of canals, but the diggings were never rich. It was a center for quartz mining as late as the 1880's.

On the Clinton Road, five miles east of Jackson, Slabtown exists only as a site. Formerly a rich mining area, it is now a prosperous agricultural community known as Milligan District. The first citizens of Slabtown were too poor to build anything better than shacks of rough slabs with the bark left on, but later the place became very prosperous and a number of brick and stone structures were erected. Not a stick or stone of the old town remains today.

Irishtown (SRL 38), seven miles northeast of Jackson at the junction of Highway 88 and the Clinton Road, has also vanished, and the story of its lively citizens is almost forgotten. The first white settlers on this spot found it a "city of wigwams," and hundreds of mortars in the rocks still testify that this was a favorite Indian camping ground. Two miles beyond is Pine Grove, once a mining center but now rapidly building up with summer cabins scattered among the pine woods. One of the early houses in Pine Grove still stands.

Ione Valley

Ione was variously known in the gold days as "Bed Bug" and "Freeze Out." But the place grew, and the more euphonious name of Ione, for a heroine of Bulwer Lytton's *The Last Days of Pompeii*, replaced the old ones.

The Methodist Episcopal church was first organized in 1853. The town was so prosperous that a larger building was planned, and in 1862 Bishop Matthew Simpson laid the cornerstone for a striking brick structure of Gothic architecture (SRL 506), which was completed in 1866 and dedicated by Bishop Calvin Kingsley. Among the old business buildings lining the streets of Ione, the D. Stewart Co. Store (SRL 788), a brick structure constructed in 1856, is noteworthy. Ione's expectations of becoming a great city were never fulfilled, but it is still a busy shopping center with a population of about 1,500. An excellent grade of potter's clay is shipped from this point, and here, also, is located the Preston School of Industry, established in 1889.

Muletown, about two miles north of Ione, was a lively camp in the 1850's, and many stories are told of the strikes in its rich foothill ravines: an Argentinean washed out $100 a day there; a Chinese, picking up a piece of gold weighing 36 ounces, was so elated that he immediately left for his homeland. After the ravines had been worked out, the surrounding hills were attacked by hydraulic power and outdid the ravines in treasure produced. Some claims paid as high as $1,000 a week per man. During its palmy days Muletown claimed several hundred inhabitants, a large proportion being Irish. The pranks and adventures of these jolly citizens of Muletown would fill a book. Most of them owned horses, and, according to one account, being neither skillful nor graceful riders, a Muletown crowd, riding out in search of fun on a Sunday afternoon, could be distinguished miles away "by the flopping limbs and furious riding." Muletown and its gay riders are no more.

The Q Ranch, about two miles northwest of Ione along Highway 104, was taken up in 1850 by several men, one of whom had been a member of Company Q of the Ohio Volunteers in the Mexican War. Being on the main highway from Jackson to Sacramento, the place became a famous hostelry in the 1850's and 1860's. Since it was the starting point for the mountain stages, the drivers always aimed to reach it at mealtime. It never became a town, but accumulated quite a colony of buildings, including hotel, stables, post office, blacksmith shop, and store. Adjoining the Q Ranch was "Doschville," located near the clay pits. The Alabama House, five miles northwest of Ione, was famous for its fine food in the early days. The house is gone and the site unmarked.

Irish Hill, situated on the north side of Dry Creek where the stream leaves the canyon, was a rich mixture of ancient river and beach deposits. Within seven months' time, four men washed out $9,000 each. As late as the 1880's, Stanford and Company and Alvinza Hayward mined this region by hydraulic process. Nothing remains here today.

The site of Quincy is virtually obliterated, but the fact of its existence has been preserved in a copy of an early newspaper published there. The main thoroughfare, a wide street called Broadway, boasted numbered houses, as well as saloons, stores, several real estate offices, and doctors' and lawyers' offices.

In memory of the many brave and self-sacrificing Wells Fargo messengers and stage drivers, a tablet was placed near Ione on September 8, 1929, which contains a replica of a six-horse stagecoach, with its driver and guard. The tablet contains the following inscription:

"Michael (Mike) Tovey, Wells Fargo messenger, was killed, and Dewitt Clinton Radcliff, stage driver, injured on this spot June 15, 1893, by a lone bandit who attempted to hold up the regular six-horse stage on the old Ione-Jackson stage road.

"A line of stages was established in 1850, running between Sacramento and Sonora via Q Ranch (near Ione), Jackson, Mokelumne Hill, Angels, and Columbia. Over $265,000,000 in gold bullion is said to have been carried in the early days over this, the main artery [from Sacramento] to the 'Mother Lode' and southern mines.

"In memory of these and many other brave, intrepid, self-sacrificing, and loyal Wells Fargo messengers and stage drivers of California, this tablet is dedicated.

"Tablet placed by Historic Landmarks Committee, Native Sons of the Golden West, and Native Sons and Native Daughters of Amador County, September 8, 1929."

SOURCES

Farquhar, Francis P., ed. *Up and Down California, 1860–1864. The Journal of William H. Brewer.* University of California Press, Berkeley, 1949.
Geologic Guidebook along Highway 49 — Sierran Gold Belt, the Mother Lode Country. State of California, Division of Mines, San Francisco, 1948.
Gold Rush Country. Lane Publishing Co., Menlo Park, 1957.
Mason, J. D. *History of Amador County, California.* Thompson and West, Oakland, 1881.
Native Sons of the Golden West. *Landmarks Committee Report, 1920–1929.*
Norboe, Major P. M. "The Maiden's Grave." Ms., dated September 26, 1916, in State Library, Sacramento.
Sargent, Mrs. Elizabeth Ann, ed. *Amador County History,* Amador County Federation of Women's Clubs, Jackson, 1927.
Tyler, Sergeant Daniel. *A Concise History of the Mormon Battalion in the Mexican War, 1846–1847.* Privately published, Salt Lake City, 1881.
Weston, Otheto. *Mother Lode Album.* Stanford University Press, Stanford, 1948.

Butte County

BUTTE COUNTY (named for the Sutter Buttes, the high hills to the south, in Sutter County) is one of the original 27 counties of the state, at first encompassing an area much larger than it does today. The first county seat was at Hamilton, but in 1853 it was moved to Bidwell Bar, and again in 1856 to Oroville.

U-I-No, the Cliff of the Giant

U-I-No, familiarly known today as Bald Rock, in the Grand Gorge of the Middle Fork of Feather River near where Fall River empties into the larger stream, was believed by ancient Indian tribes to be the home of a giant evil spirit. Towering sheer above the seething river for 3,600 feet, utterly devoid of vegetation, its white granite majesty resembles that of El Capitan in Yosemite Valley.

The entire region is one of spectacular beauty and so wild and rugged that the primeval Indians, early white explorers, and prospecting miners either avoided or failed to penetrate it. In 1889, Emery Oliver, later a great railroad engineer, ran a survey through the entire Middle Fork

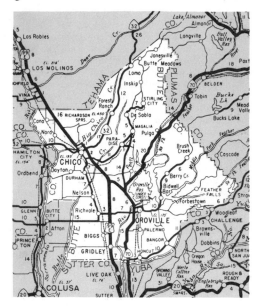

Canyon including that portion now known as Bald Rock Canyon. In 1908, two Geological Survey men also passed through it. There are immense granite boulders, deep caverns, and, above all, the superb beauty of Feather Falls, one of the most imposing of Sierra waterfalls. It is still, however, among the least known areas in California. The falls drop sheer 500 feet, with an additional 200 feet of cascades, and fill the canyon with heavy mist and iridescent lights for half a mile.

Rancho Chico

General John Bidwell came to California in 1841, as one of the leaders of the first overland company of Americans to come to California with the intention of making it their home.

On his arrival, Bidwell was employed for a time by John A. Sutter at Sutter's Fort, but in the late 1840's he bought Rancho Chico from William Dickey and Edward A. Farwell, the original grantees of Rancho Arroyo Chico (November 7, 1844) and of the Farwell Grant (March 29, 1844). On Rancho Chico Bidwell built the brick mansion that is now a State Historic Monument. On his ranch General Bidwell founded the town of Chico in 1860, later donating land for public schools, setting aside a plot of ground for each church organization, and designating a large section for the Northern Branch State Normal School, now the Chico State College, organized in 1887.

General Bidwell was one of the foremost builders of the commonwealth of California, being a member of the senate and serving in the state militia during the Civil War. He was a pioneer agriculturist and horticulturist, and a man interested in humanitarian, educational, and reform movements. He has been called "a prince among California pioneers," and became "closely identified with virtually all the important movements in the development of California." He was also a nominee for United States President on the Prohibition ticket in 1892 and received the largest

number of votes of any one ever nominated by that party.

General Bidwell was friendly to the Indians, treating them firmly and fairly, providing rancheria lands, hiring them to work on his estate, settling disputes, and making available cultural as well as material advantages. He and his wife maintained a school and a church for the use of the Indians.

On the site of the Mechoopda adobe, built for General Bidwell on Rancho Chico (SRL 329) by the Indians in 1852, a marker has been placed by the Pioneer Historical Society and the Native Sons of the Golden West, assisted by the Chico chapter of the D.A.R., in honor of General Bidwell. The marker also commemorates the fact that the Oregon Emigrant Trail passed the place.

Treaty G, one of the 18 unratified treaties of the United States government with the California Indians, was drawn up and signed at Rancho Chico, August 1, 1851. These treaties, made by duly authorized agents of the federal government under the administration of President Fillmore in 1851–52, were pigeonholed in the secret archives of Congress during the California gold fever and were not brought to light until 1905. They covered scattered areas throughout California.

Chico Landing, first known as Bidwell's Landing, where steamers plying the Sacramento River unloaded, was an important place in the 1850's. It was located on nearby Rancho de Farwell, about five miles west of the present city of Chico.

Beginning as early as 1847 and continuing until his death, General Bidwell maintained an experimental orchard near his house. It contained at least one specimen of over 400 varieties of fruit and at the time of his death included 1,800 acres of every species and variety adapted to the locality. He was the father of the raisin industry in that region as well as a pioneer in the manufacture of olive oil. He began wine making in 1864 or 1865, but in 1867 the vineyard was dug up and a wine grape was never again planted on his land. In 1886 Bidwell presented almost 30 acres of land to the state as a forestry experiment station. The gift was neglected by the State Forestry Commission and came under the care of the state university. It is now owned by the city of Chico.

The entire estate of Rancho Chico was remarkable for its splendid trees, both native and exotic. On July 10, 1905, a tract of the most desirable land along Big Chico Creek comprising more than 1,900 acres and including Oak Forest, in which may be found the Hooker Oak, Iron Canyon, and other spots of great beauty, was donated to the city of Chico by Mrs. Annie E. K. Bidwell and was named Bidwell Park. On May 11, 1911, Mrs. Bidwell added 301 acres to this gift. She also donated an area along Lindo Channel to the state of California. This is now held by Butte County as undeveloped park area. Two miles southeast of the city are 240 acres owned by the United States Department of Agriculture and used as a plant introduction garden.

Four miles northeast of downtown Chico, off

Manzanita Avenue, stands the mammoth Hooker Oak (*SRL 313*), the most famous of California's valley oaks (*Quercus lobata*, the largest of all the American oaks). This magnificent tree, partially destroyed during a storm on October 12, 1962, was named in honor of the great English botanist Sir Joseph Hooker, who visited Rancho Chico in 1877. The valley oaks were discovered in 1792 by Spanish naval officers and were often mentioned in the narratives of Vancouver, Frémont, and other early explorers. Of the many fine specimens of this oak, measurements prove the Hooker Oak to be one of the largest. Merritt B. Pratt gave the height (before the tragic storm) as 110 feet and the circumference as 28 feet.

Rancho Esquón

The headquarters of Rancho Esquón, granted to Samuel Neal and John A. Sutter in 1844, was located on Butte Creek seven miles south of Chico. Neal, a native of Pennsylvania, had come to California with Frémont earlier in 1844, and with the latter's permission had remained at Sutter's Fort as a blacksmith. Two years later, in April 1846, Neal entertained Frémont on Rancho Esquón, while the Captain was on his way to Oregon. The next month Neal helped guide Gillespie up the Sacramento Valley in an endeavor to overtake Frémont and to deliver to him certain instructions from the government at Washington.

There were other Mexican grants in Butte County: Rancho Aguas Frías (later known as the Pratt Grant), located south of the site of Durham, given to Salvador Osio in November 1844; Rancho Bosquejo, granted to Peter Lassen on December 26, 1844 (partially in Tehama County); Rancho Llano Seco (later the Parrott Grant), situated north of Rancho Aguas Frías, bestowed upon Sebastian Kayser, October 2, 1845; the Boga-Larkin Grant, occupying the southeastern part of the county, given to Charles William Flugge, February 21, 1844; and the Fernández Grant, located north of the Flugge Grant, given to Dionisio and Máximo Fernández in June 1846.

Hamilton, a Ghost Town

Hamilton was a mining town situated on a bend in the Feather River above Marysville. Its story is characteristic of many ghost towns on the Feather River and in other old mining regions. The first mining was done at this point in the early spring of 1848 by John Bidwell and others. By 1849, mining for gold in the river became active and a town grew up.

Hamilton won over Bidwell Bar in the contest for county seat in 1850, but, as the latter town (25 miles farther up the river) became richer and more prosperous, people left Hamilton, and Bidwell Bar became the county seat in 1853.

There is nothing left of Hamilton today. Part of its site disappeared as the river changed course. The old cemetery, which was the last remnant of Hamilton, has been moved to avoid inundation by an afterbay of the Oroville Dam. Just above Hamilton was a settlement of Chinese miners, who worked in the same red hills that over a

century later were the source of clay for the impervious layer in the construction of Oroville Dam.

The old stage road along the Feather River ran about one and a half miles farther east than the present highway. From Hamilton it continued north to Shasta City and the northern mines. It is said that in the middle 1850's this route had 13 roadhouses and hotels between Marysville and Hamilton.

Bidwell Bar

Bidwell Bar (*SRL 330*) was one of the many flourishing mining camps along the Feather River in the Sierra Nevada in the 1850's. Gold was discovered there by John Bidwell on July 4, 1848. The camp was located on the Middle Fork of the Feather River, 39 miles above the town of Marysville. In 1853 three daily stages ran to Bidwell Bar direct from Marysville.

As the mines at Bidwell Bar became more or less exhausted, the inhabitants moved down the river to Ophir City, later called Oroville, where rich deposits were found. Oroville captured the county seat from Bidwell Bar in 1856.

All that was left of this camp into the 1960's was the famous old suspension bridge with its stone tollhouse, an old stone store, and the "Mother Orange Tree" planted there by Judge Joseph Lewis in 1856. This tree, which still bears fruit, is probably the oldest living orange tree in California. The area was developed as Curry-Bidwell State Park, but now is to be covered by the waters rising behind Oroville Dam, scheduled for completion in 1968.

The suspension bridge (*SRL 314*) was shipped around the Horn from Troy, New York, in 1853, and placed in service in 1856. It was operated as a toll bridge until 1889, when it became a free bridge. This picturesque and historical landmark, together with the tollhouse and the Mother Orange Tree, will be relocated on Kelly Ridge overlooking Oroville Dam.

Up the South Fork of the Feather River from Bidwell Bar were other mining camps. Stringtown, about four miles east, was so called because its buildings were strung out in a narrow, rambling line along the canyon. Its history is brief and phenomenal. Dating from 1849, it had become very populous by 1850. In July 1856 the *Butte Record* published its obituary in the fol-

Old Suspension Bridge, Bidwell Bar

Masonic Hall, Forbestown

lowing words: "The string of Stringtown has been pulled out. It's 'gin' out."

A mile above Stringtown the Union Enterprise Company flumed the river in 1852, naming its camp Enterprise. An old cemetery remained here, but Enterprise, too, will be inundated as a result of Oroville Dam. About six miles beyond was Forbestown, founded in September 1850 by B. F. Forbes. It was a center of mining activities for 30 to 40 years. It was a town of some cultural importance also, with a private academy and a general assembly hall, where lectures were given during the week and where large congregations gathered for services on Sunday. This once bustling camp could be described about 1930 as "a derelict town lost in a mountain cove where a second growth of timber is fast replacing a onetime virgin forest. Heaps of debris and old foundations mark the sites of large buildings that have collapsed or been torn down. Other structures with crumbling roofs and gaping doors are verging on dissolution. The old post office is open to the weather, its grilled window and tier of letter boxes yet intact; only the curious visitor crosses its threshold." Today, however, the only noteworthy landmark remaining is the restored Masonic Hall, built in 1855. Old Forbestown is now reached by a side road, a mile or so north of the present post office and stores which perpetuate the name Forbestown. Near Forbestown is Clipper Mills, an early lumber camp, on the La Porte road.

Oroville, the City of Gold

The first miners came to the site of Oroville on the Feather River in 1849, and in 1850 they formed a mining camp there which they named, at first, Ophir City ("gold city"). By 1856 the town had been renamed Oroville, and its importance had increased so considerably that it was ambitious to be chosen as the county seat. Since Bidwell Bar, then county seat, was waning as a mining center, Oroville received the honor by popular election. The new county seat soon became a trading center for the mining towns in the surrounding hills, along Table Mountain, and up the Feather River.

Immediately east of Oroville were important river mining operations in the 1850's and 1890's. The river was diverted from its course in order that the gravel of the bed might be mined. From Oroville to the junction of the North and Middle forks of Feather River the most extensive activities of this kind in California were carried on, but all evidence of them is now inundated by the Oroville Dam project.

Several miles above Oroville was Long's Bar, founded in 1849 with the establishment of a store there by the Long brothers. The first pan of gold washed out at Long's Bar netted $400. The place became one of the principal settlements of the region during the 1850's. Opposite Long's Bar was Adamsville, where hundreds of miners gathered. At the Cape Claim, in 1855, the fluming of the river is said to have netted $1,000,000 in 60 days. Lynchburg, another thriving camp with rich surface diggings, was located in this vicinity. It was a rival of Oroville in the contest for county seat, putting forth the claim of superior climate. Centerville, or Middletown, was a camp near the site of the Southern Pacific depot in the present city of Oroville. Thompson's Flat, first called Rich Gulch and mined as early as 1848, had so increased in population by 1854 that the town, then called New Philadelphia, was moved to the top of the hill, which still bears the name of Thompson. Morris Ravine, near Thompson's Flat, also saw some of the earliest mining in the county. It was named for an employee of Samuel Neal, who in 1848 guided a party of Oregonians from the Neal Ranch to the Feather River diggings.

Because of all this activity up and down the river, Oroville had become a stage center of some importance by 1856, as is indicated by an article in the *North Californian* for November of that year: "Coaches are rattling through our streets at all hours of the day and night. We have ten, semi-daily, connecting this place with different parts of the world. There are six daily stages to Marysville, three for Spanishtown, one for Shasta, one for Bidwell, one for Forbestown, one for Bangor." Numerous pack animals also traveled up and down the highways and along the narrow trails into the higher mountains where no wagon roads yet led.

On February 26, 1857, the *Gazelle* arrived at Oroville, the first of the river steamers to penetrate that far. The last steamboats arrived there during the flood of 1862.

Beginning in the late 1850's and continuing through the 1880's, hydraulic mining was the chief activity at Oroville and Cherokee and in the surrounding country. Evidences of extensive hydraulic operations may still be seen in the form of canals, ditches, old flumes, and deeply scarred hills.

More recent years saw the development of the gold-dredging industry, which originated at Oroville and from there spread around the world. The great gravel fields about the city give some idea of the extent of the industry, which gleaned many millions in gold from the land. One dredging company offered to move the entire town of Oroville and rebuild it at the company's expense if it might be allowed to dredge beneath the town and remove the great treasure over which the city had been built. Oroville now is in the midst of a rich agricultural region. However, some mining is still carried on in neighboring towns in the hills. With the completion of Oroville Dam on the Feather River, scheduled for 1968, Oroville will become the gateway to one of California's major recreational areas, at the cost, however, of a number of interesting mining-day landmarks and natural scenic beauties. Much material for the construction of the dam has been taken from the tailings that were left by the gold dredges.

Oroville's Chinatown, once said to have housed 10,000 Chinese, was perhaps second only to San Francisco at one time in the number of its Chinese inhabitants. The Chinese Temple (SRL 770), dedicated in the spring of 1863, is now open as a museum, having been restored by Oroville women's clubs. It is located at 1500 Broderick Street. Other historical museums in Oroville are the Pioneer Museum, maintained by a private association, and the Lott House, operated by the city of Oroville.

About two miles east of Oroville, at the corner of Oak Avenue and the old Quincy road, is the site of the discovery of Ishi (SRL 809), last of the Yahi tribe and the last known wild Indian in North America. On August 29, 1911, the emaciated survivor of years of wandering and persecution stumbled into the corral of a slaughterhouse at this location. He was at first lodged in jail but fortunately came into the hands of two University of California anthropologists, T. T. Waterman and Alfred L. Kroeber, who provided a home for him until his death in 1916. Ishi made valuable contributions to our knowledge of Indian language, skills, and history.

Cherokee

The old town of Cherokee is ten miles north of Oroville and two miles west of the Feather River. Diamonds were found in the diggings around Cherokee as early as 1863. Over 300 diamonds, mostly of industrial quality, have been discovered there; at no other place in North America has an equal number been found.

Stone walls and a vault still mark the site of the Cherokee Mining Company office, built in 1873. It is a picturesque remnant of pioneer days.

Camps of the North Feather River Watershed

Scores of mining camps were once located in the hill region north of Oroville. The early locations on the river bars were followed by those on the flats somewhat back from the streams, and finally the ridges and hills were worked. In some instances, the names of these historic camps remain to mark their geographic locations, but often even the name has been forgotten. Throughout the Feather River district the remains of crudely constructed fireplaces, sometimes found in lonely and forgotten places, are almost the only evidence of pioneer habitation.

Among the many bars of the region, Potter's Bar, on the North Fork immediately above its junction with the Middle Fork, was first mined in the spring of 1848. Other bars of 1848, 1849, and the early 1850's were Kanaka, Yankee, Ohio,

Berry Creek, Huff's, Shore's, Lindsay, Bartee's, and Island.

Camps among the dry diggings of the surrounding hills included Big and Little Kimshew, Wild Yankee Ranch, Deadwood, Concow, Blairtown, Chub Gulch, Jordan Hill, Hermitage, Toadtown, and Stone House.

As early as the autumn of 1848 gold-seekers from Oregon began to arrive, the first from outside California. Their presence in the mining regions is evidenced by the names—for example, Oregon City and Oregon Gulch, halfway between Oroville and Cherokee on a side road. An old schoolhouse and cemetery remain at Oregon City (SRL 807). A member of the party that founded this place was Peter H. Burnett, who was to become the first American civil governor of California.

Perhaps the liveliest of these North Feather River camps was Spanishtown, so named because the rich diggings in the vicinity had been discovered in 1855 by a company of Chileans and Mexicans. By 1856 a town had sprung up, 20 miles north of Oroville and one mile from Frenchtown. Nearby, Yankee Hill, the successor of Rich Gulch, "fell heir to what Spanishtown and Frenchtown had to bequeath when they passed on and out."

Still farther north, 25 miles from Oroville, on the West Branch of the North Fork was Dogtown (now Magalia). The name had its origin, so one story goes, in the fact that an old French woman who lived at the place kept a kennel of poodles, hounds, and mastiffs that were known all over the countryside. The name Dogtown was applied

Honey Run Covered Bridge, near Paradise

not only to the town but to the entire ridge as well. Two miles east of the town a nugget was discovered in 1859 which is said to have been the largest gold nugget ever found in Butte County. It was known as the "Dogtown Nugget" and weighed 54 pounds in the rough and 49.5 pounds when melted into a bar. It was valued at $10,690. On the Skyway near Magalia a monument points to the site of the discovery of the Dogtown Nugget *(SRL 771)*.

About five miles southwest of Dogtown was Paradise, while to the west, on Butte Creek, was Helltown, with Whiskey Flat in close proximity. Northeast of Dogtown was Flea Valley, and several miles northwest was Nimshew.

Of all the old communities in this area, only Paradise is today numbered among the major towns of Butte County. It began to grow rapidly after the completion of the Butte County Railroad and became a center of the apple industry. Now its population has swelled primarily because of the great influx of retired people who have discovered that its clear air and wooded hills make it truly a "paradise" for their golden years. A few miles west of Paradise on an old road to Chico the picturesque Honey Run covered bridge crosses Butte Creek. It was built by George Miller in 1894.

Dogtown was only one of a number of mining camps and stage stations on the road from Oroville to Susanville. Twelve miles north of Oroville Manoah Pence and several partners located the Lyon ranch in 1850, opening a store and eating place in a tent. The place grew and became a station of some importance. By 1864 a post office, under the name of Pentz, had been established there, with Pence as postmaster. It was discontinued in 1912.

Seven or eight miles above Dogtown another station was established in 1853 by R. P. Powell, who blazed out and constructed the road to Susanville. Powell's Ranch, with its fine orchards and vineyards, was later known as Powellton, and, being at the junction of the roads from Oroville and Chico to Susanville, became an important stage station.

Exceptionally rich diggings were found in the late 1850's at Lovelock, five miles north of Dogtown, and at Inskip, seven miles above Powellton on the Susanville road. A hotel, dating probably from 1860, stands at Inskip.

Among the stage stations that once existed on the road from Oroville to Quincy were Hart's Mills, Berry Creek, Sinclair Hotel, Brush Creek, Mountain House, Junction House, Peavine, and the Hoad Ranch. Mountain House, 26 miles northeast of Oroville, still stands, but it is not the original building. The old fruit trees are still growing. About three miles farther up the road stood Junction House, the site of which is marked only by the aged apple and cherry trees, some of which are being crowded out by the pines that are growing among them. The site of Peavine, reached in another two miles or so, was occupied by a building of later construction known as the Merrimac Hotel, until it was destroyed by fire

about 1961. Last of the original stations to survive was the Hoad House, near the Plumas County line, which stood into the 1950's. Renovated and repainted, this picturesque landmark served as the Elks Retreat at Camp Wilder. The ranch was noted in the early days not only for its fine fruits but also for its excellent natural hay. Today the gnarled fruit trees and the meadow, with its luxuriant growth of wild flowers and tall grasses, present a lovely rural scene framed in a circle of dark pines. All along the highway, bits of orchard, old-fashioned wells, or portions of the original roadbed appear every mile or more, marking the path followed by the stage coaches in the 1850's and 1860's, and even as late as 1900.

Mushroom Towns

The year 1853 was an era of mushroom towns in Butte County, as elsewhere. Not only in the mining regions was this true, but in the valleys as well, and especially along the rivers. Nearly every one of the towns made enough advance to boast some kind of tavern, a blacksmith shop, and the inevitable saloon. Of those on the rivers, each claimed to be at the head of steamboat navigation on the river on which it was situated, and the usual exorbitant prices of 1849 were asked and paid for lots in their precincts.

Veazie City (named after its promoter) was laid out a short distance east of the Feather River and a few miles from the southern boundary line of the county. On the same side and a few miles farther up the river was Fredonia, and nearly opposite was Yatestown. All have long since vanished. Troy, another once hopeful "metropolis," suffered a like fate, and its site is now a matter of speculation. On the Sacramento River near the mouth of Deer Creek was Benton City, another ephemeral town; even its name has been forgotten by most people.

Bangor and Wyandotte

East and north of Veazie City was Bangor, one of a number of mining camps in that locality. It was settled in 1855 by the Lambert brothers from Bangor, Maine, and with the discovery of the Blue Lead mine it became quite important, consisting of 50 buildings, among them stores, saloons, hotels, and gambling houses. Its rival, Hylandsville, was laid out as a town in 1855, but it never attained the importance of Bangor, its promoter being the only man who ever lived there.

Northwest of Bangor was Wyandotte, named after a company of Wyandotte Indians who mined there in 1850. It reached its greatest prosperity in 1852 and 1853. In 1857 it had "a magnificent brick fireproof hotel, the only one in the county." Bangor and Wyandotte are today centers of the orange and olive industries, and the old mining ditches are being used for irrigation purposes.

Near Wyandotte is the site of the old mining camp of Evansville, first settled in 1850 by a man named Evans. By 1854 most of the place was owned by Elisha Brown. This was "one of the old towns that sprang into existence under the influence of mining, lived and flourished while mining was good, and hobbled off the theatre of life when the diggings played out" in 1870.

SOURCES

Adams, Kramer A. *Covered Bridges of the West.* Howell-North, Berkeley, 1963.

Bidwell, General John. "Echoes of the Past," *Chico Advertiser,* Chico, n.d.

Butte County Historical Society Diggin's. Vols. I–VII. 1957–63.

Commonwealth Club of California. "Indians in California," *The Commonwealth,* II, Part II, No. 23 (June 8, 1926).

Coy, Owen Cochran. *Gold Days,* of the series *California,* ed. John Russell McCarthy. Powell Publishing Co., Los Angeles, 1929.

Frémont, John C. *Memoirs of My Life, Including in the Narrative Five Journeys of Western Exploration.* Belford, Clarke & Co., Chicago, 1887.

Gold Rush Country. Lane Publishing Co., Menlo Park, 1957.

Hunt, Rockwell D., and Nellie Van de Grift Sanchez. *A Short History of California.* Crowell, New York, 1929.

Hutchinson, W. H. *One Man's West.* Hurst and Yount, Chico, 1948.

Huxley, Leonard. *Life and Letters of Sir Joseph Dalton Hooker.* Vol. II. John Murray, London, 1918.

Kroeber, Theodora. *Ishi in Two Worlds.* University of California Press, Berkeley, 1961.

Mansfield, George C. *The Feather River in '49 and the Fifties.* George C. Mansfield, Oroville, 1924.

——— *History of Butte County, California, with Biographical Sketches.* Historic Record Co., Los Angeles, 1918.

McGowan, Joseph A. *History of the Sacramento Valley.* 3 vols. Lewis Historical Publishing Co., New York, 1961.

Pratt, Merritt B. *Shade and Ornamental Trees of California.* California State Board of Forestry, 1922.

Royce, C. C. *John Bidwell, Pioneer, Statesman, Philanthropist.* Privately published, Chico, 1906.

Stephens, Kent. "Oroville Dam Railroad," *The Western Railroader,* XXVII, No. 4 (April 1964), 3–12.

Swartzlow, Ruby Johnson. *Lassen, His Life and Legacy.* Loomis Museum Association, Mineral, 1964.

Wells, Harry Laurenz, and W. L. Chambers. *History of Butte County.* H. L. Wells, San Francisco, 1882.

Calaveras County

CALAVERAS COUNTY derived its name from the river which had been named by Gabriel Moraga on his expedition of 1808. Calaveras (Spanish for "skulls") was one of the original 27 counties. Pleasant Valley, later known as Double Springs, was designated by the legislature as the first county seat on February 18, 1850, and was followed successively by Jackson, Mokelumne Hill, and finally, in 1866, by San Andreas.

Wayside Inns

Along the old Mokelumne Hill road from Stockton by way of Linden, many a wayside inn refreshed the wayfarers of early gold days. Just one-third of a mile east of the San Joaquin-Calaveras county line was the famous Red House, a two-story hostelry, no longer standing. Its stone corral (SRL 263), however, is intact today. Beyond Stone Corral, on the old river road to Jenny Lind, was the Pleasant Valley House, also a two-story building, since destroyed by fire. Halfway between Jenny Lind and Valley Springs on the north side of the main road was the North America House, where the stage horses were changed; this, too, has disappeared. On the same side of the road one and one-half miles below the North America was the Tremont House, built of lumber brought around the Horn. The Spring Valley House, between Valley Springs and San Andreas, about one-half mile above Mountain Gate, was a two-story structure with barns and corrals. Both of these historic hostelries have vanished.

The Kentucky House, about two miles south of San Andreas and the center of mining activi-

ties on the South Fork of the Calaveras River, was a stage stop between Sonora and Sacramento. At present the Calaveras Cement Company has a plant there. The original Kentucky House was destroyed by fire, but a later building was erected on the same site and has been remodeled by the cement company as a clubhouse.

Double Springs, a Once Ambitious Ghost Town

Double Springs (SRL 264), one of the ghost towns of the Mother Lode mining region, became a thriving center after it was named county seat in 1850. Neighboring towns, however, were also growing and soon wished to hold this coveted

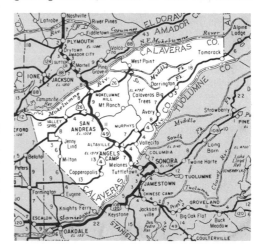

Courthouse, Double Springs

position. One of these was Jackson (then in Calaveras County), north of the Mokelumne River. The story of the contest for the position of county seat is typical of what took place in various parts of the state during the pioneer period. A few ambitious young men at Jackson drove over to Double Springs, where some of their number treated the county clerk quite liberally at the tavern bar. Meanwhile the others went to the building used as a courthouse, loaded the archives into their wagon, and hurried back across the river to Jackson. This was in July 1851. Although this high-handed action was illegal, Jackson retained its position until April 16, 1852, when by popular election Mokelumne Hill took first place. It is said that the votes cast were "out of all proportion to the number of voters."

In 1854 Amador County was separated from Calaveras County, and Jackson became the county seat of the new county. In 1866 San Andreas was given that honor in Calaveras County, in place of Mokelumne Hill, and it remains the county seat today.

At Double Springs, on a bypassed stretch of highway between Valley Springs and San Andreas, only a part of the first county courthouse remains; this building, moved from its original site, was probably erected toward the end of 1849, the material having been brought from China in October of that year. It consisted of three curiously arranged clapboard structures of camphor wood with numerous glass-paneled doors and no windows. The section still standing, although much worn by the elements, is in use as a museum. The original site of the courthouse has been marked by an eight-foot shaft of native sandstone erected by the Calaveras Chamber of Commerce.

The two springs for which the town was named still keep green the meadow that lies between the low hills. Here, surrounded by oleanders, orange trees, and aged locusts, stands the lovely old mansion of squared sandstone built in 1860 by Alexander R. Wheat. On the hill across the road, under the shadow of a great live oak, is the family cemetery where he lies.

Angels Camp

Romantic Angels Camp *(SRL 287)*, named for its founder, Henry Angel, retains several iron-shuttered stone buildings reminiscent of the early

gold days. Some of the most noteworthy landmarks are Angels Hotel, the Stickle Store (1857), and the famous Utica Mine, which was originally sold for a song and which later produced millions. This is now the site of Utica Park. The visitor to Angels Camp wanders through streets with curious names—Finnigan Lane, Hardscrabble Street, and Raspberry Lane—vivid reminders of a lively past.

In January 1865 Mark Twain, stopping at Angels Hotel *(SRL 734)*, obtained the nucleus for his famous story *The Celebrated Jumping Frog of Calaveras County*. The story was told him by Ben Coon, a bartender at the hotel. The present hotel was built in 1855, its predecessor having been destroyed by the disastrous fire of that year. Later, it was known for a time as Tryon's Hotel. In commemoration of Mark Twain's visit, Angels Camp holds an annual Jumping Frog Jubilee.

The Bret Harte Country

Scholarly investigations, unbiased by legend, have shown that it is almost impossible to attach to èxact sites most of the place names used by Bret Harte in his tales of California's early mining camps. The geography, as represented in his stories, is, for the most part, "so ridiculous as to be obviously fictitious." There is Wingdam, that illusive locale identified by some writers as Murphys but which George R. Stewart, Jr., biographer of Francis Bret Harte in 1931, characterizes as the "capital of the Bret Harte country, a place as vaguely pictured as many-towered Camelot, and as difficult to locate on any map."

Poverty Flat, and many others, "are more in the nature of figurative names than actual localities." Harte himself placed Poverty Flat contiguous to Sandy Bar on the Stanislaus River, but according to the testimony of old-timers there was no Sandy Bar with capital letters in that region. The appellative "Poverty" was prefixed to many a Sierra mining location. It was a characteristic name descriptive of the situation when thousands mined and few struck it rich. It has been suggested that Bret Harte may have borrowed the name and the "atmosphere" from the real Poverty Flat (now McDonald Flat), eight miles east of Mokelumne Hill and one mile from Whiskey Slide (now Clear View).

In spite of numerous vagaries as to individual place names and localities, the country centering about Robinson's Ferry (now Melones) on either side of the Stanislaus River, with Angels Camp and Murphys as its northern limit and Table Mountain (in Tuolumne County) as its southern extremity, is one of the few regions in the Sierra with which Harte "displayed any evidence of personal familiarity" in his stories. This was the only "Bret Harte country" that really existed. He made the Stanislaus River the scene of his humorous poem "The Society upon the Stanislaus," and charming bits of description in many of his stories fit the locality. His fondness, too, for Table Mountain is shown repeatedly. In *How Santa Claus Came to Simpson's Bar*, this characteristic picture is drawn: "Simpson's Bar on the eve of Christmas Day, 1862, clung like a swallow's nest to the rocky entablature and splintered capitals of Table Mountain."

Further evidence that Harte actually stayed in this region is found in the story of his visit to Jackass Hill (in Tuolumne County), as told to Stewart and others by William Gillis: "In December, 1855, his brother Jim was at the cabin when a very dead-beat young man came limping up. He was in city clothes, and wore patent-leather shoes which were punishing his feet. The young fellow gave his name as Harte and told a hard-luck story. . . . Gillis offered him the ready hospitality of the mountains, and Harte stayed for a night or two. . . . When he went on, Gillis gave him twenty dollars to see him through."

It is difficult to fasten with any finality Harte's nomenclature even to the sites along the Stanislaus River. Roaring Camp, for instance, has been placed at McLain's Bar, now a deserted spot five miles up the river from Melones, but other evidence indicates that no such name existed in this region. As to Poker Flat, the consensus of old-timers seems to be that it was the original name for Byrne's Ferry (the old crossing on the Stanislaus from Copperopolis to Mountain Pass); but there are others who declare that they never heard the place called by that name. Poker Flat has even been located in Sierra County, a region that Bret Harte undoubtedly never saw.

Not only was Harte's geography largely fictitious, but critics are also agreed that his stories show little intimate knowledge of mines or miners. A two months' foot journey through the southern mines looking for a school to teach, with perhaps a little amateur panning for gold (Stewart, on the testimony of Bill Gillis, favors the vicinity of Fourth Crossing as the most likely spot for the latter activity), doubtless constitutes the full measure of Francis Bret Harte's firsthand experience in the mining regions of California. The camps of his stories, moreover, are decidedly not those of 1849 and the early 1850's, but are those of the middle 1850's or even later. "The

flavor of decay hangs about his mining towns, they are just the places which he might have seen in Calaveras in 1855."

Carson Hill

Carson Hill (*SRL 274*), about four miles south of Angels Camp, has been called "the classic mining ground of California," for it was generally considered the richest camp in all the Mother Lode. There in November 1854 a mass of gold was found at the Morgan Mine weighing 195 pounds and valued at $43,534, said to be the largest nugget in the United States.

Between Carson Hill and Hanselman's Hill at Albany Flat (about two miles south of Angels Camp on Highway 49) is the elaborate James Romaggi stone house, built in 1852. It was located on the old road to Los Muertos, that wild camp on Arroyo de los Muertos ("creek of the dead") where the Battle of Six Mile Creek was waged between American and Mexican miners in the autumn of 1852. Los Muertos, with its predominant Mexican and Chilean population, was a favored haunt of Joaquín Murieta and his outlaw gang.

Morgan, on the north slope of Carson Hill, rivaled Mokelumne Hill in population and in the richness of its gold deposits. At one time in its history, over a period of two years, quartz mines at the place yielded $3,000,000. To the north of Carson Hill is Carson Flat on Carson Creek, where gold was discovered in August 1848 by James H. Carson. He was led to the place by friendly Indians and, according to his own report, panned out 180 ounces of gold in a period of ten days.

On a two-ton mine car at Carson Hill a plaque has been mounted in honor of Archie Stevenot (*SRL 769*), member of a pioneer Carson Hill family, who was born half a mile to the west in 1882. Stevenot helped publicize the attractions of California's gold country and became known as "Mr. Mother Lode."

On the south slope of Carson Hill on the Stanislaus River is Melones (Spanish for "melons"). It was originally called Robinson's Ferry (*SRL 276*), the name Melones (from the shape of the gold found in the vicinity by the Spanish and Mexican miners) having been borrowed in 1902 from a former camp midway between Carson Hill and the present town of that name. In the summer of 1849, within six weeks' time, $10,000 in tolls was collected at Robinson's Ferry.

Altaville

Altaville (*SRL 288*) dates from 1852 and was formerly known as Cherokee Flat. It is located only one mile north of Angels Camp, and the two communities have grown to meet each other. D. D. Demarest established a foundry at Altaville in 1854, producing most of the stamp mills and a large part of the mining machinery erected in Calaveras and Tuolumne counties. The foundry is still standing and in operation. The outstanding landmark at Altaville is the Prince and Garibardi Store (*SRL 735*), built in 1852 and still a strikingly handsome stone building. The old red

CENTRAL CALAVERAS COUNTY

brick grammar school *(SRL 499),* erected in 1858 and used until 1950, stands at the northwestern edge of the town.

North of Murphys Grade Road about half a mile east of Altaville is Bald Hill, on the slope of which may be seen the shaft of the old Mattison Mine. Here, at a depth of 130 feet, the famous Calaveras skull was alleged to have been found by Mr. Mattison, of Angels Camp, in February 1866. Of the many relics of prehistoric man discovered in America, "probably none has become better known than the much discussed Calaveras skull; certainly no other has been the occasion of such remarkably contradictory statements as have been recorded in reference to this specimen."

The general attention of the public was directed to this relic from Bald Hill by Professor J. D. Whitney, then state geologist of California, at a meeting of the California Academy of Sciences in San Francisco in July 1866. His final summary of the evidence in favor of the authenticity of Mattison's find in the Bald Hill Mine was not presented until 13 years later. Meantime much controversy ensued among scientists over the skull, and "the unscientific public hailed the story as a huge joke on the state geologist," put over, said the press, by fun-loving citizens of Angels Camp. Bret Harte was inspired to write a humorous poem, "To the Pliocene Skull," one of his last contributions to the *Californian.*

Scientists, however, did not dismiss the subject lightly. "Taken as a whole," says John C. Merriam, the problem "seemed ... to present as remarkable a case of absolutely contradictory evidence as ever appeared in science or in law.... After so long a lapse of years, it will probably never be possible to trace out the history of the Calaveras skull with certainty." A paper read before the American Anthropological Association in 1903 by Professor Merriam presented the general conclusion of scientists, which is still generally accepted. The genuineness of the skull as a relic of prehistoric man was established, but its origin had been shifted from the auriferous gravels of Whitney's Pliocene man to the less remote but still ancient cave deposits found in many parts of the mining regions of the Sierra Nevada. Some suggestions on how the skull might have reached Whitney's hands were also made, suggestions further elaborated upon by William J. Sinclair in 1908.

Stone Building, Happy Valley

Five miles northwest of Altaville and just west of Highway 49 is Fourth Crossing *(SRL 258).* Here stand two landmarks of the gold days, the old bridge and part of the Reddick Hotel. Between Altaville and Fourth Crossing is the site of Hawkeye.

The Mokelumne Hill Region

Mokelumne Hill *(SRL 269),* perched on the top of a mountain above Mokelumne River, is one of the most picturesque towns in the mining region. It was the county seat from 1852 to 1866 and was the leading town in the central Mother Lode at that period.

Interesting old buildings left from mining days, some of them in ruins, entice one to linger along the crooked hilltop road, where bandits and gold nuggets of fabulous worth are suggested by the solid houses of brick and stone with their heavy iron-barred doors and shuttered windows. Outstanding among them is the International Order of Odd Fellows Hall *(SRL 256),* formerly housing the Wells Fargo office and said to be the first three-story building to be erected in the Mother Lode. The two lower floors were built in 1854, and the third story was added in 1861. The Leger Hotel includes the building that served as the Courthouse of Calaveras County *(SRL 663)* from 1852 to 1866. When the county seat was moved to San Andreas, George W. Leger acquired the building and made it a part of his adjoining hotel, which had also been built in the early 1850's. The Congregational church *(SRL 261)* was erected in 1856, and is believed to be the oldest church building of that denomination in the state.

Overlooking the town of Mokelumne Hill is French Hill, the scene of one of the skirmishes in the so-called "French War." Here stood a fort erected by the Frenchmen as a barricade against the Americans. The envy of Americans had been aroused by the good fortune of the French miners throughout the region. On the pretext that they had hoisted the French flag and defied the American government, their adversaries called upon every American to arm and drive them out. The French were cowed into submission and driven from the rich diggings that they had been working. "Although the whole countryside united to evict the original holders, none can now be found to justify the expulsion, which is looked upon as a forthright robbery."

A mile and a half east of Mokelumne Hill a solid stone building at the right of Highway 26 marks the site of the settlement of Happy Valley. Just a tenth of a mile beyond this building a road branches to the right, which leads three and one-half miles to the site of Jesús María *(SRL 284),* on the creek of the same name. A small ruin by the side of the road is all that remains. Nearby were Whiskey Slide, later called Clear View, and McDonald Flat, formerly Poverty Flat.

A road going southwest from Mokelumne Hill leads to Campo Seco *(SRL 257),* a rich placer camp in early days, and in the 1860's a copper center, where the Penn Copper Mine was located. The largest cork oak *(Quercus suber)* in the state grows at Campo Seco. Stone ruins and the pioneer

Immaculate Conception Catholic Church, Camanche

cemetery are reminders of the past. The road from Mokelumne Hill to Campo Seco passes through Fosteria, an old mining town formerly called Paloma *(SRL 295)*. Beyond Campo Seco was Camanche *(SRL 254)*, a picturesque community with several old stone buildings until it was leveled in the early 1960's for the construction of Camanche Reservoir of the East Bay Municipal Utility District. Camanche was the heir of old Poverty Bar on the Mokelumne River. All that remained of Poverty Bar, now also under water, was the cemetery. The graves have been moved to the old Pioneer Cemetery near San Andreas and the People's Cemetery in San Andreas.

At Chili Gulch *(SRL 265)*, two miles south of Mokelumne Hill along Highway 49, a little group of Americans were driven from their claim by a superior force of Chileans in December 1849. The Americans had objected to the system by which Chilean leaders acquired many claims through their peon dependents, and had made laws against the practice. This in turn incensed the Chileans to such an extent that the Chilean War resulted, with the Chileans, under the leadership of one Dr. Concha, taking the aggressive. The final outcome was favorable to the Americans, but the occurrence developed considerable tension between the United States and Chile.

There are several "Rich Gulches" in Calaveras County. On the Rich Gulch that leads from Fosteria to the Mokelumne River is located the famous Gwin Mine, which was once owned and operated by Senator Gwin. Fabulous sums of gold have been taken from this Rich Gulch since early mining days.

To the east of Mokelumne Hill six miles was another Rich Gulch, a once populous camp, of which little trace is left today; while six miles beyond was Railroad Flat *(SRL 286)*, once a placer and quartz-mining center, where a store and post office and a few of the old homes still remain. A near neighbor was Independence Flat; and five miles to the north was West Point *(SRL 268)*, where numerous small but rich quartz ledges were once worked by Mexicans. It is now a quiet mountain community with many homes of retired people. A few old buildings are interspersed with newer ones in the business district. Two and one-half miles southeast of West Point on Highway 26 is Sandy Gulch *(SRL 253)*, where little more than an old cemetery remains. About nine miles northeast of Mokelumne Hill, where the road forks to West Point and Railroad Flat, is Glencoe *(SRL 280)*, once called Mosquito Gulch, of which nothing remains from pioneer days.

Murphys

At Murphys *(SRL 275)* may be seen many historic and picturesque structures, including the Wells Fargo Express Office, strongly built and guarded with iron shutters and doors; the Sperry (Mitchler) Hotel; the Traver Building; and the Jones Apothecary Shop. The Sperry Hotel *(SRL 267)*, the largest building in town in 1856, was erected by J. L. Sperry to accommodate the increased travel through Murphys, following A. T. Dowd's finding of the Big Trees of the Calaveras Grove in 1852. The Peter L. Traver Building *(SRL 466)* was constructed in 1856. It is one of the oldest buildings in Murphys and has withstood three major fires.

"For a perfect bit of unaltered atmosphere,

Murphys has few if any equals in the entire Mother Lode district.... The quaint buildings flanking its tree-lined main street have proved a delight both to the artist and to the historian. Its one surviving hotel, unchanged since it was built in the early 1850's, is a splendid example of a public house of that period."

The country about Murphys was first mined in July 1848 by two brothers, Daniel and John Murphy, who came in the same company with Henry Angel and James Carson. The Murphys, like others of the group, struck out for themselves on reaching the diggings and set up camp at a site on Angel's Creek, which soon became known as Murphy's Diggings and was later called Murphy's Camp, or, more often, simply Murphy's or Murphys.

West of Murphys was French Gulch. One mile east of Murphys on Pennsylvania Gulch Road was Brownsville (SRL 465), a thriving mining camp in the 1850's and 1860's. About one mile northwest of Murphys are the Mercer Caves, notable limestone formations.

From Murphys, Highway 4 climbs northeast up the Sierra Nevada about 20 miles to the famous Calaveras Big Trees State Park, a beautiful stand of the *Sequoia gigantea,* the larger of the two species of California sequoias. While on a scouting expedition in 1841, John Bidwell came upon one of the fallen giants of the Calaveras, the first white man known to have seen this grove. Whether he saw the North or the South Grove, however, is debatable.

Although the Big Trees had been seen by J. Marshall Wooster, Whitehead, and other miners as early as 1850, credit for their discovery has usually been given to A. T. Dowd, a hunter from Murphys. Dowd first brought the attention of the public to the Calaveras North Grove in the spring of 1852. For many years the grove continued to attract attention, numerous tourists visiting it during the 1860's and 1870's. For a time it was thought to be the only stand of the *Sequoia gigantea* in existence. The hotel that was erected in the grove by James L. Sperry soon after Dowd's discovery stood until it was destroyed by fire in August 1943. Other old hotels remain at Avery and Dorrington.

San Andreas

San Andreas (SRL 252), where the Marlette mines were located, has narrow streets and the settled air of an old town. A number of historic buildings make one think of the rugged 1850's, including the Odd Fellows Building (1856), centrally located; the Agostino Building of brick and adobe, on Court Street near St. Charles Street; and the Cassinelli adobe, just below the grade of the highway on an alley off Pixley Avenue.

East of San Andreas about eight miles is El Dorado (SRL 282), generally known as Mountain Ranch, where some of the old adobe buildings of mining days are still standing. This was the location of an early sawmill. The original Mountain Ranch post office was located about one mile west of here but was moved to the town of El Dorado in 1868. Southeast of here was Cave City. When the mines there gave out, its school was moved to El Dorado, but the district retained the name Cave City. Between Mountain Ranch and Murphys is Sheep Ranch, a quartz-mining camp where George Hearst laid the foundation of his fortune.

Six miles southeast of San Andreas are Old Gulch and Calaveritas (SRL 255). At the latter place a few adobe buildings still stand in various states of preservation. Three miles beyond is Dogtown.

Three miles northwest of San Andreas is Cottage Spring, and three miles west are North Branch and Central Hill, noted for their once rich gravel mines. Farther west is Valley Springs (SRL 251), a supply and railroad center rather than a mining town.

On the main road about two miles west of San Andreas on the north bank of the Calaveras River and near the site of North Branch is the old Pioneer Cemetery (SRL 271), the oldest known cemetery in Calaveras County. Several ancient monuments still mark the graves of early miners.

Vallecito

Vallecito ("Little Valley," SRL 273), near which the famous Moaning Caves (once an Indian burial chamber) are located, is about five miles east of Angels Camp. A few landmarks from mining days remain, among them the Dinkelspiel Store. There is also an old church bell, which was brought up from San Francisco by an itinerant preacher in the early days. The bell was mounted in a large oak tree, and every Sunday morning scores of miners answered its vigorous summons. The bell is now mounted on top of a stone monument (SRL 370).

To the north, between Vallecito and Murphys, is Douglas Flat (SRL 272), where the so-called Central Hill Channel is located, an ancient river deposit from which vast quantities of gold have been taken. The old Gilleado Building, once a store and bank, is a roadside landmark here.

Jenny Lind and Copperopolis

Jenny Lind (SRL 266), on the north bank of the Calaveras River, was once the center of most of the mining operations on the Lower Calaveras, but now it is a pleasant community of old and new homes. A few stone and adobe ruins remain as vestiges of its former activity.

Six miles south of Jenny Lind is Milton (SRL 262), first town in Calaveras County to have a railroad. The Southern Pacific arrived in 1871, and Milton was born. From here freight and passengers were conveyed by wagon and stage to other parts of the county.

Prior to the discovery of the great copper deposits in the northern part of the state, Copperopolis (SRL 296), in the southwestern part of Calaveras County, was the principal copper-producing center in California. In 1868 it boasted a population of nearly 2,000, and had three schools, two churches, four hotels, and stores and workshops of all kinds. The town of today retains a fragment of its one-time importance in the fast-disintegrating smelters, shafts, and chutes of the old mines; in the handful of brick stores straggling along the highway; and in the pioneer Congregational church (now the I.O.O.F. Building), a substantial brick structure with beautiful Gothic windows. Near Copperopolis, at Funk Hill, Black Bart, the "gentleman" bandit, committed his last stage robbery.

On the road from Copperopolis to Mountain Pass was O'Byrne's (or Byrne's) Ferry (*SRL 281*). The ferry of pioneer days was supplanted in 1862 by a covered bridge, which spanned the Stanislaus River for almost a century. The structure, 210 feet in length, was removed in 1957 when Tulloch Dam was constructed. The little triangular valley, hemmed in by steep and rugged mountain slopes covered with chaparral, is now filled with water. Above it, "like the ruins of a Rhineland castle," tower the lava-capped crags of Table Mountain.

SOURCES

Adams, Kramer A. *Covered Bridges of the West.* Howell-North, Berkeley, 1963.
Ayres, Colonel James J. *Gold and Sunshine: Reminiscences of Early California.* Richard G. Badger, Boston, 1922.
Beasley, Thomas Dykes. *A Tramp through the Bret Harte Country.* Paul Elder & Co., San Francisco, 1914.
Bidwell, General John. "Echoes of the Past," *Chico Advertiser,* Chico, n.d.
Browne, J. Ross. *Report on the Mineral Resources of the States and Territories of the Rocky Mountains.* Government Printing Office, Washington, D.C., 1868.
Buckbee, Edna Bryan. "Pioneer Days of Angels Camp," *Calaveras Californian,* Angels Camp, 1932.
Carson, James H. *Life in California, Together with a Description of the Great Tulare Valley.* 2d ed. San Joa-

quin *Republican,* Stockton, 1852; reprinted by W. Abbatt, Tarrytown, N.Y., 1931.
Coy, Owen Cochran. *Gold Days,* of the series *California,* ed. John Russell McCarthy. Powell Publishing Co., Los Angeles, 1929.
Davis, Sheldon. "On the Trail of Mark Twain and Bret Harte in the Mother Lode Country," *Stockton Record,* July 16 and 23, 1921.
Fry, Walter, and John R. White. *Big Trees.* Stanford University Press, Stanford, 1930.
Geologic Guidebook along Highway 49 — Sierran Gold Belt, the Mother Lode Country. State of California, Division of Mines, San Francisco, 1948.
Gillis, William R. *Gold Rush Days with Mark Twain.* Boni, New York, 1930.
——— *Memories of Mark Twain and Steve Gillis.* Sonora, 1924.
Gold Rush Country. Lane Publishing Co., Menlo Park, 1957.
Johnston, Philip. "Legends and Landmarks of '49 along the Mother Lode," *Touring Topics,* XXIII, No. 2 (February 1931), 12–27, 52–53.
Kerr, Mark B. *Mining Resources of Calaveras County.* Golden Jubilee Mining Fair, San Francisco, 1898.
Mason, J. D. *History of Amador County, California.* Thompson and West, Oakland, 1881.
Merriam, John C. "The True Story of the Calaveras Skull," *Sunset,* XXIV, No. 2 (February 1910), 153–58.
Paine, Albert Bigelow. *A Short Life of Mark Twain.* Garden City Publishing Co., Garden City, N.Y., 1920.
Sinclair, William J. "Recent Investigations Bearing on the Question of the Occurrence of Neocene Man in the Auriferous Gravels of the Sierra Nevada," *University of California Publications in American Archaeology and Ethnology,* VII, No. 2 (February 1908), 107–31.
Stewart, George R., Jr. *Bret Harte, Argonaut and Exile.* Houghton Mifflin, Boston, 1931.
——— "The Bret Harte Legend," *University of California Chronicle,* XXX, No. 3 (July 1928), 338–50.
Weston, Otheto. *Mother Lode Album.* Stanford University Press, Stanford, 1948.
Whitney, J. D. *The Auriferous Gravels of the Sierra Nevada.* Cambridge, Mass., 1880.
Wiltsee, Ernest A. "Double Springs, First County Seat of Calaveras County," *California Historical Society Quarterly,* XI, No. 2 (June 1932), 176–83.

Colusa County

COLUSA COUNTY (named for the Colus Indians, Colus being a corruption of the tribal name, Ko-ru-si) was one of the 27 original counties. Colusi was the older spelling of the county name. Monroeville, now in Glenn County, was the first county seat, but was superseded by Colusa in 1854.

Ko-ru-si Indian Villages

Colusa was built on the site of the ancient Indian village Ko-ru, tribal capital of the Ko-ru-si. In 1850, there were a thousand or more of these Indians living in villages scattered up and down the Sacramento River from Sycamore Slough in the south to the northern boundary of the present county. As early as 1846 Americans began to settle along this part of the river, and by the close of the nineteenth century only two of the ancient Indian villages remained, Tat-no, four miles above the town of Colusa, on what was at

that time the Colonel Hagar Ranch, and Wy-terre, on the upper end of the Rancho Jimeno.

There were at least 13 of these villages. Lochloch, at the head of Sycamore Slough, was about eight miles below the present site of Colusa, where the town of Sycamore now stands. Coo-coo came next, and beyond that was Doc-doc, just below Colusa. Colusa itself was built on the ruins of Ko-ru, the head village of the tribe. Opposite Colusa, on what afterward became Colonel Wilkins's farm, was Cow-peck, and above Colusa was Tat-no. Si-cope occupied the bend of the river east of the site of the old Five Mile House, while at the Seven Mile House was Cah-cheal. At the bend of the river, on the upper end of what became the Judge Hastings Ranch, was Si-ee ("view"), where there were no trees. On the Rancho Jimeno was Wy-terre ("turn to the north"). Cha was at the Senator Boggs Ranch and Ket-tee

was where the present town of Princeton stands, at the very northeastern corner of Colusa County. Some two miles above Princeton, at the boundary line of Colusa and Glenn counties, was Tu-tu, the northernmost village of the Ko-ru-si. A remnant of the ancient tribe still lives at the Rancheria, seven and a half miles north of Colusa.

The Larkin Grant

John Bidwell was the first recorded white explorer of Colusa County, in the years 1843–44, while in the employ of John A. Sutter at Sutter's Fort.

On July 6, 1844, Bidwell mapped out a grant of land which extended along the west bank of the Sacramento River north of what is now the town of Colusa and into the present Glenn County. This was the first land grant made in Colusa County and was known as the Larkin Grant, having been secured for the children of Thomas O. Larkin, American consul at Monterey. John S. Williams, brother of Isaac Williams, owner of Rancho Chino in southern California, was the first white settler in Colusa County. In 1847 he was employed to look after the Larkin Grant, and on it he built the first house in the county. Senator John Boggs later bought that part of the Larkin Grant on which Williams lived, just below the present town of Princeton. The town of Williams, incidentally, is named not for John S. Williams but for W. H. Williams, who laid out the townsite on the route of the Southern Pacific Railroad.

Colusa

On the spot where Ko-ru, the ancient capital of the Ko-ru-si, had been located only a few years before, Colusa was founded in 1850. The land on which the new town was laid out and two "leagues" beyond it were included in the grant made to John Bidwell in 1845. When Dr. Robert Semple, founder of Benicia, visited the country in 1847, he was so impressed with its beauty and fertility and its nearness to the great river that he saw possibilities of a future city there.

Colonel Charles D. Semple, a brother of Dr. Semple, came to California in 1849. The Doctor immediately told him of this fine country to the north and Charles was most favorably impressed. He purchased the land from Bidwell the same year, and in a small home-made launch started up the river the following spring to found a new

metropolis. Mistaking the site originally chosen by his brother, the Colonel "landed . . . at a place seven miles above the Colus rancheria and afterward known as the Seven Mile House." Later that same year, when Dr. Semple arrived, the settlement was removed "seven miles lower down the river," to the location "originally designed," which was on the site of the ancient Indian village. Barges came up the river from Sacramento and trade from the northern mines was good. Thus Semple's hopes seemed justified, and the new town prospered.

In 1853 Dr. Robert Semple and his nephew, Will S. Green, purchased Rancho Alamo on Freshwater Creek, six miles west of Williams. Dr. Semple died there on October 25, 1854, and was buried on the ranch. Later the body was removed to the Williams Cemetery. With funds raised by the people of Williams, the grave has been marked by a monument and bronze tablet. Another marker has been placed at the Semple ranch west of Williams on Highway 20. Green became well known as the crusading editor of the Colusa *Sun*.

Although Colusa did not become a great city, it prospered, and in 1854 it was made the county seat. Today it is the center of a thriving agricultural region. The Courthouse was built in 1861. Its beautiful Southern architecture reflects the taste of the early settlers who came from the South. During the Civil War Colusa County was sometimes called "the Little South" because of its strong pro-Confederate sympathies.

The brick shrine a mile and a half south of Sycamore on the Colusa-Grimes highway com-

Courthouse, Colusa

Brick Shrine, near Sycamore

memorates the first Roman Catholic service in Colusa County, a Mass celebrated on May 1, 1856, by Father Peter Magagnotto, C.P., of Marysville. According to Walsh, the service was held in the home of Jacob Meyers on the Sacramento River, an area known as Grand Island. In September 1864 a mission was preached to the people of Grand Island by Father P. G. Laufhuber, S.J., and a piece of land was donated for a church. On September 14, at the close of the mission, a 27-foot wooden cross was erected on this property. No church was ever built, but in 1883 Father Michael Walrath put up the shrine. Mass is occasionally celebrated there, and the tiny house of worship is a constant attraction for tourists. The cross was later replaced by one of concrete.

The River Road

The old River Road, following along the west bank of the Sacramento River from Colusa to Shasta City, was the only road in Colusa County in the early 1850's. Its popularity rivaled that of the river steamers, which plied as far north as Red Bluff. The volume of traffic over the road to the northern mines resulted in the building of many inns or stage stations along its course. From Wilkins' Slough in southern Colusa County to the mouth of Stony Creek in what is now Glenn County, a fringe of farms bordered the river, each with its roadhouse or inn to refresh man and beast on the long trip to the gold fields.

The most important center along the entire route was Colusa, from which as many as 50 freight wagons often started for the north in one day. Among the several stations along the River Road were the Five Mile House, where the Maxwell Road leaves the River Road; the Seven Mile House, a few hundred feet south of where the county road crosses the railroad (the original site of the town of Colusa); the Nine Mile House, erected by S. H. Cooper; the Ten Mile House, built by L. H. Helphenstine and owned by the family for over 70 years; the Eleven Mile House, originally owned by Thomas Parton; the Sterling Ranch, or Fourteen Mile House, where John S. Williams, a representative of Thomas O. Larkin, built the first house (an adobe) in Colusa County in 1847, and where Charles B. Sterling, the second settler, succeeded him in 1849; the Sixteen Mile House, two miles above the Sterling Ranch, where

Princeton now is; and the Seventeen Mile House, owned by Hiram Willits, later founder of Willits, Mendocino County.

Stone Corral

Six miles west of Maxwell is a hollow hemmed in on three sides by high hills, forming a natural site for a corral. The place may have been used by Mexican vaqueros as early as 1848, but the construction of the stone fence is generally attributed to Granville P. Swift, whose cattle operations covered a vast area of the Sacramento Valley in the early 1850's. After 1855 it was used by John Steele, who made further improvements. Settlers afterward carried away many of the stones, until only a remnant remained. The Old Stone Corral (*SRL 238*), as it was long known, has been restored by the Colusa Parlor, Native Sons of the Golden West. It is located on the ranch at the south side of the Maxwell-Sites road, where it crosses Stone Corral Creek.

Letts Valley

Jack and David Lett settled in a small valley near the northwest corner of Colusa County in 1855. Letts Valley (*SRL 736*) is now the site of a lake and campground, completed in 1959, within the Mendocino National Forest. The spillway is built on the site of a tunnel constructed by the brothers to facilitate drainage. The campground is located where, in 1877, the brothers met their death while trying to prevent squatters from settling on their land. The area is southwest of Stonyford via Fouts Springs.

Pierce Christian College

Pierce Christian College at College City was named after Andrew Pierce, who, at his death in 1874, left a large amount of land to the Christian Church for religious and educational advancement. In 1876 a board of trustees established a college on the land and laid out a town about it. For years, this was the only school of higher rank in that part of California, and at one time most of the teachers of Colusa County had received their education in it.

In 1896 the Pierce College grounds and buildings were given to the Union High School District of College City. This is what happened in many districts in northern California during the last decade of the nineteenth century, when denominational and other private schools gave their lands and buildings for the use of the newly forming high schools. The college had been discontinued because the Christian Church had decided to consolidate its various colleges scattered throughout the state into one adequately endowed institution, finally established at Los Angeles. In March 1937 Pierce Union High School was moved to its new campus in Arbuckle, and, in the three years following, the old college buildings at College City were razed.

SOURCES

Green, Will S. *Colusa County, California.* Elliott and Moore, San Francisco, 1880.
McCornish, Charles Davis, and Rebecca T. Lambert. *His-*

tory of Colusa and Glenn Counties, California. Historic Record Co., Los Angeles, 1918.

McGowan, Joseph A. *History of the Sacramento Valley.* 3 vols. Lewis Historical Publishing Co., New York, 1961.

Radcliffe, Zoe Green. "Robert Baylor Semple, Pioneer," *California Historical Society Quarterly,* VI, No. 2 (June 1927), 130–58.

Rogers, Justus H. *Colusa County, Its History Traced*

from a State of Nature through the Early Period of Settlement and Development to the Present Day. Privately published, Orland, 1891.

Sanchez, Nellie Van de Grift. *Spanish and Indian Place Names of California.* A. M. Robertson, San Francisco, 1922.

Walsh, Henry L., S.J. *Hallowed Were the Gold Dust Trails.* University of Santa Clara Press, Santa Clara, 1946.

Contra Costa County

CONTRA COSTA COUNTY was one of the original 27 counties of California, created by act of the legislature on February 18, 1850, and confirmed on April 25, 1851. Its territory included part of what is now Alameda County until March 23, 1853, but on that date the new county was formed from the southern portion of the original Contra Costa and the northern part of Santa Clara County. The town of Martinez has always been the seat of justice of Contra Costa County.

The name Contra Costa, signifying "opposite coast," was at first applied to the entire coast that lies due east of San Francisco. The significance of the name was lost when that portion directly facing San Francisco was transferred to Alameda County.

Monte del Diablo

It is doubtful whether any other place name in California has gathered about itself so many legends as has that of Monte del Diablo ("Mountain of the Devil"). Standing out all alone on a great plain and occupying almost the exact center of Contra Costa County, this storied peak is one of the most conspicuous landmarks in the state because of its isolation. The rugged grandeur of the great mountain and the strange, fantastic natural formations with which the region abounds gave rise, in earlier days, to many legends all bordering on the marvelous or diabolical. It was regarded by the Indians of the region as the home of the Puy, or devil, and their medicine men claimed to be agents of the spirit of the mountain.

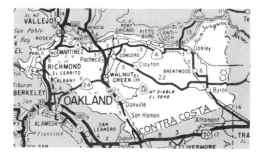

General Mariano G. Vallejo in his report to the legislature on April 16, 1850, gives the following story of the derivation of the name in its Spanish form: "In 1806 a military expedition from San Francisco marched against the tribe 'Bolgones,' who were encamped at the foot of the mount; the Indians were prepared to receive the expedition, and a hot engagement ensued in the large hollow fronting the western side of the mount. As the victory was about to be decided in favor of the Indians, an unknown personage, decorated with the most extraordinary plumage and making divers movements, suddenly appeared near the combatants. The Indians were victorious and the incognito [Puy] departed towards the mount. The defeated soldiers, on ascertaining that the spirit went through the same ceremony daily and at all hours, named the mount 'Diablo,' in allusion to its mysterious inhabitant, that continued thus to make his appearance until the tribe was subdued by the troops in command of Lieutenant Gabriel Moraga, in a second campaign of the same year. In the aboriginal tongue 'Puy' signifies 'Evil Spirit'; in Spanish it means 'Diablo,' and doubtless it signifies 'Devil' in the Anglo-American language."

General Vallejo's explanation of the origin of this intriguing place name seems to Nellie Van de Grift Sanchez the most plausible of the many presented, for "it is quite likely that the Puy, or devil, was one of the 'medicine men' who played upon the superstitions of the Indians by pretending to be the 'spirit of the mountain.'"

Erwin G. Gudde, on the other hand, is of the opinion that "Monte Diablo" referred originally to an Indian village at the present site of Concord, with "monte" used in the sense of "thicket" or "woods" rather than "mountain." Apparently, he says, early American settlers misunderstood the term and applied the name to the mountain.

An unsuccessful attempt was made by the legislature in 1865–66 to change the name of Mount Diablo. Although the legislature might say "Coal Hill," the people continued to say "Mount Diablo," and Diablo it has remained.

The mountain was a landmark for explorers and pioneers from the earliest days. In the spring of 1772 Pedro Fages and his trail blazers skirted the western side of the mountain, the first white men to touch its flowery slopes. During the spring of 1776, Juan Bautista de Anza also passed that way, after retracing Fages' steps as far as the junction of the Sacramento and San Joaquin rivers. Dr. John Marsh was led in 1836 by the great mountain to his rancho at its base. By it the Bidwell-Bartleson company, the first overland emigrant train to enter California by way of the Sierra Nevada, was guided in 1841 to Dr. Marsh's estate. Standing up boldly in splendid isolation from a broad, level plain without other mountains to limit its height, Mount Diablo is easily recognizable from a great distance by its double summit and regular conical outline, resembling that of a volcano. The view from its highest peak, 3,849 feet above the sea, is magnificent.

A government cabin and telescope were placed on the summit of Mount Diablo in 1851. This ancient landmark was chosen in that year as the base point for United States surveys in California and was established as such by Colonel Ransome. With the exception of southern California and of the Humboldt district, the locations of all lands in the state are determined by their situation with reference to the Mount Diablo "base and meridian" lines.

When the advance party of the Whitney Survey passed through Pacheco Valley in the spring of 1862 en route to Mount Diablo, the fields were studded with magnificent white oaks (*Quercus hindsu hindsii*), "their great spreading branches," writes Brewer, "often forming a head a hundred feet in diameter.... Across this great park the trail ran."

Camp was pitched on May 6 "in one of the loveliest localities, a pure rippling stream for water, plenty of wood, fine oaks around"; and behind it Mount Diablo rose grandly, its summit "burning with the Tyrian fire of evening." The town of Clayton—with tavern, store, etc.—stood scarcely 20 rods from the campsite. The discovery of coal in the region had caused the settlement to spring up only a few months before.

Toward evening Professor Whitney joined his men at this delightful spot. Thomas Starr King and other guests from San Francisco were with him. Here in the mild May evening, the party sat about a blazing campfire telling stories and marveling at the beauty of the majestic peak.

Very early in the morning of May 7, five of the Whitney party, with their guests, climbed the mountain. The day was one of those rare, crystal-clear days when the view from the summit stretched for hundreds of miles. "Probably but few views in North America," says Brewer, "are more extensive—certainly nothing in Europe.... I made an estimate from the map, based on the distances to known peaks, and found that the extent of land and sea embraced between the extreme limits of vision amounted to eighty thousand square miles, and that forty thousand square miles, or more, were spread out in tolerably plain view—over 300 miles from north to south, and 260 to 280 miles from east to west, between the extreme points."

The Whitney party remained in the region until May 28 and made scientific investigations and measurements both of the main crest and of the northeast peak, which lies about 300 feet lower. The latter was named Mount King by the Whitney party, but the name did not persist and it is now known as Eagle Point. The two cones are separated by a wild and picturesque gap, through which "the wind roared with a violence almost terrific at times... and at intervals the clouds rushed through like a torrent... [It was] a peculiarly grand spot... because of the surrounding rocks and the clouds which rushed among them."

The superb beauty of Mount Diablo, the loveliness of its wildflowers, and the profuse scattering of juniper, nut pine, oak, sycamore, and other trees very early attracted nature lovers as well as scientific explorers to its craggy summits. Two good wagon roads were laid out in early days, one from Concord to the northwest and the other from Danville on the south side of the mountain, and two stages ran daily to the Mountain House.

This famous old hostelry was erected some distance below the summit, because the last part of the trail was too steep for vehicles. The two roads met about 300 feet southwest of a spring, from which a good-sized stream issued and ran down the mountainside, to cross and recross the Concord road before joining the waters of Silver Creek above the head of Pine Canyon.

Travelers from many parts of the world signed the register at the Mountain House. Sometimes they remained for several days or even weeks, admiring the giant oak at the doorway and the magnificent views on every hand, or on foot or horseback taking the trail to the summit with its splendid panorama.

The government cabin burned in the early 1890's, and for a time the mountain lost some of its popularity. Later, after the roads were abandoned, it was shut away from the public and the old Mountain House was burned by ranchers who did not wish visitors crossing their lands. The site is still marked by a few dead almond trees which once grew near the house. The glories of Mount Diablo were again made accessible to the public on April 26, 1931, when it was made a part of the state park system.

Thus Diablo, an object of worship to an ancient people, has long been a landmark for trail breakers, gold seekers, and home makers, and the mecca of nature lovers. Today, two centuries since the coming of Fages and Juan Bautista de Anza, a powerful revolving beacon light on the summit is a guide to airplanes.

Indian Shell Mounds

One of the largest of the more than 400 shell mounds or kitchen middens which existed in the San Francisco Bay region when the first white men came to its shores was located within the present city limits of Richmond at what is now the foot of 11th Street. Twelfth Street intersects the site of the old mound as it extended across the marsh.

A large part of the Ellis Landing shell mound, as it was long called by Americans, was removed for grading purposes in 1907, and the final leveling took place in 1924. Like the one at Emeryville in Alameda County, this mound is of particular significance both on account of its unusual size and because of the extensive scientific explorations by the Department of Archaeology of the University of California. During the years 1906–8, a detailed study and report of this and other mounds was made by N. C. Nelson, and for two weeks in 1907 extensive scientific excavations were made. At that time about 67,500 cubic feet of material was removed, while 265 artifacts and 126 human skeletons were uncovered.

Before civilized man began to tear down the ancient pile, it measured 460 feet in length, 250 feet in width, and about 30 feet in height, and its volume approximated 1,260,000 cubic feet. Scientists estimate that the process of accumulation extended over a period of from 3,000 to 4,000 years. It consisted largely of broken shells, principally of the common clam and mussel variety mixed sparingly with oyster, cockle, and abalone shells. Many broken rocks, pebbles, ashes, artifacts, etc., were also found.

Fifteen house pits were visible upon the heap before it was leveled. These, together with the large number of human skeletons found there, indicate that the site was used both as a residence and as a burial place.

"The first inhabitants, however ancient they may have been," writes Nelson, "possessed some roughly made stone implements; they prepared vegetable foods; they knew the use of fire; and they painted and buried their dead. The last people to dwell on the mound had, besides . . . well-made stone implements, quite a variety of bone tools as well as several forms of ornaments made of bone and shell. There is reason to believe that they tried to fashion vessels and other objects out of clay, and that they made baskets and dressed skins. They were skilled hunters by land and sea, and consequently must have had boats of some sort.

"Progress toward perfection of manufacture is generally marked; but aside from these normal changes there are no important breaks in the culture represented. . . . If more than one people have lived on the mound . . . they were all essentially of the same type of culture, and the last occupants of the shellmound at Ellis Landing were probably Indians similar to those that have lived in middle California within historic times."

The Ellis Landing campsite seems to have afforded few of the advantages usually sought by the mound dwellers. In summer there was no fresh water for drinking, and except for drift there was no firewood, while at all times the location was exposed to strong winds. Since it lay on the shore edge directly north of Brooks Island with 600 yards of marshland at its back, access to it was difficult, and at high tide on stormy winter days it became an island completely surrounded by water.

It seems reasonable to suppose that autumn was the most likely season for aboriginal hunters to visit the site, for then the thick, low growth of *Baccharis Douglasii*, which covered it, formed coverts for numerous wild fowl. It was during the autumn hunting season, too, that white men in recent times have come for the same reason.

The natural barriers about the shell heap long served to protect it from the plow, which has ruined many of these deposits. A Mr. Ellis, who lived at the landing for about 40 years, stated that as late as 1890 the mound was still intact. His father ran a small canal from one of the marsh creeks up close to the mound on the landward side and began hauling away its rich and ancient soil.

Before man began its destruction, however, nature had already made inroads upon the mound. Because the base of the pile was from 11 to 18 feet below sea level before the leveling, the encroaching tides were yearly undermining the steep sea wall and were fast destroying the deposit itself. Since it rested upon solid gravel but was more than half buried in fine silt, Nelson estimated that "the region has sunk at least eighteen feet since the ancient inhabitants began to accumulate the refuse deposit."

The Ford Motor Company factory, now located at Milpitas, once stood on filled land just beyond the spot where the midden for ages had faced the open waters of the bay.

Archaeologists are currently working in the vast shell mounds on privately owned Brooks Island, believed to have been occupied by Indians from 3000 B.C. to A.D. 700, perhaps longer than any other spot in the Bay Area. The East Bay Regional Park District is taking steps to acquire the 73-acre island, and the public may soon be able to observe the scientists at their work.

Four moderate-sized shell mounds could still be seen at Stege within the city limits of Richmond before 1915. These mounds were located south of Seaver Avenue, on or near the bayshore in the Harborgate Tract, the largest of the group lying within the block then bounded by the waterfront, 27th, Montgomery, and 28th streets, while a smaller mound, which measured about 240 by 160 feet, stood at the foot of 25th Street.

A third deposit, covering an area about 350 by 250 feet, paralleled the head of a small slough which ran between the largest and the smallest mounds of the group. Across a small salt-water slough in the Owens Addition a fourth site was situated 200 or 300 feet north of the first shell heap. This deposit was leveled before 1915.

A real estate company laid out and graded the streets in the Harborgate Tract in the autumn of 1915. At that time Llewellyn L. Loud and Leonard Outhwaite observed operations, and about 500 artifacts were secured. These mounds, of course, were used as burial places.

The Great Discovery

The Pedro Fages expedition continued in the latter part of March 1772 up the Contra Costa in search of a land route to Point Reyes. Leaving their camp on Strawberry Creek in Alameda County and continuing past the sites of Berkeley and Albany on March 28, the little band turned into the Contra Costa County hills and descended past them into the arroyo later known as Wildcat Creek. At the Indian village on its banks, the strangers were met in a most friendly manner by the natives, who presented them with generous gifts of "cacomites, amoles, and two dead geese, dried and stuffed with grass to use as decoys." The white men reciprocated by offerings of colored beads, which were eagerly received by the Indians.

Four more arroyos "with running water" were passed before Fages at length halted his men on the bank of a fifth stream "at the foot of some hills." Before them "lay a large round bay, which resembles a great lake," wrote Fray Juan Crespí. This was San Pablo Bay, and in it they saw Mare Island close to the opposite shore. Camp was made at or near Pinole.

On the following day the explorers climbed the hills that come down close to the shore of San Pablo Bay, still confident that they could reach Point Reyes from this place. To their disappointment they found the passage completely shut off by Carquinez Strait. All day they trekked across the hills and gullies of the rough region above the strait, passing "five large villages of very mild heathen ... [where they] were well received ... and presented with some of their wild food." Many other villages could be made out on the opposite shore.

"According to scientists," says Mrs. Sanchez, "the name Carquinez is derived from Karkin, the name of an Indian village in that region.... Fray José Viader, diarist of the Moraga expedition of 1810 ... [and] other diarists speak of this Indian village and tribe under the name of the Carquines, making it fairly certain that the origin of the name is Indian." Crespí called the strait the Río de San Francisco.

Breaking camp near Martinez on March 30, the party crossed a deep arroyo "well grown with oaks, cottonwoods, alders, and laurels," which, says Professor Bolton, was probably Pacheco Creek. The expedition then entered the broad, oak-studded Concord Valley, which Crespí called Santa Angela de Fulgino. The good father thought that the valley seemed an excellent place for a settlement. Two native villages were seen in this neighborhood.

Leaving the valley behind them, the little cavalcade pressed forward over the western spur of Monte del Diablo. From one of the high hills of the range they gazed out across a vast new territory never before looked upon by any white man. Before them lay the great Sacramento Valley and the San Joaquin and Sacramento rivers, which converge at the head of Suisun Bay, and, far away to the southeast, "some high mountains," which doubtless were the great Sierra Nevada.

Thus the trail had been blazed through the Contra Costa, and although the specific goal of the expedition was never attained, a discovery of far-reaching magnitude had been made. The vast inland empire of Alta California with its great intersecting watercourses had been opened to future exploration and ultimate settlement.

Camp on this eventful evening was probably pitched "westward of Antioch, near Pittsburg." "From this place," wrote Crespí, "we decided to return to ... Monterey, in view of the fact that our passage to ... Point Reyes ... was cut off by these rivers." Before turning back, however, the expedition "went ten leagues from Pacheco Creek, reaching the Indian village near Antioch," says Bolton.

Camp near the San Joaquin River was broken early the next morning, the range was crossed north of Mount Diablo, and Concord Valley was re-entered north of Clayton. Continuing west to Walnut Creek, the party turned southeast and proceeded past the site of Danville through the San Ramon Valley. Camp was set just south of Danville.

Early on the first day of April Fages and his men traveled southward through the San Ramon Valley and on into Livermore Valley, passing "many and good arroyos, and with numerous villages of very gentle and peaceful heathen.... It is a very suitable place," Crespí's diary records, "for a good mission, having good lands, much water, firewood and many heathen."

In the Footsteps of Pedro Fages

On April 1, 1776, Fray Pedro Font mapped, from his position east of Richmond, the Richmond Peninsula, which he took to be an island. Juan Bautista de Anza was the leader of that epoch-making march up the Contra Costa. On the banks of Wildcat Creek, the "rather deep arroyo with a growth of trees and little water," the party came upon an abandoned Indian village. Crossing the creek near San Pablo, they came to a second arroyo with a "very deep" bed and a "heavy growth of live oaks, sycamores, and other trees." Here they found a native village where they were greeted by some 23 men and seven women, who presented the travelers with a feast of roasted "cacomites" (a species of iris) in exchange for the glass beads that Anza gave them.

More hills and two or three small arroyos were passed, and another village of friendly Indians greeted them. At nightfall the travelers came to a "high hill" from which they could see a wide expanse of the bay and hear the waves on the shore. This, says Bolton, was evidently one of the hills at the edge of Rodeo. Camp was made at Rodeo on Rodeo Creek.

At sunrise on the morning of April 2 the camp was visited very early by a delegation of some ten Indians from a village nearby. They came singing and dancing and bearing gifts of cacomites and chuchupate roots. After Mass had been said, Anza accepted the invitation of his visitors to go to their village. Still singing and dancing, they led the way, the padre now and then interrupting their demonstration by chanting the Alabado.

The village, which they soon reached, stood in a valley on the bank of a small arroyo at about the site of the present Tormey. The Indians welcomed their guests "with an indescribable hullabaloo"; and, with peace banners made of feathers and the skins of rabbits, they led the white men to a level spot in the center of the village, where the singers resumed the dance of welcome accompanied by "much clatter and yelling." After an exchange of gifts, Anza and his men continued their journey, apparently to the sorrow of the villagers.

The next halt was made just east of Selby and west of Carquinez Bridge. Here "at the shore of the water near to and inside the Boca del Puerto Dulce," longitudinal measurements were taken, and Father Font devoted himself to a diligent refutation of previous reports made by Fages and Crespí "that Carquinez Strait and Suisun Bay constituted a Río Grande." At this point, too, they found Indians fishing with nets from "launches" or rafts, in which the fishermen afterward crossed to the opposite shore.

The next lap of the journey followed the line of the present road from Selby to Martinez. Professor Bolton outlines the route as follows:

"Two leagues along the top of the hills took them nearly to Port Costa, where the road forks half a mile from town. From here the highway follows a canyon for two and one-half miles and comes out at the coast opposite the [former] Benicia ferry station, which evidently is built on the very farallon which Font describes." At this point the explorers looked across the long sweep of Suisun Bay to "an immense plain without any trees, through which the water extends for a long distance." They were looking upon the great interior rivers and valleys of the Sacramento and the San Joaquin, beyond which lie the Sierra Nevada.

Dropping down to the Martinez Valley, where the Indians from across the strait joined them, the little band continued southeast along the highway that goes to Walnut Creek (Santa Angela de Fulgino). Camp was made at about Pacheco on the edge of Concord Valley and somewhat more than a league from the Puerto Dulce. Father Crespí had thought that this pretty wooded spot would be an attractive place for a mission but the arroyo did not prove to have enough permanent water.

April 3 "dawned very fair and warm but with a pleasant northwest wind blowing." After Mass, the cavalcade moved forward ten leagues to Antioch Bridge. "Leaving camp, they passed the site of Concord, ascended a canyon (Willow Pass) to the top of the ridge [from which they again saw the Sierra Nevada], descending on the east side, and continued to an Indian village on the site of Antioch, swung southeast a league to or beyond Oak Grove Cemetery, and then northeast a league to the bank of San Joaquin River near Antioch Bridge where camp was made." Here the tule marsh, which still covers the river bank at this point, caused the party to turn west about a quarter of a league to the site of an abandoned Indian village. Font's observations here further convinced him that what he saw (the San Joaquin River) was a "fresh water sea," rather than a river, as Fages and Crespí believed.

Nevertheless, the commander of the expedition determined to follow the watercourse, to cross the plain, and to explore in the direction of the Sierra Nevada. With this purpose he set out on April 4 in the general direction but "to the left of the highway that runs from Antioch through

Knightsen to Tracy. Just east of the starting point," Bolton continues, "was the large marsh east of Antioch Bridge. Leaving the river, therefore, Anza swung southeastwardly past Oakley, keeping on the right the live oaks which continue to Knightsen, then suddenly disappear. At a point not far from Knightsen, Anza swung northeast for a league but encountered the tulares, perhaps at Rock Slough."

Escaping not without difficulty from the mire of the treacherous tules, the weary soldiers trudged through the blinding, wind-blown dust of the dry swamps east of Byron Hot Springs. They followed the general course of the Old River some six leagues to a point just south of Bethany, where Anza finally abandoned his plan to approach the Sierra Nevada and decided to return to Monterey instead.

Rancho San Pablo

Rancho San Pablo, at first called Rancho Cochiyumes, consisted of four leagues of land bordered on the west and north by the bays of San Francisco and San Pablo, and on the east by low verdant hills. There were no fences on all its vast acres and no roads; only divergent trails twisted through the wild oats which stretched like a vast sea on all sides. Here and there the tract was dotted by islands of huge oak trees. Numerous wild creatures made it their home—bears, coyotes, and herds of deer and elk.

Into this wilderness Don Francisco Castro drove the first herd of cattle north of Rancho San Antonio, and, like the herds of the Peraltas, it soon multiplied into roving bands of untamed animals which supplied the rancho with food and the Yankee traders with hides and tallow. Here, too, the first fruit trees in the country and grape cuttings from the mission were set out.

Francisco María Castro, a native of Mexico, was a settler at San Francisco in 1800. For 13 years he served his country as a soldier, and in 1822 he was a member of the diputación. In June 1823 he acted as diputado of the exploring expedition led by Padre José Altimira north of San Francisco Bay, and in that year also he obtained, provisionally, the grant of Rancho San Pablo on the Contra Costa.

As early as 1826, Francisco Castro took up residence on this land, and there he lived until his death in 1831, three years before the official confirmation of the grant in 1834. The estate was left half to his widow and half to his 11 children. Through years of litigation, during which, says Bancroft, the whole Castro family was "kept in a state of landed poverty," the vast grant gradually dwindled to a few acres about the adobes at El Cerrito and San Pablo.

Set in a sloping garden shaded by cedar and cypress trees, the venerable Castro adobe at El Cerrito stood until 1956 on the east side of San Pablo Avenue near the north bank of El Cerrito Creek, which here forms the northern boundary line of Contra Costa and Alameda counties. To the west rises El Cerrito ("the little hill"), long a landmark for early travelers and settlers along the northwest shore of the Contra Costa. This hill, round and smooth and high, cast a bold silhouette against the sky in the old days before it was planted with eucalyptus, and constituted one of the more substantial and permanent designations of the boundary line between Rancho San Pablo and its neighbor to the south, Rancho San Antonio.

The low southern wing, which was the older portion of the building, is thought to have been constructed by Francisco Castro, while the two-story section, with broad balconies sweeping across the front and rear, was erected some time in the 1850's by Victor Castro, the youngest of the seven sons of Don Francisco.

A unique addition to the old house was the chapel at the north wing, in which the padres periodically celebrated Mass for the family, their Indian servants, and occasional guests from neighboring ranchos. In rancho days, the hacienda was enclosed by a high wall which served as a protection from wild animals or marauding Indians. A small garden patio at the rear of the adobe sheltered the burial plot of the Castro family.

Doña Gabriela Berryessa de Castro, the widow of Don Francisco, received the adobe with 200 acres of land lying between Wildcat and El Cerrito creeks. The old residence remained in the hands of descendants of the original builder for many years, and in this century was converted into a night club and used as such for some time. Eventually the property was purchased for a shopping center. Efforts were made to secure the preservation of the adobe as part of this complex, but shortly before construction of the center was to begin, the old landmark was destroyed by fire on April 20, 1956. The site (SRL 356), within the grounds of El Cerrito Plaza, is commemorated by a plaque at sidewalk level nearby in the shopping center.

About 1842, Jesús María Castro, one of the sons of Don Francisco, built an adobe dwelling on what is now the west corner of San Pablo Avenue and Church Lane in the city of San Pablo. Martina, daughter of Francisco Castro, married Governor Juan Bautista Alvarado in 1839, and through this marriage the governor came into possession of that portion of the estate to which Martina fell heir at her mother's death in 1851. This included the adobe at San Pablo, to which the world-weary governor had retired in 1848, remaining there until his death on July 13, 1882. Gradually, the vast acreage had been relinquished until, at the time of his death, only about 50 acres of the princely estate that once surrounded the adobe remained.

The Alvarado adobe (SRL 512) stood for many years behind a grocery store at the corner, and, covered with a wooden superstructure, was used as a storeroom. In September 1954, despite the efforts of local citizens and organizations to preserve it, the old adobe was razed for the construction of a motel. A bronze plaque has been placed on an apartment house that was built later on the front portion of the lot.

In 1882 the house stood at the end of a "winding country road," which, wrote a historian of that day, "leads to the place, through hay-fields most of the way, and stops in front of the romantic old house. At present the house stands about thirty feet back from the road....

"The house is one story in height, and is ... long and low, after the manner of old California houses. Across the outer front, about one hundred feet wide, and around the northern side and rear, is a broad porch. Over this grapevines and climbing roses trail in the wildest disorder, running up to the roof ... and trying to force an entrance to the low windows. The walls are about two feet thick.... On the outside is a stairway which leads to the attic above. Huge roof joists of hewn timber project at both ends of the house and support the broad eaves.

"Many improvements were made by the Alvarados. The adobe walls were covered with clapboards, and the interior was improved in many ways. The entire yard is overrun with shrubbery and flowering plants. Over the front paths and winding walks about the house are low arbors covered with grapevines [said to have been the work of a French carpenter brought from France by Governor Alvarado]. Traces of former taste and care are visible in the arrangement of the yard, but now [1882] weeds and thistles are among the flowers, and a general appearance of ruin and neglect is about the place.

"Near the house is an old orchard of many hundred bearing trees. In the rear are old sheds and yards for poultry, and nearby is the stable with tumble-down 'lean-tos' about it."

The Gutiérrez adobe, built about 1850 and one of the finest mansions of its day, stood on the south bank of San Pablo Creek, northwest of San Pablo within the city limits of Richmond. Located west of Garden Tract Road and south of Parr Boulevard, it was razed in the summer of 1946. The home of Candido Gutiérrez and his wife, Jovita Castro Gutiérrez, was pleasantly situated on the bank of the arroyo, where schooners came up the creek to the back door, bringing supplies and taking away products from the rancho. Beneath the picturesque balcony, María Emma, the little daughter of Candido and Jovita, lay buried, and on her tombstone was an inscription in Spanish verse.

The pastoral lands once occupied by the great Rancho San Pablo are now covered by miles of residences and paved highways, humming with the noises of business and pleasure. The cities of Richmond, El Cerrito, and San Pablo have grown up around the pioneer settlements, and with the demise of the old adobes, nothing remains to remind of the pageantry of another day.

Rancho San Ramón

The vast acreage of Rancho San Ramón lay mostly within Contra Costa County, after Alameda County was separated from it in 1853. Two square leagues of this rancho were granted to Bartolomé Pacheco and Mariano Castro by Governor José Figueroa on June 5, 1833. Four leagues were granted by the same governor to José María Amador in 1834 and 1835. Leo Norris, a native of Kentucky who had come across the plains to

California from Missouri in 1846, filed claim for one square league, which he purchased from Amador, and this was confirmed and later patented to him.

Pacheco and Castro divided their grant, Pacheco taking the southern half and Castro the northern. Neither lived on the rancho. Castro lived at Rancho Pastoria de las Borregas (in Santa Clara County) and sold his share of the San Ramón to his brother-in-law, Domingo Peralta of Rancho San Antonio (in Alameda County) in 1852. Pacheco died in 1839, and his land came into the hands of his son Lorenzo, who himself died in 1846. Lorenzo's widow, Rafaela Soto de Pacheco, eventually deeded part of this southern league to Horace W. Carpentier, who had also acquired much of Domingo Peralta's land. Early American settlers on the rancho, including John M. Jones, Daniel Inman, Albert W. Stone, and James Tice, had to pay Carpentier in order to get clear title to their land.

When Leo Norris came to the rancho in the autumn of 1850, he found, according to Munro-Fraser, a branch of the Soto family residing in an adobe house then standing about 150 yards from the site of his residence. Apparently these were brothers of Rafaela Soto de Pacheco who planned to settle there, but they moved elsewhere when all their horses were stolen by Indians.

Leo Norris lived at Mission San José from June 1847 until the early autumn of 1850, when he and his son William migrated to the San Ramón Valley. With them went their cousin, William Lynch, a native of New York, who had landed in San Francisco on June 28, 1849, from the pilot boat *W. A. Hackstaff.* Lynch was a journeyman carpenter and practiced his trade in San Francisco before going out to the fertile valley of San Ramón, where he aided Norris in erecting his house, the first frame dwelling in the valley. It was constructed from lumber hauled from the San Antonio redwoods by the long and tedious route through Mission San José, Suñol Valley, and Amador's (now Dublin). In spite of this roundabout journey, the house was ready for occupancy before the winter. The old Norris dwelling, which stood on Norris Canyon Road at the mouth of the canyon, about half a mile west of San Ramon Valley Boulevard, was destroyed by fire about 1950.

In the spring of 1851, Norris fenced the field at the rear of the Lynch house. The fence posts were willow saplings taken from the banks of the adjacent stream. The willows took root and grew. The old Lynch house and its giant willow trees were destroyed when a new section of Crow Canyon Road was constructed.

Other American pioneers purchased portions of Rancho San Ramón. Joel Harlan, a native of Indiana, came to California with his parents in the spring of 1846. After a trip to the mines, followed by his marriage in April 1849, Harlan lived at different times in Napa City, Sacramento, San Francisco, San Jose, and San Lorenzo (in Alameda County) where he was one of the first settlers at "Squattersville."

Finally, in 1852, Harlan purchased a tract of land on Rancho San Ramón in Contra Costa County. There he erected a dwelling, which, when the county of Alameda was carved out of the older county, was one of the points defining the boundary line between the two counties. Notwithstanding the unique, if somewhat indefinite, position of his house, Harlan always maintained that it stood on the Contra Costa side of the line. A huge oak tree in the corner of the original Harlan yard long served as a landmark. The spot is just west of the junction of Alcosta and San Ramon Valley boulevards north of Dublin. The iron milepost erected in 1895 on the county line by Elisha Harlan and his mother, Minerva (Mrs. Joel) Harlan, has been moved to the southeast corner of this intersection.

Approximately 2,000 acres purchased from the Norris tract were added to the Harlan estate in 1856. The following year the house at the county boundary line was moved north to a site three miles south of the town of San Ramon, and there in 1858 Harlan built the fine old country mansion now known as El Nido ("The Nest"). The original dwelling was incorporated into a wing of the two-story building.

El Nido stands at 19251 San Ramon Valley Boulevard, back from the road, almost completely hidden in a leafy bower of many kinds of trees and shrubs which create a vivid contrast with the gleaming white of the house and fences. Through the ornamental gateway one peers down a stately row of Italian cypress trees to the white gabled house at the end of the path. Descendants of the genial Joel Harlan still occupy and cherish the old house and its lovely garden.

Another early settler who purchased a portion of Rancho San Ramón was David Glass, a native of Pennsylvania, who had arrived with his family in California from Iowa on August 1, 1850. After a short stay in Placerville, he came direct to Contra Costa County, where he settled in November of that year in the vicinity of Walnut Creek. It was not until some nine years later that he purchased the ranch of 718 acres located three and one-half miles south of San Ramon. The original Glass house no longer stands, but the later two-story residence built in the 1880's, now known as the Hillside Ranch Sanitarium, remains at 19801 San Ramon Valley Boulevard, half a mile south of El Nido.

Christian Wiedemann, who came to San Francisco from Germany in 1852, settled on Rancho San Ramón in 1855. He built his home, still owned by the family, in 1858 on a 400-acre tract. It is located about one-half mile south of Norris Canyon Road at a point two and one-half miles west of San Ramon Valley Boulevard.

Alamo

The towns of Alamo, Danville, and San Ramon are located on the northern (Castro-Pacheco) portion of Rancho San Ramón.

The name Alamo, which in Spanish signifies "poplar," was bestowed upon the town because poplar trees once grew abundantly in the valley and along the streams. For many years Alamo was a picturesque little community, with giant maple trees on either side of the main street and old houses from the 1850's and 1860's, but now it is thoroughly modernized and its population is mushrooming.

On the southeast corner of Stone Valley Road and Danville Boulevard long stood the old Henry Hotel. In 1854 a portion of this structure housed the Wolf store, one of the two first stores in Alamo. About the same time George Englemore started Alamo's other "first" store on the opposite corner of Stone Valley Road, and in 1854 these two establishments composed the town. They drew a large trade from the Spanish population of the neighborhood, the Garcías to the east, the Romeros to the west, and others who were interested in the San Ramón grant. With the coming of the Americans, the Spanish gradually disappeared.

An adobe was built on the site of Alamo about 1848 or 1849, and in it the first post office was located in 1852 with John M. Jones as postmaster. The old Annie Humberg house at 3170 Danville Boulevard now stands on the site. Jones, a native of Kentucky, was a typical pioneer of the early nineteenth century, who, constantly pushing westward, at last crossed the plains by ox team in 1846, bound for California. He came to the San Ramon Valley in 1851.

James Foster, a native of Maine and a mill-wright, came to California in 1856 via Panama. He followed his trade among the redwood forests of San Mateo County until February 1857, when he went to Placer County to build a gristmill on Bear River near Auburn. In the autumn of 1857 he came to Contra Costa County, opened a wheel-wright shop in Alamo, and sent East for his wife and children. Foster lived in Alamo until 1881. Always an active man, he not only practiced his trade for 12 years in that place but was postmaster during most of his stay there, was justice of the peace from 1860 to 1868, served as county assessor from 1869 to 1879, was admitted to the bar in 1872, and acted as referee at various times in important land-grant suits. Foster sold his property in Alamo in 1881 and purchased a block in Walnut Creek, where he built a fine home and became senior member of Foster and Stow, realtors. His son, Fred Lewis Foster, became one of the proprietors and the junior associate editor of the *Contra Costa Gazette.* The old Foster house at Alamo no longer stands.

The cornerstone of an academy was laid on October 19, 1859, about one and one-half miles south of Alamo, under the auspices of the Contra Costa Educational Association. The site is on the west side of Danville Boulevard almost opposite El Portal Road. A marker hidden behind a fence reads: "Site of Union Academy built 1859. Trustees: Robert Love, Silas Stone, John M. Jones. Principal: David McClure." The Rev. David McClure, first master of this short-lived educational venture, had conducted in 1857 the first services of the Presbyterian Church in the San Ramon Valley. He later became principal of the Califor-

nia Military Academy in Oakland and was succeeded at the Union Academy by Professor J. H. Braly, later of the San Jose State Normal School, who was followed by a Rev. Mr. King. In 1868, during King's administration, the building burned. It was never rebuilt.

Danville

It has been said that Danville was named for Daniel Inman, the pioneer who formerly owned the land on which the town now stands. In a way it was, but the whole story, as told in the *Danville Sentinel* of 1898, reveals a happy coincidence which satisfied a personal wish and at the same time honored a favorite son. The article quotes Inman's version of the story as follows:

"I reached Danville, or the site where it now stands, in June, 1852. I spent the summer in the valley, but returned to the mines in the fall. In the summer of 1853 I came into the valley again and remained until 1857, when I returned to the mines. In March of the following year I came into the valley once more—this time for good—and purchased a farm, where Danville is now located, of a man named Pigmore.

"I went to farming and seeded the lands with wheat that winter. In the summer of 1859 a man named Davis came along and wanted to start a blacksmith shop where the one now stands (Close's shop), and I gave him permission to do so."

With the increased life and activity, "the people," continued Inman, "wanted a post-office. Of course it had to have a name, and quite a number were suggested. At first they thought of calling it 'Inmanville,' but my brother Andrew and I objected to that.

"Finally, 'Grandma' Young, my brother's mother-in-law, said: 'Call it Danville,' and as much or more out of respect to her, as she was born and raised near Danville, Kentucky, it took that name."

In 1858, S. Wolf, M. Cohen, and Henry Hoffman dissolved the firm of Wolf and Company at Alamo and opened a store in Danville. About the same year H. W. Davis opened the first Danville Hotel at the junction of Diablo Road and Hartz Avenue. It burned in 1873, but a picturesque later version still stands nearby on Hartz Avenue near the corner of Prospect Avenue.

San Ramon (Limerick)

The northern boundary of the Norris division of Rancho San Ramón is just south of the little town of San Ramon. Originally known as Lynchville, this town, like Dublin to the south, long retained the sobriquet of Limerick because the settlers of the vicinity were primarily Irish. The first house to be erected on the site of San Ramon was put up by John White in 1852. No other was built there until 1857, when Eli Brewin constructed a smithy. With the coming of stores and homes, the citizens secured a post office in 1873, on which the name San Ramon (misspelled "San Ramoon" for the first ten years) was bestowed, although the settlement continued to be known popularly as Limerick for some time. An earlier post office named San Ramon had existed in the vicinity from 1852 to 1859. The Catholic church dedicated to St. Raymond was built in 1859 at Dublin, where it still stands.

Rancho El Sobrante de San Ramón

José and Inocencio Romero, brothers, claimed Rancho El Sobrante de San Ramón of five leagues. This was the *sobrante* or "overplus" of land "lying between the ranchos of Moraga, Pacheco and Welch." Some six or seven years before the Romeros petitioned for the grant on January 18, 1844, the tract had been claimed by Francisco Soto, but it had never been used or cultivated by him.

The large adobe residence of the Romeros, in Tice Valley southwest of Walnut Creek, was razed in 1900, but a small stone and mud house remained for some years afterward. El Sobrante de San Ramón was never confirmed to the brothers, because of certain legal complications and vagaries, but there is evidence that the land was occupied by them, probably by 1840 but at least by 1844. Petitions for a grant made by the Romeros were favorably received by the governor, who, on March 23, 1844, directed a measurement of the land to be made preparatory to the granting of the same. The measurements, however, were never taken, a provisional grant was refused, and the claim was finally rejected in 1864.

James Tice later came into ownership of the property, and the valley was named for him. Joseph Napthaly began to acquire land in the valley in 1874. He built a winery where Del Valle High School now stands. The former station of Saranap on the Sacramento Northern Railroad was a contraction of Sara Napthaly. In 1930 the Napthaly Ranch was sold to Stanley Dollar, the steamship magnate, and in 1960 it became Rossmoor Leisure World, a retirement community. About 1965 some children from Tice Valley School discovered in the hills a large sandstone rock with the chiseled inscription "J. W. Tice 1855."

The portion of San Ramón Sobrante that lies immediately east of Alamo was long known as the Stone Ranch and is still called Stone Valley. There, in 1850, Francisco García lived in an adobe, the crumbling ruins of which stood until about 1935 on the hill just below the old two-story Stone residence two-tenths of a mile north of Stone Valley Road on Austin Lane.

Albert W. Stone, a native of Pennsylvania and a blacksmith by trade, had come to California from Iowa in September 1852. After returning to Iowa the following year, he again crossed the plains to California, this time with his family. For a while he lived in Colusa County on land later occupied by Dr. Hugh J. Glenn, but in January 1858 he moved to Contra Costa County, where he purchased the farm of 800 acres adjoining Alamo. The family lived temporarily in the García adobe, but very soon a frame house was built one-half mile to the east, of redwood timbers from the Palos Colorados of San Antonio. It stood at what is now 2144 Stone Valley Road.

This was followed by the two-story house still standing on the hill above the adobe site.

Rancho Acalanes

Rancho Acalanes, lying among the fertile little valleys west of Lafayette, was granted on August 1, 1834, to Candelario Valencia, a soldier of the San Francisco Company. The name, says Kroeber, was probably derived from "Akalan" (or something similar), the name of a Costanoan Indian village in the vicinity, which was dignified by the Spaniards into the Acalanes "tribe."

Like many another native Californian of the old Spanish and Mexican regime, Valencia eventually became indebted to a foreigner and, being unable to clear himself of entanglements, was forced to sell his land. Thus it was that Rancho Acalanes fell into the hands of William A. Leidesdorff of Yerba Buena, who put it up for sale.

Meanwhile, Elam Brown, a native of New York, had arrived in California on October 10, 1846, as captain of a company of 14 families and 16 wagons which apparently had crossed the mountains in company with the Boggs and Cooper parties. Brown spent his first summer in California whipsawing lumber in the San Antonio redwoods and hauling it to the old San Antonio Landing, where it was shipped across the bay to San Francisco. Learning that Rancho Acalanes was for sale, Brown purchased it from Leidesdorff, together with 300 cows the latter had obtained from Vásquez at Half Moon Bay.

Brown took his family through the Moraga Valley to their new home, where they arrived on February 7, 1848. They were the second American family to settle in Contra Costa County. The Browns lived at first in an adobe in Lower Happy Valley, about two miles from the present town of Lafayette, on land later owned by Thomas W. Bradley. When water failed at this point, Brown was forced to move to another site. A like circumstance occurred again before he was permanently located. The final site of Elam Brown's home, built of lumber from the San Antonio redwoods, was in the present La Fiesta shopping center in Lafayette, at the southwest corner of Hough Avenue and the creek.

At first Brown had to make long, tedious trips on horseback or by ox team via the San Ramón Valley in order to carry his wheat and barley to Sansevain's mill in San José, where it was turned into flour. To eliminate the necessity for this trip, Brown purchased a horsepower mill at Benicia in 1853 and set it up near his house. The millstone was placed in the Lafayette plaza in 1955 as a memorial to Elam Brown. The gristmill was located beside the creek south of this monument, in the vacant lot next to the Park Theater.

Elam Brown, who died in 1889, was for many years a respected and prosperous citizen of Contra Costa County. He was a member of the convention that framed the State Constitution in 1849 and also of the first two legislatures after its adoption.

Conveyance of one-tenth of Rancho Acalanes was made to Nathaniel Jones in the autumn of 1847, soon after Brown had acquired the property. Jones, a native of Tennessee, had started for Oregon from Missouri in April 1846 in company with 15 or 20 other families. Circumstances diverted the immigrants to California, and Joseph Chiles induced Jones at Fort Sutter to go to Rancho Catacula in Napa County. With three or four other families the Joneses arrived in Chiles Valley on November 2, 1846. After volunteering and participating in the Battle of Santa Clara, Nathaniel Jones returned to Rancho Catacula.

Jones took his wife and small son to the San Antonio redwoods in Alameda County, and with the proceeds of the work that he did that summer he purchased a part of Rancho Acalanes from Elam Brown for $100.

Nathaniel Jones and Elam Brown moved to their new homes about the same time, and early in 1848 Jones built his house. In the spring of the following year he began to beautify his home by setting out fine, large black-locust trees which gave the name of Locust Farm to his ranch. The seed of these trees had been brought to California by Major Stephen Cooper in 1846 and subsequently presented to Jones. A few of the trees may still be seen on (Lower) Happy Valley Road, north of Lafayette.

Locust Farm in 1882 contained 372 acres, part of which was cultivated and the remainder kept for grazing. Five acres were set to choice fruit trees. The comfortable eight-room house sheltered a family of five children, the eldest of whom, Robinson, had accompanied his parents across the plains when he was only two years of age. Robinson M. Jones became a versatile and active man, being a farmer, teacher, county surveyor, newspaper man, and warehouse operator at Martinez. Nathaniel Jones himself was always interested in the affairs of his county and held such county offices as those of sheriff (he was the first), public administrator, and supervisor.

A traveler, passing by the Brown residence in 1852, was induced to remain. This was Benjamin Shreve, who taught school there during the winter of 1852–53 and later opened a store and built a home. In 1853 Milo Hugh erected a hotel, which he conducted until 1855. Other settlers came, and very early a church was built and a cemetery laid out. Thus, about Elam Brown's hospitable home the town of Lafayette grew up.

Among the first industries to be started in Lafayette was a blacksmith shop established by Jack Elston and purchased by Peter Thomson in 1859. This shop was situated at what is now 3530 Mount Diablo Boulevard. Peter Thomson, an expert blacksmith of the old school, was a Canadian by birth. Having come by sailing vessel from New York, he arrived in San Francisco with two companions on June 24, 1859. After a few months in Oakland, he went to Lafayette, where he began work as a journeyman blacksmith in the shop that he later owned.

Some of Lafayette's early buildings are still standing in the vicinity of the plaza, although they have been remodeled through the years. The oldest is Benjamin Shreve's store, built about 1856, at 3535 Plaza Way. Shreve is credited with naming the town, and he was the first postmaster.

The post office was established in his store in 1857. Lafayette's first school was located near the plaza. It no longer stands, but the second school is now used as a tavern at 3535 Mount Diablo Boulevard, and the third has been incorporated into the Lafayette Methodist Church at 955 Moraga Road.

Rancho Los Medanos (Meganos)

Father Narciso Durán, accompanied by Father Ramón Abella and Captain Luís Antonio Argüello, made a boat voyage up the Sacramento River in May 1817. It was on this expedition, according to Chapman, that the sand banks or dunes that lie along the Carquinez Straits between Pittsburg and Antioch were mentioned as *Los Medanos*, "the Sand-banks." The name was later applied to the ranchos Los Medanos (sometimes spelled "Meganos" but also interpreted as sand dunes), which embraced lands later known as the New York Ranch and the Marsh Estate.

During the late 1830's two adjoining ranchos were granted, both of which, according to Bancroft, received the name of Los Medanos, apparently because of the presence of sand dunes lying along the left bank of the San Joaquin River in their vicinity. Later writers, however, have tried somewhat ambiguously to distinguish the two by calling the rancho originally granted to José Noriega and later purchased by Dr. John Marsh "Los Meganos" and the New York Ranch "Los Medanos."

When the ship *Natalia,* bearing the Híjar and Padrés colony from Acapulco, Mexico, was wrecked at Monterey in 1834, José Noriega, supercargo, was among its passengers. The following year, Noriega was made *depositario* or receiver at Mission San José, and on October 13 of that year he also became grantee of Rancho Los Medanos (Meganos) in Contra Costa County, where he built some corrals and a few outbuildings. During 1837 Noriega sold his rancho to John Marsh, who settled upon it the same year and occupied it until his death in 1856.

Marsh, a native of Massachusetts, graduated from Harvard University with the degree of Bachelor of Arts, spent some time in Wisconsin, left the United States in 1835, and proceeded to New Mexico. After traveling through a portion of Old Mexico, he crossed the Colorado River at the Gila and entered southern California early in January 1836. He displayed his Harvard diploma to the *ayuntamiento* of Los Angeles, and it was received as a medical diploma. Marsh was given a license to practice medicine. In his sympathetic biography, Winkley points out that Marsh had completed his medical education and had practiced for some years. Although he lacked a formal medical degree, he was well qualified as a physician and surgeon.

Early in 1837 Marsh came north, and late in December he acquired the rancho in the shadow of Mount Diablo. The Indians of this region became the doctor's friends and helpers, and he even called his estate the Farm of Pulpones (evidently a corruption of Bolbones, or Bolgones), from the name of an Indian tribe or village in the vicinity

Stone House of Dr. John Marsh, near Brentwood

of Mount Diablo. The doctor was kind to his Indian neighbors—healing their sick, teaching them to trap for bear and otter, and leaving their ancient ranchería undisturbed. In return, the natives helped the "Señor Doctor" to build an adobe on the bank of the stream opposite their village. They brought grape cuttings from Mission San José and helped him to plant a vineyard and an orchard of pears, figs, and olives. They plowed his field for him and helped him to sow it to wheat. When death finally came to him, the Indians watched beside his bier and mourned his passing.

Dr. Marsh's adobe home "was a crude affair of sun-baked walls and thatched roof. Within were four large rooms and an attic . . . large enough to accommodate two of his vaqueros, who always slept there and acted as his bodyguard. . . . The walls underneath the eaves, were perforated by loopholes. Through these the doctor and his vaqueros often drove away robbers and horse thieves. . . .

"One room of the adobe had a fireplace. . . . By the light of blazing pine-knots he lay on the well-beaten floor and reflected or often read all night,—read everything that came to hand, medicine, agriculture, old newspapers and, sometimes . . . he reread his Greek and Latin books until he knew long passages by heart. . . .

"In another room, on a shelf that ran part way around the wall, were the books he had brought with him and those he had acquired from sailing ships and men-of-war. . . .

"Across the entrance to his adobe, facing the mountain and an oak grove, was a portico roofed with tules, but, like the house proper, floorless.

On either side of the door were rude benches, their backs against the wall. Here Marsh used to sit in the long summer twilights."

Disappointment and tragedy experienced during his sojourn among the Indians in Wisconsin before he came to California had left their stamp upon the life and character of John Marsh. In his new environment he became a man of mystery. To all but his Indian neighbors he was notoriously parsimonious and often unkind. When the Bidwell-Bartleson party reached his rancho in 1841, the first party to cross the Sierra Nevada into California, he received them, but he made them pay well for his services. Even the Yankee traders complained about his sharp methods when he tried to beat them at their own game. His treatment of the 1841 party is understandable in that several of the members had killed some of Marsh's trained work animals.

But there were those who admired the seemingly hard and tight-fisted doctor, and several Californians, including General Vallejo, spoke of him in terms of warm praise. To some, indeed, he had been a ministering angel, for Dr. Marsh was the first and for several years the only man to practice medicine in the San Joaquin Valley. He often traveled many leagues to minister to the sick, his services usually being paid for in cattle. "The greater the distance," writes Lyman, "the more cows he expected, but it was generally agreed that he brought comfort and relief to the households he visited. His reputation spread. Cows or no cows, his services were in demand."

Although naturalized as a Mexican citizen in 1844, Dr. Marsh joined Sutter's forces against the Californians in 1844-45 but took slight part in the troubles of 1846–47. Nevertheless, he increasingly wanted to see California come into the possession of the United States, and almost every wagon train to the East carried letters to friends praising the glories and possibilities of the land. Most of the communications were to Missourians and were published in Missouri newspapers.

These letters, interestingly written from direct observation, exerted a far-reaching influence on immigration to California, especially from Missouri. The influence of these letters, coupled with the practical efforts of Antoine Robidoux, probably helped the movement that resulted in the first emigrant party to California via the Rocky Mountains and the Sierra Nevada, led by Bidwell and Bartleson in 1841. The Marsh letters are still a valuable source of information on the life and times of pioneer California.

Dr. Marsh was married on June 24, 1851, to Miss Abbie Tuck of Chelmsford, Massachusetts. Abbie, the daughter of a minister, was a beautiful and accomplished young lady who had come to California in 1850 for her health. While she was living among friends in Santa Clara, she was invited to take a trip through Contra Costa County. On this journey she met Dr. Marsh. A strong mutual admiration immediately grew up between the two, and after a courtship of two weeks, during which Abbie was completely swept off her feet by the fascinating and compelling personality of this mysterious man, they were married. One daughter, Alice, was born to this union.

The peak of John Marsh's happiness and prosperity passed quickly. About three years after the birth of their child, his wife sickened and died. His Mexican neighbors were becoming increasingly irritated and vengeful over the doctor's parsimonious acts and unkind attitude toward the rights of others. On September 24, 1856, he was murdered by three of these desperate young Californians on the lonely road between his rancho and Martinez. Ten years later one of the murderers was apprehended and sent to prison for life. After 25 years he was pardoned. The site of the murder (SRL 722) is marked by the roadside two miles north of Pacheco on Pacheco Boulevard.

After much litigation the Marsh estate was divided between Alice and Charles, the doctor's son by Marguerite, his common-law wife of Prairie du Chien, Wisconsin, whose death had greatly changed the tenor of the doctor's life and brought him to California. It was largely through the efforts of Charles that justice was finally obtained for the two children and the property was freed from the hands of unscrupulous persons.

"Soon after the wedding," writes Lyman, "the doctor took his young wife to the old adobe to live.... She loved the broad brook that ran, deep and still, near the kitchen door.... Under the oaks and alders that fringed its bank was a favorite spot where she sat and read. Before long she had planted roses, dahlias, cinnamon pinks and peonies along its banks."

But John Marsh dreamed of greater things than the crude adobe for his beautiful wife. A stone mansion was planned with a library, marble fireplaces, a tower, and a lovely suite of rooms for Abbie and himself. Abbie selected the site "in the portal of a pretty valley and almost directly opposite the old adobe." Abbie Marsh never lived in her castle of dreams. She died before its completion, and little Alice, in the middle of litigation, among strangers, was to experience poverty and hardship before she finally came into her inheritance.

Set in wide, open fields about four miles southwest of Brentwood via Walnut Boulevard and Marsh Creek Road, the old "Stone House" has for over a century been one of the most striking landmarks of Contra Costa County. Beside the lonely road its steep English gables and solid masonry of native stone rise in picturesque solitude, reminding one of the princely acres that were Rancho Los Medanos.

A contemporary description of the mansion appeared in the *Daily Evening Bulletin* of July 19, 1856, shortly before the house was completed. Most of the details remain unchanged.

"Across the valley ... stretches a noble grove of oaks, through which vistas have been cut, affording glimpses of the broken country beyond, closed in by old Mount Diablo.... The new and beautiful edifice, now completed, is situated in the center of the plain.... From a quarry which has been opened upon the estate, an abundant supply of stone for the building has been obtained. It is of the finest quality of freestone, of a beautiful drab or cream-color, slightly variegated.... The architect, Thomas Boyd ... with a true artistic perception of the beauty of the site, and of what was wanted ... to make it harmonize with the surrounding scenery ... had adopted the old English domestic style of architecture—a pleasing and appropriate union of Manor House and Castle. The arched windows, the peaked roofs and gables, the projecting eaves, the central tower sixty-five feet in height, boldly springing from the midst and enabling the proprietor to overlook his extensive domain, must be acknowledged ... a most felicitous deviation from the prevailing style of rural architecture.

"The corners of the building as well as the door and window-jambs, sills and caps, are elaborately wrought, the spaces between the openings being laid with rubber-stone, giving a pleasing variety to the whole exterior. The building has a ground base of sixty by forty feet, and is three stories in height, with three gabled windows in the attic looking east, west, and south. On three sides of the building is a piazza, ten feet in width, supported by beautiful octagon pillars; over this is a walk on a level with the second floor, enclosed by an elaborately finished balustrade. The work has been performed ... by Messrs. Pierce and Wood ... with the utmost faithfulness and ability. The interior arrangements are as carefully planned as possible to subserve the purposes of convenience, comfort, and beautiful finish. The whole cost of the building ... will not exceed twenty thousand dollars."

The 14-room house and a few acres around it are now owned by the county. There are plans for the restoration of the beautiful old mansion

...quisition of additional property for a

...ho El Pinole

Rancho El Pinole, which stretched east from Pinole Point on San Pablo Bay to the town of Martinez at the southern end of Suisun Bay, was first given to Ignacio Martínez in 1829. It was regranted to him in 1842 and by a claim founded on the grant of the latter date was patented to his heirs in 1868.

Ignacio Martínez was born in Mexico City in 1774 and, coming to California, entered military service as cadet at Santa Barbara in 1799. He was promoted to be *alférez* of the San Diego Company in 1806 and in 1817 was again recommended for promotion, this time to go back to Santa Barbara. To his chagrin, an error in the making out of his papers sent him to San Francisco instead.

His life thereafter was spent in the central part of the state. He was retired in 1831, after having been *comandante* at San Francisco during the last four years of military service. On his retirement, he was credited with 41 years of service, was given full pay, and was allowed the continued use of his uniform.

He lived for a time at San José, where he was alderman in 1834–35, before settling on his land in Contra Costa County about 1836. In 1841 he was living on his rancho with his wife, Martina Arrellanes, and six of his daughters. Another daughter, María Antonia, had married William A. Richardson. At home Martínez threw aside the aloofness and arrogance that had marked his earlier career and became a courteous and hospitable ranchero. The town of Pinole (Mexican word meaning "cereal meal") carries the name of his rancho, and the town of Martinez at the edge of his land is named for the family.

The ruins of the Ignacio Martínez adobe were traceable as late as the Bowman-Hendry survey, published in 1942, but they have now been reclaimed by the soil. The house stood on a small ridge on the south side of Pinole Creek, about two and one-half miles southeast of Pinole. The area is identifiable by the jog in Pinole Valley Road, by which it crosses the creek twice in a short distance. The old road—now impassable but still shown on maps as Adobe Road—followed the south bank of the creek.

Two of the old El Pinole rancho houses may still be seen in the vicinity of Martinez. One is on the John Muir Ranch in Franklin Canyon about two miles south of town, and the other is farther south on the John Swett Ranch in the Alhambra Valley.

The former home of John Muir (*SRL 312*), explorer, scientist, and author, is located at Alhambra Avenue and Franklin Canyon Road. The large old-fashioned house where the writer lived from 1890 to 1914, the year of his death, stands on a knoll overlooking the orchards and homes below and the hills that hem them in on all sides. The house was built by Dr. John Strentzel, Muir's father-in-law.

John Muir was born in Dunbar, Scotland, on April 21, 1838. He came to the United States in 1849, and, while still a young man, he came to California. Most of his life was spent exploring, studying, and writing about the great mountains of California and Alaska, their valleys, glaciers, and wildlife. Many of the mountain peaks and glaciers up and down the Pacific Coast were discovered and named by him. He was one of the foremost advocates of national parks, and his books, which have literary value as well as scientific, have done much to cause people to know and love the natural wonderlands of the Pacific Coast states. Perhaps the best-known and most beautiful of his writings is *The Mountains of California*, published in 1894.

In tribute to this great man, the National Park Service is currently developing his home and property as John Muir National Historic Site. The house had previously been registered as a National Historic Landmark by the Department of the Interior. The Historic Site will also include the Vicente Martínez adobe (*SRL 511*), which was the home of ranch employees during Muir's time. It stands on Canyon Way at the western edge of the property. Vicente, a son of Ignacio Martínez, built the adobe in 1849. Four years later he sold it to Edward Franklin, for whom Franklin Canyon is named, who resided there a short time.

John Swett has been called the "father of the California public schools" because of his untiring efforts in their behalf while he was superintendent of public instruction from 1863 to 1867. He was born in New Hampshire and came to San Francisco in 1853, where he was at once employed as a teacher. Throughout his long career as a teacher and administrator he did more than any other one man to build up the public school system of California.

The John Swett Ranch, at the end of Millthwait Drive off Alhambra Valley Road, lies in the heart of the Alhambra Valley in the midst of orchards and residential developments. The big old house itself is hidden among the trees along a stream. Beside it is a little white adobe built by Abilino Altamirano about 1849 and carefully preserved by Swett and his descendants.

Rancho Monte del Diablo

Salvio Pacheco, having held high offices in the government of Mexican California, was granted the Rancho Monte del Diablo, of 18,000 acres,

Vicente Martínez Adobe, Martinez

Fernando Pacheco Adobe, Concord

in 1834. About ten years later he moved to it and soon built the adobe house *(SRL 515)* still standing in the present town of Concord, originally called by him Todos Santos, which was surveyed in 1868. The adobe is located on Adobe Street between Salvio and Central streets, and is now used as a restaurant.

The Pacheco house, with its balconies, its deep casements, shuttered windows, and thick walls, is a good example of the Spanish-Californian home. Although damaged by earthquakes, it is still well preserved. Under the pepper trees which frame the front of the house is an old brick well. By 1852 American squatters had come in large numbers to settle on this land, but in 1853 the United States government granted a patent to Pacheco; thus he was able to secure title to the estate.

The adobe home of Salvio's son Fernando Pacheco *(SRL 455)* also remains standing on the rancho. It was built in the 1840's on a 1,500-acre tract given him by his father. Long neglected, it was restored by the Contra Costa County Horsemen's Association in 1941 and serves as their headquarters. It stands at 3119 Grant Street in the northwestern outskirts of Concord.

The settlement of Pacheco lies five miles southeast of Martinez and two miles west of Concord. The first house erected in this vicinity, no longer standing, was built by G. L. Walwrath of New York in 1853. Its timbers were hewn from the Moraga redwoods. Walwrath owned it only three years and then sold it to George P. Loucks. Loucks sold his commission business in San Francisco and moved to this house in 1857, when he built a mile below his dwelling a large warehouse on Pacheco Creek, then navigable for small sternwheel steamers. He sold a piece of his land to William Hendrick, who at once erected a dwelling house and a flour mill, one of the few flour mills in the county.

In the same year, 1857, Dr. J. H. Carothers purchased a tract of land from the Pacheco family and laid out the town of Pacheco on the east bank of Pacheco (Grayson) Creek. Around the two enterprises of warehouse and flour mill a flourishing town grew up, attracting men who built for themselves houses similar to those of New England. The first business building, the "Long Store," was erected by Hale and Fassett. Shortly after, Elijah Hook put up a two-story

brick building, which housed a general-merchandise store on its ground floor and the *Contra Costa Gazette* upstairs. In 1859 a small schoolhouse was built, followed in 1863 by a larger one of two stories that was used until 1926, when it was replaced by one of cement on Aspen Drive, now a church. Pacheco's present school is on Deodar Drive.

A stage line with change of horses at Pacheco ran from Antioch to Martinez. A post office was established in 1859. Mail from San Francisco was brought to Martinez by the river steamers and on to Pacheco by stage. The town was a busy one. From the Tassajara and San Ramon valleys came great four- and six-horse wagons with grain for the mill. All traffic from the southern and eastern parts of the county passed through on its way to the county seat at Martinez. Traffic from the Sacramento Valley passed through, both going to the ferry at Martinez and returning from it. Conestoga wagons that had traveled far were familiar sights.

To accommodate travelers two hotels were built. The Eagle, on the southeast corner of Pacheco Boulevard and Center Avenue, still stands and is now the Pacheco Inn.

The flood of 1862 swept away much of the town. The Loucks warehouse fell and was never rebuilt. Within the next six years two fires destroyed many frame buildings. In 1868 came the disastrous earthquake that leveled brick and other buildings. However, the disasters of flood, fires, and earthquake did not destroy the town, which seems to have reached the peak of its prosperity in 1870, when the Contra Costa Bank of Savings and Loan was organized.

Rancho Laguna de los Palos Colorados

Rancho Laguna de los Palos Colorados ("lake of the redwoods"), comprising 13,316 acres, was granted to Joaquín Moraga and Juan Bernal in 1835. Moraga was the grandson of José Joaquín Moraga, founder and first *comandante* of the Presidio of San Francisco. Bernal was a cousin of the younger Moraga.

The picturesque adobe *(SRL 509)* built by Joaquín Moraga and completed in 1841 still stands on a hill overlooking the beautiful Moraga Valley. It was restored in the 1940's by Katherine Brown White Irvine. The old house is located one and one-half miles northwest of Moraga via

Joaquín Moraga Adobe, Moraga

Moraga Way, El Camino Moraga, Donna Maria Way, and the private Adobe Lane.

The redwoods for which the rancho was named were in the canyons between Moraga's home and Rancho San Antonio of the Peraltas. The laguna was located at the present site of Campolindo High School on Moraga Road just north of the Rheem Valley shopping center.

Rancho Arroyo de las Nueces y Bolbones

In the central part of the county is Rancho Arroyo de las Nueces y Bolbones, consisting of 17,782 acres, granted to Juana Sánchez de Pacheco in 1834. This rancho, located on the western flank of Mount Diablo, was patented to her heirs on April 18, 1866. Arroyo de las Nueces is now called Walnut Creek and has given its name to a thriving city. Bolbones was the name of a tribe of Indians in the vicinity of Mount Diablo. The rancho was also called by the name San Miguel.

One of the early American settlers on this rancho was James T. Walker, who acquired some 1,400 acres in the 1850's, and in 1868 built a home that is still standing. The previous year Walker's uncle came to live with him. This was Joseph Reddeford Walker, trapper, trailmaker, guide, and stock buyer of the 1830's and 1840's, for whom Walker Pass is named. The elder Walker moved into the new house with his nephew and lived there until his death in 1876 at the age of 77. He is buried in Alhambra Cemetery at Martinez, where his headstone recounts the highlights of his career. The old James Walker home stands at 1200 North Gate Road, on the way from Walnut Creek to Mount Diablo State Park.

Miscellaneous Ranchos

Other Mexican grants in this county that have received United States patents are Las Juntas, Boca de la Cañada del Pinole, and Cañada de los Vaqueros.

The eastern part of the town of Martinez is on what was formerly a portion of the Rancho Las Juntas, consisting of 13,292 acres granted to William Welch, a Scotsman, in 1844. In 1849, Colonel William M. Smith, agent for the Martínez family, laid out a town there, and in 1850 it became the county seat of Contra Costa County.

In the western part of the county is Rancho Boca de la Cañada del Pinole, consisting of 13,316 acres granted to María Manuel Valencia and patented to her in 1878.

In the southeastern part of the county lies Rancho Cañada de los Vaqueros, originally granted to three Spanish Californians and bought in 1847 by Robert Livermore.

Pittsburg, "The New York of the Pacific"

Colonel Jonathan D. Stevenson brought the First Regiment of New York Volunteers to California by sea, arriving in three transports in March 1847 to take part in the American occupation. In 1849 he bought Rancho Los Medanos from the original Mexican grantees, José Antonio Mesa and José Miguel García.

On this ranch, Stevenson laid out the site for a city about where Pittsburg now stands. He called it New York of the Pacific after his home city, New York, and the rancho was called the New York Ranch. The colonel hoped that his new city would become a large and prosperous seaport, and to that end he attempted to locate the state capital there in 1850, but the city of Vallejo won the honor by popular election.

As late as the 1880's, Pittsburg was a busy port for the shipment of coal from the mines discovered near Mount Diablo, and at that time was called Black Diamond. This industry was short-lived, however, because of the poor quality of the coal, and the town was never of real importance until more recent years, when it became a manufacturing center of considerable extent. The name was changed to Pittsburg in 1911.

Ghost Towns of Contra Costa

South of Antioch and Pittsburg, the lingering ghosts of coal-mining days remind one of the brief excitements and short-lived hopes, the comedies and tragedies, of human endeavor which took place there from the middle 1850's to the middle 1880's. Nortonville and Somersville, Stewartsville and Empire, West Hartley and Judsonville, with their shipping counterparts at New York and Pittsburg landings, dominated the affairs of the county for a period of 30 years, and in the case of Somersville, limited activities continued as late as 1905.

A unique and cosmopolitan population found its way into the Mount Diablo coal district from the coal fields of distant lands, especially England and Wales. In 1882 about 300 men and boys were employed in the mines at Nortonville, while the entire population of the place registered about 900.

Today the deserted ravines and hillsides bear testimony of another episode in the mining history of the state. The site of Somersville is marked by aged locust trees on the hillside. Below them are the "dumps," while meandering down the deep gullies and beside the steep, rutted roadways almond trees and rows of pepper trees indicate the former paths of progress into the hills.

High up toward the west, the white headstones of the cemetery, guarded by five stately cypress trees, gleam against the green mountain. Many of the pioneers, including Noah Norton, were buried here. This graveyard on the side of the valley is the burial place of several Welsh miners, whose epitaphs are engraved in their native language.

Nortonville long retained an old brick office building with iron doors and shutters. Now it has been torn down, and only a few bricks remain among the vivid pink and violet cinder heaps.

There are no landmarks at Empire except the dumps and a few old trees planted by early settlers.

Bancroft states that coal was discovered in Contra Costa County as early as 1848. George W. Hawxhurst located in 1855 at the place where the town of Somersville later grew up, and after prospecting for coal he discovered the Union vein in March of that year. Four years later, on December 22, 1859, Francis Somers and James T. Cruikshank discovered the famous Black Diamond vein. With his associates, H. S. Hawxhurst and Samuel Adams, Somers located the lands afterward known as the Manhattan and Eureka coal mines, which comprised, with the Union and Independent, the mines forming the basin that held the town of Somersville. In the 1880's the Pittsburg Railroad connected the district with Pittsburg Landing at the mouth of the San Joaquin River.

The Black Diamond, Cumberland, and Mount Hope mines, located about a mile west of Somersville on the same vein, were opened by Somers and another group of men. Since they were unable to finance the building of necessary roads, they never secured title to these lands. Very soon, however, Noah Norton, from whom Nortonville received its name, came upon the scene and took over the Black Diamond, while Frank Luch and others undertook to develop the Cumberland. Luch soon disposed of his share to a group of men from Martinez, who took hold of the Cumberland diggings and made a success of the enterprise and also assisted Noah Norton in getting the Black Diamond under way. Roads were opened to Clayton and New York Landing, and in the 1880's a railroad connected the latter place with the Nortonville mines.

The Black Diamond and Cumberland mines, together with adjoining lands, were at first known as the Carbondale District but later became noted as the Black Diamond coal mines. In the basin of the hills containing the Black Diamond, Cumberland, Mount Hope, and other lands the town of Nortonville still held its own as a mining center in the 1880's.

The first house in Nortonville was built by Noah Norton in 1861; its site is now covered by one of the dumps. A second house, also built by Norton, was erected the following year, while the first hotel, known as the Black Diamond Exchange, was opened in 1863 by Atwell Pray and Charles Gwynn. In 1865 a store was opened, and in 1866 a schoolhouse was established not far from the spot where the shaft was sunk later. The building was moved to the top of the hill in 1870, and there it developed to the dignity of a seminary with four departments. This school was maintained for the most part by a charge of one per cent on all moneys paid through the office of the mine superintendent. Nothing remains of these buildings today.

Somersville's first house was probably erected some time in 1860, while a boardinghouse and hotel was opened in 1861. The place grew until the slopes and dips of the canyon were dotted with cabins, and in 1865 a schoolhouse was erected for the miners' children.

The first slump in coal mining in the Mount Diablo district occurred in 1878, when the Somersville mines were closed temporarily, with the hope that they would soon reopen. Meanwhile, new locations were being made. One of these was the Empire Mine, opened near Judsonville in

Children's Grave, Somersville

1878, five miles south of Antioch and about three and one-half miles east of Somersville. A lavish outlay of capital was made, but competition demanded a cut in production cost, and this, in turn, brought the inevitable dispute between capital and labor over wages. Work was suspended early in 1880, to be continued with new men in March.

Activities speeded up in 1881, when the railroad was extended from Judsonville to the Central Mine. Fifteen new houses and a large hotel were built, and the town of Stewartsville came into existence one mile east of Somersville. Nevertheless, competition was still strangling the industry. Since the newer mines were able to pay relatively low wages for a short time and the cost of production at Nortonville was increasing, coal mining at that place was doomed by 1883.

That the industry was losing out at other points was evident when the post office was discontinued at Judsonville in 1883, "the population and business of the place having migrated to Stewartsville." One by one, men prominent in the field left for other places. As early as 1881, Mr. Pinkerton, for 16 years superintendent of the Pittsburg mines, left for Tacoma, Washington. George Hawxhurst, who had been a resident at Somersville for almost 25 years, went to British Columbia in 1883 to become superintendent of a railroad and coal mine owned by a San Francisco company.

In 1885 the famous Black Diamond Mine found that it could no longer stand the heavy expense of keeping the shaft clear of water, and by March the mines were permanently closed. Nortonville ceased to have any motive for existence and was deserted overnight. Lodges, churches, and schools were closed or moved to Martinez. Many of the houses were taken apart by their owners and moved to other places.

Activity in Mount Diablo's ancient sandstone belt has been temporarily resumed at various times. In 1923 there was renewed life when sandstone was removed from the Clark vein by the Columbia Steel Corporation. Again in 1926 there was considerable activity about the old shafts when the coal properties were surveyed and evaluated by a group of engineers with the purpose of determining the amount of coal still available in the district. In 1932 the mines at Nortonville were reopened and worked again. The coal taken out then was given to the poor and unemployed in the vicinity.

Nortonville lies south of Pittsburg, and is reached over Kirker Pass Road and Nortonville Road. Somersville is southwest of Antioch via Somersville Road. A short dirt road over a pass connects the two ghost towns, but it is not always passable in wet weather. It is on this road that the old cemetery is located.

Clayton, southwest of Nortonville and southeast of Concord, was an important center in coal-mining days. Some of its old buildings are still standing. Clayton is now an incorporated city, although still a small settlement, and will thereby retain its identity as Concord edges ever closer.

Antioch

The story of Antioch is largely the story of the devotion of two brothers, W. W. Smith and Joseph H. Smith, natives of New Hampshire. Brought up together, these twin brothers followed the same course in later life. They both learned the carpenter's trade and pursued it in their home state as well as in California; both were married at the same time and place, in their mother's home at New Market in March 1833. Together, they were the means of organizing a Christian Church at Lynn, Massachusetts, as well as two others in the same township; and both were ordained ministers of the Christian denomination, which they had first joined at the age of 12.

With the discovery of gold, the Smith brothers became fired with a desire to go to California; in company with some 50 other emigrants, they sailed on January 11, 1849, with their families from Boston harbor aboard the *Forest*, the ship *Edward Everett* sailing in company with them. The *Forest* entered the Golden Gate on July 6, 1849, and the *Edward Everett* arrived three or four hours later.

Since carpenters were in demand, the Smith brothers agreed to go to work at a place called New York of the Pacific, located at the mouth of the San Joaquin River. Arriving with their families in the schooner *Rialto* on July 11, 1849, six months after leaving Boston, the brothers took up their work as carpenters in the embryo city.

The day following their arrival Dr. John Marsh sent an invitation extending to them the hospitality of his home. Horses were provided, and the party took the well-beaten trail leading up the arroyo to the doctor's adobe house, where they received a hearty welcome. As a result of this visit, the brothers took up jointly on July 19, 1849, two quarter sections of land where Antioch now stands. Here on December 24 they broke ground and set up tents. Working their lands enough to hold them, the Smiths continued their carpenter work at New York of the Pacific, often going to Smith's Landing, as it was known at first, to cut firewood for the New York House.

The Rev. Joseph Smith died at New York of the Pacific on February 5, 1850. In September of that year a shipload of settlers arrived in San Francisco aboard the *California Packet* from Maine. This group of New England frontier families had hewn their ship out of the Maine woods, and in it they had sailed to far-off California to found a colony. They brought with them all that was best in their New England culture. A school was conducted by Deacon Pulsifer of the Christian Church.

Hearing of the new arrivals and of their wish to settle in California, the Rev. W. W. Smith hastened to San Francisco to meet them. He invited them to go with him to Smith's Landing, and, although the gold mines proved too enticing for some of the company, a number of them accepted the invitation.

A street was now laid out, and to each family that wished to settle upon the land Smith presented a lot on which to build a home. In order to keep out the animals, a fence was built the following spring from the tules on the west of the town to the tules on the east. On July 4 between 30 and 40 persons, men, women, and children, gathered for a basket picnic held at the home of W. W. Smith.

The all-absorbing topic of the day was "What shall we name our town?" One proposed "Minton," the name of a river boat, in the hope that it might be induced to stop at the landing; another proposed "Paradise," which was rejected because of the uncertainty of land titles in California, a circumstance that might result in "Paradise Lost" for the holders. At length the Rev. W. W. Smith proposed that, inasmuch as the first settlers at this spot were disciples of Christ and one of them, his own brother, had died and was buried on the land, it be given a Bible name in his honor. He proposed that they adopt the name of Antioch for their town, because "at Antioch, Syria, the followers of Christ were first called Christians." By acclamation this name was accepted.

The first house built in Antioch, the home of George W. Kimball, captain of the *California Packet*, long stood on the south side of West Third Street near E. It was constructed in 1851 by the captain, who raised barley hay, hauled it to San Francisco, and with the proceeds bought Oregon pine to use in building his home.

Other Landmarks

On the site of an old Indian village, Thomas Edwards, Sr., built a home in 1867, the nucleus of the town of Crockett. He had purchased land the previous year from Judge Joseph B. Crockett, who had earlier acquired 1,800 acres in the area. As other settlers arrived, Edwards opened the first store. "The Old Homestead" *(SRL 731)*, as the Edwards residence is called, stands, with its tall palm trees, on the south side of Loring Avenue. The timbers, some of which came around the Horn, are well preserved. For years Crockett has been the company town of the California and Hawaiian Sugar Refinery.

Three of Contra Costa County's old towns are fast becoming artist colonies. Each has a number of interesting buildings that are thereby being preserved. Port Costa, on Carquinez Strait, was an important shipping point in early days. Point Richmond antedates the city of which it is now a part. Cowell, southeast of Concord, was once a cement company town.

SOURCES

Bolton, Herbert Eugene. *Anza's California Expeditions.* University of California Press, Berkeley, 1930.
—— *Fray Juan Crespí, Missionary Explorer on the Pacific Coast, 1769–1774.* University of California Press, Berkeley, 1927.
—— *Font's Complete Diary, A Chronicle of the Founding of San Francisco.* Translated from the original Spanish manuscript. University of California Press, Berkeley, 1933.
Bowman, J. N., and G. W. Hendry. "Spanish and Mexican Houses in the Nine Bay Counties." Ms., Bancroft Library, University of California, Berkeley; State Library, Sacramento, 1942.
Chapman, Charles E. *A History of California: The Spanish Period.* Macmillan, New York, 1923.
Cleland, Robert Glass. *From Wilderness to Empire. A History of California,* ed. Glenn S. Dumke. Knopf, New York, 1959.
Farquhar, Francis P., ed. *Up and Down California in 1860–1864. The Journal of William H. Brewer.* University of California Press, Berkeley, 1949.
Fink, Leonora Galindo. "The San Ramon Valley," *Contra Costa Chronicles* (a publication of the Contra Costa County Historical Society), I, No. 3 (Spring 1966), 17–27.
Gudde, Erwin G. *California Place Names.* University of California Press, Berkeley, 1949.
Howe, Octavius Thorndike. *Argonauts of '49. History and Adventures of the Emigrant Companies from Massachusetts, 1849–1850.* Harvard University Press, Cambridge, 1923.
Hulaniski, F. J. *The History of Contra Costa County, California.* The Elias Publishing Co., Berkeley, 1917.
Kroeber, A. L. "California Place Names of Indian Origin," *University of California Publications in American Archaeology and Ethnology,* XII, No. 2 (1916–17).
Loud, Llewellyn L. "The Stege Mounds at Richmond, California," *University of California Publications in American Archaeology and Ethnology,* XVII, No. 6 (1924).
Lyman, George Dunlap. *John Marsh, Pioneer.* Scribner, New York, 1930.
McGinty, Ruth Mary. "Spanish and Mexican Ranchos in the San Francisco Bay Region." Master's thesis in history, University of California, Berkeley, 1920.
Munro-Fraser, J. P. *History of Contra Costa County, California.* W. A. Slocum & Co., San Francisco, 1882.
Nelson, N. C. "The Ellis Landing Shellmound," *University of California Publications in American Archaeology and Ethnology,* VII, No. 6 (1910).
Russi, Alice McNeil. "Elam Brown," *Contra Costa Chronicles* (a publication of the Contra Costa County Historical Society), I, No. 3 (Spring 1966), 4–16.
Sanchez, Nellie Van de Grift. *Spanish and Indian Place Names of California.* A. M. Robertson, San Francisco, 1914.
Sullivan, Maurice S. *The Travels of Jedediah Strong Smith.* The Fine Arts Press, Santa Ana, 1934.
Winkley, John W. *Dr. John Marsh, Wilderness Scout.* Parthenon Press, Nashville, Tenn., 1962.
—— *John Muir, Naturalist.* Parthenon Press, Nashville, Tenn., 1959.

Del Norte County

DEL NORTE COUNTY was organized from a portion of Klamath County in 1857, and Crescent City was made the county seat. (Del Norte is Spanish for "of the north," as the county is in the extreme northwestern corner of California.)

Trail Breakers

Taking "a northwest course across the Coast Range, through what is now Trinity and Humboldt counties, to the sea," Jedediah Strong Smith, trapper-explorer, in 1828 first "opened a line of communication from northern California to the Oregon country, a route the Hudson's Bay Company were quick to take advantage of." Crossing the Klamath River at the site of the former town of Klamath on May 25, 1828, the great pathfinder and his party traversed what is now Del Norte County slowly and with difficulty. Trails had to be blazed over steep and rugged mountains, while progress was often impeded by

heavy fogs. The scarcity of wild game, which was almost their only food, added to their hardships.

A level, grassy bottom near the mouth of the Klamath River on Hunter's Creek was reached on June 5, and camp was pitched at a spot along the present Redwood Highway near Requa. At this point, where modern tourist camps are now located, the exhausted and half-starved men and animals of this first exploring party rested for three days and nights.

Unfruitful attempts to replenish their failing food supply occupied them the first two days in camp. The last dog and a horse had, finally, to be killed for meat. On June 7, ten to 15 Indians visited camp, "bringing with them a few Muscles and Lemprey Eels and some raspberries" (thimbleberries). In a brisk trade the white men exchanged for these delicacies the glass beads brought for such occasions.

From the Hunter's Creek camp, Smith and his

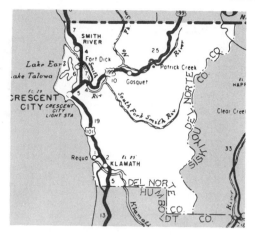

men crossed over to Wilson Creek on June 8. "We were weary and very hungry," wrote Smith; again several Indian lodges near the camp supplied them with mussels and small fish in exchange for the prized beads. They brought, also, "dried sea grass mixed with weeds and a few muscles. They were great speculators and never sold their things without dividing them into several small parcels asking more for each than the whole were worth. They also brought us some Blubber not bad tasted but dear as gold dust. But all these things served but to aggravate our hunger and having been long accustomed to living on meat and eating it in no moderate quantities nothing else could satisfy our appetites."

That afternoon Smith killed three elk, "thanks to the great Benefactor." The camp was changed from "the moody silence of hunger to the busy bustle of preparation for cooking and feasting ... Men could be seen in ev'ry part of the camp with raw meat and half roasted in their hands devouring it with the greatest alacrity while from their preparations and remarks you would suppose that nothing less than twentyfour hours constant eating would satisfy their appetites."

At the Wilson Creek camp, the explorers occupied the time making salt and cutting and drying the meat. The unblazed trail which they cut from June 11 to 16 through the wilderness of Del Norte County was rough and difficult. The route of the party during this period followed, in general, that taken later by the old county road. The prairie south and east of Crescent City was reached on June 16. Although there were no mountains on this lap of the journey, the dense redwood forest, the thick brush, and swamps made travel difficult.

They made camp in the vicinity of Crescent City on June 17, and on June 18 Earl Lake was discovered by a reconnoitering party. On June 19 Smith himself discovered the river that in later years bore his name. On the north bank of Smith River, tents of the brave little band were set up on June 20. The next day Smith pushed on northward, and on June 22, 1828, he crossed the California boundary into Oregon.

Alexander Roderick McLeod, at the head of the trapping expedition of the Hudson's Bay

Company, entered California from the north in 1829, trying vainly to follow Smith's trail but finally coming southward via the Umpqua Valley and Klamath Lake.

The River of Mystery

A mystery to early explorers and map makers was the Klamath River. Its source in the Klamath lakes and its upper course were known almost a quarter of a century before it was determined that its mouth was in the present Del Norte County. In the fall of 1826 a trapper of the Hudson's Bay Company, Peter Skene Ogden, set out from Fort Vancouver on the Columbia River for the region of the "Clamitte." His diary gives the earliest account of the visit of white men into the country north of Mount Shasta. Between 1827 and 1850, British and American trappers continued to trap for beaver on the upper Klamath and its tributaries, but not one expedition followed the river to its mouth. Thus the lower course of the river was unknown and the spot where it emptied into the sea was long a matter of conjecture. Most maps represented the Klamath as entering the ocean north of the present California-Oregon boundary line, and the lower Klamath was represented as a continuation of the present Trinity River. These two rivers, together with the South Fork of the Trinity, extended from the southeast to the northwest and on early maps were represented as one river named Smith's River.

The Klamath was the river course traveled by Jedediah Smith and his party of trappers in the spring of 1828 when he blazed a northwest trail from the Sacramento Valley into Oregon. The first Indian agent, who arrived on the Klamath in 1851, was familiar with the maps of the region that indicated its chief waterway by the name of Smith's River, and he sought to locate that stream. But, by 1851, "Smith's River" had become a lost river. The true course of the Klamath had been determined late in 1850 by a party of miners who traversed its whole length from the mouth to the junction with the Shasta River, prospecting every bar for gold. Later the name "Smith's River" was given to an unnamed stream in Del Norte County also discovered by Smith.

The early miners in northwestern California had never known of a river called Smith's but were familiar with the Trinity River, first named by Major Pierson B. Reading in 1845. Reading had discovered gold in this stream, and as a consequence the upper course of the river with its tributaries was teeming with miners in 1849–50. The approach was from the Sacramento Valley. More direct access to the sea was desirable, and soon vessels left San Francisco to explore the northern coast with the hope of finding the mouth of the Trinity River at Trinidad Bay. No river was found at Trinidad Bay, but farther north a large river was discovered (the Klamath) which many believed to be the Trinity River.

Soon all the streams of the region were being prospected for gold, and the Klamath, crossed and recrossed, was mistaken at first for the Trinity or the Salmon. Gradually, however, the true course of the Klamath was determined, and the identity of its tributaries was made known as feeders of the great stream.

Klamath City, a Dream of Yesterday

Miners came into the region in increasing numbers, and Klamath City, near the mouth of Klamath River, directly opposite the present Requa, was established in 1851. This short-lived city arose with great expectations of becoming the port of entry for the back country, rich in gold. But, because of the shifting sandbars at the mouth of the river, navigation was uncertain, and the place was deserted soon after 1852.

Bledsoe, in his *Indian Wars of the Northwest*, describes its rise and fall: "Klamath City was one of the ephemeral productions of the mining excitement. When the *Cameo*, driven from Trinidad Head by a storm in March 1850, reached Point St. George, she landed some of her passengers there. These, B. W. Bullet, Herman Ehrenberg, J. T. Tyson, A. Heepe, and a Mr. Gunn, walked down the coast, and about the middle of April arrived at the mouth of the Klamath, which they supposed was the Trinity. After travelling up the stream some distance and locating homesteads near its mouth, the explorers went down to Trinidad, their stories of discovery adding fuel to the feverish excitement which already possessed the place. They and others went up to the mouth of the river and located a new town, which they called Klamath City. Here they were met by Eugene du Bertrand, sole survivor of a boat's crew of five from the *Cameo* that had come down from Point St. George and, attempting to cross the river bar in the boat, had been upset in the breakers. Bertrand, being a good swimmer, saved himself with the timely assistance of an Indian.

"Klamath City had a rapid growth and a mushroom existence. It was supposed that the river bars from the mouth up were all rich in gold, consequently, prospectors and traders flocked to the new town in large numbers. Frames of houses, ready to be put together on arrival, were shipped from San Francisco, and it is said that one iron house was imported and erected in the town," to be used by its owners as a refuge from the attacks of the Indians.

The town of Klamath City did not prosper for several reasons. Gold seekers "did not meet with the success they had anticipated and left for other localities; the river bar was too dangerous to be crossed in safety by large vessels; traders were unable to bring in their wares by sea; explorers departed for other scenes; buildings were taken down and carried away; and in a few months from its location the site of the prospective city was the same primeval solitude broken in upon by the first white explorer. Today there is not a vestige of the town to be seen, not a single visible testimonial of the busy and exciting scenes that once transpired there."

The Lost Cabin

It has been said that a great part of northwestern California and of southern Oregon was explored, prospected, and settled as a result of the spread throughout California and the Eastern states of one or another of those "Lost Cabin" stories which thrilled and fascinated the gold-mad throngs in various sections of the state during the 1850's. The founding of Crescent City itself, according to an early account, was due to a wandering prospector in search of the "Lost Cabin." There were many versions of this romantic tale, but that told by Bledsoe has perhaps received widest currency.

"In the very earliest days of the mining excitement in California, a miner more adventurous than his fellows, armed with his rifle and supplied with necessary mining implements, crossed the Coast Range and prospected the gulches and ravines of the foot-hills near the sea-shore. One lucky day he 'struck it rich.' The rich earth yielded its yellow treasures in abundance, and the solitary miner erected a cabin in the wilderness, with the sole thought of amassing a fortune and returning to home and friends in the East. And there in the 'forest primeval' with the giant trees towering above him, the lonely gold-hunter toiled as if for life, day by day, for many weary months, adding to his store of gold until it amounted to a fabulous sum. The prowling Indians found his retreat at last, and attacking him in overwhelming numbers left him senseless on the ground, apparently dead. The treasure was too well hidden to be easily found, and failing in their search for it, the savages set fire to the cabin, burning it to ashes. When they had gone, the miner recovered consciousness, but not his reason—the light of his mind had gone out, and left a flickering flame of disconnected thought. Bereft of his reason, he wandered out of the forest and into the home of civilization. How he succeeded in finding his way back to his friends in the East the legend saith not. But (so the story goes) he did succeed in reaching home and there, after a brief period, he died. Before his death his reason returned to him, and calling his friends around him he told them the story of his hidden treasure, describing minutely the locality of the cabin, and from the account he gave, it was evident that the lost cabin was situated somewhere on the northern coast of California."

Tributary Gold Camps of Southern Oregon

Mining areas along the Klamath River, of which Happy Camp (now in Siskiyou County) was the trade center, as well as the gold camps of southern Oregon, were long tributary to Crescent City in Del Norte County, although these regions were populated and flourishing one or two years before the city itself was laid out. The Klamath section was mined and settled as early as 1851, after a party of miners, prospecting for gold on every bar, had traveled all the way up the Klamath River from its mouth. Happy Camp, Wingate Bar, Woods Bar, and Indian Creek Diggings were among the prosperous camps established as the result of the discovery of rich gold mines.

In the territory now included in southern Josephine and Jackson counties in Oregon, the first location was made near Kirbyville in 1851. Another discovery made by a group of seafaring men led to the founding of Sailor Diggings, later called Waldo after a prominent California politician. Discoveries were made in Jackson Creek in 1852, and Jacksonville became the chief center of activities, while in 1853 Philip Althouse picked up gold on a creek named after him. Soon a thousand and more miners rushed to the scene of these first locations and numerous mining companies sprang up. Strange names characteristic of the period were quickly given to the sites: Democratic Gulch, Hogtown, Browntown, Butcher Gulch, Jump-off-Joe Creek, House Creek, Hungry Hill, Galiceburg, Lucky Green, Wilderville, Quartzville, Coyote Creek, Rough and Ready Creek, Murphy's Creek, Williamsburg, Webfoot Mine, Slate Creek, Canyon Creek, Yankee-Doodle Mine.

The first port of entry to all this region was Scottsburg, in Oregon, but more direct access to the sea became desirable after the experience of high prices and famine in the winter of 1851–52. Consequently the trail to Crescent City was opened up in the spring of 1853, and pack trains soon brought in the necessary supplies. Agitation for a wagon road was started in 1854, the surveys being made by T. P. Robinson, who in June 1854 determined the Oregon-California boundary line. Work was finally commenced in 1857 by the "Crescent City and Yreka Plank and Turnpike Company," and in 1860 the wagon road between Waldo (Sailor Diggings) and Crescent City was completed. A monument commemorating this old turnpike (SRL 645) stands on Highway 199 northeast of Crescent City.

During the height of mining activity, southwestern Oregon was always connected more closely with California than with Oregon. Indeed, before the boundary line was determined, the miners considered themselves Californians. Regarding the boundary Bledsoe says: "The decision caused some excitement . . . as the miners did not like to be so suddenly transported from California to Oregon. They had before voted in both California and Oregon Territory and had refused to pay taxes to either."

Of this integral relationship between southern Oregon and northern California, Walling writes: "In every respect it resembles and is identical with the history of the mining counties of California, with which state Jackson County has far closer affiliations than with the exclusively agricultural portions of Oregon. Indeed, it is a rather striking and in some sense regrettable fact that it is not a part of the former state. Settled by the same class of enterprising, fearless and progressive miners it became the abode of a population who . . . were circumscribed precisely as those of California. The surface mining industry grew up under the same conditions, attained its maximum at the same time and has declined in the same proportion."

As the surface gold was depleted, most of the population departed. Hydraulic mining was introduced in the 1860's and 1870's, and some localities were producing as late as the 1880's. The bulk of the activity had passed long before. By 1865 Althouse, one of the most prosperous towns of the 1850's, was said to have "nearly winked out." Waldo (Sailor Diggings), on the other hand, was still an important center in the 1880's. Now it is almost extinct, being only a place on the map. The road to Crescent City was closed for many years because of the heavy cost of keeping it in repair. The present highway to Grants Pass avoids Waldo, so that it is necessary for the tourist to reach it by a side road.

Crescent City

Settlers flocked to the northwest coast of California in 1850 as a result of the discovery of gold on the Trinity. Eureka, Arcata, and Trinidad were established as trade centers, but, although a number of vessels—the *Paragon*, the *Cameo*, and the *Laura Virginia*—had anchored in the crescent-shaped bay as early as 1850, no settlement was made north of the mouth of the Klamath River until after 1852.

The site of Crescent City was first observed from the landward side in the spring of 1851, when searchers for the legendary "Lost Cabin," led by Captain McDermott, looked westward from the summit of French Hill toward the ocean and saw in the far distance an indentation like a bay. Reports of this discovery spread to the interior, where miners were eager to locate a short communication line to the sea. In September 1852 another party set out from Althouse Creek (now in Oregon), and after a perilous and fatiguing journey they cut their way to the coast. Elk Valley, located northeast of Crescent City, was named at this time from large herds of elk seen there by the miners.

Setting up camp on the beach, the party dispatched one of their number to San Francisco to charter a vessel. In due time the schooner *Pomona* arrived with prospective settlers, and in February 1853 the town of Crescent City was laid out. By the summer of 1854, 300 buildings had been erected and the town was the center of an increasing trade from the interior.

Crescent City, despite many ups and downs, continued to hold its own as the chief port of entry and as the supply center for the gold miners of southern Oregon, Siskiyou to the east, and a part of Trinity County, as well as for the camp in the vicinity of Crescent Bay. It was made the county seat of Klamath County in 1854, but in December of the following year lost this position to Orleans Bar.

During this period the citizens of this ambitious town, in their aspiration to make the city the capital of the state, gained the support of some members of the legislature by the offer of free lots, etc.—at least according to a story current at the time. The following is a choice addition to that collection of tales of would-be state capitals which are continually coming to light in the annals of California's county histories:

"What a wonderful Legislature that must have been! What a number of valuable town lots must have been offered its members to induce them to propose as the capital of the state, a town in the extreme northwest corner, and at that time almost inaccessible during the winter months. What an immense amount of ignorance must have been concentrated in that legislative body of the days of '55! ... It excites our imaginations in contemplating the sublime ignorance of the country displayed by this early Legislature.

"Unfortunately for Crescent City, the bill removing the state capital to that place failed to pass, and the visions of town lot speculators vanished into thin air. But the Crescentarians were buoyant with life and energy, and the news of the failure was but a passing cloud across their bright hopes and expectations. No doubt, as the principal men of the place discussed the matter over their wine and cigars, new speculations and day-dreams of future greatness served to 'solace the hopes that ended in smoke.' "

Indeed the business activity and social life of that early day in Crescent City were feverish in the extreme. Every day saw some new project for improvement. New hotels and business houses were opened continually. Soon the town was encroaching on the forest and even covered the beach. Fraternal organizations were established and a fire department organized.

"Saloons and billiard halls flourished in close proximity to the only house of God the place supported; in fact it soon became the type of a California mining town. The streets were filled with people and presented a busy scene—the miner from the mountains jostled the farmer from the valley; the merchant and trader vied with each other in the use of cunning arguments of trade; speculators in town lots talked loudly to new comers of the advantage of this 'garden spot of God's green earth.' God bless you, sir; young men from the states, eager to join the great army who were searching for gold, bartered for animals and outfits; pack trains just in from across the mountains, passed other trains preparing to start on their trip across the Siskiyous, heavily laden with merchandise and mining implements."

By the summer of 1855, trails were completed to the gold camps of southern Oregon and to that large area to the east which drained into the Klamath River. The trail that shortened materially the way to Yreka was long known as the Kelsey Trail.

Meanwhile new rich diggings were being uncovered in the hills immediately adjacent to Crescent City. In 1854 and 1855 the miners on Myrtle Creek 12 miles to the northeast were making from five to 15 dollars a day. New diggings were also found on the South Fork of Smith River, where individual miners were making from ten to 20 dollars a day.

Diggings were also found closer at hand. In November 1854 discoveries were made six miles from the city, on a creek that emptied into Smith River at the White and Miller Ferry, later known as Peacock's Ferry. Even the beach in front of the city was staked off into mining claims. In the Bald Hills six miles to the east gold mines were

found in 1856. Here, Villardville, named for a Frenchman, A. Villard, was laid out. Many other mining camps and districts in the neighboring hills about Crescent Bay lived their brief day and then vanished: Redwood Diggings, Big Flat, Growler Gulch, Hurdy Gurdy Creek, Blacks Ferry, Altaville, Low Divide.

Altaville was a copper- and chrome-mining center during the 1860's and was full of life and activity. In the 1880's its glory had long departed, and it lay surrounded by peace and quiet. Black mouths of tunnels appeared on the hillsides, and heaps of bluish-colored rock showed the location of mines.

Indeed, by the 1870's it could be said that "the flush days of mining in Del Norte have vanished with the years, and the halcyon days when the miner with his pick and shovel could delve into the hills and streams and bring forth the golden treasure are gone forever."

A landmark at Crescent City is the site of an old Indian village (SRL 649) on Pebble Beach at Pacific and Ocean streets. From ancient times Tolowa Indians lived near the beach, and this site was occupied as late as the latter part of the nineteenth century. At this spot were redwood huts, a *temescal* or "sweat house," a ceremonial dancing pit, and a burial place. Requa, south of Crescent City at the mouth of the Klamath River, is still an Indian settlement. The old Indian "Family House" there has been restored.

Crescent City figures, too, in modern history. A 10,745-ton General Petroleum Corporation tanker, *S.S. Emidio (SRL 497)*, was the first ship torpedoed and shelled by a Japanese submarine off the Pacific Coast during World War II. The attack took place on December 20, 1941, at a point about 200 miles north of San Francisco. Five lives were lost. The disabled vessel drifted north and foundered on the rocks off Crescent City. Some pieces of the hull, salvaged in 1950–51, are preserved on the waterfront at Front and H streets.

Two other points of historical interest in the vicinity of Crescent City are Whale Island, where in June 1855 a company engaged in the whaling business was located, and Battery Point, where three brass cannons were placed in 1855. They had been salvaged from the steamer *America*, which was burned and wrecked on June 24, 1855. The first light, a lantern fixed on top of a pole, was placed at this point before the establishment of the lighthouse by the federal government in 1856. The old lighthouse is now a museum of the Del Norte County Historical Society.

A Seacoast Cemetery:
The Tragedy of St. George's Reef

On the bluff overlooking the sea to the west of Crescent City was a neglected pioneer cemetery, in which many of the headstones revealed the terrible tragedy of the sea which occurred during the summer of 1865. On July 30 the *Brother Jonathan*, owned and operated by the California Steam Navigation Company, plying off the coast west of Point St. George under the

Commanding Officer's Quarters, Camp Lincoln

command of Captain Samuel J. De Wolfe, was overtaken by a severe storm. The immediate thought of those in command was to seek a port of safety. There was no idea of approaching death among the 100 passengers on board the vessel. But hidden just below the surface of the water, St. George's Reef lay directly in the path of the ill-fated vessel. "Suddenly," says Bledsoe, "she struck with tremendous power on a sunken rock, with such force that her foremast went through the hull, her foreyards resting across the rails. Instantly the deck became the scene of the wildest confusion. The crash was so sudden, so unexpected, so awful, that those on board had scarcely recovered from the shock when they saw that their doom was sealed—the ship was fast sinking in the embrace of the hungry waves, and short time was left to prepare for death." Between 80 and 90 persons, crew and passengers, were drowned, while only one boatload was saved. The *Brother Jonathan* Cemetery *(SRL 541)* on Pebble Beach Road has been converted into a park. Some of the old headstones have been preserved.

The Lighthouse of St. George's Reef

The St. George Reef Light, or the Northwest Seal Rock Light, has guided scores of vessels away from the treacherous, hidden reefs which lie at its base. The lighthouse is on a small, lonely isle seven miles directly off the coast and 13 miles from Crescent City. It was kept for a long time by Captain John Olsen and four assistants. Virtual prisoners the year round, the men could barely step out of doors, and in stormy periods even this was denied them. During moderate weather, however, they were permitted to take turns visiting shore.

The St. George Reef Lighthouse is one of the greatest structures of its kind ever erected by the United States government. Costing $750,000, it took four years to build, because work could be carried on only in fair weather. It was completed in 1891. The tower is of rock transported by barge to the lonely island, and it defies wind and wave. The base covers 6,000 square feet, "the enclosure within which men must work and exist and have all that is necessary to their labor." Occasionally government ships visit the island, but at times supplies cannot be delivered because

of storms. There are 20 fathoms of water on the east side of the islet, while on the west side the water is very deep.

Fort Ter-Wer

Six miles from the mouth of the Klamath River, and to the east of the present town of Klamath on Highway 101, Fort Ter-Wer *(SRL 544)* was established by First Lieutenant George Crook on October 12, 1857, as an outpost to guard the Klamath River Indian Reservation and ensure peace between the Indians and the whites. The fort was abandoned in 1862.

Camp Lincoln

Camp Lincoln *(SRL 545)*, about five miles northeast of Crescent City in Elk Valley, was an outpost on the old Smith River Indian Reservation. The military post was established September 12, 1862, by Company G, 2nd Regiment, Infantry, California Volunteers. It was abandoned in May 1870, the Indians having been removed to the Hoopa Reservation in Humboldt County. To reach the site of Camp Lincoln, one should turn north at the "Crescent City Plank and Turnpike Road" monument on Highway 199 and follow the county road about one mile. The large white house on the hill is the former commanding officer's quarters. Across the road, near the old barn, is a former barracks building of the camp. The turnpike monument is about a quarter of a mile beyond the junction of Highways 101 and 199.

Old Headstone, Brother Jonathan *Cemetery,* Crescent City

Along the Redwood Highway

Del Norte long rivaled Alpine County in the High Sierra for inaccessibility, the only passage into it being by wagon and stage or by mule-back. The Redwood Highway now crosses it, passing through the beautiful redwood groves of the Klamath River region, where the trees are larger and assume more grotesque shapes than elsewhere.

SOURCES

Bledsoe, A. J. *Indian Wars of the Northwest*. San Francisco, 1885.

Cleland, Robert Glass. *From Wilderness to Empire. A History of California*, ed. Glenn S. Dumke. Knopf, New York, 1959.
Dornin, May. "The Emigrant Trails into California." Master's thesis in history, University of California, Berkeley, 1921.
History of Southern Oregon, Comprising Jackson, Josephine, Douglas, Curry, and Coos Counties, compiled from the most authentic sources . . . A. G. Walling, Portland, Oregon, 1884.
McBeth, Frances Turner. *Lower Klamath Country*. Anchor Press, Berkeley, 1950.
——— *Pioneers of Elk Valley*. Pacific Union College Press, Angwin, 1960.
Smith, Esther Ruth. *History of Del Norte County*. Holmes Book Co., Oakland, 1953.
Sullivan, Maurice S. *The Travels of Jedediah Strong Smith*. The Fine Arts Press, Santa Ana, 1934.

El Dorado County

EL DORADO COUNTY was one of the original 27 counties. The first county seat was Coloma, but it was superseded by Placerville in 1857.

The Spanish term *El Dorado* has the connotation of "the gilded one." The general understanding is that the name was given to this county because gold was discovered there. The legend from which the name arose is significant. "The Indians of Peru, Venezuela, and New Granada, perhaps in the hope of inducing their oppressors to move on, were constantly pointing out to the Spaniards, first in one direction, then in another, a land of fabulous riches. This land was said to have a king, who caused his body to be covered every morning with gold dust, by means of an odorous resin. Each evening he washed it off, as it incommoded his sleep, and each morning had the gilding process repeated. From this fable the white men were led to believe that the country must be rich in gold, and long, costly, and fruitless expeditions were undertaken in pursuit of this phantom of *El Dorado*. In time the phrase *El Dorado* came to be applied to regions where gold and other precious metals were thought to be plentiful."

Coloma

In the latter part of 1847, John A. Sutter, founder of "New Helvetia," later Sacramento, sent James W. Marshall to find a suitable site for a sawmill. Marshall chose a spot 45 miles northeast of Sutter's Fort on the South Fork of the American River, where Coloma, the earliest of all the mining towns in California, was founded the following year.

Sutter's Mill was finished in March 1848, but on January 24, while deepening and enlarging the tailrace, Marshall discovered some shining particles in the running water. These were tested and found to be gold. The event proved to be one of the most important in the history of California. Its results were not only nationwide but world-wide and have changed the whole course of history on the Pacific Coast.

Coloma is now a quiet mountain town, but its rugged setting remains unchanged. There are a

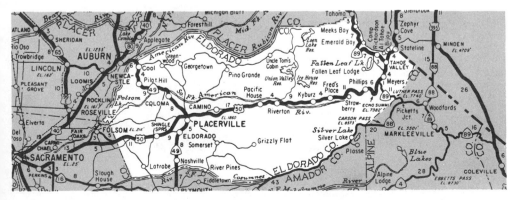

Emmanuel Episcopal Church, Coloma

few quaint buildings still to be found, which are suggestive of those wild days when thousands of gold-mad miners of many nationalities thronged the streets. Among them are Bekeart's store, the brick ruins of Bell's store, the armory of the Coloma Grays, and two small stone buildings with iron-shuttered windows and doors, originally used by Chinese and now containing State Park displays. In 1961 the state built a large museum at a cost of $150,000.

Half hidden beneath gnarled locust and apple trees, several aging, weather-worn cottages still stand in a tangle of old-fashioned flowers. One of these, at the east edge of town, was the home of the poet Edwin Markham. Snow seldom falls here, and old fig and almond trees still grow luxuriantly. During the early 1880's, Chinese miners paid high prices for gravel leads running into these orchards and gardens. One man received $800 for a tiny plot of ground on which four apple trees were growing.

On a side street is one of Coloma's historic churches, the Emmanuel Episcopal Church, which was erected in 1856. In later years the building was used also by the Methodists, as well as by the Presbyterians. The old St. John's Catholic Church is also to be found here, set amidst its tiny burial ground.

The Protestant cemetery on the hill is one of the oldest in the Sierra country and is filled with graves of members of pioneer Coloma families, some of the marble headstones dating back to the early 1850's. Beautiful wrought-iron palings surround many of the plots, while fine old shade trees and shrubbery cast quiet shadows across them.

Half a mile up the hill back of Coloma is the monument erected by the State of California in honor of James Wilson Marshall, whose discovery of gold at Coloma made California known to all the world. Although it is well established that Marshall was not the first to find gold in California—Bancroft, in his *Inter Pocula*, devotes two chapters to the subject of pre-Coloma gold discoveries—nevertheless his discovery exceeds "in human interest and historical significance every other episode" in California's history. The news of it brought an army of modern Argonauts to California, and in a short while a great new commonwealth had been created. James Marshall's Monument *(SRL 143)*, a bronze

statue on a granite base, under which he lies buried, was erected in 1890, and some distance below it on the hillside the little cabin which he built and where he lived until about 1868 has been restored. The statue overlooks the bend in the American River where the mill stood, and the right hand of the figure points to the spot where the particles of gold were first discovered *(SRL 530)*. The mill, abandoned in 1853, is gone, but the place where it stood has been marked with a monument of river stones by the Society of California Pioneers. A full-scale replica of Sutter's Mill was constructed in 1965–66. The Marshall Gold Discovery State Historic Park now comprises 143 acres, including the Marshall Monument and the actual site of the discovery. Thus continues the work begun in 1886, when the Native Sons of the Golden West first sought recognition by the state of Marshall's epochal discovery.

In view of its place in the history of the United States, Coloma has been registered as a National Historic Landmark by the Department of the Interior.

The Coloma Road

The earliest roads in the mining region (in reality, mere pack trails) were developed in El Dorado County. The first of these was marked out in 1847–48 by Sutter and his men (among whom was James Marshall) as a way to his sawmill on the South Fork. Running along the south side of the river from Sacramento to where Folsom now is, this first trail followed approximately the same line as that taken later by the railroad and the modern highway. From Folsom it continued by way of Mormon Island, Green Valley (Rescue), Rose Springs, and Uniontown (Lotus) to Sutter's Mill, later Coloma—the present route of a quiet country road along which a few of the old inns still stand, now occupied as private homes. The Pleasant Grove House *(SRL 703)*, is at the left of Green Valley Road, nine and a half miles east of Folsom. This site was a changing station for the Pony Express when it utilized this route in 1860–61. Another mile brings the traveler to the Green Valley House, on the right, an excellently preserved example of the early California roadside hotel. The Rising Sun House, with its unique design of sun rays under the east and west gables, is unfortunately no longer

James W. Marshall's Cabin, Coloma

to be seen; it stood beyond Rescue at the crest of the hill. A mile and a half northeast of Rescue, where the Green Valley Road turns to Placerville, the old Coloma Road continues north to Lotus. On the right, three-quarters of a mile from this point, the Gordon House, the material for which was brought around the Horn, still lends the charm of its quaint, old-fashioned dignity to this historic thoroughfare.

The Coloma Road evolved from a narrow pack trail into a well-beaten, crowded highway soon after Marshall's discovery of gold in 1848. Over it thousands of gold-seekers directed their eager footsteps toward that cynosure of all eyes— Coloma. Soon after the arrival of each ship at San Francisco, the Coloma Road became thronged with men afoot or on horseback, making their way to the diggings. Mexicans with long trains of pack mules loaded with freight and miners' supplies joined the procession. Oregonians, very early, brought in the first wagons. A mail business of such magnitude developed that wagon loads of letters never reached their destination and had to be sent to the dead-letter office. In 1849 the Coloma Road became the route of California's first stage line, established by James E. Birch.

Soon all available land about Coloma was staked out to claims, and newcomers were forced to seek other locations. Thus the mining area quickly expanded in all directions, with numerous trails opening up fresh diggings and newer El Doradoes for the onward-moving Argonauts.

The first, and for a long time the principal,

Marshall Monument, Coloma

branch of the Coloma Road turned north at New York Ravine three miles east of Mormon Island. Crossing the South Fork at Salmon Falls (at first by ferry and later, in 1853, by toll bridge), this road proceeded, as it still does (although realigned around Folsom Lake), to Centerville (Pilot Hill), where it branched again, one fork going through Greenwood to Georgetown. From Georgetown a road led northwest to Spanish Bar on the Middle Fork of the American River, where it crossed over into Placer County. Continuing by way of Paradise and the North Star House, this trail to Todd's Valley and Forest Hill was much traveled during the 1850's and 1860's. Another crossing farther up the Middle Fork at Volcano Bar led to Michigan Bluff (in Placer County).

Another branch road starting at Centerville took a more direct route to Forest Hill by way of Murderer's Bar, located a few miles above the confluence of the Middle and North forks of the American River. The present Mother Lode Highway follows this road, but instead of crossing the Middle Fork at Murderer's Bar it now proceeds directly to Auburn via Lyon's Bridge.

Crossing the South Fork at Mormon Island, still another branch of the Coloma Road paralleled the North Fork, connecting the populous river-bar camps. Along the 15 miles of the North Fork above its confluence with the South Fork, crossings were made at Beal's, Condemned, Whiskey, Rattlesnake, and Oregon bars.

At first crude ferries were used—ships' boats brought up from Sacramento or flimsy rafts, sometimes even beds of abandoned emigrant wagons serving the purpose. Soon, regular ferry boats, or scows, large enough to carry a wagon, were constructed, only to be supplanted by rough bridges, which were usually washed away by the succeeding winter's flood. Structures of a more substantial and permanent character ultimately replaced these first primitive ones. All, however, were built by private capital for profit. So great was the traffic to and from the mines that many fortunes were made from tolls collected by the owners of pioneer ferries and bridges.

At Whiskey and Rattlesnake bars, wire-rope bridges were constructed in 1854, and in 1856 W. C. Lyon built the Condemned Bar bridge, later torn down when he moved farther up the river.

The first regular ferry in El Dorado County was operated at Coloma early in 1849. In February 1851 this was superseded by a bridge, also the first in the county. All along the South Fork numerous bridges were erected to take the place of the ferries of an earlier date. The amount of travel was tremendous and the profit reaped from tolls was correspondingly great. At the old Uniontown Bridge it was not uncommon to collect from $600 to $800 monthly during the early 1850's, and the Rock Bridge a few miles farther downstream was almost as well patronized.

Of the maze of roads and branch roads radiating from Coloma to the scores of camps which sprang up, less than half a dozen are maintained today: the Georgetown road through Garden Valley (formerly Johntown), the little traveled Ridge Road to Kelsey, the Gold Hill Road to Cold Springs and Placerville, and the present Mother Lode Highway from Placerville via Coloma and Pilot Hill to Auburn. These few old roads, however, are rich in reminders of the historic past: scars of abandoned diggings; here and there the dark mouth of a tunnel reaching into the hillside; foundations of buildings long since vanished; crumbling walls of brick or stone standing neglected by the roadside; remnants of apple orchards; a few gnarled locust trees beneath whose shade inns or farmhouses once welcomed the wayfarer; lonely hilltop cemeteries marking once thriving communities.

Monuments signalizing the importance of the Coloma Road have been erected at Sutter's Fort, Nimbus Dam, Rescue (SRL 747), and Coloma (SRL 748).

The Carson Emigrant Road

The main route to Coloma and the gold diggings in 1849 and the early 1850's was the Carson Emigrant Road by way of the Kit Carson Pass. John C. Frémont and a few picked men led by Kit Carson himself were the first to cross the Sierra Nevada by way of this pass, in 1844, and also the first to cross the length of what is now El Dorado County. Traveling with great difficulty down the sunny side of the Silver Fork Canyon from Silver Lake to the South Fork of the American River, they forded the latter stream and climbed the opposite wall of the canyon to the southern edge of the Georgetown Divide, down which they proceeded to the Sacramento Valley and Sutter's Fort.

Only that part of Frémont's route from the Kit Carson Pass to Silver Lake is identical with the later Carson Emigrant Road. In the summer of 1848 members of the Mormon Battalion, on the way to rejoin their group in Salt Lake City, opened up this emigrant trail over the Sierra, and again, in the spring of 1849, Jefferson Hunt, a captain in the Mormon Battalion and later founder of San Bernardino, brought the first wagon that way, thus opening the Carson Emigrant Road to the host of Argonauts who entered California by this route in 1849 and the 1850's.

Winding its way over a very high pass, the Carson Emigrant Road was long and difficult, but, according to Bancroft, "the immigrants . . . in order to avoid the sharper hills and deeper gulches of a possibly lower pass, had preferred to climb to an elevation of nine thousand feet to secure a road less broken. As they arrived at the pass late in summer when the snow was off the ground this would do very well."

The course of the old road through El Dorado County may be traced on modern maps by the names of campsites, once important places along the divide between the Cosumnes River and the South Fork of the American River: Tragedy Springs, Leek Spring, Camp Springs, Sly Park, Pleasant Valley, Diamond Springs, Mud Springs (El Dorado), Shingle Springs, Clarksville, and White Rock Springs (in Sacramento County). From White Rock Springs to El Dorado, High-

way 50 follows roughly the same route today, but from El Dorado to Silver Lake in the High Sierra no through travel goes over the old road, the Carson Emigrant Road having been superseded by the Placerville Road, now the continuation of Highway 50.

Traffic over the Carson Road was enormous during the early 1850's, and a chain of wayside stations was established along its entire length between Mormon Station (later Genoa, in Nevada) and Hangtown (Placerville). Every mile had its inn or hotel. Few remnants of these early taverns remain, and even the sites of many would be difficult to determine exactly.

From the main road a number of branches diverged at various points, chiefly at Diamond Springs, where the stream of emigrants turned off to Coloma by way of Hangtown and (as new diggings were discovered) to Salmon Falls, Pilot Hill, Georgetown, Kelsey's Diggings, and numerous other camps. Two main branches led to the southern mines, one by way of Grizzly Flats to Brownsville (Mendon), Indian Diggins, and Fiddletown (in Amador County), and another via Mud Springs to Logtown, Quartzburg (Nashville), Saratoga (Yeomet), and Drytown (in Amador County). At Clarksville still another fork of the Carson Road went to Folsom, and thence to Auburn and the river-bar camps on the North Fork of the American River. Many of these arms of the old Emigrant Road may be traveled today over good county roads, with historic reminders of a glamorous past visible on every hand.

Although the Carson Road continued to be used for 20 years or more, increased transportation necessitated the development of easier routes. As an all-year road, the Carson Pass route, subject to deep snows, was impossible, and a road over a lower pass became imperative. This need led to the survey and construction of the Placerville Road over Johnson's Pass and down the canyon of the South Fork of the American River to Hangtown.

The Placerville Road

Deviations from the Carson Emigrant Road began very early, gold-seekers being impatient to reach their destination quickly, often taking great risks in trying new routes. The most popular of these shorter trails took the so-called Johnson's Cut-off, later the Placerville Road. With the construction of Bartlett's Bridge on the South Fork of the American River near the Pacific House, this route was made passable for wagons before 1854, and a large proportion of the overland emigration was early diverted to it.

The tremendous growth of population in California during the early 1850's and a corresponding increase in overland transportation hastened the demand for improved, all-year highways to take the place of those first long and precipitous trails over the higher passes of the Sierra. After much agitation, the state legislature, on April 28, 1855, passed a bill authorizing the survey and construction of such a road, the cost of which was not to exceed $105,000. No appropriation was made for the work, however, and the expense of preliminary surveys had to be met by private subscription.

Keeping to the southern exposures of the ridges and canyons, and avoiding, as much as possible, the higher altitudes in order to chart a route that could be kept open throughout the winter, Surveyor-General H. S. Marlette and his assistant, Sherman Day, finally recommended that part of the Johnson's Cut-off route that followed the canyon of the South Fork of the American River as far as Johnson's Pass and from there through Luther's Pass, Hope Valley, and the canyon of the West Carson River to the state line. This path avoided the steep eastern declivity over the western summit of the Sierra negotiated by the Carson and Johnson routes.

The construction of the Placerville Road was actually begun in 1858, with the appropriation of $50,000 by El Dorado, Sacramento, and Yolo counties. Before the road was graded or leveled, J. B. Crandall's Pioneer Stage Company began to operate between Placerville and Genoa, Nevada, making the trip in 24 hours. Meanwhile, George Chorpenning had obtained a government contract to carry the weekly mails between Placerville and Salt Lake City, with an annual stipend of $136,000, and the first overland mail via the central route arrived in California at 11:00 P.M. on July 19, 1858. With this demonstration it was proved once and for all that "a highway over the 'terrible' Sierra was both possible and practicable."

State and county governments, however, continued to be lethargic. Failing to make appropriations for further improvements or maintenance of the road, the whole enterprise, so nicely started in 1858, would have collapsed and the Placerville Road would soon have become impassable but for the timely discovery of the rich silver deposits of the Comstock Lode in Nevada. Private companies immediately obtained charters to establish toll roads, and immense sums were expended on the four or five detours routed by these companies. So great was the traffic over the Placerville turnpikes that the promoters not only cleared all expenses but made vast fortunes from the toll collections.

During the years 1859 to 1866, this "grand artery of travel" witnessed a great era of staging and freighting by horse-drawn vehicles. By day continuous streams of one- to eight-span teams moved in both directions, while at night from four to six Concord coaches rumbled in and out of Placerville loaded with bullion, passengers, and mail. Mule trains, filling the canyons with the music of their bells; cumbersome freight schooners, rumbling over the rough roads; aristocratic Concord coaches, rattling at breakneck speed over the narrow, tortuous thread of road; Pony Express riders filling the night with the clop of galloping feet—all passed over this great thoroughfare through country once traversed only by Indians.

An actual check made of this overland commerce as it passed by Swan's tollhouse during three months of 1864 revealed that 6,667 footmen, 833 horsemen, 3,164 stage passengers, 5,000 pack animals, 2,564 teams, and 4,649 head of cattle had gone that way. During the years 1864 and 1865, 320 tons of freight passed through Placerville daily, while the combined freight charges of 1863 could not have been less than $12,000,000. William H. Brewer, who camped at Slippery Ford in August 1863, says that 5,000 teams were then employed steadily in the Virginia City trade.

Mark Twain's humorous version of Horace Greeley's stage ride over the old Placerville Road in the summer of 1859 is one of the choice bits of *Roughing It*. His constant reiteration of the climax (put in the mouth of Hank Monk, most famous of the stage drivers on the Placerville Road), " 'Keep your seat, Horace, and I'll get you there on time!'—and you bet you he did, too, what was left of him!" is especially pointed after reading either Greeley's own description of the ride or the parallel masterpiece by Bancroft.

Landmarks of the Stagecoach Trail

The present Placerville Road, Highway 50, is rapidly being converted to freeway. As each new section is completed, a few more historic sites are left on side roads. The traveler in search of the past is therefore advised to follow, as far as possible, the old highway through Camino, Pollock Pines, and other settlements, where there are still some reminders of the old stage road and of the former inns along the way. Many years ago, the Forest Service of the El Dorado National Forest placed a chain of "Pioneer Days" markers designating the sites of the old landmarks, but most of these signs have disappeared at the hands of time and vandals. A number of the old stone mileposts designating the distance from Placerville can still be found. During the centennial of the Pony Express in 1960, markers were placed by the State of California at the sites of the remount stations along the route. Merely to enumerate these historic spots is thrilling and illuminating to the traveler with thought alert to the romance and drama of old trails. These markers indicate that the old Highway 50 actually touches and utilizes bits of the still older road from Placerville to Meyers at the southern end of Lake Tahoe and beyond. Other fragments of the earlier road are plainly visible on the sides of the steep canyon walls above or below the highway.

Leaving Placerville, one may take the short bypath through Smith Flat, a former mining town, before swinging again to old Highway 50. The site of the Three Mile House, later known as the Home Ranch, marks the beginning of the actual ascent of the high mountains. The sites of the Five Mile and Six Mile houses are passed successively, and a little later those of the Nine Mile and Ten Mile houses. Beyond Cedar Grove was the junction with the west end of the old Plank Road.

The next point of interest is the site of the original Sportsman's Hall (SRL 704), one of the earliest way stations. During the middle 1860's stable room for 500 horses was maintained here. The building now standing is of a later date. A short distance beyond is the site of the Thirteen Mile House.

A stone monument, erected by the Native Sons and Native Daughters of the Golden West of Placerville in honor of the brave pioneer officers of the law, stands at Bullion Bend high above the great canyon of the South Fork. This is now on a bypassed and virtually abandoned stretch of road below the highway and about a mile beyond Pollock Pines. At this point two coaches of the Pioneer Stage Line running between Virginia City and Sacramento were held up and robbed by a gang of 14 men on the night of June 30, 1869. Eight sacks of bullion and a treasure chest were taken. An attempt was made to capture the bandits, resulting in an encounter at the Sommerset House (in the southern part of El Dorado County) in which one deputy sheriff, Joseph Staples, lost his life, and another, George C. Ranney, was badly wounded. Later, one of the bandits, Thomas Poole, was captured and executed at Placerville.

Near here the first glimpse is had of the South Fork of the American River, a narrow silver ribbon gleaming amid the pines more than a thousand feet below, while far to the east snow-patched Pyramid Peak stands silhouetted against the sky. Here the road begins to drop slowly into the canyon, passing Fresh Pond and the Pacific Ranger Station before reaching the Pacific House one mile beyond Fresh Pond. Built in 1859, the original hostelry at this site harbored many a famous wanderer in the early days. Here, legend says, Horace Greeley, Mark Twain, and Thomas Starr King all stopped on their way to Sacramento over the old emigrant trail.

Passing the site of the old Brockliss Grade (used from 1859 to 1864 by stages only), one may see a bit of wild beauty in the Esmeralda Falls tumbling down the mountainside above the road. At the junction of Ice House Road a monument indicates the site of Moore's Station (SRL 705), where Baker's fast rig changed horses in toll-road days. This area was later called Riverton, and a resort developed at the very edge of the South Fork. From here the highway follows along the north bank of the river for several miles.

The site of the original White Hall watering place and saloon a few miles up the river is now occupied by the White Hall store and resort. On the right is the site of the old bridge, which once stood at the east end of the Oglesby Grade, one of the four or five detours used between 1861 and 1864 on the Placerville Road. The west end of this grade was at the Fourteen Mile House.

The sites of Sol Perrin's Road House and the Sugar Loaf House (SRL 706) are the next points of historic interest. A mile beyond Sugar Loaf is the Kyburz Hotel, successor of Dick Yarnold's Toll House. Here a community of ten inhabitants forms a center of trade for summer campers and tourists. Trails to the Silver Lake country lure the modern vacationist into the magnificent scenic highlands of this region.

Narrowing to a rocky gorge, the canyon of the South Fork becomes wilder and more spectacular as the site of the old Riverside House is approached. Mother Weltie's (or the Leon Station), the Champlain House, the Georgetown Junction House, Log Cabin No. 2, and the Watcheer House, once a well-patronized hotel, are sites passed in quick succession as one swings up the canyon.

One of the most interesting points along the entire Placerville Road is reached at Strawberry Flat, to the right of which the perpendicular walls of Lover's Leap rise more than 1,000 feet above the floor of the little valley. To the left the rocky summit of Pyramid Peak towers 4,000 feet above the river, Horsetail Falls gleaming white against the gray and barren crags far up the mountainside.

In a beautiful Sierra meadow, surrounded by river and canyon and mountain, stands the Strawberry House, formerly a popular teamsters' resort. The present building has supplanted the original Strawberry Valley House (SRL 707), which stood below the present site not far from the river. The house, a landmark itself, stands in simple dignity, inviting the summer guest to linger within its pleasant walls, to contemplate from its wide veranda the overshadowing mountains, to wander up numerous enticing trails, or to hear again the tales of long ago. The favorite legend of a Mr. Berry who sold hay, and of the oft-repeated salutation of his friends, "Have you any more straw, Berry?" is given here, as in other localities similarly designated, as the origin of the name which the valley bears. The Indian legend of the naming of Lover's Leap was a favorite tale, it is said, of Hank Monk's, a story duplicated in other parts of California where the same name is found.

At the base of Lover's Leap stood the Slippery Ford House, where William H. Brewer, of the Whitney Geological Survey, stopped for the night on August 19, 1863, climbing alone to the summit of Pyramid Peak on the following day. Brewer gives a graphic description of life at this typical hostelry on the Placerville Road:

"We stopped at the Slippery Ford House. Twenty wagons stopped there, driving over a hundred horses or mules—heavy wagons, enormous loads, scarcely any less than three tons. The harness is heavy, often with a steel bow over the hames, in the form of an arch over each horse, and supporting four or five bells, whose chime can be heard at all hours of the day. The wagons drew up on a small level place, the animals were chained to the tongue of the wagon, neighing or braying for their grain. . . .

"We are at an altitude of over six thousand feet, the nights are cold, and the dirty, dusty teamsters sit about the fire in the barroom and tell tales of how this man carried so many hundredweight with so many horses, a story which the rest disbelieve—tell stories of marvelous mules, and bad roads, and dull drivers; of fights at this bad place, where someone would not turn out, etc.—until nine o'clock, when they crawl under their wagons with their blankets and sleep, to be up at early dawn to attend to their teams."

Turning up the canyon toward Echo Summit,

the highway passes by or near several more historic sites. Toll House Flat, where today may be seen modern summer camps half hidden among the pines and luxuriant meadows of wild flowers, is the site of George Swan's Upper Toll House. Next the traveler comes to the sites of the Snow Slide House of pioneer days and of Phillips Station, where a modern store and camp are now located. The post office for this area is Little Norway, formerly Vade. Audrain Station is next, then the beginning of the old Hawley Grade into Alpine County, over Luther Pass, used from 1859 to 1861. Finally, at 7,382 feet elevation, one reaches Echo Summit. In pioneer days the Sixty Mile House was located at the summit. From this vicinity a magnificent panoramic view may be had of Lake Valley, the Upper Truckee River, the southern end of Lake Tahoe, and the barren mountains of Nevada rimming the horizon beyond.

From Echo Summit the highway drops quickly to the floor of Lake Valley. Here, near Echo Creek, once stood the Osgood Toll House. The road from Woodfords (in Alpine County) joins Highway 50 near Meyers (Tahoe Paradise). This resort is located on the site of Yank's Station (SRL 708). Following around the southern end of Lake Tahoe, the old Placerville Road here continued on into Nevada by one of two routes, the Carson Valley route via Daggett Pass, and the later road along the eastern side of the lake by way of the old Glenbrook Station in Nevada. Three-quarters of a mile east of the California-Nevada line at the south end of Lake Tahoe was Friday's Station (SRL 728), the most easterly remount station of the California Division of the Pony Express.

River Bars

In the summer of 1848, after the finding of gold by Marshall, other discoveries followed, and soon mining was being carried on along the river bars above and below Coloma. Prospectors also pushed out across the Georgetown Divide to the Middle Fork of the American River, where many stopped to pan. By 1849 thousands of newcomers were working every foot of the Middle and South forks of the American River, as well as the various branches of the Cosumnes River.

A description of a typical river-bar camp is given in an old history of Placer County:

"A rapid stream on one hand, curving around a peninsular-shaped, or rectangular, plat of land, with a sharp hilly background, down which came trails and roads, the surface of the plat being elevated but a few feet above the level of the water in the river. Next to the high ground which formed the border is the street—the main one—narrow and crowded, and upon one, or each, side are the buildings. If large enough, there may be a few square feet allotted for the plaza, near which stands the round tent where all sorts of games of hazard are played and liquors dispensed; and perhaps adjoining that is the dance-house, with squeaking violins, dark-skinned señoritas puffing cigarettes, and more liquors on sale. On the main street are found the hotels, boarding-houses, stores, bakeries, saloons, in each of which more liquors are displayed. Here are the livery stable, the butcher shop, the shoemaker, the washman, the blacksmith, all in operative order, in all sorts of structures—some stone, some shakes, some canvas, some of boards, and an occasional one of poles with brush thrown over. Pack-mules, saddle horses, donkeys, and not infrequently large freight wagons to which are hitched eight or ten mules, are seen in the street."

Practically nothing remains today to mark the exact sites of these old river camps. Some are inundated by Folsom Lake. The bars themselves have changed location, and all of the buildings have disappeared. In El Dorado County there were scores of such camps, for the Middle Fork of the American River was generally considered to be the richest river mining region in California. At least 10,000 men worked on this fork during the late summer and autumn of 1849, extracting something like ten million dollars' worth of gold dust from the river sands.

Above the junction of the North and South forks on the El Dorado side of the river were the following bars: Condemned, Long, Granite, Whiskey, and Oregon. East of the confluence of the North and Middle forks were numerous other bars: Louisiana, New York, Murderer's, Wild Cat, Willow, Hoosier, Green Mountain, Maine, Poverty, Spanish, Ford's, Volcano, Big, Rocky, Sandy, Grey Eagle, Yankee Slide, Eureka, Boston, and Alabama. The most important were Murderer's Bar, Maine Bar, Spanish Bar, and Ford's Bar. Murderer's Bar, two or three miles up the Middle Fork from its junction with the North Fork, was the scene, in the spring of 1849, of the massacre of five white men by the Indians in revenge for the killing of some Indians at the place by these same men several days before. Spanish Bar, mined as early as 1848 by men who came from Coloma, was one of several bars that produced more than a million dollars.

On the South Fork were the following bars: Dutch, Kanaka, Red, Stony, Ledge, Missouri, Michigan, and Chili. Along the Cosumnes River and its branches were a dozen or more river camps, among them Big Bar, Michigan Bar, Diving Bell Bar, Wisconsin Bar, Pittsburg Bar, and Buck's Bar.

Hangtown, or Placerville

Placerville (SRL 475), at first known as Old Dry Diggins, and then as Hangtown, was founded in 1848. James Marshall stated that in the summer of 1848 he had located the Old Dry Diggins. Usually, however, this discovery has been credited to William Daylor, owner of a ranch on the Cosumnes River not far from New Helvetia (Sacramento). Daylor did pan for gold on Hangtown Creek during that spring, in company with Perry McCoon and Jared Sheldon. With the help of a number of Indians, they took out from one small ravine or gutter, "not more than a hundred yards long by four feet wide and two or three feet deep," as much as $17,000 in one week's time. Governor R. B. Mason, who had the spot pointed out to him that July, included it in his report to the federal government, mentioning Daylor and McCoon as the men who had worked it.

The Old Dry Diggins had become quite a camp by the autumn of 1848. Practically free from crime at first, the motley society that began pouring into it by 1849 brought with it the riffraff and criminal element of all nations. Robberies and murders became prevalent, and because there was no organized government the people took matters into their own hands. Stories are told of robbers and murderers being flogged or hanged by the irate citizens of the new town, early in 1849, thus giving rise to the name Hangtown. The site of one of the hangman's trees *(SRL 141)* at which justice was meted out is at 305 Main Street. However, by 1850, Hangtown had become a well-ordered, civilized community, and on May 13, 1854, the town was incorporated under the name of Placerville in preference to Ravine City, also suggested as a substitute for the earlier designation.

The dry diggings on Hangtown Creek fluctuated with the seasons—in winter there was "water and prosperity," in summer "dullness and departures." But with the building of the South Fork Ditch prosperity became more stabilized, and the place grew to be one of the leading mining centers of the county and one of the most populous of all the early mining camps. Its voting population in 1854 was the third largest in the state, and in 1857 it was made the county seat. As early as 1856, however, a decline had begun, owing to the diminution of activity in the goldfields and the occurrence of two severe fires. A revival of fortune followed the discovery of the fabulously rich Comstock Lode in Nevada and the subsequent building of the Placerville Road. From 1859 until the building of the Central Pacific Railroad, Placerville witnessed an even greater period of activity, marked by the construction of permanent church buildings, an academy, hotels, and business houses. Placerville was a relay station of the Central Overland Pony Express *(SRL 701)* from April 4, 1860, to June 30, 1861. On July 1, 1861, it became the western terminus of the route, which it remained until its discontinuance on October 26, 1861. A Pony Express building still stands at 10 Sacramento Street, and a marker in honor of this brief episode of Western history is located nearby on Cary Alley.

The picturesque quality of the Placerville of today is chiefly attributable to the fact that its streets all conform to the topography. Following the courses of the streams and gulches and the contours of surrounding hills, the earliest settlers pitched their tents or built their first log cabins along these meandering paths. Later the builders of the permanent town were content to emulate the early example set them. As the traditional cowpaths set the pattern for the streets of Boston, so the pack-mule trails of the miners to the diggings are responsible for the intriguing course of Placerville's Main Street along Hangtown Creek, as well as for the direction of the score of little side streets and alleyways which penetrate the ra-

vines and the steep hillsides, now covered with old-fashioned homes and shaded gardens.

Placerville, with some buildings dating back to the 1860's, has an atmosphere of age. The building at 524 Main Street dates back even farther, having been erected in 1852. Built of rough native rock placed in horizontal layers (a type of construction characteristic of the early 1850's), this fine relic is one of three or four that survived the fire of 1856, and the only one still in existence. It was restored by the Pacific Gas and Electric Company, and a marker was placed on it by the Native Daughters of the Golden West and dedicated to the memory of the pioneers.

The Ivy House, no longer standing, a large, three-story brick hotel with wide verandas fronting the two lower floors, once served as the Placerville Academy, originally established as the Conklin Academy in the fall of 1861 by E. B. Conklin and his wife. With the cessation of travel to Virginia City and the subsequent lack of patronage, the academy closed its doors in 1868. Three years later, Professor George P. Tyndall, from New York, purchased the buildings, and in 1881 he enlarged them and laid out a garden. The giant ivy which grew along the front wall beneath the balcony was of a very early planting. The academy continued its activity until 1894, when the public high school was opened in the building.

Placerville's historic churches had their beginnings in the 1850's. The first religious organization in the town was that of the Methodists, established in April 1850, and their first house of worship was erected in October 1851. The ivy-clad brick structure, which long stood near the Ivy House at the intersection of Main Street and Cedar Ravine, was dedicated on September 8, 1861, during the pastorate of Adam Bland, uncle of Henry Meade Bland, California poet and educator. Now this beautiful old building is no more, but the original wooden church of 1851 *(SRL 767)* has been moved to Thompson Way and reconstructed as a pioneer memorial. It is the oldest church building in El Dorado County.

The first record of Catholic worship in El Dorado County dates back to the spring of 1851, when Father Ingoldsby traveled on foot through the mining camps, ministering to the spiritual needs of the gold-seekers, saying Mass in miners' cabins or under the open sky, visiting the sick, and conducting the last rites for the dead. The first Mass celebrated in Placerville was held in a log cabin on the site of the present Odd Fellows Hall. A substantial frame structure was erected in 1852 and the brick St. Patrick's Church in 1865. Both of these are now gone, but the sweet and sonorous tones of the old silver bell, a gift of the early miners, still call the people to prayer.

The Presbyterians, organized in 1853 by the Rev. James Pierpont, a missionary of the American Home Missionary Society, dedicated their first building on February 12, 1854, on the lot now occupied by the Episcopal church. Another structure was dedicated on April 30, 1865, on the site opposite the Courthouse, but it no longer stands. The Presbyterians have united with the Methodists to form the County Federated Church.

Episcopalians began their work in El Dorado County at Coloma in 1855, and the parish of St. Mary's in Placerville was organized in 1857. The greater part of the early history of this parish is associated with the ministry of the Rev. Charles C. Pierce, lovingly called by the church at large the "modern St. Francis," because of his years of self-sacrificing devotion as a missionary in all of El Dorado County. From 1861 until his death in 1903, the influence of Father Pierce was woven into the lives of hundreds of men, women, and children. Scattered up and down the Mother Lode, there are those who still treasure books and cards presented by him on a christening, confirmation, or wedding day. Church records show that he conducted 1,300 funerals and officiated at 600 marriages and 700 baptisms. "No home was so isolated nor schoolhouse so inaccessible as to be thrown beyond the radius of his ministry. When he died, all El Dorado mourned, schools closed, and business was suspended." With the coming of Father Pierce the name of the parish was changed to that of the Church of Our Savior; the quaint building at 42 Coloma Street, which still bears that name, was erected under his leadership and was dedicated by him in 1866.

There are a number of other interesting historic sites in Placerville, although the buildings that originally made them famous have long since disappeared. Among these was the Cary House, built in 1857 by William Cary. Mark Twain was one of the famous guests who lodged there. Horace Greeley registered there in 1859 on his overland journey to San Francisco in the interest of a transcontinental railway, and from the veranda of the hotel he delivered an address to the miners. Wells Fargo and Company had its office in this famous old hostelry, and during the Washoe silver excitement $90,000,000 in bullion is said to have passed through its doors. The present Raffles Hotel at 300 Main Street occupies the site.

Among the early settlers of Placerville was J. M. Studebaker, a wheelwright, who stuck to his trade instead of mining for gold. For five years, from 1853 to 1858, Studebaker made wheelbarrows for the miners, thus building up a nucleus for the factory that he later started with his brothers in South Bend, Indiana. There, instead of wheelbarrows, they manufactured wagons and buggies. With the advent of the automobile, the Studebakers became distributors of the car that they later bought out and manufactured for themselves under the name of Studebaker. Early in this century, J. M. Studebaker, then a very old man, revisited Placerville, the scene of his initial success. In making the visit, he kept a promise made on leaving the place that he would return at the end of 50 years. A little group of pioneers were banqueted by him on this occasion.

A marker has been placed by the Native Sons of the Golden West designating the site of the Studebaker blacksmith shop (SRL 142) at 543 Main Street.

The old Hangtown bell, used in the early days to call out the Vigilantes as well as for fire alarms, has been removed from the plaza, where it stood for many years, to the post office park on Bedford Avenue. At the intersection of Main Street and Cedar Ravine stands the Druid Monument, erected to commemorate the organization in 1859 of the first Grove of the United Ancient Order of Druids to be established west of the Rocky Mountains.

Hangtown's Neighbors

Almost the entire region about Placerville for miles in all directions was very rich in gold, particularly along the ravines and in the depressions of the hills. Yields here averaged an ounce per day per man during the early days of the gold rush. As a result of the incoming hordes of humanity, following the first discoveries, many smaller towns sprang up about Hangtown, or Placerville, always the central depot of supply and trade. So numerous were these little camps, which dotted the entire neighborhood with tents and cabins, that their names alone would cover several pages.

The basis of this immense supply of gold was the existence of several ancient auriferous river channels, which had drained the region in prehistoric times and which increased the wealth of later streams. The oldest of these river channels, the Blue Channel with its cap of lava, runs northwest and southeast at a height of several hundred feet above the bed of the present Weber Creek, which cuts through it. A number of water courses called "Gray Channels," the work of a later geologic age, intersected the Blue Channel, thus adding to the gold accumulations.

One of the richest spots in the vicinity was Diamond Springs (SRL 487), three miles south of Placerville. Its name was derived from the presence of crystal-clear springs located on the north side of Main Street on what is now mined-out ground. A camp, at first on the old Carson Emigrant Trail and for a time on the later Placerville Road, Diamond Springs grew rapidly as a mining center. With a population of 1,500, it rivaled Placerville and even aspired to become the county seat. No longer on the main artery of trade and travel, Diamond Springs is today a quiet town of several hundred inhabitants. Nevertheless, it retains a measure of importance as a horticultural and lumbering center, and on the hills near it large limekilns are still operated. The little town was once noted for its fine sandstone buildings, a few of which have survived the devastating fires that have swept it. Scars of placer diggings and remnants of early quartz mining in the outlying hills indicate the activities of other days. Among the tangled myrtle of the old graveyard just beyond the town are moss-grown obelisks bearing dates as early as 1851 and 1852.

Weber Creek bears many evidences of early mining operations, and on its banks there once flourished a number of thriving communities, now deserted. It derived its name from Captain Charles M. Weber, founder of Stockton. Weber mined along this stream in the spring of 1848, at about the same time that William Daylor discovered the rich dry diggings on Hangtown Creek. Antonio María Suñol, owner of Rancho El Valle de San José (in Alameda County), was also mining farther downstream at this time. Weber had organized the Stockton Mining Company at Tuleburg (soon to be renamed Stockton), and was working the placers at Weber Creek, assisted by a large number of Indians, 25 of whom had been sent by José Jesús, chief of the Stanislaus Indians and Weber's friend.

A store was established on the creek by Weber and his company in the summer of 1848, chiefly as a place where goods attractive to the Indians could be exchanged for the gold that they dug. The Stockton Company was disbanded in September 1848, Weber having determined to give his attention wholly to the building up of the city of Stockton. The Weber trading post, however, continued to be a center for miners, and other camps soon grew up around it. The site of Weberville, two miles from Placerville, has long since reverted to wilderness.

Coon Hollow, about a mile south of Placerville, was one of the most prosperous of the early camps, no less than $5,000,000 in gold having been mined there from an area five acres in extent, the property of the Excelsior Mine. On the Placerville side of the same ridge, at Spanish Hill and Tennessee Hill, other productive mines were located on the ancient gravel channel.

Very rich surface diggings were found at Smith's Flat, about three miles east of Placerville, in 1852, and for a decade or more the camp prospered. Many tunnels were later dug into the hills in an effort to reach the old gravel beds hidden there. Originally, the town stood on the Placerville Road, but the course of the highway has been altered and now passes to one side.

To the north of Smith's Flat, on the road to Mosquito Valley, another early camp, known as White Rock, also drew immense wealth from the ancient gravel beds, four acres alone producing $4,000,000.

Cold Springs, beyond the confluence of Hangtown and Weber creeks about five miles northwest of Placerville, was one of the liveliest of the early mining camps of El Dorado County. During its short heyday it had a population of 2,000 and enjoyed a direct stage connection with Sacramento as well as with Coloma and Placerville. From the fall of 1852 to the spring of 1853 Leland Stanford (later governor of California and founder of Stanford University), with his partner, N. T. Smith, kept a store at Cold Springs; but as business began to decline, they moved to Michigan Bluff in Placer County. As mining activities slackened in the vicinity and no new locations were found, the miners gradually left for richer fields. Stores had to close, the stage took another route, and before long the camp was left isolated and deserted on an unfrequented road. The name persists today in Cold Springs Road, but the grass-grown cemetery on the hill alone bears witness to the life that once animated the now-vanished town.

On the summit of Gold Hill north of the site of Cold Springs and seven miles northwest of Placerville, ruins of the old town of Gold Hill may be seen at the crossroads. The roofless walls of a sandstone building bearing the date 1859 mark the site of this one-time mining camp. Flourishing orchards and gardens have covered the scars of the diggings in the surrounding hills.

Mud Springs (El Dorado)

Mud Springs, later known as El Dorado (SRL 486), was an important camp on the old Carson Emigrant Trail, subsequently becoming a mining center and crossroads station for freight and stage lines. It was a remount station of the Central Overland Pony Express (SRL 700) in 1860–61. The name Mud Springs was bestowed upon the camp because the ground about the springs where the emigrants watered their stock was always muddy—a name applied likewise to a number of other old California campsites. This was changed to El Dorado when the town was incorporated during the height of the gold fever. At that time the population was counted in thousands, and the place had its "full quota of saloons, hotels, and stores, and a gold-production record that gave its citizens just cause for pride."

El Dorado was described about 1930 as "little more than a wide place in the road; a frame hotel (built in 1852), one store, and a service station comprise the entire business section, with a few cottages scattered over the surrounding hills. On one side of the main street ... stands a block of ruined buildings, roofless, with gaping windows and doors half concealed by rank vegetation." A brush fire which encroached upon the business section of the town in 1923 left only the shell of most of the old stone and brick edifices and destroyed the little Union Church on the hill, which had been erected in 1853. One of the burned-out stores, Nathan Rhine's, was repaired and still stands. The other roofless buildings stood just as they were left by the fire, until they were razed in 1956. The church has been rebuilt along its original simple lines. The old hotel has now also succumbed to fire.

With El Dorado as its center, a rich placer-mining district spread out in 1849 and 1850 to include new diggings at Loafer's Hollow, Deadman's Hollow, Slate Creek, Empire Ravine, Dry Creek, and Missouri Flat. The last place, about one mile to the north, was a camp of some importance during the 1850's. To the north and south of El Dorado, several rich Mother Lode quartz leads were also uncovered. A number of quartz mines were developed at Logtown, two and a half miles south of El Dorado, and at one of these mines, in 1851, a lessee put up a steam mill running eight immense stamps. Later on, others were built. At one time a continuous line of quartz mills extended southward to the crossing of the Cosumnes River at Saratoga, or Yeomet (later Huse Bridge).

Continuing south two miles on the road toward Nashville, one passes the site of King's Store on the North Fork of the Cosumnes River, an important trading station in the early days.

About two miles farther on is Nashville, originally called Quartzburg, one of the earliest quartz-mining districts in the state. Here the first stamp mill, brought around the Horn from Cincinnati, was used at the old Tennessee Mine, later called the Nashville. The town of Quartzburg was established on the site of an ancient Indian camping ground, and a large ranchería still existed there when the first miners arrived. Less than a mile south of Nashville and one mile north of the Forks of the Cosumnes River is a flat, east of the Mother Lode Highway and across the North Fork. Here one of the 18 unratified Indian treaties was drawn up and signed by O. M. Wozencraft, United States Indian agent, and representatives of the Cu-lu, the Yas-si, the Loc-lum-ne, and the Wo-pum-nes tribes, on September 18, 1851.

Shingle Springs

Several refreshing springs on the overland Emigrant Road and a shingle mill built in 1849 gave this historic spot the name it bears today—Shingle Springs (SRL 456). A well of very cold water is still to be found beneath an aged Missouri locust beside the Shingle Spring House, the oldest building in the town. Erected in 1850 from lumber brought around the Horn, the Shingle Spring House has been bypassed by the present Highway 50 and stands just off the Lotus road. On the highway is the Phelps Store, which was built in the 1880's of beautiful native stone, with deep-set, arched doorways in the lower and upper stories. Nearby is a monument to the Boston-Newton Company, which camped at Shingle Springs in 1849.

Mining at Shingle Springs began in 1850, and the gulches were soon dotted with cabins. At first the miners had to obtain their supplies at Buckeye Flat, one mile to the east, but in 1857 a store was established at Shingle Springs. Finally, in 1865, the Sacramento Valley Railroad was extended from Latrobe to Shingle Springs, and as the railroad terminus the place boomed for a year or two, becoming quite a stage and freight center. This prosperity was short-lived, however, for by 1867 the Central Pacific Railroad from Sacramento via Auburn had diverted the overland traffic from the Placerville Road, and Shingle Springs became a peaceful country hamlet.

Frenchtown, now called French Creek, was an

Shingle Spring House, Shingle Springs

early mining camp two miles to the southeast. It was settled largely by French and French Canadians, who later moved to Greenwood.

Clarksville, at first a way point for emigrants and later a mining camp, is marked today by a picturesque stone ruin of a building erected in the 1850's, its roof and doorways gone and a sturdy locust tree growing up within it. Half a mile west of Clarksville on the old Clarksville–White Rock Emigrant Road was Mormon Tavern (SRL 699), first opened in 1849 and a Pony Express stop in 1860–61. About the countryside linger other evidences of early habitation—an abandoned homestead with sagging roof and long-neglected garden amid the dry hills; the stone foundation of a wayside inn beside the modern highway. A deep silence, disturbed only by the tinkle of a cowbell across the pasturelands, enfolds these ghosts of yesteryear.

Latrobe

Latrobe, named in honor of the civil engineer who constructed the first railroad in the United States, was laid out in the southwestern part of the county in 1864 as the terminus of the Placerville–Sacramento Valley Railroad. The first store on the site had been opened the previous year by J. H. Miller. For a time Latrobe, with eight daily stages, was connected with all parts of El Dorado County and also controlled the entire trade of Amador County. From 1864 to 1865 it was an important way station for the vast stream of commerce that poured over the Placerville Road to Virginia City. During the first few years of its existence the town had a population of 700 or 800, with several stores, Masons and Odd Fellows halls, a school, and a hotel. Some of these buildings, including the Odd Fellows Hall, still stand, and the town continues to serve as a center for cattlemen.

Pleasant Valley

Pleasant Valley, ten miles southeast of Placerville, was named by a group of Mormons who camped there en route to Salt Lake City in the summer of 1848. At the northern end of the valley a large corral was built for some of the cattle, and a second one was placed on the South Fork of Weber Creek, one-half mile farther north. Gold was discovered while the pilgrims were at this spot, but even gold could not detain them from the real purpose of their journey, and after a three weeks' rest they resumed their march up the divide and over the Sierra Nevada.

When some of these same Mormons returned to California in 1849, news of their discovery at Pleasant Valley the year before spread quickly, and many miners were soon panning out the yellow dust in the vicinity of the old corrals, making an average of eight dollars a day. By July hundreds of Argonauts were pouring into California over the Carson Emigrant Trail. Coming by way of Stonebreaker Hill, the golden quest ended for some of these wayfarers at Pleasant Valley. Several camps of rude tents and cabins sprang up: Iowaville, on the low divide between the forks of Weber Creek; Dogtown, at the first of the Mormon corrals; and Newtown, one-half mile southwest of Dogtown. With the building of ditches to carry water to the mines, Newtown grew rapidly. Later on, hydraulic operations were carried on there, but in 1872 the town was destroyed by fire. One old stone store marks the site of this settlement, on the Newtown Road northwest of Pleasant Valley.

With the revival of quartz mining at Grizzly Flats in the 1880's, Pleasant Valley took on new life, and the Norris Hotel became an important stage station, where passengers stopped for meals and horses were changed. The old hotel is still standing.

Tiger Lily, Hanks Exchange, and Cook's were three wayside stations on the Carson Emigrant Road between Diamond Springs and Pleasant Valley.

Old Camps on the Upper Cosumnes

Grizzly Flats is located 27 miles southeast of Placerville in a wild and rugged region on the ridge between the North and Middle forks of the Cosumnes River. A company of miners who camped here in the fall of 1850 gave the place its name, suggestive of that life of adventure common to the hardy youths of '49 and of the rough country into which the lure of golden treasure had led them. The story is typical: while preparing their evening meal over a glowing campfire, the young men were surprised by the visit of a large grizzly bear, to whom the savory odors of the coffee pot and frying pan seemed also to have been attractive.

Extensive placers were worked for miles about Grizzly Flats during the spring of 1851, and by 1852 the town had grown to such an extent that it polled 600 votes. Hydraulic mining here was of some importance during the 1870's, and a number of quartz mines were also developed, among them the Eagle, the Steely, and the Mount Pleasant, a very rich mine. Lumbering, still an important industry in this neighborhood, had its beginning in 1856, when sawmills were first erected there.

Grizzly Flats today has only a few dozen inhabitants. Several wooden buildings date back to more prosperous days, and indelible scars of old mines mark the surrounding landscape. To the southwest, in a more remote and rugged region, ghosts of old gold camps, such as Dogtown and Cedarville, have found new neighbors in the mills of the Caldor Lumber Company.

Brownsville, Indian Diggins, Fair Play, and Coyoteville, once the locale of many animated scenes in the drama of the Sierra gold regions, were also located in the Cosumnes River region, where hydraulic mining was extensively carried on. Brownsville was renamed Mendon when a post office was established (there being another Brownsville, in Yuba County), but its original name was restored after the post office was discontinued. Brownsville is distinguished as the site of the rich Volcano Claim, discovered by Henry Brown and his companions, which is said to have produced hundreds of thousands of dollars in gold up to the year 1867.

Crossing the South Fork of the Cosumnes River from Fiddletown (Amador County) in 1849, a party of prospectors located near an ancient Indian village in Telegraph Gulch. A lively camp, known as Indian Diggins, soon grew up, becoming the center for mines on Indian Creek and in Drummond Gulch as well. A population of over 1,500 had gathered at Indian Diggins by 1855, and three stage lines connected the mines with the outside world. The rich gravel beds of the region were gradually worked out by tunneling and hydraulic processes, fires swept the town in 1857 and 1860, and by 1890 only a hundred people remained in the place. Today it is a ghost town, marked only by an old cemetery and an abandoned farm. The nearest settlement is Omo Ranch, whose school preserves the name Indian Diggins. East of Omo Ranch, the Indian Diggins Road, unpaved and quite rough in spots, branches to the southwest. At one and one-quarter miles along this road, the traveler should take the left fork another three miles to Indian Diggins.

Fair Play, an old camp five miles northwest of Indian Diggins, was described as late as 1890 as "a neat little village prettily situated on a sort of table-land shelving from the slope of a large mountain to the southeast." Provisions were shipped in to Fair Play, and to Slug Gulch to the east, over steep and tortuous mountain roads. The present Fair Play store is about a mile and a half from the original site of the town.

Coyoteville, south of Fair Play on Cedar Creek, received its name from the peculiar type of mining employed there, known as drift mining or coyoteing. Hittell explains the origin of the word "coyoteing" thus:

"Each miner had his separate hole, in which he delved. The men, while at work, were entirely out of sight of a person looking over the bar, flat, or slope in which they were operating, but the approach of night or any alarm or unusual noise would cause them to pop out of their holes; and their supposed resemblance under such circumstances to the Californian animal corresponding with the prairie wolf of the Mississippi states caused these pits, shafts, or tunnels to be called coyote-holes and the character of mining done in them coyote-mining.... While it was in vogue, many places were completely honeycombed by so-called coyote-holes."

Negro Hill

Negro Hill (SRL 570), first mined by Mormons in 1848, was a thriving camp located across the South Fork of the American River from Mormon Island (Sacramento County). Spaniards and Mexicans occupied ground on the south side of the hill at the mouth of Spanish Ravine in 1849, while Negroes established the camps known as Little Negro Hill and Big Negro Hill. As white miners flocked into the place, the town of Negro Hill developed, reaching a population of 1,200 by 1853. Repeating the experience of numerous mining camps throughout the Sierra Nevada, Negro Hill enjoyed its brief heyday of prosperity as a center of trade for outlying camps—Growler's Flat, Jenny Lind Flat, Massachusetts Flat,

Chile Hill, Condemned Bar (*SRL 572*), and Long Bar. That "tide of gold and trade" has long since ceased to flow, but, until the inundation of the area by Folsom Lake, the deep scars of old diggings were still plainly visible among the bushes and young trees that covered the hillsides. One or two cottages of a later date, an old-fashioned well sweep in each dooryard, stood on the site of the older camp. Across the road were extensive scars surrounding the site of the later Negro settlement, where the colored people, driven out of the former location by the whites, found even richer fields above the river.

Salmon Falls

At the mouth of Sweetwater Creek, near a cataract later known as Salmon Falls, where the Indians for many ages had come to fish, the Mormons stopped to mine in 1848. In 1849 other white men came, and in the spring of 1850 a town, named Salmon Falls (*SRL 571*), was laid out. From the few cabins built by the Mormons, the place grew rapidly to a community of some note, with a population of over 3,000 people. Many little camps in mining areas nearby contributed to this flush of prosperity, among them McDowell Hill, Jayhawk, New York House, Green Springs, and Pinchem Gut or Pinchem Tight. Pinchem Tight derived its name from the fact that Ebbert, the storekeeper, not having small enough weights to measure the gold dust for small purchases, would loosely pinch as much of the dust as he could gather between his fingers, whereupon the miners would shout, "Pinch 'em tight."

An old frame boarding house and a remnant of the pioneer cemetery on the slope of the hill were all that remained of Salmon Falls until it was covered by the waters rising behind Folsom Dam. At Jayhawk the only evidence of former habitation was the little pioneer cemetery lying amid the sheltering hills. Now speedboat enthusiasts churn the waters above these old mining towns, little realizing what sleeps below, and fishermen try their luck where once others sought a richer and often more elusive catch. A monument to the former towns of Mormon Island (Sacramento County), Negro Hill, Salmon Falls, and Condemned Bar has been erected in Folsom Lake State Park on Green Valley Road just east of the El Dorado county line. Across the road is the

Old Boarding House, Salmon Falls

cemetery to which the remains of many pioneers were moved before their original resting places were flooded.

Pilot Hill

Standing up boldly above a wide expanse of hills and forested ravines, the conical promontory of Pilot Hill has served as a landmark for ages. Probably the first white men to visit the region were John C. Frémont and his men, when, early in March 1844, they followed the well-defined Indian trails leading out of the High Sierra and down over the foothills into the Sacramento Valley.

Mining first began in the vicinity of Pilot Hill in the summer of 1849. During the following winter scores of prospectors from the river bars and higher mountains congregated at this point, and a town bearing the name of Pilot Hill grew up near the northern base of the mountain. Not far away, Centerville and Pittsfield developed simultaneously, but the three camps soon consolidated under the name of Centerville, a title that clung to the place even after the establishment of a post office officially designated as Pilot Hill. The small community of today has been bypassed by a realignment of the Mother Lode Highway, and the few businesses have relocated on the new route. On the old highway, now designated Pedro Hill Road, a decrepit hotel, historic relic of 1854, stands among a handful of old cottages and newer homes. The hotel, now cut down to one story, long served as post office, store, and service station. On the slope above the old highway one mile east of Pilot Hill is a small pioneer cemetery, where many graves of the 1850's lie beneath the locust trees, the oldest one recording the year 1850.

Hogg's Diggings, a rich and active camp three or four miles to the north of Pilot Hill, and Goose Flat to the west not far from Rattlesnake Bridge, lived briefly during the 1850's and 1860's. Today they are no more than scars upon the surface of the ancient auriferous hills. South of the site of Goose Flat is the Zantgraf Quartz Mine, dating from the 1850's. Worked to a distance of 800 feet below the river bed, its production record is estimated at $1,000,000. The old stamp mill and the settlement, for many years a mining center, were destroyed by fire in 1931.

North of the Pilot Hill Hotel a quarter of a mile stands that grand old relic of the early 1860's, the Bayley House, erected by Alcandor A. Bayley, a native of Vermont, who came to California in 1849 on the *Edward Everett*. From 1851 to 1861 Bayley owned the Oak Valley House at Pilot Hill. After it was destroyed by fire, he built the large three-story brick structure still known by his name. Believing that the overland railroad would pass that way, Bayley expended over $20,000 in the construction of this splendid old hostelry. But the dreams he so fondly cherished on that grand opening day, May 15, 1862, were never realized. The great house beneath its aged oaks and locusts is as firm and substantial as the day it was built, but the beautiful terraced garden laid out so carefully withered long ago. On the Bayley property the first grange in California was organized, Pilot Hill Grange No. 1, on August 10, 1870. A monument stands at the site of the old Grange Hall (SRL 551).

Lotus (Uniontown)

Uniontown, one and a half miles down the river from Coloma, has enjoyed a succession of names. In 1849 it was called Marshall, after James W. Marshall; in 1850 the name was changed to Uniontown, in honor of California's admission to the Union; and, finally, with the establishment of a post office, the town was assigned the exotic and poetic designation of Lotus, its former name having been preempted by Uniontown (now Arcata) in Humboldt County. Lotus it remains today.

The population of Uniontown was over 2,000 in the 1850's. It was during this peak of prosperity that Adam Lohry built the sturdy brick store with iron doors which still stands on the one street of the present town. Very soon afterward, the fine old brick mansion beside it was erected. A bit of the Old World set down here in the far, rugged West is this picturesque landmark, with its gabled roof etched against a background of spreading locust trees, a quaint garden of old-time flowers at its doorway, and a little orchard of apple, peach, and pear trees tucking it in. In sharp contrast are the scars of deserted river mines furrowing the meadows, which fringe the very dooryards of the scattered, sleepy community, indelible testimony of the gold-mad days when hope fashioned many a glowing dream—fairy castles which were only too often swept away like wisps of gossamer, leaving futility and emptiness to haunt the memory. The tragedy which often followed these broken dreams is told in the story of Adam Lohry, a story of high hopes and subsequent losses, of brooding, and, finally, of suicide.

Passing historic ground along every mile of its course, the Mother Lode Highway crosses the American River just east of Lotus. Here tourists are once more panning for gold along the old river bars, often camping out under the clear summer skies. Beyond the river the scars of countless diggings line the roadway—old claims which once had names but which now are all but forgotten. Bits of old orchards still fulfill their cycles of bloom and leaf and fruit, while occasional stone foundations cling to a gaping, weed-grown excavation made by miners in quest of treasure.

Beside Beach Court Road, just off the Mother Lode Highway, stands a striking stone ruin, roofless and windowless, a colorful relic of the days when hordes of miners of many nationalities fared up and down this old thoroughfare seeking a royal harvest from field and hill and gully. In those days Meyer's dance pavilion and saloon sat, not as a blind beggar in the wayside dust, but as a gay host enticing the lonely wayfarer to share the revelry and merrymaking within its doors. The obscure side road on which it is located was formerly part of the main route. A few miles to the northeast was Michigan Flat, now

only a memory. Red Hill, Coyote Diggings, Rich Gulch—these and others lived their brief day and passed into oblivion with the old tavern.

Kelsey's Diggings

The mining area rapidly grew outward from Coloma, soon reaching across the river and up into the higher ridges. Among other rich claims was Kelsey's Diggings, located by Benjamin Kelsey, brother of Andrew Kelsey for whom Kelseyville in Lake County was named. The two brothers had come overland with the Bidwell-Bartleson party in 1841, and early in 1848 Benjamin had come to this part of El Dorado County, discovering the diggings that took his name. Within a year the place had become a large camp, its prosperity continuing into the 1850's. Six hotels, 12 stores, 24 saloons and gambling houses, a population drawn from four continents—this was Kelsey's Diggings, a little polyglot metropolis selling its varied attractions to a wide circle of heterogeneous camps, all at one time good-sized places: Louisville, Irish Creek, Elizatown, Fleatown; and to numerous flats, such as Yankee, Chicken, Stag, American, Spanish, Union, and Columbia (later St. Lawrenceville). Spanish Flat, for many years the most important of the group, retained something of its urban appearance as late as 1883.

A solitary house hidden among the hills, remnants of scattered quartz mines, abandoned tunnels, old roads—little else remains today to mark the sites of these old camps or to tell the oft-repeated tale of fabulous treasure and of the multitudes who came to seek for it. The foundation of the old John Poor store may be seen at the site of Louisville, one and a half miles north of Kelsey at the junction of Bear Valley Road.

Today Kelsey is only a hamlet of a few dozen inhabitants, with one store, a post office, and a few scattered homesteads and farms, but with many memories vivid with the music and color of other days. James W. Marshall, the discoverer of gold at Coloma, spent his last years in Kelsey and died here. His blacksmith shop (SRL 319), built in 1872–73, was restored and carefully preserved inside the walls of a little fireproof building constructed by the state in June 1921. The contents of the shop and other museum relics have now been removed, but the structure in which they were enclosed still stands on the west side of the road at the southern edge of town. The truly remarkable collection which for a time housed here has been called a cross section of the social, industrial, political, and spiritual life of the pioneers of the 1850's and 1860's. It has now been acquired, in its entirety, by the State of California, and can be seen at the Sutter's Fort State Historical Monument in Sacramento.

Among the 3,000 and more relics that have been assembled, one of the most fascinating groups is that of the old books treasured in the little libraries of the pioneers and brought by them on the long journeys across the plains—worn Bibles, family albums, primers and copybooks of Wilson's and McGuffey's day, antiquated compendiums, copies of Godey's *Ladies' Book* and of *Leslies Magazine,* an aged volume of the *Greek Trilogy.* Quaint old prints, pictures made of brushed wool and hair, a worn writing-desk, a melodeon, the first organ used in the Placerville school—these and many other items depict the cultural and spiritual background of the pioneers who planted in this new West seeds of the old East.

Among the collection are many relics that portray the life and activities of James W. Marshall. From his shop, where he wrought as a carpenter as well as a smith, many specimens of Marshall's fine workmanship have been preserved, among others the handmade compasses with which he measured the timbers of Sutter's Mill and other buildings, the forge and anvil, and the thimbleskein uprights which supported the bellows.

Behind the blacksmith shop building in Kelsey that was restored in 1921 the tunnels of Marshall's old Grey Eagle Mine still reach 200 feet into the hillside. This property is in Kelsey Ravine, one of the richest in the county. A short distance up the road from the building is the site of the Union Hotel owned by Marshall, in which he spent his declining years and died on August 10, 1885. Next door to the Union was Siesenop's Hotel, while across the road stood Tom Allan's saloon, the windows and doors of which were brought around the Horn. Here Marshall and his friends spent their evenings. On the hill is the cemetery, with many pioneer graves. The first slate quarries in the state, working a large deposit of blue-black slate, of which almost the entire mountain seems to be composed, operated there during the 1890's and until 1915.

A quarter of a mile up the road from Kelsey, on the right opposite the Bayne Road junction, is a pleasant ranch with an old-fashioned country house surrounded by tall locusts on top of a little hill. Here, in 1851, John McClary obtained squatter's rights to the land, built a cabin, and planted an orchard at the upper end of the ravine which lies below the site of the present house. Patrick Kelly, who was a native of Ireland, also came to Kelsey in 1851. Three years later he brought his young bride from Massachusetts and purchased John McClary's orchard and the surrounding lands for a home. The log cabin in which the Kellys lived until 1858 stood in the old apple orchard, which is still in existence. The present house, which replaced a cottage built in 1860, was erected in 1887 as the fulfillment of Mrs. Kelly's long-cherished dream of a home on the hilltop. Descendants still occupy the old homestead, which was named "Drumcarn Lands" after their ancestral lands in Ireland. The late Margaret A. Kelley, who knew James Marshall, was responsible for the restoration of the blacksmith shop and the creation of the museum.

Greenwood

John Greenwood, an old trapper, established a trading post in Long Valley late in 1848. Soon other stores were built, and in 1850 the new town was christened Lewisville after the first white child born there. When the town attained the dignity of a post office, the name was changed to Greenwood. Greenwood *(SRL 521)* had social advantages not enjoyed by many of its neighbors, notably a well-patronized community theater. Like Placerville, the town had its hangman's tree and very early purged itself of unruly elements. By 1854 Greenwood was a thriving, busy place.

Situated in the midst of an old orchard community, Greenwood is still a trading center for a township of several hundred people. A number of the old houses still stand. In the cemetery a small slab of stone bearing the initials J.A.S. and the date January 24, 1863, marks the grave of John A. Stone, a pioneer song writer of the 1850's, who lived, sang, and died at Greenwood.

Spanish Dry Diggins, four miles north of Greenwood, received its name from the fact that its first miners were a party of Spaniards, under the leadership of General Andrés Pico, who prospected there early in 1848. During the following year a large number of Mexicans arrived at the camp. That same year a group of Germans also came to the vicinity and set up a trading center, which came to be known as Dutchtown. Yields of pay dirt were very rich throughout this region, and Spanish Dry Diggins was soon surrounded by subsidiary camps all along the Middle Fork of the American River: Poverty Bar, Spanish Bar, El Dorado Slide, Dutch Bar, Rock-a-Chucky, and Canyon Creek, among others. The first quartz-seam diggings were discovered in this district in 1854, among them the Grit Mine, which yielded $500,000, and the Barr Mine, with a total production of $300,000 up to 1883.

Nothing remains at the old Spanish Dry Diggins to indicate the wealth and glamor of its past save traces of old mines among the hills.

Georgetown

The first mining operations near Georgetown *(SRL 484)* were carried on along Oregon Creek and Hudson's Gulch by a party of Oregonians in 1849. A company of sailors under the leadership of George Phipps followed, and in 1850 motley camps of tents and shanties grew up on the creek at the foot of what is now Main Street. Known at first as Growlersburg, it was destroyed by fire, and the old site was deserted in 1852 for the present situation on the hill. The name, too, was changed to Georgetown in honor of its nautical founder.

U.S. Armory, Georgetown

Georgetown rivaled Placerville in the number and quality of its early social and cultural institutions. By 1855 it included in its list of attractions a school, a church, a theater, a town hall, a Sons of Temperance Hall, a Masonic Hall, and three hotels, as well as many stores. The cultural advantages of the little town, the beauty of its hill setting among the pines, oaks, and cedars of the Georgetown Divide, and the mild and tonic air of its 2,650-foot elevation won for it the title "Pride of the Mountains."

The atmosphere of the early days pervades somewhat the Georgetown of today. Its population dwindled through the years, but now people are once again beginning to realize the advantages of living there. Along the broad main street, beneath a double row of giant locusts, stand stores with fronts of brick and stone, built in the late 1850's and early 1860's after the fire of 1856. The former U.S. Armory, constructed in 1862, is especially attractive. On the corner of Main Street and the Auburn Road stands the Odd Fellows Hall, a substantial two-story brick structure formerly known as the Olmstead Hotel or Balser House, and later used as a theater. Various lodges meet in it at the present time.

Quaint clapboard houses of the 1860's and 1870's, with their neat gardens, line the streets. On Main Street, opposite the Odd Fellows Hall, is the old Knox house, a pleasant, old-fashioned country place half-hidden by gnarled apple and cherry trees. It was erected by Shannon Knox in 1864 and stands on the site of the log structure he had built about ten years earlier.

The gardens and orchards of Georgetown were remarkable for the variety of flowers, shrubs, and fruits, all grown from stock obtained from a pioneer nursery established by a native of Scotland in Georgetown in the 1860's. Many a beautiful plant, rare today and seldom seen elsewhere, may be found in the old gardens of the town, and the cemetery is filled with them. Thrifty plants of the Scotch broom, scions of this same nursery, have grown wild all over the hills, glorifying the countryside each spring with golden bloom.

In common with many other mining districts in the Sierra Nevada, locations in the vicinity of Georgetown witnessed a revival of activity in the spring and summer of 1932. Old stamp-mill methods were superseded by new processes and improved machinery. The Beebe Mine at the edge of town, as well as four or five other properties in the neighborhood, succeeded in making the low-grade quartz pay out under more up-to-date management. Fruit-raising and lumbering now maintain a considerable trade for Georgetown.

Seam mines, a formation of slate interspersed with quartz seams largely decomposed and varying in thickness from that of a knife blade to several feet, are characteristic of the Georgetown district. The Nagler or French Claim at Greenwood Valley is a seam mine that produced more than $4,000,000 from 1872 to 1885. There is another seam mine at Georgia Slide, two miles northwest of Georgetown. Here an open perpendicular bank of slate rock was found with sheets of gold-bearing quartz coursing through it. Geor-

gia Slide, however, dates back to 1849, when a group of miners from Georgia first worked the spot for its placer gold. The camp was called Georgia Flat at first, but a big mountain slide occasioned the change in name. For years it was a wild, rough place with no outside communication except by pack trail. Nothing remains of the former camp.

The ancient gravel beds of Kentucky Flat, six miles northeast of Georgetown, and of Volcanoville, three miles northwest of Kentucky Flat, once made production records. Among the many old hill camps dating back to 1851 and 1852 were Mameluke, Bottle, Cement, and Jones.

Johntown, five miles south of Georgetown, was named after a sailor who discovered its gold-bearing deposits. Later, when it become more profitable to raise vegetables there than to mine, the name was changed to Garden Valley. An old store stands there. The Empire and Manhattan creeks join at this point to form Johntown Creek. Below their confluence miners have taken out between two and three million dollars in gold.

Georgetown is situated on the old road that leads up the Georgetown Divide and from there into the wild and beautiful country of the Rubicon River. The citizens of Georgetown, and others, look forward to the fulfillment of a long-cherished dream—the complete opening up of this exceptionally fine mountain region. California's growing demand for expanding vacation lands may yet bring this to pass by the building of a through road to Lake Tahoe, since summer homes are already being built in the timbered country to the east.

SOURCES

Bancroft, Hubert Howe. *California Inter Pocula, 1846–1848.* Vol. XXX of *History of the Pacific States of North America.* The History Co., San Francisco, 1888.
——— "Routes and Transportation—California," chap. 3 in *Chronicles of the Builders of the Commonwealth,* V, 123–96.
Bekeart, Philip Baldwin. "James Wilson Marshall, Discoverer of Gold," *Quarterly of the Society of California Pioneers,* I, No. 3 (September 30, 1924).
Bowman, Amos. *Report on the Properties and Domain of the California Water Company, Situated on the Georgetown Divide.* A. L. Bancroft & Co., San Francisco, 1874.
Cleland, Robert Glass. *From Wilderness to Empire. A History of California,* ed. Glenn S. Dumke. Knopf, New York, 1959.
Clemens, Samuel L. *Roughing It.* Harper, New York, 1913.
Coy, Owen Cochran. *Gold Days,* of the series *California,* ed. John Russell McCarthy. Powell Publishing Co., Los Angeles, 1929.
Farquhar, Francis P., ed. *Up and Down California in 1860–1864. The Journal of William H. Brewer.* University of California Press, Berkeley, 1949.
Frémont, John C. *The Exploring Expedition to the Rocky Mountains, Oregon and California.* George H. Derby & Co., Buffalo, 1849.
Geologic Guidebook along Highway 49 — Sierran Gold Belt, the Mother Lode Country. State of California, Division of Mines, San Francisco, 1948.
Gold Rush Country. Lane Publishing Co., Menlo Park, 1957.
Greeley, Horace. *An Overland Journey from New York to San Francisco in the Summer of 1859.* C. M. Saxton, Barker & Co., New York, 1860.
Hittell, Theodore H. *History of California.* 4 vols. N. J. Stone & Co., San Francisco, 1897.
Hulbert, Archer Butler. *Forty-niners. The Chronicle of the California Trail.* Little, Brown, Boston, 1931.

Jerrett, Herman Daniel. *California's El Dorado Yesterday and Today*. Privately published, Sacramento, 1915.

Johnston, Philip. "Legends and Landmarks of '49 along the Mother Lode," *Touring Topics*, XXIII, No. 2 (February 1931), 12–27, 52–53.

Kelley, Margaret A. "Life, Letters, and Reminiscences of James Marshall," *The Grizzly Bear*, 1918–19.

Mountain Democrat. Seventy-fifth Anniversary Souvenir, Review Edition. Placerville, January 6, 1928.

Sanchez, Nellie Van de Grift. *Spanish and Indian Place Names of California*. A. M. Robertson, San Francisco, 1922.

Sioli, Paoli. *Historical Souvenirs of El Dorado County, California*. Paoli Sioli, Oakland, 1883.

Tyler, Daniel. *A Concise History of the Mormon Battalion in the Mexican War, 1846–1847*. Privately published, Salt Lake City, 1881.

Upton, Charles Elmer. *Pioneers of El Dorado*. Privately published, Placerville, 1906.

Weston, Otheto. *Mother Lode Album*. Stanford University Press, Stanford, 1948.

White, Chester Lee. "Surmounting the Sierras, the Campaign for a Wagon Road," *Quarterly of the California Historical Society*, VII, No. 1 (March 1928), 3–19.

Fresno County

FRESNO COUNTY was organized in 1856, with Millerton as the county seat. (Fresno is Spanish for "ash tree," a name first used in the region by the early Spanish explorers, who found many ash trees along the watercourses.) Fresno became the county seat in 1874.

The Old Los Angeles Trail (El Camino Viejo)

The oldest north-and-south trail to traverse the entire length of the San Joaquin Valley was known as the Los Angeles Trail, or El Camino Viejo, and led from San Pedro to San Antonio, now East Oakland. Following a route identical with that later known as the Stockton–Los Angeles Road as far as the later Chandler Station (Los Angeles County, between Gorman and Lebec), the road descended San Emigdio Canyon to its mouth in the extreme southwestern corner of the San Joaquin Valley. From there the trail skirted the eastern slope of the Coast Range foothills, finally passing out of the valley through Corral Hollow and Patterson Pass southwest of Tracy.

Investigation indicates that early in the nineteenth century the Spaniards drove in oxcarts over this route between San Pedro and San Antonio. Many of the old water holes along its course developed into historic places: San Emigdio in the present Kern County; Los Carneros, where there is an extremely spectacular outcropping of the famous Vaqueros sandstone, which composes also Las Tres Piedras ("The Three Rocks"), Joaquín Murieta's stronghold; and Poso de Chané, six miles east of the present Coalinga.

On the site of an Indian village, Poso ("pool") de Chané, a small agricultural community made up of a dozen or so Spanish and Mexican families, was long the only Spanish settlement in this section. Later, American pioneers came and established stores and built houses. Today nothing marks the spot where Poso de Chané stood, the pool itself having been obliterated in the flood of 1862.

Approaching Poso de Chané from the south, El Camino Viejo crossed El Arroyo de las Pol-varduras ("dust clouds"); El Arroyo de las Canoas ("troughs"); El Arroyo de Zapato Chino ("Chinese shoe"); and El Arroyo de Jacelitos, "so named by the Spanish," says F. F. Latta, "because they found there many 'Indian huts' from which the inhabitants had fled in terror." Continuing north from Poso de Chané, the road passed other camp sites on Arroyo de Cantua, Arroyo de Panoche Grande ("big sugar loaf"), and Arroyo de Panochita ("little sugar loaf").

To the northeast on an eastern branch of El Camino Viejo there were two other very early settlements—the "25" Ranch, located on or near the Laguna de Tache Mexican grant, northeast of the present community of Hub; and La Libertad, about five miles east and half a mile south of the present Burrel. The latter place was occupied by Mexicans as late as 1870.

Continuing northward other settlements were passed either on the main road or on laterals branching from it, among them Pueblo de las Juntas on the west bank of the San Joaquin River at its junction with Fresno Slough north of the present Mendota, and Rancho de los Californios on the south bank of the San Joaquin River several miles east of Fresno Slough.

El Río de los Santos Reyes

The Kings River rises in the High Sierra and flows through Fresno, Tulare, and Kings counties, forming the boundary between Fresno and Kings for a short distance. Early in the nineteenth century Spanish explorers named it El Río de los Santos Reyes (The River of the Holy Kings) in honor of the Three Wise Men. It originally emptied into Tulare Lake, but has now been controlled by Pine Flat Dam and other irrigation projects.

It is well known that Franciscan friars from the coastal missions accompanied early expeditions into the San Joaquin Valley and, while there, baptized Indians, particularly the aged, the sick, and the dying. It became a strong hope among the missionaries that eventually a chain of missions could be established in this inland area;

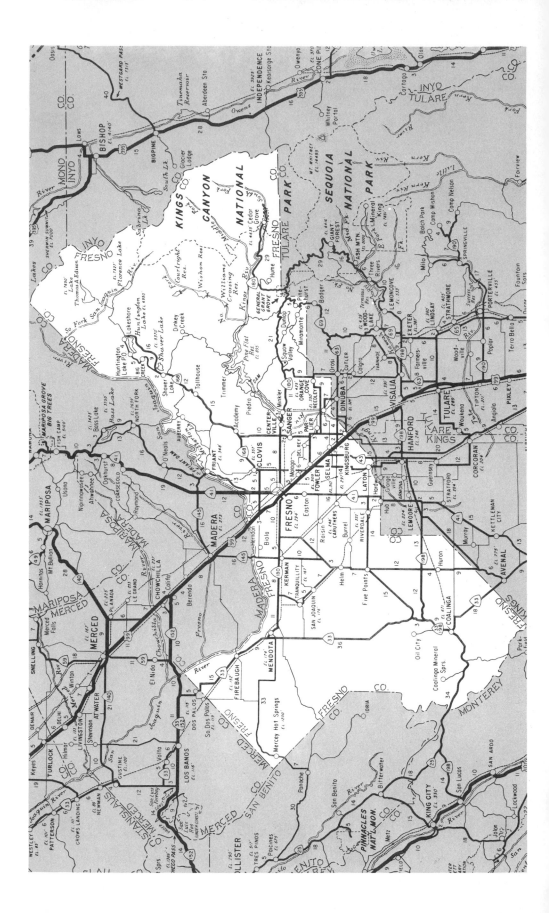

however, Franciscan historians can find no record that any such establishment was actually made. Nevertheless, Latta and others maintain that the founding of a mission was attempted near the present site of Laton on the Kings River. Evidences that work on a large adobe building had been begun at this point were noticed by the first American settlers in the region, and as late as 1852 a huge pile of adobe bricks was seen near the bank of the river. In the 1860's only a mound of earth was reported as being still visible at the site.

In one early expedition which penetrated the wild San Joaquin Valley was Caleb Strong Merrill, a stonemason who had come to San Diego in 1831 aboard a Boston hide drogher. His services were in demand first at Mission San Diego and then at Monterey. According to Latta, "The whole valley area near Laton was described as a vast jungle and swamp. The party was never able to approach Tulare Lake. After climbing the highest trees, all they could see in all directions was more trees and a sea of tules. After about three months of unsuccessful work among the Indians...the entire party returned to Monterey."

Pueblo de las Juntas

Pueblo de las Juntas, a rendezvous for adventurers, refugees, and a few pioneers from the Spanish settlements to the west, was one of the very first places in the San Joaquin Valley to be settled by Spaniards and Mexicans. The exact date when it was established will probably never be determined. Latta says, "The oldest pioneers interviewed concerning the place have said that it was first an important Indian village, and that when the Indians were taken from it to the mission at San Juan Bautista some of the Spanish returned and occupied the place."

Las Juntas ("junction" or "meeting place") was located at the confluence of the San Joaquin River and Fresno Slough, but the name may have had reference to the fact that it was a rendezvous for refugees. In the 1850's and 1860's it had a bad reputation of long standing. Horse-stealing, gambling, and drinking went unchecked, and murder was not uncommon. Murieta and Vásquez and their gangs obtained supplies here, where they were safe from the pursuit of American officers. In spite of its tough character, a number of Spanish and Mexican families lived at Las Juntas, and in the 1870's the population numbered about 250. The Butterfield Overland Stage passed this way and often stopped at the old Mexican pueblo.

Ash trees, abundant along the banks of the slough, gave the name Fresno to the locality. Two large specimens of this tree grew on the banks of the San Joaquin River at Las Juntas, so it too was sometimes called Fresno. When a settlement (near the present Tranquillity) grew up about 18 miles farther south at the head of Fresno Slough, it, too, was frequently called Fresno City. However, Las Juntas was the first Fresno.

Soon after the railroad was built down the west side of the San Joaquin Valley, most of the inhabitants of Las Juntas moved to Firebaugh. By this time Miller and Lux had acquired the land, and the remaining settlers were forced to move. The house at 1583 Twelfth Street, Firebaugh, is said to have been moved from Las Juntas about 1890.

The tule-thatched houses of brush and mud-brick at old Las Juntas have long since disappeared, and today the Delta-Mendota Canal runs through the site.

Rancho de los Californios

When things became too hot for the refugees at Las Juntas, they retreated eastward across Fresno Slough and the tule swamps to a place that became known as Rancho de los Californios. In this retreat, protected by a dense willow thicket, notorious horse thieves found themselves secure from the pursuit of the Spanish cavalry. It continued to be a hangout for robbers, murderers, and bandits, who infested the San Joaquin Valley well into the American period. From a log stockade, which was erected about 1862, sallies into the surrounding country were made.

Rancho de los Californios was probably located at or near the northwest corner of Ashlan and Lake avenues, four miles north of the present highway between Kerman and White's Bridge. The adobes on the place were destroyed by the floods of 1862 and 1868.

Old Stage Roads

In early pioneer days the Stockton–Los Angeles Road followed along the base of the Sierra Nevada, with many laterals branching off to the mines in the foothills. The route through Fresno County passed by the sites of the present towns of Reedley, Sanger, and Friant. Today only fragments remain of the old road where pack trains traced the first dim course and where the lumbering prairie schooner later beat out a well-worn trail.

The principal streams along this road were crossed by privately owned bridges or ferries. Two detours, Lower and Upper, ran parallel a few miles apart. The Lower Detour crossed the Kings River at Pool's Ferry, settled as early as 1850 or 1851, and designated as one of the two voting precincts when Tulare County was organized in 1852. However, the place has been deserted since 1855. Its location was north of Reedley and eight-tenths of a mile southeast of the intersection of Adams and LacJac avenues. The site was marked on private property on February 15, 1959, by the Jim Savage Chapter of E Clampus Vitus.

Smith's Ferry, established by James Smith in 1855, superseded Pool's and for 19 years was the most important crossing on Kings River. Because a crossing could be made at no other point along the river during high water, Smith's Ferry remained open to the public after all the others had ceased to operate. Only after the railroad was completed 12 miles to the west did business slacken, and in 1874 Smith's Ferry likewise was abandoned. This once prosperous place was located approximately one-quarter mile south of the intersection of Dinuba and Reed avenues, less than one-tenth of a mile north of the Reedley Cemetery and of the automobile bridge that crosses the river at this point. The site may be identified by the large grove of eucalyptus trees on the west side of Reed Avenue. Among these trees are two sycamores, close to the river bank. The ferry was located at this point, the sycamores, or their parent trees, having been utilized as supports for the ferry cables. The site of Smith's hotel, on the brow of the hill above, on the east side of Reed Avenue, is now occupied by a private residence.

Scottsburg was established at the ferry on the Upper Detour in 1854. It was located on the "76" Ranch, and stood on a knoll in the bottom lands of the Kings River east of the present site of Sanger. Following the devastating flood during the winter of 1861–62, when the whole town was washed away, a new site was chosen at the foot of the bluff to the northeast. Here again, in the winter of 1867, floods engulfed the settlement. Soon after, however, the town was established on the bluff and rechristened Centerville, the name it still bears.

The old Stockton–Los Angeles Road also made two crossings of the San Joaquin River, one at Brackman's on the Lower Detour, and the other at Jones's Ferry on the Upper Detour.

The route usually followed by the Butterfield stages during the years 1858–61 turned off from the Stockton–Los Angeles Road east of Visalia in Tulare County and, passing through Visalia, crossed the country to the Kings River Station, located on the south bank of the Kings River in Kings County. From there, the route ran through Fresno County to Firebaugh's Ferry, located on the west bank of the San Joaquin River approximately where the railroad station of Firebaugh now is. Latta says that two stations were established between Kingston and Firebaugh's, one being known as the Elkhorn Station, one and one-half miles southeast of Burrel, and the other as Hawthorne's Station, about one mile southeast of San Joaquin. The Elkhorn Station, operated by John Barker (later a Bakersfield newspaper publisher), was opened up in 1856 and was maintained until after the Butterfield stages had stopped running. Hawthorne's Station was named after its proprietor, who was killed there by the Mason-Henry gang of outlaws in 1865. It was established by the Butterfield Company because of the great distance intervening between Elkhorn Station and Firebaugh's.

During very wet weather, when the river was too high to cross at the Kings River Station, the Butterfield stages followed the old Stockton–Los Angeles Road along the base of the hills to Smith's Ferry. From there they took the road marked out by James Smith especially for the Butterfield stages, crossing the valley 50 miles to Fresno City.

Fresno City

This small community was established about 1855 at the head of navigation on the Fresno Slough, sometimes called the South or Fresno Branch of the San Joaquin River. A pier was built for unloading freight from flatboats and barges. There were a few warehouses, several homes, and a hotel, the "Casa Blanca," built by William H. Parker.

In 1860 the town had a brief boom. This was because of its position as a stopping place for the Butterfield Stage Lines, and because, for a few weeks, Fresno City was the southern terminus of the transcontinental telegraph line then being built through the Central Valley. Reporters swarmed down from San Francisco to Fresno City to intercept passengers arriving from the East, to obtain from them the latest news and gossip, which they relayed to San Francisco over the telegraph line, enabling their newspapers to "scoop" the arrival of the mails by about 24 hours. These reporters took up every available accommodation in the town, giving it the appearance of a "boom." It lasted, however, only until the telegraph line was extended to Tulare County, when Visalia became in its turn the headquarters for these roving reporters.

Fresno City (SRL 488) was largely abandoned by the end of the Civil War, though its memory lingered on. Today there is no trace of the community, which was located approximately one and three-quarters miles north and slightly west of the present town of Tranquillity. There is a bronze marker on the highway, five miles northeast of the site.

Millerton

Millerton, which started as a mining town called Rootville in 1850, became the county seat in 1856 when Fresno County was organized. It was located on the south bank of the San Joaquin River in the Sierra Nevada foothills, and was near the southern border of the Mother Lode gold region. The Stockton–Los Angeles Road, sometimes called the Millerton Road, crossed the San Joaquin River at this point. In 1861–62, floods from the river washed away half of the town, and in 1870 it was swept by fire.

When the Central Pacific Railroad was constructed through the San Joaquin Valley in 1872, a new site was selected for the county seat, about 25 miles southwest of Millerton. Fresno received the honor in 1874, whereupon most of the population of Millerton moved to the new city, taking their houses with them. Fresno, thus made successor of Millerton, is the largest city in the San Joaquin Valley today. It became the center of a vast agricultural belt, while Millerton lay folded in the hills, a sleeping ghost town. It has now disappeared under the waters of the artificial lake created by Friant Dam. The old brick courthouse was taken down before inundation and the materials carefully preserved. There are plans to reconstruct it nearby.

Fort Miller

In 1850 the discovery of gold in the Millerton region of the Sierra Nevada foothills attracted a large number of miners, but the Indians in the surrounding hills gave so much trouble that the

Fort Miller Blockhouse, Fresno

United States government decided to place a detachment of soldiers there in order to hold the Indians in check. The first post established was known as Camp Barbour. It was at Camp Barbour on April 29, 1851, that one of the 18 unratified treaties with the Indians was concluded by the United States Commissioner.

On May 26, 1851, a more permanent fortification was erected on or near the site of Camp Barbour. This was called Camp Miller, after Major Albert S. Miller, a former officer of the Second Infantry of the United States Army. In 1852 the name was changed to Fort Miller (*SRL 584*), possibly to distinguish it from "Miller's Camp" on the Stanislaus, 22 miles away. Even before this time, the nearby town of Rootville was changed to Millerton in honor of the military camp. Fort Miller was evacuated on September 10, 1856, but was regarrisoned in 1863 during the Civil War. It was finally abandoned on October 1, 1864.

The first school in Fresno County was conducted in the hospital building of Fort Miller in the 1850's. This building, along with all of the other buildings of the fort except the blockhouse, eventually fell into decay, and the entire site is now covered by the waters of Millerton Lake, created by the building of Friant Dam.

In 1944, as soon as it was known that the water would cover the site, the blockhouse was carefully removed piece by piece, and was re-erected in Roeding Park, in the city of Fresno. On November 14, 1954, this century-old building was formally dedicated as the Fort Miller Blockhouse Museum, and is now open free to the public on weekends. It is planned to move the blockhouse to a historical center on the grounds of the Kearney Mansion near Fresno.

The Murieta Rocks

So much fiction has been written concerning the young bandit Joaquín Murieta, and so little has been published of an authoritative nature, that it is difficult to state the facts of his career. Francis P. Farquhar says that "to trace step by step the origin and growth of the Joaquín Murieta legend, separating fact from fancy, is perhaps at this late date impossible, even if one were disposed to attempt it. After all, what difference does it make whether he was born in Sonora or in Chile, or whether his *querida* was named Carmela or Rosita? Let us be content with

Joaquín as we find him; for the story as it ultimately emerged is a good one, replete with romance, passion, color, and action. It has been novelized, dramatized, poetized; and it will bear doing over again and again, with as much embroidery as authors may choose to indulge in."

"A perusal," continues Farquhar, "of the numerous books of which Joaquín Murieta is the hero indicates that there are two principal versions of the story, distinguished by the name of the heroine. In one she is Rosita; in the other she is Carmela or Carmen . . . The significance of this distinction is that there were two 'lives' of Murieta which gained currency not long after the bandit's death. All subsequent Murieta narratives, with the exception of Burns' recent [1932] book, appear to be derived from one or the other of these versions."

Murieta began his career as outlaw in the spring of 1851, three years after the close of the Mexican War. Mexicans throughout the state secretly flocked to him or befriended him, doubtless believing that he would some day restore their independence. He ravaged all California from the upper Sacramento Valley to the Mexican border. The Sierra Nevada mining regions were also visited on his raids. But his chief stronghold (*SRL 344*) was in the Coast Range 20 miles from the old road followed later by the Butterfield stages, about 40 miles northwest of Tulare Lake and 16 miles north of the present town of Coalinga, center of Fresno County's oil industry. Here, in the Arroyo de Cantua, a place of numerous caves and rocks, he lived in a tule-thatched, loopholed adobe fort at the mouth of the creek. Massive buttes known as Tres Piedras, or Three Rocks, quite visible from the valley, protected the hiding place, and from this point the lookout could see for miles in all directions across the surrounding treeless plains. From this natural fortress, Murieta and his band of outlaws swooped down upon the unsuspecting and unprotected emigrant trains, robbing and sometimes killing their victims. Retreating to their Cantuan stronghold before a counterattack could be organized, the robbers were as safe as the birds of prey which made their homes upon the mountain's rocky ramparts.

Finally, in 1853, Murieta, at the age of 21, encountered Captain Love, a ranger, at this place. Farquhar says: "It is reasonably certain . . . that . . . Joaquín was killed by Captain Harry Love's posse in 1853, despite rumors persisting for years afterwards that the real Joaquín still lived."

The Murieta Rocks are on private property four miles by foot from the end of Monterey Avenue (locally called Repeater Station Road). There is a monument with bronze plaque near the highway junction nine miles north of Coalinga, and 14 miles farther north another marker indicates a view of the rocks.

Tollhouse

Situated in a picturesque glen of the Sierra foothills, at the foot of a very steep ascent of one of the principal ridges, lies the community of Tollhouse, 32 miles northeast of Fresno. It owes its name to the fact that at this point a building was erected in 1867 for the purpose of levying a toll upon all vehicles being driven up or down the ten-mile road leading up the steep incline to the mills in the vicinity of Shaver Lake.

The road, licensed in 1866, was finally built by J. H. and J. N. Woods, brothers, in the fall of 1867; they sold it to Henry Glass; he in turn, in 1870, sold it to M. J. Donahoo, an early Fresno financier, who greatly improved the route and the grade. It continued as a toll road until 1878, when it was purchased by the county for $5,000. The present automobile highway up the same incline was completed in 1923.

In 1882 Tollhouse was a community of about 200 people, with a school, a hotel, and a stage to Fresno every other day. Today the population is less than a hundred, and the hotel and stage-coach stop have given way to restaurants and service stations. The post office has been in almost continuous service since 1876.

The same highway passes through a small community called Academy after a private secondary school established in the vicinity in 1872.

M. Theo Kearney Mansion

Fresno is today the largest city in the San Joaquin Valley. It pioneered in the development of gravity irrigation, which changed arid land into fertile farms, and it has used its position in the geographical center of the valley to become one of the largest wholesale trade centers in California. Fresno County is one of the nation's leading producers of grapes, raisins, figs, and cotton.

During the last decades of the nineteenth cen-

tury, when Fresno was beginning its rise to agricultural prominence, one of the wealthiest landowners in the county was an eccentric Englishman of mysterious origins, M. Theo Kearney, whose estate, called "Fruit Vale," lay west of Fresno. Although he subdivided and leased much of it, he retained the central portion for his own use and built a beautiful tree-lined avenue of three lanes from Fresno to the entrance of his home grounds, seven miles from town, and continuing eight miles beyond to Kerman. To avoid the monotony of an arrow-straight drive through the level valley land, he planned the road to include two graceful curves. On both sides of the wide center lane he alternated plantings of fan palms, eucalyptus, and oleanders. Other picturesque roads he lined with orange, olive, Monterey cypress, and many other trees.

Kearney, who was president of the first California Raisin Growers Association from 1898 to 1904, planted sufficient acreage to fruit trees and crops to make the entire estate more than self-sustaining. In the 1890's he constructed a two-story residence, largely of adobe, in which he lived and conducted his business while planning a magnificent home to be modeled after the Chateau de Chenonceaux in France and to be called "Chateau Fresno." The two-story building was then to become the home of his superintendent. But Chateau Fresno was never built. In 1906, just as he was about to commence the project, Kearney died of a heart attack in mid-ocean while sailing to Europe.

By the terms of his will his entire estate was given to the University of California. The beauti-

M. Theo Kearney Mansion, near Fresno

fully planted acreage surrouding the residence is now Kearney Park, a recreation area operated by the County of Fresno. The building itself, now called the "Kearney Mansion," is open at stated times for a nominal fee as a museum of the Fresno County Historical Society. Many of Kearney's original furnishings have been preserved. The nearby carriage house has been converted into a museum of early fire-fighting equipment. The park is still approached by the pioneer's long, lovely drive, now called Kearney Boulevard.

The Underground Gardens

About six miles north of downtown Fresno, at Shaw Avenue and the 99 Freeway, is one of California's most unusual landmarks. An underground home of some 65 rooms, gardens and grottos, it is the creation of one man, Baldasare Forestiere, who tunneled and burrowed there with only the simplest of tools from 1908 until his death in 1946. Born in Sicily in 1879, he relied on the experience gained as a "sandhog" in the eastern United States, which also taught him a way of escaping the high temperatures of the Fresno area. One of the most interesting features is a tree growing more than 20 feet below the surface of the earth and grafted to bear seven different kinds of citrus fruit. The catacombs, nearly a mile in length and covering an underground area of about seven acres, display the marvelous architectural, horticultural, and engineering skills of a man with virtually no formal education. The place has been open as a commercial enterprise since 1954.

The First Junior College

Fresno can claim an important place in the educational history of California, since it was the home of the first junior college in the state. Institutions of this rank, in which California leads the nation, had their beginning as postgraduate extensions of high school. Fresno Junior College, the oldest two-year college in California, opened in 1910 in the 15-year-old Fresno High School building, with three teachers and an enrollment of 28 students. The first dean was George W. Huntting. The college was first maintained at local expense, but within several years junior colleges were made an integral part of the state school system. The original site of the junior college (SRL 803) is the block bounded by Stanislaus, O, Tuolumne, and P streets. A fountain and plaque memorialize this pioneer educational endeavor.

General Grant Grove

Fresno is one of the seven counties of the state in which the *Sequoia gigantea* is found. A small stand of magnificent trees is contained in the General Grant Grove Section of Kings Canyon National Park on the southern boundary of the county in the High Sierra. The southern portion of this park is in northern Tulare County. The General Grant, 40 feet three inches in diameter, for which the grove was named, is one of the most noted of its trees. There are seven smaller sequoia groves in Fresno County, besides the Evans Grove, east of Hume Lake, which contains 500 trees.

The Converse Basin, once containing thousands of sequoias alleged by some to have been finer than those of the Giant Forest, comprises but a small part of that vast area throughout the Sierra Nevada which was ravaged by the lumber industry during the 1860's and 1870's. One monarch alone survives of the once glorious assemblage which filled the Converse Basin. This is the Boole Tree, a close competitor of the General Sherman as the largest of all the Big Trees. It was saved by Frank Boole, foreman, for whom it was named.

SOURCES

Burns, Walter Noble. *The Robin Hood of El Dorado.* Coward McCann, New York, 1932.
Eaton, Edwin M. Article on the Kearney estate in *Fresno Home Life,* January–February 1960.
Elliott, Wallace W. *History of Fresno County, California.* Wallace W. Elliott, San Francisco, 1882.
Fry, Walter, and John R. White. *Big Trees.* Stanford University Press, Stanford, 1930.
Joaquín Murieta, the Brigand Chief of California. With Introduction and Notes by Francis P. Farquhar. The Grabhorn Press, San Francisco, 1932.
Klette, Ernest. *The Crimson Trail of Joaquín Murieta.* Wetzel Publishing Co., Los Angeles, 1928.
Latta, F. F. "El Camino Viejo," *Tulare Daily Times,* 1932.
——— "Las Tres Piedras," *Tulare Daily Times,* 1932.
——— "Poso Chané," *Tulare Daily Times,* 1932.
——— "Pueblo de las Juntas," *Tulare Daily Times,* 1932.
——— "Rancho de los Californios," *Tulare Daily Times,* 1932.
——— "San Joaquín Valley Missions," *Tulare Daily Times,* 1932.
McCubbin, J. C. *Papers on the History of the San Joaquin Valley, California.* Collected and edited by Raymund F. Wood. 1960 (Fresno State College Library).
Ridge, John Rollin. *The Life and Adventures of Joaquín Murieta, the Celebrated California Bandit.* With an introduction by Joseph Henry Jackson. University of Oklahoma Press, Norman, 1955. (Reprint of original 1854 edition.)
Vandor, Paul E. *History of Fresno County, with Biographical Sketches.* 2 vols. Historic Record Co., Los Angeles, 1919.

Glenn County

GLENN COUNTY (named after Dr. Hugh James Glenn) was organized in 1891, when it was separated from Colusa County. Willows is the county seat.

The Swift Adobe

On Hambright Creek, about a mile north of Orland, stood for many years the adobe home built by Granville P. Swift, a pioneer settler who crossed the plains in 1843 and entered California from Oregon with the Kelsey party. He served in Sutter's campaign in 1845, participated in the Bear Flag Revolt, and in 1846–47 served as captain in Frémont's California Battalion. Subsequently he settled near the confluence of Hambright and Stony creeks and made his adobe the headquarters for cattle operations extending as far south as the present Woodland. In 1849, in partnership with his brother-in-law, Frank Sears, he purchased from J. S. Williams the cattle and brand of the Larkin Children's Grant. Swift soon had vast droves of cattle, herded annually by Indian vaqueros, and extensive rodeos were held at the adobe on Hambright Creek and at a corral (no longer existing) on what later became the Murdock Ranch west of Willows. Swift also is credited with the planting of the first barley in the North Valley.

When John Bidwell discovered gold at Bidwell Bar, Swift amassed a fortune, it is claimed, by working large numbers of Stony Creek Indians on the Feather River. Legend has it that he buried his gold dust about his adobe; many have dug in the area over the years, but no one has announced success in finding this hidden fortune.

Swift moved to Sonoma County in 1854, but his name is perpetuated in Glenn County in Swift's Point, near Hamilton City, a place on the Sacramento River once fordable at low water. The river road from Red Bluff and Shasta City crossed here to points east of the Sacramento.

Swift Adobe, near Orland, before it completely disappeared

The site of Swift's adobe *(SRL 345)* is on the south bank of Hambright Creek about 100 yards east of the Southern Pacific right-of-way. Hambright Creek is between Orland and Stony Creek.

Monroeville

Monroeville, at the mouth of Stony Creek (then called Capay River) in what is now northeastern Glenn County, was the county seat of Colusa County from 1851 to 1853, before Glenn was separated from Colusa. It was situated on the old Capay Rancho, a grant made to María Josefa Soto, later the wife of Dr. James Stokes of Monterey. Out of this estate Mrs. Stokes gave a portion at the mouth of Stony Creek to a man named McGee in return for his aid in making the grant official. Part of this land was later purchased by Pierson B. Reading. A man named Bryant was the first to settle on the land, where in 1846 he built a house. After the discovery of gold in 1848, other settlers located there, among them U. P. Monroe, whose ranch and hotel became a popular stopping place on the road from Colusa to Shasta.

The hotel, which was to double as courthouse, was largely built from the remains of one of the first steamers to ascend the Sacramento River, the *California*, which was wrecked at the right-angle turn in the river on Monroeville Island, about a mile above the mouth of Stony Creek. The hotel consisted of a store, post office (established in 1853), saloon, and upstairs sleeping quarters in one large room reached by an outside stairway. Lodging was "four bits" if the lodger furnished his own blankets, but one dollar if blankets were provided by the house.

As in most of the Pacific and Middle Western states, county boundaries had scarcely been defined when the quarrel over the location of the county seat began. Monroe, who was an ambitious, aggressive man, determined that the county seat should be established on his land and be named for him. Colusa, with only one house and ten inhabitants, was equally anxious to attain the honor. Monroe's Ranch, therefore, became the active rival of Colusa and the scene of an adroit political conflict. Each side was vigilant and determined. The primary question was who should first succeed in organizing the county and so capture the county seat.

Monroe at once presented a petition to Moses Bean, a judge in Butte County, requesting that the county be organized and designating Monroe's Ranch as the only polling place for the election of county officers. This procedure—though high-handed and illegal, since Bean had no lawful authority to act—seemingly carried the day, and Monroeville assumed the role of first county seat of Colusi County, as it was orig-

inally called. The county extended from Red
Bluff southward to the Yolo County line.

No scramble for county offices followed the
election, and those chosen could be persuaded
only with difficulty to perform their duties. The
mines were too attractive and opportunity to acquire princely farmlands was too great to tempt
anyone to give his time to the irksome and un-
remunerative task of running the government.

There was, fortunately, a notable exception,
William B. Ide, primary leader of the Bear Flag
Revolt in 1846. For a time, Ide performed the
duties of judge, county clerk, auditor, treasurer,
coroner, and surveyor. Death cut short the political ambitions of this capable pioneer. A victim of smallpox, he died at Monroeville on December 20, 1852, and was buried in the local
cemetery. Today a stone monument with proper
inscription has been erected to the memory of
William B. Ide, on the River Road only a few
hundred yards from the grain field that was once
the site of Monroeville.

The county seat contest continued, and in 1853
Colusa finally won the fight. Ambitious, usurping
Monroeville was soon deserted even by her
founder. Projected avenues were turned into
broad furrows and "bearded grain . . . nodded in
autumnal contentment in places where the
founders of the defunct county seat had fondly
visioned out church spires and courthouse dome."
The name reverted to Monroe's Ranch, and the
townsite was eventually merged into a 700-acre
farm purchased by Jubal Weston.

South of Monroeville, contemporary "paper
cities," equally ambitious, rose. Among them
were Placer City, about three-quarters of a mile
north of Jacinto, and Butte City, on the east bank
of the Sacramento and formerly in Butte County.
A historian writing in 1882 had this to say of the
latter place in the early 1850's: "Butte City had
already run its race, and the spacious and only
house of sheet iron and its attractive sign of
'Rest for the Weary and Storage for Trunks' were
but ruins." All traces of Placer City have long
since been obliterated. Butte City, however, has
revived as an agricultural center for that portion
of Glenn County east of the river.

Willows

Standing out in bold relief from a vast expanse
of treeless plains, a clump of willows bordering a
large water hole fed by several springs, one mile
east of the present city of Willows, was the only
landmark in early days between the settlements
on the river and those in the western foothills.
Travelers from Princeton to the hills guided their
course by "the Willows." This place on Willow
Creek, the only live watering place from Cache
Creek (Yolo County) on the south to Stony Creek
on the north, was taken over in the late 1840's by
Granville P. Swift and was utilized by all the
cattlemen of the area at a price to the owner.

When the Central Pacific pushed its rail lines
northward to Oregon in the late 1870's, the town
of Willows was formed, taking its name from the
familiar water hole, which has since been filled
in. Strangely, the post office was known as "Wil-

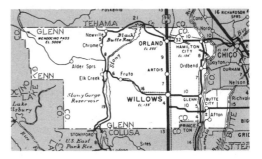

low" from its establishment in 1876 until 1916,
when the "s" was officially added by the Post
Office Department. Willows became the shipping
point for many large wheat and barley ranches,
and when Glenn County was formed in 1891 from
the northern half of Colusa County, Willows became the county seat.

Five miles east of Willows the Beehive Bend gas
fields were discovered in the 1950's, the largest in
the northern part of the state.

Jacinto and Dr. Hugh J. Glenn

Now little more than a wide space in the River
Road, which runs from Hamilton City to Colusa,
Jacinto was once the busiest river town in the
upper Sacramento Valley. This was at the time
that Dr. Hugh J. Glenn, for whom Glenn County
was named, farmed 55,000 acres of wheat land
extending in all directions except eastward from
his headquarters at Jacinto.

Dr. Glenn came to California in 1849 and
worked, for a time, a gold claim he had taken
up at Murderer's Bar on the American River.
He made a number of trips across the plains
driving herds of cattle, horses, and mules from
Missouri, but finally returned to settle permanently in California. After a few years spent in
farming in Yolo County, he purchased land in
what is now Glenn County in 1867, to which he
moved his family in 1869.

Dr. Glenn began the cultivation of wheat on a
large scale in the 1870's, purchasing large tracts
of land in Rancho Jacinto (so named after the
original grantee, Jacinto Rodríguez, who obtained the land from the Mexican government
in 1844), Rancho Capay, and the Larkin Children's Grant. The town of Jacinto, 27 miles
above Colusa, was the supply center for the huge
Glenn operations and the residence of the two
to three hundred men he employed. In the 1880's
it included a hotel, a large general store, several
blacksmith shops, a butcher shop, a post office
(1858–1910), and several immense grain warehouses. The first school in the present county
was established there. The old Glenn home stood
there in a tangle of trees and shrubbery, until it
was torn down about 1960. The site of Jacinto
is 12 miles south of Hamilton City at the junction
of the River Road and Road 39 (Bayliss Road).

Dr. Glenn was nominated for governor of California by the New Constitution and Democratic
parties in 1879 but was defeated by George C.
Perkins. The man who eventually became known
as the world's "Wheat King" did not live to see

the county named for him; he was shot to death at his Jacinto home by an employee on February 17, 1883. His great holdings have since been subdivided into small farms, now all under irrigation.

Elk Creek

Located at the base of the steep Coast Range in an open valley bisected by Stony Creek is the mountain town of Elk Creek, established in the late 1860's as a trading center for the valleys drained by Stony Creek and its tributaries. The post office was opened in 1872, and the town was the stopping place for stages from Colusa, 35 miles to the southeast, to Newville, 13 miles to the north. Elk Creek is today at the entrance to the far-flung Mendocino National Forest and is the location of a large sawmill using National Forest timber.

A conical hill of historical significance lies one mile across Stony Creek from the little town. A large redwood monument has been placed on "Bidwell Hill" by the Willows Chapter of the Daughters of the American Revolution, to mark the encampment of John Bidwell on July 4, 1844, while on an exploratory trip in search of a suitable land grant for the children of Thomas O. Larkin. The trip was unsuccessful, but a year later Bidwell located the desired lands bordering on the Sacramento River, south of the mouth of Stony Creek and north of Colusa.

W. C. Moon and Ezekiel Merritt, both of whom were members of the Bear Flag party, and Peter Lassen quarried and manufactured a large number of grindstones in 1845 on Grindstone Creek, a branch of Stony Creek several miles north of the town of Elk Creek, and packed them on mules over 20 miles to the Sacramento River. Here they loaded them into fragile canoes and drifted with them down the river, selling a number at Sutter's Fort and the rest in San Francisco. These grindstones, Bidwell concluded, were doubtless the first civilized manufacture in the far-reaching Colusa County, if not in the entire northern part of the state. On the former Grindstone Indian Reservation at the confluence of Grindstone and Stony Creeks may be seen an excellent example of an Indian sweathouse.

Orland

A child of the railroad, Orland was founded in the early 1870's and became one of the larger grain shipping points in northern California. Three pioneer settlers met to select a name for the town. One urged Comstock, another Stanford, and the third Orland, after a town in England. Unable to agree, they placed the names in a hat, and a child at the meeting drew out the slip marked Orland.

For years after the turn of the century the roadway of the Orland-Chico highway was red with brick dust just outside the city limits of Orland. This marked the site of a two-story structure that housed, in the 1880's, one of the few institutions of higher learning in the North Valley, the Orland College, a private school for students above the ninth grade. It was promoted by Professor J. B. Patch, who became its first president. On his sole solicitation, wealthy farmers throughout Colusa County furnished funds for the building. At its highest point the college had over 100 students. After a number of changes in administration, it was finally closed in the early 1890's, following the opening of the Northern Branch State Normal School, now Chico State College.

Orland's chief claim to fame is that it is the center of the Orland Federal Irrigation Project, an area of 20,000 acres watered by stored waters on the upper reaches of Stony Creek. Formed in the early part of the twentieth century, it was at the time the only irrigation project in California installed and operated entirely by the newly formed United States Reclamation Bureau. It was a pilot project for federal irrigation in the state and was the forerunner of the statewide Central Valley Project, which developed in the 1930's and 1940's.

Only eight miles northwest of Orland on the main channel of Stony Creek is the $13 million Black Butte Dam, constructed by the United States Army Engineers as a flood control project, and completed in 1963. The dam backs up a lake of 150,000 acre-feet. The proposed Newville Complex nearby will divert excess waters from the Eel River by a series of dams and tunnels to a huge lake that will provide a recreation area larger than that of the present Shasta Lake. Victim of the inundation will be the ghost town of Newville, founded in 1865, 20 miles west of Orland.

The ladino clover crop of the Orland area furnishes between 80 and 90 percent of the seed used in the nation. It is processed at a plant in the highway town of Artois (once called Germantown), south of Orland.

St. John and Hamilton City

Hamilton City, Glenn County's newest town, might well be considered the legitimate descendant of two pioneer towns that have passed into oblivion: Monroeville, about five miles south, and St. John, about three miles south.

St. John, two miles northwest of the old county seat of Monroeville, was founded by Aden C. St. John about 1856 on the banks of Stony Creek, about where it is crossed by the present River Road. It was the home of the first large general merchandise store in Colusa County, and boasted also a hotel and large warehouses and barns, built to handle the overnight ox and mule traffic bound up the west side of the river to the mines at Shasta and Weaverville.

As Monroeville was superseded by St. John, so did St. John fade when Hamilton City was founded in 1905 as the site of a large sugar beet factory, now operated by the Holly Sugar Company. The place was named for J. G. Hamilton, president of the original sugar company. At the headgates of the Central Canal on the river north of Hamilton City stands a monument to Will S. Green, guiding spirit of irrigation in the North Valley and for years editor of the Colusa *Sun*.

SOURCES

Green, Will S. *History of Colusa County*. Elliott & Moore, San Francisco, 1880. Centennial Edition reprinted in 1950 by Elizabeth Eubank, Willows.

Hittell, Theodore H. *History of California*. 4 vols. N. J. Stone & Co., San Francisco, 1897.

Ide, William Brown. *Who Conquered California?* S. Ide, Claremont, New Hampshire, 1882.

McCornish, Charles Davis, and Mrs. Rebecca T. Lambert. *History of Colusa and Glenn Counties, California*. Historic Record Co., Los Angeles, 1918.

McGowan, Joseph A. *History of the Sacramento Valley*. 3 vols. Lewis Historical Publishing Co., New York, 1961.

Rogers, Justus H. *Colusa County, Its History Traced from a State of Nature through the Early Period of Settlement and Development to the Present Day*. Privately published, Orland, 1891.

Wagon Wheels. Monthly pamphlet published by the Colusi Historical Society, Willows and Colusa.

Wigmore, L. W. *The Story of the Land of Orland*. Register, Orland, 1955.

Humboldt County

HUMBOLDT COUNTY (named, as was the Bay, for the great German scientist and traveler, Baron Alexander von Humboldt) was organized in 1853, and Union, now Arcata, was made the county seat. Before that date it had been a part of Trinity County. Eureka has been the county seat since 1856. In 1875, after Klamath County was dissolved, Humboldt County received part of its territory.

The "Arrow Tree"

One mile east of Korbel there is a redwood tree, now dead, around which an interesting Indian legend centers. When white men first passed by the ancient tree, they found it stuck full of arrows for 30 or 40 feet above the ground. It was like a mammoth porcupine. The Indians of the region had a tradition about the "Arrow Tree" (*SRL 164*) which went back to the time when it was young:

The tribes of the coast lands were at war with the tribes that dwelt in the hill country, and the two met in a great conflict. The hill tribes were defeated and peace was made at, or near, the great redwood tree, which was ever afterwards looked upon as a boundary mark between the two nations.

Both Chilulas and Wiyots passed the old tree from time to time, and, because it was sacred, they never failed to leave an arrow in its soft bark. "At first the arrows may have been real war arrows, but within the memory of living Indians, they have been merely sharpened sticks. Gradually, the original significance of the tree was partially lost sight of, and it became more and more an altar for worship and a place of prayer."

Korbel is about six miles east of Arcata off Highway 299.

The Rain Rock

Near the fishing place on Trinity River in Sugar-Bowl Valley and four miles from Hoopa is a boulder, not over four feet in diameter and not at all conspicuous, called by the white people

Thunder's Rock. By this rock, the Indians believed, dwells a spirit who, when he is displeased, sends killing frosts, or prolongs the rains till flood time, or brings drought and famine.

When heavy frosts kill the crops or when sick the "Rain Rock" and by the Hoopa the Mi, or

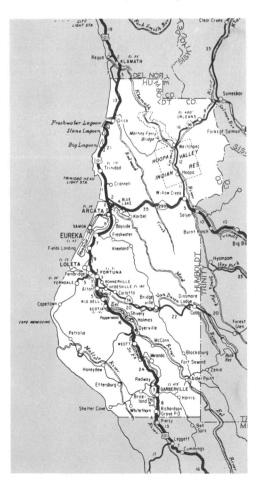

ness enters the village, the people believe that someone mourning the loss of a dear one has passed by on the road and displeased the Mi. Then a great feast is proclaimed which everyone in the village must attend. Fires are built here and there in the canyon until the Rain Rock is reached. There the last fire is kindled, and over it the feast is prepared. After the people have eaten, and the remnants of the feast have been burned, the priest makes a prayer for warm winds and gentle rains to melt the frost, while he sprinkles the sacred rock with water in which incense root has been mingled. Or, if heavy rains have washed away the little garden plot, the root is sprinkled on the rock dry.

Legend connected with Sugar Loaf Mountain is profuse, and many other mountains, as well as rocks, trees, and rivers throughout the region, have similar legends connected with them. At many of these places Indian ceremonial dances are still held, preceded by much fasting and bathing and accompanied by chanting, singing, and wailing. The climax of the festival follows in the making of "medicine." At Weitchpec, where the Trinity River runs into the Klamath, the largest of these festivals is held annually and is attended by visitors from all over the state.

Indian Wars

The Coast Indians of the Humboldt region were generally friendly and peaceful, but the mountain dwellers were often dangerous, setting fire to grass, driving off livestock, and killing or driving out, one by one, the white settlers along the Mad River and Redwood Creek and in the Bald Hills, until there were none left between Humboldt Bay and Trinity River.

"During the year of 1851 the trouble between the Indians and the whites became acute. The packers and miners used little caution in their treatment of the Indians, many regarding the latter as their natural enemies, to be shot down whenever opportunity offered. The Indians were unable to discriminate between these vicious white men and the more peaceful ones, and as a result when an Indian was killed some white man paid the penalty, and unfortunately it was seldom the man who had committed the wrong. Nor were the whites themselves at all times above this practice, for seldom was the effort made to apprehend the real offender among the Indians,

but rather a general attack followed on the nearest rancheria."

The need of military protection for the new settlements caused the establishment of a post at old Fort Humboldt (SRL 154) on Humboldt Heights within the present city limits of Eureka. The first troops arrived there in January 1853 under command of Brevet Lieutenant Colonel R. C. Buchanan. Ulysses S. Grant received the rank of captain in the 4th Regiment Infantry while he was stationed there in 1854. Used as an outpost against the Indians, the fort was not abandoned until the summer of 1870. The only structure now remaining is the building formerly used by the Commissary Department; this has been restored, and the plot of ground upon which it stands has been deeded to the state and is now Fort Humboldt State Historical Monument. A bronze tablet placed on a boulder by the Redwood Forest Chapter of the Daughters of the American Revolution, on February 7, 1925, commemorates the site.

Among the many Indian skirmishes were the following: Dow's Prairie (late in December 1858); Daby's Ferry (June 6, 1862) near Arcata on the Mad River; Oak Camp on Redwood Creek (April 6, 1862); Minor's house on Redwood Creek (early in 1863); the Bald Mountain Indian fort about five miles east of Angel's rancho on Redwood Creek (December 25–26, 1863); and at Chalk Mountain near Bridgeville on the Van Duzen River, one of the last battles.

The Mattole Valley, Hydesville, Yager Creek, and Van Duzen districts are rich in the history of Indian troubles. Many military posts were scattered throughout the region, among them Fort Baker (1862–63), where one house still stands on the Iaqua Road at Neal's Ranch, 28 miles east of Hydesville; Fort Lyons (1862), at Brehmer's Ranch on the Mad River 25 miles southeast of Eureka; Fort Iaqua (1863–66), on Yager Creek, eight miles south of Brehmer's; Martin's Ferry, on the Klamath River about three miles west of Weitchpec, where one lone house remains; Camp Grant (1863–?), on the Eel River about three miles east of Dyerville; Fort Seward (1861–63) on the Eel River, where an old log house still stands near the railroad and the county road, 20 miles southeast of Camp Grant; Camp Anderson (1862–66), near Minor's Ranch, where the road to Hoopa crosses Redwood Creek; and Fawn Prairie (1863), on the Hoopa Trail. One and one-half miles north of Arcata was Camp Curtis (SRL 215), the headquarters of the Mountain Battalion from 1863 to 1865. The Society of Pioneers of Humboldt County marked this site on October 20, 1930.

Indian Island

In 1860 a massacre of Indians who had gathered for an annual festival took place on Indian Island, now called Gunther Island, in Humboldt Bay at Eureka. Bret Harte, who was temporarily in charge of the Northern Californian, the Uniontown paper, denounced the outrage, and his attack was upheld by the majority of the community. The resentment of a "violent minority,"

Fort Humboldt, Eureka

however, was so acute that it finally caused Harte to return to San Francisco.

The massacre on Gunther Island was only one instance of numerous Indian troubles which occurred in various regions throughout California during the years 1850 to 1865. For ten years after the establishment of Fort Humboldt, the United States Army sought to pacify the Indians of Humboldt County, without success. Finally, in 1863, the Mountain Battalion of the state militia, composed of six companies of volunteers, was organized. During the two years that followed this action, almost ceaseless warfare was carried on, but the winter of 1864–65 witnessed the final establishment of reservations for the Indians and the close of the Indian hostilities.

The sites of two shell mounds are on this island. It is now designated as Gunther Island Site 67 (Tolowot) and is registered by the Department of the Interior as a National Historic Landmark.

The Hoopa Indian Reservation

The Hoopa Indian Reservation may be reached by a road from Willow Creek 56 miles northeast of Eureka. Trinity River flows through the center of the reservation, affording splendid canoeing and fishing. Most of the surviving Klamath Indians, noted for their beautiful basketry, live here in two settlements, Hoopa in the south and Weitchpec on the northern boundary. At Weitchpec representatives of 13 local Indian tribes, or bands, gathered in 1851 for the purpose of arranging a treaty with the United States government concerning their lands. This document, signed on October 6 of that year, is now included among the "Eighteen Unratified Treaties" on file at Washington, D.C.

A military post, Fort Gaston, was established in the Hoopa Valley in 1855, and in 1864 Superintendent Austin Wiley selected the valley and surrounding hills for an Indian reservation, for which Congress appropriated $60,000. The first agent placed in charge was Robert Stockton.

Cape Mendocino

Cape Mendocino, the most westerly point of the United States on the Pacific Ocean, has been for centuries a landmark for mariners along the coast of northern California. Information on its discovery and the bestowal of its name are uncertain, for, although this monumental rock may first have been seen in 1542 by Juan Rodríguez Cabrillo, the discoverer of Alta California, few writers are agreed on the exact route of his voyage; and it is more generally believed that he went only as far as the Northwest Cape. Again, the real discoverer may have been Alonso de Arellano, a deserter from the expedition commanded by Fray Andrés de Urdaneta in 1565.

In that year, too, Urdaneta had opened up the route for the Manila galleon from Asia across the Pacific to New Spain, and in 1566 the galleon made its first trading voyage. For 250 years the Spaniards followed this route, sailing across the Pacific with their holds full of rich silks, satins, and spices from the Orient, and often sighting the coast of California as far north as Cape Mendocino.

The name of the point did not appear to have been known to Bartolomé Ferrelo, pilot to Cabrillo, in 1543, but it was mentioned by Francisco de Gali, commander of the Manila galleon of 1584, in such a casual manner as to lead one to believe that it was a name well known to him, although he, himself, did not see it.

But many a famous voyager sighted Cape Mendocino and charted his course by it: Sir Francis Drake, in 1579, on his voyage around the world; Sebastián Rodríguez Cermeño, in 1595, while seeking a northern port for the Manila galleon; Sebastián Vizcaíno, during 1602–3, while exploring the coast from Cape San Lucas to Cape Mendocino; and George Vancouver, sent out by England in 1792 to investigate the extent of the Spanish possessions on the Pacific Coast; all of these, and others, passed by Cape Mendocino, or turned back southward from that point.

Cape Mendocino Light was established in the 1880's. Its Fresnel lens, made in France, was valued at $79,000. The light was located 400 feet above sea level and was visible for 28 miles. The Fresnel lens and the old mechanism are now housed in a replica of the lighthouse at the Humboldt County Fairgrounds in Ferndale.

Humboldt Bay

The first recorded discovery of Humboldt Bay was made in 1806 by Captain Jonathan Winship, an American employed by the Russian-American Fur Company to hunt seals along the coast of California. With over 40 small boats manned by Aleut Indians, Captain Winship in the *O'Cain* anchored 25 miles north of Eureka. While searching along the shore for sea otter, some of his men discovered the bay, and a few days later the *O'Cain* sailed through the long-obscured entrance and anchored opposite the present site of Eureka. Winship named the harbor the Bay of the Indians because of the numerous Indian villages found along its shore. To the entrance he gave the name Rezanov after Count Rezanov.

In 1827, Jedediah Smith, trapper and pathfinder, penetrated into Humboldt County, discovering Trinity River, but he did not see the bay. It remained for Dr. Josiah Gregg to rediscover the bay that Winship had seen and named 43 years earlier. Gregg had been employed by the government to trace the Trinity River from its source to its mouth. With his companions, he started from Rich Bar, in the vicinity of Weaverville, on November 5, 1849, and reached Trinidad Head on December 7. Here the expedition turned south and on December 20 reached the bay which Dr. Gregg named Trinity Bay. In April of the following year, Lieutenant Douglass Ottinger, in command of the *Laura Virginia*, anchored in the bay and named it Humboldt Bay.

Humboldt Bay lies halfway between Cape Trinidad on the north and Cape Mendocino on the south, a distance of 45 miles. It is very capacious, being almost the only good harbor from San Francisco to Puget Sound. "It eluded discovery with even greater success than San Francisco

Bay," Cabrillo, Heceta, Drake, and Vancouver all having passed it by without dreaming of its presence.

Trinidad

Trinidad is on the Redwood Highway 20 miles north of Eureka. It received its name from the Spanish mariners, Bodega and Heceta, who entered the bay on Trinity Sunday, June 9, 1775. In honor of the Spanish discoverers, a granite cross was placed by the women's clubs of Humboldt County near the lighthouse on Trinidad Head *(SRL 146)*.

It seems probable that Sebastián Rodríguez Cermeño may have sighted Trinidad's rocky headland on November 4, 1595, when the *San Agustin*, laden with silks and porcelain from the Orient, first sighted the coast of New Spain a little above 41° latitude. Trinidad was not visited again until April 1793, when Captain George Vancouver landed there and found the roughly hewn cross left by the Spaniards, with the inscription: "Carolus III Dei G Hyspaniarum Rex."

Trinidad *(SRL 216)*, the oldest town along the northern California coast and the first town in Humboldt County to be settled by Americans, was founded in 1850. It was then in Klamath County (later abolished) and was the county seat from 1851 to 1854.

During the 1850's, Trinidad was a port of entry and one of the principal trading posts for the mining camps in the Klamath and Trinity River drainage area. "The mining excitement of Gold Bluffs caused a veritable boom in town lots and by February of 1851 Trinidad had a population variously estimated from 1,500 to 3,000 people." It was also one of the most important whaling stations on the California coast.

The glory of Trinidad passed with the passing of mining as the chief industry. When lumbering took its place, Eureka, on the splendid Humboldt Bay, superseded all other towns in importance.

Humboldt City

The first of the several towns that hoped to become the main port of entry on Humboldt Bay and the trading center for the mines was Humboldt City. On April 14, 1850, its founders entered the bay and immediately began to lay out a town opposite the entrance, just south of what later became Bucksport. The founders of the new town, the Laura Virginia Company, were certain that it would become the metropolis of the region.

"Its water front extended [on paper] for three or four miles along Humboldt Bay and the town was capable of unlimited expansion into the interior." For a time Humboldt City held its own among the rival settlements of Uniontown, Bucksport, and Eureka, all of which were founded later in the spring of 1850. Being farther from the Klamath mines (then the center of activity) than were its rivals, Humboldt City was at a disadvantage, and in 1851 the place was almost deserted in spite of the efforts of its promoters to attract settlers.

Eureka

Eureka *(SRL 477)*, destined to be the metropolis of the Humboldt region, was the last of the towns to be established there. When the Mendocino Exploring Company arrived in May 1850, they found that the Union Company, located at Uniontown, already claimed the land. An agreement was made to share the establishment of the town, and lots were surveyed the same year under the supervision of James Ryan.

Advancement was at first very slow, since the new settlement was farther away from the Klamath mines than was Uniontown. When business shifted from the Klamath to the Trinity mining district, a road was cut to the Trinity area from Eureka, and the latter's position was improved.

Gradually mining was superseded by lumbering; and, since Eureka was situated at the head of navigation not too far from the entrance of the bay (seven miles), it soon proved to be the natural shipping center and shot ahead in the race for supremacy, while Uniontown, impeded by a vast extent of mud flats, fell behind. In 1856, the final triumph of Eureka was marked by her victory in the contest for the county seat.

Eureka's outstanding landmark is the beautiful old Carson mansion near the bay at Second and M streets. It is probably the best preserved and most photographed Victorian home in California. Built in the 1880's by lumber magnate William Carson, it consists of three stories and an ornamented tower—18 rooms in all. The redwood house remained in the Carson family until the late 1940's and subsequently became a private men's club.

Arcata

Arcata, on Humboldt Bay, eight miles northeast of Eureka, was founded in 1850 by a party of 30 men from San Francisco under the leadership of L. K. Wood. Wood was one of the Josiah Gregg party, which discovered Humboldt Bay in 1849, at the point where Arcata now stands. On April 19, 1850, Wood and his party founded their town, which they called Uniontown (Union).

When Humboldt County was organized in 1853, Uniontown became the county seat. It was the center of activity in the days of pack trains, when goods were carried to the mines over the mountain trails which began at Uniontown and followed up the Trinity and Klamath rivers. When the lumbering industry superseded mining, the lumber mills centered at Eureka, which was on deep water, making it the natural shipping point of the bay. For this reason, the county seat was removed to Eureka in 1856. In 1860 Uniontown was renamed Arcata, the original Indian name for the spot.

Arcata is beautifully situated at the northern end of Humboldt Bay, surrounded by redwood forests. The Humboldt State Normal School was established there in 1913, and it became, in 1921, the Humboldt State Teachers College, and later, Humboldt State College, the farthest west of any college in the United States. From its campus,

"Arrow Tree," near Korbel

many magnificent scenic trails lead out through the primeval redwood groves which flank the Redwood Highway in Humboldt County.

Bret Harte, California's noted short-story writer, lived at Arcata during the early part of his career, from 1857 to 1860. While there he worked on a newspaper, the *Northern Californian*, located in a building still standing. He also did tutoring at the Liscom Ranch in the suburbs of Arcata.

At Eighth and H streets is the Jacoby Building *(SRL 783)*, a pioneer business house of Arcata. Augustus Jacoby built the basement and first story in 1857, and during its early years the structure served periodically as a place of refuge in time of Indian troubles. Various firms supplying the Klamath-Trinity mines were located in it through the years.

Bucksport

The pioneer settlement of Bucksport was first located by the Gregg party. One of the members, David A. Buck, carved his name on a tree there in December 1849 and expressed a wish to settle on the spot some day. Buck did return in the summer of 1850, but the land had already been claimed by the Union Company, with headquarters at Uniontown. Buck, not to be robbed of the fulfillment of his dream, remained in spite of protests. From that time on, the place was known as Buck's Port or Bucksport.

A town was surveyed, and since it was on the main channel of the bay near its entrance, settlers were attracted to it. In 1853, the establish-ment of Fort Humboldt on the bluff overlooking the town gave the place added prestige. A campaign for the position of county seat of the newly formed Humboldt County was made in 1854 but was unsuccessful. Failure to secure this honor caused Bucksport to fall behind in the race. It is now within the southern limits of the city of Eureka.

Gold Bluffs

Gold Bluffs was the scene of great excitement in 1850 and 1851, when thousands of miners came there to extract gold from the beach sands. It was situated about 15 miles south of the mouth of Klamath River, and 35 miles north of Trinidad. Nothing remains of the old camp today.

Orleans Bar

Orleans Bar, once a thriving mining center on the Klamath River, along which the rich mines of northern California were located, was the county seat of Klamath County from 1855 to 1875, when the county was dissolved. Its predecessors were Trinidad (1851–54) and Crescent City (1854–55).

Centerville Beach Memorial Cross

On January 6, 1860, the steamer *Northerner*, which had left San Francisco the day before, struck a hidden rock off Cape Mendocino and drifted to the Centerville beach, seven miles west of Ferndale. Seventeen passengers and 21 members of the crew were lost. In 1921 Ferndale Chapter No. 93 of the Native Sons of the Golden West erected a concrete cross *(SRL 173)* to honor the memory of the 38 who lost their lives in this disaster.

Mail Ridge

Mail Ridge was once a part of the old mail stage route from San Francisco into the north western part of California before the advent of the railroad. It is about 3,500 feet above sea level with extensive views over the whole southern part of Humboldt County.

To reach the ridge, the road leaves the Redwood Highway at Fortuna, 18 miles south of Eureka, and follows up the Van Duzen River to Bridgeville, thence south through high mountain country to Blocksburg, and on to Alderpoint on the main line of the railway. Crossing the railway, the route leads uphill for eight miles to the town of Harris, then turns north again and follows along Mail Ridge, the old stage road.

Petrolia

Humboldt County claims the honor of California's first drilled oil wells, and a quiet little town in the Mattole Valley remembers the brief boom in its name, Petrolia. Prior to 1865 the area was mapped by A. J. Doolittle as "New Jerusalem," but the shipment of the first crude oil to a San Francisco refinery by the Union Mattole Oil Company in June 1865 was the occasion for the bestowal of a permanent name. A monument in the town commemorates the oil wells *(SRL 543)*, which are located on private property about three miles east on the North Fork of the Mattole River. Today, although there are occasional efforts to revive the oil industry, the main interests of Petrolia and the Mattole Valley are livestock raising, farming, and recreation.

Covered Bridges

Humboldt County contains two of California's 11 remaining covered bridges, the two most recently constructed. Both are located on the Elk River five to six miles south of Eureka, not far from Fields Landing, and both are 52 feet in length. The Berta's Ranch bridge, built in 1936, is the westernmost covered bridge in the United States. The Zane's Ranch bridge, farther upstream, was completed in 1937. About the time these bridges were constructed there were 12 covered bridges in Humboldt County alone. One of them, the Cannibal Island bridge near Eureka, was blown down in a storm on October 12, 1962. Built in 1930, the 120-foot span had been the only covered bridge in the nation over salt water, the one at lowest elevation, and the westernmost.

Redwood Groves

Along the famous Redwood Highway through Humboldt County there are many magnificent stands of primeval redwood forests (Sequoia sempervirens). An increasing number of these great groves have been made into private or public parks to be preserved for the people for all time.

There are now approximately 22,000 acres of redwood groves in state parks in Humboldt County and also about 3,000 acres of coastline and river areas in state parks. A few miles north of Scotia is Canyon Park, and just off the highway west of Dyerville on Bull Creek is the Bull Creek Grove on a road leading to Upper Mattole. The road south of Dyerville passes through numerous groves, many of which are memorials to noted men: the Perrot Grove, Sage Grove, Gould Grove, Mather Grove, Bolling Grove, Felton Grove, Stephens Grove, Fish Creek Grove (private), and the Franklin K. Lane Grove, a memorial to the Secretary of the Interior under President Wilson and first president of the Save-the-Redwoods League. The little town of Orick lies at the lower end of the Redwood Creek Grove, and north of

the town is the Humboldt Pioneer Memorial Grove, dedicated to early settlers who braved the unknown to establish their homes in the wilderness. This is also known as the Russ Grove.

The title to the world's tallest tree has long remained among the Sequoia sempervirens of Humboldt County. Until 1957 the honor belonged to the Founders Tree in Humboldt Redwoods State Park (present height 352.6 feet). Then it was discovered that the nearby Rockefeller Tree in the same park was a few feet taller. In 1963, however, Dr. Paul A. Zahl, senior naturalist of the National Geographic Society, found a redwood over 11 feet taller than the Rockefeller. This 367.8-foot giant stands in a privately owned grove on Redwood Creek southeast of Orick. In the same grove two other trees were discovered that also exceed the Rockefeller Tree in height. It is quite likely that an even taller tree yet remains to be found.

SOURCES

Adams, Kramer A. Covered Bridges of the West. Howell-North, Berkeley, 1963.
Bledsoe, A. J. Indian Wars of the Northwest. San Francisco, 1855.
Carr, John. Pioneer Days in California. Privately printed, Eureka, 1891.
Chapman, Charles E. A History of California: The Spanish Period. Macmillan, New York, 1923.
Coy, Owen C. The Humboldt Bay Region, 1850–1875: A Study in the American Colonization of California. The California State Historical Association, Los Angeles, 1929.
——— Pictorial History of California. University of California Extension Division, Berkeley, 1925.
Davidson, George. "The Discovery of Humboldt Bay," Transactions of the Geographical Society of the Pacific, II, No. 1. San Francisco, 1891.
History of Humboldt County, California. W. W. Elliott & Co., San Francisco, 1881.
Hunt, Rockwell D., and Nellie Van de Grift Sanchez. A Short History of California. Crowell, New York, 1929.
Kroeber, A. L. Handbook of the Indians of California. Smithsonian Institution, Bureau of American Ethnology, Bulletin 78, Washington, D.C., 1925.
Murdock, Charles A. A Backward Glance at Eighty. Paul Elder & Co., San Francisco, 1921.
Publications in American Archaeology and Ethnology, Vols. I and XIV, University of California, Berkeley.
Wagner, Henry R. Spanish Voyages to the Northwest Coast of America in the Sixteenth Century. California Historical Society, San Francisco, 1929.
Zahl, Paul A. "Finding the Mt. Everest of All Living Things," National Geographic, CXXVI, No. 1 (July 1964), 10–51.

Imperial County

IMPERIAL COUNTY was organized in 1907 from that part of San Diego County known as Imperial Valley. El Centro is the county seat.

A Prehistoric Wonderland

Imperial Valley is remarkable for the vast range of prehistoric and geologic relics to be found within its borders. Outlining and explaining these, as it were, is the ancient beachline extending from north to south and plainly visible at 260 feet above the surface of the Salton Sea (1963). Professor William P. Blake of the Williamson survey first observed the old beachline and examined its shells while engaged in making the first governmental survey of Imperial Valley in 1853.

Extending southward from Indio in Riverside County, past the Travertine Rock at the county line and on through western Imperial County to the Fish Creek Mountains, this ancient shoreline there turns east and south, skirting Superstition Mountain and crossing the Interstate 8 Highway about three miles west of Dixieland. Continuing south along the West Side Canal and down into Mexico as far as Black Butte, it again turns northward, re-entering Imperial County eight miles east of Calexico. Here the ancient waterline follows the East Highline Canal northward, passing east of Salton Sea into Riverside County, where the circuit is completed at a point slightly north of Indio.

This beachline, approximately 30 feet above sea level, is that of an ancient fresh-water lake which covered Imperial and Coachella valleys. Indications are that in past ages it was filled many times by waters from the Colorado River and stood at this elevation for long periods before the river shifted course again and directed its flow into the Gulf of California. Along the entire length of this ancient beach, or within a short distance from its sands, may be found curious relics of bygone ages: vast coral reefs, millions of fossils and shells, and even pottery wrought by a race long since forgotten. The beachline is not always visible south of the international border. Presumably it is buried beneath silt from the Colorado River.

In view of the difficult desert trails leading to most of the places described, and also because of the excessive heat and scarcity of water, the traveler should furnish himself with detailed information on routes and equipment before attempting any trips. It is also necessary to remember that some areas may be completely inaccessible because they have been made government-restricted areas. *Touring Topics* (October 1929), in an article entitled "Fossil Hunting about Carrizo Creek" by John Edwin Hogg, gives a good idea of the nature of some of the roads encountered.

Beginning in the north is the interesting geological upthrust known as Travertine Rock. Shared also by Riverside County, it stands near Highway 86 on the western shore of the Salton Sea. Covered by a hard crust of calcium carbonate (known as travertine), left there by receding waters at least a thousand years ago, this chalk-like surface is made even more interesting by the indelible imprint of human hands left in the Indian rock writings (petroglyphs) of a prehistoric age. Twelve miles to the south lies a petrified forest.

A group of prehistoric animal tracks, reached by a drive over rough roads and a short hike, are to be seen in a small canyon north of the Fish Creek Mountains. Presumably an ancient water hole where great prehistoric animals came to drink, it is covered by hundreds of huge tracks which geologists believe to be the footprints of mastodons, solidified and preserved by succeeding geological epochs.

Mullet Island, with its museum of curious pottery and innumerable natural relics, is five miles west of Niland and 11.5 miles northwest of Calipatria. Its bubbling oxide springs and famous mud pots or geysers cover an area of 20 acres.

Across the international boundary, ten miles southwest of Coyote Wells, lies another petrified forest, in a setting of many-tinted and fantastically shaped rocks. Pieces of petrified wood may be found scattered over an area of ten acres.

Painted Gorge, with its rugged walls tinted in "a patchwork of colors like the design of an old-fashioned quilt," is seven miles north of the Interstate 8 Highway and 30 miles west of El Centro. At the upper end of the gorge are high coral reefs and well-preserved oyster shells. In the Coyote Mountains to the northwest, valuable pieces of Indian pottery and other relics may be found, although many have already been placed in numerous valley collections.

The best and most extensive coral formations are found in Alverson Canyon (locally known as Shell Canyon) across the Coyote Mountains from Painted Gorge. These deposits are reached only by a very difficult desert road followed by three miles of hiking. Two magnificent coral canyons may also be reached from Barrett Well with less difficulty: Barrett Canyon in the Fish Creek Mountains to the north and Garnet Canyon in the Coyote Mountains on the south.

North and east of the petrified forest stretches the Yuha plain, with its myriad fish fossils, its beds of decaying oyster shells, and "the most amazing rock concretions ever discovered in the United States." These latter were first mentioned

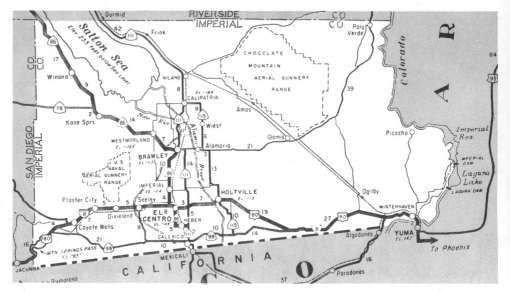

by Juan Bautista de Anza in 1774 and first described over 125 years later by George Wharton James in his *Wonders of the Colorado Desert.* They consist of "detached rocks of various shapes and sizes, chiefly spherical . . . and resembling petrified fruits, vegetables and flowers."

California's First Historic Spot

Probably the first white man to touch California soil was Hernando de Alarcón. On May 9, 1540, Alarcón started from Acapulco, Mexico, and sailed north until he reached the mouth of the Colorado River on August 17 or 18. On several occasions during the fall of 1540 he ascended the river, to a point probably a little beyond the site of Yuma. Joseph J. Hill says of Alarcón's visit: "It can hardly be doubted that he landed at various times on the California side of the river, probably being the first to do so." The point touched *(SRL 568)* was somewhere opposite Yuma. A monument in Alarcón's honor has been proposed.

The next white man to walk upon California soil was Melchior Díaz, who had left Coronado's expedition near the present site of Ures, Mexico, in October 1540, with instructions to make contact with Alarcón if possible. Díaz proceeded up the Colorado River as far as the Gila, where his party crossed over on rafts, touching California soil at about the same point as Alarcón. He then traveled down the western bank, passing historic Pilot Knob on Imperial County soil.

First Passage of the Colorado Desert

A trail from Mexico to the junction of the Colorado and Gila rivers had been blazed as early as 1700 by Father Eusebio Kino, a Jesuit priest, whose purpose was to find an overland route from Sonora to the missions of Baja California.

"Francisco Eusebio Kino . . . was the father of the cattle industry of the southwest and one of the great missionaries of New Spain." He was in Lower California from 1683 to 1685. The remainder of his life was spent in Pimería Alta, now southern Arizona and northern Sonora, where he founded some 50 missions and chapels. The desire to find a way to connect the missions of Pimería Alta with those of Lower California led to numerous exploring expeditions. In 1700 he went as far as the junction of the Colorado and Gila rivers, and the next year he descended the former nearly to its mouth, where he crossed on a raft. Descending the Colorado again in 1702, Kino reached as far as the Gulf. These explorations led him to believe that California was a peninsula and not an island, as had previously been supposed. Furthermore, the way had been opened to the great Colorado Desert, a trail followed over 70 years later by Garcés and Anza.

Fray Francisco Garcés, famous priest-explorer, was the first white man to enter the great Colorado Desert, when in 1771, believing that he was crossing the Gila River, he crossed the Colorado instead. During his wanderings he skirted the Cocopah Range to its terminus at Signal Mountain near the present Calexico. To the northwest he saw two gaps in the Sierra, which he believed could be followed into New California without great difficulty.

On this journey, Garcés gained information that exercised a profound influence on the decision of the *junta,* which eventually recommended Anza's plan to go overland to California. It was this journey, also, more than any other, that helped to determine the path taken by the subsequent expedition.

In the year 1774, Juan Bautista de Anza, one of the most heroic figures in the history of California, volunteered to find an overland route to the coast missions in order to avoid the perils and uncertainty of communication by sea, and to ensure the settlement of Alta California. Antonio María Bucareli, then viceroy of Mexico, accepted Anza's offer.

Accompanied by Fray Francisco Garcés, Fray Juan Díaz, and 20 soldiers, Anza reached the junction of the Gila and Colorado rivers on February 7, 1774, and two days later he crossed the Colorado at the ford above the Gila, camping on the California side.

On the following day, the party went four leagues along the river, passing Pilot Knob, which Anza named the Cerro de San Pablo, where the river turns south. Proceeding another league, they stopped for the night at the Ranchería de San Pablo, a Yuman Indian village at the place where the Misión San Pedro y San Pablo was established in the autumn of 1780.

This was just above the boundary line, and from here the expedition continued southwest until they reached a lake that Anza called Laguna de Santa Olaya, 12 miles south of the boundary line and eight miles west of the Colorado, "the end of the known land." Beyond lay hostile Indians and league upon league of treacherous sand dunes blocking the way into what is now southeastern Imperial County.

Undaunted, Anza set forth to cross this forbidding waste, but the dunes proved impassable and he was forced to retreat to Santa Olaya, which the party reached again on February 19. Having rested for several days among the friendly Indians at this oasis, the party resumed its journey on March 2, and finally re-entered California on March 7, camping three or four miles southwest of the Yuha Well and about two miles north of the international boundary line. The next morning they reached a little group of refreshing wells, "which, on being opened, distilled an abundant supply of most beautiful water." Here Anza rested for a day, refreshing both the footsore men and the starved horses. These life-giving springs were named by Anza the Pozas de Santa Rosa de las Lajas (the Wells of St. Rose of the Flat Rocks), because of the great number of peculiar rock formations. How the less poetic name of Yuha Well later came to be attached to them is not known. They lie in a basin of the same name six miles southwest of Dixieland and two miles north of the boundary line.

Anza's last important camp on the first journey across the desert was reached on March 10. It was made at the junction or sink of the San Felipe and Carrizo creeks, called by Anza the San Sebastián, alias del Peregrino, in honor of Sebastián Tarabal, his Indian guide, who had previously passed that way under great hardships and danger. This place, now known as Harper's Well, was at the base of the San Jacinto Mountains, where the western wall of the great Colorado Desert had been reached and where the expedition entered the San Jacinto Mountains by way of San Felipe Canyon and San Carlos Pass.

On his return to Mexico in May, Anza again crossed the desert, camping at San Sebastián on May 7, and from there making a shortcut directly across the desert. On December 11, 1775, he again stopped at the Wells of Santa Rosa, this time to rest and refresh the first caravan of emigrants to enter California, the party destined to be also the first settlers of San Francisco. This caravan, which left Tubac on October 23, 1775, was made up of 240 persons, of whom more than 30 were women and 136 were boys and girls. Only one life was lost on the entire journey of 1,000 miles, and three babies were born en route. Over a thousand animals also began the journey, but many perished on the deserts.

On his final return to Mexico in 1776, Anza again made a direct cut across the desert, paralleling Highway 86 past Kane Spring as far as Westmorland, and camping on May 8 east of Imperial.

The Desert Trail

The old desert trail across Imperial Valley, first opened by Anza and followed later by generations of explorers and trappers, traders and Argonauts, and finally by a long line of homeseekers, has been variously known as the Sonora Road, the Colorado Road, the Emigrant Trail, and the Butterfield Stage Route. That part of the route from the San Felipe Sink via San Carlos Pass was closed after 1782 and has never been used since. In July 1781 the two missions established on the Colorado River in 1780 were destroyed by Indians, and in 1781 and 1782 Pedro Fages carried dispatches to Misión San Gabriel relative to these Indian troubles. On the first of these trips he followed Anza's trail all the way, but on the second he traversed it only across the desert to the San Felipe watering place, where he turned up the Carrizo Creek into the unexplored territory to the southwest, thus opening the road which now goes by way of Warner's Ranch, a trail followed by southern emigrant trains of 1849 and the 1850's and known as the old Emigrant Trail.

Because of the hostility of the Yuma Indians, the desert trail was probably not used again until 1826, although Santiago Argüello, while pursuing Indian horse thieves in 1825, rediscovered Fages' route through the mountains. In 1826, on the approval of Romualdo Pacheco, Lieutenant of Engineers, the Mexican government adopted the desert trail as an official mail route and Pacheco established a small garrison on the Colorado River that same year. From then on, the trail was used to a small extent by traders from Sonora.

The David E. Jackson party in 1831 followed Anza's trail across the desert to Carrizo Creek, where they crossed the mountains via Warner's, probably the first Americans to pass that way.

Pilot Knob Stage Station, Araz

In 1834 Rafael Amador, a messenger for President Santa Anna of Mexico, made the trip in 48 days, record time, and in 1846 Stephen W. Kearny conducted the advanced guard of the "Army of the West" across the old desert trail and over the mountains through Warner's Pass.

The Butterfield Stage used approximately the same road from 1858 to 1861. "Winding across desert wastes, topping sand-dunes and skirting buttes, the old Butterfield trail . . . was probably the first well-defined road across the Imperial Valley. After more than seventy years [1930] of desert cloudbursts and windstorms, portions of the road still remain like a forgotten relic of yesteryear."

The ruined adobe walls of the old Pilot Knob station may still be seen at Araz on the Interstate 8 Highway a few miles west of Yuma. Except for the station at Indian Wells (also known as Sunset Springs and by various other names), the trail through the shifting dunes from Araz westward is uncertain until Carrizo Creek is reached. It led south of the international boundary line by way of the stations at Cook's Well and Alamo Mocho (both of which have disappeared), and then northwest into the present Imperial County by way of the station at Indian Wells, halfway to the Carrizo station (San Diego County). Indian Wells was located approximately eight miles south and a little west of Seeley and about two and a half miles from Silsbee. The adobe station building continued to stand there until washed away by the flood of 1906.

Another stage station in present Imperial County, though not on the Butterfield route, was at Mountain Springs (SRL 194), just east of the San Diego County line near Interstate 8. There are some ruins here and the remains of an old road. Tradition says that the Army camped at the spring here in 1846.

Seventeen miles west of Yuma in the sand dunes can be seen what is left of the old plank road built in 1916–17, one of the first automobile roads through this part of the desert. It was wide enough for only one car, with turnouts provided for passing. Nearby is a bypassed stretch of U.S. 80, built in 1927, which seems like a superhighway next to the plank road, and—providing the greatest contrast of all—the Interstate 8 Freeway carries one through the dunes in a few minutes.

Purísima and San Pedro y San Pablo

Misión La Purísima Concepción and Misión San Pedro y San Pablo once stood 12 miles apart in the southeastern corner of what was destined to become Imperial County. The two were established in the autumn of 1780, by four Franciscan padres from Mexico, Fathers Díaz, Morena, Garcés, and Barreneche. The purpose of these missions was twofold: to convert the Yuma Indians living at this point along the Colorado River, and to make a way station on the overland emigrant trail from Mexico to the California missions.

The plan followed at Purísima and at San Pedro y San Pablo was different from that followed in other parts of California. The Indians were allowed to remain on their own rancherías and the padres visited them there, ministering to their spiritual needs alone.

But this plan was not successful. The Fathers had not the means to visit the Indians often, nor had they the necessary trinkets to allure them. Moreover, the soldiers, and the few white settlers who came with them, used for themselves the scant patches of ground on which the Indians raised their melons, beans, and corn, and the white man's cattle ate up the precious pasturage which their own poor stock needed.

Naturally, the Indians soon looked upon the white people as invaders, and in July 1781 one of the most tragic occurrences in the history of California took place. Captain Fernando Rivera y Moncada, lieutenant-governor of Lower California, was bringing a party of settlers from Mexico to establish the proposed pueblo of Los Angeles in California. On reaching the Colorado River, the soldiers and settlers, over whom Rivera exercised little discipline, harassed the Yuma Indians. The families in the train were sent ahead with some of the soldiers, while Rivera remained behind to refresh his exhausted animals. From July 17 to 19, an outbreak among the Indians came to a climax. Rivera and his soldiers, as well as Father Garcés and the other priests at the two missions, and all other males were massacred. The women and children were made captive, being subsequently ransomed by Pedro Fages.

The missions and settlements were not established again on the Colorado, and the route which had been opened with such great effort by Juan Bautista de Anza in 1774 and 1775, became more dangerous to travelers than ever before. The colonists of Rivera's expedition did go on to establish the great city of Los Angeles, but the importance of the Yuma Massacre must not be underestimated. With Anza's land route effectively closed, the only means of supply from and contact with Mexico was the highly unreliable sea route. The Californians soon saw the necessity of development from within and began to draw from California's limitless natural resources. At the same time dependence upon Mexico, both economic and political, was becoming less and less, and contact was being established instead with the foreigners who came by land and sea, paving the way for an early and easy American occupation. The Yuma Massacre was thus a major turning point in California history.

The garrison located on the river in 1826 by Romualdo Pacheco served as a protection for government mail carriers and Sonoran traders. In the early 1850's, Fort Yuma was established on the spot where Mission Purísima had stood, and American troops were stationed there for several years. It was besieged by Indians in 1851. On the same spot, in later years, an Indian School, where boys and girls were taught trades as well as reading and writing, was conducted by the Sisters of St. Joseph. The school building standing today on a high hill north of the highway on the California side of the Colorado River was built by the United States government for the education of the Indians in the Yuma reservation.

Today a Catholic chapel for the Indians stands on what is thought to be at least the approximate site of Misión La Purísima Concepción *(SRL 350)*. Next to it is a statue of the martyred Father Garcés. Some of the old buildings of Fort Yuma *(SRL 806)* still stand nearby. These landmarks are on the hill just across the Colorado River from the famous Arizona Territorial Prison in Yuma, and like the prison are reached from the former routing of the main highway, which crosses the river by an old, narrow bridge. The site of Misión San Pedro y San Pablo is uncertain, but it may have been on the west side of the Colorado River near the present Imperial Dam.

Early Colorado River Ferries

Several ferries were established on the Colorado below its junction with the Gila in 1849 and 1850. The first of these was built by General Alexander Anderson, from Tennessee, in order to transport his party to the California side at a point several miles south of the Gila. Anderson afterward presented his boat to the Indians with a certificate of title, the terms of which seem to have been faithfully lived up to by the latter.

Another ferry, started in September 1849 by Lieutenant Cave J. Couts at Camp Calhoun on the California side, aided gold-seekers across the river. In December Couts sold his ferry to Dr. G. W. Lincoln, reputed to have been a distant relative of Abraham Lincoln.

This ferry was destined to come to a tragic end. When John Glanton, a renegade and blackguard, purchased a half share in Lincoln's ferry, the enterprise quickly degenerated. Lincoln was secretly done away with and the neighboring Indian ferry was destroyed in order to prevent opposition. The indignant natives retaliated by surprising and killing Glanton and his men and destroying their boat.

In the summer of the following year the ferry was re-established by L. J. F. Jaeger and others, at a point several miles below the present site of Yuma near the Hall Hanlon ranch. Lumber for Jaeger's ferry was transported across the desert from San Diego by pack train. A ferry was operated at this point until the present old highway bridge was erected in 1915. A marker commemorating these pioneer ferries stands at the

Chapel and Garcés Statue on Site of Mission La Purísima Concepción, near Yuma

old landing on the Arizona side near the Territorial Prison.

Picacho, A Ghost of the Desert

On the west or south bank of the Colorado River, 25 miles north of Yuma, is the site of Picacho, an early gold-mining camp, said to have been discovered by an Indian in 1860. It was first located by Mexican prospectors in 1862, and is said to have been one of the richest placers in California. The population was almost entirely Latin during the first few years of its existence, a bit of Old Mexico transplanted to American soil. There were arenas for bullfights, which were attended with great pomp and ceremony; and there were gay and picturesque *bailes,* accompanied by the soft music of guitars, the clatter of castanets, and the brilliant and lavish play of *cascarones* and confetti. The Americans came in later and found rich lodes in the neighboring hills, erected large stamp mills, and soon had a payroll amounting to $40,000 a month.

Near the lofty mountain from which the district is named and five miles south from Picacho, the Picacho Mine was located, being connected by railroad with the mill near the river. This railroad operated for a long time, but was eventually torn up and only the old embankments are visible today.

"Deserted by her citizens, a victim of successive floods, Picacho has all but vanished. On the flank of the mountain, out of reach of lapping waters, a few buildings still remain. Of the saloons and stores, however, there is no trace; the former townsite has been almost completely reclaimed by thorny mesquite. Within a stone's throw of the former main street, the broad Colorado flows silently toward the Gulf. On either side of it rise desert mountains, boulder-strewn and chasm-riven, composing a scene in which the forbidding is blended with wild, exotic beauty."

The old Picacho townsite is now being developed as a state park and recreation area. There are many other old mines *(SRL 193)* in the Picacho district, including the Golden Dream, close to the river east of the old camp.

Tumco

Tumco, discovered by a Swedish track-walker and known at first as Hedges, was a mining town of some importance until after the turn of the century. Nine miles north of Interstate 8 and five miles north of Ogilby Station on the Southern Pacific, it lies in a narrow desert valley hemmed in on either side by two barren mountain ranges. It received its name from the initial letters of a company that later purchased the properties: "The United Mines Co." Once inhabited by 2,000 people, Tumco is today a ghost city of ruined adobe walls and stone foundations. The Tumco mines *(SRL 182)*, originally staked as a claim in 1884, operated until about 1914. The most famous of them were the Golden Queen, the Golden Cross, and the Golden Crown. Five miles northeast of Ogilby was the American Girl Mine, developed later than Tumco and worked by fewer than 200 men. Ogilby is itself now a ghost town, with an eerie-looking cemetery by the roadside.

Water from the Colorado

The first diversion of water from the Colorado River to Imperial Valley was made through a temporary wooden gate, known as the Chaffey Gate, located several thousand feet back from the river a short distance above the Mexican border. The gate was too small and the sill too high; consequently, it was replaced in 1905 by a concrete gate, known as Hanlon Heading, which was located at the last place where rock formation is found on the lower Colorado River. This also was connected to the river by an open canal. This canal gave serious difficulty because of silting in during flood periods, and therefore, in 1918, it was replaced by another concrete gate, Rockwood Heading, several thousand feet upstream and adjacent to the Colorado River. It was through these structures that every drop of water used by the people of Imperial Valley for irrigation and domestic purposes was diverted from 1901 until 1942, when the All-American Canal was completed.

It is this water from the Colorado River, conveyed through a vast system of canals and ditches to be deposited upon the rich soil of the Salton Sink, that makes Imperial Valley what it is today, a prosperous agricultural community of over 80,000 people. It is appropriate that around this spot should cluster the memories of three pioneers of the idea of reclaiming the Colorado Desert: Dr. Oliver Meredith Wozencraft, Charles Robinson Rockwood, and George Chaffey.

Dr. Wozencraft is considered the real father of Imperial Valley, "the first man to actually plan the reclamation of the desert sink for agricultural purposes by bringing the waters of the Colorado to the arid area to the west." He came to California in the gold rush of 1849, and immediately after his arrival in San Francisco he set out on an expedition to the then little known Colorado Desert. It was there, in the year 1849, that he first conceived the idea of reclamation. The project so possessed him that he was led to devote the rest of his life to making his dream a reality.

Obtaining favorable action from the state legislature in 1859, Wozencraft was given all state rights in the Salton Sink. The next step was to get a patent from the federal government, but in spite of repeated attempts he never obtained this, chiefly because the attention of Congress was entirely taken up with the Civil War and subsequent reconstruction problems. Dr. Wozencraft died in Washington in 1887 while making a final effort to obtain Congressional action. His repeated attempts to interest capitalists in his enterprise had also been of no avail. However, an appeal made to George Chaffey for support in 1882, although not obtaining results at the time, was no doubt a factor leading to the final accomplishment of the reclamation under the latter's direction, April 1900 to February 1902.

Meanwhile, there was no one to continue the work begun by Dr. Wozencraft until Charles Robinson Rockwood, civil engineer, made a rediscov-

ery of the agricultural possibilities of Imperial Valley in 1892. The name of Rockwood will always be associated with the early history of Imperial Valley as that of one who was pre-eminent among those entertaining the idea of turning the waters of the Colorado upon the parched soil of the Salton Sink. He never gave up hope of success during the eight long years of toil, struggle, and disappointment through which he passed before finally locating the necessary man with capital to finance the work. This man was George Chaffey, "who was able to take hold of the project—and bring the water to the desert."

George Chaffey had begun his career of founding agricultural colonies based on irrigation, in 1881, at Etiwanda, where he originated the idea of a mutual water company and set up the first dynamo for developing hydroelectric power on the Pacific slope. The next year he laid out the Ontario Colony. (Both Etiwanda and the Ontario Colony are located in southwestern San Bernardino County.) In 1886 he and his brother William began their work of establishing colonies in the arid regions of Australia. There he learned that it was possible for white people to colonize hot and arid regions, provided sufficient water could be brought to them. With this experience as a background, Chaffey was ready, when approached by Rockwood in 1899, to undertake the very thing he had refused to do in 1882 when Wozencraft made his appeal.

Chaffey now became the chief factor in the actual reclamation of the desert. Entering into the work under his own terms, he built up the project from its very foundations, giving it credit by creating assets out of liabilities, and planning and directing the construction of vast canals and ditches. He not only established but also named Imperial Valley.

Water from the Colorado was first turned through the intake gate at Pilot Knob on May 14, 1901. This first heading was located about 500 feet south of the present Rockwood Gate. The water arrived at the Sharpe heading, located at the international boundary line, on June 21, 1901. In February of the following year, the construction of the canals was completed.

The necessity of bringing water to Imperial Valley by a canal located in Mexico caused considerable difficulty. Moreover, it was necessary in most years to build either brush dams or sand dams across the river in low-flood periods in an endeavor to divert a sufficient supply of water for the valley. These dams also involved complications with the Yuma Project, and it became apparent that a new location for the diversion point would have to be found. Also, there was great need for a canal located entirely within the United States.

Bills were introduced in Congress in 1918 and 1919 for a new diversion point and an All-American Canal. From 1922 through 1928, four additional bills, known as the Swing-Johnson bills, were introduced, the last one, providing for the construction of Hoover Dam and the All-American Canal, being adopted by Congress in 1928.

Imperial Dam, the diversion point for the canal, is located about 20 miles north of Yuma. The headworks for the All-American Canal are outstanding, with very large gates through which the water is diverted and a system of desilting which is one of the largest in this country. Along the canal are many large concrete structures, and at three of the drops the Imperial Irrigation District has installed power plants. The district has also installed a power plant at Pilot Knob, where surplus water is discharged back to the river through the old Rockwood Heading. Where the All-American Canal emerges from the sand dunes, a branch canal, some 120 miles in length, takes off, flowing northward on the east side of Salton Sea and around Coachella Valley, to provide supplemental water for that valley.

There are now 3,000 miles of irrigation and drainage canals serving 500,000 acres of cultivated land in Imperial Valley and all of its cities and towns. Within a period of 60 years, a vast desert waste has become "one of the world's most fruitful gardens," comprising 5,000 farms, the five major products of which were, in 1960, cattle, cotton, alfalfa, lettuce, and sugar beets. From the handful of settlers who went there in 1901, the population had become 80,000 in 1963.

In 1905–7 unusual rainfalls caused the whole flow of the Colorado River to break through the intake gates, threatening to fill the entire valley, a circumstance that had happened before in prehistoric eras. Through the almost superhuman efforts of E. H. Harriman, president of the Southern Pacific, and his agents, the flow of the river was finally turned back into its normal course February 10, 1907, thus saving the valley for the use of humanity. The runaway river had, however, left its mark in the newly formed Salton Sea, which had previously been dry land. This body of water is presently (1963) about 34 miles long and from nine to 15 miles wide. The elevation varies from year to year but averages 234 feet below sea level.

Calexico

At the present site of Calexico, adjacent to and immediately north of the international boundary, Lieutenant Cave J. Couts, escort commander with the International Boundary Commission, established Camp Salvation (SRL 808) on September 23, 1849. Until the first of December the camp served as a refuge center for the distressed emigrants who were attempting to reach the gold fields over the southern emigrant trail.

There stood in Calexico, at the international boundary line a few feet south of the Southern Pacific depot, an adobe building, not so very old, but historically an important unit in the chain of Imperial Valley's metamorphosis from desert to garden. Part of this building was originally erected in 1905 by the California Development Company, a corporation organized by Charles R. Rockwood and his associates on April 26, 1896. As a result of the devastating flood of 1906, the California Development Company failed and went into receivership. In 1916 the Imperial Irrigation District, which had been organized by the people of the valley in 1911, purchased all of the assets and property of the California Development Company and its subsidiary Compañia in Lower California. The little adobe was enlarged and remodeled as the office of the new irrigation district. In 1925 the building was abandoned by the Imperial Irrigation District and remained vacant until 1932, when it was taken over by the Veterans of Foreign Wars, and restored and dedicated by them as Rockwood Hall. It was later used by the Boy Scouts and was completely destroyed by fire in 1940. A street divides Calexico, California, from Mexicali, Mexico, being the boundary line between the two countries.

SOURCES

Adam, Joaquin. "Destruction of the Catholic Missions on the Rio Colorado in 1781," The Historical Society of Southern California Publications, III (1893), 36–40.
Ainsworth, Edward Maddin. Beckoning Desert. Prentice-Hall, Englewood Cliffs, N.J., 1962.
Banning, Captain William, and George Hugh Banning. "Dust of the 'Swift Wagon,' a Glimpse of John Butterfield and a Full Account of the Great Southern Overland Mail," Touring Topics, XXII, No. 2 (February 1930), 17–19.
——— "Wheel Tracks of the 'Jackass Mail,'" Touring Topics, XXI, No. 11 (November 1929), 21–25, 54.
Beattie, George William. Reopening Anza's Road. Ms., 1931.
Blake, William P. "Ancient Lake in the Colorado Desert," American Journal of Science, XVII (1854), No. 2, 435–38.
Bolton, Herbert Eugene. Anza's California Expeditions. 5 vols. University of California Press, Berkeley, 1930.
Davis, Arthur P. "The New Inland Sea," National Geographic Magazine, XVIII, No. 1 (January 1907), 36–49.
Dowd, M. J. Historic Salton Sea. Imperial Irrigation District, El Centro, 1960.
Eldredge, Zoeth Skinner. The Beginnings of San Francisco, from the Expedition of Anza, 1774, to the City Charter of April 15, 1850. 2 vols. Privately printed, San Francisco, 1912.
Emory, William Hemsley. Notes of a Military Reconnaissance from Fort Leavenworth, Missouri, to San Diego, California. 30th Cong., 1st Sess., Senate Exec. Doc. No. 7, Washington, D.C., 1848.
Farr, F. C. History of Imperial County. Elms and Franks, Berkeley, 1918.
Gorby, J. S. "Steamboating on the Colorado," Touring Topics, XX, No. 7 (July 1928), 14–18, 45.
Hanna, Phil Townsend. "The Wells of Santa Rosa of the Flat Rocks," Touring Topics, XX, No. 1 (January 1928), 18–20, 31.
Hill, Joseph J., compiler, and Dillon Lauritzen, painter. "A Map of Exploration in the Spanish Southwest, 1528–1793," Touring Topics, XXIV, No. 1 (January 1932), Supplement.
Hogg, John Edwin. "Fossil Hunting about Carrizo Creek," Touring Topics, XXI, No. 10 (October 1929), 14–17.
Howe, Edgar F., and Wilbur J. Hall. The Story of the First Decade in Imperial Valley, California. E. F. Howe & Sons, Imperial, 1910.
James, George Wharton. Wonders of the Colorado Desert. Little, Brown, Boston, Mass., 1906.
Johnston, Philip. "Derelicts of the California Desert," Touring Topics, XX, No. 2 (February 1928), 14–18, 37–42.
Kennan, George. The Salton Sea, an Account of Harriman's Fight with the Colorado River. Macmillan, New York, 1917.
McKenny, J. Wilson. "The Butterfield Trail." Reprinted from the Calexico Chronicle.
Romer, Margaret. "A History of Calexico, California," Publications, Historical Society of Southern California, XII, Part 2 (1922), 26–66.
Steward, Julian. "Words Writ on Stone," Touring Topics, XIX, No. 5 (May 1927), 18–20, 36–38.
Tout, Otis B. The First Thirty Years. Otis B. Tout, San Diego, 1931.

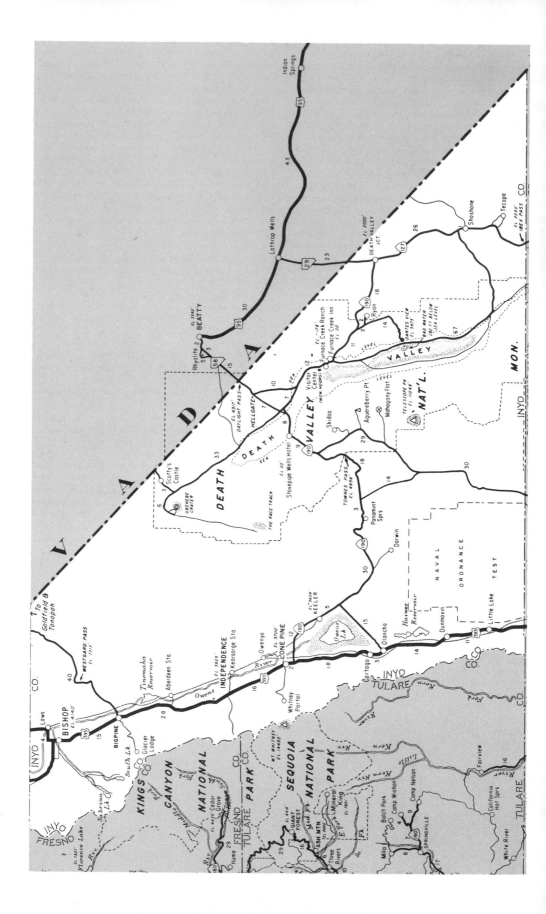

Inyo County

INYO COUNTY (according to W. A. Chalfant, the meaning of Inyo, as given to early white settlers, is "dwelling place of a great spirit") was organized in 1866 from territory that had been set aside two years earlier from Mono and Tulare counties and called Coso County. However, Coso County was never organized and Inyo took its place. Independence has been the county seat since the organization of the county.

Inyo County contains within its borders a more varied topography than any other equal area on this continent, probably than any other in the world. On its western boundary stands Mount Whitney, the highest peak in the United States outside of Alaska, while Death Valley, the lowest spot on the continent, is also included within its borders. Death Valley abounds in scenic as well as historic interest: Marble Canyon, Mosaic Canyon, the Sand Dunes, Grotto Canyon, Stovepipe Wells, Furnace Creek Ranch (a veritable oasis in the desert), Golden Canyon, Mushroom Rock, Pluto's Salt Pools, Bad Water, Ashford Mill, the Devil's Golf Course, Old Confidence Mill, and other places of equal interest. While the summers are very hot, "the late fall, winter, and early spring months find the valley in a friendly and approachable mood . . . a favorite spot for those who love the unique, the colorful, and the spectacular."

Mount Whitney

Mount Whitney is the highest peak in the United States outside Alaska and one of a group of splendid mountains of 13,000–14,000 feet elevation situated in the High Sierra at the headwaters of the Kings and Kern rivers. For many years it was thought that Mount Shasta was the highest summit in California, but in 1864 the Whitney Geological Survey discovered the fact that the summit of Mount Whitney was the highest point in the Sierra and higher than Shasta. The latest accurate measurement of the altitude of Mount Whitney is 14,495 feet.

The mountain was named in 1864 by the Brewer party, in honor of Josiah Dwight Whitney, state geologist and leader of the Geological Survey. Clarence King wrote: "For years our Chief, Professor Whitney, has made brave campaigns into the unknown realm of Nature. There stand for him two monuments: one a great report, made by his own hand; another the loftiest peak in the Union, begun for him in the planet's youth and sculptured of enduring granite by the slow hand of time."

King, attempting to climb the peak in 1871, missed it on account of obscuring storm clouds and climbed Mount Langley by mistake. Learning of his error in 1873, he hastened West to climb the real Mount Whitney on September 19. He was too late, however, for on August 18 John Lucas, A. H. Johnson, and C. D. Begole had made the first ascent of the great mountain.

Since July 1881 Mount Whitney has been the base of operations for many scientific astronomical observations, the astronomical expedition under Professor S. P. Langley that year being the first.

Approach to Mount Whitney was formerly made by way of Lone Pine in Owens Valley, up Cottonwood Creek, through Cottonwood Pass, and from there north through Whitney Meadows in Tulare County to Crabtree Meadow, which is at the base of the ascent. A new trail by way of Lone Pine was opened for travel in the spring of 1931, with a base camp in Lone Pine Canyon. The mountain can also be approached from the west via Sequoia National Park.

The Bishop Petroglyphs

Indian petroglyphs, or rock markings, may be found throughout much of the arid West. Those of one area are unlike those of others, and so it is thought that they were made by different tribes. All, however, are similar in their crudeness and simplicity of design. They are generally made in soft tufa by chipping, and are usually found near springs or streams on natural routes of travel, but sometimes are discovered in secluded mountain nooks.

A few miles north of Bishop, in northern Inyo County and southern Mono County, the largest group of markings in this part of the state is found on the courses of stream beds or near ancient springs. Among the petroglyphs found here are crude pictures of what appear to be deer, human and animal footprints, snakes, many-legged bugs, and numerous geometrical designs. At Deep Springs Valley, on the Midland Trail, is a great round boulder covered with these carved pictures: sun symbols, snakes, a bird, a rabbit (possibly), and concentric circles which may represent sweat houses. At Little Lake, Coso Hot Springs, and Keeler are more rocks, on which animal figures predominate. Other petroglyphs are found covering the granite walls at the base of the Inyo Mountains at a point near Swansea.

Scientists generally do not believe that these rocks show great antiquity, but rather that they were done by the ancestors of the present Piutes at no far-removed period. Probably some were made by priests or medicine men and had a religious significance. Others acted as signposts to mark water holes, trails, or other important places, and a few may have been made to represent some important event.

Similar carvings have been found from Alaska

to South America, and scientists have sought for years to understand their mystery. With few exceptions, however, the most penetrating study has failed to lift the veil of obscurity from their origin. Their age is still speculative and their meaning enigmatic.

Big and Little Petroglyph Canyons, in Inyo County on the property of the U.S. Naval Ordnance Test Station, China Lake, have been registered as a National Historic Landmark by the Department of the Interior. The petroglyphs are accessible by a well-maintained road leading north from the China Lake housing area, but permission to visit them must be obtained from the Security Police at NOTS.

Winnedumah

Directly east of Independence on the extreme crest of the White Mountains stands a remarkable monolith of granite commonly known as the Piute Monument. It is 80 feet high and is visible on the skyline for many miles. The legend of Winnedumah, the best known of all the legends of the Owens Valley Indians, is associated with this gigantic rock. According to it, the rock for many ages stood as an enduring symbol of faithfulness to the Indians who lived at the base of the mountains.

The Owens Valley Emigrant Trail

Although trappers may have penerated Owens Valley south to Inyo County as early as 1826, the first authentic record we have is that of Joseph Reddeford Walker, who led a party north through Owens Valley in 1834. He entered the valley again in 1843, this time from the north; following his old trail, he led the Chiles emigrant party, the second wagon train to enter California from the east, southward through the pass that was later named for him. In 1845 Walker accompanied the main body of John C. Frémont's second expedition into California over the same route. Frémont himself went by way of Donner Pass with Kit Carson, Richard Owens, and 12 others. Frémont considered Owens a very valuable man, and after the two divisions of the expedition reached the San Joaquin Valley he gave Owens' name to the Inyo river, valley, and lake which still bear it, although the man for whom they were named never saw this region.

Resting Springs

The old "Spanish Trail" into California from the northeast, opened up by William Wolfskill in 1831 and followed later by caravans from New Mexico, became the route adopted by Mormon emigrants to San Bernardino, and was used by them from 1847 until after the Mountain Meadows massacre. A branch of this trail passed by Resting Springs, Inyo County, where the Mormon caravans stopped to rest their livestock on journeys across the desert.

The Resting Springs were first known as the Archilette, and to them John C. Frémont came on April 19, 1844, on his way out of California. Frémont called the place Agua de Hernández, in honor of the Mexican boy Pablo Hernández, who had come to his camp on the Mojave River on April 24 with Andrés Fuentes, a Mexican, the two being the lone survivors of a small party of traders, victims of an Indian raid at the Archilette. More than 40 years afterward an old rusty sword, of the pattern used in Frémont's day, was found at this spot, supposedly lost by one of Frémont's party.

Death Valley

Death Valley, on the southeastern border of California, is a long, sunken desert, surrounded by fairly high mountains. It is the lowest spot in the United States, its minimum elevation as established by the latest U.S. Geological Survey being 282 feet below sea level. Its grim name is believed to have been given after the William Lewis Manly and Jayhawker parties attempted to cross the valley into California in 1849, tragic episodes in California's history. Manly himself writes on the origin of the name:

"We took off our hats, and then overlooking the scene of so much trial, suffering, and death spoke the thought uppermost in our minds, saying: 'Goodbye, Death Valley!' . . . Many accounts have been given to the world as to the origin of the name, but ours were the first visible footsteps, and we the party which gave it the saddest and most dreadful name that came to us first from our memories."

During Christmas week of 1849 more than a hundred half-starved emigrants, seeking a shortcut to the California gold fields, entered the Valley of Burning Silence at the mouth of what was later known as Furnace Creek. This gateway (SRL 442) is now commemorated by a stone monument and bronze plaque. From this point the Manly party proceeded southward, while the Jayhawkers and other groups turned to the northwest. Manly's group crossed the salt flats and found a good spring at what was without doubt Tule Spring, on the west side of the Death Valley sink. They called this place the Last Camp (SRL 444), for their situation was so critical that it was decided that the party should remain in camp while Manly and John Rogers set out over the mountains to seek help. After incredible suffering and almost insurmountable difficulties, these two brave men finally reached their destination and returned to Death Valley after almost a month to rescue their friends. At Last Camp (or Long Camp) it was found that only the Bennett and Arcane families remained, the others having attempted to go on alone. Some were never accounted for, but one, a Captain Culverwell, who had joined the last party out, died not far from camp. He is the only one of the entire party known to have perished within the limits of Death Valley itself.

Of the Jayhawkers, those gay young men who set out from Galesburg, Illinois, in the spring of 1849, and other persons associated with them, the story is even more tragic. Travelling, for the most part, by themselves, the Jayhawkers were often closely associated with the Manly-Bennett-

Arcane group in their grim march across the desert, being together at some camps and apart at others. Accounts of the journey by participants in these two main parties differ, but the best authority seems to be that nine of the Jayhawkers perished to the east of Death Valley and four died after leaving it but while still in the desert. One of these, a man named Robinson, died within sight of deliverance not far from the foot of the Sierra. Having separated from Manly's party at Furnace Creek, the Jayhawkers and allied groups proceeded northwest to a point near the present Stovepipe Wells Hotel. This place has become known as Burned Wagons Point (*SRL 441*), for here the emigrants abandoned and burned most of their equipment before they continued westward on foot and, after suffering tremendous hardships, reached safety.

Manly's route lay over the mountain barrier, through Red Rock Canyon, into the Mojave Desert, and on to the San Gabriel Mountains. There the party passed through Soledad Canyon and over Newhall Pass into the San Fernando Valley.

Some contingents of escaping Forty-niners, suffering from the thirst of Death Valley which they had just left, attempted to secure water from Searles Lake. Finding it unpotable, they despaired and turned northward and westward across the Argus Range and other mountains in their search for civilization. This bitter disappointment is commemorated at Valley Wells (*SRL 443*), about six miles north of Trona.

Although the story of this trek across Death Valley is the first recorded tragedy to be associated with it, there were doubtless other lone wanderers who had met death there before. Since then, too, emigrant parties, gold seekers, and lone wayfarers, almost every element of society, have entered the valley, many of them never to return. One of the earliest expeditions from the west was a mining company headed by Dr. Darwin French, in the spring of 1860. These men discovered and named Furnace Creek, the presence of a crude furnace at the stream being the occasion for the name. It has been generally believed that this was built by Mormons, but it may have been set up by Mexican miners.

The first scientific expedition was made by Dr. Owen and other members of the State Boundary Commission in 1861. It was followed in 1871 by the Wheeler expedition and in 1875 by Lieutenant Birney, who crossed the valley several times.

The ruins of the Harmony Borax Works (*SRL 773*) may still be seen in Death Valley just north of Furnace Creek Ranch and west of the highway. There, in 1880, large deposits of borate were discovered by Aaron Winters and his frail Spanish-American wife, Rosie, who were located at Ash Meadows, a place just eastward across the Funeral Mountains from Death Valley, 200 miles from the nearest railroad. A short while before this, Isidore Daunet, a prospector, had discovered white marshes in Death Valley a few miles north of Bennett's Wells and 20 miles southwest of Furnace Creek. On hearing of Winters' find, Daunet opened up the Eagle Borax Works, the

first borax corporation in the valley. The product, however, proved to be impure and the plant was closed, passing into oblivion. Remnants of the old works may still be seen.

The Winters deposits of borate were finally acquired by F. M. ("Borax") Smith and his partner, W. T. Coleman, who started the old Harmony Borax Works. In 1889, after the marshes had been thoroughly worked out, Coleman assigned his property to the Pacific Coast Borax Company and work at the old Harmony plant ceased. Smith then entered the picture in earnest, working his way to the head of the company. A deposit at the base of Monte Blanco, a thousand-foot peak southeast of Furnace Creek, proved to be in a purer state than that previously worked and so rich that even today the mountain seems to be composed of almost solid colemanite, as the deposit was called. The miles of tunnels and drifts into the mountain did not begin to exhaust the supply. A picture of the 20-mule team used to haul the borates 200 miles across the desert to Mojave became the trademark of the company and is used to this day, although the teams were replaced by the Tonopah and Tidewater Railroad in 1907. New borax deposits as rich as those of Death Valley and far more accessible were found in Nevada, Oregon, and at Trona near Searles Lake in San Bernardino County, California. Borax is still present in Death Valley in great quantities, but the ever-present handicap of the valley itself is too great and the mines are no longer worked.

In the extreme northern part of Death Valley National Monument, near the Nevada line, is the fabulous castle built in the 1920's by Walter Scott, a "desert rat," once a cowboy with Buffalo Bill Cody's Wild West show, and his partner Albert M. Johnson, a Chicago financier. Said to have cost $3,000,000, it is now open to the public for guided tours, for which a fee is charged. "Death Valley Scotty," who died on January 5, 1954, at the age of 91, is buried nearby. A few miles to the west is interesting Ubehebe Crater.

Death Valley, with its many scenic wonders and old ghost towns, is now a great playground in the winter months and is visited by thousands of tourists annually. It became a National Monument in 1933.

The First White Man's Dwelling

Prior to 1861 the only white population in Owens Valley was composed of transient prospectors, mountain men, and travelers to the West Coast, who took a shortcut through the valley or who used this route to reach the gold fields without going over the high Sierra Nevada. In August 1861 A. Van Fleet with three other men drove cattle into the northern end of the Owens Valley from Nevada Territory. A cabin of sod and stone was built, the site (*SRL 230*) of which is at the big bend of Owens River about four miles northeast of Bishop, not far from the little community of Laws. The same month Charles Putnam built a stone cabin on Little Pine Creek (now Independence Creek) and started a trading post. These were the first white dwellings in Owens Valley.

Camp Independence

On July 4, 1862, Lieutenant Colonel George S. Evans with 201 men of the Second Cavalry California Volunteers arrived on Oak Creek, raised the "Stars and Stripes" and established a military post, naming it Camp Independence in honor of the day. The purpose of this post was to protect the few white people in Owens Valley and to act as a barrier in case of an invasion by the Secessionists from the Territories of Nevada and Arizona. With the exception of the year 1864, troops were maintained at Camp Independence until July of 1877, when the post was abandoned. The site *(SRL 349)* is about two miles north of the town of Independence, off Highway 395. The caves occupied by soldiers and the old cemetery are all that remain, and they are difficult to reach.

A relic of the old post may be seen, however, in the town of Independence. The Commander's House was purchased and moved to the corner of Edwards and Main streets in 1883. It was constructed following the great earthquake of 1872, which rendered the earlier adobe buildings unsafe. The two-story, ten-room frame house with its adobe fireplace has been renovated and is open to the public.

Independence

The town of Independence was started with the building of the stone trading post by Charles Putnam in August 1861 and was at first called "Putnam's," or Little Pine after the creek so named. Town and creek derived their new name from the nearby army post. The stone cabin was used as a residence, store, hospital, and fort, and stood on a site *(SRL 223)* southwest of the present courthouse until torn down in 1876. In 1862 gold was discovered in the Inyo Mountains to the east, and for some years the town was the center of a rich mining area. On February 13, 1866, the platting of the townsite was completed, the first to be found in the county records. Upon the organization of Inyo County that year, Independence became the county seat and has remained so.

The home of Mary Austin *(SRL 229)*, said to have been designed and supervised by the author herself, still stands at Independence. There she

Site of Japanese War Relocation Center, Manzanar

wrote *The Land of Little Rain* and other books which picture the beauty of Owens Valley and Inyo desert regions.

Independence is headquarters for the offices and shops of the Northern Division, Department of Water and Power, City of Los Angeles–Owens Valley Aqueduct, which extends the full length of Inyo County and into Mono County on the north. The town is now an outfitting point for trips over Kearsarge Pass into the Kings River region and other points in the back country of the Sierra Nevada.

Bell's Mill was the oldest flour mill in Owens Valley and served a vast, sparsely settled territory. Its wooden ruins may still be seen on Oak Creek, northwest of Independence, about half a mile west of the main highway, by a road that branches from the road leading to the Mount Whitney Fish Hatchery.

About midway between Independence and Big Pine, Harry Wright's stage station on Taboose Creek, one and one-half miles north of Aberdeen and a mile west of the highway, was a popular gathering place in the 1860's and 1870's. Only a few locusts and black willow trees mark the site. The area is now a public campground.

While there are no traces left of the Shepherd ranch house, it was said to be the first two-story frame dwelling in Owens Valley. The house stood one-half mile west of Manzanar crossroads on the north side of the road. It was built in 1873 by John Shepherd from materials brought by horse- or mule-drawn wagons from San Pedro, 250 miles away. An even earlier house stood at this site, having been built in 1864 of shakes made in the locality. Shepherd bought the property from a man named Coburn, but whether he built the first house is not known. The Shepherd ranch house was a stage stop for a number of years, and was one of the most imposing in the area, with its green shutters, lacy front trimmings, white fence, and spacious grounds. The settlement of Manzanar grew up in this area after the turn of the century, but was abandoned when the City of Los Angeles bought the land. In 1942 the same area became the site of a Japanese War Relocation Center, housing 10,000 people. A pair of ornamental stone Japanese-style gates and a large garage remain beside the highway six miles southeast of Independence to

Commander's House, Camp Independence

remind us of this sad chapter in California history.

The San Francis Ranch and Bishop

Samuel A. Bishop, for whom the town of Bishop was named, came to California in 1849. He was associated with General Edward F. Beale at Rancho Tejón before coming to Inyo County and later, in 1866, he became one of Kern County's first supervisors.

Bishop and his wife came to Inyo from Rancho Tejón in 1861, settling on the creek that now bears his name. Here, where the stream leaves the foothills and enters the valley, about three miles southwest of the present town of Bishop, two small cabins of rough pine slabs were erected on August 22, and the new settlement was named the San Francis Ranch (SRL 208). However, Bishop did not remain here long, moving in 1864 to the abandoned fort at Tejón.

Settlers were in and around the area from the time Bishop arrived. The town of Bishop, now the largest in the county, prospered mainly because of the rich farming land surrounding it, but early mining in the White-Inyo Range also contributed to its growth. With the building of good roads, Bishop has occupied a strategic place at the intersection of U. S. Highways 395 and 6, making it a commercial hub for all of northern Inyo County as well as Mono County and parts of Nevada. The area is becoming known as a vacation paradise for campers, fishermen, and hunters, and the increasing number of ski lifts in the area is bringing a great new winter recreation.

Indian Troubles

A large party of Indians threatened San Francis Ranch in the autumn of 1861, greatly alarming the settlers. Knowing that they could not withstand a siege, they agreed to hold a council with the natives. Accordingly, on January 31, 1862, the Indian chiefs met with the white settlers at the ranch and concluded a treaty, which was signed by both parties.

The San Francis treaty proved to be only an episode in the Indian wars of Inyo County, for within two months the natives started hostilities in earnest. In March, Warren Wasson, Nevada Indian agent, asked for aid from the United States troops in order to prevent a long and bloody war. He made every effort to settle the difficulty by peaceful means, but without success.

On April 6, between 50 and 60 pioneers under John T. Kellogg and a settler named Mayfield engaged in battle with 500 to 1,000 Piutes lined up from a small black butte in the valley across Bishop Creek to the foothills in the south. Three white men were killed, and after the moon had set, the pioneers retreated to Big Pine. A marker has been placed at the Bishop Creek battleground (SRL 811), southwest of Bishop.

Troops arrived at Owens Lake on April 2, and on April 8 they joined with the citizens in an engagement with the Indians. Trooper Christopher Gillespie and Mayfield were killed. The site of this battleground (SRL 211) is at the mouth

of what was later named Mayfield Canyon, about one-half mile north of the former Wells Meadow Ranger Station, northwest of Bishop near the Mono County line. Temporary peace followed, but by May the valley was in almost undisputed possession of the Piutes and many of the white settlers left the region. On July 4, 1862, Camp Independence was established. By the fall of 1863 settlers in increasing numbers were coming into the valley, and new camps sprang up. Not until 1866, however, was the valley pronounced safe from Indian hostilities, and troops were maintained at the post until 1877.

Camps on East Side of Owens River

Notwithstanding Indian hostilities, new settlements were made in 1862 and 1863. Among these was Owensville, on the east bank of Owens River four miles northeast of Bishop, close to where Van Fleet had built his cabin in 1861. For a few years it held the distinction of being the chief settlement in the northern part of the valley. In its vicinity more than 50 homestead claims of 160 acres each were taken up; in the White Mountains to the northeast were a number of mines, among them the Golden Wedge and the Yellow Jacket. By the end of 1864, however, Owensville had started to decline. Its buildings were being torn down and rafted down the river to Independence and Lone Pine. By 1871 the last inhabitant had vanished.

San Carlos has been marked for many years by the stone foundations of old houses and by a lone smokestack, now fallen into ruins, where the old mill once stood. It was started by miners in 1862 on the east bank of Owens River near the mouth of Oak Creek and was a mining camp until 1865. A letter from the district dated September 4, 1863, contains this item: "Our miners, who are generally men of education, vie with each other in selecting refined names for their mines. Silver Cloud, Norma, Olympic, Golden Era, Welcome, Chrysopolis, Gem, Green Monster, Blue Bird, Red Bird, Evadne, Fleta, Bonnie Blossom, Calliope, Romelia, Lucerne, Pluto's Pet, Birousa, Proserpine, Atahualpa, and Ida are among the mines here."

Bend City (SRL 209), a mining camp established in the early 1860's, was named by the legislature as the seat of Coso County (which, however, was never organized). It was located near the Owens River, four miles east of the town of Independence. Nearly all of the 60-odd houses originally built at the camp were adobe. Near Kearsarge their ruins may be seen, one of the many ghost towns that still haunt California's romantic mining regions. The first county bridge across Owens River was erected at Bend City, but the earthquake of 1872 changed the river's course and left the already deserted townsite on the bank of an empty ravine.

Several ambitious mining camps farther up the river existed during the 1860's and 1870's, among them Galena and Riverside (alias Graham City), "now so completely buried in oblivion that even their sites cannot be learned by the enquirer." Chrysopolis, a mining camp on the east side of Owens River south of Aberdeen Station, flourished briefly in the 1860's, but the election of 1867 found the place entirely dead, and the voting precinct was abolished.

Kearsarge Peak and the town that followed the strike made in the Sierra Nevada in 1864 were named for the *U.S.S. Kearsarge*, which sank the *C.S.S. Alabama* off the coast of France the same year. The miners were Northern sympathizers and jubilant over the sinking. They named their mine the Kearsarge, and soon the peak, a pass, and the town that grew up under the boom took the same name.

Kearsarge city was built at the southern base of Kearsarge's highest crest, and had developed into a considerable camp by the end of 1865. Violent storms raged about the peak in February 1867, bringing rain, snow, freezing, and thawing. An avalanche swept down the side of the mountain, which almost wiped out the settlement. A woman was killed and several men injured. Despite such setbacks, the Kearsarge, Silver Sprout, Virginia Consolidated, and other mines on the slopes of the great mountain continued to be worked for a number of years. The town was moved to a safer location, but today only crumbling foundations remain of a place that once vied with Independence for the county seat.

Lone Pine

The first cabin at Lone Pine was built in the early part of the winter of 1861–62, and a "fine settlement" was reported there two years later. The town was so named because of a large pine tree that stood at the confluence of Lone Pine and Tuttle creeks. Its shade provided a meeting place for the early settlers and had been used in this manner by the Indians long before the white man came. It blew down in a storm in 1876.

On March 26, 1872, a severe earthquake shook Owens Valley, opening a great fault 12 miles long, paralleling the present highway and running north from Lone Pine. Along this crevice, land dropped from four to 12 feet, and at Lone Pine, a town of adobe houses and stores, 27 persons were killed and dozens injured. On the edge of the fault north of Lone Pine, 16 of the disaster victims were buried in a single large grave (*SRL 507*). The earthquake was felt throughout Inyo County, and two other deaths occurred in other areas, but the major damage was done between Olancha and Big Pine. Lone Pine is now a thriving tourist town, an outfitting station for parties ascending Mount Whitney and packing into some of the most beautiful back country in the Sierra Nevada.

The Alabama Hills run generally north and south and are just west of Lone Pine and east of the alluvial apron at the base of the Sierra Nevada. Southern sympathizers, mining in a gulch at the north end of this strange and unique stretch of hills in 1863, heard of the damage the *C.S.S. Alabama* was inflicting upon Northern shipping and, in their elation over the news, named the hills for the ship, which was to be sunk by Northern forces the following year. These hills have now become a major attraction

for tourists visiting Lone Pine, and a new county road running through them from north to south makes many of the scenic areas easily accessible. A movement is under way to make the Alabama Hills into a State Park.

The White Mountain District

From the earliest coming of the white settlers to Inyo, more than one aspiring city was staked out in the White Mountains east of Bishop, only to be forgotten. Just over the summit of the range from Owens Valley, town plots were actually surveyed for two "would-be mining centers," which figured in an attempted election fraud in the fall of 1861. The "Big Springs precinct," with its alleged polling place at what is now known as Deep Springs, was created less than two weeks before the election. In spite of the fact that virtually no population existed in the region, election returns showed a total of 521 votes cast. Investigation finally revealed that the names had been copied from the passenger list of a steamer at San Francisco. White Mountain City, neatly laid out on Wyman Creek on the Deep Spring slope, and its rival, Roachville, on Cottonwood Creek, were only paper cities in 1864, and never became any more.

The White Mountain area is now known principally for the ancient bristlecone pines, the oldest living things, which grow on its windswept slopes. The late Dr. Edmund Schulman, associate professor of dendrochronology at the University of Arizona, made the discovery of the age of these trees in 1953, and in April 1958 the Forest Service set aside 28,000 acres of land in the White Mountains as the "Ancient Bristlecone Pine Area." Rangers now patrol the area and stop anyone from removing parts of living or dead trees. Some of the trees are as much as 4,600 years old.

Settlements were made near Big Pine Creek in 1861, and the rich farming land fed by the creek was an early attraction to those wanting to locate in the new area. The town of Big Pine, on Highway 395, is near the famous Palisade Glacier, the most southerly glacier in the United States. A road leads eastward from Big Pine over scenic Westgard Pass, and the south branch of this road, leading to Eureka and Saline valleys, has been extended into Death Valley, making this recreation area accessible from the north end of Inyo County. Big Pine is also the gateway to the Ancient Bristlecone Pine Area, a new road having been built north from the Westgard Pass road to the age-old bristlecones.

The Cerro Gordo Mines

Twenty miles northeast of Olancha, on the ridge of the Inyo Mountains, are the famous Cerro Gordo Mines, believed to have been discovered in 1865 by a Mexican named Pablo Flores and two companions, who later in the same year located the Ygnacio, San Felipe, and San Francisco claims. The Cerro Gordo ("fat mountain") Mines produced silver, lead, and zinc, and were without doubt the most productive mines in Inyo County. During the 1870's the region had a population of several thousand. Some estimate that the mines yielded $28 million. The Cerro Gordo Mines have not produced for many years. A number of buildings, including the old hotel, remain at the camp, which is reached only by a tortuous road from Keeler on the east side of Owens Lake. Later discoveries include the Waucoba, discovery date unknown but worked as early as 1872 (the old road is still in use); Pigeon Springs, Log Springs, and Sylvania, 1873; Lucky Jim and Ubehebe, 1875; Beveridge District, 1877; and Poleta, 1881.

Landmarks around Owens Lake

Ore from Cerro Gordo was hauled to the foot of the Inyo Mountains, where a town named Keeler grew up on the eastern shore of Owens Lake, now dry. From here it was taken across the lake by such steamboats as the *Bessie Brady* and the *Molly Stevens* to Cartago on the far shore, and thence to San Pedro. This process cost more than $50 a ton, thus necessitating the building of smelters in the area. One of these was constructed at Cerro Gordo itself and another at what became known as Swansea, a short distance northwest of Keeler. This place derived its name from the famous smelter town of Swansea in Wales. At California's Swansea, all that remains of the furnace of the Owens Lake Silver-Lead Company *(SRL 752)* is the old firebox. Across the highway stands part of the adobe house of James Brady, a superintendent of the company and the town's founder. The furnace operated from 1869 to 1874, and, together with the one at Cerro Gordo, produced about 150 bars of silver a day, each weighing 83 pounds. Salt was brought from nearby Saline Dry Lake to Swansea and then shipped across Owens Lake to Cartago, on to San Pedro, and finally over to Swansea, Wales, for refining.

From Keeler to Laws (near Bishop), a distance of 71 miles, the last remnant of the narrow-gauge Carson and Colorado Railroad, founded by D. O. Mills, operated until 1958. Mills had sold out to Southern Pacific, and through the years various sections of the line were abandoned, finally leaving only the stretch along the east side of Owens River. Some of the old equipment is on exhibition at Laws.

On the western shore of Owens Lake, 15 miles south of Lone Pine and east of the highway, stand two of the Cottonwood charcoal kilns *(SRL 537)*.

Cottonwood Charcoal Kilns, Owens Lake

Here wood was turned into charcoal and taken across the lake by steamboat to the Cerro Gordo furnaces. These kilns were vital to the smelting operations, for all the available wood in the Cerro Gordo area had been used. The kilns are similar to those in Wildrose Canyon, Death Valley.

The town of Olancha is near the southern tip of Owens Lake. Near here M. H. Farley, working for the Silver Mountain Mining Company in the Coso Mountains, completed the first mill and furnace in the Owens Valley by December 1862. Two years earlier he had explored and named Olancha Pass and had conceived the idea of his mill. The site *(SRL 796)* is on Olancha Creek, about a mile west of the historical marker that stands on Highway 395 at Williams Road. East of Olancha and southeast of Keeler is another interesting old town, Darwin, named for Darwin French, early explorer of Death Valley.

Today the *Bessie Brady* and the *Molly Stevens* are to be seen no more on Owens Lake. Relics of them are in the museum at Independence. The once beautiful Owens Lake is now dry, but from its bed the Pittsburgh Glass Company takes many minerals for processing in its large plant near the shore.

Old Panamint

"Tucked away in a remote section of a wild, unexplored range of mountains, separated from the more populous districts of the State by league upon league of hostile wilderness, Panamint was a law unto itself—a law of lead and steel.... Here was a Gargantuan range of barren mountains, taking root in a shimmering desert, rising almost perpendicular for two miles, gashed and cleft with abysmal gorges, colored with bizarre tints. Death by thirst and starvation lurked in the dread valley to the east, that claimed the lives of many audacious pioneers who sought to cross it. A small edition of Death Valley bounded these weird mountains on the west, less deadly, perhaps, but holding a menace that few men cared to face. Small wonder, then, that Ishmaels of society found perfect safety within these mountains."

High on a rocky promontory southwest of the spot where Panamint later sprang up, outlaw gangs as early as 1870 had their lookout, known as Robber's Roost. Any effort to track them here would have been futile.

In 1875, the Panamint Mining Company was organized by Senators William M. Stewart and John P. Jones. Other companies were formed, but most of them either died out or united in the Surprise Valley Mill and Mining Company. Panamint became one of the wildest camps in the history of California, with a population of 1,500. Inability to make a profit from the ore was the chief cause of Panamint's failure. After 1877 it reverted to the wilderness.

Through Randsburg, by the edge of Searles Lake with its vast deposits of potash and borax, up over the Slate Range, and down into the Panamint Valley, the road leads past the picturesque adobe ruins of Ballarat, a "wraith of the desert." From here the road leads on to Pan-amint, entering the gateway to the mighty chasm four miles from Ballarat.

Where the canyon widens to several hundred feet is the site of old Panamint, now wrecked by cloudbursts, floods, and vandals. A tall brick chimney rises from a smelter, and high above it hangs an aerial tram. A few skeleton houses of wood stand among the juniper and mesquite bushes, while the thick stone walls of former saloons and gambling houses cluster along the base of the cliffs. And over all hangs the stillness, the grandeur, and the desolation of the wilderness.

Greenwater and Skidoo

Two later boom camps, Greenwater and Skidoo, had their start in the 1880's. The former, discovered in 1884 on the eastern side of the Funeral Mountains and just over the summit from where the slope into Death Valley begins, has had few parallels in the "sudden rise, great outlays, small returns and quick decline" which have attended its brief periods of excitement. Gold, silver, and copper finds each had their day, the latter as late as 1906, when the population increased from 70 to over 1,000 within a month. Over a 30-mile stretch of mountain range 2,500 claims were staked within four months' time, and from them the "copper kings" reaped a rich harvest. But the camps were surrounded by hundreds of miles of barren mountain and desert, so their inaccessibility ultimately caused all claims to be abandoned. A letter written by a cheerful wag from somewhere in the locality voiced the situation in vivid terms when he said that he was employed on the "graveyard shift (miners' slang for the shift including midnight) in the Coffin Mine, Tombstone Mountains, Funeral Range, overlooking Death Valley."

Greenwater is remembered not only for its mining but for one of its favorite residents, Charley Brown. He came to the mining camp as a very young man and followed various types of work, one of his jobs being town marshal, which was not easy in this "rip-roaring town." While living there Charley fell in love with Stella Fairbanks, daughter of "Dad" Fairbanks, famed for saving many a life from the torrid heat of Death Valley. The young couple married after Greenwater was abandoned. Charley was superintendent of the Lila C for a time and finally settled in Shoshone. From this area he was elected to the Board of Supervisors of the County of Inyo, in which capacity he served for 17 years. He left this office to become Senator from the 28th District of California and was re-elected many times, serving in all 24 years. Charley Brown died in the spring of 1963. He is remembered as the great man from Greenwater and the desert area, and was affectionately known as the "Tall Joshua from Shoshone."

Skidoo, located on the summit of the mountain on the western edge of Death Valley, was Greenwater's nearest neighbor. It had the luxury of pure mountain water piped many miles from a spring near the top of Telescope Peak. It continued to produce gold and silver ores years after its sister mine was deserted. Although Skidoo never attained the fame that fell to Greenwater, nor was it known for its "wide-open" saloons and dance halls as were most of the early mining towns, yet it received notoriety for a cold-blooded murder. On April 19, 1908, Joe Simpson (familiarly known as Joe Hootch) shot and killed the manager of the local store, Jim Arnold. Simpson was immediately jailed. On Wednesday night following, while most of the town slept or refused to be aroused by stealthy footsteps, Simpson was taken out of jail and hanged, his swaying body found the next morning. The headlines of the next *Skidoo News*, a weekly paper, read in bold letters: "Murder in Camp, Murderer Lynched with General Approval." As if this didn't create enough excitement, when reporters from daily newspapers arrived shortly, the body of Joe Simpson was dug up and hanged all over again, with appropriate pictures made of the event. With this exception, Skidoo was a rather peaceful town until, its mines worked out, it was abandoned. A few buildings still stand.

Modern Inyo

Life in Inyo County has undergone many changes. It was known first as a great mining area. When the mines gave out, the people turned to farming and cattle raising. This too passed when the City of Los Angeles Department of Water and Power acquired most of the farming land and water rights, soon after the turn of the century. The Owens River, which heretofore had poured into Owens Lake, was diverted to the Los Angeles–Owens Valley Aqueduct, which finally came to be extended all the way through Inyo County and far up into Mono. The water is carried in a large siphon some 250 miles to Los Angeles. The loss of the water caused many people, particularly farmers, to leave the county. Some remained, however, and new people came. Cattlemen lease much of the city-owned land for grazing, and there is some mining in nonmetallics, but today tourism is big business in Inyo County. The people appreciate the area's highly varied topography. Each year from two to three million people hunt, fish, camp, and study nature in the Inyo National Forest. Several hundred thousand visit the great desert playground of Death Valley each winter, and there is travel through it all year. Eureka and Saline valleys are becoming well known, and these areas are being considered as recreation sites.

In Owens Valley, the four larger settlements of Bishop, Big Pine, Independence, and Lone Pine are modern, with fine facilities for tourists. From each, people can pack into the back country of the Sierra Nevada. Some of the smaller towns are beginning to grow and share in the general prosperity. The rich history of Inyo County is just being discovered and appreciated, much aided by the Eastern California Museum, whose headquarters and displays are at the County Courthouse in Independence.

Perhaps Inyo County has at last hit its stride and is becoming "a wonderland of scenic and historic interest."

SOURCES

Austin, Mary. *The Land of Little Rain.* Houghton Mifflin, Boston, 1903.
Bowie, William. "Levelling up Mount Whitney," *Sierra Club Bulletin,* XIV, No. 1 (February 1929), 53–57.
Chalfant, W. A. *Death Valley, the Facts.* Stanford University Press, Stanford, 1930.
——— *The Story of Inyo.* Privately published, 1922.
Cragen, Dorothy C. *My Land. San Bernardino Sun,* San Bernardino, 1954.
——— Articles in *Inyo Independent* and *Inyo Register,* 1953–65.
Farquhar, Francis P. "The Story of Mt. Whitney," *Sierra Club Bulletin,* XIV, No. 1 (February 1929), 39–52.
Florin, Lambert. *Western Ghost Towns.* Superior Publishing Co., Seattle, 1961.
Johnston, Philip. "Days and Nights in Old Panamint," *Touring Topics,* XX, No. 12 (December 1928), 22–25, 50–51.

King, Clarence. *Mountaineering in the Sierra Nevada.* James R. Osgood & Co., Boston, 1872.
Kirk, Ruth. *Exploring Death Valley.* 2d ed. Stanford University Press, Stanford, 1965.
Manly, William L. *Death Valley in 1849.* Privately printed, San Jose, 1894.
Nadeau, Remi A. *City Makers.* Doubleday, New York, 1948.
——— *The Water Seekers.* Doubleday, New York, 1950.
Richards, Frederick L. "The Commander's House," *Westways,* LVII, No. 2 (February 1965), 16–17.
Rose, Dan. "The Legend of Winnedumah," *Touring Topics,* XIX, No. 8 (August 1927), 35, 39.
Schumacher, Genny, ed. *Deepest Valley.* Sierra Club, San Francisco, 1962.
Steward, Julian. "Words Writ on Stone," *Touring Topics,* XIX, No. 5 (May 1927), 18–20, 36–38.
Wilson, Neill C. *Silver Stampede.* Macmillan, New York, 1937.

Kern County

KERN COUNTY (so called after the Kern River, which Frémont named in honor of Edward M. Kern, topographer of the expedition of 1845–46) was organized in 1866 from parts of Los Angeles and Tulare counties. Havilah was made the county seat, but it was changed to Bakersfield in 1874.

Garlock's Prehistoric Village

On Black Mountain, about five miles northwest of Garlock, at the edge of the Mojave Desert, are the remains of a prehistoric Indian village, discovered in the 1880's. From the nature of these ruins scientists have concluded that no recent tribe of Indians could have erected the village. On the inside of one of the doorways are stone carvings resembling those found on the famous Posten Butte near Florence, Arizona. From this evidence it is believed by some that the village may have been occupied centuries ago by the same race of men that built the extinct and buried cities of Arizona and Mexico. Other authorities hold that the site was not a true village but rather a religious center used during certain periods of the year and not otherwise occupied. A large-scale archaeological investigation of this area is planned.

In neighboring mountains and valleys there are many evidences of more recent tribes, among the most notable being the painted rocks (pictographs) on the Kern River near Lake Isabella.

Grizzly Gulch

Grizzly Gulch, in northeastern Kern County, about seven miles south of the old mining town of White River (Tailholt), was noted in early days for its large number of grizzly bears. Several prospectors were reported killed or crippled by them, and active mining operations could not be carried on until they had been killed.

The prevalence of fossil bones of prehistoric animals and of archaeological remains of the Yokuts Indians adds greatly to the interest of this region. South of Grizzly Gulch, and particularly in Rag Gulch and north of the Kern River, marks of an ancient shoreline are plainly visible, showing that this was, in past geological ages, the eastern margin of a vast ocean. For miles, the waterline may be traced by the remains of shellfish and other sea life, and at Shark Tooth Mountain, north of the Kern River, the bones and teeth of prehistoric sharks exist in great numbers.

An Indian ranchería once existed in Grizzly Gulch a little less than half a mile east of the Woody road. Hundreds of Indian mortars, many of them deeply worn into the granite through the grinding of acorns and seeds for generations, may still be seen in the bedrock and outcropping granite surrounding the little valley. During the 1890's, while prospectors were attempting to mine the flat on which the ranchería had been situated, the digging of a ditch for sluices disclosed the remains of an Indian burial ground. In 1928 three undisturbed graves of great archaeological importance were uncovered at this site.

Passes to the South

"The Tehachapi Mountains form an east and west link at about the 35th parallel, between the southern end of the Sierra Nevada on the east and the Coast Range on the west. They mark the southern limit (head) of the San Joaquin Valley, which is walled in on three sides by these three mountain groups. South and east lie the Mojave and Colorado deserts. Lieutenant Williamson, who, under orders from the War Department,

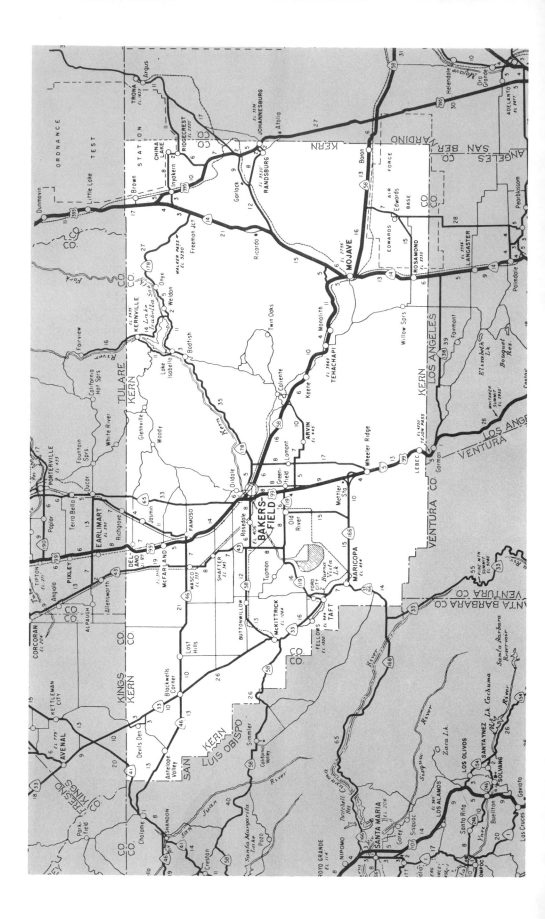

examined these Tehachapi Mountains in 1853 for purposes of finding the most practical passage for a railway, discovered six more or less available passes through them, of varying degrees of difficulty. Beginning with the most easterly, they were as follows: Walker's Pass (near Freeman); Tehachapi Pass (traversed by the railways); Oak Creek Road (Willow Springs north to Tehachapi); Tejón Pass (original pass of that name, along Cottonwood and Tejón creeks); Canyon de las Uvas (present Tejón Pass); San Emidio Pass (San Emidio Creek to Cuddy Valley). . . . Much confusion has arisen in published accounts, owing to the fact that each of three of these names, Walker's, Tehachapi, and Tejón, has been applied to two different passes in succession."

Walker Pass

One of the pioneer trails to California followed down the Owens River valley through what is now western Inyo County, passing by Owens Lake, and thence through Walker Pass (SRL 99) to the South Fork of the Kern River, and down the South Fork to its junction with the North Fork at Isabella.

There the trail divided, one branch going south by way of Bodfish, Havilah, and Walker's Basin, and then west by several routes to the ferry on the Kern River (for many years called Gordon's Ferry) about five miles northeast of Bakersfield, and the other branch crossing the Kern River near Isabella, passing over the Greenhorn Mountains either to Poso Flat or to Linn's Valley (near Glennville), and then turning north to the White River and Visalia.

In 1834 Joseph Walker, captain of an exploring party, left California by the latter route, via the White River and the Greenhorn Mountains, and in 1843 he followed the same trail in, while leading the Chiles emigrant party, the second wagon train to enter California from the East. In 1845 John C. Frémont, on his second expedition into California, sent his main party, accompanied by Joseph Walker, via this route, while he and a few others crossed the Sierra at Donner Pass. It was on this expedition that Edward Kern mapped the Kern River, which Frémont subsequently named for him. Kern's campsite (SRL 742) at the junction of the North and South forks is now inundated by Lake Isabella, but a monument has been placed on Highway 178 on the east side of the lake. The summit of Walker Pass on the same highway is also marked, and it received an additional plaque in 1963 when it was designated a National Historic Landmark by the Department of the Interior.

A marker has been erected at Freeman Junction (SRL 766), a meeting place of old Indian trails that was passed by Walker in 1834 after his discovery of the pass to the northwest. At this point the Death Valley '49er parties diverged west and south after their escape from that inferno of suffering. Later the place became a favorite haunt of the bandit Tiburcio Vásquez. It is now the junction of State Highways 14 and 178. A few miles north of this point on Highway 14 is Indian Wells (SRL 457), a station on the Walker Trail and later on the freight line from Los Angeles to the Cerro Gordo Mines in Inyo County. It derives its name from a rock-walled spring, still in existence, the former location of an Indian village.

The Tejón Passes

The pass that at present bears the name of Tejón ("badger") was first penetrated by Pedro Fages, then acting governor of Alta California, in 1772, while pursuing deserters from the Spanish Army. A manuscript penned by Fages himself and discovered only in modern times describes his inland expedition from San Diego to San Luis Obispo. Concerning the manuscript, Professor Herbert E. Bolton says that "it is a surprising story of an entirely unknown California expedition, ahead of Anza, from Imperial Valley over the mountains to San Bernardino Valley, thence through Cajón Pass, along the edge of Mojave Desert, through Antelope Valley through a pass into the southern end of San Joaquin Valley, northwest across it to Buena Vista Hills and Lake, and through the mountains to San Luis Obispo, four years before Garcés entered the Valley. . . . It gives Captain Pedro Fages a distinctive position, hitherto unrecognized, as far-travelling trail blazer, and as pioneer in the South San Joaquin."

The pass and canyon through which Fages blazed this trail has had various names. Fages himself called it Buena Vista ("beautiful view"). The Spaniards who came later designated the canyon as La Cañada de las Uvas ("the canyon of the grapes"), and it is known today as Grapevine Canyon. The route over the summit, however, is designated on modern maps as Tejón Pass. A monument (SRL 283) has been placed at Lebec, near the summit, in memory of Pedro Fages, the first white man to cross the Tehachapi Mountains by this pass and the first to enter the San Joaquin Valley from the south.

Leaving Grapevine Canyon, Fages traveled 30 miles northwest across the southwestern corner of the San Joaquin Valley to the Buena Vista Hills in the Coast Range, perhaps taking a short cut by way of the low gap at the neck of Wheeler Ridge. A marker on Highway 166, about seven miles west of Highway 99, indicates the point (SRL 291) at which Fages' trail was crossed in 1806 by the expedition, in search of mission sites, that included Father José María Zalvidea. This party traveled from Santa Barbara Mission to San Gabriel Mission, passing the site of present Bakersfield.

Reaching the foot of the hills on the southwestern shore of Buena Vista Lake, Fages found an Indian village, the existence of which is still attested by vast kitchen middens. Across the floor of the valley and about the lake itself Fages found a "labyrinth of lakes and tulares."

"Anyone who has stood even today on this spot and looked off to the east and south will yield ungrudging approval of the name which Fages gave to the same, but more liquid, panorama nearly one hundred and sixty years ago [1931]. The survival of Fages' place name here is most significant. Manifestly, Buena Vista Lake, the Buena Vista

Hills, and the village at their foot all got their name from the same circumstance." The name has been applied to the lake ever since the earliest maps, and is the oldest Spanish place name in the San Joaquin Valley.

The site of the principal Tulamniu Indian encampment *(SRL 374)* visited by Fages is indicated by a marker on the former western shore of the lake, now virtually dry. This was the scene of excavation work done in 1933–34 under the auspices of the Smithsonian Institution. In attempting to find the marker, one will almost certainly become lost in the veritable maze of dirt roads on the west side of the lake bed unless one has exact directions. The following is perhaps the easiest and most direct route to the monument. About nine or ten miles northeast of Taft on Highway 119 a main paved road turns left (due north) to the Navy Headquarters of the Elk Hills Petroleum Reserve and the town of Tupman. About one-tenth mile beyond this junction a dirt road turns right (due south) from Highway 119 (this corner was identifiable in 1963 by an old wooden building bearing the name "Nine-Mile Station"). One should take this dirt road, which follows the power poles, a distance of approximately three and three-fourths miles to a four-way intersection of dirt roads, marked by a number of large blue boxes. Turning left (east) at this intersection, one follows the old lakeshore, passing an isolated tree in about three-fourths mile. Another half-mile will bring the traveler to the Tulamniu marker.

The second Spaniard to enter the San Joaquin Valley from the south was a Franciscan friar, Father Francisco Garcés, in 1776. Garcés left San Gabriel in April of that year and, ascending San Fernando Valley, crossed over the Newhall grade to the vicinity of the present town of Castaic, in Los Angeles County, where he swung northeast over the mountains by a trail running east of the present Ridge Route. Near Hughes Lake on the edge of Antelope Valley he crossed Fages' trail of 1772, and then proceeded north across the valley to Cottonwood Creek, up which he climbed to the pass above. From there he descended into the San Joaquin Valley by way of Tejón Creek. To this pass, 15 miles to the east of the pass over which Fages had entered the great central valley four years before, rightly belongs the name Tejón.

On April 30, 1776, Garcés visited the locality of the present Arvin, a fact commemorated by a

statue of him *(SRL 371)* in front of St. Thomas Church on Bear Mountain Boulevard at the eastern limit of the town. On May 1 he crossed the Kern River, which he named Río de San Felipe, at a point *(SRL 278)* about one mile north of the marker on Highway 178, eight miles east of Bakersfield. Since the priest could not swim, friendly Indians carried him across the river, much as did his beloved Yuma Indians of the Colorado, who later revolted and martyred him in 1781.

The padre traversed the valley as far north as the White River, near which on May 3 he baptized a dying Indian boy. This site of the first baptism in the south San Joaquin Valley *(SRL 631)* is marked by a cross on the private Vincent ranch three miles north of the monument that stands on Garcés Highway seven miles east of Highway 65 and 16 miles east of Delano. Outdoor pageants dramatizing the visit of the pioneer Franciscan have been held in a natural amphitheater on the ranch. On his return trip, Father Garcés visited, on May 7, an Indian ranchería at or near the site of the present city of Bakersfield. This city has commemorated the first white man known to have been within its present limits by a statue in the traffic circle *(SRL 277)* at Chester and Golden State avenues. A Catholic high school in Bakersfield has been named in Garcés' honor. The explorer returned by way of Arvin on May 10 and 11 en route to the Tehachapi region and the Mojave Desert.

Hudson's Bay Company trappers came as far south as the Tejón region in the 1830's, and in the name of the town of Lebec is preserved the memory of Peter Lebeck, possibly one of these trappers, who was killed on October 17, 1837, by a grizzly bear, which he had shot and wounded near the site of Fort Tejón. The tree near which Lebeck died and under which he lies buried stands at the northeast corner of the old Fort Tejón parade grounds, three and one-half miles north of Lebec.

Across the highway from Lebec lies Castaic (Castac) Lake, "with its waters so blue and its fringe of snow-white salt." It is now dry.

Rancho El Tejón

Rancho El Tejón is one of the most interesting and important of all the historic spots in the San Joaquin Valley. Here are the sites of several Indian villages which dated back to prehistoric times. They were occupied until the last quarter of the nineteenth century.

The first historic record of the region was made by Fray Francisco Garcés, who, on his expedition in April 1776, visited and named the Indian village of San Pascual, probably the one located at the mouth of Tejón Creek, later the site of the Los Alamos Butterfield Stage station. For many years this village was the center for the ancient Indian ceremonies described by Bishop Kip, who visited the place on October 15, 1855: "It was a wild scene as the glare of the fire fell upon the dancers and a thousand Indians gathered in a circle around them."

General Edward Beale, while Superintendent of

Adobe Store, Rancho El Tejón

Indian Affairs, established a government Indian reservation on Rancho Tejón in the early 1850's, erecting stone and adobe buildings as headquarters for the agency on the site later occupied by the headquarters of the rancho on Arroyo del Paso. One of these buildings, erected in 1856 and formerly used as a store, still stands, in part, although it has been extensively modernized. The thickness of its adobe walls is evident, and the old front doors, bearing the symbol of the Tejón brand, are still in use, having been replaced on the building after its original front portion was torn down. Most of the old buildings were razed following serious damage in the Tehachapi earthquake of 1952. At this location there were also later adobe buildings constructed from bricks salvaged from some of the old structures at Fort Tejón after its abandonment, but these too are gone. After the earthquake new ranch headquarters were built on the east side of Interstate 5 three and one-half miles north of Lebec, opposite Fort Tejón State Historical Monument and on a portion of the old fort site. The old rancho headquarters are 15 miles east of the highway. Entrance to Tejón Ranch Co. properties requires a written permit from the headquarters near Fort Tejón.

A marker beside the highway north of Grapevine (together with the Rose Station marker) commemorates the government reservation, originally called Tejón but later renamed Sebastian Indian Reservation (SRL 133) in honor of William King Sebastian of Arkansas, Chairman of the Senate Committee on Indian Affairs. Although the reservation failed, General Beale, as owner of Rancho Tejón, encouraged the Indians to remain on the land, employing them as vaqueros and laborers. It is said that when the rancho was finally sold, it was stipulated that the Indian residents should be allowed to remain and that they should be well treated. For years many Indians lived in the little adobe houses scattered up and down Arroyo del Tejón for a distance of several miles, but only one family was to be found there in the summer of 1963. Their house was wooden, the remaining adobes having been demolished following the 1952 earthquake. The Tejón Ranch Co. provides housing for the Indians in its employ.

Rancho El Tejón was a grant made in November 1843 to José Antonio Aguirre, a Spanish Basque who was a wealthy trader, and to Ignacio del Valle. The largest Mexican grant in the San Joaquin Valley, it included 97,616 acres of land. It lay in the extreme southeastern corner of the valley, a section largely mountainous, hilly, or rolling. After the failure of the Indian reservation General Beale purchased the rancho in 1865 from Del Valle and Juan Temple (who had acquired Aguirre's share) and retired to it after his term as United States Surveyor-General. The irregularity of the rancho is due to the fact that an attempt was made to include sufficient water facilities to support the land.

Rancho Tejón today is one of the several combined ranchos owned by the Tejón Ranch Co., incorporated in 1936, totaling over a quarter of a million acres of cattle range. This corporation succeeded a southern California syndicate that had purchased the ranch in 1912 from Truxtun

Restored Barracks and Ruins, Fort Tejón

Beale, son of the General. Other old Mexican land grants, each with an interesting history, are included in this vast domain: Rancho de los Alamos y Agua Caliente (partly in Los Angeles County), Rancho de Castac, and Rancho de la Liebre (also partly in Los Angeles County).

Rancho de los Alamos y Agua Caliente was purchased by Beale in 1865 from Agustín Olvera, Cristobal Aguilar, and James L. Gibbens. It had been granted in 1843 and 1846 to Francisco López, Luís Jordan, and Vicente Botello.

Rancho Castac, traversed throughout nearly its entire length by the Ridge Route, extends northward from Castac Lake, near Lebec, to a distance of two miles beyond Grapevine Station. It was granted on November 22, 1843, to José María Covarrubias, a French citizen of Mexico, who came to California as a teacher in 1834 and later took a prominent part in public affairs. He served as secretary to Governor Pío Pico, and in the autumn of 1849 became a member of the first State Constitutional Convention and later of the state legislature.

The first settler at the mouth of El Arroyo de los Encinos (Live Oak Canyon) was Samuel A. Bishop, who erected adobe corrals and an adobe house beside a large white oak. Bishop did not at first know that he was on the old Mexican land grant, Rancho de Castac. He purchased the grant in 1860, and in 1864 moved to Fort Tejón, thus acquiring possession of the buildings that had cost the government over half a million dollars. Here Bishop lived before selling in June 1866 to Colonel Robert S. Baker of Los Angeles, who, in October of the same year, resold to Beale.

Rancho de la Liebre was the first of Beale's acquisitions in this area, in 1855. His old adobe still stands in Los Angeles County on property of the Tejón Ranch Co. The rancho had been granted to José María Flores in 1846.

In a description of historic Rancho Tejón one cannot omit mention of the vast wild-flower gardens which each spring fling their gorgeous colors along the upland canyons and mountain meadows. Formerly, the broad valley floor, too, was covered with miles of bloom, but now the huge acreages under cultivation have caused the wild flowers to become restricted largely to the foothills.

Fort Tejón

Romantic, alluring in its sylvan setting, old Fort Tejón (*SRL 129*) stands amid a grove of ancient oaks and sycamores beside the winding mountain stream known on modern maps as Grapevine Creek (Arroyo de las Uvas). It was established in 1854 as the headquarters of the United States Army's First Dragoons, to protect the Indians from extermination and to deter cattle and horse stealing, and it became quite important in the early days of the American occupation.

In 1858 the fort became a station on the Butterfield Overland Mail route, when six-horse stages covered the distance between St. Louis and San Francisco in 23 days. Soldiers from the fort went

Hamilton Saloon, Willow Springs

out to meet the stages and escorted them through the pass, where protection from Indians and bandits was needed. The post, as a military station, was abandoned on September 11, 1864, and the buildings fell into the possession of Samuel A. Bishop, who had acquired the land in 1860 from Albert Packard, owner of Rancho Castac, on which they were located.

On Armistice Day in 1923 the Bakersfield Chapter of the D.A.R. placed a bronze tablet at old Fort Tejón, which is now owned by the State of California. It was taken over by the Division of Beaches and Parks in 1939, and a park ranger was first stationed there during the winter of 1947–48. Two buildings, an enlisted men's barracks and an officers' quarters, both of adobe, have thus far been restored by the state, in cooperation with a lay group known as the Fort Tejón Restoration Committee. Ruins of other adobes are in evidence. A reception building housing the ranger office and exhibit room has been erected on the grounds.

On the old road between Fort Tejón and Lebec is an adobe building known as "The Dairy." It is owned by the Tejón Ranch Co., and was erected in 1886 of adobe bricks salvaged from disintegrating buildings at Fort Tejón. Its circular gable windows are said to have been removed from the fort's original guardhouse.

The Tehachapi Passes

From Bakersfield, a road leads across the Sierra Nevada to the Mojave Desert, by way of Tehachapi Pass. Tehachapi is an Indian word, the meaning of which is uncertain, but Powers, in his *Tribes of California,* asserts that it was named for a now extinct tribe of Indians who once lived in the pass. Tradition gives the meaning "land of plenty of acorns and good water" to the name, and the abundance of artesian well water and sturdy oaks seems to justify the interpretation.

The summit of the Sierra is reached just beyond the town of Tehachapi, and from there the road descends into the Mojave Desert. The first white man to go through the Tehachapi region was Father Garcés, in 1776. On this expedition Garcés crossed the mountains from the south via Cottonwood and Tejón creeks, and penetrated into the San Joaquin Valley as far north as the White River, passing en route the present site of Bakersfield. Retracing his steps he crossed the Sierra into the Mojave Desert. His route varied considerably from that followed by the present state highway and the railroad. Instead of going up Tehachapi Creek, Garcés reached Tehachapi Valley via Rancho Tejón and Cummings Valley, where he turned south into the desert, probably by way of Oak Creek Pass (*SRL 97*). A monument has been placed at the summit of this pass, seven miles southeast of Tehachapi on the road to Willow Springs.

Historians have not yet determined which of the passes through the Tehachapi Mountains Jedediah S. Smith traversed in finding his way into the San Joaquin Valley in 1827. Whether he went by way of one of the passes which have borne the name of Tejón or by one of the Tehachapi passes, no record has yet disclosed. Kern County has not forgotten Smith, however. A monument has been erected on Highway 58 about 12 miles east of Bakersfield. He traveled where water was obtainable for his party, and, being primarily a trapper, he investigated the possibility of fur animals being on the several water courses emerging from the mountains, and so kept close to the foothills. Considering the topography of the area, there is little doubt that he passed at or very near the site of the monument (*SRL 660*).

Other trappers and hunters went this way from time to time. John C. Frémont, on his way out of California in April 1844, went into the Mojave Desert by way of Tehachapi Creek and Oak Creek Pass, called Tehachapi Pass until the building of the railroad in 1876, when the name was transferred to the present Tehachapi Pass. Later the old trail and wagon road used by the early emigrants followed closely along the trail taken by Frémont through the original Tehachapi Pass (now Oak Creek Pass). Frémont himself called this Walker's Pass.

This became an important stage road from Los Angeles to Havilah when the Kern River mines were centers of activity during the 1860's. Its importance continued during the 1870's, since it was the route between San Fernando and Caliente, which was at that time the southern terminus of the railroad under construction down the San Joaquin Valley from Stockton.

The first permanent settlers came to Tehachapi, in Tehachapi Valley, about 1854. Gold in the China Hill placers brought a large number of miners to the region, but it was not until 1869 that a post office was established there. Before this, the settlers had to get their mail from Los Angeles, 100 miles away, whenever they or their neighbors went there for provisions.

The original town of Tehachapi was about three and one-half miles west of the present town, originally called Greenwich, which supplanted it when the railroad was built in 1876. At the first location, still known as Old Town (*SRL 643*), no buildings remain, but a monument indicates the site. The entire countryside is made fragrant each spring with the scent of millions of fruit blossoms, for in hidden nooks and upon sunny plateaus, often lying more than 3,000 feet above sea level, orchards of prize-winning apples and pears flourish.

San Emigdio

In San Emigdio Canyon there remained for many years the ruins of the headquarters of Rancho San Emigdio. Among these were a stone foundation, 30 × 60 feet, thought by some to have been the beginnings of a church. It is not definitely known whether work was ever started on the walls. Ruins of several buildings actually brought to completion also remained, including living quarters, a blacksmith shop, and a structure "occupied as late as 1870 by Alexis Godey, noted plainsman and guide, who accompanied Frémont on several of his trips to California." Latta believes these buildings were originally an attempted establishment of a San Joaquin Valley outpost of Mission Santa Barbara, but mission historians do not generally concur in this opinion. It is known that the Franciscans looked upon the valley as being a fruitful place for their future endeavors, but nothing has been discovered in mission records to substantiate any actual or attempted establishments before secularization. Both Father Zephyrin Engelhardt, O.F.M., and Father Maynard Geiger, O.F.M., repudiate the existence of a mission station at San Emigdio. Whatever the original purpose of these buildings, nothing remains to be seen today.

Rancho San Emigdio (Emidio) was granted to José Antonio Domínguez in the summer of 1842. Domínguez died in 1843 or 1844 and his son, Francisco Domínguez, thereupon fell heir to the rancho. Don Francisco, however, did not occupy it because of its remoteness, and he had the cattle removed to a location where they would be safer from Indian attacks. On November 29, 1851, John C. Frémont bought a half interest in Rancho San Emigdio. Later Alexis Godey occupied the ranch and ran cattle.

Among the scattered boulders of Arroyo de San Emigdio, several miles from its mouth and three miles north of the headquarters site, is the site of the Mexican settlement of San Emigdio. Remnants of several adobe buildings stood for many years in this once beautiful spot, where rows of poplar and cottonwood trees shaded the homes of the Mexicans and Indians who lived there, while streams of water running in many directions irrigated their tiny vegetable gardens.

Between the pueblo and headquarters sites are the buildings of the present headquarters of Rancho San Emidio, now owned by the Kern County Land Company. The house erected by Godey is still standing, although it is a reconstructed version dating from the 1890's.

On the west fork of San Emigdio Creek near the head of the arroyo stood the Mill Potrero, on the site of the first steam sawmill in this part of the San Joaquin region. Here Joseph Gale milled lumber for Fort Tejón and other early neighborhood improvements, bringing the lumber down from the pine forests on the slopes of San Emigdio Peak two miles north of the mill. Joseph Gale's homestead, where he settled in 1858, was at the mouth of Grapevine Canyon, at the site of an Indian ranchería, 400 yards north of Grapevine Station. His house and orchard have disappeared. His daughter married John Fletcher Cuddy, who came to Fort Tejón with the soldiers, and they settled in Cuddy Valley above the mouth of Uvas Creek, where their first log cabin still stands.

El Camino Viejo

The western San Joaquin Valley retains much of the atmosphere of the early Indians and Spaniards. Even today the sites of hundreds of ancient rancherías may be identified, and for years there were many old Spaniards still living along the dry creeks and among the oak-covered hills bordering El Camino Viejo who remembered the location of every water hole along its course. The very names of those numerous arroyos and *aguajes* ("water holes") suggest a significant but little-known Spanish-Californian background.

El Camino Viejo of the Spanish period, which followed the prehistoric Indian trails and the still older paths of antelope as they wandered from *aguaje* to *aguaje* over hill and gully, through tule swamps and plains of blistering alkali, was used chiefly by Spanish and Mexican refugees. They passed over it unobserved from San Pedro to San Antonio (now East Oakland)—horse thieves and cattle rustlers, following their nefarious trade in comparative safety; bandits of the 1840's and the 1850's; and even the daring young lovers Ramón Solorcono and his beautiful bride, who, in 1823, according to legend, fled over this path in a creaking carreta, while agents of the bride's irate father followed in a fruitless chase all the way from Chile to Fort Ross.

For eight months of the year El Camino Viejo crossed a desert waste, to be traveled only when unavoidable; but in springtime it wound through one vast wild-flower garden, where every arroyo flowed with abundant, crystal-clear water. Beyond El Arroyo de San Emigdio, the old road passed a second campsite at the sink of El Arroyo de Armargosa ("bitter water"), located southwest of Buena Vista Lake at a spot occupied until the late 1880's by an ancient adobe. At Pelican Island, one and a half miles from the normal shore of the lake, relics of an Indian camp and burial ground have been uncovered. Composed largely of the shells of fresh-water mussels, this island mound also contained dozens of artifacts and other materials of archaeological value. Pelican Island no longer exists, having been leveled off and placed under cultivation. It had been occupied by a cattle camp of the Miller and Lux Company for a number of years.

On El Camino Viejo, 20 miles to the northwest of Armargosa, was La Brea, a site later occupied by one of several oil camps that have borne the name of Asphalto, five miles east of McKittrick. Many bones of prehistoric animals have been taken from the asphalt deposits at this point, as well as from the spot southwest of McKittrick that is now a registered landmark. Another three miles to the northwest was Aguaje de Santa María, while still farther on was El Arroyo de los

Temblores ("earthquake"), where were found living springs said to have first issued from the canyon floor as a result of a severe earthquake. An old adobe house surrounded by giant fig and cottonwood trees stood on the Temblor Ranch until destroyed by fire about 1950. The old trees still thrive in the sequestered hillside nook.

Beyond the Creek of the Earthquake, El Camino Viejo crossed El Arroyo de Chico Martínez, near the mouth of which rise glistening white chalklike bluffs and hills which may be seen for miles across the plains. The arroyo was named for Chico Martínez, a Spanish pioneer in this region, who was known as "king of the mustang-runners" because of his skill in herding wild horses into the corrals built for their capture at Aguaje Mesteño ("mustang springs") and elsewhere.

Traversing an elevated and broken country, El Camino Viejo wound along from El Arroyo de Chico Martínez to El Arroyo de los Carneros ("sheep"). Two chimney-like rocks rising 800 feet above the valley piloted travelers to this water hole. Among these rocks are caves covered with Indian pictographs. Passing successively the Aguajes de en Media ("middle water") and del Diablo ("of the Devil"), and Arroyo de Matarano, the road now ran two miles east of the Point of Rocks, known to the Spanish as Las Tinajas ("tanks") de los Indios, evidently the site of an important Indian encampment. Rock formations here acted as natural reservoirs to hold the water that collected during the winter rains. These cisterns bear evidence of having been improved by the Indians, for deeply worn steps cut into the rock lead down to the water. Indian mortars, rock writings, and other evidence that this was a prehistoric campsite have been found about the rocks.

The next water hole to be reached was at a second Aguaje de la Brea ("tar springs") near the present Paso Robles–Wasco highway three miles southwest of Devils Den. The oil that covered the water of this spring doubtless deceived many a thirsty wayfarer, who passed it by thinking it only a pool of oil.

At Alamo Solo ("lone cottonwood"), three and a half miles north of La Brea, El Camino Viejo forked, a branch going northeast four miles to Alamo Mocho ("trimmed cottonwood") and thence on to several early Spanish settlements on the west banks of Tulare Lake, Fresno Slough, and the San Joaquin River. The main road continued northward to Poso de Chané and thence to San Antonio. At Alamo Solo, probably the most unfailing water hole on the entire west side of the valley, there was at one time an Indian encampment that covered approximately 100 acres.

Edward F. Beale

In 1852 General Edward Fitzgerald Beale was made Superintendent of Indian Affairs for California and Nevada. He at once initiated a policy of honest and humane dealings with the Indians. He established a government reservation and later employed them on his ranch.

Edward Beale "deserves to be classed with Kit Carson and others as a pathfinder of the West."

He was famous for his exploit in reaching San Diego with Kit Carson after the Battle of San Pasqual, to warn Stockton of General Kearny's dangerous situation. He was the first to carry California gold to the East, after the discovery of 1848. He explored mountain passes, surveyed routes, and built roads over them, and in 1861 he was appointed Surveyor-General of California and Nevada. He also acquired the extensive Rancho El Tejón, south of Bakersfield, to which he retired after the Civil War.

Beale, who was an enthusiastic advocate of the camel as a means of transportation across the deserts of the Southwest, brought the first caravan to California, a trying journey of more than 1,200 miles, taking from June 1857 to the following January. This feat proved beyond a doubt the great endurance of the animals. After crossing the Colorado River (where Beale proved that camels can swim), the caravan was driven to Fort Tejón, where some of the animals remained for more than a year.

The camel experiment, however, proved to be a failure, although the animals were used to a limited extent for about two years. Dislike of the animals and lack of understanding in their care and management, the Civil War, and, finally, the coming of the railroad, all combined to bring about the ultimate abandonment of the project. In 1863 the camels were sold at auction at Benicia Arsenal, and were soon dispersed to different parts of the country, gradually disappearing altogether. Rumors were long current that descendants of the original camel corps were occasionally encountered upon the deserts, but the only physical evidence of them today is the skeleton of one of the animals preserved in the Smithsonian Institution.

The Beale Memorial Library was given to the city of Bakersfield by Mrs. Mary E. Beale in memory of her husband, General Beale. It was located on the northwest corner of Chester Avenue and Seventeenth Street, but was so badly damaged by the earthquake of 1952 that it was torn down.

Butterfield Stage Stations

Following along the old Stockton–Los Angeles Road, the Butterfield stages rumbled back and forth through the Cañada de las Uvas and up the southern San Joaquin Valley on their periodical trips between Los Angeles and San Francisco, during the years from 1858 to 1861. Most of the stations along the way have long since disappeared, and little remains today even to indicate their sites. Through Kern County one may trace the trail by the following names: Fort Tejón, Sink (or Sinks) of the Tejón, Kern River Slough, Gordon's Ferry, Posey, and Mountain House.

The Sinks of the Tejón, called Agua de los Alamos, or Los Alamitos by the Mexicans, was located at the mouth of Tejón Creek. Here, where the water of the arroyo sinks into the dry sands, there was a perpetual spring, long a gathering place of the Indians. From 1858 to 1861 it was an important station for the Butterfield stages. Several buildings, including a barn, hostlers'

quarters, and a combined general store, drugstore, and post office, were erected. This site (SRL 540), on the property of the Tejón Ranch Co., is now under cultivation, but a monument with bronze plaque stands six miles west at the intersection of David Road and the Weed Patch–Wheeler Ridge road.

The old stage road continued north past the station at Kern River Slough (SRL 588), where horses were changed. This location is now marked two miles east of Greenfield on Panama Road. The stage road then crossed the Kern River at Gordon's Ferry (the Kern River Station), about four miles northeast of Bakersfield near the foot of China Grade. No remnant of the Kern River Station (SRL 137) can be seen today, but there is a marker at the south end of the bridge. This place was active as a ferry operated by Major Aneas B. Gordon for several years before the establishment of the Butterfield route.

According to Banning, the next station was located at Posey (Poso) Creek (SRL 539), two and one-half miles east of the marker that stands at the junction of Round Mountain Road and the Bakersfield–Glennville highway. To the north was Mountain House (SRL 589), sometimes called Willow Springs, but not to be confused with the Willow Springs near Rosamond in eastern Kern County. Mountain House had a bad reputation because of several murders which had been committed there, and weird tales developed around it—of the white ox that came to the spring to drink and then mysteriously disappeared; of the possum that hid at the watering trough, disturbing the flow of water in an uncanny manner; and many others. The site of the Mountain House Station is on private property about one and one-half miles north of the marker that stands on the Bakersfield–Glennville highway eight miles southwest of Woody.

Other Landmarks of Stagecoach Days

Six miles due north of Mountain House over very rough country was Coyote Springs, located in a branch of the barren Grizzly Gulch where there was a good source of water. Marks of the old stage road may yet be seen and parts of it are still in use.

William H. Brewer, on April 14, 1863, described the route from Tule River to Coyote Springs thus: "The road this day was through a desolate waste. . . . The soil was barren and, this dry year, almost destitute of vegetation. A part of the way was through low barren hills. . . . We stopped at a miserable hut, where there is a spring, and a man keeps a few cattle." In stagecoach days a barn and a cabin served the needs of travelers at this point.

Rose Station (SRL 300), about four miles north of the present Grapevine Station and one mile east of Interstate 5, was an important stopping place for travel between Bakersfield and Los Angeles during the late 1860's and early 1870's. A monument stands on the highway at a point from which the site, on Tejón Ranch Co. property, can easily be seen in the distance. An inspection of the site in 1963 disclosed that the adobe station house erected in 1876 by William B. Rose had vanished completely, although the spot on which it stood was still identifiable. According to Earl Rowland, former Director of the San Joaquin Pioneer Museum in Stockton, a portion of one wall remained standing in the summer of 1946. The building was intact and in good condition in 1933 when this section of the book was first published. So pass our California landmarks.

The history of the Rose Station goes back to 1857, when the first building was erected at the sink of Arroyo del Rancho Viejo or Arroyo de los Encinos (Live Oak Creek), 200 yards southeast of the future site of Rose's adobe. The place was first known as Rancho Canoa ("trough"), and was operated by W. W. Hudson and James C. Rosemeier. William B. Rose and J. J. López purchased the station in 1872.

Willow Springs (SRL 130), about eight miles west of Rosamond, was once an important watering place on the trail connecting the southern San Joaquin Valley and the desert. The springs were used by Indians from ancient times and numerous artifacts have been found there. The site was visited by Padre Garcés in 1776, John C. Frémont in 1846, and the Death Valley '49ers. On the old Tehachapi Pass route (Oak Creek Pass), it was a stage and freight station until the coming of the railroad in 1876. It was the dividing place for the ordinary stage travel to the Kern River mines by way of Oak Creek and the heavier ox-team traffic by way of Red Rock Canyon, Jawbone Canyon, and the South Fork of the Kern River. Ox teams bound for Inyo County also turned northeast at Willow Springs. Later, it became famous as a resort and still boasts a number of picturesque stone and adobe structures erected about the turn of the century under the direction of Ezra Hamilton, who discovered the nearby Tropico Gold Mine in 1896. One crumbling adobe wall belonging to the original stage station is still standing just off the main street of Willow Springs behind an occupied building.

Another Death Valley '49er water hole that later became a freight station is Desert Spring (SRL 476), one and three-quarters miles southeast of the desolate hamlet of Cantil, which is east of Highway 14 and one and one-half miles south of the Red Rock–Randsburg road. Just east of Cantil is the three-way intersection of Cantil, Valley, and Norton roads. One should follow Valley Road east one mile to the junction of Pappas Road. Turning right (south) on Pappas for half a mile, one reaches a dirt road that branches to the right and leads a quarter of a mile to Desert Spring. The historical monument stands on the far side of the wooded clump that surrounds the spring.

North of the junction with the Randsburg road, Highway 14 passes through beautiful Red Rock Canyon, an area of highly colored cliffs that have been eroded into pillars, temples, and other fantastic formations. The coloration appears more vivid in early morning or late afternoon. Some of the formations have been given names, including the Great Temple and the Phantom City.

Glennville

Forty-two miles northeast of Bakersfield is the pioneer community of Glennville, named for the Glenn brothers, who settled there in the early 1850's. Already at the spot when they arrived was Thomas Fitzgerald, who had built an adobe (SRL 495), still standing and the oldest known residence in Kern County. The tamped-earth structure, restored by the Kern County Museum, was originally a trading post at the intersection of two ancient Indian trails. Fitzgerald traded with the Indians and also with white trappers. The building still has its original ceiling rafters and a hand-hewn oak door hung on hand-forged iron hinges.

One mile from Glennville on the White River Road a marker indicates the site of Lavers Crossing (SRL 672), community center for the settlers in Linn's Valley. Here miners and emigrants stopped en route across Greenhorn Mountain to the gold strike of 1854 at Keyesville on the Kern River.

Keyesville

Kern River, with towering granite walls, banks lined with brilliant green, and "deep-throated roar," is the gateway to one of California's most fascinating mountain regions. Here, in this stupendous natural setting, romance, comedy, and tragedy were enacted during one of California's most important gold rushes.

Robert Glass Cleland said of the discovery of gold on Kern River and of its importance to Los Angeles and southern California:

"Perhaps the most serious drawback to the material development of the south was its deplorable lack of money . . . and under such a handicap economic progress was necessarily slow. . . . In 1855 gold was discovered in considerable quantities on the Kern River. This at once attracted miners from the entire State, and led to a rush of no mean proportions. The southern California merchants were naturally jubilant over this event in which they saw an opportunity of reaping some of the rich harvest their San Francisco, Stockton and Sacramento rivals had previously monopolized."

The first town to spring up in this new field was known as Keyesville (SRL 98), after Richard Keyes, who had opened up a mine likewise named for him. The town was situated in a semicircular cove of the Greenhorn Mountains at the edge of a rocky gulch, and its few stores were scattered about the middle of this flat. There were no streets and the dwelling houses went straying up the slope in a most informal way.

Keyesville was the scene of gambling resorts and gunmen as wild as in any of the larger camps in the north. The surrounding mountains, too, were wild in the extreme. In 1856 the settlers, expecting an attack from Indians who were waging war in neighboring counties, erected a rude fort on the sage-covered hill just outside of town. The Indians, however, never came and the fort was never used, but a vestige of the trenches may be traced there today.

The passage of time and the depredations of vandals have almost obliterated Keyesville, and fewer than half a dozen of the old roughly hewn board houses, with their shake roofs, remain. The townsite is four miles west of Lake Isabella.

Quartzburg and Whiskey Flat—Rivals

In 1860, Lovely Rogers (this was indeed his first name), a miner from Keyesville, was out looking for a lost mule. In a gulch eight miles north of home, he found his mule and also a magnificent piece of quartz where the famous Big Blue Mine was later located. That was the beginning of Quartzburg and of its rival, Whiskey Flat, later known as Kernville. The rush to the gulches and mountainsides around Rogers' mine soon resulted in the opening of a dozen quartz mills, and the region became the richest in the state during that period.

On a small ledge above the river the town of Quartzburg sprang up. Water from the mine pumps irrigated the trees and gardens and alfalfa patches and a homey atmosphere clung about the place from the beginning. Moreover, the influential citizens of Quartzburg believed in local option, and when an attempt was made to start a bar in town, that unwelcome feature was forced to move a mile down the river to a place thereafter known as Whiskey Flat.

Kernville (SRL 132) eventually became the most important town in the Kern River mining region, but for several years it had a rival in the little town up the river. If one tired of the quiet, orderly Quartzburg, it was but a short walk along the riverbank to the bars and gambling resorts of Whiskey Flat; and, according to Johnston, "if the iniquity of the latter town outraged him, he could find more congenial atmosphere among the devotees of prohibition in the former town."

By 1879 the Kern River region had reached the height of its prosperity, and most of the mines around Quartzburg had been acquired by Senator John P. Jones, who consolidated them into the Big Blue. Soon after this, the Senator met with reverses and the mine closed down, thus shutting off the water supply for Quartzburg's houses and gardens. The former were gradually torn down and carted away, while the latter were left to run wild or die. Nothing remains at Quartzburg today to remind one of its past.

Old Town of Kernville, now under water

Kernville remained until the early 1950's a pleasant town of quaint houses and tree-shaded streets. Now it sleeps beneath the waters of Lake Isabella, created when two dams were completed in 1953. A new Kernville was built in 1951 on the bank of the Kern River several miles north of the original site. Some of the old houses were moved to the new community.

The old Kernville Cemetery, however, was not inundated by the lake, and may be seen bordering the highway to new Kernville near the site of vanished Quartzburg. A monument that used to stand at old Kernville is now located in front of the cemetery.

Havilah

Havilah (SRL 100), named for the Biblical land "where there is gold" by Asbury Harpending, a man who became involved in a Civil War plot to prey on San Francisco shipping for the benefit of the Confederate cause, was the fourth town opened up in the Kern River country. It produced a high grade of ore, which attracted miners from all over the state. Havilah, eight miles south of Bodfish, was already quite a populous town when Kern County was created, April 2, 1866, and was chosen as the county seat.

Soon after 1879, however, the mines in Kern Canyon became exhausted and the population moved down from the hill regions to the valley, where railroads were already being constructed and agriculture was taking the place of mining. Meanwhile the county seat had been changed from Havilah in the hills to Bakersfield in the valley.

Havilah, where a few adobe walls still stand, has a population of less than a hundred today, while Bakersfield numbers over 50,000. But, although little more than memories, these former cities of the Sierra—Keyesville, Quartzburg, Kernville, and Havilah played a tremendous role in the building of the greater and more enduring cities in the southern part of the state.

Forgotten Camps of the Piute Mountains

High in the Piute Mountains above the Mojave Desert, in a land of singular charm, lies isolated Kelso Valley surrounded by high peaks and primeval forests of pine and fir. This almost forgotten outpost of Kern County's feverish mining activities of the 1860's, which have been replaced today by the more placid small cattle ranches, "constitutes one of the few remaining frontier sections in southern California."

Eight miles north of the center of the valley is the site of Sageland, once a flourishing mining camp, now marked only by a lonely cemetery.

A fair dirt road ascends the mountain from Kelso Valley to the former site of Claraville, at an elevation of 6,000 feet. This beautiful wooded flat can also be reached by three poor roads, which wind up other parts of the mountain. Claraville was once the metropolis of the region, conceding a larger population only to Havilah and Kernville, in the lower mountains to the northwest. In all other matters Claraville had "all the concomitants of the proverbial mining camps." The last dilapidated building marking the site has been removed to the Kern County Museum's Pioneer Village in Bakersfield. It had served as the Claraville court of justice.

Of all the mines in the region, the Bright Star, about six or seven miles north of Claraville, was the richest. It was owned by three brothers, who finally dissipated the vast fortune in gold taken from the mine, causing its collapse. The passing of the Bright Star "marked the beginning of a decline for the whole district. Abandoned by the hordes of miners, Piute Mountain has reverted to wilderness."

Mining in the Mojave

A mining boom was inaugurated at the eastern edge of Kern County with the discovery of gold in 1895 in a group of rounded hills rising out of the Mojave Desert. The mine became known as the Rand, and a town called Randsburg sprang up nearby, to become the center of several camps, including Johannesburg, Red Mountain, and Atolia, the latter two being in San Bernardino County. Tungsten and silver were later discovered in the area, and there is still some mining activity amid the remnants of boom days. The Rand Mine has been renamed the Yellow Aster. There is located in Randsburg the interesting Desert Museum, a branch of the Kern County Museum in Bakersfield. Randsburg is one of the most picturesque old mining towns in California.

On Garlock Road, one mile north of the Red Rock–Randsburg road and ten miles west of Randsburg, a marker indicates the ghost town of Garlock (SRL 671), one-time location of four stamp mills serving the Rand Mining District. The first of these was set up in 1895 by Eugene Garlock near a water hole known as Cow Wells. The post office, established in the following year, took his name. The Randsburg area was supplied by freight wagons hauling from the railroad town of Mojave, and Garlock became a regular stopping place. The town quickly grew to a population of 300 and promised further growth, but the completion of a railroad to the Rand area and the erection of a stamp mill at the Yellow Aster caused Garlock to dwindle in importance and its people gradually moved elsewhere.

Bakersfield

Colonel Thomas Baker and his family came from Visalia, crossed the Kern River at Gordon's Ferry, and, on September 10, 1863, arrived and settled in a swampy, forested area that is now the city of Bakersfield. They moved into a tule-thatched log cabin vacated by an earlier settler and Baker began to reclaim the land. Soon he built an adobe house that became a community center for the incoming population and planted ten acres of his reclamation land to alfalfa. The place that had been known as "Kern Island," for its location between the channels and sloughs of the Kern River, was now being called "Baker's Field."

One of the first visitors the Bakers had received after their arrival was Captain Elisha Stevens of the Murphy-Townsend-Stevens over-

Old Town of Randsburg

land party of 1844, who made his final home in the area and is buried in Bakersfield. He brought the Colonel and his family a welcoming gift of some hogs and chickens from the ranch he had established below the China Grade Bluff. Stevens' homesite (SRL 732) is on 34th Street just east of the Bakersfield Memorial Hospital.

In 1870 Bakersfield had a population of 600 and was fast becoming the most important town in newly created (1866) Kern County. In 1873 it was incorporated as a city, an event that Colonel Baker, who had planned and mapped the townsite, did not live to see. He had died a victim of the typhoid epidemic the previous year. In 1874 Bakersfield displaced the dying gold town of Havilah as county seat. Railroads, agriculture, cattle ranching, oil, and highway transportation have continued the boom until Bakersfield is today one of the major cities of California, with a population in the greater area of over 150,000.

Alexis Godey, explorer with the Frémont expeditions, made his last home in Bakersfield, having acquired about 66 acres there in 1873. He disposed of much of this land but retained a favorite spot of high ground as his home. This site (SRL 690), facing 19th Street, is now occupied partly by Central Park and partly by business and residential property.

The most interesting historical attraction of present-day Bakersfield is the Pioneer Village of the Kern County Museum at 3801 Chester Avenue, three blocks north of Garcés Circle. An outgrowth of the museum, which was established in 1945 as a tax-supported county department, the 12-acre Village is a reconstruction of a typical valley town of the period 1860–1900. Most of the buildings are authentic early-day structures that have been moved to the site from various parts of Kern County to be preserved from inevitable destruction in the name of progress. Among these are a log cabin built in 1868, a one-room school from 1882, an early Bakersfield home built the same year, a firehouse of the 1890's, and the general store (1899) from the town of Woody. A replica of the first county courthouse at Havilah has been built. The ranching, agricultural, railroad, and oil eras of county history are also represented. Next to the museum has been constructed a replica of the famous Beale Clock Tower, which stood in the intersection of 17th Street and Chester Avenue for almost 50 years, until it was razed following the earthquakes of 1952. The original had been given to the city by Truxtun Beale, son of the pioneer General Beale, in memory of his mother. The Pioneer Village is the largest outdoor museum on the Pacific Coast operated and maintained by a branch of government, and it continues to grow. Other parts of California will do well to emulate the example set by Kern County in its preservation of historic values. The museum and Pioneer Village are open to the public daily.

Bakersfield boasts a fine set of modern public buildings housing the city and county departments. These were constructed following the earthquake of August 22, 1952, which wrecked the city hall and courthouse beyond repair. This shock followed one on July 21, which devastated the town of Tehachapi. In front of the Bakersfield city hall, at Truxtun and Chester avenues, stands a statue of Colonel Thomas Baker (*SRL 382*).

The Railroad

Construction had started in the spring of 1870 on the San Joaquin Valley branch of the Central Pacific Railroad, now Southern Pacific, but the tracks did not reach Kern County until 1873. The first station, at the northern boundary, was called Delano for Columbus Delano, then Secretary of the Interior. The railroad bypassed Bakersfield—since its citizens, led by Colonel Baker, had refused to give the customary subsidy—and established a station called Sumner just northeast of the city. (This place, later called Kern, was consolidated with Bakersfield in 1909, and by that time the Santa Fe Railroad had already established itself in Bakersfield.)

The Tehachapi Mountains presented a major engineering obstacle to the continuation of the railroad to Los Angeles County. Construction reached Caliente in April 1875, and here the engineers were faced with the task of raising the railroad 2,734 feet to scale the pass at a height of 4,025 feet in 16 air-line miles. Caliente (*SRL 757*) thus became the terminal for about 16 months while a force of up to 3,000 men, mostly Chinese, labored in the mountains. A station just beyond Caliente was named Bealville (*SRL 741*) for Edward F. Beale, on whose Rancho El Tejón it was located. (An automobile shortcut from Highway 58 to Caliente crosses the railroad at this point.)

The Tehachapis were conquered in 28 miles of track laid on gradual curves and through 18 tunnels. At one point the track is looped over itself in a remarkable manner, an engineering marvel directed by William Hood, who later became chief engineer for the entire Southern Pacific system. A portion of the famous "Tehachapi Loop" (*SRL 508*) may be glimpsed from the Woodford–Tehachapi road at a point about two miles southeast of Woodford (Keene). A monument has been erected at this spot, and with luck one may see the locomotive of a long train at the top of the "loop" and the caboose just entering the tunnel below.

A station called Greenwich was established near the summit of the pass, but this soon developed into a town and stole the name and population of nearby Tehachapi (the place now called "Old Town"). At this time also the name "Tehachapi Pass" was transferred from the pioneer Oak Creek route to the new railroad pass. The railroad was opened through the Tehachapis and across the desert to Mojave on August 8, 1876. Today the trackage between East Bakersfield and Mojave is used jointly by the Southern Pacific and Santa Fe railroads. At the latter town the S.P. goes south and the Santa Fe east. With the coming of the railroad to Kern County, the modern era began and agriculture and livestock raising replaced mining as the principal industry.

The desert town of Mojave, child of the railroad, was the rail terminus for the 20-Mule-Team borax wagons that operated from Death Valley in the years 1884–89. The route, over 165 miles of mountains and desert, ran from the Harmony Borax Works to the railroad loading dock in Mojave. A round trip required 20 days. A monument has been placed in front of the County Building across from the terminus site (*SRL 652*).

Black Gold

The story of oil in Kern County is essential to a complete picture of the modern era. The county today contributes about one-fourth of the oil produced in the entire state. Few realize, however, that oil was being refined in Kern even as the county came into existence in 1866. The Buena Vista Petroleum Company was organized and incorporated in 1864, and soon thereafter a refinery was built at the foot of the Temblor Range eight miles west of the marker that stands at the intersection of Highway 33 and Lokern Road, about seven miles north of McKittrick. The refinery site (*SRL 504*) is quite close to the tree-shaded spot on the Temblor Ranch where for many years an old adobe stood in which the Buena Vista workers are said to have taken their meals. The refinery operated until April 1867, producing 3,000 gallons of refined oil, but work ceased when freight charges were found to be prohibitive.

There were a number of relatively early discoveries in the McKittrick Field. The California Standard Oil Well No. 1 (*SRL 376*), not completed until 1899, has thus been incorrectly designated as the discovery well of that field. The McKittrick area is more famous for the refining of asphalt, the original name of the settlement being Asphalto. About one-half mile south of McKittrick a marker stands near the location of a brea pit (*SRL 498*) of the Pleistocene Period (15,000 to 50,000 years ago), from which the bones of many long-dead animals and birds, trapped in the sticky asphalt, have been recovered. These relics, first brought to the attention of scientists in 1929, may be seen in the Kern County Museum in Bakersfield. The pit has now been filled in.

Although the west side of the county, with its thriving petroleum communities of Maricopa, Taft, and Ford City (the last deriving its name from the preponderance of Model-T's there in

1921), is generally associated with Kern's industry, it was in the Bakersfield area in 1899 that the discovery was made that zoomed the county to prominence as an oil producer. Several miles northeast of the city on Round Mountain Road (not far from the site of Gordon's Ferry but across the Kern River) a marker indicates the discovery well of the Kern River oil field (SRL 290), dug by hand in the summer of 1899. The first commercial well of the area was drilled a few hundred feet away several weeks later, and soon the towns of Oil City, Oil Center, and Oildale came into existence, communicating their prosperity to nearby Bakersfield.

Fellows was a railroad terminal in 1908 but experienced its greatest boom when the Midway Gusher, Well 2-6 (SRL 581), blew in on November 27, 1909, with a production of 2,000 barrels a day. It is located one-fourth mile west of Fellows on Broadway Road.

Although the Midway Gusher started the West Side oil rush, it was eclipsed a few months later when Lakeview Gusher No. 1 (SRL 485), the greatest gusher in the history of the world, blew in on the evening of March 14, 1910, producing an unprecedented 18,000 barrels in the first 24 hours. This Union Oil Company well flowed for 18 months and nine million barrels and presented a major control problem and fire danger, forcing residents of the nearby camp to abandon their homes for a time. At its peak production the output reached 68,000 barrels a day. It is said that the tremendous flow of this gusher brought down the price of oil. Its location is marked one and one-half miles north of Maricopa on Division Road off Highway 33.

The town of Buttonwillow, also on the West Side, antedates the oil boom. It derives its name from a lone buttonwillow tree (SRL 492), still standing and marked one mile north of town on Buttonwillow Avenue, which was a landmark for early-day cowboys in the area and the location of their spring rodeos. It had been an ancient Indian campsite. Henry Miller established headquarters of Miller and Lux at this spot and bestowed the name of the tree on the railroad station and the post office, started in 1895.

Edwards and China Lake

The largest dry lake in the United States is 65-square-mile Muroc Dry Lake, also known by the name of Rodrigues or Rogers, after a silver- and gold-mining company that operated there early in the twentieth century. The name "Muroc," which was also given to a settlement of homesteaders there in 1910, is not an Indian word, but the reversed spelling of the name of Ralph and Clifford Corum, pioneer settlers. The hard lake bed has been much used in the past for sports car racing. Its first use by the military was in 1933 as a bombing and gunnery range. In 1942, shortly after the outbreak of World War II, the north end of the lake was used for testing the Air Force's first jet plane, the P-59. Muroc Air Force Base was established to include the dry lake bed, and since then most of the testing of experimental and production aircraft by the Air

Force has been done here and a number of world speed records have been set. The base was renamed Edwards Air Force Base in 1950, in memory of Glen W. Edwards, who was fatally injured a year and a half earlier in the crash of his test plane. The Muroc post office has also been renamed Edwards. The base has brought prosperity to the railroad towns of Mojave and Rosamond and to the community of Boron, already thriving as producer of half the world's borax.

North of Edwards, but also on the eastern border of the county and also extending into San Bernardino County, is China Lake, site of the United States Naval Ordnance Test Station. The dry lake nearby derives its name from the Chinese who searched Indian Wells Valley for borax in the years following their construction work on the Central Pacific Railroad. The station was established in November 1943 for the development and testing of rockets. Its first headquarters, while the station itself was under construction, were at Inyokern Airport, called Harvey Field by the Navy until its deactivation in 1946–47 in favor of Armitage Field. The N.O.T.S., often pronounced "nots," is the location of the $8 million Michelson Laboratory, named for the first American to receive the Nobel prize for physics. About 1,000 square miles in area and with a population of approximately 12,500, the station has boomed the new town of Ridgecrest, where a post office had been established in 1941, and has brought new life to Inyokern, which had originated as a supply station during the construction of the Owens Valley Aqueduct early in this century.

SOURCES

Albright, George Leslie. "Official Explorations for Pacific Railroads, 1853–1855," University of California Publications in History, Vol. XI (October 1921). University of California Press, Berkeley, 1921.
Bailey, Richard C. Explorations in Kern. Kern County Historical Society, Bakersfield, 1962.
——— Heritage of Kern. Kern County Historical Society, Bakersfield, 1957.
Banning, Captain William, and George Hugh Banning. Six Horses. Century Co., New York, 1930.
Bolton, Herbert Eugene. "In the South San Joaquin Ahead of Garcés," California Historical Society Quarterly, X, No. 3 (September 1931), 211–19.
Bonsal, Steven. Edward Fitzgerald Beale, A Pioneer in the Path of Empire, 1822–1903. Putnam, New York, 1912.
Boyd, William Harland. Land of Havilah. Kern County Historical Society, Bakersfield, 1952.
Cleland, Robert Glass. From Wilderness to Empire. A History of California, ed. Glenn S. Dumke. Knopf, New York, 1959.
Crowe, Earle. Men of El Tejón. The Ward Ritchie Press, Los Angeles, 1957.
Farquhar, Francis P., ed. Up and Down California in 1860–1864. The Journal of William H. Brewer. University of California Press, Berkeley, 1949.
Frémont, J. C. The Exploring Expedition to the Rocky Mountains, Oregon and California. 1st ed., 1847. George H. Derby & Co., Buffalo, 1849.
Gifford, E. W., and W. Egbert Schenck. "Archaeology of the Southern San Joaquin Valley, California," University of California Publications in American Archaeology and Ethnology, XXIII, No. 1 (1926), 1–122.
Gray, A. A. "Camels in California," California Historical Society Quarterly, IX, No. 4 (December 1930), 299–317.
Harpending, Asbury. The Great Diamond Hoax. The James H. Barry Co., San Francisco, 1913.

Johnson, Henry Warren. "Where Did Frémont Cross the Tehachapi Mountains in 1844?" *Annual Publications of the Historical Society of Southern California*, XII, Part IV (1927), 365–73.

Johnston, Philip. "When the Kern Bore Gold," *Touring Topics*, XIX, No. 11 (November 1927), 26–28, 36–37.

——— "Beyond the Gray Mountains," *Touring Topics*, XX, No. 8 (August 1928), 24–26.

Kip, Right Rev. William Ingraham. *The Early Days of My Episcopate.* Thomas Whittaker, New York, 1892.

Kreiser, Ralph F., and Thomas Hunt. *Kern County Panorama.* Kern County Historical Society, Bakersfield, 1961.

Latta, F. F. "San Joaquin Primeval—Archaeology," *Tulare Times*, 1931.

——— "San Joaquin Primeval—Spanish," *Tulare Times*, 1932.

Lesley, Lewis B., ed. *Uncle Sam's Camels.* Harvard University Press, Cambridge, 1929.

Miller, Thelma B. *History of Kern County, California.* 2 vols. S. J. Clarke Publishing Co., Chicago, 1929.

Morgan, Wallace M. *History of Kern County.* Historic Record Company, Los Angeles, 1914.

Peirson, Erma. *Kern's Desert.* Kern County Historical Society, Bakersfield, 1956.

Powers, Stephen. *Tribes of California*, Vol. III of *Contributions to North American Ethnology.* Department of the Interior, Government Printing Office, Washington, D.C., 1877.

Robinson, W. W. *The Story of Kern County.* Title Insurance and Trust Company, Bakersfield, 1961.

Saunders, Charles Francis. *The Southern Sierras of California.* Houghton Mifflin, Boston, 1923.

Williamson, Robert S. "Report of Explorations in California for Railroad Routes," *Explorations and Surveys for a Railroad Route to the Pacific.* Vol. V (1853).

Wynne, Marcia. *Desert Bonanza.* M. W. Samelson, Publisher, Culver City, 1949.

Kings County

KINGS COUNTY (named for the river called El Río de los Santos Reyes, "River of the Holy Kings," in honor of the Three Wise Men, by a Spanish explorer, probably Gabriel Moraga, in 1805) was organized in 1893 from territory set off from Tulare County. Hanford was made the county seat. Two small additions from Fresno County were made in 1909.

Tulare, a Vanished Lake

Tulare Lake was discovered in 1772 by Pedro Fages, who called the vast marshlands of the San Joaquin Valley Los Tulares ("the place of rushes"). Chapman says that as early as 1804 Father Juan Martín of Mission San Miguel crossed the Coast Range into the San Joaquin Valley, penetrating as far as an Indian village on Lake Tulare. Again Chapman says that "in October 1814 a fresh search for a mission site in the tulares was made. The commander of the expedition was a sergeant (Juan Ortega?), whose name does not appear. The account comes from Father Juan Cabot, who was a member of the party. They went from San Miguel to Lake Tulare." Crossing the lake by way of the Alpaugh sand ridge to a place where there was a large Indian village, "they got into some difficulties when they attempted to serve as peacemakers between two warring tribes. In a 'battle' with one of them the Spaniards lost two horses and the Indians one old woman. Peace was restored, and the party went on to the vicinity of Visalia. On their return they crossed Kings River, and made their way to San Miguel by a more northerly route than that by which they had come." The fur-trapping "mountain men" also visited Tulare Lake as early as 1827.

Tulare Lake comprises the natural drainage area in the valley for the Kings and Tule rivers and other watercourses. According to government surveys, the lowest point in the bed of Tulare Lake is 175 feet above sea level. The highest water on record reached 220 feet above sea level. In 1865, when its waters covered the present site of the town of Corcoran, it was 35 miles wide and 60 miles long. Its maximum depth has never been more than 45 feet. Commercial boats for fish and game, as well as many pleasure boats, operated on the lake in times past. Sloughs fed a swamp area much larger than the actual lake. Streams that formerly flowed into the lake have gradually been drained for irrigation purposes. The entire area has been farmed, and grain and cotton have been grown on the land for years. The building of Pine Flat Dam has assured flood and irrigation control.

The Cross Creek Stage Station

A stage station known as the Head of Cross Creek was established at Cross Creek in 1856. The

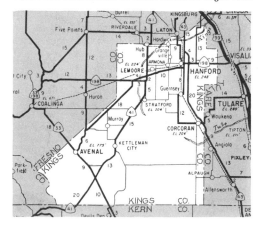

site is four miles northwest of Goshen in Tulare County, and in stagecoach days it was the half-way point between Visalia and the Kings River Station at Whitmore's Ferry. After the coming of the Butterfield stages in 1858, the station was called Cross Creek Station. Similar to the other stations of this section, the Cross Creek post consisted of a small board-and-batten barn and a cabin of the same construction for the use of the hostlers, generally two in number.

During the drought of 1864, Peter Van Valer built a toll bridge over Cross Creek. It is said to have been the only bridge between Visalia and Stockton at the time. Today the site of that early structure, six and one-half miles northeast of Hanford, is marked by a large mulberry tree beside the old stage road. Planted about 1870, the tree stands on a spot that is now on the extreme eastern edge of Kings County but which was in Tulare County until 1893.

Kingston, a Ghost Town

Kingston *(SRL 270)*, a ghost town on the south bank of the Lower Kings River eight and one-half miles northwest of Hanford, was founded in 1856 at Whitmore's Ferry, which had been put into operation in 1854 by L. A. Whitmore. After 1858 the town became a stopping place for the Butterfield stages, which established a regular route through the San Joaquin Valley by way of Kingston and Whitmore's Ferry (the Bliss Ferry in later years) after leaving the old Stockton–Los Angeles Road at a point east of Visalia.

A toll bridge superseded the ferry in 1873, and its piers remain near the riverbank, about a quarter of a mile below the Santa Fe railroad bridge at Laton. On the evening of December 26, 1873, before the tollgates of the bridge were in place, Tiburcio Vásquez and his bandit gang made a bold raid on the little town of Kingston. They bound 39 men and robbed three stores before the alarm was spread, when they fled across the new bridge to horses waiting in a corral on the north side of the river and escaped. But not before two of the bandits and a horse were killed.

All that remains of the town today is the black walnut trees that stood in front of the old stage barn, beside a little-frequented road one-half mile west of the Hanford-Laton highway.

El Adobe de los Robles Rancho

One of the oldest houses still in use in the central San Joaquin Valley is a long low adobe *(SRL 206)* with casement windows of Spanish design, which stands beneath the shade of immense oaks and blue gums on Highway 41 three miles north of Lemoore. It was built in 1856 by Daniel Rhoads, who arrived in California in 1846, having come over the Oregon Trail with the caravan of pioneers from which the Donner party separated to take the fateful Hastings Cut-Off, later becoming snowbound in the High Sierra. In February 1847 Dan Rhoads became a member of the first relief party, which in the face of untold hardships and even death left Johnson's Rancho to go to the rescue of the starving emigrants at Donner

El Adobe de los Robles Rancho

Lake. Much of the material used by Bancroft for his account of the Donner tragedy was drawn from an interview with Daniel Rhoads.

Carefully preserved, and containing relics of pioneer days, the old adobe is opened to interested visitors by the owners, Carroll V. and Leona K. Buckner, who are responsible for its restoration. The roof is of modern construction, and a small portion of the original adobe has been removed and replaced by an addition in character with the old and forming a patio. The old house, originally 122 feet in length, contains a living room, dining room, kitchen, and bedroom —each with a fireplace. There is also a storeroom and the wine room, its windows stoutly barred with willow to protect its contents from bandits. "El Adobe" is maintained strictly as a home and not as a museum, and it is easy to capture the spirit of pioneer days there.

Evidences of the industry and ingenuity of its builder may still be seen about the old dwelling. Remnants of footbridges across the nearby slough indicate where he obtained the clay from which the Indians, under his supervision, fashioned the 18-inch adobe bricks, without the customary straw binding, which went into the construction of the house. The other ranch buildings, all made of lumber which Rhoads laboriously freighted from Stockton—a trip of three weeks—have succumbed to earthquake and the elements, but some of the lumber has been saved. The huge millstone which once was used to grind grain into meal; the mausoleum erected by Rhoads a quarter of a mile from his home, where "Uncle Dan" and "Aunt Mandy" lie at rest; the site of an ancient Indian sweat hole, the "medicine house" of the Yokuts—these are some of the reminders of that busy pioneer California homestead, telling a vivid story of its past.

Signs of thrift and industry are also preserved in the aged trees about the place—stately Australian blue gums and tall cypress trees planted by Rhoads himself, black old olive trees lining the driveway—these still flourish amid the 40 native oaks from which the house derived its name of "El Adobe de los Robles." About a mile east of the adobe grows a lone, three-trunked sycamore tree that could be seen for miles in former days and served as a landmark for traders and cattlemen.

Avenal Ranch

The town of Avenal takes its name from the Spanish word for wild oats. Much older than the town is the Avenal Ranch, now operated by the Crescent Meat Company, 14 miles south of Avenal and six miles off Highway 41 toward the mountains. The ranch headquarters stand on the site of a prehistoric Indian village. The mission padres from San Miguel passed this way in their search for a mission site in the tulares. Here is located an adobe barn, built probably in the early 1850's by the original owners, Welch and Cahill from Missouri. There is also the old ranch house, most of the original lumber of which is redwood brought by oxen from the Santa Cruz Mountains. The second owner of the ranch was Caleb Strong Merrill.

An Adobe Trading Post

On the west shore of Tulare Lake an adobe trading post was established in 1870 by Cox and Clark. As it was the only building on that side of the lake at the time, it served as a landing place for the lake boats and as a trading center for the Indians. The site of the old post is three miles south of Kettleman City on Highway 41. About three miles north of Kettleman City is the site of another adobe known as the Vaca dugout, built in 1863 by Juan Perría and Pablo Vaca. This was a vaquero headquarters, never a boat landing.

Both of these buildings were on the eastern branch of El Camino Viejo, which left the main road at Alamo Solo, a campsite 20 miles to the south of the Cox and Clark adobe. Alamo Mocho ("trimmed cottonwood") was another campsite on this road, located just south of Kettleman Hills within a short distance of Highway 41. Here a large cottonwood stood, a landmark for wayfarers. The story told is that a traveler along the road, needing forage for his cattle, trimmed the cottonwood of all its foliage. The tree has long since disappeared, and the spot where it stood is now part of an extensive cattle ranch.

At the mouth of El Arroyo de las Garzas ("herons") a camp on the western branch of El Camino Viejo was located. It was here that Dave Kettleman first settled. His name is remembered in Kettleman City and Kettleman Hills, as well as Kettleman Oil Fields, which achieved prominence in 1928.

Lemoore and Hanford

Dr. Lavern Lee Moore proposed that a post office should be established at the small agricultural community of La Tache, which was growing up north of Tulare Lake. The Post Office Department acceded to his request in September 1875, but gave the new office a name coined from that of the petitioner. Two years later the center of population moved a short distance to the branch railroad built through the area and across the Kings River to the Huron Plains and the important sheep-shearing center at Poso Chanea trading post. In 1890 Lemoore was considered the largest wool-shipping center in the United States. The older pre-railroad crossing of the river to the west side was at what is still called Murphy's Bridge, one-quarter mile south of Jackson Avenue (former routing of Highway 198). Lemoore is now the site of a large Naval Air Station.

The same branch railroad gave birth in 1877 to Hanford, named for James M. Hanford, a Southern Pacific official, and destined to become the county seat when Kings County was formed. Landmarks here include the old County Jail on Court Street, an architectural wonder, and "China Alley," a short street with picturesque brick buildings and sturdy old iron doors, north of East Seventh Street between North Green and North White streets. The large Chinese population of Hanford was due, in part, to the great number of Chinese employed in railroad construction.

The Mussel Slough Tragedy Oak

The Tragedy Oak (SRL 245), six and one-half miles northwest of Hanford and one-half mile east of the Grangeville-Hardwick highway, marks the site of the old homestead built by Dick Brewer in 1872. It was here on May 11, 1880, that the first shooting in the Mussel Slough Tragedy occurred, an episode during the warfare between the early settlers and the railroad agents. Five settlers and one railroad agent were killed in that encounter in less than one minute, and a second railroad agent was killed an hour later. Frank Norris, in The Octopus, has drawn a somewhat exaggerated picture of this warfare. A monument stands at the roadside, within sight of the oak.

SOURCES

Banning, Captain William, and George Hugh Banning. Six Horses. Century Co., New York, 1930.

Bolton, Herbert Eugene. "In the South San Joaquin Ahead of Garcés," California Historical Society Quarterly, X, No. 3 (September 1931), 211–19.

Bragg, William F. "Old Adobe Home Built Seventy-one Years Ago, Standing at Lemoore." Ms., 1928.

Brown, J. L. The Mussel Slough Tragedy. Privately printed, Hanford, 1958.

——— The Story of Kings County, California. Lederer, Street & Zeus Co., Berkeley, in cooperation with Art Print Shop, Hanford, 1941.

Brown, Robert R. History of Kings County. A. H. Cawston, Hanford, 1940.

Buckner, Leona Kreyenhagen. The Lemoore Story. Lemoore Chamber of Commerce, [1962.]

Chapman, Charles E. A History of California: The Spanish Period. Macmillan, New York, 1923.

Hoyle, M. F. "Crimes and Career of Tiburcio Vásquez," Evening Free Lance, Hollister, 1927.

Latta, F. F. "El Camino Viejo," Tulare Times, February 8 and 10, 1932.

McCubbin, J. C. "Papers on the History of the San Joaquin Valley, California." Collected and edited by Raymund F. Wood. Fresno State College Library, 1960.

Lake County

LAKE COUNTY (so named because of the presence within its confines of a large body of fresh water known as Clear Lake) was set off from Napa County on May 2, 1861, and Lakeport was made the county seat. In 1867 the courthouse and all its records were burned. Another was built in 1870–71, but in the meantime the county seat was temporarily located at Lower Lake.

Indians and Their Legends

Accessibility to a convenient food supply is the prime requisite for the habitation of a primitive people. Throughout Lake County the abundance of fish, fowl, berries, nuts, and game met this need and attracted a large Indian population, possibly the densest in what is now California.

Tule roots grew abundantly along the shores of the lakes, and here the Indians camped in great numbers during the digging season. One lake, located midway between the Blue Lakes and the upper end of Clear Lake, is today known as Tule Lake. Also of economic value were the massive bodies of obsidian found southwest of Mount Konocti and used for making knives and razors, and those found near the east and northeast shores of Lower Lake and used for making spearheads and arrowheads. From the numerous game birds feathers were taken for decoration. George Gibbs, writing in his journal in 1851, says: "At Clear Lake the women generally wear a small round bowl-shaped basket on their heads, and this is frequently interwoven with the red feathers of the woodpecker and edged with the plume tufts of the blue quail."

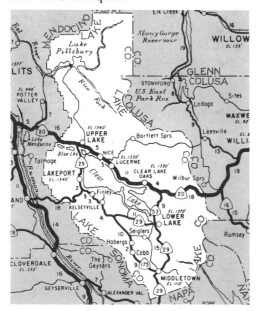

A legend of the area concerns the most notable feature of the landscape, Mount Konocti: Lupiyomi, daughter of the proud and powerful Chief Konocti, was sought in marriage by a rival chieftain, Kahbel. Chief Konocti, refusing consent to the union of his beautiful daughter with this suitor, was challenged to battle. He took up his stand on one side of the Narrows of Clear Lake, while his opponent took a position on the opposite side. The rocks hurled across the water by these warriors during the combat are the immense boulders that now cover the mountainside. The maiden's tears formed a pool—now Little Borax Lake—a lasting memorial of her grief. The lover Kahbel was killed; his blood is seen in the red splashes on the gashed side of Red Hill, rising on the north shore. Chief Konocti also succumbed and, sinking back, formed the rugged mountain that now bears his name. The maiden was so distraught that she threw herself into the lake; her unfailing tears bubble up in Omarocharbe, the Big Soda Spring, gushing out of the waters of Clear Lake at Soda Bay.

Clear Lake

Clear Lake was known to the Indians as Hokhas-ha and Ka-ba-tin, names given to it by two different tribes. It is the largest natural body of fresh water lying wholly in the state and is near the geographical center of the county. Ewing Young and his party of trappers crossed the Coast Range in 1832 by way of this lake on their journey from the Sacramento River to the Pacific Ocean. James Clyman, in his diary for December 1845, wrote that he camped on the outlet of Clear Lake and feasted on bear ribs and liver. Edwin Bryant, a traveler in California in 1846–47, wrote: "A lake not laid down in any map and known as the Laguna among the Californians, is situated about sixty miles north of the Bay of San Francisco. It is between forty and sixty miles in length. The valleys in its vicinity are highly fertile and romantically beautiful. In the vicinity of this lake there is a mountain of pure sulphur. There are also soda springs and a great variety of the mineral waters and minerals."

Lieutenant Joseph Warren Revere, in command of the northern district for some months after the raising of the United States flag at Sonoma, made a tour to Clear Lake and wrote his experiences for publication. "Few white men have visited this magnificent Laguna." About sunset one evening, he and his men arrived at the narrowest part of Clear Lake, "opposite a pretty islet" upon which was a native village. The Indians, at first fearful because of the many raids made upon them in search of servants, were finally persuaded to ferry the travelers across on tule balsas. The island village, protected by this natural moat, had between two and three hundred inhabitants.

Clear Lake is actually now 19.5 miles long. It is shaped like a double-tailed polliwog. The fat body part is Clear Lake proper. The two tails are called East Lake and Lower Lake, and are joined to the body by the Narrows. According to Mauldin, "Reclamation in the 1920's ended Upper Lake as a body of water, although it occasionally rebels and returns to its original status when the rains are generous. But it still yields such rich crops that these floods are forgiven. Upper Lake is now a series of canals and a wide slough formed by Scotts Creek."

Mount Konocti, formerly sometimes called "Uncle Sam Mountain," rises in solitary fashion to the southwest almost 3,000 feet above the level of the water, a majestic guardian of the scene. Settlement near the summit of this mountain was attempted in the 1870's by O. S. Morford, who built the first wagon road and completed it in 1878 with the intention of establishing a public summer resort far up on the mountainside. On May 1, 1878, Morford, with two companions, ascended to the pinnacle and there unfurled the Stars and Stripes. His plans for a summer resort were never carried out. The first permanent settlers near the summit were the Euvelle Howard family early in the twentieth century. Orchards now grace the slopes of the mountain, but the shores of the lake are dotted with summer settlements, and at Lakeport and other locations annual water carnivals are held.

Kelseyville

General Mariano G. Vallejo founded and was placed in command of Sonoma in 1835. In 1836 an expedition led by his brother Salvador and Ramón Carrillo was made into the Clear Lake country, the first military expedition to enter that region. Salvador Vallejo and his brother Antonio, as early as 1839, applied for a grant of land covering what are now known as the Big, Scotts, Upper Lake, and Bachelor valleys. For several years the Vallejo cattle were herded over its fertile ranges, where they multiplied and became exceedingly wild. A log cabin and corral were built in Big Valley near the present site of Kelseyville, with a mayordomo and ten vaqueros to look after the ranch.

In 1847, Vallejo drove some of his cattle out of the valley and sold the remainder to four men, Charles Stone, a man named Shirland, and two Kelsey brothers, Andrew and Benjamin, who had arrived in California with the Bidwell-Bartleson party in 1841. Stone and Andrew Kelsey took possession of the ranch and employed Indians to erect an adobe house for them west across Kelsey Creek from where Kelseyville now stands. Apparently Kelsey earned their ill will, for he and Stone were killed by the Indians in the fall of 1849.

In January 1850 an expedition under the command of Lieutenant Davidson came to punish the offenders, but found that the Indians had taken refuge on various islands in Clear Lake and could not be reached. In May Captain Nathaniel Lyon was sent from Benicia for the same purpose. He brought with him two whaleboats on the running gears of wagons and two mountain howitzers. The only Indians they found were gathered on an island in Upper Lake. By a strategic use of the boats, cannon, and bayonets, the soldiers practically annihilated the group. About a hundred Indians were killed, none of whom, in all probability, had taken any part in the Stone and Kelsey incident. Since that time the place has been called "Bloody Island" (SRL 427), although land reclamation projects have eliminated its water boundaries. There are differing versions of this massacre. A monument with bronze plaque marks the site, about one and one-half miles southeast of the town of Upper Lake. There is also a tablet at the base of the hill that was formerly an island.

The remains of Stone and Andy Kelsey were moved in May 1950 to a monument near the site of their adobe home (SRL 426), west of Kelseyville near the Kelsey Creek bridge. The adobe stood on the bluff one hundred yards west of the monument.

The graves of John Kelsey (Kelsay), a cousin of Ben and Andy, and his wife, are one mile northwest of the monument, in the intersection of Merritt Road and Renfro Drive. This location was originally the corner of a field. The couple were buried there because of the wife's wish to be close to her son's grave, which was in a cemetery (a short distance north on Renfro) which had been closed by law against further burials. The later building of roads caused the graves of John and his wife to be in the center of a crossroads.

The town of Kelseyville began in 1857 with Denham's store and blacksmith shop. The oldest business building presently standing is an ivy-covered brick tavern, built in the 1870's, on the main street. Kelseyville is now a flourishing place with a Union High School and is the center of the pear industry of the county.

A Lost Treaty

To meet the problem of the Indian, a commission to negotiate treaties was appointed by President Millard Fillmore shortly after the admission of the State of California into the Union.

Commissioner Redick McKee, representing the United States government, and the chiefs and headmen of eight local Indian tribes signed a Treaty of Peace and Friendship on August 20, 1851, at Camp Lu-Pi-Yu-Mi on the south shore of Clear Lake. This treaty consisted of eight articles setting forth details of the promises on both sides, and a careful description of the lands to be given, in perpetuity, to these tribes, as well as certain benefits to be derived by them in recompense for their renunciation, as set forth in Article III of the treaty: "The said tribes, or bands, hereby jointly and severally relinquish, cede, and forever quitclaim to the United States all their right, title, claim, or interest of any kind, which they, or either of them, hold to the lands or soil in California." At this council a gift was made to the assembled Indians of "ten head of beef cattle, three sacks of bread, and sundry clothing."

This treaty, along with 17 others, was sent to the Senate by President Fillmore on June 1, 1852, for constitutional action. Never ratified, it is now referred to as one of the "Eighteen Lost Treaties." Attempts have been made to secure compensation for the Indians of California from the United States in lieu of the values granted them in the treaties, and some reimbursement has been given.

Mexican Grants

Three grants of land were made by the Mexican government within the territory now included in Lake County.

Rancho Lupyomi, about which there was much litigation, was originally granted to Salvador and Juan Antonio Vallejo by Governor Micheltorena on September 5, 1844. The map accompanying this grant showed the territory of Laguna de Lu-Pi-Yo-Mi as extending 16 leagues and embracing Upper Lake, Bachelor, Scotts and Big valleys. In 1854 settlers began to arrive, and by 1861 many families had located on the land, although their titles to it could not be made valid until certain claims were decided. After many delays, Judge Ogden Hoffman rendered a decision that gave satisfaction, and the potential owners met for a "jollification" at Lakeport on October 6, 1866. Soon after this, the land was surveyed and each man secured his home. Kelseyville is on a part of this grant.

Rancho Callayomi, consisting of three leagues of land in Loconoma Valley, was given to Robert T. Ridley on June 17, 1844, by Governor Micheltorena. Ridley, an English sailor, became captain of the Port of San Francisco in 1846, a position that he held but a short time. He had been naturalized as a Mexican citizen in 1844 and married to Presentación Briones. Within a few years, in 1852, the claim of Colonel A. A. Ritchie and Paul S. Forbes was confirmed to this land, and a patent was issued to them in 1863. This grant was divided in 1871 and disposed of to actual settlers.

Rancho Guenoc, containing six leagues in Coyote Valley, was ceded by Governor Pío Pico to George Rock (Roch) in 1845. Coyote Valley extends for several miles along the banks of Putah Creek. According to Bancroft, George Rock came into the valley as early as 1837. For a time he was agent there for Jacob P. Leese, who kept cattle both there and in Loconoma Valley. Rock

Stone House, Rancho Guenoc

lived in a cabin on the north side of the valley before 1850. The stone house (SRL 450) now standing on the site of Rock's cabin was originally built in 1853–54 by Captain R. Steele and Robert Sterling, the wife of the latter being the first white woman in the valley. Colonel Ritchie and his partner, Paul S. Forbes, who had acquired Rancho Callayomi, also received the United States patent for the Guenoc grant in 1865. The stone house was torn down and rebuilt of the same stone about 1894 by Charles M. Young. It stands on private property, on the Frank Hartmann Ranch about six miles north of Middletown at the lower of two junctions that Spruce Grove Road makes with the Middletown–Lower Lake highway.

A small ephemeral settlement, called Guenoc, was situated on the south bank of Putah Creek on the road between Middletown and Lower Lake, in 1866; but when Middletown with its superior central position with respect to roads sprang up, all activity was transferred to the new site.

Mineral Springs

A number of medicinal springs are found in Lake County. The Harbin Springs, four miles from Middletown, were visited by A. A. Ritchie in 1852, but were known to the Indians long before that time. They were already famous when the water was examined by Dr. Winslow Anderson in 1889, and a fashionable resort grew up about them as the population of the state increased. They have been well maintained to the present time.

Seigler Springs are in Seigler Valley at the foot of Seigler Mountain. Crude bathing pools, in which the temperature of the water could be regulated, were in use by the aborigines before the place was settled by Seigler. Among the names of prominent people connected with the development of these springs are Dr. J. T. Boone, in 1868, and Alvinza Hayward and W. Cole of San Francisco, in 1870. It has long been a well-kept place with attractive buildings.

Anderson Springs, at the head of Loconoma Valley, were also notable in the early days. They were opened to the public in 1874 by Dr. Anderson and L. S. Patriquin.

Bartlett Springs, at an elevation of 2,100 feet, are renowned for the curative properties of their water. They were found in 1868 by Greene Bartlett in the Middle Fork of Cache Creek. Suffering from a severe attack of rheumatism contracted while herding sheep in Berryessa Valley, he revisited them in 1870 and found relief from his ailment by drinking the water. To this place he later led his friends, and a health resort grew up. Bartlett homesteaded the land about the springs, built a log house, and, in association with others, erected a hotel and cottages. The old log cabin was restored in later years and used as a museum in which relics of pioneer days were stored. This resort was kept up until a fire in September 1934 practically destroyed the hotels and cottages. The log cabin also was burned, but a trunk formerly owned by Greene Bartlett was rescued from the flames.

Other springs that have been well known for

many years are Witter (no longer in existence) and Saratoga, both near Blue Lakes; Highland, now the location of a reservoir, six miles west of Kelseyville; and Adams, in the mountains between Kelseyville and Middletown.

Old Mills

The many streams of Lake County afforded power for two industries of great importance in a pioneer community: the grinding of grain for food, and, in a few instances, the sawing of lumber for houses. Thomas Boyd built the first mill in the county on the south shore of Boggs Lake. It was a steam gristmill and sawmill combined and was put in operation in 1858. In 1866, H. C. Boggs purchased the mill, which from this date was known as the Boggs Mill, although its location was changed several times. A few remnants mark its last location, three miles north of Harbin Springs.

Another mill, originally known as Elliott's Mill, was erected in Upper Lake Township in 1855 by William B. Elliott, who had come overland from North Carolina, arriving in California in 1845 with his wife and children. He and his sons became successful hunters of the grizzly bears then so prevalent in the mountain regions. His mill was in operation until 1867. In time it became known by the odd cognomen of "Whittle-Busy," because, since it ground very slowly, its patrons whiled away the time by whittling.

The old Brown Mill (earlier called the Allison Mill) stood on Kelsey Creek about three miles above Kelseyville. Joel Stoddard's Mill, about three and one-half miles west of Middletown, was known in the 1880's as "one of the neatest and best mills in Lake County." A later mill at the same location was operated by the McKinley family until 1935. The site, on the highway to Lakeport, is marked by an old millstone and a plaque placed by the Native Daughters of the Golden West. The Upper Lake Planing and Grist Mill was erected in 1875 with an 8½-horsepower steam engine. The proprietor at that time was "prepared for planing, grinding grain, manufacturing doors, sash, and furniture." Lower Lake Flouring-Mill was built in 1869 by J. M. Evarts and William Davy on the west bank of Seigler Creek. It was run by steam and had a reputation in the 1880's for making good flour.

Mines

Although a great variety of minerals have been discovered in the county, the quantities usually have been too small for economic development. Mercury, sulfur, and borax have been mined. The Great Western, a cinnabar (mercury) deposit, first produced in 1873. It is four miles south of Middletown.

The old Sulphur Bank Mine *(SRL 428)* grew out of the works of the California Borax Company. This was the location of the mountain of sulfur referred to in the journal of Edwin Bryant. It was 40 feet high and some 300 feet long, and was completely removed by mining in 1865–69, having produced two million pounds of sulfur. The first mercury was mined here in 1873, and the place became a steady and important

St. Anthony's Church, Sulphur Bank

producer. It has been idle since World War II. The Sulphur Bank Mine is on the eastern end of East Lake south and across the lake from the town of Clearlake Oaks. A monument of native obsidian stands on the highway about one and one-half miles from the town at the junction of the road leading to the mine. In the hills, about one mile east of the monument and on the same side of the highway, stands the Saint Anthony (or Sulphur Bank) Church, which was erected in 1909 as a place of worship for workers in the mine. For many years previous to that time, the Catholic families of the vicinity had been in the habit of holding Mass in private dwellings. When it was decided to construct a church building, bricks, probably well impregnated with mercury, were obtained from the old furnaces on the Sulphur Bank property. The Catholics of the district donated their services in transporting the brick and laying the walls, assisted by local Indians. Regular services are conducted in this church of Saint Anthony, although the realignment of the highway has left it on a small side road.

There are several other old mercury mines in the county, including the Abbott, the Mirabel, and the Helen.

The first source of borax in Alta California was Big Borax Lake, more commonly called simply Borax Lake, discovery of the mineral having been made in 1856 by Dr. John A. Veatch. The California Borax Company began operation there in 1864. In 1868 all work was transferred to Little Borax Lake, where Dr. Veatch had found borax eight years earlier. Operations were carried on successfully until 1873.

Lower Lake

The first house in the town of Lower Lake, two miles southeast of the body of water for which it is named, was built by E. Mitchell in 1858, although there had been settlers in the area as early as 1848. The town became important for its location on crossroads and was the center of business activity for the surrounding agricultural interests, mountain resorts, and mercury mines. It was a station on the stage line running from Calistoga in later years and was the county seat for two years. Still standing in the town is a tiny stone jail *(SRL 429)* dating from the late 1870's.

Upper Lake

Dr. Josiah Gregg, scientist, explorer, and author of *The Commerce of the Prairies,* died near Upper Lake on February 25, 1850, of starvation and exposure. He was returning from an exploring trip to Humboldt Bay with a few of his men when he fell from his horse because of weakness. He was buried, "according to the custom of the prairies," in a shallow grave with a blanket for his coffin, and a pile of stones was placed over his body to protect it from prowling animals.

Two business establishments, one above and one below the town of Upper Lake, were made before 1865, when the present site near the junction of Clover, Middle, and Scotts creeks was settled. Benjamin Dewell, one of the makers of the first Bear Flag, settled on the west side of Clover Creek in 1854, as did his father-in-law, William B. Elliott, in whose company young Dewell had made the overland trip to California. Benjamin Dewell's house, occupied by his descendants, stood for many years on the outskirts of the present thriving town. Now it has been demolished.

Lakeport

Lakeport, on the western shore of Clear Lake, was first named Forbestown. William Forbes owned 160 acres here before the formation of the county in 1861 and deeded 40 acres as a site for the county seat in the vicinity of his previously erected house and blacksmith shop. Forbes Street now commemorates his name. The first place of business in the county was a short distance south of Lakeport, at Stony Point, where Dr. E. D. Boynton built a store and put in a stock of goods in 1856.

Clear Lake College opened its doors in Lakeport on the first Thursday in September 1876 in a two-story frame building still standing at 102 Clear Lake Avenue (Twelfth Street), at the corner of Main Street. Seven students matriculated on the opening day. The upholding of the classics in a frontier community met with many difficulties; nevertheless, by 1881, at the end of the fifth year, the entire classical course had been "successfully mastered by one of its students," who was granted the degree of Bachelor of Arts in June. At the same time two honorary degrees of Master of Arts and one honorary degree of Doctor of Laws were conferred. The president of the institution, Rev. John A. Kelley, said at that time:

"It proves itself to be one of the permanent institutions of Lake County, and the only college in the state that places the advantages of a broad and liberal education within easy reach of all parties who may aspire to the rank of learned men." After having been in existence about 20 years, the college was forced to close its doors because it was unable to compete with the State University. Its fate was similar to that of most of the private and local colleges in California.

Lakeport Academy was founded in 1884 by Professor John Overholser in a discarded grammar school building on Forbes Street between Third and Fourth. This building was destroyed after being vacated by the academy, and a mortuary now occupies the site. A small plaque has been placed at the corner of Forbes and Fourth. Moving to its own new quarters in the northwest part of the town, the academy continued until the formation of the Clear Lake Union High School District in 1901, when the place was rented by the high school. With the erection of a new high school building, the academy building was vacated and was later purchased by H. S. Spillers, who made alterations that transformed it into a hospital. The building, which stood on a knoll in the 1800 block of Hartley Street, was burned in 1928.

The ivy-covered courthouse, completed in the fall of 1871, is still in use, and adjacent to it is the Lake County Museum. A small marker has been placed on the grounds of the grammar school on Main Street to commemorate the first Lakeport boat landing in 1873. Lakeport is the nerve center of a county that now contains, in addition to countless resorts and vacation places, several modern pear-packing plants, one walnut-packing plant, an up-to-date cannery, and four airfields.

Middletown

Middletown, near the center of the Callayomi land grant and midway between Lower Lake and Calistoga (Napa County) at the junction of roads leading to several important mineral springs, was first settled in 1868. The oldest building now standing in the town was the O. Armstrong house in 1870. It is on the left side of a bypassed stretch of road between the high school and the old bridge on the way to Lower Lake, and is still occupied by members of the Armstrong family. The site of the old Lake County House, built in 1875, is now occupied by the Herrick Hotel. The present hotel incorporates some of the brick walls of the earlier building, which was destroyed by fire in 1918. A small house built on this same site by J. H. Berry in 1870 was the first hotel in Middletown.

The last years of a distinguished European scholar, Dr. James Blake, were spent in Middletown, where he died and was buried in 1893. Native of England, writer of medical books, California pioneer of 1849, one-time president of the California Academy of Sciences, Dr. Blake retired in 1876 to Lake County because of impaired health. He took up his residence near a large spring, where he built a cottage east of Mount

St. Helena and just south of the county line in Napa County, about two miles east of the present highway connecting Middletown and Calistoga. Feeling his health vastly improved here, he erected simple buildings where others might be helped, and where he carried on his medical research until he finally moved to Middletown. The main building used for this sanatorium is still in existence, but the cottage that he occupied was destroyed by fire about 1943. The sanatorium stands within the grounds of the private estate of the Livermore family. Dr. Blake's house in Middletown also remains, at the southeast corner of Barnes and Young streets.

At the edge of Middletown on the highway to Calistoga a stone monument with bronze plaque commemorates the old toll road over Mount St. Helena (*SRL 467*), built in the 1860's by John Lawley, and the earlier and steeper "bull trail" which it replaced. The Lawley road passed out of existence as a toll road in 1924.

The Cache Creek Dam

In 1866 a dam was constructed across Cache Creek near the outlet of Clear Lake by the Clear Lake Water Company. The level of the water in the lake was raised to such an extent that the rich farmland, the established orchards, and the houses within a large radius were flooded. Reasonable appeals to the Water Company had been ignored and no compensation for damage was allowed. On Sunday morning, November 15, 1868, after being led in prayer by the Baptist minister, Rev. B. Ogle, a crowd began the demolition of the dam. The work was completed the following Tuesday morning. Litigation ensued, but the dam was never rebuilt on this spot. Another dam on Cache Creek, below the town of Lower Lake, was completed in 1914 and is in use at the present time.

Langtry Farm

Lily Langtry, English actress known as the "Jersey Lily," became joint owner of a property in the southern part of the county. "Freddy" Gebhard, wealthy clubman of New York, was the co-partner in the purchase of this 7,500-acre portion of the old Guenoc grant. At the time of the purchase, a winery was in operation and a few dwellings were on the premises.

Extensive improvements were made, and large sums were invested in fine race horses by the new owners. "Doc" Abbey, former manager of the Santa Anita ranch of "Lucky" Baldwin, was put

in charge, and a one-mile race track was constructed. Mrs. Langtry visited the place only once, for about two weeks in May 1888. For some years all went well; then in 1897 the partnership was dissolved. Barns, race track, and general operations were concentrated on the Gebhard land, and a stout fence was built to define the two holdings.

This place, known to stock raisers of that time as the home of the Guenoc Stud, is seven miles east of Middletown at the point where the road to Pope Valley makes a sharp turn to the south. The Langtry house still stands on the present ranch and is occupied.

SOURCES

Anderson, Winslow. *Mineral Springs and Health Resorts of California.* Bancroft Co., San Francisco, 1892.
Bancroft, Hubert Howe. "California," of the series *History of the Pacific States of North America.* Vols. 18–24. History Co., San Francisco, 1884–90.
Benson, William Ralganal. "Narrative of the Stone and Kelsey Massacre," *California Historical Society Quarterly*, XI, No. 3 (September 1932), 266–73.
Bryant, Edwin. *What I Saw in California, Being a Journal of a Tour in the Years 1846–47.* D. Appleton Co., New York, 1849.
Carpenter, Aurelius, and Percy H. Millberry. *History of Mendocino and Lake Counties.* Historical Record Co., Los Angeles, 1914.
Clyman, James. "Diaries." Ms. in Huntington Library, San Marino.
Corrected Report of Spanish and Mexican Grants in California. Complete to February 25, 1886. Prepared by Surveyor General, State of California. Supplement to official *Report of 1883–84.* Sacramento, 1886.
"The End of the Langtry Farm," *San Francisco Call*, August 28, 1898.
Gibbs, George. "Journal of the Expedition of Col. Redick McKee, U.S. Indian Agent, through Northwestern California. Performed in the summer and fall of 1851," in Henry R. Schoolcraft, *History of the Indian Tribes of the United States*, Vol. III. Lippincott, Grambo & Co., Philadelphia, 1853.
Goss, Helen Rocca. *The Life and Death of a Quicksilver Mine* (Great Western). Historical Society of Southern California, Los Angeles, 1958.
Harris, Henry. *California's Medical Story.* J. W. Stacey, San Francisco, 1932.
History of Napa and Lake Counties, California. Slocum, Bowen & Co., San Francisco, 1881.
History of Northern California. Illustrated. Lewis Publishing Co., Chicago, 1891.
Indian Tribes of California . . . , Hearings. U.S. Cong., H.R., March 23, 1920.
"Langtry Story," *New York Times*, February 13, 1929.
Mauldin, Henry K. *Your Lakes, Valleys & Mountains: History of Lake County.* East Wind Printers, San Francisco, 1960.
Menefee, C. A. *Historical and Descriptive Sketch Book of Napa, Sonoma, Lake, and Mendocino.* Reporter Publishing House, Napa City, 1873.
Quayle, Mrs. James A. Manuscript notes.
"Visit to Lake County," *San Francisco Post*, July 1877.

Lassen County

LASSEN COUNTY, named for the pioneer Peter Lassen, was organized in 1864 from parts of Plumas and Shasta counties. Susanville has been the county seat from the beginning. The eastern portion of the Lassen Volcanic National Park is in Lassen County, but the greater part of the park, as well as Lassen Peak, is in Shasta County.

Nobles' Pass

Nobles' Road, one of the so-called northern cutoffs used by emigrants in the early 1850's, passed by the site of the present town of Susanville in Lassen County. In 1851 William H. Nobles, member of a prospecting party, saw the value of the route over the pass followed by his party and enlisted the interest of the businessmen of Shasta, then an important mining town on this trail. In 1852 he succeeded in raising $2,000 for surveying a wagon road over the new route, with its terminus at Shasta. Both Nobles' Pass (about ten miles northwest of Lassen Peak) and Nobles' Road were named in honor of the one man whose foresight and energy made this route possible.

The trail through Nobles' Pass started from the Humboldt River and followed the Applegate-Lassen Trail for about 60 miles; then the newer trail turned southwest across the Smoke Creek Desert to Honey Lake Valley, three miles north of Honey Lake; passing the spot where the pres-

ent town of Susanville stands, it continued west up the canyon of the Susan River until it reached Lassen's Trail, which it followed in a northwesterly direction as far as Poison Lake. At this point Lassen's Trail continued north, skirting the western end of Dixie Valley and following up the Pit River to Big Valley, where the present town of Bieber is located. Turning west at Poison Lake, Nobles' Road reached Butte Creek, where it swerved to the south, following along the west side of the creek as far as Butte Lake. There it entered Shasta County, passing to the north of Lassen Peak and proceeding over Nobles' Pass, where it continued westward as far as the city of Shasta.

At first, emigrants were persuaded with difficulty to use the new road, but, within a year or two, improvements were made and much of the travel for the northern end of the Sacramento Valley then passed over it. Nobles' Road became more important than the more widely known but more dangerous Lassen's Trail.

Early in the summer of 1854, while Isaac Roop and his men were yet the sole occupants of Honey Lake Valley, Lieutenant E. G. Beckwith, in the interest of a transcontinental railroad, surveyed the road over Nobles' Pass, one of the various Sierran passes that he explored between Goose Lake and Beckwourth's Pass.

North of Honey Lake, on Highway 395 near Viewland, a marker has been erected to designate the route of the Nobles Trail (SRL 677). Another was placed in the Susanville city park (SRL 675), once a meadow and a welcome stopping place for emigrants along this route. The Lassen Trail has been marked at the Clara Bieber Memorial Park in Bieber (SRL 763) and at a point (SRL 678) on Highway 36, two and one-half miles west of Westwood.

Lassen's Monument

About six miles south of Susanville via Richmond and Wingfield roads, at the upper end of Elysian Valley, a monument was erected by the Masons on June 24, 1862, over the grave of Peter Lassen (SRL 565). An inscription on the tablet reads: "In memory of Peter Lassen, the pioneer, who was killed by Indians, April 26, 1859. Aged 66 years." It was in this vicinity that Lassen mined in the summer and fall of 1855. His first cabin was located "on the south side of Lassen Creek, about one-third of a mile west of where the mountain road from Susanville to Janesville crosses that stream." This cabin was burned in 1896.

A native of Denmark, Peter Lassen came to America at 29 years of age. In 1839 he journeyed overland to Oregon, and from there he went

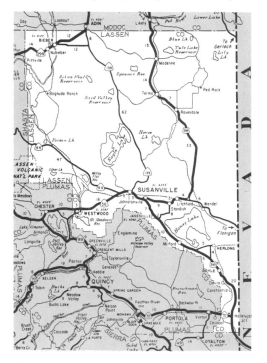

down the coast by boat to Fort Ross in 1840. One of the first white settlers in the upper Sacramento Valley, Peter Lassen settled in 1844 on what came to be known as the Lassen Ranch. In 1848 he brought a party of emigrants to California from Missouri, over the Lassen Trail, and attempted to found Benton City on his ranch in Tehama County. He was the first settler in Indian Valley, Plumas County, coming there in 1851, but in 1855 he located in Lassen County, where he played an influential part in the early history of the area.

Susanville

Susanville was named after the only daughter of Isaac Roop, the first white settler in Honey Lake Valley and the founder of Lassen County as well as of the county seat, Susanville. Roop came to Honey Lake from Shasta in 1853, and returned in 1854 to build a store on the Nobles Emigrant Trail, which had been recently opened up through that region. Early in 1855 Peter Lassen discovered gold in Honey Lake Valley, and news of the find brought in a number of men from the Feather River mining region. Several land claims were staked out there at that time.

Honey Lake Valley was so isolated during the pioneer period that a local government was set up on the initiative of the people themselves. About 20 signers, all original settlers in Honey Lake Valley, met at the Roop cabin on April 26, 1856, and formed the "Territory of Nataqua," with Roop as secretary and recorder and Lassen as surveyor. With the eastern boundary of California not definitely determined, the organizers of the new territory included much of the present state of Nevada in "Nataqua." However, "they made a wild shot at their location. They didn't even live in the territory they had created. It was nearly thirty-five miles from their place of meeting to the western line of Nataqua, and the settlers furthest down the lake were almost twenty miles west of it." Moreover, the citizens of the Carson, Eagle, and Washoe valleys were not even notified that they were included within the boundaries of the new political division. Actually, "Nataqua" existed for a short time only, and then merely in the minds of a few men.

Finally, in 1857, the citizens of the would-be "Nataqua" decided to cast their lot with those who were petitioning Congress for separation from Utah Territory with its Mormon dominance. While awaiting Congressional action on their petition for the formation of a new territory, the settlers met again in 1858 to set up a local government. As a result, a constitutional convention was held at Genoa, Nevada, on July 18, 1859, and in the following September Isaac Roop was chosen provisional governor of the proposed territory.

Roop's Fort, Susanville

On March 2, 1861, Congress passed the bill creating the Nevada Territory, which, only with California's consent, was to include the eastern slope of the Sierra Nevada from Inyo to Modoc counties. In creating its first counties the same year, however, the territory extended Lake County to include Honey Lake Valley. In 1862 both Plumas County and Lake County held elections in the valley. The Sagebrush or Boundary Line War in February 1863, waged by 40 or 50 of the original settlers of Honey Lake Valley against Plumas County officers, resulted from the attempt of the Plumas County sheriff to uphold the authority of his county in the valley. The difficulty was finally settled by the creation of Lassen County on April 1, 1864.

Isaac Roop's old log cabin (SRL 76), called Fort Defiance because it was used as a fort during the Sagebrush War, still stands on the east side of Weatherlow Street in the Susanville city park. Next to it is the William H. Pratt Memorial Museum.

Another Lassen County fort was located three-fourths of a mile from Janesville. Fort Janesville (SRL 758), as it was called, was built by the people of Honey Lake Valley in preparation for an Indian attack that never materialized.

SOURCES

Albright, George Leslie, "Official Explorations for Pacific Railroads," *University of California Publications in History*, II. University of California Press, Berkeley, 1921.
Beckwith, Lieutenant E. G. His report in *Pacific Railroad Reports*, Vol. II. Beverly Tucker, printer, Washington, D.C., 1855.
Dornin, May. "The Emigrant Trails into California." Master's thesis in history, University of California, Berkeley, 1921.
Fairfield, Asa Merrill. *Fairfield's History of Lassen County, California*. H. S. Crocker, San Francisco, 1916.
The Illustrated History of Plumas, Lassen and Sierra Counties. Fariss & Smith, San Francisco, 1882.
Swartzlow, Ruby Johnson. *Lassen, His Life and Legacy*. Loomis Museum Association, Mineral, 1964.

Los Angeles County

LOS ANGELES COUNTY (Los Angeles is Spanish for "the angels") was one of the original 27 counties. Its boundaries have been changed many times. At one period the county covered an area of 31,000 square miles. The city of Los Angeles has been the county seat from the beginning, and its archives contain many pre-state records in Spanish.

The Cabrillo Memorial

The Cabrillo Memorial in honor of Juan Rodríguez Cabrillo, discoverer of California, was placed in Exposition Park, Los Angeles, September 19, 1915, by the Cabrillo Chapter, D.A.R. Cabrillo first sighted the coast of Alta California at San Diego on September 28, 1542.

A replica of this tablet was placed at Avalon, Catalina Island. Catalina had been named San Salvador by Cabrillo on October 7, 1542, but Sebastián Vizcaíno, who sighted it on November 20, 1603, St. Catherine's Day, named it Santa Catalina. Vizcaíno anchored there on November 27, en route north in search of suitable ports for the protection of Spain's Manila galleon.

Portolá's Trail

In 1769, Gaspar de Portolá left San Diego to find a trail up the coast to the port of Monterey, where the second mission was to be established. Traveling through what are now San Diego and Orange counties, he entered Los Angeles County on July 30, making camp at or just east of present La Puente. The following day the party moved west and made camp in an open space in the valley north of the Whittier Narrows, not far from where Mission San Gabriel was later established.

On August 2 the party reached a spot on the Los Angeles River occupied by the ancient Indian village of Yang-na, where central Los Angeles stands today. Camp was probably made near what is now North Spring Street, at the juncture of the Los Angeles River and North Broadway. This site (SRL 655) was marked in 1930 by a bronze tablet mounted on a granite boulder placed in Elysian Park by the Daughters of the American Colonists. The plaque was stolen four years later, but has now been replaced by an official state marker. The hill, around which the Los Angeles River turns to the south at the point where it is bridged by North Broadway, is mentioned in the journal written by Lieutenant Miguel Costansó of Portolá's expedition. Under the same date, Wednesday, August 2, 1769, the diary of Father Crespí tells how he named the campsite and the village across the river Nuestra Señora la Reina de los Angeles de la Porciúncula (Our Lady, the Queen of the Angels, of the Portiuncula), in

honor of the Franciscan feast of the day. To this incident, the city of Los Angeles owes its name.

Leaving their camp and crossing to the west side of the river, Portolá and his party bypassed the La Brea tarpits, which were discovered by their scouts, and camped the night of August 3 at springs surrounded by sycamores. The approximate site (SRL 665) has been marked on La Cienega Boulevard, between Olympic Boulevard and Gregory Way, in Beverly Hills. The next day they moved on to two hillside springs where friendly Indians made them welcome. This campsite was apparently on or near the grounds of the Veterans Administration Center in West Los Angeles. From there the scouts went as far as the beach west of Santa Monica. On the campus of the University High School at 11800 Texas Avenue in West Los Angeles are springs that some believe are the ones at which Portolá camped on August 4. Many Indian artifacts have been uncovered on the grounds. The springs are known as "Serra Springs" (SRL 522) because of a tradition that Father Serra said Mass in the locality in 1770.

On August 5 the Portolá party followed the route of the San Diego Freeway up Sepúlveda Canyon, and after pausing to view the San Fernando Valley from the mountaintop, they descended to camp at the warm springs now included in Los Encinos State Historical Monument at Encino. (The large Indian village here was revisited by Portolá's party on January 15 and April 27, 1770, when they established the east-west route along the south side of the valley and through Cahuenga Pass.) On August 7 they camped northwest of the site of Mission San Fernando, and the next day they traveled over San Fernando Pass to Newhall, pitching camp at an Indian village on the Santa Clara River near Castaic. From there, they proceeded northward by way of the Santa Clara Valley, so named by Portolá.

Mission San Gabriel Arcángel

On August 6, 1771, a party set out from San Diego, consisting of two friars, Pedro Benito Cambón and Angel Somera, and ten soldiers, to found a mission 40 leagues to the north. On September 8, 1771, Misión San Gabriel Arcángel was founded.

The new mission, being on the direct overland route from Mexico to Monterey, was the first stopping place and supply station after the desert and mountains had been crossed. This strategic location was protected with special care by the padres, and the mission prospered, growing rich and populous. It survived the period of secularization and withstood the tide of American immigration, and has continued its usefulness to the present time.

The original site of the mission (*SRL 161*) was about five miles south of the present site, on a bluff overlooking the Río Hondo, then called the San Gabriel, about one-half mile north of the present Montebello oil district. Nothing remains of the old buildings. A granite marker has been placed by Walter P. Temple at the corner of San Gabriel Boulevard and Lincoln Avenue near the old mission site.

Floods from the Río Hondo eventually forced the fathers to seek another location for their mission, and the old site was abandoned about five years after its founding. The new land chosen was higher and dryer but no less fertile, and luxuriant gardens and orchards soon flourished about the new buildings. An extensive vineyard, olive groves, and orchards of orange, fig, and pear trees covered several hundred acres of ground, and were protected from wild animals and unfriendly Indians by a high, thick cactus hedge. Remnants of this old hedge, as well as of the mission orchard, may still be seen about the town of San Gabriel. Other vineyards were planted from cuttings taken from the Mother Vineyard ("Viña Madre") at San Gabriel.

The first church building on the second site of California's fourth mission was dedicated in 1776. However, this was only temporary. The present church (*SRL 158*) was started in 1791 and completed in 1803, under the supervision of Padre José María Zalvidea. It was solidly constructed of stone and cement as far up as the windows, and of brick above that. Its massive walls and flying buttresses, its outside stairway leading to choir and belfry, and the bell tower with its several arches quaintly built to corre-spond to the different sizes of the bells make it one of the most unusual and interesting of all the missions.

In the yard just back of the church there are extensive ruins, which include ancient soap vats, a smithy, and the kitchen, solid testimonials of that practical industrial education everywhere given the natives by the zealous Franciscan fathers.

About two miles north of Mission San Gabriel near the site of the present Huntington Hotel, Claudio López, under supervision of Padre Zalvidea, sometime between 1810 and 1812 built the first water-operated gristmill in California. The old mill, "El Molino Viejo" (*SRL 302*), was constructed of solid masonry and still stands at 1120 Old Mill Road in western San Marino. It has been marked by the Martin Severance Chapter, D.A.R., of Pasadena. In 1903, H. E. Huntington bought the building and restored it to its former proportions, retaining the ancient picturesqueness of mission days. For a time after 1923 it was used as a real estate office. Long a private residence, it is now the Southern California headquarters of the California Historical Society.

Anza's Route

Juan Bautista de Anza reached the Santa Ana River on March 20, 1774, crossing it by an improvised bridge the following morning. That night he camped in a wooded valley near San Antonio Creek a little west of the present town of Ontario. At sunset of March 22 the party reached Mission San Gabriel (then located at its original site), where they were received with great rejoicing.

Anza remained at San Gabriel for nearly three weeks, awaiting necessary supplies for the jour-

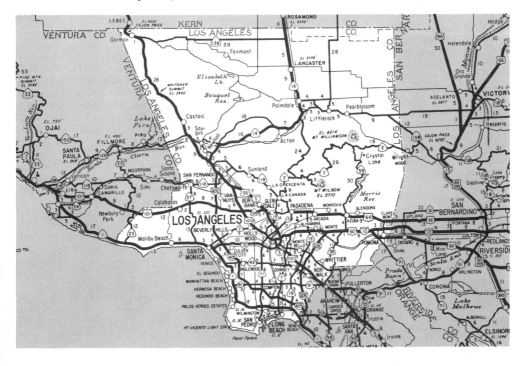

ney to Monterey. On the morning of April 10 he proceeded to the Río de la Porciúncula (Los Angeles River), followed it into the San Fernando Valley, and there turned west around the point of the mountain west of Glendale. Camp was made that night in Russell Valley, in what is now Ventura County.

Anza followed much the same route in 1776 with the band of emigrants who settled San Francisco, the first settlers to come overland to California. The caravan reached the San Antonio campsite on January 2, and on the 3rd they halted at the San Gabriel Wash, reaching Mission San Gabriel on the 4th. There they rested until February 21, when, refreshed by the welcome hospitality of the mission fathers, they set out once more. Swinging westward to the Los Angeles River, they followed it northwest to a campsite west of Glendale. Crossing the southern edge of the San Fernando Valley on February 22, the party entered the Simi Hills at Calabasas (an important stage station in the early American period) and continued to the vicinity of Las Virgines Creek. There tents were pitched for the night, and on the following day the pilgrims continued beyond the Santa Clara River, camping near El Rio in Ventura County.

Where the Trails of Two Spanish Pathfinders Crossed

Early in 1772 Pedro Fages passed the site of Hughes Lake on his notable inland journey from San Diego to San Luis Obispo, while in pursuit of deserters from the Spanish army.

In April 1776 the intrepid friar Francisco Garcés crossed Fages' path at Hughes Lake. Leaving San Gabriel he "ascended San Fernando Valley, crossed over Newhall Grade to the vicinity of Castaic and swung northeast over the mountains by a trail east of the present 'Ridge Route.' Just before he entered the plains, on the edge of Antelope Valley, he mentioned a lake, evidently Hughes Lake, 'and near thereto a village where, according to the signs, Señor Capitan Faxes had been.' "

Such trailmakers as Pedro Fages and Fray Francisco Garcés "should be held in memory through monuments by the wayside," said Bolton, and he suggested that a "joint monument" be placed for both of these men at Hughes Lake. "On one face put 1772 and an arrow pointing west to commemorate Fages' discovery of Antelope Valley. On another face put 1776 and an arrow pointing north in honor of Garcés' crossing of Antelope Valley to Cottonwood Creek, Tejón Canyon, and San Joaquin Valley."

Antelope Valley

Antelope Valley, geographically a part of the Mojave Desert, was the hunting paradise of Andrés Pico and other Californios, lured there by the immense herds of antelopes that roamed through it and from which it derived its name. In the heart of this valley one of the state's most glorious poppy fields adds its flame to the spectacular carpet of wild flowers that each spring spreads out across the valley floor at the foot of Portal Ridge from Palmdale to Del Sur.

Northwest of Fairmont there is a splendid forest of tree yuccas (yucca arborescens), with their spires of exquisite waxen lily bells. These strange inhabitants of the desert, more commonly known as Joshua trees, so impressed the first emigrants to California with their resemblance to the praying prophet that they bestowed his name upon them.

John C. Frémont, coming down from the north by way of Oak Creek Pass, on April 15, 1844, crossed Antelope Valley to the base of the Sierra Madre, following Fages' trail as far as Cajón Pass, where he connected with the Spanish Trail near Victorville. It is interesting to note that on this trip Frémont wrote in his diary of the "strange and singular" yucca forests and the fields of California poppies, as well as other shrubs and flowers in Antelope Valley.

St. Ann

Jedediah Strong Smith, the first American pathfinder to blaze an overland trail into California, camped at a spot designated by Harrison Rogers, Smith's diarist, as "St. Ann, an Indian farm house." This place, George W. Beattie assumes, was on the San Gabriel mission rancho known as San Antonio, and "at a ciénega formerly existing within the limits of what is now Claremont.... Emory's map in the Report of the U.S.–Mexico Boundary Commission shows nothing but San Antonio between Los Angeles and San Bernardino. Duflot de Mofras includes San Antonio among the seventeen ranchos for cattle and horses possessed by Mission San Gabriel. The Mexican grant of San José on which both Pomona and Claremont are situated was a combination of the San José and the San Antonio ranchos of Mission San Gabriel."

Ciénega

One mile southeast of the center of San Dimas, on Palomares Avenue at its junction with San Dimas Canyon Road, is the site of an ancient Indian camping place. In early mission days, the Indians who frequented this spot hauled logs from the neighboring San Bernardino Mountains for the building of the San Gabriel Mission. Their campground became the stopping place for the Spaniards, who called it Ciénega ("a wet place"), because of the presence of natural springs that were perpetually seeping up out of the earth. Later, American pathfinders and emigrants stopped there en route from San Bernardino to San Gabriel and Los Angeles, and they called it Mud Springs.

Before 1870 there was a stage station at the springs on the road from San Bernardino to Los Angeles. This station was probably located near the site of the pumping plant on the present Palomares Avenue. All that is left of the old San Bernardino road, however, is a short strip of the present road less than one-half mile east of the springs, where Palomares Avenue turns southeast at Grand Avenue for a short distance. Only a few willows and tules wave over the site of the Indians' ancient watering place at Ciénega, the seeping springs of which have long since been pumped dry for irrigation purposes.

The Old Adobes of San Gabriel

Of the many quaint adobe homes that made the little town of San Gabriel unique and picturesque a number of years ago, only a handful remain. Indeed, six adobes described in the first edition of this book (1932) have since disappeared.

Perhaps the oldest adobe in this region is the former home of Colonel Purcell, located between West Mission Drive and Orange Street, near Anderson Way, at the end of a short, curving lane. Part of it is said to have been built as a home for the mission friars three years before the mission church was erected. Many indications of great age have been discovered, such as the old hand-planed doors and the original rafters blackened by the passing years. The present ceiling was originally the roof, while under three successive board floors the old tiles of the original floor have been found. In the yard outside there are indications of other rooms having once extended beyond the present walls.

In the garden and orchard, too, were many famous old trees bearing testimony to the age of the place, most of which are now gone. They doubtless formed a part of the old mission orchard, which was walled in by a cactus hedge. It was from this hedge that the ranch received its name, Las Tunas ("the cactus"). The history of Las Tunas Ranch is uncertain. In 1852 it was purchased by Judge Volney E. Howard from a Mr. Hildreth. It was occupied earlier by Henry Dalton, when he was mission administrator. There is evidence, also, that Hugo Reid was once the owner. Reid, a Scotsman who married an Indian woman, is noted for his splendid account of the life and customs of California Indians, which has been much quoted by later writers.

La Casa Vieja de López, located at 330 North Santa Anita Avenue, is doubtless one of the former mission buildings, being of the type of adobe construction used during mission days. It has been redecorated, in keeping with its ancient quaintness, by Doña María López de Lowther, whose family occupied the place for many years. A museum is planned there.

The "Grapevine adobe," one block west of the mission on the corner of Santa Anita Avenue and Mission Drive, next to the Mission Playhouse, has been torn down, but its mammoth grapevine remains. Extending over an area with a circumference of 100 feet, it has lured the passing generations into its shade, and even today tourists often linger there on hot summer days.

The Vígare adobe (SRL 451), at 616 Ramona Street, was for many years the home of Doña Luz Vígare, great-granddaughter of a soldier of the mission guard. The old house is generously proportioned, with rather high walls. The ancient beams have been covered by a modern roof above and a ceiling below. An old adobe lean-to kitchen, or *cocina*, in the rear has disappeared, and the *corredor* is now a front porch.

Pueblo de Los Angeles

El Pueblo de Nuestra Señora la Reina de los Angeles de la Porciúncula, second of the three pueblos to be established in Alta California, was founded on September 4, 1781. A carved wooden cross, placed on the north side of the present plaza at the entrance to Olvera Street, commemorates the founding. An idealized bronze statue of Governor Felipe de Neve, who ordered the establishment of the settlement, was erected in the plaza in commemoration of the 150th anniversary of the founding of Los Angeles, by the California Parlor, No. 247, Native Daughters of the Golden West. Felipe de Neve governed California from 1775 to 1782.

The northwest corner of the present plaza was the southeast corner of the old plaza. From this point the boundary of the old plaza followed along the east side of North Main Street to Bellevue Avenue, thence across to New High Street, south to Sunset Boulevard, and thence back to the point of beginning.

The settlement slowly progressed. In 1784 a chapel was built on the plaza, and in 1785 new settlers began to come in. By 1800 there were 30 small adobe homes clustered within the pueblo walls.

That year, floods from the Los Angeles River forced the colonists to abandon the settlement on its banks and to move to higher ground. The new plaza (SRL 156), which remains today, was established, and about it the life of Los Angeles and of southern California centered during the Spanish and Mexican periods. The old Spanish aristocracy built their homes around it—the Del Valles, the Coronels, the Lugos, the Carrillos, the Ávilas, and others. Gradually the settlement grew outward from the plaza, which remained the center of life even after the coming of the Americans.

None of the adobe homes that clustered about the old plaza remains today. The original site was gradually built up with other adobes after the plaza was moved to its present site. This district, which came to be known as Sonora Town and part of which is Chinatown today, still harbored

Church of Nuestra Señora la Reina de los Angeles, Los Angeles Plaza

a couple of these historic dwellings until the 1960's.

Only one adobe residence remains in the area of the second plaza. This is the Ávila adobe (SRL 145) at 14 Olvera Street, the oldest dwelling house in Los Angeles, which dates back probably to the year 1818. Originally twice as long as it is now and L-shaped, it still retains much of its ancient appearance. With its high ceilings, spacious rooms, numerous windows, and *corredor* facing the patio, it was a real mansion in its day, richly furnished and draped with imported satin damasks from France. However, the portion of the house that remains today was the less important part in its heyday. Doña Encarnación Ávila was its first mistress, and for over a century it was in possession of the Ávila and Rimpau families. For five days during the American occupation—January 10–14, 1847—it served as Commodore Robert F. Stockton's headquarters.

The restoration of the Ávila adobe and Olvera Street, under the leadership of the late Christine Sterling, was the beginning of historical preservation in Los Angeles. These efforts in the late 1920's and early 1930's culminated in 1953 in the establishment of Pueblo de Los Angeles State Historical Monument, encompassing much of the area surrounding the old and new plazas. Acquisition of property and restoration of buildings will proceed according to a master plan over a period of years. In 1962 the City of Los Angeles established a Cultural Heritage Board with power to declare historic-cultural monuments, and to delay the issuance of demolition permits should the property owners seek to destroy such historic-cultural monuments. Its powers are limited, however, to property that is privately owned or owned by the city. Landmarks on federal, state, or county property are officially recognized and listed in a separate inventory. Through the Cultural Heritage Board, Los Angeles has implemented historical preservation not only in the downtown area but throughout the sprawling city.

The Ávila adobe is now a museum about which centers the Paseo de Los Angeles along Olvera Street, with its picturesque Mexican shops arranged irregularly on either side or scattered down the middle and sheltered from the summer sun by gay umbrellas. A diagonal band of brick in the paving of Olvera Street marks the line of the ancient *zanja madre* (mother ditch) that furnished water to the pueblo. La Casa Pelanconi, at 33–35 Olvera Street, was built in 1855 and is one of the first brick houses constructed in Los Angeles. During La Fiesta de Los Angeles in September 1931, the Los Angeles Chapters, D.A.R., united in placing a sundial in Olvera Street in honor of Kit Carson, the famous scout. It was unveiled by his great-granddaughter, Teresa Carson Beach.

The Church of Nuestra Señora la Reina de los Angeles (SRL 144) was begun about 1818–19 and dedicated in 1822. Services are still held in this church, where all Los Angeles once worshiped. It stands on the west side of the plaza at 535 North Main Street. The historic bronze bells in the tower still chime the Angelus above the noise of the city streets, as they did above the sleepy pueblo over a century ago. Adjacent to the church at 521 North Main is the site of Los Angeles' first cemetery, in use from 1823 to 1844.

The Lugo adobe (SRL 301) stood until the 1940's on the east side of the plaza on Los Angeles Street. It was one of the few two-story houses in the pueblo and was the last remaining two-story adobe in the city of Los Angeles. It was probably built before 1840 by Vicente Lugo, who lived there until 1850, when he retired to Rancho San Antonio. He later donated the house on the plaza to St. Vincent's College (now Loyola University), the first college in southern California, founded in 1865. After a short time, however, the college moved to the block bounded by Broadway, Hill, Sixth, and Seventh streets, where it remained until 1887. St. Vincent's Place (SRL 567), off Seventh Street between Broadway and Hill, commemorates the site. The spot on which Vicente Lugo's town house stood is now a small park.

There are also landmarks of the early American period in the plaza area, and these, too, are being restored as parts of Pueblo de Los Angeles State Historical Monument. The Pico House (SRL 159) was built by ex-Governor Pío Pico in 1869 on the site of the Carrillo adobe, and was the finest hotel in the Southwest at that time. It stands at 430 North Main Street, on the south side of the plaza. Next door, at 420–22, is the Merced Theater (SRL 171), built in 1870, the first theater in Los Angeles. The Masonic Hall at 416 North Main was erected in 1858. The old firehouse (SRL 730) on the south side of the plaza was built in 1884.

The Plaza Church and the site of the cemetery have been declared historic-cultural monuments by the Cultural Heritage Board of the City of Los Angeles. The Ávila and Pelanconi houses, the Pico House, Merced Theater, Masonic Hall, and firehouse—all owned by the state—have been officially recognized by the same board.

Rancho San Rafael

One of the first grants made in Alta California was the great Rancho San Rafael granted to José María Verdugo on October 20, 1784, and on January 12, 1798. It was also one of the largest of all the grants, comprising 36,000 acres of fertile pasture land from the Arroyo Seco to Mission San Fernando. Many modern towns have since been established within what were once the confines of the old rancho, including Glendale, Eagle Rock, and Verdugo City.

Don José died in 1831, leaving the estate to his son Julio and his daughter Catalina, who, 30 years later, divided it between them. Julio took the southern portion, while his sister took the more rugged and mountainous section in the north.

Doña Catalina, who had been blind from girlhood, never married, and as she grew old she tired of living here and there with her nephews, and wished a home of her own. Accordingly, Teodoro, one of the nephews, built for her what is now the last Verdugo adobe *(SRL 637)*, one of the five that were once erected by the Verdugos on Rancho San Rafael. This modest but charming little house, half-hidden under a giant rose vine and set in the midst of its historic garden of oleander, pomegranate, orange, and olive trees, is lovingly cared for and in excellent condition, being used as a private residence. It is located two miles northeast of downtown Glendale off Cañada Boulevard at 2211 Bonita Drive. Near it is a mammoth oak under which General Andrés Pico made his last camp before surrendering to Frémont at Cahuenga.

Another Verdugo adobe became the famous Casa Verdugo Inn, at the end of Brand Boulevard near the base of the Verdugo Mountains in Glendale. This had been the home of Fernando Sepúlveda, son-in-law of Julio Verdugo. It was torn down about 1915, and the site is marked only by the aged trees of the garden.

The adobe of Tomás Sánchez *(SRL 235)*, who married María Sepúlveda, still stands on Rancho San Rafael, at 1330 Dorothy Drive. It is now owned by the City of Glendale, and the house and its sunken gardens are open to the public.

Eagle Rock takes its name from a massive rock distinguished by a natural formation resembling an eagle in flight. It was an important landmark in Spanish and Mexican days. The rock, located at the northern end of Figueroa Street, has been declared a historic-cultural monument by the City of Los Angeles.

Rancho Los Nietos

Another early grant in California was made to Manuel Nieto in 1784, just three years after the founding of the Pueblo de Los Angeles. At first it included all the land lying between the Santa Ana and San Gabriel rivers from the mountains to the sea, but this vast tract was later divided among Don Manuel's five heirs. The ranchos thus created were Los Alamitos, Los Cerritos, Santa Gertrudes, Los Coyotes, and Las Bolsas. Los Alamitos, Santa Gertrudes, and Los Coyotes lie partly within Orange County, and Las Bolsas is wholly within it. Old adobes still stand on Ranchos Los Alamitos and Los Cerritos.

Rancho Los Alamitos

Don Abel Stearns, a native of Massachusetts and one of the first American settlers in California, helped to introduce energetic American business methods into the slow and unenterprising life of the sleepy pueblo of Los Angeles. He opened a general merchandise store and became prosperous.

Don Abel married Arcadia Bandini, the beautiful daughter of a noble Spanish family in Alta California. Doña Arcadia reigned as social leader at El Palacio ("the palace"), Don Abel's home, built on the site of his general store. In 1858 he built the Arcadia Block at the rear of El Palacio, fronting on Los Angeles Street. It was a center of business for many years. After Don Abel's death, Doña Arcadia married Colonel R. S. Baker. The Baker Block was built about 1878 on the site of El Palacio and stood at the southeast corner of the former intersection of Arcadia and Main streets. It has now been demolished for a freeway.

Stearns was very active in public affairs after California became part of the United States, being a member of the first Constitutional Convention, a city councilman, state assemblyman, and county supervisor.

Through his marriage to Arcadia Bandini, Abel Stearns came into possession in 1840 of Rancho Los Alamitos, on a part of which the eastern section of the city of Long Beach now stands. Don Abel suffered financial reverses when he abandoned the cattle business following the great drought of 1863–64 in which cattle died by the thousands. Michael Reese, who held a mortgage on the ranch, foreclosed, and in the early 1870's Reese's heirs sold the Rancho Los Alamitos to the Bixbys. The Los Alamitos ranch house has remained the property of one branch of the Bixby family for these many years. Although it has undergone alterations and additions through the years, the old house has never lost its charm and remains today an excellent example of the adobe ranch house. The spacious proportions and simple plan of the older portion lead authorities on its history to believe that the original owners built it very early in the nineteenth century.

The Bixby ranch house, half-hidden among the fine old trees and shrubs planted by Mrs. John Bixby many years ago, is located on a hill at 6511 East Seventh Street, five and one-half miles east of downtown Long Beach.

The oil well "Alamitos 1" *(SRL 580)*, discovery well of the important Signal Hill field, takes its name from the old rancho. Drilled to a depth of 3,114 feet in 1921, it is located at Hill Street and Temple Avenue in Signal Hill.

Rancho Los Cerritos

La Casa del Rancho Los Cerritos, with its broad balcony stretching the full length of the front above and below, its great patio enclosed on three sides by the long wings of the house and on the fourth by a high adobe wall, is the largest and most magnificent extant adobe in southern California. On the balcony side is a beautiful garden dating from early days, and in the patio is another planted in modern times. Below is the river, and beyond lies the valley. In the distance, on a clear night, the lights of downtown Los Angeles can be seen. The shaded *corredores,* the many and varied rooms, the hand-finished woodwork, and the evidences of rude fortification make a veritable castle of the old house. The present tile roof is misleading, because the original roof was of brea, which was later replaced with redwood shakes.

This splendid adobe mansion was built in 1844 by Don Juan Temple, another energetic young Yankee and a native of Massachusetts, who, finding life in Alta California most agreeable and profitable, married Rafaela Cota and bought out the shares that the grandchildren of Manuel

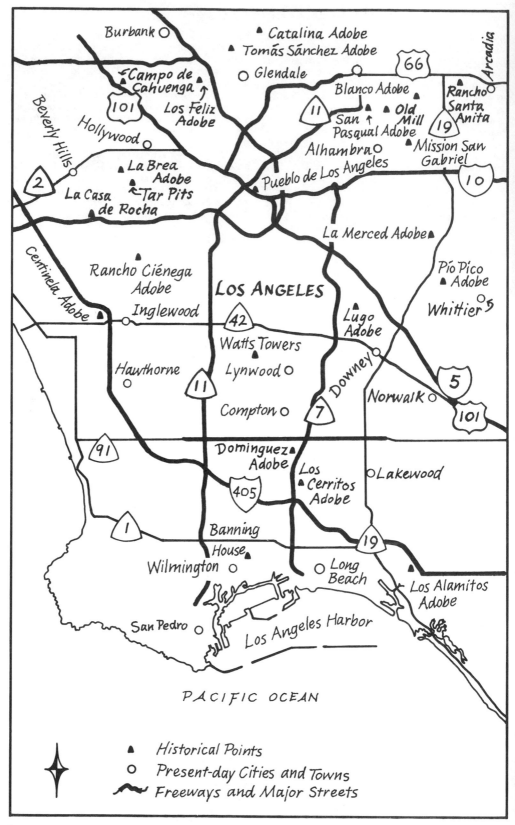

LOS ANGELES METROPOLITAN AREA

Nieto held in Rancho Los Cerritos. He built his mansion about four miles north of the center of the present city of Long Beach, the main part of which stands within the confines of the old rancho. Adjoining the Virginia Country Club in the rear, Los Cerritos stands at 4600 Virginia Road. It is now owned by the City of Long Beach and is open to the public at stated times. For years it had been in the Bixby family and was restored by Llewellyn Bixby (son of the pioneer Llewellyn) in 1930.

Everything Juan Temple did was successful. He opened the first general store in the Pueblo de Los Angeles, and in front of it he planted pepper trees. His was the first market in the city. He and his brother built the Temple Block, Los Angeles' first office building. Juan Temple's establishments were located in what is now the Civic Center. The Federal Building stands on the site of his general store. The market later became the courthouse, and the Temple Block stood just to the north. The sites of these two buildings are now occupied by the City Hall.

Rancho Santa Gertrudes

Antonio María Nieto received that part of Rancho Los Nietos designated as Rancho Santa Gertrudes, and in 1834 the Mexican government confirmed the title to his widow, Doña Josefa Cota de Nieto. Later, the rancho was sold to Lemuel Carpenter, a Kentuckian, who married the beautiful María de los Angeles Domínguez. Carpenter and his wife conveyed a portion of Rancho Santa Gertrudes to José M. Ramírez on July 14, 1855. This section became known as the Ramírez Tract. The Carpenters had been happy and prosperous under Mexican rule, but they failed under the more difficult business methods of the Yankees. On November 14, 1859, the rancho was sold by the sheriff; John G. Downey and James P. Mc-Farland were the fortunate bidders. Carpenter took his own life.

Santa Gertrudes was one of the first ranchos to be subdivided. Out of it grew the town of Downey, established in 1873. Later, when the rich oil wells toward the eastern boundary were discovered, the town of Santa Fe Springs emerged, "a city of derricks with black gold." In 1963 it was estimated that close to half a million people were living within the former boundaries of Rancho Santa Gertrudes. Oil production at Santa Fe Springs has waned, and it is now given over largely to manufacturing plants and residential subdivisions.

The northernmost part of the rancho had been occupied by Tomás Sánchez Colima since 1841. Don Tomás received a patent for the land from the United States government, and the estate was afterward designated as the Colima Tract of Rancho Santa Gertrudes. Until about 1965 an old adobe still stood at 8547 Norwalk Boulevard in Los Nietos. Tradition says that it belonged to some of the Nieto grandchildren and was later occupied for a time by Governor Downey. Still later, it was bought by Colonel Swain, an Army officer. Swain's son remodeled the old adobe. It retained something of its original simple California design, with low roof, thick walls, and deep casements, but was otherwise much altered.

Rancho San Pedro

The rich grazing lands of Rancho San Pedro covered 43,119 acres, extending from the coast near Wilmington up the estuary halfway to Los Angeles. Gardena and Compton are situated on the northern boundary of the grant. San Pedro is one of the earliest grants in California, and has continued in part in the hands of descendants of the original grantee. First granted to Juan José Domínguez before 1799 and again in 1822 to his heir, Sargento Cristobal Domínguez, Rancho San Pedro came into the charge of Manuel Domínguez in 1826. Don Manuel lived on the estate until his death in 1882, and his vigorous management as well as his integrity and hospitality made the rancho famous.

Only the shaded eastern *corredor* of the Domínguez adobe (*SRL 152*) and the historic trees in the garden recall the atmosphere of gay rancho days long past. Arches and stucco have made the west front decidedly modern. In the chapel of Don Manuel's casa there is a stained-glass window bearing the inscription "Domínguez, 1826." Where many guests once enjoyed the hospitality of Manuel Domínguez and his lovely daughters, young seminarians now have their classrooms and dormitories. A descendant of the Domínguez family presented the old place to the Claretian Order to be a memorial seminary for the training of priests. It stands on a low hillside south of Compton at 18127 South Alameda Street.

Rancho San Pedro was the scene of a battle between the Californians and the Americans on October 9, 1846. After the citizens of Los Angeles had given their allegiance to the United States, Commodore Robert F. Stockton (acting commander of American forces in California) and Colonel John C. Frémont left the city early in September, leaving Captain Archibald Gillespie in charge of 50 men. But such a small garrison proved a mistake. A revolt occurred among the Californians of the city, and the garrison, forced to surrender on September 30, retreated to San Pedro. Meanwhile, Commodore Stockton had heard of the revolt and sent Captain William Mervine with 300 men from San Francisco.

Gillespie arrived in San Pedro on October 7, and was about to embark when Captain Mervine arrived on the *Savannah* with reinforcements. The two commanders then joined forces and marched toward Los Angeles. They were halted on October 9 at the Domínguez rancho, by a force of 120 mounted Mexicans commanded by José Carrillo.

"Here began a pretty game in which the Californians used a four-pounder, known as 'The Cannon of the White Mule.' They would fire it until the Americans, charging, would almost capture it, when they would drag it away with their riatas. Mervine, worn out with charging, and discouraged by the loss of six killed and a number wounded, retired again to San Pedro."

The American dead were buried on a little island near the mouth of San Pedro Bay. Dead Man's Island, as it was christened by the burial party of the American forces, long remained a landmark in that vicinity, but it has now been entirely removed by harbor construction work.

As a result of their victory on the Domínguez rancho, the revolt of the Californians quickly spread all over California, and the Americans were confronted with the semblance of a real war.

At this point in the game, that clever leader of the Californians, José Carrillo, played a trick on the Americans which temporarily kept them out of Los Angeles. Setting his troopers to rounding up all the wild horses of the neighboring ranchos, he herded them back and forth across a gap in the hills where they kicked up such a dust that Stockton, watching from San Pedro harbor three miles away, took it to be a great body of mounted Californians. Knowing their daring and marvelous horsemanship, he weighed anchor and sailed for San Diego.

An official state marker at the Claretian seminary recounts the history of the Domínguez ranch house and the Battle of the Domínguez Rancho.

The first air meet in the United States was held atop Domínguez Hill on the old rancho from January 10 to 20, 1910. The initial competitive meeting of pioneer fliers was held at a time when aviation was considered by many as a passing novelty. Glenn H. Curtiss set a new air speed record—60 miles per hour. The site (SRL 718) was marked in 1941 by the Compton Parlors of the Native Sons and Native Daughters of the Golden West, but the marker is relatively inaccessible. Another monument has been placed one-half mile to the northwest, on Wilmington Avenue, one mile north of Del Amo Boulevard.

Wilmington, near the southern edge of Rancho San Pedro, was founded in 1858 by General Phineas Banning, "Father of Los Angeles Transportation." He was famous first as an operator of stage lines and later as the builder of the first local railroads. His 30-room mansion in Banning Park (SRL 147), at 401 East M Street, was built in 1864. It has been owned by the City of Los Angeles since 1927. Drum Barracks (SRL 169) at Wilmington was the central supply station for the Union Army in southern California during the years 1861–68. It was named in honor of Richard Coulter Drum, a general of the Mexican War. The last surviving building of Drum Barracks is the officers' quarters at 1053–55 Cary Avenue. In the early 1870's Don Benito Wilson donated it to the Southern Methodists to be used as a college. The institution was called Wilson College in honor of its donor. The building is privately owned and was marked by the Native Daughters of the Golden West on October 2, 1927. The Banning mansion and Drum Barracks have been declared historic-cultural monuments by the City of Los Angeles.

Heritage House (SRL 664), at 205 South Willowbrook Avenue, is the oldest house in Compton. The original two rooms were built in 1869 by A. R. Loomis. The house, which originally stood at 209 South Acacia Street, was purchased by the City of Compton and moved to its present site in 1957.

Redondo Beach is at the northwest corner of Rancho San Pedro. At this point it adjoins Rancho Sausal Redondo, 22,459 acres. Between Pacific and Francisca avenues at the north end of Redondo Beach is the site of an old salt lake (SRL 373) from which the Indians of the area obtained salt. Messrs. Johnson and Allanson erected a salt works here in the 1850's.

Rancho Los Palos Verdes

The great Rancho Los Palos Verdes was given to the Sepúlveda family in 1827, and the grant was ratified to José Loreto and Juan Sepúlveda on June 3, 1846. It contained 31,629 acres, extending from south of Redondo Beach to San Pedro. At Sepúlveda's Landing, later called Timm's Point, a port grew up, which ultimately developed into San Pedro. San Pedro is now a part of the city of Los Angeles, and it is interesting to note that "almost the entire district was carved not out of Rancho San Pedro, as is generally understood, but out of Rancho Los Palos Verdes."

According to Chapman, Cabrillo discovered San Pedro Bay on October 8, 1542, calling it Bahía de los Fumos ("the Bay of Smokes"), because of the dense smoke arising from burning grass during the Indians' periodic rabbit hunts. However, the Bahía de los Fumos, or Fuegos, has also been identified as Santa Monica Bay.

Sixty years later, Vizcaíno entered the bay, and as early as 1793 San Pedro had become the port of entry for the Pueblo of Los Angeles, three missions, and several ranchos. In that year George Vancouver, the English navigator, on his second voyage to California, named the points at the two extremities of the bay Point Fermín and Point Lasuén, in honor of his friend Father Fermín Francisco de Lasuén, permanent successor to Junípero Serra as Padre Presidente of the missions. The names given by Vancouver were retained on modern maps.

The first Yankee ship to anchor at San Pedro was the *Lelia Byrd* in 1805, with Captain Shaler in command, on his return voyage from the Sandwich (Hawaiian) Islands to Boston. This was the beginning of a brisk trade between Californians and Yankee ships from New England. After this, Yankee brigs as well as ships from other nations called regularly at San Pedro, first in quest of otter skins and later of hides and tallow. This was contraband trade until 1821, when Mexico, having freed herself from Spain, made it legal. From then on, the port of San Pedro grew in importance.

The first harbor improvement was begun in 1877, and in 1892 steps were taken for the creation of a deep-water port. Scarcely any of the old landmarks remain today. There is a lighthouse on Point Fermín, built in 1874 and officially recognized by the Cultural Heritage Board of the City of Los Angeles. Point Lasuén, however, has been incorporated into the harbor. Timm's Point (SRL 384), mentioned by Richard Henry Dana in *Two Years Before the Mast* as the place down which the cargoes of hides and tallow were lowered to Yankee trading ships below, has disappeared with harbor improvements. The point and landing were located off the south end of Beacon Street near present Fisherman's Dock. Halfway between Timm's Point and Point Fermín, on the Naval Reservation grounds, was the hide-drogher's warehouse, erected in the 1820's and long the only building in San Pedro.

The Palos Verdes Peninsula, with its beautiful homes and an outstanding tourist attraction, Marineland of the Pacific, occupies much of old Rancho Los Palos Verdes. At Portuguese Bend, now the site of a private residential community, a whaling station (SRL 381) was located from about 1864 to 1885.

None of the old Sepúlveda adobes stands today. The home of Diego Sepúlveda (SRL 380) was located in the 700 block of Channel Street in San Pedro and faced on Gaffey Street. Built about 1853, it was the first two-story Monterey-type adobe in southern California. An even earlier adobe stood southeast of Walteria at the foot of the Palos Verdes Hills. The home of José Dolores Sepúlveda (SRL 383), father of Diego, is said to have been built in 1818. The exact site is unknown, but the general area is indicated by old pepper trees at the mouth of the canyon into which Madison Street runs. The elder Sepúlveda was killed by an Indian arrow at Mission La Purísima Concepción in the 1820's.

Mission San Fernando Rey de España

Misión San Fernando Rey de España (SRL 157) was founded on September 8, 1797, by Padre Fermín Francisco de Lasuén. The spot chosen had been provisionally granted to Alcalde Francisco Reyes of Los Angeles. The padres took over the adobe house the alcalde had built, and within two months erected the first small chapel. Another church was completed in 1799, and the present church in 1806. It was heavily damaged by the earthquake of 1812 and subsequently repaired. The mission was secularized in October 1834.

The vast lands of Mission San Fernando were leased in December 1845 to Andrés Pico, brother of Governor Pío Pico. In order to obtain money to defend California against the Americans, the governor sold Rancho Ex-Mission de San Fernando in June 1846 to Eulogio de Celís for $14,000. Celís recognized Andrés Pico's lease, and in 1854 Pico bought a half-interest in the rancho. He continued to make the old mission his country home and to herd his cattle on its vast ranges. Rómulo Pico, the son or adopted son of Andrés, also came to live on the rancho.

In 1874 Senators Charles Maclay and George K. Porter purchased the northern half of the rancho; B. F. Porter became associated with them in 1879. The southern half had already been bought by a group headed by Isaac Lankershim and I. N. Van Nuys, and with these two purchases the era of small farms and the building up of the town of San Fernando and the San Fernando Valley began. The old mission days were ended forever.

For many years the only intact building of Mission San Fernando was the convento, often called simply the "long building," 243 feet in length with 19 arches. At the east end is the chapel room containing several ancient paintings and relics of mission days, and the building also includes the refectory, kitchens, and underground wine vats. In 1938, under the leadership of Mark R. Harrington of the Southwest Museum, restoration of the other buildings began. The mission church had fallen into ruin, and very little remained of the workshops and living quarters. Now the church is fully restored and part of the quadrangle has been rebuilt. On the northwest side of the mission is the graveyard where 2,000 Indians lie buried.

In what is now Brand Park (SRL 150), across San Fernando Mission Boulevard from the convento, are the immense stone soap vats constructed by the mission fathers and also two beautiful fountains. One of the fountains, a replica of one in Cordova, Spain, was moved 300 feet from its original location in the mission courtyard in 1922. Both of them were a part of the old mission water system.

The Pico Reserve, a portion of Rancho San Fernando near the mission not sold to the subdividers, had on it the adobe occupied by Eulogio de Celís. The original of this building probably had been part of the mission establishment. Some years after Celís returned to his native Spain in 1853, Rómulo Pico restored and enlarged the adobe. The house again fell into ruin, but in 1929 it was purchased by Mr. and Mrs. Mark R. Harrington, who restored it as their home. The beautiful two-story adobe (SRL 362) stands a quarter of a mile southwest of the old mission at 10940 Sepulveda Boulevard, where it serves as headquarters for the North Valley Y.M.C.A. This adobe and Mission San Fernando have been declared historic-cultural monuments by the City of Los Angeles.

Gerónimo López had erected an adobe home on Rancho San Fernando at an early period when the mission, some distance to the southeast, was just about the only other building for miles in any direction. The adobe became a stage station, and in 1869 the first post office in the San Fernando Valley was established there. The old house was dynamited when the San Fernando Reservoir was built, and the site is now inundated.

The town of San Fernando began to boom about 1874, and Don Gerónimo decided to move to town. This he did in 1878, and his son Valentino built the house that still stands at the corner of Pico Street and Maclay Avenue. The López adobe has been restored somewhat elaborately, but it retains its quaint and picturesque upper balcony and outside stairway, and an old-fashioned garden that keeps well the spirit of the past.

The oldest nonsectarian cemetery (SRL 753) in the San Fernando Valley is located at Foothill Boulevard and Bledsoe Street in Sylmar.

On the Workman Ranch, now called the Shadow Ranch, at 22633 Vanowen Street in Canoga Park, there is an adobe-and-redwood ranch house built between 1869 and 1872 and now owned by the City of Los Angeles. In the same area is "Rancho Sombra de Robles," the adobe house and estate of W. W. Orcutt, the oil magnate, at 23555 Justice Street. Both ranches have been declared historic-cultural monuments by the Cultural Heritage Board.

Rancho El Encino

Fray Juan Crespí, who with Gaspar de Portolá and his band of explorers first marched through the beautiful valley of San Fernando in 1769, named it El Valle de Santa Catalina de Bononia de los Encinos ("the Valley of Saint Catherine of Bologna of the Oaks"). The presence of these native trees also inspired the name for Rancho El Encino, which was granted in 1845 to three Indians, Ramón, Francisco, and Roque. It was purchased by Don Vicente de la Osa, who erected there in 1849 the long, low adobe house that still stands a few hundred yards north of the present Ventura Boulevard. The house shows evidences of having been extensively repaired and improved during the 1870's or early 1880's.

Rita de la Osa, on March 6, 1867, conveyed to James Thompson ("Don Santiago" of Rancho La Brea) all of her interest and that of Don Vicente in Rancho El Encino. Two years later it was purchased from Don Santiago by Eugene Garnier, a hard-working French Basque, who made of El Encino a great sheep ranch.

The broad pool or reservoir in front of the old adobe was constructed by Garnier in 1867 or 1868, and just to the north of it in 1872 he built the quaint two-story house of stone and adobe that still stands beneath magnificent eucalyptus trees.

In spite of his thrift and industry, Eugene Garnier was not able to hold Rancho El Encino. It passed to Gaston Oxarart, a Frenchman, in 1878, then to Juan Bernard, and in December 1891 to Domingo Amestoy. At one period the place was a stagecoach stop.

The rancho headquarters are now Los Encinos State Historical Monument (SRL 689), at 16756 Moorpark Street in Encino. It includes the springs that feed the lake and at which the Portolá expedition camped on August 5, 1769. On Louise Avenue just south of Ventura Boulevard is a huge oak tree, estimated to be 1,000 years old, typical of the many that gave the area its name. The oak has been declared a historic-cultural monument by the Cultural Heritage Board of the City of Los Angeles, and the rancho headquarters have been officially recognized by the same body.

Besides Rancho Ex-Mission de San Fernando and Rancho El Encino, there were other Mexican grants in the San Fernando Valley. One was Rancho El Escorpión, 1,110 acres, granted to three Indians, Urbano, Odon, and Manuel, and to Joaquín Romero. It came into the hands of Miguel Leonis, a Basque who arrived in California about 1858. Leonis enlarged an old adobe on public land outside the confines of his rancho. It still stands at 23537 Calabasas Road in Calabasas, a well-preserved two-story house of Monterey style. It has been declared a historic-cultural monument by the City of Los Angeles.

Rancho San Antonio

"No horses so fast, no cattle so fine, no land so fertile, no rancho more famous than the Rancho San Antonio. No family more prominent, no hospitality more welcome or as freely partaken, no hacienda more lovely, happy or prosperous than that of the Lugos."

Rancho San Antonio was granted to Antonio María Lugo in 1810, and for 50 years it remained in the possession of the family. It consisted of 29,513 acres of land which adjoined the original pueblo grant of the city of Los Angeles on the southeast. Don Antonio and his bride lived at first in a tule house on the site of the present station of Bell. In 1819 he built an adobe dwelling in Los Angeles on what is now the east side of San Pedro Street between First and Second. Here his sons, José del Carmen, José María, and Vicente, were born.

Later, Don Vicente Lugo, sometimes called the "Beau Brummel of Los Angeles," because of his fine wardrobe, built a two-story house which was long the center of social life in the pueblo. In 1844 he erected a two-story casa in the country at what is now 6360 East Gage Avenue (at Garfield), east of the city of Bell. Don Antonio's original homestead no longer exists, nor does Vicente's town house on the plaza, but the adobe on Gage Avenue is in good condition today, being occupied by a descendant of Vicente Lugo.

Ultimately, the pressure of American business closed in upon the great Rancho San Antonio until, bit by bit, it was lost to its original owners. In 1927 a part of the land was sold to the Firestone Tire and Rubber Company for a factory site at $7,000 an acre. On other portions of the old rancho, prosperous communities have grown up, including Huntington Park, Vernon, Walnut Park, South Gate, and Lynwood.

Rancho La Brea

Rancho La Brea, originally a part of the Los Angeles pueblo lands, was granted in 1828 to Antonio José Rocha and Nemicio Domínguez by José Antonio Carrillo, alcalde of Los Angeles and brother-in-law of Pío Pico. Later, the grant was confirmed by Governor Echeandía. The rancho derived its name from La Brea Pits, where brea, or crude oil, oozed out of the ground in great quantities. Early conveyances of this land all provided that the owners were to allow the inhabitants of Los Angeles to take from the pits as much brea as they needed for the roofs of their adobe houses.

Antonio José Rocha was a Portuguese who came to California in 1815 and became one of the most respected citizens of the Pueblo of Los Angeles. He was naturalized in 1831, and in 1836 he was a resident of Santa Barbara. On November 16, 1860, José Jorge Rocha, a son of Antonio José, deeded Rancho La Brea to Major Henry Hancock. Parts of the estate were later conveyed to Cornelius Cole, James Thompson, and Arthur

Gilmore, but much of it remained in the hands of the Hancocks. For years, the Hancocks extracted immense quantities of oil from the rancho lands, but the oil gradually decreased, until today the derricks of the once wealthy oil fields have been replaced by the beautiful homes of the Wilshire District. The site of the old pits has become Hancock Park (*SRL 170*), with smooth green lawns and only occasional pools of black asphalt.

In the heavy crude oil that has oozed out of the ground at La Brea Pits from time immemorial, animals, once caught, were unable to free themselves. For this reason the area became an invaluable mine to scientists in the early years of the twentieth century, and the specimens, numbering into thousands, of prehistoric animals that have been exhumed from these natural preserving beds and deposited in the Hancock Room of the Museum of History and Art at Exposition Park, Los Angeles, constitute one of the world's most remarkable exhibits of its kind. Bones and skeletons of many strange prehistoric animals may be seen there, including those of the American mastodon, saber-toothed tiger, giant ground sloth, Imperial elephant, ancient bison, and the prehistoric camel, bear, lion, and giant vulture. Scientists are still finding bones of great interest in the neighborhood.

Although Major Hancock began to uncover some of these bones during the 1870's, their importance was not recognized until 1906, when Professor J. C. Merriam of the University of California investigated them. Professor Merriam and other scientists made extensive studies at the rancho. On June 23, 1913, G. Allan Hancock gave the exclusive right to excavate the beds to the City of Los Angeles, and the Hancock Room was set aside as a memorial to his parents, Major Henry Hancock and Ida Hancock Ross.

Rancho La Brea (Hancock Park) has been registered as a National Natural Landmark by the Department of the Interior.

The adobe house that remains standing approximately ten blocks north of the pits was built by Antonio José Rocha about 1828–30. It is one of the original adobes of the rancho and has been restored with exceptional care by Earl B. Gilmore, oil magnate, who was born in the old house in the 1880's and who died there on February 27, 1964. It stands at the address 6301 West Third Street, on a private drive between the Farmers Market and the CBS television studio. The adobe has been officially recognized by the Cultural Heritage Board of the City of Los Angeles.

Rancho Rincón de los Bueyes

Rancho Rincón de los Bueyes ("the corner of the oxen"), which lay southwest of Rancho La Brea, was granted to Bernardo Higuera and Camilo López on December 7, 1821, a very early Mexican grant. It was confirmed by Governor Micheltorena on July 10, 1843, and in 1872 Don Bernardo's sons, Francisco and Secundino, were granted a patent to the land by the United States government. On November 8, 1872, Francisco Higuera conveyed 100 acres of the rancho to Antonio José Rocha, the son of Antonio José I, owner of Rancho La Brea.

Since then Rancho Rincón de los Bueyes has been divided many times, but that portion on which the old home place stood has remained in possession of Antonio José Rocha's descendants until the present. La Casa de Rocha, "an ample, pleasant place, with a big square ground plan and a gringo stairway inside," erected by Don Antonio José II in 1865, has seen the broad ranges that surrounded it on all sides change gradually from country to city life. Robertson Boulevard crosses the once fertile farmlands, and the city has moved up to the very doors of the old adobe.

Abandoned for many years, La Casa de Rocha has now been restored in keeping with its simple, pastoral charm, and stands today, very much as it was when built, at 2400 Shenandoah Street in Los Angeles. A second story of redwood ship siding, of the original construction, is superimposed on the outer adobe wall, while the roof projects from the bottom of this superstructure, forming a wide *corredor* all around the house. This quaint landmark, still showing evidences of its romantic past, is the home of a descendant of Antonio José Rocha. Located back from the street on a private lane, it has been declared a historic-cultural monument by the City of Los Angeles.

Culver City and Palms are located on the old rancho. The abandoned Southern Pacific depot at Palms, built in 1888 and now used by the Boy Scouts, has been declared a Los Angeles historic-cultural monument. It is situated on National Boulevard at Vinton Avenue.

Rancho Rincón de San Pasqual

At the foot of Raymond Hill in South Pasadena is a charming adobe beautifully restored and now used as a private residence. Begun in 1839, it was the first house built on Rancho San Pasqual, originally that part of the extensive lands of Mission San Gabriel granted first in 1835 to Juan Mariné, husband of Eulalia Pérez de Guillén, reputedly the oldest white woman in California at the time. This land was a gift made as a recompense for Doña Eulalia's long services at the mission as nurse, overseer of spinning and tailoring, cashier, and accountant. Today, the cities of Pasadena, South Pasadena, and Altadena cover the former rancho lands.

The rancho was regranted provisionally to José Pérez, who died in 1840 before he had completed the building and stocked the rancho according to the requirements of Mexican law. The land subsequently reverted to public ownership, but was granted to Manuel Gárfias, son-in-law of Doña Encarnación Ávila, in 1843.

The casa at Raymond Hill has come to be known as the Flores adobe because it was there that General José María Flores, provisional governor of California, took refuge in January 1847 after the Battle of La Mesa, while Kearny and

Stockton took final possession of Los Angeles and Frémont held the San Fernando Valley. General Flores and his staff held their last council within the San Pasqual rancho house on the night of January 9, while the California horsemen kept watch and guard on the hills outside. Knowing that surrender was inevitable, they made final plans, leaving Andrés Pico in command while Flores and Manuel Gárfias, both commissioned officers of the Mexican Army, fled to Mexico under cover of darkness on the night of January 11. On the 13th the Cahuenga Capitulation Treaty was signed by Frémont and Andrés Pico, and all hostilities came to an end.

The Flores adobe stands on Foothill Street, near the junction of Garfield Avenue and Clark Place. A bronze tablet was placed on September 14, 1919, by the Oneonta Park Chapter, D.A.R.

The Blanco Adobe

Standing behind San Marino High School on the north side of Huntington Drive is an old story-and-a-half adobe, now restored, that was once the home of Michael White, alias Miguel Blanco, a sailor who came to California in 1829 and married one of the daughters of Doña Eulalia de Guillén. Blanco obtained a grant of 77 acres directly north of Mission San Gabriel and lived there for many years after 1843.

At San Marino is the estate of Henry E. Huntington, now the location of the Huntington Library and Art Gallery. The Huntington Library is one of the foremost depositories of historical material in California.

For many years another adobe house stood in San Marino. It was the home of George Stoneman, governor of California from 1883 to 1887. Stoneman's 400-acre estate was called "Los Robles." A monument at the site of the house (SRL 669) on Montrobles Place incorporates some of the old adobe bricks.

Rancho Paso de Bartolo Viejo

At first a part of the lands belonging to Mission San Gabriel, Rancho Paso de Bartolo was granted to Juan Crispín Pérez on June 12, 1835, the year of the secularization. Pérez had been alcalde auxiliar of Rancho Santa Gertrudes from 1831 to 1836, and was later mayordomo of the mission, during its declining years. Following the original grant, Paso de Bartolo Viejo was finally divided among four claimants, Juan Crispín Pérez, Bernardino Guirado, Joaquina Sepúlveda, and Pío Pico. Pico and Pérez finally received their patent to 8,891 acres in 1881.

Pío Pico, last Mexican governor of California, did not inherit his wealth but obtained it by his own efforts. The vast ranchos of Las Flores and Santa Margarita were his, as well as several other extensive properties. He called the 8,000-acre rancho of Paso de Bartolo by the title "El Ranchito," both because of its diminutive size in comparison to his vaster estates and because of the affectionate regard in which he always held it. It was his favorite home place, and at the close of that pitiful struggle to compete with American business methods which finally reduced Don Pío Pico

from the position of the wealthiest man in California to a pauper's grave, El Ranchito was his last possession in Los Angeles County.

It is uncertain just when the adobe house of Pío Pico (SRL 127) was constructed, but it is likely that it was in the middle of the nineteenth century. Capacious and full of a quiet charm, the old house stands on the east bank of the San Gabriel River, which, in the flood of 1867, swept away a portion of the adobe. When Don Pío lived at El Ranchito, the house was the scene of lavish hospitality, and even in the years of his poverty, he still entertained with gracious courtesy. In 1891 he "passed through the portals of El Ranchito for the last time," and went to Los Angeles to spend his final years.

Concerted efforts to preserve the Pico adobe were begun in 1906 by the Governor Pico Museum and Historical Society of Whittier, and the Landmarks Club. The house was leased from the City of Whittier and much-needed repairs were made. Later, it was turned over to the state and is now restored as Pío Pico State Historical Monument, at 6003 Pioneer Boulevard, off Whittier Boulevard between Montebello and Whittier.

What is now the city of Whittier became the ranch of John M. Thomas in 1880–81. Whittier was founded as a Quaker colony in 1887, and Jonathan Bailey, one of the founders, moved into the Thomas ranch house, which still stands at 522 East Camilla Street. In Whittier's Mt. Olive Cemetery at Broadway and Citrus Avenue is the grave of "Greek George" (SRL 646). George Caralambo came to the United States from Asia Minor as a camel driver when the Army was experimenting with the use of camels in the southwestern desert. He settled in the Los Angeles area after the venture was abandoned, and in 1867 became a naturalized citizen under the name of George Allen. Another Whittier landmark is the huge paradox hybrid walnut tree (SRL 681) in the 600–800 block of West Whittier Boulevard. It was planted in 1907 as part of an agricultural experiment by the University of California.

Rancho San José

In the beautiful valley of Pomona west of the Arroyo de San Antonio, the boundaries of the great Rancho San José were first laid out by Ygnacio Palomares and Ricardo Vejar on March 19, 1837, the feast of St. Joseph. Father Zalvidea, who accompanied the party from Mission San Gabriel, performed the first Christian religious service ever held in the valley when he pronounced a benediction upon the two families about to establish their homes in the wilderness of San José. The ceremony was held under an oak tree, the stump of which still stands in the city of Pomona at 458 Kenoak Place, about two blocks from Ganesha Park. A bronze tablet commemorating this event was placed on the historic tree by the Pomona Chapter, D.A.R., in 1922. For many years the old Preciado adobe stood beneath the sheltering branches of this oak, but it has long since been torn down.

To Ygnacio Palomares was given the upper portion of Rancho San José, or San José de Arriba, while Ricardo Vejar received the lower half, known as San José de Abajo. Four adobes remain on the rancho, in the city of Pomona and in the foothills to the west.

The Palomares adobe, built by Don Ygnacio after 1837, still stands among the orange trees at 1569 North Park Avenue, although the older part of it has been torn down. It is a place full of quaint charm and peace, calling forth pleasant thoughts. The low roof of the little house projects over a broad *corridor* extending down the full length of the side that faces the old-fashioned garden. Masses of oleanders and cape jasmine, peach and orange trees diffuse their fragrance on the soft southern air and cast a welcome shade over the lilies and roses in the little garden.

About 300 yards southwest of the Palomares adobe, at 1459 Old Settlers' Lane, stands the Alvarado house, once the home of Ygnacio Alvarado, the close friend of Palomares. In those days when neighbors lived many miles apart, the hospitality of Spanish settlers was proverbial, but in few other instances was it expressed in so friendly and intimate a manner as in the case of Ygnacio Palomares and Ygnacio Alvarado. At the urgent invitation of the former, Alvarado came to Rancho San José and built his home within a stone's throw of his friend, the only stipulation in the arrangement being that Alvarado should build a chapel in his house, an agreement that was accordingly fulfilled. The chapel room is still an interesting part of the old house. Both of these unique adobes are private houses today, cared for and prized by their owners.

In 1854 Ygnacio Palomares built another adobe (*SRL 372*) at what is now the corner of Arrow Highway and Orange Grove Avenue. Leaving the old home to his son Francisco, Don Ygnacio made his home at the newer place on the road to Chino and San Bernardino. The adobe became a popular stage station and tavern, where a huge fireplace welcomed many a wayfarer on chill nights. For many years it stood among the fragrant orange groves, deserted and neglected, the *corridor* half-fallen, the walls crumbling with each winter rain, with only the untended rose vines and wisteria to cover the scars of the passing years. Fortunately, it has now been restored; since 1940 it has been open to the public as a museum of the Historical Society of Pomona Valley.

At 919 Puddingstone Drive above Pudding-

stone Dam, about two miles southeast of San Dimas, the Carrión adobe (*SRL 386*) stands on the lower reaches of the hills amid a natural setting of sagebrush and schmizl, with an occasional tuna cactus and broad-spreading sycamore breaking the clean and pleasant monotony of the landscape. Here on the old San Bernardino road, where the padres and caballeros of Spanish and Mexican times were followed by the pioneers of the early American period, Saturnino Carrión built one of the most attractive of the smaller adobes in southern California. This portion of Rancho San José de Arriba was given to Carrión by his uncle and aunt, Don Ygnacio and Doña Concepción López de Palomares, in 1843, when he was only a boy of 11, but it was not until 1863 (at the time of the great drought) that he finally came to San José to live. The little house was for many years threatened with decay, but fortunately it has now been restored to its former loveliness and is occupied as a private residence.

On Rancho San José de Abajo, Ricardo Vejar built an adobe that disappeared long ago. A second house, built about 1850 for his son Ramón on the adjoining Rancho Los Nogales, was, until its destruction in the 1950's, one of the best examples of the adobe mansion to be found in southern California. This splendid two-story ranch house, with the soft and graceful tracery of aged pepper trees flecking its mellow walls with ever-changing shadows, occupied a commanding position on one of the lower slopes of the rocky hills, whose rugged form made a picturesque background for the stately old house. The broad *corredores*, home-made doors, and other details of skillful and conscientious craftsmanship and fine taste gave Casa Vejar a charm and interest surpassing many other adobes of the period. In 1852 the Vejar family, like others, was swept into poverty by inability to cope with American business methods, but the pleasant customs, graciousness, and hospitality of a bygone era lingered at Casa Vejar. A historical marker, featuring a scale model of the old adobe, has been erected near the site, but this seems small compensation for the loss of the original. The marker stands at Diamond Bar and Richardson roads within the grounds of the Pacific State Hospital at Spadra.

The first American settlement in Pomona Valley was at Spadra, located on Rancho San José de Abajo. Spadra was a stage station on the old Colorado Emigrant Road via Chino in the 1850's and 1860's. Here "Uncle Billy" Rubottom, the first American settler in the valley, built a tavern in the 1860's, and the place was named Spadra after his native home in Arkansas. The old Spadra station has disappeared. The stage road is not followed by the highway today and has been obliterated.

About a mile east of Spadra at 2640 Pomona Boulevard is the two-story mansion built by Louis Phillips in the late 1860's. It was the first brick house in Pomona Valley and is still in good condition. Ricardo Vejar, easy-going and trustful, had lost Rancho San José de Abajo to Tischler and Schlesinger by foreclosure in 1864. A year or

Ygnacio Palomares Adobe, Pomona

two later, they sold it to Phillips, who proved to be an excellent manager, and in his hands and those of his descendants the great rancho prospered.

Pomona College, founded in 1887, held its first class on September 12, 1888, in a small cottage, the site (SRL 289) of which is at the southwest corner of Fifth and White avenues in Pomona. Five months later, the college moved to Claremont. Dr. Cyrus Grandison Baldwin, president of Pomona College, organized the San Antonio Light and Power Company, which built, in 1892, the first hydroelectric installation in California for long-distance transmission of alternating current at high voltage. A monument to this pioneer power plant (SRL 514) stands on the upper road in San Antonio Canyon northeast of Pomona, while the foundations of the plant can still be found on San Antonio Creek near the lower road. Pomona College is now one of the Associated Colleges of Claremont—a landmark in the history of education.

Rancho La Puente

"The arrival of the Bidwell-Bartleson company at Marsh's ranch ushered in . . . the period of organized immigration to California. Almost contemporaneous with the coming of this party, some twenty-five immigrants, recruited partly in Missouri, and partly from American residents in New Mexico, reached Los Angeles by way of the Gila and Colorado. This company was known, from the names of its leaders, as the Workman-Rowland party; and while Bidwell and his companions, for the most part, settled along the coast north of Monterey, or in the Sacramento Valley, the immigrants who came from Santa Fe established themselves in the south. Here many of them, like Rowland and Workman, the leaders, and Benjamin D. Wilson, the [second] mayor of Los Angeles under American rule, acquired large grants of land, upon which they dwelt in entire harmony with the California authorities and became respected citizens of the province. Other parties were not slow to follow the lead of Bidwell and of Rowland."

The Workman-Rowland party arrived in Los Angeles on November 5, 1841, and almost immediately the two partners, William Workman and John Rowland, began to look for a permanent home. Both had lived in New Mexico for more than ten years and were married to New Mexican women, and both had become Mexican citizens there. This entitled them to petition for grants of land in California, which they did in the spring of 1842, receiving the land formally in 1845.

At first the two friends seem to have owned the great ranges of Rancho La Puente jointly, their herds sharing the unfenced pastures and their adobe dwelling houses standing less than a mile apart. Later, the land was formally divided, William Workman retaining the western section of the rancho and John Rowland taking the eastern half.

On a slight knoll overlooking the valley, with higher mountains rising in the background, the old Workman adobe built in 1842 still stands about a mile west of the town of La Puente. Don Julián, as he was known to the Spanish, erected an adobe home similar in picturesqueness and baronial grandeur to that of Juan Temple at Los Cerritos. There he lived a quiet, industrious life, little concerned with the affairs of the world beyond the hills of his rancho.

But on September 7, 1845, a change was ushered in when Francisco P. F. Temple, younger brother of Juan Temple, became the son-in-law of William Workman. Francisco Temple, or "Templito," as the Californians called him, was greatly trusted by this proud and taciturn old Englishman whose daughter he had married. Young Templito, being ambitious and capable, brought many changes with him into the quiet life of the rancho.

After his brother's death in 1866, Templito bought the famous Temple Block in Los Angeles, and there, between 1866 and 1870, he added the middle section, the last or northern part of which housed the bank which eventually wrecked the entire fortunes of both Templito and Don Julián Workman.

It was during this period that, enamored of the splendid new buildings of the Temple Block, Don Julián remodeled his simple adobe house according to the mode of the time. Much of the original U-shaped structure was torn down and replaced by additions more suitable to the fancy of the day. Although greatly altered and modernized, it retained a certain old-fashioned air from its old adobe days.

Marks of many interesting features of Rancho La Puente survive today on the remaining portion of the estate which immediately surrounded the Workman home. The Indian retainers of the place were allowed to keep their hereditary ranchería during Don Julián's time, and at a short distance from the ranch house the cluster of tule huts stood on the banks of San José Creek, the ancient course of which is still visible where it runs parallel with the hills to the south. Just west of the village was the Indian burial ground. This was first set aside by Workman in 1850, principally as a family cemetery.

On San José Creek also stood two gristmills erected by Workman and Rowland before 1850, and extensively patronized by farmers of the neighborhood in the 1850's and 1860's. Some of the old millstones have been incorporated into the fountain in the patio of the modern adobe erected in the 1920's by Walter P. Temple just across the drive from the old home. Remembrance of the mills is preserved also in the name of a road that passes through the region, Workman Mill Road.

One of the most interesting remnants of early days is the tunnel, now blocked up, that started under the east wing of the rancho house and extended to the family cemetery several hundred feet to the east. It is said that Don Julián used to send his servants on errands down this underground passageway, and tales of ghosts and witches arose among the simple Indians who chanced to see these messengers emerge mysteriously from the ground. Tales of buried treasure came to be connected with this rancho, as with many another where no treasure has ever been found other than the treasures of fancy and romance.

In 1870 Francisco Temple built the third portion of the Temple Block and there, on November 23, 1871, he opened the Temple-Workman Bank. Templito was held in the highest regard by all who knew him, and his venture was backed by both his own and his father-in-law's fortunes. But the generous nature of the one and the simple trust of the other, when confronted by the financial panic which swept California after the failure of the California Bank in San Francisco in 1875, finally involved them in a net of mortgages and foreclosures. All the fortune that Don Julián Workman and Francisco Temple together had built was finally lost in 1876—all, that is, except the 75 acres of the old home place, which passed to Don Julián's grandchildren. This, too, was lost on a mortgage in the 1890's, but in 1919 it was bought back by Templito's youngest son, Walter P. Temple, who restored the Workman home and cemetery and built the modern adobe mansion, for which he imported artisans from Mexico. In the cemetery, on the site of a brick chapel that Workman had erected in 1857, Walter P. Temple built a marble and concrete mausoleum for the remains of members of the Workman and Temple families. He also provided a place in it for the bodies of Don Pío Pico and his wife, which were brought from an abandoned cemetery in Los Angeles. The Workman homestead is now the location of a private sanitarium, the entrance to which is on Turnbull Canyon Road.

The adobe of John Rowland has long vanished, but about 100 yards south of its site a two-story brick house built by him in 1855 still stands. It is located behind the buildings of the Hudson School District on Gale Avenue east of Hacienda Boulevard. At the rear of the brick house, which is now covered with stucco, is its first kitchen, a separate adobe building. The site of Rowland's original adobe house near the south bank of San José Creek is marked by two ash trees and an olive tree, planted by him about 1850. A mile or so east of the brick house, and on the same side of Gale Avenue, stands the three-story wooden house of early date that belonged to John Reed, Rowland's son-in-law. It later became the home of William R. Rowland, John Rowland's son, who was sheriff of Los Angeles County for a time in the 1870's and 1880's. John Rowland is buried in the cemetery at the Workman place. Workman himself was laid to rest beside his partner, but his remains have now been placed in the mausoleum.

Southeast of La Puente in the hills stands the Grazide adobe, officially recognized by the Cultural Heritage Board of the City of Los Angeles. It was built in 1875 by Francisco Grazide for his bride, Isabel Rowland, a granddaughter of John Rowland. The adobe is located just south of Fifth Avenue off South Batson Avenue, to the east of the road. Stately trees, beautiful gardens, and a small lake fed by natural springs give the place a charming atmosphere.

Rancho La Merced

Rancho La Merced lay west of Rancho La Puente. It was originally granted to Doña Casilda Soto in 1846. In 1850 she sold the ranch and her adobe house to William Workman, who in 1851 gave it to Francisco P. F. Temple, his son-in-law, and Juan Matías Sánchez. The place was then, as now, called Misión Vieja, because the first site of Mission San Gabriel had been established in 1771 less than a mile from the spot where Francisco Temple later built his adobe home. In the same region today, but across the river to the west, is the rich Montebello oil field, and intersecting it is San Gabriel Boulevard, which crosses the Río Hondo bridge at this point.

The spot where the Temple adobe stood is near the corner of San Gabriel Boulevard and Durfee Avenue. The splendid gardens and vineyards of former days have vanished, as has the settlement of Temple's Corners just across the river from the oil wells. Both the adobe and the later brick mansion erected by Templito were destroyed by fire early in the twentieth century. Francisco Temple died there on April 27, 1888, and the little home tract at Temple's Corners became the property of his widow, Doña Antonia Margarita. This portion of Rancho La Merced remained in the Temple family for many years, thus escaping the grasp of "Lucky" Baldwin, who acquired much land in this area.

One day in the spring of 1914, a grandson of Francisco Temple, Thomas Workman Temple II —then a boy of nine, now the historian of Mission San Gabriel and an authority on the genealogies of old California families—was looking for tall wild oats, which he used to snare lizards, on the hillside across the Río Hondo from his home at Temple's Corners. On the search he discovered an outcropping of natural gas in a pool of water on the property his father, Walter P. Temple, had purchased in 1912. Operations were begun there in April 1917 by the Standard Oil Company. Thus was the famous Montebello oil field established.

In this district an old adobe stood for many years. It was built in 1869 by Jesús Andrade and Rafael Bayse and was used first as a store and later as a saloon. Walter Temple remodeled "La Casita de Rafael Bayse," then much disfigured by time and use, and he and his family were living in it at the time of the oil discovery. It was torn down in the early 1930's. From the tract on which it stood, a large oil company continues to extract a fortune in black gold. Such are the changes wrought by the passing years in the lives of men and in their dwelling places.

On Lincoln Avenue near La Merced Avenue, about two miles southwest of the site of the home of Francisco Temple, stands a fine adobe mansion on a pleasant hill above the Río Hondo. The older wing, facing the river, was erected by Casilda Soto in the late 1840's. The house was enlarged in the early 1850's by Juan Matías Sánchez, who built the wing facing the hills. Although elaborately remodeled within, the old Sánchez adobe retains some of its original exterior lines and character. Juan Matías Sánchez had owned 2,200 acres of excellent land about Misión Vieja, as well as the Potrero Grande and the Potrero de Felipe Lugo. His friendship for William Workman and Francisco Temple, however, caused him to sacrifice all his possessions in a heroic effort to save the honor of his friends. His last years were spent in poverty, while rich oil wells about his adobe made later owners wealthy and preserved the old adobe house in lavishness.

First Discovery of Gold in California

The first discovery of gold in commercial quantities in California was made in 1842 by Francisco López at Placerita Canyon. In the following year he found gold in San Feliciano Canyon. The story of the first discovery is as follows.

One day in March 1842, López rode into the canyon. While resting in the shade of an oak tree, he became engaged in gathering wild onions. He suddenly noticed some shining particles clinging to the roots of the plants. Plucking up more of the roots, he found the same kind of pebbles fastened on them. Later, in Los Angeles, he was assured that they were gold nuggets.

This discovery not only caused considerable excitement throughout the south but also brought numbers of prospectors from Sonora, Mexico. On November 22, 1842, Don Abel Stearns sent the first California gold from the mines at Placerita to the United States Mint at Philadelphia. For many years thereafter he continued to send to Philadelphia gold dust and nuggets from this same region.

Placerita Canyon State Park is located about four miles east of Newhall in the San Fernando Hills, and about 40 miles northwest of Los Angeles. In the vicinity of the old placers on the west side of the canyon proper, a boulder with a bronze plate was placed on March 9, 1930, by the Kiwanis Club and the Native Sons of the Golden West to mark the site of the first discovery of gold in California. Near the marker, the old oak tree under which López rested still grows, below the level of the present main park road. It has been styled the "Oak of the Golden Dream" (*SRL 168*).

Rancho Ciénega o Paso de la Tijera

There were many natural springs and marsh lands (*ciénegas*) below the hills at Rancho Ciénega, and two narrow valleys between the Baldwin Hills formed a pass, which, to the imaginative Spaniards, resembled a pair of opened scissors (*paso de la tijera*). Thus originated the double name of the great Rancho Ciénega o Paso de la Tijera, granted to Vicente Sánchez, alcalde of Los Angeles, in 1843.

Rancho Ciénega was a long day's journey into the country in those days, and Don Vicente's official duties caused him to live in Los Angeles. The vast ranges of his country estate were, therefore, used merely for cattle grazing.

After Don Vicente's death, about 1850, his landholdings were partitioned among his heirs, and Tomás A. Sánchez, famous as sheriff of Los An-

Casilda Soto–Juan Matías Sánchez Adobe, near Montebello

geles for nearly ten years, received Rancho Ciénega, while his sisters took the property on Calle de los Negros in Los Angeles.

Don Tomás married María Sepúlveda, who received a portion of Rancho San Rafael after Fernando Sepúlveda's death. Tomás Sánchez sold Rancho Ciénega and made his home on his wife's little estate at the present Glendale, where a handsome adobe, still standing, was built near the site of the original home.

E. J. (Lucky) Baldwin finally became the owner of Rancho Ciénega, and when the estate was settled after his death in 1909, this rancho was listed as one of the most valuable of all his extensive holdings. "Seemingly, no matter how fast this old rancho has been subdivided, the remaining unsubdivided part grows in value by leaps and bounds directly contrary to its diminishing size."

Although some of the adobes erected at Ciénega in rancho days were in ruins when the Sunset Golf Corporation leased the estate from the Baldwin heirs in the 1920's, a number of them were still standing. Unusual restraint and appreciation were used in the restoration of these buildings, and the clubhouse was laid out along the lines of the original plans, as nearly as they could be ascertained. The smooth, green slopes which lay before the casa, where the herds of Lucky Baldwin and, before his time, those of Vicente and Tomás Sánchez once grazed, became the broad links of a public golf course. Now this, too, has disappeared, to be replaced by curving streets and modern homes. The golfers' clubhouse buildings, into which the old adobes were incorporated, have become the home of a women's club. There is still a definite Spanish flavor there at 3725 Don Felipe Drive, above South Crenshaw Boulevard.

It was in this Crenshaw or Angeles Mesa district that the world's greatest athletes were housed during the Olympic Games in 1932. The Olympic village, including over 600 two-room dwellings, was built in the hills to the west of Crenshaw Boulevard south of Vernon Avenue. The area's brief world fame is commemorated in the names of Olympiad Drive and Athenian Way.

Rancho Aguaje de Centinela

Rancho Aguaje de Centinela was granted to Ignacio Machado in 1844. The very next year, Machado traded his new estate, which was good only for cattle grazing, to Bruno Ábila (Ávila) for a small adobe house and vineyard in Los Angeles. Since the latter was considered of more value than the half-league of pasture land, Machado gave, in addition, two barrels of *aguardiente* (brandy) in exchange for the town house. Today, most of the pastures of Centinela are covered by the thriving city of Inglewood, one of the prosperous suburbs of Los Angeles.

The *aguaje* ("water hole") of Centinela was located in what is now Inglewood's Centinela Park. Known to the Indians from ancient times, it became the principal water supply for early settlers in the area. The Centinela Springs *(SRL*

363) are commemorated by a drinking fountain in the park below the swimming pool.

Rancho Centinela had a varied history. Bruno Ábila finally lost it in 1857, at a sheriff's sale, when it was purchased by Hilliard P. Dorsey for about a dollar an acre. Two years later, his widow sold it for 35 cents an acre to Francis J. Carpenter. Meanwhile, Fernando, a Frenchman and the son-in-law of Bruno Ábila, had refused to give up the land and it became the duty of Carpenter to dispossess him of it.

Joseph Lancaster Brent, a Southerner by birth, but a prominent citizen of Los Angeles for many years, and later brigadier general in the Confederate Army, next came into ownership of Rancho Centinela. He sold it in 1860, however, in order to join the Confederate Army, and his successors were Sir Robert Burnett and his wife from Crathes Castle, Scotland.

Land values in this region increased in the years following, and in 1885 the baronet sold the rancho to Daniel Freeman, founder of Inglewood, for $140,000. During the land boom of 1886–88, it became one of the most spectacular of the boom subdivisions, ultimately developing into the modern city of Inglewood.

The Centinela rancho house, at 7634 Midfield Avenue, is one of the most beautifully preserved of the smaller adobes of Los Angeles County. Its simple lines, vine-clad *corredores*, and deeply recessed windows have remained unmarred by modern "improvements." The owners have cared for it well and no signs of deterioration spoil its beauty. The adobe is open to the public at stated times.

Rancho Los Feliz

Rancho Los Feliz was granted to María Ygnacia Verdugo in 1843, but was occupied by her as early as 1841. The United States government issued a patent in her name for 6,647 acres. The rancho passed successively through the hands of Antonio Coronel, famous pioneer of Los Angeles; James Lick, an equally famous pioneer of San Francisco and the founder of Lick Observatory; and Colonel Griffith Jenkins Griffith, who, in 1898, deeded 3,015 acres of the rancho to the City of Los Angeles. This is now Griffith Park. An old adobe still stands in this exquisitely wooded mountain park, at 4730 Crystal Springs Drive.

Rancho Santa Anita

Rancho Santa Anita, comprising 13,319 acres, was granted to Hugo Reid in 1845. He later sold it to Henry Dalton, an Englishman, for 20 cents an acre. For a time it was in the hands of William Wolfskill, but in 1872 his son, Lewis Wolfskill, sold it to H. Newmark and Company for $85,000. In 1875 Elias Jackson (Lucky) Baldwin, San Francisco mining operator and horseman, purchased it for three times the amount paid by Newmark. Baldwin had made millions, it is said, in the Ophir Mines of Nevada. He soon moved from San Francisco into the ranch house at Santa Anita. Here he continued to win fortunes not only by developing a world-famous breed of racing horses

Los Feliz Adobe, Griffith Park

but also by acquiring and selling great landed estates.

Lucky Baldwin was a lover of trees as well as of horses. "He bordered every road within his rancho with trees and jealously fostered and guarded them. The towering lines of eucalyptus trees along Huntington Drive and Santa Anita Avenue through the Rancho Santa Anita" stood for many years as evidence of his planting.

The heart of the Baldwin estate is now the Los Angeles State and County Arboretum at Arcadia. Here, surrounded by beautiful trees, flowers, and lakes, stands the original Hugo Reid adobe *(SRL 368)*, built in 1839 and later occupied by Baldwin as his home. It was restored by the state and dedicated in 1961. The "Queen Anne Cottage" *(SRL 367)* was built by Baldwin in 1881 as a guest house. It was restored and dedicated in 1954. Still another landmark is the old carriage house, also built by Lucky Baldwin.

Landmarks of the Mexican War

The Battle of San Gabriel occurred on January 8, 1847, ten miles southeast of Los Angeles at a place *(SRL 385)* on the San Gabriel River (now Río Hondo) in the southern part of the present city of Montebello. There were quicksands at this point and a high bluff opposite the ford, making passage of the stream difficult. Here the Californians, with 500 or 600 men under command of General José Flores, held the bluff, while the Americans under Commodore Robert F. Stockton and General Stephen W. Kearny, with 600 men, had the difficult task of fording the river with their heavy artillery under fire of the enemy. Within an hour and a half, however, the feat was accomplished and the Californians were retiring toward Los Angeles. A monument has been erected at the corner of Washington Boulevard and Bluff Road.

On January 9 the two forces met again at La Mesa, the site of the present Union Stockyards in the great central manufacturing district of Los Angeles. A group of four granite boulders, set with bronze tablets, was placed on the spot *(SRL 167)* on September 9, 1926, by the Native Sons and the Native Daughters of the Golden West. This is now in front of a bank building at Downey Road and Exchange Avenue.

La Mesa was of slight importance in itself, merely confirming the course of events at San Gabriel. Like all the so-called "battles" of the American occupation, it amounted to little more than a skirmish. The Californians, realizing the hopelessness of resistance, soon withdrew to Rancho San Pasqual, where their final decision to surrender was made. Camping that night on the outskirts of Los Angeles, Stockton and Kearny marched to the plaza on the following day, the city having already surrendered. With this action, control passed forever from the hands of Mexico.

With Kearny and Stockton in control of Los Angeles and Frémont occupying the San Fernando Valley, the Californians offered no further resistance. Frémont at once sent Jesús Pico to persuade the Californians to lay down their arms, which they were eager to do. Ready to make peace if favorable terms were arranged, the two parties met on January 13, 1847, at the Cahuenga adobe, about a mile from the entrance to Cahuenga Pass. Here Andrés Pico and John C. Frémont signed the Cahuenga Capitulation Treaty, which ended all hostilities throughout California.

Liberal terms and common sense characterized this agreement by which the entire course of history on the Pacific slope was changed. Henceforth, Mexican laws and customs were to be replaced by those of Anglo-Saxon origin. Large cities were to arise where pueblos stood, a vast school system was to take the place of the illiteracy of the past, and the undreamed-of wealth of California's mines and forests and fertile soil was to be discovered.

The site of the old treaty adobe *(SRL 151)* has been preserved by the City of Los Angeles as a memorial park called "Campo de Cahuenga." It is at 3919 Lankershim Boulevard in North Hollywood, and has been declared a historic-cultural monument by the Cultural Heritage Board. Not far from the site, below Lookout Mountain, at a place called Los Alamos, a skirmish took place on February 20–21, 1845, between a band of rebel Californians, under José Castro and Juan Bautista Alvarado, and Governor Manuel Micheltorena's *cholo* army. The governor was forced to retreat to Rancho Los Feliz, where he surrendered, and Pío Pico was made governor in his stead.

The site of Lieutenant Colonel John C. Frémont's headquarters in Los Angeles in January 1847 was at the southeast corner of Aliso and Los Angeles streets. There he established himself in the Alexander Bell adobe, after Commodore Stockton had appointed him military governor of the territory on January 19, an office he held for 50 days. The old Bell adobe was torn down long ago, and the site is now occupied by a modern public building.

When Stockton and Kearny entered Los Angeles on January 10, 1847, after the Battle of La Mesa, their troops, numbering 600 men in all, were stationed on a hill west of the plaza. On January 11, Frémont and his men came down from Monterey, via Cahuenga Pass, and for several weeks 1,000 American soldiers were quartered on the hill. At this time, work was begun by Lieutenant William H. Emory on a temporary fort, but it was never completed. Later, in the summer of 1847, Lieutenant Davidson erected another fort on this same spot overlooking the pueblo. It was dedicated on July 4 and was named Fort Moore, in honor of Captain B. D. Moore, who was killed in the Battle of San Pasqual. Nothing of the old fort remains today, and much of Fort Moore Hill was leveled for construction of the Hollywood Freeway. What remains of the hill is occupied by the Los Angeles City Board of Education. At the base is the Pioneer Memorial, a heroic bas-relief constructed in the 1950's. On it is chiseled the following inscription: "On this site stood Fort Moore, built by the Mormon Battalion.... The flag of the United States was raised here on July 4, 1847, by United States troops at the first Independence Day celebration in Los Angeles. This memorial honors the troops who helped to win the Southwest: the United States First Dragoons..., the New York Volunteers..., and the Mormon Battalion ..."

El Monte

The "Old Spanish Trail" into California, followed by William Wolfskill in 1830–31, has been proved "to be neither old nor strictly Spanish." The trail was first traversed by a New Mexican, Antonio Armijo, in 1829–30, although his route, before reaching California, varied considerably from that followed by Wolfskill the following year. Later, it came to be known also as the Santa Fe Trail, and was used by many early American pioneers who came into California by the southern route. In the late 1840's and early 1850's, this trail, as far as Salt Lake, Utah, was also known as the Mormon Trail. For many of the covered-wagon emigrants, El Monte became the end of the trail, and here on the banks of the San Gabriel River, where natural springs made agriculture easy and where the land remained unappropriated by Spanish or Mexican grants, they made their homes. At first El Monte was only a camping place, but as early as 1849 Ira Thompson had established a stage station at a place called "Willow Grove." By 1852 the Dodson and Ryan families had arrived by ox team and Dodson had erected the first dwelling in El Monte, a crude adobe of "sticks and mud." Soon other emigrants arrived, and permanent homes were established in this green oasis.

In 1852 the first schoolhouse was erected on a site now in the bed of the San Gabriel River, the flood of 1909 having washed out a new channel farther east. The building had previously been removed to what is now 3436 Granada Avenue, where it still stands, remodeled and used as a private house. John Prior, a Baptist minister, organized the first Protestant evangelical church in southern California in this old schoolhouse in 1853. The first church building, however, was not erected until the early 1860's.

Angeles National Forest

Angeles National Forest (SRL 717), in the San Gabriel Mountains of Los Angeles and San Bernardino counties, was the first national forest in California and the second in the United States. President Benjamin Harrison set the area aside on December 20, 1892, and it was first called San Gabriel Timberland Reserve. In 1907 it became San Gabriel National Forest, and the following year it acquired its present name. The most scenic road in the forest is the Angeles Crest Highway from La Cañada to Big Pines. A historical monument commemorating the early forest preserve stands on this highway.

The side road to Mount Wilson and the observatory branches from the Angeles Crest Highway at the Red Box ranger station. Just south of Red Box a dirt road leads east into the canyon of the West Fork of the San Gabriel River. About six miles along this road is "Old Short Cut" (SRL 632), the oldest building in the Angeles National Forest, erected in 1900. The log structure was the original West Fork ranger station and is said to be the first United States Forest Service ranger station in the nation built with government funds. It takes its name from the Short Cut Canyon Trail, on which it is one of the main stopping points.

Tujunga is a community along Foothill Boulevard near the boundary of Angeles National Forest. It was once an incorporated city but is now a part of the city of Los Angeles. Bolton Hall, a unique building of native stone built in 1913 and at one time the Tujunga City Hall, has been declared a historic-cultural monument by the Cultural Heritage Board. It stands at 10116 Commerce Avenue.

Hollywood and Motion Pictures

In the minds of many at home and abroad, Los Angeles and Hollywood are one and the same. The motion picture industry brought fame and wealth to southern California, and Hollywood—only one district of the huge city—became the glamor capital of the world.

The oldest house in Hollywood (SRL 160) is located in Plummer Park at Santa Monica Boulevard and Vista Street. It was built in the 1870's by Eugene R. Plummer, a rancher who acquired part of Rancho La Brea in 1874.

The first feature-length motion picture made in Hollywood was The Squaw Man, filmed in 1913–14 by Cecil B. DeMille, Samuel Goldwyn, and Jesse Lasky, Sr. The studio in which the picture was made was a barn at the corner of Selma Avenue and Vine Street. In 1927 the historic barn (SRL 554) was moved to the property of Paramount Studios on Marathon Street, where it stands today, although not accessible to the general public. A few years before his death, DeMille participated in the dedication of a plaque on Hollywood's first major film company studio.

Barnsdall Park, on Olive Hill at 4800 Hollywood Boulevard, is owned by the City of Los Angeles and is a major cultural center. Here stands Hollyhock House, the first California residence designed by Frank Lloyd Wright. It was built for Aline Barnsdall in 1918–20. The Arts and Crafts Building, by the same architect, was constructed about the same time. In 1927 Miss Barnsdall deeded her property to the city, and in 1954 Wright was engaged to design another building, the Municipal Gallery. Hollyhock House, the

Arts and Crafts Building, and the park itself have been declared historic-cultural monuments by the Cultural Heritage Board.

For years, bus tours past the homes of motion picture stars in Beverly Hills, Bel-Air, and other exclusive districts have been a major attraction for tourists to Los Angeles. Two such homes, in outlying areas, have now been set aside as public parks. Will Rogers State Historic Park, at 14253 Sunset Boulevard in Pacific Palisades, includes the home built by the famed humorist in the 1920's. The William S. Hart Ranch, at San Fernando Road and Newhall Avenue in Newhall, is now a Los Angeles County Park. Here stand the original ranch house, built about 1910 by an earlier owner, and the mansion completed by the cowboy actor in 1928.

The Griffith Ranch (SRL 716), privately owned, was the home of the pioneer film producer D. W. Griffith and the locale of many of his pictures. A marker stands one and a half miles east of San Fernando at Foothill Boulevard and Vaughn Street.

Other Landmarks in the City of Los Angeles

The first commercial orange grove in California was planted in 1857 by William Wolfskill on his ranch near the Pueblo of Los Angeles. For a number of years it was the largest citrus grove in the United States and yielded very heavy crops. In 1885 the owners of the Wolfskill Ranch donated to the Southern Pacific Railroad the site for the Arcade depot, no longer in existence, at Fifth Street and Central Avenue. Soon after, the remainder of the famous orchard was sold and subdivided.

The site of the Coronel ranch house, where Helen Hunt Jackson was hospitably entertained by Antonio Coronel in the winter of 1881-82, and where she conceived her novel Ramona, is at Seventh and Alameda streets.

In April 1950 an official state marker was placed on Temple Street at the Federal Building to commemorate the centennial of the establishment of the Los Angeles post office. Two markers have been placed on the bank building at Main and Commercial streets. One honors southern California's first newspaper, the Los Angeles Star (SRL 789), founded on May 17, 1851. The newspaper office stood at Los Angeles Street and the Santa Ana Freeway, and the plaque has been placed nearby on the Commercial Street side of the bank. The other marker indicates the site of the Bella Union Hotel (SRL 656), Los Angeles' pioneer hostelry, where the first Butterfield stage arrived from St. Louis on October 7, 1858. The Butterfield Overland Mail Company soon acquired the property at 145 South Spring Street and built there its Los Angeles station (SRL 744), one of the best equipped on the route. A plaque marks the site.

Bunker Hill, west of the present Civic Center, was one of Los Angeles' most fashionable residential districts in the last quarter of the nineteenth century. Now, practically all of its beautiful old Victorian homes have been razed in an urban redevelopment project. Still standing are "The Castle" at 325 Bunker Hill Avenue, built in 1882, and its neighbor at 339. On the northern fringe of the hill, at 1012 West Temple Street, is an ornate three-story house built about 1887. Angel's Flight, a diminutive cable railway, climbs the eastern slope of Bunker Hill from Third and Hill streets. Built by Colonel J. W. Eddy in 1901, Angel's Flight has been declared a historic-cultural monument by the Cultural Heritage Board, as have the three old homes mentioned above. Another such monument is the Samuel Calvert Foy residence. Now located at 633 South Witmer Street, west of the Bunker Hill area, it was originally constructed in 1873 on Grasshopper Street (now Figueroa) at the present site of the Statler Hilton Hotel.

The Bradbury Building at 304 South Broadway, another historic-cultural monument, is Los Angeles' most interesting old business building. The exterior of the five-story structure, built in 1893, is undistinguished, but the interior is unique, with a court, open corridors, ornamental rails and stairs, and exposed elevator cages.

The original building of the University of Southern California (SRL 536), opened in 1880, is the oldest university building in southern California in continuous use for educational purposes. It was moved in 1956 to Childs Way (formerly 36th Street) between Hoover Boulevard and University Avenue. In the same part of Los Angeles is the former mansion of Edward L. Doheny, oil magnate, at 8 Chester Place, now occupied by the Sisters of St. Joseph of Carondelet. It was built in 1899-1900 and acquired by Doheny in 1901. A little-known fact is that Los Angeles was the birthplace of Adlai E. Stevenson, late Ambassador to the United Nations. He was born on February 5, 1900, at 2639 Monmouth Avenue, while his father was employed by the Los Angeles Examiner. The Doheny mansion and the site of the Stevenson birthplace have been declared historic-cultural monuments by the Cultural Heritage Board.

The same board has officially recognized several old buildings at Sawtelle, the Veterans Administration Center in West Los Angeles, originally the Pacific branch of the National Home for Disabled Volunteer Soldiers. Among the oldest structures is the chapel, built about 1888.

La Casa de Adobe, at 4605 North Figueroa Street, part of the Southwest Museum, is a faithful and charming replica of an early California home. Built of adobe around a patio planted exclusively with shrubs and plants grown in early California gardens, it is furnished with genuine antiques of the period, most of which were provided by Spanish and American pioneer families. It is open to the public.

El Alisal ("the sycamore"), former home of the writer Charles F. Lummis (SRL 531), has been the objective of more pilgrimages of famous people than perhaps any other home in southern California. "Don Carlos" Lummis wrote and lectured vividly on the Southwest, of which he was a lifelong student. In 1893 he edited the Land of Sunshine, later the Outwest Magazine. In 1897 he founded the California History and Landmarks

Club, which was largely responsible for the preservation of the old missions and the bettering of conditions among the mission Indians. He and others founded the Southwest Museum for the housing of the collections of the Society of the Archaeological Institute of America, which he also founded. He was Los Angeles city librarian from 1905 to 1911. At his death at El Alisal on November 26, 1928, this tribute was paid to him: "He was Southern California—he was the Great Southwest."

With his own hands, Lummis built his home of native stone in 1898 around a giant sycamore in the vicinity of Sycamore Grove in northeastern Los Angeles. The old tree is gone, but the home is now open to the public. Lummis Home State Historical Monument is located at 200 East Avenue 43, near the Pasadena Freeway. It has been officially recognized by the Cultural Heritage Board of the City of Los Angeles.

The Pasadena Freeway, originally called Arroyo Seco Parkway, is California's first freeway. A six-mile stretch was opened on December 30, 1940, and in the next few days California suffered its first freeway congestion—traffic to and from the Tournament of Roses parade and the Rose Bowl game at Pasadena.

At 1765 East 107th Street in the Watts district of Los Angeles is one of California's most unusual landmarks, the Watts Towers. The three spires, highest of which is 104 feet, were the work of one man from 1921 to 1954. Simon Rodia, an Italian immigrant, using only simple tools, constructed what has been called "a paramount achievement of twentieth-century folk art" of steel rods, wire mesh, seashells, broken dishes and bottles, and cement. He intended it as a tribute to his adopted land. In 1959 the towers were threatened with demolition, but a severe stress test proved their solidity and safety, and the city allowed them to remain. Since then, they have been declared a historic-cultural monument by the Cultural Heritage Board and are open to the public. Rodia died in obscurity in Martinez, California, on July 17, 1965, at the age of 90.

Landmarks of Northern Los Angeles County

Early in the twentieth century the City of Los Angeles acquired the water rights to the Owens Valley, in Inyo County some 250 miles to the north. Under the direction of City Engineer William Mulholland, an aqueduct was begun in 1905 and completed in 1913. The terminus of the aqueduct is about four miles north of San Fernando beside Interstate Highway 5. It is called "The Cascades" *(SRL 653)*, and here water from the eastern slope of the Sierra Nevada may be seen coursing into reservoirs to slake the thirst of the metropolis. The Western Hotel *(SRL 658)* in Lancaster was one place where crews were housed during the construction of the aqueduct. It was built in 1874 and still stands at 557 West Lancaster Boulevard in the Antelope Valley town. The St. Francis Dam was built in 1926 as part of the same water project. Two years later, on March 12, 1928, the 185-foot-high dam broke, sending a wall of water down San Francisquito Canyon and the valley of the Santa Clara River. Hundreds of homes were washed away and nearly 500 persons were killed in one of California's worst disasters. Many had been asleep, for it was after midnight. The dam was never rebuilt. A heap of rubble marks the site, on the west side of San Francisquito Canyon Road between Powerhouse No. 2 and Los Angeles County Detention Camp 17.

On the east side of Highway 14, about a mile north of its junction with Interstate 5, is a parking area with several historical markers. John C. Frémont went this way in January 1847 on his way from Santa Barbara to Los Angeles, and the crossing of the mountains became known as Frémont Pass. In 1859 General E. F. Beale and his men cut 50 feet of rock and earth from the gap to enable vehicles to make the crossing more easily. One may still see Beale's Cut by hiking about a quarter of a mile east and north of the parking area, across a dry wash. Modern engineers consider it a remarkable feat of pioneer engineering. Frémont Pass was replaced by the Newhall Tunnel, directly west, and this, in turn, has been superseded by the present giant cut and modern highway.

Until 1915 a trip from Los Angeles to Bakersfield entailed a circuitous route up either Bouquet Canyon or San Francisquito Canyon, and then past Elizabeth Lake, Neenach, and Quail Lake, to Gorman. In 1914 the famous Ridge Route was built—48 miles of twisting, turning pavement between Castaic and the Grapevine, much of it along the crest of a ridge. It was opened ahead of schedule in the latter part of 1915. The degrees of curve in the road, if totaled, are said to equal 110 complete circles, but it was nevertheless a remarkable improvement over the older roundabout route. Soon many service stations and inns sprang up along the Ridge Route; some, such as Tumble Inn and Sandberg's Lodge, became famous stopping places. The road was superseded in 1933 by the present Highway 99 between Castaic and Gorman, which, though it follows the canyons instead of the ridges, has kept the venerable name of Ridge Route. This, in turn, is being replaced in the mid-1960's by the Interstate 5 freeway. The old Ridge Route was deserted practically overnight in 1933 and the food and gasoline stops were closed. The "ghost highway" is still passable to cautious drivers, although parts of it are not maintained as public road, and a trip along its steep, narrow course is like a step backward in time. Through the years the old stopping places have virtually all burned down or been torn down, but the ribbon of concrete is still there. The original Ridge Route branches left from Lake Hughes Road (the Elizabeth Lake Canyon road) at a point one mile north of Castaic.

Several historical places are located in the vicinity of Newhall, besides the "Oak of the Golden Dream" and the William S. Hart Ranch, described earlier. South on San Fernando Road is the site of Lyons Station *(SRL 688)*, an old stage stop. A small community grew up here in the 1860's, and the pioneer cemetery has been expanded into Eternal Valley Memorial Park.

The discovery well of the Newhall oil field, CSO-4 or Pico 4 *(SRL 516)*, is located in Pico Canyon west of Newhall beyond Interstate 5. It was spudded early in 1876, completed at 300 feet in September of the same year, and deepened to 600 feet still later in 1876, at which time it produced 150 barrels a day. The success of this well led to the construction of the first commercial oil refinery in California *(SRL 172)* at Newhall, also in 1876. The refinery, now restored, is one-half mile west of San Fernando Road via Pine Street and a side road to the left.

Lang Station *(SRL 590)*, ten miles east of Saugus on the Southern Pacific Railroad and Soledad Canyon Road, is the site of the driving of the "last spike" that united the two sections of the railroad approaching each other at this point, one coming north from Los Angeles and the other south from San Francisco through Tehachapi Pass. Here on September 5, 1876, with Governor Leland Stanford, Collis P. Huntington, Charles Crocker, and other officials in attendance, the last spike was driven, ending the period of isolation that had hitherto kept Los Angeles a sleepy, unprogressive town, and ushering in the new era in which it would become one of the great cities of the West.

Robbers' Roost, better known as Vásquez Rocks, is an interesting geologic formation on a high ridge between Soledad and Mint canyons, northeast of Lang and west of Acton. It is said that this was one of the hiding places of Tiburcio Vásquez, the most feared of all the outlaws in southern California during the 1860's and early 1870's. He was captured in the Santa Monica foothills and executed in San Jose on March 19, 1875. The Vásquez Rocks form a part of the great San Andreas Fault, which extends, in California, from the Mendocino coast to the Imperial Valley. The disaster of 1906 in San Francisco and many other earthquakes in California were caused by this fault system. The Vásquez Rocks are composed of sandstone in which many kinds of rocks are embedded. One formation is in the shape of a huge elephant's head. Ancient Indian legends are associated with these rocks. The Antelope Valley Freeway (Route 14), opened in September 1963, bisects the area of the Vásquez Rocks.

Rancho San Francisco *(SRL 556)*, comprising 48,612 acres, was granted to Antonio del Valle in 1839. A marker stands near the junction of Interstate 5 and State 126, half a mile north of the site of the old rancho headquarters. William Lewis Manly and John Rogers obtained supplies here in January 1850, whereupon they returned to Death Valley to rescue their starving comrades. Rancho Camulos, to the west in Ventura County, is part of Rancho San Francisco, and Del Valle's beautiful adobe house still stands there.

Several adobe homes were built by Martín Ruiz and his sons in the Cañon del Buque, erroneously called "Bouquet Canyon" by General Beale and other early topographers, whose mistake persists on modern maps and road signs. It was in this same region that Francisco ("Chico") López, nephew of the Francisco López who discovered gold in Placerita Canyon, pastured his cattle during the 1840's. Later, Francisco Chari, one of his herdsmen, took up land here. Chari was a French sailor whom the Californians nicknamed "El Buque" ("the ship"), because of his many tales of the sea and of the ships in which he had sailed. Martín Ruiz sold the rancho to Battista Suraco, a Genoan, in 1874. The last surviving adobe stood a few miles up the canyon at the point where it widens into a narrow valley. The low, rambling one-story building was long neglected and finally crumbled under the inroads of the elements. Nothing remains, but the Suraco family still live on the property.

La Casa de Miguel Ortiz, a long one-story adobe, stands at the left of the old stage road that came up from San Francisquito Canyon and passed by Lake Elizabeth (known to the Spaniards as La Laguna de Chico López) on its way north to Fort Tejón. It is said that this was the first building erected at the lake and that it was built by Miguel Ortiz, a muleteer in the employ of General Beale. The land was given him by the general. This region also comprised one of the grazing lands of Chico López in the 1840's, and was a haunt of Tiburcio Vásquez, the bandit, during the 1870's. The modern address of the adobe is 13980 Elizabeth Lake Road.

The Andrada stage station, built of adobe in the 1880's by Pedro Andrada, still stands at the point where the old Fort Tejón road entered San Francisquito Canyon, south of Lake Elizabeth. It is located at 13850 Elizabeth Lake Road, only a short distance from the Ortiz adobe. However, it has been modernized to serve as a physician's office and residence and is not recognizable as an old adobe.

An old adobe stage station stood into the 1960's at 38839 San Francisquito Canyon Road, about two miles west of the community of Green Valley. It has been torn down, but a later two-story adobe stands next to the site and is occupied. The older building is believed to have been in use at the time the Butterfield stage line used this route from 1858 to 1861.

On Highway 138 in Antelope Valley is a small post office called Llano. It preserves the name of an ill-fated socialistic colony, Llano del Rio, that existed in the area from 1914 to 1918. The founder was Job Harriman, unsuccessful candidate for mayor of Los Angeles in 1910. He was associated with Clarence Darrow in the defense

Ruins of Hotel, Llano del Rio

Beale Adobe, Rancho La Liebre

of James B. and John J. McNamara, brothers, arrested for the bombing of the *Los Angeles Times* building on October 1, 1910, during a tense period in the organization of labor. Harriman could well have been elected mayor if the McNamaras had been acquitted, but the brothers unexpectedly changed their pleas to guilty, and Harriman's political career was over. The desert colony he founded in 1914 moved to Louisiana four years later because of insufficient water supply at the California site. A few ruins, notably the stone pillars and chimneys of the colony's hotel, stand along the highway half a mile west of the Llano post office.

Another utopian colony, this one with a religious basis, was located in Los Angeles County about the same time. Pisgah Grande was founded by Finis E. Yoakum in the mountains northwest of Chatsworth, very close to the Ventura County line. A number of substantial brick buildings were erected, most of which are still standing, including a two-story headquarters, a post office, and a prayer tower high on a hill. Las Llajas Canyon Road and its private extension (with locked gate) lead from Santa Susana to the site of the settlement.

La Casa del Rancho La Liebre stands on property of the Tejón Ranch Co. in the northwestern corner of Los Angeles County. It is located about one-half mile south of Highway 138 at a point about ten miles east of its junction with Interstate 5 near Gorman. It stands on the floor of a small canyon known as the Cañon de las Osas ("canyon of the she-bears"). The adobe, which was built by General Edward F. Beale after he acquired the property in 1855, was the headquarters for his Rancho La Liebre ("ranch of the jack rabbit"), 48,800 acres, a part of his vast estate composed of several ranchos and extending north well into Kern County. The house is strong and commodious, suggestive of the efficiency and thoroughness of its builder, and is said to have been his home for two or three years while he was surveyor-general. This region was another of the haunts of Tiburcio Vásquez.

SOURCES

Belderrain, Francisca Lopez. "First to Find Gold in California," *Touring Topics*, XXII, No. 11 (November 1930), 32–34.
Bolton, Herbert Eugene. *Anza's California Expeditions.* 5 vols. University of California Press, Berkeley, 1930.

——— *Fray Juan Crespí, Missionary Explorer on the Pacific Coast, 1769–1774.* University of California Press, Berkeley, 1927.
——— "In the South San Joaquín Ahead of Garcés," *California Historical Society Quarterly*, X, No. 3 (September 1931), 211–19.
——— "Spanish Exploration in the Southwest, 1542–1706," *Original Narratives of Early American History*, XVII. Scribner, New York, 1916.
Brackett, Frank Parkhurst. *History of San José Rancho.* Historic Record Co., Los Angeles, 1920.
The California Missions, a Pictorial History. By the editorial staff of Sunset Books. Lane Book Co., Menlo Park, 1964.
Chapin, Lon F. *Thirty Years in Pasadena, with an Historical Sketch of Previous Eras.* 2 vols. Southwest Publishing Co., 1924.
Cleland, Robert Glass. *From Wilderness to Empire. A History of California*, ed. Glenn S. Dumke. Knopf, New York, 1959.
Conner, E. Palmer. *The Romance of the Ranchos.* Title Insurance and Trust Co., Los Angeles, 1930.
Cultural Heritage Board, Department of Municipal Art, City of Los Angeles. Reports. 1962–65.
Dakin, Susanna Bryant. "San Gabriel Days of Hugo Reid," *Touring Topics*, XXIII, No. 11 (November 1931), 24–26, 48.
Dektar, Cliff. "Ghost Highway in the Mountains," *Westways*, XLVII, No. 3 (March 1955), 8–9.
Dennis, Frederick James. "A Pioneer among Water Wheels," *Touring Topics*, XXIV, No. 2 (February 1932), 19, 36.
Elder, David Paul. *The Old Spanish Missions of California.* Paul Elder & Co., San Francisco, 1913.
Emory, William H. *Notes of a Military Reconnaissance from Fort Leavenworth, Missouri, to San Diego, California*, 30th Cong., 1st Sess., Senate Exec. Doc. No. 7, Washington, D.C., 1848.
Engelhardt, Zephyrin. *The Missions and Missionaries of California.* 4 vols. (1st ed. 1913.) 2d ed., Mission Santa Barbara, Santa Barbara, 1930.
——— *San Fernando Rey, the Mission of the Valley.* Franciscan Herald Press, Chicago, 1927.
——— *San Gabriel Mission and the Beginnings of Los Angeles.* Mission San Gabriel, San Gabriel, 1927.
First of the Ranchos, the Story of Glendale. Security Trust and Savings Bank, Glendale, 1927.
Frémont, John C. *The Exploring Expedition to the Rocky Mountains, Oregon and California.* Geo. H. Derby & Co., Buffalo, 1849.
Guinn, James Miller. *History of the State of California and an Extended History of Its Southern Coast Counties.* Historic Record Co., Los Angeles, 1907.
Hanna, Phil Townsend. "Our Lady in the Beginning," *Touring Topics*, XXIII, No. 9 (September 1931), 12–17, 40.
Harrington, M. R. "A House of Adobe," *Touring Topics*, XXII, No. 11 (November 1930), 50–51, 55.
Hill, Laurance L. *La Reina Los Angeles in Three Centuries.* Security First National Bank, Los Angeles, 1929.
——— *Six Collegiate Decades: The Growth of Higher Education in Southern California.* Security First National Bank, Los Angeles, 1929.
Hine, Robert V. *California's Utopian Colonies.* Huntington Library, San Marino, 1953.
Keaveney, Thomas. "Early Days in Los Angeles County," *Grizzly Bear Magazine*, February, March, April, 1917.
Leadabrand, Russ. *A Guidebook to the San Gabriel Mountains of California.* Ward Ritchie Press, Los Angeles, 1963.
Nevins, Allan. *Frémont, the West's Greatest Adventurer.* 2 vols. Harper, New York, 1928.
Newmark, Harris. *Sixty Years in Southern California 1853–1913*, ed. Maurice H. and Marco R. Newmark. The Knickerbocker Press, New York, 1916.
Older, Mrs. Fremont. *California Missions and Their Romances.* Coward-McCann, New York, 1938.
Owen, J. Thomas. "The Church by the Plaza, a History of the Pueblo Church of Los Angeles," *The Historical Society of Southern California Quarterly*, XLII, No. 1 (March 1960), 5–28; No. 2 (June 1960), 186–204.
Parks, Marion. "In Pursuit of Vanished Days, Visits to the Extant Historic Adobe Houses of Los Angeles County," *Annual Publications of the Historical Society of Southern California*, Vol. XIV, Parts I and II (1928–29), 7–63, 135–207.
Prudhomme, Charles J. "Gold Discovery in California; Who Was the First Real Discoverer of Gold in the

State?" *Annual Publications of the Historical Society of Southern California*, Vol. XII, Part II (1922), 18–25.

—— "Early Days in Los Angeles," *The Grizzly Bear*, November 1918.

—— "Old Plaza Site in Los Angeles," *The Grizzly Bear*, January 1919.

—— "Reminiscences of Old Days," *El Monte Gazette*, March 23, 1923.

Rider, Fremont, ed. *Rider's California; A Guide Book for Travelers*. Macmillan, New York, 1925.

Robinson, W. W. *Los Angeles from the Days of the Pueblo*. California Historical Society, San Francisco, 1959.

—— *Ranchos Become Cities*. San Pasqual Press, Pasadena, 1939.

—— *The Story of San Fernando Valley*. Title Insurance & Trust Co., Los Angeles, 1961.

Rogers, Warren S. *Mesa to Metropolis; The Crenshaw Area, Los Angeles*. Lorrin L. Morrison, Los Angeles, 1959.

Rowland, Leonore. *Bits of Californiana*. Privately printed, 1963.

—— *The Romance of La Puente Rancho*. Neilson Press, Covina, 1958.

Smith, Sarah Bixby. *Adobe Days, Being the Truthful Narrative of the Events in the Life of a California Girl on a Sheep Ranch and in El Pueblo de Nuestra Señora de Los Angeles While It Was Yet a Small and Humble Town*. Enlarged edition, Jake Zeitlin, Los Angeles, 1931.

Stock, Chester. *Rancho La Brea, A Record of Pleistocene Life in California*. Los Angeles Museum, in History, Science, and Art Publication No. 1, 1930.

Willard, Charles Dwight. *History of Los Angeles City*. Kingsley-Barnes & Neuner Co., Los Angeles, 1901.

Madera County

MADERA COUNTY was organized from a part of Fresno County in 1893. (Madera is Spanish for "wood" or "timber.") It was given the same name as its principal town, Madera, which was made the county seat.

The Big Trees

There is but one living group of *Sequoia gigantea* within Madera County and that is the Nelder Grove, formerly called Fresno Grove, which stands about five miles south of the Mariposa Grove. Partly cut over during the years 1888–90, it is now covered with a fine second growth. It derives its present name from John A. Nelder, who had a cabin there in the 1870's. The Dead Grove, part of an ancient forest located between the Mariposa and Nelder groves, consists of ten big trees cut many years ago and still lying where they were felled.

The Devil's Postpile

The Devil's Postpile, a spectacular mass of basaltic columns like an immense pile of posts, is located near where the Mammoth (French) Trail from Fresno Flats (Oakhurst) to Mammoth Lakes crosses the Middle Fork of the San Joaquin River. These columns vary in size from ten to 30 inches in diameter and in some cases stand as high as 60 feet. In shape they are irregular polygons with from three to seven sides each but all closely and perfectly fitted together like a vast mosaic.

"In every scenic freak the sheep-herder recognizes the handiwork of his Satanic majesty. This formation is therefore known to local fame as the Devil's Woodpile." It was officially designated as the Devil Postpile National Monument by President Taft on July 6, 1911. It ranks with the famous Giant's Causeway in Ireland.

Old Trails

It is unlikely that many of the early Spanish expeditions entered the confines of Madera County, and no Spanish settlements were ever made there. This isolation was due, first of all, to the fact that it was practically impossible to penetrate the tulares from the west or to cross the sloughs which covered the whole central portion of the San Joaquin Valley at high water. In addition to this general inaccessibility, the streams throughout the area of the county were little more than dry, sandy washes except during and immediately following a heavy rainfall. Furthermore, the water holes along the foothills of Madera County were few as compared with the broad, perennial streams to the north and south. For many years these conditions repelled both exploration and settlement. This impenetrable barrier is described by F. F. Latta:

"Between Martinez on the north and San Emigdio, two hundred and fifty miles to the south, there were only two places where the San Joaquin Valley could be crossed from east to west except at time of low water. Throughout the course of the San Joaquin River and bordering the lakes to the south was an impenetrable sea of tule, sloughs, mud flats, and water, which, until as late as 1880, was passable only at these same places. When Tulare Lake was below the extreme high water mark the sand ridge which crossed it from east to west formed a bridge over which we know the Spanish crossed. The other point at which they were able to cross during time of high water was at the head of Fresno Slough near the present town of Tranquillity."

There is evidence, however, that the Pico expedition to the San Joaquin and Kings rivers in 1825–26 entered Madera County, crossing the rivers on tule rafts. Monte Redondo, a Madera

County landmark, apparently was familiar to people on the coast as early as 1825.

Jedediah Strong Smith passed through what is now Madera County in 1827 and again in 1828. He was soon followed by Hudson's Bay Company trappers and later by Ewing Young, Kit Carson, and other Americans, who followed the trail of the beaver along the numerous streams which come down from the High Sierra on the eastern side of the valley. A member of one of the Hudson's Bay Company expeditions may even have left a souvenir of their visit. Dr. Raymund F. Wood of Fresno State College believes this to be the origin of the rock carving on the Herrick Brown Ranch near Kelshaw Corners (Highway 41 south of Coarse Gold). The bust and head of a woman, with the inscription "To J. M. 1841," has become known as "The Lady of the Rock." Unfortunately, it has been defaced by vandals.

The first definite record that we have of a trail across Madera County is that left by John C. Frémont on April 4–6, 1844. By means of rafts the party ferried Bear Creek (in Merced County) on the 4th, and then proceeded southward, their progress being greatly impeded by the numerous sloughs of this section. Continuing up the San Joaquin River, they passed "elk . . . running in bands over the prairie, and . . . along the left bank . . . immense droves of wild horses." Camp was made on the San Joaquin River on the 4th and 5th. On the 6th the party crossed the San Joaquin at Gravelly Ford, a crossing still in use.

The Millerton or Stockton–Los Angeles Road, the only north and south route that passed through Madera County during the 1850's and 1860's, ran along the base of the foothills, crossing the Chowchilla River at the Home Ranch a little west of where the Merced-Mariposa boundary line intersects the Madera County line. The San Joaquin River was crossed at Millerton by means of the Converse Ferry, which fell into disuse after the building of the railroad.

Most of the miners at Coarse Gold and other mining centers in Madera County migrated south from Mariposa County. Others came from Gilroy via Pacheco Pass, crossed the San Joaquin River just south of the mouth of Fresno River, and from there proceeded to the Sierra Nevada mines. Alexis Godey, famous plainsman and guide to Frémont, operated a ferry at this point for a short time during the early 1850's.

In the late 1870's a stage road from Madera to the Yosemite Valley was constructed, passing through Bates Station, Kelshaw Corners, Coarse Gold, Fresno Flats, Fish Camp, and Clark's Station (Wawona).

The Madera and Mammoth Trail is generally called the French Trail after its promoter, John French, who sought a better route to his mining interests in the Mammoth area. Biweekly trips from Fresno Flats (Oakhurst) to Mammoth City were started about 1880; the travelers were met at the stagecoach and continued the trip to Mammoth by saddle train. The French Trail proper began at the ranch of Jesse B. Ross, who settled there about 1858. This ranch later passed into the hands of George Francis (Frank) Hallock, Ross's son-in-law, and in 1910 was sold to Samuel L. Hogue. The Joseph E. Foster family acquired it in 1930, and today it is known as Foster's Hogue Ranch. The log house built by Jesse B. Ross about 1860 still stands. Ross's Indian wife died in 1949 in her 109th year. A good automobile road from North Fork now follows the course of the French Trail past the old Ross ranch (elevation 4,500 feet) and for some distance beyond.

Fresno Indian Reservation

Living water and Indian rock writings near the headquarters of the present Adobe Ranch,

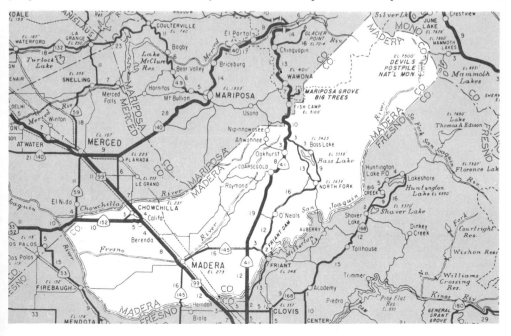

"The Lady of the Rock," before it was vandalized

ten miles northeast of Madera on the River Road, mark the site of the old Fresno Indian Reservation established at this point on the Fresno River during the early 1850's. It is mentioned by J. Ross Browne among similar projects in his *California, Washoe and Crusoe Island,* and the following item in the *Mariposa Chronicle* of October 6, 1854, bears out his statement:

"We learn that Mr. Henley, the Superintendent of Indian Affairs, has leased the Adobe House and Ranch of Capt. Vinsonhaler on the Frezno, and intends locating there for the present all the Indians originally belonging in that section, many of whom have heretofore refused to remove to the Tejón."

The Savage Monument

A monument in honor of Major James D. Savage, pioneer trader and one of the explorers of the Yosemite Valley in 1851, was erected above Fresno River about 18 miles northeast of Madera. Savage was murdered on the Kings River in 1855; his friend and partner, Dr. Lewis Leach, marked the grave by a ten-foot shaft of granite brought from Vermont. The Native Sons of the Golden West purchased a plot of ground about the monument to ensure its preservation.

This monument was placed near the site of the fourth and last trading post established in this region by Savage, who came to the mines early in 1848 with the Woods party, the first discoverers of gold in Tuolumne County. He later enlisted the aid of Indians in mining at Big Oak Flat (Tuolumne County) and soon developed an extensive trade with the various Indian tribes of the Sierra. His first post was at the mouth of the South Fork of the Merced River (in Mariposa County), but this was abandoned when the Yosemite Indians went on the warpath. A second post was then established at the mouth of Agua Fria Creek, near the site of Buckeye, while a branch station was started on the Fresno River near Fresno Flats. The last post of Major Savage was near Fresno Crossing, where the monument was later erected. The adobe ruins in the vicinity, sometimes pointed out as the old Savage trading post, are those of a structure built by Chinese and used as a store as early as 1872.

The Savage Monument, reached only by a private road with a locked gate, will be relocated, along with the remains of Major Savage, because the area is to be inundated when the Hidden River Dam on the Fresno River is completed.

A Bit of the Mother Lode

Extending from the northwest to the southeast through Madera County, the Mother Lode is marked by the shafts and tunnels of old mines and the sites of one-time mining camps. Before the quartz ledges were opened up in the 1870's and 1880's, however, placer mining began. As early as 1849 settlements sprang up in flats and ravines and along the bars of the San Joaquin and Fresno rivers.

Among the early prosperous placer-mining camps, Coarse Gold (at first known as Texas Flat) was the largest in Madera County. There in 1849 five Texans found diggings on the creek where sand yielded particles of gold so coarse that the stream was named Coarse Gold Creek. Many fortunes were taken from the surrounding hills and the settlement grew rapidly.

Other placer-mining centers quickly developed: Grub Gulch, six miles northwest, and Fresno Flats (now Oakhurst), seven miles northeast of Coarse Gold; Fine Gold, about six miles southeast near Mountain View Peak; Temperance Flat, on the San Joaquin River four miles east of Fine Gold Gulch; Cassidy's Bar, also on the San Joaquin River in the vicinity of old Fort Miller; Soldier Bar; and Rootville—these made up a round of lively little camps which, during the 1850's, composed a small but rich mining district. However, little trace of them is left today.

Throughout this section of the Mother Lode a number of quartz mines likewise earned records as big producers during the 1870's and 1880's. The old mining camp of Coarse Gold was located at the confluence of Coarse Gold Gulch and Deadwood Gulch, 32 miles northeast of Madera. Radiating from it in all directions were quartz mines, traces of some of which remain today: the Texas Flat Mine, one mile to the northwest, and Topp's Mine (located in 1880), three miles north; the D'Or de Quartz, four and a half miles south; the Five Oaks, one and one-half miles southeast; the Waterloo, one and one-half miles farther on; and Last Chance, located in 1880 five miles by road from Coarse Gold.

At the Grub Gulch camp the Josephine Mine (1880) and the Gambetta (which included the

Arkansas Traveler Claim) were located, while two miles to the northeast was the Enterprise Mine.

Other mines located in the Potter Ridge District east of Grub Gulch included the Flying Dutchman, the Crystal Spring, the Rattlesnake, the King's Gulch, and the Victoria. The Potter Ridge Mine was two miles southwest of Fresno Flats.

The Hildreth Mining District was named after Tom Hildreth and his brother, who operated butcher shops in various Sierra mining camps and who ranged their cattle on Madera County foothills. The district, extending ten miles or so northward from the mouth of Fine Gold Creek, which was three miles northeast of old Fort Miller and is now inundated by Millerton Lake, was located in the southern part of the county, with Fine Gold Gulch as the western and northern boundary line of the section. Here were the Abbey Mine, a quarter of a mile east of the small camp of Hildreth; the Morrow Mine, located in May 1881, in the same section and township as the Abbey Mine; the Hanover, the Golconda, and the Standard. One mile east of Fine Gold, too, was the Mountain View Mine, located in 1880 in the vicinity of Mountain View Peak.

During the 1860's, while the copper excitement was at its height in California, a few copper mines were developed in the foothills of Madera County, notably the Daulton, located on the railroad about 12 miles southwest from Raymond, and the Daisy Bell. Productive in early days, the copper mines ceased to be worked when prices fell. The Daulton was again in operation about 1960.

The Town of Madera

With the construction of the railroad in 1870 an increasing demand came from the East for lumber from the great sugar pine forests of the Sierra Nevada, while some trade developed also in yellow pine, fir, cedar, and other woods. Quick transit from the mountains to the railroad was accomplished by the construction of a V-shaped flume 60 inches wide and 63 miles in length running from the Soquel Basin. This flume, built in 1874 at a cost of half a million dollars and later extended as far as Sugar Pine, carried countless millions of feet of lumber annually from the higher mountains to the railroad. The Sugar Pine Lumber Company and the Madera Sugar Pine Company, with a monthly payroll of $140,-000, employed from 900 to 1,000 men.

A settlement grew up at the lower end of the flume where it terminated near the Central Pacific Railroad on the south side of Fresno River. There in 1876 the California Lumber Company laid out the town of Madera, the Spanish word for "wood" or "timber" having been adopted as its name. When the county was created in 1893,

Ross Log Cabin, Foster's Hogue Ranch

the same name was chosen for it, and the city of Madera became the county seat.

Borden, an Early Farm Community

The little town of Borden (originally known as the "Alabama Settlement"), located 17 miles northwest of Fresno, was the center for a thriving agricultural community before Fresno and Madera even came into existence. It was the earliest farm center in this part of the valley, having been founded in 1868–69 by families from Alabama. Borden had become quite a pretentious place by 1873–74, with two hotels, two stores, and other buildings, and it even aspired to become the county seat. However, as early as 1881 it was described as already beginning to wear a deserted air.

SOURCES

Bunnell, Lafayette Houghton. *Discovery of the Yosemite and the Indian War of 1851.* Privately published, Chicago, 1880.
Cook, S. F. *Expeditions to the Interior of California Central Valley 1820–1840.* University of California Press, Berkeley, 1962.
Elliott, Wallace W. *History of Fresno County.* Wallace W. Elliott, San Francisco, 1882.
Farquhar, Francis P. *Place Names of the High Sierra.* Sierra Club, San Francisco, 1926.
Foster, Doris, and Clyde Foster. "One Hundred Years of History—Foster's Hogue Ranch," *The Madera County Historian* (Madera County Historical Society Quarterly), I, No. 4 (October 1961), 1–7.
Frémont, John C. *The Exploring Expedition to the Rocky Mountains, Oregon, and California.* George H. Derby & Co., Buffalo, 1849.
Fry, Walter, and John R. White. *Big Trees.* Stanford University Press, Stanford, 1930.
Latta, F. F. "Pah-Mit's Story," *Tulare Daily Times*, 1931.
Le Conte, J. N. "The Devil's Postpile," *Sierra Club Bulletin*, VIII, No. 3 (January 1912), 170–73.
The Mariposa Indian War, 1850–51. Eccleston Diaries, C. Gregory Crampton, ed. University of Utah Press, Salt Lake City, 1957.
Matthes, François E. "Devil's Postpile and Its Strange Setting," *Sierra Club Bulletin*, XV, No. 1 (February 1930), 1–8.
Russell, Carl P. *One Hundred Years in Yosemite. The Story of a Great Park and Its Friends.* University of California Press, Berkeley, 1947.
Vandor, Paul E. *History of Fresno County, with Biographical Sketches.* Privately published, Los Angeles, 1919.

Marin County

MARIN COUNTY was one of the original 27 counties, San Rafael being the county seat. (Marin is thought to be a corruption of El Marinero, "the sailor," a name given to a Christian Indian who rendered excellent service as a ferryman on San Francisco Bay before 1834.)

Indian Shell Mounds

Marin County was once well populated with Indians. The picturesque, indented shoreline of its entire coast, particularly that part along San Pablo Bay (the "Round Bay" of the early Spanish explorers), San Pablo Strait, and Richardson's Bay, attracted them because of the ample supply of shellfish, one of their main foods. In this region shell mounds were numerous. Mounds of animal and vegetable residue are sometimes found on hillsides around springs and small streams. Those composed mainly of shell are nearer to the salt marshes, or even on the edge of the water, and it is from these more enduring mounds that information can best be gathered regarding the primitive people who occupied these village sites.

Two large mounds were near Novato; creeks between Ignacio and San Rafael are studded with smaller ones. Santa Venetia has the remains of a mound that was probably at one time 15 feet high and 80 feet in diameter, although most of it has been hauled away as fertilizer for gardens. There were several on the McNear estate between Santa Venetia and China Camp; the coastline extending back from San Pedro Point in both directions and also the irregular coast of Tiburon Peninsula and Richardson's Bay had dozens more. Across the flat north of Belvedere at the edge of a hill there was a large shell mound, through one side of which a street was constructed.

Shells, mortars, pestles, and bowls were found in a shell heap formerly on the site now occupied by the building at 107 Caledonia Street in Sausalito. One mound accidentally discovered at the bottom of Elk Canyon, northwest of Sausalito, and three others below Mill Valley completely covered with natural deposits were from one to three feet deep and of unknown lateral extent. A large mound at the highland edge of the marsh below Mill Valley, when measured in 1908, was 200 by 450 feet through the base, having a height of 20 feet to a truncated top 90 feet in diameter. Southeast of Kentfield and on the southeast side of the high hill along the road to Greenbrae was a notable shell mound from which hundreds of tons of material were hauled away.

Utensils, beads, and arrowheads have been taken from various mounds in the county and placed in museums of the Bay region, and from two large mounds at Greenbrae archaeological material is said to have been sent many years ago to London. Obsidian arrow points have been found frequently near the library of the College of Marin at Kentfield. In the leveling of ground on Hamilton Air Force Base, two mounds were razed, bringing to light stone and shell ornaments and conical polished stones pierced at one end and believed to be ceremonial pieces used by a medicine man or possibly the insignia of a chief. When the pit for a gas tank at Fourth and Irwin streets in San Rafael was dug, workmen found the skeleton of a chief decorated with strings of stone beads and ornaments made of abalone and other shells. Many small mounds have been found on the shores of Bolinas and Tomales bays—making a total of well over 200 mounds in this county.

In the Drakes Bay region, sixteenth-century mounds containing European and Oriental material from visiting or wrecked ships have been explored by University of California archaeologists and members of the Drake Navigators Guild.

Drakes Bay

On November 15, 1577, sponsored by Queen Elizabeth I, Francis Drake (afterward Sir Francis) set out westward from England in command of five sailing vessels. His destination was the Orient and his mission the achievement of honor and riches for his queen and country. His vessel the *Pellican,* renamed the *Golden Hind* the following year, was the only one of the five to make the entire voyage and to return with acclaim to the starting point.

According to contemporary authorities of the sixteenth century, all on board suffered from severe cold in the summer of 1579 as they sailed along the coast of California: "we fell with a conuenient and fit harborough, and June 17 came to anchor therein, where we continued till the 23 day of July following. During all which time . . . were wee continually visited with like nipping colds as we had felt before; . . . neither could we at any time in whole fourteene dayes together, find the aire so cleare as to be able to take the height of sunne or starre." The dates are those of the Julian Calendar; June 17 would be June 28 by today's reckoning.

Here the vessel was reconditioned and contact was made with the natives—Indians, who were deeply impressed by their white visitors. Word of the strange arrival passed from village to village. The number of natives who came down to the harbor daily increased. One day, before a week had passed, a great number of Indians came with their leader.

On this occasion the natives placed a crown upon the head of Drake: "inriched his neck with all their chains, and offering unto him many

other things, honoured him by the name of 'Hyoh.' Adding thereunto (as it might seeme) a song and dance of triumph; because they were not onely visited of the gods (for so they still judged us to be), but the great and chiefe God was now become their God, their king and patron, and themselues the onely happie and blessed people in the world."

Some days later, Drake with a large company of men journeyed on land and found "a goodly country and fruitfull soyle, stored with many blessings fit for the vse of man." The account continues: "This country our Generall named *Albion,* and that for two causes; the one in respect of the white bancks and cliffes, which lie toward the sea; the other, that it might haue some affinity, euen in name also, with our own country, which was sometimes so called."

And further: "Before we went from thence, our Generall caused to be set vp a monument of our being there, as also of her maiesties and successors right and title to that kingdom; namely, a plate of brasse, fast nailed to a great and firme post; whereon is engrauen her graces name, and the day and yeare of our arriuall there, and of the free giuing vp of the prouince and kingdom, both by the king and people, into her maiesties hands: together with her highnesse picture and armes, in a piece of sixpence currant English monie, shewing itselfe by a hole made of purpose through the plate; underneath was likewise engrauen the name of our Generall, etc."

Authorities have differed about the identity of this harbor. The present-day Drakes Bay, Bodega Bay, San Francisco Bay, and other places have been mentioned as Drake's probable landing place. On June 25, 1916, the Sir Francis Drake Association of California placed a marker upon a rocky eminence on the western shore of Drakes Bay in an area now known as Drakes Beach.

About midsummer of 1936 chance brought to the notice of historians the plate described in the narrative. The discovery was made public at a meeting of the California Historical Society in the Sir Francis Drake Hotel in San Francisco on April 6, 1937. Careful study of the plate was made by Dr. Herbert E. Bolton, of the University of California, and others, and it was subjected to rigorous scientific tests. It was judged to be authentic.

The plate is of solid 16th-century brass. It is

five inches wide, eight inches long, and one-eighth inch thick, with square holes at top and bottom to admit the nails that secured it to the post. A jagged hole near the lower right corner fits an Elizabethan sixpence. The words engraved upon the plate are as follows:

BEE IT KNOWNE VNTO ALL MEN BY THESE PRESENTS
IVNE 17 1579
BY THE GRACE OF GOD AND IN THE NAME OF HERR
MAIESTY QVEEN ELIZABETH OF ENGLAND AND HERR
SVCCESSORS FOREVER I TAKE POSSESSION OF THIS
KINGDOME WHOSE KING AND PEOPLE FREELY RESIGNE
THEIR RIGHT AND TITLE IN THE WHOLE LAND VNTO
   HERR
MAIESTIES KEEPEING NOW NAMED BY ME AN TO BEE
KNOWN VNTO ALL MEN AS NOVA ALBION.
      FRANCIS DRAKE

$$\left(\begin{array}{c}\text{Hole for}\\\text{silver}\\\text{sixpence}\end{array}\right)$$

This ancient relic was picked up by Beryle Shinn, a young motorist, near Greenbrae, south of San Rafael and about one and one-half miles northwest of Point San Quentin. William Caldiera, a chauffeur, claimed that he had found the plate in 1933 in the Drakes Bay area and later discarded it in the San Quentin area where Shinn found it three years afterward. In any case, the discovery or discoveries cannot be used to prove conclusively that Drake landed in either San Francisco Bay or Drakes Bay, since the easily portable plate might well have been carried about through the centuries by Indians and others. The site where the "great and firme post" originally displayed it may never be located.

The Drake plate is now the property of the University of California and is kept on display in the Bancroft Library on the Berkeley campus.

The Prayer Book Cross in Golden Gate Park, San Francisco, commemorates the religious services held in 1579 by Francis Fletcher, Drake's chaplain, somewhere in the Bay region.

In January 1594, King Philip II of Spain ordered an exploration of the northwest coast of North America. The viceroy of New Spain commissioned Sebastián Rodríguez Cermeño, a Portuguese, to take a ship to the Philippines, fill it with Oriental treasure, explore the northern coasts, and then return to Acapulco. On November 4, 1595, the *San Agustín,* a Manila galleon which Cermeño had secured in the Philippines and filled with merchandise, arrived off the California coast at about 41° latitude. Three days later, the treasure-laden galleon entered Drakes Bay, just 16 years after the great Englishman had raised his country's flag upon California's shore. Here the vessel was wrecked by a storm and Cermeño and his men were forced to proceed in a launch they had constructed there as an auxiliary boat. Before sailing, they explored inland a distance of four leagues and found several rancherías of Indians from whom acorns were obtained for food. Cermeño named the harbor the "Bay of San Francisco," a name that for many years caused great confusion among historians. Hunt and Sanchez say: "The present Drake's Bay was the place first known as 'San Francisco' to the Spaniards, and the name was not transferred to the great inland sea which now bears it until after 1769."

Rancho Olómpali

Rancho Olómpali, named for a former Coast Miwok Indian village, Olemaloke, consisted of two square leagues granted by Governor Manuel Micheltorena on October 22, 1843, to Camilo Ynitia (Ynito), who filed claim for it on February 26, 1852, and received a United States patent in 1862. The tract was bounded by the "Arroyo de San Antonio and the Portezuela de Novato."

Camilo Ynitia was the son of the last chief of the Olómpali Indians, who lived there as early as 1776 and for whom, according to General Mariano G. Vallejo, an adobe was constructed, the first house to be erected north of San Francisco Bay. Grateful for friendly treatment given an expedition sent out from the San Francisco Presidio earlier in the year, the Spaniards instructed the Indians in making adobe bricks and building the house for their chief. (This statement by Vallejo is discounted as legend by Bowman and other historians.) Near this dwelling Camilo, the son of the chief and an industrious Christian Indian, also erected an adobe. The older one is gone. When its walls fell and lay in a heap and were rained on, weeds grew up over them.

Eugène Duflot de Mofras, a representative of the French government who journeyed through California in the years 1840–42, probably had reference to this place when he wrote: "On leaving San Rafael and turning away from the great salt marshes, one finds himself passing in front of the Rancho del Indio composed of some free Indians."

On June 24, 1846, there was a surprise skirmish at this point, when Lieutenant Henry L. Ford, of the Bear Flag movement, unaware of the presence of the enemy, made a charge upon the horse corrals while a force of Californians under Joaquín de la Torre and Juan N. Padilla were at breakfast in the ranch house. The Californians retreated after a few shots had been exchanged, one man being killed and another badly wounded.

The greater part of this rancho was purchased in 1852 by James Black from Ynitia and his wife Suzane for the sum of $5,200. Black, originally from Scotland, was the owner of many other tracts of land. He afterward gave this one to his daughter Mary.

In 1863 the daughter and her husband, Dr. Galen Burdell, came there to live. They developed one of the earliest and finest of Marin County gardens. When Mrs. Burdell returned from a trip to the Orient in a sailing vessel, she brought with her an extensive collection of trees and shrubs, of which many choice specimens, among them camellias and Japanese maples, now flourish. The place, to the west of Highway 101, is approached by a wooded drive three miles north of Novato. The second adobe house (SRL 210), that of the son Camilo, was used by Dr. and Mrs. Burdell as their home, and three of the rooms are incorporated in the stucco house

erected by their son James B. Burdell in 1915. The former living room, now used as a storeroom, is large, with a moderately high ceiling. When the original small windows were enlarged to admit more light, the workmanship was found to be first-rate and the walls in excellent condition.

On the trunk of a huge oak on the grounds could long be seen a deep gash in the shape of a cross, such as early Californians made to mark the spot where a death occurred. It is supposed that this was made to mark the one casualty in the surprise skirmish of June 1846, mentioned above. The cross is now overgrown with bark. A large copper cauldron supposedly used for cooking food for Frémont's men during their encampment at this spot remained on the property for many years, but is now in the museum at San Rafael. Another treasured relic on this old Rancho Olómpali was a bell that originally hung, according to family tradition, at the San Rafael Mission, to which it has now been returned.

There is now a recreation center at Rancho Olómpali.

Mission San Rafael Arcángel

Because the mortality rate of the Indians at Mission Dolores had become alarming, it was suggested that some of the neophytes be sent across the bay to a somewhat more equable climate. A trial move proved the wisdom of that measure, and it was determined to establish there a kind of rancho with chapel, baptistry, and cemetery. The name San Rafael Arcángel was chosen in order that the angel "who in his name expresses 'the healing of God' might care for bodies as well as souls." The mission was founded on December 14, 1817, on a spot called by the natives "Nanaguani."

An adobe building 79 feet long, 38 feet wide, and 16 feet high was erected and divided by partitions into chapel, padres' house, and other required apartments. San Rafael was at first nothing more than an *asistencia* to Mission San Francisco de Asís, but by 1823 it had become self-supporting. Although there is no record that it was raised to the position of an independent mission, all the reports of the fathers refer to it as such, and it is so considered by historians. Padre Juan Amorós, known for the zeal with which he undertook every task, served as missionary there from 1819 to his death in 1832. During this period the mission attained maximum strength, although Duhaut-Cilly, passing within sight of it in 1827 on his way to Sonoma, did not "deem this poor establishment worth stopping at for purposes of trade." Two years after the death of Padre Amorós came the secularization, when Ignacio Martínez, a distinguished military officer retired since 1831, was made *comisionado*. For two years he managed the affairs of San Rafael and established the boundaries of the pueblo.

The long, low adobe structure erected at San Rafael was much plainer and simpler than most of the mission structures. Old pictures show that the bells were hung in a wooden frame placed outside the chapel entrance. After the secularization the uncared-for walls melted away, and no sign of them now remains. On the site of the chapel *(SRL 220)* stands the present St. Raphael's Catholic Church. A map of 1852, found among Marin County records, shows the extreme southerly point of the mission at the corner of Fifth and A streets, with one side of the building paralleling the later De Heiry Street. The mission garden extended from the present courthouse to Irwin Street. An old pear tree from the mission orchard survived until the 1950's at the rear of the apartment house at the southeast corner of Fifth Avenue and Lootens Place.

A replica of Mission San Rafael has been built of modern materials near the original site. In front is a wooden standard in which the old bells are hung in the same way as in the days of the mission. The bells were returned from various places in which they had been kept through the years.

The Mission San Rafael rancho, consisting of 16 square leagues, was sold by Governor Pío Pico on June 8, 1846, to Antonio Suñol, a Spanish member of the San José Council, and Antonio María Pico for $8,000, but they failed to get possession and their title was later decided to be invalid. In 1859 Bishop J. S. Alemany obtained patent for something over six acres of this land for the church.

The Mission Embarcadero and the City of San Rafael

The farthest inland meanderings of Estero San Rafael de Aguanni are now lost beneath the pavements and buildings of the city of San Rafael. On A Street at Third is the probable landing place used by the padres, the mission embarcadero. This was the scene of a tragic episode in the Bear Flag Rebellion. Frémont and his men had arrived for a week's stay at the buildings of Mission San Rafael on June 26, 1846. On June 28, a boat was seen approaching the shore from the direction of San Pablo, where two divisions of Castro's army were stationed. It was assumed that the passengers were carrying messages to Castro's aides. When the three occupants of the boat stepped on land, before any words were spoken or their errand ascertained, they were shot down by Kit Carson and his two companions, who had been sent to intercept the travelers. The men killed were Francisco and Ramón, twin sons of Don Francisco de Haro, former alcalde of San Francisco, and their uncle, Don José de los Reyes Berryessa, owner of Rancho San Vicente near Santa Clara.

On C and D streets between First and Second, bridges span the old channel of San Rafael Creek. A post to which small craft had formerly tied stood as a landmark near the intersection of E and First streets for many years after canoes and small rafts had ceased to come up so far. At the corner of C and Second streets freight was received in 1850.

The oldest part of the city of San Rafael lies west of a line drawn between the site of the mission and that of the mission embarcadero. The adobe residence of Don Timoteo Murphy, started in 1839, two years after he assumed charge of the mission estate and the Indians there, stood at the northwest corner of Fourth and C streets. It was the most pretentious building in the county at the time and the center of social activities. In 1844, it was occupied by Don Antonio María Osio, grantee of Angel Island, a man who held important positions in different parts of California previous to the American conquest.

The alcaldes transacted the business of their offices in the old mission building up to 1850. In 1851 a hall, called the Juzgado, was set aside for the holding of the sessions of the newly established county court. In 1853, the year of the death of Don Timoteo, the seat of justice was moved to his house and there remained until the completion, in 1873, of the present courthouse. The road leading from this adobe house to the freight landing of the 1850's became C Street, and on the east side of this road, between what are now Third and Fourth streets, a general merchandise store was opened in 1850 by Davis and Taylor.

On April 14, 1871, a corporation known as the Mechanics Institute was organized for the purpose of conducting a library and reading room "for literary, beneficial, moral, and educational purposes unconnected with other Societies, religious denominations, or political parties." For this, a one-story frame building was erected, almost covering the 30 × 50 foot lot that the corporation had purchased. This library existed but a short time; the building stood at 1016 C Street. One of the sponsors of the Mechanics Institute was William T. Coleman, chosen leader of the San Francisco Vigilantes of 1856. In addition to his San Francisco interests, he owned a vast tract of land in Marin County, and his home at 1130 Mission Avenue was one of the first frame buildings of San Rafael. It had been erected by Walter Skidmore, and Coleman, after purchasing it, took great pains to preserve it intact while making suitable additions. It is still standing.

In 1853 Paul de Heiry bought a tract of land just back of the old mission and sent to his native France for seeds, fruit trees, roses, and grapes, which even today are enriching the gardens of San Rafael. A street in the vicinity was later given his name. In 1863 the De Heiry property passed to Henry Wilkins, who made a swimming pool, using redwood planks to confine the water flowing from the old mission spring. This spring is now in Boyd Park, donated by Captain Robert Dollar to the City of San Rafael. Dollar's old mansion stands at 1408 Mission Avenue.

Several houses were erected in San Rafael by convict labor in the years 1859 and 1860, at which period prisoners were hired under contract to a firm known as Sims and McCauley. Two of these houses were on the public square: one, used as a pharmacy in 1859 by Dr. Taliaferro, stood in the middle of the block on Fourth Street between B and C streets; the other, the old Central Hotel, a brick building quite famous in the early days, was located at 720 Fourth Street. A third house was built for an official of the prison on the block bounded by Second, Third, B, and C streets.

North of San Rafael on the east side of the Redwood Highway is the beautiful Marin County Civic Center, one of the final masterpieces created by Frank Lloyd Wright. The first unit was completed in 1962.

Rancho Corte de Madera del Presidio

Rancho Corte de Madera del Presidio was granted by Governor José Figueroa to Juan (John) Read (Reed, Reid) on October 2, 1834. It lies on the peninsula northwest of Raccoon Straits and extends inland between the Punta de Quentín and Saucelito ranchos. On December 23, 1852, his widow, Hilaria Sánchez de Read, and her four children, Juan, Hilaria, Inéz, and Ricardo, filed petition for it; 7,845 acres were confirmed to them in 1884.

Read, an Irish sailor, arrived in the area in 1826. As opportunity arose, he ran a boat for hire to Yerba Buena, antedating the regular ferry services by many years. He was naturalized as a Mexican citizen in September 1834, one month before he received the grant of his rancho. For an interim of about five months between the Martínez and Murphy administrations of the affairs of the secularized San Rafael Mission, he filled that position, beginning on November 30, 1836. His first house was a temporary structure near the beach in the vicinity of Sausalito in 1832. He later erected an adobe dwelling on a knoll one mile west of Highway 101 at La Goma Street and Locke Lane in Mill Valley. The ruins of this adobe were removed in 1918, and the site is now occupied by houses near which some of the old pear trees stand. Juan Read died in 1843 and was buried in the Catholic cemetery in San Rafael. Hilaria Sánchez lived until 1872.

The timbers of Read's old sawmill *(SRL 207)*, after which Mill Valley was named, stand in Old Mill Park on Cascade Drive in Mill Valley. This mill, built sometime in the ten years previous to Read's death, has been marked by the Native Daughters of the Golden West.

One of the early settlements in this vicinity was Blithedale. This sunny place, through which ran the Arroyo del Corte de Madera del Presidio, was chosen in 1873 by Dr. John Cushing and his wife for the location of a sanatorium. The idealistic agricultural community portrayed by Hawthorne in *The Blithedale Romance*, written 20 years earlier, inspired Dr. Cushing to give the name

Read's Sawmill, Mill Valley

Blithedale to this place. Because of difficulty in obtaining title to the property, Dr. Cushing did not succeed in actually establishing the sanatorium before his death in 1879, but his wife and son remained on the property and managed it as a summer resort for years afterward. The extensive cement walks that were then made on the place now surround private homes on the site in the 200 block of West Blithedale Avenue near the creek. The original Blithedale Glen, between Eldridge and Cottage avenues, has been subdivided and built up as a part of the town of Mill Valley.

The town of Larkspur is located in the north corner of Rancho Corte de Madera del Presidio. Here an Indian shell mound formed a knoll, then practically surrounded by marshes, upon which Captain Frémont and some of his soldiers are said to have camped for a time in the summer of 1846. On this knoll, just northwest of the Larkspur Nurseries, the first dwelling in Larkspur was erected of brick in 1852—by convict labor, so tradition says. In 1850 a steamboat, plying by way of Corte Madera Creek between what is now Larkspur and San Francisco, made three or four trips a week to carry lumber, hides, beef, and other produce from the country and to return with goods purchased in the city.

St. Hilary's Catholic Church at Tiburon was named for the patron saint of Hilaria Read. The former church, a frame structure dedicated in 1888 and used for services until 1954, was the first church in the Tiburon area. Located on a hilltop covered with wildflowers, it was purchased and restored by the Belvedere-Tiburon Landmarks Society in 1959–60.

Rancho Saucelito

Rancho Saucelito, according to legend granted in 1835 to José Antonio Galindo, afterward a corporal in the San Francisco militia, was granted on February 11, 1838, to Guillermo Antonio (William A.) Richardson by Governor Alvarado.

Richardson, born in England in 1795, arrived in San Francisco as first mate on the whaling vessel *L'Orient* in 1822. He procured papers allowing him to remain on land, and thereafter became active in the region of San Francisco Bay, spending some time also at San Gabriel, Sonoma, and Monterey. In 1823 he was baptized at the mission in San Francisco. On May 12, 1825, he married María Antonia, daughter of Ignacio Martínez, at that time *comandante* of the presidio. In 1830 he obtained naturalization as a citizen, his name being placed on record as pilot and shipbuilder with a knowledge of the Spanish language. From 1835 to 1844 he was first Captain of the Port of San Francisco, having been appointed by General Vallejo. After 1836 he made his home at Rancho Saucelito, filing his petition as claimant for it with the Land Commission on March 16, 1852. The final patent for 19,572 acres was issued August 7, 1879, long after his death in 1858. His private business was the collection of country produce by means of a launch which visited the various embarcaderos about the bay. The shore of his own rancho was washed by the waters of

Richardson's Bay, thus named at the time of his land ownership there. The site of Richardson's adobe home, built about 1841, is at the northeast corner of Bonita and Pine streets in Sausalito.

Fine hillside springs on Rancho Saucelito gave life to the *sausal* or willows, from which the name is derived, and in 1850 Captain Richardson piped water from these springs to a great cistern 30 feet square and 15 feet deep which he had dug for the purpose. From this cistern (located on Richardson Street, Hurricane Gulch, Sausalito) pipes were run on a trestle to the waterfront and thence to a boat, the *Water Nixie,* equipped with tanks and casks for transporting the water to Meiggs' Wharf at San Francisco. From this point Marin County spring water was distributed to dwellers in the growing city by means of horse- and mule-drawn carts for the price of 50 cents a bucket. The mooring place of the old *Water Nixie* is on Richardson Street near Bridgeway, not far from the place of the first settlement of the town of Sausalito, where in 1862 there were a half-dozen houses.

San Carlos Avenue in Sausalito is named for the first known ship to sail through the Golden Gate, on August 5, 1775, under command of Juan Manuel de Ayala. The *San Carlos,* after moving cautiously into the unknown strait, taking frequent soundings, first dropped anchor off Sausalito, and later moved to Angel Island.

For many years the Sausalito waterfront was widely known as an anchorage and supply station for whaling vessels and men-of-war. Captain Beechey, in 1826, saw "seven whalers" anchored there. Sir George Simpson, governor-in-chief of the Hudson's Bay Company territories in North America, on entering San Francisco Bay in December 1841, wrote: "We saw on our left in a deep bay known as 'Whaler's Harbor,' two vessels, the Government schooner California and the Russian brig Constantine, now bound to Sitka with the last remnants of Bodega and Ross on board, . . . about a hundred souls, men, women, and children, all patriotically delighted to exchange the lovely climate of California for the uncongenial skies of Sitka, and that, too, at the expense of making a long voyage in an old, crazy, clumsy tub at the stormiest season of the year."

Captain Richardson in 1855 sold a piece of property near Sausalito to S. R. Throckmorton, who in turn sold it to the Sausalito Land and Ferry Company. This company built wharves, filled in marshy places, and put on a reliable boat for frequent rapid transit across the bay to San Francisco. Their first boat, the *Princess,* made four round trips daily. It is in the vicinity of this wharf that the newer part of Sausalito has grown up. On the opening of the line of the North Pacific Railway in 1875, the franchise of the ferry company was leased to the railway company.

The Golden Gate Bridge has in effect brought Sausalito closer to San Francisco. The town has spread far up the hills above the landing, and from the homes located on the steep, curving streets, magnificent views of islands and bay are obtained—views undreamed of by the motorists speeding up the Redwood Highway.

On Bulkley Avenue, near Harrison Avenue, on the drive above the wharf, a crescent-shaped cement seat has been placed honoring the memory of a poet who had a retreat in these hills, Daniel O'Connell, grandnephew of the Irish patriot of the same name. He came to California after resigning from the British Navy and was a teacher in Santa Clara College in 1868; later he taught Greek in St. Ignatius College in San Francisco before devoting his entire time to newspaper and other writing. He was one of the early members of the Bohemian Club in San Francisco. Two of his poetical works are *Lyrics* and *Sweethearts and Wives.* He lived in Wildwood Glen with his family in "the little house on the hill." The house, now remodeled and modernized, is at 41 Cazneau Avenue. The memorial seat, on the back of which are inscribed three stanzas of the poem "The Castle of Silence," written ten days before his death, rests upon a tiled platform shaded by pepper trees overlooking the bay from Bulkley Avenue.

In 1869, James H. Gardner, former state senator from Downieville and custom house broker, purchased from the Sausalito Land and Ferry Company a parcel of land in Sausalito now identified as 47 Girard Avenue. The same year, he constructed his home, known as "The Bower," which is the oldest standing residence in Sausalito.

Rancho Punta de los Reyes

When on December 28, 1841, the *Cowlitz* lay becalmed offshore at Drakes Bay after coming from the north, its passengers "began sensibly to feel the influence of a more congenial climate. The sails flapped listlessly against the mast, the vessel heaved reluctantly on the sluggish waters." Sir George Simpson, one of the passengers, continues: "During the whole of the 29th we lay in this state of inactivity about five miles from shore which presented a level sward of about a mile in depth, backed by a high ridge of grassy slopes— the whole pastured by numerous herds of cattle and horses, which, without a keeper and without a fold, were growing and fattening, whether their owners waked or slept, in the very middle of winter, and in the coldest nook of the province. Here, on the very threshold of the country, was California in a nutshell, Nature doing everything and man doing nothing—a text on which our whole sojourn proved to be little but a running com-

James H. Gardner Home, Sausalito

mentary. While we lay like a log in the sea, we were glad to be surrounded by large flights of birds—ducks, pelicans, cormorants, gulls, etc."

The land so described is that of Rancho Punta de los Reyes Sobrante, which after the advent of the American settlers became the first great dairy center of the state.

The names of several outstanding men are connected with Rancho Punta de los Reyes on the western slopes of Marin County. James Richard Berry, an Irish gentleman who in his travels had spent much time in Spanish countries, arrived in 1836 and received, on St. Patrick's Day, a grant of land in the vicinity of Inverness from Governor Nicolás Gutiérrez. He was known to be in Sonoma in 1844, but in the meantime he had sold this rancho to Joseph Francis Snook, who received a grant of it from Governor Juan B. Alvarado on June 8, 1839. About 1837, the grantee had built a house of logs and mud on this land. Snook, an English shipping master, whose boats plied the California coast, married María Antonia, daughter of Governor Alvarado. He retired from active service to spend his last years with his family on a rancho near San Diego, granted to him in 1842. His death came suddenly in 1847.

In 1843 Rancho Punta de los Reyes Sobrante was granted to Antonio María Osio, a public official under Mexican authority, who held it for but a few years and who probably never lived upon it. In 1844, the fourth year of his position as justice, Osio occupied the dwelling of Don Timoteo Murphy near the San Rafael Mission, while the owner of the house lived at the mission itself. Two years later, in 1846, Osio escaped the Bear Flag disturbance by taking his family to Honolulu. On his return he moved to his former home in Lower California and wrote *Historia de California*.

Early in the 1850's, Rancho Punta de los Reyes and Rancho Punta de los Reyes Sobrante ("surplus") were acquired by Andrew Randall, and on March 2, 1853, he filed a petition for them, basing his claim on the grant of 11 Spanish leagues formerly made to Osio. Randall had arrived on the West Coast as a gunner on the *U.S.S. Portsmouth*, and was reputed to be a doctor and a scientist. He received patents for the two pieces of land, a total of 57,067 acres, on June 4, 1860.

From Randall these two grants passed into the hands of three men who were notable in the early development of the state: Justice Oscar L. Shafter, of the State Supreme Court; his brother, Judge James McMillan Shafter; and Charles Webb Howard, president of the Spring Valley Water Company. To their large holding was later added Rancho Tomales y Baulenes, which had been granted in 1836 by Governor Nicolás Gutiérrez to Rafael García. The combined property stretched from the coast north of Point Reyes south and east to include the top of Mount Tamalpais.

Judge James McMillan Shafter, after a distinguished career in the East, arrived in California in 1853. He became State Senator and was a member of the Constitutional Convention of 1878. He

was a regent of the University of California, and at the time of the founding of Leland Stanford Junior University he delivered the dedicatory address and became a trustee of the new institution. His house, "The Oaks," located on this extensive holding, was built of lumber ferried out of the Golden Gate and into Tomales Bay, then hauled by oxen to the site two miles south of Olema. The rough timbers for the buildings on the many farms into which his land was divided were sawed by his own mill on the place. The house still stands, surrounded by old trees. Judge Shafter's town house was at 951 Chestnut Street in San Francisco.

Dairying became the major business in this part of Marin County. Almost the entire area of this rancho was leased out by the grantees to dairy farmers, and houses were built for them near clear-flowing springs, of which there were a considerable number. Butter was shipped by schooner to San Francisco. Judge Shafter was greatly interested in blooded stock, horses as well as cattle, and he frequently entertained friends at his private race track, where his fine horses were trained and shown. After his death many of the customs of the family were continued, for the son, Payne Jewett Shafter, "Squire" Shafter as he was generally known, was also interested in agriculture and the country life. Squire Shafter's daughter Mary had similar interests, pursuing courses at the University of California along those lines. Her book *American Indian and Other Folk Dances* reveals a historical interest in the native peoples who inhabited the grass-covered hills up to the time the white man came.

The three ranchos that were combined into the one vast property are now divided into many parts; some passed to descendants of Charles W. Howard and the Shafters, and others have been purchased by newer residents.

The lighthouse on Point Reyes was built in 1870. Point Reyes Peninsula is now being developed as Point Reyes National Seashore, approved by Congress in 1962.

Rancho Punta de Quentín

The name of this rancho is derived from a point off the coast which received its name from an episode that occurred on an island at the mouth of the Estero de San Rafael. A hostile Indian chief, Marín, and his companion in flight, Quentín, both sought by Spanish soldiers under Lieutenants Ignacio Martínez and José Sánchez, were captured in their hiding place on this small island and taken to San Francisco as prisoners. A good sailor, Quentín was there employed by the fathers at Mission Dolores as skipper of one of the lighters trading in the bay. He was later employed by General Vallejo for making trips between Sonoma and Yerba Buena. General Vallejo is the authority for this explanation of the name "Punta San Quentín." The island on which the fugitives hid was named Marín for the chief.

Rancho Punta de Quentín consisted of two square leagues, extending west from the shore of the bay into the mountains lying north of Mount Tamalpais. Larkspur is near its southern line, and San Anselmo its northern. It was granted in 1840 to Juan Bautista Roger Cooper, who received at various times other ranchos in the state and does not seem to have held this one for very long. A claim for the confirmation of ownership of this rancho was filed in 1853 by Benjamin R. Buckelew, who based his action on a grant made to him by Governor Alvarado on September 24, 1844. He received the confirmation in 1855, and the patent for 8,878 acres was issued to his heirs on April 10, 1866. Publisher and editor of the *Californian* during the brief existence of that newspaper, Buckelew died in 1859 at the early age of 37.

On the eastern part of this rancho stands San Quentin Prison, begun in 1853. Before its erection the state's convicted criminals were confined on hulks of ships anchored off Angel Island. It stands on the site of the projected but never built Marion City. In the vicinity were found beds of a medium quality clay. In 1888, the State Mineralogist reported: "At San Quentin there are manufactured from clay on the prison ground 500,000 common and 80,000 pressed brick, annually." This industry ended after a few years when the clay deposit was exhausted.

Rancho San Pedro, Santa Margarita y las Gallinas

This rancho, extending northwest from Point San Pedro and the Gallinas canal and consisting of five square leagues, was granted on February 14, 1844, by Governor Manuel Micheltorena to Timoteo Murphy. The grantee was a tall blue-eyed man from Ireland, good-natured and generous, who after some commercial experience had come to California in 1828 to supervise the packing and exporting of beef for Hartnell and Company at Monterey. He brought with him letters to the Mexican authorities. From 1833 to 1835 he was engaged in otter hunting. Shortly afterward, having made the acquaintance of the Vallejo family, this Irishman of commanding presence was chosen by General Vallejo as prospective husband of one of his attractive sisters. The General gave him some property and established him as administrator of the mission at San Rafael. The sister, however, did not agree to the arrangements and married Jacob P. Leese—if Sir George Simpson, a visitor to both Don Timoteo and the Vallejo family in 1841, was correctly informed.

From 1837 to 1842, Timoteo held the position at the mission and was a faithful guardian of the neophytes, who were otherwise abandoned to their own devices after the secularization of the mission and who were in need of wise supervision. In 1839, while in charge of affairs of the mission, he became naturalized. Before receiving this grant in 1844, he began building an adobe house, probably the first dwelling outside of the mission that was built on the site of the present town of San Rafael. Here he dispensed hospitality, his house being widely known. Lieutenant William Tecumseh Sherman and party, on their way to Sutter's Fort in June 1848, spent one night with him. The house is said to have been Frémont's headquarters for a time, possibly when he marched with 130 men to the mission on June 26, 1846, and made a stay of a few days. After Don Timoteo's death in 1853 the adobe was used as a place of justice until the erection of the present courthouse in 1873, when a piece of adobe from the Murphy house was sealed within the cornerstone of the new building.

On his deathbed Don Timoteo deeded 317 acres of land to Archbishop Joseph Sadoc Alemany, O.P., of San Francisco for the foundation of a school. In 1855 the Sisters of Charity of St. Vincent de Paul established what is now St. Vincent's School for Boys (*SRL 630*). For years it was administered by the Christian Brothers, but now it is operated by priests of the Archdiocese of San Francisco and Dominican Sisters of Mission San Jose. The approach to the school is through a long eucalyptus-lined drive east of the Redwood Highway about four miles north of San Rafael. Don Timoteo Murphy left the bulk of his estate to his brother Matthew and a nephew, John Lucas.

Rancho Cañada de Herrera

Rancho Cañada de Herrera (Vale of the Blacksmith), or La Providencia, was granted by Manuel Jimeno, acting governor, to Domingo Sais (Saez) in 1839 at the end of the latter's two-year term as elector and *regidor* of San Francisco. The Sais heirs received United States patent for 6,658 acres in 1876.

Dr. A. W. Taliaferro, a skilled surgeon and physician who had come to Marin County in 1849 with a group of young men from Virginia, while wandering one day up San Anselmo Valley "came upon a tract of park-like land, shaded by ancient trees with a sparkling stream of water running through it." He at once began negotiations for its purchase. When Don Domingo learned that he wanted only 40 acres he said: "It is worth forty acres to us to have a good neighbor. Select your forty acres, we give it to you thankfully." The doctor fenced in his land and built a spacious house on the bank of the "sparkling stream," cleared a considerable area of brush, built outbuildings, and settled into the life of a gentleman, as his forebears had done in Virginia. The abundance of wild game and his unstinted hospitality at once made the place popular with his sportsman friends.

Among his visitors in 1856 were Charles S. Fairfax and his wife. Fairfax was a lineal descendant of the barons of that name in England, and his wife, famous for her wit and beauty, was the niece of Senator John C. Calhoun. Both these visitors became fascinated with the place; some sort of deed of gift was made; they took over the property, and Dr. Taliaferro remained as their permanent guest. Fairfax, in later years always called "Lord Fairfax" because of his line of descent, had come in 1849 as a youth of 20 from the county of Fairfax in Virginia and had spent his first winter in a cabin near Grass Valley. A young man of good education and pleasing address, he became a member of the Assembly from Yuba County in 1853 and in 1856 was clerk of the State Supreme Court, which position he held for five years.

The Fairfax home (*SRL 679*) was located not far from the present business district of Fairfax. Presided over by the gracious Southern lady, it became a center of the social life of the period where notables of the state and nation were entertained. Here a luncheon party gathered on May 21, 1861, the day following the close of the state legislature, where hot political debate had resulted in a challenge to a duel. The prompt action of an official at that time had prevented the duel from taking place, and the principals, their seconds, and the surgeon had gone to the house of "Lord Fairfax," where their host attempted a reconciliation. The antagonists, Daniel Showalter of Kentucky and Charles W. Piercy of Illinois, had crossed the continent in the same small company some years before but on arriving in California had gone different ways. They had met again as members of the legislature in opposing factions of one of the political parties—the Breckinridge and Douglas factions of the Democrats. After the luncheon, when all hope of preventing the conflict was abandoned, the hour of three o'clock was set for the duel. Following the first shots, in which neither had been injured, Fairfax again attempted to pacify the hot-tempered men, but without success. On resuming their positions and firing, Piercy was instantly killed. Showalter, immediately filled with remorse, pleaded with the surgeon to save his opponent. He was killed not long afterward in ambush by Apaches as he journeyed through Texas on his way to join the Confederate Army.

In May 1868 the heirs of Domingo Sais deeded this 40-acre tract to the Fairfaxes. In that year Charles Fairfax was made chairman of the California delegation to the Democratic National Convention in New York. He attended the convention, but died the following year at Baltimore. After his death his Marin County home became the restaurant of Madame Adele Pastori, who, on the decline of her career in Italian opera, came here with her husband, a former master of stagecraft. Her attractive personality and the fine table set by her husband soon drew many artists from San Francisco.

This wooded spot now belongs to the Marin Town and Country Club on Pastori Avenue. Although the original buildings used by Dr. Taliaferro and "Lord and Lady" Fairfax are no longer there, the houses erected by the Pastoris still stand and are distinguishable from the newer buildings of the country club by their shingled roofs.

Rancho San José

Don Ignacio Pacheco, whose father of the same name was a Mexican soldier in San Francisco in 1790, was born in San José in 1808. When he was 19 years old, he became a soldier in the San Francisco Company, and he was a sergeant ten years later. At the expiration of his military service in 1838 he settled on a tract of land bordering San Pablo Bay south of the Feliz grant of Rancho de Novato, and on October 3, 1840, the tract was granted to him by Governor Alvarado. A year or so later he began erection of an adobe house of one story like those of old Mexico, using Indians from Mendocino County as laborers.

Don Ignacio was married three times: first to Josefa Higuera, a pious woman, who named the rancho for her patron saint; second to Guadalupe Duarte; and third to María Loreto Duarte. In 1846, as alcalde at San Rafael, he held his court in the large hall of the mission. During the Mexican War he was briefly held prisoner by Frémont until he agreed to relinquish all his horses to the Bear Flag troops. Don Ignacio is remembered as a man who used his influence for the best interest of town, county, and state. He received United States patent for his rancho of 6,659 acres on May 14, 1861. When he died in 1864, he left it to his five sons and his daughter Catalina. To the daughter, child of his third wife, he gave the family home and 600 acres of land. The sons—Salvador, Gumesindo, Augustin F., Juan F., and Benjamin—divided the rest. Catalina married a Valencia, and the four-room adobe home of her parents became known as the Valencia adobe. It stood protected by a wooden sheathing until destroyed by fire on May 23, 1916; its foundations remained for many years beside the main highway north of San Rafael and not far from Ignacio, the town founded by the original grantee and named for him. The site is now Galli's restaurant.

Hamilton Air Force Base has been established on a part of Rancho San José. Pacheco Point on San Pablo Bay is the eastern extent of the grant.

Rancho Nicasio

Attempts were made to give three grants in the county to Christian Indians. Rancho Olómpali was successfully patented to Camilo Ynitia, but the other two, ranchos Nicasio and Tenicasia, were not confirmed. Twenty square leagues of Nicasio had been granted to Teodosio Quilajuequi and others of his tribe in 1835 by Governor Figueroa, but it was rejected by the Land Commission in 1855. Tenicasia, given by General M. G. Vallejo to the San Rafael Mission Indians in 1841, was rejected by the Commission in 1854 because of "failure of prosecution." Vallejo was a valiant friend of the neophytes, but he alone could not carry through the plan of obtaining farms for them where they could use the agricultural knowledge received at the mission. Timoteo Murphy, his friend and co-worker who held the confidence of the Indians and was furthering their interests, had died the year before the matter was settled, and no one else remained to intercede in behalf of the native claimants.

In 1844, another part of Rancho Nicasio, containing ten square leagues, was granted by Governor Micheltorena to Pablo de la Guerra and Juan Cooper, men prominent in political and business affairs, who seem to have parted with the land before 1852. In that year a claim for it was filed by H. W. Halleck and James Black, and a supplementary claim was filed the following year by Benjamin R. Buckelew, Daniel Frink, and William Reynolds. The long and comparatively narrow stretch of this rancho reached from Keyes Creek, flowing into Tomales Bay, to the western boundary of Murphy's Rancho San Pedro, Santa Margarita y las Gallinas. It was surveyed in the autumn of 1859 and found to contain 56,621 acres, for which patent, signed by President Abraham Lincoln, was issued to all five claimants on November 1, 1861.

The extreme northwestern and northeastern ends were claimed by and patented to Henry Wager Halleck, a graduate of West Point, who had come in 1847 with a company of United States artillery to inspect Pacific Coast fortifications. He resigned his commission, was an active and influential member of the Constitutional Convention of 1849, acted as inspector of lighthouses on the coast, became the leading member of a law firm in San Francisco, prepared a report on California land titles, and was the author of several law books. Halleck resumed his military career and as a general during much of the Civil War was greatly relied on by Lincoln. The southeastern corner of this large grant was patented to Benjamin R. Buckelew, who was also the owner of Punta de Quentín. The two middle tracts, along the eastern shore of Tomales Bay, were patented to the other three claimants, Frink and Reynolds owning the northern piece, and James Black, who also had Rancho Olómpali, the southern.

A few interesting buildings stand in the old town of Nicasio, notably the little Church of Our Lady of Loretto, established in 1867.

Other Mexican Grants

The official map of Marin County, published in 1892, shows several old ranchos about which little material is available. The northern line of the county runs through the southern part of two grants, Blucher and Laguna de San Antonio, lying partly in Sonoma County to the north. From the angle between these two extends the Bolsa de Tomales, of 22,193 acres, west to the shore from Keyes Creek to the Estero de San Antonio, a property formerly granted to Juan Padilla, who was in command of a party of Californians north of San Francisco Bay at the time of the raising of the Bear Flag.

Rancho Soulajule, south of Rancho Laguna de San Antonio, was granted in 1844 by Governor Micheltorena to Ramón Mesa, a former soldier in the San Francisco Company. In 1879 the patent to this rancho was issued to five men: G. N. Cornwall, L. D. Watkins, Pedro J. Vásquez, J. S. Brackett, and M. F. Gormley.

Rancho Corte de Madera de Novato, of two square leagues, granted October 16, 1839, by Governor Alvarado to John Martin, to whom 8,879 acres were patented on May 23, 1863, lies to the east of Soulajule.

Rancho de Novato extends south from Black Point along San Pablo Bay. It was granted in 1839 by Governor Alvarado to Fernando Felis (Feliz), and afterward it was owned jointly by Frederick Billings, James R. Bolton, and Henry W. Halleck, assignees of Bezar Simmons, who died in 1850. Archibald Peachy purchased the rancho from these assignees, one of whom, Billings, was a brother-in-law of Simmons.

Rancho Los Baulenes, granted in November 1845 by Governor Pío Pico to Gregorio Briones, extends around Bolinas Bay. Don Gregorio's house stood on the west shore of the bay near an embarcadero. The house of Pablo Briones, undoubtedly his son, stood near the northeast boundary line of the rancho.

Rancho Tomales y Baulenes was owned by two men to whom patents were issued. The northern part was claimed by Rafael García, to whom Nicolás Gutiérrez, political chief of Alta California, granted two square leagues on March 18, 1836. It was surveyed in October 1865, and a final patent was issued to García on October 15, 1883, for 9,468 acres. At the time the survey was made, a number of houses stood along his eastern line, which lay along Gerónimo Creek. He and his wife, María Loreto, raised eight children to maturity. The southern portion of Rancho Tomales y Baulenes was claimed by Bethuel Phelps; 12,000 acres of this was afterward owned by Shafter and Howard.

Rancho San Gerónimo, lying west of Cañada de Herrera, was granted to Rafael Cacho by Governor Micheltorena in 1844 and patented to Joseph Warren Revere in 1860. Revere, a native of Massachusetts and grandson of Paul Revere, came to California in 1846 as a lieutenant in the United States Navy and was commander of the northern district for several months. In his *Tour of Duty*, published in 1849, he wrote of his adventures and observations in California. Becoming colonel of a New Jersey regiment, he lived in Morristown after his return to the East.

Islands of Marin County

The eastern boundary line of Marin County runs from Petaluma Point in San Pablo Bay south into San Francisco Bay far enough to include almost all of Angel Island. Within the water area lie small islands of some interest. The Sisters lie a little to the northwest of Point San Pedro. The Marin Islands, upon which Chief Marín hid when escaping from his white pursuers, lie midway between San Pedro Point and San Quentin Point. Just south of the mouth of San Rafael Creek is San Rafael Rock. Directly northwest of California

Church of Our Lady of Loretto, Nicasio

Point is Red Rock, called on some maps "Golden Rock," an uninhabited area of one or two acres through which pass the boundary lines of three counties, Marin, San Francisco, and Contra Costa, and about which cling traditions of buried treasure. The largest of all, Angel Island, opposite Tiburon Point, is separated from the mainland by Raccoon Strait.

On August 13, 1775, Lieutenant Juan Manuel de Ayala reached an island in San Francisco Bay to which he gave the name of Nuestra Señora de los Angeles—today known as Angel Island. Ayala's mission at that time was to explore in the interest of Spain the estuaries of San Francisco Bay and to discover whether or not a strait connected Drakes Bay and San Francisco Bay. Finding good anchorage and plenty of wood and water, the explorers based at the island for several weeks while making careful surveys of the surrounding topography. The chaplain of the expedition, Padre Santa María, and some of the officers landed several times upon the Marin shore, where they visited a hospitable ranchería, undoubtedly that of the Olómpali.

"The grants of this and other islands were made by the express direction of the Superior Government of Mexico and the governor [of Alta California] was enjoined to grant the islands to Mexicans in order to prevent their occupation by foreigners who might injure the commerce and the fisheries of the Republic, and who, especially the Russians, might acquire otherwise a permanent foothold upon them." This Island of Los Angeles, or Angel Island, was granted February 19, 1838, by Governor Juan B. Alvarado to Antonio María Osio, who used it for raising horses and cattle. He did not live upon it himself, but he subdivided it, built four houses, made a dam for the conservation of water for his stock, and placed part of the land under cultivation. His claim was recognized at the time but later rejected by the courts.

According to Bancroft, Angel Island was ceded by the State of California to the federal government as early as 1852 or 1853. Osio, then living in Mexico, where he had gone when Mexican authority ceased in Alta California, put in a claim for it in 1855, but the claim was adjusted.

Except for two tiny points of land in the City and County of San Francisco, Angel Island lies wholly within Marin County and the city limits of Tiburon. It is gradually being developed and opened to the public as Angel Island State Park. After the establishment of the park in 1954, the first area opened was Hospital Cove (SRL 529) on the northwest coast of the island, until 1940 the site of the U.S. Public Health Service Quarantine Station for immigrants entering the United States through the Port of San Francisco. It has now been renamed Ayala Cove, for it was here in 1775 that Ayala anchored the San Carlos. The island has known other uses, principally military, and eventually the historic buildings at North, East, and West garrisons will be restored and made accessible to the public. During World War II, Japanese and Italian prisoners of war were detained on Angel Island. The 781-foot summit of Mount Livermore provides a spectacular 360° view. Boat service to Angel Island is available at Tiburon, Sausalito, and Fisherman's Wharf at San Francisco.

Old Lime Kilns near Olema

An outcropping of limestone on Olema Creek was worked in the early 1850's by James A. Shorb and William F. Mercer, who held a lease on the property and presumably shipped lime to San Francisco. This lease, dated July 13, 1850, is on file in the book of mining claims in the county recorder's office. The operation lasted only a few years.

The mossy, fern-decked remnants of three old stone lime kilns (SRL 222) are situated on the east side of the creek about 100 yards west of State Highway 1 at a point four and two-tenths miles south of Olema. They are not visible from the highway. What remains of the common façade of the kilns is about 39 feet long and 15 feet high. Its arches show the skill of experienced craftsmen. A ledge of limestone can be seen nearby.

Pits for three fires extend some feet into the earth below the façade. In one of these pits a Douglas fir seed has sprouted and grown into a sizable tree. Above the pits tower two almost intact chimneys built against a cut in the hillside and standing adjacent to each other with a common wall between them. In a crevice at the very top of the common wall another Douglas fir seed long ago took root. The trunk of this tree had grown to a diameter of 42 inches when, in 1935, borings were made by the County Agricultural Commission and its age was estimated at 128 years. This gave rise to speculation that the kilns had been built by the Russians or Spanish. The age of the tree was computed incorrectly because of insufficient equipment. In 1949 Professor Adan E. Treganza of San Francisco State College obtained a more complete sample of the growth rings, and it was determined that the tree took root no earlier than the 1860's.

A number of interesting frame buildings remain at the old town of Olema, including the Nelson Hotel, once a stagecoach stop.

Bolinas and the Lighter Wharf

Otter hunting, the first occupation engaged in by settlers in the vicinity of the town of Bolinas, was followed by lumbering in the 1850's, when many sawmills were operating in the tree-filled

Old Town of Olema

canyons back from the shore. The only evidence left is the few piles that mark the site of the lighter wharf *(SRL 221)*, about two miles north of Bolinas at the head of Bolinas Lagoon, not far from the junction with State Highway 1.

From the mills the wood was hauled to the wharf by ox-drawn wagons, which creaked along the uneven roads on wooden wheels made from sawn sections of huge trees. The loads were transferred at the wharf to flat-bottomed boats, or lighters, that carried the cargo to seaworthy vessels offshore. These vessels, in turn, transported the lumber and fuel to the growing city of San Francisco. It is estimated that 13 million feet of lumber were shipped to the city for building purposes from the lighter wharf at Bolinas before the supply was exhausted. After the large trees had been used for lumber, the smaller trees were felled for domestic fuel and sent to the same market.

On the afternoon of April 9, 1853, a schooner leaving with a load of lumber was hailed by Lieutenant William Tecumseh Sherman, who was on his way to summon assistance for the stranded steamer *Lewis*, sailing from San Juan del Sur, on which he had been a passenger. A fog had carried the *Lewis* past the port of San Francisco and had grounded it on Duxbury Reef a few miles from Bolinas Bay. When all had safely reached a bleak beach by means of small boats, Lieutenant Sherman and a young companion set out for assistance. By walking about three miles, they reached a board shanty, where lumbermen told them of the schooner about to depart. They hastened to it and were accommodated on top of the lumber. But before the vessel had reached its destination, it too was submerged by a heavy ebb tide and a strong wind. The remainder of the journey to San Francisco was made in a rowboat that appeared on the scene of the second disaster.

Nothing in the topography of the west shore of Bolinas Bay softened the force of ocean gales for the settlement of Bolinas. Cypress hedges had to be planted as windbreaks before the cottage gardens of the pioneers could grow. In some parts of the town, the roses, fuchsias, and lemon verbenas of the early days have now attained treelike proportions.

Tomales

"Tomales" is a word in the Coast Miwok Indian dialect meaning "bay."

Lieutenant Juan Francisco de la Bodega y Cuadra, commander of the schooner *Sonora*, discovered Bodega Bay by chance and "soon afterwards distinguished the mouth of a considerable river, and some way up a large port exactly resembling a dock," according to the Daines Barrington translation of the account of Don Antonio Mourelle. At first members of the expedition thought that Tomales Bay was the harbor of San Francisco, but they later realized that it was not, because the Farallon Islands were not visible. Indians came in great number and rowed their tule rafts between Tomales Point (Punta del Cordon) and Sand Point (Punta de Arenas). They came alongside the ship to present gifts of "rosaries of bone," "seeds," and "plumes of feathers." Bodega gave "in return bugles, looking glasses and pieces of cloth."

Bodega named Tomales Bay and today's Bodega Bay for himself—Puerto de la Bodega. The *Sonora* anchored in the mouth of Tomales Bay on October 3, 1775. After midnight, on the first flow of the tide, the full force of a northeast swell struck the ship and covered it with breaking water. The discovery "boat on the side of her was broken into shivers." By nine o'clock in the morning the *Sonora* set sail for Monterey. The following day, October 5, the expedition passed two miles from the Golden Gate, unaware that only a month earlier the *San Carlos* had departed for Monterey. Bodega was afraid to enter San Francisco Bay because of the loss of the discovery boat.

The vicinity of Tomales is a favorite vacation place, particularly toward the southern end of Tomales Bay. The town of Tomales, originally located at the head of Keyes Creek, which flows from the northeast into this bay, had its beginning in a store located there in 1852. The site of its old steamer landing is now covered by pastureland. The North Pacific Coast Railroad, in which Governor Milton S. Latham was financially interested, ran its first freight train from a warehouse there on December 3, 1874, with a load of 300 sacks of potatoes shipped by James Fallon. This was the forerunner of many trainloads of produce raised in the vicinity and shipped over this line to Sausalito and thence to San Francisco. The railroad has now been discontinued.

Ross and Kentfield

Ross is situated in an area of beautiful country homes. The Katharine Branson School, a preparatory school for Bryn Mawr College, is located here. The town received its name from James Ross, who settled on this part of Rancho Punta de Quentín in 1859, the year of the death of the former owner of the rancho, Benjamin R. Buckelew. There was an old house standing on the property which was thought to have been "built by convict labor, from the old leg-irons found in the cellar." The house was renovated and enlarged for the Ross family.

In 1869 the name of James Ross is listed among directors of the local railroad, a line of three and one-half miles between San Rafael and San Quentin, afterward incorporated in the system managed by Peter Donahue. After Ross's death, the family home burned, and his widow moved to the site that is now a park opposite the former location of the Ross railroad station.

Kentfield is on land that passed from the estate of James Ross to Albert Emmet Kent when Kent came to California in 1871 for his health. It was called Ross Landing in earlier days, when steamers came up Corte Madera Creek above the present Highway 101 bridge to load the thousands of cords of wood which they carried to San Francisco. The original spacious colonial house built by the Kents faced due east and had an old-fashioned formal garden on the south with a fountain in the middle and numerous box-edged flower beds; vineyards and orchards were at a little distance. On these grounds in the autumn the annual Grape Festival for the benefit of the Presbyterian Orphanage at San Anselmo used to be held.

A canyon on the Kent estate is called Baltimore Gulch, and a station on the former railway was called Baltimore Park. Both names are reminiscent of the group of young men from Maryland, sponsored by the Baltimore and Frederick Trading Company, who came to Marin County in 1849 and erected a sawmill on Rancho Corte de Madera. Their venture, made in high hope, was not a financial success and was of short duration, but such stable citizens as Judge Barney, Daniel Taylor, David Clingan, and S. S. and Harry S. Baechtal settled in different parts of the county. Judge Barney founded the *Marin Journal* in 1861.

Tennessee Cove

Tennessee Cove at the foot of Elk Valley and just outside the outer limits of the Golden Gate received its name after the disaster of March 6, 1853, when the steamer *Tennessee,* plying between Panama and San Francisco, went aground in a dense fog. At that date no lighthouse had been erected on the Pacific Coast; in trying to enter the Golden Gate, this boat, with 600 passengers, struck the beach about two and a half miles north of Point Bonita. No lives were lost. The first light station on the coast was erected at Alcatraz the following year. Near Tennessee Cove and Point Bonita are the old military posts Forts Baker, Barry, and Cronkhite.

Point Bonita Light Station

The southwestern extremity of Marin County and the outer north headland of the Golden Gate is Point Bonita, where a much-needed light station was established by the United States government in 1855. When it was first placed, great difficulty was experienced in keeping this isolated, fog-ridden station manned; at the end of the first nine months, seven different keepers had been employed.

Here, also, was established in the same year the first fog signal on the Pacific Coast: an iron cannon transferred from the Benicia Arsenal. Sergeant Maloney, placed in charge at the point with instructions to "fire the gun every half hour during fogs," reported two months later that as there was almost continual fog and no one to relieve him "for even five minutes" he had been unable to get the "two hours' sleep necessary out of the twenty-four." The gun remained in use for two years before its expense and ineffectiveness caused it to be abandoned in favor of another type of fog signal. However, it remained on the point until the Panama-Pacific Exposition of 1915, when it was displayed in San Francisco and afterward stored, along with its wheels and part of the framework, in the Lighthouse Service storehouse on Yerba Buena Island.

The Pioneer Paper Mill

Samuel Penfield Taylor erected a paper mill in 1856 on Daniels Creek, afterward known as Paper Mill Creek. It was the first paper mill on the Pacific Coast and was run by water carried by a flume from a dam in the creek one-half mile above. The warehouse was situated at the end of Tomales Bay, where Point Reyes Station is now.

Rags to supply this mill were gathered by Chinese in San Francisco, made into great bales, and shipped by schooner to the head of Tomales Bay. They were then loaded on a scow and floated on the tide to Taylor's warehouse, from which a team of oxen completed the transportation to the factory. The finished paper was conveyed in reverse manner to San Francisco, where the product found a ready sale and was sent to all parts of the Pacific Coast. The undertaking was prosperous from the beginning and was especially so during the Civil War period. By 1884 the demand for paper had become so great that a larger mill was built at a cost of $165,000 and employment there furnished a livelihood for about 100 families. Steam power was added, and the mill did a flourishing business until the depression of 1893.

After lying idle for over 20 years, the red-painted building with windows and doors outlined in white was destroyed by fire. Now only the damaged foundations remain; the columns that acted as supports for the water wheel are still standing, and crumbling bricks mark the site of the boiler.

The site of the first paper mill (*SRL* 552) is marked by a stone monument with bronze plaque in Samuel P. Taylor State Park, off Sir Francis Drake Boulevard between Lagunitas and Olema. A few yards from the marker are the ruins of the later mill.

Another mill, the Pacific Powder Mill, built for a different purpose, was erected in 1866 about three miles upstream from the paper mill. These buildings were vacant in 1880, and even the exact site is now lost.

Dominican College

The convent grounds on which stand the buildings of Dominican College occupy a large and beautiful tract northeast of the center of San Rafael. While the establishment of the convent in this locality is of this century, its beginnings are to be found in the earliest days of the state.

The Dominican Sisters, originally from Paris, located on the West Coast first in Monterey in 1851. From Monterey they moved to Benicia in Solano County and from Benicia to San Rafael, where they acquired, by gift and purchase, property that belonged to families prominent in early days. Forest Meadows, the outdoor auditorium, is on land which was owned by William T. Coleman; Meadowlands, the dormitory on Palm Avenue, was the country home of the M. H. de Young family of San Francisco. On the same avenue is the home formerly owned by William Babcock, also of San Francisco. His widow gave this completely furnished house to the convent.

San Francisco Theological Seminary

When William Anderson Scott, D.D., a native of Tennessee, first sailed through the Golden

Gate in 1854, he resolved to establish a school to be a training center on the coast for the Presbyterian ministry, somewhere on the land surrounding the harbor. The realization of his ideal took years of endeavor and saw several changes of location.

The seminary was started in two rooms of the City College in San Francisco, but was moved twice later. For its third location, a building, which still stands at 121 Haight Street, was erected in 1877 by the trustees. Here the seminary remained until its removal to the permanent site in San Anselmo in 1891. The piece of land upon which it is now situated was the gift of a generous citizen of San Rafael, A. W. Foster. The small hill upon which the substantial buildings have been placed overlooks the town. The Montgomery Memorial Chapel, built at the foot of the hill, was the gift of the chief benefactor of the institution, Alexander Montgomery, whose remains were interred there.

Mount Tamalpais State Park

Two Indian words, *tamal* (bay) and *pais* (mountain or country), form the name of the heavily wooded elevation that dominates the landscape on the north side of San Francisco Bay. In the 1860's it was occasionally called Table Mountain. Its three peaks, East, West, and Middle, are all over 2,500 feet high, the highest being the West Peak, 2,604 feet above sea level.

Pedestrian trails, some of which were made originally by Indians and others blazed by white men in the early years, are still used by hiking parties. These pathways begin at different places around the base of the mountain; a favorite one starts beneath the shadows of the trees back of the old mill at Mill Valley. In 1896 the eight-mile Mount Tamalpais and Muir Woods Railroad was laid out, and after its completion a train drawn by a steam engine carried passengers over 283 curves, giving rise to the title "the crookedest railroad in the world." About halfway to the top, at Mesa, the track described a double bowknot to accomplish a 100-foot rise within a distance of 1,000 feet. The railway is a thing of the past since 1930, but a highway following another route makes it possible for people to enjoy the extensive panorama displayed at every turn.

From the broad trail that circles the summit of East Peak one may see close at hand bays, islands, cities, and bridges. If atmospheric conditions are good, one can see to the north Mount Saint Helena and Mount Shasta, to the east Mount Diablo with the snow-capped Sierra Nevada in the distance, to the south Mount Hamilton and Loma Prieta, and to the west the limitless Pacific Ocean.

Mount Tamalpais State Park, a wooded area of about 2,000 acres with unusually comprehensive flora, includes the East Peak. Below Rock Spring lies the natural amphitheater where plays, legendary ,and historical in character, are enacted annually in May. Steep Ravine in this park, a gift of the Honorable William Kent shortly before his death in 1928, is an abrupt descent, with redwoods, firs, and thickets of underbrush.

Muir Woods National Monument

Adjoining Mount Tamalpais State Park on the south is a stand of *Sequoia sempervirens*. These coast redwoods have been growing in this sheltered canyon on the lower western slope of Mount Tamalpais for centuries. Some of the trees, whose ages are estimated at up to 1,700 years, have a diameter of 12 feet and a height of 240 feet.

This forest area was made a National Monument by presidential proclamation on January 9, 1908, a gift to the nation from William Kent, a member of the 62d Congress, and his wife, Elizabeth Thacher Kent of Kentfield. Although President Theodore Roosevelt expressed his désire in accepting the gift to name it for the donors, they wanted it named for John Muir, California's noted naturalist, explorer, and writer, who had long worked in the cause of forest conservation. John Muir was at that time 70 years of age. He lived for six years to enjoy the honor conferred upon him in the naming of Muir Woods. It is known that Muir visited the woods, but the cabin traditionally associated with him no longer stands. The original gift has been supplemented until the area is now 491 acres.

SOURCES

Bancroft, Hubert Howe. *History of California.* A. L. Bancroft Co., San Francisco, 1884.
Barber, Roger. "Mill Valley Yesterdays," *Mill Valley Record*, XXXV, No. 47 (February 16, 1934), 1.
Bingham, Helen. *In Tamal Land.* Calkins Publishing House, San Francisco, 1906.
Bolton, Herbert Eugene. "Francis Drake's Plate of Brass," *California Historical Society Quarterly*, XVI, No. 1, Part 2 (March 1937), 1–16.
——— "Spanish Explorations in the Southwest, 1542–1706," *Original Narratives of Early American History*, XVII. Scribner, New York, 1916.
Bowman, J. N., and G. W. Hendry. "Spanish and Mexican Houses in the Nine Bay Counties." Ms., Bancroft Library, University of California, Berkeley; State Library, Sacramento, 1942.
Boyd, Margaret Kittle. *Reminiscences of Early Marin County Gardens.* Privately printed, 1934.
Brown, Belle C. "Findings of Marin County Historical Landmarks Committee." Ms., 1935.
The California Missions, a Pictorial History. By the editorial staff of Sunset Books. Lane Book Co., Menlo Park, 1964.
California State Mineralogist, Report of. State Printing Office, Sacramento, 1888.
Davidson, George M. *Identification of Sir Francis Drake's Anchorage on the Coast of California in the Year 1579.* Includes maps. California State Historical Society, San Francisco, 1890.
Dodge, George M. *Official Map of Marin County.* Schmidt Label and Lithograph Co., 1892.
Drake, Sir Francis. *The World Encompassed.* Hakluyt Society, London, 1854.
Duflot de Mofras, Eugène. *Exploration du territoire de l'Orégon, des Californies et de la mer Vermeille, exécutée pendant les années 1840, 1841 et 1842.* 2 vols. and atlas. A. Bertrand, Paris, 1844.
Dwyer, John T. *One Hundred Years an Orphan.* St. Vincent's Home for Boys at San Rafael, 1855–1955. Academy Library Guild, Fresno, 1955.
Eckel, Edwin C. "Limestone Deposits of the San Francisco Region," *Report of California State Mineralogist*, XXIX. State Printing Office, Sacramento, 1934.
Edwards, Philip Leget. *Diary.* "The Great Cattle Drive from California to Oregon in 1837." Grabhorn Press, San Francisco, 1932.
Elder, David Paul. *The Old Spanish Missions of California.* Paul Elder & Co., San Francisco, 1913.

John Muir Cabin, Muir Woods National Monument

Frémont, John Charles. *Memoirs of My Life*. Bedford Clarke & Co., Chicago, 1887.

Glimpses of Belvedere & Tiburon, the Early Decades. The Landmarks Society, Belvedere-Tiburon, 1964.

Greene, Clay M. "Life and Death of Daniel O'Connell, 1899," Annals of the Bohemian Club, IV. Recorder Printing and Publishing Co., San Francisco, 1930.

Guinn, J. M. *History of the State of California, Memorial and Biographical Record of Coast Counties of California*. Chapman Publishing Co., Chicago, 1904.

Harpending, Asbury. *The Great Diamond Hoax and Other Stirring Incidents*. The James H. Barry Co., San Francisco, 1913.

History of Northern California, Memorial and Biographical. Lewis Publishing Co., Chicago, 1891.

James, George Wharton. *In and Out of the Missions of California*. Little, Brown, Boston, 1906.

Land Grants, Book of Patents. Ms. Marin County Recorder's Office, San Rafael.

Mourelle, Antonio. *Voyage of the* Sonora *in the Second Bucareli Expedition*, trans. The Hon. Daines Barrington. Reprinted by Thomas C. Russell, San Francisco, 1920.

Munro-Fraser, J. P. *History of Marin County*. Illustrated. Alley, Bowen & Co., San Francisco, 1880.

Nelson, N. C. "Shellmounds of the San Francisco Bay Region," *University of California Publications in American Archaeology and Ethnology*, XVII, No. 4 (1909).

Nevins, Allan. *Frémont, the West's Greatest Adventurer*. Harper, New York, 1928.

Older, Mrs. Fremont. *California Missions and Their Romances*. Coward-McCann, New York, 1938.

Royce, Josiah. *California from the Conquest in 1846 to the Second Vigilance Committee in San Francisco*. Houghton Mifflin, Boston, 1917.

Shafter, Payne J. "Reminiscences." Ms.

Sherman, W. T. *Memoirs*. D. Appleton & Co., New York, 1875.

Simpson, Sir George. *Narrative of a Journey round the World during the Years 1841–42*. 2 vols. Henry Colburn, London, 1847.

Treganza, Adan E. "Old Lime Kilns near Olema," *Geologic Guidebook of the San Francisco Bay Counties*. State of California, Division of Mines, San Francisco, 1951, 65–72.

Wagner, Henry R. *Sir Francis Drake's Voyage around the World, Its Aims and Achievements*. John Howell, San Francisco, 1926.

––– *Spanish Voyages to the Northwest Coast of America*. California Historical Society, San Francisco, 1929.

Wilkins, James H. "The Story of Fairfax," *Marin County Leader*, I, No. 2 (March 6, 1926).

––– "The Duel at Fairfax," *Marin County Leader*, I, No. 2 (March 6, 1926).

Winn, W. B. *Souvenir of Marin County*. Published by Marin County Journal, San Rafael, 1893.

Mariposa County

THE NAME MARIPOSA (Spanish for "butterfly") was first given in the plural form, Las Mariposas, to a spot in Merced County visited by the expedition of Gabriel Moraga in 1806. The old Mexican grant conferred upon Juan Bautista Alvarado in 1844 and purchased for Frémont on February 10, 1847, by his agent, Thomas O. Larkin, likewise took the plural form of the name, while the singular form, Mariposa, was bestowed first upon the creek and later upon the town and the county.

Some have erroneously thought that this place name was derived from "Mariposa Lily," the common name of the many-hued lilies (*Calochortus luteus* and other varieties) which in late spring and early summer give color to the hills of this region. But it is to the butterfly, which at certain seasons of the year is found here in countless numbers, that the source of the delightful place name must be traced.

Mariposa County was one of the original 27 counties. With an area of about 30,000 square miles, it covered one-fifth of the state. Stretching from the Coast Range to the present Nevada state line, and touching Los Angeles County on the south, it contained land now included within ten other counties. The area of the present county is 1,455 square miles. Agua Fria was the first county seat, in 1850–51, after which Mariposa became the seat of government.

Walker's Trail over the Sierra

Joseph Reddeford Walker, as early as 1833, came into California over the Sierra Nevada through what are now Mono, Mariposa, and Tuolumne counties. "Reliable knowledge of the Sierra Nevada," says Francis P. Farquhar, "really begins with this expedition."

Passing down the Humboldt River Valley in Nevada and thence south by Carson Lake, Walker and his men struck westward across the Sierra, probably ascending its eastern slope by one of the southern tributaries of the East Walker River. After crossing the summit of the pass, the party was lost for several days "in a maze of lakes and mountains." The description of this region, as given by Zenas Leonard, chronicler of the expedition, accords well with the character of the country in the vicinity of Virginia Canyon.

From this point, Farquhar says "they would have crossed the Tuolumne, perhaps near Conness Creek. Passing Tenaya Lake, they probably followed the general course of the present Tioga road" (mostly in Tuolumne County) down the divide between the Tuolumne and Merced rivers. On this stage of the journey the party saw either the Merced Grove or the Tuolumne Grove of *Sequoia gigantea*, thus being the first known white men to see the Big Trees of the Sierra Nevada.

Yosemite Valley

"It is now known with reasonable certainty that Yosemite Valley was seen by the Walker party in 1833." Zenas Leonard, clerk of the expedition, recorded in his diary what is thought to be the first mention of Yosemite Valley by a white man. He writes:

"Some of these precipices appeared to us to be more than a mile high. Some of the men thought that if we could succeed in descending one of these precipices to the bottom, we might thus work our way into the valley below—but on making several attempts we found it utterly impossible for a man to descend, to say nothing of our horses."

The diary of William Penn Abrams, a Gold Rush pioneer, reveals that he and his companion, U. N. Reamer, saw Yosemite Valley in October 1849. They were following the tracks of a grizzly bear when they came upon the spectacular scene. Bridal Veil Falls was described as dropping "from a cliff below three jagged peaks into the valley." Half Dome looked to the men "as though it had been sliced with a knife as one would slice a loaf of bread." They called it "Rock of Ages." It is possible that historical research may yet uncover other early accounts of Yosemite.

However, "it was not until 1851 that the valley can properly be said to have been discovered and made widely known." This, the first effective discovery, was made by Major James D. Savage and Captain John Boling, who, with a strong detachment of mounted volunteers and friendly Indian guides, entered the valley in March of that year to capture the resident Indians in order to put them on the Fresno Indian Reservation. One of this party of discoverers was Dr. L. H. Bunnell, the first man to make the wonders of the Yosemite Valley known to the world.

Major Savage had come to the mines in 1848, enlisted Indian labor in his diggings in Tuolumne County, and soon developed extensive trading relations with the natives. His first post (SRL 527) was set up at or near the mouth of the South Fork of the Merced River in Mariposa County, but this was abandoned when the Yo-semite Indians went on the warpath against the whites in 1850. (The approximate site of Savage's trading post is indicated by a marker on the All-Year Highway.)

In 1851 and 1852 a number of punitive expeditions against the Indians entered the valley, the last, led by Lieutenant Moore, finally driving the remnant of the tribe over the mountains, where they took refuge with the Monos.

The tourist history of Yosemite Valley began in 1855, when J. M. Hutchings, in company with three friends, formed the first tourist expedition to enter it. Five days of "scenic banqueting" were spent in exploring the region and sketching its wonders. "The publicity given to Hutchings' writings and to Ayers' drawings was what really called public attention to the existence of Yosemite Valley.... From that time on not a year passed but that tourists found their way there in ever increasing numbers." The first improved pack trail into Yosemite Valley was made in 1856 by the Mann Brothers, a livery firm in Mariposa. It led from Mariposa to the valley by way of the South Fork of the Merced River, crossing at Wawona.

Regular tourist travel to Yosemite Valley began in 1857. The first house was built there in the autumn of 1856, and the first hotel in 1859. The latter was, until its destruction in 1940, a part of the Sentinel Hotel establishment known as Cedar Cottage.

Nearly all of the early visitors to Yosemite Valley were Californians, mostly campers. Only a few hundred came yearly until the completion of the Union Pacific and Central Pacific railroads. Today thousands come annually from all parts of the world. Although the Yosemite Valley Railroad from Merced to El Portal no longer exists, there are four main automobile roads which lead to the valley: the All-Year Highway from Merced through Mariposa and El Portal, the Big Oak Flat Road, the Tioga Pass route from the east, and the southern route from Fresno through Wawona. Besides these, there are two old routes for the traveler with plenty of time and an indifference to steep, rough roads: the old highway from the west that passes south of

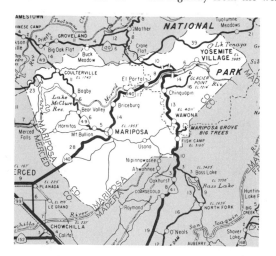

Mariposa, through Mormon Bar and Bootjack, and over Chowchilla Mountain to Wawona; and the Coulterville road past Bower Cave and the Merced Grove of Big Trees, the first stagecoach route into Yosemite Valley. Part of the old road to Wawona is to become a segment of State Highway 49. The Coulterville road is gradually being improved and may someday regain its former importance.

Yosemite Valley (*SRL 790*) was made a state park on June 30, 1864. A national park surrounding the valley was established in 1890, and the present Yosemite National Park was constituted in 1906, when the State of California ceded back the Yosemite Valley and the Mariposa Grove of Big Trees.

The numerous trails and roads in the valley, as well as specific points of interest such as Bridal Veil Falls, El Capitan, Cathedral Rocks, Glacier Point, Half Dome, Inspiration Point, and Yosemite Falls, are thoroughly dealt with in the current government publications, as are the hotels, camps, and lodges open to visitors. At Government Center a museum, established in 1921, and comprising four departments—history, ethnology, zoölogy, and botany—houses natural history exhibits and treasured relics of early days in Yosemite.

The center of activity in Yosemite Valley prior to 1916 is now called Old Village. Here stands the chapel, built in 1879 from pennies donated by Sunday school children.

Wawona (Clark's Station)

At Wawona is the site of the log cabin built by Galen Clark in 1857, the same year in which he officially discovered the Mariposa Grove, only eight miles from his cabin and now within the Yosemite National Park. Galen Clark was a member of the first Board of Commissioners for the care of Yosemite Valley and the Mariposa Grove, and was for many years known as the "Guardian of the Valley." For more than 50 years he lived either in Yosemite or at Wawona. At the latter place his cabin was known to all travelers as Clark's Station, where kindly hospitality never failed to be extended.

Galen Clark in 1904, at the age of 90 years, published his first book, *Indians of Yosemite*, and in 1907 another, *Big Trees of California*. Clark finished his last book, *The Yosemite Valley*, just two weeks before his death on March 24, 1910, at the age of 96 years.

Wawona is now the home of the Pioneer Yosemite History Center, a collection of the park's oldest structures, most of which were moved here from other areas for permanent preservation. Through this outdoor museum the interesting history of Yosemite National Park is meaningfully interpreted for visitors. Among the buildings are a Wells Fargo office, a jail, a wagon shop, and several cabins, including one built by a trail blazer, another by a homesteader, one built by the U.S. Army, and another by the National Park Service. The historical displays center around the old Wawona covered bridge, begun about 1858 by Galen Clark, covered in 1875, and restored in

Old Village Chapel, Yosemite Valley

1956. Nearby is the Wawona Hotel, still in operation. The main building was constructed in 1885, but one structure of the group, the "Long White," dates from 1879.

Historic Spots along the All-Year Highway

The All-Year Highway from Merced to the Yosemite Valley passes through one of the most interesting and romantic of California's historic regions. Many of the landmarks of mining days have been obliterated, but here and there stark ruined walls of brick or stone marking the site of some ghost city of the hills may be seen, or an occasional hamlet invites the passer-by to linger and picture for himself the lively scenes enacted there in the stirring heyday of its past.

Where the modern highway crosses the Merced-Mariposa county line, the route of the old Stockton–Los Angeles Road (locally known as the Millerton Road) is intersected. Following the base of the lower foothills along what is now the boundary line of the two counties, this old road (now almost lost in the grass-grown hills) avoided the winter freshets and the labyrinthine tulares then covering the floor of the valley. Along its route, at first but faintly marked and shifting, the commerce of the rich southern mines flowed in the days of pack trains and stagecoaches. This road was antedated only by the Los Angeles Trail, or El Camino Viejo, on the western side of the valley.

About seven miles from the Merced county line the old Yosemite highway branches to the east. A little to the northwest is Indian Gulch, while to the northeast is Guadalupe, both flourishing mining camps at one time. A few interesting old adobes still stand along the main street of Indian Gulch, now a road through the Solari Ranch. After traversing Cathey's Valley, first settled in the early 1850's and still claiming among its inhabitants descendants of the original families, the All-Year Highway passes through the lower mountains of Mariposa County. A few miles west of Mariposa, the Agua Fria Road turns north to Mount Bullion. The road to the south, part of the same old road, joins the old highway at Buckeye. The site of Carson, at the junction of the All-Year Highway and the road to Buckeye, is marked by a few stone ruins. One-half mile above Carson on the All-Year Highway is Arkansas Flat. During the depression of the 1930's both these sites were taken over by modern miners, who gleaned from ten cents to a dollar a day in the neighboring gulches.

Agua Fria

Until 1852, while mining was the main industry of the area, Mariposa County included what are now Merced, Madera, Fresno, Tulare, and Kings counties, and parts of Kern, Inyo, Mono, Ventura, and San Benito counties. As agriculture developed, new counties were gradually carved out of the territory included in the original county. The first county seat of Mariposa County, in 1850–51, was at Agua Fria (SRL 518) on Agua Fria Creek. Today scarcely a trace of the place is left except a few foundation stones and abandoned diggings, and it is hard to believe that this place was once the seat of government for one-fifth of California. The site has been marked.

Mariposa

Mariposa, founded on Frémont's Rancho Las Mariposas, a grant that occupied a unique position in the mining history of the state, became the county seat of Mariposa County on September 7, 1851, and was long the center of trade for the rich mining area covered by the rancho. The town of today has preserved some of the features typical of early mining camps—buildings with substantial walls of brick and stone supplemented by iron doors and shutters, with an occasional overhanging balcony.

Among the several old buildings dating from early mining days the one of greatest interest is

Courthouse, Mariposa

the courthouse (SRL 670). Lumber from the neighboring forests was used in its construction and the timbers were fitted together with mortise and tenon and held in place by wooden pegs. Built in 1854, it is the oldest courthouse in California still in use. The clock in its tower has been running since 1866. In spite of their years of service the seats and the bar in the courtroom remain unchanged. Adding to the historic interest of the building are many quaint documents and newspaper files of priceless value, which are kept within a fireproof vault. Court was conducted in rented quarters in Mariposa from September 1851 until about May 1855, when it moved into the new courthouse.

Other picturesque and historic buildings in Mariposa are St. Joseph's Catholic Church (1862), the old stone jail, the Trabucco Warehouse, the Schlageter Hotel (1866), the Trabucco Store, and the Odd Fellows Hall (1867). Directly across the street from the Schlageter Hotel is an adobe building that was used by Frémont as an assay office on his grant of 44,500 acres. The Historical Center operated by the Mariposa County Historical Society is considered one of the finest in the Mother Lode country.

Mormon Bar

Mormon Bar (SRL 323), one and a half miles southeast of Mariposa on Mariposa Creek, was first settled in 1849 by Mormons, who stayed, however, only a short time. Their places were taken at once by other miners, while at a later period the same ground was worked over by thousands of Chinese. The site of Mormon Bar has been obliterated by the widening of the highway, but the Mariposa County Fairgrounds are today located close to the old townsite. No longer to be seen is the Chinese graveyard from which the bones of the dead were carried by friends or relatives back to the ancestral burial grounds in China.

Buckeye to the west, where James Savage had one of his trading posts, Bootjack to the east, and Ben Hur, about ten miles to the south, all shared with Mormon Bar the prosperity of their neighbor, the town of Mariposa. The site of the last Ben Hur post office on the Quick Ranch is located about a mile southeast of the older site on the hill. The post office was discontinued in 1951. Not far away is the Quick ranch house, into which has been incorporated a portion of the original house built by Morgan W. Quick, who purchased the original 160 acres of his ranch in 1859 from two men having squatters' rights. The garden and orchard about the present house are still watered from the perpetual spring which attracted the first settlers. The 4,000 acres that comprise the present ranch, still owned by the family, are fenced by a stone wall, built with infinite labor and remarkable skill by Chinese coolies in 1862. According to the contract with Quick, each coolie was forced to lay a rod and a half daily or forfeit his job. For this he was paid at the rate of two bits a day, while the Chinese contractor received one dollar and six bits per rod. The old wall, which extends for five miles up hill and down, is a truly marvelous piece of workmanship, and is as perfect today as when it was laid.

At the foot of Becknell Hill, two and a half miles south of Ben Hur, stand the remains of the once picturesque Becknell adobe, one of the oldest original dwellings in Mariposa County. About 1950 it was intact, roofed, and in fairly good condition; when visited 15 years later, only fragmentary ruins marked the spot. These are located behind a residence on the east side of the road.

Mount Bullion

Mount Bullion, located on the mountain of that name and reached by the Mother Lode Highway, is about five miles northwest of Mariposa on a part of the former Frémont estate. The peak was named in honor of Senator Thomas H. Benton, Frémont's father-in-law, whose nickname was "Old Bullion." Only a few buildings reminiscent of the gold days remain in the town. On the left side of the road is a deserted saloon, faded lettering on the front still proclaiming it "The Princeton." Farther along the same side is the Trabucco store, a remodeled frame building, now closed. Across the street long stood the Marre store, a one-story adobe with heavy iron shutters and doors closely barred, its sturdy walls shaded by two tall cottonwood trees. It gradually fell into ruin and disappeared in the 1950's. The old Princeton Mine, located on Mount Bullion just south of town, was originally owned by Frémont. Its total production exceeded $3 million in gold, and although it has long since been closed down, many believe that is still capable of producing wealth.

Hornitos

Hornitos ("little ovens"), 13 miles west of Mount Bullion, probably derived its name from the presence of many odd Mexican graves or tombs built of stone in the shape of little square bake ovens and set on top of the ground. On the hillside just below the Catholic church and cemetery the ruins of two or three of these interesting relics may still be seen. Some authorities believe the name came rather from the outdoor ovens on which the Mexican women cooked.

Hornitos seems to have been settled by Mexicans driven out of the adjoining town of Quartzburg. The old plaza was the scene of many a lively fiesta. "Gamblers, girls and roughnecks . . . they were a tough lot, the worst in the southern mines. They reverenced nothing but money, cards and wine. . . . Blood was upon nearly every doorstep and the sand was caked with it." It is said that Joaquín Murieta, the noted bandit, on his frequent visits found friends here.

In time, however, a change came over the place. When the placers at Quartzburg (a short distance up the creek) gave out, many of its citizens came to Hornitos, where the diggings were very rich. In 1870 it became the first and only incorporated town in Mariposa County. Ordinances were passed remedying many of the old social abuses, the gambling dens became stores,

Princeton Saloon, Mount Bullion

and children played on the streets. The "city" has never been officially disincorporated, but it has not exercised its municipal functions for many years.

Hornitos (SRL 333) appears today much as it was years ago—no pavements, no plate glass, and no gasoline signs to mar the atmosphere of other days. The long bars are dry and deserted, and in the door casings significant bullet holes still show. A decided Mexican influence is evident in the quaint adobe and stone structures with their massive iron doors, many of them in ruins and others closed and deserted. A few of the more interesting buildings from mining days are the stone jail, the Cassaretto and Gagliardo stores, George Reeb's butcher shop on the plaza, and the one remaining wall of the Ghirardelli store, where a pioneer merchant "whose name has since become a household word" had an early merchandising business. The dance hall once had an underground passage—"for escape when things grew too hot"—and it is said that Joaquín Murieta found it useful on more than one occasion when he was in danger of being captured by the officers of the law. The Masonic Hall, a single-story building erected in 1860 and still in use, was once the only one in California with its meeting room on the ground floor. The frame Hornitos Hotel, erected about 1860 and torn down in the 1930's, hosted many prominent men of the day, including President Grant.

Quartzburg, at one time a populous center of placer mining in Mariposa County, with fraternal societies and all the organizations that made up the social life of the time, consists today of an adobe ruin and a few fruit and shade trees plainly showing the neglect of many years. The old Thorn house, with its tall brick chimney and adobe walls fashioned from the dark red soil native to the vicinity, was for years a picturesque landmark on the present Hornitos–Bear Valley road. It was built by Colonel Thorn in the early 1850's and served as store and post office at Quartzburg. Now only a crumbling fragment remains.

The Mount Ophir Mint

Another vanished town of the Mother Lode is Mount Ophir, which is located one and a half miles northwest of Mount Bullion near the old highway. Nothing remains of this once busy set-

Ruins of Thorn House, Quartzburg

tlement except the ruins of a private mint, one of several such early mints in California, in which hexagonal fifty-dollar slugs were coined. Today one of these slugs, if it could be found, might be valued at $10,000. Near the ruins of the mint is an arched stone vault, broken and ravaged by treasure hunters, where the raw gold is said to have been stored. Just beyond Mount Ophir, on the way to Bear Valley, walls of the Trabucco Store stand at the left of the road, "as pretty a ruin as most of the missions can show," as one traveler has described it. This old trading post of the Mother Lode was erected by Louis Trabucco in the early 1850's.

Bear Valley

The present Mariposa County includes what was once Rancho Las Mariposas, sometimes spoken of as the Frémont Grant, a vast estate constituting one of several so-called "floating grants," and located originally in what is now Merced County. After gold was discovered in the Mariposa region in the spring of 1848, Frémont "floated" his rancho up into the hills. The new location proved to be very rich in gold, and for several years large operations were carried on there by Frémont.

The center of Frémont's activities was Bear Valley *(SRL 331)*, about 11 miles northwest of Mariposa. At one time it was practically Frémont's own town, built by him and owned by him, and he lived there. Diggings were all about it, and on Saturday night hundreds of miners thronged the streets.

Along the Mother Lode Highway from Mariposa northwest to the site of Benton Mills, evidences of mining activities and of Frémont's associations may still be found. In the town of Bear Valley itself can be seen remnants of past glory, a few stone and adobe structures, including saloons, stores, and public houses, some fast crumbling into decay. The large, jagged ruins of the old Frémont Company store stand across the road from the site of the Oso House, a two-story wooden structure with wide upper and lower balconies which burned to the ground in the 1930's. It was built by Frémont in 1850, from lumber brought around the Horn, and was the main hotel of the camp as well as the headquarters for the Frémont Company. Many noted names, that of Ulysses S. Grant among others, were on its register. The Frémont residence,

which stood some distance back from the main street, is also gone. At Bear Valley there is an Odd Fellows Hall, once graced by a balcony, only the iron framework of which remains.

Just beyond Bear Valley on the road to Coulterville stand the ruins of Bear Valley's once thriving Chinatown. The climb up the ridge road from this point is so gradual that one is startled, on making a sudden turn, to look down a thousand feet into the heart of Hell's Hollow. It is "a sight different from all other grades, with a play of light and shadow, rolling contour upon contour until lost to sight in the long distance." When covered with a carpet of purple godetias from base to summit, the beauty of this canyon is something never to be forgotten.

The winding grade down into the hollow passes the Pine Tree and Josephine mines, once big producers for Frémont. The next place of historic interest was Bagby, formerly Benton Mills, the site of one of Frémont's largest mills and river dams, portions of which were visible into the 1960's. Bagby, on the Merced River and once a station on the Yosemite Valley Railroad, has been inundated by the expanded Exchequer Dam project.

On the North Fork of the Merced River northeast of Benton Mills was another Indian Gulch of Mariposa County, while to the northwest, also on the river, was Horseshoe Bend, once a rich and populous mining camp. Between them was Split Rock, on the south bank of the river. To the southeast in Sherlock Gulch was one of the numerous Whiskey Flats with which the mining regions abounded.

Exchequer Dam has created Lake McClure, where water is impounded for generating electric power and for irrigating the farms of Merced County. Exchequer was formerly a mining area, and was on the route of the Yosemite Valley Railroad.

Coulterville

The old mining town of Coulterville *(SRL 332)* is one of the most picturesque and interesting on the Mother Lode. It was called "Banderita" by the first American miners who came there, because of the small red flags used by the Mexican inhabitants. Although Coulterville has suffered from several devastating fires, there are still many old stone and brick buildings to be seen, some of them roofless and in ruins. The main street, lined with umbrella trees, is the location of the Jeffery Hotel, the adjoining saloon with its old swinging doors, and the Bruschi and Gazzolo buildings. Across the highway from the Jeffery Hotel are the remains of George Coulter's hotel and the Wells Fargo building, in front of which stand an old mine locomotive and the ubiquitous hangman's tree. At the far end of town, where the Chinese once lived, is the old adobe Sun Sun Wo store, now a museum.

About four miles west of Coulterville near Highway 132 is the beautiful old Wheeler mansion, built in 1860 by a man for his fiancée, who jilted him before the house was completed. A mile and a half south of Coulterville and three-quarters of a mile west of Highway 49 are the foundations of the French Mills, built along classic lines of architecture in the early 1850's. Also in the vicinity of Coulterville are Maxwell Creek and Piñon Blanco (misspelled "Penon" on the maps), one-time flourishing mining camps.

Interesting Names

In the early mining days millions of dollars in gold was washed from the gravel beds of Mariposa County's many streams. Quartz mining succeeded placer mining, and veins of fabulous wealth were located in the great Mother Lode, which stretches throughout the width of the county. Numerous camps, many of them with odd or unusual names, sprang up all over the county, such as Texas Tent, Cow-and-Calf, Drunken Gulch, Red Cloud, Poison Springs, Hog Canyon, Fly Away, Boneyard, White Rock, Mariposita, Chowchilla, Sherlock's Diggings, Whitlock, Pleasant Valley, Bridgeport, and Chamisal.

El Portal

For years this gateway on the west to Yosemite Valley was the terminus of the railroad line from Merced. Now it is the last major settlement on the All-Year Highway before it enters the park boundaries. The Yosemite Valley Railroad operated from 1906 to 1942, but the quaint log El Portal station continued to stand for some years afterward. Now it is gone, as is the beautiful hotel. From El Portal, passengers traveled by stage into the Yosemite Valley. The town is now the headquarters for Yosemite Valley employees, and many new homes have been built for the rangers. Under development here is the Pioneer Yosemite Transportation Center, which will display the story of early travel to Yosemite by exhibiting various vehicles from different eras.

SOURCES

Adams, Edgar H. *Private Gold Coinage of California, 1849–1855, Its History and Its Issues.* Privately published by Edgar H. Adams, Brooklyn, N.Y., 1912.

Adams, Kramer A. *Covered Bridges of the West.* Howell-North, Berkeley, 1963.

Badè, Frederic William, *The Life and Letters of John Muir.* 2 vols. Houghton Mifflin, Boston, 1924.

Browne, J. Ross. *The Mariposa Estate.* Russell's American Steam Printing House, New York, 1868.

Bunnell, Lafayette Houghton. *Discovery of the Yosemite and the Indian War of 1851.* Privately published, Chicago, 1880.

Chamberlain, Newell D. *The Call of Gold.* Gazette Press, Mariposa, 1936.

Clark, Galen. *The Yosemite Valley.* Yosemite Valley, 1911.

Corcoran, May S. *A History of the San Joaquin Valley Counties.* Ms., 1921.

Cossley-Batt, Jill Lillie Emma. *The Last of the California Rangers.* Funk & Wagnalls Co., New York, 1928.

"The Early Days in Yosemite," reprinted from the *Mariposa Democrat* of August 5, 1856, with Introduction by Ansel F. Hall, in *California Historical Society Quarterly,* I, No. 3 (January 1923), 271–85.

Farquhar, Francis P. "Exploration of the Sierra Nevada," *California Historical Society Quarterly,* IV, No. 1 (March 1925), 2–58.

Geologic Guidebook along Highway 49 — Sierran Gold Belt, the Mother Lode Country. State of California, Division of Mines, San Francisco, 1948.

Gold Rush Country. Lane Publishing Co., Menlo Park, 1957.

Heald, Weldon F. "The Forgotten Pioneer," *Westways,* XLIII, No. 3 (March 1954), 6–7.

Hutchings, James Mason. *In the Heart of the Sierras.* Pacific Press Publishing House, Oakland, 1886.

——— *Scenes of Wonder and Curiosity in California.* Hutchings & Rosenfield, San Francisco, 1860.

Johnston, Philip. "Legends and Landmarks of '49 along the Mother Lode," *Touring Topics,* XXIII, No. 2 (February 1931), 12–27, 52–53.

Leonard, Zenas. *Narrative of the Adventures of Zenas Leonard . . .* Original edition, Clearfield, Pennsylvania, 1839. Later edition ed. W. F. Wagner. The Burrows Brothers Co., Cleveland, 1904.

Muir, John. *Mountains of California.* 2 vols. Houghton Mifflin, Boston, 1917.

——— *The Yosemite.* Century Co., New York, 1912.

Peterson, Henry C. "Relics of Early Days to be Seen on Sierra Landmark Expedition," *Oakland Tribune,* May 14, 1922.

Russell, Carl P. *One Hundred Years in Yosemite. The Story of a Great Park and Its Friends.* University of California Press, Berkeley, 1947.

Weston, Otheto. *Mother Lode Album.* Stanford University Press, Stanford, 1948.

Wood, Raymund F. *California's Agua Fria.* Academy Library Guild, Fresno, 1954.

Mendocino County

MENDOCINO COUNTY was one of the original 27 counties, but until 1859 the government was administered by Sonoma County officials. (The name was first applied to Cape Mendocino, so named in honor of Antonio de Mendoza, the first viceroy of New Spain.) Ukiah has always been the county seat.

Point Arena

Point Arena, or Punta de Arenas (Sandy Point), is a prominent headland on the coast in the southwestern part of the county. Offshore at this point Captain George Vancouver spent the night of Friday, November 10, 1792, in his ship *Discovery,* while on his way from Nootka to San Francisco. Captain Vancouver called the place "Punta Barro de Arena."

The land stretching back from this point was included in an unnamed and unconfirmed grant made in 1844 to Rafael García, an early soldier of the San Francisco Company and already owner of two grants in what is now Marin County, who stocked the land with cattle. The Garcia River flowing through the tract bears his name. This grantee and Antonio Castro were reported to have been the leaders of a party of white men

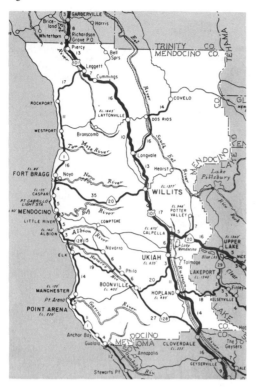

who raided the Indians in the vicinity of Ross in 1845 in search of laborers.

Although a store was built and goods were sold on the site in 1859, the town of Point Arena was not incorporated until 1908. It is said that, when the lumbering industry was at its height, Point Arena was the busiest town between San Francisco and Eureka. Asphalt, which exuded from an ocean bluff nearby in quantities insufficient for commercial exploitation—as was proved during the oil excitement of 1865—is used on the streets of the town and makes a satisfactory road surface.

In 1870 a light station was erected well out on the point. The tower, built of brick, was destroyed in the earthquake of 1906; another, of reinforced concrete, was built subsequently a little distance back from the point. The present tower is 115 feet high, one of the two highest on the coast of California, and supports a light of 380,000 candlepower. Before the establishment of this light, many vessels were lost near here. The night of November 20, 1865, is memorable as that of a most disastrous storm in which ten vessels went ashore within a few miles of the point.

The Sanel Grant, Sanel, and Hopland

Fernando Felix (Feliz), a former *regidor* at the Pueblo San José and already owner of Rancho Novato, received in 1844 a large tract of land in Sanel Valley lying along the Russian River. He erected an adobe house, 30 by 50 feet, and lived with his family just south of where Hopland now stands. He had lived there for seven years when in 1860 he received the United States patent for the 17,754 acres comprised in his estate.

The settlement that grew up around the Felix home was known by 1859 as Sanel. Then a toll road was built down the east side of the river, which rerouted all the traffic that way, and the town gradually moved over to the road, leaving only one building, a brick store, behind. The new site was called Hopland. Later the building of a railroad drew business back to the original site; and eventually the two places consolidated as Hopland, being called by the residents Old Hopland and New Hopland.

A populous Indian village once existed just south of Old Hopland on the south bank of Mc-Dowell Creek. It was called "Sanel," and from this village the grant, the township, and the town preceding Hopland all inherited the name Sanel. Six miles south of Hopland on the Redwood Highway is Squaw Rock (*SRL 549*), also called "Lover's Leap," associated with a Sanel Indian legend. Sotuka, an Indian maiden, is supposed to have jumped from the precipice upon her faithless lover and the girl for whom he had deserted her, as they lay sleeping below, bringing death to all three.

The first hops grown in this once famous hop-raising center were planted by Stephen Warren Knowles, who settled in Sanel Township in 1858, after arriving in San Francisco on the steamer *Northern Light* a few years earlier. He sold his first crop, dried in the loft of his barn, in Petaluma for 30 cents a pound. The Hermitage post office of early days was on the Knowles's place. Hop growing has now been replaced by the pear industry in this area.

The Yokaya Grant and Ukiah

The Indian word *yokaya* means "south valley" or "deep valley between high hills." This rancho of 11 square leagues lay in the fertile valley of the Russian River. It was given by Governor Pío Pico in 1845 to Cayetano Juárez, a native Californian who was a captain of militia and had engaged in many Indian forays. Captain Juárez was also the grantee of Rancho Tulucay in the Napa Valley four years earlier. He had built an adobe there for a permanent home, where he died in 1883 at the age of 75. He distinguished himself somewhat, at the time of the capture of General Vallejo, by his offer (which was rejected) to rescue that officer. The message to Vallejo regarding his release was carried by a brother of Captain Juárez disguised as a woman. Patent to this land was received by Juárez from the United States in 1867. Later owners (Hastings, Curry, and Carpenter) surveyed the property and sold it in tracts to suit purchasers.

The town of Ukiah, within the boundary of the grant and taking its name phonetically, had its origin in the 1850's. The first settler on the site, S. Lowry, had established himself there by 1856, but sold out within a year to A. T. Perkins, who became a permanent resident. In 1859, when Sonoma County officials were relieved of the administration of county affairs, the little town was chosen as the county seat. At that time only 100 people were dwelling in the Russian River Valley. Ukiah is easily accessible today by means of the scenic Redwood Highway, which each year brings thousands of tourists through the town. The valley is now devoted almost entirely to the raising of pears, prunes, and grapes.

Three institutions of interest to scientists were established in or near Ukiah. The first one, biological, brought there in 1894, was the Fish Hatchery. Through the joint efforts of the Northwestern Pacific Railway and Mendocino County, this scientific exhibit had been placed in the Midwinter Fair in San Francisco. After the close of the fair, it was brought to Ukiah and maintained at the expense of the railway company until eventually it was taken over by the State Fish and Game Commission and moved to a more suitable location eight miles out of town. The hatchery no longer exists. The second of these scientific institutions, a geodetic one, was established in Ukiah in 1898 and is still in use. It is the International Latitude Observatory, one of four established by the International Geodetic Association. The third, which was botanical, was the pioneer project, started in 1900, for the preservation and propagation of native Western wildflowers, bulbs, shrubs, and trees. The originator of this interesting venture, Carl A. Purdy, arrived with his parents in the Ukiah Valley in 1870. In 1878, while still on the home farm, chance gave him the opportunity to gather native bulbs and plants for an Eastern firm. The interest thus stimulated in the youth led to the development of the once internationally known gardens, The Terraces, eight miles east of Ukiah. The gardens are now no more.

Early Sawmills

A vessel carrying a cargo of silk and tea to San Francisco in 1851 encountered a severe storm and was driven ashore at the mouth of Noyo River. A party sent from Bodega to salvage the freight saw the timber along this part of the coast, with its readily available lumber supply, and carried the information to Alderman Harry Meiggs of San Francisco. Meiggs, in addition to his political interests, was a mill owner and lumberman, with his main depot at North Beach in San Francisco. Finding his equipment inadequate for handling such large logs, he immediately ordered more substantial machinery from the East, procuring an engine and boiler from Norwich, Connecticut, and other parts from Painted Post, New York. When the goods arrived in San Francisco, he chartered the brig *Ontario* and with the new outfit entered the mouth of Big River, or Booldam, as the Indians had named it, on July 19, 1852. Finding that William Kasten, one of those who had been driven ashore by the foul weather, claimed the waterfront, he purchased Kasten's claim, giving him some of the first product of his mill as part payment. With this lumber, Kasten built a dwelling house on what is now Kasten Street in Mendocino City, the first house of sawed lumber in the town. The house was occupied for many years by William Heeser, a pioneer.

The California Lumber Company was immedi-ately formed, with Harry Meiggs the most active member of the firm, and J. B. Ford, who had arrived with eight yoke of oxen ten days before the brig, one of its important employees.

During the height of the lumbering activity, a number of towns grew up along the coast, each one a shipping point. Twenty mills, including some for making shingles only, were erected in Beaver Township before 1880. In almost every mile, along a creek or gulch or river, could be found a mill with its narrow-gauge railway built up the canyon a few miles for the purpose of bringing lumber or logs from the mountains down to the landing places. Ox teams dragged the logs from where they were felled to the railways. Most of these mills along the coast were operated with no loading facilities other than chutes from the cliffs, down which the lumber was slipped to the vessels lying at anchor below.

From north to south these coast towns and hamlets were Usal, Rockport, Hardy Creek, Westport, Cleone, Fort Bragg, Noyo, Caspar, Mendocino City, Little River, Albion, Navarro, Greenwood, Elk River, and, on the very southern edge of the county, Gualala. With the decline of lumbering, many of the old towns have been abandoned, and their railways and wharves have become only memories.

Such an abandoned place is Rockport. Hardy Creek, with its score or two of cottages scattered along a deep canyon opening into a "triangle of bluest sea," has become a ghost town. Caspar, a community of 200 persons, is invitingly situated

Masonic Hall, Mendocino

Presbyterian Church, Mendocino

beside a millpond with wooded canyon walls rising in the background. Noyo, lying on a neck of land between Noyo and Hare creeks just south of Fort Bragg, is making a name for itself again, this time by its fishing industry. Plants for canning and drying fish are now located in its picturesque deep-water harbor.

Mendocino City, "with its red and white houses, schools, and churches ranged on a long promontory above the bay at the mouth of Big River," remains a thriving community and a promising artists' colony with a population of about 1,000. Here are an interesting old Masonic temple with carved wood figures, and a historic Presbyterian church (*SRL 714*), both dating from the 1860's. The cliffs at the harbor hide deep caves around which legends of disappearing ships are woven. The lumbering operations which were started there in 1853 by the California Lumber Company are now controlled by the Union Lumber Company, with a main plant at Fort Bragg.

South of Mendocino City is Little River, location of the old Silas W. Coombs house, built in 1853 and now famed as the Little River Inn. Between Little River and Albion, the coast is cut by wooded headlands, fiords, and islets.

Albion today is a quiet town, with no lumbering operations. The second mill in the county was erected there during the winter of 1852–53, on contract with Captain William Richardson of Marin County. In 1845 Captain Richardson had applied for a grant of land covering this area, which extended from the Albion River to the

Garcia River. This estate, known as the Albion Grant, was never confirmed by the United States.

Navarro, set in a deep valley at the mouth of a broad, winding river, was thus described by J. Smeaton Chase in 1913: "Most of the buildings were out of plumb; the church leaned at an alarming angle; and a loon, swimming leisurely in the middle of the stream, seemed to certify the solitude of the place." Today little remains of this old town, but another community 14 miles up the river preserves the name. Greenwood is the location of the Elk post office, while Elk River, two miles south, is deserted. Gualala, at the mouth of the picturesque Gualala River, had its lumbering heyday in the 1860's and 1870's.

Spy Rock

About two miles south of Twin Rocks Creek and 33 miles north of Willits a road branches east from the Redwood Highway. About eight miles distant along this road is Spy Rock, an isolated peak in the Eel River Canyon, where Indians in early days built smoke signal fires.

Round Valley

East of Spy Rock and north of the town of Covelo is Round Valley (*SRL 674*), so named because it has about the same diameter (seven miles) in any direction. Here is the Round Valley Indian Reservation, where in 1856, early in the administration of Thomas J. Henley, superintendent of Indian affairs, a farm called the Nome Cult Station (*Nomcult* being a Wintun word meaning "West Tribe") was established by the government, pricipally as a breeding and fattening station for beef to supply the reservation at Fort Bragg on the coast. Round Valley was declared a reservation in 1858. In 1863 a military post was established there with 70 soldiers under the command of Captain Douglas. Soon afterward a company of cavalry came as reinforcement. This post was maintained until the reservation was turned over to the care of the Methodist Episcopal Church, in pursuance of the policy of General U. S. Grant toward the Indians.

The Round Valley Indian Reservation is now under the jurisdiction of the Sacramento Indian Agency. In 1932 representatives of 15 different tribes resided there. The Round Valley historical monument is located at Inspiration Point on the main road between Dos Rios and Covelo.

Fort Bragg

Lieutenant Horatio Gates Gibson was ordered in June 1857 to establish a military post on the Mendocino Indian Reservation. The post was placed one and one-half miles north of the mouth of the Noyo River and was named Fort Bragg (*SRL 615*) in honor of General Braxton Bragg of Mexican War fame. Lieutenant Gibson, who afterward attained the rank of brigadier general, remained there for one year. For some years before his death in his nineties he had the distinction of being the oldest living graduate of West Point.

Fort Bragg was located within the city limits

of the thriving town that grew up on its site. A historical marker at 321 Main Street stands upon land that was once part of the fort. Fort Bragg is still one of the largest cities in the county and the only one on the coast to have a rail connection. The route of the California Western Railroad is one of the most scenic in the state, passing along the Noyo River through magnificent redwood forests to Willits on the Redwood Highway. The railroad, over which the Union Lumber Company ships its product, also offers a passenger service, the "Skunk," which has become immensely popular with tourists. The town is also a shipping point for fish and farm and dairy products. Located there is the nursery which was started by the Union Lumber Company in 1922 to raise seedling trees for reforestation work, giving the nursery the distinction of conducting the first private venture of this kind in the state. From it a systematic planting of cutover land is carried on.

From Fort Bragg the coast road runs north through several miles of sand dunes. At Ten Mile River the shore becomes rugged with high cliffs and surf-beaten rocks honeycombed with caves.

Willits

The town of Willits, now a railway junction 40 miles east of Fort Bragg, lies on the Redwood Highway between Ukiah and Eureka. It had its origin in a store opened in 1865 by Kirk Brier from Petaluma, whose venture was followed by a blacksmith shop and saloon. Hiram Willits, who had come to the county in 1857, purchased the store; and the town, incorporated in 1888, was called by his name.

Mineral Springs

Ukiah Vichy Springs, known and used by the Indians before the arrival of the white man, are three miles east of Ukiah. These waters are said to be similar to the Vichy Waters of France, noted since Roman times. Anderson's report of 1888 mentions these springs as the "Doolan Ukiah Vichy" and says: "Bathing in the vichy renders the skin soft and clear and very soon heals up any skin irritation." The place was developed into a summer resort and continued popular until the buildings were destroyed by fire.

Orr's Hot Sulphur Springs, equipped with a small hotel and a number of cabins, are located on the edge of the redwood belt 14 miles west of Ukiah. At Duncan Springs, on a hillside south of Hopland, also are a summer hotel and cottages with mineral-water baths.

Redwood Groves

The humid coast belt in which this county lies is the natural habitat of the coast redwood *(Sequoia sempervirens)*. The rugged shoreline, famous for its vistas of the Pacific Ocean, is cut by wooded canyons formed by numerous mountain streams flowing seaward through fine stands of these and other native trees. Fortunately, some of these forests escaped the axe and saw of the pioneer lumberman.

In the interior, also, are many timbered areas either publicly or privately owned. Among these are the Coolidge Redwood Park; the Devoy, or Tuomey, Grove; Hickey Memorial Grove; Hartsook's Grove; and Lane's Redwood Flat, containing very beautifully placed trees on a bluff above Eel River. Just west of Ukiah, on the Orr's Springs Road, is the Montgomery Redwood Grove, a stand of virgin timber. The Paul Dimmick Memorial Grove of 11.8 acres of second-growth redwood on a part of the old Albion Grant, "logged off" many years ago, lies on the MacDonald-to-the-Sea Highway.

On the coast is the Russian Gulch Redwood Park, containing 1,103 acres, and nearby is the Van Damme Park, a sandy beach tract, willed to the state by the late C. G. Van Damme. Certain areas east of Fort Bragg and Albion are famous for their magnificent display of wild rhododendrons in the spring.

The southern part of Mendocino National Forest is in this county. It extends into the adjacent counties of Humboldt and Trinity. Formerly known as the California National Forest, to avoid confusion the name was changed on July 12, 1932, by executive order from Washington.

The Nature Conservancy is preserving an area of about 3,000 acres in the Elder Creek basin, four miles due north of Branscomb. The tract includes magnificent stands of ancient Douglas fir, as well as coast redwood and other trees. The Elder Creek area has been registered as a National Natural Landmark by the Department of the Interior.

A Bandit's Rock

A huge boulder on the old highway near Willits, known as the Black Bart Rock, is said to have been the hideout of Black Bart, the bandit, who robbed the mail stage there in pioneer days. As intriguing as Sherlock Holmes is the story of Black Bart, who, between the years 1875 and 1883, became "a synonym for elusiveness and mystery." During that time he robbed 27 coaches, traveling on foot for thousands of miles in rough mountain country from the Sierra to the Coast Range. Calaveras, Sierra, Plumas, Yuba, Butte, Shasta, Sonoma, Mendocino and Trinity, all knew the terror of this lone highwayman in the linen duster and mask who eluded years of diligent search by detectives. His endurance seemed uncanny, for, although he always traveled on foot, he was known to have robbed two coaches 60 miles apart in a rough mountain region within 24 hours.

Black Bart was never vicious and seemed averse to taking human life. He was immaculate in dress and extremely polite, a man of refinement and education. Because he was such a quiet, respectable, delicate-looking person, he lived in San Francisco for years under the very eyes of the detectives without once being suspected. He even frequented the favorite restaurant of the police headquarters staff, a bakery on Kearny Street, sometimes eating at the same table with the officers. Black Bart seemed thoroughly to enjoy his own cleverness and notoriety, and a decided sense of humor often expressed itself in facetious rhymes left on empty mail or express boxes for the baffled officers to read.

The mystery of Black Bart's identity was finally unraveled through the combined efforts of Sheriff Thorne of San Andreas, Detective Harry N. Morse, and James B. Hume, special agent of the Wells Fargo Company, whose iron-bound boxes were so frequently rifled in transit. The bandit's propensity for cleanliness finally proved his undoing, for on November 3, 1883, at Funk Hill, on the stage run between Sonora and Milton (Calaveras County), not far from the scene of the first robbery of his career, he dropped a handkerchief while he was busily engaged in opening an express box containing $4,100 in coin. The mark "F.X.o.7." on this piece of linen led Detective Morse, specially hired by Hume, after a most careful search to a laundry on Bush Street in San Francisco to which the fastidious Black Bart had for years carried his little bundle. He had lived in San Francisco all that time under the name of Charles E. Bolton, ostensibly a mining man, who made periodic trips to the mines. He was lodged in jail at San Andreas and was shortly sentenced to San Quentin, where he started his term November 21, 1883, and was released January 23, 1888. His whereabouts after that date are unknown.

SOURCES

Anderson, Winslow, M.D. *Mineral Springs and Health Resorts of California.* The Bancroft Co., San Francisco, 1892.
Ayers, Robert W., and Wallace Hutchinson. *National Forests of California.* U.S. Dept. of Agriculture, Circular No. 94, Washington, D.C., n.d.
Bellew, Tom. "Laundry Mark Ends Career of Black Bart, Gentleman Stage Robber," *San Francisco Chronicle,* May 20, 1934.
California, State of. *Corrected Report of Spanish and Mexican Grants in California, Complete to February 25, 1886.* Prepared by State Surveyor-General. Supplement to *Official Report of 1883–1884.* Sacramento, 1886.
California State Mineralogist. *Report, 1887–1888, 1889–1890.* Sacramento.
Carpenter, A. O., and P. H. Millberry. *History of Mendocino and Lake Counties.* Historic Record Co., Los Angeles, 1914.
Chase, J. Smeaton. *California Coast Trails.* Houghton Mifflin, Boston, 1913.
Dane, Ezra, and Beatrice Dane. "New Strikes in Old Diggins." Ms., 1932.
Gibson, Brig. Gen. Horatio Gates. "Letter to the Mayor of Fort Bragg," *Fort Bragg News,* March 2, 1923.
History of Northern California. Illustrated. Lewis Publishing Co., Chicago, 1891.
Johnston, Philip. "Gentleman Black Bart," *Touring Topics,* October 1929.
Lane, D. R. "State Parks, a Heritage for All," *Motor Land,* XXXII, No. 6 (June 1933), 3–5.
Menefee, C. A. *Historical and Descriptive Sketch Book of Napa, Sonoma, Lake, and Mendocino.* Reporter Publishing House, Napa, 1873.
Munro-Fraser, J. P. *History of Mendocino County.* Illustrated. Alley, Bowen & Co., San Francisco, 1880.
Purdy, Carl A. Notes. Ms., 1934.
Putnam, George R. *Lights and Lightships of the United States.* Houghton Mifflin, Boston; Riverside Press, Cambridge, 1917.
Russell, Carl Parcher. *One Hundred Years in Yosemite.* University of California Press, Berkeley, 1947.
Sanchez, Nellie Van de Grift. *Spanish and Indian Place Names of California.* A. M. Robertson, San Francisco, 1922.
Union Lumber Company. *Historical Files.* San Francisco, 1934.
Woods, Ruth Kedzie. *The Tourist's California.* Dodd, Mead, New York, 1914.

Merced County

MERCED COUNTY (named from the river that Gabriel Moraga, in 1806, had called El Río de Nuestra Señora de la Merced, "The River of Our Lady of Mercy") was organized in 1855 from a part of Mariposa County. The county seat first chosen was located on the Turner and Osborn Ranch, but in 1857 it was moved to Snelling's Ranch, and in 1872 to Merced.

Ranchería in Menjoulet Canyon

Elevated some 40 feet above El Arroyo de los Baños just before it issues from the hills is a plateau on which an Indian ranchería flourished three to four hundred years ago. The smooth and regular surface of the little tableland (approximately 80 acres in extent), sheltered from the cold valley winds by a ledge of rocks and a low hill, slopes gently to the stream with its fringe of cottonwoods.

Excavations were made at the ranchería site in 1925, when the entire plateau was found to be covered with relics of the Stone Age. A ton or more of artifacts were removed, and the remains of some 40 bodies were taken from the cemetery. At this time well-defined outlines of six Indian houses were discovered, one of them being 67 feet across and six feet in depth. Circular basins, almost perfect in form and grouped closely together, indicated the foundations of those prehistoric dwellings, in which remains of fire pits were found with blackened rocks and quantities of charcoal just as the long-forgotten occupants of the houses had left them. Near an old barn about one mile from these larger huts, four or more smaller and older basins were found filled with dust. Here, too, excavations disclosed old fire beds and fire rocks. These have been plowed up and are now only faintly visible.

The site, about eight miles southwest of the city of Los Banos, was the subject of further and more detailed scientific excavations in 1964. At this time, the remains of two cremated burials were discovered on the floor of the largest house pit. They are said to be the first cremations ever found in this region. The canyon is to be the site of a dam built to hold back the waters of Los Banos Creek.

The land on which this village was situated was owned for a short time in the early 1870's by Anthony Pfitzer, who had purchased the possessory right of Nelson Wood, an earlier settler. Pfitzer soon sold to John Menjoulet, a French sheepman, after whom the ranch and the canyon were named.

First Trails

Little was known of the great interior valleys of the San Joaquin and Sacramento until the beginning of the nineteenth century. During the second administration of Governor José Joaquín de Arrillaga, active exploration of the interior began, the motives being to check the Indians, who were becoming troublesome, and to establish missions for their conversion. A number of minor expeditions were made into the tulares, or swamps, of the San Joaquin in 1805 and 1806, but scant record is left of these. The first expeditions of which we have much knowledge, as well as the most important from the standpoint of accomplishments, were those made by Gabriel Moraga, the "greatest pathfinder and Indian fighter of his day."

Moraga, with 25 men and Father Pedro Muñoz as chaplain and diarist, left San Juan Bautista on September 21, 1806, probably entering the valley of the tules by way of San Luis Creek in Merced County. Proceeding across the San Joaquin River, they reached a slough, the haunt of numerous butterflies, which Moraga named "Las Mariposas." Father Muñoz says that here one of the soldiers was sorely afflicted by the lodging of a butter-

fly in his ear. The name, in the singular form, survives in Mariposa Slough, Mariposa Creek, and Mariposa County. The creek has its source in Mariposa County, which lay east of Moraga's march.

Proceeding north and northwest, the party toiled for 40 miles through a parched and treeless plain. Coming suddenly upon a clear, sparkling stream, they expressed their gratitude by naming it El Río de Nuestra Señora de la Merced, a name that was applied not only to Merced River but later to the county and to the present largest city and county seat. The place seemed so beautiful to the tired travelers that Father Muñoz enthusiastically declared it to be an excellent site for a mission.

Moraga explored the lower course of the Merced River in the fall of 1808. He again touched the county in 1810 on his way down the west side of the San Joaquin River from the north. Turning west along San Luis Creek, he returned to San Juan Bautista by way of Pacheco Pass.

The magnitude of Moraga's achievement was never realized by himself or the mission fathers. To them the expedition was a failure since it had discovered no sites suitable for the building of an inland mission chain.

The first American to pass through the San Joaquin Valley, although he may not have touched on what is now Merced County, and the first white man to cross the Sierra Nevada, was Jedediah Strong Smith, the great pathfinder and trailbreaker of the West. In 1827 he and his party camped on various rivers in the San Joaquin Valley while engaged in trapping beaver. Smith called one of these the Wimmulche (Wimilche) after a tribe of Indians living there. Some historians identify this river with the present Kings River. At any rate, Smith trapped there for a time and then, leaving some of his men encamped on the Wimilche, he crossed the mountains by a route not definitely determined.

Following in Smith's footsteps came other ad-

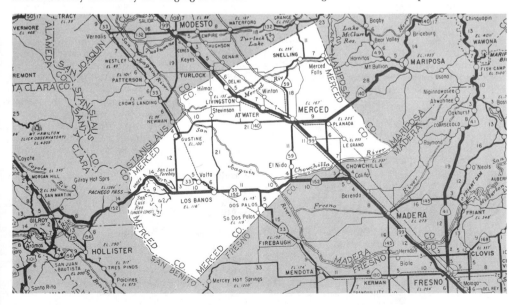

venturers, and from 1828 until the American oc-
cupation, beaver skins may have been gathered
along the rivers of Merced County by Hudson's
Bay Company trappers and others, among them
Peter Skene Ogden, Michel La Framboise, and
Ewing Young.

John C. Frémont, on his way out of California
in 1844, proceeded southward from Sutter's Fort,
passing through what is now Merced County, and
reached the Merced River on April 1. On the
following day a "boat" was constructed, with
which the party crossed the river somewhere near
its junction with the San Joaquin. Camp was
made on the far bank. On April 3 the expedition
stopped on the north bank of Bear Creek five
miles from its mouth, and the next day they
ferried the stream, continuing up the San Joaquin
River to Madera County.

Westside Trails

Where the foothills of the Mount Diablo Range
meet the western rim of the Great Valley, El
Camino Viejo, the old westside trail from San
Pedro to San Antonio (now part of East Oakland),
crossed El Arroyo del Ortigalito ("little nettle"),
a link in that long chain of arroyos and *aguajes*
about which the huts of the red men had clustered for ages, and along which the Spaniards
later laid out their ranchos. From the water
holes of Ortigalito, El Camino Viejo proceeded
northwestward to El Arroyo de los Baños del
Padre Arroyo, where fresh water was again found.
Still farther to the north the road crossed El
Arroyo de San Luís Gonzaga at Rancho Centinela, where another water hole was found 50
yards to the north. Leaving Centinela, El Camino
Viejo skirted the abrupt foothills which led to
El Arroyo de Romero, named after a Spaniard
from San Juan Bautista who was killed there by
Indians. Finally, El Arroyo de Quinto ("fifth
creek"), the last watering place in Merced County,
was reached. An adobe, probably built before
1840, stood on the plains among the cottonwoods
of Quinto Creek as late as 1915.

With the coming of the Americans and the
growth of transportation from Stockton to points
southward, the Stockton–Visalia Road was developed parallel to El Camino Viejo. It followed
along the west side of the San Joaquin River, the
exact route varying according to the seasonal
changes in the river country. The one-story adobe

Adobe at San Luis Camp, Wolfsen Road

which still stands in good condition at San Luis
Camp on Wolfsen Road, seven and one-half miles
north of Los Banos via Highway J-14, was once
an important low-water station on this road. This
adobe and other structures built in the early
1840's later came under the control of Miller and
Lux. Henry Miller customarily slept in this house
whenever he visited this part of his estate.

Joining the Stockton–Visalia Road eight miles
northeast of Los Banos, the older Pacheco Pass
stage road came in from the west. Long before
the Americans came, Indians had worn a deep
trail over the hills by way of Pacheco Pass, and
Spanish explorers in search of mission sites, as
well as Spanish officers in pursuit of deserting
soldiers or runaway mission Indians, made use
of this ancient mountain path.

A toll road was built over the Pacheco Pass in
1856–57 by A. D. Firebaugh. Two miles west of
the summit (in Santa Clara County), and a mile
from where the Mountain House later stood, he
built a toll station. Portions of the old rock walls
of the toll house may still be seen in the narrow
defile below the present highway. Along the
rocky creek bed, marks of the former stage road
lead past the ruins and up the steep hillside,
where the route is marked by the remnant of a
picturesque split-rail fence of the 1860's. Above
it is the "New Road," built in 1878 by Santa
Clara and Merced counties and still in good condition, although unused. It was considered a
marvelous road in its day and was traveled until
1923, when the state built the present highway,
which has since been straightened and widened.

The early stage road was used by the Butterfield overland stages from 1858 to 1861; on it San
Luis Station was an important stopping place. It
was 18 miles from San Luis Ranch east to the
Lone Willow Station, and from there the stages
passed through a long stretch of desolate alkali
wastes to Temple's Ranch and on to Firebaugh's
Ferry in Fresno County. During the middle 1860's
the loneliness of this part of the road was relieved
by the little cabin of David Mortimer Wood at
Dos Palos, where a lantern was placed in the
window at night to guide the drivers of the Gilroy–Visalia stages. Water for the horses was available too, and in return Wood received supplies
and mail brought by the stagecoaches. The part
of the old road that lay between Los Banos Creek
and Santa Rita ran about one mile and a half
north of the present highway. Along it were the
earliest pioneer American settlements of the Los
Banos district. Very little remains to mark any
of these places except an occasional black and
gnarled tree or faint traces of the former roadbed.

A branch of the Pacheco Pass Road crossed El
Camino Viejo at Rancho Centinela. From this
point it continued northeast to the ford on the
San Joaquin River where Hill's Ferry (Stanislaus
County) was established during the gold rush.

Rancho San Luís Gonzaga

Juan Pérez Pacheco and José María Mejía were
granted Rancho San Luís Gonzaga in 1843. Captain Mejía's name had been added to the petition
to lend prestige, and by agreement he conveyed

his interest to Pacheco. The rancho had previously been granted in 1841 to Francisco Rivera, but he had not met the conditions of the grant, having left the land unoccupied for two years. Grants of land were often made to prominent men, who in return were to help prevent the roving Tulare Indians from raiding the stock at the coast missions. The petitioners, Pacheco and Mejía, indicated that they were prepared to do this, and they received the grant. Juan Pacheco died in the early 1850's, and his property reverted to his father, Francisco Pérez Pacheco, already the holder of much land in present San Benito County.

The Arroyo de San Luís Gonzaga, which had received its name very early in the nineteenth century from Spanish explorers, was chosen by Juan Pérez Pacheco as his homesite. He built his adobe on the ancient *aguaje*, or water hole, the site of Lis-nay-yuk, a prehistoric Indian village, which had existed long before the coming of the mission fathers. To it herds of antelope came to drink, and traveling tribes of Indians rested by its springs on their journeys over Pacheco Pass. Later came the Spanish explorers and rancheros, then the stagecoach drivers of the American period, and, finally, the motorists of the twentieth century.

The one-story adobe built by the younger Pacheco soon after he took possession of the rancho stood in good condition at San Luis Station on Highway 152 until 1962. It was marked by the Native Sons of the Golden West of Merced on May 3, 1931. Still displaying in its walls the loopholes through which guns could be fired, the adobe served various purposes through the years, including, in the 1920's and 1930's, a roadside refreshment stand. In 1948 it became the lovely home of Miss Paula Fatjo, a fifth-generation direct descendant of Don Francisco Pérez Pacheco and owner of much of the old rancho. With such good care the ancient structure seemed destined to survive many more years. But the rancho was chosen as the site of the San Luis Dam, and the old water hole was to be under several hundred feet of water in the new reservoir. Excavations (which, incidentally, disclosed prehistoric burials estimated to be between 1,000 and 1,500 years old) were begun, with President John F. Kennedy present at the inaugural ceremonies in August 1962. Rather than allow her adobe to disappear, Miss Fatjo decided to move it, at her own expense, to her new ranch headquarters on the western part of the old rancho, just across Pacheco Pass in Santa Clara County, a distance of ten miles. Every precaution was taken to ensure the safety of the building in transit, and, on December 6, 1962, it was inched up the steep grade by truck. Less than a mile short of its destination, the oldest existing adobe in the San Joaquin Valley collapsed into the highway. The two ends of the building survived, together with its new reinforced concrete foundation, and it was put into place at the chosen site. Many of the bricks from the side walls were salvaged and are now stored on the ranch. The owner has tentative plans to rebuild the old adobe.

Rancho San Luís Gonzaga Adobe, at Original Site

Pacheco also built a two-story adobe at San Luís, but it was destroyed by the earthquake of 1868. It had served as a station on the Butterfield Overland Stage Line from 1858 to 1861. Later a frame structure, modeled after the original, was erected on the site. This stood until it was destroyed by fire in 1935. Nearby was a barn, built in the early 1870's, in which steep, winding stairs led up to a huge hayloft, in the early days often made to serve as a ballroom. This, too, disappeared in the 1930's.

Until land was sold to the federal government and the State of California, the entire rancho was owned by direct descendants of the Pachecos.

Rancho Centinela was originally a part of San Luís Gonzaga. Here for many years stood a two-story adobe, erected by Basque sheepherders who occupied the rancho during the 1860's and 1870's, and an even older one-story adobe. The two-story house was torn down in 1890 and a frame structure was erected in its place by Miller and Lux. This later house and the barn, built in 1872 across the road, were long local landmarks, but now both have been removed. Until construction of San Luis Dam began, bits of the old road could be traced among the grass-grown hillocks and gullies of the open pastures stretching between Centinela and San Luís Gonzaga. Centinela, on the road to Gustine at the crossing of San Luis Creek, is one of many places in California where legends of buried treasure long persisted. The name of the current roadside stop at the old site has been corrupted to "Santa Nella."

Rancho Sanjón de Santa Rita

Santa Rita, as well as San Luís Gonzaga, was a place name familiar to Gabriel Moraga as early as 1806; they were both mentioned in the journal of his expedition of that year. Rancho Sanjón ("deep slough") de Santa Rita was granted to Francisco Soberanes on September 7, 1841. With the coming of the Americans the grant changed hands a number of times. Nine leagues were sold to Manuel Castro in 1853, and in 1858 he sold two leagues to Salisbury Haly, who in turn, in 1861, sold it to William Dumphy, the latter deeding a half-interest to Tom Hildreth. Finally, on May 22, 1863, the land of Dumphy and Hildreth came into the possession of Henry Miller, and with it the "double H" cattle brand used by the firm of Miller and Lux. Miller thus secured his first foothold in the San Joaquin Valley.

By 1866 the remainder of Rancho Sanjón de Santa Rita had been purchased by Henry Miller. From that year the firm of Miller and Lux gradually increased their holdings in this section until, in the 1880's and the 1890's, they owned land extending for 68 miles along the west side of the San Joaquin Valley, from Firebaugh's Ferry in Fresno County to Arroyo de Orestimba in Stanislaus County. In addition, they held thousands of acres in the Buena Vista Lake district of Kern County, 200,000 on the east side of the valley, as well as thousands of acres in other parts of California (including their original holdings in the Santa Clara Valley) and in Oregon and Nevada. At the time of Miller's death on October 14, 1916, it was estimated that the "Kingdom of Miller and Lux" included a million acres, with control of a million and a half.

The Miller and Lux headquarters were at the old Rancho Santa Rita. A few of the buildings erected during Henry Miller's lifetime remained into the 1950's, but now all have been demolished except the old company store. The site is north of Highway 152 via Indiana Road, four miles west of the San Joaquin River, and 13 miles east of Los Banos. A little town called Santa Rita Park has grown up nearby.

Henry Miller did more than acquire lands and cattle. By means of irrigation he turned desert tracts into flourishing fields. It is true he fought all who tried to forestall his seizure of waters and lands, but he also offered part of his water rights to adjacent towns and ranches for a consideration, thus making adjoining lands fertile as well as his own. In this way he built up the wealth of the entire state. The immense Miller and Lux holdings are now divided into small farms.

Rancho Panoche de San Juan y de los Carrisolitos

Throughout the southwestern portion of Merced County ancient Indian trails may still be traced, and the remains of prehistoric Indian villages have been uncovered at various water holes. In this section, too, early in the nineteenth century, Spanish settlers evidently had sought homes, for it is said that when the survey of Rancho Panoche de San Juan (granted to Julián Ursua on February 10, 1844) was completed in 1866, adobes, already of a considerable age, stood on the rancho, which covered five square leagues, over 20,000 acres.

West of Rancho Panoche is the pleasant mountain valley known as Saucelitos ("little willows"). At the lower end of this valley, Vásquez and his gang of outlaws had a hangout during the late 1860's and the early 1870's. Here Juan Soto, a member of the gang, was killed by a deputy in the posse of Sheriff Harry Morse of Alameda County in 1871. The scene of the gun duel between the bandit and the deputy sheriff was at the old adobe now used as headquarters of the Pfeifer Cattle Company. According to one version of the story, 25 members of the band were hold-ing a fiesta at the Alvarado adobe two miles above the Pfeifer adobe. Soto, who had gone to the Pfeifer place to get onions and salt for the barbecue, was there accosted by the lawman, and the fatal shooting followed. Standing in the shadow of beautiful St. Mary's Peak, this adobe, now part of a much larger two-story house, is still well preserved. In the adjoining meadow, kept green by a perpetual spring, Soto's grave lies about a half-mile from the house. This area is on the South Fork of Los Banos Creek and is accessible only by private ranch roads from Hollister.

At the upper end of the Saucelitos Valley, three or four miles from the Pfeifer house, is a long, narrow adobe owned by the Storm family and used as headquarters for the Storm Ranch. Beside it is the spring "Lying Water," famed among early pioneers in the region, around which legends have been woven.

El Arroyo de los Baños

Los Baños (SRL 550) is a Spanish place name meaning "the baths," and was applied to the deep, clear pools on El Arroyo de los Baños near its source. Tradition says that here Padre Arroyo de la Cuesta refreshed himself when on missionary trips to the San Joaquin Valley. The name El Arroyo de los Baños del Padre Arroyo (now Los Banos Creek) was derived from this circumstance. Padre Arroyo, who served Mission San Juan Bautista for 25 years, from 1808 to 1833, was an accomplished man. He invented a perpetual calendar and became familiar with as many as 13 Indian dialects, preaching in seven different Indian tongues. He also wrote an Indian grammar and recorded many facts concerning the Indians and their manner of life.

The present town of Los Banos, located about two miles from the creek, has its origins in the Lone Willow Stage Station, built in 1858 on the west bank of what is now called Mud Slough. This place, consisting of a small house for the station keeper and a large barn for the relays of horses, prospered until the Butterfield stages between San Francisco and St. Louis stopped running in 1861, and then it became a mere way station on the San Francisco–Los Angeles route and later the shortened Gilroy–Visalia run. By 1865 the countryside was becoming sufficiently settled to require a store, and an enterprising German named Gustave Kreyenhagen opened one in the former residence of the station keeper. He soon realized, however, that he would have better trade if he moved to the junction of the stage road and the Stockton–Visalia freight road; he therefore moved three miles east, taking the store building with him. (This junction is eight miles northeast of present-day Los Banos.)

Kreyenhagen was not destined to remain there long. Miller and Lux fenced in their property and required that teamsters drive around it. In the summer of 1870, therefore, the storekeeper relocated his trading post 12 miles to the west and still on the Gilroy–Visalia road. (This location is about two miles south of the present Volta.) Kreyenhagen had long served as unofficial postmaster, bringing his customers' mail each week from Gilroy, and in 1873 an official post office was established in his store under the name of Los Banos. Other businesses followed, and soon there was a little town. Eventually Miller and Lux took over the settlement, and, when the railroad came in 1889, moved post office and businesses five miles east to the tracks. The town is now the center of diversified industry, including fruit and dairy products, and is the second city in importance in Merced County, although exceeded in population by Atwater as well as by Merced.

Beginning in 1873, the headquarters of Henry Miller for his Los Banos Division were at Canal Farm (SRL 548), just across the railroad east of the Los Banos business district. None of the original buildings remain at Canal Farm, since many of them were sold and the last of them were destroyed by fire in 1932. In that year the present inn was constructed on the foundations of the old ranch superintendent's residence, which itself had been built on the ruins of the 1873 ranch house of Henry Miller. Canal Farm derived its name from an irrigation canal, not a Miller and Lux enterprise, built from Mendota Dam to Los Banos Creek in 1871. The orange and olive orchards planted by Miller at Canal Farm still flourish.

Rancho Las Mariposas

In 1847 John C. Frémont again figured briefly in Merced history when on February 14 he purchased the Rancho Las Mariposas from Juan Bautista Alvarado, who had received it from Governor Micheltorena on February 22, 1844. This grant, of ten leagues, stipulated that the land be located within the area bounded on the west by the San Joaquin River, on the east by the Sierra Nevada foothills, on the north by the Merced River, and on the south by the Chowchilla River. Alvarado never complied with the usual legal requirements by building a house on the grant and inhabiting it within a year. In fact, he never saw the land, but on account of the hostility of the Indians he did apply to the governor for a military force to enable him to take possession, and in answer to this request General José Castro was sent to the region with a company of mounted Californios. Fortifications were begun on the east bank of the San Joaquin River about six miles south of the Merced River, at or near the place where the town of Dover was later located. In December 1844 the Indians stole most of the horses, and the Californios, "always averse to walking, had to return to Monterey as best they might." A final effort to take possession of the grant was made by Alvarado in August 1845, but this attempt was frustrated by the revolution against Governor Micheltorena, of which Alvarado was one of the leaders.

According to tradition, Frémont first attempted to locate his grant near the site of the present town of Stevinson, a tradition that seems to be substantiated by the name Frémont's Ford, which still exists at a point on the San Joaquin River near this town. More tangible evidence shows that Frémont endeavored to locate his ranch near the site of the present Le Grand on Mariposa Creek. Early surveyors' maps show a house called Frémont's Ranch south of Mariposa Creek, and it is possible that he lived there in 1848. When gold was discovered in the foothills above this ranch, in 1849, Frémont established himself in the hills of what is now Mariposa County. Through personal influence Frémont was able to secure confirmation of his grant as located by him in the mining regions. The precedent thus set was to cost the United States government many thousand square miles of territory claimed in other grants of a similar nature.

The First "Cattle King of Merced"

The first bona fide American settlers in Merced County were John M. Montgomery and his partner, Colonel Samuel Scott, two young Kentuckians. In the fall of 1849 they camped under one of the large water oaks on the banks of the Merced River a short distance north of the Cox Ferry Bridge on the left side of Highway 59, not far from the present town of Snelling.

John Montgomery became the richest man in Merced County during his time and was known as the "Land and Cattle King of Merced," the predecessor of Henry Miller and others. Before 1852 he had established a permanent home on Bear Creek, on what later became the Wolfsen Ranch, six miles east of Merced.

The Courthouse Tree

The first county seat of Merced was located on the Turner and Osborn Ranch on Mariposa Creek, a place that afterward became known as the Givens Ranch. The Courthouse Tree, under which the first county meetings were held, stood on the bank of the old channel of Mariposa Creek, which was considerably to the south of the present channel. The spot is one and a half miles to the west of Highway 99 and the Southern Pacific Railroad, and about seven miles southeast of Merced. The old course of the creek runs out a very short distance below where the tree stood. This historic tree was killed by floods in the winter of 1868–69 and was subsequently used for firewood.

Snelling's Ranch

Early in the spring of 1851, Montgomery, Scott, and Dr. David Wallace Lewis established a house of entertainment, which was the beginning of the town of Snelling. At first it was only a brush shelter, but Dr. Lewis very soon built what was later known as Snelling's Hotel. In the fall of 1851 the Snelling family arrived and purchased the property.

In 1857 Snelling's Ranch replaced the Turner and Osborn Ranch as the site of the county seat, but in 1872 it was in turn superseded by the new town of Merced, located in the valley 15 miles to the south. By that time the mines in the mountain regions were giving out, while agriculture was steadily growing in importance. New towns sprang up in the fertile valley regions where railroads were being built, and the old hill towns soon became almost deserted.

Snelling, although not a mining town, was an

overflow from the mining regions, and was of considerable importance at one time, being on the well-traveled road to the Mariposa mines. Settled largely by people from the South, it was noted for its spirit of hospitality. Today Snelling is a quiet place, picturesquely situated, where the visitor may find a link with the past in the old courthouse *(SRL 409)*, which was erected in 1857. The lower story, part of which is now used as a women's club room, is of stone. The thick walls of that section, which was once used as a jail, are pierced by narrow windows heavily barred. A stone monument dedicated to the memory of the pioneers and commemorating the seventy-fifth anniversary of the organization of Merced County was placed in front of the courthouse by the Native Sons of the Golden West in 1930.

Old River Towns

As early as 1850 settlers came to the rivers and streams of Merced County and established homes. The vast fertile areas along the streams were used for livestock raising and agriculture, and almost invariably the ranch houses on the through roads became inns. Finally, centers of trade grew up about some of them. After the advent of the railroad, however, trade deserted the old river towns and they became little more than memories.

Located on the Merced River six miles below Snelling was Hopeton, at first known as the "Forlorn Hope." It was chiefly notable for the fact that it possessed two churches before Snelling had any.

Merced Falls was one of the principal crossings on the Merced River along the route of the old Stockton–Fort Miller Road. A flour mill and a woolen mill, indicative of two of the county's most important early industries, were located there until 1893, when they were destroyed by fire. The lumber mills of the Yosemite Lumber Company were later located there, but now Merced Falls is a ghost town.

Dover was a landing place on the San Joaquin River five miles above the mouth of the Merced. Freight was brought by water to this point. The first settlement at the site of Dover was made in the fall of 1844, when General José Castro attempted to build a fort there to facilitate the location of Alvarado's grant, Las Mariposas. Dover was occupied by Americans in 1866. Better boat-landing facilities later led to the abandonment of the site in favor of Hill's Ferry (Stanislaus County), six miles down the San Joaquin River.

Plainsburg, first settled in 1853 and once a thriving settlement on Mariposa Creek 12 miles southeast of Merced, began to decline when the railroad came in 1872.

The Old Stage Road

The numerous rivers and streams running from the Sierra Nevada into the San Joaquin Valley made it necessary for the early roads to follow along the base of the foothills and thus avoid the tules or swamps of the lowlands. These foothill roads afforded solid foundation even in rainy seasons. Also, the streams were more easily forded before they spread out over the level valley floor. Population during the 1850's and 1860's was centered around the mines, and supplies had to be freighted into the southern Mother Lode from Stockton along the stage route at the base of the hills. At the time of the formation of Merced County in 1855, the legislature placed the eastern boundary along this old Stockton–Fort Miller Road, which was a part of the Stockton–Los Angeles stage road.

At first but "a dim and shifting pack trail, as travel increased, the hoofs of the oxen and the wheels of the emigrants' covered wagons marked out a roadway that was finally worn into a deep gash by the long freight teams as they drew the big heavy prairie schooners along its meandering course. Laterals, both pack trails and wagon roads, branched off to the various mining camps in the adjacent hills."

Across the Merced River, the Stockton–Fort Miller Road had a choice of three ferries, Murray's, Young's, and Phillips', grouped within two miles, from Merced Falls down. The smaller creeks had to be forded, a feat that would have been impossible among the tules of the valley.

After the coming of the railroad in 1872, the rich bottom lands of the San Joaquin soon became an agricultural region. Not only were the hill towns deserted, but the old stage road also lapsed into a dim and forgotten trail, of which only a vestige here and there is visible today. At the Merced-Mariposa county line the intersection of the old Fort Miller Road with the present highway from Merced to Yosemite may be seen.

SOURCES

Frémont, John C. *The Exploring Expedition to the Rocky Mountains, Oregon and California.* George H. Derby & Co., Buffalo, 1849.
"History Falls by the Wayside," *San Francisco Examiner,* December 9, 1962.
Latta, F. F. "San Joaquin Primeval—Archaeology," *Tulare Daily Times,* 1931.
——— "San Joaquin Primeval—Spanish," *Tulare Daily Times,* 1932.
McCubbin, J. C. *Papers on the History of the San Joaquin Valley, California.* Collected and edited by Raymund F. Wood. (Fresno State College Library.) 1960.
Milliken, Ralph LeRoy. *Henry Miller Slept Here. Los Banos Enterprise,* Los Banos, n.d.
——— "San Luís Gonzaga Rancho History Dates from Earliest Civilization of San Joaquin," *The Los Banos Enterprise,* January 27, 1933.
——— *West Side Centennials of 1958.* Speedprint Advertising, Los Banos, 1957.
Outcalt, John. *History of Merced County.* Historic Record Co., Los Angeles, 1925.
Thome, Joe. "Indian Town's Relics Found near Los Banos," *Merced Sun-Star,* August 21, 1964.
Treadwell, Edward F. *The Cattle King.* Macmillan, New York, 1931.

Modoc County

MODOC COUNTY was formed in 1874 from a part of Siskiyou County. There are different opinions as to the meaning of the name, but ethnologists generally agree that Modoc means "south people," and was probably the name given the natives of this region by the Klamaths, their kinsmen on the north.

Alturas, the first and only county seat of Modoc County, was originally called Dorris' Bridge after the owner of the ranch on which it was located. The town is still bordered on the south by this ranch.

The Tule Lake Petroglyphs

At the southeastern corner of Tule Lake, in the Lava Beds National Monument, a high bluff of smooth sandstone projects into the dry lake bed, and a chain of Indian petroglyphs, chiseled deep into the sandstone, extends for several hundred yards along its face. The carvings of these unusual rock writings, which have been painted, are undoubtedly the work of early Indian tribes. The Indians living in the region in the early 1850's disclaimed all knowledge of them, regarding them with awe and surrounding them with legends. The elements have obliterated some of the carvings, but most of them remain as clear-cut, and the black and ochre colorings apparently as undimmed, as the day they were put there.

Some authorities believe that the carvings were made by the last of the Rock Indians. These Indians antedated and were exterminated by the fiercer Modocs, who took possession of the lava beds with their many hiding places and abundant water supply.

Frémont in Modoc County

John C. Frémont passed through Modoc County when he traveled from Fort Sutter to Upper Klamath Lake over what was later known as the eastern branch of the California–Oregon Trail. In the vicinity of Cornell, on the present Dan McAuliffe Ranch, the party camped May 1–4, 1846. Among the group were Kit Carson, Alexis Godey, and Richard Owens. Tule Lake is designated as Rhett Lake on Frémont's map. The campsite (SRL 6) is about 11 miles southeast of Tulelake, on the old highway seven-tenths of a mile north of its junction with the present Highway 139.

The Applegate Cut-Off and Lassen's Trail

The Applegate Cut-Off from Oregon across the northeast corner of California to the Humboldt River in Nevada was opened up by Jesse and Lindsey (Lindsley) Applegate with the help of 13 others in June and July of 1846. In the autumn of the same year 90 or 100 wagons were piloted by the Applegates from Fort Hall into Oregon over the new road. In 1848 Peter Lassen followed this route across Nevada via High Rock Canyon and Massacre Lake and through the '49 Canyon into California by way of Surprise Valley. Passing between Upper and Middle lakes and up the west side of the valley to Fandango Pass (SRL 546), long known as Lassen's Pass, the old trail led down into Goose Lake Valley, where it followed the eastern shore of the lake to a narrow neck at the southern end of the basin a few miles from Sugar Loaf Hill.

Across this neck at a point on the west shore of Goose Lake, the Applegate Road turned toward Oregon, passing around the north end of both Clear Lake and Tule Lake into the Klamath country. At this same point on Goose Lake the true Lassen's Trail began. Running in an almost southerly direction across the Devil's Garden and striking the Pit River near the mouth of Rattlesnake Creek four miles west of the present town of Alturas, it continued along the north side of the Pit, crossing the river near the mouth of a canyon below the site of Canby. Passing south and west, its course lay through Stone Coal Valley, where it went due west for a few miles and then turned south along the Pit River. Crossing and recrossing the stream several times or following along the sides of the hills above it, the trail finally led across the river for the last time ten miles above the site of Lookout. From there it proceeded down the east side of the Pit River to Big Valley in Lassen County. Joseph B. Chiles with a company of 12 men, among whom was Pierson B. Reading, had followed much the same route into California, by way of Goose Lake and the Pit River, in October 1843.

Tradition has it that the Pit River was so named because of the many holes or pits which had been dug in the region by Indians for trapping wild animals. Reading, who entered California by the Pit River route in 1843, makes mention in his journal of these treacherous pitfalls, into which one of his party fell. It should be noted in this connection, however, that Commodore Charles Wilkes, in his report and on his map of 1841, designated this stream as "Pitt's River" and Goose Lake as "Pitt's Lake," which indicates a different origin for the name. Hudson's Bay Company trappers had penetrated this region before 1830, a fact recorded by Peter Skene Ogden in his diary of 1829. In this record, also, we find mention of "Pitt's River" under the entries of May 21 and 28.

From 1846 on, the Applegate Cut-Off was used by emigrants from Oregon, and in August 1848 the first wagon train to enter California from the north came in over the Applegate and Lassen roads. The Oregonians, captained by Peter Burnett (afterward the first American civil governor of California) and piloted by Thomas McKay, an old Hudson's Bay Company trapper, followed the Applegate Road to Clear Lake, where the party branched off, blazing a new road south to the Pit River. There, Burnett writes, "to our utter surprise and astonishment, we found a new wagon road. Who made this road we could not at first imagine." It was later found that this was the trail over which Peter Lassen and his band of emigrants had just passed on their way to Lassen's Ranch in Tehama County. Southeast of Lassen Peak at the headwaters of the North Fork of the Feather River, the Oregonians came upon Lassen and his party, whom they found stranded and in dire distress, their provisions almost exhausted.

The general course of Burnett's trail was followed by gold seekers in 1849 and the early 1850's, and the present highway from Klamath Falls to Bieber in Lassen County follows closely the trail of the Forty-niners.

A section of the old emigrant trail *(SRL 111)* may be seen near the Pit River–Happy Camp road, five and one-half miles west of Highway 299. This road branches from the highway four and two-tenths miles southwest of Canby.

The Fandango Pass Massacre

Fandango Pass, over which the Applegate Cut-Off and Lassen's Trail crossed the Warner Mountains, is thought by some to have been the scene of an Indian massacre in the early 1850's. The story is that a large emigrant train coming into California over this trail was encamped near a large spring at the edge of the valley beyond the mountains. Rejoicing over the arrival of much-needed supplies, the party was indulging in a fandango (a lively Spanish dance) when the camp was suddenly attacked by Indians and almost the entire company killed. Because of this tragic occurrence the name Fandango was given to the valley, as well as to the mountain and pass.

Another and more credible explanation of the origin of the name involves the Wolverine Rangers, a company of California-bound gold seekers, who camped overnight in the valley and disbanded there, burning some of their abandoned wagons. According to one member of the group, the night was so cold that "the men had to dance to keep warm, and named their wild camping place 'Fandango Valley.'" Later emigrants, seeing the remains of the burned wagons, assumed that an Indian massacre had occurred there.

At the head of Fandango Valley in 1866 a battle took place between a group of settlers and soldiers from Surprise Valley and a band of Piute Indians, in which the Indians were badly defeated.

Evidences of another early massacre were found on the old Lassen Trail four miles west of Alturas on what was later known as Rattlesnake Ranch. Here in 1870 the Hess family and other pioneer settlers came upon a large circle of burned wagons in a flat on the north side of the Pit River close to the present Redding–Alturas highway.

Bloody Point

One of the most terrible of the emigrant massacres in Modoc County took place in 1850 at Bloody Point *(SRL 8)*, seven miles east of Tulelake on the Johnson Ranch and three and one-half miles south of the California–Oregon line. Passing over the old Oregon Trail, a band of more than 90 emigrants, men, women, and children, were attacked by the Modoc Indians, and all were killed except one man, who, badly wounded, escaped to the settlements in southern Oregon with his tragic tale of disaster. Old wagon parts were picked up at the spot for many years.

Members of a second emigrant train narrowly escaped death at this point in 1851, and were rescued only by the timely arrival of Oregon Volunteers. The spot apparently was a natural ambush, as several other parties were killed there by the Indians, and for many years it was called "the Dark and Bloody Ground of the Pacific."

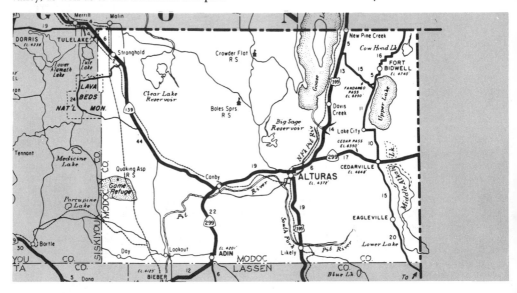

The Cressler and Bonner Trading Post

In Surprise Valley there are still standing some of the first log cabins built by white settlers, all loopholed for defense against the Indians. Among these is the log trading post (SRL 14) which was conducted by William T. Cressler and John H. Bonner. The oldest structure in Modoc County, it was built in 1865 by James Townsend, who shortly afterward was killed by Indians. Townsend's widow sold the building to Cressler and Bonner, and in it the partners set up the first mercantile establishment in the county. A thriving trade was carried on, first with emigrants en route to California and Oregon and later with the early settlers of Surprise Valley.

This interesting relic, surrounded by a magnificent grove of trees planted by the original owners, stands in a semipublic park in the center of Cedarville.

The first road from Cedarville to Alturas followed, in a general way, the course of the present scenic highway over the Warner Mountains from Surprise Valley. John H. Bonner, in 1869, was largely instrumental in securing the construction of this road over the Bonner Grade (SRL 15), which was named in his honor. This route, which became an important stage and freight road to Yreka, was maintained by Bonner until 1871, when Siskiyou County took it over.

Indian Battles

The battle of Infernal Caverns, one of the most famous Indian fights in California, took place on September 26–27, 1867, between 110 soldiers led by Lieutenant Colonel George Crook and a band of 75 Piutes, 30 Pit Rivers, and a few Modocs. For some time the Indians, well equipped with arms and ammunition, had been terrorizing the settlers throughout southern Idaho, western Nevada, and northeastern California, and Colonel Crook and his men had been sent to subdue them. The Indians were finally driven into a rough region on the South Fork of the Pit River. Here, before a seemingly impregnable fortress of caves and rocks, a pitched battle took place. The Indians were eventually driven from their stronghold, leaving many of their number dead, but not before eight of Crook's command were killed and 14 wounded.

Cressler & Bonner Trading Post, Cedarville

The battleground of Infernal Caverns (SRL 16), where the old fortifications may still be seen, is on the Monroe Ranch about 17 miles south of Alturas. At the foot of the slope the graves of six of the soldiers killed in action have been marked by regulation Army headstones. Lieutenant John Madigan, 1st Cav., who was among those killed, was brevetted posthumously for conspicuous bravery. His body was secretly buried at a spot near the forks of the Pit River not far from Alturas. To reach Infernal Caverns drive 14.5 miles south on Highway 395 from the south limits of Alturas, turning right for one mile on a good road leading to ranch homes. Turn right again at the sign reading "Pit River Ranch Headquarters." Follow this road, keeping to the right, for three and one-half miles to the Monroe ranch house. The six graves are about a mile from this point, and above, in very difficult terrain, are the caverns.

One of the engagements of the Modoc War took place on December 21, 1872, on what was then known as Land's Ranch, at a spot (SRL 108) located within a stone's throw of the old Frémont campsite on the Oregon Trail. Army supply wagons, escorted by a detachment of cavalrymen, had reached camp in safety, but several of the soldiers who had dropped behind were suddenly attacked by Indians in hiding among the rocks above the road. Two men were killed and several wounded.

The last of the engagements which occurred during the Modoc War was fought at daybreak on May 10, 1873, when Captain Jack, leader of the Modocs, led a charge on the military camp at Dry Lake. The soldiers were aroused to a realization of danger by the stampeding of their horses and mules. Wanting vengeance after the long and bitter campaign of the winter and spring, they led a fierce counterattack seldom equaled in the annals of Indian warfare. This battle resulted in a decisive defeat for the Indians and the capture of Captain Jack, thus putting an end to the Modoc War. The site of this important Indian battle is located about half a mile west of the Dry Lake guard station on Highway 139.

Fort Bidwell

Fort Bidwell (SRL 430), at the head of Upper Lake in Surprise Valley, about 30 miles northeast of Alturas and ten miles south of the Oregon boundary line, was named in honor of General John Bidwell. It was established in 1865, and cavalrymen were stationed there to hold in check the marauding Indians of northeastern California, southern Oregon, and western Nevada. Fort Bidwell was finally abandoned as a military outpost in 1893, but until 1930 it was used as a government school for Indians. The boarding school was discontinued that year and the military barracks, formerly used for dormitories, were torn down. The old military graveyard is about all that remains. Newer homes have taken the place of the old quarters in which the Indians long lived, and the 200 acres of fine bottom lands which had been used for the school farm continue to be used by the Indians.

Chimney Rock, near Alturas

Other Historic Sites

Four and seven-tenths miles southeast of Canby on the Centerville Road to Alturas is the site of an Indian attack that has come to be known as the Evans and Bailey fight *(SRL 125)*. S. D. Evans, Sr., and Joe Bailey were killed here in July 1861, while they and their men were driving 900 head of beef cattle from Oregon to the mines at Virginia City, Nevada. A white obelisk stands on a hill to the right of the road.

About seven miles north of Alturas near Highway 395 is Chimney Rock *(SRL 109)*, the remains of the second building to be erected in Pit River Valley. Thomas L. Denson, a California pioneer of 1852, built his cabin here in 1860, utilizing the rock as a chimney by cutting the fireplace and flue out of it.

Seven miles southeast of Tulelake off Highway 139, near the junction of one of the roads leading to the Lava Beds National Monument, are the barracks buildings of Newell, one of the Japanese internment camps of World War II.

SOURCES

Bancroft, Hubert Howe. *History of California,* Vol. V (1846–48). History Co., San Francisco, 1886.
Brown, William S. "The Land of Burned Out Fires," *Touring Topics,* XIX, No. 8 (August 1927).
Bruff, J. Goldsborough. *Gold Rush: The Journals, Drawings and Other Papers of J. Goldsborough Bruff, April 2, 1849–July 20, 1851,* ed. Georgia Willis Read and Ruth Gaines. New York, 1944.
Burnett, Peter H. *Recollections and Opinions of an Old Pioneer.* D. Appleton & Co., New York, 1880.
Cleland, Robert Glass. *Pathfinders,* Vol. I of the series *California,* ed. John Russell McCarthy. Powell Publishing Co., Los Angeles, 1929.
Delano, A. *Life on the Plains and among the Diggings.* Miller, Orton & Mulligan, Auburn and Buffalo, New York, 1854.
Dornin, May. "The Emigrant Trails into California." Master's thesis in history. University of California, Berkeley, 1921.
Frémont, John C. *Memoirs of My Life.* Chicago and New York, 1887.
French, R. A., comp., and Gertrude P. French, ed. *A Historical, Biographical and Pictorial Magazine Devoted to Modoc County.* Alturas, 1912.
Goldsmith, Oliver. *Overland in Forty-Nine. The Recollections of a Wolverine Ranger after a Lapse of Forty-Seven Years.* Detroit, 1896.
Lipps, Oscar H. *The Case of the California Indians.* United States Indian School Print Shop, Chemawa, Oregon, 1932.
Ogden, Peter Skene. "Journals of Snake Expeditions, 1827–28; 1828–29, with Editorial Notes by T. C. Elliott," *Quarterly of the Oregon Historical Society,* XI (December 1910), 355–97.
Reading, Pierson B. "Journal of Pierson B. Reading, Written during His Journey from Westport, Missouri, to Monterey, California, in 1843," *Quarterly of the Society of California Pioneers,* VII, No. 3 (September 1930), 148–98.
Riddle, Jeff C. *The Indian History of the Modoc War.* Privately published, 1914.
Sanchez, Nellie Van de Grift. *Spanish and Indian Place Names in California.* A. M. Robertson, San Francisco, 1922.
Wilkes, Charles. *Narrative of the United States Exploring Expedition during the Years 1838, 1839, 1840, 1841, 1842.* 5 vols. and an atlas. Lea & Blanchard, Philadelphia, 1845.

Mono County

MONO COUNTY was formed in 1861 of territory taken from Calaveras and Fresno counties. (Mono is possibly a corruption of Monache, a name of obscure meaning but said to have been applied to the Indians of the region.) The eastern boundaries were undetermined for several years, and in 1863 Aurora, the first county seat, was found to be in the state of Nevada. Bridgeport then became the seat of government and has since retained that position. The old and beautiful courthouse is still in use. From 1863 to 1870 the boundary lines of Mono County were changed four times, Alpine and Inyo counties each obtaining a portion of it in 1864 and 1870, respectively.

Rock Writings

"Among all the strange symbols inscribed on rock, up and down the globe, and especially in Southwestern America, by peoples since passed utterly out of human knowledge, it would be difficult to designate any more mysterious or fascinating than certain specimens now revealed just without our own doors."

Facing Chalfant Valley 17 miles north of Bishop, there is a high volcanic tableland between the lofty Sierra on the west and the White Mountains on the east. Cut into the eastern escarpment of this rough ridge of rock are the remarkable petroglyphs known as the Chalfant Valley Group.

These major rock writings are so well hidden that their presence could easily lie unguessed for years, and yet they are just two miles from where the old Bishop-Benton stage route intersects Chidago Canyon, and about the same distance from Highway 6 running northward via Laws.

At this point, the Owens River cuts through a great plateau comprising the Piute Indian Reservation. No Indians live there today, but the region embraces most of this amazing group of ancient rock writings. A towering wall nearly half a mile in length and almost unscalable is covered with carvings (petroglyphs) and a very few paintings (pictographs). The petroglyphs are principally circular in form and are the largest, it is believed, of any of this type yet found in the United States. The most conspicuous of the group is about five and one-half feet in diameter, the other figures being carved in proportion and seemingly connected with the larger one, constituting a series more than 20 feet long.

In the same vicinity there is a smaller group, also circular, but not drawn in proportion and arranged vertically. This entire group is three times as tall as a man and presents a weird appearance with its crisscrossings, wavy parallels, serpentine figures, and other odd shapes woven into an intricate maze, which only infinite patience and labor could have accomplished.

The "masterpiece" of this "inscriptive wall" is a mysterious carved projection which may be designated as the Sun Dial, but whether intended as sun dial, flood gauge, calendar, or simply landmark, no one can say. The excellence of the workmanship displayed is scarcely less cause for wonder. The projection is eight feet beyond the solid rock wall and surmountable only by a ladder. The edge is sharp and vertical, "extending eighteen feet from top to bottom and the blade cutting due east." This edge is notched its entire length with great accuracy, and, although worn by the elements, the horizontal lines on both sides are very clear, and many writings can be traced over the entire surface.

Chidago Canyon at this point is a labyrinth of carvings and paintings in many strange combinations. Many of the minor carvings represent a great variety of animal figures, bighorn sheep, bear, deer, a dragon fly, chicken or turkey tracks, lizards, snakes, and human figures, as well as geometrical designs.

Just above the Benton road, 20 miles from Bishop and six from the Chalfant Group, is a unique procession of tracks on the rock: "For full a hundred yards along the crest, sometimes narrow, of a broken ridge . . . the dramatic procession of footprints wends its precarious way, almost every individual headed northward. It conjures up a dark lost trail into another world. There are literally hundreds of tracks, prominent among others those of a giant . . . the soft baby feet of a child of three years and those of a boy and girl of seven. . . . Heavy marks of bears' paws, the lighter steps of dogs and coyotes, cats and indistinguishable beasts and wriggling serpents com-

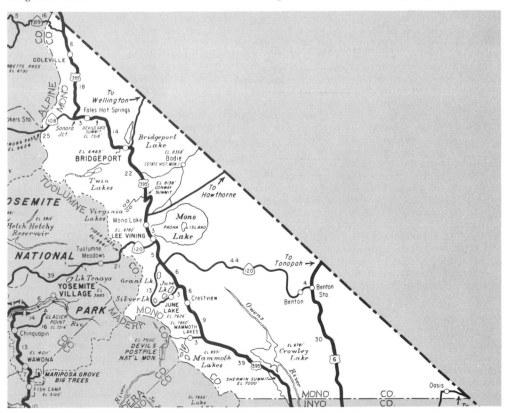

plete the queer march, which begins and ends abruptly where the stone has broken off and crumbled or been swept away by a deluge."

What pressing need caused the participants in this mysterious procession to tread so carefully along the rocky ledge? Were they fleeing from a flood or trying to evade their enemies? "The balls and toes of the feet sunk in more than half an inch and some of the heels deeper and they look perfect, but—those footprints are hand made! Close scrutiny brings to light plain proofs of chiseling.... It is marvelously done and the toil its execution entailed almost inconceivable."

Julian H. Steward of the Department of Anthropology, University of California, studied the Indians of eastern California very closely, and stated his belief that the rock pictures were made by the ancestors of living Indians, but what tribes were responsible for the work is unknown.

Indian Rock Houses

"The discovery of the principal groups of ancient stone houses or rather the foundations of brush or skin huts which they believe sheltered the rock message people" is accredited to Charles T. Forbes and Frank M. Parcher of Bishop, at one time respectively secretary-treasurer and curator of the Eastern California Museum at Independence, Inyo County.

The largest of these rock villages "is a cluster of 150 on the barren plateau ten miles north of Chalk Bluff. Perched high above the Owens River and half a mile back upon the uninviting, windswept mesa is another group. At Fish Springs, near the toppled walls of the Stage Station, are forty; and two sets of former habitations comprise forty–five each, making up a total of several hundred....

"The individual 'residences' are sometimes a hundred yards apart while in other instances they adjoined and assumed communal form, thus effecting an economy in labor. They are invariably round, average twelve feet in diameter, and open on the east. Usually the natural bedrock is the floor but occasionally sand serves the purpose. The walls, in which no mortar was used, are two or three feet high where not tumbled by the elements. The prevalent tufa was employed, frequently big blocks. With the single exception of those at Fish Slough these simple dwellings are remote from water and from petroglyphs and pictographs.... These were there on the arrival of the Piutes, who admit the use of the walled circles for winter camps years ago, but profess to know nothing about their origin."

It is interesting to note that these remains are similar to those of Coachella Valley, 350 miles away.

The Sonora Trail

In October 1841 the Bidwell-Bartleson party, much weakened and disheartened after many months of hardship, finally ascended "the Sierras on the north side of the Walker, [and] came at last to a little stream which flowed westward instead of toward the east. This proved to be the headwaters of the Stanislaus, one of the largest tributaries of the San Joaquin. The course of the river through the mountains was too rough and precipitous to furnish an easy route of travel. The emigrants became entangled in gorges and cañons ...food became scarce...and the emigrants, as they dragged themselves down the last weary ridge of the Sierras, were too worn with fatigue to realize that the San Joaquin Valley lay before them, and that California itself was at hand."

Nevertheless, the arrival of this first overland party of American settlers to enter California "ushered in ... the period of organized immigration," and nine or ten years later the first faint trail left by the Bidwell-Bartleson party (varied somewhat, of course, from the original route) had become beaten down and widened into a fairly well-defined road, which led through the very heart of the Mother Lode country and was a close rival in popularity to the Truckee Road.

The Sonora Trail is thought by some historians to have been traversed for the first time by Jedediah Strong Smith, "Pathfinder of the Sierras." At any rate, it is certain that Smith not only was the first American to come overland to California but was also the first white man to cross the Sierra Nevada, blazing a trail through one of the high Sierran passes on his way back to the Great Salt Lake in 1827.

Harrison C. Dale, an authority on this expedition, the record of which is very incomplete, "identifies 'Mount Joseph' with Mount Stanislaus, and tentatively fixes Smith's course along the Middle Fork of the Stanislaus River to the divide. ...From the eastern slope of the Sierras, Smith and his companions probably followed the course of Walker River to the vicinity of Walker Lake and then turned northeasterly toward the Great Salt Lake." Other students of Smith's travels have various explanations concerning "Mount Joseph," which is still a good deal of a mystery.

Sonora Pass lies high up in the Sierra at the converging point of what are now Mono, Alpine, and Tuolumne counties. It was one of the highest wagon roads over the Sierra Nevada.

Monoville

Monoville was the first settlement of any consequence east of the Sierra and south of Lake Tahoe, although some mining had probably been carried on in the region from the time of Lieutenant Tredwell Moore's discovery in 1852. Continued reports that the Mormons from Nevada were washing out gold in Dog Creek near Mono Lake brought a number of prospectors into the region in 1857, and Dog Town (SRL 792) quickly came into existence as a camp and trading center. This was a popular miner's term for a camp built of huts or hovels. The site of Dog Town is along Highway 395 seven miles south of Bridgeport. After 1859 Dog Town was deserted for its more promising neighbor, Monoville, which soon boasted a population of 700, made up mostly of arrivals from Tuolumne County who came in via the Sonora Pass.

Monoville was different from the majority of

mining camps in that it "left no notable record of crime." Although the town soon disappeared, it is noteworthy as the starting point from which the discoverers of other mining locations in the region set out. From it many an adventurer went forth in quest of the "lost cement mines," long the legendary "El Dorado" of the High Sierra. As late as 1864 Monoville was an ambitious contestant for the position of county seat.

The once noted Sinnamon cut, a long, deep gash in the earth from which it is said that $90,000 in gold was washed out by a hydraulic process, is the chief landmark in the region today. By it one may locate the spot where "the once largest town of the western Great Basin lived its little day." Nothing else remains save "a forlorn, rickety windlass over a shaft sunk by a hopeful mining company."

"The Lost Cement Mines"

Three brothers, Germans (according to the accepted version of the story), on their way to California in the early 1850's, finally reached the headwaters of the Owens River after many trials. While camping somewhere between Mammoth Peak and Mono Lake, one of the party found a vein of cement in which "lumps of gold were set like raisins in a pudding."

Approaching winter drove the three from the place, and only one of them survived the hardships of the journey over the Sierra. Half insane from his sufferings but still carrying some of the rich cement, he reached the settlements to the west. The story of his experiences started "the great hunt," and through the years many have sought the long-lost treasure.

Here in the Mono country, in a region of magnificent mountain scenery in the northern section of the High Sierra, the summer vacationist with a bent for "treasure hunting" may find a place of superb enjoyment. In the neighborhood are the Minarets, Gem Lake, June Lake, Silver Lake, Shadow Creek, Rainbow Falls, Thousand Island Lake, and Pond Lily Lake, while, "like a tombstone in a scene of revelry," is Deadman Creek, its name calling up incidents connected with the persistent search for the "lost cement mines."

"The Bad Men from Bodie"

Bodie (SRL 341), "one-time metropolis of the Mono country" and the best preserved ghost town of that region, became Bodie State Historic Park on September 12, 1964. "Bodie's story dates back to the discovery of gold in that region during the '50's, but the old town's claim to fame [was] based upon the wild later years when Mono gold poured forth in millions and the 'bad men from Bodie' gained a nation-wide reputation."

Gold ore was first discovered in the Mono region in 1852 by members of Lieutenant Tredwell Moore's detachment of the Second Infantry, U.S.A., while searching for recalcitrant Yosemite Valley Indians. This discovery led to some excitement, and a party needed by Lee Vining subsequently found gold in Lee Vining Canyon, through which the Tioga Road now passes.

Knowledge of the Mono diggings reached the Tuolumne mines in 1857, resulting in a rush to the new field and the blazing of the Mono Trail from Big Oak Flat in Tuolumne County through the present Yosemite National Park. In 1859, William S. Bodey made a find, and the district was named Bodie after him.

The sensational Aurora discovery made in 1860 affected Bodie, which was 12 miles southwest, and the Mono Trail became a much-traveled highway for pack trains and miners until 1864, when the Sonora Pass wagon road was opened.

The Standard Mine, discovered in 1861, the first of Bodie's mines to become famous, is typical of the fluctuating fortunes of mining ventures. During Aurora's boom, the owners of the Standard sought to create interest in it, but with little success. In 1870, when the Aurora mines became exhausted, Bodie also suffered a relapse, and it was not until 1876 that its fortunes again cleared. The adjacent Bodie Mine, at first considered a "wild cat," also rose in value, to the great surprise of its promoters. Between the years 1876 and 1880 the town of Bodie was at the height of its success, although it continued to hold its interest until 1881. Its population during this period numbered between 10,000 and 12,000, and it was known as one of the wildest mining camps in the West.

By 1883 all of the mines except the Bodie and the Standard closed down, and in 1887 these were consolidated. Of all the numerous ventures of the region, this was almost the only one that continued to uphold the fame of Bodie. Operations in later years were sporadic.

Although Bodie has suffered heavily through the years from fires, the most serious one on June 23, 1932, there are still 168 buildings standing in various degrees of preservation. It is the intention of the Division of Beaches and Parks to maintain Bodie in a state of arrested decay, whereas the buildings in Columbia State Historic Park (Tuolumne County) are being restored to their original grandeur. Bodie is a complete ghost town, the only residents being the State Park rangers and their families. Among the landmarks to be seen are the Methodist church, the James Stuart Cain home, the jail, the Miners' Union and Odd Fellows halls, and several interesting cemeteries. Located 18 miles east of Bridgeport and 11 miles

Panorama of Bodie

from the junction of Highway 395 by a good dirt road, Bodie is one of the most fascinating old towns to be found anywhere in the West. It has been registered by the Department of the Interior as a National Historic Landmark.

The neighboring camps at Mono Lake, Masonic, Benton, Tioga, Lundy, and Mammoth City in California, and Aurora in Nevada, are also long deserted. Abandoned miners' cabins, built of massive logs, still linger in Mono's mountain regions, telling tales of primitive life when "great populations" flourished there. At the settlement on the west shore of Mono Lake are two old wooden buildings that were moved from Bodie. Masonic, best reached by a nine-mile dirt road that leaves Highway 182 three miles north of Bridgeport, is a photogenic conglomeration of old cabins lying close to the Nevada line. Here is an interesting tram system leading from the mines to the ruined stamp mill. At Benton, four miles west of Highway 6 on Highway 120, are a jail, a schoolhouse, and a thick-walled general store with iron shutters, that housed the Wells Fargo office. The population here at Benton once reached 6,000.

From Bodie a road, sometimes impassable, leads northeast to Aurora, the first county seat of Mono County before it was determined to be in Nevada. At the state line are the ruins of the Sunshine stage station. Until about 1950 Aurora was a very well-preserved ghost town with many buildings standing, but since then most of the old structures have been torn down for their bricks.

Little Cities of the High Sierra

East of Yosemite Valley high up in the mountains, relics of early silver-mining ventures may still be seen. One of the old camps in the region is Tioga (formerly Bennettville), a mile or two north of Tioga Pass. Here the Tioga Mine was located in 1860 as the Sheepherder Mine, and in 1874 William Brusky, a prospector, came upon the abandoned diggings and relocated the old claim under its original name.

The Tioga Mining District was organized in 1878 by the Great Sierra Mining Company, made up of men from Sonora. The old Sheepherder Mine was renamed the Tioga Mine and Bennettville was made the headquarters for the company. Great quantities of supplies and equipment were brought to the camp over very difficult roads from the east side of the mountain, at enormous expenditure of labor and money.

The pressing need for a good road over which to transport heavy machinery from the west side of the Sierra occasioned the expenditure of $64,000 for the construction of the Tioga Road, which was completed in 1883. However, the total expenditure of $300,000 brought about a financial collapse in 1884, and the project was abandoned before any of the ore had been milled.

To reach Bennettville, drive eight-tenths of a mile north on Highway 120 from the Tioga Pass entrance to Yosemite National Park. At this point, opposite the head of Tioga Lake, a dirt road branches to the left. A short distance along this road, a rough mining road turns left. A hike

Old Town of Masonic

of about a mile on this road will bring one to the site of Bennettville, where the old livery stable and assayer's building are still standing.

The Mount Dana Summit Mine (in Tuolumne County), opened in 1878, lay to the south of the Tioga Mine. Here "long-deserted rock cabins clustered about a deep mine shaft" are the remains of a once thriving camp. Hikers and fishermen from Yosemite Valley often come upon this interesting mountain ghost town, which is located within Yosemite National Park. The Gaylor Lakes trail, which begins at the Tioga entrance to the park, leads two miles to the remains, which are located on the slope above upper Gaylor Lake.

Lundy, another deserted mining camp a few miles north of Tioga, was established in 1879. Prior to that date W. J. Lundy had a sawmill there from which he helped supply the enormous demand for lumber at Bodie. Approximately $3 million was taken from the Lundy Mine and the place remained a substantial town for several years. Lundy has now been deserted for years, and the building of a dam, with the raising of Lundy Lake, has partly submerged the townsite. An old cemetery remains. Lundy is best reached from Highway 395.

In Tuolumne County at the head of Bloody Canyon (in Mono Pass), strongly built log cabins in various stages of decay remain as evidence of a one-time mining camp. Here in 1879 the Golden Crown silver mine was discovered by Fuller and Hayt (or Hoyt), and this as well as surrounding mines attracted considerable attention for a time. Today the entire district is deserted. It is located within Yosemite National Park, and is reached over the Mono Pass trail, which branches right from the highway at a point five and eight-tenths miles east of the Tuolumne Meadows ranger station. The hike is about three and one-half miles in length.

About 20 miles south of Tioga in the Lake District (a region of spectacular scenic grandeur), Mammoth and Pine City flourished for a brief period. The first discoveries were made there in 1877, but the greatest activity took place in 1879–80. A mill was erected and a trail constructed from Fresno Flats (now Oakhurst, 54 miles west), but the expected ore was not forthcoming. Like many other camps in which enormous capital was expended, little or nothing was produced in return, and in the winter of 1880–81 the place was closed up.

A Vacationer's Paradise

Mammoth lies in the heart of one of the most superb recreation centers in the Sierra. From it interesting short trips may be taken to the hot mineral springs at Whitmore Tubs, the ice-cold or boiling springs of Casa Diablo, the Hot Creek Geyser, Mammoth Rock and the Old Mammoth Mill, the Devil Postpile National Monument (in Madera County), the Earthquake Fault, Minaret Pass, and Shohonk Pass. Pack trips may be taken to Shadow Lake, Thousand Island Lake, and the Upper San Joaquin, while good trails lead to

splendid camping and fishing spots about the numerous lakes of the region.

The country is rough and mountainous, rising to the snowy summits of the Sierra crest on the west, while lower slopes to the east are covered with forests. Mount Dana and Mount Lyell with their splendid residual glaciers, that of the latter being the second largest in the Sierra, and Castle Peak are among the highest of the crests. In the center of the county lies Mono Lake. Having no perceptible outlet, its waters, which hold many chemical substances in solution, are apparently without life, giving rise to the name "Dead Sea of America."

Crossing a low divide several miles beyond Mammoth, the road drops down toward Mono Lake, passing the Mono Craters on the right. "A beautiful, slightly crescent-shaped range of twenty distinguishable volcanic cones," the Mono Craters have the appearance of sand dunes, the delicate colors of the smooth pumice-stone slopes creating a picture of exceptional symmetry and beauty of form. The story of Mono's sleeping craters forms one of the fascinating chapters of California's geological epic.

Convict Lake

In the vicinity of Convict Lake and Convict Creek in southern Mono County a gun battle took place in September 1871 between some desperate fugitives from the prison at Carson City, Nevada, and a posse from Benton. On September 17, 1871, 29 convicts—murderers, robbers, and horse thieves—had broken through the prison guard and escaped. Six of them headed south. On their way they met William A. Poor, a mail carrier, whom they robbed and murdered.

When news of this outrage reached Aurora and Benton, a posse was organized. The men from Benton followed the convicts into southern Mono County, the fugitives having been sighted by Robert Morrison, a Benton merchant, who saw them going up Monte Diablo Creek, henceforth called Convict Creek.

On the following morning the posse followed up the canyon to the lake at its head. There, on September 24, they came upon three of the desperadoes, and in the gun fight that followed, Morrison (for whom Mount Morrison was afterward named) was killed. The convicts escaped toward Round Valley, where they were later captured. They were taken to Bishop by irate citizens, where the two who had committed murder were hanged and the third was returned to the prison at Carson City.

SOURCES

Cain, Ella M. *The Story of Bodie.* Fearon Publishers, San Francisco, 1956.
Chalfant, W. A. *Outposts of Civilization.* The Christopher Publishing House, Boston, 1928.
Cleland, Robert Glass. *From Wilderness to Empire. A History of California,* ed. Glenn S. Dumke. Knopf, New York, 1959.
Farquhar, Francis P. *Place Names of the High Sierra.* Sierra Club, San Francisco, 1926.
Florin, Lambert. *Western Ghost Towns.* Superior Publishing Co., Seattle, 1961.

Miller, H. C. "Mono's Slumbering Craters," *Touring Topics*, XXII, No. 2 (February 1930), 46–47, 56.

Russell, Carl P. "The Bodie That Was," *Touring Topics*, XXI, No. 11 (November 1929), 14–20.

——— "Early Mining Excitements East of Yosemite," *Sierra Club Bulletin*, XIII, No. 1 (February 1928), 40–53.

——— *One Hundred Years in Yosemite. The Story of a Great Park and Its Friends*. University of California Press, Berkeley, 1947.

Von Blon, John L. "Rock Writings of the Owens Valley," *Touring Topics*, XXI, No. 5 (May 1929), 14–17, 51.

Wasson, Joseph. *Complete Guide to the Mono County Mines*. San Francisco, 1879.

Monterey County

MONTEREY COUNTY was one of the original 27 counties. (Monterey is Spanish for "hill or wood of the king," so named in honor of Gaspar de Zúñiga, Count of Monterey, viceroy of Mexico.) Monterey was the original county seat, but in 1873 the honor was given to Salinas. The county archives contain many pre-state records in Spanish.

The Discovery of Monterey Bay

Juan Rodríguez Cabrillo, in command of the *San Salvador* and the frigate *Victoria,* discovered California in 1542 and sailed up the coast as far as the Northwest Cape. On his return voyage, his chronicle records that, on November 18, "they ran along the coast, and at night found themselves off Cape San Martín [Point Pinos]." This entry would indicate that, although Cabrillo may have seen what we know as Point Pinos, the southern headland of Monterey Bay, he did not actually see the bay itself.

The Pacific Grove Lighthouse was established on Point Pinos in 1872, and a marker has been placed there by the Pacific Grove Chapter, D.A.R., in honor of Cabrillo, the first European to see the coast of Alta California.

Probably the first white man to see Monterey Bay itself was Sebastián Rodríguez Cermeño, a Portuguese in command of the Spanish galleon *San Agustín,* in 1595. Cermeño had been sent out to discover a northern port on the California coast where the Manila ships might find protection and supplies and receive warning of enemies. On November 30, the *San Agustín* was wrecked at Drake's Bay, but Cermeño continued his voyage in the *San Buenaventura,* a little launch, or open sailboat, which he had constructed. In this frail craft he saw Monterey Bay on December 10, 1595, seven years before Vizcaíno, the so-called discoverer, landed there. Cermeño called it San Pedro Bay.

The Vizcaíno-Serra Landing Place

Sebastián Vizcaíno was a merchant trader who had had much experience on the Spanish galleon route, and who had also been a shipmate of Rodríguez Cermeño on his voyage of discovery in 1595. In the flagship *San Diego,* Vizcaíno entered Monterey Bay on December 15, 1602, the second European to enter its waters, and the first to make a landing there.

Vizcaíno was so enchanted with the beauty of the bay that "he wrote almost too enthusiastically to his Majesty concerning it." He spoke of it as a harbor "sheltered from all winds," and a legend grew up concerning the port of Monterey, which became "one of the moving factors for a century and a half in Spanish expansion to the northwest." It explains, too, the difficulty that later Spanish explorers had in finding it.

The entrance into Monterey Bay and the act of taking possession of it were the principal events of Vizcaíno's voyage. The ceremony was performed under a live oak very close to the shore, the same oak under which Padre Junípero Serra performed a similar ceremony in 1770, when Mission San Carlos and the Presidio of Monterey were founded.

The Vizcaíno-Serra Oak died in 1905, but the trunk was removed to the San Carlos Church, where it is preserved in the rear garden. The site of the tree and of the landing place *(SRL 128),* now a unit of Monterey State Historical Monument, is marked by the Junípero Serra Cross, on the south side of the main gateway to the Monterey Presidio. On Presidio Hill, overlooking the bay, is the Junípero Serra Monument erected by Mrs. Leland Stanford in 1891. A monument in honor of Gaspar de Portolá, founder of the presidio, has been erected at the landing place, near the Serra Cross, by the state of California.

Portolá's Trail Through Monterey

Starting from San Diego on July 14, 1769, Gaspar de Portolá started north with his men to search for the Bay of Monterey, described in such glowing terms by Vizcaíno in 1602. Traveling up the coast by way of Gaviota Pass, the expedition entered the confines of what is now Monterey County and camped, September 21–24, on the banks of the Nacimiento River, near its source. The high ridges of the Coast Range had just been crossed with great difficulty, and the men were in need of rest.

After they had somewhat recuperated, the party pushed on and reached the San Antonio River at a point near Jolon, where they camped on September 24. The next day they camped in the upper Jolon Valley, and on September 26 they descended Quinado Canyon, reaching the Salinas River near King City.

During the days following they camped successively near Metz, Camphora, and Chualar, and on September 30, below what is now Hill Town. From October 1 to October 6 they camped near Blanco and from this point they explored the Monterey Bay region and saw the river and bay at Carmel.

During all this week the party did not recognize Vizcaíno's wonderful harbor "sheltered from all winds" and described in Cabrero Bueno's sailing directions as a bay "round like an O" for which they sought. It was doubtless shrouded in gray fog, and not until a year later did they know what they had missed.

Leaving a cross planted upon the beach, near Monterey, the party continued the journey northward, camping on October 7 near Del Monte Junction and then proceeding across Pajaro River and camping near the present site of Watsonville, in Santa Cruz County.

Misión San Carlos Borroméo (El Carmelo)

The settlement of Monterey was at the point farthest north in the original plan for the colonization of California, and there the presidio and the mission were to be established. Portolá's party had failed to find the bay in 1769, but a second expedition was organized the following year, Portolá and Father Crespí going by land and Father Serra, who was ill, proceeding by boat.

Portolá reached the Bay of Monterey for the second time on May 24, 1770, to find the cross that he had erected there the year before still standing near the beach, but curiously decorated, "with arrows stuck in the ground and sticks with many feathers, which the gentiles had placed there; suspended from a pole beside the cross was a string of small fish, all fairly fresh, while pieces of meat were deposited at the foot of the cross and a pile of mussels." The Indians later told the padres how, at night, the cross had become wonderfully illuminated, reaching far up into the heavens, and they were afraid and brought peace offerings to the foreigners' god. The day being calm and clear, the entire sweep of the bay was visible, and Crespí and Fages exclaimed: "Why, this is the Port of Monterey, for it is as Sebastián Vizcaíno tells, to the very letter!"

Father Serra arrived in the *San Antonio* seven days later, and on June 3, 1770, under the same oak where Vizcaíno had held services 168 years before, the Misión San Carlos Borroméo and the Presidio of Monterey were dedicated.

The first mission building was erected at the presidio on the site where the San Carlos Church stands today. But the presence of the soldiers and the lack of good agricultural land caused Father Serra to look about for a more suitable location. This was found five miles to the south in a fertile valley watered by the Río Carmelo (so named for the Carmelite Fathers who accompanied Vizcaíno), which empties into the ocean at this point, and the formal transfer of the mission site was made in December 1771. Misión San Carlos Borroméo del Carmelo (*SRL 135*) became the favorite of Father Serra, and there he lies buried within the sanctuary today.

The present building at Carmel was begun in

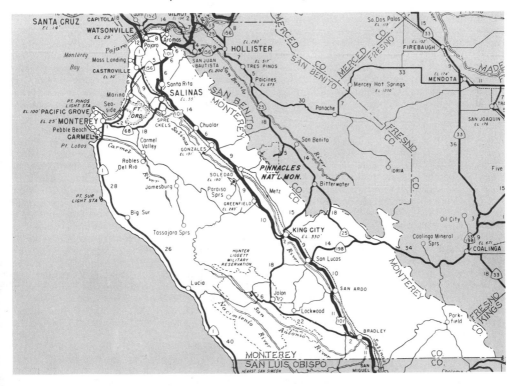

1793 and dedicated in September 1797. Being beautifully situated and prosperous, it was the headquarters for the Padre Presidente of the California missions until 1803. After 1836, it was not kept in repair and quickly fell into ruins, but in 1882, through the efforts of Father Casanova, the graves of Presidentes Serra and Lasuén and Fathers Crespí and López were discovered within the church. Public interest was then aroused and funds were raised for the restoration, which was accomplished and the church rededicated in 1884. Restoration of the other buildings of the mission has continued to the present. Carmel Mission, as it is popularly known, has been registered as a National Historic Landmark. In 1960 it was raised to the rank of a minor basilica by the Vatican. The cause for the canonization of Junípero Serra is being considered by Roman Catholic authorities.

Robert Louis Stevenson in "The Old Pacific Capital," written shortly before the restoration of San Carlos, calls the valley drained by the Carmel River "a true Californian valley, bare, dotted with chaparral, overlooked by quaint, unfinished hills. The Carmel runs by many pleasant farms, a clear and shallow river, loved by wading kine; and at last, as it is falling towards a quicksand and the great Pacific, passes a ruined Mission on a hill. From the Mission church the eye embraces a great field of ocean, and the ear is filled with a continuous sound of distant breakers on the shore. The roof has fallen; the groundsquirrel scampers on the grass; the holy bell of St. Charles is long dismounted; yet one day in every year the church awakes from silence, and the Indians return to worship in the church of their converted fathers. I have seen them trooping thither, young and old, in their clean print dresses, with those strange, handsome, melancholy features, which seem predestined to a national calamity; the Mission church is in ruins; the ranchería, they tell me, encroached upon by Yankee newcomers; the little age of gold is over for the Indian; but he has had a breathing-space in Carmel Valley before he goes down to the dust with his red fathers."

The Presidio of Monterey

The Presidio of Monterey and Misión San Carlos were founded on the same day, June 3, 1770, when Gaspar de Portolá took possession of the land in the name of King Carlos III of Spain. A fort of rude palisades and a few huts were erected at once and the second presidio in Alta California was instituted.

Late in the eighteenth century, Spain erected a fort on the hill overlooking Monterey Bay, where the present presidio grounds are located. Count de la Pérouse, who visited Monterey in September 1786, says that the guns of the Castillo greeted him; and in 1793, when George Vancouver sailed into the harbor, he also noted the battery on the hill. Vancouver's party was long and gratefully remembered by residents of the Monterey vicinity (who numbered fewer than 500 by 1800), for they "left fruit stones, or seeds of trees . . . extending their generosity by leaving likewise different grains of the best quality," which, planted and tended, added greatly to the variety of foods available in later years.

During the Spanish and Mexican periods, Monterey held first place as the military and social capital of Alta California. It was also the port of entry where "Boston ships" and whaling vessels came to trade with the colonists, finally breaking down the barriers placed by the reluctant Spanish government on foreign trade.

The little port, set like a jewel within pine-clad hills beside the blue bay, is charmingly described by Richard Henry Dana in *Two Years Before the Mast*. When Dana sailed into the harbor on the brig *Pilgrim* in the year 1834, "the town lay directly before [him], making a very pretty appearance, its houses being of whitewashed adobe. . . . The red tiles, too, on the roofs, contrasted well with the white sides and with the extreme greenness of the lawn upon which the houses—about a hundred in number—were dotted about, here and there, irregularly. . . . This, as they are of one story, and of the cottage form, gives them a pretty effect when seen from a little distance. . . .

"In the centre of it is an open square, surrounded by four lines of one-story buildings, with half a dozen cannon in the centre. . . . This is the Presidio, or fort."

In 1822 the Mexican government built a fort on the present presidio grounds on the hill overlooking Monterey Bay. In 1846, after the American occupation, a blockhouse was erected there and ship guns were mounted. It was named Fort Stockton at first, but later in the same year the name was changed to Fort Mervine in honor of the officer in charge. The old fort is no longer there, but the place where it stood has been marked.

The Sloat Monument, erected in honor of Commodore John Drake Sloat, U.S.N., commemorates the act of taking possession of California for the United States, July 7, 1846, and the raising of the United States flag over the Custom House at Monterey. The base of the monument was erected by the people of California through popular subscription, and the superstructure was added by the United States government. It was dedicated and unveiled on the hilltop on the present presidio grounds, June 14, 1910.

Fort Halleck was built at the present presidio in 1847 and named in honor of Lieutenant H. W. Halleck of the corps of engineers which laid out the fort. Halleck later became secretary of state in California during Governor Bennett Riley's military rule, and was a prominent general in the Civil War. He was a man of considerable influence during the period of transition from Mexican to American rule, interpreting the Spanish and Mexican law for the Americans, and thus helping to prevent much confusion and disorder. In the early 1850's he was a prominent lawyer in San Francisco. Fort Halleck no longer exists, but the site is marked.

Misión San Antonio de Padua

Father Junípero Serra, as soon as he had explored the Río Carmelo and had set his people to work building the Misión San Carlos on the new site, set out for the Santa Lucía Mountains to found the third of the missions in Alta California. At length he came to the beautiful valley covered with oaks which was named Los Robles, and which Portolá, in 1769, had called La Hoya de la Sierra de Santa Lucía.

Close by the little river, which Father Serra named the San Antonio, the bells were hung from the branch of a live oak. Grasping the rope and ringing the bells loud and long, the venerable father cried: "Hear, O Gentiles! Come! Oh come to the holy Church of God! Come, oh come, and receive the Faith of Christ!" And to his companion's plea that it was useless to ring the bells he replied: "Let me give vent to my heart's desires; for I would that these bells were heard all over the world, or at least by all the pagan people who live in this sierra."

And, as though a miracle had been wrought, after the rustic *enramada* had been raised and the simple altar placed, one dark native hesitatingly approached to witness the celebration of the Mass. This was the first instance of a native being present at the founding of a mission. By 1805 there were 1,296 neophytes from the neighboring rancherías.

Misión San Antonio de Padua was founded July 14, 1771, at a site one and one-half miles from the present church, which was begun in 1810. The latter is said to have been not only one of the largest but also one of the most picturesque and interesting of all the missions, unsurpassed in its artistic arrangement and the loveliness of its rural setting. The beautiful brick *fachada* withstood the neglect of years and the stress of storm and earthquake, even after the body of the main building and the roofs of the long corridors had crumbled.

Standing in a well-watered valley through which the San Antonio flows in a southeast direction to join the Salinas River, the mission became famous for its excellent wheat and its fine horses. A stone mill for grinding the wheat was constructed and operated by water brought for many miles through a stone-walled ditch, or *zanja*. Remains of this marvelous, if primitive, engineering feat still exist in the valley a few hundred yards from the mission, in what was once the garden, or orchard.

After the death of the Reverend Dorotéo Ambris, the last resident priest at San Antonio, the mission structures were deserted and from year to year became a more complete ruin. Finally, in 1903, the California Historic Landmarks League and the Historic Landmarks Committee of the Native Sons of the Golden West, under the leadership of Joseph R. Knowland, made a plea for restoration, and in September of that year it was begun. In 1906 much of their effort was destroyed by the earthquake, but the following year renovation of the church proper was completed. The mission stood in loneliness—a vacant but intact church and a long row of brick arches fronting heaps of adobe mud that were once the main wing—until 1948, when the Franciscan Order, aided by the Hearst Foundation, commenced restoration on a large scale. Renewal of the principal buildings was completed in the early 1950's,

Threshing Floor, Mission San Antonio

but the project will continue until the entire mission establishment is re-created. An example of the thoroughness of this work is the unearthing of the old threshing floor that lay buried and invisible beneath the dust of decades.

Mission San Antonio (*SRL 232*) is 20 miles southwest of King City and about six miles northwest of Jolon, near the Hunter Liggett Military Reservation. It is one of four missions under the care of the Franciscans, the founding order.

Anza's March Through Monterey

Anza and his band of settlers crossed the Río del Nacimiento on March 5, 1776, and proceeded another mile to El Primo Vado (the First Ford) of the Río de San Antonio, near King Well in what is now Monterey County. Here they camped for the night, continuing up the river valley the following day to Misión San Antonio de Padua, where Anza had made a brief stop on his previous journey in 1774 and where they now remained two days. The fathers welcomed them as royally as had their brothers at San Gabriel and San Luís Obispo.

On the morning of March 8, the expedition once more resumed its march, following up Sulphur Spring Canyon northeast to Upper Milpitas Road, east to the Jolon Road, northeast over the ridge, and down Kent Canyon to the valley of what was then known as the Río de Monterey and is now called the Salinas River. Camp was made northwest of the site of King City at Los Ositos (the "little bears"), where Anza had stopped on April 17, 1774. On March 9 they rested at Los Correos (west and across the river from the present town of Gonzales), and the next day, in a pouring rain, they reached the Presidio of Monterey.

Father Junípero Serra welcomed the travelers and escorted them to Misión San Carlos del Carmelo, where Anza was very ill. Before recovering fully he insisted on fulfilling his mission and proceeded north to explore and to map out the site for the new settlement to be established at San Francisco, leaving his people at Monterey until arrangements could be made for their final migration to the new presidio.

On his way north, Anza followed along to the left of what is now the road to Salinas and San Juan Bautista. He made his final camp in Monterey County on March 23, at a place called La Natividad, near Sugar Loaf Mountain. A town

Soledad Mission, 1952

Soledad Mission, 1962

and a rancho of that name were later located in the vicinity.

Having finished his work at San Francisco, Anza returned to Monterey on April 8. Governor Rivera was opposed to the settlement of San Francisco and refused to allow Anza to settle his people there. Greatly disappointed, Anza finally set out on his return march to Mexico on April 14, after bidding a sad farewell to the people who on the long and perilous journey from Sonora had learned to love him and who wept bitterly at his departure. On the return trip Anza had several unpleasant encounters with Rivera. The latter maintained his obstructionist policy until an order from the viceroy forced him to proceed with the founding of a presidio and mission at San Francisco. Others led the settlers to the new outpost, but Anza was the founder in all but name.

Monterey has recognized Juan Bautista de Anza by a monument, dedicated by the California Centennials Commission, in El Estero Park.

Misión Nuestra Señora Dolorosísima de la Soledad

Misión Soledad (SRL 233) was founded by Father Lasuén on October 9, 1791, 30 miles southeast of Monterey and about a mile west of the Salinas River, with thousands of acres of bare, brown plains stretching away on every side. Although very nearly limitless in acreage, soil and pasturage were only fairly good, and the growth in the number of neophytes was very slow.

Gradually, however, the faithful labors of the fathers surmounted these handicaps, until the Mission of Our Most Sorrowful Lady of Solitude was quite prosperous, and its occupants lived peacefully for about 40 years. Governor Arrillaga died at Soledad in 1814 and was buried under the center of the church, and in 1818 the mission became a refuge for the coast missions during the appearance of the pirate Bouchard. After the decree of secularization, Soledad became impoverished, and Father Sarría, who refused to forsake his little flock of Indians, died there, destitute and enfeebled by age.

The first temporary adobe structure at Soledad was erected in 1797, and a new church was begun in 1808. The buildings fell into ruin until finally only mud walls stood desolately beside the roadway. Great haystacks towered above them and roaming cattle pastured there. Wrapped in solitude, the remnants of the old church for many years saddened those who knew and loved its story of sacrifice and devotion. Now, with work still continuing, it has become the last of the extant California missions to be restored. The remaining walls were carefully incorporated into the renovated structure. The work, carried out under the auspices of the Native Daughters of the Golden West, was begun in 1954.

Royal Presidio Chapel

After the removal of Mission San Carlos Borroméo to Carmel, the old mission building at the Presidio of Monterey became the Presidio Chapel. (SRL 105). The present building was erected in 1794 and was then called the Royal Chapel because the king's representative worshiped there. At the time of the secularization of the mission at Carmel, in 1836, the chapel at Monterey became the parish church.

The San Carlos Parish Church, now a registered National Historic Landmark, is well preserved and in regular use today. In 1836 many of the furnishings from the old mission at Carmel were brought to the parish church, where they are still treasured.

The Custom House

The old Custom House (SRL 1) in Monterey occupies a prominent place in California's history. The flags of three nations have floated over this building: Spain until 1822, Mexico from 1822 to 1846, and the United States from 1846 on. Cleland says, "California history is vastly more significant because of its national and international aspects than for any local interest it may possess. From this standpoint, the event of primary importance in the history of California is its transformation from a Mexican province into an American state. To this event, as Dr. Chapman shows, the Spanish period looks forward; from this event, dates the California of today and the greater California of tomorrow."

The Custom House at Monterey was the most important in the province of Alta California, and all trading vessels were compelled to enter their cargo on its records. To this quiet harbor came the hunters of seal and sea otter, the pioneers of trade on the Pacific Coast, followed closely by battered whaling vessels, to be reconditioned after perilous voyages in far northern seas. Most important of all, the "Boston ships" from New England came early, seeking hides and tallow, and with their coming a new era on the coast of Alta California was foreshadowed.

The American flag was raised over the Custom House, temporarily, on October 19, 1842, by Commodore Thomas ap Catesby Jones, owing to misapprehension of the seriousness of affairs between the United States and Mexico and of the much feared invasion of England. However, he took it down again the following day and apologized for his mistake. But on July 7, 1846, the American flag was raised permanently by Commodore John Drake Sloat, signalizing, by that act, the passing of California from Mexican rule.

The Custom House is a picturesque structure

Old Custom House, Monterey

of stone and adobe begun by the Spanish and added to by the Mexican and American governments. Statements as to the dates of construction differ. Some authorities say that the low central portion was begun first, the foundations being laid in 1814 by the Spanish and the walls and roof being completed by the Mexicans after 1822, while the two square, balconied towers, one at the north end and one at the south, were erected during the Mexican and American periods, the north tower having been built first. Gertrude Atherton used the Custom House and the rocks in front of its veranda as the setting for a dramatic incident in *The Pearls of Loretto*.

The Custom House once belonged to the United States government, but was sold to a group of private citizens, who deeded it to the state of California. It was restored by the state and marked by the Monterey History and Art Association. A museum of local relics is housed in it, and it is open to the public as a unit of Monterey State Historical Monument. Because of its importance to the history of the United States, the Monterey Custom House has been registered by the Department of the Interior as a National Historic Landmark.

Land Grants

In 1773 the Spanish Viceroy Bucareli, in preparation for the establishment of future pueblos, authorized Captain Rivera to distribute lands to worthy persons, either native or Spanish, who would devote themselves to farming and stock raising. Among those considered to be worthy persons were Spaniards who had married baptized Indian girls.

Such a man was Manuel Butron, a soldier, who married Margarita María of the San Carlos Mission and to whom Rivera gave a plot of land 140 varas square near the mission in 1775. This was the first grant of land made by the Spanish in Alta California. The grantee, however, abandoned it later and was living in the Pueblo de San José in 1786.

After the Butron grant, pueblo lots were given to settlers, and by 1784 other tracts of larger dimensions were temporarily granted to individuals by Don Pedro Fages. By 1786 grants of land up to three square leagues were authorized, provided that they did not overlap the boundaries of already established missions, pueblos, or rancherías. By 1793 a few had been granted provisionally to *inválido* soldiers and other settlers on the Salinas River.

By January 1795 a half-dozen provisional ranchos were held in the Monterey district, none of which seem to have been made permanent at a later date: Buena Vista, five leagues, near Monterey, held by José Soberanes and Joaquín Castro; Salinas, four leagues, held by Antonio Aceves and Antonio Romero; Bajada a Huerta Viega, one-half league, by Antonio Montano; Cañada de Huerta, three-quarters league, by Antonio Buelna; Mesa de la Polvora, "a musket shot," by Eugenio Rosalio; and Chupadero, "1 mile," by Bernardo Heredia and Juan Padilla.

Rancho Bolsa de San Cayetano

Don Ignacio Vicente Ferrer Vallejo, a Spanish native of Jalisco, Mexico, came to Alta California in 1774 with Lieutenant Ortega (or possibly even with the Portolá expedition in 1769) and became the progenitor of the Vallejo family in the state. He had a brother, Juan José, who was a priest, but he himself inclined to a military rather than an ecclesiastical life and enlisted in that service. Records show that he was praised for his bravery on many occasions. After the termination of his enlistment he was employed at San Carlos, where he directed agriculture and irrigation. He reenlisted in military service in the Monterey Company and held positions at Soledad, San José, and Branciforte. In 1824 he was at San Luís Obispo for the purpose of preventing an Indian revolt, and while there he received the grant of Rancho Bolsa de San Cayetano. The limit of this tract on the north was the Pajaro River; on the west, Monterey Bay; on the east, Rancho Vega del Río del Pájaro; and on the south, an estuary separating it from the Carneros Rancho. Because it was the first land owned by the Vallejo family within the boundary of California, the original house built on it has been termed the "Casa Materna of the Vallejos" ("mother house").

This adobe was also known as the "Glass House," because of the many glass windows that once enclosed the upper porch. Built on a hill overlooking the Pajaro Valley, supposedly about 1824, the house was occupied up to 1870 or perhaps later. For a while it served as a barn, and at length it fell into ruin. Each winter saw the adobe walls further eroded by the weather. One end finally collapsed, but there always remained enough of the building to serve as a basis for restoration. The Pajaro Valley Historical Association, with the cooperation of the owner, Arthur Trafton, spearheaded efforts to renovate the old structure and make it a State Park, but in vain. Finally, in the spring of 1962, a later owner removed the remains with a bulldozer. The loss of the "Glass House," first permanent home of the eminent Vallejo family in California, is one of the most tragic in the annals of the landmarks of the state.

The site (*SRL 387*), thus far unmarked, is in an open field, actually the edge of a bluff, about two and three-quarters miles south of the Pajaro River bridge at Watsonville. It is beyond the Watsonville Golf Club and on the opposite side of Highway 1, almost opposite the end of Hillcrest Road. A lone tree and an orange-colored tank indicate the approximate location.

The structure was 44 feet long, and the outer walls were 20 inches thick. The joists, 4×6 inches, and the window frames were of hewn redwood. A shingle roof, upheld by a 6×8 inch beam extending the whole length of the building, covered the structure. Two large rooms with floors of hard earth made up the first floor; the upper story was without partitions and formed one large room with a floor of hewn boards.

Two versions of the placing of the windows

have become traditions: one story is to the effect that the glass, which is said to have come from Spain, was intended for use in the house of General Vallejo at Sonoma but proved unsuitable for that purpose. The other story relates that the owner of this adobe ordered one dozen glass windows, but found, when the shipment arrived, that 12 dozen were in the consignment. He refused them at first, but finally accepted them and glassed in the entire upper veranda. An extensive view is obtained from the spot.

In 1790 Don Ignacio married María Antonia, daughter of Francisco Lugo. Their family consisted of five sons and eight daughters. Five of the daughters married men of more than ordinary position in the country: Mariano Soberanes, José Amesti, J. B. R. Cooper, J. P. Leese, and José F. Alvarado, all of whom received large grants of government land. Four of the five sons survived the father, who died at Monterey in 1831 at the age of 83. The most distinguished of the sons was Mariano, a leading figure in the annals of California.

José de Jesús, probably the eldest son in the family, as his birthdate is ten years before that of Mariano, lived on his father's rancho and became the owner of it by grant from José Figueroa, then political chief or governor of Alta California. It was confirmed to him as executor of his father's estate, and he received final patent to it in 1865. That this son had been interested in the land for many years is proved by a petition that he signed on October 27, 1826, in which he asks for two *sitios* at San Cayetano. He states in this document that his father and Dolores Pico had earlier received a grant for the property and that his father had used it for a cattle range but that Don Dolores had not fulfilled the conditions essential to its possession and had therefore forfeited his right, which the petitioner now desired and had need of. He apparently lived upon this rancho only a few years after settling the estate, as he became the grantee of Rancho Arroyo de la Alameda in 1842. He spent the last years of his life at Misión San José, where he died in 1882 at the age of 84 years.

In 1847 another son, Juan Antonio, was still living on the rancho, for in the spring of that year Lieutenant William Tecumseh Sherman, who claimed him as a friend, attempted to call upon him at the breakfast hour. At this time Lieutenant Sherman was accompanying Governor Richard B. Mason to Monterey. Sherman states that by "nine o'clock we had reached the ranch. It was on a high point of the plateau, overlooking the plain of the Pajaro, on which were grazing numbers of horses and cattle. The house was of adobe, with a long range of adobe-huts occupied by semi-civilized Indians, who at that time did all the labor of a ranch, the herding and marking of cattle, the breaking of horses, and cultivating the little patches of wheat and vegetables which constituted all the farming of that day. Everything about the house looked deserted, and, seeing a small Indian boy leaning up against a post, I approached him and asked him in

"Glass House," near Watsonville

Spanish, 'Where is the master?' 'Gone to the Presidio' [Monterey]. 'Is anybody in the house?' 'No.' 'Is it locked up?' 'Yes.' 'Is no one about who can get in?' 'No.' 'Have you any meat?' 'No.' 'Any flour or grain?' 'No.' 'Any chickens?' 'No.' 'Any eggs?' 'No.' 'What do you live on?' *'Nada'* ['nothing']." As a result, the travelers went a short distance to a pond and made a slim breakfast from the contents of their knapsacks.

An adobe house of two stories, sometimes called the Hipólito adobe and sometimes the Pope adobe, originally constructed four miles from Watsonville on this rancho, was badly wrecked in the 1906 earthquake, but its material afterward was used in the construction of a small one-story cottage at 514 Blackburn Street in the town of Watsonville, where it is now used as a private residence. When in use on the rancho, the structure housed a gristmill in its northwest corner, with millstones on the second floor turned by ox power from the ground floor.

It is not definitely known how many adobes were built on this rancho in early days. Two Vallejo houses are indicated on the map of the 1859 survey: that of A. Vallejo, situated near the Watsonville Road; and that of José de Jesús Vallejo, situated a little south of the center of the property. Whether or not General Vallejo lived on the rancho after he became famous is not definitely known, although it is said that a black and white sign on the "Glass House" once bore the name "General Vallejo."

Rancho El Alisal and El Colegio de San José

Rancho El Alisal, consisting of one and one-third square leagues, was granted by Governor Figueroa to Feliciano and Mariano Soberanes on June 26, 1834. Through this tract runs Alisal Creek, on the bank of which W. E. P. Hartnell had established a school of higher learning a few months earlier.

Hartnell, an Englishman who had married María Teresa de la Guerra in 1825, obtained a grant of land in this vicinity in 1834 for the purpose of building a summer home to be called El Patrocinto de San José. Seeing the need of education for the youth of the country, he decided to establish at his home a place where certain studies might be pursued, and on December 10, 1833, he sent out a prospectus inviting a limited number of students to attend. One young man who availed himself of this opportunity was Pablo de la Guerra, later a member of the Constitutional Convention and after that a state senator and chairman of the committee on counties and their boundaries.

The school, called El Colegio de San José, opened on January 1, 1834, with 15 pupils enrolled, and continued for a few years. Two adobe buildings used in this undertaking stood for many years: the smaller one was the dormitory, dining room, and kitchen, and contained a fireplace, deep and broad, where the cooking may have been done; the larger, oblong structure served as the family residence and housed Hartnell's private library and the classrooms. Both were of two stories with roofs made of shingles split by Indians under the instruction of the mission fathers. Although no trace remained of the flower gardens, orchards, and vineyards that once beautified the site, the buildings themselves stood in a relatively good state of preservation until late in 1960, when they were destroyed by their owner, who became annoyed at the frequent intrusion of sightseers. Such was the tragic end of the Hartnell adobes, an important and irreplaceable landmark of California education. The name Hartnell has been taken by a Salinas college, in memory of the pioneer educator of El Alisal.

The genial Hartnell established picnic grounds a few hundred yards distant, to which his invited guests from far and near came to partake of his hospitality. El Colegio was the scene of many gay social festivities held by its host for the entertainment of his many friends. The grounds were known as the Alisal Picnic Grounds and were a favorite gathering place. They were kept open by later owners until the privilege, too often abused, had to be withdrawn. The grounds and the site of the two adobes are now a part of a private stock ranch five miles east of Salinas at 955 Old Stage Road. The rancho, consisting of 2,971 acres, was patented to M. T. de la Hartnell on February 2, 1882, and afterward passed from the Hartnell heirs to the Spreckels Sugar Company, which has since disposed of the property.

Frémont, on March 3, 1846, camped on the rancho. He approached it over the Salinas plain, where "the wild oats were three feet high and well headed." It was while here that he received the peremptory order from Castro to "return with your people out of the limits of this territory," an order that he refused to obey. He fortified himself in the Gabilan (Gavilan) Mountains and raised the American flag.

A part of Rancho El Alisal was purchased by the Bernal family, who owned Rancho Santa Teresa in Santa Clara County. Bruno Bernal, son of Don Joaquín, filed his claim for 5,941 acres of it in 1853. For this tract, patent was issued to him in 1866. The house in which he lived, a long, low adobe from which the traditional Bernal hospitality was dispensed, has disappeared. Its ruins could long be seen from the Natividad-Gonzales Road (Old Stage Road) in a field lying to the east of that thoroughfare, not far from the Hart-

nell adobes, although the latter could not be seen from the road.

The house of the original grantees, the Soberanes adobe, is in the same vicinity but to the west of the road. Hidden by trees, fences, and farm buildings, it is approached by a pathway lined with fruit trees in a fenced garden. The path leads to a sheltered ell corner where fuchsias and citrus trees grow between the two-story part of the house and a one-story extension. Roofed by the original tiles, the place is still used as a family residence on the Silacci Ranch at 960 Old Stage Road.

Rancho Sausal

Although a large part of the city of Salinas lies on Rancho Nacional, the northern part lies on the adjoining Rancho Sausal, which extends north and east of the city. Over this area the Natividad and Gabilan creeks find their way into some of the sloughs that abound in this part of Monterey County.

The American pioneer Jacob P. Leese, who was a landholder in several parts of the state, acquired this property. He filed claim for a confirmation of his right on February 5, 1853, and two amendatory petitions on July 12 and August 4, 1854. He founded his claim on two Mexican grants: the first, made August 2, 1834, by Governor José Figueroa; and the second, August 10, 1845, by Governor Pío Pico. He received a patent for 10,241 acres in September 1859.

Earlier mention of this rancho goes back to 1823; in this year a certain Soberanes was its occupant. In 1828 it was used, along with Alisal and Cañada de Natividad, by Manuel Butron and Nicolás Alviso as a range for their cattle.

Although the grant was made to José Tiburcio Castro in 1834, he seems to have resided there much earlier, for his house, only a small part of which is still standing, is said to have been built in 1823. The remnant of the adobe residence is in excellent condition, with leather thongs still binding the hand-hewn rafters. It is located two miles from the Salinas Rodeo Field and a short distance north of the Monterey County Hospital, at 803 Sausal Drive, near the corner of Cambrian Drive. Surrounded by a few of the old eucalyptus and cypress trees, it is used as a private residence. A modern subdivision hides it from Natividad Road. In more recent times the property was known as the Sherwood Ranch.

Rancho Bolsa Nueva y Moro Cojo

According to *Spanish and Indian Place Names in California* by Sanchez, the name Moro Cojo literally means "lame Moor"; but, as the Spaniards used *moro* to mean anything black, tradition says that a lame black horse gave the name to this particular tract of land.

This rancho of eight square leagues was granted to Simeón Castro in three parts: the first, called Moro Cojo, was granted February 14, 1825, by Governor Luís Argüello; the second, Bolsa Nueva, May 14, 1836, by Governor Chico; and the third by Governor Alvarado November 20, 1837. The last one, according to Bancroft, had been given first to John Milligan, an Irishman who taught weaving at San Juan Mission. The whole was revalidated to the heirs of Castro by Governor Micheltorena on September 26, 1844. Irregular in shape, it reached from the swamp near Monterey Bay to rolling, timbered hills. Its southeastern corner is Lagunita, a lake on which three other ranchos touched: Bolsa de las Escarpinas, La Natividad, and Los Vergeles.

The widow, Doña María Antonia Pico de Castro, and her nine children filed claim for this land in 1853. In December 1872 a survey was made, and a patent was thereafter issued to these claimants for 30,901 acres.

The northwestern corner of this grant is near the Elkhorn Slough and the railway station of Elkhorn. The town of Castroville, founded in 1864 by Juan Castro, son of the grantee, is situated within the bounds of this old grant.

Ranchos Santa Rita and Bolsa de las Escarpinas

José Trinidad Espinosa had received a provisional grant to Rancho Los Gatos, or Santa Rita, many years before September 30, 1837, the date on which the land was formally made his by act of Governor Alvarado. Its location may be identified approximately by the town of Santa Rita, which is in the eastern part of the old rancho, and by Lake Espinosa, which lies on the northwest border.

Salvador Espinosa filed petition for Rancho Bolsa de las Escarpinas on September 22, 1852, basing his claim on a grant received by himself on October 7, 1837. This tract lay north of Rancho Santa Rita, which was granted the same year to José Trinidad Espinosa. The line dividing the two runs through Espinosa Lake.

The Espinosa adobe, of which nothing now remains, was erected on the brow of a hill between Lake Espinosa and the "Tembladera" (quaking bog). Don José married Jacinta Archuleta; their daughter, Fermina, married Domingo Pérez, who is mentioned in records as having lived on Rancho Nacional in 1836, when he was 27 years of age.

The date of the death of José Trinidad Espinosa lies between the year 1845, when he took part in the battle of Cahuenga, and January 29, 1853, when his daughter filed her petition with the Land Commission as claimant for Rancho Santa Rita. Doña Fermina's death occurred before the confirmation of her claim. The final papers of ownership to the 4,424 acres were made out to the surviving husband, Domingo Pérez and the children, Fermina, María Trinidad, Mateo Asunción, Pedro, José Manuel, and Crysogono. Patent was issued to these claimants on April 4, 1870.

Rancho La Natividad

Rancho La Natividad consisted of two square leagues of land south of a stretch of Gabilan Creek. The tract was granted to Manuel Butron and Nicolás Alviso by Governor Alvarado on November 16, 1837, and their ownership was confirmed by the United States in 1853.

Old Saloon, Natividad

A site on this land near the town of Natividad was leased in 1836 to "Ysaac Graham, Enrique Nale y Guillermo Dockey" for the erection of a plant for manufacturing *aguardiente*. The signing of this lease by Manuel Butron proves that he, at least, was considered owner of the tract before his formal receipt of the grant from the governor.

In 1853 the children of Butron and of Alviso filed claim for this rancho. A patent for 8,641 acres was issued to them by the United States in that same year.

Natividad, six miles northeast of Salinas, became a flourishing station on the Coast Stage Line in the 1850's. After the discontinuance of the line and the routing of the main traffic between the northern and southern parts of California through Salinas, it disintegrated into a deserted crossroads with its vacant frame buildings falling to ruin. Now there are several newer homes in the area, one of which (at 661 Old Stage Road) is the former schoolhouse remodeled. The deserted saloon at the corner of Old Stage and Old Natividad roads is about all that remains to remind one of the town's bustling days.

Rancho El Sur

In March 1852 Juan Bautista Roger Cooper, then harbor master at Monterey, filed claim to two ranchos in Monterey County: Bolsa del Potrero y Moro Cojo in the vicinity of Salinas, and Rancho El Sur on the seacoast south of the town of Monterey. To the former he received patent in 1859; and to the latter, in 1866.

Rancho El Sur had been granted to Juan B. Alvarado, Cooper's wife's nephew, July 30, 1834, by Governor José Figueroa and thereafter was approved by the Territorial *Diputación*. The grantee was the son of Sergeant José F. Alvarado and his wife, María Josefa Vallejo. He was born on February 14, 1809. His official life began in his twentieth year, when he became secretary of the *Diputación*—the first step toward the central position in California history which he eventually held, the governorship of Alta California from 1836 to 1842. At the age of 25 he was elected a member of the *Diputación,* and two years later he became president of that body. In 1839 he married Martina, daughter of Francisco Castro, and later he went to live on her Rancho San Pablo in Contra Costa County.

Before 1852 Juan Bautista Roger Cooper, the owner of other ranchos, became the owner of this one also. Cooper Point on the coast is the most southerly extension of this tract, and the mouth of the Little Sur River is the northern limit. The son, John Baptist Henry Cooper, later relieved his father of a great part of the burden of managing his property and eventually inherited it. The headquarters of this rancho were in a frame house, which is still standing, constructed of timbers brought around the Horn. This area, located near the mouth of Big Sur River, will eventually be developed as Andrew Molera State Park. Molera was a grandson of J. B. R. Cooper. Frances M. Molera, Andrew's sister, retains a life interest in the property.

Rancho Milpitas

Rancho Milpitas, the grant extending for many miles along the San Antonio River, has its comparatively narrow northwest boundary within Los Padres National Forest. In the fertile level areas along the river and along some of its tributaries were probably located those small plots, cultivated by the natives in a crude manner, that gave rise to the name Milpitas—"little gardens."

Mission Creek was the name given to one of these tributary streams after the establishment of the San Antonio Mission near its bank. From it a supply of water was obtained.

The southeast corner of the rancho is at Jolon (said to be an Indian word for "valley of dead oaks"), once an Indian settlement and later a settlement of white people served by early stagecoaches. Here now stands what remains of the two-story adobe hotel then kept by Dutton, an American. The barroom at one end of the building has been torn down, and the larger part of the hotel left standing has been abandoned and allowed to fall into ruin. An ancient grapevine once spread its leaves over the upper balcony that extended across the entire front, but now both grapevine and balcony have disappeared. For the protection of the adobe walls, a coat of cement plaster marked out in squares to simulate stone covered the long front of the building next to the road. Today there is only fragmentary evidence of this covering.

Ygnacio Pastor, a neophyte of the San Antonio Mission, received the grant of Rancho Milpitas

from Governor Alvarado on May 5, 1838. He filed claim for it with the United States Land Commission in August 1852, and the patent for 43,281 acres was issued to him on February 18, 1875. A small area, 33 acres, in the immediate vicinity of the mission, was patented to the Catholic Bishop J. S. Alemany in 1862 during the administration of President Abraham Lincoln.

For many years the lack of a definite understanding concerning the boundaries of this grant led to considerable squatter trouble. Faxon D. Atherton, whose home was on a subdivision of Rancho de las Pulgas (San Mateo County), became the owner, and evictions of undesired tenants became general. Many families of the dispossessed sought refuge temporarily at San Antonio Mission.

Atherton sent his son George to be manager of the rancho. George and his wife, the novelist Gertrude Atherton, their small son and a Chinese servant took up residence for a time in an adobe vacated by a squatter and whitewashed for their use: "an adobe mansion with three rooms, an attic, and a lean-to that served as kitchen." Mrs. Atherton's *Los Cerritos* drew its local color from the period spent here.

This rancho later became a part of the holdings of William Randolph Hearst, whose elaborate Milpitas ranch house on the hill overlooks the San Antonio Mission. Hearst's buildings are now the headquarters of the Hunter Liggett Military Reservation, which occupies large portions of Milpitas and adjoining ranchos.

Rancho Los Ojitos

Rancho Los Ojitos (in free translation, "ranch of little springs"), adjoining the southern tip of Rancho Milpitas, is a long narrow strip of land lying along the San Antonio River. A few hills and canyons are in the south-central part, but in the main it is composed of bottom land. A part of the herds belonging to the San Antonio Mission were pastured there; and it is recorded that in 1823 an adobe house of two rooms was built and roofed with tiles, supposedly for the use of neophyte herders. Ruins of this building still remain, as do those of another larger one, near the San Antonio River. It is estimated that they were built before 1825.

Both of these houses came into the hands of Mariano Soberanes on April 5, 1842, when, after the secularization of the mission, the grant of Los Ojitos was given to him by Governor Alvarado.

Because the grantee had been active against the American invaders, the place was pillaged by Frémont's men on their way to Los Angeles in 1846. Don Mariano later put in a claim for $40,000 damages, of which he finally received by court decree a mere pittance. In 1871 patent for 8,900 acres was issued to him. Previous to that time (in the 1860's), the Roth family became the owners of a part of the rancho.

The two old houses remained in good repair, until they were deliberately spoiled by Hunter Liggett soldiers on practice maneuvers during World War II. Interesting features of the construction of these houses were the upper floors.

They were fashioned of logs and poles laced together with rawhide. On top of this rude frame was placed a layer of cornstalks, which in turn was covered with mud and thoroughly tamped to make a hard, smooth surface. Such floors were used in the earliest construction of the missions. The ruins can be seen from the Jolon-Pleyto road on the north side of the river. This road branches to the right from the main Bradley road about three and one-half miles southeast of Jolon.

Rancho Pleyto

Early Spanish travelers through the San Antonio River Valley remarked upon the groups of natives frequently seen engaged in earnest conversation there. To all appearances, they were endeavoring to settle disagreements that had arisen among themselves, and this valley seemed to be a customary meeting place for that purpose. The Spanish word *pleito* means "lawsuit," and from it the name of Rancho Pleyto is supposed to have been derived.

The grant of this land was made on July 18, 1845, by Governor Pico to Antonio Chavez (Chavis), who two years previously had received Rancho Ciénega del Gabilán.

A claim founded on this grant was filed with the Land Commission in 1853 by W. S. Johnson and Preston K. Woodside. The two were members of the regiment of New York Volunteers brought to California by Colonel Stevenson in 1847. Their claim, first rejected, was settled upon appeal in their favor, and 13,299 acres were confirmed to them in 1872.

Through the long narrow valley that comprises this rancho ran the trail between Missions San Antonio and San Miguel; when the days of the stagecoach arrived, it was still the main line of travel between these two points. At the settlement of Pleyto lived J. T. Betts, who was for many years responsible for keeping the horses on the line properly shod. His children grew up in the little town, and his sister kept the hotel there. The town has disappeared; its site is the junction of Pleyto Road and the road to Bradley along the south side of the San Antonio River.

A part of this rancho was sold to a Mr. Pinkerton, whose children were all born in an adobe ranch house a little way from the town. The old adobe is in ruins, the result of the same army maneuvers that ended the Los Ojitos adobes. The remnants are on the south side of the river, about a mile east of the site of Pleyto, just beyond and opposite the junction of Lynch Road but not visible from the Bradley road.

Ranchos along the Salinas River

Of the 32 private land grants in the Salinas Valley, 26 lie adjacent to the Salinas River. The fertile acres in this region successively attracted the Spaniard, Mexican, and American as they traveled over the level country.

Near the mouth of the Salinas River is Rancho Rincón de las Salinas ("corner of the salt marshes"), extending from just east of Twin Bridges (Neponset) to the ocean. This was granted by Governor Figueroa to Cristina Delgado on June 13, 1833; and Rafael Estrada, having occupied it in 1853, received United States patent for it in 1881. The ranch house, situated on the hillside about half a mile southeast of the Neponset railway station, fell to ruin, but its foundations were visible for many years.

Across the river from the Rincón de las Salinas was the Bolsa del Potrero y Moro Cojo, or La Sagrada Familia, originally granted to José Joaquín de la Torre, who had arrived in Alta California in 1801. He thereafter had served long and well in the Monterey Company, much of the time as secretary to the governor. In a petition to Governor Pablo Vicente de Solá, dated June 20, 1822, Don José Joaquín stated that he had served his nation for 21 years as cadet and corporal and that, as his pay was inadequate for the proper support of his wife and seven children, the eldest of whom was then 16 years old, he desired "most humbly" a piece of land that he might call his own and that he might pass on to his descendants. He further stated that he owned horses and cattle and that, having been allowed to pasture them on the Bolsa del Potrero y Moro Cojo, he would be pleased to receive a grant of that particular piece of land in order to build houses and fences. Having been afflicted with a paralysis on his left side, he was fearful that his life might be cut short or that he might become entirely disabled. Furthermore it was his belief that the land in question belonged to the government and that no one else had claim upon it. Such apparently was the case, for within two days after the signing of the petition the grant was made to him by the governor.

The tract was almost surrounded by water, lying between the Salinas River and the "Tembladera" (quaking bog), with branching sloughs meandering through it. In 1829 Don José Joaquín sold the entire property, consisting of nearly 7,000 acres, to Juan Bautista Roger Cooper, the older half-brother of Thomas O. Larkin. After Cooper had filed claim for it on March 30, 1852, a survey was made. Cooper's house stood about a mile from the Cooper Switch on the railroad.

Southeast of Don Joaquín de la Torre's Rancho La Sagrada Familia lay the Rinconada del Sanjón (*zanjón*, "deep ditch") of 2,230 acres. Its boundary line on the south and southwest was made up of the curves of the Salinas River and the adjacent sloughs.

The grant of this property was given by Governor Alvarado to José Eusebio Boronda on February 1, 1840. After being confirmed by the United States government in 1854, the grant was surveyed in December 1858 and patented in July 1860. At the time of the survey, five houses were standing across the Salinas River from the southwest boundary of the grant.

Don José Eusebio was 30 years old when he received this rancho; four years earlier he had been mayordomo of Rancho Vergeles, that lay along the road from Monterey to San José. He married Josefa Buelna. Their home, built on a hill (across the road and the railroad from the present Graves School), was so situated that it could be seen for miles over the Salinas plain. Horsemen traveling through the rank growth of wild mustard, could see, by standing on their saddles, the red tiles of the Boronda adobe over the yellow blossoms, as Lieutenant William Tecumseh Sherman did in 1846 after crossing the Salinas River on his way from Monterey. Cultivation of the land has now largely eliminated the wild mustard. The house no longer stands, but a second adobe erected by Don Eusebio in a more protected location may be seen less than three miles northwest of the city of Salinas at 333 Boronda Road, where it is in use as a private residence. It is reached by traveling the Salinas–Castroville road and turning due north opposite the Catholic Cemetery for a distance of about one mile.

Rancho El Tucho, part of which was patented to David Jacks in 1867, had been granted to José Joaquín Gómez in December 1843. It was in the heart of the Blanco country, where the Portolá expedition of 1769 had maintained a base camp during the first week of October, while scouts tried to find the port of Monterey. Another part was granted in 1841 to Simeón Castro.

Antonio Aceves and Antonio Romero had held a four-league grant, called Las Salinas, before 1795. But, as was frequently the case with grants given at that period, when the entire area was unoccupied except by roving bands of Indians, the grantees made little effort to hold their lands.

On April 15, 1836, Governor Nicolás Gutiérrez gave one square league out of this area to Gabriel Espinosa. The western tip of his rancho reached almost to the Bay of Monterey, and the rancho stretched in the opposite direction to the Salinas opposite Blanco. Lucinda E. Pogue and the heirs of Don Gabriel filed claim for this property on February 9, 1853, and the patent was issued in 1867. Lucinda Pogue received two-sevenths, and the children of Gabriel Espinosa—José María, María Jesús, Barbara Lucille, Juan José Jesús, and José Manuel—each received one-seventh.

To the south of Rancho Las Salinas lay part of the City Lands of Monterey, the vast tract extending from the Bay of Monterey to the Salinas, with title dating back to 1830. Divided from these City Lands of Monterey by the Pilarcitos Canyon was Rancho El Chamisal, granted by Governor Castro to Felipe Vásquez on November 15, 1835. Nicanor Lugo, widow of Don Felipe, and his three children, Pedro, Dionisio, and Manuel, filed their claim on January 31, 1853, and received patent for 2,737 acres in 1877.

Lying parallel with El Chamisal and on the same side of the Salinas River was Rancho El Toro, along which ran Toro Creek. Hill Town is near the northeastern corner of this tract. The rancho was granted to José Ramón Estrada on October 17, 1835, by Governor Castro. The grantee had attended school at Monterey for five years up to 1820. Don José Ramón married María Castro and was administrator at Santa Clara for two years after receiving this grant. In 1852 Charles Walters filed claim to the grant and in 1862 received patent for 5,668 acres.

Rancho Nacional lay northeast of the narrow ends of El Chamisal and El Toro across the river.

Its corner was at Hill Town, and it extended from the river into Salinas. The cattle, horses, and sheep belonging to Carmel Mission and the Presidio of Monterey were once pastured here. It was one of the *ranchos del rey*, land belonging to the King of Spain, to be used as directed by the government. The grazing was particularly good because of the rich bottom land and the many streams and sloughs. When the Argentine pirate Bouchard was a threat in 1818, the people sought refuge here.

On April 4, 1839, Governor Alvarado granted two square leagues of Rancho Nacional to Vicente Cantua. United States patent was obtained by the grantee on April 7, 1866, for 6,633 acres.

Hill Town is at the junction of Highway 68 and the Spreckels road, a few miles south of Salinas. Near here there used to be a ford called Paso del Quinto. In later years Hill Town was the site of one of the first ferries to cross the Salinas River. Operated by Hiram Cory, it was guided across the river by a cable and propelled by the force of the current. Hill Town Ferry *(SRL 560)* operated until a bridge was built in 1889. A marker commemorates the pioneer ferry, and nearby is a picturesque old roadside hotel.

Up the river from Hill Town stretched two ranchos belonging to the Estrada family—Buena Vista and Llano de Buena Vista. Llano de Buena Vista was granted to José Mariano Estrada in 1823. Don José Mariano had come to Alta California in 1797 and was at once made *alférez* of the Monterey Company, a position he held for 12 years. He was rewarded for his service in 1818 against Bouchard by being made brevet lieutenant, and in 1824 he was made full lieutenant for his services in suppressing Indian uprisings. He retired from military service in 1829, and the following year he was made executor of the Luís Argüello estate. His daughter Adelaide married David Spence, to whom this rancho, consisting of 8,446 acres, was patented in 1860. On this grant is the town of Spreckels.

Rancho Buena Vista was granted to José Santiago Estrada and his father, José Mariano Estrada, by Governor Pablo Vicente de Solá on May 28, 1822. It consisted of two square leagues. José Santiago and his brothers filed claim for this rancho in April 1852, and through the offices of their attorney, Mariano Malarin, they received patent in 1869. Fragmentary ruins of the adobe ranch house on Buena Vista may be glimpsed from the River Road at a point about two and one-half miles southeast of its junction with the Salinas–Monterey highway. This point is almost directly across the river from the Spreckels sugar factory. The tiny remnant is on a hillside to the right of the road on the Violini Ranch. Two old pear trees which long guarded the ruins fell in 1963.

Southeast of Llano de Buena Vista was Rancho Encinal y Buena Esperanza, also bordering on the roving Salinas River. It was granted to the son-in-law of Don José Mariano Estrada, David Spence, by Governor Figueroa on November 29, 1834. At this date the governor stipulated that "within a year at latest he shall build a house thereon and it must be habitable." It was also provided that, when the property was confirmed, the corners should be marked not only by boundary stones but by planting fruit trees, "either wild or tame, of some utility." Any violation of these and other conditions would cause him to forfeit his right to the land. Another square league was granted on April 15, 1839, by Juan B. Alvarado, governor ad interim. Both of these grants were approved in due time, and a patent for 13,352 acres was issued on May 23, 1862.

David Spence was a conservative and much-respected man from Scotland. After living in Peru for a few years he had come to California, where he lived until his death in 1875. Debarking at Monterey in 1824 from the *Pizarro*, he superintended meat packing for Begg and Company for three years. At the end of that time he went into business for himself and was successful from the first. In 1828 he was baptized at Santa Cruz as David Estévan Spence, and the following year he married Señorita Adelaide Estrada. After nearly 40 years of life together, they died within one month of each other. Since their son David, who had been educated in Honolulu, had died seven years previously, their large estate was left to the three grandsons and a granddaughter. The station of Spence on the Southern Pacific Railroad is in the northwestern part of this rancho.

South of Don David's property were Ranchos Chualar and Zanjones, both of which finally came into the possession of Don Juan Malarin. On the western bank of the river along this stretch lies the land once contained in Rancho Guadalupe y Llanitos de los Correos, granted to Don Juan between 1831 and 1835. The three grants contained a total of 24,470 acres.

Juan Malarin, the grantee, was a native of Peru. He came to California as master of the *Señoriana* in 1820 and came again in 1824 as master of the *Apolonia*. In 1825 he was chosen by Governor Argüello to take the prizes *Asia* and *Constante* to Acapulco; for this service, which he performed for the government, he was made a lieutenant in the Mexican Navy. He thereafter made Monterey his home between sea voyages and married Josefa Estrada. The fine character of Don Juan and his unobtrusive manner made him an influential citizen and he became president of the Monterey Council. He died at the age of 60, leaving a large family. His eldest son, Mariano, who had been sent to Peru to be educated, was made executor of the estate. The son succeeded in obtaining patents for all three of the ranchos, for Zanjones in 1866, Guadalupe in 1869, and Chualar in 1872.

The town of Chualar with its pepper trees stretches along Highway 101 for a quarter of a mile near the western boundary of Rancho Chualar. The next rancho to the south was Zanjones.

The Malarin house stood on Rancho Guadalupe, the first grant made to Don Juan. In the property settlement, Josefa Estrada, the widow, received one-half of the whole property. The remainder went to the ten children: Mariano, Ysabel, Concepción, Ramona, Urbano, María, Refugio, Josefa, Cristino, and Ignacio.

Along the river southeast of the Malarin estate

was Rancho Rincón de la Puente del Monte, four square leagues granted by Governor Gutiérrez to Teodoro Gonzales on September 20, 1836. A patent for 15,219 acres was given to him in 1866. Don Teodoro, a Mexican otter hunter, became a man of good standing and wealth and at one time served as *alcalde* in Monterey. His widow and sons later resided in San Francisco. The town of Gonzales, named for this family, lies within the bounds of this irregularly shaped rancho.

Southwest and across the river from the Gonzales property was Rancho Paraje de Sánchez. El Camino Real ran through this grant between Soledad Mission and the missions to the north. The 6,584 acres in this rancho were patented to C. Lugo and others in 1866.

The Salinas River curves in and out of the southwestern line of Rancho San Vicente. The town of Soledad is in the southern part of this nearly 20,000-acre grant made to Francisco Soto, Francisco Figueroa, and Estévan Munras (Munraz). On April 1, 1852, when the seven children and heirs of Estévan Munras filed their claim, it was stated that "possession had been had and enjoyed" under the grant.

Estévan Munras was an early Spanish trader at Monterey. His wife was Catalina Manzanelli of Tepic, Mexico, under whose name Ranchos Laguna Seca and San Francisquito were held. Don Estévan, unlike many of his compatriots, was prominent in aiding foreigners and quite ready for a change from Mexican political intrigues.

Across the river from Soledad and Rancho San Vicente lay the lands of Soledad Mission. In behalf of the church, Bishop J. S. Alemany was given patent in 1859 to 34 acres, containing orchards, vineyards, and springs. Feliciano Soberanes purchased 8,900 acres of the mission lands in June 1846, reputedly for $800, and his title to them was confirmed. It was reported at the time that the mission was in ruins and that travelers stopping there were grossly overcharged.

Three adobes occupied by members of the Soberanes family, which were located along the old thoroughfare El Camino Real, are still standing. Although the largest residence was almost destroyed by fire on January 5, 1935, three of the original 11 rooms were left standing and are in use. This remnant is hidden from view by a modern residence that has been erected on the site of the burned building. These structures stand, with other farm buildings, at the far left of the River Road near a bend in the road three-quarters of a mile east of its junction with Foothill Road. Less than half a mile farther down the River Road (this section of it is officially designated Fort Romie Road) stands another Soberanes adobe, also at the left, a charming cottage with blue walls and red roof. Another mile or less brings one to the restored Mission Nuestra Señora de la Soledad.

On Rancho Los Coches ("the pigs"), east of the mission beyond the turnoff to Paraiso Springs and Arroyo Seco, is an adobe structure that is being preserved by the state of California. It stands directly on the corner of the north–south freeway between Soledad and King City at the junction of the Arroyo Seco Road. This story-and-a-half building *(SRL 494)*, known as the Richardson adobe, faces the branch road. A porch extends along the entire front. The structure has had various uses: a family residence, a post office, a stage station, a house used by tenant farmers, and now the residence of the ranger in charge of Los Coches Rancho State Historical Monument. Bancroft says the grant of Los Coches was made in 1841 to María Josefa, daughter of Feliciano Soberanes. She was married to William Brunner Richardson, who built the adobe in 1843 and planted the row of black locusts in front in 1846.

Rancho Arroyo Seco, which adjoined Los Coches on the south, consisted of 16,523 acres. Its northwest corner was near the present junction of Paraiso Springs Road and Clark Road. For this property Joaquín de la Torre filed a claim founded on a grant of four square leagues that Governor Alvarado made to him on December 30, 1840. Don Joaquín was a Mexican patriot of energy and courage, active against incoming foreigners. Greenfield has grown up on the southeast boundary of this rancho. Southeast of Arroyo Seco was Rancho Poza de los Ositos, which was granted to Carlos Cayetano Espinosa by Governor Alvarado on April 16, 1839. This tract, consisting of 16,939 acres of rolling land lying on the west side of the Salinas River, was patented to the grantee on June 29, 1865.

Across the river from Arroyo Seco and Poza de los Ositos was Rancho San Lorenzo, stretching south along the river as far as San Lorenzo Creek. King City is located on the southern part. This grant of 21,884 acres, made by Governor Alvarado to Feliciano Soberanes in 1841, was in addition to Rancho Alisal already held by the grantee, who later purchased some of the land formerly belonging to Soledad Mission.

South of King City lay Rancho San Bernabe. Through it flowed the Salinas River. From its banks the rancho lands extended back to the hills on both sides. Two old grants made by Governor Alvarado were consolidated in this one rancho. The first grant was made to José Molina on March 10, 1841, and the second to Petronelo Ríos on April 6, 1842. Don Petronelo was a Mexican sergeant of artillery in San Francisco from 1827 to 1840. His wife was Caterina Ávila.

From the westernmost point of this rancho, a trail led up Pine Canyon and through the forest down to Rancho Milpitas. Somewhere along that trail near the summit is an immense pile of jagged rocks and within them a cave frequently used by early travelers as a shelter at night. On top of these rocks, unseen until the perilous ascent is made, is a flat piece of ground several acres in extent. This is said to be the hidden pasture where the bandit Vásquez concealed his stolen horses.

The King City–Jolon road passes through this rancho. At the left, two miles after crossing the river bridge at King City, one may see a fragment of the thick adobe walls of an abandoned ranch house originally covered by a shingle roof. In this building lived David Leese, son of Jacob P., as manager of the ranch. During his residence there

with his family, the place was struck by lightning and burned to such an extent that it was never repaired.

San Bernabe, consisting of 13,296 acres, was confirmed in 1855 to Henry Cocks, a famous justice of the peace in the county, and was patented to him in 1873. Before the destruction of the adobe, the land had been purchased by J. B. R. Cooper. David Leese, to whom the management of the ranch had been given, was the nephew of Cooper's wife.

South of the San Bernabe lay Rancho San Benito, extending on both sides of the river. The little town of San Lucas is situated in its southeastern corner. Here, one and one-half square leagues were granted to Francisco García by Governor Alvarado on March 11, 1842. The patent for 6,671 acres was given in 1869 in the name of James Watson, deceased claimant. Watson was an Englishman engaged in trading in Monterey who had married Mariana Escamilla. The original grantee, Francisco García, built an adobe house of eight rooms with a tile roof on the bank of the Salinas River about two miles northwest from San Lucas. The river has so changed its course since that time that it no longer flows near the house, a tiny remnant of which still stands on an embankment in an open field about one mile west of Highway 101. One wall of the house was constructed with openings to shoot through. A 20-year-old son of the family was ambushed by Indians and killed on his return journey from Monterey, where he had gone with an ox-team load of hides to be sold. The house was occupied by the patentee until the year before his death in 1865. The sharp-eyed may see the ruin from the highway, far in the distance across the river, but there is no access to it at this point. A private farm road leads one and one-half miles to it along the west side of the river from the far end of the bridge southwest of San Lucas.

The southernmost rancho in the Salinas River region was San Bernardo, composed of 13,346 acres of rich bottom lands which reached up the river to Sargent's Canyon. It was founded on a grant made by Governor Alvarado to Mariano and Juan Soberanes on June 16, 1841. At its northern line it joined Rancho San Lucas. San Ardo, a station on the Southern Pacific Railroad, is about midway of the long narrow tract. The property was owned by M. Brandenstein at the time the right of way was purchased for the railroad, and he stipulated that trains must stop at the town when flagged.

Rancho San Lucas

The group of adobe buildings composing the headquarters of Rancho San Lucas lies about six miles south and west of the town of San Lucas. The grant of this land was made to Rafael Estrada in 1842, and the original ranch house, no longer standing, was built near the northern line of the rancho west of the Salinas River. The present headquarters are at the southwestern corner of the grant.

James McKinley, a Scottish sailor who deserted ship at Monterey in the 1820's, came into possession of 8,875 acres, according to the patent of February 23, 1872. Alberto Trescony, who came to California from Italy in 1842, purchased the land in 1862 and moved there with his family. He added adjoining properties to his holdings until he possessed many thousand acres over which his herds of cattle ranged. The patent for the branding iron used in roundups was issued by the last Mexican governor of Alta California. The iron is a treasured relic of those early years. Descendants of Alberto Trescony, who still own a large part of the estate, now give their attention to grain farming as well as cattle raising.

The six adobe structures built by the Tresconys lie in a pocket valley protected by hills and trees, one and one-half miles from the Paris Valley Road. The main dwelling house, built in 1865, consists of one story only. It has thick walls and is nearly surrounded by porches. The barn is of two stories, both made of adobe bricks. The blacksmith shop is roofed with handmade tiles removed from a building on Rancho San Benito, also purchased by Alberto Trescony.

Ranchos El Pescadero and Punta de Pinos

The land contained in these two grants occupies the greater part of the area of the Monterey Peninsula, and through both of them runs the scenic Seventeen-Mile Drive.

Rancho Punta de Pinos was the more northern of the two. For this tract three men, Jacob P. Leese, Milton Little, and Santiago Gleason, as joint claimants, petitioned the Land Commission on September 2, 1852, their claim being founded upon a grant made by Governor Figueroa to José María Armenta on May 13, 1833. Later other names were substituted for these claimants: Henry de Graw for Leese, and Charles Brown for James H. Gleason. Finally Milton Little's interest, in addition to that of Leese, was absorbed by De Graw. The courts approved the claim, and patent for 2,667 acres was issued on November 19, 1880. Point Pinos, southwest headland of Monterey Bay, early and present site of the Light Station, is the north limit of the rancho.

The whole shoreline of Rancho El Pescadero, extending from near Seal Rocks to Carmel, is threaded by the Seventeen-Mile Drive, of which Cypress Point is the most western limit and the most famous spot on the route. At this point on the rugged shoreline are found the picturesque Monterey cypress trees, whose branches have been grotesquely bent and gnarled through long exposure to ocean winds. Few species of cypress—trees of ancient origin—are found in the state, and *Cupressus macrocarpa Hartweg* (commonly known as the Monterey cypress) has a restricted habitat and is found only on the coast adjacent to the mouth of the Carmel River.

Because of early fishing activities carried on at the water's edge on the southern part of Monterey Peninsula, the name Pescadero ("place where fishing is done") was given to the rocks off the shore in Carmel Bay, to a point to the west of them, and to the rancho itself.

The grant, containing one league, was made by Nicolás Gutiérrez to Fabian Barreto on February 29, 1836. Other names associated with its ownership were John Frederick Romie, who came to California in 1841 and bought the rancho before he died in 1848; John C. Gore, who filed a claim for it on February 9, 1853, which was rejected by the court; and David Jacks, whose name was substituted for that of Gore and to whom a patent for 4,426 acres was given in 1868. The grantee, Fabian Barreto, a Mexican who came to Monterey in 1827, became a permanent resident of the place and married Carmen García, who outlived him. As an aftermath of the Bear Flag depredations the widow filed a claim for $2,582.

That Gore actually lived on the land is proved by the map made by the survey of 1864, which shows the location of his house near the present Pebble Beach. A cistern, remembered as being filled about 1926, was in an open space among the trees near the Gore home.

Both of these ranchos, Punta de Pinos and El Pescadero, became part of the large holdings of David Jacks, who also owned Rancho Aguajito adjoining El Pescadero on the east. In the 1870's Jacks developed a tent city in the cove on the bayshore northwest of the city of Monterey. He patterned it after one on the Atlantic Coast and named it Pacific Grove. This tent city has grown to be a city of broad paved streets lined with houses.

Standing two miles southeast of downtown Monterey in the suburbs is the old Castro adobe of Rancho Aguajito, now restored by the Jacks family. It stands at 1224 Castro Road facing the Del Monte Golf Course.

Ranchos along the Río Carmelo

The novelist Mary Austin used this region as the setting for *Ysidro,* an idyl of mission days in the quiet Carmel Valley. Six land grants were recognized and patented by the United States.

Los Tularcitos, the great triangular tract of 26,581 acres covering the Buckeye Ridge and Burnt Mountain, contains a short stretch of the upper part of the Carmel River. As the river flows through the southwestern corner of the rancho, Los Tularcitos Creek drains into it. This rancho was granted by Governor Figueroa to Rafael Gómez on December 1, 1834. In April 1852 his widow, Josefa Antonia Gómez de Walters, and his children filed claim for the property; they received a patent in 1866.

Some time later, Rancho Los Tularcitos was acquired by Andrew J. Ogletree, and in the late 1880's it passed into the hands of Alberto Trescony, owner of Rancho San Lucas. Although he sold portions of it, Trescony still owned about 14,500 acres of the original grant at the time of his death. Some 2,000 acres remain in the Trescony family today. The main portion, however, which still bears the name Rancho Tularcitos, was acquired by the Marble family in 1924. This consists of about 8,000 acres, to which the Marbles added 6,000 acres of adjacent land that was not part of the Tularcitos grant. On a hill south and across the road from the Marble residence is a fragment of adobe wall, all that is left of the original ranch house of Los Tularcitos. The Marble home overlooks a seven-acre tule-bordered lake, from which the ranch received its name of "the little tules." These landmarks are on Tularcitos Road, about two miles east of the junction with Carmel Valley Road.

There were two ranchos Los Laureles along the river: the larger one, through which the river flows, joined Los Tularcitos on the west; the smaller rancho lay to the west of the larger. The larger, granted to José Manuel Boronda and Vicente Blas Martínez by Manuel Jimeno on September 19, 1839, contained one and one-half square leagues, which were patented to Don José Manuel and his son, Juan de Mata, on August 9, 1866. The original adobe home, with later additions, is still standing between Carmel Valley Road and the river to the east of Los Laureles Grade junction. It is on the west side of Boronda Road one-tenth of a mile south of Carmel Valley Road and is occupied as a private residence. The old part of it is of unusual architectural interest. It is 64 feet long and 19 feet wide. The thick-walled rooms are well preserved; roughly squared beams of the simple ceilings are carefully fitted. The ceiling of one room shows an interesting example of veneering done in soft wood.

The smaller Laureles rancho lay wholly north of the river. It was given by Governor Micheltorena to José Agricio on March 4, 1844, and its 718 acres were patented to Leander Ransom on April 18, 1871.

Also on the north side of the river, beyond the oblong tract granted to James Meadows, an Englishman who married a native Indian woman, was Rancho Cañada de la Segunda, which reached west to Carmel. It originally consisted of one league given by the prefect Castro to Lazaro Soto in 1839. The eastern end lies in the Cañada de la Segunda. Patent for this was issued to Fletcher M. Haight in 1859, after the death of Andrew Randall, who had filed a claim for it on February 5, 1853.

On the south bank of the river was Rancho Potrero de San Carlos, granted by Governor Alvarado to Fructuoso del Real on December 12, 1839. In 1852 claim to this was filed with the Land Commission by Joaquín Gutiérrez and María Estefana, daughter of the original grantee, to whom patent for 4,307 acres was issued on June 9, 1862. This property was purchased by Bradley V. Sargent in 1858. Back from the river this land becomes hilly. Potrero Canyon, stretching down from the mountains, opens out upon a place that was once an Indian ranchería, composed of a cluster of small and very plain adobe structures. The adobe house in which the owners of the rancho lived, formerly standing a half-mile farther up the canyon, has disappeared. It was a symmetrical, five-room dwelling with the usual wooden kitchen addition in which Indian servants prepared food for the household. Rancho San Carlos and Potrero Canyon are now closed to the general public. Residents have access by a private bridge across the Carmel River.

Bradley Sargent purchased other lands adjoining Rancho Potrero de San Carlos. One of his purchases was Rancho San José y Sur Chiquito, located west of Rancho Potrero de San Carlos and stretching from the lower reaches of the Carmel River along the coast southward. This rancho had been granted on April 16, 1839, to Marcelino Escobar, and for it José Castro filed claim on February 2, 1853. After lengthy litigation this tract was finally patented May 4, 1888, to J. S. Emery and N. W. Spaulding as administrators for the will of Abner Bassett and his widow, successors in interest to the deceased José Castro. In the northern part of this rancho near the river stood an adobe called "Las Virgenes," because tradition says that local Indians saw there apparitions of the Virgin Mary.

Sargent also purchased Rancho San Francisquito, lying to the southeast of Rancho Potrero de San Carlos. Rancho San Francisquito, two square leagues, had been granted by Governor Castro to Doña Catalina Manzanelli, wife of Estévan Munras, on November 7, 1835. For this land, a joint petition had been filed by José Abrego for himself and by Milton Little for the minor heirs of William R. Garner. To these claimants patent was given in 1862 for 8,814 acres.

The San Francisquito ranch house is mentioned in the writings of Robert Louis Stevenson as the place where he, an invalid, was visited by Captain Wright. There is a tumbledown cabin in Robinson Canyon that some believe is the building in which Stevenson stayed. It is nine miles south of Carmel Valley Road via Robinson Canyon Road.

Ranchos on the Eastern Boundary of the County

Following the boundary line between Monterey and San Benito counties from north to south, one locates Ranchos Vega del Río del Pájaro, Cañada de la Carpintería, Los Carneros, Los Vergeles, and Ciénega del Gabilán.

Vega del Río del Pájaro ("a meadow along the Pajaro River") covered the level plain along the river and stretched south into the hills, none of which reach an altitude much higher than 500 feet. It was granted to Antonio María Castro on April 17, 1820, by Don Pablo Vicente de Solá under the Spanish régime and was recognized and confirmed by Don José Figueroa, political chief under the Mexican rule, on June 14, 1833. The grantee was probably the first permanent settler in the now productive Pajaro Valley. He was a soldier retired from military life in 1809, and about the time of receiving this land from the Spanish authorities he was one of the alternates for the five electors of the province.

Thirty years after the Spanish grant, Juan Miguel Anzar filed a petition on June 28, 1852, as claimant for this rancho but died before his title was clear. His widow married Frederick A. McDougal. She too died, leaving as heirs her husband and her four children, to whom the 4,310 acres of the rancho were patented on January 18, 1864. Not far from the river, the highway and railway now run a parallel course across the rancho, the name of which is perpetuated in Vega Road. This road runs westward into the San Cayetano ranch of the Vallejos, as do the highway and railroad.

Adjoining the southeastern corner of Rancho Vega del Río del Pájaro lay Rancho Cañada de la Carpinteria, a tract of hilly and mountainous land granted by Governor José Castro to Joaquín Soto on September 25, 1835. The patent for 2,236 acres was given to the heirs of the grantee in 1873. At Carpinteria Avenue and the highway, near the center of this area, there was once a small settlement called Dunbarton.

The next rancho to the south, Los Carneros, extended a little way across the present county line. This, like Vega del Río del Pájaro, was finally patented to Frederick A. McDougal and his stepchildren after the death of his wife, who was the claimant.

To the southeast of Los Carneros was Rancho Los Vergeles with its eastern boundary across the county line. This rancho was founded upon two grants to José Joaquín Gómez, one made on August 2, 1834, by Governor Figueroa, the other on August 28 of the following year, by Governor Castro. The original name of the two combined was "Cañada en Medio y la Cañada de Ceboda." José Joaquín Gómez was a Mexican trader who, after coming to California in 1830 on the *Leonor*, became a customs officer in Monterey and thereafter held many positions of trust. His adobe, located on the direct route between Monterey and San José, was a favorite stopping place for travelers. It stood about six miles from Salinas at the bottom of the San Juan Grade.

Consul Thomas O. Larkin, on his way from Monterey to Yerba Buena, where he had sent his family for safety during the troubled months of the Bear Flag Rebellion, stopped at Los Vergeles on the night of November 15, 1846. When his whereabouts became known to the Californians camped in the Salinas Valley, one of them, José Antonio Chavez, determined to capture him. About midnight the consul was awakened and forced to accompany his captor to Castro's camp, where he was treated kindly but detained as a hostage.

Another visitor at Don Joaquín's home was William Tecumseh Sherman, who relates the circumstances in his memoirs. In the course of duty Sherman was in Monterey for a short time in the winter of 1847. Wishing to see something of the country back from the coast, he set out on February 1 with one companion. "In the morning we crossed the Salinas Plain, about fifteen miles of level ground, taking a shot occasionally at wild-geese, which abounded there, and entering the well-wooded valley that comes out from the floor of the Gavillano. We had cruised about all day, and it was almost dark when we reached the house of a Señor Gomez, father of those who at Monterey [the evening before at an entertainment] had performed the parts of Adam and Eve. His house was a two-story adobe, and had a fence in front. It was situated well up among the foothills of the Gavillano, and could not be seen until within a few yards. We hitched our horses to the fence and went in just as Gomez was about to sit down to a tempting supper of stewed hare and tortillas. We were officers and *caballeros* and could not be ignored. After turning our horses to

grass, at his invitation we joined him at supper. The allowance, though ample for one, was rather short for three, and I thought the Spanish grandiloquent politeness of Gomez, who was fat and old, was not over-cordial. However, down we sat, and I was helped to a dish of rabbit, with what I thought to be an abundant sauce of tomato. Taking a good mouthful, I felt as though I had taken liquid fire; the tomato was *chili colorado*, or red pepper, of the purest kind. It nearly killed me, and I saw Gomez's eyes twinkle for he saw that his share of supper was increased. I contented myself with bits of meat, and an abundant supply of tortillas. Ord was better case-hardened and, stood it better. We staid at Gomez's that night, sleeping, as all did, on the ground, and the next morning we crossed the hill by the bridle-path to the old Mission of San Juan Bautista."

South of Los Vergeles and lying between Gabilan Creek and Gabilan Peak, which rises to an elevation of 3,169 feet on the eastern line of the grant, was the Ciénega del Gabilán, with its southern end extending into the Salinas Valley. (*Ciénaga* means "swamp or morass" and *gavilán* means "hawk." *Ciénega* and *gabilán* are variant Californian spellings.) This rancho was granted on October 26, 1843, by Governor Micheltorena to Antonio Chavez, who three years later captured Thomas O. Larkin at the neighboring Rancho Los Vergeles, as above related.

José Antonio Chavez had been brought to California from Mexico by Figueroa. In 1843, the year of receiving the grant, he was tax collector at Monterey and in 1846 he was a lieutenant under Castro. He was wounded in the battle of Natividad, but, befriended by prominent Californians, he escaped capture by remaining hidden. In 1848 he left Alta California and was afterward with Castro in Baja California. José Y. Limantour filed claim for this rancho in 1853, but Thomas O. Larkin received confirmation of it and afterward turned it over to Jesse D. Carr, who received patent to 48,781 acres in the 1860's.

Miscellaneous Ranchos

One square league of land called Rancho Noche Buena, lying near the bay northeast of the town of Monterey, was granted to Juan Antonio Muñoz on November 15, 1835, by Governor Castro. At that date, the grantee was 35 years old, a captain in the Mexican artillery with a wife, Manuela Cruz, and three children. The year following, he was exiled with Gutiérrez. In March 1853 José Monomany and Jaime de Rinz Monomany filed a claim for the property; and in 1854 five-sixths of it was confirmed to them. The other sixth was held for José Muñoz, infant heir of the original grantee. Both the railway and the highway which lead into Monterey from the north cross the entire length of this rancho, on which is now located part of the Fort Ord Military Reservation.

Governor José Figueroa granted the one square league of Rancho Saucito to Graciano Manjares on May 22, 1833; and for it John Wilson, Josiah H. Swain, and George C. Harris filed claim on February 23, 1853. This land was surveyed in

October 1858 and found to contain 2,212 acres, which were patented to them on October 7, 1862.

Little is known of Don Graciano, the original grantee, except that he married Maximiana Gongora and that, in 1836, their family consisted of five children. In 1842 he was *juez auxiliar*. The Saucito ranch house stood in the Canyon del Rey east of Monterey, on the northern part of the rancho close to the remains of a pear orchard said to have been planted in the 1880's. The Monterey–Salinas highway runs through the property from west to east. The aged pear trees are near the junction of this highway and Canyon del Rey Road.

East of Rancho Saucito lay Rancho Laguna Seca, granted to Doña Catalina Manzanelli in 1833 and 1834. Doña Catalina was the wife of Estévan Munras, grantee of San Vicente. She received patent for Rancho Laguna Seca, 2,180 acres, on November 24, 1865. The Laguna Seca ("dry lake") lies in the northeastern corner and the Canyon del Rey runs through the middle of the grant.

Two ranchos given out by Governor Alvarado lay along the Nacimiento River: the San Miguelito, to José Rafael Gonzales on July 21, 1841; and El Piojo, to Joaquín Soto on August 20, 1842. After José Rafael Gonzales filed his claim to San Miguelito, the court found that he had divested himself of all rights by a deed to his son Mauricio Gonzales; therefore, a patent for the 22,136 acres in question was issued to the latter in 1867. Stony Creek, rising in Los Padres National Forest, threads the mountainous northern part of this rancho and empties into the Nacimiento River, which lies along the southwestern line. The patentee had also another tract of land, Rancho Cholame, in the southern edge of the county, about one-half of the grant lying across the boundary in San Luis Obispo County. It had been given to him in 1844 by Governor Micheltorena; and in 1852 Ellen, widow of Charles White, filed claim upon it. The ranch house was on the Monterey County end of the grant south of Gold Hill.

Rancho El Piojo, lying adjacent to both San Miguelito and Los Ojitos, has a stretch of the Nacimiento River in its southwestern corner. The San Carpojo Trail enters the rancho from the west, crosses the river, and continues almost due east the entire length of the rancho. El Piojo ("louse") Creek, a tributary of the Nacimiento, makes its way from the middle of the rancho to the southeastern corner.

There were two ranchos Los Carneros in Monterey County: one (mentioned in the previous section) was in a hilly part near the eastern boundary, the other was just east of the Elkhorn Slough. The latter consisted of 4,482 acres granted to David Littlejohn in 1834 and patented to his heirs in 1866.

Rancho Corral de Tierra lay south of Rancho El Toro and adjoined the northern boundary of Los Laureles. It was patented in 1876 to Henry McCobb, whose claim was founded on a grant made by Nicolás Gutiérrez to Francisco Figueroa for his daughter Guadalupe.

Three grants named San Lorenzo were given in the county, one on the Salinas River, one on the San Benito County boundary line, and one in the upper part of the San Lorenzo Canyon. The last-named, 22,264 acres, covered Peach Tree Valley and extended from both sides of it into rough broken hills. It was granted to Francisco Rico on November 16, 1842, and was patented to the heirs of Andrew Randall on June 4, 1870.

The Battle of Natividad

The battle of Natividad took place on November 16, 1846, about 20 miles northeast of Monterey and seven miles from the present town of Salinas. A bronze plaque now marks the site (*SRL 651*), at the foot of the old San Juan Grade, over which the stagecoach traveled from Monterey to San Juan Bautista in the 1850's.

There was nothing decisive about the battle of Natividad, its chief significance being that it was the only severe engagement that took place in the north during the revolt of the Californians against the military occupation of the Americans under Commodore Stockton. It was different from the southern engagements, in that no regular United States troops took part in it, the participants being an American recruiting and foraging party under Captains Charles D. Burrass and Bluford K. Thompson and a small band of Californian patriots.

Burrass with 500 horses and Thompson with about 35 men were on their way to Monterey to join Frémont, who was preparing to go to Los Angeles to reinforce Stockton. On hearing of this, a group of native Californians under Manuel Castro determined to hamper Frémont. Making a night march from Monterey toward San Juan, Castro and his men met Burrass and Thompson at Natividad. In the skirmish that followed, four Americans were killed and as many wounded, while the Californians sustained a somewhat greater loss.

The marker is near the junction of the San Juan Grade and Crazy Horse Road. The original San Juan Grade is now called Old Stage Road.

Colton Hall

Colton Hall (*SRL 126*) was erected in 1847–49 by Rev. Walter Colton, chaplain of the United States frigate *Congress* and named alcalde of Monterey by Commodore Stockton. On August 15, 1846, in company with Robert Semple, he established the *Californian*, the first newspaper to be published in California. His journal, *Three Years in California*, published in New York in 1850, is one of the most fascinating books on the early American period in California and is a mine of information for the historian.

Colton Hall "was for many years the most useful building in the city, having been used as a constitutional hall, a schoolhouse, a courthouse, a public assembly hall and a place of religious worship." California's first Constitutional Convention met at the hall September 1 to October 13, 1849. The 48 delegates held their sessions on the upper floor, which ran the length of the main building. Robert Semple was chairman and William G. Marcy, secretary. While Monterey was county seat of Monterey County from 1850 to 1873, Colton Hall was used as the county courthouse. One of the first schools in California was held in this building, in 1849, by Rev. Samuel H. Willey, later prominent in the founding of the College of California, predecessor of the University of California.

Unlike most of Monterey's early buildings, Colton Hall was distinctly of the old New England academy style. Rev. Mr. Willey, who was one of the chaplains of the Constitutional Convention, says in his reminiscences that when he landed from the steamship *California,* on February 3, 1849, he was struck by the contrast between the architecture of this plain white building and the many Spanish adobe cottages and mansions around it. "It might have dropped down from a New England village," was his comment.

The building itself is a two-story structure of stone and remains today in excellent condition. The state of California made provisions in 1903 for its preservation, protection, and improvement, and it is now owned by the city of Monterey. It was permanently marked by a bronze tablet placed by the Native Sons of the Golden West on June 3, 1931.

California's First Convent School

The first convent school in California was established at Monterey in the spring of 1851 by three Dominican Sisters who had arrived in California in 1850. The old adobe building in which the school was held proved to be in very bad condition, and, as population in Monterey was diminishing while that around San Francisco Bay was rapidly increasing, the sisters, in 1854, decided to move to Benicia, then a more central location.

Concepción Argüello, the story of whose life is closely associated with San Francisco and Benicia, was the first novice to enter the Convent of St. Catherine at Monterey, and when the school was moved to its new location, she was transferred to Benicia.

After the removal of the convent to Benicia, the old building at Monterey was used as a chapel and parish house for a time. Later, it was rented to private parties and rapidly fell into decay. Soon after 1885 it was torn down. The site where it stood is on the northwest corner of Calle Principal and Franklin Street and is now occupied by the San Carlos Hotel.

The Moss Landing Whaling Station

One of the most important whaling stations on the coast of California in early days was at Moss Landing, about 15 miles northeast of Monterey. The whale fishery, one of the chief industries on the coast for a period of nearly 35 years, was finally abandoned in 1888. The old Moss Landing station has now disappeared. This landing was named for Charles Moss, who had a farm near the Five-Mile House on the Santa Cruz–Watsonville road. He and a partner, Beadle, after starting a line of schooners at the landing in 1865, constructed a wharf to facilitate the loading of freight. Within a year, Moss moved his family from the ranch to a house near the landing, and later he moved to Texas.

The Adobes of Old Monterey

At the western entrance to Old Monterey stands one of the earliest of its historic dwellings, the Casa Munras, one of the first homes to be built outside the original presidio grounds. It was erected by Estévan Munras, who came to California as a merchant. Considerably remodeled and incorporated into a hotel, the Munras adobe stands at 656 Munras Avenue, opposite what was once the southwest corner of the old presidio grounds.

Alvarado Street is the main street of Monterey, where the old and the new mingle and into which run other streets with memories of Spanish California. From the waterfront it leads up the hill to a group of dwellings rich in historic interest, centering about the Larkin House.

The Larkin House *(SRL 106),* located on the corner of Calle Principal and Jefferson Street, is typical of the Spanish-Californian type of architecture which prevailed throughout Alta California: softly tinted adobe walls, cool veranda and picturesque upper balcony, iron-barred windows, and walled gardens, with rose and fig trees. It was built in 1834 by Thomas Oliver Larkin, who had come to Monterey as a merchant in 1832 and was appointed American consul in 1843. Being thoroughly acquainted with conditions in the province, he rendered important service as consul and confidential agent, and his policies helped to prepare the way for annexation of California. The old house is now a unit of Monterey State Historical Monument, and has been registered by the Department of the Interior as a National Historic Landmark.

The House of the Four Winds *(SRL 353),* built about 1830, stands at 540 Calle Principal. It was used as a residence for many years, but in 1846 the first hall of records in the state of California was housed there, and the first recorder in Monterey had his home as well as his office in the building. Now the Monterey Civic Club uses it. The picturesque name was derived from the fact that it had a weathervane, the first in Monterey.

Between the Larkin House and the House of the Four Winds is a small one-room adobe built by Larkin in 1834 and known as Sherman's Head-

Sherman's Headquarters and Larkin House, Monterey

quarters. It is an integral part of the architecture of the old Larkin garden, with its redwoods and palms and fig trees, and may be reached through the walled patio of the big house. Here, in 1847–49, Lieutenant William Tecumseh Sherman of Civil War fame had his civil and military headquarters.

The Cooper House, located at 508 Munras Avenue, formerly California Street, is one of the largest adobes left in northern California. It was built in 1826 by Captain J. B. R. Cooper, who was a native of Alderney Island, England, and a pioneer in California in 1823. Cooper influenced Thomas O. Larkin, his half-brother by his mother's second marriage, to come to California and to establish himself at Monterey as a merchant. Cooper himself married Encarnación Vallejo, a sister of Mariano G. Vallejo. In 1864 he moved to San Francisco, taking up residence at 821 Bush Street. The Cooper adobe is now more generally known as the Molera House.

A quaint adobe at 599 Polk Street, with a delightful garden opening at the side on Hartnell Street, was built about 1832 by José de la Torre, a Mexican alcalde, and was the first federal court building in California. The Cooper House and barn are near neighbors on the northeast at Munras Avenue, while across the way on the north side of Polk is the Casa Amesti, a two-story, balconied adobe built about 1825 by José Amesti. Don José was a Catalonian who had come to California in 1822 and who, in 1824, had married Mariano G. Vallejo's sister Prudenciana. The adobe is now owned by the National Trust for Historic Preservation.

On the northwest corner of Webster and Abrego streets is the one-story Abrego adobe, built by José Abrego in the 1830's. Bayard Taylor, in his *Eldorado,* describes an evening party that he attended in this house in 1849, and also comments that José Abrego, having amassed a substantial fortune within a few years, was the most industrious Californian he had seen in the country.

The Francisco Pacheco House, later known as the Malarin House because his son-in-law Mariano Malarin, son of Juan Malarin, resided there, is a picturesque two-story adobe located on the southwest corner of Abrego and Webster streets opposite the Abrego House. It was used for a time as a hospital but is now a private men's club. It was built in 1840 by Francisco Pérez Pacheco, a wealthy landowner who came from Mexico in 1819. He is buried in the San Carlos Church directly in front of the main altar.

On Houston Street between Pearl and Webster is the Robert Louis Stevenson House *(SRL 352),* where the Scottish poet and author of *Treasure Island* lived for nearly three months in the autumn of 1879. His attachment for Mrs. Fannie Van de Grift Osbourne, whom he had met in France, brought Stevenson to California. This proved to be one of the most decisive steps he had ever taken, for both his character and the entire trend of his life were influenced by this visit to the West. In Monterey some of his greatest friendships were matured; among them were those of Fannie Osbourne, who became his wife; her sister, Nellie Sanchez, his amanuensis; and Jules Simoneau, his lifelong friend. Stevenson occupied two airy rooms in the ell of the house, with five sunny windows opening on the balcony to the west. The place is now a unit of Monterey State Historical Monument.

Directly back of Colton Hall on Dutra Street is one of Monterey's most picturesque adobes, the Casa Vásquez *(SRL 351),* set in an old-fashioned garden amid a bower of trees. Now a city office building, it was once the home of Dolores Vásquez, sister of Tiburcio Vásquez, California's most ruthless bandit, who terrorized the stage roads up and down the state in the 1870's.

On the northwest corner of Alvarado and Pearl streets is a two-story adobe *(SRL 348)* now used for stores. Here, it is said, lived Juan Bautista Alvarado, provisional governor of California under Mexican rule from 1836 to 1842 and known to his contemporaries as the "silver-tongued" orator because of his brilliant eloquence and great personal magnetism. This Alvarado house is only one of several in various parts of the state in which Don Juan is said to have lived. Another in Monterey is at 510 Dutra Street.

On Monterey's quaint and picturesque waterfront is the so-called Old Whaling Station with its vivid memories of high adventure on many seas. It was built in 1855 by David Wight as a residence. Later it became a boardinghouse for Portuguese whalers. Today it is again a private home. The sidewalk in front of the house, at 391 Decatur Street, is still paved with whalebones, placed there by gallant sea captains many years ago. A stone wall, crowned with red tile, encloses an old-fashioned flower garden at the rear, while a balcony in front looks out from the second story over the encircling harbor with its multitude of gay yachts and fishing boats.

One door to the west, at 351 Decatur Street, stands the first brick house in California. It was built for Gallant Duncan Dickenson, son of a Virginia planter, who came overland to California from Missouri in 1846. The main part of the house was erected in 1847, but the wings were never completed, as the gold rush took the owner away to the mines.

California's first theater *(SRL 136),* a long rectangular adobe built by Jack Swan in 1843, was originally a sailors' boardinghouse and saloon, and was first used for amateur dramatics by four soldiers and a small local group in 1847, and later by members of Colonel J. D. Stevenson's regiment of New York Volunteers. The building, which was restored in 1917, is now part of Monterey State Historical Monument and stands at the corner of Pacific and Scott streets about one block northwest of the Pacific Building. It was reopened as a theater in 1937.

The Pacific House *(SRL 354),* at the junction of Alvarado Street, Calle Principal, and Scott Street, was originally a hotel built in 1835–47 by James McKinley, a Scotsman who had come to California in the 1820's. For many years the Presbyterian Church held services in this building. Now it belongs to Monterey State Historical Monument and is open to the public as a historical and Indian museum. At the rear, a beautiful patio, bright with flowers and trees and musical with the murmur of a fountain, breathes the spirit of old Spain. A short distance away, at Scott and Olivier streets, is the Casa del Oro (SRL 532), also a part of Monterey State Historical Monument. It is said that gold dust was left here for safekeeping—hence the name "house of gold."

The Casas Gutiérrez (SRL 713), adjoining adobes on Calle Principal near Madison Street, became part of Monterey State Historical Monument in 1954 but are currently being leased to businesses. One of Monterey's—and California's—most beautiful adobe homes is also part of the State Monument but is not open to the public. This is the Casa Soberanes (SRL 712), the "House with the Blue Gate," at 336 Pacific Street. Built about 1830 by José Estrada, it derives its name from Feliciano Soberanes, who purchased it from Estrada. Since 1941 it has been the home of Mayo Hayes O'Donnell, noted Monterey historian. She presented it to the state in 1953 but retained a life interest in the property.

The House of the Sherman Rose was the setting for a legendary romance linking the names of General William Tecumseh Sherman and the pretty Señorita María Ygnacia Bonifacio, or Doña Nachita, as she was sometimes called. The gallant young American, then a lieutenant, called several times at the rose-bowered casa where the señorita lived. On one of these visits, so the story goes, he unpinned a rose from his uniform and planted it in her garden, saying that if it took root and grew, their love would endure. The flower did grow into a marvelous rose tree which almost covered the adobe and which was, for years, the admiration of hundreds of tourists. But because Sherman never returned and Señorita Bonifacio never married, the legendary threads of romance were gradually woven about the old house. A bank building now stands in its place on Alvarado Street at Bonifacio Place. The house was reconstructed in 1922 on Mesa Road as the home of the artist Percy Gray, and a part of the original rose tree was transplanted to the Municipal Rose Garden.

The House of the Sherman Rose, however, has a more real association with the name of Robert Louis Stevenson, for it was here that his fiancée, Mrs. Fannie Van de Grift Osbourne, and her sister, Nellie Sanchez, lived with Señorita Bonifacio. Stevenson was a frequent visitor at the place, and there he began The Amateur Emigrant, gathered notes for "The Old Pacific Capital," and wrote The Pavilion on the Links, as well as the unfinished work "A Vendetta of the West."

In addition to the adobes and other structures mentioned above, the following are still standing. At 177 Van Buren Street is the Doud House (frame). Pierce Street has the Gordon House (frame) at 526, another Casa de la Torre at 502, and the Casa de Jesús Soto at 460. On Pacific Street one finds the Merritt House at 386, and the

Casa Madariaga, Monterey

Casa Serrano (headquarters of the Monterey History and Art Association) at 412. At the corner of Pacific and Franklin streets is the Capitular Hall, and at the south end of Friendly Plaza facing Pacific Street is the Underwood-Brown adobe. Hartnell Street has the Stokes House at 500 and Frémont's Headquarters at 539. Alvarado Street contains the Casa Sánchez at 412, and the Casa Rodríguez-Osio at 378. The Estrada adobe, restored in the 1960's, is at 456 Tyler Street. The first French Consulate, an adobe originally standing at Fremont and Abrego streets, was reconstructed in 1932 at the edge of Lake El Estero. The Casa Madariaga stands on Abrego Street opposite the Casa Pacheco, and the Casa Buelna is on Mesa Road. Casa Joaquín Soto is at 5 Via Joaquin off El Dorado Street. Casa Boronda (1817), one of Monterey's oldest buildings, is at the end of Boronda Lane south of Fremont Street.

These are only a few of the many adobes built in Monterey during the time that it flourished. As late as the 1890's, Pacific Street, Alvarado Street, and Calle Principal were lined with adobe buildings, most of which have been demolished to give way to more modern structures, and now not a half-dozen can be found on any one of these thoroughfares. Nevertheless, Monterey has done more than most California cities to preserve the tangible evidence of its past, and in this it has set an example that others would do well to follow. The Monterey History and Art Association has marked virtually all of the city's historic buildings, and a "path of history" has been painted on the streets to enable the traveler to find them with ease.

The Pear Orchard

Since its name is given on few maps, the location of the "Pear Orchard" on Dutra Creek is known principally to persons residing in the coast area south of Monterey Bay. Only one pear tree, with a diameter of 40 inches, now remains to give reason for the name, but it has as companions perhaps a dozen old olive trees. J. Smeaton Chase, in his classic ramble on horseback along the California coast trails early in the twentieth century, turned aside to visit this pear orchard. He found the pear tree to be oaklike in its dimensions, "the Nestor of mortal pears"; and in comparing the olive trees with those at the missions he decided that they could be little less than a century old.

The origin of the place is given by tradition to the period of the first missions. It is said that the priests maintained there a station and residential quarters for the workers in a silver mine farther up Dutra Creek, the northwest fork of San Carpojo Creek, which enters the Pacific in San Luis Obispo County.

This mine is locally called the "Priest Mine." It is said that the Indians took silver from it before the Spaniards came, and that afterward, under the direction of the fathers, it was mined more systematically and the ore carried over the trail to the San Antonio Mission. Aged Indians described the location of the mineral deposit as being north of the Pear Orchard, where the trail passes a pine tree. At this point, a distant view of the ocean is obtained.

Prospectors of a later day have found evidence of a small amount of excavation but have discovered no silver. The region is accessible only by rough trails.

Los Burros Gold Mines

The Los Burros Mining District in the Santa Lucia Range was organized in 1876. There were many Indian tales of gold being mined there by the Spaniards prior to that date, but nothing definite is known of such old workings. Placer mining had been carried on for years in the surface gravels of the Jolon area, where at one time over 100 Chinese were engaged in gold mining. It is difficult to estimate the amount of gold taken there, but Dutton and Tidball, who owned a store at Jolon patronized by the Chinese, took in $2,500 in gold dust in 1877–78. After the land where the washing was done was proved to be a part of Rancho Milpitas and the title to it was cleared, placer mining by the public was forbidden.

In 1887 W. D. Cruikshank, prospecting in Alder Creek over the summit of the range, found gold ore. Here he established Alder Creek Camp and developed the mine that he called the "Last Chance." Other mines opened later in the same area were the Mars, Manchester, Queen, King, and Grizzly. All supplies had to be brought from Jolon by pack train over the 3,600-foot summit, down the western slope to the Alder Creek Camp, at 2,800 feet. Mining of ore that ran under $12 a ton was not profitable.

Tassajara Hot Springs

From early records and folklore it appears that Tassajara (probably a corruption of "tasajera," a place where jerked meat is hung up to cure) has long been a gathering place for many peoples: first, the Indians, who made annual pilgrimages to receive the benefit of its waters; later, pioneer white men, who built a rough log cabin and baths; and today, the modern vacationist, who seeks the Tassajara Springs for his summer's outing.

The Tassajara Hot Springs are in the heart of Los Padres National Forest, 45 miles south of Salinas. Somewhere in the wilderness to the south the coast redwood (Sequoia sempervirens) finds its most southerly native habitat.

SOURCES

Andresen, Anna Geil. Historic Landmarks of Monterey, California. Privately printed, Salinas, 1917.

Bland, Henry Meade. Stevenson's California. The Pacific Short Story Club, San Jose, 1924.

Bolton, Herbert Eugene. Anza's California Expeditions. 5 vols. University of California Press, Berkeley, 1930.

——— Fray Juan Crespí, Missionary Explorer on the Pacific Coast, 1769–1774. University of California Press, Berkeley, 1927.

——— "Spanish Explorations in the Southwest," 1542–1706," Original Narratives of Early American History, XVII. Scribner, New York, 1916.

The California Missions, a Pictorial History. By the editorial staff of Sunset Books. Lane Book Co., Menlo Park, 1964.

Chapman, Charles E. A History of California: The Spanish Period. Macmillan, New York, 1921.

Chase, J. Smeaton. California Coast Trails. Houghton Mifflin, Boston, 1913.

Cleland, Robert Glass. From Wilderness to Empire. A History of California, ed. Glenn S. Dumke. Knopf, New York, 1959.

Colton, Walter. Three Years in California. A. S. Barnes & Co., New York, 1850.

Dana, Richard Henry, Jr. Two Years Before the Mast, a Personal Narrative of Life at Sea, ed. John Haskell Kemble. 2 vols. The Ward Ritchie Press, Los Angeles, 1964.

Davenport, William. The Monterey Peninsula. Lane Books, Menlo Park, 1964.

Davis, William Heath. Seventy-five Years in California (a reissue and enlarged, illustrated edition of Sixty Years in California). Ed: Douglas S. Watson. John Howell, San Francisco, 1929.

Elder, David Paul. The Old Spanish Missions of California. Paul Elder & Co., San Francisco, 1913.

Eldredge, Zoeth Skinner. The Beginnings of San Francisco from the Expedition of Anza, 1774, to the City Charter of April 15, 1850. Privately printed, San Francisco, 1912.

Engelhardt, Zephyrin. Mission Nuestra Señora de la Soledad. Mission Santa Barbara, Santa Barbara, 1929.

——— San Antonio de Padua, the Mission in the Sierra. Mission Santa Barbara, Santa Barbara, 1929.

Fisher, Anne B. The Salinas, Upside-Down River. Rinehart, New York, 1945.

Guinn, James Miller. History and Biographical Record of Monterey and San Benito Counties. Historic Record Co., Los Angeles, 1910.

Hunt, Rockwell D., and Nellie Van de Grift Sanchez. A Short History of California. Crowell, New York, 1929.

James, George Wharton. In and Out of the Old Missions of California. Little, Brown, Boston, 1916.

Jochmus, A. C. The City of Monterey, Its People, Its Connection with the World, Anecdotes, Legends, Romances, Achievements, 1542–1930. Privately published, Pacific Grove, 1930.

O'Donnell, Mayo Hayes. Monterey's Adobe Heritage. Monterey Savings & Loan Assn., Monterey, 1965.

Older, Mrs. Fremont. California Missions and Their Romances. Coward-McCann, New York, 1938.

Osbourne, Katharine D. Robert Louis Stevenson in California. A. C. McClurg & Co., Chicago, 1911.

Palou, Francisco. Historical Memoirs of New California. Translated into English from the manuscript in the archives of Mexico; ed. Herbert Eugene Bolton. University of California Press, Berkeley, 1926.

Peixotto, Ernest Clifford. Romantic California. Scribner, New York, 1910.

(Robinson, Alfred). Life in California. (H. G. Collins, Paternoster Row, London, 1845.) Wiley & Putnam, New York, 1846; republished in part by W. Doxey, San Francisco, 1891.

Robinson, W. W. "Mellow Monterey," Touring Topics, August 1927.

Smith, Frances Rand. The Mission of San Antonio de Padua. Stanford University Press, Stanford, 1932.

Stevenson, Robert Louis. "The Old Pacific Capital," in Across the Plains. Scribner, New York, 1905.

Taylor, Bayard. Eldorado, or Adventures in the Path of

Empire; Comprising a Voyage to California, Via Panama; Life in San Francisco and Monterey. H. G. Bohn, London, 1850; G. P. Putnam, New York, 1850 and 1864.

Wagner, Henry R. *Spanish Voyages to the Northwest*

Coast of America in the Sixteenth Century. California Historical Society, San Francisco, 1929.

Willey, Samuel Hopkins. Ms. of reminiscences, in possession of Native Sons of the Golden West Landmarking Committee.

Napa County

NAPA COUNTY was one of the original 27 counties. (Napa, accented as Napá in old documents, was the name of a tribe of Indians, said to be the bravest of all the California tribes, who once occupied the valley. They were almost completely annihilated by smallpox in 1838.) The city of Napa has always been the county seat.

The first courthouse was a two-story frame building erected in 1850, material for which is said to have been brought around the Horn from the East.

The First Trail

The first recorded expedition into what is now Napa County was made in 1823, when a party led by Francisco Castro, and accompanied by José Sánchez and Father José Altimira, made explorations north of San Francisco Bay preliminary to the founding of Mission San Francisco Solano.

The party left San Francisco in a launch on June 25 and went north to Mission San Rafael. Then they explored the valley from Petaluma to Sonoma, Napa, and Suisun. Sites at Petaluma, Sonoma, and Napa were favorably considered, but Sonoma was finally chosen for the mission, while Petaluma and Napa were to be used as mission cattle ranches.

Ranchos Caymus and La Jota

George Calvert Yount, "representative American pioneer, soldier, hunter, trapper, overlander and frontiersman," and a native of North Carolina, came to California from New Mexico with the Wolfskill party in 1831. After he had traveled almost the entire breadth of the continent, his name was linked with many early events in the history of the American occupation of the West. Soon after his arrival in California, he was engaged (1831–33) in hunting sea otter on the Santa Barbara Channel Islands and along the coast of the mainland. While at Santa Barbara in 1833 he made for Captain A. B. Thompson probably the first shingles that were fashioned in California. During the same year, Yount trapped beaver in San Francisco Bay and along the San Joaquin River. Toward the end of the year he proceeded to the missions at San Rafael and Sonoma, where his resourcefulness and ingenuity appealed to the padres, who engaged him to repair the mission buildings. General Vallejo had him make shingles for his house in Sonoma.

Mission life pleased Yount, and he stayed for almost three years. In 1835, when he was baptized into the Catholic faith at Mission San Rafael, his name, as was the custom in Alta California on such occasions, was rendered in the Spanish as Jorge Concepción Yount.

It was during this eventful year of Yount's career that he penetrated the Napa Valley with the purpose of making it his home. Here this hardy pioneer lived for many years practically alone except for his Indian neighbors. From the nearest tribe was derived the name "Caymus" which he bestowed upon his estate. Within a territory 50 miles long and 20 miles wide, there were six distinct Indian nations: the Napa, whose villages were situated near the site of the present city of Napa; the Ulucas, on Rancho Tulucay; the Caymus, near Yount's house two miles north of the site of Yountville; the Mayacomas, with their villages located near the mineral hot springs of Calistoga; the Calajomanas, at the Bale ranch; and the Soscols, on Soscol Creek and Rancho Soscol (in Solano County).

Through the influence of Father José L. Guigas of Mission San Francisco Solano at Sonoma and

of General M. G. Vallejo, Yount obtained the princely grant of Rancho Caymus on March 23, 1836. It consisted of 11,814 acres, lying in the heart of Napa Valley and including within its southern boundary a bit of what was later to become the northern edge of the town named in his honor, Yountville. Rancho Caymus was the first grant made in Napa County, and Yount's first dwelling was, at the time it was built in 1835 or 1836, the only white habitation inland between Sonoma and the settlements on the Columbia River.

A second grant, known as Rancho de la Jota, was made to Yount on October 23, 1843, and comprised 4,543 acres of timberland lying on Howell Mountain north of his first estate. The Seventh-Day Adventists founded Pacific Union College high on the western slope of the mountain. About four miles west of this thriving institution is the St. Helena Sanitarium, located on the lower slopes of the mountain overlooking Napa Valley.

Some of the mission Indians accompanied Yount to Rancho Caymus, where they helped him to build his first dwelling, a Kentucky blockhouse (probably the only one of its kind ever erected in California), as well as subsequent buildings. During his first years on the rancho, this blockhouse apparently served as a fort. It consisted of an upper room 22 feet square used as living quarters and a lower one 18 feet square fitted with portholes for protection against unfriendly tribes from the mountains.

The blockhouse, well stocked with food and other supplies, could have withstood a siege. Yount, however, found it unnecessary to use his fort except on rare occasions, because of his experience with the Indians, his fearlessness, and his ability to form alliances with the strongest rancherías.

In 1837 the blockhouse was superseded by a low, narrow building, its massive adobe walls, about 100 feet long, pierced by portholes. This so-called adobe "fort" antedated Sutter's by two years. It is said that the "fort" was torn down in 1870, but a map of that year shows it standing just below the point where the old road to Chiles Valley crossed the Napa River. Charles L. Camp of the University of California, who made a study of some of California's earliest pioneers, says that after Yount moved into his new adobe house (later the location of the Napa State Farm buildings), his daughter, Mrs. Vines, lived in the old fort.

The warm red tiles of this old adobe long remained a vivid memory to Mary E. Bucknall, Yount's granddaughter, who spoke of the place as the scene of pleasant childhood days. Before the broad veranda a little stream flowed; a tall hedge of sweet-scented Castilian roses enclosed the garden plot, while a clump of weeping willows gave shade on warm summer days.

James Clyman, adventurous surveyor-trapper from Virginia, visited Yount's homestead at three different times. The first date recorded was July 14, 1845, when he wrote in his diary that he had "passed a low range of hills and arrived at Mr.

Younts ranch or farm on a small stream running a saw and grist mill here we sat down to a Breakfast of good mutton and coffee having rode 60 miles without food and mostly without water."

Clyman remained with his hospitable host three days, resting his animals and watching the threshing activities of the Indians, who used half-wild horses, in the old Mexican manner. Leaving the ranch, Clyman "took a northern direction up the valley of the creek of which Mr. Younts mills are located."

The hunter again stopped at Yount's in August; in March of the following year, he "finally lift on the 31 the head of Napa valley and proceeded down 18 miles to Mr. Yount ... [who] has a Flouring and saw mill in opperation ... as far as I could learn this [is] the only Flouring mill in the province."

Although these references to Yount's mills are vague as to location, they prove beyond a doubt that he had both a flour mill and a sawmill on his property as early as 1845. Bancroft's statement that Yount had built a sawmill on Rancho de la Jota soon after 1843 seems to agree with the belief that he brought pine and redwood timbers from Howell Mountain for rebuilding his flour mill in 1854–55. Run by waterpower with a wide overshot wheel, this mill had a capacity of 30 bushels a day.

Fred Ellis, Yount's miller, leased the mill from 1865 to 1870, and later purchased it from the Yount heirs. The property was sold by Ellis's widow in 1915.

The locations of Yount's blockhouse, adobe, and mills (SRL 564) on Napa River are indicated by a stone monument with bronze plaque on Yount Mill Road about one and one-half miles east of State Highway 29, at a point about two miles northwest of Yountville. Nothing remains of the old flour mill except a few of the millstones fashioned by William Gordon, which are preserved on the ranch at this site. The location of Yount's later home is on the former Napa State Farm property to the west of Silverado Trail, north of the confluence of Conn and Rector creeks and east of Oakville. At this site the frame house Yount built for his wife still stands, although damaged by a fallen tree. The hardy pioneer died in 1865, and his grave (SRL 693) is in the cemetery at the northern outskirts of Yountville.

Rancho Carne Humana

In the 1830's a young English surgeon, Edward Turner Bale, landed at Monterey, where he practiced medicine for five or six years; for part of that time (1840–43) he was surgeon of the California forces by appointment of General Vallejo. Dr. Bale married Carolina Soberanes, a niece of the General, and became a naturalized citizen of Alta California. He received the grant of Rancho Carne Humana in Napa County, to which he went in 1843. By the time of his death in 1849, he was able to leave a rich estate to his widow, two sons, and four daughters.

Dr. Bale was a man of good education, hardy, bold, and adventurous. Unfortunately, "his debts and personal quarrels," says Bancroft, got him into many difficulties. One such complication arose between himself and Salvador Vallejo, the reckless, hot-tempered brother of the General and uncle of Bale's wife. The story goes that in 1844 Don Salvador paid the doctor and his wife a visit. "It seemed to Dr. Bale that the captain and the charming Señora . . . greeted each other too heartily. Their close family relationship and the fact that Salvador had just returned from dangerous Indian fighting did not seem sufficient reason for the warmth of those Latin embraces.

"The irate doctor quarrelled with Vallejo and challenged him to a duel. Well might the soldier smile: he was the best swordsman in the land.

"The duel was a farce. Vallejo skillfully twisted his cumbersome opponent into ridiculous knots. Then sardonically, he beat the Englishman with his sword as though it were a whip. In a rage, Bale drew a revolver and fired.

"Luckily, the attempted Murder was a failure. The intention, however, was counted more important than the deed. The doctor found himself in jail."

It was rumored that the Kelseys and other foreigners planned to rescue Bale, and there was much excitement for a time. Narrowly escaping with his life, Bale was finally released.

Rancho Carne Humana, within the confines of which the towns of St. Helena and Calistoga grew up in the 1850's, comprised the whole of that part of Napa Valley lying north of Rancho Caymus. It consisted of two leagues of fertile land skirted on the west and east by wooded hills and overshadowed on the north by the purple crags of Mount St. Helena.

An idyllic spot on the west side of Napa Valley beside a small stream was chosen for the Bale adobe. The site is on Whitehall Lane two miles south of St. Helena and one mile west of the highway. In the background a low, round hill covered with native woods once sheltered numerous wild creatures, among which the grizzly bear was the most formidable. To the south and east of the house site are a few ancient pear trees. To the west, beyond a huge, twisted oak tree, the half-obliterated roadway leads to the ford, beyond which lie the woods and the protecting hill. Between the hill and the stream are the remnants of a second orchard.

The Bale adobe is mentioned in the diary of James Clyman, who passed that way on July 16, 1845, to hunt wild game in Lake County. The orchards and cultivated fields which resulted later from Dr. Bale's efforts were not at all in evidence on that blistering hot summer day, if we are to judge from the hunter's rather disgusted account:

"Passed the farm house of Dr. Bales this hous looked desolate Enough standing on a dry plane near a dry black volcanis mountain allmost destitute [of] vegitation no fields garden of any kind of cultivation to be seen and about 10 or 12 Indians lying naked in the scorching sun finished the scenery of this rural domain."

The old adobe collapsed in 1931, and the ruins were subsequently cleared away.

The enterprising doctor had two mills on his land, a sawmill and a gristmill. The former, long since disappeared, was constructed for Bale by Ralph L. Kilburn in 1846. This mill was located north of St. Helena on the Napa River just a little northeast of Krug's wine cellar. As payment for its construction and subsequent operation, Bale gave Kilburn three-fourths of a league of land. During the winter of 1847, lumber for six buildings was cut and framed at this mill and shipped to Benicia and San Francisco. It also supplied the lumber for the first frame structure put up in the city of Napa. John York, who came to the valley in 1845, cut the first logs for Bale's sawmill.

The gristmill *(SRL 359)*, that picturesque landmark which stands beside the highway three miles northwest of St. Helena, was constructed in 1846, some of the work being done by F. E. Kellogg, who also was paid for his services in land. Fred W. Ellis, who afterward operated George Yount's mill on Rancho Caymus, worked at the Bale mill during the early 1860's.

While the Forty-niners were eagerly searching for gold in the hills and ravines of the Sierra Nevada, the great water wheel of Bale's mill was daily grinding the golden grain of the Upper Napa Valley into flour for the settlers, who, for a period of over 25 years, brought their grist here to be ground. The construction of this mill is interesting to the student of pioneer days. The lumber that went into the building (ultimately of three stories with a false store front) was cut from neighboring forests. The millstones were taken from the hill back of the mill, while the cogs in the great wheel, which made such a clatter when in operation, were all made of wood.

This mill, together with surrounding land, was at length given to the Native Sons of the Golden West by the widow of W. W. Lyman, owner of the mill for many years. It was restored through the efforts of the combined parlors of the Native Sons in Napa County, under the leadership of Past Grand President Bismarck Bruck, a grandson of Dr. Bale, and the Historic Landmarks Committee of the Native Sons. The restored mill was dedicated on June 21, 1925, and a large native boulder surmounted by a bronze plaque was placed at the site. As the years passed, however, it became evident that the mill was in need of permanent maintenance and protection from vandalism and fire. Through the efforts of Ivy M. Loeber, St. Helena historian, it became a Napa County Park with a resident caretaker, the Native Sons having deeded the property to the county in 1941. Living quarters for the caretaker were built inside the old granary. The old Bale Mill has become a tourist mecca, visited by thousands annually.

A number of American pioneers settled on Bale's rancho in the middle 1840's; among them in 1845 were John York, William and David Hudson, William Elliott and sons, William Fowler with sons William and Henry, William Hargrave, and Benjamin Dewell. They found Benjamin and Nancy Kelsey already living on what was soon to become the Kilburn place, owned in later years

Old Bale Mill, near St. Helena

by Peter Teal and located one mile southeast of Calistoga at 4531 Foothill Boulevard. This is now the Rockstroh property, and on it may be seen the hearthstone of the Kelsey house *(SRL 686)*. Nancy Kelsey, the first woman to cross the plains, arrived in California in 1841 with the Bidwell-Bartleson party. Ralph Kilburn came to Napa Valley in 1844. After Kilburn became established on the tract of land that he had received from Dr. Bale, Peter Storm, a Norwegian sailor, lived with him.

The incoming settlers of 1845 also found Samuel Kelsey living near Bale's mill with his wife and two or three children, while Elias Barnett already had a log cabin on what later became the George Tucker place. The Tucker house once stood across the highway from the Napa Valley State Park. This park, incidentally, is the site of the first church in the valley, the old White Church. Behind the marker for the church is the oldest cemetery in the valley. The church, Methodist Episcopal, was built in 1853 and named for its organizer and minister, the Rev. Asa White. The small structure had two separate front entrances, one for the men and one for the women, who sat on opposite sides of the church.

During the winter of 1845–46 John York built a log cabin for himself within the present city limits of Calistoga. This cabin, remodeled and incorporated in a larger house, stood until 1930 at Foothill Boulevard and Lincoln Avenue on the site *(SRL 682)* now occupied by a gasoline station. York had the distinction of planting the first wheat crop in this section of Napa County. Diagonally across the street, where another service station now stands, was David Hudson's cabin *(SRL 683)*, built about the same time as York's. Later Hudson fashioned a split-redwood house on the north side of Hudson Creek, where he lived with his wife and boy. On the south side of the creek but higher up in the hills, York took his wife and three boys, putting up a little split-redwood cabin 10 by 15 feet.

It is interesting to note the number of women and children mentioned in the records of the pioneers. The experience of one mother and grandmother, who came early to the valley, is typical of the strenuous life. She was the wife of William B. Elliott, and with her came several grown children and grandchildren. For a time the family lived in a cloth tent, a frail protection against the elements and the wild animals. The entire family had to spend the nights on a platform built in the forks of a mammoth oak tree, often watching helplessly while their uninvited guests below plundered the tent for food. During the day the men frequently went on hunting expeditions; and in their absence Mrs. Elliott and the smaller children often had to take refuge in the trees to get away from prowling bears. Mrs. Elliott, however, was herself an excellent shot.

At the head of the valley one and one-half miles northwest of Calistoga on the road to Knight's Valley was the log cabin of Enoch Cyrus, who came to California with his wife and six children in 1846. Then came the Fowlers, who lived with William Hargrave in a log house at the foot of the Mayacamas Range west of Calistoga. Calvin Musgrove and his wife also lived on the Fowler ranch. Wells and Ralph Kilburn lived with their families one mile south of Calistoga.

In 1849 the Owsley family—husband, wife, and eight children—erected a log cabin. That same year they set out an orchard and put up a frame house two miles south of Calistoga. One-half mile farther south was the home of William Nash, who had come with his wife and 14 children to California in 1846. Purchasing 330 acres of land from R. L. Kilburn in 1847, Nash settled on his ranch on November 26, 1847, naming it Walnut Grove. There he put up a house of boards cut at Bale's mill, and in January of the following year planted an orchard from seedlings brought by Elias Barnett from Kentucky. Nash was among the first to inaugurate new and better methods of agriculture in California, practicing, among other things, deep plowing and cultivation. He sold Walnut Grove in 1868 and moved to his Magnolia Farm five and one-half miles north of the city of Napa.

The chain of pioneer homesteads continued southward to the log house of M. D. Ritchie, who lived with his wife and five children across the road from Reasin P. Tucker. The latter had a split-redwood house for his wife and three or four boys. F. E. Kellogg had a frame house one-half mile beyond. Having arrived in the valley in 1846 with a wife and seven children, he had obtained this land for services rendered in building Dr. Bale's gristmill. Kellogg's house still stands, just south of the mill, very much as it was when built in 1849 of lumber cut at Bale's sawmill. It is now owned by the Lyman family, also important in the history of the old Bale Mill.

Across the road from the gristmill Sarah Graves Fosdick opened the second American school in California, in July 1847. The first had been established earlier that same year by Olive Mann Isbell in the old mission buildings at Santa Clara. Mrs. Fosdick was a survivor of the Reed-Donner party who had been brought to the Napa Valley by Reasin P. Tucker, one of the rescuers of that tragic group. The school was a mere shelter of branches and could be used only during good weather. It was replaced in 1849 by a real building, erected for Mrs. Fosdick by William Nash, which was used for about five years until the first public school was opened.

Rancho Yajome

On an elevated shelf of land above a branch of the Napa River where a splendid view of the valley stretches westward, the mellow buff walls of the old Salvador Vallejo adobe stand amid the orchards and gardens of the present Longwood ranch, north of Napa at 1006 Monticello Road. This was the third of three adobes built by Don Salvador, the other two (no longer in existence) having been located on Rancho Napa. In excellent condition today, the adobe is an outstanding example of an early Californian rancho house. The first floor comprises the original structure, with thick walls and deeply recessed doors and windows, while the second story, added at a later date, is of wood. On the east veranda, overlooking the garden, one may see the old hand-hewn redwood pillars with the round redwood beams overhead. Indian mortars, dug from the soil about the house, attest the presence of a native ranchería at the site before the white man took it over.

This adobe was built by Don Salvador on Rancho Yajome, an estate of 6,652 acres of fertile land lying on either side of the Napa River north of Rancho Tulucay. The grant was made to Damaso Antonio Rodríguez, a soldier, on March 13, 1841. It appears, however, that Rodríguez never lived on the land, and claim to it was filed by Salvador Vallejo on April 20, 1852, and confirmed to him on February 21, 1853.

That part of the grant now contained in the Longwood farm was purchased in 1932 by the Clifford E. Albert family from William Watt, who had lived on it for 25 years. In the early 1860's the long row of native trees, which still border the river below the house, gave the estate its present name.

Rancho Napa

On March 2, 1853, Don Salvador Vallejo and his wife, María de la Cruz Carrillo, filed a claim for about 3,000 acres of the much larger Rancho Napa originally granted to them on September 21, 1838, by Governor Alvarado. From time to time they had sold parts of their land that lay some distance back from the Napa River.

The part retained and for which confirmation was now asked was called "Trancas and Jalapa," which may be translated to mean "Sticks and Morning-glories" (trancas means "sticks," and jalapa is the name of a Mexican trailing plant in appearance like a wild morning-glory). A Mexican settlement lay in the south end of this area between the road and the river. South of this community was Pueblo de Salvador, a piece of the original grant, where James Clyman purchased a piece of land in 1850 shortly after his marriage to Hannah McComb, a member of the party that he had guided across the plains and mountains in the autumn of 1848.

Rancho Tulucay

A Napa County historian lamented in 1881 the disappearance of California's historic landmarks, saying: "And so the old landmarks are passing away, and the links which bind the present, or

Cayetano Juárez Adobe, Napa

American regime to the Spanish-Mexican or past, are disappearing one by one.... The few relics of that people will, in another half-century, be matters of legend and history."

More than 80 years have now passed since those words were written, and the prophecy has been almost fulfilled in many sections of California. In the Napa Valley only three of the many adobes which stood there are extant today. One of these, built in the 1840's by Cayetano Juárez, stands at the junction of Soscol Avenue and Silverado Trail in the southeastern part of the city of Napa on what was once known as Rancho Tulucay.

Rancho Tulucay, comprising two square leagues of land just east of the city of Napa, was granted to Cayetano Juárez on October 26, 1841. He had stocked the land as early as 1837 and became a permanent settler there before 1840, having built a small adobe house, no longer standing, and brought his family from Sonoma. About 1847 he built a second and larger adobe house, which stands today.

Juárez, a native of California and a military man of some importance, had been a soldier of the San Francisco Company during the years 1828–31, had been promoted to the rank of corporal in 1832, and apparently had served as sergeant from 1833. He had engaged in many Indian expeditions, was made mayordomo at Sonoma in 1836, and later served as captain of the militia. In 1845 he was appointed alcalde at Sonoma, the same year in which he received the grant of Rancho Yokaya (Ukiah, in Mendocino County). He distinguished himself somewhat in 1846 by his plans to rescue the Bear Flag prisoners and by a famous swim of nine miles which he made to escape capture. Juárez, who died in Napa in 1883, lies buried in the Tulocay Cemetery, for which he had donated the land to the city as early as 1859. The cemetery is in the eastern part of the city and is surrounded by a high wall of exceptionally fine native stone.

Just south of the city of Napa stands the Napa State Hospital, on a site that once lay within the confines of Rancho Tulucay. This institution was initiated by the legislature in 1869–70, when a commission was appointed to visit asylums throughout the United States and Europe and to report on management, modes of treatment of the mentally ill, etc. Dr. E. T. Wilkins was appointed to head the commission. A second commission was appointed in March 1872 for the purpose of selecting a site for the building. Napa was chosen on August 2 of that year, and in March 1873 the cornerstone was laid, while the first patient was admitted on November 15, 1875.

A few miles farther south, on Soscol Creek, the old Soscol House still stands beside the highway to Vallejo, much as it did in stagecoach days. Rancho Soscol, on which it is located, lay mostly within present Solano County.

Other Land Grants

Nicolás Higuera, a soldier in San Francisco from 1819 to 1823 and afterward *alcalde auxiliar* at Sonoma, received two grants from Governor Mariano Chico on May 9, 1836. One was Rancho Entre Napa, which lay to the west of Napa Creek. The northeast section of this was bought by Nathan Coombs in 1848 and later patented to him; here he laid out plans for the present city of Napa. The other was Rancho Rincón de los Carneros, a tract of 2,558 acres lying to the north and west of the confluence of Carneros Creek and the Napa River. This afterward passed into the possession of Julius Martin, who received United States patent for it on April 3, 1858.

Rancho Las Putas, on Putah Creek, covering most of the Berryessa Valley, consisted of eight square leagues. It was granted by Governor Micheltorena in October 1843 to two men, probably brothers, who had served as soldiers at San Francisco in the 1830's. The grantees were José de Jesús and Sixto (Sisto) Berryessa, whose wives, probably sisters, were María Anastasia and María Nicolasa Higuera. With the consent of their husbands, the wives filed claim for this tract on May 21, 1852, and received confirmation of their rights to 35,516 acres in January 1863. Here Lake Berryessa, created by the construction of Monticello Dam, has inundated the sites of the old Spanish adobes, as well as the quaint old stage-stop town of Monticello.

Joseph B. Chiles, who came to California first alone in 1841 and for the third time in 1848, bringing family and friends, received a grant of Rancho Catacula in November 1844. The grant covered 8,877 acres along the Arroyo de Napa (Chiles Creek), east of Yount's Rancho La Jota. Near the arroyo, Chiles built a house and a gristmill. The old mill (*SRL 547*) stood unused for many years and has now collapsed into the creek. The heavy timbers, part of the wheel, and the dam can still be seen. A bronze plaque has been mounted on a boulder on the hillside across the road from the ruins. This location is in Chiles Valley, at the junction of the Chiles and Pope Valley Road with the Lower Chiles Valley Road, three and three-quarters miles north of State Highway 128, at a point seven miles east of Rutherford. On a ranch just north of the mill ruins on the road to Pope Valley stands, in excellent condition, the old adobe Chiles built in 1846. The place remained in the possession of the Chiles family for many years. Chiles' home at Rutherford is near the Inglenook Winery; his town house in St. Helena still stands at 1343 Spring Street, but it has been remodeled into a church.

Old Stable, Monticello

In 1841 Manuel Jimeno granted Rancho Loco-allomi, consisting of 8,872 acres, to Julian Pope and Rancho Huichica, of two square leagues, to Jacob P. Leese. Leese received an extension of his property three years later, when Governor Micheltorena gave him another three and a half leagues. The Huichica grant lay southeast of Pueblo de Sonoma and the Buena Vista tract of Colonel Haraszthy. Carneros Creek formed its northeastern boundary, with Ranchos Napa and Rincón de los Carneros as neighbors across the stream.

William Gordon and Nathan Coombs filed claim for the four square leagues of Rancho Chimiles, granted to José Ignacio Berryessa on May 2, 1846. In 1859 the route of the county road between Suisun and the Berryessa Valley lay along the creek.

Calistoga

Samuel Brannan, active in several parts of California, purchased in 1859 a tract of land in the region around the hot springs at the foot of Mount St. Helena, with the intention of establishing a summer resort there. He coined the word Calistoga from "California" and "Saratoga" (an Eastern watering place) as a name for his resort, and built a hotel and 25 cottages near the springs. One of these cottages (SRL 685) and a row of old palm trees still stand on the grounds of the resort, now called Pacheteau's Hot Springs, in northern Calistoga. Nearby, at Wappo Avenue and Grant Street, Brannan's old store (SRL 684), in which he made $50,000 in one year, is now used as a rooming house. Sam Brannan interested people in the Napa Valley and elsewhere in financing a branch railroad to his resort. Its first trip brought some three thousand persons from San Francisco to the grand opening of Calistoga Hot Springs in October 1868. The Napa Valley Railroad Depot (SRL 687), built the same year, is now the Southern Pacific Depot. Brannan also turned his attention to the adjacent hillsides. Encouraged by the example of Colonel Agoston Haraszthy in Sonoma County and by a few growers near Napa, he planted the slopes with cuttings of superior wine and table grapes. Northwest of Calistoga, on Tubbs Lane, an "Old Faithful" geyser is a tourist attraction.

Vineyards and Wineries

On the wooded hillsides in Napa County, famous for its 15,000 acres of vineyards, stand picturesque structures of stone and brick similar to those built long ago in Germany and France. These wineries, however, date back only to the 1860's, when it was realized that the climate and soil were favorable to the culture of the vine.

Both the Spanish and early American settlers had made wine from Napa County vineyards. A notable year, however, was 1859, when Sam Brannan planted his hillside. The previous autumn Charles Krug had made about 1,200 gallons for a Mr. Patchett at Napa. In the year following, he went to the Bale Mill place north of St. Helena and made wine for Louis Bruck, and in 1860 he made 5,000 gallons at Yount's place at Yount-ville. His reputation now established, Krug began in 1868 to build a stone wine cellar (SRL 563) north of St. Helena on the floor of the valley. Additions were made periodically to this winery until it was finally completed in 1884. Standing amid plantings of shrubbery in a large grove of oaks, it is in splendid condition today and is still in operation, although not under the original ownership. Not far away is "Larkmead," the winery of the late Mrs. Howard Coit, better known in San Francisco as Lillie Hitchcock—the friend of the firemen.

The wine industry of the county is centered at St. Helena, where, in its infancy, the custom of a vintage festival was established. About six miles north of St. Helena, Jacob Schram planted vineyards in 1862 in the western hills of Napa Valley. His winery was a series of tunnels built into the hill a half mile up the canyon to the southwest of the present highway. The place is called "Schramsberg" (SRL 561), and the beautiful old home and two of the tunnels are still in existence, but it is not now in operation and presently is closed to visitors.

In 1869 Charles Wheeler purchased property two miles south of St. Helena at Pine Station, later known as Bell Station and now as Zinfandel, and here a stone winery was built by W. P. Weeks and J. Weinburger. Wheeler's son, John W., was secretary of the State Board of Viticulture in 1861 and its executive head in 1888. During this time another son, Rollo, was associated with his father in the management of the Wheeler Winery. In 1889 John W. took his brother's place with the father. This winery has now been torn down. It was near the highway about two miles south of St. Helena.

In 1870 Seneca Ewer came to live at St. Helena. In 1882 he and a partner, Atkinson, built a stone winery near Rutherford. The son, Fred S. Ewer, afterward carried on his father's business and about 1915 sold the wine cellar to Georges de Latour, who enlarged the original stone building by an addition built of cement. Since then much attention has been given to the gardens of the estate. Sacramental wines made here have received the approval of the Roman Catholic Church. This, now called the Beaulieu Winery, stands on the main highway at Rutherford.

In the foothills directly west of Rutherford is the beautifully designed Inglenook Winery. The land for this vineyard, formerly the property of a sanatorium, was purchased by Gustave Niebaum in 1880 and planted with cuttings of the finest kinds of wine grapes brought from Europe. The winery, built of stone quarried on the estate, was completed in 1887. It is a three-story structure of chateau type, its walls now festooned with trailing greenery. The taproom contains a rare collection of tankards, pewter and pottery mugs, and valuable old glass.

An interesting winery stands upon the site selected in 1875 by Jacob L. Beringer, who had been foreman of the Charles Krug cellar. This stands on the north side of St. Helena and is built into the west hills, where the limestone formation is peculiarly adapted to the storing and aging of wines. The winery and 800 feet of cellars are cut through the stone. The tunnels running 250 feet directly into the hill are connected by several laterals, honeycombing the entire hill. This underground storage space is filled with oval oak casks, each with a capacity of about 500 gallons. At the entrance to the cellar is a large oval cask, with a capacity of 2,700 gallons, built in the early 1880's by a San Francisco cooper and decorated by a wood carver from Germany. The management of this business has always remained in the Beringer family.

The Christian Brothers Winery, formerly Greystone Winery, situated a mile north of St. Helena and a few hundred feet away from the main highway on the western side of the hill, is one of the largest stone wineries in the world. It was built in 1889 by W. B. Brown and Everett Wise. The ownership changed in 1894, 1896, 1925, and again in 1943. It is a magnificent building 400 feet long, with tunnels into the hills at the rear.

The Montelena Winery, on Tubbs Lane about three miles north of Calistoga at the foot of Mount St. Helena, was built of wood in 1880. In 1881 the owner, A. L. Tubbs, had the stone cellar built, copying the Chateau Lafitte of France. This huge cellar is built into the hill and was filled with large oak ovals for the storing of wines. In 1897 the son, William B. Tubbs, succeeded his father in the management and, in turn, passed the control on to a later generation. The wooden winery no longer exists, and the stone building has been converted into a beautiful home.

Among the most beautiful homes in the Napa Valley are those that have been built from former wineries. Besides the former Tubbs winery at Calistoga, two such stone homes may be seen just north of St. Helena's Christian Brothers Winery on the same side of the highway. Another evidence of beautiful pioneer stone work in the Napa Valley is to be found in the large number of stone bridges still in use. Although they are narrow by today's standards and many will eventually have to be replaced, it is to be hoped that some of this fine artisanship will be spared for posterity. The first stone bridge built in Napa County, constructed in the late 1880's, is in eastern St. Helena at the Pope Street crossing of Napa River to Silverado Trail.

Stevenson's Silverado

In the spring of 1880, Robert Louis Stevenson brought his bride to Silverado. There, in the woody canyon filled with the scent of sweet bay trees and wild azaleas, he lived from May 19 to June 9. That delightful collection of descriptive and narrative essays, *Silverado Squatters*, completed in France, came from the memories of that health-giving summer on the heights of St. Helena.

From Calistoga, with its geysers and hot springs and orchards, it is a scant nine miles to the site of the old Toll House, nestled in a little glen high on the mountain. A steep and winding stage road, vestiges of which still remain, climbed the mountain in Stevenson's day, and the coach,

driven by the reckless Foss, bumped perilously over the zigzag trail, to come at last to a halt before the Toll House Hotel, "dozing in sun and dust and silence, like a place enchanted." The old gray inn was much the same for many years, as it slept behind the green thicket which isolated it from the modern highway leisurely circling the mountain grades. Finally it collapsed, and it and the old Toll House are to be seen no more.

The old mining camp of Silverado had already, in Stevenson's day, "been carted from the scene; one of the houses was now the schoolhouse far down the road; one was gone here, one there, but all were gone away. It was now a sylvan solitude."

A quarter of a mile along the rutted, tortuous road through the forest, one comes to the canyon, where "a rusty iron chute on wooden legs came flying, like a monstrous gargoyle, across the parapet" down which the ore was poured.

Proceeding another quarter-mile, one reaches the "triangular platform, filling up the whole glen, and shut in on either hand by bold projections of the mountain. Only in front the place was open like the proscenium of a theatre," and one looks forth, as Stevenson did, "into a great realm of air, and down upon treetops and hilltops, and far and near on wild and varied country."

Here Stevenson took possession of a deserted miner's cabin with its sashless windows "chocked with the green and sweetly smelling foliage of a bay," and its three rooms "so plastered against the hill, that one room was right atop of another." The old cabin is gone, its place marked by the Stevenson Monument carved from polished granite in the form of an open book, on a base of ore taken from the Silverado Mine.

One hundred yards from the cabin site, the trail leads abruptly up the mountainside and around a sharp bend to the cavernous tunnel of the Silverado Mine, going down into the bowels of the mountain from which "a cold, wet draught tempestuously blew." Abandoned ore cars and a narrow-gauge railroad testify to activities through the years, for there have been sporadic and not highly profitable mining efforts at Silverado since the early 1870's.

Here in this deeply wooded glen filled with a thousand mountain fragrances and lifted high above the valley fogs, Robert Louis Stevenson

Manhattan Mine Headquarters, Knoxville

spent his honeymoon with Fannie Van de Grift Osbourne, and then returned to France with rich memories and restored health.

The Robert Louis Stevenson Memorial State Park (*SRL 710*) has been established here, but it has yet to be developed by the state.

The highway along the eastern side of Napa Valley bears the name "Silverado Trail" and provides a beautiful alternate route between Napa and Calistoga.

Silverado was not the only mining camp in Napa County. The Manhattan quicksilver mine was located at the old ghost town of Knoxville, in the extreme northern part of Napa County near the Lake and Yolo county boundaries. A number of interesting structures, including the old headquarters building, remain at this site, which is about midway between Clear Lake and Lake Berryessa. Also in Napa County is the Oat Hill quicksilver mine, near the Lake County line.

SOURCES

Bancroft, Hubert Howe. "California," of the series *History of the Pacific States of North America*. Vols. 18–24. The History Co., San Francisco, 1884–90.

Bucknall, Mary E. *Early Days*. Pamphlet, privately printed, n.d.

Chapman, Charles E. *A History of California: The Spanish Period*. Macmillan, New York, 1921.

Clyman, James. *James Clyman, American Frontiersman, 1792–1881*. California Historical Society, San Francisco, 1928.

History of Napa and Lake Counties. Slocum, Bowen & Co., San Francisco, 1881.

Hyatt, T. Hart. *Handbook of Grape Culture*. H. H. Bancroft & Co., San Francisco, 1867.

Kanaga, Tillie. *History of Napa County*. Privately printed, Oakland, 1901.

Loeber, Ivy M. Articles in Calistoga Centennial souvenir book, 1959, and personal interview.

Stevenson, Robert Louis. *The Silverado Squatters*. Scribner, New York, 1904.

Tuomey, Honoria, and Louisa Vallejo Emparan. "History of the Mission, Presidio, and Pueblo of Sonoma," *Press-Democrat*, Santa Rosa, 1923.

Wheeler, Mrs. Elliott H. Ms. notes.

Nevada County

NEVADA COUNTY (Nevada is Spanish for "snow-covered") was formed in 1851 from territory that had been originally a part of Yuba County. Nevada City was made the county seat. Situated in a region where the entire upper country wears a heavy mantle of snow during the winter months, the name Nevada was appropriately chosen by its citizens for the town of Nevada City. Later the same name was given to the county.

The Donner Tragedy

One of the routes into California most frequently used by the emigrants of 1849 and the 1850's was known as the California Trail, or the Truckee Pass Emigrant Road, which followed up the Truckee River valley in Nevada through Donner Pass in the High Sierra.

The first overland party of emigrants to follow the California Trail was the Murphy-Townsend-Stevens party, in the autumn of 1844. In 1845, John C. Frémont, with a small detachment of his company, entered California by this same trail. But the most famous group to negotiate it was the ill-fated Donner party, whose experiences in the High Sierra during the winter of 1846–47 constitute the most heart-rending tragedy in the history of California.

In the spring of 1846 a party of emigrants, led by George and Jacob Donner and James F. Reed, was organized in Sangamon County, Illinois, and started on what proved to be the most terrible trek westward in all the annals of American history. When the party reached Independence, Missouri, the first week in May, it had grown to such proportions that between 200 and 300 wagons were included in the train.

Upon arriving at Fort Bridger, the Reed-Donner party proper took the fatal step of breaking off from the larger group and following the Hastings Cut-Off, a supposed shortcut that passed south of the Great Salt Lake. Instead of taking one week as expected, a whole month of valuable time was consumed in reaching Salt Lake. Struggling on over the great salt deserts west of the lake, where the party suffered terrible hardships, they finally reached the site of Reno, Nevada, entirely exhausted. Finding forage for their emaciated animals here, the party rested for three or four days. This delay, however, proved to be disastrous, for the storm clouds were already gathering when they reached the mountains. The little band hastened up the eastern side of the Sierra as fast as possible, but on October 28, 1846, before they could reach the summit, heavy snow began to fall—a month earlier than usual.

The emigrants, already weakened and spent, soon found it almost impossible to make progress through the rapidly deepening snow, which quickly obliterated all semblance of a trail. Several valiant attempts were made to cross the mountain barrier, but all ended in bitter defeat. With fear growing in their hearts, the party hastened to make what pitiful preparations they could for winter camp on the shores of Donner Lake. Here most of them found shelter—such as it was—in three log cabins and a few hastily constructed shacks. However, the families of George and Jacob Donner, owing to an accident which

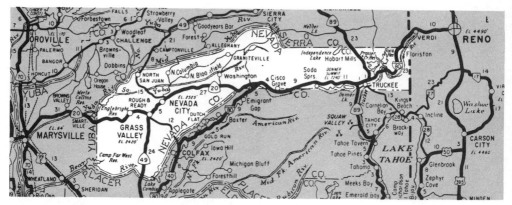

delayed them, had been forced into camp at Alder Creek, about six miles below the lake. Here their only shelters were crude huts of canvas and boughs banked with snow. With such meager protection from the elements, during what proved to be the most severe winter in 30 years, and with actual famine staring them in the face, the members of the unfortunate party would all have perished had no aid come to them.

On December 10 or, according to some authorities, on the 16th, a party of ten men and five women, who were afterward known as the "Forlorn Hope," started out in a desperate attempt to obtain help. Struggling on for 32 days over the snow-covered mountains and enduring almost unbelievable hardships, the five women and two of the men, William Eddy and William Foster, finally succeeded in reaching Johnson's Rancho, near the present site of Wheatland, some 35 miles north of Sutter's Fort.

With the aid of John A. Sutter and others, four relief parties were subsequently organized to attempt the rescue of those remaining in the mountains. With great stamina and courage, the men comprising these parties succeeded in carrying in provisions and brought from their frightful camps of death the emaciated survivors, many of them children.

Of the 82 persons who began the winter at Donner Lake and on Alder Creek, 35 perished. Suffering, despair, and death stalked the camps, but the unselfishness and courage of many members of the party make the story one of greatness as well as tragedy. Of the many acts of heroism, none surpasses that of Tamsen Donner, wife of George Donner, who refused to leave her dying husband alone in the camp. Knowing she had sealed her own fate, she watched her children go out with the third relief party. "For heroism ennobled and glorified by love and sacrifice one looks in vain in the annals of California history for a finer example than that of Tamsen Donner."

The old emigrant road, over which the Reed-Donner party passed, was first marked in the 1920's by P. M. Weddell, a San Jose high school teacher, with homemade signs, on some of which the picture of a covered wagon was traced. A few of these still exist. Later permanent bronze plaques were placed by the Native Sons and other

groups. The tablet on the bridge near the summit of Donner Pass on the old Highway 40 bears the inscription "Donner Summit Bridge dedicated to the pioneers who blazed the Overland Trail through these mountains."

The Pioneer Monument (SRL 134), erected by the Native Sons and Daughters of the Golden West, stands at the lower end of Donner Lake, and marks the site of the Breen cabin, one of the shelters used by the Donner party. It consists of a rock pedestal supporting a group of four figures in bronze representing a pioneer family. On the front of the pedestal is the inscription "Virile to risk and find—Kindly withal and a ready help—Facing the brunt of fate—Indomitable—Unafraid." On the back of the pedestal are the words "In commemoration of the pioneers who crossed the plains to settle California. Erected under the auspices of the Native Sons of the Golden West and Native Daughters of the Golden West. Dedicated June 6, 1918."

The Breen cabin, located about a quarter of a mile below the foot of the lake, had been erected in November 1844 by Moses Schallenberger, Joseph Foster, and Allen Montgomery, and in it Schallenberger, then a boy of 17, spent the winter alone, guarding the goods stored there by the Elisha Stevens party, until their return March 1, 1845. The Murphy-Townsend-Stevens expedition had been led across the plains in 1844 by Caleb Greenwood, trapper and mountaineer, and his two sons, Britain and John. The company had about a dozen wagons, which were the first to cross the Sierra Nevada into the central valley of California.

About half a mile east of the Pioneer Monument and just south of the old highway near the Truckee Elementary School stands the so-called Donner Cross. A bronze tablet 195 feet south of the cross marks the site of the Graves cabin. It was placed by the Native Sons of the Golden West.

Where the Murphy cabin stood, a huge boulder bears a bronze tablet with the words "Donner Party, 1846–47. The face of this rock formed the north end of the fireplace of the Murphy Cabin. General Stephen W. Kearny, on June 22, 1847, buried under the middle of the cabin the bodies found in the vicinity." The tablet lists the names of the members of the Donner party, those who survived and those who perished. This boulder is 200 yards by trail from the Emigrant Trail Museum, opened in 1963. The Pioneer Monument, museum, and Murphy boulder are all included in Donner Memorial State Park. The area has been recognized also for its significance to the history of the nation, and has been registered and marked by the Department of the Interior as a National Historic Landmark.

McGlashan places the site of the Donner tents at the head of Alder Creek about a mile and a half above its junction with Prosser Creek. Somewhere in the vicinity the body of George Donner was buried, in June 1847, by some of Kearny's men, according to Edwin Bryant, who accompanied that expedition.

The Old Emigrant Trail

One of the first permanent markers along the old emigrant trail was placed near Truckee, and stands today in front of the Tahoe-Truckee High School, about a mile east of the Pioneer Monument on the old highway. The tablet contains the following inscription:

"The emigrant trail in the pioneer days of California came through the low pass to the north facing this monument. The trail turned west at this point for a distance of approximately twenty-six hundred feet, where a tablet describes the route then followed.

"Placed by Historic Landmarks Committee, Native Sons of the Golden West, September 14, 1929."

The second tablet, mentioned in the first and placed on the same day, has apparently disappeared in the course of highway construction. It read:

"The emigrant trail in the pioneer days of California turned to the south at this point for approximately three miles, then west across the summit of the Sierras about a mile south of the present railroad. It was here that the Donner party missed the trail, owing to the early snows, resulting in tragedy."

The Donner party and most of the other early emigrants who crossed the Sierra Nevada by way of the Truckee River and the Donner Pass traveled down the ridge north of the Bear River, entering the Sacramento Valley by using approximately the same trail as that opened by the Murphy-Townsend-Stevens party in 1844-45.

The point at which the emigrant trail (*SRL* 799) crossed present Highway 49, midway between Auburn and Grass Valley, has been marked.

Later a much-traveled emigrant road came down the San Juan Ridge between the Middle and South forks of the Yuba River. This was used mostly by those who had come via the Henness Pass route in Sierra County. This trail followed down the ridge over a soil formation and was preferable to the route over Donner Pass, which was extremely rough and rocky. During the 1860's this route became one of the stage and freight roads for the mines of the famous Comstock Lode in Nevada. In the 1920's a section of this road above Graniteville was rebuilt and utilized during construction of the Bowman Dam.

Toll Roads

During the 1850's and 1860's the rapid development of mines in the recesses of the mountains resulted in an imperative need for the construction of roads—a need that the counties could not meet because of the expense. Consequently, most of the roads and bridges that replaced the pack trails were constructed and owned by individuals or by turnpike companies, and were operated for profit.

The development of a system of state and national highways following roughly the early roads and trails has almost completely eliminated the toll-road system in the state. Nevada County bought the last of its toll roads and bridges about 1890.

Among the privately owned turnpikes leading from Nevada City were the following: the Nevada–Washington; the Nevada–Little York; the Nevada–Grass Valley; and the South Yuba Road, which went from Nevada City to Lake City on the San Juan Ridge, crossing the South Fork of the Yuba at Robinson's Crossing, later known as Black's and then as Edward's Bridge. Today a good scenic road follows this early stage route.

Another important turnpike followed approximately, in part, the route taken by the present state highway from Nevada City to Downieville. The first ten-mile stretch of the road, now bypassed on the west by several miles, was known as Purdon's Grade, and is today called Purdon Road. The bridge across the South Fork was at first known as Wall's, then as Webber's, and

Pioneer Monument, Donner Lake

finally as Purdon's, before its purchase by the county. The bridge at the Middle Fork of the Yuba River was and still is known as Freeman's Crossing. Thomas Freeman, in 1854, purchased the property from Thomas Hess, who built the first bridge at this point in 1851. The winter floods carried it away, and a second structure, subsequently taken over by Freeman, was erected in 1852. After the flood of 1862, Freeman built a substantial structure which he owned for some 30 years. Two of the old pilings of this bridge may still be seen in the river, less than half a mile west of the present bridge via Moonshine Road. That portion of the tollhouse which served as a stable also stands and has been restored. Between its walls the stagecoaches passed on their way up the mountain.

Just above the massive concrete bridge which carries the modern motorist across the river into Yuba County, Oregon Creek runs into the Middle Yuba. Here is the junction of three roads, one leading up Oregon Creek to Downieville, a second turning right across the creek through an old covered bridge to Alleghany, Forest, and the Henness Pass in Sierra County, and a third proceeding to the left across Moonshine Creek to the Bullards Bar Dam in Yuba County—modern roads of superb scenic grandeur following the routes of historic trails and turnpikes.

The covered bridge across Oregon Creek (in Yuba County) was built probably in 1862. A flood in 1883 swept it off its foundations and turned it around, depositing it on the bank 150 feet downstream. By means of ox teams it was inched back to its site on logs and planks, but since no way could be found to reverse it, what had been the south end is now the north. It was at this time, presumably, that the portals at either end of the bridge were curved to meet the road.

Yuba River Bars

Early in 1849 John Rose, who gave his name to Rose's Bar in Yuba County, built a cattle corral at a spot in Pleasant Valley on the lower San Juan Ridge between the sites later occupied by the Anthony House on Deer Creek and Bridgeport on the South Yuba. Apparently Rose's original purpose was to trade with the Indians of the region, but during the early summer prospectors found their way up the South and Middle forks of the Yuba River and Deer Creek, crevassing for

Anthony House, Old Stage Station

gold and finding many rich gravel deposits on the bars along the margins of these streams. The news of these discoveries spread quickly, and by late summer and early fall of 1849 scores of miners were working the Deer Creek and Yuba River surface diggings. In order to accommodate the increasing trade, Rose established a trading post in a small adobe he had built.

As in practically all of the mining regions of the Sierra Nevada, the first prospecting in Nevada County was confined to the gravel bars and the beds of running streams. Scores of river-bar camps sprang up almost overnight. Typical of these mining camps was Bridgeport, on the South Fork of the Yuba, about one and a half miles from its mouth. For two years the town was exceedingly prosperous, but after river mining ceased to be profitable the camp declined. Today the name is preserved only in Bridgeport Township.

The present road to French Corral leaves Highway 20 midway between Smartsville and Rough and Ready. In slightly less than three miles it passes the Anthony House, still standing, a stage station on the old turnpike up the San Juan Ridge. After another five miles it crosses the river at Bridgeport (Nye's Crossing) by means of an old covered bridge (SRL 390), known to have been erected in 1862 by David I. Wood. It is the oldest housed span in the West and, at 233 feet, the longest single-span covered bridge in the nation. The road continues to French Corral, less than three miles, and in another five miles joins Highway 49 near North San Juan.

On the Middle Fork of the Yuba additional camps were established in 1850, among them Rice's Crossing (at first known by the rather dubious title of Liar's Flat and then as Lousy Level), Frenchman's Bar, and Condemned Bar (Yuba County). On the South Fork was Jones's Bar, once famous among the river camps.

Panning for gold was, of course, the first and most primitive method of washing the metal from the gravel. The first machine to be employed for the purpose was the rocker, which was introduced in the summer of 1848. This was, in turn, superseded by the long tom. Gradually the miners extended their activities to the gravel of the dry gulches, flats, and hillsides; then ground-sluicing, introduced by William Elwell at Nevada City in February or March of 1850, came into practice. With this innovation an elaborate system of ditches and sluice boxes was developed, out of which, in time, grew the more powerful and extensive hydraulic methods of the 1860's and 1870's. Many old mining ditches today serve the irrigation needs of orchards and gardens in the hill country of the Sierra Nevada.

Rough and Ready

Coming up from Marysville to Grass Valley, the motorist passes near Timbuctoo and Smartsville in Yuba County and climbs the wooded hills through a country that grows richer in historic interest with each curving vista of the highway. The early farmhouses, tucked among gnarled apple trees, give to the countryside that hint of old New England found nowhere in California except in the Sierra gold regions. Touching elbows with these fast-vanishing bits of pastoral beauty are the deeply scarred gullies and gravelly hillocks which mark the abandoned diggings of the 1850's and 1860's.

Another turn in the road brings one to a place of green upland meadows where a tiny hamlet lies sheltered among aging shade and orchard trees. This peaceful spot, with its weatherbeaten, shake-roofed houses, belies its name—Rough and Ready—but in the feverish days of the 1850's it was a busy mining town, one of the first to be established in Nevada County. A party of men calling themselves the Rough and Ready Company arrived in the vicinity on September 9, 1849, under the leadership of Captain A. A. Townsend, who had served under General Zachary Taylor ("Old Rough and Ready"), hero of the Mexican War. For several months the Rough and Readys were able to keep the richness of this region a secret, preempting all the land round about, but by 1850 the incoming tide of miners could not be held back and the place developed into a good-sized town.

One episode in the history of the town makes it unique. During the uncertain days of 1850, while state sovereignty was still in abeyance, E. F. Brundage conceived the idea of a separate and independent government. Issuing a high-sounding manifesto, he called a mass meeting to organize the State of Rough and Ready. For a short period he had a following of about 100, but the whole affair met with so much ridicule that the State of Rough and Ready soon dissolved into thin air.

On June 28, 1850, Rough and Ready (SRL 294) had its first devastating fire. But in spite of this discouraging experience, in October it polled 1,000 votes and even aspired to become the county seat of the newly organized Nevada County. A committee to preserve law and order had been elected, a Christian Association was holding services in a little clapboard shanty, and the Masons and the Odd Fellows had joined in forming a benevolent association. The town continued to grow, and during the early 1850's there were more than 300 substantial frame buildings.

Its decline began with the gradual exhaustion of the gold in the creeks and on the flats, and by 1870, after the fires of 1856 and 1859 had all but wiped out the place, only 24 houses were left in the town. A few of these are still standing. On the hill is the I.O.O.F. building, deeded by the society (now joined with the Grass Valley lodge) to the town of Rough and Ready as a community hall. The old hotel, built about 1853, was the community's outstanding landmark for nearly a century, until, unfortunately, it was razed in July 1948. The present post office contains stained-glass windows from the old office, which was in the hotel.

As one leaves the town, the old Fippin blacksmith shop, deserted and dilapidated, stands on the left of the road, and just beyond is the fallen "Slave Girl Tree," which legend says sprouted from a switch planted there by the daughter of a slave brought to the diggings by his master.

A little farther on to the right is the Toll House, now an antique shop. Scars of old diggings are passed on either side of the road as one leaves Rough and Ready behind and climbs the hills toward Grass Valley, four miles away.

In 1865–66 during the copper-mining excitement, a boom occurred southwest of Rough and Ready, and the towns of Spenceville, Hacketville, Wilsonville, and Queen City were laid out. Only Spenceville endured, being the location of a post office from 1872 to 1932 and the center of a small agricultural community. It is said to have had a population of 150 in the 1920's. During World War II it was used by neighboring Camp Beale as a model German village for war maneuvers. The few remaining old buildings were posted with German signs and became targets for the soldiers' guns. Now the site is practically inaccessible, although a piece of the old road southwest of Rough and Ready is still called Spenceville Road.

About three and a half miles northeast of Rough and Ready, via Beckman Hill Road and Newtown Road, is Newtown, formerly Sailor Flat, while ten miles west and one mile north of Highway 20 is Mooney Flat. Both were mining camps in the 1850's but now consist largely of newer homes. The Mooney Flat Road continues past Englebright Reservoir to join the Pleasant Valley Road (to French Corral) at Anthony House.

Grass Valley

The town of Grass Valley, full of memories of the colorful gold-mining days, received its name from the well-watered valley in which it lies. The valley was named by a company of emigrants who in 1849 found their way into the meadows kept green by perpetual springs, after toiling over the Truckee Pass Trail with their half-starved cattle. The poor, gaunt beasts had strayed from camp during the night and in the morning were found enjoying the abundant grass and water of the meadow.

The first white men known to have seen this valley were Claude Chana and a party of French emigrants in 1846. In the summer of 1848, David Stump and two other prospectors came from Oregon to the diggings of El Dorado County, drifting northward into Grass Valley in October. Here they crevassed for gold near the sites of the Eureka and Idaho mines until approaching winter drove them from the mountains.

In August 1849 a party of five men headed by a Dr. Saunders built a cabin on Badger Hill near the eastern edge of what is now the city of Grass Valley. The Saunders party was soon joined by others, making a colony of 20 men who spent the winter in the valley. This became the nucleus of the present city.

Another settlement, which also became a part of the modern Grass Valley, was established in what came to be known as Boston Ravine, named after the company that arrived there on September 23, 1849, under the leadership of the Rev. H. H. Cummings, its president. Four cabins were erected on the south side of the ravine, where they spent the winter. On September 28, 1849, the first Christian burial in Nevada County took place in Boston Ravine, with Cummings officiating, when an emigrant who had toiled across the plains only to die on the threshold of his destination, was buried on the southern slope of the ravine.

For two years Boston Ravine, at the south end of present Mill Street, was the chief settlement in the vicinity, laying the foundation for the flourishing trade of the town which ultimately grew out from it. Today only one old brick building, at Mill and Empire streets, remains from this once thriving community.

Among the many rich placer mines in the Grass Valley district during the 1850's were the Pike and Humbug flats, Grass Valley Slide, Rhode Island Ravine, Kentucky Ravine, and the Lola Montez, the Kate Hardy, and other diggings.

Beneath the pines on Gold Hill, at Jenkins Street and Hocking Avenue, stands a monument (SRL 297) bearing the following inscription:

"This tablet commemorates the discovery of gold-bearing quartz and the beginning of quartz mining in California. The discovery was made on Gold Hill by George Knight, October 1850. The occurrence of gold-bearing quartz was undoubtedly noted here and elsewhere about the same time or previously, but the above discovery created the great excitement that started the development of quartz mining into a great industry. The Gold Hill Mine, 1850–1857, is credited with a total production of $4,000,000. This monument dedicated by Quartz Parlor, N.S.G.W., and Manzanita Parlor, N.D.G.W., October 20, 1929." This discovery aided the development of the city of Grass Valley, although its first prosperity came from the rich placer fields.

Other rich veins about Grass Valley were soon discovered, and crude mills for the reduction of the ore were built. Besides the Gold Hill Mine, where the discovery was first made, there were the Massachusetts Hill; the Eureka, located in 1851 on Wolf Creek; the Allison Ranch, located in 1853 two and a half miles south of the town and for a time one of the richest in the state; the North Star, opened in 1851 on Lafayette Hill; the Empire (SRL 298), located in 1850 on Ophir Hill one mile southeast of town, via East Empire Street, one of the world's major gold mines and still producing on a limited scale; and the Idaho, located in 1863 just across Wolf Creek from the Eureka.

About a mile from the scene of Knight's (or McKnight's) discovery, the hoists and stamp mills of the consolidated North Star and Empire mines (the one to the south and the other to the east of Gold Hill) stand today amid the millions of tons of tailings accumulated from operations extending over a period of more than a century—for these mines have produced since the early 1850's. From the seemingly inexhaustible lode upon which the tunnels, shafts, stopes, and winzes are situated, more than $80 million has been taken. These two mines, like others in the county, are now consolidated under one management. One vein alone extends for a distance of more than 9,000 feet—nearly two miles. The longest

shaft has been sunk to an inclined depth of approximately 7,000 feet, the bottom of the shaft being 4,000 feet below the earth's surface and 1,500 feet below sea level. The Idaho-Maryland and the Brunswick are other old producers that have been worked off and on in more recent years.

The atmosphere of early mining days still clings to the town of Grass Valley, and even pavements and modern stores along its narrow, irregular streets cannot entirely destroy it, accented as it is by outlying aged farmsteads and by the vivid scars of diggings flanking the roadsides and bordering the very town itself.

The churches of Grass Valley reflect a significant historical background. Isaac Owen, the first commissioned Methodist minister in California and later the founder, at Santa Clara, of the University of the Pacific (now located at Stockton), preached his first sermon on California soil under the shade of an oak tree in Grass Valley on the north portion of Clark's Ranch in September 1849, having just come overland by ox team. In January 1852, while Owen was presiding elder of the district, a church was organized in Grass Valley in a building that had been used as a meeting place by the Presbyterians and as a schoolhouse. This building was superseded by a larger one in 1854, by another in 1872, and finally by the present one.

Opposite the Methodist church on Church Street is the Emmanuel Episcopal Church. Bishop Kip held the first Episcopal services in Grass Valley on April 23, 1854, and the parish was organized in 1855. The present building, erected in 1858, has served the community all these years. A few blocks up Church Street, old Mount St. Mary's Academy still stands, but stately old St. Patrick's Catholic Church was replaced by a modern structure in 1949. The Congregationalists, under the leadership of Rev. J. D. Hale, a worker from the American Home Missionary Society, erected their first building in December 1853 on the corner of Neal and Church streets, where the present edifice now stands. In the original building the first Woman's Christian Temperance Union to be organized in California was formed in 1874 by the women of the Methodist and Congregational churches.

On April 9, 1933, the Harvard Club of San Francisco dedicated a tablet in the Public Library

Lola Montez House, Grass Valley

to Josiah Royce, philosopher, historian of California, and noted Harvard professor, who was born in Grass Valley in 1855.

Lola Montez, Countess of Landsfeld, Bavaria, born in Ireland in 1818, came to Grass Valley in 1854. A woman of marked intellectual ability, of almost angelic beauty and with regal grace, Maria Dolores Eliza Rosanna Gilbert, alias Lola Montez, had been the personal friend of George Sand, Alexander Dumas, Victor Hugo, Lamartine, and Liszt, and the favorite of kings and queens throughout Europe. "A woman of loves, marriages, divorces, adventures," the magnetic and daring Lola, while she had charmed with the grace and originality of her dancing, had also exerted a considerable political influence throughout Bavaria.

A furor was created by the appearance of this extraordinary woman in San Francisco, where her Spider Dance took the rough miners by storm. Her subsequent sojourn in the obscure mining camp of Grass Valley was of romantic significance to that community, where the charm of her personality was widely felt.

Surrounded by magnificent poplar trees, the old house (SRL 292) in which she lived with her pet bear—at that time a one-story cottage—with its brick-lined cellar, rose garden, and quaint dovecote, may still be seen at 248 Mill Street. The site was originally occupied by the first school in Grass Valley, a private institution opened in 1852 by Rosa Farrington. However, the school was soon moved to the site where the Methodist church now stands.

Three doors from the cottage where lived the beautiful and dashing Lola stands a two-story building (SRL 293) that once served as a boardinghouse. There a small, precocious child of six shyly admired the distinguished dancer, and between the two there ultimately developed an attachment that "laid a foundation for the success of that little girl in years to come, when, as Lotta Crabtree, she endeared herself to the heart of a nation." The address is 238 Mill Street.

There are many ghost towns of the past east and southeast of Grass Valley, with strangely incongruous names reminiscent of the rough-and-ready life of the miners who created them: You Bet, Red Dog, Gouge Eye, Little York, Walloupa, and Quaker Hill. At the summit midway between Grass Valley and Nevada City is the site of the old mining community of Town Talk.

Nevada City

James W. Marshall, the discoverer of gold at Coloma, came to Deer Creek, a tributary of the Yuba River, in the summer of 1848. The first white man to pan for gold at this spot, Marshall did not suspect that the stream contained phenomenal wealth, nor did he dream that just two years later more than 10,000 miners would be at work within a radius of three miles from the spot where he had found the first shining grains of metal.

Early in September 1849 Captain John Pennington and two companions built the first cabin on Gold Run above where that stream empties

Lotta Crabtree House, Grass Valley

into Deer Creek and just above the site of the bridge now known as the Gault Bridge. In October Dr. A. B. Caldwell erected a log cabin and set up a store on the slope of Aristocracy Hill. (The old Episcopal church still stands in this area; nearby in 1854 the first public school in the city was erected.) For a time the place was known as Caldwell's Upper Store (or Deer Creek Dry Diggings), as Dr. Caldwell previously had had a store seven miles below on Deer Creek at Pleasant Flat, where the town of Deer Creek grew up. Its inhabitants later removed to Newtown, where a number of springs furnished a good water supply.

In that same month the town's first family, the Stampses, settled in a ravine back of the present Coyote Street. In the fall Madam Penn came; an indefatigable worker who customarily took her turn at the rocker. In the spring of 1850 this enterprising woman built a boardinghouse on a site which was continuously occupied by a hotel or lodging house for 109 years and on which the Union Hotel stood from 1863 to 1959.

In March 1850 the miners elected Stamps alcalde of Caldwell's Upper Store, and at the same time they changed the name of the place. In the census of 1850 the name of the town is given as Nevada City, although in an unofficial list of post offices for the year 1851 it appears as Nevada. When a county was established in that section of the Sierra country in 1851, it was also called Nevada, and the town of that name was made the county seat. Ten years later, when the state of Nevada was formed, the citizens of the town of Nevada in California bitterly protested that they had first claim to the name. The matter was appealed to Congress, but that body refused to act. Consequently, its citizens decided that their town should henceforth be known as Nevada City, the name always borne officially by the post office.

The phenomenal growth of this region was due at first almost entirely to surface placers. So eager were the miners to find rich strikes that even the streets of the town were not secure from operations. Finally one irate storekeeper protested these liberties. Approaching a miner in the act of digging up the street, the merchant demanded that he stop. The miner refused, pleading that there was no law to prevent him from digging in the streets. "Then I'll make a law," said the indignant merchant, producing a revolver, whereupon the miner beat a hasty retreat. Thereafter the streets of Nevada City were not disturbed.

On the eastern end of Lost Hill gold was discovered early in 1850. The gravel ranges of this section proved extraordinarily rich, and news of the diggings spread rapidly, causing a city to mushroom almost overnight. It was not uncommon for the miners to take out a quart of gold (worth $6,000) in a single day in this region. Because the peculiar method of mining called "coyoteing," or tunneling, was adopted here, the town was called Coyoteville. During the two years of its existence, a total of $8 million is said to have been taken from the surrounding gravel banks. The site of the old settlement constitutes the northwestern section of present Nevada City.

Many quartz mines in the neighborhood have notable production records: the Champion, Providence, Merrifield, Wyoming, Murchie, Pittsburg, New England, Sneath and Clay, and dozens of others. Adjacent areas, too, have their quota, the Willow Valley, Blue Tent, Canada Hill, and Banner being among the most productive.

At the foot of a panorama of mountains nestles Nevada City, its roofs and tall church spires gleaming white through the shade trees. In spite of paved streets and modern stores, Nevada City remained a storybook town until the 1960's, when construction of a freeway shattered much of its original charm. Still, in those parts of the city removed from the bustle of traffic, there may be found picturesque relics vividly recalling its historic past. Aged, steep-roofed houses, three or four stories high, cling to the precipitous walls of Deer Creek canyon. One of them, a gabled structure of substantial brick at Clay and Prospect streets, has long been known as "The Castle."

The back streets of this quaint and colorful county seat are so crooked, and wander across the narrow valley in such confusion, that one wonders if they were "surveyed by burro trains of prospectors, meandering from the surrounding hills." Here and there along these labyrinthine thoroughfares interesting iron-barred stores of brick and stone, erected after the first shack city

had been swept by fire in the early days, suggest the stirring scenes once familiar to the Argonauts. The National Hotel, a balconied brick structure with iron shutters, remains much as it was in the 1850's and is still one of the gold country's outstanding hostelries.

Through the doors of Ott's assay office, established in 1853 and still standing, a miner from across the Sierra entered one memorable day in 1859 with puzzling specimens from a new "strike" made near Washoe Lake in Nevada. The ore was examined, and the assayer's report carried out from this building proved to be the most sensational bit of news since the announcement of Marshall's discovery of gold at Coloma in 1848, for it heralded the fabulous wealth of the Comstock silver mines, which within a few years produced almost one billion dollars.

Next door to the assayer's office, the Native Sons of the Golden West, together with the Wells Fargo Bank and Union Trust Company, have placed a bronze plaque on the site of the early Wells Fargo Express office, established in 1853. To the right of this location is the site of the Union Hotel. Other pioneer landmarks of the town include two firehouses of the 1860's, with their quaint steeples.

On Commercial Street, which led from Coyoteville to the creek, a few old brick stores are standing in the two blocks that formerly made up Chinatown. Shacks had stood there before an ordinance was passed requiring brick buildings as a protection against fire. The Chinese responded to this action by moving almost en masse to another site just northeast of town, where a new wooden Chinatown was built—and subsequently burned. A few of the more enterprising Chinese, however, remained on the original site and erected these surviving brick structures.

The first religious services in Nevada City, as in many other mining camps throughout the Sierra, were held under the spreading branches of a tree. In the summer of 1850, at the instance of Alcalde Stamps and Mr. Lamden, a former minister, money was raised by popular subscription for the first church. This was a crude affair built of shakes, and in this simple house of worship services were held for a time by the various denominations represented in the community.

The Congregationalists, organized September 28, 1851, by Rev. James H. Warren, took over the little shake church building, but replaced it in the autumn of 1855 by a frame structure. This edifice, with its fine bell, was destroyed by fire in 1856. The following year a brick church was erected, but in the conflagration of 1863 this building likewise, with a library of 1,000 volumes, was lost. The structure erected in 1864 during the pastorate of Rev. H. H. Cummings is still standing at Main and Church streets and is now a Baptist church.

The history of this Congregational church is connected with a circumstance of statewide significance, and illustrates the broad influence that radiated from the pioneer ministries of many of these mountain charges. W. W. Ferrier says of this event: "The movement out of which was to

SAN JUAN RIDGE COUNTRY

come the College of California [forerunner of the University of California] had its inception in May 1853, a few days after the arrival of Professor Henry Durant, in the little mountain town of Nevada City." There, on May 9, a joint session of the Congregational Association of California and the Presbytery of San Francisco (New School) was held, and on the 17th a plan was adopted for establishing an institution of learning in California.

The little pioneer shake church building in which this meeting was held is known historically as the Washington Monument Church—"contributions for its erection having been made by men in the mines thereabout from every state in the Union.... The pastor, James H. Warren, was a graduate of Knox College.... Pastor in 1853 in that little mountain town, participator in that early educational movement ... James H. Warren was destined as Congregational Home Missionary Superintendent ... to lay by his memorable service the foundations of enduring churches over all the State."

Another pioneer church of Nevada City is St. Canice's Catholic Church, built in 1864 and still in use.

Washington and Its Neighbors

Climbing the Washington Ridge over Highway 20, one passes a solitary grave at the right, seven miles northeast of Nevada City. Here in 1858 an emigrant family buried their two-year-old boy, Julius Alfred Appertson. For years this grave, marked by an inscribed wooden plaque nailed to the overshadowing pine tree, was tended by unknown hands, and after that by the Native Sons and Daughters of the Golden West. The California State Highway Commission ignored the original specifications for the road at this point sufficiently to leave the grave of this child undisturbed beneath its sentinel pine.

About seven miles further, the motorist suddenly comes upon a marvelous view of rugged mountain scenery dominated by the majestic Sierra Buttes, which rise above the pine-clad ridges to the north and are visible for 100 miles in every direction. From this point a road winds down six miles through magnificent pines to the old mining town of Washington, picturesquely situated on the bank of the South Yuba River. Seeming to belie its memories of the stirring "days of '49," the quiet little town of today has a population of less than 150. Next to the frame hotel stands an old store with massive stone walls, and across the street is another. Just outside the town are immense piles of huge granite boulders carried there stone by stone by patient Chinese miners of long ago.

In the vicinity of the town during the gold days, numerous mining camps were located at the wealth-producing bars and flats along the river. While many of these camps never attained the dignity of towns, some of them developed into trading centers of considerable activity. At the mouth of Canyon Creek about three miles up the river from Washington was Canal Bar, from which the line of camps extended downstream past Long Bar, Keno Bar, Jimmy Brown's Bar, and Boulder Bar to Rocky Bar, a prosperous place, opposite which was Grissell Bar, worked by Chinese. Across the river from Washington was the Brass Wire Bar, which in 1880 was worked entirely by Chinese miners. Below the town the chain of camps was continued by Whiskey Bar, Brandy Flat, Jackass Flat, and Lizard Flat, opposite which was the once thriving settlement of Jefferson.

Four miles east of the Washington turnoff, a monument has been erected near a viewpoint overlooking the diggings of Alpha and Omega, now ghost towns. Alpha (SRL 628) was the birthplace of the noted prima donna Emma Nevada. The Alpha mines became exhausted in 1880, but up to that time they had produced no less than $1,500,000 in gold. To the east was its sister camp, Omega (SRL 629), where the deep pit washed out by hydraulic mining reveals the old diggings from which $2,500,000 was taken during the same period. This mine operated off and on until 1949. Across the river from Washington a road winds up the canyon to the famous Eagle Bird Mine, while from the Washington bridge another road leads about three miles to the Spanish Mine, where Patrick Dillon first panned for gold on Poorman's Creek in 1851.

"Bring Me Men to Match My Mountains"

Along the San Juan Ridge are the gravel deposits of an ancient river channel left high and dry above the present drainage system. These accumulations, washed down in some past geologic age and containing fossil wood and nearly every kind of rock known to the Sierra region, "were partly formed from the degradation of quartz veins," the result being a richly auriferous mass. The gold, however, is disseminated unevenly throughout the whole, the lower levels being the richest. The only way in which this gold can be extracted in paying quantities is by hydraulic mining, a method prohibited by the federal Anti-Debris Act of 1883 because of its destructiveness to agriculture, but later allowed again with certain restrictions.

It was along the San Juan Ridge that the most spectacular hydraulic operations took place. In this gigantic search for gold, an enterprise and ingenuity were combined which "left as mementoes the great hydraulic pits that appear to be the work of a Brobdingnagian race." Three companies owned vast mines in the region, which were operated at a tremendous outlay. High up in the Sierra, 6,000 feet above sea level, reservoirs were constructed from which the water supply for hundreds of mines along the ridge was obtained through a system of canals and flumes. Although constructed in 1850–80 merely with pick and shovel and carpenter's level, they are still intact, exhibiting a marvel of workmanship upon which modern engineers could scarcely improve.

These three companies were the Eureka Lake and Yuba Canal Company, with headquarters at North Columbia, which owned four reservoirs and a system of ditches 200 miles long; the North

Bloomfield Mining Company, with 43 miles of ditches; and the Milton Mining and Water Company, with offices at French Corral, which owned 80 miles of ditches. The total expenditure of these companies for construction and equipment amounted to $5,568,000.

In order to obtain the most effective management of the ditches and flumes along the ridge, the companies in 1878 built, cooperatively, the world's first long-distance telephone line, at a cost of $6,000. This line was 60 miles long and extended up the ridge from French Corral through Birchville, Sweetland, North San Juan, Cherokee, North Columbia, Lake City, North Bloomfield, Moore's Flat, Graniteville, Milton, and Bowman Lake. It was managed by the Ridge Telephone Company and owned jointly by the three named mining companies. Edison instruments manufactured in Boston in 1876 were used.

"Along the route of that telephone line, one may see the results of hydraulic mining operations—hillsides washed away and gutted for gold which cradles and long-toms could never have recovered. The terrain, mountainous and extremely rugged, is traversed by roads that are narrow and tortuous; but incomparable vistas of forested heights and verdant valleys pass in a review that is never to be forgotten.... Below the mountain rims are livid scars, where age-old formations crumbled before the onslaught of great jets of water, searching the very bowels of the earth for gold."

The largest of these colossal excavations, the Malakoff, near North Bloomfield, is second in size only to the La Grange Mine near Weaverville (Trinity County). Its sheer cliffs, multicolored pinnacles, and fantastic minarets are exquisitely molded, reminding one of those weird and spectacular formations found in the desert canyons of the arid Southwest. It is difficult to realize that this marvel is man's handiwork, and one feels that the stirring call "Bring me men to match my mountains" has been indeed fulfilled here. There are plans to make the Malakoff diggings a state park.

Enormous profits in gold were being washed out along San Juan Ridge when the famous Sawyer decision of January 23, 1884, finally closed all hydraulic mines of the state. A mining engineer, resident in the district many years and eminently qualified to make such a statement, once said that

$400 million, at the very least, remains locked in the vast storehouse of San Juan Ridge.

Certain vitalizing sections of the Caminetti Act, passed by Congress in 1893, make it possible to regulate hydraulic mining by impounding the debris under the regulations of the California Debris Commission. Through the efforts of the late Harry L. Englebright, member of the U.S. House of Representatives, this act was amended to permit the building of debris control dams, such as Englebright Dam on the Yuba River near Mooney Flat and North Fork Dam on the American River near Auburn, so that hydraulic mining would not be directly destructive to the farmlands of the Sacramento Valley.

Many of the old dams and canals constructed so laboriously with pick and shovel for the development of placer and hydraulic mining along the San Juan Ridge were relocated and rebuilt by the Nevada Irrigation District along larger and more massive lines. The dam at Bowman Lake, built in 1868 and raised to higher levels in 1872 and 1876, was superseded by a massive rock fill built of granite taken from the old dam and from quarries nearby. To the credit of the builders of the original dam, the Nevada Irrigation District, after six years of careful study and survey, decided to locate the new dam on the site of the old and to use the same type of construction as in the original one. Furthermore, the irrigation district officials attributed much of their success in carrying out the new project to the reliable and extensive records of the early mining companies.

French Corral

Equal to the wealth of the gold ridges is the treasure of history and romance that lies in the rugged San Juan Ridge. Not only from the pits of the long-deserted mines and the hundreds of miles of rotting flumes and overgrown, debris-filled ditches, but still more from the picturesque towns that are found along the mountain roads, one gets a sense of the comedy and tragedy that made up one of the most stirring periods in the great epic of California's mining era. Some of these cities of the past can claim about 100 inhabitants today, while others, far off the usual routes of travel, are mere ghosts, deserted, crumbling, or entirely obliterated, and unmarked except by the inevitable diggings, which are everywhere visible in spite of the smoothing over by the passage of time.

Beginning at the lower tip of the ridge, the road passes through French Corral, the first of the historic mining camps to spring up along the ancient San Juan River channel. There in 1849 the first settler, a Frenchman, built a corral for his mules. Very soon it was discovered that the locality was rich in placer gold, and a town grew up on the site of the Frenchman's corral. Later, as hydraulic mining developed, French Corral became second only to North San Juan in size and importance, numbering its population in the thousands.

Now a hamlet of only a few dozen persons, French Corral retains a flavor of romance in its historic landmarks. The office of the Milton Min-

Hotel (later schoolhouse), French Corral

ing and Water Company, in which one terminus of the first long-distance telephone line *(SRL 247)* was located, has been torn down, but the site is marked. The brick walls of the old Wells Fargo Express office, built in the 1850's and equipped with iron doors and window shutters that once guarded millions of dollars of gold against possible robbers, look as though they would stand for generations to come. The former schoolhouse was a hotel in the 1850's. A number of old homes are still in use.

Beyond French Corral are Birchville and Sweetland, both of which were quite populous centers from the 1850's to the 1880's. Birchville, three miles northeast of French Corral, still has St. Columcille's Catholic Church, which was once the Bridgeport Union Guard Hall.

North San Juan

On the state highway from Nevada City to Downieville lies North San Juan, still the metropolis of the San Juan Ridge country, although its one block of picturesque old buildings, its scattered homes, and its 125 inhabitants are but a remnant of the city which boasted a population of several thousand until the 1880's.

San Juan Hill to the north was first mined in 1853 by Christian Kientz, who, according to tradition, was the originator of the name. The several stories purporting to explain why a Castilian name, so unusual in the northern mines, was bestowed upon this locality by a German at least indicate that the story-telling propensities of these sturdy mountaineers were not undeveloped. The most likely of the tales is that Kientz, who had been with General Scott's army in Mexico, supposedly saw a resemblance between this hill in the Sierra Nevada and the hill on which stands the old Mexican prison, San Juan de Ulloa, and named it accordingly. Later, when the whole hill had been staked out to rich claims, the name was given to the promising camp that grew up close by. By 1857 San Juan was of sufficient importance to be assigned a post office, an advance that necessitated prefixing "North" to the name in order to distinguish it from the much older San Juan in San Benito County.

This quaint hamlet retains a number of historic landmarks, although the ancient frame National Hotel, to which "weighty presidents and secretaries" from San Francisco came "with their gold-headed canes and frock coats to seriously confer with their superintendents at the mines," has succumbed to fire. The Masonic Hall, built in 1862, is now a grocery store and bar. In the firehouse is an ancient hosecart, brought around the Horn in the early 1850's and transported by ox-drawn wagons from San Francisco after that city had abandoned its two-wheel carts for the more up-to-date four-wheel wagons. To the walls of a large brick structure still clings a heavy steel railing which once supported an upper veranda, reminiscent of the days when the town band gave summer-evening concerts from the gallery.

Many houses had been built on the hill above town, but when these were found to stand on "pay gravel" they were bought by mining companies and "piped away." A high cliff forms the southern wall of the chasm washed out by hydraulic operations, along the rim of which today a road winds, while in the distance rise the snow-crested peaks of the Sierra.

Cherokee and North Columbia

Passing along the scenic Ridge Road, now through groves of pine, now above them, one comes to Cherokee, also called Tyler, five miles east of North San Juan. This ghost town of the 1850's consists today of a little Catholic church and a handful of weatherworn houses which stand at the edge of the diggings. Just north of Cherokee is the old Badger Hill Mine, once a famous producer.

At North Columbia, originally known as Columbia Hill, three miles beyond Cherokee, a few of the old homes still stand, notably that of the Coughlan family. The old schoolhouse also remains. At North Columbia begins the famous Foote's Crossing Road to Alleghany in Sierra County.

North Columbia was originally built on the Pliocene gravel bed of the ancient river channel, but in 1878, when the site was found to contain rich gold deposits, the town was moved to its present location. Its neighbors, Grizzly Hill and Lake City, shared in its changing fortunes. The former is but a memory, while Lake City, four miles to the southeast on the way to North Bloomfield, is now a ghost town.

A forlorn-looking frame hotel built by the Bell Brothers in 1855, two years before the founding of Lake City, long stood at the crossroads, with lace curtains still at the dust-covered windows. An upper balcony fell to ruins, the little garden under the locust trees became a dense thicket, and the building was finally removed. Beyond the site the old reservoir, or "lake," is nothing more than a grass-grown depression where cattle feed. A rickety old boardinghouse and a collapsed barn complete the picture of general dissolution.

North Bloomfield

Entering the broad, locust-lined street of North Bloomfield one is overcome by a feeling of remoteness. Surrounded by wild and rugged mountains, the charming little town nestles almost at the brink of a huge hydraulic canyon, pinnacled and castellated and touched with vivid colors like a place enchanted. A few of the old homes are still occupied, and have neat gardens at their doors. The McKillian and Mobley store, still standing unoccupied, was built in 1852 and housed the post office until it was discontinued in 1942. The little firehouse also remains.

At the office of the Malakoff Mine gold used to be made into bars for transportation to the mint. The largest single bar produced there weighed 512 pounds, more than a quarter of a ton, with a value exceeding $114,000. A model of this famous bar may be seen at the Ferry Building in San Francisco, while another is on exhibit in the courthouse at Nevada City.

Humbug, the name first given to North Bloomfield, was not accepted by the Postal Department when the town applied for a post office. Upon the origin of the name there hangs a tale typical of those told of the various other localities to which this name was applied:

"In the winter of 1851–1852 a party, composed of the incongruous elements of two Irishmen and a German, prospected along the creek, near which they discovered a rich deposit of gravel, yielding them a goodly quantity of dust. When their supplies became exhausted, one of the sons of Erin was despatched to Nevada City for provisions, being strictly enjoined to preserve due silence in regard to their good fortune ... After purchasing the supplies and a mule to carry them, he invested liberally in 'corn juice,' his purse strings and his tongue both becoming loosened at the same time ... and he boasted of his rich 'strike,' declining, however, to give the location. When he took his departure the next morning, a crowd of ravenous gold seekers tracked him to camp. Up and down the creek they wandered, panning a little here and a little there, but in no place finding the rich diggings they anticipated. Disgusted, the crowd returned to the city, calling the creek 'Humbug,' which name has always clung to it, and which it later bequeathed to the town."

North Bloomfield, with its neighboring camps at Derbec and Relief Hill, once had a population of about 2,000. Situated three miles to the east, Relief Hill, long a ghost town, has now been virtually obliterated by mining operations. Farther to the northeast were three rival settlements in the 1850's: Moore's Flat on the Middle Fork of the Yuba River, established as early as 1851 and named for H. H. Moore, who built the first store and house there; Orleans Flat, settled about the same time; and Woolsey's Flat. Moore's Flat and its rivals have little left but names.

Graniteville

Graniteville, a town on the line of the old Ridge Telephone Company, lies in a beautiful forested region near the summit of the mountains 26 miles northeast of Nevada City. Gold was mined in the gulches here as early as 1850, and because the diggings were shallow a number of miners were soon attracted to the spot. The original name of the place was Eureka South, to distinguish it from Eureka in Humboldt County and Eureka North in Sierra County, but when the post office was established there in 1867, the present name was adopted.

Graniteville was threatened with extinction when the surface diggings became exhausted, but during the middle 1860's gold-bearing quartz was found in the vicinity and the town again became a thriving place. A severe fire swept through it in 1878, but because hydraulic-mining companies had reservoirs in the mountains above the town, Graniteville was rebuilt and until 1883 was an active distributing point for these companies. After that date, however, its existence depended on quartz mining and lumbering. Now its schoolhouse and many of its old residences have been beautifully renovated as summer homes. The post office was closed in 1959.

SOURCES

Adams, Kramer A. *Covered Bridges of the West.* Howell-North, Berkeley, 1963.
Bean, Edwin F., compiler. *Bean's History and Directory of Nevada County, California.* Nevada City, 1867.
Bryant, Edwin. *What I Saw in California.* D. Appleton & Co., New York, 1848, 1849.
Buckbee, Edna. "Thespis in El Dorado. A Sketch and Something of a Defense of Lola Montez," *Touring Topics,* XX, No. 10 (October 1928), 32–34, 47–48.
California Mining Journal, featuring Nevada and Sierra County mines, I, No. 1 (August 1931).
Ferrier, W. W. *Origin and Development of the University of California.* Sather Gate Book Shop, Berkeley, 1930.
Geologic Guidebook along Highway 49—Sierran Gold Belt, the Mother Lode Country. State of California, Division of Mines, San Francisco, 1948.
Gold Rush Country. Lane Publishing Co., Menlo Park, 1957.
Hanson, George Emmanuel. "The Early History of Yuba River Valley." Master's thesis in history. University of California, Berkeley, August 1924.
Houghton, Mrs. Eliza Poor (Donner). *The Expedition of the Donner Party and Its Tragic Fate.* A. C. McClurg & Co., Chicago, 1911.
Johnston, Philip. "Relics of the Gold-Rush among the Northern Diggin's," *Touring Topics,* XXIV, No. 1 (January 1932), 10–25, 45–46.
Lardner, W. B., and M. J. Brock. *History of Placer and Nevada Counties, California.* Historic Record Co., Los Angeles, 1924.
McGlashan, C. F. *History of the Donner Party. A Tragedy of the Sierra.* A. L. Bancroft, San Francisco, 1881.
The Morning Union. Commemorative Edition. Grass Valley, July 1, 1927.
Rourke, Constance. *Troopers of the Gold Coast, or the Rise of Lotta Crabtree.* Harcourt, Brace, New York, 1928.
Spencer, Mrs. Dorcas James. *A History of the Woman's Christian Temperance Union of Northern and Central California.* West Coast Printing Co., Oakland, 1911.
Stewart, George R., Jr. *The California Trail.* McGraw-Hill, New York, 1962.
——— *Ordeal by Hunger.* Holt, New York, 1936.
Thompson, Hugh B. *Directory of the City of Nevada and Grass Valley.* Charles F. Robbins, San Francisco, 1861.
Wells, Harry L. *History of Nevada County, California.* Thompson & West, Oakland, 1880.
Weston, Otheto. *Mother Lode Album.* Stanford University Press, Stanford, 1948.
Wolff, J. L. "The Yuba River Canyon Country." Ms., 1932.

Orange County

ORANGE COUNTY, named by the legislature after the orange groves that had made the district famous, was created in 1889 from a portion of Los Angeles County. Santa Ana has always been the county seat.

Portolá's Trail

A little company of soldiers and priests led by Gaspar de Portolá entered what is now Orange County on July 22, 1769, on their way north to seek the port of Monterey. Passing through low, open mountain country, they made camp for the night near an Indian village north of San Onofre. Here two little Indian girls, who were very ill, were baptized by the fathers—the first administration of baptism in Alta California. The soldiers named the place Los Cristianitos ("the little Christians"), and it is still called Cristianitos Canyon. The site of the first baptism (*SRL 562*) is the spring called Aguaje de la Piedra, now within the boundaries of Camp Joseph H. Pendleton. A marker stands there, off Cristianitos Road, and another has been placed at the city hall in San Clemente.

On July 23 the Portolá party "came to a very pleasant green valley, full of willows, alders, live oaks, and other trees not known to us. It has a large arroyo, which at the point where we crossed it carried a good stream of fresh and good water, which, after running a little way, formed in pools in some large patches of tules. We halted there, calling it the valley of Santa María Magdalena."

Thus does Fray Juan Crespí describe the valley of San Juan Capistrano, in which Portolá and his men stopped. The spot chosen was within a few hundred yards of the present Mission San Juan Capistrano. At this same spot, the explorers camped again on January 20 and April 21, 1770. Juan Bautista de Anza camped there on January 8, 1776, on his way from Mission San Gabriel to San Diego to lend aid to Governor Rivera during the Indian uprising.

From this point, Portolá's trail lay along the foothills east of the Santa Ana Valley, and across the Puente Hills into Los Angeles County. On July 24, camp was made on Aliso Creek, near the present site of the hamlet of El Toro, where there was a village of friendly Indians. Here the party rested for two days, moving on a short distance to Tomato Spring on the Irvine Ranch on July 26. Again they pitched camp "near a dry lagoon on a slope, from which [they] examined the spacious plain, the end of which [they] could not see."

On the following day, after crossing the plain, camp was made near a stream, which to this day is called Santiago Creek. This campsite was near or just above the modern city of Orange, at a spot that the Spaniards considered suitable for the building of a city.

Skirting the mountains to the north, Portolá reached the Santa Ana River on July 28. There he pitched camp near the west bank opposite an Indian village. The site of this camp is due east of Anaheim. Here Anza camped on January 7, 1776.

Crossing the swiftly flowing river with great difficulty on July 29, the pilgrims traveled northwest until they reached "a very green little valley, which has a small pool of water, on whose bank there is a very large village of very friendly heathen." Camp was made on a hill near the pool and the place was called Santa Marta, now on the south side of La Habra.

Descending the hill on July 30, the little band proceeded north across the valley and over the Puente Hills, probably by Hacienda Boulevard, coming into the spacious and fertile valley of the San Gabriel. The later main highway, which came from Whittier to La Habra, and then through the hills along Harbor Boulevard, was opened by the Portolá party on their return trips in January and April 1770.

Mission San Juan Capistrano

Owing to the zeal of Padre Presidente Junípero Serra, the founding of Mission San Juan Capistrano was first attempted as early as October 1775. Palou writes:

"The little troop, composed of Fr. Lasuén, Lieutenant Ortega, a sergeant, and the necessary soldiers, left San Diego toward the end of October. On arriving at the site, an enramada or arbor was hastily erected, near which a large cross was constructed, raised, blessed, and venerated by all. On an altar prepared in the arbor, Fr. Lasuén offered up the first holy Mass. This happened on

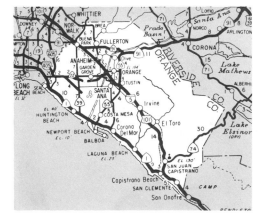

October 30, 1775, the last day of the octave after the feast of San Juan Capistrano, the patron of the mission. Formal possession was then taken of the lands and thus the beginning was made amid the rejoicings of numerous pagans who had flocked thither. They proved their satisfaction by helping to cut and bring down the timber for the chapel and the dwelling."

Hardly had the first founding of San Juan Capistrano taken place than news of the Indian uprising at San Diego forced the fathers to give up the undertaking temporarily. It was not until October of the following year that they returned, this time in company with Father Serra himself. Palou relates that the cross erected by Father Lasuén the year before was found to be still in place and that the two bells which had been left in hiding were disinterred, hung in position, and rung joyously to tell the Indians of the missionaries' return. An arbor was quickly erected and on November 1, 1776, the formal founding of Mission San Juan Capistrano took place.

The work of building and conversion was left in the care of Fathers Pablo Mugártegui and Gregório Amúrrio, both good and efficient men, who constructed the first chapel and dwelling houses and who increased the prosperity of the mission both materially and spiritually.

It was long believed by some that the first mission church was erected up the stream four or five miles from the present site at a place known as Misión Vieja, or La Vieja—The Old Mission. Engelhardt, however, believes that the facts point to one location rather than to two, citing statements of Father Palou regarding the finding of the cross and bells and the distance of the first

church from the sea as evidence. "From the buildings," writes Palou, "the ocean can be seen and the ships when they cruise there; for the beach is only about half a league [rather, a league, says Engelhardt] distant." There is no mention in any of the diaries of a change of location. Engelhardt states that Misión Vieja was only a rancho of the mission.

San Juan Capistrano, which was planned by Father Gregório, was over nine years in the building, the first stone having been laid in 1796, and consecration taking place on September 8, 1806. On December 8, 1812, a great earthquake undid the work of years and took the lives of 40 neophytes. Little attempt was made to rebuild the fallen church until 1860, when some adobe restorations were made, only to be washed away by the first heavy rainstorms. In later years, the Landmarks Club restored the beautiful arched corridors of the patio, the old *pozolera* with its quaint chimney, and Serra's church, the long building that still stands on the east side of the patio. It is said to be the oldest part of the mission, probably having been erected as early as 1777, and the only church left standing in California in which Father Serra celebrated Mass. Extensive restorations were also carried on by the Catholic Church under the direction of Father St. John O'Sullivan.

San Juan Capistrano *(SRL 200)* was perhaps the grandest and most beautiful of all the missions. Today the great stone church, which was its crowning glory, lies in magnificent ruins, the delight of artists and poets. Its exquisite carvings, done by a master mason over a period of nine years; the great dome, one of the original seven,

Mission San Juan Capistrano

within which was once the altar; the semi-Moorish architecture, set in a frame of green hills and purple mountains, and softened by the old garden still lingering within its walls, make of San Juan Capistrano an unforgettable picture, an Old World poem. The romance of the old mission is enhanced by the legend, celebrated in song, of the return of the swallows each year on St. Joseph's Day, March 19. The largest part of the flock does in fact arrive on that day in most years.

The quaint little town of San Juan Capistrano, which today clusters about the old mission, was described by J. Smeaton Chase in 1913 as "the most interesting small town in California. The reason is that it has remained Californian in the old sense, that is to say, Spanish, Mexican, and Indian . . . Capistrano's threescore or so of houses are mostly adobes, its stores are 'tiendas,' its meat-markets 'carnicerías,' its weekly function a 'baile,' its celebrations 'fiestas,' and the autumnal employment of its people 'pizcando nueces' in the walnut orchards."

The town retains much of its interest and some of its old buildings even today. The original registration of San Juan Capistrano as a State Historical Landmark included, for this reason, the town as well as the mission. The restaurant known as "El Adobe de Capistrano" incorporates two old adobes, the Miguel Yorba on the north and the *juzgado* (justice court and jail) on the south. The two buildings were originally remodeled as the Van der Leck residence in 1910. To the east across the street is the brick house of Judge Richard Egan, built in the 1880's on the site of an old Aguilar adobe. The Domingo Yorba adobe stands at 31871 Camino Capistrano. Next door is La Casa de Tepenco, built after 1840, with lower story of adobe and upper of frame construction. The picturesque carved balcony was added in the 1880's. Part of the Juan Ávila adobe, once a huge structure, still stands at 31831 Camino Capistrano. The Blas Aguilar adobe is located at 31806 El Camino Real. Part of it is said to have been built in 1794 and occupied by the mayordomos of the mission.

At Verdugo and Los Rios streets is the Ríos adobe, built in 1794. It stands on the tiny grant, a fraction more than seven acres, made to Santiago Ríos by Governor Manuel Micheltorena on July 5, 1843. The *ranchito* was located on San Juan Creek between the mission and the beach and was entirely surrounded by Rancho Boca de la Playa. The adobe is still the home of the Ríos family and has been marked by E Clampus Vitus, a social organization of historians, as the oldest single-family residence in California continuously occupied by the same family. Rancho Boca de la Playa, 6,607 acres, was granted to Emigdio Vejar by Governor Pío Pico on May 7, 1846. It was later owned by Juan Ávila and then by Pablo Pryor. The old adobe ranch house still stands in its lovely location at 33751 Camino Capistrano in Capistrano Beach—under a little point of hill overlooking the ocean at the mouth of San Juan Creek.

On the heights of Adams Avenue in Costa Mesa, half a mile east of the Santa Ana River, stands an adobe *(SRL 227)* built about 1823–25 as an *estancia,* or station, of Mission San Juan Capistrano. An *estancia* was a less important outpost of a mission than an *asistencia.* The adobe was located on Rancho Santiago de Santa Ana, and, when the rancho was later subdivided, it became the home of Diego Sepúlveda, an auxiliary alcalde of Pueblo de Los Angeles. There are plans to utilize the old adobe as a museum and library.

The Henry Siever adobe, in Sievers Canyon one-quarter mile east of the San Juan Guard Station on Highway 74, is said to have been another *estancia* of San Juan Capistrano. It is located 13 miles northeast of the mission. The Trabuco adobe, whose ruins were long visible in Trabuco Canyon, was probably another mission station.

Dana's Cove

On the coast seven and one-half miles southeast of Laguna Beach, west of the outlet of San Juan Creek into the sea, lies Dana's Cove. The promontory on the west is Dana Point *(SRL 189),* and farther west are San Juan Capistrano Point and the San Juan Rocks. In Spanish and Mexican days the cove was the site of the embarcadero, which played an important part in the material life of Mission San Juan Capistrano. Here, in 1818, the pirate Hippolyte de Bouchard landed to raid the mission.

This cove and the high cliff above it are described by Richard Henry Dana in *Two Years Before the Mast,* and they were later named in his honor. The name is also preserved by a modern seaside resort, Dana Point, to the north. It is easy to identify the perilous cliff over which the cowhides were thrown to the beach below, during the first visit of the *Pilgrim* in the spring of 1835. Dana describes the loading thus:

"Down this height we pitched the hides, throwing them as far out into the air as we could; and as they were all large, stiff, and doubled, like the cover of a book, the wind took them, and they swayed and eddied about, plunging and rising in the air, like a kite when it has broken its string. As it was now low tide, there was no danger of their falling into the water; and, as fast as they came to ground, the men below picked them up, and, taking them on their heads, walked off with them to the boat. It was really a picturesque sight: the great height, the scaling of the hides, and the continual walking to and fro of the men, who looked like mites, on the beach. This was the romance of hide droghing!"

Rancho Santiago de Santa Ana

Rancho Santiago de Santa Ana extended along the east bank of the Santa Ana River from the mountains to the sea. It was bounded on the east by a line extending from Red Hill to the sea and running parallel to the present Newport Boulevard one mile to the southeast. It is the only rancho lying entirely within Orange County the history of which goes back to the Spanish period, some portion of it always having been in the hands of the Yorbas.

José Antonio Yorba first saw this land when he passed over it in 1769 as a corporal in Portolá's company. His father-in-law, Juan Pablo Grijalva, was awarded pasturage rights to the area in 1801, but there is some doubt whether he actually lived on the land. Grijalva had come to California with Anza in 1776. On July 1, 1810, the rancho of 11 leagues was formally granted to Yorba and his nephew, Juan Pablo Peralta, by Governor Arrillaga.

The site of the first adobe erected on Rancho Santiago de Santa Ana is on Hoyt Hill, the most westerly point of El Modeno Hills, between El Modeno and Villa Park. Hoyt Hill is on the south side of Santiago Creek directly overlooking the Santiago Boulevard bridge. Another adobe site was west of Orange. A cluster of adobes stood in the vicinity of the present town of Olive. The community became known as Santa Ana, or Santa Ana Abajo ("lower") to distinguish it from Santa Ana Arriba ("upper") on Bernardo Yorba's Rancho Cañon de Santa Ana, farther up the river. A marker has been placed at the crossroads at Olive to commemorate the former settlement as Old Santa Ana *(SRL 204)*. An old map designates an adobe just south of Olive as the "Casa de Yorba y tierras."

Red Hill *(SRL 203)*, or Cerrito de las Ranas ("hill of the frogs"), as it was known to the Spaniards, was an ancient landmark followed by Indians, padres, rancheros, and early map makers. It became the dividing line between ranchos. Between it and the Santiago Hills nearby ran the old trail. Later the stage route also followed this road, crossing the Santa Ana River near Olive and dividing north of the river, one route going through La Habra Valley via Don Pío Pico's rancho, and the other west of Anaheim, via Rancho Los Coyotes, on which Buena Park is now situated, and Santa Fe Springs. One of the old stage stations, a mile or two east of Red Hill, was a landmark for many years but has long since disappeared. Another stood at Olive, where there was also an early flour mill. Red Hill is a prominent landmark three miles northeast of Tustin, near Browning Avenue and La Colina Drive.

In Santa Ana Canyon stands the Ramón Peralta adobe, built in 1871, one of the latest and best preserved of Orange County's adobes. It is located at the rear of a restaurant on the south side of the Riverside Freeway, one and one-quarter miles east of the Imperial Highway junction. Behind it stands the old Peralta School. Two other

adobes stand on the north side of the freeway within a short distance of the Peralta house, but they are difficult to recognize because of extensive remodeling. To the west is the small and very old Manuel Felíz adobe. Felíz married a daughter of Juan Pablo Peralta. To the east is the adobe of Carlos Domínguez, another son-in-law of Juan Pablo Peralta, which has the appearance of a two-story frame house.

The present city of Santa Ana was founded by William Henry Spurgeon, who settled in the area in 1869. He gave his town the name that had formerly been applied to the settlement near Olive. In 1913, two years before his death, Spurgeon built the present W. H. Spurgeon Block, at the southwest corner of Sycamore and Fourth streets, the first four-story building in Orange County. It replaced a two-story wooden structure on the same site, built by Spurgeon in 1883. As late as the early 1880's, an old adobe called the "Policarpia," after St. Polycarp, a disciple of St. John the Evangelist, stood at the corner of Seventeenth and Bristol streets.

Rancho Santiago de Santa Ana was bounded on the southeast by Rancho Lomas de Santiago, toward the mountains, and Rancho San Joaquín, toward the sea. Lomas de Santiago, 47,227 acres, was granted to Teodocio Yorba by Governor Pío Pico on May 26, 1846. San Joaquín was owned by José Sepúlveda, to whom it was granted by Governor Juan B. Alvarado on April 15, 1837, and May 13, 1842. The United States issued a patent to 48,803 acres. Sepúlveda's adobe home once stood at the head of Newport Bay. Later, he built another in what is now the southwestern part of Santa Ana, near Willits and Bristol streets. This he called "Refugio," and there in the 1850's and 1860's he lived in true baronial style.

Ranchos Lomas de Santiago and San Joaquín, together with a strip along the southeast line of Rancho Santiago de Santa Ana, ultimately came into the hands of James Irvine, and most of this land—close to 100,000 acres—remains today as the Irvine Ranch, one of the last great ranches in California. It covers almost one-fifth of Orange County and stretches from the mountains to the sea. James Irvine, born in Belfast, Ireland, in 1827, came to California during the gold rush, but made his fortune in merchandising rather than mining. In the 1860's he entered into partnership with Flint, Bixby and Company, and by 1876 was sole owner of what became known as the Irvine Ranch. Irvine died in 1886, and management of the huge estate eventually passed to his son, James Irvine, Jr., who formed the Irvine Company in 1894. This company holds title to the ranch today, but the lands are gradually being subdivided and converted to other uses, including a campus of the University of California. The small town of Irvine (post office, East Irvine) is near the center of the ranch, and five miles north at Irvine Boulevard and Myford Road are the offices of the Irvine Company. Across Myford Road from the headquarters stands the home built by James Irvine, Jr., shortly after the turn of the century. The old residence, with its double row of palm trees, has been converted to offices.

Ramón Peralta Adobe, Santa Ana Canyon

In the northern part of the ranch are Irvine Park and Irvine Lake.

Rancho Cañon de Santa Ana

The most important ranch house in Orange County during the Mexican period was that of Don Bernardo Yorba, one of California's greatest landowners. It was situated on Rancho Cañon de Santa Ana on the north bank of the Santa Ana River, and was a very large establishment. A spacious patio was entirely surrounded by adobe buildings, those on two sides being two stories high. Don Bernardo, a son of José Antonio Yorba of Rancho Santiago de Santa Ana, received his grant of 13,329 acres from Governor José Figueroa on August 1, 1834, and construction of the great hacienda began soon after.

The old house stood for years unoccupied and neglected. An effort to restore this fine landmark failed, and the owner razed its walls about 1927. Nothing but a historical marker is now left to show where once stood what was one of the greatest of the Mexican rancho houses in California. The site (SRL 226) in Santa Ana Canyon is on Esperanza Road about half a mile east of its junction with Imperial Highway north of the Riverside Freeway. Bits of tile and stone from the mansion have been incorporated into the monument. Not far away is the old Yorba Cemetery in which Don Bernardo lies buried.

Rancho Cañada de los Alisos

Rancho Cañada de los Alisos, an area of 10,668 acres according to the United States patent, was granted to José Serrano by Governor Juan B. Alvarado on May 3, 1842, and by Governor Pío Pico on May 27, 1846. It was acquired in the 1880's by Dwight Whiting. One of Serrano's adobes (SRL 199) still stands about two miles northeast of the little town of El Toro, on a private drive to the left of Trabuco Road. It is eight-tenths of a mile north of the junction of Trabuco and El Toro roads. The adobe was restored by the Whiting family in 1932. Across Aliso Creek once stood an adobe house belonging to Serrano's father-in-law, Juan Ávila, resident of San Juan Capistrano and grantee of Rancho Niguel.

Anaheim

Anaheim is the pioneer town of the American period in Orange County. It is antedated in the county only by the communities of San Juan Capistrano, Santa Ana Arriba, and Santa Ana Abajo. It is also one of the oldest colony experiments in the state, having been started in 1857 by Germans, chiefly from San Francisco. The plan was to purchase a tract of land in common, lay it out in small farms and vineyards, and work it under supervision of a general manager. There were 50 charter members, who purchased a part of the Rancho San Juan Cajón de Santa Ana from the family of Don Juan Pacífico Ontiveros, the original Mexican grantee.

This fertile tract of 1,165 acres on the north bank of the Santa Ana River, about 12 miles from the ocean, was divided into 50 twenty-acre lots for the little farms and vineyards, and 50 house

Mother Colony House, Anaheim

lots that were to make up the nucleus of the community. Besides these, there was enough public land for schoolhouses and public buildings. A fence made of 40,000 willow poles and five and a half miles long enclosed the entire colony. Most of the willows took root, forming a living wall about the place. Gates were erected at the north, south, west, and east ends of the two principal streets of the colony. The north gate (SRL 112), located at what is now the intersection of Los Angeles Street (Anaheim Boulevard) and North Street, was the main entrance to the settlement, being on the road from Los Angeles.

" 'The colonists,' says one writer," quoted by Lucile E. Dickson, " 'were a curious mixture ... two or three carpenters, four blacksmiths, three watchmakers, a brewer, an engraver, a shoemaker, a poet, a miller, a bookbinder, two or three merchants, a hatter, and a musician.'

"But in spite of this medley of professions, the colony flourished almost from the beginning, and for many years its name was almost a synonym for prosperity and industry throughout the south."

For many years the town was known as the "Campo Alemán" to its Spanish neighbors, because of the continued predominance of Germans. And, in spite of the hardships and struggle of the early years while the little colony was getting established financially, only one of the 50 settlers moved away.

At first supplies to Anaheim came through the port of San Pedro. By 1864, however, the colonists had organized the Anaheim Lighter Company and developed a port, with warehouse and dock, closer to the colony. Anaheim Landing (SRL 219), which served the entire Santa Ana Valley until the opening of the railroad in 1875, was located on Anaheim Bay at what is presently called Seal Beach. A historical marker has been placed 600 yards southwest of the intersection of Highway 1 and Bay Boulevard.

The Pioneer House of the Mother Colony (SRL 201) is said to be the first house built in Anaheim Colony, in 1857 by George Hansen, a leader of the group. It has been moved from its original location on North Los Angeles Street and placed at 414 West Street. It contains an interesting collection of relics of pioneer days gathered in the neighborhood. The museum was opened in 1929 by the Mother Colony Chapter,

Ontiveros-Kraemer Adobe, Placentia

D.A.R., and is now administered by the Anaheim Public Library.

In more recent years Anaheim has enjoyed international fame as the location of Disneyland. A rival attraction at nearby Buena Park (on Rancho Los Coyotes) is Knott's Berry Farm, to which Walter Knott has moved a number of old buildings from various towns in the West. One of these is the Maizeland School *(SRL 729)*, first school in the Rivera district (Los Angeles County). It was originally built in 1868 on Shugg Lane, now Slauson Avenue. Knott has also restored the ghost town of Calico in the Mojave Desert.

Rancho San Juan Cajón de Santa Ana, on which Anaheim is situated, was granted to Juan Pacífico Ontiveros by Governor Juan B. Alvarado on May 13, 1837. The United States patent was issued for 35,970 acres. One of the Ontiveros adobes is still standing at 330 East Crowther Avenue in Placentia and is known as the Kraemer adobe. Hidden from the road by dense foliage, it was once an L-shaped structure, but the wing built about 1850 was razed in the 1930's. The older part, which remains, was probably built soon after the rancho was granted. Ontiveros later moved to Santa Barbara County and died at the age of 95.

Newport Beach

About 1865 Captain S. S. Dunnells of San Diego brought the *Vaquero* into Newport Bay for the first time. It is believed that he named the "new port" he had found. In 1872 he and D. M. Dorman established a small dock and warehouse called Newport Landing. The following year James, Robert, and John McFadden, brothers, received a shipment of lumber at the landing for their personal use. Other settlers, however, prevailed upon them to sell the cargo, and the McFaddens decided to enter into the lumber business. They purchased Newport Landing the same year, 1873, and made it their headquarters. It later became known as McFadden's Landing and Port Orange. It was located just below the bluff that divides upper and lower Newport Bay, or near the intersection of Highway 1 and Dover Drive in Newport Beach. Eventually it became known as the Old Landing *(SRL 198)* when the McFaddens built a wharf on the ocean side of the peninsula at the present location of the Newport pier. The original wharf *(SRL 794)* on this site was completed in 1888, and in 1892, the same year

the town of Newport was laid out, it became the terminus of the Santa Ana and Newport Railroad. Until 1907 it was the major commercial port for Orange, San Bernardino, and Riverside counties.

On May 10, 1912, Glenn L. Martin flew a hydroplane from the waters of the Pacific Ocean at Balboa to Santa Catalina Island. It was the first water-to-water flight *(SRL 775)* and the longest and fastest overwater flight to that date. A monument at the foot of the Balboa pier commemorates this historic event. The Martin Aviation Company had its beginning in an abandoned church that stood on the present site of McLean's Garage near Second and Bush streets in Santa Ana. Here in 1909 Martin built his first airplane.

Landmarks of the Santa Ana Mountains

In the late 1870's and early 1880's Orange County (still a part of Los Angeles County at the time) experienced a short-lived mining boom. Hank Smith and William Curry discovered silver in 1877 in a canyon east of Santa Ana that was to become known as Silverado Canyon. The mining camp of Silverado *(SRL 202)* sprang up the following year and prospered for three or four years. The Blue Light was the principal mine in the district. The canyon is now filled with summer cabins.

In 1878 Ramón Mesquida discovered coal nearby, and the town of Carbondale *(SRL 228)* was built on the flat at the intersection of Santiago and Silverado canyons. The Southern Pacific Railroad operated the mine for a few years. In 1879 August Witte also discovered coal, this time in the Cañon de los Indios (Canyon of the Indians) to the north. His mine was named the Black Star, and the canyon, a branch of Santiago Canyon, was soon known by the same name as the mine. Black Star Canyon was the scene of a battle between William Wolfskill and other trappers and a band of Indian horse thieves in the early 1830's. The site of the Indian village *(SRL 217)* is marked by mounds and grinding rocks. It is six and two-tenths miles up Black Star Canyon Road from the intersection of this road with Silverado Canyon and Santiago Canyon roads.

Rugged Santiago Canyon was chosen by Madame Helena Modjeska, the famous Polish tragédienne, as the home to which she retired after a long dramatic career that took her all over the world. She had come to California in 1876 as a member of a small and short-lived Polish colony that attempted to establish itself at Anaheim. Another member was Henryk Sienkiewicz, the author of *Quo Vadis*. After the colony disbanded, Madame Modjeska returned to the stage for a few years. In 1883 she bought the canyon property from Joseph Edward Pleasants and named it "Forest of Arden." About four years later she began construction of a large and beautiful home, under the direction of Stanford White, famed architect. Madame Modjeska sold her property in 1906, three years before her death. The old home *(SRL 205)* is located near Highway S-18 and the boundary of the Cleveland National Forest. It is entirely hidden by the forest and the estate is heavily fenced against intruders. A historical marker is located on the public road nearby.

Across the creek from Modjeska's home is Flores Peak (SRL 225), scene of the capture of a group of bandits in January 1857 by a posse led by General Andrés Pico. Juan Flores, leader of the gang, escaped but was later captured by Pico. Pico's posse was organized after the killing of Sheriff James Barton of Los Angeles by the Flores gang. Flores had escaped from San Quentin Prison earlier in the month. The sheriff's posse encountered the outlaws at what became known as Barton Mound (SRL 218), and there Barton and three others met death. Barton Mound is located beyond the southwest end of Sand Canyon Avenue, about two miles from the East Irvine post office.

SOURCES

American Institute of Architects, Orange County Chapter. "Historical Summaries of Buildings on Select List of Historical Buildings Preservation Committee." Ms., n.d.

Armor, Samuel. *History of Orange County.* Historic Record Co., Los Angeles, 1921.

Ashby, Gladys E. *Study of Primitive Man in Orange County and Some of Its Coastal Areas.* Board of Education, Santa Ana, 1939.

Bolton, Herbert Eugene. *Fray Juan Crespí, Missionary Explorer on the Pacific Coast, 1769–1774.* University of California Press, Berkeley, 1927.

The California Missions, a Pictorial History. By the editorial staff of Sunset Books. Lane Book Co., Menlo Park, 1964.

Chase, Joseph Smeaton. *California Coast Trails; A Horse-back Ride from Mexico to Oregon.* Houghton Mifflin, Boston, 1913.

Cleland, Robert Glass. *From Wilderness to Empire. A History of California,* ed. Glenn S. Dumke. Knopf, New York, 1959.

——— *Irvine Ranch of Orange County, 1810–1950.* Huntington Library, San Marino, 1952.

Dana, Richard Henry, Jr. *Two Years Before the Mast; A Personal Narrative of Life at Sea,* ed. John Haskell Kemble. 2 vols. Ward Ritchie Press, Los Angeles, 1964.

Davis, William Heath. *Seventy-five Years in California,* ed. Douglas S. Watson. John Howell, San Francisco, 1929.

Dickson, Lucile E. "The Founding and Early History of Anaheim, California," *Annual Publications, Historical Society of Southern California,* II, Part I (1918).

Engelhardt, Zephyrin. *San Juan Capistrano Mission.* The Standard Printing Co., Los Angeles, 1922.

Grumshaw, Alice. "History of Orange County, 1779–1889." Thesis, University of Southern California, Los Angeles, May 1937.

Older, Mrs. Fremont. *California Missions and Their Romances.* Coward-McCann, New York, 1938.

Orange County History Series, a collection of historical papers about Orange County. Orange County Historical Society, 1931–32.

Parker, C. E., and Marilyn Parker. *Orange County: Indians to Industry.* First American Title Insurance & Trust Co., Santa Ana, 1963.

Pleasants, Mrs. Adelina B. *History of Orange County.* Finnell & Sons, Los Angeles, 1931.

Robinson, W. W. *The Old Spanish & Mexican Ranchos of Orange County.* Title Insurance & Trust Co., Los Angeles, 1964.

Rush, Philip S. *Some Old Ranchos and Adobes.* Privately published, San Diego, 1965.

Saunders, Charles Francis, and Father St. John O'Sullivan. *Capistrano Nights, Tales of a California Mission Town.* Robert M. McBride & Co., New York, 1930.

Smith, Bill. *The Capistrano Story.* John T. McInnis, Orange, 1965.

Stephenson, Terry E. *Caminos Viejos.* T. E. Williams, Santa Ana, 1930.

——— *Shadows of Old Saddleback.* Santa Ana High School & Junior College Press, Santa Ana, 1931.

Placer County

PLACER COUNTY was organized in 1851 from parts of Sutter and Yuba counties. Auburn was made the county seat. The name Placer is an old Spanish word, the origin of which has never been satisfactorily explained, which came to be applied in Spanish countries to surface mining. At the time the name was adopted for this county, placer mining was the principal method employed there, and the placers of the region were among the richest in the state.

Lake Tahoe

Lake Tahoe, located partly in Placer and El Dorado counties and partly in the state of Nevada, lies 6,228 feet above the sea. It is remarkable for its great depth, which, together with its variable bottom, seems to account for the rare and exquisite color of its waters. "It is never twice the same...sometimes the blue is lapis lazuli, then it is jade, then it is purple, and when the breeze gently ruffles the surface it is silvery-gray." The exact meaning of the old Indian name Tahoe, sometimes interpreted in poetic phraseology as "Big Water" and considered by modern Indians of the region to mean "deep" and "blue," remains undetermined. The lake has also been known by other names for short periods.

Passing through Alpine County on his way into California in 1844, John C. Frémont climbed the ridge to Carson Pass. From his encampment under the shadow of the Sierra he explored, in company with Charles Preuss, the highest peak to the right, probably Stevens Peak, more than 10,000 feet above the sea. From its lofty summit on February 14, 1844, Frémont and his companion gained the first view of Lake Tahoe ever enjoyed by a white man. In his narrative of the expedition Frémont called the newly discovered sheet of water simply the "mountain lake," but on his later map of the expedition he named it Lake Bonpland. Of this circumstance he writes: "I gave to the basin river its name of Humboldt and to the mountain lake the name of his companion traveler, Bonpland [the noted French botanist], and so put it in the map of that expedition."

Frémont's name for the exquisite body of water he had discovered has been practically forgotten except by a few historians. The official mapmaker of the new state of California gave to it in 1853 the name of Lake Bigler, after John Bigler, the third governor of California, and people undoubtedly used this official designation for some years. An attempt to change the name to the fanciful Tula Tulia was made in 1861. A successful attempt to find a more appropriate name for this beautiful lake was made in 1862 through the efforts of William Henry Knight.

Knight had come overland to California from Missouri in 1859, according to the Power account, and it was on this journey that he had his first view of Lake Tahoe, "from a projecting cliff 1,000 feet above its surface." The scene, wrote Knight, "embraced not only the entire outline of the Lake with its charming bays and rocky headlands but also the magnificent forest of giant pines and firs in which it was embosomed, and the dozen or more lofty mountain peaks thrusting their white summits into the sky at altitudes varying from 8,000 to 11,000 feet above sea level." "No imagination," he continues, "can conceive the beauty, sublimity and inspiration of that scene, especially to one who had for weary months been traversing dusty, treeless, and barren plains. The contrast was overwhelming."

In 1861 Knight gathered data for compiling the first general map of the Pacific States, and in 1862 this map was published by the Bancroft Publishing House in San Francisco. On it the name of Lake Bigler had been changed to Lake Tahoe. Knight, who deliberately omitted the name of Bigler, urged John S. Hittell and Dr. Henry De Groot to support him in a change of names. At his request, also, Dr. De Groot had suggested "Tahoe," the Indian name for the lake, as a fit substitute. De Groot had heard the name for the first time in 1859 while on an exploring trip.

Knight at once obtained the approval of the Land Office at Washington, D.C., and the new name appeared on all subsequent maps and in printed matter issued from the Department of the Interior.

Thomas Starr King, who visited the lake in 1863, used it as the inspiration for one of his famous sermons, "Living Water from Lake Tahoe." Undoubtedly this sermon helped introduce the name to the public. That it was quickly and definitely approved by the people is shown by the almost universal usage of the name from that time on, and this in spite of the fact that it was still "officially" Lake Bigler. The state legislature, oblivious to the popular acceptance of the name "Tahoe," legalized "Bigler" in 1870 and this act was not repealed until 1945.

Mark Twain, in comparing Lake Tahoe with Lake Como in northern Italy, wrote: "As I go back in spirit and recall that noble sea, reposing among the snow peaks 6,000 feet above the ocean, the conviction comes strong upon me again that Como would only seem a bedizened little courtier in that august presence.... A sea, whose royal seclusion is guarded by a cordon of sentinel peaks that lift their frosty fronts 9,000 feet above the level world; a sea whose every aspect is impressive, whose belongings are all beautiful, whose lonely majesty types the Deity."

Very early there were those who sensed the possibilities of the Lake Tahoe region as a pleasure and health resort. With increasing frequency pioneer vacationists from Nevada and elsewhere were lured to the place by the beauty of the lake as well as by its fishing and hunting facilities. The earliest permanent settlements on the lakeshore were those at the mouth of McKinney Creek, at Ward Creek, at Glenbrook (in Nevada), and at Tahoe City. In the summer of 1862 William Ferguson and Ward Rust built a cabin on the lake at the mouth of Ward Creek. Two other men, John W. McKinney and Thomas Wren, had located a hay ranch on the summit near the county line in 1861, and in 1862 McKinney moved down from his ranch and settled on the shore of Lake Tahoe near the creek that bears his name. There he established a hunting and fishing resort

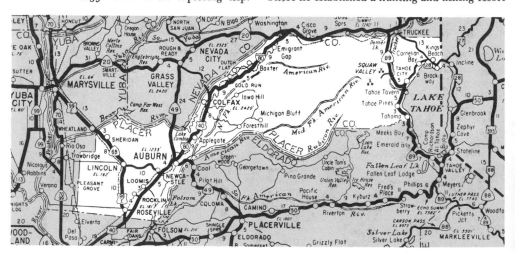

known as Hunter's Home, or Hunter's Retreat, which as late as 1882 was patronized by tourists. An old cabin and barn built by McKinney still stand at Chambers Lodge.

The first survey for Tahoe City was made in 1863, and the Tahoe House was erected by William Pomin the following year. While the nature lover and tourist contributed to the early prosperity of Tahoe City, the town at first was essentially a lumbering center. After the completion of the Central Pacific Railroad as far as Truckee, a wagon road was constructed from that point to the lake, resulting in the need for another hotel, which was met by A. J. Bayley, who established the Grand Central Hotel at Tahoe City.

Near Tahoe City are the Lake Tahoe outlet gates (SRL 797), first constructed in 1870. A monument on Highway 89 near the Truckee River bridge commemorates the work of Dr. James E. Church, Jr., who in 1910–11 made possible the accurate prediction and control of seasonal rise in the lake and river levels, thus ending a long dispute between lakeshore owners and downstream Truckee River water users over control of the gates.

After the decline of the lumber industry, the fame of Lake Tahoe as a summer resort increased. Now it is an all-year playground with an impressive permanent population, but, unfortunately, much of its beauty has been spoiled by commercialization. Winter sports at nearby Squaw Valley and other resorts draw many visitors during the snowy months. At Squaw Valley (SRL 724) the VIII Olympic Winter Games of 1960 commemorated a century of sport skiing in California. By 1860 ski clubs and races were being organized in the mining towns of Plumas County, 60 miles to the north.

Emigrant Gap and the Old Emigrant Trail

Emigrant Gap, an old lumbering camp and a station on the Central Pacific Railroad, established in the late 1860's, derives its name from a low opening in the mountains at the head of Bear River. A branch of the old California emigrant trail went down into Bear Valley by way of this pass, a region of wild and magnificent scenery.

West of the turnoff to the settlement of Emigrant Gap, a monument at a viewpoint adjacent to the westbound lanes of Interstate 80 commemorates the Emigrant Gap (SRL 403), where the covered wagons were lowered over the precipitous cliff to the floor of Bear Valley by means of rope and tackle held by iron spikes driven into the solid rock. It was first used by wagons in the spring of 1845 and continued as a part of the emigrant trail during and after the gold rush.

The early California emigrant trail over Donner Pass skirted the present boundary line between Placer and Nevada counties, following mainly along the Nevada County side. The easier route out of the mountains led north of the Bear River, since the narrow divide between that stream and the North Fork of the American River offered no roadway without improvements, which the emigrants were unable to make.

The Dutch Flat-Donner Lake Road

It was not until the building of the Central Pacific Railroad up the divide between the Bear River and the North Fork of the American River in 1864–66 that a wagon road was constructed along its entire length. In 1849 the head of "wagon navigation" up this ridge was at Illinoistown, and within a few years vehicles had reached as far as Dutch Flat. By 1860, after the discovery of the rich Comstock Lode in Nevada, a great demand had developed for adequate means of transportation over the mountains, and the people of Placer County became anxious to have this very profitable traffic diverted their way. Several attempts made by groups of local citizens to build roads met with failure. Finally, in the fall of 1861, the "Big Four" and others who were building the Central Pacific Railroad over the mountains organized the Dutch Flat and Donner Lake Wagon Road Company, their purpose being to attract as much of the Nevada traffic as possible. This road was completed in June 1864.

By June 1865 the railroad had been constructed as far as Clipper Gap, and in July the California Stage Company began running coaches from that point to Virginia City, Nevada. As the railroad progressed up the ridge, stations were placed at various points, while the stages and forwarding houses moved on simultaneously, making connections at each terminus. Thus the railroad company forced the stages and freight wagons over its own road. By the time Colfax had become the terminus, in September 1865, the Central Pacific had acquired the greater part of the passenger and freight business between Nevada and California, most of which, up to that time, had gone largely to the Placerville Road in El Dorado County.

Sicard's Ranch

The first settlement in Placer County was Sicard's Ranch, a Mexican grant on the south bank of Bear River. This grant was given to Theodore Sicard, a French sailor, in 1844, and here in 1845 he built an adobe house about one-half mile above Johnson's Crossing.

Being located on the overland emigrant trail which crossed the valley via Sinclair's Ranch to Sutter's Fort, Sicard's Ranch became of some importance as a stopping place. A fellow countryman of Sicard, Claude Chana (Chanay, Chané), arrived at the ranch in October 1846. That same fall, Chana and Sicard planted a few pits of dried peaches brought by an emigrant family and some almonds which Chana himself had; from this beginning came the pioneer commercial orchard of the Sacramento Valley. Chana was also the discoverer of gold in Placer County. After mining at Auburn Ravine, where the discovery was made, and later on the Yuba River, he purchased the Sicard Grant and sold the products of his orchard, vegetable garden, and vineyard to the miners at great profit. The site of Claude Chana's pioneer orchard now lies beneath the debris brought down by the Bear River from the hydraulic diggings in the foothills.

Johnson's Crossing, on the Bear River about three miles east of Wheatland, received a post office in 1853, and for some years it was a lively settlement, being a stopping place for emigrants, as well as for many of the teams engaged in hauling freight from Sacramento to the northern mining camps. The great flood of 1862 nearly destroyed the place, but the real cause of its final desertion was the later avalanche of debris which poured down upon it from the hydraulic mines higher up the river.

Rogers' "Shed," a Crossroads Station

About half a mile south of present Sheridan stood a very busy crossroads station during the days of stagecoaches and freighters. It was situated on the Sacramento–Nevada road at a point where four other roads diverged: one running west to Nicolaus in Sutter County (13 miles); one running northwest to Marysville (15 miles) via Kempton's Crossing; a third going northeast toward Grass Valley (28 miles) via McCourtney's Crossing; and a fourth following east to Auburn (20 miles) via Danetown.

At this strategic location, in 1857, a man named E. C. Rogers built a one-story house with a 150-foot shed in front. The "Shed"—"Union Shed" as it was called—soon became a place of importance. Here the long freight teams which then thronged the roads received shelter from the heat in summer and the rain in winter, and here the farmers of the surrounding country brought hay and grain to supply the teams.

The bustling activity about the Shed did not last long, for the building of the California Central Railroad northward from Folsom did away with staging and teaming up and down the valley. In 1861 the railroad had been built as far as Lincoln, named for one of the promoters of the railroad, Charles Lincoln Wilson. From 1861 to 1866 Lincoln was a thriving stage and freight center; but when the terminus of the railroad was changed to Wheatland in 1866, the stage and teaming business was transferred also, and both Lincoln and Rogers' Shed lost their importance as stage centers. In 1868 the Shed, with all its buildings, was consumed by fire. Lincoln, a town of some 3,000 inhabitants, is today the trading and shipping point for an industrial and agricultural region, while Sheridan is a mere hamlet of fewer than 200 people.

Manzanita Grove, situated on a wooded knoll in the middle of broad, open fields halfway between Lincoln and Sheridan and east of the highway between them, gained notoriety in early days as a stronghold for thieves. Here, hidden in the center of a thick growth of trees, was a corral where the bandits kept their stolen stock. The robbers were eventually cleared out, and by 1855 the grove had been made the cemetery for the countryside. Today there are only a few of the low-growing manzanitas left among the native oaks, which cast their shadows over the graves of the pioneers buried at this spot. The cemetery is reached over Chamberlain Road, which turns to the right from Highway 65 about four miles north of Lincoln. Chamberlain Road joins the Manzanita Cemetery Road in less than two miles, and from this point it is one mile to the left to the cemetery.

About five miles northeast of Lincoln is the site of Newtown, a former mining camp established near Doty's Ravine in 1855. Many claims here paid big while others brought little. It was what was known as a "spotted" area, where "once you find it, and twice you don't." Like others of its class, Newtown has ceased to exist as a place of habitation.

River Bars

Placer County, embracing several branches of the American River besides Bear River, included scores of river-bar camps. Beal's Bar was the first camp above the confluence of the North and South forks of the river. As late as 1853 it polled a vote of 96, and was an active center of trade for surrounding mines. When the old bar immediately upon the river was worked out, the town was moved to a high bench adjoining, and the former site was dug out and its gravel washed for gold.

In this vicinity John Sinclair and some 50 Indian retainers, in the spring and summer of 1848, were among the first to mine on the North Fork of the American River. Governor Richard B. Mason, in his report to Washington in 1848, says: "He [Sinclair] had been engaged about five weeks when I saw him, and up to that time his Indians had used simply closely-woven willow baskets. His net proceeds . . . were about $16,000 worth of gold."

Beal's Bar is now under Folsom Lake, but a marker near Beals Point in Folsom Lake State Park recalls the old express trail (SRL 585) of 1849–54 that led to this and other camps. The Folsom–Auburn road now parallels this route.

Following up the stream from Beal's Bar to the mouth of the Middle Fork, one encountered a strange variety of names, such as Doton's, Smith's (settled by Mormons in 1848), Horseshoe, Rattlesnake, Beaver, Milk Punch, Deadman's, Lacy's, Manhattan, and Tamaroo bars. All of these camps were at one time densely populated, and each had an interesting history of its own.

Horseshoe Bar, seven miles above Beal's, was first worked in 1849, when the entire bar was divided into claims of 20 × 30 feet. It became a trading center for adjacent bars, and as late as 1858 still claimed 300 voters, although many of the houses had by that time been moved away. A number of permanent settlers, however, remained in the vicinity for many years.

Robert E. Capson, a sea captain, came to Smith's Bar in 1848, followed seven months later by his wife and 15-year-old daughter. J. W. Smyth, a young Irishman, arrived in 1849. With the union of these two families, a home was established at Horseshoe Bar. This event resulted in the preservation of that part of the old bar which remained until it was inundated by Folsom Lake, for when Smyth finally patented this remnant of land and planted it to orchard, he saved it from further depredations by the miners.

Rattlesnake Bar had become the principal

town along the river by 1853, when it was moved to the flat bench known as Rattlesnake Flat, high up and back of the low bar from which it derived its name. By 1861 gardens, orchards, and vineyards had made of it a very pretty place, but the town started to decline after the fire of 1863 destroyed much of it. Nevertheless, in 1865 it still had a population of more than 1,000, a post office, a Wells Fargo Express building, a theater, and the usual hotels, stores, and saloons. Like all of the river mining towns, Rattlesnake Bar became deserted, the site being marked only by piles of rock from the diggings, by the old toll house, and by a picturesque wire bridge, which replaced the earlier one washed away in the flood of 1862. Rattlesnake Bridge is no more, and the surrounding lands are now covered by Folsom Lake.

Beyond the junction of the Middle and North forks are the sites of numerous other bars. On the North Fork, Calf Bar comes first, followed by Kelly's, Rich, Jones', Barnes', Mineral, Pickering, and Euchre, with a score of others long since washed away or buried out of sight by the mass of debris washed down by the hydraulic mines of Gold Run and other places. On the north bank of the Middle Fork the following camps were located: Sailor Claim, Buckner's, Rocky Point Slide, Mammoth, Texas, Quail, Brown's, Kennebec, Buckeye, American, Sardine, Yankee, Dutch, African, Drunkard's, Horseshoe (No. 2), Pleasant, American, Junction, Stony, Rector's, and a score of others, each noted at one time for its production of gold and for some interesting occurrence, comic or tragic, in the early history of the county.

Humbug Bar was located in Humbug Canyon, a tributary of the South Branch of the North Fork of the American River. The canyon, at first known as Mississippi Canyon, was rechristened Humbug early in 1850 when a group of miners became disgusted with their luck at this place. Later these same prospectors returned with others and "struck it rich," proving it to be no "humbug" after all.

The Iron Mine

On the bars of the lower American River early miners from Pennsylvania noticed that many boulders contained iron ore. In 1857 the chief center for the ore was found to be on the ranch of S. W. Lovell, near Clipper Gap, about six miles northeast of Auburn. Although tests proved the ore to be of high quality, no mining was done until 1869, when the firm of Brown and Company began shipping ore to San Francisco. In December of that year the Iron Mountain Company was organized to develop the mine, but nothing was accomplished. The property remained undeveloped until 1880, when smelting works were erected and the town of Hotaling, named in honor of one of the owners, was founded nearby. The old buildings no longer stand at Hotaling, and mining operations have long since ceased.

Auburn

Early in 1849, Auburn (SRL 404) was known as Woods Dry Diggings. It was one of the earliest mining camps in California, gold having been

Rattlesnake Bridge, Now under Water

first discovered there in Auburn Ravine on May 16, 1848, by Claude Chana and a party of Indians en route to Coloma from Sicard's Ranch on the Bear River. Chana was soon followed by Nicolaus Allgeier, who had come up from his ranch in Sutter County with his Indian retainers.

Hordes of prospectors and adventurers began to pour in by 1849 and camps sprang up everywhere. According to some authorities, Woods Dry Diggings was called for a time North Fork Dry Diggings. A large group of the miners in the vicinity had come to California in 1846, in Stevenson's Volunteer Regiment from Auburn, New York. It is thought that they changed the name of North Fork Dry Diggings to Auburn in the summer of 1849. Records show that the early diggings here were very rich. During the peak of productiveness it was not unusual for a man to take out $1,000 to $1,500 a day. There is one instance of four cartloads of earth yielding as much as $16,000.

Auburn became the county seat of Sutter County in the spring of 1850. Its favorable location, "its preponderance of population, and the inexhaustible powers of voting possessed by its citizens and partisans, decided the contest in its favor by a majority considerably exceeding the entire population of the county." On April 25, 1851, when Placer County was created from a portion of Sutter County, Auburn was made the seat of justice of the new county. The city was incorporated April 14, 1860, disincorporated about 1866, and reincorporated May 2, 1888. During the 1860's and the 1870's, Auburn became quite a cultural and social center, having a private normal school and college and enjoying a reputation as a health resort, the pure air of the lower Sierra being both mild and invigorating.

Devastating fires swept many of the mining camps several times during the early years of their history. After Auburn's first experience, its citizens determined to rebuild of more substantial material. None of the very first houses remain, but in the older section there are a number of solid brick structures dating from the 1850's and 1860's, with the heavy iron doors and iron-shuttered windows common to that period. Some of the buildings of "Old Town" have been remodeled, and a few of the finest ones, notably the Orleans Hotel, were razed as late as the 1950's.

As one writer has said: "The Auburn of today

Orleans Hotel, Auburn

is a city of contrasts. Entering it from the south, one descries a narrow street, flanked by old brick buildings, and overlooked by the high bell tower of a fire station. A half-mile beyond, upon the summit of a hill, is the modern portion of the community with up-to-date establishments and public buildings. It is plain to see that Auburn, like the chambered nautilus, outgrew the site upon which it was first located. But the shell that it left behind is still a part of its metropolitan area."

The Placer County Historical Museum is located in the 20th District Fairgrounds at Auburn.

Auburn, a Turnpike Center

Auburn has always been the center of extensive staging and freighting operations. In its early days a network of trails radiated from it to the numerous camps springing up in all directions, and over these trails miners' supplies were carried by pack-mule trains and their Mexican drivers. During the 1850's and 1860's these rough and narrow trails were gradually, and in large measure, superseded by toll roads scarcely less rude and precarious, over which daring "knights of the whip" drove the old stagecoaches at reckless speed, or piloted the swaying, creaking freight wagons, aided by the uncanny intelligence of from six to ten horses or mules.

Even after the building of the Central Pacific Railway up the ridge, the staging and freighting business continued over the many roads reaching out from Auburn. The first passenger train arrived in Auburn on May 13, 1865. The advent of the railroad created a demand for additional wagon traffic into Nevada County and, in 1866, brought about the opening of a new and more direct stage route into El Dorado County, via Lyon's Bridge, where the Mother Lode Highway now crosses the river. Today, buses and trucks still carry their quota of passengers, mail, and freight over the old mountain roads, most of them improved or reconstructed into modern highways leading to and from Auburn.

There were five main wagon roads centering in Auburn, while many laterals led out from these to all parts of Placer County. The highway from Sacramento up the ridge to Illinoistown went through Auburn, and a branch of this road was one of the main routes to Grass Valley and Ne-

vada City, crossing Bear River at a place later known as English Bridge and then as Gautier Bridge, ten miles north of Auburn on present Highway 49. A third road extended northeast to mining camps along the Forest Hill ridge, while a fourth turned west, passing down Auburn Ravine to Ophir and Virginiatown. Still another ran south along the ridge above the American River to Folsom and Sacramento, and connected with roads coming from El Dorado County. On this road six and a half miles south of Auburn stood the Mountaineer House, on the site of which the stone mansion of J. J. Brennan has been built, over the foundations of the old stage station. Four miles beyond is the site of the Franklin House, another stage station. Near the Brennan ranch was Auburn Station, the final terminus of California's first passenger railroad, the Sacramento Valley, originally built from Sacramento to Folsom in 1855–56. It was to be extended to Auburn, but the Central Pacific arrived first, and so the Sacramento Valley Railroad was discontinued. Auburn disincorporated to keep from paying the bonds on the railroad that never reached it.

Stupendous difficulties were encountered in transforming devious, threadlike pack trails into roads. The turnpike from Auburn to Forest Hill furnishes an excellent example of the problems met by the builders of these old "High Ways." Leading down into the canyon of the North Fork of the American River where the traveler crossed the stream by means of a crude ferry, the Auburn–Forest Hill trail climbed another steep and meandering path up the opposite canyon wall. Only by a great expenditure of money and labor could the obstacles presented by these mighty canyons be surmounted. Since the county government was unable to raise sufficient funds for the enterprise, the work was taken up by private turnpike companies, the new routes of travel thus becoming toll roads.

The grade of the North Fork Hill Road, as it was called, was improved in 1855 at a cost of $12,000, and in the early 1860's an additional sum of $50,000 was expended upon it. Over a distance of more than 20 miles from Auburn to Yankee Jim's—winding up the deep gorge of the North Fork or clinging to the sides of a mountain far above the stream—this road was carved out of the canyon walls only through Herculean effort.

Over this old highland thoroughfare, a continuous stream of traffic from Auburn poured into the mining camps along the Forest Hill Divide, passing a number of stations and roadhouses along the way, among them the Junction House two and a half miles from Auburn, the Grizzly Bear House, Butcher's Ranch, Sheridan's, Mile Hill Toll House, and Spring Garden.

In the medley of humanity which passed that way, there were two types in particular which might well figure as leading characters in a dramatic epic of the road, the hero and the villain par excellence: the former, that "original and fantastic" tyrant of "the brotherhood of Jehu," the stage driver; the latter, his equal in daring but forever his enemy, the bold, bad bandit. The stage driver was an expert in his profession and usually possessed a steadiness of nerve, a courage, and an inherent integrity which not even his veneer of crude bravado and indifference could entirely conceal. Matched at least in daring, this jehu of the Sierra and his natural enemy, the highwayman and stage robber, often faced each other upon the lonely roads, and many a thrilling episode in the drama of gold-rush days was enacted by them, a group of frightened fellow travelers usually completing the cast.

South of the site of the Grizzly Bear House one can look across the river to Lime Rock (near Clipper Gap), at the right of which is a burner where lime was formerly made from the rock. In the early days a woman used to signal from this rock to the bandits when the stage was coming on the Forest Hill road. Even as late as 1901, bandits were numerous along this road.

Auburn Ravine

Extending west from Auburn, down what was once the old Auburn Ravine turnpike, are a number of historic sites reminiscent of early mining activities. Ophir (*SRL 463*), three miles west of Auburn and north of Interstate 80, was first known as Spanish Corral. Like the biblical Land of Ophir whence came the gold to adorn the temple of Solomon, the region about Spanish Corral was found to be fabulously rich, and the name of the settlement was changed to Ophir. In 1852 it was the most populous community in the county. Today the district about Ophir numbers not many more than 200 inhabitants. Orchards and vineyards abound in the surrounding hills, and the town itself is bowered in giant fig trees. A fragment of stone archway is said to be part of a pioneer bakery built sometime in the 1850's. About a mile up the road is the site of the Oro Fino House. The hills are scarred with diggings, old pits and dumps, and the foundations of abandoned stamp mills. The Paramount Mine, two miles from Ophir, was once a major producer.

Two miles west of Ophir was Frytown, a "mushroom city" settled in 1849. Although its palmy days were few, "'t was lively while it lasted." Gold Hill, four miles west of Ophir, was organized as a town in April 1852, when the presidential vote numbered 444. The rich surface diggings of this earlier period were later replaced by fine orchards and vineyards, which continue to flourish today. The little town now consists of newer homes. Only a small cemetery remains from earlier days. Two miles west of Gold Hill is Virginiatown (*SRL 400*), a typical ghost town, with the abandoned shells of two adobes standing beside the road. The one next to which the historical monument has been erected is said to have been Philip Armour's first butcher shop. Another mile and the traveler passes the site of the ephemeral Fort Trojan (pronounced "Troejam" by the miners), settled in 1858. When Lincoln was established three miles farther down in the valley in 1861–62, the citizens of Fort Trojan moved to the new town.

Secret Ravine

Secret Ravine, extending southwest from Auburn, was the scene of extensive placer mining operations during the 1850's and 1860's, and of later granite quarrying in the 1870's and 1880's. Commercial orchards were planted up and down the ridges as early as 1870, and these continue to be the chief source of income in the region today. Old mining camps which flourished in the ravine during the gold-rush days were soon superseded after the coming of the railroad by other towns built along the ridge. Brick stores, in use as late as 1880 but mostly vacated by 1900, have since been torn down; often the ground on which they stood has been plowed and planted to fruit trees.

Newcastle, at the head of Secret Ravine, is the only one of the old 1850 mining camps which thrives today, being a fruit-shipping center on the railroad with a population of about 800. In the ravine to the north long stood picturesque Chinatown, its balconied upper stories overshadowed by an avenue of giant cottonwoods; it has now been destroyed by freeway construction.

Stewart's Flat, a mining town of some importance before the coming of the railroad, was located in Secret Ravine east of Penryn. The Stewart's Flat Mine was worked from 1862 to 1864. After Penryn was established in 1864, with the opening of granite quarries in the vicinity, Stewart's Flat dwindled until it was abandoned in 1867, the old graveyard being all that marks the site today. It is located to the right of a dirt road,

Griffith Building, Penryn

a quarter of a mile north of the Penryn–Rock Springs Road one and a half miles east of Penryn.

Penryn (or Penrhyn, after its patronym in Wales) was established and named in 1864 by Griffith Griffith, a Welshman, whose extensive granite quarries for a number of years supplied the building material for many structures in San Francisco, Stockton, and elsewhere, and which employed as many as 250 workmen. A two-story building of hewn granite blocks, erected in Penryn by Griffith in 1878, is still standing in perfect condition. David Griffith succeeded his uncle in 1889 and operated a much smaller granite works until his death in 1918.

About two and one-half miles southwest of Penryn is Loomis, the successor of Pino. Pino had derived its name from the old mining camp of Pine Grove, which was established in Secret Ravine about a mile and a half from the site of Loomis, before the coming of the railroad. Mining began at Pine Grove (or Smithville) in 1850, and a store was set up by L. G. Smith. By 1860 the place had 1 500 people.

Gold Run

The Gold Run region, 25 miles northeast of Auburn, on the ridge south of Dutch Flat between Bear River and the North Fork of the American River, is a good example of early hydraulic mining. A vast bed of auriferous blue gravel two miles long, half a mile wide, and 250 feet deep, with pay dirt all the way down, it yielded immense profit until the early 1880's. O. W. Hollenbeck came to the region in 1854 and mined at a place called Mountain Springs. In 1859 hydraulic mining was begun on the Gold Run claim. In 1862 Hollenbeck laid out a town on Cold Spring Mountain, calling it Mountain Springs. A post office had been established in 1854 under that name, but the name was changed to Gold Run in 1863. The place developed into a mining center long after the other towns of the county, and was very flourishing during the 1860's and 1870's. Squire's Canyon, Canyon Creek, Goosling Ravine, Gold Run Canyon, Potato Ravine, and Indiana Canyon all had productive hydraulic mines. After 1883, when the courts decided against hydraulic mining, the town became almost deserted.

The original town of Gold Run (SRL 405) is near Interstate 80 south of the present Gold Run railway station. The old Union Church built by the miners has been preserved. Deep ravines and high cliffs in the canyon below present striking evidence of the hydraulic forces that once operated there. It is estimated that the total production of the Gold Run mines reached $15 million.

Dutch Flat

Dutch Flat (SRL 397), quaint, colorful, quiet, among the pine-covered mountains, is unique among the old camps of Placer County. Its main street, lined by huge poplar and locust trees, climbs abruptly from the hollow where the town had its beginning, to a narrow, sloping terrace, on which perches the settlement of later growth, and on up past the summer homes of those who,

in ever-increasing numbers, seek the invigorating air and romantic flavor of the place.

Thousands of miners, in years past, have worked the ridges and hills about Dutch Flat, until the entire region is deeply torn by hydraulic operations. Aside from its prominence as a mining center, Dutch Flat was a stage station, making it one of the largest and most important towns of the county in 1864 to 1866.

The town was first settled by a group of Germans, among them Joseph and Charles Dornbach, in 1851. The name "Dutch" may have been derived from the nationality of these first settlers, but one looks in vain for the "Flat." In 1856 the town was granted a post office under its present designation.

From the town runs the old road, which from 1864 to 1866 was a much-traveled turnpike; over it the well-braced Concord coaches ran to the rich Washoe silver mines of Nevada, one branch going by way of Bear Valley, Bowman Lake, and Henness Pass, and the other via Donner Lake. The latter route, known as the Dutch Flat-Donner Lake Road, was built by the men who were at that time constructing the Central Pacific Railway. The names of Governor Leland Stanford, Dr. D. W. Strong, and other promoters of the railway thus became linked with the history of this toll road and with the town. Strong, a resident of Dutch Flat, was the only one of the nine promoters of the railway who lived outside of Sacramento. It was he who from the beginning advocated the advantage of the Dutch Flat–Donner Pass route for the railway even when others doubted its feasibility. In the fall of 1866, after the railway had reached Cisco about 20 miles farther up the ridge, Dutch Flat lost much of its importance as a stage center.

Just over the hill about 100 feet north of town "lie the 'diggin's,' miles in extent, rugged man-made canyons and deep amphitheatres abounding with rocks and stones and pebbles of various shapes and colors, among them not infrequently beautiful hexagonal crystals. Gold nuggets are there also, but are rarely found." Beds of ashes, charcoal, and partly charred wood have also been discovered under 100 feet or more of gravel in this fascinating geological hunting ground.

During the 1870's hydraulic mining operations at Dutch Flat reached their height. In 1872, the Cedar Creek Company of London purchased as many as 32 claims and worked them on a gigantic scale. Millions in gold were taken from the extensive placers of Dutch Flat, one nugget alone being worth more than $5,000. It is estimated that $30 million more remain in this gravelly ridge awaiting new and less destructive hydraulic methods to release them.

The tide of gold has long since ebbed from Dutch Flat, and its citizens, "contented with what they have . . . go their quiet peaceful way. They delight in talking of the old days when life socially was on a par with the best in California." Every old building in the block that comprises the business section has a history. There is the hotel with its long mirror, a relic of the one-time bar, and its old ledgers tabulating the ounces of

Chinese Adobe Store, Dutch Flat

gold taken from adjoining diggings. Begun in 1852, this was a quite pretentious hostelry, with some 30 rooms more than those represented in the present structure, including an annex which extended across the road. The I.O.O.F. Building, erected in 1858, is still in use, as is also the old stone store built in 1854. The Masonic Hall dates from 1856, and the Methodist Episcopal church from 1859–61.

In the hollow as one approaches the town from the south, a lone Chinese store stands guard. It is built of solid adobe with a stone foundation and a superstructure of wood. The tiny air holes that serve as windows give the structure the appearance more of a jail or fort than of a place of trade. Adjoining the pioneer American cemetery just above the town is the Chinese burial grounds, half hidden among the pines. Most of the bodies have been removed from the graves and taken back to China. The old site of Chinatown, with a population of 1,000, was on the railroad one mile above Dutch Flat.

Colfax and Illinoistown

Colfax, named after Ulysses S. Grant's running mate, Schuyler Colfax, is a small town about 15 miles northeast of Auburn in the center of a once prosperous mining region. The Central Pacific Railroad from Sacramento reached as far as Colfax in September 1865. Today, the town is an important shipping point for lumber and fruit.

Across the railroad southeast of Colfax, and now completely absorbed by it, is the site of Illinoistown, first settled early in 1849 under the name of Alder Grove. That year the town became the distributing point for supplies to neighboring camps, and quickly assumed an importance as a business and trading center second only to that of Auburn.

Goods brought in wagons to Illinoistown were there loaded on pack mules and carried to remote camps over steep and winding mountain trails, later widened into toll roads. One of the most intriguing of these old roads is the one that leads from Illinoistown to Iowa Hill and was known as the Mineral Bar Bridge and Road. The cost of constructing the seven miles entering and leaving the canyon of the North Fork of the American River, which, at this point, is 1,500 feet deep, was $75,000. The scenery is magnificent—steep mountainsides seemingly ever threatening to precipi-

tate the traveler into the abyss, where, far below, the sparkling river can be seen with the canyon walls towering above it.

Iowa Hill

The site of the little old town of Iowa Hill *(SRL 401)* is on the narrow neck of a high ridge between the North Fork of the American River on the north and Indian Canyon on the south. Gold was first discovered there in 1853, and in 1856 the weekly product was estimated at $100,000. The rich cement of the Blue Lead Channel running under the town has been all drifted out, while later hydraulic operations on either side of the town have all but washed the site away. The total gold production up to 1880 has been estimated at $20 million.

Like most of the early mining camps, Iowa Hill had its baptisms of fire. In 1857 a conflagration swept away all of the buildings "from Temperance Hall to McCall & Company's Brewery," as an old news item puts it. The last serious fire occurred in 1922, destroying most of the remaining houses in this much-stricken place. An old brick store and a Wells Fargo vault still stand.

Numerous camps flourished within a radius of five miles of Iowa Hill during the 1850's and 1860's. Independence Hill, Roach Hill, Bird's Flat, Stephen's Hill, Elizabethtown, Wisconsin Hill, Grizzly Flat at the head of Grizzly Canyon, Monona Flat, and Succor Flat—each lived its little day of colorful, polyglot life, only to become again a part of the enveloping wilderness after a few short years. Hundreds of tunnels honeycomb the mountains about these old campsites, constituting tangible evidence of the few extremely profitable claims that were once worked there: the Jamison, the pioneer of the district, producing $500,000; the North Star, $400,000; the Sailor Union, $300,000; and the Iowa Hill, $250,000.

Elizabethtown, on the south side of Indian Canyon from Iowa Hill, was the most important camp north of Shirt-tail Canyon and south of the North Fork in the years 1850–54. Wisconsin Hill, separated from Elizabethtown by a deep ravine, was first settled in 1854 and soon had a population of 700, but after 1856 the miners began to scatter. With the completion of a turnpike across Indian Canyon from Iowa Hill and another across Shirt-tail Canyon from Yankee Jim's, the hopes of Wisconsin Hill's businessmen temporarily revived. But instead of bringing more people in, the road furnished the remaining inhabitants with an easy method of transportation to more favored localities.

Todd's Valley

Few more inviting places existed in the Sierra of Placer County than Todd's Valley, southwest of Forest Hill, before it was overrun with Argonauts, "washing away the beautiful ridges and seaming up the gently sloping vales" in their feverish quest for gold. Even the forests of pine and maple and flowering dogwood were not free from the encroachments of the early placer diggings and the tunnels and shafts of drift mining, as well as the more gigantic scars of later hydraulic action.

Among the few men who wintered on the Forest Hill Ridge in 1849–50 were Dr. F. W. Todd and three or four companions. Dr. Todd had established a store at his ranch in June 1849, in the valley that later bore his name. By 1850 Todd's store had become a stopping place for miners seeking new locations on the ridges and in the canyons to the north and northeast. The old pack trail that passed by its door was an extension of the Sacramento Road to Greenwood and Georgetown via Pilot Hill in El Dorado County, crossing the Middle Fork of the American River near the Spanish Dry Diggings. Climbing the precipitous canyon walls from this point via Paradise and the North Star House, the trail continued through Todd's Valley to the diggings at Forest Hill and camps beyond.

Forest Hill

Forest Hill (SRL 399), a mining and lumbering camp of some importance in the 1850's and 1860's, was located in a region reported by J. Ross Browne in 1868 as "the most productive cement tunnel-mining district in the state." Situated at an elevation of 3,400 feet, on the summit of the Forest Hill Divide between the Middle Fork of the American River and Shirt-tail Canyon, the town is 2,500 feet above the river. Thousands of acres of virgin pine forests surround it and the canyon scenery is superb. The auriferous gravel of the Forest Hill Diggings is a part of the Blue Lead Channel, and the early claims, limited to 50 feet each, extended along the side of the hill. The tunnels penetrated the mountain to a distance of from 200 to 5,000 feet.

Early in the spring of 1850 a great rush of miners came to the Forest Hill Ridge, lured by the news of rich diggings uncovered there. Coming from the south via Coloma and Greenwood Valley and from the west by way of Auburn, the two streams met about three miles northeast of Todd's store at the place that later became Forest Hill. The brush shanty set up at the latter site as a trading post in 1850 was replaced about 1858 by a substantial house and hotel. The Forest House, as it was known, became the nucleus of an important center of trade and of travel to and from the numerous camps in all directions. The historic hostelry was destroyed by fire on Christmas Day, 1918, with the turkey dinner in the oven. Another hotel replaced it and bears the same name.

The height of activity began early in 1853, after the winter storms had brought down a great mass of loose gravel at the head of Jenny Lind Canyon, exposing many glistening chunks of gold. The Jenny Lind Mine alone later yielded $2,000 or $2,500 daily, the total yield reaching approximately $1,100,000 by 1880. The aggregate production of all the mines in the immediate vicinity of Forest Hill or within rifle shot of the express office was estimated at $10,000,000 up to 1868. Rich mines in the region were the Dardanelles, New Jersey, Independence, Deideshei-

mer, Fast and Nortwood, Rough and Ready, Gore, and Alabama.

Forest Hill had already assumed a metropolitan air in the late 1850's, boasting a newspaper, fireproof hotels and stores, banks and elegant saloons, as well as neat homes surrounded by gardens and orchards. It was still one of the larger towns of Placer County in 1880, numbering about 700 inhabitants at that date. The population later dwindled to about 400, but now the place is once again beginning to prosper. Many of the buildings along the broad main street are new, but two old brick stores with iron shutters are still open for business. The old church burned in 1952, but its bell has been preserved on a monument. An exceptionally clear, sweet-toned bell, it could be heard at times, it is said, 20 miles away through the forest.

A mile northeast of Forest Hill the Bath road turns south a mile to the site of Bath, first settled in the summer of 1850 by a merchant named John Bradford, who built a cabin and started a stock ranch. In the fall some miners came in and bought the place for a small sum. Wintering there, the party discovered gold in the dry gulches debouching into Volcano Canyon. Miners flocked to the place, and the camp that sprang up that same fall took the name of Volcano. The next year the town grew rapidly after the Mint Drop and Snodgrass claims were located. Since another camp just across the Middle Fork to the south also bore the name of Volcano, the town on the Forest Hill Ridge chose to call itself Sarahsville, in honor of the first woman in the camp. When a post office was established there in 1858, the name of Bath was finally bestowed upon the place.

The Bath claims which adjoined those of the Forest Hill district, beginning with 1852, included the San Francisco, Oro, Rip, Golden Gate, Rough Gold, Paragon, Greek, New York, and Sebastopol claims. Bath declined after 1858, owing to the increasing importance of its neighbor, Forest Hill, but since its mines were still rich it continued to exist as a town for a number of years. Forest fires have devastated the area, and only the diggings and a few old locust trees remain at Bath.

Yankee Jim's and Shirt-tail Canyon

A road from Forest Hill leads northwest three miles to Yankee Jim's (SRL 398), high up on the same ridge between the North and Middle forks of the American River. A number of the old weather-worn houses at Yankee Jim's are still standing, reminders of the stirring days when it was one of the largest mining camps in Placer County. Extensive diggings lie on its outskirts. Not far away is Shirt-tail Canyon, which Bayard Taylor thought should be called "Spartan Canyon"—"but we were not classical enough for the change in those days," was the comment of an old pioneer.

The origin of the name Yankee Jim's is one of those riddles often encountered in the mining regions. Some hold that the person from whom the camp derived its title was, indeed, a Yankee. The majority, however, believe that he was "a son of the Emerald Isle" who, because of his luck in striking rich diggings, popularly attributed to shrewdness, had become known as "Yankee Jim."

In any case, Yankee Jim, who seems to have been somewhat given to banditry, was the first to mine away from the river bars of the North Fork and to find the rich diggings along the ridges. He sought to keep these discoveries a secret, but rumors spread quickly, and by 1850 miners swarmed over the entire ridge country. At the place of Yankee Jim's chief activities a town sprang up, was named for him, and became famous as a rich mining center.

Shirt-tail Canyon and its several branches— Brimstone Canyon, Brushy Canyon, Grizzly Canyon, Refuge Canyon, and Devil's Canyon—were all the scene of extensive gold excitement during the 1850's. The stream bed in each of these canyons was worked and numerous tunnels were dug into the rocky walls above.

The following story is told of how Shirt-tail Canyon got its name. "Early in the summer of 1849 two men, one named Tuttle, formerly from the state of Connecticut, and the other Van Zandt, from Oregon, were prospecting upon Brushy Canyon and in that locality, and at the time supposed there was no one nearer to them than the people who were at work along the river bars. From Brushy they emerged into the valley of the larger stream into which it emptied. It was sultry and hot, and no sound but their own suppressed voices broke the silence of the gorge. A bend in the creek a short distance below them obstructed the view, and they walked down the stream to overcome it. Abruptly turning the point, they were astonished to see before them, but a little way off, a solitary individual—whether white or red they could not at first determine —engaged in primitive mining operations, with crevicing spoon, and sheath-knife and pan. The apparition was perfectly nude, with the exception of a shirt, and that was not overly lengthy. The lone miner was in the edge of the water, and, happening to look up, saw the two men who had intruded upon his domain at about the same time that they discovered him. Had this not been so ... they ... would have stepped back, made some noise, and given the man a chance to don his overalls. As it was, the eyes of both parties met, and an involuntary 'Hello' came from all three mouths. 'What in the devil's name do you call this place?' queried one of the intruders of the *sans cullottes,* who proved to be an American. He glanced at his bare legs, and from them to his questioners, took in at a moment the ludicrous appearance he made, and laughingly answered: 'Don't know any name for it yet, but we might as well call it Shirt-tail as anything else.'"

Michigan Bluff

Looking over into El Dorado County to the south, Michigan Bluff (*SRL 402*), seven miles east of Forest Hill, clings to the steep slope of the Forest Hill Ridge from 1,500 to 2,000 feet above the yawning gorges of the Middle Fork and the North Fork of the Middle Fork of the American River and El Dorado Canyon. Behind it old Sugar Loaf towers 250 feet or more above the main street of the settlement, which sits directly at its southern base. The first town, commonly known as Michigan City, was located about half a mile below the present site, on the stretch of comparatively level ground once existing there and later mined out. Scars of hydraulic operations may be seen all up and down the mountainside. Only an old well remains today at Michigan City.

The first settlement on this ridge was made one mile to the west at Bird's Valley, where a party of sailors located in the summer of 1848. Later, these men reported at Sutter's Fort the rich diggings which they had worked at Rector's Bar and other places below their camp. A second company, under the leadership of J. D. Hoppe, came up from Sutter's Fort the same fall. Following the trail made by the sailors up the mountainside, they too set up camp in Bird's Valley, crevassing for gold along the rivers in the canyons below. Seeking for the precious metal only upon and in the crevices of the bedrock, these first miners used the most primitive tools for their operations —butcher knives, iron spoons, an occasional steel bar, and a pan. As the rainy season approached, the men returned to the valley, believing it to be impossible to winter in that wild country.

In the spring of 1849, hundreds of miners trekked over the rugged mountain trails to the new diggings and a few stayed through the winter of 1849–50, among them being two men at Bird's Valley. Rich discoveries had been found in El Dorado Canyon and along the bars of the Middle Fork during the summer of 1849, and with the coming of another spring a general stampede began, in February 1850. Thousands of men thronged over the trails from Hangtown, Coloma, Georgetown, Pilot Hill, and other places in El Dorado County already overrun with gold seekers. Finding it impossible to mine along the streams, the rivers still being too high, they camped along the ridges, and Bird's Store became an important rendezvous, with up to 3,000 impatient Argonauts gathered there to wait for the snow to recede and the water to subside.

A few ambitious men camped on the little flat to the east where Michigan City grew up. While grading out the mountainside for enough level ground for their cabins to stand upon, they struck a bed of auriferous gravel. Lack of water delayed the working of the find until 1853, when ditches were dug from the upper reaches of El Dorado and Volcano canyons, 12 and five miles to the north. Until 1858 the town enjoyed a period of great prosperity, shipping $100,000 worth of gold per month. The North American Mine alone yielded $300,000 up to 1868.

Michigan City had no sooner become established on the narrow shelf at the edge of the diggings than the shelf began to settle and to slip down the mountainside, cracking the walls of the houses and threatening to precipitate the entire settlement into the abyss. This was in 1858, and in 1859 the settlers moved en masse to the present site of Michigan Bluff higher up on the brow of the mountain. Hydraulic mining began in the vicinity in 1858, and during the 1860's and 1870's the town was one of the most prosperous centers on the Forest Hill Ridge. By 1880 the numerous smaller claims had been bought up by the owners of the Big Gun Mine, and then, in 1883, came the Anti-Debris Act and the cessation of hydraulic activities.

The decline of Michigan Bluff followed quickly, until today little of its former prosperity is apparent. Shaded by old locust and fruit trees, the tiny hamlet of a few dozen people still clings to the mountainside. Some of the old frame houses are empty and rotting on their foundations, while others have been attractively renovated. The only business operation is a bar and restaurant housed in a sturdy structure built of native stone many years ago. A decrepit clapboard cottage, to the left of the main street at its end, is still pointed out as the one-time residence of Leland Stanford, though George T. Clark gives several very conclusive reasons why it is improbable that any building still standing in Michigan Bluff dates from the period that Leland Stanford was there, from 1853 to 1855. Stanford himself stated that for the three years he was in Michigan Bluff "he slept on a counter" in his store, his wife being still in the East. Moreover, Michigan Bluff then stood on its first site, and in 1857 it was swept by a fire that destroyed the entire business block, in which Leland Stanford's store was doubtless located. Elijah and Lyman Stanford and their families, cousins of Leland, did live at Michigan Bluff in 1857, Lyman being listed as a merchant in the Placer County directory for 1861.

Ghost Towns of the High Sierra

Some of the most awe-inspiring scenery in California is found on the ridge route as one travels east from Iowa Hill past the site of Damascus and north to Soda Springs. This road, very rough in spots, parallels the North Fork of the American River, which lies far below to the north; from it several branches lead south along narrow ridges high above deep canyons, each of them wild and rugged. These canyons were long ago the scene of many a quest for El Dorado, and the roads above them led to old camps now obliterated by the returning forest. Little travel goes this way, and one can almost imagine being a member of that first band to penetrate the area.

The ridge route was constructed in 1852 by the citizens of Placer County in the hope that it would draw the tide of immigration through their territory. To some extent, emigrants did come this way for a few years, but traffic was never great, and since the road was not maintained, it soon fell into disuse. During the 1860's, as a result of the rush to the silver mines of Nevada, travel over the old ridge road revived. Even during this period, however, it never reached the extent of popularity enjoyed by the Placerville and Dutch Flat–Donner Lake roads.

The old ridge road connected a chain of camps and way stations running eastward from Iowa Hill: Monona Flat, where a branch led to Succor Flat; Damascus; the Forks House, where the emigrant road from Yankee Jim's, Forest Hill, and Michigan Bluff came in from the south; Westville, beyond which a road goes south to Deadwood; the Secret Canyon station at the head of Secret Canyon; and Robertson's Flat, where one road turned north past the Lost Emigrant Mine and across the North Fork of the American River to Soda Springs and Donner Pass, and another led south to Last Chance and the North Grove of Big Trees. The main road crossed the summit at the head of Squaw Valley, but this route is not passable by automobile.

Damascus and Sunny South

Ten miles east of Iowa Hill was Damascus, located on a steep mountainside more than 1,000 feet above the waters of Humbug Creek. When the site was first settled in 1852, it was known as Strong's Diggings, but with the establishment there of a post office in 1856, the more dignified title of Damascus was adopted. Here the Mountain Gate, a tunnel drift mine with a 2,000-foot frontage which pierced the mountain to a distance of 4,000 feet, was long the chief location in the district. The Damascus claim, which adjoined it, with a 500-foot frontage and a 3,000-foot tunnel, was the only other mine in that locality. For many years during the 1870's and early 1880's hydraulic operations in the vicinity produced great wealth.

Damascus, with its scattered cottages and little garden plots, its schoolhouse, and its few stores, was completely destroyed by a forest fire many years ago.

Seven miles to the south another hamlet clung to the warm, sunny slopes of the mountain in a sheltered nook that in winter seemed always to escape the heavy snows covering the surrounding country. This phenomenon gave to the place the pleasant name of Sunny South. Here the Hidden Treasure, a very rich mine during its heyday, was worked as late as the 1880's. Nothing but happy memories of Sunny South and its old mine remain today.

Deadwood

At the tip of a narrow mountain spur high above the yawning chasms of El Dorado Canyon and the North Fork of the Middle Fork of the American River is the site of Deadwood, a one-time mining camp located seven miles from Michigan Bluff by pack trail. It is 25 miles by the long circuitous road that winds around the head of El Dorado Canyon past the Forks House, continuing across the head of Indian Creek at Westville, and thence down the Deadwood spur.

Gold was first found at Deadwood in 1852 by a group of miners who had previously experienced very indifferent success in the prospecting game. Being greatly elated over this sudden change for the better, the party remarked to all subsequent comers that they "now assuredly had the 'deadwood' upon securing a fortune"—in other words, it was a cinch. Thus Deadwood got its name.

The heartening news of the Deadwood discovery soon spread and a bustling camp sprang up, composed of over 500 miners who had toiled over fearful canyon trails to this remote spot. It was a wild, austere habitat, to which only the most venturesome came. A few even built their flimsy cabins along the precipitous canyon walls on the outskirts of the camp. Here they dwelt in almost constant danger of winter snows and avalanches. About these lonely domiciles cluster tales suggesting Hawthorne's *Ambitious Guest* in their tenderness of human relationships and the dramatic quality of setting and circumstances.

Deadwood's transient glory had departed by 1855, although mining with moderate returns was carried on in the vicinity for many years. Only a small cemetery and an old well remain at the site.

A high bench or bar in the canyon of the North Fork of the Middle Fork some two or three miles from Deadwood bears the delightful title of Bogus Thunder. A mile or more up the canyon from this place is a waterfall the sound of which reverberates throughout the gorge with such terrific roar that the first comers there thought it was thunder. When they finally discovered the real cause of the noise, they proclaimed the thunder bogus.

Last Chance

Almost as difficult of access as Deadwood is Last Chance, above the canyon of the North Fork of the Middle Fork and that great network of narrow gorges and immense canyons which runs into it from the north. Perched at the tip of a promontory on the very brink of this tremendous drop-off, the Last Chance area seems like the jumping-off place.

The search for treasure had led a little group of prospectors into this remote region in 1850. Several rich deposits discovered in the vicinity caused them to linger until all the provisions were gone and starvation threatened. One of the company possessed a good rifle. Saying to his companions, "This is our last chance to make a grub-stake," he went into the forest, and returned with a large buck. Thus the miners were able to return to their diggings and a new camp earned its name. This at least is one of several versions of the origin of this name.

Last Chance had become a real town by 1852, and by 1859 the Masons, the Odd Fellows, and the Sons of Temperance had erected halls. Forty-two of the 70 voters of the town were members of the last-named organization. Remnants of its short-lived glory are still visible at Last Chance in the old cemetery and a handful of scattered cabins.

Across Peavine Canyon from Last Chance and about five airline miles to the southeast, the northernmost group of *Sequoia gigantea* in California stands in a well-watered vale on Duncan Ridge overlooking the Middle Fork of the American River. These trees, known as the North Grove (American River Grove, Placer County Grove),

consist of six old living trees and two large fallen ones. They are a part of the Tahoe National Forest. At the instance of the owner of the Blue Eyes Mine nearby, the Placer County Chamber of Commerce in 1920 reopened the old road into this grove.

The motorist to Last Chance and the Placer County Big Trees should take the Mosquito Ridge Road, which branches from the Auburn–Forest Hill road half a mile west of Forest Hill. The Mosquito Ridge Road, paved for the first 19 miles and with a wide, graded surface beyond, intersects the road to Last Chance at 24 miles and the road to the Big Trees at 25 miles. The Last Chance road turns north and goes five miles to a junction, thence west a little over three miles to the townsite. The Big Trees road turns south and goes about half a mile to a parking area, from which a trail leads less than a mile to the grove. Other routes to Last Chance are not recommended.

At the base of Duncan Ridge is Duncan Canyon, its story similar to that of the famous Gold Lake expedition in Plumas County. James W. Marshall is authority for the statement that the name was derived from Thomas Duncan, who came overland from Missouri with Captain Winter in 1848, entering California by way of the mountain trail that diverged from American Valley and followed down the ridge south of the North Fork.

Late in the fall of 1850, while mining in Shirttail Canyon, Duncan regaled his companions with tales of rich diggings, which he claimed he had found upon entering California. Taking the tales seriously, his listeners persuaded him to lead them to the favored spot. When they arrived in the vicinity of the supposed treasure, the canyons all looked so much alike that Tom was unable to locate the right one. His followers became suspicious, threatening to shoot him unless he located the promised bonanza. Fortunately for Thomas Duncan, he did discover a fairly exciting deposit above Sailor Bar, and vigilance over him was temporarily relaxed. Duncan made the best of his opportunity and escaped that night. His misguided friends never saw him again, but they named the place where they had camped Duncan's Canyon.

About six miles west of the Big Tree Grove is Big Oak Flat, a parklike plateau covered with oaks, where there is now a flight strip. Here in the fall of 1850 James W. Marshall and a companion dug for gold, evidences of previous diggings being found by them at that spot. Prospecting all up and down the Sierra from 1848 to 1850, Marshall was one "of that human mass who carried the advancing ripple of civilization into the canyons of the California highlands." In the summer of 1850 he had been at Antoine Canyon, just northeast of Last Chance, a location first worked earlier in the season by a half-breed Crow Indian named Antoine.

Numerous other canyons throughout this highland country were penetrated by miners in the early 1850's, their names suggesting the nature of the region: Lost Canyon, Secret Canyon, Dark Canyon, Black Canyon, and Deep Canyon.

"Donner County"

Several efforts were made to cut new counties out of the territory already belonging to Placer and other counties. The last such attempt was made in 1869–70, when it was proposed to create "Donner County" from the High Sierra regions of Placer, Nevada, and Sierra counties. The movement met with much disfavor. One opposing editor, a former resident of Placer County, expressed his opinion of the project in the following words:

"If Donner County is created, Placer County will lose several well-known places, and the glory of much of her history. 'Ground Hog's Glory,' 'Hell's Delight,' 'Miller's Defeat,' 'Ladies' Canyon,' 'Devil's Basin,' 'Hell's Half Acre,' and a few other places of like significance will be in the new county... Placer County should fight the new county, in order to retain her glorious nomenclature of towns."

SOURCES

Angel, Myron. *History of Placer County, California.* Thompson & West, Oakland, 1882.
Browne, J. Ross. *Report on the Mineral Resources of the States and Territories of the Rocky Mountains.* Government Printing Office, Washington, D.C., 1868.
––– *Resources of the Pacific Slope.* H. H. Bancroft & Co., San Francisco, 1869.
Clark, George T. *Leland Stanford, War Governor of California, Railroad Builder and Founder of Stanford University.* Stanford University Press, Stanford, 1931.
Ferrier, W. W. "Berkeleyans Enjoy an Old Mining Town," *Berkeley Daily Gazette,* July 10, 1925.
Fulton, Robert Lardin, *The Epic of the Overland.* A. M. Robertson, San Francisco, 1924.
Geologic Guidebook along Highway 49–Sierran Gold Belt, the Mother Lode Country. State of California, Division of Mines, San Francisco, 1948.
Gold Rush Country. Lane Publishing Co., Menlo Park, 1957.
Hemphill, Vivia. *Down the Mother Lode.* Purnell's, Sacramento, 1922.
James, George Wharton. *The Lake of the Sky, Lake Tahoe.* Pasadena, 1915.
Johnston, Philip. "Relics of the Gold-Rush among the Northern Diggin's," *Touring Topics,* XXIV, No. 1 (January 1932), 10–25, 45, 46.
Lardner, W. B., and M. J. Brock. *History of Placer and Nevada Counties, California.* Historic Record Co., Los Angeles, 1924.
McGowan, Joseph A. *History of the Sacramento Valley.* 3 vols. Lewis Historical Publishing Co., New York, 1961.
Power, Bertha Knight. *William Henry Knight, California Pioneer.* Privately published, 1932.
Steele, R. J., James P. Bull and F. I. Houston. *Directory of the County of Placer, for the Year 1861.* Charles F. Robbins, San Francisco, 1861.
Weston, Otheto. *Mother Lode Album.* Stanford University Press, Stanford, 1948.

Plumas County

PLUMAS COUNTY was organized in 1854 from a portion of Butte County. (The name was derived from El Río de las Plumas, "the river of the feathers," so named by Captain Luís A. Argüello, who led an exploring party up the valley of the Feather River in 1820, and who was impressed by the many feathers of wild fowl which he saw floating on the water.) Quincy, originally known as American Ranch, has been the only county seat.

Beckwourth Pass

Beckwourth Pass *(SRL 336)* over the High Sierra was discovered in 1851 by James Beckwourth, trapper, scout, and honorary chief of the Crow Indians, while on a prospecting expedition as he and his party crossed the mountains from the American River valley to the Pit River valley. This pass, at 5,212 feet, is the lowest over the summit of the Sierra. It is about 15 miles east of the present town of Beckwourth. Through the error of a postal clerk, the town was for many years designated by the name "Beckwith," but a 1932 ruling restored the original spelling of "Beckwourth." The old brick Masonic Hall is a landmark in the little community.

Jim Beckwourth subsequently proposed to interested citizens at Bidwell Bar and Marysville that a wagon road be made through this pass, across the Sierra Valley to the Middle Fork of the Feather River, and down the ridge east of the river past Bidwell Bar to Marysville. His plan was eventually adopted, and soon after the completion of the trail, Beckwourth, while at Truckee in the Sierra Nevada, succeeded in persuading a passing emigrant train to try the new road. The party liked it, and others followed in their footsteps until it became a well-beaten trail. Beckwourth Pass is still in use by "present-day emigrants" who cross the Sierra on the Western Pacific Railroad or on State Highway 70.

Many emigrants came through this region in 1852. During the spring of that year Jim Beckwourth built a cabin, the first house in Sierra Valley, which served as trading post and hotel. It stood on a hillside just west of the site later occupied by the residence of Alexander Kirby, and two and a half miles west of the town of Beckwourth. A second cabin was built nearby, but both were burned by Indians. A third log cabin soon replaced the first two, and a part of this historic relic still stands on the Ramelli Ranch at Walker Mine Road and Highway 70.

It was in 1852 that Ina Coolbrith, destined to

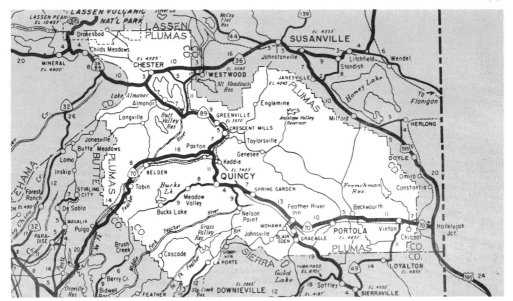

become California's first poet laureate, then a child of 11, came through Beckwourth Pass. The party had trekked across the plains and mountains from St. Louis, Missouri, in ox-drawn schooners.

Speaking at a luncheon given in her honor in San Francisco on April 24, 1927, Ina Coolbrith gave this account of the trip:

"Ours was the first of the covered-wagon trains to break the trail through Beckwourth Pass into California. We were guided by the famous scout, Jim Beckwourth, who was an historical figure, and to my mind one of the most beautiful creatures that ever lived. He was rather dark and wore his hair in two long braids, twisted with colored cord that gave him a picturesque appearance. He wore a leather coat and moccasins and rode a horse without a saddle.

"When we made that long journey toward the West over the deserts and mountains, our wagontrain was driven over ground without a single mark of a wagon wheel until it was broken by ours. And when Jim Beckwourth said he would like to have my mother's little girls ride into California on his horse in front of him, I was the happiest little girl in the world.

"After two or three days of heavy riding we came at last in sight of California and there on the boundary line he stopped, and pointing forward, said:

"'Here is California, little girls, here is your kingdom.' . . .

"This wagon train arrived in California in September, 1852. In the Spring of that year, Jim Beckwourth, according to his own story, had established himself in Beckwourth Valley, and finally found himself transformed into a hotel keeper and chief of a trading post. His house, he said, was considered the emigrant's landing place."

By action of the United States Geographic Board, through the efforts of officials of the Western Pacific Railroad, a high peak, formerly known as Summit Peak, located six miles due south of Beckwourth Pass, was renamed Mount Ina Coolbrith, in honor of the late poet laureate. The peak, which rises to an elevation of 8,000 feet in Sierra County, is plainly visible from the pass through which young Ina Coolbrith rode with the famous scout. It lies near the intersection of the county lines of Plumas, Lassen, and Sierra counties, with its slopes reaching out into Plumas and Lassen counties.

The Gold Lake Excitement

The higher regions of the Sierra Nevada were the last to be prospected during the early days of the gold rush. Several hundred Argonauts in 1849 passed over the Lassen Trail through what is now northwestern Plumas County, but not one stayed to work its streams. One man, however, was instrumental in opening up the country to a later influx of miners. This was J. R. Stoddard, the hero of an adventure whose beginnings are shrouded in mystery. The facts of its later developments and the resulting Gold Lake migration are well known, however.

Stoddard, according to his own account, had stumbled upon a lake in the higher mountains somewhere between Downieville and Sierra Valley. The shores of this lake, he declared, were literally covered with chunks of gold. His recital of its exact location and of the circumstances attending its supposed discovery was conflicting and uncertain. The spirit of the times, however, was such as to make the wildest extravaganza seem plausible to credulous gold seekers, and soon Stoddard found himself the leader not only of the small group originally chosen to go with him to relocate the fabled lake of gold but of several hundred others, all eager and determined to share in the imagined riches. The number increased, as rumor spread, until 1,000 or more miners left their diggings on the lower reaches of the rivers to join the migration to the new El Dorado.

Gold Lake was never found. Nevertheless, the influx of prospectors into the highlands of the upper Feather River canyons resulted in the opening of the entire region, and many of the tributary streams were found to be very rich. The Gold Lake in Sierra County just across the line from Plumas County, and the much smaller Gold Lake just northwest of Spanish Peak in Plumas County, are reminiscent of this early excitement over the mythical lake with its gold-pebbled shores.

Intersected by the various forks of the Feather River, the land of the fabled "Gold Lake" is one of rugged scenic grandeur. The sculpturing waters have here chiseled the Sierra with canyons 2,000 feet deep, flanked by lofty, forested ridges, magnificent and awe-inspiring. Green and fertile valleys, watered by countless streams, nestle among giant hills and are made still more lovely by the mirrored beauty of numerous lakes. These valleys include Indian, American, Big Meadows, Buck's, Humbug, Mohawk, Genesee, Sierra, Long, Red Clover, Round, Last Chance, and Onion. Near the southern boundary of the county the South Fork of the Feather River rises in the neighborhood of Pilot Peak, while the Middle Fork, a much longer stream with many tributaries, has its headwaters in Sierra Valley. The North Fork rises in the northwestern corner of the county southeast of Lassen Peak. Flowing almost due south through Big Meadows, now largely occupied by Lake Almanor, it waters a considerable section of Plumas County before joining the Middle Fork of the Feather River one and a half miles west of Bidwell Bar in Butte County, an area to be inundated upon completion of Oroville Dam.

Beginning with the gold excitement of the 1850's, mining, lumbering, and agriculture have played important roles in the history of Plumas County. With an increasing horde of gold seekers pouring into every corner of the region in the early days, mushroom cities of log cabins sprang up almost overnight. Soon there was a great demand for milled lumber with which to erect better buildings. Farmers saw the need for farm and dairy products, and ranches were established in the fertile valleys, where water and pasturelands were abundant. Although many of the old mining camps have since become ghost towns, a few remain, forming a link in the chain reaching back into the historic past. Today, also, many of the pioneer ranches are being farmed by descendants of the original owners.

Plumas County contains scores of mineral springs located in various parts of the county: in Humbug Valley, on the North Fork of the Feather River; at Soda Bar on the East Branch of the North Fork; in Indian Valley near Greenville, where there are warm bathing springs; in Mohawk Valley at the Sulphur Springs Ranch, where both hot and cold water are found; and in many other places. Numerous jets of steam and hot mud accompanied by rumbling noises suggest volcanic activities in Hot Springs Valley near the northwestern corner of the county. Since early days these places have attracted many visitors.

Onion Valley

Early in July 1850 a party of about 130 prospectors stopped in a lofty valley 15 miles northwest of Downieville. Because of the thick growth

Old Trading Post, near Beckwourth

of wild onions carpeting the place it was called Onion Valley. Here a member of the party known familiarly as "One-Eyed Moore" discovered rich diggings, and a camp was at once set up. Other discoveries were made, and soon the region was swarming with diggings: Dixon's Creek, Poorman's Creek, Nelson's Creek, Sawpit Flat, and many others. To the west, at the tip of a high ridge above the Middle Fork of the Feather River, was one of the several places in Plumas County called Last Chance.

At Onion Valley, Moore took out several thousand dollars' worth of gold and then moved on to fresher fields. However, others soon took his place, and by 1851 the camp had a population of 1,500. On January 1 of that year a rich deposit was uncovered from which over $6,000 in gold was taken out in an hour and a half, including one nugget worth $1,800 and several smaller ones valued at $500 each. A few days later a large quartz boulder was turned over, and from the soil beneath it "half a man's hat full" of gold was picked up.

Just south of Onion Valley near Pilot Peak an uncommonly rich quartz vein was found sometime in the late 1850's or early 1860's. This extraordinary story is told of its discovery: "A Frenchman, who had gone out shooting with a Spaniard, fired at a bird but missed and struck a piece of quartz rock, which came rolling down the hill. The Spaniard picked it up and noticed that it was studded with gold. Upon going to the spot from which it had been detached, they found an outcropping of auriferous quartz, from which they broke off and carried to Pine Grove [Sierra County] a large piece that turned out to be about two-thirds solid metal." Following this discovery, a company was formed and the new vein worked. For many years it continued to yield large profits.

Onion Valley is a few miles north of Gibsonville on the Quincy road.

Nelson's Point

In the wake of the fabulous Gold Lake expedition, hundreds of miners invaded the Middle Fork of the Feather River early in the summer of 1850. Claims were soon staked out all along the tributary streams by the disappointed searchers for Gold Lake. The first of these locations was made on Nelson's Creek, a branch of the Feather River named after one of its two discoverers. The town of Nelson's Point, at the mouth of the creek, was established soon afterward and became the trading center for the camps along the Middle Fork, such as Hottentot Bar, Sailor Bar, Poverty Flat, Sunny Bar, English Bar, Bell's Bar, and Henpeck Flat.

Hittell describes Nelson's Point as "one of the roughest places in California. It consisted of a few houses, piled as it were without form or shape against one another on the sides of the precipices where the spurs of three steep mountains met at the junction of Nelson's Creek. . . . As a place of carousal and wassail on Sundays for the miners of the rough and rocky regions round about, it became famous in the early times." Nelson's Point was later moved about a mile up the river to the stage road running from La Porte to Quincy. The site is marked today by a few old trees. The town, with its hotel and store kept by the Pauly family, was destroyed by a forest fire in 1924.

Rich Bar

Stragglers of the Gold Lake influx made one of the foremost discoveries in Plumas County, about July 1, 1850, on the East Branch of the North Fork of the Feather River at a place afterward called Rich Bar. Enormous production records were made at this point, where pans of dirt frequently yielded from $100 to $1,000. It is said that three Germans took out $36,000 in nuggets and gold dust during four days' time. Claims were so rich that they were limited to ten square feet. During the first two years after its discovery, Rich Bar yielded a total of from three to four million dollars in gold, thus earning its name. With the approach of the winter of 1850–51, most of the claims at Rich Bar were deserted, although a few log cabins were erected and occupied until the spring of 1851, when a host of miners again flocked to the region.

A vivid and colorful picture of life in this old river camp in the early 1850's has been preserved for us in the letters of a New England woman, Mrs. Louise Amelia Knapp Smith Clappe, who lived at Rich Bar from 1851 to 1852. Written to her sister Molly, in the old home at Amherst, Massachusetts, these letters, playfully signed "Dame Shirley," were penned merely to give her sister "a true picture . . . of mining life," with no thought of subsequent publication. However, two years later they appeared in print, when a friend, the Rev. Ferdinand C. Ewer of San Francisco, made use of them in *The Pioneer*, a monthly magazine of which he was the publisher and in which the "Shirley Letters" appeared during the two years of its existence.

Later writers, notably Bancroft, Hittell, and Royce, have acknowledged their indebtedness to these letters. Certainly the delightful pen pictures, written on the spot, glossing nothing over, form the best firsthand account we have of life in the early gold camps. "It is easy indeed," says Carl I. Wheat, "to credit the legend that from her Bret Harte obtained many ideas, and wrought from them undying tales of California's youth. *The Luck of Roaring Camp* and *The Outcasts of Poker Flat* contain mute evidence of Harte's great debt to her."

With her husband, Dr. Fayette Clappe, "Dame Shirley" came to Rich Bar in the fall of 1851. The journey from Marysville to Bidwell Bar was made in an "excruciatingly springless wagon," with the second stage of the trip negotiated on muleback over winding mountain trails, passing, at long intervals, a rare and thrice-welcome farmhouse— the Wild Yankee's (Butte County), the Buckeye Ranch, and the Pleasant Valley Ranch—where fresh butter, cream, and other luxuries might be had. The Berry Creek House (Butte County) was missed, the two pilgrims having strayed out of their way over a devious and confusing Indian trail in the mountainous region near the North Fork of the Feather River. "Who knows," Mrs. Clappe afterward wrote, "how narrowly I escaped becoming an Indian chieftainess, and feeding for the rest of my life upon roasted grasshoppers, acorns, and flower-seeds?"

Coming at length to the summit of the high ridge overlooking Rich Bar, she was enchanted with the exquisite beauty of the scene which lay before her: "shadowy nooks" and "far down valleys...half a dozen blue-bosomed lagoons.... It was worth the whole wearisome journey, danger from Indians, grizzly bears, sleeping under the stars, and all."

On the last stretch of her journey Mrs. Clappe had a narrow escape from death. Although warned that she should walk rather than ride down the precipice, since even the hardiest miners did so, she was determined to ride, for, as she told her sister, "I had much more confidence in my mule's power of picking the way and keeping his footing than in my own." At one point on the trail her saddle slipped and she landed on the tiniest of ledges far above the river bed. "Had the accident happened at any other part of the hill," she writes, "I must have been dashed, a piece of shapeless nothingness, into the dim valleys beneath."

Mrs. Clappe at length found herself safely at "Barra Rica," as the Mexicans called it. The third of the series of letters describes it in vivid tone. "Imagine a tiny valley, about eight hundred yards in length and, perhaps, thirty in width ... apparently hemmed in by lofty hills, almost perpendicular, draperied to their very summits with beautiful fir trees, the blue-bosomed 'Plumas,' or Feather River, I suppose I must call it, undulating along their base.... Through the middle of Rich Bar runs the street, thickly planted with about forty tenements, among which figure round tents, square tents, plank hovels, log cabins, etc. —the residences, varying in elegance and convenience from the palatial splendor of 'the Empire' down to a 'local habitation,' formed of pine boughs, and covered with old calico shirts."

Although numerous shanties on the bar claimed the grandiloquent title of "hotel," the Empire was *the* hostelry of the place, and Mrs. Clappe's portrayal of its whimsical splendor equals if not excels her other descriptions: "You first enter a long apartment, level with the street, part of which is fitted up as a bar-room, with that eternal crimson calico which flushes the whole social life of the 'Golden State' with its everlasting red—in the center of a fluted mass of which gleams a really elegant mirror, set off by a background of decanters, cigar vases, and jars of brandied fruit, the whole forming a *tout ensemble* of dazzling splendor.... The entire building is lined with purple calico, alternating with a delicate blue, and the effect is really quite pretty. The floors are so uneven that you are always ascending a hill or descending into a valley." Such was "this impertinent apology for a house," a one-time gambler's palace costing its original owners more than $8,000.

On the steep hillside behind the Empire Hotel lay the lonely graveyard where Nancy Ann Bailey, "the second 'Mrs. B.'," one of the two women who preceded Mrs. Clappe at Rich Bar, was buried a week after "Dame Shirley's" arrival. At the head of the bar was the little windowless log cabin in which this pioneer mother died September 30, 1851, according to the date on the headstone.

Nothing of the mining period remains at Rich Bar *(SRL 337)* except the decaying headstones in the tiny cemetery on the hill and the heaps of boulders along the river where miners once worked this richest of the northern diggings. Overlooking the river stands the Rich Bar monument dedicated by the Native Sons of the Golden West on August 7, 1915, in memory of the pioneers who settled at this spot, some of whom found rest on the hillside nearby, and in special honor of Nancy Ann Bailey. The townsite is on the Western Pacific Railroad three miles east of Belden and just south of Highway 70.

Indian Bar

In 1852 the Clappes moved to Indian Bar. Mrs. Clappe thus describes the river trail leading to her new home: "The crossings are formed of logs, often moss-grown....At every step gold diggers or their operations greet your vision, sometimes in the form of a dam, sometimes in that of a river turned slightly from its channel, to aid the indefatigable gold hunters in their mining projects....As we approached Indian Bar, the path led several times fearfully near deep holes from which the laborers were gathering their yellow harvest."

A little below Indian Bar was Missouri Bar, reached by a log bridge, while half a mile beyond on the same side of the river was Smith's Bar, also reached over a bridge formed by two logs. Within a few miles were Frenchman's, Taylor's, Brown's, The Junction, Wyandotte, and Muggins' bars.

Just across from Indian Bar was Pea Soup Bar (not yet named when Mrs. Clappe wrote her letters), while opposite Rich Bar was a narrow diggings later known as Poverty Bar. It was on this bar that builders of the Feather River Highway established camp while blasting out a roadway from the cliffs of the gorge. The road reached the point opposite Rich Bar in the autumn of 1932. The Western Pacific Railroad was constructed up the canyon in 1909, under the leadership of Arthur W. Keddie, although such a route had been considered as early as 1867.

Spanish Ranch

A quarter of a mile north of the old Oroville–Quincy road, and about six miles west of Quincy, two Mexicans in July 1850 set up an early camp in that part of Meadow Valley. This circumstance gave rise to the names Spanish Ranch, Spanish Creek, and Spanish Peak. Miners customarily left their horses and pack mules in the care of these Mexicans, who also engaged in cattle raising and slaughtering, selling the meat at one dollar a pound.

Spanish Ranch soon became a distributing center for surrounding camps. The first hotel, blacksmith shop, and store were erected there in 1852 by Lloyd and Snodgrass. A Wells Fargo Express office was established in 1868. Millions of dollars in gold dust and nuggets passed through its doors. As late as 1881 the year's output in coin and bullion amounted to $114,076. Directly above the townsite towers Spanish Peak (7,047 feet), pierced by the tunnel of the Monte Cristo Mine at an altitude of 6,288 feet, or within 759 feet of the summit.

Two miles southwest of Spanish Ranch is Meadow Valley, an old camp where W. S. Dean settled as early as 1852. A post office called Meadow Valley was established in 1855, but its name was changed to Spanish Ranch in 1861. A change of location may also have been involved. The present Meadow Valley post office was established in 1864. None of the old business buildings remain standing at Spanish Ranch and Meadow Valley (SRL 481). Two and a quarter miles west of Meadow Valley on the old stage road between Quincy and Oroville is the site of Toll Gate, where tolls were collected on one of the first turnpikes in Plumas County. The buildings here, too, have all disappeared.

Seven miles farther southwest the road passed Buck's Ranch, which was first occupied in the fall of 1850 by Horace Bucklin and Francis Walker. It later developed into another important stage station. All of the original buildings have been destroyed by fire, and the site is under the waters of Bucks Lake (SRL 197), which now covers most of Buck's Valley. The dam was constructed in 1925–27. On a large boulder on the lakeshore below Bucks Lodge a bronze tablet was placed by the Native Sons and Daughters of the Golden West of Plumas County on August 9, 1931. This marker designates the site of the Buck's Ranch hotel, which stood 100 yards to the northeast at a point immediately in front of the dead pine tree which still stands in the lake. If standing, the building would be submerged by 20 feet of water when the lake is full. The Buck's Ranch hotel and store served for years as a stage station and express and post office. In the early days it was a haven for pioneers, where miners' pack trains stopped en route to the Feather River mines, while later it became an important point in the passenger, express, and mail service to and from Quincy and other towns. In the rich Gravel Range District near Buck's Ranch, miners were known to have found gold, silver, and copper all in one ledge.

Beyond Grizzly Creek, about three and one-half miles west of Buck's Ranch, is a meadow hemmed in by the forest. Here, visible from the road, stands a granite monument marking the grave (SRL 212) of P. Linthiouh, a 19-year-old pioneer who was killed by bandits and buried under a pine tree at this spot by his comrade in September 1852. The tree, on which his name and age were carved, no longer stands.

The site of the old Letter Box House in another pine-fringed hollow, about three miles farther on, has been marked by the Forest Service. Five miles beyond is another site designated as Palmetto, where a miner's cabin and corral once stood and where a public campground is now located. Soon after leaving this point, the road enters the famous Walker's Plains or lava beds, where in pioneer days difficulty was experienced in keeping spokes in the stagecoach wheels. A good dirt road now crosses this region of interesting geological formations. The site of the Buckeye Hotel, the last stage station before entering Butte County, is passed soon after leaving the lava beds.

La Porte

La Porte, an old mining camp located on flat benches on both sides of Rabbit Creek, a tributary of Slate Creek in the southwest corner of Plumas County, was known as Rabbit Creek or Rabbit Town from 1850 to 1857. This area was part of Yuba County until 1852 and Sierra County until 1868. During the 1860's and 1870's it developed into a populous center for hydraulic mining. But after 1883, when hydraulic mining became illegal, La Porte dwindled in population, until today it is a quiet mountain hamlet with only a few dozen inhabitants. The frame Union Hotel and the brick Wells Fargo office with its heavy iron doors lend an atmosphere of age to the place. The house in which Lotta Crabtree lived for a time as a child has been destroyed by fire. At the west entrance to the town a granite monument (SRL 213) was placed by the Native Sons and Daughters of the Golden West of Plumas County on June 24, 1928, to mark the site of the Rabbit Creek Hotel and the old emigrant trail, and to commemorate the discovery of gold on Rabbit Creek in 1850 and the subsequent founding of La Porte.

Little Grass Valley, about four miles north of La Porte on the South Fork of the Feather River, was at the head of wagon traffic in pioneer days. Along the old stage road from Marysville to La Porte a number of inns were built, one of the most famous being the American House. The Lexington House, the Winthrop House, and the Buckeye House also stood on this road.

Elizabethtown, or Betsyburg

Miners flocked to the region of Elizabethtown (SRL 231) in 1852 in search of gold. There being only one unmarried lady in the new camp, Elizabeth Stark, the chivalrous miners named the new town in her honor. Elizabethtown or Betsyburg, as it was sometimes humorously called, was a large camp by 1853, and in March 1855 a post office was established there. However, the sur-

Union Hotel, La Porte (Wells Fargo Office at Left)

rounding gulches were soon exhausted. After Quincy was made the county seat of Plumas County in 1854, and the post office was moved there in December 1855, Elizabethtown began to decline. Today only tailings from the old mines indicate its one-time activity. The site of the former town was marked by a monument placed by the Native Sons and Daughters of Quincy on September 9, 1927. Highway 70 passes through the Elizabethtown area two miles north of Quincy.

American Ranch—Quincy

The American Ranch was owned by James H. Bradley, one of the three commissioners who organized Plumas County. Owing to his influence, the seat of justice was placed by statute at the hotel on his ranch. With this as a nucleus, he laid out a town, calling it Quincy after his home city in Illinois, and the people were induced to vote for Quincy as the county seat. The site of Bradley's hotel (SRL 479) is at Fillmore and Main streets.

The oldest buildings in Quincy are the Masonic Hall, on Harbison Avenue between Jackson and Main streets, moved from Elizabethtown in 1855, the lower floor being used at first as a schoolroom; and the Methodist Episcopal Church, built in 1877, at Jackson and Church streets. Several homes still standing were constructed of lumber brought from abandoned houses in Elizabethtown.

The Plumas House (SRL 480), built in 1866 by James and Jane Edwards at Court and Main streets, replaced an earlier log structure on the

Masonic Hall, Quincy

site. The famous old hotel was destroyed by fire in 1923, and the present Hotel Quincy took its place in 1925.

Quincy was one of the stations of Whiting and Company's Dog Express, which, in the early days, brought the mails over the snowy Sierra. For stretches of 20 miles through snow-covered mountain country, Newfoundlands or St. Bernards, driven tandem, two or four to a team, pulled sledges often carrying loads of over 600 pounds. Passengers, express, and mail were all transported. Distinguished service was rendered by these faithful animals and their masters from 1858 until the invention of the horse snowshoe in 1865.

Two miles east of downtown Quincy and just north of Highway 70 the first schoolhouse in Plumas County (SRL 625) has been preserved on the grounds of a modern school. It was built in 1857 by the residents of the eastern end of American Valley.

The Plumas-Eureka Mine

A few miles west of Blairsden and Graeagle (on Highway 89) is Plumas-Eureka State Park, which includes or surrounds several important landmarks of mining days—Jamison City, Johnsville, Eureka Mills, and the Plumas-Eureka Mine (SRL 196).

Operations started at the Plumas-Eureka Mine, situated on the east slope of Eureka Peak, in the summer of 1851. A company of 36 men was formed, but instead of setting up stamp mills at once, they wisely mined with arrastras, or drag stones, until sufficient money had been made to warrant improvements. Chili wheels, heavy wheels rotated around a pivot, superseded the arrastras, and finally, in 1856, a mill with 12 stamps was erected. Improvements continued to be made and profits were still accruing in 1870.

In the vicinity of the Plumas-Eureka other quartz mines were opened at various times. To the northeast was the Mammoth Mine, worked by a company of 80 men with the use of arrastras until 1856, when a 12-stamp mill was erected. Two other mines in the vicinity, the Washington and the Rough-and-Ready, were not financially successful, because their promoters spent all their profits on equipment. The Washington Mine was owned by a company of 76 men, who laid out an ephemeral town on Jamison Creek, calling it the City of 76.

All of these claims—the Plumas-Eureka, Mammoth, Washington, and Rough-and-Ready—were bought by John Parrott in the early 1870's. Parrott, in turn, sold them to the Sierra Buttes Company of London. Johnstown, now called Johnsville, was laid out in 1876 on Jamison Creek one-half mile east of the Plumas-Eureka Mine. A number of the old buildings still stand in this town of a few dozen inhabitants, notably the little firehouse and the rustic Catholic church. Johnsville is not part of Plumas-Eureka State Park, and its buildings are private property. Near the upper works of the mine was located the once prosperous settlement of Eureka Mills. About two miles north of Johnsville on Jamison Creek was Jamison, a mining camp first settled in 1853. Jamison has disappeared, and its site is traced now only by old trails and piles of stones indicating the vast extent of the early mining operations carried on there. All along Jamison Creek, too, traces of early quartz mills and arrastras may still be found.

The headquarters of Plumas-Eureka State Park are a short distance from Johnsville, at the beginning of the old road to Gibsonville and La Porte. Across from the museum (the former mine bunkhouse and office) and other buildings stands the massive Eureka Mill, a wooden structure 72 feet high, where millions of dollars in gold were produced. The old 48-stamp mill, once leaning precariously and falling into ruin, is being carefully restored by the State of California.

At park headquarters is a plaque designating Johnsville as a pioneer ski area of America (*SRL 723*). Winter sports events in the High Sierra were run off annually as early as 1860. La Porte, Onion Valley, Jamison City, and Johnsville, as well as the Sierra County towns of Whiskey Diggings, Poker Flat, Port Wine, and Howland Flat, organized the earliest ski clubs and held thrilling ski-racing contests that resulted in some notable speed records. The VIII Olympic Winter Games of 1960, held at Squaw Valley near Lake Tahoe, some 60 miles to the south, commemorated a century of sport skiing in California.

A short distance from park headquarters along the road to Gibsonville is a monument marking the old trail from Jamison City to Marysville. It consists of a stone taken from one of the earliest Jamison Creek arrastras and was dedicated by the Native Sons and Daughters of the Golden West of Plumas County on October 25, 1932. A second marker was placed at Split Rock, now on an abandoned piece of road between Johnsville and Mohawk. From this rock early miners obtained the arrastra stones which formed the primitive mills used to grind out the gold. The pioneer trail to Mohawk Valley passed near the site of this marker.

Mohawk, a hamlet near Blairsden and Graeagle, was once a prosperous agricultural center for surrounding mines. It is about three miles east of the site of Jamison. All of the early buildings at Mohawk have been destroyed by fire.

Other Historic Spots

At Greenville, long a center of quartz-mining activity, a bullion ledge was discovered in 1851 and first mined with profit by John W. Ellis in 1856. The Lone Star Mine was first worked there in 1857. At Round Valley, south of Greenville, John Ellis opened up the Ellis Mine in 1862, and quite a camp grew up about the stamp mill. With the abandonment of the mine, the town faded out completely within a few years. Tunnels and rock piles are the only evidence of early-day activity in the locality. Southeast of Greenville at Crescent Mills quartz-mining and milling operations were carried on as late as 1926.

Two famous copper mines in the mountains east of Indian Valley have made fine production

Catholic Church, Johnsville

records, and continued to employ a large number of men until they were shut down. One of these was the Engel Mine, closed in 1930, 15 miles northeast of Crescent Mills. The other was the Walker Mine, northwest of Portola and Beckwourth, which yielded $1,099,000 in copper in 1931, but was closed down in 1932.

Peter Lassen, the first pioneer to settle in Indian Valley, came there with Isadore Meyerwitz in the fall of 1850. Lassen called the spot Cache Valley, but later settlers gave it its permanent name of Indian Valley, because of the many Indians living there. Lassen returned to the region in 1851 accompanied by a Mr. Burton. The two men built a log cabin four and a half miles east of the site of Greenville, and developed a thriving trading post. Vegetables were raised and sold to the miners at high prices. The site of the old Lassen cabin (*SRL 184*), which stood for many years, has been permanently marked by the Native Sons and Daughters of the Golden West of Plumas County.

Between the broad meadows of Indian Valley and the dense evergreen forests of Mount Hough lies Taylorsville, founded by Jobe T. Taylor, who settled there in 1852. A quaint charm pervades the town, with its great barns, shady streets, white-steepled church, old houses, substantial and dignified, and, close against the hill in a tiny oak wood, the burial ground of the pioneers. A monument here marks the grave of Jobe Taylor. The school stands on the site of the Vernon House or Taylor Hotel, the third hostelry built by Jobe Taylor on the same site. It was erected soon after the fire of 1859 had destroyed the second structure. The Young Hotel, now the Grange Hall, is of later date. The Odd Fellows Hall was built in 1874.

SOURCES

Beckwourth, James P. *The Life and Adventures of James P. Beckwourth*, ed. T. D. Bonner. Harper, 1856. New ed., Knopf, New York, 1931.
Clappe, Mrs. Louise Amelia Knapp (Smith). *California in 1851–1852. The Letters of Dame Shirley.* Introduction and Notes by Carl I. Wheat. 2 vols. The Grabhorn Press, San Francisco, 1932. Originally appearing as "The Shirley Letters from California Mines, 1851–52," in *The Pioneer* I–IV (January 1854–December 1855). Reprinted by Thomas C. Russell at his private press, San Francisco, 1922.
Dornin, May. "The Emigrant Trails into California."
Master's thesis in history. University of California, Berkeley, 1921.
Fariss and Smith. *Illustrated History of Plumas, Lassen, and Sierra Counties.* Fariss & Smith, San Francisco, 1882.
Gold Rush Country. Lane Publishing Co., Menlo Park, 1957.
Hittell, Theodore H. *History of California.* 4 vols. N. J. Stone & Co., San Francisco, 1898.
Purdy, Helen Throop. "The Shirley Letters from California Mines, 1851–1852," a review in *California Historical Society Quarterly*, I, No. 3 (January 1923), 299–301.
Rider, Fremont, ed. *Rider's California: A Guide-Book for Travellers.* Macmillan, New York, 1925.
Rourke, Constance. *Troupers of the Gold Coast, or the Rise of Lotta Crabtree.* Harcourt, Brace, New York, 1928.
Royce, Josiah. *California.* Houghton Mifflin, Boston, 1886.

Riverside County

RIVERSIDE COUNTY was created in 1893 from territory originally belonging to San Bernardino and San Diego counties. Riverside has been the county seat from the beginning.

Indian Rocks

Riverside County is exceptionally rich in Indian rock writings, those mysterious carvings and drawings of a people long since passed away, depicting stories of hunts, of fires, and of battles. Most of them are painted in that vivid red pigment, the secret of which has been lost. Others are in red and white, and a few in red, black, and white. Nearly always they command a spring or watering place, the camping grounds of the ancients, where these rock pictures were often left as sign boards. Modern Indian tribes do not know their origin or meaning and scientists have deciphered only a few of them. Some have traced in them the Montezuma frog and hold the theory that these people were of the same race as the Aztecs of Mexico.

There were once seven Indian villages in San Jacinto Valley: Ivah; Soboba, near the Soboba Lithia Springs; Jusispah, where the town of San Jacinto now is; Ararah, in Webster's Canyon on the road to Idyllwild; Pahsitnah, the largest in the valley, near Big Springs Ranch; Corova, the most northern, in Castle Canyon; and a small settlement of the Serranos from San Bernardino, near Eden Hot Springs. It is believed that the tribes who lived here were among the most powerful of any in the Southwest, and this region about the great peaks of San Jacinto and Tahquitz has an abundance of Indian lore. There are doubtless many carved and painted rocks (petroglyphs and pictographs) in this region that still remain undiscovered.

One of the finest of the Riverside group of pictographs is found in Fern Valley, a canyon of San Jacinto Peak, a short walk from the road by an easy trail. Painted in vivid red on the face of a huge rock, the color is apparently unfaded in spite of the action of the elements upon it. The design, too, is unusual and constitutes a remarkable piece of workmanship, conforming, so scientists say, to rock paintings and designs found among the early Aztecs of Mexico. According to one theory, it tells the story of a great hunt: the long trail which the hunters follow, their encounter with a bear, the crossing of streams and the climbing of mountains, a skirmish with members of a hostile tribe, the trail again, the final kill, and the great feast.

There is a very striking petroglyph in Reinhart Canyon, three miles north of the Perris–Hemet highway, carved into a massive granite boulder in the form of a huge swastika. This marvelous rock, called the Maze Stone (SRL 557), is reached via California Avenue, which leaves the highway at a point five miles west of Hemet. The area is now a county park, and the petroglyph is assured of preservation. The larger figure is made up of four smaller swastikas, the whole being about four feet in diameter. Many anthropologists have theorized about it. Some believe that a little group of Orientals, blown in frail craft across the Pacific before the beginning of history, left their imprint upon the ancient tribes of the Southwest. There is only one other carved rock in the United States known to be like this one, and that is far in the Northwest.

"About a mile west of the Ramona Bowl, near Hemet, on the Big Springs Ranch, are many flat boulders covered with metate holes, and one object of very unusual interest. This is a table-like rock about five feet square and three feet high with slanting top surface covered with many small round depressions arranged in a series of circles, usually a central depression and five around the circumference of the circle. These depressions were not metates. They are too near together and are only deep enough to hold a small nut or stone. Whether this was for an ancient Indian game or was used as some sort of ballot box, or for something else, is unknown.

"Along the bench east and west of the Ramona Bowl, the site of the ancient village of Pahsitnah, are a number of flat granite rocks with their surface quite covered with metate grinding holes. One boulder on the property of Captain F. L. Hoffman, east of the Bowl, contains over forty metates." This rock marks the site of the village of Pochea (SRL 104), one of the "Seven Villages of Pahsitnah." It is about seven-tenths of a mile east of the Ramona Bowl, which is located south of Hemet.

There are many other Indian rocks, both pictographs and petroglyphs, scattered throughout Riverside County. In Dawson Canyon there is an interesting painted rock (SRL 190) which has been marked by the Corona Women's Improvement Club. This rock, found on the right of way of the Santa Fe Railroad, was threatened with destruction until saved by the History and Landmarks Committee of the club. Placed in a cement base by the Santa Fe Railway Company, it was unveiled on May 4, 1927, displaying a bronze tablet bearing the following legend: "In tribute to the earliest record of any people in this region, the Santa Fe Railroad has preserved this rock with ancient Indian pictographs, and the History and Landmarks Committee of the Corona Women's Improvement Club has placed this tablet, May 4, 1927."

Chief Lafio of Temecula said the painted rock was the work of the Temecula (Luiseño) Indians, perhaps telling of a three-day fiesta or a religious celebration. Again, it may have been a flood warning, as the San Jacinto River formerly flowed beside the rock and on it are four water signs similar to those found on other rocks listed in the report of the United States Bureau of Ethnography. The painted rock is reached by the Dawson Canyon Fireroad, which turns to the east from the Temescal Canyon Road at a point seven and one-half miles southeast of the intersection of Ontario Avenue and Main Street south of Corona. A distance of only a quarter of a mile along the Dawson Canyon road brings one to the old Serrano tanning vats, immediately adjacent to the road on the right. From this point the painted rock may be seen across the field on the opposite side of the road. It stands next to the railroad track and is reached by an easy hike. In this same vicinity there is also a carved rock (SRL 187), which is reached by the winding road through the clay pits that turns right from the Dawson Canyon Fireroad just one-tenth of a mile past the old tanning vats. A mile or more of twisting and turning along the clay pit road will bring one into clear view of a great natural amphitheater, in the midst of which stands the rock. Its top has been damaged, presumably by lightning, but

Maze Stone, near Hemet

many of the carvings are still intact. Near it is found the black basaltic stone which will cut the petroglyphs.

In Mockingbird Canyon, between Riverside and Perris, there are two groups of painted rocks near the Mockingbird Springs. One group is in the form of a cave. Here the five basic colors used in the Indian sign language, red, blue, green, yellow, and black, have been worked into the designs which cover the under side of the roof. This is probably the only instance in this area where all five colors have been employed. Just east of this unusual group is another one consisting of several huge boulders painted in red in various simple designs.

In the hills about Perris many Indian relics and painted rocks have been found. Some of the most interesting of these are located on the old Penny Ranch, two miles north of Perris, where there is also an ancient Indian council cave. Others are found on the Sill Ranch, three miles south of Perris, on the Roberts Ranch, between Perris and Winchester, and on the Guthridge Ranch, at the south end of Leon Street on the western edge of Homeland. There are still others near Highway 395 three miles south of Temecula; at Rabbit Point, or Travertine Rock, at the Imperial-Riverside county line south of Oasis in the eastern end of the county; and in the mountains to the north of Lake Elsinore.

Just off the road through Bernasconi Pass, a couple of miles west of Lakeview, are the Lakeview Hot Springs, formerly Bernasconi Hot Springs, the site of three ancient Indian battles. Here are many metate holes, where corn was ground by the women of ancient tribes.

About ten miles southwest of Coachella, and west of Highway 86 via Avenue 66, on the south slope of the Coachella Valley, once populated only by the Cahuilla Indians, is a remarkable group of "circular depressions among a maze of boulders just below the ancient shoreline," thought by some archaeologists to be ancient Indian fish traps. They are made in the form of circular stone walls with an opening on the ocean side, so that, as the water receded with the outgoing tides, fish could be caught in the stone traps. Others say that they were foundations for ancient houses. At least, they were made by human hands a long time ago. All along the southern side of the valley the ancient shoreline is plainly visible,

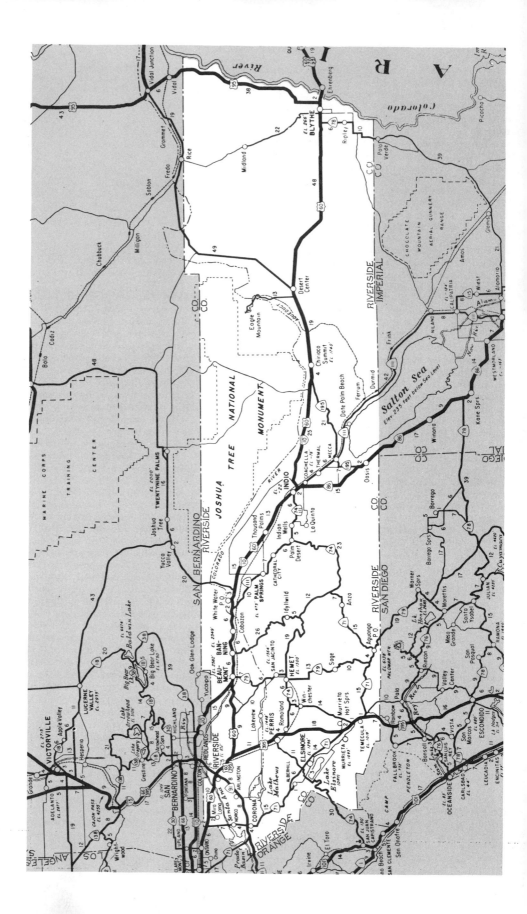

and it extends down through Imperial Valley into northern Mexico.

The ancient village of Ivah once thrived in the region of the present town of San Jacinto, near Massacre Canyon, on the Gilman Hot Springs Road. Many years ago a battle was fought there over a crop of chia, a grain that grew wild on nearly all of the mesa lands. The story goes that a severe drought in southern California caused the total failure of the chia crop in Temecula Valley. Now, the Temeculas, who were a tribe distinctly separate from the seven tribes at San Jacinto, and more warlike, came in search of grain. Proceeding to gather the crop belonging to the village of Ivah, they precipitated a fierce battle. The Ivahs fought valiantly, but being outnumbered they were forced to flee into the narrow ravine now known as Massacre Canyon. There, with their backs against a vertical wall, they fought to their death. Long afterward Massacre Canyon received its name from the white settlers, who had heard the story from old Indians.

Perhaps the most inexplicable prehistoric relics in the county, both as to age and as to purpose or meaning, are the giant desert figures (SRL 101) just west of the Colorado River. They represent both man and animals and are best seen from the air, from which they were discovered. The largest of them is 167 feet long. The mesa is covered with sandstone pebbles which were moved by prehistoric man in such a way that bare earth was left to form the figures, the pebbles being placed in windrows about the edge as an outline. These ancient remnants of an unknown civilization are about half a mile west of Highway 95 at a point 16 miles north of Blythe.

Palm Springs, now the foremost desert resort in the United States, was once the exclusive domain of the Cahuilla Indians. Two miles to the south of Palm Springs in the Palm, Murray, and Andreas canyons are magnificent groves of the native date palms, one of the grandest spectacles in all the Southwest. Here, too, in certain spring seasons after heavy rains, may be witnessed the miracle of vast wild flower gardens springing as if by magic from the dry sands of the desert.

The first permanent white settler in the Palm Springs area was John Guthrie McCallum, who arrived in 1884 and put up an adobe house. This building is still standing, but it has been moved south from its original location on Palm Canyon Drive, once a rough dirt road, and now stands at 223 South Palm Canyon Drive. The first resort hotel was opened in the late 1880's and others followed. Much of the land, including the ancient hot springs called "Agua Caliente" by the Spaniards, is still owned by the Indians, who have prospered by renting their property for plush resorts.

The Pechanga Burial Ground

About five miles southeast of Temecula lies the Pechanga chapel and burial ground, where, it is supposed, Alessandro, hero of Helen Hunt Jackson's *Ramona*, buried his father after the massacre at Temecula. According to the story, the 200 Indians who had been driven "from their poor homes at Temecula staggered with their dead to this little sanctuary in the hollow of the hills. Later, creeping back through the river sands to Temecula at night time, many removed their dead from the old Temecula graveyard to the security of Pechanga.

"The cemetery is quaint.... Broken bits of pottery and household utensils are placed on the graves, whether in decoration or with the thought of possible need by those buried there, is debatable ... small metates, bits of colored glass, parts of lamps, children's toys ..."

The old chapel and cemetery are on the Pechanga Indian Reservation about a mile east of Highway S-16 leading to Pala.

San Carlos Pass and Anza's Trail

San Carlos Pass, the first inland gateway to the coast of California, was discovered by Captain Juan Bautista de Anza in 1774 on the first continuous overland journey into the state. The trail and the pass were located by Professor Herbert E. Bolton of the University of California, and in 1924 the Native Sons of the Golden West marked them with a tablet bearing the following inscription: "On March 16, 1774, Juan Bautista de Anza, Indian fighter, explorer and colonizer, led through this Pass (named by him, San Carlos) the first white explorers to cross the mountains into California. The party travelled from Tubac, Arizona, to Monterey, California. On December 27, 1775, on a second expedition into California, Anza led through the Pass the party of Spaniards from Sonora who became the founders of San Francisco."

The pass was at what later became Fred Clark's horse corral near the southern boundary of Riverside County, 20 miles west of the junction of Riverside, Imperial, and San Diego counties. Camp on the previous night, March 15, was on a flat in Nance Canyon, 200 yards below the Royal Pass of San Carlos. Anza entered the San Jacinto Mountains from the desert via San Felipe Creek and the Borrego Valley in San Diego County, and from there passed into Riverside County through Coyote Canyon.

The marker (SRL 103) described above stands on the Anza trail about eight miles southeast of the little town of Anza on the present Cary Ranch. About a mile and a half east of Anza the Terwilliger Road turns south from Highway 71. At a point just under five miles along Terwilliger Road the Coyote Canyon Road turns east one and one-half miles to the Cary Ranch.

On March 16 the travelers marched through Cahuilla Valley to Laguna Príncipe, now known as Dry Lake and located on the Contreras Ranch. Another short march on the following day took them as far as San Patricio, at the head of Bautista Canyon. Following this canyon, the expedition descended the mountain to Río de San Joseph, now the San Jacinto River. This was on March 18, and camp was pitched in a leafy cottonwood grove about three miles above the site of San Jacinto.

On March 19 Anza and his party passed San

OLD TEMESCAL ROAD

Jacinto Lake, now dry, camping at its western end. Turning west on the 20th, they proceeded past the site of Moreno through Alessandro Valley, and descended the ridge probably by way of Sycamore Canyon. Crossing the site of Riverside, the expedition stopped near an Indian village on the banks of the Santa Ana River about three miles southwest of Mount Rubidoux near the Union Pacific railroad bridge. Here, on the 20th a bridge of logs was thrown across the river, and on the 21st the party crossed the river. On the 22d they entered San Bernardino County and on the 24th they arrived at Mission San Gabriel.

Returning from Monterey in April 1774, Anza retraced his steps through Riverside County early in May, stopping again at some of his previous campsites. On May 10 he was once more at Yuma.

In December 1775, Anza again passed over this route as the leader of that remarkable band of pioneers who first settled San Francisco. On Christmas Eve, camp was made near the upper end of Coyote Canyon at Upper Willows, or Fig Tree Spring.

Here, shortly before midnight, a baby boy, Salvador Ignacio Linares, was born, the third and last since leaving Tubac. The colonists, forgetting their misery for a time, spent that first Christmas Eve in California singing and dancing and partaking a little too freely, perhaps, of the aguardiente which Anza had given them against the good priest's protests. On Christmas morning, the train being held in the canyon for another day on account of little Salvador, Father Font took the opportunity to rebuke his now repentant flock by a sermon, at the close of which he wished everybody a happy Christmas.

In 1950 the California Centennials Commission erected a monument in Coyote Canyon to commemorate the birth of the first white child in California.

From here, the route was, with one variation, the same as on Anza's previous trip. After leaving Lake San Jacinto, the company went past the site of Lakeview, through Bernasconi Pass, and across Alessandro Valley by way of March Field to the old campsite on the Santa Ana River *(SRL 787)*. The location of this crossing has been marked near the Union Pacific bridge.

The route which Anza opened up at this time was used infrequently until 1782. By it came the colonists for Los Angeles, and the troops for the presidio of Santa Barbara, but after Fages' expedition in 1782 it was closed because of the hostility of the Yuma Indians.

A statue of Anza stands at Fourteenth and Market streets in Riverside.

The Old Emigrant Trail

Anza's route across the mountains was superseded by another trail opened up by Pedro Fages in 1782, who, instead of following the older path back to San Gabriel after his expedition against the Yuma Indians, blazed a new one, coming into San Diego County by way of the Carrizo Creek, Vallecito, and over the Cuyamaca Mountains to San Diego Mission.

Santiago Argüello, while in pursuit of Indian horse thieves, rediscovered this trail in 1825. In January 1826 the Mexican government sent Romualdo Pacheco, Lieutenant of Engineers, to investigate it, and with his approval an official mail route was adopted via Carrizo Creek, Vallecito, San Felipe Valley, and Warner's Pass. A small garrison was established on the Colorado River to protect the road, and from then on it was used occasionally by mail carriers and traders from Sonora. Probably the first Americans to come this way were David E. Jackson and his party of fur traders, who had come overland from Santa Fe in 1831. Later it came to be known as the Emigrant Trail and formed a part of the Southern Overland Trail, a much-traveled route from the East into California during the 1840's and 1850's. In Riverside and San Bernardino counties there were two branches of the old Emigrant Trail. From the Colorado River to Warner's Ranch and continuing west to Aguanga there was one road. There the San Bernardino–Sonora Road branched north along the western base of the San Jacinto Mountains, while the Colorado Road went directly west and then northwest through the valley north of the Santa Ana Mountains. This section of the road through San Bernardino and Riverside counties to San Gabriel was called the Canyon Road by the mission fathers, who opened it up immediately after Romualdo Pacheco had reestablished the overland route by way of Warner's. It was by the latter route that Jackson traversed Riverside County on his way to San Gabriel, going by way of Temecula, Elsinore, Temescal Canyon, and Corona.

The San Bernardino–Sonora Road

"After reaching San Gorgonio [near the present town of Beaumont], the San Bernardino–Sonora Road turned southward and ran, via the present Lamb Canyon, to San Jacinto; thence to what is now Hemet; then through the hills, following approximately the line of the present St. John's Grade; and on until near what is now Aguanga, west of Warner's Ranch, it merged with another road from San Gabriel that was designated . . . as the Colorado Road. From this point of junction on to the desert and Sonora, the San Bernardino–Sonora Road and the Colorado Road were one and the same.

"... This region had been inhabited by Indians for generations, and was traversed by well-established trails. When Sonorans and Americans began coming in to California, they naturally followed the old paths whenever possible.

"The very name of this road is intriguing. It leads back into history more than two [and a half] centuries, and recalls innumerable romances and adventures, though, up to comparatively recent times, it was but little more than a trail for horsemen and pack animals, traveled by ox carts only through the stretches that were open and fairly level. Starting in the Mexican state of Sonora, it had stretched to the northwest, over courses many of which are now almost or entirely forgotten. The name brings to mind Father Kino, the missionary who was perhaps responsible for the road's beginning; it recalls the Anzas and Pedro Fages, the adventurous soldiers and explorers; it recalls the race against time of Amador to head off the delivery of California missions to scheming colonizers; it brings to mind journeys of the 'Santa Fe Traders'; over a part of it, guided by Kit Carson, marched General Kearny and his men on their way from Santa Fe to San Diego; over it crawled thousands of Argonauts on their way to the gold fields; over long stretches of it raced Overland Mail stages on their run from St. Louis to San Francisco; over part of it Crabb and his misguided colonists—or filibusters—marched to their death; over it traveled engineers on their search for a route by which a railway could reach the Pacific. A historic road, indeed."

The Butterfield Overland Stage Route

"In 1858, the road from Los Angeles to the Colorado attained national importance when the Butterfield Company adopted it for their stages carrying mail between St. Louis and San Francisco, continuing its use until the outbreak of the Civil War. They did not travel through the San Bernardino Valley, but, after leaving Warner's Ranch, went to Los Angeles by way of Temecula, Sierra Rancho, and Chino. This latter route was the military road between California and Arizona during the Civil War, and an army post, Camp Wright, was maintained at Oak Grove [San Diego County], the first of the stage stations west of Warner's."

The adobe ruins of one of the few extant stage stations could long be seen at 20730 Temescal Canyon Road, four and one-half miles southeast of the intersection of Ontario Avenue and Main Street south of Corona. Horses were changed here in the stable behind the station, and, for a time, mail was delivered in the front room of the inn. A very old pepper tree formerly shaded the place, but this has disappeared, and now the ruins, too, have been cleared away. The site *(SRL 188)* has been marked. After the Civil War the Banning and Tomlinson stages passed over this road. Half-hidden among a sheltering grove of trees, the Aguanga station stood a few hundred feet from

the road which winds down the mountain from Warner's Ranch to Temecula.

One of the few intact portions of the old Butterfield Trail in the state lies in the Alberhill section of Elsinore Valley. William Collier, one of the owners of the Rancho Laguna in the early 1880's, said that he went over this old trail by the following route:

"I passed over this stage route from Coyote Wells on the desert to the Carriso stage station and through the range to San Phillipi, thence over to Warner's Ranch and across it to the base of the mountain, passing one mile from the present Warner's Hot Springs and down from the divide northerly of the Palomar mountains through Oak Grove to the Temecula stage station, at that time about two or three miles from the present town of Temecula, on the Little Temecula Ranch.

"The stage route lay from Temecula station, as it is now known, up the valley, passing through the town-site of Murrieta, Wildomar and west, along the westerly side of the lake of Elsinore as now known and reached the Machado ranch house. From there diagonally across the northwesterly end of Laguna ranch, and after crossing the Laguna ranch line about midway of what is now known as Block 'B' of Elsinore, passed through the unimproved country covered largely by chaparral, over the hills until it reached the southerly section line of Section 22, at a point across the valley to the west half of the southwest quarter of Section 22, Township 5 south, Range 5 west. It reached the level ground now occupied by the Los Angeles Pressed Brick Company.

"The line of the old stage route is still visible on the hill and going up the hill. In the valley it has been so disturbed as to be impossible to locate it."

One of the old Machado adobes, possibly the one used as a Butterfield stage station, stood until 1964 at 32912 Macy Street near Grand Avenue on the southwest side of Lake Elsinore. It and a small adobe outbuilding have been razed, but three tall palm trees have been retained. The adobe had known various uses through the years, and a frame addition and frame second story had been built onto it. At the turn of the century the Willard post office was located there. Two rooms of another Machado adobe have been incorporated into the home at 15410 Grand Avenue. Agustín Machado acquired the Rancho La Laguna in 1858 from Abel Stearns, who had purchased it from the heirs of the original grantee, Julián Manríquez. The grant of over 13,000 acres was made by Governor Micheltorena in 1844.

The path of the old Butterfield trail may still be seen near Rome Hill (between the Machado place and Wildomar) on the way to Temecula. There it probably skirted the chapel and the graveyard with its adobe wall, a region replete with the romance of Ramona and Alessandro.

Old Temescal Road

A monument has been placed at the junction of the Temescal Canyon Road and the road to Glen Ivy Hot Springs, eight and eight-tenths miles southeast of the intersection of Ontario Avenue and Main Street south of Corona, to commemorate the old Temescal Road *(SRL 638)*, which has seen the transition from Indian trail to automobile highway, with many an explorer, Argonaut, stagecoach, and military caravan between. Highway 71 was long routed this way, but now a wider, more modern thoroughfare is being built.

There is another historical marker in this vicinity, but it is very small and difficult to find. About half a mile north of the Temescal Road monument and 800 feet west of the road is a low hill with lacy pepper trees, near Lawson–Hunt Road. Here is the Serrano Memorial *(SRL 185)*, a small granite boulder bearing a bronze tablet which reads: "Boulder placed by residents of Temescal Valley to mark the site of the first house in Riverside County, erected by Leandro Serrano about 1824."

Inquiry as to the location of this marker can be made at the nearby office of the Temescal Water Company, on whose property it is located.

The spot on which this old adobe once stood was located by Dolores Serrano, daughter of Don Leandro, and while the foundation for the memorial was being placed the hearthstone of the old house was unearthed.

Leandro Serrano was the son of a soldier who had come to San Diego with Father Junípero Serra in 1769. He became mayordomo of Pala Chapel, and in 1818, because of his long and faithful service and his influence over the Indians, the priest at Mission San Luís Rey sent him to locate on the mission lands in Temescal Valley where many Indians were then living.

The valley was fair with groves of oak and sycamore, green *ciénegas* or marshes, and myriad wild flowers, and at the largest of the *ciénegas*, Serrano built his first adobe home in 1824. A large Indian ranchería and sweathouse were located nearby, and Serrano enlisted the natives in a drive against the bears and mountain cats of the region before bringing in his sheep and cattle.

A mile from the site of Don Leandro's original adobe, two stone tanning vats *(SRL 186)*, a double one and a single one, may still be seen. These, according to P. Aguilar, who came to Temescal Valley in 1864, had been in use since 1819, and were, without doubt, used by the Indians of Serrano's rancho for the tanning of hides. They are reached by the Dawson Canyon Fireroad, which also gives access to the well-known Indian painted rock and carved rock. The fireroad turns to the east from the Temescal Canyon Road at a point seven and one-half miles southeast of the intersection of Ontario Avenue and Main Street south of Corona. The vats, which have been fenced for protection, are very close to the right side of the fireroad one-quarter mile from the Temescal road. Near the tanning vats stood another and later adobe dwelling of Leandro Serrano *(SRL 224)*, the ruins of which were long in evidence. Now even the aged olive trees which would indicate the site have vanished, and the location is marked only in the memories of old-timers and local historians. Although a formal grant was never applied for, Leandro Ser-

rano occupied the land at Temescal until his death in 1852.

The city of Corona, largely situated on the Rancho La Sierra of Bernardo Yorba, has honored its founders of 1886 by a monument *(SRL 738)* in the city park on Sixth Street between Rimpau Avenue and East Grand Boulevard. Corona was formerly called South Riverside.

The Temescal Tin Mine

The history of the Temescal (or Cajalco) Tin Mine, discovered about 1856 in the Temescal Mountains to the east, "would fill a volume." Litigation between the claimants of the mine, on the one hand, and the Serrano heirs and Abel Stearns, on the other, was long and bitter. The decision was finally made in favor of the claimants.

At the Mechanics Fair in San Francisco in 1869, bars of tin from Temescal were exhibited. Specimens were also sent to England, where they were pronounced of the purest quality. It was the opinion of many investigators that "here was a body of tin, unlimited in quantity and of the finest quality—the richest and, indeed, the only workable body of tin ore in the United States."

Little was done at the Temescal Mine until after the clearing of the title in 1888. English experts examined the region repeatedly, and in 1890 two English companies were incorporated and more than two million dollars were invested within the two years following.

Why the mine was closed down in 1892 and has never been permanently reopened has not been satisfactorily explained: a tariff on tin, the competition of Cornwall interests, or a mistaken estimate of the real value of the property by English tin experts all have been offered as possible explanations of the brief heyday of tin mining at Temescal. The old mine workings are two miles west of Lake Mathews, formerly the Cajalco basin.

Rancho El Rincón

This rancho, of one square league, was granted to Juan Bandini by Governor Alvarado in 1839. It is located partly in San Bernardino County, where the Yorba–Slaughter adobe still stands in a fine state of preservation.

Bandini built an adobe home on El Rincón

Ruins of Bandini-Cota Adobe,
Rancho El Rincón

about 1840–41, but after a few years he sold it and the rancho to Bernardo Yorba, who gave it to his daughter Bernarda, who married Leonardo Cota. Thus the adobe came down in history as the Cota house. Of two stories, it was a fine example of Spanish colonial architecture, standing on a high bluff above the Santa Ana River bottom. A magnificent view of broad rolling fields, of the bottom lands with their luxuriant cottonwood groves, and of the distant mountains made this one of the finest of all the old homesites.

The old adobe has been falling to pieces since about 1930, but there are still some ruins to be seen. One can catch a glimpse of them in the distance to the east of Highway 71 four miles north of its junction with Highway 91. The ruins are located within the Prado Flood Control Basin, on a hill behind a hog ranch, through which, with permission, they can be reached. This ranch is between Prado Dam and the California Institution for Women.

Rancho Jurupa

Rancho Jurupa, a portion of which later became the Rubidoux Ranch, and on a part of which the city of Riverside now stands, was granted to Juan Bandini in 1838. Don Juan was a well-educated Peruvian gentleman of Italian descent who came to this part of California in 1828. A man of unusual ability, he was a member of the Territorial Assembly and a delegate to Congress, and at various times held many important offices in California.

Juan Bandini was one of the first white settlers in Riverside County, and in 1839 he built his first home on the Rancho Jurupa. The site was on a high bluff along the northwest side of the Santa Ana River, about one thousand feet west of Hamner Boulevard at a point one-half mile north of the Santa Ana River bridge and five and one-half miles north of Corona—a site occupied in 1963 by Excelsior Dairy Farms. Traces of the adobe could be seen as late as 1928, but now nothing remains. This house was three and one-half miles upstream from Bandini's later adobe (the Cota house). Rancho Jurupa consisted of over 32,000 acres of land, which extended for 20 miles along both sides of the Santa Ana River. The plains to the east of the river were considered worthless, being left wild and uncultivated or used for the pasturage of thousands of sheep. Today, the city of Riverside covers the old Jurupa "bench lands." Extensive orange groves replaced the sheep ranges, but these, in turn, have given way in large part to homes. The southeast corner of Rancho Jurupa is easily identifiable. It is the prominent Pachappa Hill at the eastern end of Jurupa Avenue in Riverside. Most of Rancho Jurupa was sold in 1859 to Abel Stearns.

Rubidoux Ranch

Juan Bandini, on May 6, 1843, sold one and a half leagues of Rancho Jurupa to Benjamin D. Wilson, a native of Tennessee. Wilson, affectionately known as "Don Benito" among the Californians, had been a trader in New Mexico, but on coming to California he bought this ranch and settled down as a ranchero, marrying Ramona Yorba, daughter of Bernardo Yorba, his nearest neighbor. He was held in high regard by the Californians, and among the American pioneers he was a notable friend of the Indians. Robert Glass Cleland said of him: "A man of brave and adventurous spirit, who dealt justly and walked uprightly throughout the entire course of his romantic and richly varied life. B. D. Wilson might well be selected as an example of the most admirable type of manhood bred on the western border in the period immediately preceding the Mexican War. He lived through stirring times in the history of California and contributed abundantly to the making of the state."

Wilson built for himself a fine adobe house, which he sold to Louis Rubidoux. By 1850, Rubidoux had purchased the remainder of the land which Bandini had sold to Wilson in 1843, obtaining a deed from Wilson on May 3, 1848, for a half-interest in his land, and a deed from Isaac Williams for the other half-interest on December 13, 1849. Louis Rubidoux, a native of St. Louis, was of French descent, his family being prominent in the early history of Missouri. The name was originally Robidoux but was corrupted to Rubidoux in Mexican California. His father was a pioneer merchant in St. Louis and his brother Joseph was the founder of the city of St. Joseph. Louis himself, as well as other members of the family, had been active in the trapping and fur trading industry in the Southwest before coming to California. Louis Rubidoux exercised considerable influence in building up his community and served as local judge and supervisor. He was a well-educated, genial, kindly man, and his home became a haven for many pioneer families in southern California.

A tablet was placed by the State Society, D.A.R., on the Santa Ana River bridge at the west entrance to Riverside to memorialize the name of Louis Rubidoux, pioneer builder and one of the first permanent American citizens in the valley. This bridge was destroyed by the county in 1958, and the Rubidoux plaque has been removed to the community center on Limonite Avenue in Rubidoux, a community once known as West Riverside. The old Rubidoux adobe *(SRL 102)* faced the north side of Mission Boulevard in Rubidoux, about one hundred yards east of Bloomington Boulevard. It fell into ruins early in this century and the walls were cleared away about 1930. The last trace of it was an auxiliary building, reputedly made of original adobe bricks, which was razed in 1962 when a shopping center was constructed on the old homesite.

One of the first gristmills in that part of southern California was built by Rubidoux on the Rancho Jurupa in 1846–47. Being at that time the only mill of its kind in all that region, it supplied a great need. It is said that the troops of the Mormon Battalion and Frémont's Battalion, in 1847, were the enthusiastic recipients of flour from the Jurupa Mill and beans from the rancho. One of the old millstones has been preserved at the Mission Inn, and another adorns the Rubidoux–Frémont Monument, which stands near the site of the mill *(SRL 303)* at the intersection of Fort Drive and Molino Way, across Mission Boulevard from the site of the Rubidoux home. The monument, erected in 1926, honors two great figures of California history, but John C. Frémont had no direct connection with the Riverside area. Molino Way recalls Rubidoux's industry in the Spanish word for "mill," and Fort Drive commemorates a small military post that never deserved or officially received the title of fort. A United States Army post was established at this spot on Rancho Jurupa in 1852 by Captain Lovell and Lieutenant Smith, and a small body of troops, never more than 20, was kept there until 1854, chiefly as a protection against the Piute and Mojave Indians. The site of the post is sometimes called "Fort Frémont," although Frémont himself never visited this spot.

The death of Louis Rubidoux occurred in 1868, and in 1870 a brick house was built on former Rubidoux land—a house that still stands and is one of the Riverside area's oldest. Cornelius Jensen, a native of Denmark who married Mercedes Alvarado, became the storekeeper at Agua Mansa (San Bernardino County) in 1854. His adobe house there was one of the few to survive the great flood of 1862. A few years later Jensen came to the Rubidoux ranch, purchased some of it, and built a fine brick home in Danish style. This landmark, with two old brick wineries, stands at the end of a lane of cottonwoods at 4350 Riverview Drive, Rubidoux. Cornelius Jensen became one of the most respected citizens of Riverside. He is buried in the old cemetery at Agua Mansa, as also, reputedly, is Louis Rubidoux.

La Placita, or Spanish Town

There were two settlements on the "Bandini Donation" of Rancho Jurupa—Agua Mansa on the northwest side of the Santa Ana River and San Salvador on the southeast—to which the New Mexican colonists moved from Politana on the Lugo rancho in the mid-1840's. These towns were devastated by flood in 1862, but both were rebuilt on higher ground. Of Agua Mansa only the cemetery remains, but of the second location of San Salvador, better known as La Placita and called "Spanish Town" by the American pioneers, there are still a few old adobes in existence. These stand in the shade of giant cottonwoods along Center and North Orange streets, northeast of Riverside and just south of the San Bernardino county line. The most prominent one, facing Orange slightly north of Center, is probably the newest, constructed shortly before 1900, reputedly from bricks of an older building, and once used as a *cantina*. Directly behind it, with an Orange Street address, is another adobe, a more modest structure but far older. This was the home of Lorenzo Trujillo, leader of the New Mexicans who settled at Politana, Agua Mansa, and San Salvador.

When Trujillo's group left the Lugo rancho for the Bandini Donation, the Lugos replaced them at Politana with Juan Antonio and his band of Cahuilla Indians. This Indian leader also founded the village of Sahatapa *(SRL 749)* in San Timoteo Canyon, a few miles northwest of Beaumont near El Casco Station on the Southern Pacific Railroad.

San Jacinto

Rancho San Jacinto Viejo, an area of over 35,000 acres, was granted by Manuel Jimeno, governor *pro tem*, to José Antonio Estudillo in 1842. Estudillo was a member of the California family which held land also in San Diego and San Leandro. The city of San Jacinto, now located on this old grant, is Riverside County's second oldest city, having been incorporated in 1888.

George W. Beattie said of Casa Loma:

"In his report to Governor Echeandía, in 1827, Fr. Antonio Peyrí of Mission San Luís Rey, wrote, 'In the direction of northeast, in the sierra, at a distance of twelve leagues, the Mission has the Rancho of San Jacinto with a house of adobes for the mayordomos.'

"When José Antonio Estudillo, in 1842, applied to the Mexican Government for a grant of a portion of San Jacinto Rancho, he said:

" 'The land for which I petition has upon it a dilapidated, earthen roofed house ten varas long—a menacing ruin.'

"The walls of this house were enclosed in a larger structure built by Estudillo and known as 'Casa Loma.' A year ago, Miss Pico showed me the part of their present residence represented by the old walls." The reference is to Miss Dolores Pico, a descendant of Governor Pío Pico, who lived at Casa Loma at the time of Beattie's visit. Casa Loma, now in other hands, still stands, about five miles northwest of San Jacinto on the road to Lakeview.

Two other homes of the Estudillo family stand on the old grant. One is the impressive mansion located on Seventh Street in San Jacinto; the other is on the Althouse property on Soboba Road, close to the hot springs resort and formerly a part of it.

San Jacinto received national publicity when, on July 14, 1937, a Russian plane flying nonstop over the Polar route from Moscow missed March Field and landed in Earl Smith's cow pasture.

The Judge North Memorial Park

In 1870 the town of Riverside was founded on the eastern portion of the old Jurupa Grant by Judge J. W. North, a pioneer settler from New York.

John W. North, born in New York in 1815, and educated as a lawyer, took a prominent part in the material and cultural foundations of three American commonwealths, Minnesota, Nevada, and California. In Minnesota he was active in the territorial legislature, founded the town of Northfield, promoted the Minneapolis and Cedar Valley Railway, and helped to establish the University of Minnesota. He was active in the Republican Convention and the nomination of Abraham Lincoln in 1860; he was subsequently appointed Surveyor-General of the Territory of Nevada, and, soon after, he became a territorial judge. He was president of the Nevada State Constitutional Convention.

Judge North went to Knoxville, Tennessee, to open up foundries after the Civil War. While there he became interested in organizing a colony in California. Associating with him men from Massachusetts, Michigan, Iowa, and New York, he went with a committee to California over the Central Pacific Railroad, which had just been opened up. He examined sites in southern California, purchasing a portion of the Rancho Jurupa. In 1870, Riverside was founded on the old rancho. Judge North later moved to Fresno County, where he had acquired land. He died there in 1880.

The old North residence once stood on the city block now bounded on the west by the Union Pacific depot, on the east by the Santa Fe depot, on the north by Seventh Street, and on the south by Eighth Street. The site was set aside as a city park in 1927, and was named in honor of the founder of Riverside the Judge North Memorial Park.

The city of Riverside was incorporated in 1883. Ten years later it became the seat of a new county. The first courthouse is still standing; it is the old Hotel Riverside at Eighth and Lime streets. Riverside County rented office space in the hotel, then called the Arlington, until the courthouse was built in 1903-4.

The Tibbets Memorial

The Tibbets Memorial in honor of Mrs. Eliza Tibbets, the woman who raised the first navel orange trees in California, was placed by Aurantia Chapter, D.A.R., in a small park at the head of Magnolia and Arlington avenues, Riverside, in 1920. Two seedling orange trees were sent to Mrs. Tibbets from Washington, D.C., in 1873 or later by Professor William A. Saunders, the husband of an old friend. Budlings had been sent to Professor Saunders from Bahia, Brazil. Two of these he sent to a friend in Florida, and two he sent to Mrs. Tibbets in Riverside.

The two budlings sent to Florida did not survive, but, owing to Mrs. Tibbets' care and in spite of somewhat adverse circumstances, the two trees entrusted to her lived. From these two budlings grew the great navel orange industry of southern California, adding millions of dollars annually to the state's resources.

The trees were originally planted at the Tibbets home, the site of which is at Central Avenue and Navel Court. At this spot a marker was placed in honor of Eliza's husband, Luther C. Tibbets, in 1935. In 1903 one of the trees (SRL 20) was transplanted a short distance away, at Magnolia and Arlington, and in front of this tree, still producing fruit, is the memorial to Mrs. Tibbets. The other tree was transplanted to the courtyard of Mission Inn by President Theodore Roosevelt at the time of his visit there, also in 1903. It died in the late 1920's, but the trunk is preserved at the inn.

Mission Inn

Captain C. C. Miller came to southern California when it was first emerging from its "hacienda days." In 1873 he was made engineer of the new colony of Riverside, which had been established on the old Rancho Jurupa in 1870. As his salary, he received a block of land in the new colony, and there, in 1875, he built an adobe cottage, one of the first solid-walled houses in town, which later became the nucleus of the famous Mission Inn.

The Miller family began to receive guests in the adobe as early as 1876, and the name Glenwood Cottage was given to it. The old-fashioned, homely hospitality of the Millers drew an increasing number of patrons, and a small group of frame buildings grew up around Glenwood Cottage. With this growth, the name was changed to Glenwood Tavern, and later to Glenwood Hotel.

Almost from the beginning, Frank A. Miller, son of the pioneer, was proprietor and manager at Glenwood. In 1902 he replaced the old wooden cottages by a new structure of concrete and brick, the building that now surrounds the Court of the Birds. The old adobe cottage stood on its original site in this same court until 1952, when it gave way to the swimming pool. Around these two grew the famous Glenwood Mission Inn (now simply Mission Inn), modeled after the old missions of California, and containing rare art treasures from all over the world. The Cloister, built in 1911, with its Music Room and Cathedral Organ; the Spanish Art Gallery, built in 1915, with the Patio of the Fountains, and the Garden of Bells, with 650 bells of many shapes and sizes from all over the world; the Rotunda with its Galeria, St. Francis Wedding Chapel, and Oriental Court, built in 1931—these are only a few of the beautiful treasures of Mission Inn (SRL 761).

Mount Rubidoux

Tradition tells us that the Indians long ago held an annual sunrise service on Mount Rubidoux in honor of the sun. About the sacred sacrificial altar (now in the patio at Mission Inn), all the tribes of the valley pledged themselves to live in peace under the leadership of the Jurupas, whose name is said to have meant "peace," and whose home was at the foot of the mountain.

The mountain was named in honor of Louis Rubidoux, who owned part of the Rancho Jurupa, on which it was located, from the 1840's until his death in 1868. In 1906 the Huntington Park Association acquired Mount Rubidoux and developed it as a public park. On April 26, 1907, the Serra Cross was raised on the highest point of the mountain and consecrated to Fray Junípero Serra, founder of the California missions. The first annual sunrise pilgrimage to the top of Mount Rubidoux on Easter Sunday was held in 1909, and from that service have come all the subsequent Easter sunrise services of southern California. Every Easter morning thousands of worshipers climb Mount Rubidoux and other mountains to pray for universal peace and brotherhood.

Temecula

On Rancho California, formerly the Vail Ranch, about three and one-half miles east of Temecula and just south of Highway 71, stands the old adobe trading post and tavern once kept by the husband of Ramona Wolff. Helen Hunt Jackson stayed there in 1879 while investigating the condition of the Temecula Indians, whose tragic eviction from their homes had stirred her deeply. Mrs. Wolff, whose knowledge of the situation and whose sympathy with the Indians won Mrs. Jackson's confidence and admiration, became Mrs. Hartsel of the novel *Ramona*. Mrs. Wolff was also one of those bearing the musical name which was given to the heroine of the tale. The author had, however, heard it before and, it is said, was so impressed by it that she decided to use it in her story.

This building is now used as a storeroom, but the interior of the large room which once served as a trading post and tavern is changed but little. Visitors may gain admittance to this very interesting place on application at the office of the ranch superintendent.

In this adobe, on January 5, 1852, the United States entered into a treaty of peace and friendship, the Treaty of Temecula, with several tribes of southern California Indians. This treaty was of importance in establishing friendly relations between the Indians and the incoming settlers. The adobe was a station on the main military road between Los Angeles and Arizona during the Civil War, and had served as a Butterfield Stage station from 1858 to 1861. It was marked by the State of California on October 1, 1950, but has never been officially registered or given a landmark number. The land on which it stands was once a part of the "Little Temecula" Rancho of one-half league, granted by Governor Pío Pico to Pablo Apis in 1845. The much larger Rancho Temecula, on which the present town is located, was given to Felix Valdez in 1844 by Governor Manuel Micheltorena.

Ramona's Country

Many were the old adobes in southern California posted as the "birthplace" or the "marriage place" of Ramona. Many were the homely Indian women advertised as "the real Ramona." In actual life, the real Ramona was a complex personality, and as one visits the various places described by the author, one is able to live again the scenes that she pictured so faithfully and to catch the spirit of romance that colored that long-ago time in which her Ramona lived.

On the journey through Orange and Riverside counties to San Diego, gathering data which would strengthen her appeal to the United States government in behalf of the mission Indians, Mrs. Jackson kept in memory many of the vivid scenes and incidents and appealing personalities that she later immortalized in her novel *Ramona*. Pala Chapel, where the Indians still go to pray; Old Town, San Jacinto, where Aunt Ri's cabin stood; Temecula and the Pechanga burial ground with their memories; the old Wolff trading post on the former Vail Ranch; these and other places are used by the author in her romance.

And each spring, one may journey to Hemet, where the Ramona pageant is given at Ramona Bowl, a rugged natural stage set in the hills where this California romance is supposed to have taken place. An unregistered state plaque has been placed at Ramona Bowl.

SOURCES

Beattie, George William. "Development of Travel between Southern Arizona and Los Angeles as Related to the San Bernardino Valley," *Annual Publications, Historical Society of Southern California*, XIII (1924–27).
——— "Reopening Anza's Road." Ms., 1931.
Bolton, Herbert Eugene. *Anza's California Expeditions.* 5 vols. University of California, Berkeley, 1930.
Cleland, Robert Glass. "Pathfinders," in the series *California*, ed. John Russell McCarthy. Powell Publishing Co., Los Angeles, 1929.
Davis, Carlyle Channing, and William A. Alderson. *The True Story of "Ramona," Its Facts and Fictions, Inspiration and Purpose.* Dodge Publishing Co., New York, 1914.
Ellerbe, Rose L. "History of Temescal Valley," *Annual Publications, Historical Society of Southern California*, XI, Part III (1920).
Gould, Janet Williams. "Notes on the Historical Spots of the Country around Corona." Ms., 1930.
Hornbeck, Robert. *Roubidoux's Ranch in the '70's.* Riverside, 1913.
Hutchings, De Witt V. "Outline of Riverside County History." Ms., 1930.
Jackson, Helen Hunt. *Ramona.* Roberts Brothers, Boston, 1884; Little, Brown, Boston, 1900.
James, George Wharton. *Through Ramona's Country.* Little, Brown, Boston, 1909.
McCoy, Edna. "The Butterfield Trail," and "Historical Background of Elsinore and Vicinity," *Elsinore Leader Press*, 1930.
Morrison, Evaline. "Elsinore Valley's Oldest Landmark to be Razed," *Riverside Daily Enterprise*, Valley Edition, July 21, 1964.
——— "They Called It Willard—Forgotten Community Once Occupied Lake Front Site," *Riverside Daily Enterprise*, April 24, 1955.
Patterson, Tom. *Landmarks of Riverside.* Press-Enterprise Company, Riverside, 1964.
"Pictorial Map of Historical Corona and Its Environs." Prepared by Corona Women's Improvement Club, History and Landmarks Committee, Mrs. R. L. Hampton, Chairman, 1963–64.
Robinson, W. W. *The Story of Riverside County.* Title Insurance and Trust Co., Riverside, 1957.
Slaughter, E. Marguerite. "Historical Riverside County." Ms., 1936.

Old Adobe, "Little Temecula" Rancho

Sacramento County

SACRAMENTO COUNTY (named for the river so called by the first Spanish explorers of that region in honor of the Holy Sacrament) was one of the original 27 counties. The only changes made in its boundaries have been those necessitated by the shifting of the stream beds of the Mokelumne and Sacramento rivers. Sacramento has always been the county seat.

Old Spanish Trails

Five Spanish expeditions entered or saw the Sacramento–San Joaquin delta before 1800. In 1772 Pedro Fages, while exploring the "Port of San Francisco" for the purpose of finding a suitable mission site, went up the eastern shore of San Francisco Bay as far as the San Joaquin River and saw the great Sacramento River "from a point of vantage." In 1793 Francisco Eliza sailed into the Sacramento River and stated that this river had not yet been explored. Sometime before 1808 it was given the name Sacramento.

Long after the mission had been founded at San Francisco, and after 19 of the 21 missions had been established along the coast of Alta California, several expeditions were organized and sent into the river country of the great interior valley to search for suitable sites for new missions. One of the most remarkable of these expeditions was that commanded by Gabriel Moraga in 1808. On October 9 Moraga's party camped on the lower Feather River, which Moraga called the Sacramento, a name he applied also to the great river into which it flows farther down, showing that he believed that the two composed the main stream. He considered the upper Sacramento, which he reached a little later, to be a branch of the main river and called it the Jesús María, a name long retained for that part of its course. It is easy to understand why Moraga reached this conclusion, for at the point where the Sacramento and the Feather come together, it is the Feather that makes a straight line north and south with the lower Sacramento, while the upper Sacramento flows at that point from the west.

An attempt to explore the river country by boat was made by José Antonio Sánchez in 1811, when he proceeded a little way up the Sacramento River. However, an expedition of more importance in the history of Sacramento took place in 1817, led by Father Narciso Durán, accompanied by Luís Argüello and Father Ramón Abella. Various channels which they followed, as well as a number of the places at which they camped, have been identified. At one time a fierce windstorm drove them behind the Montezuma Hills in the vicinity of the present town of Rio Vista (Solano County), and, again, from a vantage point on the site of Clarksburg they had a fine view of the Sierra Nevada. Soon afterward they passed the site of what is now the city of Sacramento, probably being its discoverers.

Opening of the Sacramento Trail

The Sacramento Trail was opened to trade and immigration by an American, Jedediah Strong Smith, who had made the first overland journey into California in 1826. Smith came again, in 1827, to rejoin that part of his company which he had left encamped on one of the rivers of the San Joaquin Valley. Although the Mexican government had demanded his departure from the province, he did not leave the country at once by the way he had come. Instead, he opened a new route which led north up the Sacramento River, called by Smith the Buenaventura.

After several unsuccessful attempts to find a pass through the Sierra Nevada from the river, the Smith party finally left the Sacramento about the middle of April 1828. Going northwest across the Coast Range through the wild region now included in Trinity and Humboldt counties, Smith and his men came to the seacoast and proceeded along it to Oregon. The route thus opened by this tireless pathfinder of the Far West was soon followed by Hudson's Bay Company hunters and traders from Vancouver by way of Oregon.

A tablet in honor of Jedediah Strong Smith, the man who first opened the doors to California from the north, has been placed by the Sacramento Chapter, D.A.R., at the west end of the bridge over the American River just out of Sacramento, on Highway 160.

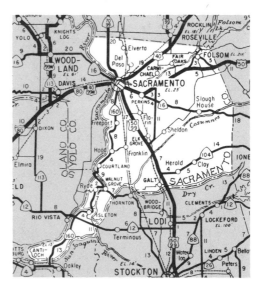

New Helvetia

The first white settlement in the great central valley of California was made by John A. Sutter in 1839. Sutter, who was born in 1803 in Baden, Germany, of Swiss parents, came to America when still a young man. Eventually, he drifted to St. Louis and from there to the Pacific Coast by way of the Columbia River.

Slowly, the idea of founding a colony in California took form in the mind of this enterprising young pioneer. Sailing from Vancouver to the Sandwich Islands, he aroused the interest of a handful of Americans and native Kanakas in his project and, with this as a nucleus for the future independent state of which he dreamed, Sutter reached California early in July 1839. There he became a citizen of the province and obtained permission of Governor Juan B. Alvarado to establish his settlement.

The great Sacramento Valley was at that time unfortified and unsettled. A few Spanish expeditions had been made into the interior to search for mission sites or runaway Indians, Jedediah Smith had explored it in 1828, and Hudson's Bay Company trappers had hunted on its streams. The natives who inhabited the river country and the surrounding mountains were a constant problem to the scattered coastal settlements, and Sutter's proposal to establish a frontier outpost that would act as a buffer to this ever present annoyance was welcomed by the Mexican government, especially since it meant no expense on their part, other than the granting of a few leagues of wilderness land for the proposed settlement.

With high hopes for the future, Sutter embarked in August 1839 from Yerba Buena up the Sacramento River to choose a location for his estate. About August 15 he landed at what was then the south bank of the American River, just north of B Street between 28th and 29th streets. A marker has been erected to commemorate the landing place (SRL 591). Soon he moved to a site nearby, where he established a permanent camp and later built his fort.

In 1841 Sutter was granted 11 leagues of land in the great valley of the Sacramento. The construction of a pretentious adobe fort was begun in that year, the outside walls being completed in 1844. In December 1841 Sutter purchased the equipment of the Russian settlement at Fort Ross, then being disbanded. This purchase included a large number of horses and cattle, a small launch, and several pieces of artillery. The cannon was set up at Sutter's Fort, and armed guards and daily drill became a feature of the place, giving it a decidedly military aspect. Sutter named the little settlement New Helvetia, undoubtedly hoping one day to make of this semifeudal barony an independent state.

Sutter's Fort

Sutter's Fort, as it soon came to be known, was not merely a fort; it was a trading post and a place of refuge as well. Cleland says that "in addition to Sutter's military activities, he displayed a vast amount of energy in more peaceful endeavors. To care for the ever growing needs of his colony, and especially to meet the pressing demands of his Russian debt, he branched out into a great variety of pursuits and tried all sorts of experiments, most of which impoverished, rather than enriched him. He planted large areas to wheat; built a flour mill; diverted water from the American River for irrigation purposes; grazed large herds of cattle and horses; sent hunters into the mountains and along the rivers for furs and elk skins; set up a distillery; began the weaving of coarse woolen blankets; ran a launch regularly for freight and passengers between his settlement and San Francisco Bay; employed nearly all foreigners who came to him for work, whether he needed them or not; trained the Indians to useful occupations; at times chastised the thieving, war-inclined tribes which the Spanish Californians could not subdue; administered justice as an official of the provincial government; and, in short, made his colony the nucleus of all activity, whether political or economic, in what was then the only settled portion of interior California.

"In addition to these varied activities, with their decided local and personal interest, Sutter contributed in a much larger way to the making of California history through his aid to American immigration. Few people today realize how large a part this hospitable, visionary, improvident land baron of the Sacramento played in the American advance to California. His fort occupied the most strategic position in all Northern California, so far as the overland trails were concerned, and became the natural objective for parties crossing the Sierras, by the central and northern routes, or coming into the province by way of Oregon.

"At Sutter's, these immigrants, exhausted and half-starved as many of them were, found shelter, food and clothing, and an opportunity to learn something of the new land and people to which they had come. More than one company [the most famous of which was the Donner party], caught in the mountain snows, was saved from destruction by a rescue party sent from Sutter's Fort. The situation of the latter also made it impossible for the California authorities, had they been so inclined, to check or turn aside the stream of overland migration. The passes and trails of the northern Sierras lay open to American frontiersmen so long as Sutter maintained his position on the Sacramento."

Sutter's dream of New Helvetia was ruined by the discovery of gold at his mill at Coloma in 1848. His workers left him to go to the mines. The gold rush was a wave of humanity that swept over his lands. A bustling city grew up on the Sacramento. His splendid isolation was gone. Eventually Sutter moved to Lititz, Pennsylvania, where he spent his last years. He died in 1880 in Washington, D. C., where he had gone to defend his land titles, and was buried at Lititz.

Sutter's Fort fell into the hands of other owners after 1850, and the buildings began to deteriorate. Final destruction was threatening when, in 1889, it was proposed to open 27th Street from

K to L. This disaster was averted by the efforts of General James G. Martine. The fort was restored by the state in 1891–93, and is now Sutter's Fort State Historical Monument *(SRL 525).* It is located between K and L streets on the north and south and 26th and 28th streets on the west and east, about two and one-quarter miles from the waterfront. It has been registered as a National Historic Landmark by the Department of the Interior.

The original adobe bricks, made by Sutter's Indians, may be seen in the central building, which is all that remained of the original fort when reconstruction got under way following donation of the property to the state by the Native Sons of the Golden West. This two-story building, with basement, has walls about 30 inches thick, and the original hand-hewn oaken floor joists. Other walls within the fort were reconstructed of kiln-baked bricks, as were the outer walls. The fort was reproduced in its approximate original form and dimensions, with shops, storerooms, living quarters, etc. Peter Slater's saloon, Sutter's bedroom, office and kitchen, and an old-time print shop have been reproduced, as has the blacksmith shop. About 22 rooms or sections are devoted to museum purposes, for storage of reserve material, workshops, or displays of historical objects. Several cannon dating back to Sutter's time preserve the military aspect of the place. A park, beautifully landscaped, is included in the grounds, which cover two city blocks.

Many interesting objects of pioneer days are housed in Sutter's Fort. These include an outstanding collection of Reed-Donner party items; firearms; stagecoaches and other vehicles; mining tools; costumes; objects made or used by James W. Marshall, who is credited with the discovery of gold at Coloma; equipment used by early fire departments; household furnishings; musical instruments; maps, documents, diaries of forty-niners, paintings, prints, and rare photographs. The curator's office has files of information relating to California pioneers.

Labels placed on various rooms about the quadrangle of the fort give the visitor a vivid picture of the social and industrial life of the settlement. Sites of the former flour mill, granary, stores, and emigrant quarters are marked.

During the restoration of the fort some of the workmen panned dirt near the east gate and recovered a quantity of gold dust which had been dropped years before by miners, or swept from gambling rooms and stores on the premises. Doubtless this was some of the first gold mined after the discovery at Sutter's sawmill in 1848.

Sutter's Fort State Historical Monument collects, preserves, and exhibits objects used in California by the pioneers and early settlers between the years 1839, when the fort was founded, and 1869, when the driving of the gold spike marked the completion of the transcontinental railroad and the decline of the stagecoach era.

The State Indian Museum is located on the property, with the entrance at 2618 K Street. Here is one of the finest and most complete collections of relics representing the workmanship of the

Sutter's Fort, Sacramento, before Restoration

prehistoric California Indian. The artifacts were gathered from the ancient campsites and burial grounds of the San Joaquin and Sacramento valleys. Arranged with scientific order and skill, the display will long serve as an educational archive for scholars wishing to study the habits and handicraft of an extinct people. In this remarkable array one sees striking evidence that the California Indian was a skilled craftsman as well as an artist of rare ability. There are pipes, serrated arrow points, and bowls, scores of baskets from all sections, ornaments and implements of stone, bone, and shell—all fashioned with a perfection of line and a niceness of detail that the modern artisan, with all his up-to-date tools, could not duplicate.

A plaque has been placed at Sutter's Fort to mark the western end of the Coloma Road *(SRL 745).* The route was first used in 1847 to reach the site of Sutter's sawmill. In January 1848 James W. Marshall brought to Sutter's Fort over this road the first gold discovered at Coloma. In 1849 James E. Birch established California's first stage line along this route. Other markers on the Coloma Road have been placed near Alder Springs at Nimbus Dam *(SRL 746),* and at Rescue and Coloma in El Dorado County.

Mexican Land Grants

John A. Sutter was not the first person to receive a land grant in the Sacramento Valley. In 1833 J. B. R. Cooper was granted the land "known by the name of Río Ojotska," on the present American River three leagues east of the Sacramento. Cooper did not develop the property and renounced the grant in 1835. Four years later Sutter arrived at New Helvetia.

Sutter did not long remain the sole land baron in the Sacramento Valley. The beginning of the American occupation found him already surrounded by neighbors. Many of his former employees had occupied ranchos up and down the length of the Sacramento and San Joaquin valleys.

John Sinclair, a Scotsman, settled on Rancho del Paso as early as 1841. On this estate of 44,000 acres, granted to Eliab Grimes in December 1844, Sinclair built a house on the right bank of the American River two and one-half miles from Sutter's Fort. This house was, for a time, the first civilized dwelling reached by the overland emigrant trains after crossing the Sierra Nevada. Sinclair was hospitable and kindly in his treatment of those in need, and as alcalde of the Sacramento district he was especially instrumental in sending aid to the Donner party.

Rancho Río de los Americanos, extending over 35,500 acres on the south side of the American River east of New Helvetia, was granted on October 1, 1844, to William A. Leidesdorff, vice-consul of the United States by appointment of Thomas O. Larkin. Leidesdorff died in 1848, leaving the rancho and other valuable property in San Francisco. Captain Joseph L. Folsom, who had come to California as assistant quartermaster of Stevenson's New York Volunteers, purchased the vast Leidesdorff estate from the heirs for a song, thus becoming one of the wealthiest men in California. The town of Folsom was laid out on his rancho in 1855 and named in his honor. The site of the old Leidesdorff adobe, erected in 1846, is about ten miles east of Sacramento at Routier, just west of modern Rancho Cordova.

One summer evening in 1840, William Daylor, an employee of Sutter, climbed a hill southeast of New Helvetia and saw for the first time the rich valley of the Cosumnes River, then thickly populated with Indians. Daylor decided then and there that the lands bordering the north bank of the river were to be his. On returning to the fort he talked the matter over with his friend, Jared Sheldon, also an employee of Sutter. Sheldon, a native of Vermont, had become a naturalized Mexican citizen and held claims against the Mexican government for services in building the Custom House at Monterey. The two men formed a partnership whereby Sheldon was to obtain the grant of land through W. E. P. Hartnell in liquidation of his claim, and also to supply the cattle, while Daylor was to settle upon the land and look after the stock. The first grant, made in 1841, proved to be defective, and a second was drawn up and approved on January 8, 1844, under the designation "Rancho Omochumnes."

The Delta Region

The rich delta lands of the Sacramento and San Joaquin rivers cover more than 425,000 acres of immensely productive country. It is a section suggestive of the dikes and canals of old Holland. First settled in the early 1850's by gold seekers who had failed to make a living in the mines and who had squatted on the river delta in order to raise enough food for their subsistence, the land early demonstrated its extraordinary fertility. After the completion of the Central Pacific Railroad thousands of unemployed Chinese were glad to work, for very low wages, reclaiming the delta country for agriculture. They built the first system of levees along the various islands, working laboriously with wheelbarrows. Today, 90 per cent of the world's asparagus comes from the delta region of the Sacramento and San Joaquin rivers.

Mining Camps of the American River

Mormon Island (SRL 569), in the northeast corner of Sacramento County, was the site of the second important gold discovery in California. Early in the spring of 1848 two Mormons, on their way to Sutter's Mill at Coloma, camped for the night at a bar on the South Fork near its confluence with the North Fork. One of the men remarked: "They are taking out gold above us on the river. Let's see if we can find some at this place." Panning out a little dirt in one of their cooking utensils, they revealed a fine prospect. The two Mormons returned to the fort the next day and reported their find to Samuel Brannan, leader of the Mormons in California and associated with C. C. Smith, who kept a store at New Helvetia. Brannan immediately proceeded to the place where the discovery had been made and set up a preemptive claim, demanding a royalty of one-third on all the gold taken out at the bar. This fee continued to be paid to Brannan as long as the Mormons were in the majority. Later, when unbelievers outnumbered those of the faith, the tithe could no longer be collected. Meanwhile, Brannan had accumulated thousands of dollars, which he invested in merchandising, becoming one of the wealthiest men in California.

By 1853 Mormon Island had become a city of over 2,500 inhabitants, but a fire in 1856 destroyed most of the town and it was never rebuilt. A few rock cellars and the ubiquitous locust tree were all that remained to locate the site of this historic gold town when it was inundated by Folsom Lake. A marker has been placed on Green Valley Road just over the El Dorado County line, near the cemetery to which graves were moved from the Folsom Dam project area.

Down the American River from Mormon Island were numerous camps, some of which were important towns in the early 1850's. In quick succession came Alabama Bar, on the north bank of the river; Slate Bar, opposite Folsom State Prison, where several stores were located; and Sailor Bar. Bean's Bar was one-half mile below Alabama Bar on the opposite side of the river.

Negro Bar was first mined by Negroes in 1849. By 1851 it had a population of 700. The town of Folsom was laid out there in 1855. In the same year, at Sacramento, Theodore D. Judah began construction of California's first passenger railroad, the Sacramento Valley Railroad, which was completed as far as Folsom—a distance of 22 miles—in 1856. Historical markers have been placed at the Sacramento terminal (SRL 526) at Third and R streets, and at Folsom (SRL 558). The new town became an important center for stage and freight lines running to the northern mining camps and to Virginia City, Nevada. The greatest prosperity was enjoyed in the early 1860's, when many substantial hotels and business houses were established, as well as an academy and several churches. Some of these sturdy stone and brick buildings still stand along Folsom's main street. Likewise reminiscent of an earlier period are the town's old-fashioned homes, surrounded by beautiful old trees. Unfortunately, Folsom's finest old building, the Wells Fargo office, has been torn down. The Folsom Powerhouse (SRL 633), a landmark in the history of long-distance high-voltage transmission, operated continuously from 1895 to 1952. It has been presented to the state by the Pacific Gas and Electric Company for preservation.

Earlier mining methods were replaced by giant dredges which have piled high with boulders hundreds of acres for miles about the town. Although the dredges are no longer in operation, the evidence of their work is inescapable. The Natoma district totaled $45 million in gold from about 1880 to 1930, of which amount the dredges produced $40 million. In the 1920's and early 1930's the average annual production from gold dredging in Sacramento County was $1,300,000.

Construction of the California Central Railroad to Marysville was begun in 1857 at Folsom, and was completed to Lincoln in 1861. That part of the line between Folsom and Roseville was abandoned in 1866, but portions of the old roadbed are still visible.

On or near Alder Creek, two miles south of Folsom, was Prairie City (SRL 464), a mining camp that reached the height of its prosperity in 1853, after the Natoma Water and Mining Company's ditch was completed to that point. A large quartz mill was also erected there in 1857 at a cost of $50,000. For a time, Prairie City was a city in fact as well as in name, being a center of trade for a number of other camps, including Rhoads' Diggings, Alder Creek, and Willow Springs Hill Diggings. The last-named place covered about 2,000 acres and yielded several million dollars' worth of gold.

The history of Big Gulch, a mining camp opposite Folsom, was peculiarly colorful. The arrival of Colonel Russ at this quiet place in 1857 was quite an event, and the town was renamed Russville in his honor. Possessing a "speculative genius," Russ induced a number of San Francisco capitalists to form a company to mine the rock for the gold it never contained. Tons of quartz were crushed, but no "color" was ever produced. Russ invented a machine to plane the granite. It did not work. The company failed, and then Colonel Russ was elected justice of the peace. "He put up a small flag pole and an elevated platform about six feet high, and when a case was to be tried, up went the stars and stripes on the flag pole and the Colonel mounted the seat of justice. Law statutes were of no use to him. He dispensed his own brand of justice. Any person asking for an appeal was immediately fined for contempt. He soon became unpopular, went broke, and departed." For a time the town was called Bowlesville, but in 1860 the citizens renamed it Ashland.

Just below Big Gulch was Mississippi Bar, the name surviving today as Mississippi Township. Opposite it was Texas Hill, from which cobblestones were shipped to pave the streets of San Francisco.

Cosumnes River Mining Camps

Michigan Bar (SRL 468) was the most prominent of all the early gold camps on the Cosumnes River in Sacramento County. Founded in 1849 by two men from Michigan, it reached a population of 1,500 or more in the early 1850's. The

Wells Fargo Office, Folsom

original townsite has since been washed out by hydraulic mining, destroying the last remaining landmarks—the old Heath store and the Wells Fargo Express office. The Addington Pottery Works at Michigan Bar was one of the earliest and largest in the state. The town was located one mile north of the historical marker that stands on Highway 16.

Fleeting towns developed in the vicinity of Michigan Bar during those feverish days of 1849 and the 1850's. Cook's Bar, founded in 1849 by Dennis Cook two miles below Michigan Bar, became quite a town in the early 1850's, but by 1860 it had ceased to exist. Five miles southwest of Michigan Bar on the Ione Valley road was Sebastopol, named during the Crimean War, and a lively camp from 1854 to 1859. Katesville, near Cook's Bar, another mining center that arose in 1854, had several stores and saloons, a hotel, and a boardinghouse. By 1862 the place was deserted. Live Oak, northeast of Sebastopol, had rich returns from its diggings from 1854 to 1861. An old brick building stands at this point on the south side of Highway 16, about a mile west of the Michigan Bar marker. The McKinstry trading post on the Cosumnes River was opened in 1849 by George McKinstry, who had been associated with John A. Sutter, Pierson B. Reading, and John Bidwell at Sutter's Fort.

Several roads to the southern mines passed through the Cosumnes River region, and ferries, succeeded by toll bridges, as well as a number of hotels, were established by enterprising men at a very early date. William Daylor and Jared Sheldon, as owners of the Omochumnes Mexican grant, were strategically situated and made great profits from mining, ranching, trading, and hotelkeeping. In 1850 Sheldon built the Slough House *(SRL 575)* on Deer Creek (a branch of the Cosumnes River) where the Jackson road crossed that stream. It was destroyed by fire in 1890 and rebuilt the same year on the old site. The second hotel still stands, with gigantic black walnut trees bordering the old highway, and an old cemetery on the knoll above the orchards. The little town of Sloughhouse has a population of about 50.

Daylor established himself as a trader and hotelkeeper on the Cosumnes River about a mile east of Slough House. This place, which was at first known as Daylor's Ranch, later became the Cosumne post office, and the site is still known as Cosumne.

In 1846–47 Jared Sheldon built a gristmill on Rancho Omochumnes. Four years later he constructed a dam to provide water to operate the mill. It caused flooding of the claims of miners working along the river below the dam. The miners threatened violence, and Sheldon erected a small fort, placing a cannon there by way of warning. On July 11, 1851, the indignant miners captured the fort, and when Sheldon arrived with reinforcements two hours later, a battle ensued in which he and two of his men were killed. The dam was swept away by high water in the winter of 1851–52. The site of Sheldon's gristmill *(SRL 439)* is about one mile southeast of Slough House on Meiss Road.

On the west side of Highway 99, where it crosses the Cosumnes River between Elk Grove and Galt, was the ranch of Martin Murphy, Jr. *(SRL 680)*. Here the initial action took place in the conquest of California by the United States. On June 10, 1846, Ezekiel Merritt and a band of settlers overpowered the soldiers of Lieutenant Francisco Arce of the Mexican army and took their horses from the Murphy corral on the north side of the river. Four days later the Bear Flag was raised at Sonoma.

In the Masonic Cemetery at Elk Grove is the grave of Mrs. Benjamin W. Wilder, nee Elitha Cumi Donner *(SRL 719)*. Born in 1832, she came to California in 1846 in the ill-fated party of which her father, George Donner, was one of the leaders. She died in 1923.

Sutterville

Sutter laid out a townsite in 1844 on his ranch, about two miles below the Sacramento River embarcadero. Here, on high ground overlooking the river, he and his friends built a few dwellings and called the place Suttersville, later Sutterville. The location boasted one of the few elevations above the treacherous waters of the river, and the future of the little settlement seemed promising. It flourished until 1848 as the friendly rival of the fort and the embarcadero. George Zins built a brick building there in 1847, one of the first brick structures erected in California.

The discovery of gold by James W. Marshall in the tailrace of Sutter's Mill at Coloma in 1848 changed the course of events for Sutterville as it did for all California. Sutter's Fort became too small for the business demands which soon crowded in upon it from every side, and the old embarcadero continued to hold its own while Sutterville declined.

The site of Sutterville *(SRL 593)*, across Sutterville Road from the zoo of the William Land Park, was long marked by one of its original brick buildings. It was built by R. H. Vance in 1853 and cost $27,000. In later years it was known as the Sutterville Brewery.

During the Civil War, Camp Union *(SRL 666)* of the California Volunteers was located at Sutterville. A marker has been placed at Sutterville and Del Rio roads.

"Paper Cities"

Mushroom cities were not confined to California's mining areas. "The spirit of venture and speculation" invaded tributary regions in the valley also. Aside from Sutterville and Sacramento there were other towns laid out with the same high hope of becoming commercial centers for the mining camps. Coming up the Sacramento River from the San Francisco Bay region, the gold seekers of 1849 passed the sites of several towns below Sacramento: Onisbo, opposite the mouth of Steamboat Slough; Webster, on the east bank about ten miles below the mouth of the American River; and Washington (Yolo County), on the western shore opposite Sutter's embarcadero. Just below Sacramento was Sutterville and to the north was Boston. Leaving Boston, one arrived, it is said, at a second Washington about 12 miles farther up the river. (This place may never have existed.) Beyond were Springfield and Vernon (Sutter County), the latter situated at the mouth of the Feather River opposite its rival, Fremont (Yolo County).

Boston, typical of these "paper cities," was described by E. G. Buffum, who visited the region in 1849. "It extends upon the banks of both rivers for several miles and is destined to become a flourishing town.... [It] is situated upon a broad and well-watered plain covered with many groves of magnificent oaks, and the largest class of steamers and all vessels navigating the Sacramento River can lie and discharge directly at its banks. Boston ... is laid in squares ... subdivided each into eight building lots eighty feet by one hundred twenty feet, with large public squares and reservations for schoolhouses, churches and public buildings.... Lots are selling rapidly at $200 to $1,000 each, and before many months the city of Boston on the golden banks of the Rio Sacramento will rival its New England namesake in business and importance." According to McGowan, Boston was located near the mouth of the American River, at the present site of the Sacramento Filtration Plant.

A group of speculators laid out the town of Brighton in 1849 on the west bank of the American River about three miles east of Sutter's Fort. Mormons in the employ of Sutter had built a flour mill there in 1847, but with the discovery of gold at Coloma the mill was left unfinished. The frame was purchased in 1849 for $10,000. It was then moved to Sacramento, where it went into the construction of the City Hotel, Sacramento's first major hotel, on Front Street between I and J streets. The town of Brighton never came to anything and was abandoned in 1852, but its hostelry, the Five Mile House, existed for several years on the Coloma Road. The site of Brighton is now the campus of Sacramento State College. The present community of Brighton was located one mile south of the old site in 1861.

Norristown was established in 1850 on the American River, north or west of old Brighton in the present Riverpark area. To the north was the Norris Ferry. A few years later Hoboken came into existence in the vicinity of Norristown. During the great flood of 1853 all teaming was cut off between Sacramento and the mining regions. The merchants of Sacramento, being forced to move to higher ground, established temporary branches at Hoboken, and the town claimed 1,500 residents.

The Founding of Sacramento

It was around the embarcadero at the foot of the long road leading to Sutter's Fort that the new city of Sacramento first grew up. Sutter had fallen heavily into debt, and finally, in order to evade his creditors, he turned his property over to his son John A. Sutter, Jr., who had arrived at the fort on September 14, 1848. In December the younger Sutter laid out a town at the embarcadero, naming it Sacramento after the river. By the first part of January 1849 two log cabins had been built, followed soon by the first frame building and a canvas house. In April there were 30 buildings, and by June over 100. On August 1 the first town election was held. Situated at the entrance to the gold regions, Sacramento profited tremendously from the mining trade. By October 1849 it had a resident population of about 2,000 and a floating population of 5,000. Sacramento was incorporated as a city in 1850.

Many home seekers arrived at Sacramento in 1849, expecting to take up homesteads there as they had done in Oregon and the Middle West. Sacramento was being built on the Sutter grant, but these settlers did not see why the laws of a foreign government should have more weight than the rights of free American citizens in the assigning of land. They claimed the right to at least one free city lot each. However, those men who had been buying from Sutter hotly contested this claim, and the Squatters' Riot was the result.

A lot at the southeast corner of Second and N streets was put to the test, when Dr. Robinson, one of the outstanding leaders of the squatters, erected a shanty there, only to have it removed by the city authorities. On May 10, 1850, judgment was rendered in favor of Sutter's title, but on August 15 a body of about 40 squatters contested this decision by attempting to regain possession of the lot from which Robinson had been ousted. When prevented from doing so, they retired up I Street to Third and thence to J near Fourth, where they were met by Major Bigelow with a small band of citizens. The squatters then threw a line across Fourth Street at J and fired upon the citizen group.

In the fight that followed, Major Bigelow was seriously wounded, as was Dr. Robinson, while Maloney, the leader of the squatters, and the city assessor were killed. This so frightened the insurgents that they quickly dispersed. On August 19 a proclamation was issued calling for law and order, and the Squatters' Riot was ended. For a number of years, however, it was echoed in the city elections.

The Capitol

The state capital, after a brief career in various ambitious young cities, was finally established at Sacramento in 1854. The site of the first courthouse, completed on December 24, 1851, is on the north side of I Street between Sixth and Seventh, and is now occupied by the present Sacramento County Courthouse, dedicated in 1913. The first courthouse was offered for use as the state capitol and the legislative sessions of 1852 and 1854 were held there. The building was destroyed by fire in 1854, but was immediately replaced by a second structure in which the state officials and the legislature were housed until the late fall of 1869.

The foundations of the state capitol buildings were laid on the present site in the fall of 1860, only to be washed away by the flood of January 10, 1861. As a protection against recurring floods, two great terraces were constructed, and on this elevation the cornerstone was laid on May 15, 1861, under the auspices of the Masonic Grand Lodge of California. The unfinished structure was occupied by the government late in the fall of 1869, but the building was not finally completed until 1874. The total cost of construction with subsequent improvements was estimated in 1933 at $3,400,000. In 1951 an annex was completed at a cost of about $12 million. The offices of the governor and the legislators are housed, along with other departments, in this building. With the construction of the annex, the terraces were removed and the ground was graded to a gentle slope from the building to the street.

On the first floor of the rotunda of the Capitol is the beautiful marble statue of Queen Isabella presenting her jewels to Columbus, executed by Larkin Goldsmith Mead, an American sculptor, and presented to the state by D. O. Mills in 1883. The walls of the rotunda are decorated by 12 mural paintings done by Arthur F. Mathews and depicting four epochs in the history of California. On the second floor of the rotunda, flags carried by California units in the Civil, Spanish-American, and World wars are displayed.

Surrounding the capitol buildings a park covering 33 acres has been planted to thousands of varieties of trees and shrubs contributed by every continent and climate in the world. Grecian laurels, pomegranates from Europe and Asia, the Australian bottle-brush and silk oak, camellias from Asia, the strawberry bush from Europe, pampas grass from South America, and the varnish tree from Asia—these and many more seem to thrive equally well in this unusual arboretum. Fronting the building is a row of ten fine deodars, natives of India, planted in 1873. Almost as spectacular are the giant stone pines of Italy, the Norway spruce, Lawson's cypress, giant arbor vitae, cedar of Lebanon, cryptomeria from China and Japan, and a row of superb magnolias, flanking the stately white walls of the Capitol with dark green masses of foliage.

A semicircle of giant elm trees was planted in 1872 between 12th and 14th streets, marking the old bridle path or exercising track for saddle and carriage horses. Near the center of the park is the Memorial Grove, composed of eastern North American trees transplanted as saplings from the most prominent battlefields of the Civil War by the women's auxiliary of the Grand Army of the Republic and dedicated by them to the state. Many varieties of such well-known Eastern trees as the walnut, ash, oak, maple, elm, tulip tree, dogwood, mulberry, and locust are represented in this interesting group.

A space of three acres at the southeast corner of the park is devoted entirely to California flora, where cactus, yucca, and desert willow are close neighbors of fern, azalea, huckleberry, and tiger lily, which thrive in the shade of sequoia and oak and pine, whose native habitat ranges from the Coast Range to the Sierra Nevada.

The work of classifying and labeling the trees and shrubs in the park was begun in July 1905 by Miss Alice Eastwood, head of the Horticultural Department of the California Academy of Sciences in San Francisco. Hundreds of specimens have been tagged, each with its botanical as well as its common name and native habitat, making this grove unique in its educational value as well as in the beauty of its assembled trees.

The State Fairgrounds, located on Stockton Boulevard, cover an area of 207 acres and comprise an outlay of equipment and buildings aggregating an investment of $7 million. The State Fair originated in 1854, when the California State Agricultural Society was organized in San Francisco. From that time it has been an annual event. For the first five years of its existence it was held in various cities, but since 1859 it has been held continuously at Sacramento. The grounds, first located at Sixth and M streets, were later moved to 15th and N, and finally to the present location.

The State Library

The California State Library was created on January 24, 1850, by act of the legislature. By July it had acquired 135 volumes, the first donations being made by Colonel J. D. Stevenson, Senator Thomas Jefferson Green, and General John C. Frémont. The collection grew steadily, although at first there was no fund available for the purchase of books. From 1853 to 1901 all fees collected by the secretary of state were paid into the Library Fund. A monthly appropriation is now made.

For many years the State Library occupied the semicircular central wing of the Capitol, additional rooms being assigned to it until it covered about 30 per cent of the entire floor space of the building. It is now housed in a building of its own on Capitol Mall (M Street) between Ninth and Tenth streets.

The State Library has a California department comprising a vast amount of information on the history, resources, and natural wonders, the industrial, social, and intellectual life of the state. It houses also a unique collection of early newspaper files, a newspaper index, and interesting indexed information about the old pioneers and early settlers of the state, as well as about California authors, artists, actors, and musicians, all of which is important to the student of California history.

The Pioneer Memorial Congregational Church

The Pioneer Memorial Congregational Church, presently located facing Sutter's Fort, is recorded as having been the first church to be organized in Sacramento, on September 16, 1849, and to hold regular services. The first building was erected in 1850 on a site *(SRL 613)* on Sixth Street at the southwest corner of the alley between I and J streets. It was destroyed by fire in 1854, and another building was constructed the same year across the street almost opposite the first site. For over 70 years this historic edifice sheltered many significant gatherings, serving as a rallying point "for Christian forces through many a stormy period." Its open forum, where some of the most distinguished orators of the day spoke, satisfied the intellectual needs of the community.

The founder of the First Congregational Church was the Rev. Joseph A. Benton, who began his long and beneficent career in Sacramento in July 1849. Joseph Benton's parish, however, was boundless and his missionary journeys were often of several weeks' duration. His interests, too, were broad and included education as well as religion. He taught one of the first schools in Sacramento, and in 1849 he and Samuel Willey, with several others, were already planning for public schools and a college in California. Benton was one of the founders of the College of California (forerunner of the University of California), and he later became a professor in the Pacific Theological Seminary in Oakland (now the Pacific School of Religion in Berkeley).

Benton's life is typical of that of many pioneer ministers of the churches of early California, Protestant as well as Catholic. Full of the earnest desire to serve and to build up a Christian civilization in a primitive land, unselfish, tireless, boundless in enthusiasm, large of vision, and great in endeavor, they were missionary heroes in every sense of the word.

Other religious bodies also organized congregations early in the history of Sacramento. The first Roman Catholic parish was St. Rose of Lima; the church building, which stood at Seventh and K streets, was opened in 1851, although Mass had been said at various locations in 1850. The present Cathedral of the Blessed Sacrament, seat of the Bishop of Sacramento, was erected in 1887.

The Methodist Episcopal Church was housed in a prefabricated building shipped around the Horn from Baltimore in 1849. It was located on the east side of Seventh Street between L and Capitol. In 1852 the Methodists sold the building to the local Jewish congregation and it became the first congregationally owned synagogue on the Pacific Coast (SRL 654). A historical marker is located at sidewalk level.

Old Sacramento

Sacramento has more historic business buildings dating from the American pioneer period than any other city in California. Most of them stand in the area bounded by Front, Third, I, and L streets. This was the heart of the city for several decades. As the business center moved closer to the Capitol, the old district declined and ultimately became a slum area. Cheap hotels and diners occupied the solid old brick buildings where much of California's history was made; now, of course, they were modernized beyond recognition by the addition of cement veneers and the removal of ornamentation of an earlier era.

For years, some proponents of slum clearance urged the complete demolition of the blighted area; others, conscious of the priceless heritage at stake, said that the same end could be achieved by restoring the pioneer structures and attracting new businesses to occupy them. But little was done in either way. Finally, the issue came to a head when the State Division of Highways announced plans to build a freeway through the old "skid row." The decision was welcomed in some quarters as the answer to two of Sacramento's major problems—transportation and beautification—but historians and historically minded persons insisted that the loss of Old Sacramento would be irreparable, and urged an alternate freeway route along the Yolo County side of the Sacramento River. Inventories of the ancient structures were taken and plans drawn up for the renovation of the area as a historic district. At length a compromise was reached whereby the freeway, although routed through Old Sacramento, would be deflected to spare as many of the important buildings as possible. Their victory at least partly achieved, the historians began to plan in earnest for the careful re-creation of pioneer Sacramento. Construction of the freeway began in the middle 1960's.

At last Old Sacramento (SRL 812) is once more to come into its own. A cooperative effort of the State Division of Beaches and Parks, the Redevelopment Agency of the City of Sacramento, and private investors, over a period of years, will culminate in the restoration of most of the old buildings, the relocation of others doomed by the freeway, and the reconstruction of still others that disappeared long ago. Part of the area will be a State Park, but largely it will be privately owned and used for business purposes in keeping with the historic theme. Sutter's embarcadero will also be re-created. The entire project will tie in perfectly with the Capitol Mall and the redevelopment of the downtown area. The plan should serve as a model for cities throughout the United States. It is regrettable that a similar technique was not followed in the old sections of Stockton and Marysville, two other major supply centers during the gold rush, and that more of early San Francisco was not included in the Jackson Square restoration.

Front and Second streets, and J and K streets between Front and Second, have been left unscathed by the freeway, and the buildings in this area can be restored on their original sites. Structures on J and K east of Second, and on the west side of Third Street, were demolished in 1966 or earlier. Ornaments and fixtures from the buildings that are lost will be used in the restoration of others. Exploration has revealed that the basements of the oldest buildings were originally the first floors. As the level of the Sacramento River rose, the street levels were correspondingly raised.

One of the most important buildings was the two-story D. O. Mills bank (SRL 609) at 226 J Street, built in 1852. It is proposed that this structure, in the freeway area, be rebuilt, with the adjoining Figg building (1852) at 224 J, on the south side of L Street between Front and Second. The original bank at the J Street site was a small one-story frame building with a stone front; it was destroyed by fire in 1852. A picture of it was used for many years on the bank's checks. In 1865 the bank was moved to the Heywood building (1857), still standing at the southeast corner of Second and J. In 1912 the Mills bank found a new location at the northwest corner of Seventh and J.

Darius Ogden Mills came to Sacramento in 1849 and began his career as a merchant in the new, chaotic city. He was a man who was keen to see a big opportunity and quick to take it, and on October 18, 1849, he opened the first banking house on the Pacific Coast. Mills was not only an astute financier but a man of sound principles and steady, conservative judgment as well. He became a leading figure in the financial life of California, building up the bank at Sacramento on a sound basis and becoming the first president of the Bank of California, established in San Francisco in 1864. He was also interested in educational and philanthropic movements and gave much of his wealth to these activities. Later, he became a prominent figure in the Bank of New York, and was famous for the three Mills Hotels that he established in New York City for the comfort of homeless men of limited means.

The B. F. Hastings bank building (SRL 606), built in 1852–53 at the southwest corner of Second and J streets, is better known as the western terminus of the Pony Express. Here began the first overland journey eastward on April 4, 1860.

The Central Overland Pony Express was inaugurated by the firm of Russell, Majors, and Waddell, in April 1860, thus preceding the telegraph and the railroad in opening overland communication between the East and the West. Before this, mail had been carried by steamer via Panama, the official mail ship arriving at San Francisco once a month. The Butterfield stages had begun to carry mail overland via the southern route in 1858, requiring from 20 to 24 days for the trip. In the same year George Chorpenning operated over the central route between Placerville and Salt Lake City. The Pony Express inaugurated a special semiweekly mail service on horseback. Stations were erected about every 25 miles, each rider spanning three stations at the rate of about eight miles an hour. Ten days from St. Joseph, Missouri, to Sacramento was the usual time required.

There were two Pony Express remount stations in Sacramento County. The first was at the Five Mile House (SRL 697), near the present Sacramento State College and the town of Perkins. The Fifteen Mile House (SRL 698), four miles east of Mills on White Rock Road, was next, followed by Mormon Tavern, just over the El Dorado County line. From July 1, 1860, to July 1, 1861, Folsom, rather than Sacramento, was the western terminus of the Pony Express (SRL 702). The mail was carried between the two places by the Sacramento Valley Railroad.

The ponies and their riders, who were picked with care from among the hardiest of Western men, kept the long trail open between the East and the West until October 26, 1861, when the service was discontinued with the completion of the overland telegraph. The romance of these riders daringly pursuing their path regardless of snow, storm, or hostile Indians has been graphically, and except for a few minor details accurately, portrayed by Mark Twain in Roughing It. Although not a financial success for its promoters, the Pony Express was nevertheless a substantial aid to business and undoubtedly helped to hold California, isolated as it was, in the Union.

Another Sacramento building associated with the Pony Express is the stately three-story Adams and Company building (SRL 607), erected in 1853 at 1014 Second Street. Wells Fargo and Company occupied this structure at the time that it was agent for the western portion of the Pony Express. Across the street at 1015 is the old telegraph building (SRL 366), long thought incorrectly to have been the Pony Express terminus.

Sacramento's first major hotel was the City Hotel, built in 1849 at about 915–17 Front Street. Nearby, at about 923–25, was the Eagle Theater (SRL 595), Sacramento's first, opened the same year. The city's very first buildings were not solidly constructed and fell victim to fire and flood. These two and others, however, will be reconstructed, as accurately as old drawings permit, in a section of the Old Sacramento project devoted to portraying the city as it was in its earliest days.

Another early hostelry was the Orleans Hotel (SRL 608), which stood from 1852 to the late 1870's at 1018 Second Street. The building presently occupying the site will be converted into a replica of the old Orleans. Typical of the "days of '49," when thousands of miners thronged the place, was the What Cheer House (SRL 597). The site of this famous hotel is at the southeast corner of Front and K streets. It was built in 1853 and was destroyed by fire on February 10, 1931. Now it is to be reconstructed. Ebner's Hotel (SRL 602), built in 1856, still stands at 116 K. Soon its three stories will once again be crowned with a cupola, as in its heyday. The Western Hotel (SRL 601) at 209–21 K, once one of the largest hotels in the West, is a victim of the freeway. It was built by William Land in 1875 after a fire that year had destroyed the earlier hotel built in 1853. A variety of materials from the Western will be preserved in the restoration of other buildings.

The Sacramento Theater was opened in March 1853 on Third Street between I and J streets. Ole Bull, Maurice Strakosh, Madame Anna Bishop, and the Robinson family were among the celebrities who played there. A stock company, including Edwin Booth, took it over in 1855. The old building no longer stands, but nearby, at 917 Third, is the Pioneer Mutual Volunteer Firehouse (SRL 612), erected in 1854 and occupied by Engine Company No. 1. The No. 3 firehouse is at 1112 Second Street. It is now a fine restaurant, having been restored in 1959 in one of the first efforts to rehabilitate Old Sacramento.

The Sacramento Union issued its first edition on March 19, 1851, from a site (SRL 605) at 121 J Street. The building no longer stands but will be reconstructed. The Union is still published, as is the Sacramento Bee, founded in 1857. One of the early buildings occupied by the Bee (SRL 611) stood at 1016–20 Third Street, but it was demolished for the freeway, since it lacked a sponsor for its relocation. It is regrettable, also, that no plans were made for the adjoining Aschenauer building at 1022 Third, built in 1850 and believed to be, at the time of the inventory, the oldest building in Sacramento after the central building of Sutter's Fort. It was very much in its original condition and probably could have been moved intact to a new site.

Sam Brannan's buildings are located at the southeast corner of Front and J streets. Some of the seven structures built between 1853 and 1865 are still standing; the others will be reconstructed. The building (SRL 604) at 112 J was built on Brannan's property by Henry E. Robinson in 1853. Across the alley is the slim four-story City Market, a later building (about 1870–80) but one of Old Sacramento's most attractive. Newton Booth, elected governor of California in 1871 and later United States senator, maintained his home, headquarters, and wholesale grocery business (SRL 596) on Front Street. The buildings in which he lived, at 1015–17, are gone but will be rebuilt. Part of his block still stands at 1019–21 Front. The beautiful narrow three-story building at

Western Hotel, Sacramento

1023 was also owned by Booth. He entered business in Sacramento in 1851. Leland Stanford's wholesale warehouse, built in 1856, still stands at the southeast corner of Front and L. The Lady Adams building *(SRL 603)* is one of Sacramento's oldest. It was built in 1852 at 113–15 K Street and was named after a ship. The Fashion Saloon at 209 J, barely within the freeway area, is slated to be relocated on the south side of L between Front and Second. Built in 1855, it had an unusual ornamental cast iron, brick, and plaster façade. The Overton-Read building *(SRL 610),* at the northwest corner of Third and J, was gone many years before the site was obliterated by the freeway. It housed the Sacramento post office from 1852 to 1859.

Perhaps the most important building, historically, in Old Sacramento fell within the limits of the route finally chosen for the freeway. According to plan, however, the "Big Four" building *(SRL 600)* at 220–26 K Street will be rebuilt on the north side of I Street between Front and Second. Built in 1852 but drastically altered through the years, it consisted originally of three buildings—the Stanford store at 224–26, and the Huntington-Hopkins buildings (a hardware store) at 220 and 222. From their offices here, Leland Stanford, Collis P. Huntington, Mark Hopkins, and Charles Crocker financed and built the Central Pacific Railroad, western end of the first transcontinental railway, later gaining control of the political and financial affairs of California.

These are only a few of the historic buildings and sites in the old section of California's capital. Old Sacramento has been registered as a National Historic Landmark by the Department of the Interior, and the B. F. Hastings (Pony Express) and "Big Four" buildings have been declared individually eligible for the same status.

First Transcontinental Railroad

On January 8, 1963, Governor Edmund G. Brown dedicated a bronze plaque *(SRL 780)* at Front and K streets in Sacramento. It was 100 years to the day since Governor Leland Stanford, at the same spot, turned the first spade of earth to begin construction of the Central Pacific Railroad. An earlier plaque had been dedicated by retired railroad employees on the 50th anniversary, January 8, 1913.

Six years and four months after construction began, having conquered seemingly insurmountable obstacles, crews of the Central Pacific met those of the Union Pacific, which had been building westward, at Promontory, a lonely spot in northern Utah. There, on May 10, 1869, the gold spike was driven to signify completion of the first transcontinental railroad. "The successful completion of this great project, one of the most stupendous engineering works undertaken by man, brought to an end the frontier era of California history."

It must not be thought that the "Big Four" alone were responsible for this remarkable achievement. The man who planned the Central Pacific, and who earlier had built the first passenger railroad in California, did not live to see the last spike driven. In his memory a splendid

"Big Four" Building, Sacramento

monument of granite boulders stands in front of the Southern Pacific depot at Fourth and I streets. A bronze tablet on the face of the rock bears this inscription: "That the West may remember Theodore Dehone Judah, pioneer civil engineer and the tireless advocate of a great transcontinental railroad—America's first, this monument was erected by the men and women of the Southern Pacific Company, who, in 1930, were carrying on the work he began in 1860. He convinced four Sacramento merchants that his plan was practicable and enlisted their help. Ground was broken for the railroad, January 8, 1863, at the foot of K Street nearby. Judah died November 2, 1863. The road was built past the site of this monument over the lofty Sierra—along the line of Judah's survey—to a junction with the Union Pacific at Promontory, Utah, where on May 10, 1869, the 'last spike' was driven."

The Southern Pacific depot is built on what in gold rush days was China Slough *(SRL 594).*

Even before the Central Pacific was begun, the corner of Front and K streets was a transportation center. In the early 1850's it was the terminal *(SRL 598)* for stagecoaches to various points in the Mother Lode country. At this same location, the first successful commercial fruit cannery in the Sacramento Valley, Capitol Packing Company, was established on January 1, 1882.

Old Sacramento Homes

Sacramento has many early residences of brick or frame construction, sheltered by fine old trees.

The Stanford-Lathrop home *(SRL 614)* at 800 N Street was originally built in the late 1850's. It was purchased by Leland Stanford in 1861 and occupied by him and his wife, Jane Lathrop Stanford, as their residence until 1874. Stanford was governor of California in 1862–63 and United States senator from 1885 until his death in 1893. Leland Stanford, Jr., their only child, who died at the age of 16 and for whom Stanford University is named, was born in this house in 1868. The house was extensively remodeled by Stanford and was presented by his widow to the Roman Catholic Diocese of Sacramento in 1900.

The stately white Victorian house at 16th and H streets was built about 1877 as the residence of Albert Gallatin. It was acquired by the State of California in 1903 to be used as the Governor's Mansion. If a new Executive Mansion is built, as is contemplated, it is to be hoped that this fine old house will be preserved as a land-mark.

The Crocker Art Gallery *(SRL 599)* stands at 216 O Street. Judge E. B. Crocker and his wife collected many fine paintings and drawings during their travels in Europe, especially during the Franco-Prussian War. In the early 1870's a building was erected at the southeast corner of Second and O streets, next to their residence, to house this private collection. In 1884 Crocker's widow donated the building and its contents to the City of Sacramento, with the California Museum Association as co-tenant and administrator. After Mrs. Crocker's death, the old home at the southwest corner of Third and O, built by B. F. Hastings about 1853 and purchased by Crocker about 1868, was also acquired and converted into the gallery annex. Judge Crocker was a brother of Charles Crocker and was legal counsel for the Central Pacific Railroad.

Sacramento Cemeteries

Sacramento's first cemetery *(SRL 592)* was established by John A. Sutter in 1849. It was located on Alhambra Boulevard between I and J streets, and is now the campus of Sutter Junior High School.

In the same year Sutter and H. A. Schoolcraft gave the land for the Sacramento City Cemetery *(SRL 566)*, at Broadway and Riverside Boulevard. Many pioneers and important persons are buried here, including Governors John Bigler, Newton Booth, and William Irwin; Mark Hopkins; E. B. Crocker; and William S. Hamilton.

William Stephen Hamilton, youngest son of Alexander Hamilton, the distinguished Revolutionary statesman, came to California in 1849. Previous to that time he had served as surveyor of public lands in Illinois, discovered the Hamilton Diggings in southwestern Wisconsin in 1827, engaged in the Black Hawk War, when as colonel he distinguished himself for efficiency and bravery, and was several times a member of the Territorial Legislature of Wisconsin. On coming to California, Hamilton engaged in mining for about a year, after which he went to Sacramento to trade. He died in that city on October 7, 1850.

An unmarked grave in the city cemetery constituted the resting place of William Hamilton until 1879, when friends had the body removed to a more appropriate part of the cemetery and a slab of polished Quincy granite placed over it. In 1889, at the suggestion of John O. Brown, mayor of Sacramento, the remains were again moved, this time to a new plot in the cemetery named in honor of the deceased, Hamilton Square. At this time the handsome, oddly shaped monument of massive Quincy granite that still marks the grave was sent out from Massachusetts by a grand-nephew of the pioneer. On one side it bears a bronze medallion of Alexander Hamilton. A small plate below the medallion indicates that the grave is now cared for by the Sacramento Chapter, D.A.R., who thus keep in memory the worthy life of a great man's son.

Down the Sacramento River

The little town of Franklin lies about four miles east of the Sacramento River, and may be reached from Hood, or directly from Sacramento by Highway J-8, a distance of about 15 miles. In the Franklin Cemetery is the grave of Alexander Hamilton Willard *(SRL 657)*, one of the last surviving members of the Lewis and Clark Expedition of 1804–6. Willard was born in New Hampshire in 1777, came to California in 1852, and died on March 6, 1865.

Farther south along the river is the unique town of Locke, which could easily pass for a Mother Lode mining camp or a Western movie set. It is neither. Locke is a community composed entirely of Chinese and was built as late as 1916, when fire destroyed the Chinatown of neighboring Walnut Grove. The narrow main street, flanked by balconied two-story wooden buildings, lies below the level of the highway. The structures fronting the highway are actually the upper stories of the buildings below.

Main Street, Locke

SOURCES

Benton, J. A. *The California Pilgrim: A Series of Lectures.* Solomon Alter, Sacramento; Marvin & Hitchcock, San Francisco, 1855.
Bidleman, H. J. *The Sacramento Directory, for the Years 1861–62.* H. S. Crocker & Co., Sacramento, 1861.
Bradley, Glen D. *The Story of the Pony Express.* A. C. McClurg & Co., Chicago, 1913.
Bryant, Edwin. *What I Saw in California.* Appleton, New York, 1848, 1849.
Buffum, E. Gould. *Six Months in the Gold Mines.* Lea & Blanchard, Philadelphia, 1850.

Chapman, Arthur. *The Pony Express: The Record of a Romantic Adventure in Business.* Putnam, New York, 1932.

Clark, George T. *Leland Stanford, War Governor of California, Railroad Builder, and Founder of Stanford University.* Stanford University Press, Stanford, 1931.

Cleland, Robert Glass. *From Wilderness to Empire. A History of California,* ed. Glenn S. Dumke. Knopf, New York, 1959.

Clemens, Samuel. *Roughing It.* Harper, New York, 1913.

Colville, Samuel. *Sacramento Directory, 1856.* Manson, Valentine & Co., San Francisco, 1856.

Coy, Owen Cochran. *Gold Days,* of the series *California,* ed. John Russell McCarthy. Powell Publishing Co., Los Angeles, 1929.

Dale, Harrison Clifford. *The Ashley-Smith Explorations and the Discovery of a Central Route to the Pacific, 1822–1829, with the Original Journals.* The Arthur H. Clark Co., Cleveland, 1918.

Davis, Winfield J. *Illustrated History of Sacramento County, California.* Lewis Publishing Co., Chicago, 1890.

Delano, Alonzo. *Life on the Plains and at the Diggings: Being Scenes and Adventures of an Overland Journey to California.* Miller, Orton, & Mulligan, Buffalo, 1854.

Hall, Carroll D., Hero Eugene Rensch, Jack R. Dyson, and Norman L. Wilson. *Old Sacramento, a Report on Its Significance to the City, State and Nation, with Recommendations for the Preservation and Use of Its Principal Historical Structures and Sites.* 3 vols. Division of Beaches and Parks, Sacramento, 1958 and 1960.

Historic Old Sacramento. Redevelopment Agency of the City of Sacramento, 1964.

History of Sacramento County, California. Thompson & West, Oakland, 1880.

Krysto, Christina. *The Romance of Sacramento.* Weinstock, Lubin & Co., Sacramento, 1923.

McGowan, Joseph A. *History of the Sacramento Valley.* 3 vols. Lewis Historical Publishing Co., New York, 1961.

Morse, Dr. John F. "History of Sacramento" in Colville's *Sacramento Directory for the Year 1853–54.* Printed at the *Union* Office, Sacramento, 1853.

Muldoon, Sylvan. *Alexander Hamilton's Pioneer Son.* Aurand Press, Harrisburg, Pa., 1930.

Neasham, V. Aubrey. *Old Sacramento, a Reference Point in Time.* Sacramento Historic Landmarks Commission, in cooperation with the Redevelopment Agency of the City of Sacramento, 1965.

Old Sacramento Historic Area and Riverfront Park. Technical report prepared for the Redevelopment Agency of the City of Sacramento. Candeub, Fleissig and Associates, San Francisco, 1964.

Old Sacramento, Inventory of Historical Buildings. Prepared by Western Heritage Inc. Division of Beaches and Parks, Sacramento, 1962.

Peterson, H. C. "List of Historic Spots in Sacramento County." Ms., 1930.

Reed, Walter G. *History of Sacramento County, California.* Historic Record Co., Los Angeles, 1923.

Sacramento Bee. Seventy-fifth Anniversary Number, February 3, 1932.

Sacramento Directory for the Year 1871. H. S. Crocker & Co., Sacramento, 1871.

Sacramento Illustrated. Barber & Baker, Sacramento, 1855.

Sidewalk History—Pioneer Sites of Old Sacramento. Published by the City of Sacramento, 1958.

Wheat, Carl I. "A Sketch of the Life of Theodore D. Judah," *California Historical Society Quarterly,* IV, No. 3 (September 1925), 219–71.

San Benito County

SAN BENITO COUNTY derived its name from San Benito Creek, which was named by Father Crespí in 1772. (San Benito is Spanish for St. Benedict.) The county was formed in 1874 from a part of Monterey County, and the county seat was placed at Hollister. By act of the state legislature in 1887, the area of the county was increased by additions from the adjoining counties of Fresno and Merced.

Mission San Juan Bautista

Following the expressed wish of the viceroy, missions were established as fast as possible to fill gaps in the chain from San Diego to San Francisco. Soon after the dedication of Mission San José, Father Lasuén proceeded to the San Benito Valley, where on the feast day of St. John the Baptist, June 24, 1797, Mission San Juan Bautista was founded. The father had chosen this spot from others suggested to him because this location "promised the most abundant harvest of souls."

Assisting in the ceremonies at the dedication were Father Magín Catalá from Mission Santa Clara and Father Manuel Martiarena, who was to be left in charge of the new establishment.

The rites took place before a large assemblage of Indians from the plains nearby. These were peaceful Indians, but there were others who inhabited the mountains to the east, including the warlike Ausaymas tribe, who gave trouble for several years.

The temporary building constructed for use as a church had a "mud roof." It was not until June 13, 1803, that the cornerstone of the new church was laid. Within this stone were placed coins and a sealed bottle containing a narrative of the proceedings at the celebration.

The new building was "about one hundred ninety feet long from the entrance door in front to the altar at the rear, thirty feet wide and forty feet high from floor to ceiling, having the chancel separated from the nave by a railing, over which was sprung an arch spanning the full width of the church. The nave was subdivided on either side into seven sections by as many arches. The church and adjacent buildings, which as usual throughout the country were of adobe, occupied two sides of a court-yard which was completed by a wall; and in front, next the church, there was a corridor of twenty arches, resting on pillars of brick."

The new group of buildings was completed in 1812, and Father Estévan Tápis, who had succeeded to the office of Padre Presidente on the death of Father Lasuén, officiated at the dedication on June 25 of that year. Later in the year, at the end of his term of office, Father Tápis went to live at San Juan, remaining there until his death in 1825 at the age of 71. Under his influence, population figures at the mission reached their highest point in 1823. Father Tápis was an excellent man for his position. He was familiar with several Indian dialects, took an interest in the neophytes as individuals, and enjoyed teaching the boys to read and write. After his death, it was said that he had been remarkably wise in his dealings with the superior officers and the civil governors who also lived at San Juan. As a result of this ability to get along with people, "all friars, military, civilians, and Indians loved him."

In 1831, the mission was visited by Captain Alfred Robinson, who wrote: "It is conveniently located in the center of a large valley, with an abundance of rich land and large stocks of cattle. Padre Felipe Arroyo [de la Cuesta] was the missionary, whose infirm state of health kept him confined closely to his chamber. For amusement, when tired of study, he called in the children of the place and set them to dancing and playing their games. In his eccentric taste he had given them the names of all the renowned personages of antiquity, and Ciceros, Platos, and Alexanders were to be found in abundance."

In 1835, when Mission San Juan Bautista was secularized, José Tiburcio Castro, grantee of Rancho Sausal not far away, was made mayordomo. Sixty-three families of Indians were released from mission discipline at the time, and payments were made to them amounting to over $8,000. The value of the remaining mission property was estimated to be $138,973, with a debt of only $250 standing against it.

The mayordomo, aside from a few problems with the Indians and the padres, on the whole settled the mission affairs promptly and well. He gave his final report in 1836. There were at that date 900 head of cattle and 4,000 sheep belonging to the mission and an account of $1,300 against the property.

The mission (SRL 195), sadly neglected for many years, was restored in 1884. Only one of the original nine bells remains. The long, arched corridors, extending the entire length of the building, still give grace and charm to the ancient chapel, which is now used as the parish church for the town of San Juan Bautista.

San Juan

In 1835 José Castro became interim governor of California, and in 1836 he and Juan B. Alvarado made San Juan their headquarters in the revolt that resulted in the exile of Governor Gutiérrez and in the election of Alvarado in his place.

From 1837 on, after the affairs of the mission had been settled, continual depredations from the Indians contributed to its ruin. However, a small group of Spanish and Mexicans were joined by others, until by 1846 probably 50 persons were living in San Juan de Castro, as the place was called for a time.

Don José Castro petitioned on April 4, 1839, for land: "Being the owner of a considerable quantity of cattle and horses without possessing any land of my own whereon to place them to increase and prosper I have become acquainted with a suitable place in the neighborhood of this pueblo known by the name of San Justo which does not belong to any owner and is entirely unoccupied." The request was granted. In July 1844, Castro transferred the property to Francisco Pérez Pacheco.

In 1840–41 Castro built a two-story adobe house (SRL 179) on the south side of the plaza diagonally opposite the mission church. With its overhanging balcony, it is considered one of the finest examples of California adobe construction re-

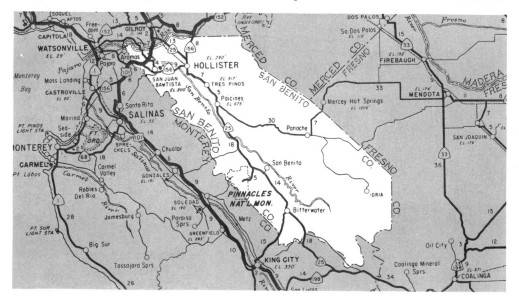

maining from the Mexican era. The large dining room and living room are on either side of the central hallway. Upstairs are the bedrooms, each opening onto the balcony.

In 1846, while interim *comandante general*, Castro again organized forces at San Juan; this time he wished to expel Frémont from his temporary stronghold on Gabilan Peak, where the American captain of topographical engineers maintained his forces from March 6 to March 9. On July 17, 1846, Frémont raised the United States flag on the plaza at San Juan and there drilled his ten companies of volunteer troops before starting for Los Angeles to support Commodore Stockton in suppressing the revolt of General Flores.

Castro's house in the pueblo of San Juan was acquired by Patrick Breen and finally deeded to him in 1854. Breen and his family, the first English-speaking settlers in San Juan, were among the members of the Reed-Donner party who survived the tragic winter at Donner Lake. Breen purchased some of the mission property in addition to the Castro house and established an inn, which became famous as a stopping place for travelers between Monterey and the mines in 1849–50. Years later, Helen Hunt Jackson began to write *Ramona* while staying there.

In the 1850's and 1860's San Juan was the site of an exchange station on the route between San Francisco and Los Angeles. At one time 11 lines made it a stopping place. During the Civil War the United States established military headquarters in the National Hotel in the town. At that time the place was called Camp Low in honor of California's governor, Frederick F. Low.

On the same side of the plaza as the Castro house stands the Plaza Hotel (*SRL 180*). This building consists of two one-story adobes, which were combined, and a second story of wood. The larger of the adobes was built in 1813–14 as armory and barracks for the soldiers of the mission guard. Angelo Zanetta added the second story in 1858 and opened the building as the Plaza Hotel. For many years it was the stopping place for stagecoaches on the well-traveled route that eventually became Highway 101. The old livery stable, built in the 1870's, is also still standing and contains an interesting display of old vehicles. Next to it is the Zanetta house. In 1868 Angelo Zanetta had the old mission nunnery torn down. This was an adobe building, built in 1815 and enlarged in 1832, in which the Indian girls were housed. Zanetta used bricks from the nunnery to build the lower story of a new building on the site. This served as his residence, and the upper story of wood was a public hall.

The Plaza Hotel, Castro adobe, stable, and Zanetta house are all included in the San Juan Bautista State Historical Park, which was dedicated on September 29, 1935, by the State Park Commission and the San Juan Preservation League. A few other adobes stand along the streets of the old town, as well as several interesting wooden structures from the early American period. Notable among the adobes are the "Casa Juan de Anza" at Third and Franklin streets, and the two-story adobe restored by the Native Daughters on Fourth Street near Washington. Highway 101 long ago bypassed the little community, and, being off the main line of travel, it has been able to preserve its air of antiquity.

Mission San Juan Bautista

The Pacheco Ranchos

Francisco Pérez Pacheco was a Mexican carriage maker, who came to California in 1819 with the artillery detachment under Ramírez. His bravery and success in quelling Indian revolts won his promotion to *brevet-alférez* in 1824. Afterward, he was commander of the Custom House guard and then of the military post at Monterey.

Since the mission fathers at San Juan Bautista did not need all the land set aside for mission use, they allowed Pacheco to settle upon a part of it before 1833. This part was apparently the Bolsa de San Felípe, which came by the name Bolsa ("pocket") because it was nearly enclosed by a swamp, a willow grove, and a ravine called Sanjón de Tesquisquite. He let the family of the mayordomo of the mission and some of the mission Indians who were living upon it remain.

The formalities that attended the legal taking possession of land at that period included pulling up grass, cutting a few tree branches, throwing a few stones, and taking up a handful of earth. After taking possession, Pacheco built a stone house, where he and José María Sánchez, owner of the adjoining Rancho Llano del Tesquisquite, lived together for a time.

On petition to Governor Figueroa for adjoining property, the Ausaymas tract of two leagues was granted to Pacheco on November 21, 1833. In 1836 he petitioned for another two leagues, which he called Guadalaxarita but which the padres called San Felipe, and this tract was probably included in the grant of six leagues made by Governor Gutiérrez on April 1, 1836. With a good start the first year, his herds gradually increased, in spite of a raid by Indians in 1838. Pacheco became an extensive landowner, eventually having in his possession the San Justo, conveyed to him by José Castro in July 1844; the Bolsa de San Felipe, near Hollister; the Ausaymas y San Felipe, extending into Santa Clara County; and the San Luís Gonzaga, lying in the counties of Santa Clara and Merced, including the Pacheco Pass and several miles of the Pacheco Pass Road. All of these ranchos were later patented to him by the United States.

In 1844 Don Francisco Pacheco was captain of *defensores* and in 1846 tithe collector. Testimony given in 1852 states that he was then the owner of a house valued at between $15,000 and $20,000,

ten cabins for laborers, and thousands of horses, cattle, and hogs, with pens and corrals, and that enough of his land was in cultivation to provide for all living upon it.

Rancho San Justo, through which runs the San Benito River, was sold by Pacheco in 1855, three years before his death, to W. W. Hollister and Flint, Bixby and Company, men who brought a flock of sheep from the East and turned the place into a sheep ranch. Some years later Colonel Hollister sold the eastern portion to the San Justo Homestead Association, a group of businessmen who established the town of Hollister. On the western part, Flint, Bixby and Company built a three-family ranch house, which still stands as a part of St. Francis Retreat in the hills above San Juan Bautista. The old house and surrounding land were sold to the Franciscan Fathers in 1947. Diversified farming and fruit raising gradually replaced grazing, and much of the rancho is now owned by Ferry-Morse Seed Company and is used for growing flowers for seed, making a beautiful sight in summer.

The only child surviving Don Francisco Pacheco was a daughter, Isadora, who married Mariano Malarin. Pacheco's house on Rancho Ausaymas y San Felipe stood near Pacheco Creek in the area in which it is crossed by the present highway seven miles north of Hollister. This later became the Smith Ranch. When Malarin came into possession of the rancho, he moved the old Pacheco frame house by sawing it into sections and reassembling it about two miles east on Las Viboras Creek. There it still stands, a large two-story house painted dark red. This portion of the grant is now owned by the Hawkins Cattle Company.

Rancho Llano del Tesquisquite

José María Sánchez, who came from Mexico in 1824, received a grant of land situated in San Benito and Santa Clara counties from Governor Castro on October 10, 1835. With Thomas O. Larkin the grantee instituted an early soap-making enterprise near the northern end of his grant. A rough frame building was erected by them on the edge of Soap (now San Felipe) Lake, into which the Tesquisquita Slough drains. The kettle used for boiling soap was a cauldron from an old whaling vessel enlarged by slabs of wood extending upward from the edges until its capacity was increased many times. The slabs were held in place by iron hoops, and an adobe foundation was built around it. The soap works, superintended by an Englishman, were in operation until 1848, when they were deserted in the rush to the gold region.

Don José María was still living in 1852, when he filed claim with the Land Commission for this rancho and for Rancho Las Animas in Santa Clara County. In 1871 patents for both of these tracts were issued to the children of José María Sánchez and Encarnación Ortega—Vicente, Refugio, Candelaria, Gregorio, and Guadalupe. The last-named daughter married into the Roche family and lived until 1935. Don José is supposed to have buried a fortune on his estate, but no trea-

Zanetta House, San Juan Bautista

sure has been found, although his rancho has been cut up into many small farms and has long been cultivated.

Rancho Santa Ana y Quien Sabe

Rancho Santa Ana y Quien Sabe, consisting of over 48,000 acres, covered the Santa Ana and the Quien Sabe valleys. Quien Sabe had been granted to Francisco J. C. Negrete, one of the Híjar colonists of 1834, who petitioned for this land in December of that year. He received the grant of six leagues in April 1836, after serving as secretary of the *ayuntamiento* at Monterey. Some time later that same year, as secretary to Governor Chico, he went to Mexico. Since he did not return to Alta California, his land was granted on April 8, 1839, to two men who held it in a sort of partnership for a number of years.

One of these partners was Juan Miguel Anzar, brother of Father José Antonio Anzar. He did not live on the land but furnished 800 head of cattle and paid Manuel Larios, the other partner, to oversee the property. Manuel Larios was a native of San José who had spent his early years as a soldier and, like his father, Don José Larios, was a famous bear hunter. He was married three times: first to María A. Pacheco, second to Guadalupe Castro, both of whom died, and finally to Rosario Arnas, who bore him 22 children, four of whom were born on this rancho.

Larios furnished 300 head of cattle in the partnership and cultivated land for garden crops, but no orchard was planted because of lack of water. His adobe house was built beside the road leading to San Juan Bautista, where he was *juez* (judge) in 1840. Under his supervision, cheese was made, and in shops erected for the purpose a primitive sort of manufacturing was done by weavers, shoemakers, saddlers, silversmiths, and blacksmiths. A guard was posted to prevent raids by hostile Indians.

A chapel was built on the rancho in the early 1840's. After its completion, the celebration of St. Ann's Day on July 26 became an annual event. On those occasions Mass was said in the chapel, followed by out-of-door festivities common to that period: bull-and-bear fighting, horse-racing, feasting, and dancing.

The other owner, Miguel Anzar, had three children. Although he did not live on the rancho, some of his employees lived in a house in the northern part. In the late 1840's the two men divided their joint grant: Larios, who died in 1865, took Santa Ana; and Anzar, who also owned Ranchos Carneros and Real de Aguillas, took Quien Sabe.

No trace of the old buildings remains on either part of the property. A modern barn in which relics of Mexican days were stored was destroyed by fire on May 2, 1933. Among the heirlooms lost at that time were Spanish worked-leather bridles, bronze-studded harness, and carriages.

Rancho Ciénega de los Paicines

Rancho Ciénega de los Paicines was granted by Governor Alvarado to Angel Castro and José Antonio Rodríguez on October 5, 1842. Rodríguez died before 1853, when a claim to the property was filed by Angel Castro and Hilaria Castro de Rodríguez, widow of the co-grantee, and her three children. A patent for 8,918 acres was issued to these claimants on September 23, 1869.

This grant covered the land extending from Tres Pinos Creek on the east to the Cienega Valley at the foot of the Gabilan Mountains on the west. Through it runs a stretch of the San Benito River and its tributary, Pescadero Creek. The southeastern boundary of the rancho is near the site of the former Paicines School, which was located on the old stage road to San Benito, south of the little settlement of Paicines.

Before receiving the grant of this land, Angel Castro, a native Californian, had married Isabel Butron. In 1835 he had been sub-mayordomo of Mission San Juan Bautista, and at the time of receiving this grant he was the commander of a militia company at San José and Branciforte.

Castro's house, a two-story adobe, was built about two miles south of the town of Paicines. The large living room was reproduced and used as the setting for the ballroom scene in David Belasco's stage production of *The Rose of the Rancho,* in which a daughter, one of the eight children of Angel Castro, was the heroine. In 1916 the adobe, no longer used as a family residence, had been reduced to the position of bunkhouse for farm laborers.

Rancho Ciénega de los Paicines has passed through the hands of several owners since the day of Angel Castro. The first of these was Alexander B. Grogan, who built the large white ranch house occupied by the present owner. Grogan made extensive improvements to the ranch during his ownership, and his large Red Durham cattle were the prize herd of the county. He sold the ranch to Captain Sudden, a retired English sea captain, who leased it as a cattle and grain ranch. It was then sold to A. Kingsley Macomber, who restored the Grogan ranch house, built a beautiful mansion, and landscaped the grounds extensively. Macomber's ranch became famous for its purebred horses and prize-winning cattle. His private Pullman car stood on a special siding at Tres Pinos, ready for use whenever he wished to travel. Soon after purchasing the ranch, Macomber sold 1,000 acres east of the old stage road to San Benito and Bitterwater, and south of Tres Pinos Creek, to Colonel George Sykes, who planted part of this acreage to prunes and English walnuts, using the hills for a cattle range. The Sykes Ranch is now owned by Almaden Vineyards, who have planted the hills to wine grapes. The Macomber Ranch proper passed into the hands of Walter P. Murphy, and his estate, in turn, sold it to the present owner, Robert B. Law.

Cienega Road, south of Hollister, follows the main line of the awesome San Andreas Fault for a distance of about 15 miles. This fault is subject to sudden movement, such as caused the 1906 earthquake, and to slow creep or gradual movement. Evidence of fault movement may be seen in the Cienega Winery of Almaden Vineyards, which is slowly being pulled apart and requires constant repair. It was built in 1939 to replace the former winery, which was so weakened by fault movement that it eventually collapsed. The San Andreas Fault at Cienega Winery has been registered by the Department of the Interior as a National Natural Landmark.

Other Ranchos

Two other ranchos in this county received recognition from the United States in the form of patents. Lomerias Muertas, along the Pajaro River, consisting of one and a half square leagues, was granted to José Antonio Castro in 1842 and patented in 1866 to the heirs of José María Sánchez, who was the claimant in 1842. San Joaquín, or Rosa Morada, consisted of 7,424 acres lying northeast of Hollister and granted by Governor Gutiérrez to Cruz Cervantes in 1836. The grant followed Cervantes' petition of the previous year. At the end of ten years Cervantes had horses, cattle, and sheep, with corrals for them, on his land. He also had four or five acres under cultivation.

Ranchos lying on the boundary line and extending far into Monterey County were Los Vergeles, Ciénega del Gabilán, and San Lorenzo.

Gabilan Peak

The highest peak in the Gabilan range of mountains on the border between the counties of San Benito and Monterey is called Gabilan (Gavilan) Peak, and sometimes Hawk's Peak, *gavilán* being Spanish for "sparrow hawk." It is also referred to as Frémont Peak *(SRL 181)*. To this spot Frémont took his little band of followers, after being ordered by Mexican officials to leave the country.

Taking possession of the peak, he erected a log fort there on March 6, 1846. The United States flag was raised over the fort, and Frémont held it for four days. General José Castro prepared to dislodge the Americans, and Frémont, with his forces outnumbered five to one, slowly retreated north to Sutter's Fort.

On the outcome of the Gabilan episode, Hunt and Sanchez have this to say: "The affair of Hawk's Peak amounted to but little in itself, but the results were unfortunate, both in stirring up antipathy on the part of the Americans toward the Californians and in outraging the feelings of the Californians and giving color to the persistent rumor that the Mexican Government had purposed expelling all foreign residents from the province. In the light of subsequent events, the episode may be regarded as a direct cause of the Bear Flag revolt."

A memorial flagstaff of iron was erected in 1908 on Gabilan Peak. There are no traces of the old fort left. The site is now Frémont Peak State Park.

The New Idria Mines

The New Idria Quicksilver Mine *(SRL 324)*, where work began in the 1850's, lies on the slope below San Carlos Peak. The date of the discovery of this ore deposit is unknown, but tradition says that the mission fathers, before the coming of the Americans, made assays of it and determined

it to be cinnabar. Bret Harte, in his *Story of a Mine,* attributes the accidental discovery of the first quicksilver in the region to a group of prospectors who were burning specimens of rock to test it for silver and were surprised to find a pool of "liquid silver" in the ashes of their improvised furnace.

With actual records that go back to 1854, it ranks among the most famous quicksilver mines of the world. The name, New Idria, was copied from the Idrija Mine in Austria, and the same square type of furnace was used, but it was supplanted long ago by a more effective type.

In 1861 William Brewer of the Whitney Geologic Survey kept a record of the findings of that party on a visit to this region. They visited three mines, the New Idria, the San Carlos, and the Aurora, all within a radius of a few miles. They found the square furnaces of the New Idria at an approximate elevation of 2,500 feet and the excavation of the San Carlos at almost double that elevation. The two mines were later consolidated into one company. Ore from the higher mine, however, was treated at the New Idria works even at that early time, when it was hauled down the mountainside by means of ox teams. In later years iron buckets suspended from a cable have lowered the ore to be treated.

By July 1861 many miles of tunnels had been driven into the mountainside, among them the 700-foot Sleeman tunnel, in 1859, and the Day and Myers tunnel. Through these dark passages Brewer and his party wandered "mole-like" for six hours; a part of this time they were "a thousand feet from daylight."

In the 1850's and 1860's the town nearest to the mine was San Juan, 68 miles away. The stage route between them became a well-traveled road livened by the jangle of bells on the freight teams. From six to 12 horses or mules constituted a team. The driver sat on a wheel horse and guided the team by means of a jerk line that was fastened to the bit of one of the lead horses.

The road from the mine followed San Carlos Creek down to Griswold Creek, named for a rancher who lived there. It passed several adobe houses, a few of which stand vacant or in ruins beside the route today, and cabins constructed of rough lumber, most of which have disappeared. Next it came to Panoche Creek and ran through

Old Adobe on New Idria Road

the Panoche Valley, famous for cattle pasture, until it reached Tres Pinos Creek, which it crossed and recrossed by means of fords. That part of the road has long been called the "wiggletail." The roadbed of today has been somewhat improved and, for a part of the distance, is now cut out of the canyon side at a higher level. Finally, the settlement that was then called Tres Pinos, now called Paicines, was reached, and the remainder of the journey to San Juan was on a more even grade.

At the time of Brewer's visit, between 200 and 300 men were employed at the New Idria mines. Work has continued there practically all these years. The mines were sold in 1898 to a company of men who formed the New Idria Quicksilver Mining Company. During World War I the place was policed by a company of soldiers. The mines are now operated by the New Idria Mining and Chemical Company, formed July 3, 1936.

Supplies are now received by truck from Hollister and Fresno. Many of the old cabins are vacant, but those that are occupied have electricity. Descendants of some of the early miners live and work here. The paths and roads of the town are covered with red slag, or burnt ore.

Eight miles from New Idria are the Picacho mines, which were discovered in 1858. The huge red peaks in the vicinity rise out of a wild and picturesque country, 75 miles south of Hollister, where grizzly bears were once numerous. The town of Picacho had disappeared by 1880.

Tres Pinos; Paicines

The settlement of Paicines, little more than a post office and general store, stands at the junction of Highway 25 and the road to New Idria. This spot used to be called Tres Pinos, named for three stunted pine trees on the bank of Tres Pinos Creek. It was known as Tres Pinos when Tiburcio Vásquez made his last robbery, at Snyder's store, which still stands, remodeled, at this junction. The robbery occurred in August 1873. Three men were killed by the bandit at that time: one a deaf man, who did not hear the peremptory orders given by the bandit; one a Portuguese, who did not understand the language; and third, the hotelkeeper across the street, who refused to open his door and was felled by a bullet through it. The residents of the county became so incensed at the callous crime that Vásquez and his gang sought safety in the south. Trailed by sheriffs, they were brought back to Hollister in May 1874, and after trial in San Jose, Vásquez was executed there on March 19, 1875.

When the railroad was built out from Hollister to a point west of the original settlement of Tres Pinos, a town grew up at the station and it also was called Tres Pinos. After a time the older settlement came to be called Paicines, for Rancho Ciénega de los Paicines nearby. The word itself is supposed to be the name of a tribe of Indians that once lived in the region. The main activity of the new Tres Pinos was handling freight for the New Idria mines. The railroad was abandoned in 1927, but the town still prospers on Highway 25.

Hollister

In the autumn of 1868 the San Justo Homestead Association was formed by a group of 50 farmers, who each held one share. They purchased from Colonel W. W. Hollister the eastern part of Rancho San Justo, containing 21,000 acres, for the sum of $400,000 and divided the best part of the land into 50 homestead lots—one for each member. One hundred acres in the middle was reserved for a townsite and was laid out in blocks, lots, and streets. This is now the center of Hollister.

A man prominent in the formation of the association and the town was T. S. Hawkins, who came to California from Missouri in 1860. He settled first in Santa Clara County but came to what is now San Benito County in 1867, renting 1,000 acres of virgin soil and planting it to grain. He hauled seed for this planting from Gilroy over a robber-infested road. The produce of his planting was hauled by wagon to Alviso, whence it was carried by boat to San Francisco. In the following year, Hawkins helped to form the San Justo Homestead Association, of which he was made secretary and general manager in 1870. At that time he gave up farming and turned his attention wholly to the advancement of the town.

Because it seemed a waste of time to go all the way to the coast to transact legal business at the county seat in Monterey, the suggestion of forming a new county met with approval. Agitation of the subject resulted in the organization of San Benito County on February 12, 1874, with the new town of Hollister as the county seat.

The Hazel Hawkins Memorial Hospital, completed in Hollister in 1907, was erected by Hawkins as a tribute to his granddaughter, who had died in 1902. It is now a rest home.

The Pinnacles

On November 19, 1794, George Vancouver, the English navigator, who had been ill for some time in Monterey, had sufficiently recovered to go on an exploring expedition. With a small party on horseback, he set out across the Salinas Valley and reached a point, possibly the southern termination of the Gabilan Range, where he "was gratified with the sight of the most extraordinary mountains" that he had ever beheld. One side "presented the appearance of a sumptuous edifice fallen into decay; the columns, which looked as if they had been raised with much labor and industry, were of great magnitude, seemed to be of an excellent form, and seemed to be composed of . . . cream coloured stone." It is thought by some that Vancouver reached the Pinnacles. If so, his would be the earliest record of a visit to this region. The curious rocks that he supposedly saw were occasionally called "Vancouver's Pinnacles" on the basis of this conjecture. There is evidence, however, that Vancouver actually saw a flat-topped hill supported by column-like projections near El Toro Lake north of Monterey.

In *The Days of a Man*, David Starr Jordan wrote: "From 1904 to 1908 it was my pleasure to assist an ardent mountain lover, Mr. C. S. Hain of Tres Pinos, in securing for the people as a Government Forest Reserve, a singular district known as the 'Pinnacles' lying in the Gavilan Range on the line between San Benito and Monterey counties. There the mountain range of yellow Miocene sandstone has been scored into deep gulches by the long action of small streams unaided by frost or ice. The cuts are very narrow and regular, scarcely widened even at the top, and the cliffs assume varied fantastic and picturesque forms. The forests are of little consequence, being of scant oak and digger pines, but many rare flowers are found in the tract, and some of the precipitous walls bear nests of the great California Condor—*Gymnogyps*—a majestic vulture with wing spread of from nine to ten feet."

This area was set aside as a National Monument by proclamation of President Theodore Roosevelt on January 16, 1908. By grants made in 1923 and 1924, the area was increased to 2,980 acres. In 1931 the County of San Benito purchased land from private owners that increased the total acreage to 4,609 acres, and by the acquisition of Chalone Peak in July 1933 the monument reached nearly 10,000 acres. Further additions brought it to 14,498 acres by 1963, of which only 880 acres are not federal-owned. The spire-like formations of the Pinnacles rise to a height of from 600 to 1,000 feet, and beneath them are caves and subterranean passages. An amphitheater enclosed by smaller pinnacles has been named in honor of Jordan.

The Pinnacles National Monument is located in San Benito County, except for a very small corner in Monterey County, and is entered about 35 miles south of Hollister.

SOURCES

The California Missions, a Pictorial History. Lane Book Co., Menlo Park, 1964.

Elder, David Paul. *The Old Spanish Missions of California.* Paul Elder & Co., San Francisco, 1913.

Goodwin, Cardinal. *John Charles Frémont: An Explanation of His Career.* Stanford University Press, Stanford, 1930.

Harte, Bret. *The Story of a Mine.* Houghton Mifflin, New York, n.d.

Hittell, Theodore H. *History of California.* 4 vols. Pacific Press Publishing House and Occidental Publishing Co., San Francisco, 1885.

Hoyle, M. F. *Crimes and Career of Tiburcio Vasquez, the Bandit of San Benito County and Notorious Early California Outlaw.* Evening Free Lance, Hollister, 1927.

Hunt, Rockwell D., and Nellie Van de Grift Sanchez. *A Short History of California.* Crowell, New York, 1929.

Iacopi, Robert. *Earthquake Country.* Lane Book Co., Menlo Park, 1964.

Jordan, David Starr. *The Days of a Man.* 2 vols. World Book Co., Yonkers, N.Y., 1922.

Milliken, Ralph LeRoy. *San Juan Bautista, California, the City of History.* Los Banos Enterprise, Los Banos, 1961.

Miser, Ross J. *The Pinnacles Story.* Privately printed, San Jose, 1962.

Nevins, Allan. *Frémont, the West's Greatest Adventurer.* 2 vols. Harper, New York, 1928.

Older, Mrs. Fremont. *California Missions and Their Romances.* Coward-McCann, Inc., New York, 1938.

(Robinson, Alfred). *Life in California.* H. G. Collins, Paternoster Row, London, 1845.

Smith, Sarah Bixby. *Adobe Days, Being the Truthful Narrative of the Events in the Life of a California Girl on a Sheep Ranch and in El Pueblo de Nuestra Señora de Los Angeles While It Was Yet a Small and Humble Town.* Enlarged edition, Jake Zeitlin, Los Angeles, 1931.

San Bernardino County

SAN BERNARDINO COUNTY was organized as a county in 1853 from territory that was at first a part of Los Angeles and San Diego counties. (The name comes from the Spanish for St. Bernardine of Siena.) The city of San Bernardino has been the county seat since the county's organization.

Pueblo Settlements and Turquoise Mines

"Pueblo settlements, turquoise mines, and weapon manufactories" were discovered on the edge of the Mojave River sink, southwest of Death Valley and 140 miles from the Pacific Coast of California, in the winter of 1928–29. This remarkable discovery was made by the San Diego Museum of Archaeology under the direction of Malcolm J. Rogers, field archaeologist. Pottery and other artifacts unmistakably peculiar to the Pueblo peoples were found as testimony that the Pueblo culture once spread "about two hundred miles west of the limit heretofore attached to it. . . . Not even a guess is hazarded at the age of these recent findings . . . but few archaeologists believe them to be less than twenty centuries old."

Dr. Rogers expressed little doubt that "what is now the Mojave River sink region once had a permanent Pueblan population. Besides the East Cronise Lake site, several other widely separated sites on the south end of the sink produced dominant percentages of Pueblo-type pottery. . . . On the northwest shore of East Cronise Lake is a site whose Pueblan attributes are sufficiently strong as to identify it as a permanent village of these people."

"Petroglyphs [rock carvings]," Dr. Rogers said,

"are fairly common in these mountains. . . . Some of these appear to be guide boards, and it was by following one of them that we came on the largest of the Pueblan settlements on East Cronise Lake, somewhat west of the sink of the Mojave River, and northwest from Crucero."

The line of turquoise deposits was followed by Dr. Rogers and his associates from Mineral Park, Arizona, to Granite Wells in San Bernardino County, 22 miles east of Johannesburg. In the Turquoise Mountains one of the largest mines was located. Here many tools of the Pueblo type were found. The most extensive digging was 30 feet long, 12 feet wide, and 12 feet deep, and from it more than a dozen smaller tunnels branched off.

Dr. Rogers said of the 50 or more ancient mines discovered: "Throughout this extensive terrain, I seldom visited an outcropping of turquoise without finding distinct evidence of the stone having been mined by the aborigines, as evidenced by ancient open cuts, pits, and stone hammers. In cases where I have failed to find such evidence, I have been assured by modern miners that the 'Indian workings' were there, but had been obliterated by the white man's methods and machinery.

"In and about the undisturbed turquoise mines of the Himalaya group," Dr. Rogers continued, "some twenty-five pieces of Pueblan pottery were found," but "of all the sites in this region, excluding the mines, the Halloran Spring site produced the most Pueblan artifacts, and, possibly, was the temporary camp of the turquoise miners."

Archaeological investigation of the Mojave Desert continues, and research indicates that man may have lived there as long ago as 30,000 years.

Cajón Pass and Mojave Indian Trail

Professor Herbert Eugene Bolton established that, as early as 1772, Pedro Fages traversed the region of the Cajón Pass, while on his way north into the San Joaquin Valley in pursuit of deserters.

The first white man to cross the San Bernardino Mountains into the San Bernardino Valley was Padre Francisco Garcés, the famous Spanish priest-explorer, who came in 1776 from the Colorado River. Jedediah Strong Smith, the first American to enter California overland, traveled the same trail from the Colorado in 1826 and again in 1827.

At the eastern entrance to the city of Needles, in a small parkway, a monument (SRL 781) has been placed, calling attention to an old Indian trail, still visible in some places, that ran roughly parallel to the Colorado River on the California side. It was over this route that Garcés and Smith traveled.

Study of the diaries of the Garcés and Smith expeditions has shown that the route taken by these two men did not lead directly through Cajón Pass, as had been supposed. Mojave Indians served as guides from the Colorado on both occasions, and they used the ancient Indian trail, which led across the desert and up the Mojave River to its western headwaters in the San Bernardino Mountains. Crossing the range eight miles east of the present Cajón Pass, it came down into San Bernardino Valley on the ridge between Devil and Cable canyons, crossing Cajón Creek between Devore and Verdemont. From here it skirted the base of the foothills to Cucamonga, and led on to San Gabriel and the sea. The old Mojave Indian Trail is therefore extremely important historically, as it antedates the Cajón as a mountain crossing for white men.

Smith's expedition was one of the most important in all the annals of Western trail-breaking. It did for California what the expedition of Lewis and Clark did for the Pacific Northwest and what Pike's expedition did for the Southwest. It opened up the first of the great transcontinental routes to California and covered a vast stretch of country, most of which Smith was the first to explore. It "made known the valleys of the San Joaquin and Sacramento to American trappers, and, through them, to American settlers; opened a line of communication from Northern California to the Oregon country, a route the Hudson's Bay Company was quick to take advantage of; and traversed the Pacific Slope from the Mojave Desert to Puget Sound." On September 19, 1931, the San Bernardino County Historical Society placed a monument and tablet to Father Garcés and Jedediah Smith (SRL 618) at the place where the Mojave Trail crossed the summit of the mountains. This marker is located on a peak between the headwaters of Devil and Cable canyons, about eight and one-half miles northwest of Crestline, on a dirt road leading to Cajón Mountain Lookout.

During the years 1830–31 three pioneer pack trains from New Mexico crossed the San Bernardino Mountains into the valley beyond. The first, forerunner of the Santa Fe caravans, was led by Antonio Armijo, a New Mexican trader, who came in January 1830 by what he called the "San Bernardino Canyon," probably the present Cajón Pass. Ewing Young and his trappers came a little later in the same year, but the trail by which he crossed the mountains is not mentioned. In the fall of 1830 William Wolfskill left Santa Fe with still another band of trappers, and, according to J. J. Warner, went through the Cajón in February 1831. Certainly the last, and possibly all three, of these parties made use of the Cajón.

Wolfskill's trip, with its course over the mountains so clearly defined, is notable. His route from Santa Fe to California was more nearly that followed later by the New Mexican caravans than was that of either Armijo or Young. It was he who established the famous pack-train route known as the "Spanish Trail," used by the Santa Fe–Los Angeles caravans for nearly two decades, until the establishment of the wagon road from Salt Lake, practically along the same line from Utah south.

The caravan route up Cajón Canyon crossed and recrossed the wash, following the general direction taken later by the railroad and still later by the highway. The route continued for a distance of about eight miles from the mouth of the canyon, until it reached the "Narrows," where

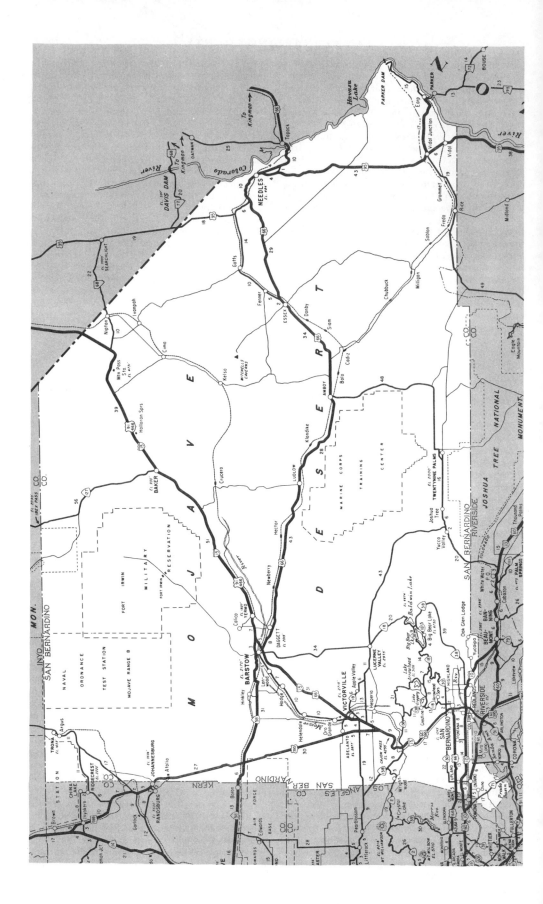

it turned northeast. At this junction a monument *(SRL 576)* was placed in 1917 by the Pioneer Society of San Bernardino commemorating the early explorers, traders, and pioneer settlers who used this trail. This marker stands adjacent to the southbound lanes of the freeway (Interstate 15) through Cajón Pass. Nearby, about 200 yards north of Cajón Station on the main line of the Santa Fe Railroad, a similar monument *(SRL 578)* was placed in 1912. Sheldon Stoddard and Sydney P. Waite, who came over the trail in 1849, helped to erect these monuments.

Captain Jefferson Hunt of the Mormon Battalion left California by way of Cajón Pass in 1847. In 1851 a company of Mormons, on their way to settle San Bernardino Valley, came by way of Cajón Canyon, and in 1857 a large number of the same settlers left that way, when recalled to Salt Lake City by Brigham Young.

The Mormons, with their heavy wagons, could not use the "Narrows," but came out of the desert into Cajón Canyon four or five miles farther west than does the present highway. A monument *(SRL 577)* commemorating this route was placed in 1937 in West Cajón Canyon beside Highway 138, several miles to the northwest of the Stoddard-Waite monuments. While negotiating for lands in San Bernardino Valley, the Mormons camped at Sycamore Grove *(SRL 573)*, a small, verdant valley about one and one-half miles southwest of what is now Devore Station, near the mouth of Cajón Canyon. The Pioneer Monument erected at this spot to commemorate these emigrants was washed away in 1938, but has since been replaced.

Lieutenant A. W. Whipple, with the United States topographical engineers, came through Cajón Pass in March 1854 while on a government exploring expedition.

Across the dry wash of Cajón Creek, about one-half mile from Devore on the way to Sycamore Grove, was a picturesque stone tavern, once a station on the emigrant wagon road which went along the west bank of the river at this point in the canyon. The tavern, standing in the midst of fine old trees, with a perpetual spring at its doorstep, was until its destruction by flood in 1938 a memorial to that long line of settlers, stagecoach drivers, gold seekers, and adventurers who passed its doors in pioneer days.

Horsethief Canyon, which extends into Cajón Canyon from Summit Valley, is reminiscent of the days (1830–60) when stolen animals were pastured in this region, before the long drive across the Mojave Desert. From the time of the opening up of the "Spanish Trail" by William Wolfskill, a brisk trade in California mules and horses was carried on with Santa Fe, New Mexico. Most of the mules were destined for Missouri, where there was a great demand for the superior type of animal produced in California. While a large proportion of this trade was lawful, there was also much illegitimate and clandestine traffic carried on by renegade Indians, New Mexicans, Americans, and others. Hardly a year passed that the mission fathers and the rancheros did not lose valuable livestock, which was driven off

through Cajón Pass by raiding parties of outlaws. Even after the American occupation, Indians continued these raids.

Old Trails across Euclid Avenue

Four historic trails once crossed what is now Euclid Avenue, that long, tree-lined drive that extends north and south through the modern towns of Ontario and Upland.

1. The first of these trails to be traversed by white men was the Anza Trail, over which Juan Bautista de Anza in 1774 led the first overland party into California, and again in 1775 the first overland band of settlers, the founders of San Francisco. The Boy Scouts of America and service organizations of Ontario have placed a memorial boulder in honor of Anza in a small park on the corner of Euclid Avenue and Phillips Street. On it a bronze tablet bears the inscription: "To the honor and glory of Juan Bautista D'Anza, Trailmaker, and his band of intrepid followers, who, on March 21, 1774, passed near this spot on their way to San Gabriel and Monterey, the first white men to break a trail overland to California."

The San Gabriel Mission fathers used this trail as far as the Santa Ana River in order to reach their mission station in the San Bernardino Valley until a more direct route was cut shortly after 1822.

2. The oldest of the four trails crossing Euclid Avenue was the Mojave Indian Trail, which was well established when Father Garcés traveled it in 1776. Smith, and probably Ewing Young, followed the same route. The Spanish Trail, sometimes called the Santa Fe Trail, opened in 1831, made use of the line of the Mojave Indian Trail from the mouth of Cajón Canyon to San Gabriel, and also from "Fork of Roads" (east of Barstow) to "Lane's Crossing" (Oro Grande) along the Mojave River. This old Spanish Trail was followed by a long line of explorers, hunters, and traders; pioneer settlers of El Monte and Los Angeles who came close in the wake of these adventurers; later emigrants of covered-wagon days and the gold seekers bound for the north; and, last of all, the daring stagecoach drivers of the 1860's and 1870's, forerunners of the "iron horse" and the modern motor car. This trail followed the base of the mountains in San Bernardino Valley even more closely than does the Foothill Boulevard of today. Where it crossed the site of the modern town of Upland at Euclid Avenue, just at the beginning of "Ye Bridle Path," one of the several statues of the Pioneer Mother which mark the National Old Trails Road has been placed in honor of the mothers of covered-wagon days who passed over this part of the old road. The National Old Trails Committee of the D.A.R. has erected one of these monuments in each state through which the National Old Trails Road passed from Maryland to California.

3. The old Emigrant Trail, which followed Anza's route across the Colorado Desert as far as Carrizo Creek and crossed the mountains via Warner's Ranch, branched in two directions after leaving Aguanga: one branch, known as the San

Yorba-Slaughter Adobe, near Chino

Bernardino–Sonora Road, followed north to San Gorgonio Pass and west through the San Bernardino Valley, while the other, known in mission days as the Canyon Road to the Colorado, and designated by the Los Angeles Court of Sessions, May 19, 1851, as the Colorado Road, took its course along the western mountains via Temecula, Elsinore, Temescal Canyon, Corona, and the Santa Ana River.

The San Bernardino–Sonora Road, the upper branch of the old Emigrant Trail, came from Warner's Ranch via Aguanga and passed down the San Jacinto Valley and across the hills to the site of what is now Beaumont in Riverside County. From there, it continued northwest and west through San Bernardino County via Redlands and Old San Bernardino, or Guachama, to what is now Colton. From that point the road went southwest past Slover Mountain to Agua Mansa, where it again proceeded westward to what is now Ontario, crossing Euclid Avenue one mile north of the Southern Pacific Railroad. From there it continued west across San Bernardino County to Los Angeles County via Ciénega (Mud Springs) near San Dimas.

The padres, after 1822 and before 1827, were the first to use this road on their way from San Gabriel to their mission outpost at Guachama. Smith took this route in 1827 on his journey out of California, camping at Jumuba Ranchería a few miles west of the Guachama Mission Station. Here he awaited the much-needed supplies which Padre Sánchez, of Mission San Gabriel, had ordered the mayordomo at Guachama to furnish him for his journey.

4. The last of the four roads crossing Euclid Avenue was Colorado Road. This was opened from Carrizo Creek to Warner's in 1826 by Romualdo Pacheco, leader of a government expedition seeking an official mail route. Immediately thereafter the missionaries of San Gabriel opened up the road all the way from Warner's to San Gabriel via the canyon route. The first American to use this route was David E. Jackson in 1831, and it was used by other trappers and by those emigrants from Mexico and the East who followed the southern route via Santa Fe and the Gila River, of which the Colorado Road was a continuation. As this southern trail was the only all-year route into California from the East, it

was also used by the Butterfield Stage from 1858 to 1861 for carrying passengers and mails.

The route of the Butterfield Stage over this section of the Colorado Road may be traced by the adobes that it passed. After crossing the Santa Ana River near the Cota House, in what is now Riverside County, the road followed the base of the hills along Chino Creek, above which the highway from Chino to Santa Ana now runs. About three miles northwest of the Cota House, the stage passed the Raimundo Yorba adobe on Rancho Rincón, now in San Bernardino County. Although it was not one of the official stations along this route, doubtless stages did halt at the old adobe house, which still stands on the brow of the hill, beautifully restored. In 1868 Fenton M. Slaughter purchased this building from Yorba, and lived in it until his death in 1897. His daughter, Julia Slaughter Fuqua, saved it from ruin and brought it back to its former glory as a memorial to her father. The Yorba-Slaughter adobe *(SRL 191)*, built in the early 1850's, stands at 17127 Pomona–Rincon Road, about five and one-half miles south of Chino; it is one of the outstanding examples of adobe architecture in California.

At Rancho Rincón, the Butterfield route ran along the base of the hill, crossing the extreme southern terminus of Euclid Avenue at that point. From there it continued northwest along Chino Creek for seven miles to Rancho Chino, where a station was maintained on what is now the southern part of the Boys Republic property.

A marker commemorating this old trail has been placed on one of the buildings of the Boys Republic. The inscription reads: "This tablet is placed by Pomona Chapter, Daughters of American Revolution, in memory of the pioneers who first broke this trail, known as the Canyon Trail, from Fort Yuma via Warners Hot Springs, Temecula, Lake Elsinore, Rancho del Chino, by this place, thence, to Mission San Gabriel. In 1858 the Butterfield stages from San Francisco to St. Louis, Missouri, traveled this way."

Rancho and Asistencia de San Bernardino

It was on May 20, 1810, that Franciscan Padre Francisco Dumetz celebrated Mass in a temporary chapel west of present-day Redlands. It was the feast day of St. Bernardine of Siena, and the priest called the chapel "San Bernardino." The name was later to become that of a ranch, a branch mission, a city, a county, a valley, and a mountain range.

In a report on the missions issued in 1822 in connection with the transfer of California from Spain to Mexico, there is this statement from Mission San Gabriel regarding the origin of Rancho San Bernardino:

"In the year 1819, at the request of the unchristianized Indians of the place they call Guachama and which we call San Bernardino, we began the introduction of cattle raising and farming, in order to induce the natives to become Christians."

When Father Payéras visited Guachama (the

"place of plenty to eat") in 1821, he found that Mission San Gabriel had cattle grazing in the valley and that there were a number of old houses, probably for the herdsmen of the rancho, at Jumuba, a few miles west of the rancho headquarters. In 1827, Father Sánchez of Mission San Gabriel reported:

"Rancho of San Bernardino—The house is of adobe. It consists of one long building. It has an enramada or structure of boughs which serves for a chapel. It has also a building with compartments for keeping grain. The walls of this structure are of adobe."

This was the Guachama Mission Station (*SRL 95*), or the rancho headquarters, on Rancho San Bernardino, which was owned by Mission San Gabriel. The little mission station was located north of what is now Mission Road and east of where it intersects Mountain View Avenue, while the site of the Guachama Indian village was on the south side of this road. The entire region is today covered with extensive orange groves. The remains of the old adobe station were leveled in 1875, but the site was located by the fact that the orange trees growing where the old buildings once stood did not thrive as well as the other trees in the same orchard. It has been marked by the State of California.

On what is now known as Barton Hill, one and one-half miles southeast of the old rancho buildings, and about two miles west of the present city of Redlands on Barton Road, an extensive adobe structure was begun about 1830. This was the Asistencia San Bernardino, to which Father Durán, in 1837, referred thus:

"San Gabriel founded the beautiful San Bernardino Asistencia, which has lately been given to some private individual."

From other testimonies of the times, we know that San Bernardino, like San Antonio de Pala and Santa Ysabel, was to have been one of that inland mission chain that the fathers contemplated before the decree of secularization, which ended all mission activity in California.

After secularization, all work on the asistencia ceased and the buildings remained practically deserted until 1842, when a large section of the mission lands was granted to three sons and a nephew of Antonio María Lugo of Los Angeles. The cities of San Bernardino, Redlands, and Colton now stand on the Rancho San Bernardino of the Lugos. One of Don Antonio's sons, José del Carmen Lugo, came to live in the old asistencia buildings, thus saving them from complete disintegration for a time.

After the Rancho San Bernardino was sold to the Mormons by the Lugo brothers in 1851, Bishop Nathan C. Tenney, manager of agricultural operations on the lands formerly cultivated by the mission, occupied the old asistencia buildings. Upon the withdrawal of the Mormons in 1857, Dr. Benjamin Barton, a prominent pioneer settler, and his family took over the buildings, occupying them until 1867. From this date, the old adobes, untenanted and uncared for, gradually succumbed to the weather, until only a few mud walls remained.

The Asistencia San Bernardino (*SRL 42*) has been restored by the citizens of San Bernardino County under the instructions of George W. Beattie of East Highlands. Every effort has been made to be historically accurate in the work of restoration, old court records, diaries, and mission archives being utilized in working out the original details of construction. A native of Mexico, expert in the making of real adobe bricks, was brought to the asistencia, where he lived. Here he molded the adobe bricks and tiles out of na-

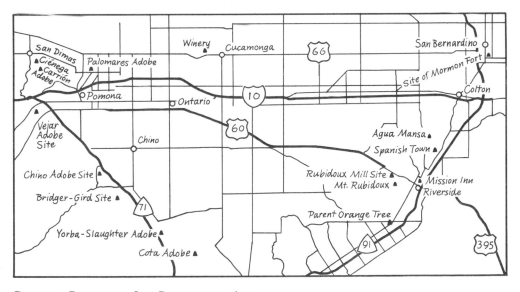

POMONA–RIVERSIDE–SAN BERNARDINO AREA

Asistencia de San Bernardino

tive clay, just as was done in the days of the mission. The whole project (1928–37) was extremely illuminating and fascinating, both in its picturesque and in its historical aspects, a notable example for similar projects in other parts of the state.

North of the asistencia, and just beyond the Southern Pacific tracks, may be seen the old *zanja,* or water ditch *(SRL 43),* built in 1819–20 by the Indians under the direction of the Spaniards, to bring water for irrigation from Mill Creek Canyon to the Guachama Ranchería. The ditch passes under the business district of Redlands. Just north of the asistencia is the large brick mansion built in 1866–67, to which the Barton family moved after leaving the adobes.

Mission Ranchòs

Mission San Gabriel had three ranchos in the San Bernardino Valley: Rancho San Bernardino, already mentioned as the location of the mission station Guachama and later the asistencia; Rancho Agua Caliente, on which the present city of San Bernardino is located; and Rancho Jumuba, located between the present Loma Linda and Colton. Rancho Jumuba was named after an Indian ranchería which occupied the site beside a bubbling spring of water. It was here that Jedediah S. Smith camped in 1827 while being outfitted by the generosity of the mission fathers just before starting on his return trip to Salt Lake, via the San Joaquin Valley.

San Bernardino

"The city of San Bernardino, now making claim to [some 100,000] inhabitants, owes its beginning to a colony of Mormons from Salt Lake City, who arrived in June of 1851 and laid the foundation of a thriving community in the six years before they were recalled by their leader, Brigham Young."

Gradually, the lands purchased from the Lugo brothers were subdivided and sold to the individual members of the Mormon community, who established homes and farms. The town of San Bernardino was founded; in the San Bernardino Mountains, sawmills were erected; roads were constructed, the Mormons opening up the present Foothill Boulevard as far as Cucamonga; extensive agricultural activities were started; churches and schools were founded.

Adobe and log houses were soon erected on a site originally known as "Agua Caliente," but the name of the neighboring Asistencia San Bernardino was transferred to the new town. Here, because of rumored Indian uprisings, a fort and stockade enclosing eight acres of ground was erected in the form of a parallelogram, 300 feet wide and 720 feet long. The north and south ends were made of cottonwood and willow tree trunks closely fitted together and set three feet in the ground and 12 feet above, while the log houses were moved along the west side, forming a solid wall finished with logs in blockhouse fashion, with loopholes, bastions at the corners, and indentured gateways. Within this stockade about a hundred families lived; a few, however, remained outside, camping at a spot now occupied by the old cemetery at Seventh Street and Sierra Way.

The site of the old Mormon fort *(SRL 44),* now occupied in part by the courthouse, included the present Arrowhead Avenue from Third Street nearly to Fourth Street, and lands to the east, west, and south. On the courthouse site also stood the José María Lugo adobe, while on the present Third Street and Arrowhead Avenue was a two-story adobe built by the Mormons and used as the first courthouse of San Bernardino County. This was torn down in 1867.

In 1851, the year of their arrival, the Mormons built the first road from San Bernardino Valley to the summit of the mountains, over which they hauled lumber from their sawmills to be sold in Los Angeles and other expanding communities of southern California. Much of the cost of their colony at San Bernardino was defrayed by the sale of lumber, and, of course, it was needed for construction of their own buildings. Where the Rim of the World Drive crosses the old Mormon lumber road *(SRL 96),* a monument has been erected.

Although they were by and large a peaceable people, there did develop a dispute over a land title between Mormon factions. The "Independent" group even put up an adobe fortification, Fort Benson *(SRL 617),* in 1856-57 and maintained it about a year. Its site is indicated by a monument east of Colton, on the west side of Hunt's Lane between the freeway (Interstate 10) and the Southern Pacific tracks. This was also the site of the Indian village of Jumuba, where Jedediah Smith camped in 1827.

In 1857 the Mormon activity was halted by the decree of Brigham Young, which recalled the "faithful" to Salt Lake City because of the threatened invasion of Utah by the United States forces under General Albert Sidney Johnston. The majority of the settlers obeyed the call and left their homes in the San Bernardino Valley, often selling them for very little. Their departure greatly decreased the population of the county and seriously hindered its prosperity for some time. The Mormons had been industrious citizens with great organizing ability, and they had been largely responsible for the development of the agricultural resources of the valley as well as for the sound basis of the city of San Bernardino.

Rancho Santa Ana del Chino

Rancho Santa Ana del Chino was another of the Mission San Gabriel ranchos. Soon after the secularization of the missions it was granted to Antonio María Lugo. About three miles southwest of the modern town of Chino, the Chino ranch house once stood on what is now the southern part of the Boys Republic property. It was built by Colonel Isaac Williams (known as Don Julián to the Californians), who came to California with Ewing Young in 1832 and became one of the leading citizens of Los Angeles. He married a daughter of Antonio María Lugo, one of the finest of the old Spanish settlers, who, in 1841, deeded a half-interest in the great Rancho Santa Ana del Chino to his son-in-law. There Williams built the adobe mansion which became a refuge for every wayfarer who came into Alta California over the southern emigrant trail. Orchards and vineyards were planted; barns, shearing sheds, and adobe huts for a great army of Mexican and Indian laborers were erected; a gristmill, one of the earliest in southern California, was built; the rancho was stocked with fine cattle, horses, and imported sheep; and an extensive trade in hides and tallow was carried on. In 1851, Lugo deeded his remaining interest in this rancho to Williams.

Very soon after the death of Isaac Williams in 1856, his daughter Francisca married Robert Carlisle, a young southerner, and Mercedes Williams married John Rains, who had been mayordomo at Chino. John Rains and his wife moved to Rancho Cucamonga, while the Carlisles remained at Chino. Robert Carlisle was an energetic, well-educated man and a good business manager, and under his control the prosperity of Rancho del Chino continued until his death in 1865.

Francisca Williams Carlisle married again, and the Chino estate was managed by trustees. In 1881 it was sold to Richard Gird, a miner and engineer, one of the most picturesque characters of the early American period. On Rancho del Chino, Gird lived lavishly in a fine adobe built by Joseph Bridger (the site is on the grounds of the Los Serranos Country Club), and added to his estate until it contained 45,000 acres. The land boom of 1887, however, ruined Richard Gird, and in 1894 the rancho was sold to Charles H. Phillips, of San Luis Obispo. In 1896 it came into the hands of English investors, when it was broken up into small tracts and sold.

Much of historical interest centered in the Chino adobe. During the Mexican War it was the scene of a battle between the Americans and the Californians. While Colonel Gillespie was shut up in Los Angeles in 1846, a score of Americans, commanded by B. D. Wilson, took refuge on Rancho del Chino, which was 25 miles east of Los Angeles. On September 27 the Chino house was surrounded by a force of 70 mounted Californians. During the short skirmish that followed, one of the Californians, Carlos Ballesteros, was killed and several Americans were wounded. The Californians, incensed by the death of their friend, who was very popular, set fire to the brea roof of the adobe. At this point, Isaac Williams appeared with a white flag and his two little daughters, whom he insisted on placing in the hands of their uncle Felipe Lugo, one of the attacking party, so they could be taken to their Grandfather Lugo in Los Angeles. The leaders of the Californians, however, persuaded the Americans to surrender, promising them protection as prisoners of war. The success of the Californians in this encounter encouraged them in their attack upon Gillespie.

During the years 1858–61, the Chino adobe assumed additional historical importance as a station on the old Butterfield Stage route, which passed its door.

The lands once belonging to Rancho del Chino are now occupied by the town of Chino and the Boys Republic, as well as by many small farms. The old adobe ranch house, so long dominated by the personality of Isaac Williams and the scene of so much of historical significance, has long since disappeared. A monument commemorating the rancho, the Williams adobe, the battle site, and the Butterfield Stage station has been proposed.

Rancho Cucamonga

Rancho Cucamonga derived its name from an Indian village which was on the land when the first white men came there. Tradition tells us that the Cucamonga Indians were unusually intelligent and industrious and that they learned much from the padres, who sometimes came down from Mission San Gabriel to visit them. Gradually they acquired cattle and horses and raised good crops of corn and melons in the fertile hills and valleys of "Nuestra Señora del Pilar de Cucamonga," as the padres called the locality.

Tiburcio Tapia, a leading citizen of Los Angeles, petitioned for a grant to the Cucamonga lands in 1839. This grant was made on April 16, 1839, and Don Tiburcio immediately began the building of an adobe house on the crest of Cucamonga's highest hill. Its roof was covered with brea from Rancho La Brea near Los Angeles. It was as "massive as a fortress, facing south, with east and west wings and a gateway on the north side." The Tapia mansion was indeed well built for the rugged, romantic years through which it was destined to stand.

The Indians, who were employed in the building operations, rebelled when they realized that the newcomers were taking their rich grazing lands from them. Retreating to the foothills and canyons, they made occasional raids upon the stock of the white men. Desert Indians, too, frequently invaded the rancho lands, and many tales were told by old residents of raids and battles and even of attacks upon the Tapia "fortress" on "Red Hill."

In the beginning, Don Tiburcio left his rancho largely in the care of his mayordomo, José María Valdez, who is said to have set out the "mother vineyard." This later developed into one of the large plantings of grapes in California, the first cuttings probably having been obtained at Mission San Gabriel. The history of the old rancho

Diego Sepúlveda Adobe, Yucaipa

is closely associated with the development of its vineyard.

Among other traditions of those hectic days at Cucamonga is that of the chest of coins which Don Tiburcio is said to have hidden when rumors of war began to herald the aggression of the United States in Alta California. It is said that this chest contained not only Señor Tapia's own money but that entrusted to him by friends, and also a sum collected for the building of a chapel at Cucamonga.

Not long after this, in 1845, Tiburcio Tapia died suddenly. No one knew where the chest had been hidden, except an Indian servant whom Don Tiburcio had sworn to secrecy. Nor would the Indian disclose the whereabouts of the hidden treasure, so great was his fear of the fulfillment of the terrifying oath that Señor Tiburcio had placed upon him.

A few years later, Tiburcio Tapia's daughter, María Merced, married Leon V. Prudhomme, and moved with him to the adobe on Red Hill. Doña María, who knew the story of the hidden treasure, slept in her father's room. One night, so the story goes, she saw a mysterious light move across the chamber wall, resting upon a particular spot. The apparition was repeated a number of times, greatly disturbing the young wife. In order to prove that the vision was entirely imaginary, her husband plunged a knife into the adobe wall. To his amazement, it went through the wall, disclosing a hollow space behind. In the aperture was a purse containing some silver coins and a scrap of paper with its message faded with age. The paper was studied very carefully and much search followed. But all in vain. No treasure was ever found, though searchers have not been lacking through the years. The Tapia adobe has long since returned to its native clay.

In 1858, Victor Prudhomme sold Rancho Cucamonga to John Rains and his wife, Mercedes Williams. An unpublished history of the 1890's says:

"The coming of John Rains to this place marked not only a new but a progressive epoch in its history. The old Tapia residence on the hill was abandoned and a new one built at the highest point of the east bank of the arroyo, north of the vineyard. Labor and expense was not spared in its construction. . . . The walls were built of heavy brick made of the red clay dug

from the hills and roofed with thatches covered with brea mixed with tallow. . . .

"A little to the east of the Valdez residence was built the store and nearby a blacksmith shop, stables and several dwellings. . . . The rancho was stocked by Mr. Rains with sheep, horses and cattle, and 160 acres was set to vines. The small still and winery were proportionately enlarged and improved. The road from Los Angeles to San Bernardino by way of the Chino having been abandoned by the stage for the Arroyo San José routes to Bear Valley and the mines, this be came a regular station, where the horses were changed and the traveler enabled to obtain refreshments.

"With the vaqueros in charge of the flocks and herds, the laborers in the vineyards and winery, the stable hands in charge of stage relays, mechanics at work on buildings, teamsters, the blacksmiths and a trader and postmaster, the place became not only a hive of industry, but noted as the chief trading post and assembly point for all classes and nationalities east of Los Angeles. The Rains home was a center of social life, and, attracted by the hospitality of its master, the beauty of its mistress, the sparkling wines and festivities, here frequently gathered the representative wealthy and élite of the south."

John Rains was murdered on November 17, 1862, and his widow was left with four small children and many heavy obligations to meet. In 1864 she married José C. Carrillo, and the gay life of the rancho was revived for a few years, until, in 1870, debt forced Mrs. Rains-Carrillo to sell a part of the rancho. The Hellmans and their associates finally acquired the greater part of the rancho, and Mrs. Carrillo lost all title to the estate.

The old adobe winery (*SRL 490*) built by John Rains stands in western Cucamonga on Foothill Boulevard. Although abandoned for many years, California's first commercial winery was restored by H. H. Thomas and is open for business daily. Next to it is the adobe residence, among the occupants of which was E. K. Dunlap, who had charge of planting the vineyard and building the winery. Splendid trees, walnut, sycamore, and eucalyptus, planted in John Rains's time, still surround the place. To the north, the brick Rains house, at 7869 Vineyard Avenue, has been repaired and is now used as a residence. The Valdez house, "Ritchie's Store," and the blacksmith shop have all disappeared. To the west of the winery, across Cucamonga Creek, is the site of the Tapia adobe (*SRL 360*) on the southeastern slope of Red Hill, which is now built up with homes and a large country club.

Yucaipa

The oldest dwelling still standing in San Bernardino County is located at 32183 Kentucky Street, near Dunlap Boulevard and Sixteenth Street, about four miles east of Redlands at the western outskirts of Yucaipa. The two-story Diego Sepúlveda adobe (*SRL 528*) was built in 1842 in the southeastern corner of the Rancho San Bernardino. Sepúlveda was a nephew of Antonio

María Lugo, three of whose sons were co-grantees of the rancho with Sepúlveda. Later owners of the adobe included John Brown, Sr., James W. Waters, and the Dunlap family, after whom the nearby street is named. In the early 1950's the old house, rapidly falling to ruin, was saved from threatened demolition by a group of public-spirited citizens, who effected its purchase and restoration. Since 1955 it has been the property of the County of San Bernardino, with a resident caretaker, and is open to the public daily.

Yucaipa is the site of an Indian ranchería (SRL 620), from which it received its name. On the hillside just above the Charles W. Simpson ranch house, at 33142 Avenue E, excavations by the San Bernardino County Historical Society have revealed metates, fireplaces, and implements used by the peaceful Serrano Indians before and during the Spanish period. The place, well watered by springs, a ciénega, and a creek, was a logical site for habitation.

Politana

George W. Beattie summarizes the story of Politana as follows:

"From the time that the holders of Mexican land grants in the San Bernardino valley began raising stock there, raids by wild Indians were the most serious difficulty with which the rancheros had to contend. Counter attacks by the whites were made frequently, but the most effective defense of the rancheros was through the establishment of colonies of immigrants from New Mexico that were friendly.

"From 1833 to 1848, trading caravans from Santa Fe passed through the valley twice a year, and the Santa Ana river bottoms and the adjacent damp lands afforded feed for their animals. At a point northeast of the present Colton there lived a man called Hipólito [Espinosa], and his house was a stopping place for the caravan people." The Lugo family "realized that a populated center where the caravans stopped would afford very effective protection for the stock of the region, and offered half a league (2,200 acres) near the home of Hipólito to a group of New Mexicans who were thereby induced to settle there. They occupied the land in [or about] 1843, and built adobe houses" at Bunker Hill, now on Colton Avenue just inside the San Bernardino city limits. "The settlement was called Politana because Hipólito, or Polito, as he was familiarly called, lived near and had been instrumental in bringing the colonists from New Mexico. The settlement consisted largely of families that arrived in California in the winter of 1842 . . . , although some had come the preceding year with the Rowland-Workman party. Many of the men had been long in the employ of the caravan traders and were experienced Indian fighters. In return for the land on which they settled, they agreed to defend the stock of the region in case of Indian raids.

"The colonists secured water from a spring northwest of the present San Bernardino Valley . . . College grounds. Vicente Lugo, however, soon established a rodeo center north of the colony and diverted the water of the spring. The New Mexicans became dissatisfied at this, and, in 1845, abandoned their settlement at Politana, and accepted a more favorable offer from Juan Bandini, grantee of the Jurupa Rancho, to occupy a new location on his lands south of the present cement plant at Slover Mountain. The Lugos replaced the New Mexicans with Juan Antonio and his band of Cahuilla Indians. They located their ranchería near the establishment of Vicente Lugo on Bunker Hill ridge, and the name Politana, or Apolitana, as it was more commonly termed, was transferred to their home."

Agua Mansa and San Salvador

These settlements on the "Bandini Donation" on Rancho Jurupa were composed of New Mexican colonists who had moved there in 1845 from Politana on Rancho San Bernardino. Colonists were desirable at that time as protectors against the inroads of unfriendly Indians; and when dissatisfaction with certain conditions at Politana arose, Juan Bandini invited the settlers to leave that place and locate on a parcel of land he donated. It lay on both sides of the Santa Ana River, and later formed part of San Salvador parish. Agua Mansa was on the north and west bank of the river, while the settlement on the south and east side was known as San Salvador. The original parish capilla was erected in San Salvador, but collapsed before it was completed because it had been built on quicksand. Another capilla was erected in 1851–52 at Agua Mansa and used until 1893. This, too, has now disappeared.

Nothing remains of Agua Mansa (SRL 121) today except the little burial ground on the hill above the river, near which once stood the chapel. It is the oldest cemetery in the county, and many members of the old Spanish and Mexican families are buried there. Agua Mansa means "gentle water," but the Santa Ana River was anything but gentle in 1862 when it washed away the homes of Agua Mansa and San Salvador on its banks. The chapel and cemetery were on high enough ground to escape the rampaging river. Long neglected and overgrown with weeds, the cemetery was restored in the 1950's by a group of interested citizens, including descendants of those buried there. It is located about three miles southwest of Colton on Agua Mansa Road, east of its intersection with Riverside Avenue.

Agua Mansa Cemetery, near Colton

While, as we have said, the part of the "Bandini Donation" on the south and east bank of the river was originally called San Salvador, it was known later to American pioneers as "Spanish Town." It has also been called "La Placita de Trujillo." In both Agua Mansa and San Salvador the settlers immediately built new adobe homes on higher ground after the flood. A remnant of Spanish Town remains today, but since it is now in Riverside County, it is described in that chapter.

The San Bernardino Mountains

High above the San Bernardino Valley the Rim of the World Drive takes motorists to the mountain resorts of Lake Arrowhead and Big Bear Lake, among many others. There are also historic spots to be seen, and markers are being erected to direct the tourist.

About three miles north of Big Bear Lake, and roughly parallel to it, lies Holcomb Valley (*SRL 619*), now a peaceful cattle ranch but in the 1860's the scene of a full-scale gold rush. It derives its name from William Francis "Bill" Holcomb, who made the first strikes there in 1860. The area is crisscrossed with good dirt roads, along which Forest Service signs have been placed, indicating the principal landmarks, including the site of Belleville, the valley's largest town, reputed to have reached 10,000 population and to have been a hotbed of Secessionists during the Civil War years. A contemporary gold rush occurred in the Lytle Creek–Glenn Ranch area far to the west.

There were a number of other lumber roads between the mountains and the valley, besides the one built by the Mormons in 1851, and one

of the most important was the Daley Toll Road (*SRL 579*), built in 1870 by Edward Daley and Co. from Del Rosa to the crest near Strawberry Peak. After 20 years as a toll road, it became a county road. Presently it is in use only by the Forest Service as a fire road, but a stretch of it can be seen where it crosses the Rim of the World Drive. The Native Sons and Daughters placed a monument there in 1935.

Like Lake Arrowhead, Big Bear Lake was created by the impounding of mountain waters behind a dam. The first Bear Valley Dam (*SRL 725*) was built in the mid-1880's by the Bear Valley Irrigation Company to provide water for Redlands and Highland. It is still in evidence beside the present dam, which was built in 1911.

Ghost Cities of the Mojave

The Calico Mountains, vivid with ever changing colors, their wild and lofty grandeur wrought by age-old volcanic action, lie in the middle of the Mojave Desert five miles north of the town of Daggett (a supply station for mines and a few ranches) and two miles northwest of Yermo. At their base is the once famous mining town of Calico (*SRL 782*), today a ghost of the desert. In the 1880's the wealth of the silver mines discovered in this region brought 3,500 people to the place, and Calico became one of the most prosperous as well as one of the wildest camps of the great Southwest. A sensational drop in the price of silver was the cause of its abandonment, and the fury of desert storms caused its final desolation.

A few adobes still crouch at the foot of the mountain looming above them. Old diggings are everywhere visible, while across the canyon in the

Old Bear Valley Dam, Big Bear Lake

cemetery heaps of stone guard the shallow graves of the dead upon the lonely hillside. Among the wooden slabs that serve as headstones is one whose painted letters stand out in startling relief against erosion from wind-driven sand. The inscription reads: "In Memory of Minnie B. Whitfield, Born 1881, Died 1885." The old town of Calico has now been restored by Walter Knott of Knott's Berry Farm.

At Daggett the Walter Alf Blacksmith Shop is still standing and contains the old tools and equipment used to repair the vehicles and machinery of miners and pioneers.

Northwest of Calico and about eight miles north of Barstow is Rainbow Basin, considered by the Department of the Interior as eligible for registration as a National Natural Landmark. The area "contains significant fossil evidence of the development of life on the earth and outstanding illustrations of geologic processes," according to the government report. The fossilized insect specimens are among the best preserved to be found anywhere.

Dale, a ghost town 40 miles north of the Salton Sea, in the most desolate section of the Colorado Desert, was a prosperous mining camp at the turn of the century, but today its site is reached by roads that are faint and sometimes almost impassable. Only a few grim reminders are left to tell the story of its inhabitants, who became discouraged by the scarcity of water and the difficulty of transportation.

The Spring Ranch, three miles from the modern town of Adelanto, is located on the Mojave River at a place where many cottonwoods grow. The ranch dates back to covered-wagon days, when it was the stopping place for ox and mule trains hauling freight from Prescott, Arizona, to Los Angeles. The old ranch house is still standing.

Chimney Rock (SRL 737), north of Highway 18 at Rabbit Dry Lake in Lucerne Valley, is the site of the last Indian fight in southern California. In January 1867 Indians from this area raided a lumber camp in the San Bernardino Mountains, looting and burning a number of cabins and a sawmill. A retaliatory posse descended upon the Indians at their Chimney Rock camp and killed and wounded many of them.

John Searles discovered borax in 1862 on the surface of the lake that now bears his name. In 1873 he and his brother Dennis formed the San Bernardino Borax Mining Company, which they operated until 1897. The now-dry lake today yields many other chemicals besides borax, and the significance of the Searles discovery is indicated by a historical marker (SRL 774) beside the highway at Trona. Borax was also mined near Calico; it maintained that old camp in existence for a few years after the end of the silver boom.

Not far from Trona the picturesque remains of the towns of Atolia and Red Mountain mark the Rand Mining District, which straddles the San Bernardino–Kern county line. Across the line, Johannesburg and Randsburg also contain much evidence of a flourishing past.

One of the Argonauts trapped in Death Valley in 1849 led his family to safety by following the dry course of the Amargosa River south to Salt Spring, where they encountered the old Spanish Trail. A monument has been erected in honor of Harry Wade at the site (SRL 622), which is 30 miles northwest of Baker.

Wyatt Earp of Tombstone, Arizona, fame, and now an almost legendary character via television, mined gold in the Whipple Mountains near the Colorado River from the early 1900's until his death in 1929. In his honor the little town of Drennan in the southeastern corner of the county renamed itself Earp.

There are many other interesting old towns in the desert area of San Bernardino County, including the railroad towns of Kelso, Cima, and Ivanpah. At Kelso stands a beautiful Spanish-style Union Pacific depot built about 1906, surrounded by shade trees, a welcome rarity in the hot, barren desert.

SOURCES

"Agua Mansa," in Quarterly of San Bernardino County Museum Association, VIII, No. 4 (Summer, 1961), 1–34.

Beattie, George William. "An Old Road to New Mexico," paper read before the Historical Society of Southern California, 1929.

——— "Development of Travel between Southern Arizona and Los Angeles, as Related to the San Bernardino Valley," Annual Publications, Historical Society of Southern California, XIII, Part II (1925), 228–57.

——— "Historic Crossing Places in the San Bernardino Mountains." Ms., 1931.

——— "San Bernardino Valley before the Americans Came." Ms., 1931.

——— "San Bernardino Valley in the Spanish Period," Annual Publications, Historical Society of Southern California, XII, Part III (1923), 10–28.

——— "Spanish Plans for an Inland Chain of Missions in California," Annual Publications, Historical Society of Southern California, XIX, Part II (1929), 243–64.

Bolton, Herbert Eugene. "In the South San Joaquin Ahead of Garcés," California Historical Society Quarterly, X, No. 3 (September 1931), 211–19.

Cleland, Robert Glass. From Wilderness to Empire. A History of California, ed. Glenn S. Dumke. Knopf, New York, 1959.

——— Pathfinders, Vol. I of the series California, ed. John Russell McCarthy. Powell Publishing Co., Los Angeles, 1929.

Coues, Elliott. On the Trail of a Spanish Pioneer, Garcés Diary, 1775–1776. 2 vols. Francis P. Harper, New York, 1900.

Crafts, Mrs. Eliza Persis (Russell) Robbins. Pioneer Days in the San Bernardino Valley. Redlands, 1906.

Dale, Harrison C. The Ashley-Smith Explorations and the Discovery of a Central Route to the Pacific, 1822–1829. The Arthur H. Clark Co., Cleveland, 1918.

Dunn, H. H. "Tracing the Pueblos to the Pacific," Touring Topics, XXII, No. 10 (October 1930), 48–50, 53.

Ellerbe, Rose L. "The Mother Vineyard," Touring Topics, XX, No. 11 (November 1928), 18–20.

Haenszel, Arda M. "Historic Sites in San Bernardino County," San Bernardino County Museum Association Quarterly, V, No. 2 (Winter, 1957), 1–36.

Hill, Joseph J. "Ewing Young in the Fur Trade of the Far Southwest, 1822–1839," Oregon Historical Society Quarterly, XXIV, No. 1 (March 1923), 1–35.

——— The History of Warner's Ranch and Its Environs. Privately printed, Los Angeles, 1927.

——— "The Old Spanish Trail, a Study of Spanish and Mexican Trade and Exploration Northwest from New Mexico to the Great Basin and California," Hispanic American Historical Review, IV, No. 3 (August 1921), 444–73.

Houston, Flora Belle. "When the Mormons Settled San Bernardino," Touring Topics, XXII, No. 4 (April 1930), 32–34, 52.

Lawrence, Eleanor. "Horse Thieves on the Spanish Trail," Touring Topics, XXIII, No. 1 (January 1931), 22–25, 55.

———— "Mexican Trade between Santa Fe and Los Angeles, 1830–1848," *California Historical Society Quarterly*, X, No. 1 (March 1931), 27–39.

Leadabrand, Russ. "Let's Explore a Byway . . . through Historic Holcomb Valley," *Westways*, LI, No. 9 (September 1959), 12–14.

Robinson, W. W. *The Story of San Bernardino County.* Title Insurance and Trust Company, San Bernardino, 1962.

Van Dyke, Dix. "A Modern Interpretation of the Garcés Route," *Publications, Historical Society of Southern California*, XIII, Part IV (1927), 353–59.

San Diego County

SAN DIEGO COUNTY was named after the harbor that Vizcaíno christened in 1602. It was one of the original 27 counties, and the city of San Diego has always been the county seat. (San Diego is Spanish for St. Didacus, a native of Spain and a Franciscan saint.) Many pre-state records of deeds and wills in Spanish are housed in the courthouse.

The Torrey Pines

Along the Torrey Pines grade and the plateau above, about two miles south of Del Mar, the famous Torrey Pines (*Pinus torreyana* Parry) cling to the precipitous cliffs in strangely twisted, wind-blown shapes. A distinct species, the only other place where these trees may be found is on Santa Rosa Island off the coast of southern California. Dr. Joseph L. Le Conte, in 1850, recognized them as a new species. Dr. C. C. Parry, then engaged with the Mexican Boundary Survey, was told of the find, and the two men named the aged trees after their former instructor at Columbia University, Dr. John Torrey.

The Painted Rocks of Poway

From Escondido south to the Mexican border, and possibly beyond, distinct and remarkable Indian pictographs can be found. Extending over a distance of about 50 miles in the Poway Valley region, they comprise not only the 11 rock paintings of the "maze" or "square" type already located by white men, but, according to old resident Indians, almost a score more of like design and workmanship in the hills above Poway Valley.

The Poway pictographs are distinct from any others in southern California, constituting a series of designs made up of squares and rectangles with occasional rows of concentric crosses. They are so uniform in "pattern, width of lines, coloring, thickness of paint, selection of sites and durability of color" that some students believe them to have all been made by one prehistoric artist.

The patterns used in these designs are of three types: "the square; the running, right-angled scroll; and the series of concentric crosses. The squares may be concentric in one pattern, and broken to fit each into the other in the next, but their lines are never crossed." The squares or the right angles of any one of these designs are so nearly of the same dimensions as to suggest the use of a measuring unit.

There is a marked similarity between these paintings in squares and rectangles in San Diego County and the more nearly perfect figures of the same type in Mitla and at San Juan de Teotihuacan, Mexico, where the temples of the Sun and Moon are located. Moreover, although the more common Indian paintings of many-legged bugs, birds, animals, and curious curved figures also occur in the Poway region, they never appear on the same boulders with these peculiar "maze" patterns, as they are commonly called. It would seem that these paintings were sacred to the Sun God, keeping guard over the precious water holes of that semi-desert region. Always in red pigment of a marvelously enduring quality, they were painted on the flat surface of granite boulders facing the east, and always they overlooked the approach to a spring.

The country around this area has many low hills with spurs running down from the higher elevations into Poway Valley, the basin of Lake Hodges, and other little valleys from north to south. Here, men of the Stone Age lived in crude rock houses above the springs. Remains of uncemented rock walls may still be seen at some of these ancient campsites. There, also, many implements of crude workmanship have been found, such as arrowheads, stone scrapers, knives, and hammers.

Near the western end of Lake Hodges, a large campsite of this type has been located where a "granite-lined creek bed" comes down into the lake. Here, also, are two of the rock paintings belonging to this special group. One consists of the scroll design only, while the other is of a very dim pattern of concentric squares. The latter, which overlooks a perpetual spring, is about three feet wide at the base and five feet high. Facing eastward, it stands about 20 feet back from the pool and the spring.

Across the narrow canyon from this rock is the entrance to a large cave, now closed in by landslides. On the western side of this cave, facing the east, the right-angled scroll design has been placed on an overhanging wall of the cavern overlooking an arm of the lake. It is about six by three feet in size, but was probably larger originally, since much of it has been worn away by the elements.

Another perpetual spring, far up in the Poway Valley, is guarded by the crude remains of two fortresses, crowning the summits of two low, isolated hills on either side of the spring. Ruins of uncemented stone walls still stand two or three feet high, some of them marking off small rooms. On one hill an entire room, about 16 × 16 feet, was built. Back of it is a cave, the entrance to which was evidently once walled in. Below this room a stone stockade reached nearly to the spring, which it was evidently built to protect, while the fortress on the opposite hill guarded that side of the spring.

At this camp a smaller series of painted squares, facing east, overlooks the spring. Its exposed position has caused the work to be gradually erased by the action of sun and rain and blowing sands. In time it will be completely obliterated.

Other rock pictures of this unusual group are located, roughly speaking: (1) about a mile west of Escondido; (2) in Highland Valley about three miles east of Highway 395; (3) about four miles west of the Poway post office near the Peñasquitos or Poway Creek; (4) about two miles east of the Lakeside–Ramona highway just northwest of San Vicente Creek, and about two miles southeast of the Earl School; (5) near El Cajón Mountain, about six miles northeast of Lakeside; (6) about two miles east of Alpine near The Willows; (7) on Sweetwater River just north of Lawson Valley and about halfway between Dehesa and the Japatul School; (8) about three miles northeast of

Dulzura near Barber Mountain; and (9) about three miles southwest of Dulzura near Otay Mountain in the San Ysidro Range.

The Discovery and Naming of San Diego

The bay of San Diego was first seen on September 28, 1542, by Juan Rodríguez Cabrillo, a Portuguese navigator sent out by Antonio de Mendoza, viceroy of Mexico, to explore the coast of New Spain and to discover, if possible, the elusive strait of Anián. Cabrillo, with his chief pilot, Bartolomé Ferrelo, in the tiny vessels *San Salvador* and *Victoria* anchored in that "port, closed and very good, which they named San Miguel" and which Sebastián Vizcaíno in 1602 renamed San Diego. It is believed by local historians who have made an intensive study of the topography of the region that Ballast Point was the most likely place for Cabrillo to have landed. One-half acre of land within the Fort Rosecrans Military Reservation on Point Loma was set aside by the government in 1913 as Cabrillo National Monument. It is near the end of Point Loma, south and slightly west of Ballast Point. The main feature of the little park is the old Point Loma lighthouse.

It was not until 60 years later that the bay of San Diego was again visited by white men. On May 5, 1602, Sebastián Vizcaíno, with the two ships *San Diego* and *Santo Tomás* and the little frigate *Tres Reyes*, sailed north from Acapulco. He had been sent out by the new viceroy, the Conde de Monterey, to explore the coast of Alta California for safe and convenient harbors in which the Manila galleon might stop for repairs and the recuperation of scurvy-stricken crews,

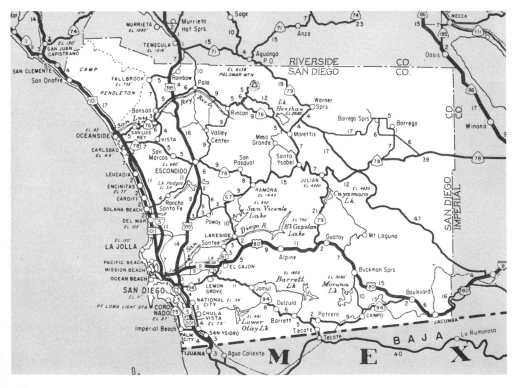

and from which observations on the whereabouts of English pirate ships might be made.

Early in November, Vizcaíno reached the port that Cabrillo had seen before him. In his diary this entry is found:

"On the twelfth of the said month, which was the day of the glorious San Diego, the general, admiral, religious, captains, ensigns, and almost all the men went on shore. A hut was built and mass was said in celebration of the feast of Señor San Diego."

Thus was San Diego Bay named, and the first recorded house of Christian worship in Alta California, although a crude and humble one, was erected.

The Settlement of San Diego

In the 1760's, rumors that the Russians were planning to extend their colonies from Alaska down the Pacific Coast to Upper California caused King Carlos III of Spain to order the viceroy of New Spain to investigate the danger. The viceroy transmitted the order to José de Gálvez, visitador general, and Gálvez put into effect what had long been contemplated—the settlement of Alta California. His decision was influenced by personal ambition as well as by fear that the land might become the possession of Russia or England. In 1768, 226 years after the discovery of San Diego by Juan Rodríguez Cabrillo, Gálvez organized the first colonizing project. Gaspar de Portolá was appointed military governor of Alta California and was placed in command of the entire expedition, and Father Junípero Serra was named Padre Presidente of the missions that were to be established in the new province. Officers, priests, soldiers, sailors, laborers, and southern Indian retainers, perhaps 300 men in all, made up the personnel of this, the first band of settlers dispatched to California. The primary aim of the expedition was the protection of the port of Monterey, but a base was also to be established at San Diego. The Franciscan friars were to found missions and convert the Indians, and the soldiers were to guard the country and protect the mission settlements.

The expedition was divided into five companies, three of which went by sea in the ships *San Carlos, San Antonio,* and *San José,* and two by land, one under command of Portolá himself and the other under Fernando Rivera y Moncada, his second in command. The second of the sea expeditions to leave La Paz, under command of Juan Pérez in the ship *San Antonio,* was the first to arrive at San Diego, on April 11, 1769, after a voyage of 55 days. On April 19, the *San Carlos,* with Vicente Vila in command and Pedro Fages with his 25 Catalonian volunteers, arrived after a voyage of great suffering, lasting 110 days. Rivera, accompanied by Father Crespí, the famous diarist, arrived on May 14, after a march of 51 days from Velicatá in Baja California. Governor Portolá and a few men of the second land expedition arrived June 29. The rest of this division, with Father Serra, who had made the journey while suffering from an ulcered foot and leg, arrived last, on July 1. The *San José* and all

aboard were lost at sea. Ninety-three had died aboard the other ships, and many of the Indians had died or deserted. There were left only 126 settlers at San Diego.

Already advanced in years, Father Serra endured experiences of great hardship and privation with a cheerfulness that ignored all physical ills and dangers for the cause to which he gave his life. His fiery enthusiasm for the conversion of the Indians of California was never dampened by any amount of suffering or discouragement.

With him, in that first gathering at San Diego, were Father Crespí (the friend of his youth, with whom he had studied in the convent of Majorca, and with whom he had come to Mexico in 1749), and Fathers Vizcaíno, Parrón, and Gómez, besides Portolá and several other government officers. Immediately after the assembling of the expedition, Portolá, with Captain Rivera and a band of soldiers, accompanied by Fathers Crespí and Gómez, and Miguel Costansó, cosmographer, engineer, and diarist, set out northward to search for the port of Monterey, where the first northern mission was to be established. Father Serra remained at San Diego to undertake the founding of the first of the Franciscan missions to be established in the wilderness of Alta California.

Mission San Diego de Alcalá, Mother of the Alta California Missions

Immediately after the departure of Portolá and his men, Padre Junípero Serra, on July 16, just 15 days after his arrival at the port of San Diego, founded Misión San Diego de Alcalá. The ceremony was performed in the presence of 20 or 30 men, on what later came to be known as Presidio Hill. Here, overlooking the bay and the river, the first temporary chapel was erected and the first cross was raised.

The order of ceremony followed at this first founding was much the same as that subsequently used in establishing all of the 20 other missions that finally composed the chain. Helen Hunt Jackson describes the procedure: "The routine was the same in all cases. A cross was set up; a booth of branches built; the ground and the booth were consecrated by holy water, and christened by the name of a saint; a mass was performed; the neighboring Indians, if there were any, were roused and summoned by the ringing of bells swung on limbs of trees; presents of cloth and trinkets were given them to inspire them with trust, and thus a Mission was founded. Two monks (never, at first, more) were appointed to take charge of the cross and booth, and to win, baptize, convert, and teach all the Indians to be reached in the region. They had for guard and help a few soldiers, and sometimes a few already partly civilized and Christianized Indians; several head of cattle, some tools and seeds, and holy vessels for the church service, completed their store of weapons . . . with which to conquer the wilderness and its savages."

The little settlement at San Diego had, perhaps, greater hardships to endure in the beginning than any of the missions that followed. For a whole year Father Serra labored in vain among the Indians before even one child was baptized. Supplies, too, were insufficient and at the end of six months the whole enterprise was threatened with failure.

Meanwhile, Portolá and his men, under great hardships, were struggling northward on what proved to be an unsuccessful endeavor.

Portolá's Trail to Monterey

Leaving the port of San Diego on July 14, 1769, Portolá, with Fray Juan Crespí as chronicler of the expedition, had started north on the long journey to Monterey, where the second mission was to be established.

Passing what is now called Mission Bay, the party came to an Indian village near the northeast point of the cove. Leaving the shore here, they passed into Rose Canyon and camped at some pools. The following day the route lay through Soledad Valley with its Indian villages, one of which was located near the site of Sorrento. Camp was again made in San Dieguito Canyon, near Del Mar, with another Indian village not far distant.

On July 16 and 17 the trail led by way of the present county road called El Camino Real (the main highway all through the nineteenth century) past San Elijo Lagoon, Batequitos Lagoon, Agua Hedionda Creek, and Buena Vista Creek, near Carlsbad. Many Indian villages were passed along the way, all of them friendly. On July 18 the verdant valley of San Juan Capistrano, the first name given to the valley of San Luís Rey, was reached and camp made. The location was pronounced by Fray Crespí to be an excellent site for the placing of a mission, and several years later Mission San Luís Rey was indeed founded near this very spot.

From the valley of San Juan Capistrano northward Portolá passed, successively, the campsites near Home Ranch and Las Pulgas Canyon, called by the explorers the valley of Santa Margarita and the valley of Santa Praxedis de los Rosales (because of the numerous Castilian roses and other flowers growing there). These sites are commemorated in the name of the old Rancho Santa Margarita y Las Flores, north and west of Mission San Luís Rey.

Passing into the region of what is now Orange County on July 22, the party continued north. Six months later, returning from their fruitless search for the port of Monterey, sick and weary, their provisions nearly gone, the little company passed over much the same route as on the earlier trip, but the homeward marches were long, and several of the old camps were passed without stopping. On January 21, 1770, camp was made apparently on San Onofre Creek, and on January 24 the party rejoined the group anxiously awaiting their return at the newly established Mission of San Diego.

There, Portolá found that the supply ship, which had left for San Blas six months before, had not returned and that provisions were almost exhausted. In his discouragement he considered abandonment of the colony, but he would not yet admit defeat. Father Serra, although greatly concerned about the critical state of affairs, had no intention of giving up the enterprise, and, when the hour seemed darkest, his faith and determination were rewarded by the arrival of the San Antonio, and the immediate settlement of Alta California was assured.

The search for the lost port of Monterey was renewed as soon as possible. Father Serra went north by sea, leaving Fathers Luís Jayme and Francisco Dumetz to carry on the work at San Diego. The land expedition under Portolá camped again at Sorrento on April 17, Agua Hedionda on the 18th, Home Ranch on the 19th, San Onofre Canyon on the 20th, and entered Orange County the next day.

El Camino Real, the Royal Road

"It will be interesting to many to know that the original El Camino Real, or Royal Road, stretched from Guatemala to Mexico City and thence to Sonoma. The most modern section, established in the late eighteenth century by Spanish soldiers and missionary friars, is the route from San Diego to Sonoma, in California.

"In attempting to re-trace that section of the California route between San Diego and Los Angeles, it has become apparent that there was no single road, but that, in fact, there were many routes, all used at one period or another by friars, Indians, and rancheros."

The modern highway called El Camino Real follows quite closely in some places the old road between the missions, but in other places it varies greatly from the original route. Nevertheless, "the motorist who drives from San Diego to San Francisco over the King's Highway can rightfully feel that he is re-tracing the paths of the padres."

At one time the highway was marked by several hundred mission-bell guideposts, each one bearing a sign directing the traveler to the next mission and also to the next town. Each guidepost was surmounted by a bell weighing 100 pounds or more. These markers were placed in 1906 and the years following by historians Mr. and Mrs. A. S. C. Forbes and the El Camino Real Association. Through the years they have disappeared until only a few of the originals are left. A program to place along El Camino Real new guideposts of the same style began in the early 1960's.

On November 24, 1963, the 250th anniversary of the birth of Father Serra, bronze plaques were dedicated at the northern and southern terminals of El Camino Real (SRL 784) as he knew it and helped to blaze it. One was placed at Mission San Diego de Alcalá and the other at Mission Dolores in San Francisco.

The Second Mission Site

The first site of the mission at San Diego proved to be unsatisfactory because of its proximity to the presidio, and the fathers soon realized that it would be better for the Indian neophytes to be removed some distance from the influence of the soldiers. Furthermore, a location affording more water for agricultural purposes was desirable.

Mission buildings of wood were constructed in 1774 five miles up the valley from the presidio, and considerable progress had been made in the conversion of the Indians by October 1775. At that time, the number of neophytes totaled 76, and 60 additional converts were baptized by the fathers on the day before the feast of St. Francis, October 4, 1775.

The hatred of the unconverted Indians, however, finally culminated in a fierce attack upon the unprotected mission on the night of November 4, 1775. Father Jayme, who, "with the shining light of martyrdom in his eyes, and the fierce joy of fearlessness in his heart," sought to quiet the mob by walking toward them, his hand extended in blessing and with his usual salutation, "Love God, my children!" was ruthlessly slain. A stone cross has been erected to Padre Luís Jayme, Alta California's first martyr priest.

The mission buildings were all destroyed at the time of this insurrection, but a temporary church of adobe was soon begun and was ready for use in October 1776. A more spacious and substantial building was completed in 1780. By 1800 San Diego had become the most populous as well as one of the wealthiest of all the California missions. A more elaborate church was dedicated on November 12, 1813. Within a few years extensive fields and vineyards were being irrigated by water brought over an aqueduct through Mission Valley. The old mission dam (SRL 52) built across San Diego River gorge in 1807–16 and constructed of granite and cement 12 feet thick is still in fair condition, although choked with drift. It stands as a remarkable testimony to the excellence of California's first irrigation and engineering venture. Recognized by the Department of the Interior as a National Historic Landmark, the dam

is located six miles north of Interstate 8 on Old Mission Gorge Road. The old route branches left from the present Mission Gorge Road at a point about four miles from the freeway.

The second Mission San Diego de Alcalá (SRL 242) stands just north of Interstate 8 on Friars Road, off Murphy Canyon Road. Little of the original mission except the façade and the base of the belfry remains today, but the church and tower were restored by the Native Sons of the Golden West and other organizations in 1931. Under the scholarly supervision of J. Marshall Miller, restoration was made true to the old mission in design and decorations and is exact in every detail. A few old palm and olive trees are still standing near the mission.

The First Presidio in Alta California

Father Serra had dedicated the cross, July 16, 1769, on what later came to be known as Presidio Hill. In the shadow of this first cross to be raised in Alta California, the first mission was begun and the first presidio was established. On the same spot, on July 16, 1915, 146 years later, a group of earnest San Diegans placed the Serra Cross, which stands on Presidio Hill today. From the heap of clay upon which it was raised, old tile from early buildings had been dug up and incorporated into the memorial cross. On it is a bronze tablet bearing this legend:

Here the First Citizen, Fray Junípero Serra,
Planted Civilization in California.
Here he First Raised the Cross,
Here Began the First Mission,
Here Founded the First Town—San Diego,
    July 16, 1769.

Serra Cross, Presidio Hill, San Diego

Presidio Hill, being situated a little back from the river and the bay, afforded an excellent outlook over the surrounding country and made fortification easy as well. It was near the site of the ancient Indian village of Cosoy, ranchería of the Diegueños, and here, for over 60 years, San Diego was located within the adobe walls of the Spanish garrison.

The presidio, an essential feature of Spanish colonization, was usually a fortified square, constructed at first of wood and later of brick or stone, inside of which the commander's residence and the chapel formed the central points around which the garrison for the soldiers, the officers' quarters, and adobe houses for provisions and military supplies were located.

On January 11, 1776, the Presidio of San Diego became the meeting place of three men intimately associated with the beginnings of Alta California, Juan Bautista de Anza, Fernando Rivera y Moncada, and José Francisco de Ortega, who arrived there with Fathers Vicente Fuster and Pedro Font to discuss what measures should be taken to punish the Indians responsible for the burning of the mission and the death of Father Jayme.

On his way into San Diego, Anza and his men had camped on January 9 at the San Luís Rey River, then called the Arroyo de San Juan Capistrano. On January 10 they stopped in Soledad Valley, south of Del Mar about at Sorrento and some ten miles north of San Diego.

Finding that Governor Rivera expected him to remain at San Diego until danger from further Indian uprisings was past, Anza tarried until February, when word from San Gabriel informed him that there were no longer sufficient supplies for the band of San Francisco colonists he had left there. On February 9, in spite of storms and swollen streams, Anza left San Diego, camping that night on the Arroyo de Agua Hedionda, a creek that enters the ocean just south of Carlsbad. On February 12 he rejoined the settlers anxiously awaiting his return at San Gabriel.

San Diego passed, with the rest of California, from Spanish to Mexican control in 1822, "without much more than a ripple." Under Mexican rule it entered a little more turbulent period, when frequent revolts occurred both between the Californians and the Mexican governors and between the rival factions of the Californians themselves. José María Echeandía, the first governor sent from Mexico, established his headquarters at the Presidio of San Diego, which remained the capital of Alta California during his administration, 1825–31.

It was during this time that the second overland party of Americans to enter California came by way of San Diego County under the leadership of Sylvester Pattie and his son, James Ohio Pattie. The journal of this perilous westward trek of American trappers, written by the younger Pattie, constitutes one of the most stirring narratives of frontier history. This expedition, moreover, opened up a new overland route to the coast and added much to the knowledge of the great Southwest.

Coming down the Gila and Colorado rivers as far as the tidewaters of the Gulf of California, the party crossed the desert to the Spanish settlements on the northern coast of Baja California. At Mission Santa Catalina, they were harshly received and conducted to San Diego in Alta California under heavy guard, arriving there on March 27, 1828.

Governor Echeandía was fearful and suspicious because of the recent expedition of Jedediah Strong Smith, who on January 1, 1827, had come to San Diego to apply for a passport and was peremptorily refused. Consequently, the governor treated the newcomers cruelly, imprisoning them for several months. Under this harsh treatment, the elder Pattie, already weakened by long privation, died.

Gradually, the younger Pattie was able to soften the governor's attitude by serving as interpreter and by using his knowledge of vaccination to save the population in a smallpox epidemic. Finally, in 1830, he was given passage to Mexico City, whence he made his way back to his native Kentucky.

After Echeandía's administration the presidio was gradually abandoned. The retired soldiers were often given grants of land and went to live on their ranchos or built homes in the town at the foot of the hill. Within a decade the old garrison was deserted and dismantled.

On December 25, 1838, earthworks were thrown up on Presidio Hill preparatory to an expected attack from José Castro, leader of the northern faction then supposedly threatening the San Diegans. Two cannon from Fort Guijarros were mounted, but the anticipated attack did not materialize.

The earthworks on Presidio Hill were never used by the Mexicans. On the coming of the Americans in 1846, they were improved by Commodore Robert F. Stockton, and United States troops, including Company B of the famous Mormon Battalion, were stationed there during the brief period of military rule before California's entrance into the Union. The old American fort, of which scarcely a vestige remains, was called Fort Stockton (SRL 54) during that period. The Native Sons of the Golden West have placed a flagstaff and bronze tablet on the site to commemorate it.

The presidio has been almost completely obliterated by storms, earthquakes, and settlers, who used the materials for their homes. The walls of the presidio chapel, the old Spanish garrison, and the first civilian houses long ago crumbled into shapeless mounds of earth, but in 1929 plans were completed for preserving the hill and marking some of its ancient landmarks. Through the consistent and indefatigable efforts of George W. Marston, extending over a period of years, the land was gradually purchased and ultimately presented to the city. Thus, "the cradle of the state's civilization" was finally rescued from complete oblivion and made a public park.

Here, on July 16, 1929, the 160th anniversary of the founding of San Diego, the Junípero Serra Museum was dedicated. The museum, the Junípero Serra Cross, the site of the first mission building, the site of the old Spanish garrison, and the site of Fort Stockton are included within Presidio Park. Beside Taylor Street at the foot of the hill, also within the park, is the site of the first two date palms planted in California *(SRL 67)*. These historic trees are thought to have been planted by Father Serra in 1769. Neglected and abused for many years, they were finally enclosed in a picket fence in 1887. One of the palms stood until June 6, 1957, when it had to be removed. It was near this spot that the four divisions of the Sacred Expedition of Gálvez were reunited July 1, 1769, when Father Serra limped into the Spanish camp located near this spot. This is also the area where the victims of scurvy were buried in 1769.

The site of the Presidio of San Diego *(SRL 59)*, first non-Indian settlement in the nation's most populous state, has been registered as a National Historic Landmark by the Department of the Interior.

Mission San Luís Rey de Francia

"The stately magnificence of San Luís Rey, more typically Moorish than any other mission, is impressive [even] today ... and in the time of its greatest wealth and power it might easily startle and arrest the attention of the traveller." It is situated on a slight eminence in a beautiful, secluded valley four miles inland from Oceanside. There, on June 13, 1798, Father Fermín Francisco de Lasuén, permanent successor to Father Serra as Padre Presidente of the missions, led the solemn ceremonies that celebrated the founding of Misión San Luís Rey de Francia *(SRL 239)*.

The first substantial church building, which was completed in 1802, was planned by Father Antonio Peyrí and erected under his direction. In 1811 the foundations for the present structure were laid, and on the feast of St. Francis, October 4, 1815, the completed church was dedicated. It was constructed of adobe and faced with burnt brick. Its beautifully proportioned façade, its graceful doorway and massive bell tower, its corridors and quadrangular patio filled with flowers and shrubs, long ago called forth the admiration of Duhaut-Cilly, who visited it in 1827. His description creates for us a picture of unusual splendor set in the midst of the wilderness of old California:

"The buildings were drawn on a large and

Mission San Luís Rey de Francia

ample plan, wholly the idea of the Padre (Peyrí); he directed the execution of it, in which he was assisted by a very skillful man, who had contributed also to the building of those at Santa Barbara; so, although these are much more sumptuous, at that place may be recognized the same hand. This building forms a large square of five hundred feet on each side. The main façade is a long peristyle borne on thirty-two square pillars supporting round arches. The edifice is composed, indeed, of only a ground-floor, but its elevation, of fine proportions, gives it as much grace as nobleness. It is covered with a tiled roof, flattened, around which reaches, as much without as within the square, a terrace with an elegant balustrade, which stimulates still more the height. Within is seen a large court, neat and leveled, around which pillars and arches similar to those of the peristyle support a long cloister, by which one communicates with all the dependencies of the Mission."

Under the efficient management of Father Peyrí, lasting over a period of 30 years, San Luís Rey prospered and became "a model of energetic, well directed endeavor and growth." By the close of 1801 over 300 neophytes had been enrolled. Numerous cattle, sheep, and horses grazed the surrounding fields, and large gardens supplied the inhabitants of the mission with food.

Not only was Father Peyrí materially successful in his mission; the love and veneration of his Indian charges was a still greater token of his worth. It has been said that he excelled all the other missionaries in his record of achievement. "He was zealous, sensible, and energetic. He knew what he wanted and how to secure it. The Indians worked willingly for him."

When the law expelling all Spaniards from Alta California was passed in 1829, Father Peyrí stole sorrowfully away to San Diego during the night in order to avoid saying goodbye to his Indians. He boarded the ship, which was already weighing anchor. But the Indians, who had followed him with swift ponies, arrived just in time to receive his farewell blessing. He stood with outstretched arms on the ship's deck, while the Indians begged him to remain.

George Wharton James says that "for many years the Indians left behind at San Luís Rey were in the habit of placing candles and flowers before the picture of Father Peyrí and offering prayers to him, pleading with him to return. Even after his death this was kept up, the simplehearted Indians preferring to pray to a Saint whose goodness they had known and felt, rather than to those of whom they knew nothing but what they were told."

After secularization, the Indians at San Luís Rey were scattered and the property was sold. It was later returned to the Church by the United States government, but it had suffered much from neglect and misuse, its garden court even having been used for bullfights. United States troops used it as a military post during the Mexican War and for some time afterwards.

San Luís Rey was later restored, and on May 12, 1893, it was rededicated as a Franciscan seminary. It is one of four missions still in the hands of the founding order. Something of the original simple beauty of the old mission buildings has been lost in the process of restoration, but continuing work is aimed toward a re-creation of the original establishment.

Rancho Santa Margarita y Las Flores

For many miles around, Mission San Luís Rey possessed great ranchos on which thousands of head of cattle grazed in mission days. Among these vast domains was Rancho Santa Margarita y Las Flores, to the north, long one of the princely estates of California and now, since 1942, Camp Joseph H. Pendleton of the United States Marine Corps.

Fragmentary ruins of the stout adobe walls of the outpost of San Pedro, or Las Flores *(SRL 616)*, built by the mission fathers about 1823, may still be seen on a knoll overlooking the blue waters of the Pacific. For many years this building was the hospice where travelers between Missions San Luís Rey and San Juan Capistrano stopped to rest. Nearby, below the hill, is the Las Flores rancho house erected by Marcos A. Forster, son of Don Juan Forster who had purchased the estate of 133,441 acres from Pío and Andrés Pico in 1864. It is a large two-story adobe of the Monterey type, with inviting patio, verandas below and above extending across front and sides, and in the rear a low, one-story wing rambling from room to room. Set amid age-old trees, facing the ocean, this delightful old house, with its sense of peace and tranquillity, presents a fine picture of early rancho life. These landmarks are quite close to Interstate Highway 5 between San Clemente and Oceanside, but the access road at this point has been closed by Camp Pendleton. However, they may be reached, with permission, through the main gate of Camp Pendleton near Oceanside. At a point one mile north of the gate, Stuart Mesa Road branches left from Vandegrift Boulevard, the main highway through the base, and leads about seven miles to a junction with Pulgas Road. Here stands the old Marcos Forster adobe, which later became the residence of the Magee family. On a hillside above are the ruins of the mission outpost.

Overlooking the valley of the Santa Margarita River stands the 20-room adobe Santa Margarita rancho house, now the private residence of the commanding general of Camp Pendleton. It is at the left of Vandegrift Boulevard, about seven and one-half miles north of the main gate. Parts of this building, as well as the nearby chapel, once a winery and blacksmith shop, are said to have been built in mission days. Juan Forster and later owners enlarged the house, and finally it was remodeled by the Marine Corps.

Asistencia de San Antonio de Pala

The most distinctive of Father Peyrí's activities was the founding in 1816 of the Asistencia de San Antonio de Pala *(SRL 243)* as a branch of Mission San Luís Rey, located in the Valley of Pala about 20 miles from the mission. A thousand Indian neophytes were soon enrolled from the rancherías of the district.

Pala Chapel is especially noted for its picturesque campanile and for its original Indian frescoes, for many years hidden by a coat of whitewash. The campanile stands apart from the main chapel building, in the old cemetery. It has been restored and is now joined to the main building by a little arched gateway. In its two graceful arches still hang the ancient bells which, for many generations, have called the Indians to prayer.

The Indian population of mission days has disappeared from Pala, but the evicted Palatinguas from Warner's Ranch who now live there and other Indians from rancherías for many miles around still attend the services of the chapel and give freely of their labor for its restoration and preservation.

Pala Chapel stands at the base of Palomar Mountain about six miles east of Highway 395. A modern highway up the mountain follows somewhat the same route that the old Emigrant Trail took to Warner's Ranch.

Santa Ysabel

The Chapel of Santa Ysabel *(SRL 369)* was established by Father Fernando Martín on September 20, 1818, as an asistencia or outpost of the mission at San Diego. A permanent structure was erected later, but at what date is unknown. For many years a portion of one of the walls remained, and each spring this was used to form one end of an improvised chapel of branches and tules where Mass was said for the Indians of the region. Two ancient bells hung on a rude wooden beam nearby and a tall cross made of saplings marked the consecrated spot. The appearance of the chapel has been described thus:

"When the festival time approaches, this picturesque church springs into beauty as if by magic. The walls are made of verdant boughs, interwoven with branches of green, and wild flowers are brought in to decorate the altar—a pathetic evidence of the sincerity of the worshippers of the district."

Nothing remains of the original buildings. The present chapel, built in 1924, is just south of the site of the old structure. Nearby is the picturesque and ancient cemetery. The historic bells vanished mysteriously in 1926. The Chapel of Santa Ysabel is on Highway 79 one and one-half miles north of the town of the same name.

Old Town

The old San Diego Presidio left an heir in the tiny town that had grown up at the foot of Presidio Hill as an overflow from the garrison. As the tide of immigration increased, the settlement on the lowlands grew and prospered, and there the romantic, pastoral life of San Diego was lived, leaving its imprint upon the adobe houses which still cluster about the plaza.

The Old Town Plaza *(SRL 63)*, once noisy and dusty with bullfights, Judas-hangings, and other entertainments typical of its Spanish-Mexican population, today lies in a perpetual siesta amid the refreshing green of lawns and shrubbery. Above it floats the American flag, reminding one of that memorable day, July 29, 1846, when a group of men under Lieutenant Stephen C. Rowan was ordered by Captain Samuel F. du Pont of the *Cyane* to raise the Stars and Stripes on the flagpole at the plaza. Twenty minutes later, Frémont and his California Battalion arrived on the spot. Old Glory was raised again in November 1846, when, according to Winifred Davidson, "amid shots from the California Rangers, young Albert B. Smith nailed up the flag to the flagpole, Señora María Antonia Machado de Silvas having boldly rushed out from her home and cut away the halyards, rescuing the Mexican flag which had been flying there for some unknown period."

The incoming practical Yankees soon saw that the old San Diego was unsuitable for a seaport town, and New San Diego, located on San Diego Bay, at length superseded it. William Heath Davis built the first wharf there in 1850, but his venture was a financial failure and nothing more was attempted until 1867, when Alonzo E. Horton arrived and soon afterward laid out the nucleus of the present city. But something of the peace and simple charm of the past still lingers about the little plaza at Old Town, and the lure of its quaint adobes brings many a visitor to the gates of the modern city.

Of the older adobe buildings that once stood about the plaza, none remain today. A few of the later ones, with low tiled roofs and cool corridors, flower-filled patios and many memories, still face the quiet plaza: on the east corner, the Bandini house, much altered; on the southeast, the Estudillo house, popularly but erroneously known as "Ramona's Marriage Place"; and on the southwest, the Machado adobe with its romantic and colorful associations. Nearby are other old buildings of equal interest: Casa de Soto, Casa de Pedrorena, Casa de Stewart, Casa de Alvarez, and the little Chapel of the Immaculate Conception. And, mingled with these, are places that are associated with the coming of the Americans and the building of a new order.

Casa de Carrillo

Casa de Carrillo stood on the southwest side of Calhoun Street between Taylor and Wallace streets. It was variously known as the Pear Garden House, the Fitch House, and Rose's Garden House, according to the different owners. It was one of the earliest and largest of the great casas in which the aristocratic Spanish families of the period lived. Begun as early as 1810 in the old pear orchard planted in 1807 by Francisco María Ruiz, it became the home of Joaquín Carrillo and Ignacia López de Carrillo. It was the social center of their day. From its doors, that remarkable double wedding journey set forth in the spring of 1827 for Monterey, Agustín Zamorano and Luisa Argüello, and Romualdo Pacheco and Ramona Carrillo, the principals, together with Governor Echeandía and nearly all of San Diego forming its train. Here, too, Henry Delano Fitch, the gallant New Bedford sea captain, met and wooed the beautiful Josefa Carrillo and eloped with her to South America in 1829. The house was purchased in 1866 by Louis Rose, a pioneer businessman prominent in the affairs of Old San Diego after 1850. In 1874, while occupied by Judge Benjamin Hayes, great authority on Span-

ish land grants, the old home was revisited by Josefa Carrillo de Fitch, nearly 50 years after her dramatic elopement.

For years a small restored adobe *(SRL 74)* at the northeast end of Wallace Street has been pointed out as a remnant of Casa de Carrillo. Further research has now established this identification as erroneous. The little structure, which is now a clubhouse on the Presidio Hills Golf Course, was probably built by Lorenzo Soto after 1849. It does not appear on a map drawn that year by Cave J. Couts.

The Estudillo Adobe

The Estudillo adobe *(SRL 53)* was built about 1827 by José Antonio Estudillo. It was a center of hospitality, receiving a brilliant company of friends from San Diego to Monterey, and Don José's wife, Doña Victoria, was known as Lady Bountiful to the entire countryside.

The house was once topped by a cupola from which the family and guests could in safety watch the bullfights and other entertainments staged on the adjoining plaza. In 1846 it "became a sanctuary" for all the women and children while Old Town was occupied by American troops and guns from Fort Stockton startled the sleepy pueblo.

The old house, with its 12 rooms and long beamed chapel, all opening onto a spacious inner court, is well preserved, and the lovely patio garden, with its fountain and many varieties of trees and shrubs bright with fruit and flowers, affords a vivid picture of pastoral California. Within its walls are many valuable Spanish, Indian, and early American antiquities, gathered early in this century by T. P. Getz.

The Bandini House

The Bandini house *(SRL 72)*, at 2660 Calhoun Street, built also about 1827, was originally a one-story adobe, a second story being added when it passed into the hands of the Seeley family. Broad balconies encircle it above and below, retaining the old-time grace and charm of Spanish Californian architecture despite modernization of the building. Juan Bandini, a native of Peru, was for nearly 40 years one of the leading citizens of Alta California. He took a prominent part in its affairs and saw it pass from Spanish to Mexican control in 1822.

Juan Bandini's daughters were noted for their

Casa de Bandini, Old Town, San Diego

beauty, and his home was a center of social gaiety as well as of political affairs for nearly 20 years. Arcadia Bandini married the young pioneer Yankee, Abel Stearns, and her sister Ysidora married another American, Cave J. Couts, while Josefa married Pedro Carrillo. Juan Bandini, himself a famous dancer, introduced the waltz to Alta California society.

Don Juan was friendly to the American cause, and his house was used by Robert F. Stockton as his headquarters during the period of American occupation in 1846. His daughters there made one of the first American flags in California. Here, too, on December 9, 1846, after a harrowing three nights' journey of 35 miles made in bare feet over country luxuriantly covered with prickly pears and guarded by mounted Californians, Lieutenant Edward Beale, with his Indian servant and Kit Carson, the scout, delivered the message from General Stephen W. Kearny to Commodore Stockton calling for sadly needed reinforcements after the battle of San Pasqual. As a result of the bravery of these men, Kearny and his soldiers, hungry and footsore, many of them wounded, arrived at Old Town, San Diego, December 12, 1846. There on the plaza, opposite the old Bandini and Estudillo houses, the D.A.R., in 1920, placed a granite boulder bearing a bronze tablet marking the end of the Kearny trail.

The Bandini house was used as a stage station by A. L. Seeley in the 1860's and was then known as the Cosmopolitan Hotel. The building was restored about 1930 by Cave J. Couts, Jr., grandson of Juan Bandini. It has since passed out of the Bandini family.

Other Old Town Adobes

Casa de Pedrorena (SRL 70), at 2616 San Diego Avenue, was the home of Miguel de Pedrorena, a native of Madrid and a man of high birth and excellent education. He came to San Diego in 1838, and, being courteous and polite in manner and of a gracious bearing, won the heart and hand of María Antonia Estudillo. Don Miguel was a member of the Constitutional Convention at Monterey in 1849.

Casa de Machado (SRL 71), at 2741 San Diego Avenue, is one of four or five similar adobe houses built by José Manuel Machado for himself and his married daughters on the large town place where he first settled. This, one of two such homes which survive, was built for María Antonia Machado de Silvas and is almost an exact duplicate of the old Wrightington house, razed in the 1890's. This historic spot, at the south corner of San Diego Avenue and Wallace Street, served as Colonel John C. Frémont's headquarters in 1846.

The Stewart house (SRL 73) was built by José Manuel Machado for his daughter, Rosa, who married John C. Stewart, a shipmate of Richard Henry Dana, Jr. Dana describes his visit to the house in 1859 in his book *Two Years Before the Mast*. It was still occupied in 1932 by Jack Stewart's eldest daughter, Rosa. Casa de Stewart, a clapboard-covered adobe, is located on the northeast side of Congress Street northwest of Mason Street.

Casa de Pedrorena, Old Town, San Diego

Casa de López, known as "La Casa Larga" ("the long house"), was built about 1835 by Juan Francisco López, a member of one of the older San Diegan families. It was located on what later became the northeast side of Jefferson Street between Mason and Twiggs streets, with one corner in the path of Jefferson Street. One room of this house served as quarters for Father Antonio Ubach, pastor of Old Town. Another occupant at two different times was Matías Moreno, secretary to Pío Pico, last Mexican governor of Alta California. Jefferson Street has been obliterated by freeway construction at this point. A nearby adobe (SRL 60) has long been identified incorrectly as the Casa de López. It is located at 3890 Twiggs Street, at the southwest end of the street. In reality, it was built by Miguel Alvarez in 1851.

Casa de Cota (SRL 75) stood on the north corner of Twiggs and Congress streets until World War II, when it was destroyed by United States Army bulldozers. It was said to have been built about 1835 by Juan or Ramón Cota, but construction may have taken place some years later.

Chapel of the Immaculate Conception

One of the most interesting buildings in Old Town is the Chapel of the Immaculate Conception (SRL 49), on Conde Street southwest of San Diego Avenue. The adobe chapel was originally built in the 1850's as the home of John Brown and was sold by him to José Antonio Aguirre, who presented it to the Catholic congregation, after restoring and altering it to fit the needs of a church. It was dedicated on November 21, 1858.

The chapel was the special charge of Father Antonio D. Ubach, a native of Catalonia, who was educated at Cape Girardeau, Missouri. He traveled thousands of miles as a missionary among the Indians, and came to San Diego in 1866, where he was placed in charge of the Catholic parish. He brought the first organ to San Diego, and also a football with which he played with the boys on the plaza. He had charge of many valuable relics and records of early Spanish days, but the greater part of his work was among the Indians, by whom he was greatly beloved, and with whom he had much influence. It is said that he was the original of the "Father Gaspara" of Helen Hunt Jackson's novel *Ramona*, and he claimed to have known the originals of the char-

acters in the story and their families. Father
Ubach's death in March 1907 "was the sundering
of the last link which connected the new day with
the olden time." He had seen the final transfer of
the church's activities from Old Town to New
San Diego in 1875, and had lived to see the dawn-
ing of a new era and a new century.

The chapel was replaced in 1916 by the present
mission-style church on San Diego Avenue. In
1937 the old adobe was restored and rebuilt a few
feet away from its original site.

Pioneer Americans at Old Town

One of the pioneer newspapers in California
and the earliest to be published in San Diego
was the *San Diego Herald*, edited by J. Judson
Ames. It began in New Town, San Diego, May 29,
1851, but was moved to Old Town in 1853, where
it appeared until April 7, 1860. In August 1853,
when Ames made one of his frequent trips to
San Francisco, he left the *Herald* in charge of
George Horatio Derby ("John Phoenix"), who
converted it into a humorous sheet, reversed its
politics, and brought himself increased fame as a
humorist. The *Herald* office occupied the second
floor of a building that formerly stood on the
west corner of the plaza.

Closely associated with the *Herald* office, where
"John Phoenix" continued to make contributions
to Judson Ames's paper until 1855, is the Pendleton house, still standing but altered, on Harney
Street in Old Town, next door to the Whaley
house. The Pendleton house was built in 1852
by Juan Bandini for his daughter Dolores, the
wife of Captain Charles Johnson. Captain George
Allan Pendleton, a member of the State Constitutional Convention in 1849, purchased the place
in the 1860's and lived there with his wife, Concepción B. Estudillo. At that time the house was
used as the office of the county recorder and the
county clerk, both offices being held by the Captain himself, until his death in 1871.

But it is as the home of Lieutenant George
Derby of the U. S. Corps of Topographical Engineers that the old house became famous. He lived
there during the years 1853–55 while engineering
the first turning of the San Diego River into False
Bay (now Mission Bay), and, during leisure hours,
writing bits for the *Herald*. The "naive humor
and exquisite drollery" of *Phoenixiana*, compiled
and published by the author's friend, J. Judson
Ames, has since become classic.

Derby Dike *(SRL 244)* can no longer be seen
because of the development of the San Diego
River Flood Control Channel. It was a levee or
earth embankment built west from Old Town
1,190 yards across the flats to the opposite high
land. Deflection of the river was deemed necessary to avoid silting of the harbor in San Diego
Bay. Derby himself, writing as "John Phoenix,"
described his government appointment in these
words: "He was sent from Washington some
months since to dam the San Diego River, and
he informed me with a deep sigh and mournful
smile that he had done it (mentally) several
times since his arrival."

El Desembarcadero, or the Old Landing

(SRL 64), at the mouth of the San Diego River,
was the usual landing place for small boats carrying passengers or goods to Old Town. The site,
now filled in, is off the ends of Udall and Voltaire
streets, just below Rosecrans Street.

Congress Hall *(SRL 66)* was a two-story public
house built by George Dewitt Clinton Washington Robinson about 1867 on the site of the
Aguilar adobe. It is thought that it was named
after Robert F. Stockton's ship, *Congress*. From
this building one of the last Pony Express sys-
tems was operated. During the 1860's and 1870's
it was the meeting place for "all those colorful
early transients who kept San Diego lively with
their crude games, shooting affrays, etc." It was
razed in 1939. The site is at 4016 Wallace Street.

The Whaley house *(SRL 65),* at 2482 San Diego
Avenue, in which the San Diego County court
met for about 20 years, was the first brick building to be erected in San Diego County. The white
cedar woodwork and all of the hardware used in
its construction were brought around Cape Horn,
but the bricks were made at Thomas Whaley's
own kiln in Old Town in 1856, and the walls
were finished with plaster made from ground seashells. Mrs. Whaley came to this house as a 16-
year-old bride and the place became a center of
culture, for Whaley was a man of excellent education and his wife was of pure French extraction.
Five generations of the Whaley family have occupied the old home. It has been beautifully restored.

Other Old Town places of interest include the
site of Governor Pío Pico's early home, built in
1824, on the southwest side of Juan Street between Wallace and Mason streets. The old Catholic cemetery, El Campo Santo ("the holy field"),
was used from 1850 to 1880 and is the resting
place of some of Old San Diego's most distinguished citizens, including Miguel de Pedrorena,
José Antonio Estudillo, and Santiago Argüello.
The cemetery *(SRL 68)* is on the east side of
San Diego Avenue at Arista Street. The ruins of
the cobblestone jail, built in 1850, are evidence
of possibly the first instance of graft in California.
The jail cost the taxpayers over $7,000 and housed
but one prisoner, who promptly cut his way out.
The Mason Street School *(SRL 538),* now restored
at 3960 Mason Street, was built in 1865 and is
thought to be the first publicly owned schoolhouse in San Diego County. The frame José An-

Whaley House, Old Town, San Diego

tonio Altamirano house, at 2602 San Diego Avenue, was the first office of the *San Diego Union* in 1868–70. The Exchange Hotel *(SRL 491)* stood at 2731 San Diego Avenue. The San Diego Lodge of the Masons was organized here in 1851. In 1855 it became the first three-story building in the city, with two frame stories surmounting the adobe first floor, and was renamed the Franklin House. The hotel was destroyed by fire in 1872.

Historic Point Loma

The ancient Playa trail of the Indians, later used by oxcarts and carretas, horseback riders and pedestrians from the mission, followed the curving eastern shore of the bay. It may be roughly identified today as Roscrans Street, especially that part of it which, after crossing Cañon Street in Roseville, runs through modern La Playa and terminates beyond the Fort Rosecrans barracks.

This ancient road today leads to historic ground, for "it is within the United States Government Military Reservation of Fort Rosecrans that lie the sun-drenched, unspoiled acres where he whom we incorrectly name Juan Cabrillo [his surname was Rodríguez] in 1542 first walked in Upper California; where in 1602 Sebastián Vizcaíno built on smooth sands a temporary house of prayer; where the first Spanish graves were heaped; where in 1769 the first California coast beacon was lighted; off which early in the nineteenth century the first . . . California naval battle was fought." These and other beginnings make of Point Loma a place of history, adventure, and romance. Ballast Point, Fort Guijarros, the old lighthouse, and La Playa are some of the historic spots that witnessed those beginnings. A number of the landmarks on Point Loma are located in restricted military areas.

La Punta de Guijarros

La Punta de Guijarros ("The Point of Cobblestones"), probable landing place of Cabrillo in 1542, was named by Vizcaíno in 1602 and was so designated until early in the nineteenth century when English-speaking men began to arrive at Old San Diego and La Playa. Captain George Vancouver, who anchored there in 1793, referred to it as "Punta de Guiranos." But it is the memory of long vanished Boston ships steadied on their stormy homeward voyages around Cape Horn by cargoes of cobblestones within their holds that is preserved for all time by the Yankee translation of the old Spanish name, Ballast Point *(SRL 56)*. The point is within the military area, reached by the lower road which starts where Rosecrans Street ends. The present lighthouse on Ballast Point was established in 1890.

It was on this small jutting headland that the Spanish castillo, Fort Guijarros *(SRL 69)*, designed by Alberto de Cordoba, was begun about 1797, under the direction of Comandante Manuel Rodríguez. It was completed by the beginning of the nineteenth century and manned by Catalonian soldiers from the San Diego Presidio. Here was fought the so-called "Battle of San Diego" on March 22, 1803, when the American brig *Lelia Byrd,* commanded by Captain William Shaler,

was fired on by the Spaniards under command of José Velásquez. The Yankees were attempting to carry on a barter in furs contrary to the Spanish law forbidding foreign trade. "El Júpiter," a cannon cast in Manila in 1783 and used at Fort Guijarros in this early Spanish-American naval engagement, is now mounted on the site of old Fort Stockton on Presidio Hill. Fort Guijarros, built of adobe bricks made by the Indians, stood at the foot of the short hill which runs down to the sea from the later Fort Rosecrans barracks. It was abandoned in 1838.

The Old Point Loma Lighthouse

"The . . . first light on California's shores was . . . a lantern hung on a pole erected at the tip of Ballast Point; and was the signal for supply ships coming northward after 1769." The first United States government beacon to be placed on this section of the California coast stood on a ridge less than half a mile from the tip of Point Loma. Point Loma Light, No. 355, as it is known, was erected in 1854–55 and was used for the first time at sunset on November 15, 1855. A few floor tiles from the ruins of Fort Guijarros were incorporated into the building. Because of the heavy fogs which obscured the beacon light at this point, the station was abandoned in 1891 for a lower and more suitable site located at the extreme southwestern tip of Point Loma. The old Point Loma lighthouse *(SRL 51)*, sometimes erroneously called "the old Spanish lighthouse," is now the central feature of Cabrillo National Monument.

La Playa

The canyons of Point Loma "have remained haunts of rare beauty even to this day . . . They are secret places, the canyons . . . Even now it is easy to understand how in them it was long ago safe for runaways to hide; for smugglers to trade; for thieves to conceal loot; for cut-throats to rendezvous."

But not only was lonely Loma a hiding place for smugglers and bandits. "The scene of the most flourishing hide-droghing business on the Pacific Coast during the period 1824–1846 was old La Playa on Point Loma." Here a cosmopolitan town of about 800 men grew up about the ten or 12 great barnlike hide houses established there by the captains of Boston trading ships and named for the vessels they commanded. The most famous of these, the *Brookline,* under Captain James O. Locke, was the first to be erected and the last to disappear. Here the American flag was first raised over California, unofficially, in 1829. The *Brookline* was located near the seawall before the south buildings of the Quarantine Station *(SRL 61)*, the place where ships inbound from foreign ports were examined for contagion. Vessels from almost every maritime nation in the world found anchorage in the little harbor. The crude but colorful life of the day is vividly described by Richard Henry Dana, Jr., in *Two Years Before the Mast,* and by Alfred Robinson in *Life in California.* Old "Hide Park," as the Yankees called it, occupied the sandy tableland which extends from modern La Playa through the

Quarantine Station and beyond, and which reaches back to the barren ridge on the west. The site is now within the Naval Electronic Laboratory area off Rosecrans Street.

The site of the old Mexican custom house maintained on Point Loma during this period was probably identified by ruins at the former address, 1036 Bay Street in Roseville, just north of modern La Playa. Don Juan Bandini was the first custom house keeper.

About halfway out on the inner beach of Ballast Point, headquarters for two New England whaling companies *(SRL 50)*, the Packard Brothers and the Johnson Brothers, were established during the middle of the nineteenth century. "The remains of the try-pot fires, the sand still impregnated with oil and soot," could long be seen in this locality, which is also within the Naval Electronic Laboratory.

Other Sites on Historic Loma

Loma's acres include other sites worthy of note. The all but forgotten "Mormon Well" was a futile attempt at coal mining said to have been carried on by members of the industrious Mormon Battalion while stationed at Fort Stockton in 1847. The spot, about halfway between the sea cliffs and the crest of Point Loma, was filled in about 1962 and is now covered by a parking lot on the government reservation.

Military reservation of the outermost three miles of Point Loma was ordered by the United States government on February 26, 1852. Possession of the property was not taken, however, until February 28, 1870. The post established in 1898 was named Fort Rosecrans *(SRL 62)* for General William S. Rosecrans, who died the same year; he had come to San Diego with Alonzo E. Horton in 1867. The last remnants of the old Fort Rosecrans are reached by driving to the end of Rosecrans Street. The Fort Rosecrans National Cemetery *(SRL 55)*, on the crest of Point Loma along the highway to Cabrillo National Monument, was designated Cemetery of San Diego Barracks in the late 1870's, although there had been earlier burials in the general area. Here, marked by a granite boulder from the battlefield of San Pasqual, are the graves of the heroes who fell there on December 6, 1846. The remains were transferred from the first American burial ground at Old Town, to which they had been moved in 1850. A granite obelisk memorializes the 60 sailors and marines who lost their lives on July 21, 1905, in a boiler explosion aboard the gunboat *U.S.S. Bennington* at anchor in San Diego Bay, and most of whom are buried here.

Landmarks of New San Diego

Long before the establishment of New San Diego, La Punta de los Muertos, or Dead Man's Point *(SRL 57)*, appeared on maps of the area. In 1782, when the first survey of the harbor was made, several men from the two ships engaged in the exploration, *La Princesa* and *La Favorita*, died of scurvy and were buried at this spot. The point is at the corner of Pacific Highway and

Market Street and is now surrounded by filled-in lands.

San Diego Barracks *(SRL 523)*, of which no buildings remain, was located on the block bounded by Kettner Boulevard, Market, G, and California streets. It was established in 1851 by Captain Nathaniel Lyon as a supply depot for frontier troops and was first called Post New San Diego. It became subject to Fort Rosecrans around the turn of the century and was abandoned in 1921. A marker is located on Market Street.

Balboa Park, home of the Panama-California International Exposition in 1915–16 and the California-Pacific International Exposition in 1935–36, was set aside as a park in 1868. The first improvements were made in 1889, and three years later the city rented 36 acres in the northwest corner to Kate O. Sessions for a nursery. She paid the rent by landscaping the west portion of the park, and credit is due to her for much of the beauty of San Diego. The Botanical Building and the striking California Tower are among the structures remaining in Balboa Park from the earlier exposition. The famous San Diego Zoo was founded in 1916.

A beautiful park in Pacific Beach, north of Mission Bay, has been dedicated to the memory of Kate Sessions. Nearby, at Pico Street and Garnet Avenue, a plaque marks the site *(SRL 764)* of another of her nurseries.

The oldest iron-hulled sailing ship afloat, *Star of India*, is berthed at the San Diego Embarcadero. It was restored in 1963, exactly one hundred years after it was first launched as the British ship *Euterpe*.

San Diego State College *(SRL 798)*, off Interstate 8 past the old mission, was established in 1897 as a two-year normal school. Four years later it became San Diego State Teachers College, and in 1935 it was fully recognized as a liberal arts college. In 1960 the California State Colleges were authorized to grant doctoral degrees jointly with the University of California, and honorary doctorates independently. On June 7, 1963, San Diego State College conferred upon President John F. Kennedy the first doctorate to be granted by the California State College system.

The Old Emigrant Trail

Juan Bautista de Anza, who opened the route across the Colorado Desert into California in 1774, entered the mountains from the desert via San Felipe Creek. On March 12–13, 1774, he camped at San Gregorio *(SRL 673)* at the entrance to Borrego Valley, where welcome forage refreshed the half-starved animals. A jeep trail to the site proceeds east from the junction of Yaqui Pass Road and Rango Way, six-tenths of a mile north of the intersection of Yaqui Pass and Borrego Springs roads.

Passing through the valley on the 14th, Anza's party halted at Santa Catarina *(SRL 785)* in Coyote Canyon at Reed's Springs, or Lower Willows, just above Beatty's Ranch. The following day the wayfarers entered Riverside County.

Anza's colonizing expedition of 1775–76 camped

near San Felipe Creek on December 18, 1775. The next day they marched through the little pass called Los Puertecitos (SRL 635), a short distance west of the campsite. A historical marker stands at Los Puertecitos on Highway 78, one and seven-tenths miles east of Ocotillo Wells. That night they camped at San Gregorio. From December 20 to 22, the party stopped at El Vado ("the ford") at the mouth of Coyote Canyon, and on the 23d at Santa Catarina. These sites are within Anza-Borrego Desert State Park. El Vado (SRL 634) is about seven miles north of the town of Borrego Springs via Di Giorgio Road and its dirt continuation. Santa Catarina is several miles farther northwest by a jeep trail.

Anza's route was superseded by another trail opened by Pedro Fages on an expedition against the Yuma Indians in 1782. Instead of taking the old path back to San Gabriel, Fages blazed a new one by way of Carrizo Creek and Vallecito and over the Cuyamaca Mountains to San Diego. This route was rediscovered in 1825 by Santiago Argüello in pursuit of Indian horse thieves, and in January 1826 the Mexican government sent Romualdo Pacheco, Lieutenant of Engineers, to investigate it. As a result of his findings, an official mail route was adopted via Carrizo Creek, Vallecito, San Felipe Valley, and Warner's Pass, and from then on it was used occasionally by mail carriers and traders from Sonora. Probably the first Americans to come this way were David E. Jackson and his fur-trading party, who came overland from Santa Fe in 1831. This road, which came to be known as the Emigrant Trail, formed a part of the Southern Overland Trail and was a much-traveled path during the 1840's and 1850's. From September 1858 until the beginning of the Civil War it was also the route of the famous Butterfield Stage.

This trail, after crossing the deserts a little south of the international boundary line, entered what is now San Diego County via the Carrizo Creek and Warner's Ranch. Passing down the mountain by the old Canyon Road to Sonora, the route proceeded by way of what is now Oak Grove in San Diego County to Temecula and Elsinore in Riverside County, and thence northwest to Mission San Gabriel and Los Angeles.

Another branch of the southern Emigrant Trail passed from Warner's down Palomar Mountain by the old Indian trail back of Pala Chapel to Mission San Luís Rey. Still another route, followed by General Stephen W. Kearny in 1846, led from Warner's to San Diego via Santa Ysabel and San Pasqual.

Warner's Ranch

When the Spaniards first visited Agua Caliente (the "hot springs"), they found an Indian ranchería there. All of the land surrounding the springs, about 49,000 acres in all, later came under the joint control of Missions San Diego and San Luís Rey, remaining in their possession until the secularization and confiscation of the missions in 1836. At that time the whole valley, known as the Valle de San José, was granted to

Silvestre de la Portilla, but his grant seems to have lapsed later, for when Jonathan Trumbull (Juan José) Warner, a Connecticut Yankee, applied for the land in 1844 the missions still laid claim to it.

Warner, who had come to California with the David E. Jackson party in 1831, was one of the first Americans to become an extensive landholder in California. He dispensed liberal hospitality on his great estate, and Warner's Ranch became an objective for all of those early wayfarers who entered California over the old Emigrant Trail, which crossed the Colorado Desert from Yuma. It was the camping place for various divisions of the Army of the West, notably Stephen W. Kearny's regiment and the Mormon Battalion, in 1846 and 1847. Again in 1853, explorers for a Pacific railroad passed and re-passed it in their search for a suitable route.

The old headquarters of Warner's Ranch (SRL 311) are located about four miles southwest of Warner Springs and just east of Highway 79 on the road to Ranchita and Borrego Springs. Here, fast falling into ruin, stand the old ranch house and barn, both built of adobe. The house served Warner as trading post as well as residence. Warner's Ranch, now registered as a National Historic Landmark by the Department of the Interior, became a stopping place for the Butterfield Overland Stages in 1858.

About one and one-half miles east of the headquarters is another crumbling adobe. For years this building was pointed out as the Butterfield stage station and was even marked as such by the Native Daughters and Native Sons of the Golden West. The late historian William Lawton Wright proved, however, that it was built no earlier than 1862–63, after the discontinuance of the stage line, and that the actual Butterfield station was Warner's ranch house. The later adobe was the Kimble-Wilson store. It stands about a quarter of a mile to the north of the Ranchita road, behind a knoll and in the midst of wide, sloping fields near a group of giant cottonwoods. Below it lie extensive meadows, where the famous herds of Warner's Ranch grazed.

At Warner Springs, the old Agua Caliente, is an adobe thought to have been built in the 1830's by an Indian named Chungalunga. This is the dwelling in which Warner is supposed to have lived when he first took possession of his ranch in 1844. It is now restored as the Kupa House, a guest house of the resort. Also standing is the picturesque adobe St. Francis Chapel, built about 1830.

The Butterfield Stage Route

On September 16, 1857, the Butterfield Overland Mail Company (closely affiliated with Wells Fargo Express Company) was awarded the contract for the first transcontinental mail and passenger line to California, winning over eight other bidders.

A southern route through Yuma, Arizona, was selected because it was open all year round, and St. Louis was chosen as the central supply depot.

Coaches or spring wagons were used, and they carried passengers as well as mail. Stations were erected along the entire route at 20-mile intervals, horses being changed at every station and drivers every 200 or 300 miles.

The first stage on the Butterfield line left St. Louis on September 15, 1858, and a second followed the next day. "If the chronicle of the Butterfield Stage Line could be fully told it would include stories of Indian raids, hold-ups, robberies, accidents, cloudbursts and sandstorms. . . . Most of the relics of the days of the Butterfield stage have been swept away, but there are still standing on the southern route that crosses the Colorado desert some ruins which mark the stations of the fifties."

One of the chief remaining landmarks of the famous old Butterfield Stage route is at Vallecito ("Little Valley"). This section of the route goes northwest to Warner's Ranch and southeast through Carrizo Canyon, joining the highway from San Diego to Yuma, Arizona, near Dixieland. In 1847 the men of the Mormon Battalion, under command of Lieutenant Colonel Philip St. George Cooke, passed this way on their journey to San Diego. Their wagons were the first vehicles to use this route.

The Vallecito stage station (SRL 304) was built of blocks of sod rather than adobe bricks. For long it stood deserted, a prey to vandals and earthquakes, its walls rapidly crumbling before the elements. In 1934 it was rebuilt and is now a county park. Nearby are a number of graves. The only remaining early gravestone records the death of one John Hart, at the age of 31 years in 1867. Vallecito is 19 miles southeast of Scissors Crossing, which is 12 miles east of Julian on Highway 78.

Vallecito was one of six stations along the stretch of the Butterfield route through present San Diego County. The first was at Carrizo Creek, just west of the Imperial County line. The next was Palm Spring (SRL 639), shown on some maps as Pamitas Spring. This site is about 14 miles southeast of Vallecito by road and jeep trail. Vallecito was the third station.

About ten miles northwest of Vallecito the Butterfield stages passed through Box Canyon (SRL 472), a narrow defile about a mile in length. Here, on January 19, 1847, Cooke's men of the Mormon Battalion had to use axes to hack a wagon road out of solid rock. A trail leads from the historical marker to the edge of Box Canyon. By climbing down into the canyon, one may see the cut made by the Mormon Battalion well over a century ago.

The Butterfield route (SRL 647) is still visible at the puerta, or pass, between Blair and Earthquake valleys, through which the old stages crossed. The hill six miles south of Scissors Crossing on the Vallecito road is the divide between the valleys. On the south side, in Blair Valley, a dirt road branches from the main route and circles around to the pass, where a historical marker is located. In this area the Butterfield route passes through Anza–Borrego Desert State Park.

The fourth station was at San Felipe (SRL 793), where Kearny and his men had camped in 1846 on their march to San Diego and the battle of San Pasqual. The site is in San Felipe Valley, about a mile northwest of Scissors Crossing. The fifth station, still standing, was the Warner ranch house.

The last station before Aguanga in Riverside County still stands at Oak Grove on Highway 79. It is a long, well-preserved adobe in use as a store and bar—one of the few Butterfield stations still occupied. Although the building has been enlarged through the years, at least the northern part dates from Butterfield days. The Oak Grove station (SRL 502) has been declared eligible for registration as a National Historic Landmark by the Department of the Interior. Across the road, from 1861 to 1866, was Camp Wright (SRL 482), established to guard communication between California and Arizona and to cut off traffic to the Confederate States. Troops from this post engaged in the only military action of the Civil War on California soil, the capture of a group of Southern sympathizers en route from El Monte to join the Confederate army. The Oak Grove stage station served as a hospital for Camp Wright.

The Kearny Trail

The trail that General Stephen W. Kearny and the Army of the West followed through Imperial and San Diego counties, on their way to the fatal battle of San Pasqual, has been traced by Arthur Woodward, one-time curator of history of the Los Angeles Museum, who went over this section of the old Kearny trail, tracing its route and locating the campsites one by one. He describes the route as follows:

"On November 28, [1846,] they pressed on slowly and came to the large spring near which in later days the Carrizo stage station was erected. . . . From Carrizo, where they camped on the night of the 28th, they pushed on up the dry creek bed to Vallecito, where they camped on the night of the 29th and 30th. . . .

"Beyond Vallecito the road winds across the valley to the base of a small rocky ridge, 4.3 miles distant. On the other side of this low ridge lies Mason Valley. Up this valley marched the troops for a distance of 4.8 miles until they came to the entrance of Box Canyon, a narrow rocky defile through the hills. . . . Here the road emerges and swings west again and after passing over a low ridge of hills drops into San Felipe Valley. The troops marched for about twelve or thirteen miles along this route until they came to the Indian village of San Felipe, which was on the creek. They camped here on the night of December 1 and the next day pressed on up the valley, topped the divide and dropped down to Warner's Ranch. The present road to Vallecito from Warner's probably follows fairly accurately the old trail; indeed, in Box Canyon (the spot where the Mormon Battalion under Cooke had so much trouble early in 1847) it cannot have changed very much.

"The army camped a trifle south of Warner's Ranch house. . . . The place upon which they camped is probably the rather level grassy flat a few hundred yards south of the house.

"Here they remained recuperating during the days of December 2 and 3. They started for Santa Isabel the morning of December 4th and, after marching for thirteen and a half miles, they camped near the old Mission station of Santa Isabel (probably in the flats southeast of the present site of the chapel on the edge of the creek).

"On the morning of the 5th, the army marched south-southwest to the rancheria of Santa María. They were delayed en route by a parley with Captain Gillespie and the naval reinforcements from San Diego, probably at Ballena, about six miles from Santa Isabel. Thence through the hills they travelled southwest, skirting the western edge of what is now the Valley of Santa Maria (in which the town of Ramona is situated) and probably camping at the head of Clevenger's Canyon. . . . It is about nine or ten miles via the hill trail to the point where they probably emerged into the valley of San Pascual on the morning of the 6th.

"Their trail to San Pascual lay along a rolling brush covered ridge and probably emerged into San Pascual at a point . . . [about half a mile from] the spot where the Santa Maria river empties into San Pascual Valley."

The Battle of San Pasqual

The battle of San Pasqual was fought in San Pasqual Valley near an Indian village of that name, east of the site of the present town of Escondido. It was the bloodiest of all the battles fought on California soil (aside from Indian massacres), and took place on December 6, 1846, during the period of American occupation.

A detachment of regulars under command of General Stephen W. Kearny had, after crossing the desert, reached Warner's Ranch worn and footsore. From there they marched on toward San Diego. "In the narrow San Pascual valley they were met by General Andrés Pico with a superb body of horsemen, recruited mostly from the ranchos." After severe losses, Kearny rallied his men the next day on the top of a hill, from where Kit Carson and Lieutenant Edward F. Beale slipped out into the darkness to seek reinforcements from San Diego. The army remained on the hill until December 11, and the men were forced to eat their mules to keep from starvation. Mule Hill (SRL 452) is east of Highway 395, four miles south of Escondido. A historical marker has been placed on a side road at a point from which Mule Hill is easily visible, three-quarters of a mile to the northeast. It is a low, boulder-studded hill, identifiable by white rocks near the top.

Twenty-one Americans were killed in the battle of San Pasqual, and nearly that number were seriously wounded, among the latter being General Kearny and Captain Archibald Gillespie. A monument erected on the site on December 20, 1925, by the State of California memorializes the men who gave their lives in this battle. A bronze tablet was also placed, on February 22, 1924, by the Daughters of the American Revolution of California. The site, about seven miles east of Escondido on Highway 78, is now San Pasqual Battlefield State Historical Monument (SRL 533), the land having been donated by Colonel Edward Fletcher and other public-spirited citizens of San Diego.

Rancho Los Peñasquitos

The first land grant in present San Diego County was made to Francisco María Ruiz by Governor Luís Antonio Argüello on June 15, 1823. Rancho Los Peñasquitos, 8,486 acres, lies along the creek of the same name. Ownership was transferred in 1837 to Francisco María Alvarado. The Alvarado adobe, possibly built by Ruiz as early as 1827, is mentioned in Major Emory's report of General Kearny's expedition in 1846. The soldiers reached the ranch house on the evening of December 11, after reinforcements from San Diego had enabled them to leave their forced camp on Mule Hill. Emory's report vividly describes the welcome abundance of food that the half-starved soldiers found at Peñasquitos.

The ruins of the adobe are located one mile northeast of Sorrento Station (Santa Fe Railroad) on a private ranch road with two gates. The ruins are visible from the Interstate 5 freeway bridge across Los Peñasquitos Canyon. In 1962 the entire ranch was sold to a corporation which has built a golf course and a senior citizens' development on Highway 395, near the center of the rancho.

Rancho Guajome

Although erected after the Mexican period, one of the most typical of the old adobe ranch houses still standing is that on Rancho Guajome (the "Ranch of the Big Frog").

Guajome was a part of the original mission lands of San Luís Rey. In 1845 it was granted to two Indians, Andrés and José Manuel. A few years later they sold it to Abel Stearns, who gave it as a wedding gift to his sister-in-law, Ysidora Bandini, when she married the American Colonel Cave J. Couts in 1851. The house was built in 1852–53.

Added historic interest is attached to the Guajome adobe because it was one of the several Spanish-Californian homes in which Helen Hunt Jackson was a guest while gathering material for her novel Ramona. Sitting with its back to the highway, five miles east of Mission San Luís Rey, the house is entered through a courtyard surrounded by corrals, barns, stables, and servants' quarters. Snow-white doves strut upon the red-tiled roofs or coo among the eaves. Passing through an open doorway to the inner patio, one is greeted by the murmur of a fountain and the scent of oranges and limes mingled with that of old-fashioned flowers. Beyond are the living room and other rooms opening on to the patio, nearly all with fireplaces. In one corner is the old schoolroom with its many windows, erected by Ysidora Bandini Couts, and outside, a few feet south of the house, stands the quaint chapel, filled with quiet memories.

On July 15, 1943, Cave J. Couts, Jr., son of Cave and Ysidora Couts, died in the same room and the same bed in which he had been born in 1856. The old adobe is still a private residence. It is located two miles southeast of Highway 76 on North Santa Fe Avenue (Highway S-14 to Vista). The junction of highways is three miles northeast of San Luis Rey.

South of Rancho Guajome was Rancho Buena Vista, also owned by Cave J. Couts, Sr. The adobe ranch house stands at the rear of the Rancho Buena Vista Medical Center, at the corner of East Vista Way and Escondido Avenue in the town of Vista.

Other Ranchos in San Diego County

Old adobes still stand on a number of the other ranchos in San Diego County. Rancho Monserate is northeast of Guajome in the vicinity of the junction of Highways 76 and 395. The Tomás Alvarado adobe is located on the south bank of the San Luis Rey River, just west of Highway 395. The dirt road that leads to it branches from the highway at the south end of the Keys Canyon bridge, less than a mile south of Highway 76. The beautiful old house has been restored, but, in the summer of 1966, it stood vacant and showed signs of vandalism. Beside it are the ruins of another adobe.

East of Monserate beyond the Pala Asistencia is Rancho Pauma. Here stands the old Serrano adobe, from which 11 Californians were abducted by Indians and massacred shortly after the battle of San Pasqual in December 1846. The ranchers, some of whom had fought in the battle, had driven their horses and cattle to Pauma for safekeeping, fearing reprisals from the Americans. The adobe is located on the Arthur Cook ranch, to the left of Highway 76 three miles northwest of the Pauma Valley post office.

Rancho Agua Hedionda borders the coast and includes the town of Carlsbad. Several adobes built by the Marrón family are still in existence. The oldest, built about 1842–43, stands several miles inland and is remodeled as a private residence. It is on a hill to the left of Sunny Creek Road just off El Camino Real, four miles south of Highway 78. Two other adobes stand close to the highway. One is in ruins, to the left of Highway 78 half a mile east of the El Camino Real junction. A quarter of a mile beyond the ruins, to the right of Highway 78 on a piece of the old highway, is the third Marrón adobe, remodeled as a private home. Robert Kelly, a later owner of Agua Hedionda, built a ranch house about 1882. It still stands, elaborately rebuilt by the

late actor Leo Carrillo, a descendant of prominent early Californians. The Carrillo ranch is located off Palomar Airport Road (Highway S-12), two miles east of El Camino Real. El Camino Real, the original highway through the region, is now a county road and runs parallel to Interstate 5 but several miles inland.

Rancho Las Encinitas lies wholly inland and several miles east of the town of Encinitas. Ruins of two old adobes, possibly built by the grantee, Andrés Ybarra, are located about five and one-half miles northeast of Encinitas along the road to San Marcos, or one and one-half miles east of El Camino Real. The place served as a station on the old San Diego–Los Angeles stage route. Part of the cactus fence also remains. A German colony called Olivenhain was founded on Rancho Las Encinitas in 1884. Some of the old buildings are still standing. Rancho San Dieguito adjoins Las Encinitas on the south. The area is now called Rancho Santa Fe. Two of the three San Dieguito adobes are still in existence, restored as beautiful country homes. The one built by Leandro Osuna is located on the H. C. Morton ranch, on Via de Santa Fe opposite El Sicomoro. A little more than a mile south, off Via de la Valle, is the Juan María Osuna adobe, restored by Bing Crosby and now owned by George B. Willoughby.

To the east of Encinitas and San Dieguito ranchos lies Rancho San Bernardo. An old adobe stands near the north shore of Lake Hodges; another, a mile farther north, was torn down in 1960. One of these may have been the home of Captain Joseph F. Snook, the grantee, to which Kearny and his men came after the battle of San Pasqual to get food before barricading themselves on Mule Hill, also on the rancho. The extant adobe, with a wooden addition and guarded by two palm trees, stands on the ranch at the southeast corner of Highway 395 and Sunset Drive, about three miles south of Escondido. The site of the other adobe is marked by the fireplace and old palm and eucalyptus trees. It is on the left side of Sunset Drive, a quarter of a mile north of the junction with San Pasqual Road.

East of San Bernardo is Rancho Santa María, which includes the town of Ramona. The adobe house of Captain Edward Stokes still stands on the left side of Highway 78 one and one-half miles east of Ramona, just beyond the junction with Magnolia Avenue. Kearny's army spent the night before the battle of San Pasqual on Rancho Santa María. North of Santa María, isolated Rancho Guejito y Cañada de Palomia, over 13,000 acres, remains intact. The ruins of the Cazaurang and Maxcy adobes are in evidence on the ranch, which is located in the area between Lakes Wohlford and Henshaw.

In southern San Diego County, Rancho de la Nación, which gave its name to National City in the northwest corner of the grant, was once the property of Juan Forster. A remodeled adobe stands on the old ranch of Dr. Frank Dunbar, which later became the Rohr Recreational Center and now belongs to the Bonita Valley Country Club on Sweetwater Road in Bonita. Highway 94 passes through Rancho Jamul, which stretches southeasterly from Jamul to Dulzura. An adobe

Stokes Adobe, near Ramona

built about 1852, remodeled beyond recognition, serves as the main residence at the headquarters of the Daley Ranch, just north of the highway three miles southeast of Jamul.

Rancho La Cañada de los Coches *(SRL 425)* is said to be the smallest full-fledged rancho granted in California. A fraction over 28 acres, it was completely surrounded by Rancho El Cajón, 48,800 acres. The little grant was made to Apolinaria Lorenzana by Governor Manuel Micheltorena in 1843. The adobe ranch house was demolished by treasure-seekers many years ago. The rancho lies along old Highway 80, five miles northeast of El Cajon.

Rancho Cuyamaca, 35,501 acres in eastern San Diego County, was long the subject of litigation. In 1933, 25,000 acres became Cuyamaca Rancho State Park.

Julian, a Town That Came Back

Julian *(SRL 412)*, a little alpine town nestled among forests of oak and conifer, is today the center of a modest agricultural community, where apples, pears, and honey supplant the gold of former days. The first discovery of gold in the region was made shortly before February 22, 1870, when the first mine was named the "George Washington." The Julian gold stampede followed this discovery, and the Golden Chariot, Cuyamaca, Stonewall Jackson, and other locations proved to be very rich. These mines, now inactive, have produced over $5 million.

Gold in the mines near Julian had about played out in 1880. Then came the boom at Tombstone, Arizona. "When Tombstone came up, Julian went down like a punctured tire," says an old-timer of the California town. "They loaded most of the camp on to wagons, cracked the whips, and drove off to Arizona with it."

But Julian was not dead, and with the departure of the miners the surrounding hills and valleys were homesteaded. The region proved exceptionally suitable for fruit growing, bees, and livestock, and Julian was soon a busy trading center for the farmers. The modern motorist, too, is finding this little mountain town to be an alluring playground, with cool woods and tempered air in summer, and in winter a touch of snow.

Miscellaneous Landmarks of San Diego County

In Anza–Borrego Desert State Park, besides the numerous landmarks of Anza and the Butterfield Stage, there is a most unusual monument *(SRL 750)* in honor of Thomas L. "Peg Leg" Smith, who is supposed to have discovered gold in the vicinity about 1830. Many have sought the "lost" mine in vain. Legend has it that anyone who adds a stone to the monument will have good luck, while the removal of a stone will bring the opposite result. The monument is located about seven miles northeast of Borrego Springs via Palm Canyon Drive and Peg Leg Road.

At Spring Valley, ten miles east of San Diego, is the Bancroft ranch house *(SRL 626)*. The adobe was built about 1856 by A. S. Ensworth and came into the hands of Hubert Howe Ban-

Gaskill Stone Store, Campo

croft, the great California historian, in 1885. Because of the importance of this occupant, the house has been registered by the Department of the Interior as a National Historic Landmark. It stands on Memory Lane, off Bancroft Drive.

Campo is a small settlement along Highway 94, a mile north of the Mexican border. Here, on December 5, 1875, a gunfight took place to rival the famous incident at the O.K. Corral in Tombstone, Arizona. The battle pitted Silas E. and Luman H. Gaskill, the Campo storekeepers, against a gang of Mexican bandits from Tecate. Several of the outlaws were killed or mortally wounded. The Gaskill brothers were injured but recovered. Several years later they built a stone store *(SRL 411)*, still standing across the wash from the site of the earlier store where the gunfight began.

West of San Ysidro via Dairy Mart Road and Monument Road and reached through a private ranch is a granite shaft marking the southwest corner of the United States and the northwest corner of Mexico. The monument was first set up on June 16, 1851, following the signing of the Treaty of Guadalupe Hidalgo, which ended the Mexican War, on February 2, 1848. The landmark, overlooking the ocean, was later taken down, restored, and replaced in August 1894.

At Coronado, across the bay from San Diego, is the Hotel del Coronado, a relic of the Victorian era that is still a showplace. It was designed by the famous architect Stanford White and was formally opened on February 14, 1888.

Eleven miles south of San Diego via National Avenue is Montgomery Memorial State Park *(SRL 711)*, set aside in honor of John Joseph Montgomery, whose glider flight at Otay Mesa in 1883, 20 years before the Wright brothers, was the first successful flight of heavier-than-air craft. A monument in the shape of a wing has been erected near the site of the historic event. Montgomery died in a glider crash near Evergreen in Santa Clara County in 1911.

SOURCES

Beattie, George William. "Reopening Anza's Road." Ms., 1931.
Bolton, Herbert Eugene. *Fray Juan Crespí, Missionary Explorer on the Pacific Coast, 1769–1774.* University of California Press, Berkeley, 1927.
——— "Spanish Exploration in the Southwest, 1542–

1706," in *Original Narratives of Early American History*, Vol. XVII. Scribner, New York, 1916.

Brackett, R. W. *The History of San Diego County Ranchos*. Union Title Insurance Co., San Diego, 1960.

The California Missions, a Pictorial History. By the editorial staff of Sunset Books. Lane Book Co., Menlo Park, 1964.

Cleland, Robert Glass. "Pathfinders," in the series *California*, ed. John Russell McCarthy. Powell Publishing Co., Los Angeles, 1929.

Davidson, Winifred. "Historic Spots in San Diego." Ms., 1931.

—— *Where California Began*. McIntyre Publishing Co., San Diego, 1929.

Dunn, H. H. "The Prehistoric Painter of Poway," *Touring Topics*, XXII, No. 5 (May 1930), 36–38, 56.

Elder, David Paul. *The Spanish Missions of California*. Paul Elder & Co., San Francisco, 1913.

Emory, William H. *Notes of a Military Reconnaissance from Fort Leavenworth, Missouri, to San Diego, California*. 30th Congress, 1st Session, Senate Exec. Doc. No. 7, Washington, D.C., 1848.

Engelhardt, Zephyrin. *San Diego Mission*. The James H. Barry Co., San Francisco, 1920.

—— *San Luis Rey Mission*. The James H. Barry Co., San Francisco, 1921.

Gorby, John S. "After Serra on California's Royal Road," *Touring Topics*, XXIII, No. 8 (August 1931), 12–17, 36.

Hill, Joseph J. *The History of Warner's Ranch and Its Environs*. Privately published, Los Angeles, 1927.

Jackson, Helen Hunt. *Glimpses of California and the Missions*. Little, Brown & Co., Boston, 1903.

James, George Wharton. *In and Out of the Old Missions of California*. Little, Brown & Co., Boston, 1906.

Loop, A. M. "The Fight of the Paso del Mar," *The Silver Gate*, II, No. 1 (January 1900), ed. James A. Jasper, San Diego.

Mills, James. *Historical Landmarks of San Diego County*. San Diego Historical Society, San Diego, 1960.

Morrison, Lorrin L. *Warner, the Man and the Ranch*. Privately published, Los Angeles, 1962.

"The Old Ames Press—A Venerable Pioneer," a letter by Edwin A. Sherman, March 22, 1873, with introductory note by Carl I. Wheat, *Quarterly of the California Historical Society*, IX, No. 3 (September 1930), 193–200.

Older, Mrs. Fremont. *California Missions and Their Romances*. Coward-McCann, New York, 1938.

"Pattie, James Ohio, A Personal Narrative of," *Early Western Travels, 1748–1846*, ed. by Reuben Gold Thwaites, Vol. XVIII. The Arthur H. Clarke Co., Cleveland, Ohio, 1905.

Pourade, Richard F. *The Explorers*. Union-Tribune Publishing Co., San Diego, 1960.

—— *The Glory Years*. Union-Tribune Publishing Co., San Diego, 1964.

—— *Gold in the Sun*. Union-Tribune Publishing Co., San Diego, 1965.

—— *The Silver Dons*. Union-Tribune Publishing Co., San Diego, 1963.

—— *Time of the Bells*. Union-Tribune Publishing Co., San Diego, 1961.

Robinson, Alfred. *Life in California During a Residence of Several Years in That Territory*. William Doxey, San Francisco, 1891.

Rush, Philip S. *Some Old Ranchos and Adobes*. Privately published, San Diego, 1965.

San Diego Magazine. Souvenir Number Commemorating Restoration of Old Mission. VII, No. 9 (September 1931).

Smythe, William E. *History of San Diego, 1542–1908*. 2 vols. Vol. I, *Old Town*. The History Co., San Diego, 1908.

Taylor, Bayard. *Eldorado, or Adventures in the Path of Empire*. H. G. Bohn, London, 1850; G. P. Putnam's Sons, New York, 1850 and 1864.

Wilcox, Horace Fenton. "Memories of the Gold Stampede to Julian," as told to John Edwin Hogg, *Touring Topics*, XXIV, No. 2 (February 1932), 16–18, 38–39.

Wolcott, Marjorie T. "The House near the Frog Pond," *Touring Topics*, XX, No. 12 (December 1928), 40–41, 53–56.

Woodward, Arthur. "The Kearny Trail Through Imperial and San Diego Counties." Ms., 1931.

San Francisco County

SAN FRANCISCO COUNTY (San Francisco is Spanish for St. Francis) derived its name from Mission San Francisco de Asís, established within the present boundary lines of the city in 1776. San Francisco County was one of the original 27 counties. Until 1856 the county included what is now San Mateo County, and the city of San Francisco was the county seat of the entire section. After that date, the government was consolidated, operating as the City and County of San Francisco. Most of the city records were destroyed in the fire that followed the earthquake of April 18, 1906. Fortunately, however, many of the pre-state records in Spanish were saved.

Discovery of the Golden Gate

The entrance to San Francisco Bay, La Boca del Puerto de San Francisco, was discovered November 1, 1769, by Sergeant José de Ortega, pathfinder of Gaspar de Portolá's expedition and the first white man to see San Francisco Bay.

The expedition was searching for the lost bay of Monterey and had proceeded up the coast as far as San Pedro Valley. From this point, Portolá had commissioned Ortega to explore as far north as Point Reyes, which he had seen from the summit of the Montara Mountains just east of Point San Pedro. The channel of the Golden Gate, however, prevented Ortega and his party from reaching their objective. They were obliged to return without reaching Point Reyes; but, unknowingly, they had discovered the greatest harbor on the Pacific Coast.

Ortega's trail had covered the coast from San Pedro to Point Lobos, but when his way was blocked by the deep waters of the Golden Gate, he proceeded along the south shore of the channel and climbed La Loma Alta (later called Telegraph Hill). From this vantage point, he could see the whole expanse of the bay, its islands, and the Contra Costa hills beyond.

Having made his observations, Ortega returned

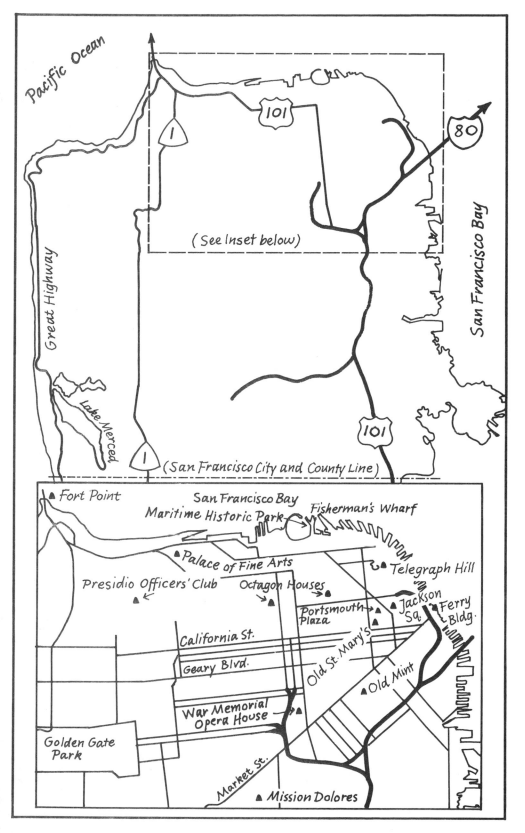

SAN FRANCISCO

to camp to report. Portolá, however, did not realize the tremendous importance of his discovery. He was looking for the bay of Monterey.

The Spaniards had called the gateway to the newly discovered bay "La Boca del Puerto de San Francisco," but an American gave it the name of "Golden Gate." In his *Memoirs* General John Charles Frémont says: "To this gate I gave the name of Chrysopylae, or Golden Gate; for the same reason that the harbor of Byzantium [afterward Constantinople] was called Chrysoceras, or Golden Horn." In a footnote he adds: "The form of the entrance into the bay of San Francisco and its advantages for commerce, Asiatic included, suggested to me the name which I gave to this entrance and which I put upon the map that accompanied a geographical Memoir addressed to the Senate of the United States in June 1848."

Juan Manuel de Ayala, in the historic ship *San Carlos,* and José Cañizares, his subordinate, were the first white men to enter San Francisco Bay. In the spring of 1769 the *San Carlos* had carried supplies and colonists for the new pueblo to be founded in San Diego. Again, in 1775, with Ayala in command, it sailed with the fleet sent from Mexico to explore San Francisco Bay. On August 4 the entrance to the bay was reached. Ayala, suffering from a wound accidentally incurred on the voyage, sent Cañizares ahead to find anchorage. The latter did not return all that day, the currents and tides of the Golden Gate being too strong for the little launch in which he made the reconnoitering expedition. On the evening of August 5, therefore, Ayala, in the *San Carlos,* passed through the Golden Gate and into the great port of the West. Cañizares and Ayala had thus jointly gained the honor of making the first recorded entrance into San Francisco Bay by way of the Golden Gate. Ayala and his men remained in the bay for 44 days, exploring every arm and inlet and going as far as the mouth of the San Joaquin River, at the same time taking soundings and making a map. Two of the names given at this time are in use today in slightly different forms. One is that of the island just inside the strait, which was called Isla de Nuestra Señora de los Angeles, "Island of Our Lady of the Angels," and is known today as Angel Island. In a sheltered cove of this island, the *San Carlos* remained during most of its stay in the bay. Another island was named Isla de los Alcatraces, "Island of the Pelicans," and we have the name today in Alcatraz Island. The first lighthouse to be put to use on the coast of California by the United States Light Service was placed on Alcatraz Island in 1854.

It was Ayala's exploration of San Francisco Bay that established the suitability of its shores for a settlement, and the location at San Francisco of the mission and presidio was largely influenced by this expedition. A plaque commemorating the entrance of the *San Carlos* into San Francisco Bay (*SRL 236*) was placed at Fort Point by the D.A.R. in 1955.

The Founding of San Francisco

Juan Bautista de Anza, "one of the most remarkable men who ever appeared on the field of California history . . . , was a member of the presidial aristocracy of the frontier provinces of New Spain." He early distinguished himself not only as a valiant Indian fighter but as an officer of unusual abilities and irreproachable character.

Anza's ambition to find a practicable overland route to California began in early boyhood, but it was realized only after meeting and overcoming many delays and difficulties. The great need for a land route for carrying supplies to the struggling colonies in Alta California and the inadequacy of the route by way of Baja California were clearly pointed out by Padre Junípero Serra. This, together with the growing menace of foreign aggression in California, finally influenced Antonio María Bucareli, viceroy of New Spain, to push Anza's proposed expedition.

Anza successfully accomplished his first journey overland to California in 1774, opening the route and paving the way for the real colonization of California and the founding of San Francisco. The success of Anza's expedition caused Bucareli to do everything in his power to strengthen Alta California, both within itself and against any possible attacks from without, and to utilize the new route to the fullest extent possible. All plans finally culminated in the project to settle San Francisco and the region round about what was known to the Spaniards as the Río Grande de San Francisco (now known as the mouth of the Sacramento and San Joaquin rivers). These settlements were to serve not only as buffers against possible outside enemies, but as a base for further settlements to the north.

Accordingly, a second expedition was planned on which Anza was to take settlers and supplies with him to found a presidio and mission at San Francisco. After fearful hardships encountered in desert and mountains, and needless delays caused by Governor Fernando Rivera, who was opposed to the settlement of San Francisco, this remarkable undertaking was accomplished. Anza himself reached San Francisco on March 27, 1776, but Rivera's dilatory movements made it necessary for him to leave his settlers temporarily at Monterey. The final lap of the journey had led along the hills, by way of Ingleside, with a "good-sized lake of fresh water," clearly what is now called Lake Merced, lying to the westward. From this point the little company marched through what is now Golden Gate Park to the southern edge of the Presidio of San Francisco military reservation, a mile and a half south of Fort Point. His camp at San Francisco was made at what was later called by the Spaniards Laguna del Presidio and is now known as Mountain Lake. The creek, which Anza called Arroyo del Puerto, is now known as Lobos Creek and forms the southern boundary of the presidio reservation. Anza made a thorough survey of the region, marking out the sites for the presidio and mission. For the presidio fort he chose a location which the Spaniards called Cantil Blanco ("White Cliff"), but which is today known as Fort Point, where the old American fort now stands. Here Anza planted a cross "on the extreme point of the white cliff" to mark the place where the fort should be built. He selected a place for the mission near a little rivulet that he named Nuestra Señora de los Dolores. The mesa or tableland between the Laguna del Presidio and the Cantil Blanco was where the presidio town was to be.

After exploring the Bay and the River of San Francisco to the junction of the San Joaquín and Sacramento rivers, Anza returned to Monterey. He was greatly disappointed not to be able to settle his colonists in San Francisco, but since he could not do so without the aid of Rivera, he left Monterey amid "the tears and lamentations of the settlers, who had learned to revere and love him in the course of their long march from Sonora."

The final settling of the colonists at San Francisco was accomplished by José Joaquín Moraga, Anza's faithful and capable lieutenant, and Padre Francisco Palou in the summer of 1776. The presidio was dedicated on September 17, and less than a month later Mission San Francisco de Asís was founded.

"Thus had the great port been occupied, and the vitally needed settlers, with their equally needed herds of domestic animals, were now in Alta California to stay. For the first time it was possible to say that the province had been placed upon a permanent basis. There was no longer any likelihood that it would be abandoned and left open for another power."

Anza never returned to California, but his work there had "an enduring importance beyond anything that had ever happened in the history of the Californias." Back of his work, too, stood that other great figure, Antonio Bucareli, viceroy of Mexico, who had aided, encouraged, and pushed the enterprise in every way within his power from beginning to end.

The Presidio of San Francisco

The site of the Presidio of San Francisco (SRL 79) was selected by Juan Bautista de Anza on March 28, 1776. On June 27 Lieutenant José Joaquín Moraga and the band of settlers, who had traveled all the way from Sonora to Monterey with Anza, made temporary camp on the Laguna de Manantial, now Eighteenth and Dolores streets. The next day a shelter of branches was built to serve as a chapel, and on June 29 the first Mass was said. On July 26 most of the expedition moved to the presidio site, where shelters were erected, and Mass was offered on July 28. On September 17 the presidio was dedicated and Moraga took formal possession in the name of the King of Spain.

The Spanish and Mexican governments never supported the Presidio of San Francisco adequately, and consequently it was never well garrisoned. After 1835 regular troops were no longer stationed there, and by 1840 it was in ruins. Since the American occupation on July 9, 1846, it has been one of the principal United States Army reservations on the Pacific Coast. The presidio was formally occupied by American troops under command of Major A. Hardie on March 27, 1847.

The presidio reservation consists of approximately 1,400 acres, originally bare sand hills. In the 1880's large areas were planted with eucalyptus and pine trees.

The sites of the old Spanish presidio buildings have been marked. A bronze tablet set in a granite block was placed by the California Chapter, D.A.R., in 1928 at the southwest corner of the original presidio building, and the other three corners were also located and marked by concrete posts bearing bronze inscriptions. The only building left from the Spanish period is the adobe *comandante* headquarters on the south side of the parade ground, near the corner of Moraga Avenue and Arguello Boulevard. Built about 1810–20, this was the officers' quarters under Spanish and Mexican rule. What remained of the old adobe was incorporated into the Officers' Club in 1934. Four old Spanish cannon, dated as early as 1673, stand in front of this building. Several structures from the early American days of the presidio also remain on the grounds. In 1963 the Presidio of San Francisco was registered as a National Historic Landmark by the Department of the Interior, and a plaque was unveiled a short distance northwest of the Officers' Club.

Mission San Francisco de Asís (Dolores)

The first plans of the Visitador General of Mexico, José de Gálvez, did not call for a mission dedicated to St. Francis of Assisi, founder of the Franciscan Order. The Padre Presidente, Junípero Serra, protested this omission, but Gálvez replied, "If Saint Francis wishes a mission, let him show you a good port, and then let it bear his name." Accordingly, when Portolá's party discovered San Francisco Bay, the Franciscan chroniclers in the party exclaimed, "This is the port to which the Visitador referred and to which the Saint has led us."

But it was not until seven years later, in 1776, that Misión San Francisco de Asís was founded. Juan Bautista de Anza had selected the site of the mission in the spring. This was on the bank of the little lake that Anza called Laguna de Manantial, now filled in. The stream that flowed into it he called Arroyo de Nuestra Señora de los Dolores, because it was on the Friday of Our Lady of Sorrows (Viernes de los Dolores) that he examined it. The name of the mission itself in later years became popularized to "Mission Dolores." Laguna de Manantial covered roughly the city blocks bounded by Fifteenth, Twenty-third, Guerrero, and Harrison streets. They are now filled with residences.

Father Francisco Palou arrived at the lake on June 27, 1776, and two days later celebrated the first Mass in a temporary chapel. Dr. Herbert E. Bolton has written: "Dolores was continuously occupied from June 27 ... [it] became the cradle of the city erected to the honor of St. Francis." San Francisco celebrates its birthday each year on June 29, the anniversary of the first Mass at the mission site, and thus claims to be five days older than the Declaration of Independence.

The mission was not formally dedicated, however, until early October, probably October 9. The present mission church (SRL 327) was begun, a few hundred yards from the original site, on April 25, 1782, when the first stone was put in place, and dedicated on April 3, 1791. Mission Dolores, with its simple yet massive façade, its bells, and its overhanging roof—all well pre-

Mission San Francisco de Asís (Dolores)

served—has a quaint individuality that sets it apart from the more elaborate missions. It has none of the usual arches, arcades, and towers that adorn most of the others, but its massive simplicity makes it none the less impressive.

The infant María de la Concepción Marcela Argüello, daughter of José Darío Argüello, was baptized at Mission Dolores on February 26, 1791. Her story is told below and in the section on Solano County, her burial place.

The shadow of a redwood cross in the enclosed cemetery beside the mission falls across old graves. Here lie the remains of Don Luís Antonio Argüello, governor of Alta California from November 1822 to November 1825; he died in 1830. Don Francisco de Haro, first alcalde of San Francisco, is also buried here. Other graves include those of James P. Casey and Charles Cora, both hanged by the Vigilantes. The grotto of Our Lady of Lourdes stands in memory of forgotten dead. Within the church itself are buried Don José Joaquín Moraga, follower of Anza and founder of the San Francisco Presidio, who died in 1785; the Noé family; and William Alexander Leidesdorff, "the first pioneer of Negro origin who came to San Francisco."

On the south wall of the mission is a plaque erected by the California Historical Society to honor Fray Francisco Palou, founder of Mission Dolores and California's first historian. On November 24, 1963, the 250th anniversary of the birth of Father Junípero Serra, a tablet was placed at Mission Dolores to mark the northern terminus of El Camino Real (SRL 784) as Serra knew it and helped to blaze it. A similar plaque was placed at the southern terminus, Mission San Diego de Alcalá.

Today, Mission Dolores is overshadowed by a large parish church built in 1913–18. This church, because of its associations with the old mission, was honored by the Vatican in 1952 with the title of minor basilica. It is in the quiet aisles and peaceful graveyard of the mission, however, that one will find rich memories of San Francisco's picturesque and romantic beginnings.

Castillo de San Joaquín

Castillo de San Joaquín (SRL 82) was a Spanish fort located on Fort Point near the old presidio but separate from it. It was completed and dedicated on December 9, 1794. Castillo de San Joaquín would never have withstood a siege, for "the structure rested mainly on sand; the brick-faced walls crumbled at the shock whenever a salute was fired; the guns were badly mounted, and, for the most part, worn out." The fort, built principally of adobe in the form of an immense horseshoe, gradually became a ruin, and after 1835 no troops were stationed there.

On July 1, 1846, as an aftermath of the Bear Flag Revolt, John C. Frémont and 12 of his men crossed over from Sausalito in the launch Moscow and spiked the guns of the Castillo de San Joaquín. In telling of this affair in his Memoirs, Frémont says that the guns he spiked were large handsome pieces, but he fails to add that they were dismounted and lying on the ground.

During the years 1854 to 1860 the old site of the Castillo de San Joaquín was dug down to sea level, and Fort Point was built of brick and granite on the leveled site. It was renamed Fort Winfield Scott in 1882, but a new fort, built after the turn of the century, was also given that name. Old Fort Point was finally abandoned in 1914, but it still stands, within the present presidio reservation and overshadowed by the Golden Gate Bridge. There is a movement to preserve it as a historical monument. The D.A.R. tablet, placed in 1955 to mark the entrance of Ayala's ship San Carlos into the bay in 1775, also honors Castillo de San Joaquín and Fort Point.

Yerba Buena Cove

The first Englishman to sail into San Francisco Bay was Captain George Vancouver, who came on the night of November 14, 1792, in the sloop of war Discovery, dropping anchor "about a league below the Presidio in a place they called Yerba Buena." Eldredge says that this "is the first reference we have to the little cove where, forty-three years later, Richardson's tent marked the beginning of the modern city. Vancouver's map ... shows the anchorage in Yerba Buena Cove, in other words, off the foot of Market Street."

Vancouver was received hospitably by the priest of the mission, Father Antonio Danti, and by the comandante of the presidio, Hermenegildo Sal. He has left an interesting description of the country, the bay, the presidio, and his trip to Mission Santa Clara.

When Vancouver came again the next year, he was not received so warmly, for Don Hermenegildo had been reprimanded for letting an Englishman see the defenseless condition of the Spanish possessions on the bay.

The Russians in San Francisco

Count Nikolai Rezanov came to San Francisco in 1806. The colonists in Russia's Alaska settlements were starving and could no longer survive unless a permanent source of food supply could be found. With this purpose in mind, Rezanov sailed south to seek negotiations with the Spanish officials of San Francisco, well knowing that trade with foreigners was forbidden and that entry into San Francisco Bay was against Spanish law. He was desperate, however, for his voyage was a race with death, and on April 5, 1806, he sailed past the presidio and entered the harbor.

José Darío Argüello, a very influential man and the best friend of Governor José Joaquín de Arrillaga, was comandante of San Francisco at this time. His daughter, Concepción, or Concha, as she was affectionately called by her family, was reputed to be the most beautiful woman in Alta California. Count Rezanov was entertained in the Argüello household during his entire stay in San Francisco. While there he not only was captivated by the lovely Concepción but also won her heart.

Meanwhile, by gifts and a display of the eagerly sought Russian wares, he had won the favor of the settlers, and especially of the mission fathers. With such powerful allies to aid him, Rezanov at length overcame Governor Arrillaga's reluctance to grant the exchange of goods which he so desperately sought.

On May 21, six weeks after his coming, Rezanov sailed back to the aid of his starving people in Alaska and presumably to obtain royal and ecclesiastical permission for his marriage to Concepción. The mission in Alaska was accomplished, but Rezanov's untimely death on the steppes of Siberia frustrated all further plans.

The aftermath of this romance rightfully belongs to Benicia, Solano County, the place where Concepción spent the closing years of her life and where she lies buried. Its political significance concerns the Russian settlements at Bodega and Fort Ross.

The Farallones

The Farallon Islands were probably discovered in 1543 by the Cabrillo-Ferrelo expedition, although no mention was made of them. In 1579 Sir Francis Drake landed there to secure a supply of seal meat, birds, and eggs. He named them the Islands of St. James. In 1595 Cermeño called them simply "the islands," but the Vizcaíno expedition in 1603 gave them the name of the "Frayles," in honor of the Carmelite friars on board. In 1743 George Anson, an English freebooter, captured a Manila galleon on which there was a chart indicating the islands as "Los Farollones," but when or by whom they were so named is not known. In 1775 Bodega called them by a combination of the two Spanish names, the "Farallones de los Frailes."

In the period 1809 to 1812, these islands were developed as a station for the Russian-American Fur Company, and a Russian settlement was made there. San Francisco Bay was full of sea otter, and the Russians entered the harbor in canoes, hunting under the very guns of the Spanish fort.

The Farallones have always been a natural rookery. In 1849, when food soared to fabulous prices in San Francisco, they became a profitable source of supply for egg hunters. This traffic continued for 40 years, until the quarrels of rival egg companies caused the United States marshals to interfere. Bird lovers were later aided by Admiral George Dewey in their efforts to have the islands declared a bird sanctuary. It is now one of four in the state.

In 1855 a lighthouse was erected on the Farallon Islands. The place has a long disastrous record of shipwrecks, its bays and inlets bearing the names of many lost steamers and sailing vessels.

Yerba Buena, the Forerunner of San Francisco

Captain William A. Richardson was the founder of Yerba Buena ("good herb," Spanish for wild mint), which became the nucleus of the modern city of San Francisco. Richardson, an Englishman by birth, came to San Francisco in 1822, when the Mexican flag was floating over the presidio, and Governor Pablo Vicente de Solá, the last Spanish ruler, was just leaving California. From Solá, Richardson had gained permission to settle permanently at San Francisco, and in return for this privilege he was to teach the young Spaniards the arts of navigation and carpentering, two skills that were much needed. In 1825 Richardson married María Antonia, daughter of Don Ignacio Martínez, *comandante* of the San Francisco Presidio.

Richardson was a master mariner, and not only taught the Spaniards and Indians at the San Francisco Presidio the trades of carpenter and shipwright, as well as navigation, but was also the first to develop extensively trade and communication by water on San Francisco Bay. For three years he was manager of the transporters which traded between San Francisco and the embarcadero at Mission San José. He piloted vessels in and out of the bay, and later became Captain of the Port and Bay of San Francisco under the direction of Mariano Guadalupe Vallejo, *comandante general*.

It was Richardson's plan to found a port town on San Francisco Bay at the best possible anchoring place. For this purpose he chose Yerba Buena Cove. José Figueroa, California's most enlightened Mexican governor, acted upon these plans and made Richardson San Francisco's first harbor master.

In 1835 Richardson moved to Yerba Buena with his family, living in a tent for three months. "This tent was the first habitation ever erected in Yerba Buena. At the time, Richardson's only neighbors were bears, coyotes and wolves. The nearest people lived either at the Presidio or at Mission Dolores." In October 1835 he replaced the tent by a board house. He was the "solitary settler" described by Richard Henry Dana, Jr., in his *Two Years Before the Mast*. This region is now in the heart of Chinatown, and the site where Richardson's tent stood is now at 823–27 Grant Avenue (formerly Dupont Street) between Clay and Washington streets.

In 1836 he built a more elaborate dwelling, an adobe house, "which contained a parlor, commodious bedrooms, and a sitting and dining room which was used at times as a ballroom. The walls were thick with blinds or massive shutters closing the windows on the inside." This was the "Casa Grande" of Yerba Buena until 1848, it being the largest and most pretentious building there. It withstood several devastating fires, but was taken down in 1852 and replaced by the Adelphi Theater.

The settlement at Yerba Buena Cove was, from the first, predominantly Anglo-Saxon and American, a group of foreigners surrounded by Spanish, Mexicans, and Indians.

The next settler there was Jacob Primer Leese, an American trader, who erected a second substantial frame house in the settlement in 1836. The site of the Jacob Leese house is "in Grant on the west side, mostly in the intersection of Grant and Clay," according to J. N. Bowman. The first Fourth of July celebration in San Francisco was held at this house in 1836. Many notable families about the bay attended the festivities, among them being the Estudillo, Martínez, Castro, Guerrero, and De Haro families. General Vallejo himself was present, and several ships, anchored in the cove, took part in the celebration.

This house, which was built of redwood, was the center for a large trading business which Leese and his partners, Spear and Hinckley, carried on with the ranchos bordering San Francisco Bay. To commemorate this house, the Tamalpais Chapter, D.A.R., placed a tablet on October 3, 1931.

Mexican Land Grants

Within the original boundary of San Francisco County lay private ranchos obtained through Mexican governors. When the county was divided in 1856, by far the greater part of the land thus granted was given to San Mateo County. The diminished county of San Francisco occupied the tip of the peninsula, where lands had been reserved for mission and presidio use and where little had been granted to private individuals. The line drawn to separate the two counties passed due west from a point on San Francisco Bay a little east of Visitación Valley to the Pacific Ocean and cut the southern end of Lake Merced.

Two of the old ranchos were cut by this line. Rancho Laguna de la Merced, consisting of one-half a square league, was one of these. It was granted in 1835 to José Antonio Galindo, a corporal in the San Francisco militia. After holding it for two years, he sold it on May 12, 1837, to Francisco de Haro for 100 cows and $25 in goods.

Francisco de Haro arrived in California with Governor Argüello in 1819, as a sublieutenant in the San Blas Infantry. In 1824 he was one of the leaders in the suppression of a revolt among Indian neophytes. In that year, too, he married Josefa, daughter of José Antonio Sánchez, and thereafter lived in San Francisco, where they raised their family. In 1838, within a year after purchasing the rancho, he was made alcalde. In that office he was responsible for the guardianship of persons arrested for offenses against law and order. A problem arose when Galindo, former owner of the rancho, was taken into custody for the murder of José Peralta. Lack of a jail compelled Alcalde de Haro to order his fellow townsmen to act as guards. After holding the prisoner under trying circumstances for three months, he finally appealed to Governor Alvarado on February 27, 1839, for permission to send Galindo to San José, where prison facilities were available.

Francisco de Haro held many important positions under the Mexican regime and is frequently mentioned in the annals of San Francisco. He died at a comparatively early age in 1849, his death being hastened by grief over the tragic deaths of his twin sons at the San Rafael Mission embarcadero across the bay.

The second rancho cut by the new county boundary line was the Cañada de Guadalupe, la Visitación y Rodeo Viejo, only a small portion of which was left in San Francisco County. It consisted of two leagues and was granted by Governor Alvarado in 1841 to the well-known early resident of San Francisco, Jacob Primer Leese. As the grantee had a house in Yerba Buena, forerunner of San Francisco, he and his family resided for only a short time upon the rancho property, which he afterward sold. The United States patent for the tract was issued in 1865 to Henry R. Payson and William Pierce; the former possessed the larger part, 5,473 acres, the latter, 942 acres.

A tract of 12,643 acres of pueblo land was patented to the City of San Francisco in June 1884.

Other grants of land in the San Francisco area recognized by the United States government were few in number and small in extent. One of these was the Ojo de Agua de Figueroa, 100 varas, granted to Apolinario Miranda in 1833. Miranda was a soldier in the San Francisco Company from 1819 to 1836. He constructed an adobe house to replace an earlier temporary structure in 1834. His wife was Juana Briones. Her house in the North Beach section, about where Filbert and Powell streets intersect, was the only dwelling between Yerba Buena and the presidio. Her husband was at one time brought before the alcalde for mistreating his wife. She long outlived her husband, who was buried at Mission Dolores, and ended her days in Santa Clara County.

Among the other small grants were Las Camaritas, about 19 acres, patented to Ferdinand Vassault; two lots in the pueblo land patented to J. P. Leese in 1858; Mission Dolores, eight and one-half acres, patented to Bishop J. S. Alemany in 1858; and a few others, varying from half an acre to 25 acres, given to various persons.

In 1853 José Y. Limantour made a fantastic claim to the United States Land Commission that he had been granted four leagues of land within and adjoining what had become the city of San Francisco. The citizens were aroused and astounded, but the claim was proved to be fraudulent, and Limantour fled the country.

The Old Custom House

The building of a custom house at San Francisco was authorized by the Mexican governor in 1844. Work was begun that summer and completed in September 1845. It was a one-story, four-room adobe with veranda and tile roof and was erected mostly by Indian labor. It fronted the northwest corner of the plaza (later called Portsmouth Square), while its north end faced what is now Washington Street.

During the American occupation, the Custom House was used as barracks, and in front stood the flagpole on which Captain John B. Montgomery raised the American flag on July 9, 1846. The alcalde and revenue officers used it later, and in 1850 it was occupied by a bank and law offices. It was destroyed by fire in 1851.

Portsmouth Plaza

Captain John B. Montgomery, of the *U.S.S. Portsmouth*, received orders from Commodore John Drake Sloat on July 8, 1846, to take possession of Yerba Buena and the northern frontier. On the morning of July 9, Montgomery and his men landed at what is now the corner of Clay and Leidesdorff streets. Nearby, at the southeast corner of Clay and Montgomery streets, is a tablet placed by the Native Sons of the Golden West in 1916. This plaque not only commemorates Montgomery's landing place (SRL 81) but also brings to the attention of all who view it the fact that the water of San Francisco Bay once came up to the foot of Clay Street almost as far as Montgomery Street. (On this site the Bank of Italy, now Bank of America, which had been founded in San Francisco by A. P. Giannini in 1904, built its first head office in 1908. For this reason, the *Portsmouth* is pictured on the bank's seal.)

Montgomery Street was named after Captain Montgomery, and the plaza, where the first American flag was raised in San Francisco, was afterward called Portsmouth Square in honor of the United States sloop of war *Portsmouth*. Now, it is officially Portsmouth Plaza (SRL 119).

In 1849 and the 1850's Portsmouth Square became the place where the principal gambling houses were situated. "Neither tree, shrub, nor grass adorned it, but it contained a rude platform for public speaking, a tall flag staff, and a cow pen enclosed by rough board." Today, Portsmouth Plaza, location of an underground parking garage since 1962, is planted with trees and grass. The fantastic pagoda roofs of Chinatown look down upon it, and Chinese mothers sun their babies on its green slope. As in the days of Robert Louis Stevenson and Jack London, men of all nations still seek its hospitable benches, where they may let the wheels of progress roll by unheeded for a few brief moments.

On the plaza near the corner of Clay and Kearny streets is a monument commemorating the Clay Street Hill Railroad Company (SRL 500), first cable railroad system in the world. Andrew S. Hallidie, English builder of aerial cables for use in Western mines, invented an arrangement whereby heavy cables could be laid underground to draw cars uphill. The first successful car thus equipped ran from Kearny Street to Leavenworth Street on Clay Street on August 1, 1873, and soon thereafter such lines were in general use. At one time San Francisco had eight lines, but now there are only three. The Clay Street line had its final run on February 15, 1942. San Francisco's cable cars, perhaps its most famous tourist attraction, have been registered as a National Historic Landmark by the Department of the Interior.

Portsmouth Plaza "is now the chief center of Stevenson associations in the city; for it was here Robert Louis went to observe at close range and to talk to the flotsam and jetsam of humanity drifting in from the mighty Pacific Ocean. Who knows but he found here Long John Silver and Blind Pew? The monument in Portsmouth Square, planned and executed by Bruce Porter and Willis Polk, is the perpetual memorial of San Francisco to Stevenson." This is the first monument (1897) to be erected anywhere to him, and of all the landmarks in San Francisco, it is the one most closely connected with Stevenson. It stands in the middle of the part of the city he found most interesting, which he portrayed in *The Wrecker*.

Much of the work that Stevenson began in Monterey was finished in San Francisco, notably *Across the Plains* and *The Amateur Emigrant*. Some of his dearest friendships were formed there, with Virgil Williams, painter and founder of the California School of Art, and his wife; Judge Rearden and Judge John Boalt; and Charles Warren Stoddard, professor and author. Stoddard was influential in centering Stevenson's interest in the South Seas, where he spent the latter part of his life.

"No other Stevenson land-mark remains in the city. The old Carson House (608 Bush Street) was torn down long before the great fire and a new building erected, and this, with all that section, was eventually burned. The house at No. 7 Montgomery Street, in which he lived a few days after his marriage, is gone, as well as Donadieu's (the restaurant on Bush Street, between Kearny and Dupont—now Grant) and the Sixth Street Coffee House (near Market)—all gone! And the Stoddard Studio on Rincon Hill where Stevenson visited the author of the 'South Sea Idylls'—this has been swallowed up by ravenous time too. No other building was frequented by Robert Louis in his San Francisco sojourn, which in truth was doubtless not more than five months," from December 1879 to May 1880. At the northwest corner of Hyde and Lombard streets is a house that survived the fire of 1906 and was once the home of Mrs. Robert Louis Stevenson, who resided there after her famous husband's death. The house is now owned by descendants of the pioneer James Phelan and John Sullivan families.

San Francisco's First Schools

Soon after the American occupation in 1846, the need of a school for the children of the rapidly growing town began to be agitated. In April 1847 the first private school in San Francisco was opened by J. D. Marston in a shanty on the west side of Grant Avenue between Broadway and Pacific Avenue. It was attended by some 20 or 30 children, but it lasted only a few months.

The site of what has been called San Francisco's first public school (SRL 587) is on the southwest corner of Portsmouth Plaza, and has been marked by the Grand Lodge of Free and Accepted Masons. In the autumn of 1847 a committee met to plan the building, and on April 3, 1848, school was opened by Thomas Douglas, a graduate of Yale. The gold excitement took Douglas away to the mines six weeks later, but the school was resumed in April 1849 by Rev. Albert Williams, a Presbyterian minister.

This small shanty of a schoolhouse was used for various purposes, "town hall, court house, people's court for trial of culprits by the first vigilance committee, school, church, and finally, jail. Owing to the range and variety of its uses, the building was dignified by the name of Public Institute." The Public Institute School, however (like others in that early period), was not a public school in the modern sense, for it was obliged to charge some tuition and was not under complete government control.

In October 1849, John Cotter Pelton, a young New England schoolteacher and a layman of the Baptist church, came to California to establish free public schools. On December 26, 1849, he opened a school in the First Baptist Church at 878-A Washington Street east of Stockton. There were only three children present the first day, but within a few days the number had increased to 50. In spite of financial discouragements, Pelton would accept no tuition in his school and worked indefatigably to arouse public interest and action in behalf of the free public school as an established institution.

As a result of Pelton's efforts, his school was adopted by the city in March 1850, and the first public school in California became a reality. On April 8, 1850, the first school ordinance in the state was passed. This site has been marked with a bronze tablet placed by the Northern California Baptist Convention.

Another early school was established in Happy Valley in 1850, as noted below.

At the entrance to The Emporium, on the south side of Market Street between Fourth and Fifth streets, is a plaque noting that St. Ignatius College was founded on the site in 1855. The Jesuit school was moved to Van Ness Avenue and Hayes Street, near the present Civic Center, in 1880. It is now the University of San Francisco and is located west of the downtown area between Lone Mountain and the Panhandle of Golden Gate Park.

St. Mary's College (SRL 772) was founded in San Francisco in 1863 by Archbishop Joseph Sadoc Alemany, O.P. A marker at College and Crescent avenues near Mission Street indicates the original site. The Christian Brothers took charge of the college in 1868, and in 1889 it was moved to Oakland. In 1928 it became located at its present campus in Moraga.

The First Churches

The Mormons, under Sam Brannan, held religious services in Captain Richardson's "Casa Grande" on Dupont Street soon after their arrival, and a Sunday school was organized by a Methodist missionary, Rev. James H. Wilbur, on May 16, 1847. The former organization did not hold together long, and the Sunday school was soon disrupted by the gold stampede. But other organizations at once took their places.

On July 25, 1847, Chaplain Chester Newell, of the United States frigate *Independence*, preached in the C. L. Ross store, on the northwest corner of Washington and Montgomery streets. Although there were probably other services held by ships' chaplains, this is the first recorded Protestant divine service in San Francisco.

The first record of a sermon preached after the opening of the mines was that of Rev. Elihu Anthony, a Methodist from New York. It was delivered in the Public Institute on September 3, 1848. Other services were held in this building that month, and in October Rev. Timothy Dwight Hunt, a native of New York, who had just returned from missionary work in the Sandwich Islands, was appointed chaplain of the town for one year. Services were held in the Institute, this being the only organized institution for Protestant worship in the city until the spring of 1849. It was patronized by members of every religious persuasion.

The first ships landing at San Francisco in the year 1849 brought not only feverish Argonauts seeking the golden fleece but several missionary preachers as well. These men, together with the teachers and some of the merchants, such as C. L. Ross, W. D. M. Howard, Nathan Spear, and C. E. Wetmore, were the real builders and founders of San Francisco. They were the molders of the spiritual life of the city, working in the middle of the rough, mad turmoil of the gold days to plant the finest traditions of the American nation in this new and chaotic commonwealth. In many cases these missionaries and their successors were both preachers and teachers and played a considerable part in the government as well.

In August 1849 the following Protestant organizations were holding services in the city: (1) The Chaplaincy, Rev. T. D. Hunt, Public Institute; (2) First Presbyterian, Rev. Albert Williams, in a large tent on Dupont Street, near Pacific; (3) First Baptist, Rev. O. C. Wheeler, church on Washington Street, near Stockton; (4) Protestant Episcopal, Rev. Flavil S. Mines, in the house of J. H. Merrill. It is interesting, also, to learn that "on the 8th of October, a Methodist Episcopal Church, shipped from Oregon and set up on a Powell Street lot, was dedicated by the missionary minister, the Rev. William Taylor, assisted by the Rev. Mr. Hunt, Rev. Albert Williams, and Rev. O. C. Wheeler."

At 100 McAllister Street, near the Civic Center, stands a structure originally named in honor of San Francisco's pioneer Methodist preacher, William Taylor, whose "unique career as street preacher earned for him the nickname 'California Taylor.'" This building was erected in 1927–30 as the William Taylor Church and Hotel by the united efforts of the Methodist churches of San Francisco and their friends, at a cost of over $3,000,000. The Methodists vacated the building in 1937, and it is now used for federal offices. Taylor and the Rev. Isaac Owen did much to establish religious and educational institutions in California, in the years between 1849 and 1856.

St. Francis Church at the northeast corner of Vallejo Street and Columbus Avenue is, after Mission Dolores, the oldest Roman Catholic parish in San Francisco, having been established in 1849. The present building was erected in 1859. Its interior was destroyed by the great fire of 1906, but the walls remained intact and it is now fully restored. St. Patrick's Church was founded in 1851. The old wooden building that stood on Market Street about where the Palace Hotel was later built has been moved several times and now stands on the north side of Eddy Street east of Divisadero, where it is in use as the parish hall of Holy Cross Church. It is one of the oldest frame buildings in the city. The present St. Patrick's at 756 Mission Street was rebuilt after the 1906 disaster but incorporates portions of the structure erected about 1870.

Old St. Mary's Church (SRL 810), at California Street and Grant Avenue, San Francisco's first Catholic cathedral, was dedicated in 1854. The bricks came around the Horn, and some of the stone from China. It was replaced in 1891 by a new cathedral at Van Ness Avenue and O'Farrell Street, and three years later was put under the charge of the Paulist Fathers. Only the walls survived the fire of 1906. The church was rebuilt within them and rededicated in 1909. St. Mary's Cathedral on Van Ness Avenue was spared in 1906 but was destroyed by fire on September 7, 1962, and was subsequently torn down. A new cathedral of contemporary style is to be built in the block bounded by Gough, Ellis, Octavia, and Geary streets.

St. Ignatius Church was established with the college in 1855 on the present site of The Emporium on Market Street. It now stands on the campus of the University of San Francisco, facing Fulton Street.

Thomas Starr King, beloved Unitarian preacher and "apostle of the Union cause, toured the State in a remarkably effective campaign to arouse the spirit of loyalty" throughout California. He "threw himself with his marvelous talent into the breach to champion his country's cause with an irresistible eloquence.... It was the eloquence of Starr King that saved the [Sanitary] Commission's work from financial ruin." (The Sanitary Commission was the Civil War counterpart of the Red Cross.) Starr King's portrait was hung in the state capitol and bears the inscription: "The man whose matchless oratory saved California to the Union."

Starr King came to San Francisco from Boston in 1860, a young man already winning fame. Until his death in 1864 he served as pastor of the First Unitarian Church, the first site of which was on Stockton Street near Sacramento. Since the town was growing southward, a new church was built at 133 Geary Street near Stockton soon after King's arrival. In this church he preached and there he was buried. Later, the city's growth necessitated the removal of the church to its present site at Geary and Franklin streets. Here the body of Starr King now lies in a white marble tomb (SRL 691) before the door of the church. A bronze statue was erected in Golden Gate Park as an expression of San Francisco's appreciation of his life and services. A statue of him done by Haig Patigian has been placed, along with one of Father Junípero Serra done by Ettore Cadorin, to represent California in Statuary Hall in the Capitol Building at Washington, D.C.

On the west side of Montgomery Street near Columbus Avenue a plaque has been placed to mark the site of the first Jewish religious services in San Francisco (SRL 462). Here 40 pioneers gathered to celebrate Yom Kippur on September 26, 1849.

Monuments on Market Street

Perhaps the best known and most beloved monument on Market Street is Lotta's Fountain, at the intersection of Geary and Kearny streets. This ungainly shaft was presented to the city in 1875 by Lotta Crabtree, famed entertainer who began her career as a child in gold rush days. In 1910 Luisa Tetrazzini sang at midnight on Christmas Eve before hushed thousands massed around the fountain. In commemoration of this event a bas-relief portrait of Tetrazzini by Haig Patigian was added to the fountain.

At Market, Battery, and Bush streets is the Mechanics Monument, dedicated about the turn of the century to Peter Donahue, pioneer industrialist. The sculptor was the deaf-mute Douglas Tilden. The Pioneer Monument, a gift of James Lick, was erected in 1894 at Market, Hyde, and Grove streets.

The Native Sons' Monument in Golden Gate Park originally stood at Market, Turk, and Mason streets. It was given to the city by James D. Phelan to commemorate the admission of California to the Union, and was unveiled on Admission Day, September 9, 1897, dedicated to the Native Sons of the Golden West. It is in the form of a drinking fountain surmounted by the bronze figure of an angel holding aloft an open book on which is inscribed the date of California's admission to the Union. At the base of the shaft stands a miner with a pick in his right hand, while in his left he holds high an American flag, with California's new star in the field.

Happy Valley

"The space from California Street to the line of Market Street was a region of high sand-hills covered with a scattering growth of brush and scrub oak; but following the curving shore of the cove to the south, one came to a little valley protected on the west by the sand-hills of Market Street. Here, sheltered from the harsh winds, tents had been set up and the place named Happy Valley. This was between First, Second, Market, and Mission streets. It was supplied with a good spring of water and contained in the winter of 1849–50, about one thousand tents.... In Happy Valley, W. D. M. Howard put up a number of cottages that he had made in Boston, in one of which he lived."

In 1850 a school was opened in this district, which, through the efforts of those interested, became very flourishing. One of its founders was Rev. Samuel H. Willey, pastor of the Howard Presbyterian Church in Happy Valley, and later one of the founders of the College of California in Oakland. W. D. M. Howard, a prominent merchant, and Thomas J. Nevins greatly aided Willey in building up this school, which became known as the Happy Valley Public School. In November 1851 it became the first school opened under the city public school system.

The San Francisco Post Office

According to Harry L. Todd, "the establishment of the San Francisco Post Office became effective November 9, 1848, when William Van Vorheis was commissioned Assistant Postmaster General for California, by President Polk, and Samuel York, at Lee, was appointed first Postmaster. For some reason, York [Yorke] never entered upon the discharge of his duties, and Stephen J. Dallas was appointed, November 21, 1848, serving for the brief period of two months only. General John W. Geary, for whom Geary Street was named, became Postmaster on January 22, 1849, and served for less than three months, when he was chosen . . . Alcalde of San Francisco. He was succeeded by Jacob B. Moore, who was appointed April 17, 1849. Mr. Moore was the real organizer of the Postal Service in San Francisco.

"The first post office was located at the northeast corner of Stockton and Washington streets. The office consisted of one room only, in which there were two clerks. It remained there but a short time, when it was moved to the corner of Clay and Pike streets, the latter now called Waverly Place. There it remained for a few years and was the scene of many memorable events in San Francisco's postal history. From Clay and Pike streets it was moved to a location on Clay Street just above Kearny facing Portsmouth Square. It remained in this location until 1857, when it was transferred to the ground floor of the Custom House building, and from that place it was moved to its present location at Seventh and Mission, in 1905."

During the days when mails arrived only at long intervals, the post office was still located on the Waverly Place site. It was then "a place of popular interest not only for San Francisco but for all the mining district. When [a person left] home for the mines the only known address to give was San Francisco. So, notwithstanding the fact that the man might be two hundred miles away, his mail came to the San Francisco Post Office. The building was small and could accommodate but few clerks within. Outside there was little space for standing room. The mail arrived once a month. The task of sorting the mail kept the clerks busy for many hours. Meanwhile the anxious were awaiting their letters. Often they would hold their place in line all night in the rain in order to reach the window early in the morning. The lines often extended many blocks even out into the brush-covered sand-hills. Many desirous of adding to their funds, would secure good positions only to be able to sell them to others with more money than time. Ten to twenty dollars are said to have been paid for positions near the delivery window. Express carriers from the mines gathered up letters for their patrons and delivered them at one dollar each. The Postmaster at San Francisco was given twenty-five cents of this amount for permitting the sorting of the mail."

The Shoreline Markers

The location of the shoreline on Market Street as it was at the time of the discovery of gold at Coloma, in 1848, was marked by two bronze tablets *(SRL 83)* on April 16, 1921, by the Landmarks Committee of the Native Sons of the Golden West.

One of the tablets was placed on the corner of Market and First streets and reads as follows: "The Shore-line of San Francisco reached a point twenty-five feet northeasterly from this spot at the time gold was discovered by James W. Marshall at Coloma, California, January 24, 1848."

The other tablet was placed across the street at the base of the Donahue Monument, where

Battery and Bush streets run into Market Street. On this tablet is reproduced a map of the old shoreline from Howard Street to Pacific Street.

The Tidelands of Yerba Buena Cove

Eldredge says that "San Francisco began to improve immediately after the American occupation and its future greatness as the metropolis of the Pacific was clearly foreseen. The people recognized the necessity for wharves to deep water and for filling in and building upon the mud flats lying before the town."

On February 15, 1847, a petition was made to the Governor asking that the tidelands of Yerba Buena Cove be granted to the town. On March 10, 1847, General Stephen W. Kearny, military governor, released to the town all government claims of title to the beach and water lots between what was formerly Clark's Point and the Rincon, except the claims to a few lots reserved for government use. Although it was thought that General Kearny did not have the right to make such a grant, the state in 1851 ceded this section "to the city for a period of ninety-nine years and confirmed previous sales."

The First Wharves

A little pier for the landing of small boats at high tide was built at the foot of Clay Street in 1846. The principal landing place, however, was at the Punta del Embarcadero, or Clark's Point, now the corner of Broadway and Battery streets. A small wharf was built there in 1847 by William S. Clark, replacing the town's first permanent wharf built there in the year 1839. Clark's Point was at first known as the Punta de la Loma Alta. In 1839 this land was granted to Jacob Primer Leese and Salvador Vallejo, who later transferred his interest to Leese. The grant was bounded by what are now Vallejo, Front, Pacific, and Davis streets.

In 1848 William S. Clark came to Yerba Buena and occupied this same land. Years of litigation followed, which resulted unfavorably to Leese, while Clark enjoyed the rich proceeds of the property. Bordering on the new city's best waterfront where deep-sea vessels could discharge, its value became very great. Today, it is covered by extensive warehouses and receives the bulk of storage merchandise from ships.

All of San Francisco's present streets below Montgomery between California and Broadway were originally wharves.

In the spring of 1848 the Central Wharf was built "from the bank in the middle of the block between Sacramento and Clay streets, where Leidesdorff Street now is, eight hundred feet into the Bay." After 1850 it was extended 2,000 feet, and the Pacific Mail steamers and other large vessels anchored there. At the shore end of Leidesdorff Street was the office of the Pacific Mail Steamship Company.

Central Wharf, or Long Wharf *(SRL 328)*, as it was called, soon "became the favorite promenade. Buildings perched on piles sprang up quickly on either side, and commission houses, groceries, saloons, mock auctions, cheap-John shops, and ped-

Commercial Street (Long Wharf)

dlers did a thriving business. Central Wharf is now Commercial Street."

The success of Central Wharf caused other wharves to be built, until the whole area was covered with wharves and alleyways. Gradually the entire cove was filled in, mostly with sand from the great dunes stretching behind Yerba Buena.

In 1853 Meiggs Wharf was built in the area between the foot of Mason Street and the foot of Powell Street. It was constructed by Henry (Honest Harry) Meiggs, a prominent city official and businessman, who fled San Francisco to South America in 1859 to escape thousands of dollars of bad debts. He became prosperous for a time by building railroads in Chile and Peru. By 1881 Meiggs Wharf was enclosed by a seawall. The present Fisherman's Wharf is in the vicinity.

Nearby are Aquatic Park and the Maritime Museum. At the foot of Hyde Street is the San Francisco Maritime State Historic Park, consisting of a number of old ships, restored and open to the public. Among them are the lumber schooner *C. A. Thayer* (1895), the San Francisco Bay ferry *Eureka* (1890), the steam schooner *Wapama* (1915), and the schooner-scow *Alma* (1891). The park was opened in the fall of 1963. Anchored nearby at Pier 43 is the old square-rigger *Balclutha* (1886), the last of the fleet of grain ships that called San Francisco home port. It sailed around Cape Horn 17 times and around the Cape of Good Hope four times.

West of Aquatic Park is Fort Mason, called Black Point in the early days. Several buildings

from the 1850's still stand, among them McDonald Hall, the officers' club off the entrance from Bay Street and Van Ness Avenue, which was once the commanding general's quarters. The Haskell house (Quarters 3), east of the north end of Franklin Street, is the home in which Senator David C. Broderick died in 1859 after his duel with Judge David S. Terry. The home of General and Mrs. John C. Frémont no longer stands. The area was set aside as a military reservation in 1850 and was later named for Colonel Richard Barnes Mason.

As population increased in both San Francisco and the East Bay, the question of convenient transbay travel arose. Ferry lines increased in number, as did the docks along the Embarcadero, the name given to the street at the water's edge.

On the Embarcadero at the foot of Market Street, where a shed had been erected in 1877, the Ferry Building of Colusa sandstone, located about midway between Black Point and Mission Rock, was constructed in 1896–1903. Through it poured the morning and evening throngs of local commuters as well as overland passengers to and from the transcontinental trains at their Oakland terminal. This building is flanked by wharves and docks for the use of vessels of all descriptions—from tugboats to ocean liners flying flags of foreign nations. Ferry service to Oakland was sharply curtailed after January 1939, but the Southern Pacific Railroad operated some ferryboats until 1959. The old Ferry Building, now converted to other uses, remains as one of San Francisco's best known and most revered landmarks.

San Francisco Bay, long crossed only by boats, is now crossed by means of six bridges. The most southerly bridge, completed in 1911 by the Southern Pacific Railroad Company, is used mainly for freight trains. Completed respectively in 1927 and 1929, the Dumbarton Bridge and the San Mateo Bridge, connecting the counties of Alameda and San Mateo, are designed for motor traffic.

Two bridges have been built across the bay to meet the demands of modern travel between San Francisco and the regions to the north and east. These are the San Francisco–Oakland Bay Bridge and the Golden Gate Bridge.

The San Francisco–Oakland Bay Bridge was opened to traffic by a gala celebration on November 15, 1936. This giant structure of steel and concrete is approached at its western end by ramps that lead over certain downtown streets in San Francisco to the first span over the water near Pier 26 at the Embarcadero. A land link of this bridge is constructed on Yerba Buena Island, midway between the two cities and just within the boundary of San Francisco City and County.

The Golden Gate Bridge crosses the channel between old Fort Point in San Francisco and Lime Point on the Marin County side. Construction was begun in January 1933 and the bridge was opened on May 27, 1937. Converging roadways at either end lead to the single suspension span, which is 4,200 feet long and at its center is 230 feet above the water.

The newest and northernmost bridge across

San Francisco Bay is the Richmond–San Rafael Bridge, connecting Contra Costa and Marin counties. It was constructed in 1952–56.

Niantic Hotel

The site of the old Niantic Hotel *(SRL 88)* is on the northwest corner of Clay and Sansome streets. Early in the spring of 1849 the ship *Niantic* was anchored on this spot, after it had brought 250 emigrants from Panama at $150 a head. Since it was impossible to obtain a crew for the return voyage because of the lure of the gold mines, it was necessary to leave the ship where it was.

Storeroom and lodging accommodations were very meager in San Francisco at that time, and any sort of space covered with a roof brought enormous rents. Thus it was not long before the old ship was leased out to various occupants, who used it as stores and offices. The hull was used as a warehouse. This ship was connected with the land by the Clay Street Wharf, which before long was lined with structures built on piles.

On May 4, 1851, the *Niantic* was burned to the water's edge in one of the great fires that devastated San Francisco in the early 1850's. On the hulk of the ship was erected the Niantic Hotel, which gave place in 1872 to the Niantic Block.

On September 8, 1919, the Native Sons of the Golden West placed a marker on the building now standing on the site of the old emigrant ship *Niantic*. The legend reads as follows: "The emigrant ship, 'Niantic,' stood on this spot in the early days, 'when the water came up to Montgomery Street.' Converted to other uses, it was covered with a shingle roof, with offices and stores on deck, at the level of which was constructed a wide balcony surmounted by a veranda. The hull was divided into warehouses, entered by doorways on the side."

Many other ships were abandoned in Yerba Buena Cove in 1849. Although some of them were unseaworthy, even sound ships often had to remain where they had been anchored, owing to the inability of their owners to obtain a crew for the return voyage. Besides the *Niantic* there were the *General Harrison* (northwest corner of Clay and Battery streets), the *Apollo* (northwest corner of Sacramento and Battery streets), the *Georgian* (between Washington and Jackson streets, west of Battery Street), and the *Euphemia* (near Battery and Sacramento). Most of them were used as warehouses until the fire of May 1851, when they were destroyed. Before 1851 the *Euphemia* was purchased by the city government and used as a prison. Balance Street, off Jackson Square, received its name from the ship *Balance* buried there. Lower Market Street covers the remains of three sailing vessels, *Callao*, *Bryon*, and *Galen*. At the southwest corner of Sacramento and Front streets is the *Thomas Bennett*. The English brig *Hardie* and the ships *Noble* and *Inez* are in the block bounded by Pacific Avenue, Drumm, Davis, and Jackson streets. The bark *Elizabeth* is under the Embarcadero between Clay and Merchant streets, while the ship *Alida* is beneath Davis Street between Washington and Jackson streets. These are a few of the gold rush fleet buried beneath the streets of old San Francisco.

Pioneer Buildings and Sites

Several pioneer buildings known to be standing in San Francisco at the present time are in the vicinity of Montgomery Street. Others were torn down during the 1950's and 1960's, but this same period saw the restoration of a number of the finest ones in the Jackson Square project.

San Francisco's outstanding attempt at historic preservation takes its name from Jackson Street. It began with the renovation by wholesale interior decorating firms of several old brick warehouses on what was once the waterfront. Cement veneers and other evidences of modernization were removed, and the buildings stood once again as they had in the 1850's and 1860's. Before long, other businesses were attracted, and a once shabby district was transformed into a handsome, useful center. Jackson Square is proof that historic values need not be lost, that renewal and redevelopment can be accomplished without the bulldozer.

On the east side of Montgomery Street between Washington and Jackson streets are several buildings erected in the 1850's, notably those at 722–28 Montgomery. At 722–24 is the building opened as a variety theater on December 15, 1857. A plaque at 728 indicates the site of the first recorded meeting of Free and Accepted Masons in California *(SRL 408)*, on October 17, 1849. The old warehouse of F. L. A. Pioche, pioneer French

722–28 Montgomery Street, Jackson Square

merchant, is one of the most recent San Francisco landmarks to perish. It stood into the 1960's at the southeast corner of Montgomery and Jackson streets and was among the very oldest buildings in the area.

At the northeast corner of Montgomery and Jackson is the building *(SRL 453)* to which William Tecumseh Sherman moved the branch bank of Lucas, Turner and Company in 1854. He had established the branch the year before and headed its operation until 1857. The corner buildings at Jackson Street and Hotaling Place were built about 1860 and served as warehouses for the Hotaling liquor business. The fact that they, like the other solid structures in the present Jackson Square area, escaped the disaster of 1906, inspired a popular jingle by Charles K. Field:

> "If, as they say, God spanked the town
> For being over-frisky,
> Why did He burn the churches down
> And save Hotaling's whisky?"

Remnants of the old Hotaling stables are in evidence in the building at 38 Hotaling Place, and in the basement of No. 42 is the entrance to a brick tunnel said to have been used by smugglers to bring contraband from the wharf to downtown San Francisco.

The building at 432 Jackson Street has served as the Tremont Hotel and the French consulate. The Ghirardelli Chocolate Company was once located in the building at 435–41 Jackson. (This is not to be confused with Ghirardelli Square, another historical center, at 900 North Point Street near Fort Mason.) The Jackson Square area has been extended to include the old Barbary Coast on Pacific Avenue, one of the most infamous sections of any city in the world. Some of the Barbary Coast landmarks still standing are the former Hippodrome Dance Hall and Bar at 555 Pacific, the House of Blue Lights at 551, and the firehouse at 449.

The Montgomery Block *(SRL 80)*, first known as the Washington Block, stood on the east side of Montgomery Street with sides on Washington and Merchant streets. It was begun in July 1853 and was opened in December of that year. The architect was Gordon C. Cummings. It was a four-story-and-basement brick structure with iron shutters at the windows and a doorway flanked by cut-stone pillars. The chief features of the

Montgomery Block, San Francisco

Sherman's Bank, Jackson Square

building were cast-iron keystones with portrait heads. Above the heavy doors of the main entrance on Montgomery Street was carved the head of George Washington. While the building was new, the owners, the law firm of Halleck, Peachy and Billings, had their offices on the second floor. Among the tenants were other law firms and financiers. For 30 years a part of the Sutro Library was housed there. In more recent times the old redwood foundations were replaced by concrete and the exterior was somewhat modernized, but the old block, which survived the earthquake and fire of 1906, stood solidly for well over a century. In 1959 this fine landmark gave way to a parking lot.

On the southwest corner of Montgomery and Merchant (617 Montgomery) stood the western business headquarters of Russell, Majors, and Waddell—a Leavenworth, Kansas, firm that operated the Pony Express *(SRL 696)*. On April 14, 1860, the first westbound rider arrived here from St. Joseph, Missouri. The Pony Express ceased operation in 1861.

At 608 Commercial Street is the old U.S. Subtreasury Building, now reduced from three stories to one. At this site in 1854 the first U.S. branch mint in California *(SRL 87)* was established.

Under the rule of Spain, and later of Mexico, business in California had been transacted mainly through barter; for a time after the American occupation and the discovery of great quantities of gold, payment was made with gold dust. This led to the coining of the metal. In 1849–50 there were 15 different institutions making coins of various kinds in California. One of these establishments was situated on the south side of Portsmouth Plaza. O. P. Dutton was the director and F. D. Kohler the assayer. Coins made here were stamped with the name of the Pacific Company and dated 1849.

Although private coins were legal tender until 1856, an act passed by the United States Congress on July 3, 1852, directed the establishment of a government branch mint in San Francisco. The building on Commercial Street opened on April 3, 1854. The first assayer was Agoston Haraszthy, later famous for his vineyards at Sonoma. Bret Harte was employed at the mint as bookkeeper for a time.

Another mint was constructed in 1870–74 at Fifth and Mission streets. Designed by government architect A. B. Mullet, it is a fine example of the Greek Revival style typical of federal buildings in Washington, D.C. It survived the 1906 fire, only to be supplanted by a new mint in 1937. Today, the timeworn yet still beautiful structure is occupied by various federal offices. It has been declared eligible for registration as a National Historic Landmark by the Department of the Interior. The new mint at Buchanan Street and Duboce Avenue closed in 1955, but reopened in 1965.

In the early 1840's the Hudson's Bay Company had an establishment on Montgomery Street between Clay and Sacramento streets. William Glen Rae was sent to San Francisco as agent for the company, with Robert Birnie as a clerk. The lot was bought from Jacob P. Leese, the purchase price being $4,600, of which half was paid in money and the other half in goods. The building already standing upon the site occupied a space of about 30 × 80 feet and was divided in the middle by a hall into store and dwelling. The Hudson's Bay Company business was carried on there until 1846, when the San Francisco office was abandoned and the property was sold to Mellus and Howard. The building was afterward the United States Hotel. The Mellus and Howard Warehouse (SRL 459), built in 1848, once stood at the southwest corner of Montgomery and Clay. Here, on August 31, 1850, the Society of California Pioneers, oldest historical society in the state, was organized. W. D. M. Howard was the first president.

The office of the California Star, the first newspaper published in San Francisco (SRL 85), was on Brenham Place at the southwest corner of Washington Street, just west of Portsmouth Plaza. It stood behind the house of its publisher, Sam Brannan. Elbert P. Jones was the editor, and the first number was issued on January 9, 1847. The name of this paper was twice changed. From 1849 until it was discontinued in the late 1880's it was called the Alta California. The site is now identifiable by the building at 743 Washington Street, the first Oriental-style structure to be built in Chinatown. Erected in 1909, it long served as the Chinese telephone exchange and is now a branch of the Bank of Canton.

At 405 Montgomery Street, at the corner of California, is the site of the Parrott Block (SRL

89), San Francisco's first fireproof building. Constructed in 1852 of granite blocks brought from China, the three-story building came through the earthquake and fire of 1906 relatively unscathed, but in 1926 it was demolished to make way for the Financial Center Building.

On the south side of Clay Street, between Kearny and Montgomery, is the site of the Portsmouth House opened as California's first hotel in 1846.

The El Dorado and the Parker House (SRL 192), once on the east side of Portsmouth Plaza, were among the most famous of the saloons and gambling resorts clustered about the center of the city's activity in 1849 and the early 1850's. The Parker House was destroyed by fire three times and as many times rebuilt. Later it was incorporated into the Jenny Lind Theater, which, after two fires, became the City Hall in 1852. This was finally taken down in 1895 to make way for the Hall of Justice. This in turn was destroyed by the fire of 1906 but was rebuilt. It now stands vacant since the construction of a new Hall of Justice at Seventh and Bryant streets in 1961. The four-story El Dorado, also destroyed by fires and rebuilt, was eventually incorporated into the old City Hall as the Hall of Records.

Another hotel, the What Cheer House (SRL 650), opened in 1852 by R. B. Woodward, stood between Montgomery and Leidesdorff streets on the south side of Sacramento Street; the Oriental Hotel (1854) stood on the southwest corner of Battery and Bush streets; the Tehama House (1851), frequented by the elite of the town, stood at the northwest corner of California and Sansome streets where now the Bank of California is located.

The International Hotel (1854) stood on the north side of Jackson Street east of Kearny. The Russ Building on Montgomery Street between Bush and Pine today occupies the site of the Russ home and hotel owned by J. C. Christian Russ, who came to California with Company C, New York Volunteers, in 1847.

The American Theater was built on the northeast corner of Sansome and Halleck in 1851. Maguire's Opera House was built in 1852 on Washington Street between Montgomery and Kearny. The Olympic Theater, built in 1853 and known until October of that year as Armory Hall, stood at the northwest corner of Washington and Sansome streets.

The site of the old California Theater (SRL 86) is at 444 Bush Street. It was built by a syndicate headed by William C. Ralston, William Sharon, C. N. Felton, and H. P. Wakelee. The architect, S. C. Bugbee, was ordered to construct a building seating 1,600 and guaranteed to withstand earthquake and fire. Its grand opening was on January 15, 1869, under the direction of the actor-managers Lawrence Barrett and John McCullough, who presented Lytton's comedy Money with a distinguished cast. A tablet installed by the Commonwealth Club at the suggestion of the last surviving member of the cast, Emelie Melville, marks the site.

The first bridge erected in San Francisco was

Old Mint, Fifth and Mission Streets

placed over the tidal inlet to a salt-water lagoon on the east side of Montgomery Street at Jackson by Alcalde William S. Hinckley.

The site of the first Mechanics Fair (1857) is on the west side of Montgomery Street between Post and Sutter. The site of the first Pioneer Hall, built in 1863, is at the corner of Montgomery and Gold streets.

Union Square (SRL 623), bounded by Post, Geary, Stockton, and Powell streets, was set aside for public use on January 3, 1850, during the administration of John White Geary, the first mayor. Geary had served a short time as postmaster the year before, and later he became governor of Kansas and of Pennsylvania. The square received its name in 1860 when pro-Union meetings were held there. An underground parking garage was built beneath the square in 1942.

The main entrance to Woodward's Gardens (SRL 454), a pioneer amusement resort, was on the west side of Mission Street between Duboce Avenue and Fourteenth Street. R. B. Woodward built here his private home about 1866 and filled it with art pieces. Finding that his collections would be appreciated by the public, he opened his grounds and built an octagonal pavilion with a seating capacity of more than 5,000, to be used for plays, dances, and skating. He added a zoological department across Fourteenth Street, with wild animals and an aquarium. A tunnel beneath the street connected the two parts.

Hubert Howe Bancroft began in 1859 to collect material on the history of California, the basis for his voluminous writings. The Bancroft Building on Market Street was destroyed by fire in 1886, but the historian's vast library did not perish, for in 1881 he had built a special depository for it. The first Bancroft Library (SRL 791) was located at 1538 Valencia Street. In 1905 the collection was purchased by the University of California, and the following year it was moved to Berkeley. It is now housed in an annex to the main library on campus, and much material has been added to it through the years.

One of San Francisco's oldest houses stands back from the street at 329 Divisadero, hidden by a commercial building. It was built by John Middleton in 1850 of materials brought around the Horn.

"Fort Gunnybags"

The site of old "Fort Gunnybags," or Fort Vigilance, the headquarters of the San Francisco Vigilance Committee of the year 1856, is located at 243 Sacramento Street. The city at that time was given over to a reign of terror, the officials themselves being corrupt and in league with the lower elements, so that crime remained unpunished.

The occasion for the formation of the Second Vigilance Committee of 1856 was the murder of James King of William, free-lance editor of the Bulletin, by James P. Casey, whom King had denounced in his paper because of his political corruption.

The people of San Francisco demanded immediate punishment of the murderer, and since the regularly elected officials could not be depended upon, a committee of prominent citizens undertook to see that justice was meted out. William T. Coleman, organizer and leader of this Vigilance Committee, was made chairman, and thousands of citizens gave him their support. The committee not only brought Casey to justice, but it made a general clean-up of the city, and many notorious criminals were banished.

Hubert Howe Bancroft has called the work of the committee "one of the grandest moral revolutions the world has ever witnessed."

The Second Vigilance Committee was succeeded by the reform People's party, which governed San Francisco so well that, for years, it was one of the best regulated cities of the country.

The site of "Fort Gunnybags" (SRL 90) was first marked on March 21, 1903, by the California Landmarks League. In the fire of 1906 the old building was destroyed, and by the time the tablet was replaced on June 1, 1918, by the Native Sons of the Golden West, almost all who had taken part in the work of 1856 had died. At the top of the tablet is a representation of the all-seeing eye that adorned official documents issued by the committee.

Hills of San Francisco

The hills upon which San Francisco is built separated three original settlements now lying within the one great city. These settlements were the presidio, where soldiers were stationed for the protection of the interests of Spain; the mission, where the Spanish fathers carried on the work of civilizing and Christianizing the native Indians; and Yerba Buena, where persons of several nationalities who were mainly interested in commercial pursuits made early headquarters. Yerba Buena was the youngest and soon became the strongest. It grew and spread, up and over the hills, so that today's streets ascend and descend the heights, although the steepest parts have been somewhat lowered by grading for the pavements that now cover them.

Telegraph Hill (SRL 91), called by the Spaniards "Loma Alta" (high hill), with an elevation of 275 feet, is first in historic interest. It stands at the extreme northeast corner of the San Francisco Peninsula and extends back and upward from the Clark's Point of early days. From its top, on October 29, 1850, a fire signal was given to announce the news, brought by the steamer Oregon, of the admission of California as the 31st state of the Union.

The area considered a part of this hill up to 1850 was bounded by a line that runs, roughly, from the intersection of Broadway and Battery streets north and then west to Powell and Francisco streets, thence to the corner of Broadway and Kearny, and along Broadway to the point of beginning at Battery. A battery built in 1846 under the direction of Captain John B. Montgomery on the east side of Telegraph Hill gave the name to Battery Street.

Many people of Chilean origin in the San Francisco of early days had homes near the base of the hill, and in later years Italians predominated.

This section was often called the "Latin Quarter." On the slopes and summit lived the Irish. The part between Kearny and Montgomery and Green and Greenwich streets housed what was called the "Artist Colony" in the 1890's. Since the early 1930's the hill has become the site of expensive homes and apartment houses.

As early as 1849, Loma Alta was used as a station from which to observe incoming vessels and was sometimes called "Signal Hill." In September 1849 a two-story house, 25 × 18 feet, was erected on the top, and this was soon purchased by George Sweeny and Theodore E. Baugh, founders of the Merchants' Exchange. Within this house lived the observers who reported the nature of the approaching vessel—whether side-wheel steamer, sailing vessel, or other craft—to the people in the city below. Upon the top of this house stood a sort of semaphore by which an elaborate system of signals could be given. The place was known as the Inner Signal Station. The Outer Signal Station was then established near Point Lobos, where incoming craft could first be seen and reported by telegraph to the Inner Station. This was California's first telegraph line, opened in 1853. The same year the North Point Docks were constructed below the hill and Sansome Street was cut through it. The house that had stood on the top of the hill since 1849 blew down in a storm in 1870 and was not replaced.

Among the writers who have lived on Telegraph Hill are Mark Twain, Joaquin Miller, Frank Norris, Ambrose Bierce, "cynical poet and philosopher of old San Francisco," and Bret Harte, who complained that goats browsed on the geraniums in his second-story windows and tramped over the roof at night "like heavy hailstones." His story "The Secret of Telegraph Hill" is associated with this historic landmark. Charles Warren Stoddard called the goats that wandered here the "mascots of the hill," and Robert Louis Stevenson called the summit the "Peak of the Wind."

Actors have also lived on this hill. Among them perhaps the most famous was Edwin Booth, who lived in a house, no longer standing, on Calhoun Street.

"At 31 Alta Street is a little house built about 1852, with red brick foundation and frame superstructure, and narrow balcony with spindle railing. . . . At 228 Filbert Street opening on the terraced staircase of the hill is a very old and interesting house of slate-gray color, with several balconies. . . . The location, . . . the architectural ornaments at the gable and eaves make it quite unusual. . . . At the [northwest] corner of Montgomery and Union streets . . . is a square, flat-roofed house called 'the old Spanish House.' It has very thick walls, no window mouldings, deep window embrasures. The local inhabitants say it is the oldest house on Telegraph Hill, and that the modern . . . stucco covers a foundation of red brick." Some of the oldest houses on the hill, and in the city, stand on Napier Lane, off the Filbert Street stairway.

In 1876 a group of leading citizens donated to San Francisco a tract 275 feet square between Kearny, Greenwich, and Filbert streets, extending almost to Montgomery Street, as a park; later the city purchased an area of about the same size to extend the park to the summit. In the 1880's a "castle" stood on the top and a funicular railway ran up Greenwich Street. In the early 1900's the top of the hill was cleared and the area was named Pioneer Park.

On March 15, 1929, a ceremony attended the placing of a marker on this summit. The Sequoia Chapter, D.A.R., presented to the city a bronze tablet memorializing the Inner Signal Station and the first Western telegraph station. The tablet at that time was placed outdoors, but at the erection of the Coit Tower upon the top of Telegraph Hill, it was placed within that structure near the entrance. In 1939 a monument in honor of Guglielmo Marconi, inventor of the wireless, was erected on the northern face of Telegraph Hill.

The Coit Tower, about 210 feet in height, was constructed in 1933 with funds left by Mrs. Lillie Hitchcock Coit for the beautification of the city. Lillie, daughter of Dr. Hitchcock, arrived in San Francisco in 1851 at the age of eight. In her girlhood she was made an honorary member of one of the fire companies, the Knickerbocker Number Five. She died in July 1929. The view from the tower, or even from the ample parking space below it, is magnificent.

Russian Hill, probably so named because of an early unenclosed Russian sailors' graveyard upon its summit at the crest of Vallejo Street, is now a favored residential section. The growth of scrub oaks and chaparral that used to flourish on the lower western side of Telegraph Hill continued to the top of Russian Hill, not far beyond, where a few of the oaks may still be seen. The summit has an elevation of 360 feet, with wonderful sunset views. An observatory that stood there as early as 1863 was reached by means of a spiral staircase.

Among writers who have resided on this hill was Helen Hunt Jackson, who died there in 1886. Near her home on the eastern brow a mast was erected for use in the early days of wireless telegraphy. At Vallejo and Taylor streets is the site of Ina Coolbrith's home, now a tiny park named in her honor. She, Bret Harte, and Charles Warren Stoddard were known as the "Golden Gate Trinity" in the early days of the *Overland Monthly*. Beloved by all of California's poets and writers, Ina Coolbrith became the state poet laureate. Off Greenwich Street (stairway) between Hyde and Larkin streets is another small park, this one dedicated to the San Francisco poet George Sterling.

On the 1000 block of Green Street are several houses that escaped the fire of 1906. The Feusier Octagon House at 1067 Green, built in 1855, is one of two in San Francisco. The former firehouse at 1088, now an elegant residence, was built two years after the great fire. The famous architect Willis Polk built the house at 1013–17 Vallejo Street as his own residence in 1893. At 1023 Vallejo, far back from the street, is a house said to have been built in 1860. Hidden by trees and shrubbery at 1052 Broadway is one of the city's oldest houses, built by Joseph Atkinson in 1853.

Gallows for the first official execution in San Francisco were erected 100 feet west of the summit of Russian Hill, and there José Forni, a Spaniard who had committed murder in Happy Valley—now the vicinity of Mission Street between First and Third streets—was hanged in 1852.

Rincon Hill (SRL 84), which, along with Telegraph Hill, was recommended by Robert Louis Stevenson to the city dilettantes, rose from Rincon ("corner") Point shown on old maps of San Francisco. On the sheltered southern side of this point was a wooded area favored for picnic outings, and in that region George Gordon laid out South Park in 1852, patterning it somewhat after the squares in London. Each man who purchased a lot there was required to erect a fireproof house of brick. The center of the place was planted to grass and trees and was protected by an oval curbing that still remains. In South Park lived many people of education and social position, including Lloyd Tevis, David Colton, Isaac Friedlander, Reverend William A. Scott, Robert B. Woodward, Dr. Beverly Cole, Judge William T. Wallace, Judge Elisha W. McKinstry, and Mayor James Otis.

Higher upon Rincon Hill grander homes were built, among others those of William C. Ralston, Milton Latham, General Henry W. Halleck, John Parrott, Peter Donahue, General Albert Sidney Johnston, Senator William A. Gwin, Henry Miller, Mayor Thomas Selby, Joseph Donohoe, General William Tecumseh Sherman, H. W. Newhall, and the McAllisters. In 1852 the United States Marine Hospital was built on the eastern extremity, and in 1860 St. Mary's Hospital, first Catholic hospital on the Pacific Coast (now located on Hayes Street), was built on the hill to the south.

In 1869 Rincon Hill was cut at Second Street, after which the social prestige of the place declined. Some of the wealthy remained in their mansions, however, until the fire of 1906. In The Wrecker Stevenson tells of seeing the hill in its decline in 1879, when he visited Charles Warren Stoddard's residence, which at that time was on Vernon (now Dow Place) off Second Street. The economist Henry George lived at 420 Second Street, just south of Harrison, from 1861 to 1880, and here he wrote Progress and Poverty. The "Battle of Rincon Hill" between strike-breakers and striking longshoremen took place on the waterfront nearby on "Bloody Thursday," July 5, 1934. Two maritime workers were killed, several hundred persons were injured, and a general strike followed.

Rincon Hill occupied the area roughly bounded by Spear, Second, Folsom, and Brannan streets. The western anchorage and ramps of the San Francisco–Oakland Bay Bridge have necessitated the almost complete leveling of the hill.

West of Kearny Street is the elevation originally called Fern Hill, now called Nob Hill. Not until the cable car was perfected was it possible to make this ascent in comfort and safety. Pretentious homes erected on the hill by early financiers whose fortunes had been carved out of Western enterprises probably gave rise to the name "Nob Hill." Some of these homes were too lavish to be in good taste; others were beautiful. Most of them were destroyed in the fire of 1906. After the fire the pillars of the Grecian doorway of the A. N. Towne residence were left standing among the ruins. These "Portals of the Past" have been placed in Golden Gate Park on the banks of Lloyd Lake near the main drive.

On Nob Hill stood the homes of four of the builders of the Central Pacific Railroad, the "Big Four"—Stanford, Hopkins, Crocker, and Huntington. The mansion of Governor Leland Stanford was on the site now occupied by the Stanford Court Apartments at 901 California Street. The Mark Hopkins Hotel marks the site of Hopkins' mansion, and the carriage entrance and Mason Street retaining walls are from the original. In 1893 Edward F. Searles donated the mansion to the University of California, in trust for the San Francisco Art Institute, and it became San Francisco's first cultural center, the Mark Hopkins Institute of Art (SRL 754) "for instruction in and illustration of the fine arts, music and literature." (The San Francisco Art Institute is now located on Russian Hill at Chestnut and Jones streets.) Charles Crocker's mansion stood at the present site of Grace Cathedral of the Episcopal Diocese of California, now the crowning edifice of Nob Hill. Across California Street is the stately Masonic Temple, dedicated in 1958. Collis P. Huntington lived in the mansion built by David D. Colton, now the location of Huntington Park, bequeathed to the city by Huntington's widow in 1915.

Among other notable residents on Nob Hill were the "Silver Kings" of the Comstock Lode, James G. Fair and James C. Flood. On the Fair property has risen the Fairmont Hotel. At its top the time ball, placed there in 1909, daily descends to mark the hour of noon. The time ball was originally placed on the top of Telegraph Hill, then on the Ferry Building until 1909. The Flood residence is the only one of the great mansions remaining on Nob Hill. This brownstone structure is now the home of the Pacific Union Club at the northwest corner of California and Mason streets.

Lone Mountain rises to an elevation of 468 feet between Golden Gate Park and the Presidio. For years it was surmounted by a cross, first erected in 1862, which was removed to make room for the buildings of the San Francisco College for Women, a Catholic institution established in 1932. At the base of the mountain were four old cemeteries: to the north, Laurel Hill; to the east, Calvary; to the south, the Masonic; and to the west, the Odd Fellows. In 1937 the city voted to remove them.

Laurel Hill Cemetery (SRL 760) was laid out in 1854 when earlier burial places in the city were abandoned. Two earlier ones had been on Telegraph Hill, one on the southern slope near the corner of the present Sansome and Vallejo streets and one on the North Beach slope in an area bounded by Grant Avenue, Powell, Chestnut, and Francisco streets. Another small one had been near the top of Russian Hill and still another in an area at present Fulton and Hyde streets near the Civic Center. The oldest of these early cemeteries was the Catholic one at the mission, still intact.

Ultimately, the only burials permitted within the city limits were in the National Cemetery at the Presidio. This was superseded by the Golden Gate National Cemetery at San Bruno in 1941. Most of San Francisco's cemeteries are now located in the small city of Colma in San Mateo County. Laurel Hill Cemetery, the former burial place of many of the most distinguished figures of California's early days, is commemorated by a marker at 3333 California Street.

Twin Peaks has, as its name implies, two distinct elevations at its top: a north one of 903 feet and a south one of 910 feet. These were early called the "Mission Peaks" and, sometimes, "Los Pechos de la Choca" (the breasts of the Indian maiden). Here an extensive view repays a pleasant drive over a winding roadway to the top. From this vantage point may be seen Mount Hamilton and the Lick Observatory, Loma Prieta, stretching from Santa Clara County into Santa Cruz County, Mount Diablo in Contra Costa County, Mount Tamalpais and Point Reyes in Marin County, and the Farallones, off the coast.

Mount Davidson, with an elevation of 938 feet, is the highest peak in San Francisco. It was surveyed in 1852 by the United States Geodetic Survey under George Davidson and was named "Blue Mountain." It was included in Rancho San Miguel, afterward purchased by Adolph Sutro, outstanding citizen of San Francisco, who began the planting of the trees that now form Sutro Forest. Mount Sutro, with an elevation of 920 feet, is also in this forest. By 1911 the saplings had grown into trees and the highest peak was renamed Mount Davidson in honor of its original surveyor. In 1923 a cross was erected upon its summit and the first Easter sunrise service held there, now an annual event.

Sponsored by the City and County Federation of Women's Clubs, 26 acres of land on the mountain were acquired by the city of San Francisco. This area was dedicated and named Mount Davidson Park on December 20, 1929, the dedication being a part of the celebration of the 83d birthday of John McLaren, creator of Golden Gate Park and superintendent of the city's parks for 53 years. The first two crosses erected on Mount Davidson were destroyed by fire. A third cross, 103 feet in height and made of concrete, was set up in March 1934.

Some of San Francisco's finest old homes stand on Pacific Heights. One of the city's two remaining octagonal houses is located at 2645 Gough Street. It is owned by the National Society of Colonial Dames and is open to the public occasionally. Built in 1857, it was moved from its original site at 2618 Gough in 1953. In the same area, the house at 1782 Pacific Avenue was built in 1869, the one at 2439 Buchanan Street in 1859, and the one at 2209 Jackson Street in 1861. The headquarters of the California Historical Society are in a beautiful stone mansion completed in 1896 at 2090 Jackson. It is open to the public.

One source states that there are 42 hills in San Francisco. Among the others, not mentioned above, are Bernal Heights, Castro Hill, Mount St. Joseph, and Strawberry Hill.

Old Cisterns

In the early days of San Francisco many sunken water tanks or cisterns were constructed in the town. One of these, elliptical in form and having a capacity of 32,000 gallons, is located at the corner of California and Montgomery streets. Made originally of tar-drenched plank in 1852, it was rebuilt with brick four years later. Another, known as the Plaza Cistern, at Kearny and Merchant streets, with a capacity of 36,000 gallons, has a similar history, having been built and rebuilt of similar materials at approximately the same dates.

Thirty-six such cisterns were in use by 1856. Most of them were square or oblong in shape and not more than 15 feet in depth. They were first filled with water hauled in carts from springs on the hillsides of regions nearby. In later years they have been filled from the city water mains.

When, on April 18, 1906, the great earthquake broke the modern water pipes supplying San Francisco, water from these old underground receptacles was used to fight the fire that eventually consumed a great part of the city. Since that date modern cisterns have been constructed beneath street pavements throughout the city.

Chinatown

From the vicinity of its intersection with Sacramento Street, Grant Avenue leads into one of the largest colonies of Chinese outside of China itself. This colony originated on Sacramento Street west of Kearny, and by 1885 it had expanded to cover about ten blocks, "closely packed," says Bancroft, "with some 25,000 souls." The same authority states that the first Chinese to enter California under American rule were two men and one woman who came on the clipper bark *Eagle* in 1848.

On April 1, 1848, the *California Star* published in San Francisco said in an editorial: "We have received information from a very reliable source, that a large immigration from China may be expected here. We already have two or three of the 'Celestials' among us who have found ready employment."

By about 1876 labor troubles were precipitated, in the mining districts and elsewhere, by the presence of the 116,000 Chinese who were scattered over the state. These troubles arose partly on account of race prejudice and partly because of the low scale of wages accepted by these immigrants. At length drastic laws governing the entry of these aliens were enacted, laws revoked in 1943.

A description of the Chinatown of the late 1870's comes from Benjamin F. Taylor, a visitor from the eastern part of the United States: "Fancy yourself walking along the gay streets of San Francisco in the edge of the evening—streets bright with light, pleasant with familiar forms, musical with English speech, and feeling all the while, that under the patriotic flight of July flags as thick as pigeons and as gay as redbirds, you were still at home though thousands of miles away—fancy this, and then at the turn of a corner and the breadth of a street, think of dropping with the abruptness of a shifting dream into China, beneath the standard of Hoang-ti who sits upon the dragon throne . . .

"A strange chatter as of foreign birds in an aviary confuses the air. A surf of blue and black shirts and inky heads with tails to them is rolling along the sidewalks. Colored lanterns begin to twinkle. Black-lettered red signs all length and no breadth, the gnarled and crooked characters heaped one above another like a pile of ebony chair-frames, catch the eye. You halt at a building tinseled into cheap magnificence, and hung with gaudy paper glims . . .

"The creak of a Chinese fiddle shaped a little like a barometer, all bulb and no body, scrapes through a crack in the door. . . . Lights stream up from cellar stairs . . .

"You enter the restaurant. It is the 'Banquet Saloon' of Yune Fong. And there is Yune Fong himself, a benign, double-chinned old boy who is of a bigness from end to end. He sits by a counter. . . . Under his hand is a well-thumbed arithmeticon, a family of boys' marbles strung like beads upon parallel wires and set in a frame, wherewith Fong ciphers out your indebtedness and his profits. . . . The lights are feeble, as if there were nothing worth their while to shine on.

"You climb stairs into an improved edition of the ground floor. The furniture is faintly tidier and better, the tableware costlier. . . . One more lift and you are in large and elegant apartments with partitions of glass. . . . The furniture is of Chinese wood dark as mahogany at a hundred years old. . . . Lacquered boxes and curious cabinets abound."

After taking tea in the restaurant, Taylor and his friends, returning to the street, set out to see the Joss House: "Up a few steps, down a few steps, round a corner, up a whole flight, along a gallery as dumb as a tomb," they reach the "Joss-House, one of eleven heathen temples in San Francisco. It is never closed and we enter. . . . In the great shrines are rows of sinister gods with trailing black beard and moustache . . . the god of War . . . the deity of Medicine . . . the god of Fortune."

Then on to an opium den and afterward to the Chinese theater, whose orchestra consisted of "ticks and clucks and jingles and squeaks, and tinkles of bells, and a frog and locust interlude, and emaciated fiddles," followed by a roar of gongs and a clash of cymbals. "The music and the acting were alike—a marvelous jumble. It was as if a medley had swallowed itself."

Much of the labyrinth of old Chinatown was destroyed by the fire of 1906. A large part has been rebuilt, under modern conditions, and is one of San Francisco's principal tourist attractions.

The pedestrian wandering north along Grant Avenue suddenly finds that he has reached Chinatown. The windows are filled with curios and beads and jewelry; shops with young English-speaking Chinese attendants display silks and wearing apparel from the Orient. Strange foods with their unusual odors are in some of the doorways leading to similarly filled interiors. Both sides of the streets in this section are lined with shops, some large, some small. Chinese costumes are worn by some of the older men and women on the street. A few old men with queues appear. The younger generation are usually clothed in modern American dress.

The remains of many of San Francisco's early Chinese were returned for burial in their native land, but there is a Chinese cemetery near Colma.

Other Landmarks

The oldest buildings in Golden Gate Park are the Conservatory, a gift of James Lick in 1878 but rebuilt after a fire four years later with funds from Charles Crocker; the Children's House in Children's Playground, built in 1885; the gate and tea house at the Japanese Tea Garden, relic of the Midwinter Exposition of 1894; and McLaren Lodge, the city's park headquarters, built in 1895. The California Academy of Sciences, founded in 1853, is the oldest scientific institution on the Pacific Coast. Across the Music Concourse from the Academy is the Michael H. de Young Memorial Museum. Golden Gate Park consisted of 1,017 acres of sand dunes when the city acquired the land in 1868. The first superintendent was William Hammond Hall, appointed in 1871. The beautiful park of today is largely the creation of John McLaren, who became assistant superintendent in 1887 and was superintendent from 1890 until his death in 1943.

The Southern Pacific Building at 65 Market Street stands on the site of the famous Preparedness Day bombing of July 22, 1916, in which ten persons were killed and 40 injured. Labor leaders Thomas J. Mooney and Warren K. Billings were falsely convicted of the bombing, but after many years in prison they were finally pardoned.

San Francisco has been host to two world fairs. The Panama-Pacific International Exposition of 1915 was held in the Marina. One of the major buildings, a temporary structure as they all were, was allowed to remain after the fair had ended, and it became a San Francisco landmark. This was the huge Palace of Fine Arts, designed by Bernard Maybeck. It crumbled away until the 1960's, when it was taken down in order that it might be reconstructed of permanent materials. Spurred by a gift of $2 million from Walter Johnson, a local tycoon, the city and state have cooperated to re-create the last relic of the 1915 fair as the Palace of Fine Arts State Historical Monument. The Golden Gate International Exposition was held in 1939–40 on man-made Treasure Island, specially created in San Francisco Bay for the event. The island was later taken over by the United States Navy. A few structures from the fair still stand among the buildings erected by the Navy. Treasure Island adjoins Yerba Buena Island (Goat Island), through which the San Francisco–Oakland Bay Bridge passes.

The federal prison on Alcatraz Island was established in 1934, but the Army had used it for detention purposes since the 1850's. The buildings are of early date. The prison was closed in the 1960's, and the future of the island and the fate of its buildings are as yet uncertain.

The War Memorial Opera House in the Civic Center, opened in 1932 as a memorial to those who served in World War I, is the birthplace of the United Nations. Here, in April 1945, representatives of 46 nations met to determine ways of maintaining peace, once World War II came to an end. On June 26 they signed the United Nations Charter. It was also in this building that the treaty of peace with Japan was signed on September 8, 1951.

One of California's most interesting museums is the History Room of the Wells Fargo Bank, next to the bank's side entrance at 420 Montgomery Street. Here are displayed relics of the days when the Wells Fargo Express Company was one of the mainstays of California.

SOURCES

Annals of San Francisco. Frank Soulé, John H. Gihon, and James Nisbet, comp. Appleton, New York, 1855; Authors and Newspapers Association, New York and London, 1906.

Benét, James. *A Guide to San Francisco and the Bay Region.* Random House, New York, 1963.

Bland, Henry Meade. *Stevenson's California.* The Pacific Short Story Club, San Jose, 1924.

Bolton, Herbert Eugene. *Anza's California Expeditions.* 5 vols. University of California Press, Berkeley, 1930.

Bowman, J. N., and G. W. Hendry. "Spanish and Mexican Houses in the Nine Bay Counties." Ms., Bancroft Library, University of California, Berkeley, and State Library, Sacramento, 1942.

California Historical Society Quarterly, San Francisco, 1922–36.

The California Missions, a Pictorial History. By the editorial staff of Sunset Books. Lane Book Co., Menlo Park, 1964.

Chapman, Charles E. *A History of California: The Spanish Period.* Macmillan, New York, 1921.

Cleland, Robert Glass. *From Wilderness to Empire. A History of California,* ed. Glenn S. Dumke. Knopf, New York, 1959.

Coy, Owen C. *Pictorial History of California.* University of California Extension Division, Berkeley, 1925.

Davis, William Heath. *Seventy-five Years in California.* (A reissue and enlarged illustrated edition of *Sixty*

Years in California.) Ed. Douglas S. Watson. John Howell, San Francisco, 1929.

Deering, Margaret Perkins. *The Hills of San Francisco.* Privately printed, San Francisco, 1936.

Elder, David Paul. *The Old Spanish Missions of California.* Paul Elder & Co., San Francisco, 1913.

Eldredge, Zoeth Skinner. *The Beginnings of San Francisco from the Expedition of Anza, 1774, to the City Charter of April 15, 1850.* 2 vols. Privately printed, San Francisco, 1912.

Engelhardt, Zephyrin. *San Francisco, or Mission Dolores.* Franciscan Herald Press, Chicago, 1924.

Frémont, John Charles. *Memoirs of My Life.* Bedford Clarke & Co., Chicago, 1887.

Hills of San Francisco. Foreword by Herb Caen. Chronicle Publishing Co., San Francisco, 1959.

Hittell, John S. *A History of the City of San Francisco, and Incidentally of the State of California.* A. L. Bancroft & Co., San Francisco, 1878.

Hunt, Rockwell D., and Nellie Van de Grift Sanchez. *A Short History of California.* Crowell, New York, 1929.

Kelly, D. O. *History of the Diocese of California from 1849 to 1914.* San Francisco, 1915.

McSweeney, Thomas Denis. *Cathedral on California Street.* Academy of California Church History, Fresno, 1952.

Native Sons of the Golden West. Landmarks Committee Report, 1920–29.

Older, Mrs. Fremont. *California Missions and Their Romances.* Coward-McCann, New York, 1938.

——— *San Francisco, Magic City.* David McKay, New York, 1961.

Palou, Francisco. *Life and Apostolic Labors of the Venerable Father Junipero Serra, Founder of the Franciscan Missions of California.* With an Introduction and Notes by George Wharton James; English translation by C. Scott Williams. Pasadena, 1913.

Purdy, Helen Throop. *San Francisco, as It Was, as It Is, and How to See It.* Paul Elder & Co., San Francisco, 1912.

Rensch, Hero Eugene. *Educational Activities of the Protestant Churches in California, 1849–1860.* Master's thesis in history, Stanford University, 1929.

Stevenson, Robert Louis. *The Wrecker.* Scribner, New York, 1898.

——— *Across the Plains, Essays and Reviews.* Vol. IX of his *Works,* ed. de luxe. The Davos Press, New York, 1906.

Taylor, Benjamin F. *Between the Gates.* Ninth ed. S. C. Griggs & Co., Chicago, 1882.

Taylor, William. *California Life Illustrated.* English ed. Jackson, Walford & Hodder, London, 1867.

Todd, Harry L. "The San Francisco Post Office," Ms.

Watkins, Eleanor Preston. *The Builders of San Francisco.* Privately printed, San Francisco, 1935.

San Joaquin County

SAN JOAQUIN COUNTY was one of the original 27 counties. (San Joaquín, Spanish for St. Joachim, was the name given by Gabriel Moraga to the river in 1813, and was later used to designate the county.) Stockton, which is centrally located, has been the county seat from the first.

Indian Villages

More than 100 Indian mounds, or kitchen middens, have been located in San Joaquin County, and new discoveries continue to be made from

time to time. These mounds, many of which have been leveled, are the sites of aboriginal villages and burial places. They are found on relatively high ground along the banks of the numerous watercourses of the San Joaquin Delta region, such as the San Joaquin, Cosumnes, Mokelumne, and Calaveras rivers, and the Mormon, French Camp, and other sloughs, which furnished almost inexhaustible hunting grounds for the Indians. W. Egbert Schenck said that "apparently it would be hard to exaggerate the number of water fowl that were formerly present in the marshy area of the Great Central valley. Early accounts indicate an abundance and a tameness which it is hard to conceive."

To the inexperienced eye an Indian mound appears much the same as the land about it. The archaeologist, however, quickly perceives an appreciable difference. "Upon a mound's base," said Schenck, "there is found a mass of earth essentially the same as the base and the surrounding land, but which has been acted upon by man until in color, texture, constituents, or all of these it is readily distinguishable from the base . . . In color the mounds are characteristically blacker than the surrounding soil . . . Presumably this darker color is due to the greater amount of organic matter which man has accumulated upon them."

James A. Barr, for many years superintendent of schools in the city of Stockton, became interested in the archaeology of the Stockton region and during the years 1898–1901 made a large collection of specimens. His excellent field notes and carefully catalogued specimens form the main source of information on the archaeology and ethnology of the Stockton region. Of the nearly 4,000 specimens he gathered, 1,870 came from this section.

The principal aboriginal sites explored by Barr were the Stockton Channel, Walker Slough, Ott, Pool, and Island mounds. There were also three on the Woods Ranch on Robert's Island; one on the Copperopolis road; and others on Martin's Ranch and the O. R. Smith Ranch, at Brant's Ferry, on the Lewis Ranch, and on French Camp Slough.

The Stockton Channel Mound, located in Stockton between Edison and Harrison streets on the north bank of the Stockton Channel, is probably the site of the Passasimas village described by the 1817 Spanish expedition led by Padre Narciso Durán and accompanied by Luís Argüello. It is

possible, however, that this village may have been the one covered by the Walker Slough Mound. The latter, being only an eighth of a mile from the Island Mound, may be regarded as part of the same settlement.

The Ott Mound (southeast of Stockton and north of French Camp Slough) and the Pool Mound (nine miles southwest of Stockton) were undoubtedly inhabited when the Spanish visited the region in 1805, in 1810, and again in 1811. One of the most interesting localities worked by Barr was that of Union Island near Bethany, where the Spanish expeditions of 1810 and 1811 found the Yokuts village of Pescadero ("fisherman"), so named because they saw Indians catching fish there. Rancho Pescadero (35,446 acres), which is located north of Tracy, received its name from this settlement.

One of the most notable archaeological finds in the Stockton region was made quite by accident in a field where dirt was being obtained for a bridge approach at Garwood Ferry on the San Joaquin River southwest of Stockton.

The Stanislaus River was the scene of one of the most notable series of battles fought in Alta California between the Mexicans and the Indians. The encounters took place near the mouth of the river in May and June 1829. The leader of the Indians was Chief Estanislao, who had been educated at Mission San José but who had become a renegade, inciting his tribe against the Mexicans. The Mexican troops, under command of General Mariano G. Vallejo, were victorious. It was one of the few instances in California in which cannons were used in battle. For years farmers in the vicinity plowed up cannon balls and other relics of the Battle of the Stanislaus. The site (SRL 214) is thought to be the north side of the Stanislaus within two miles of its junction with the San Joaquin River.

Rancho del Campo de los Franceses

French Camp, four miles south of Stockton, was first occupied about 1832 by French-Canadian hunters employed by the Hudson's Bay Company to trap beaver, mink, bear, and other fur-bearing animals then numerous along the San Joaquin River and adjoining sloughs. Evidences of beaver may still be traced along French Camp Slough. The site of the present town of French Camp was the terminus of the Oregon Trail, used by these trappers from 1832 to 1845. This trail led from the north across the county along a route later followed by the Sutter's Fort–San José Trail, over which Frémont passed in 1844. Michel La Framboise, leader of the fur hunters, came annually to French Camp (SRL 668), and James Alexander Forbes, agent for the company after 1836, likewise made many trips to it. As late as 1845 the place was occupied from spring until fall by the Canadians and their families, who had constructed rude cabins of tules and willow brush, many of which were plastered with mud.

Abandoning their camp hurriedly in the summer of 1845, the trappers left their arms buried in a wood-lined hole or cache on a knoll situated one block and a half northeast of the present

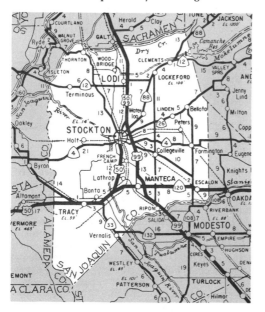

French Camp School and one block from the present road through town. Colonel P. W. Noble, who later kept a store at French Camp, told the story of the buried arms, only to be laughed at. The Reynolds brothers, Eldridge, Edward, and James, then children at the French Camp School, took the story seriously enough to dig for the hidden treasure, and uncovered 40 sabers and muskets. This was in 1856 or 1857. Many years later two of the sabers were presented to the museum at Victory Park in Stockton. Mrs. Alice B. Maloney made a study of the weapons and concluded that they were rather sailors' swords left by an 1846 punitive expedition.

Charles M. Weber, a native of Germany, who was later to become the founder of Stockton, stopped at French Camp in the fall of 1841 while on his way into California with the Bidwell-Bartleson party. Weber was much impressed with the fertile, oak-studded lands that bordered the San Joaquin River. Subsequently, in 1842, he settled in Pueblo de San José and soon after went into partnership with William Gulnac, a blacksmith. Gulnac came to California in 1833, perhaps with the French-Canadian trappers, and later married a Mexican woman, after becoming a naturalized Mexican citizen. For a time the two men engaged in merchandising, manufacturing, and ranching at San José. In the spring of 1843 they organized a company of 12 men for the purpose of forming a colony at French Camp. On July 14 Gulnac, being a Mexican citizen, petitioned for a grant of land in the region, and on January 13, 1844, he and others received a large tract, which included both French Camp and the site of the later Stockton. This was named Rancho del Campo de los Franceses. The company organized by Weber and Gulnac was the first colony of white settlers to take up lands in the San Joaquin Valley.

In August 1844, under the leadership of Gulnac, the first settlers arrived at Rancho del Campo de los Franceses. One of the company, Thomas Lindsay, built a tule hut on what is now Lindsay Point back of the City Hall at the west end of East Lindsay Street in Stockton, the first dwelling (SRL 178) to be erected by an American within the present city limits. However, in the spring of 1845, Lindsay was killed by Indians, his hut was burned, and his stock and tools were stolen.

To encourage other colonists, Gulnac offered a square mile of land at French Camp to any prospective settler. One of the first to accept the offer was David Kelsey, who, soon after Gulnac's arrival, reached the settlement with his wife and two children from Oregon en route to Pueblo de San José. Stricken with smallpox within a few months, Kelsey died at the Lindsay cabin and was buried near the present southwest corner of El Dorado and Fremont streets in Stockton. Only one member of the family did not contract the disease. This was America, a child whose care in nursing her family unaided places her among the pioneer heroines of California.

The task of inducing settlers to remain on Rancho del Campo de los Franceses was rather difficult with its problems of contending with hostile Indians, plague, poor food, and primitive conditions. Before many months Gulnac became disgusted with the project, and on April 3, 1845, he sold the entire estate to Weber for $60, the amount of a grocery bill he owed his partner. In order to persuade settlers to come to the region, Weber virtually gave away the major portion of his estate to those who would settle on it. The testimony and influence of dozens of these colonists ultimately forced the land commissioners to recognize Weber's claim to the grant, the whole of which would otherwise have been lost to him.

Stockton

Captain Weber, in 1847, laid out the town of Tuleburg on the south side of the Laguna, later known as the Stockton Channel. The dense tule swamps which then bordered every watercourse fully justified the name. Even the roofs of the first rude huts were thatched with tules. The head of the channel soon came to be known as the Embarcadero, the location of which was about where Weber Avenue now "approaches the water." For a time, Weber continued to make his home at Pueblo de San José, occasionally going to Tuleburg to carry supplies to his vaqueros, who lived in a tule hut on the north side of Stockton Slough. More houses and corrals were built in the spring of 1848, and wheat was planted.

After the discovery of gold at Coloma, Weber organized the Stockton Mining and Trading Company, which operated for a time on Weber Creek in El Dorado County. José Jesús, an Indian chieftain with whom Weber had made a treaty in 1844 and who remained his lifelong friend, sent many of his own tribesmen to work for Weber in the mines. Believing that it would be more profitable to devote all his time to the building of a city that would serve as an entrepôt to the southern mines, Weber dissolved his mining company in September 1848 and took up residence in Tuleburg. In the spring of 1849 the town was resurveyed and renamed Stockton, in honor of Commodore Robert F. Stockton, whom Weber had met in Los Angeles in 1846 and admired. By the winter of 1849 Stockton had a population of approximately 1,000, and in 1850 it became the county seat of San Joaquin County, having been incorporated on August 15 of that year.

Thousands of Argonauts bound for the southern mines passed through Stockton in the early 1850's. Some came up the river by boat; others traveled over the Livermore Pass from San Jose and crossed the San Joaquin River at Doak and Bonsell's Ferry, located about where the highway between Tracy and Manteca crosses today. From Stockton this restless tide of humanity branched out over the various trails leading to the gold fields—the Mariposa, French Camp, Sonora, Mokelumne Hill, and Lockeford roads, all teeming with life and each one leading to a hoped-for El Dorado. Stockton soon became a flourishing center of trade and commerce. Freighting and staging activities developed to enormous proportions, agriculture and stock-raising in the vicinity increased, local commerce grew, and the town became a fixed settlement.

The first house built on Weber Point was of adobe. Adjacent to it Weber erected a second dwelling in 1850 or 1851. This was a two-story frame structure, the lumber for which had been brought around the Horn. To this house the Captain brought his bride, Helen Murphy, daughter of Martin Murphy, a large landowner in Santa Clara County. The Weber house, surrounded by gardens, was a notable show place during the 1850's and 1860's. Some time after Weber's death in 1881 it was destroyed by fire, to be replaced by a second frame house built by the family on the southeast corner of the property facing Stockton Channel. This building has since been moved to West Lane just beyond the Diversion Canal outside of Stockton, and stands at the rear of the large red house that is the home of Helen Weber Kennedy. The foundation piers which supported the first mansion and which were made of brick brought around the Horn could long be seen at the original site on Weber Point (SRL 165), but now only a few old oak and locust trees are visible among great piles of earth moved to the point when the basement for the new San Joaquin County courthouse was dug. Weber Point is at the west end of Channel Street, and there are plans to convert it into a convention center. The Stockton Channel, which borders the old homesite, is today lined with warehouses, wharves, coal bunkers, mills, and factories, and its waters are filled with barges, ferries, and river steamers. Since the completion of the Stockton Deep Water Project, oceangoing vessels have plied the river from San Francisco to the Port of Stockton.

A few of Stockton's early buildings, dating from the 1850's, remained in the old business section until the 1960's, but most of these were destroyed by the redevelopment project encompassing the nine blocks bordered by Weber Avenue and Hunter, Washington, and Commerce streets. Old St. Mary's Catholic Church at 201 East Washington Street was built in 1861 but includes later additions. The parish was established in 1851.

The principal landmarks of the city today are its old cemeteries. Stockton Rural Cemetery, at the end of Cemetery Lane, was dedicated on August 31, 1862. Among the pioneers buried there is David S. Terry, famed for the 1859 duel in which he killed Senator David C. Broderick. Judge Terry's violent life came to an end in 1889 at the railroad station in Lathrop, south of Stockton, where he was shot by the bodyguard of Justice Stephen J. Field. Terry had threatened Field because of the latter's decision against Terry's wife and client, Sarah Althea Hill, in her suit for a part of the fortune of her putative husband, William Sharon. Mrs. Terry went insane a few years later and died in the Stockton State Hospital in 1937.

The monument to Reuel Colt Gridley (SRL 801), erected in 1887, marks the grave of a man who raised $275,000 for the Sanitary Commission, Civil War counterpart of the Red Cross, by selling and reselling a sack of flour. Stockton Rural Cemetery also contains the remains of persons originally buried in the city cemetery located on the block bounded by Weber Avenue and Pilgrim, Main, and Union streets. When this cemetery was abandoned in the 1890's, the body of one John Brown was among those left at the old site, since he had no relatives to pay for the move. Brown, known as "Juan Flaco" ("John the Lean"), was California's Paul Revere. In September 1846 he rode 500 miles in five days on horseback to bring word of the siege of Los Angeles to Commodore Stockton in San Francisco. A marker has been proposed to mark the last resting place of this forgotten hero of California history (SRL 513), who died at Stockton in 1859.

Another early cemetery is the Temple Israel Cemetery (SRL 765), located on the block bounded by Acacia, Pilgrim, Poplar, and Union streets. It was given to the Jewish community of Stockton by Captain Weber in 1851 and is the oldest Jewish cemetery in continuous use in California and west of the Rockies.

Even in pioneer days, although life in Stockton was full of excitement and gaiety, cultural development was not neglected. Churches and schools were established as early as 1850, and during the 1850's and 1860's a number of prosperous private academies existed. Today, it is the home of the University (formerly College) of the Pacific, which was transferred to Stockton from San Jose in 1924. The Pioneer Museum and Haggin Art Galleries, in Victory Park, contain many interesting relics of San Joaquin County's early days.

The Mariposa Road

Leading from Stockton to the southern mines are various roads which were first used during the days of the gold rush. Along these thoroughfares the first settlements outside of the city were established. Every house was a wayside inn for the accommodation of travelers. The cost of a meal was usually $1.50, the regular menu comprising pork and beans, with bread and coffee.

Dr. L. R. Chalmers, who settled at the site of Collegeville as early as 1850, persuaded the government teams en route to Fort Miller to pass by his ranch, thereby establishing the Mariposa Road, which became the main route to the southern mines. By 1851 the principal stopping places along this road were Chalmers' Ranch, George Kerr's House, the Fifteen Mile House, the Lone Tree House, and Heath and Emory's Ferry, on the Stanislaus River (since 1860 in Stanislaus County). A settlement grew up at Chalmers' Ranch, and because a college was located there from 1866 to 1874, the name of Collegeville became permanently attached to the place. The college was housed in a three-story frame structure erected by members of the Cumberland Presbyterian Church at a cost of $8,000. The building was destroyed by fire in 1874. At the corner of the Mariposa Road and the Jack Tone Road is a remnant of the pioneer Collegeville cemetery, now grass-grown and deserted.

The Lone Tree House, built in the early 1850's from lumber brought around the Horn, stood on the W. P. H. Campbell farm until about 1910.

The ranch and hotel were purchased in 1854 by Campbell. The site of the hostelry is on Lone Tree Road near the Lone Tree School, about three miles north of Escalon. In the early days the road at this point branched off to the several ferries on the Stanislaus River—Burney's, Cottle's, and Heath and Emory's.

Of the many hotels and stage stations erected along the Mariposa Road during the 1850's, 1860's, and 1870's, one remained into the 1960's. This was the two-story building that stood about four miles from downtown Stockton near the junction of the Sonora (now the Farmington) and Mariposa roads. Near the present Mariposa Road are the sites of some of these early buildings, such as the Fifteen Mile House, marked by groups of old trees.

The French Camp Road

During flood years and always during the winter months the Mariposa Road became impassable—a veritable mire of adobe. Then the stagecoaches and freighters were routed over the French Camp Road, which had a sandy loam base. This winter traffic made of French Camp an important staging and freighting center during the early 1850's. Boats landed at the end of French Camp Slough, where goods destined for the mining camps were unloaded. In the summer of 1850 Major Richard P. Hammond laid out a town on the site for Charles Weber, calling it Castoria ("place of beavers"). Colonel P. W. Noble and A. Stevinson, who had come to French Camp in August 1849 and who became agents for the sale of lots in the new town, built a two-story adobe structure in 1850, using it as a hotel and trading post. As late as 1880 the building was occupied as a home by Noble's widow. This hotel, with its broad fields for the pasturage of livestock, was thronged by travelers during the first years of its existence, but its patronage declined when a second hotel, owned by Le Barron and Company, was erected—this hostelry likewise offering extensive pasturage facilities.

In the French Camp of today, a town of 580 inhabitants in 1960, none of the early buildings are to be found. Even the cemetery has disappeared.

The principal stopping place on the French Camp Road between French Camp and Heath and Emory's Ferry, and almost the only one in 1852, was the "Zinc House," the material for which had been brought around the Horn from New York early in 1850. The fame of the Zinc House, which stood just east of Simms and just south of the highway off Wagner Road, lent color to the French Camp Road, sometimes known as the Zinc House Road. The house was a small affair, "12 × 16 out of the wet," as an old history quaintly puts it, with one room seven feet in height. The owner, E. Allen, paid "for this frontier luxury . . . one dollar for every year that had elapsed since Christ was born; that was $1850." Here the traveler could get pie for one dollar, or the regular pork and beans, bread and coffee, for the same price. "He paid his money and took his choice." The first school in this part of the county was held in the Zinc House, and for many years the school district retained the name of the unique old hostelry in which it had its beginning.

In October 1852 Ernest Wagner rented the Zinc House for a period of five months for $800, purchasing it soon afterward. Seven years later he erected a two-story house on the site. This served as the Wagner home until 1910, when another house took its place. Opposite the house are two sturdy brick barns, where for many years stage horses were stabled. The bricks used in their construction were fashioned on the spot and are as solid today as when they were first made.

In the course of time the number of public houses along the French Camp Road increased. Among them were the Liesy Station, a few miles east of the Zinc House, and the Minges Station, a mile to the northwest, where the old brick barn is still standing.

The Atlanta Store, built in 1866 by Lee Wilson on a site about two miles northwest of the Zinc House, was a station for the accommodation of the Fisher stages during the late 1860's and 1870's. William Dempsey bought the place in 1867, and in 1868 the Atlanta post office was established there. In 1874 the property was acquired by the Murphy family. The store no longer stands.

At Five Corners, the junction of the French Camp, Jack Tone, and Lone Tree roads, stands the little white Community Church built by the Methodists in 1878. Nearby, on Lone Tree Road, is the old Protestant cemetery. A few miles to the southeast, and a mile east of Simms, stood St. Patrick's Catholic Church, built the same year, its quiet churchyard dotted with the graves of pioneers. The church has been replaced by a modern structure, but the cemetery is still there.

Pioneer Farmhouses

San Joaquin County is noteworthy for the number of pioneer farmhouses dating from the 1850's and 1860's still owned by descendants of the original builders. Many of these houses are in excellent condition and are occupied by their owners, while others which have been replaced by more modern structures are being allowed to disintegrate. This is especially true of the frame structures built close to the ground without the protection of stone or brick foundations.

Community Church, Five Corners

Among the historic homesteads found north of the Calaveras River, one of the most interesting is the Dodge house situated on the bank of the river and the Waterloo Road to Lockeford (Highway 88). A few giant oaks, all that are left of the hundreds that once flourished in the region, surround this fine old mansion. One of the oldest trees stands near the highway and bears a bronze tablet placed by El Toyon Chapter, D.A.R., in 1923 in commemoration of the camp made in that vicinity on March 26, 1844, by John C. Frémont. "This place is beautiful," Frémont wrote, "with open groves of oak, and a grassy sward beneath, with many plants in bloom."

Following a shady path along the levee above the stream, now drained periodically for irrigation, past the Dodge cherry orchard, one comes to a spot about half a mile from the house. Here on the levee above a dirt road a crooked apple tree marks the site of the log cabin erected by Dr. J. C. Isbell soon after he took up land there in November 1846. In 1848 Dr. Isbell sold the ranch to the Hutchinson brothers, who ten years later sold it to Jonathan A. Dodge. The log house at that time was furnished with fine old mahogany pieces brought around the Horn. The present Dodge house was built in 1866. Slight alterations have been made on the interior, while the exterior has assumed a rather modern appearance. It is still remarkably well preserved.

The J. H. Cole house, which stands just north of Eight Mile Road and half a mile east of Highway 88, was erected in 1863. Much of the original "fancy work" along the eaves has been removed; a front porch, over which a giant rose tree had become inextricably entwined, has been torn down; and some of the shingles have been renewed. Otherwise this fine pioneer farmhouse remains much as it was when built. Old elms and Italian cypresses, which may be seen a long distance across the open fields, lend a quiet dignity to the garden.

The former McCall house, on the west side of Highway 88 about one and seven-tenths miles north of the Jonathan Dodge house, apparently stands on an ancient Indian mound, as many relics have been dug up in the garden from time to time. The original house, which was built by Samuel Martin about 1858, has been incorporated into the present structure and now serves as a bedroom. From its doors many changing scenes have been witnessed: in the winter, mud-spattered teamsters, with eight to 16 horses, each striving to pass the other on the miry road, which gradually widened at this point to 200 feet; in the summer, grimy stagecoaches lurching along that same lane, now deeply rutted and choked with dust; and always, long lines of Chinese marching single file to and from the mines, and cowboys with their lowing, milling herds.

A two-story brick ranch house stands on the Jack Tone Road and the north bank of the Calaveras River about 11 miles northeast of Stockton. John H. (Jack) Tone and two associates came to California as members of the Webb-Audubon party, under the leadership of Colonel Henry L. Webb and John Woodhouse Audubon, youngest son of the famous ornithologist. Most of the party were bound for the gold fields, but Audubon made the trip to gather specimens of birds and mammals. When Colonel Webb deserted his men in the Rio Grande Valley, Audubon was made leader of the party, which after many hardships reached Stockton in December 1849.

Jack Tone and his partners, in the autumn of 1850, settled on the Calaveras River, where they attempted to raise potatoes. Owing to lack of skill in irrigating, their initial experiment in California ranching resulted in failure, so the three men tried their luck at mining for a time. In 1851, however, they returned to locate permanently on the Calaveras River, where they built a one-story adobe house on the high part of the river bank about one-half mile west of the present brick house. The three partners were known thereafter as the "Dobey Boys" by the settlers who had meanwhile taken up land about them. This adobe stood for several years after the brick house was erected in 1873. The homestead is today owned and occupied by descendants of Jack Tone, who treasure the stories of pioneer life on the ranch and are especially proud of that part of the *Audubon Journal* which mentions their ancestor. Tone's wife, Alice Walsh Tone, daughter of Nicholas J. Walsh, another of the original Audubon party, aided Maria R. Audubon in the biographical sketch of her father.

Many settlers came to the Mokelumne River in 1851 and took up homesteads along the rich river bottoms. Among these was B. F. Langford, a native of Tennessee, who became a California State Senator in the 1880's. This enterprising pioneer built the picturesque one-story brick house which stands in the midst of orchards and vineyards on the north side of the river due west of Lockeford. It is located on a segment of Woodbridge Road, just west of Tretheway Road. The bricks used in its construction were burned on the place. The house is well preserved, although changes through the years have considerably altered its original appearance. The schoolhouse built by Langford for his children still stands unaltered. A long grape arbor which extended from the front door of the house has been eliminated, but some of the trees which were planted at the time the house was built are still flourishing—a knotted pear tree, two magnificent old fig trees, and several pomegranates. Between the house and the present walnut orchard are a few ancient oaks, remnants of the splendid groves that once covered the surrounding fields. Beyond the walnut orchard on the opposite side of the river is the site of Staples' Ferry.

South of Lodi and back from the corner of Kettelman and Cherokee lanes stands the ten-room David H. Kettelman house, built in 1858 of brick kilned nearby. Kettelman purchased the place soon after it was built and developed an extensive grain and cattle ranch before the town of Lodi came into existence with the railroad in 1869. He was treasurer and chief promoter of the Mokelumne Ditch and Irrigation Company in 1876. Descendants of David Kettelman own and occupy the old residence, which is sometimes called the "sunbonnet house" because of three deeply recessed windows in the second story.

The John Lyman Beecher house is located east of Stockton on Berne Road near the intersection of Alpine and Copperopolis roads. It was erected in 1860 and stands well preserved today, still in the Beecher family. Beecher crossed the plains from Massachusetts during the gold rush, but soon gave up mining in favor of teaming and freighting out of Stockton, and ultimately purchased the large ranch where he lived the rest of his life. His son John L. became a member of the California legislature.

Seventeen miles east of Stockton was the "Oregon Ranch," first settled by George Theyer and David Wells, who built a tule house there in 1848. When traffic began to flow over the Sonora Road to the southern mines the partners opened the "Oregon Tent," the first stopping place along the road, on a site in what is now Farmington. In 1852 Nathaniel Siggons Harrold, a native of Pennsylvania, who had come by ox team to Woods' Creek, Tuolumne County, in November 1849, purchased the Oregon Ranch, and in 1868 he built a large brick house, still standing at the southern limits of Farmington. Harrold, who engaged in cattle-raising, gradually increased the size of his ranch from 320 to 5,400 acres. He owned thousands of acres in other sections also.

In 1850, about three-fourths of a mile west of the Oregon Tent, James Wasley built the Wisconsin House, which later was moved to Peters, where it was used as a boardinghouse as late as 1890. The Marietta House, three miles east, and the Texas Tent, four miles west, were other taverns on the Sonora Road in the 1850's. Harrold served as a cook at the latter establishment before purchasing the Oregon Ranch.

A town was laid out on the Oregon Ranch in 1858 by Dr. W. B. Stamper. It is said that he named the place Farmington because it was the center of an extensive and rich farming country.

After passing Simms, the present French Camp Road becomes part of Highway 120 and runs about one-half mile north of the course of the early-day thoroughfare. The original road can be traced, however, by the old-fashioned farmhouses surrounded by tall shade trees which stand south of the present highway. On the north side of the highway, three-fourths of a mile east of Simms, is the J. O'Malley homestead, with its treasured locust trees planted in the 1850's. The house stands today in a thick grove of orange, olive, and walnut trees. The O'Malley sisters, daughters of the original owner, told how ranchers walked the fences all the way to Stockton during the flood of 1862 and came back in boats.

At Park and Pioneer Streets in Escalon is the John Jones house, a square, two-story mansion built in 1867 of bricks fired on the place. John Wheeler Jones, a native of North Carolina, came to California with his family in 1852, and at first kept the Blue Tent Tavern on the French Camp Road one mile east of the site of Escalon. In 1855 he purchased the ranch of 160 acres on which the brick mansion was later built. By 1875 Jones had increased the size of his ranch to 7,000

acres, and in addition he owned several thousand acres in other parts of the valley. In 1894 the town of Escalon was laid out on the home ranch by James W. Jones, son of the original owner.

Near the north bank of the Stanislaus River, about five miles southeast of Escalon, a picturesque two-story brick house stands at the bend of Burwood Road off the River Road. It was built in 1868 by Euphrates Monroe. Nearby, also on Burwood Road, is a two-story white frame house, built in 1862, in which Ishmael Monroe lived and kept the Burwood post office, which operated from 1859 to 1898.

Mokelumne River Ferries

John C. Frémont says that on March 25, 1844, his men "halted in a beautiful bottom at the ford of the Río de los Mukelemnes," which received its name from an "Indian tribe living on the river." "The bottoms on the stream," he continued, "are broad, rich, and extremely fertile, and the uplands are shaded with oak groves." Most of these ancient woodlands have disappeared, having been supplanted by verdant orchards and vineyards. The Indian ranchería, which existed at the ford when the first white settlers came, has likewise vanished, but the site has been fixed on the Langford ranch some 200 yards east of the present brick house by relics unearthed at the spot.

Among the early wayfarers and emigrants who made use of the ford mentioned by Frémont were Captain Weber, on his journeys between Sutter's Fort and Stockton, and the Murphy-Townsend-

Euphrates Monroe House, Burwood

Stevens party, who in 1844 were the first to drive wagons along the trail and across the stream at this point. The next few years saw increased travel from Sutter's Fort to Pueblo de San José via this route, which soon came to be known as the Sutter's Fort–San José Trail. Later it was designated as the Upper Sacramento Road.

Although the first to settle at the ford was Thomas Pyle in November 1846, records show that in 1849 the place was known as Laird's Ferry. That year David J. Staples, J. F. Staples, and W. H. Nichols took up residence there. Organizing a company known as Staples, Nichols and Company, they acquired possession in February 1850 of the ferry, which was thereafter known as Staples' Ferry. In the fall of 1850 the company built a toll bridge—perhaps the first in the county—across the river west of the ferry. The first to cross on the new bridge, so the story goes, was a grizzly bear, which was given free passage without question. A post office was established at Staples' Ferry in 1851, and until 1854 all stagecoach travel to Sacramento passed that way. After that date the route by way of Woods' Ferry (Woodbridge) was used except in times of flood. Staples' Ferry, however, continued to serve travelers for many years—even as late as 1880, although by that time it was known as Miller's Ferry. The site of the old Staples' Hotel, built from lumber brought around the Horn in 1850, is on the south side of the river, about two miles west of Lockeford via Locke Road and Tretheway Road. In the former river bed, just south of the present channel, the steamboat Pert lies buried under 12 feet of sand.

After crossing the Calaveras River at the Isbell cabin, the Upper Sacramento Road proceeded via Staples' Ferry to Dry Creek, where in 1849 a Mr. Davis established a crossing which he operated for a few years. Turner Elder, one of the first settlers in the county, had erected a log cabin at this point in the fall of 1846. In 1852 the now extinct Liberty City was established there by C. C. Fugitt. Sixteen years later, when the Central Pacific Railroad was under construction, the town was moved one mile south in the hope that it would be made a station on the new line. This dream, however, was never realized, and before long Liberty became a ghost town. Neither townsite is definitely marked today, although the first location can be approximated from the old pioneer cemetery on Liberty Road just west of Elliott Road, about six miles north of Lockeford.

Benedict's Ferry, about halfway between Woods' and Staples' ferries, was established in 1850 by C. L. Benedict, who had a ranch on the north side of the Mokelumne River at this point. In 1852 the government opened a post office at Benedict's Ferry, and during the same year the Bramlett and Langford sawmill was built there.

Benson's Ferry (SRL 149), started in 1849 by Edward Stokes and A. M. Woods, was purchased by John A. Benson in 1850. After the murder of Benson in February 1859 by Green C. Palmer, an employee, and the latter's subsequent suicide, E. P. Gayetty, Benson's son-in-law, took over the operation of the ferry. The two-story Gayetty

house, built in the 1870's, still stands near the levee 300 yards west of the present bridge. During the flood of 1862 the earlier Benson house was lashed to a large tree, which stood nearby, and was thus saved from being washed down the river. A little to the south is a large pond, which fills the pit where clay was dug for the manufacture of brick during the active days of Mokelumne City, one-third mile to the east. The Benson property later became part of the Barber ranch.

Mokelumne City (SRL 162) was laid out at the junction of the Cosumnes and Mokelumne rivers in 1854 shortly after the Snap brothers had opened a store there. High hopes were cherished that the place might be made the head of navigation and a center of trade for the mines. For a time the town grew and prospered: boats unloaded at the landing; lots were sold; hotels, stores, shops, warehouses, and dwellings were erected. Then came the flood of 1862. The town was submerged, and as many as 19 houses were swept away by the rushing, swirling river. Mokelumne City never fully recovered from the disaster, although there was some business activity in the place and people continued to live there until 1878, when the townsite was included in the property purchased by the Barber family for a ranch. The hotel was converted into a barn and stood until replaced by the present structure sometime in the 1890's. The site of the town is on an old stretch of road just east of Benson's Ferry, and three miles north of Thornton via the road to Franklin.

Some of the houses of Mokelumne City were removed to other localities, and a few still stand. One of these is the Jesse Thornton house, situated in a dense grove of oak trees at a beautiful spot on the Mokelumne River directly below the present bridge on the road from Thornton to Galt.

Lockeford

Dr. Dean J. Locke, a native of New Hampshire and a graduate of the Harvard Medical School, came to California in 1849 as physician for the Boston and Newton Joint-Stock Association. For a few months he engaged in mining with his brother George at Mississippi Bar on the American River, but in December 1850 they both came to the Mokelumne River, where another brother, Elmer, had already become an enthusiastic settler. The Lockes purchased 360 acres of land from D. J. Staples for one dollar an acre, and in 1851 they erected a log cabin, since destroyed, on a knoll thickly sprinkled with oaks. Grizzly bears were plentiful in those days, and when night came the hired men "roosted high in the trees like turkeys," for fear of them. The cabin site is now occupied by a pleasant modern farmhouse on La Lomita Rancho about half a mile northwest of Lockeford on Elliott Road.

Lockeford (SRL 365) was laid out on the D. J. Locke ranch and named in 1859. Its founders envisioned the town as becoming the head of navigation on the Mokelumne River, an ambition that was strengthened when the little pioneer steamer Pert tied up to the Lockeford landing on

April 5, 1862. Eventually the Mokelumne Steam Navigation Company was organized, and for three or four years it carried on some business. After 1865, however, the mining population gradually scattered, and the coming of the railroad ultimately put an end to all navigation on the Mokelumne.

Dr. Locke was very influential in the development of the new town, and was especially active in organizing schools, churches, and temperance societies. Even before the town was officially laid out, Locke interested himself in the cultural life of the community. On the second floor of his adobe granary, built in 1858 just west of the site of the present brick house, he fitted up a hall for public gatherings, and here the Sons of Temperance were organized. As early as November 24, 1861, the Congregationalists held services in this same hall. In 1869 they erected the building on Elliott Road that is now the Grace Church. The first house on the site of Lockeford was a frame structure erected in 1855, and to it Dr. Locke brought his bride that same year. This first house was outgrown in the succeeding years, and in 1865 the front part of the present two-story brick dwelling on Elliott Road was constructed on the same site. The old brick barn also remains.

Luther Locke, father of the Locke brothers, came to California when Dr. Locke returned with his bride. The following year he built himself a home, a frame structure, in which the first store in Lockeford was opened in 1862. The post office, established in 1861, was located in this building, with Luther Locke as the first postmaster. This landmark, long known as the "White House," stands, very much remodeled, at the northeast corner of Main Street and Elliott Road.

One and one-half miles southwest of Lockeford on Locke Road is an old brick church erected by community effort in the late 1850's. The building was afterward acquired by the Methodists, who still own it as well as the cemetery adjoining the Odd Fellows and Catholic cemeteries to the east. Unused since 1912, with its tall Gothic windows and doors boarded up, the old church is fast falling to decay.

Four miles northeast of Lockeford is the little town of Clements. One mile north of here via the old Ione road stood the Lone Star Mill (SRL 155) on the Mokelumne River. To this site the Bramlett and Langford sawmill, built near Benedict's Ferry in 1852, was removed in 1854 by the new proprietors, David S. Terry and a man named Hodge. Terry was raised in the "Lone Star" state of Texas. In 1855 Hodge and Terry added a flour mill. The establishment was destroyed by fire in 1856 and rebuilt on the same site. S. L. Magee bought the Lone Star Mill in 1860 and continued to operate it until its abandonment about 1885. The present site of Clements was purchased by Thomas Clements from David S. Terry in 1871.

Woodbridge

The first permanent settlers in the vicinity of Woodbridge were George W. Emerson and Ross C. and J. P. Sargent, all from New England. When they arrived in 1850, it is said that they found huts of rived oak left by Hudson's Bay Company trappers. In 1852 Jeremiah H. Woods and Alexander McQueen established a ferry across the Mokelumne River at this point, about where the present bridge and dam span the stream, with the result that before long a new road from Stockton to Sacramento was routed by way of Woods' Ferry. After 1854 the stages that had formerly traveled via Staples' Ferry on the Upper Sacramento Road adopted this more direct route. In 1858 Woods, a very energetic and enterprising man, built a bridge at the site of the ferry (SRL 163), which for years was known as Woods' Bridge. From it the town, which was laid out on the south side of the river in April 1859, took the name Woodbridge. For several years the place showed considerable activity, but with the death of Jeremiah Woods in 1864 Woodbridge lost its chief promoter.

Several of the early houses and business buildings are still to be found at Woodbridge (SRL 358). On the main street is the I.O.O.F. building, a two-story brick structure, the lower part of which was built in the early 1860's, while the upper story dates from 1874. The older portion was at first the Lavinsky store; then later for a time it served as a school. The Masonic Hall was built in 1882. A pioneer cemetery contains the grave of William Lewis Manly, hero of the rescue of the Death Valley '49ers.

The Woodbridge Academy, a two-story frame structure erected in the winter of 1878–79 under the leadership of Professor S. L. Morehead, was taken over by the United Brethren in 1881, when it became known as the San Joaquin Valley College (SRL 520). As such it continued to function until the beginning of the twentieth century, when it was superseded by the public grammar school. Today another school building occupies the site on Lilac Street.

The Mokelumne Hill Road

In 1850, 17 public houses, all located within a distance of 24 miles from Stockton, lined the Mokelumne Hill Road, now the Linden Road or Highway 26. Not a vestige of these early inns can be found today, but one such building, erected in 1853 by Masterson and Cogswell at a cost of $8,000, survived into the 1950's. This two-story brick structure stood a few feet from the histori-

D. J. Locke Home, Lockeford

cal marker on the highway about halfway between Linden and Bellota. For a time during the 1860's the building housed a young ladies' seminary. The sturdy old landmark was ruined by fire and subsequently removed.

The town of Linden, which was laid out in 1862, had its beginnings in the little community that grew up around the Fifteen Mile House. This tavern had been established by Dr. W. D. Treblecock in the fall of 1849. Some years later C. C. Rynerson erected a flour mill in the vicinity. Soon after, John and James Wasley, cousins of Treblecock, and later brothers-in-law to Rynerson, joined the group and were among the founders of the town. John Wasley named the new settlement, presumably after his old home at Linden, Ohio. The Rynerson flour mill was destroyed by fire in 1865 but was replaced by a second structure, which met a similar fate in 1868. A three-story brick mill, erected in 1871 but no longer used as such, now occupies the site.

Bellota, four and a half miles northeast of Linden, was originally known as Fisher's Bridge, for at this point William V. Fisher had erected a bridge and stage station on his farm, purchased in 1861. The old hotel, a decaying one-story rambling structure, stands on the west side of the present highway near the north bank of the Calaveras River.

Before the building of Fisher's Bridge, the Mokelumne Hill Road crossed the Calaveras River a few miles east of the site of Bellota at the Davis and Atherton Ferry. The first settler in this section, David F. Douglas, took up land between Bellota and the ferry, where he built a shake house, one of the 17 inns along the old Mokelumne Hill Road in 1850. Douglas, who had come to California from Mexico with Graham's Dragoons in 1848, became a member of the Constitutional Convention in 1849, and was Secretary of State under Governor J. Neely Johnson from 1855 to 1857.

San Joaquin and Stanislaus River Crossings

In pioneer days river crossings were important points in the San Joaquin Valley, and it was on the various watercourses that the earliest settlements were planted. Among these first attempts at colonization was New Hope (SRL 436), later known as Stanislaus City, established on the Stanislaus River in November 1846 by a party of Mormons under the leadership of Samuel Brannan. About 20 colonists came up the San Joaquin River in the sailing launch Comet, landing on the east branch near the site at which John Doak and Jacob Bonsell established a ferry two years later. From this point the party proceeded overland to a spot previously selected by Brannan on the north bank of the Stanislaus River one and a half miles from the river's mouth.

Soon after their arrival three log houses, constructed after the Western manner and covered with oak shingles fashioned on the spot, were put up. With a crudely improvised sawmill, boards were hewn from oak logs for the cabin floors. Elk, bear, and wild geese were so abundant that one man with a rifle could bring in enough game

in three hours' time to supply the colony for a week. Wheat, farm implements, and other necessary supplies had been brought, and by the middle of January 1847, 80 acres of grain had been sown. The little settlement did, indeed, seem full of hope and promise.

But with the coming of the winter rains the whole aspect was changed. The season was so stormy that the river overflowed its banks, causing the little band of pioneers much suffering and hardship. Then, too, serious dissension arose among the colonists. So completely disheartened did they become that gradually the group disbanded. By the summer of 1847 only one man, a Mr. Buckland, remained, and he, too, was gone by November.

An attempt to re-establish a settlement at Stanislaus City seems to have been made during the gold rush of 1849. Buffum in 1850 made the prophecy that "this point ... being nearer the southern mining region than Stockton, will doubtless become a great resort for miners and traders." Stanislaus City appears on a map published in 1851, which also indicates that the road from Stockton to Tuolumne City crossed the Stanislaus River at that point. Nevertheless, no substantial revival ever took place, for Henry Grissim, who took up land on the old site in May 1851, apparently was not aware that he was farming on ground occupied four years earlier by the town of Sam Brannan's "new hope." A monument commemorating New Hope stands at Ripon, six miles northeast of the site. A similar marker indicating the landing place of the Comet (SRL 437) is located on Highway 120, west of Manteca near the San Joaquin River.

Various ferries along the Stanislaus River are mentioned in the journals of early travelers and in old newspapers and county records: Knight's (established in the spring of 1849), the first of the chain; George Keeler's (1849); Heath and Emory's (1849); Leitch and Cottle's; Islip's, mentioned in the Audubon Journal, under the date of January 6, 1850, as the "Middle Ferry"; Boland (1850); Burney's; Murphy's; Sirey's (1849); and Belcher's (1849).

After attempts to establish Stanislaus City failed, a settlement was started on the west side of the San Joaquin River a little below the mouth of the Stanislaus. Hoping to become a rival of Stockton, San Joaquin City (SRL 777), as it was called, persisted for a number of years. As late as 1880 it had a hotel, a warehouse, and two saloons, as well as stores and homes. Nothing but a historic plaque marks the location today, although the name is found on some recent maps. North of the site a bridge crosses the river in the vicinity of the old Durham Ferry crossing, established by Titus and Manly in 1850, and later successively owned by Durham and Fiske. San Joaquin City is about ten miles southeast of Banta via Kasson Road.

The first ferry to be operated on the San Joaquin River was that of John Doak and Jacob Bonsell, who in 1848 began to convey passengers in a small yawl across the river at a spot located about where the Southern Pacific Railroad and the highway from Tracy to Manteca cross today. It was here that the old Sutter's Fort–San José Trail crossed the river. Traffic to the mines soon grew so heavy that it became necessary to have a larger and more substantial ferryboat, so Doak went to Corte Madera in Marin County, where he built the new craft. With their increased carrying facilities, the partners did an enormous business, reaping equally large returns, for charges on this pioneer ferry were high—one dollar for footmen, three dollars for horsemen, and eight dollars for horses and wagons. In 1852, however, Doak sold his share in the business to Hiram Scott, and later in the same year Bonsell died. With the subsequent marriage of Bonsell's widow to James A. Shepherd, the ferry became known as Shepherd's Ferry and was so called until 1856, when it was sold to William T. Moss. The place is still referred to as Mossdale.

Three miles south of Bonsell's Ferry was Slocum's Ferry, established in 1849, while to the north was Johnson's Ferry. In later years Frewert's and Lindstrom's ferries were put into operation still farther to the north.

Corral Hollow

Corral Hollow (SRL 755) may be reached over the Corral Hollow Road, which turns south from the highway one mile west of Tracy. Many Indian relics, including arrowheads, pestles, and beautifully shaped bowls, have been uncovered along the dry bed of the arroyo, indicating the probable existence of a former Indian encampment in the vicinity. Petrified cedar, as well as fossil leaves and shells, have been found in the arroyo and in the neighboring hills. Two miles up the canyon is Castle Rock, a Vaqueros sandstone formation pierced with so-called "caves" or prospect holes, which tradition says was one of Joaquín Murieta's numerous hideouts.

In early days the hollow was known as El Arroyo de los Buenos Aires, through which an old Spanish trail, El Camino Viejo, ran. According to Bolton, Juan Bautista de Anza passed that way in April 1776. Later, Spanish and Mexican vaqueros made customary use of the trail, along which they drove their herds of cattle. Still later, during the gold days, the old trail was much traveled as a road to the southern mines.

One of the first white settlers in the hollow, and certainly the most famous, was Edward B. (Ned) Carrell, who in 1850 took up government land there. For many years it was believed that the present "Corral Hollow" was a corruption of "Carrell's Hollow," but Carrell's diaries prove this to be untrue. Probably the hollow was named for a corral built there in early days for captured wild horses.

Down on the arroyo among the cottonwoods, directly on the line of the old Spanish trail, Carrell and three associates, Horatio P. Wright, William Breyton, and John A. Stockholm, built, under the leadership of Wright, a tavern called the "Zink House"· where the buildings of the present sheep ranch stand. Here for several years meals and liquor were served to wayfarers. A famous visitor to stop at the Zink House was

James Capen Adams, or "Grizzly" Adams, as he was popularly known. With his two bears, "Lady Washington" and "Ben Franklin," and his dog "Rambler," famous actors in Adams' "Mountaineer Museum" in San Francisco, he spent several months in 1855 hunting in the region, his experiences afterward figuring in Theodore Hittell's biographical narrative.

In 1856 John O'Brien, a sheepman who had established his camp in Corral Hollow, discovered an outcropping of a black mineral at the upper end of the canyon about nine miles from the Zink House which when tested proved to be coal. The Pacific Coal Mining Company was subsequently organized, and this became, in turn, the Commercial Mine and the Eureka Mine.

Carrell at once began to erect a two-story house of resawed siding to serve as a boardinghouse for the teamsters, who hauled coal from the mines to the San Joaquin River, where it was loaded on barges at Mohr's Landing (on Old River near Bethany). A monument marks the site of the old Carrell house, completed in 1861, which stood for many years at the mouth of the canyon just above the gravel pits of Pacific Cement and Aggregates, the bleakness of its surroundings softened by vividly green pepper trees planted by Carrell and by a few magnificent old cottonwoods, all that were left of the many that flourished in the region when the first white settlers came. This historic landmark was the home of Carrell's stepdaughter, Mrs. Mamie Burns, until her death in 1935. It was destroyed by fire in 1938.

When Carrell, the only surviving owner of the Eureka Coal Company, died in 1880 at the homestead in the hollow, John and James Treadwell of the famous Bears' Nest Mine, Alaska, purchased the Corral Hollow coal property, naming it the Tesla Mine in honor of Nikola Tesla, the great electrical inventor. During the early 1890's, under the management of the San Francisco and San Joaquin Coal Company, the yield from the Tesla Mine averaged 500 tons of coal daily. From six to ten carloads were shipped each day over the Alameda and San Joaquin, a branch railroad to Stockton, where the coal was transferred to river boats bound for San Francisco.

About this time the Treadwells built a brick and pottery plant, called Pottery, two miles down the gulch at Walden Spur on their railroad. It employed about 65 men. Later they built a larger plant four miles down the gulch and organized it as the Carnegie Brick and Pottery Company to manufacture white glazed firebrick. Carnegie (SRL 740) became a town of some 2,000 inhabitants and flourished until 1906, when the earthquake and the failure of the California Safe Deposit Bank in San Francisco ruined the Treadwells financially and caused the abandonment of Carnegie. A great boiler explosion in 1907 and, finally, the floods of 1911, which washed out the railroad, sealed its doom.

Corral Hollow, partly in Alameda County, today presents a forlorn appearance. Only the wreckage of abandoned dumps marks the site of the Tesla Mine. The housing settlements of

Tesla, Fry's Flat, Jimtown, Treadwell Row, and Harrietville, with its Silk Stocking Row, are gone, as are the hotels and stores. Not a trace remains of the fine brick houses that lined the hills between Pottery and Carnegie, and only a few broken foundation bricks at the sites of the two great plants themselves. A monument, similar to the one at the Carrell homesite, stands at Carnegie. Southeast of Carnegie, just above the site of the former Camp Thomas of the Hetch Hetchy project, is a manganese mine, first developed by Aurelius Ladd in 1863. A company of Frenchmen worked it further in the 1890's. During World War I, interest again centered on this mine, when about $80,000 was recovered from the tailings. It was again worked during World War II and the Korean war.

SOURCES

Audubon, John W. *Audubon's Western Journal: 1849–1850.* The Arthur H. Clark Co., Cleveland, 1906.

Bogardus, J. P. "A Historical Sketch of Stockton," *Stockton City Directory for the Year 1856.* Harris, Joseph & Co., San Francisco, 1856.

Bolton, Herbert Eugene. *Anza's California Expeditions.* 5 vols. University of California, Berkeley, 1930.

Bonta, Robert Eugene. *The Cross in the Valley.* Academy Library Guild, Fresno, 1963.

Buffum, E. Gould. *Six Months in the Gold Mines.* Lea & Blanchard, Philadelphia, 1850.

Carrell, Edward B. Diaries for 1846, 1850–51, 1856–58, 1860–62, in the possession of Earle E. Williams, Tracy.

Carson, James H. *Life in California, Together with a Description of the Great Tulare Valley.* 2d ed. San Joaquin Republican, Stockton, 1852; reprinted by W. Abbatt, Tarrytown, N.Y., 1931.

Curtis, Mrs. Dwight. *Old Cemeteries of San Joaquin County.* 2 vols. San Joaquin Genealogical Society, Stockton, 1960.

Davis, Shelden. "Tesla, a Coast Range 'Ghost Town,'" *Stockton Record,* February 7, 1931, pp. 25–28.

Finkbohner, Agnes Steiny (Mrs. George). "History and Landmarks of San Joaquin County." Ms., 1924.

Frémont, Brevet Colonel John C. *The Exploring Expedition to the Rocky Mountains, Oregon and California.* George H. Derby & Co., Buffalo, 1849.

Gilbert, Colonel F. T. *History of San Joaquin County, California.* Thompson & West, Oakland, 1879.

Hittell, Theodore H. *The Adventures of James Capen Adams, Mountaineer and Grizzly Bear Hunter of California.* Towne & Bacon, San Francisco, 1860. New ed. Scribner, 1911.

Hubbard, Harry D. *Building the Heart of an Empire.* Meador Publishing Co., Boston, 1938.

Illustrated History of San Joaquin County, California. The Lewis Publishing Co., Chicago, 1890.

Latta, F. F. "San Joaquin Primeval—Spanish," *Tulare Daily Times,* 1932.

Maloney, Alice B. "California Rendezvous," *Beaver,* December 1944.

Martin, V. Covert. *Stockton Album through the Years.* Simard Printing Co., Stockton, 1959.

Reynolds, James. Statement on French Camp, made to F. F. Latta, August 12, 1933.

Schenck, W. Egbert. "Historic Aboriginal Groups of the California Delta Region," *University of California Publications in American Archaeology and Ethnology,* XXV, No. 4 (1929), 289–413.

Stockholm, John A. Diary for 1846, in the possession of Earle E. Williams, Tracy.

Taylor, Bayard. *Eldorado, or Adventures in the Path of Empire.* Putnam, New York, 1850, 1864.

Tinkham, George H. *History of San Joaquin County, California.* The Historic Record Co., Los Angeles, 1923.

——— *History of Stockton.* W. M. Hinton & Co., San Francisco, 1880.

Wright, Horatio P. Zink House account book, later used by Edward B. Carrell until 1875, in the possession of Earle E. Williams, Tracy.

San Luis Obispo County

SAN LUIS OBISPO COUNTY (named for the Mission of St. Louis, Bishop of Toulouse) was one of the original 27 counties of the state. San Luis Obispo has been the county seat continuously.

The Carrizo Plain and the Painted Rock

A singular geologic formation in the southeastern part of the county is the elevated plateau, or basin, over 1,600 feet above sea level. It can be reached by taking the road that runs east from Santa Margarita and passes through the little settlements of Pozo ("cup," "well") and La Panza ("the paunch"). This highway passes through the Carrizo Plain, which extends to the east and south.

The plateau is about 50 miles long and from eight to 20 miles wide. The drainage appears to be entirely to the center, where an area of four square miles, dry and white, bears the name Soda Lake. Farmers and stockmen used to get their supply of salt from this place. General Parkes, in his report of the Pacific Railroad survey in 1853 and 1854, says: "The hills on either side supply it with water, small in quantity, which collects in lagoons or ponds in the center of the plain, which is uninhabited by man, and occupied by only herds of deer, antelope, and wild horses, with which it abounds." However, by 1890, the plain had become private property, with many prosperous settlements upon it.

In the southwestern part of the plain is an isolated butte, roughly 1,000 feet in diameter and rising to a height of 140 feet. It is conical, like the crater of a volcano, but has a narrow opening toward the east on a level with the plain. The opening is 24 feet wide and leads to a vast oval cavity 225 feet in its greatest diameter and 120 feet in the smallest, the walls rising to a height of 132 feet at the highest point. The rock is of coarse sandstone, and the walls are irregular and overhang in places, making the inner space like a cave. In these recesses, covering a space 12 feet high and 60 feet long, are many paintings, representing men, suns, birds, and other designs not easily described, probably writings of meaning to the prehistoric people who made them. Early settlers said the paintings were unchanged since the pioneer Spanish missionaries discovered them. The Indians knew nothing of their origin.

The paintings are in three lines of red, white, and black; the colors are remarkably bright and distinct but now much defaced by vandals. The spot has been used as a cattle corral, and no care has been taken to preserve it. The rock, called La Piedra Pintada (The Painted Rock) by the early Spanish settlers, is located about 15 miles southeast of Simmler. The turnoff is a mile west of that community, and the road is paved for the first nine miles.

Unamuno and Cermeño

The coast of San Luis Obispo County was first seen by white men in 1542, but there is no evidence that the Cabrillo expedition landed at any point within the present county. At least two Manila galleon captains, however, paid brief visits. In 1587 Pedro de Unamuno brought his ship into Morro Bay and, according to Henry R. Wagner, penetrated inland about to the present city of San Luis Obispo. Possession was taken in the name of the king of Spain and a cross was erected. The first Indians encountered by the party were extremely timid, but later the Spaniards were caught off guard by an Indian attack in which two of the explorers were killed and several others wounded. Eight years later Sebastián Rodríguez Cermeño, returning to Mexico in an open launch after the loss of his galleon *San Agustín*

at what is today called Drake's Bay, put in at San Luis Obispo Bay. The hungry crew traded with the Indians, who, they recorded, shouted "Cristianos" and "Mexico," evidently memories of their contact with Unamuno. It is probable that Vizcaíno, who named the Santa Lucía Mountains, entered the same bay in 1602.

The Portolá Trail

The present Oso Flaco (Lean Bear) Lake, situated near the coast in southwestern San Luis Obispo County, was so named by the soldiers of Gaspar de Portolá's expedition on September 3, 1769, when a very lean bear was killed near their camp on the shore of the lake. On the 4th, a halt was made in Price Canyon north of Pismo Beach, and on the 5th, one in San Luís Canyon, where the party rested on the 6th. Again the tents were pitched on the 7th, this time at the lower end of Los Osos Creek, where the soldiers spent the day replenishing their food supply with bear meat. This was the occasion for naming the valley La Cañada de los Osos (The Canyon of the Bears), a name it retains today.

On a site within the present town of Morro Bay, opposite the bay's entrance and majestic Morro Rock, camp was made on September 8. Again the expedition was halted on the 9th, on this date at Ellysly's Creek just east of Point Estero. Continuing up Ellysly's Creek and over Dawson Grade, the band stopped on the 10th somewhat south of present Cambria; and on the 11th, at Little Pico Creek east of San Simeon Point. The following day the party went inland over the hills and stopped above Arroyo de la Cruz. Reaching Ragged Point on San Carpóforo Creek (now shortened to San Carpojo) on the 13th, Portolá found that further progress up the coast was barred by steep mountain precipices. The 14th and 15th were spent in preparing a

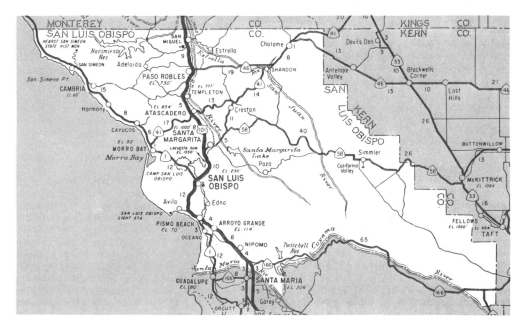

trail over a most difficult pass by way of San Carpojo Creek to its junction with Dutra Creek, where camp was made on the 16th. On the 17th the march was resumed over very rough country to Wagner Creek, within the present confines of Monterey County.

Three years later Pedro Fages, who had been a leader on the Portolá trek and was now commander of the Presidio of Monterey, had good reason to recall La Cañada de los Osos. The unpredictable supply ships had failed to reach the presidio, and near-famine conditions prevailed there and at Misión San Antonio de Padua. Fages organized California's greatest grizzly bear hunt and, with 13 soldiers, was able to supply the settlements for months.

The Anza Trail

As far as the site of Mission San Luís Obispo, Juan Bautista de Anza passed over practically the same trail in San Luis Obispo County as Portolá had before him in 1769. The Southern Pacific Railroad follows much the same route today. From the mission, Anza crossed the Santa Lucía Range through Cuesta Pass over the present highway route. Continuing along its course to Paso Robles, he turned northwest over the hills along Oak Flat Road (Paso de los Robles) to San Marcos Creek. There the road went almost due north to Nacimiento River about at Rancho Nacimiento and proceeded to the first crossing of the San Antonio River, about at King Well, now in Monterey County.

On Anza's first trip, in 1774, two stops were made in San Luis Obispo County, one at the mission on April 15, and a second at the Nacimiento River on April 16. On his second trip, in 1776, as leader of the San Francisco colonists, he camped at the following places: the Indian village of El Buchon, in Price Canyon two miles north of Pismo Beach on March 1; Misión San Luís Obispo on March 2 and 3; and La Asunción, a short distance beyond Atascadero, on March 4.

Cave Landing

Cave Landing is situated on San Luis Obispo Bay about one-half mile east of the resort town of Avila Beach, and can be reached from the freeway via Cave Landing Road northwest of Shell Beach. The padres used this landing place for shipping tallow and grain.

According to Velva G. Darling: "The boat came as close in shore as it could and the freight was let down from the cliff by means of a rude crane. Later, along in the sixties, when settlers began coming into the county, the schooners and sailing vessels stopped at Cave Landing and the pioneers climbed rope ladders to the top of the cliff after being brought ashore in little rowboats. Sometimes the surf and spray dashed far up the side of the cliff.

"A path leads down the side of the cliff to a pretty curving beach. From the beach you can see the great Arch Rock and the mouth of Robbers' Cave. This cave was the hiding place for many a bandit's loot. It is said there is much treasure still buried there and often do the treasure seekers dig and delve for it." Between Arch Rock and Robbers' Cave lies tiny Moonstone Beach, so called from the moonstones among the pebbles and shells washed up by the waves.

From the white sands of Moonstone Beach one may climb over the rocks, ducking through tunnels made by the sea, until, rounding a corner, one comes suddenly upon an immense level rock which juts out 150 feet into deep water and beneath which the tide swirls. This is Cave Landing, an excellent natural pier for deep-sea fishing. Here Indians fished for hundreds of years and buried their dead in crude graves along the rugged cliffs facing the east. After them came smugglers and bandits, priests and sea captains.

About 1860 David Mallagh, an Irish sea captain, erected a warehouse on the cliffs above the sea, with a long wooden chute leading down to the water. Huge iron spikes, with immense rings of iron fastened to them, were driven into the solid rock at the top of the cliff. To these rings, the great ship cables were fastened. For a decade, Captain Mallagh handled all of the shipping at the cove and hauled passengers and freight to San Luis Obispo. After his death and the advent of the railroad a mile farther north on the coast, Cave Landing was abandoned and gradually fell into decay. Only the rusted iron rings and spikes and the great postholes remain to tell the tale of adventure, pirates, and treasure.

Misión San Luís Obispo de Tolosa

Misión San Luís Obispo de Tolosa (SRL 325) was founded by Padre Junípero Serra on September 1, 1772, while on his notable journey from Monterey to Mexico. Since no other priest was available at the time, Father José Cavaller was left in sole charge of the new post, contrary to the rule that two priests must be stationed at each mission. He continued to serve there until his death in 1789.

The first attempt to manufacture tile in California was made at San Luís Obispo, after the buildings, thatched with tule, had been three times badly damaged by fire. The first of these disasters occurred in November 1776, when hostile Indians shot burning arrows into the roofs. This first experiment in tile making proved successful, and after 1784 all the missions used this method of roofing. At San Luís Obispo an adobe church, completed in 1794, replaced the original chapel.

Helen Hunt Jackson in her novel *Ramona* gives a pleasing picture of Father Luís Martínez, who began his long services at the mission in 1798. The story tells how, when he wished to entertain General Moreno and his bride, he "caused to be driven past the corridors, for their inspection, all the poultry belonging to the Mission. The procession took an hour to pass. The Indians had been hard at work all night capturing, sorting, and guarding the rank and file of their novel pageant. It would be safe to say that a droller sight never was seen, and never will be, on the Pacific Coast or any other. Before it was done with, the General and his bride had nearly died with laughter." Father Martínez was one of the best known of the friars to serve at San Luís Obispo. "Portly of figure and gruff of speech," he was very jovial and much loved by Indians and Spaniards alike.

The mission is now an active parish church in the city of San Luis Obispo. Alterations and makeshift restorations over the years included the boarding over of crumbling walls and the erection of an incongruous steeple. Efforts have been made since 1934 to restore the whole establishment to its original appearance. The steeple has been removed and red tiles again cover the roof of the old church. As funds are available, adjoining buildings are restored, and the garden at the rear, where great old grapevines have survived long neglect, is receiving attention and will be fittingly enclosed as it was in earlier years.

San Luis Obispo County, one of the original 27 counties, was created on February 18, 1850, even before California was admitted to the union. San Luis Obispo was made the county seat, and a courthouse was erected on the site of the present building. The original courthouse was commemorated by an official State marker on February 18, 1950, but the spot has not been registered nor assigned a number.

San Luis Obispo was organized as a town in 1856 and incorporated as a city on March 20, 1876. It is a city of beautiful old adobe homes, although it is not so well known as either Monterey or Santa Barbara for this feature. Outstanding among them is the Pierre Hyppolite Dallidet adobe *(SRL 720)* on San Luis Obispo Creek at 1185 Pacific Street. This was the home of a French vineyardist who came to the area in 1853. His son Paul presented the old residence and gardens to the San Luis Obispo County Historical Society, and they are now open to the public on Sunday afternoons. The estate is fast becoming a historical center to complement the museum operated by the society at Monterey and Broad streets near the old mission.

Among the other adobes in San Luis Obispo are the old Sauer home at 964 Chorro Street and the nearby art gallery at 970. The Cortesi adobe stands at 669 Chorro. At 642 Monterey Street is the Hays adobe, and the Murray is at 747. The

old Simmler home is located at 466 Dana Street, and the Fisher is at 883 Nipomo Street. The Andrews adobe, built for the mayordomo of the mission, stands at 1451 Andrews Street near Conejo. At the end of Lizzie Street, splendid in its isolation, is the two-story Quintana adobe.

Some of the city's old business buildings are still in use. These include the Sinsheimer store at 849 Monterey Street, Sauer's Bakery across the street at 848, and Kluver's cigar factory (1897), now a restaurant, at 726 Higuera Street. The Ah Louis store *(SRL 802)* at 800 Palm Street was the first Chinese store in San Luis Obispo County. It was established in 1874 and the present iron-shuttered brick structure was completed ten years later. In addition to selling herbs and general merchandise, the place served as a bank and post office for the numerous Chinese coolies employed in digging railroad tunnels through Cuesta Pass in the 1880's and 1890's. Ah Louis died in 1916 in his 99th year.

Misión San Miguel Arcángel

Misión San Miguel Arcángel *(SRL 326)* was founded July 25, 1797, by Father Fermín Francisco de Lasuén, assisted by Father Buenaventura Sitjar. It was located on a beautiful spot on the Salinas River where there was plenty of water for irrigation. Some of the canals and dams built by the fathers for irrigating their orchards and crops may still be seen around the mission.

The first temporary wooden buildings were gradually replaced, from 1799 to 1804, by adobe structures. Fire almost destroyed the entire establishment in 1806, and plans were made for reconstruction on a more spacious scale. The church building which was begun in 1816 and completed in 1818 still stands. Secularization took place in 1836, followed by confiscation and neglect. In later years, the building was restored, and services are now held there by the Franciscan Fathers, who maintain the old place as a novitiate. It is one of four California missions still in the hands of the Franciscan Order.

San Miguel remains less spoiled by restoration than most of the missions, and contains perhaps the finest examples of the original decorations done by the Indians under supervision of the padres, and, in this case, under the particular direction of Estévan Munras of Monterey. They are crude, but plainly a work of love and sincerity.

Great rafters and corbels hewn from solid trees, carried by Indians 40 miles from the mountains, support the ceiling, and all are colored in light green, pink, blue, and white. The walls are designed to represent fluted pillars tinted in blue, while between these are conventionalized designs of leaves and carved figures. A frieze in reddish brown represents a gallery with railings and pillars. The ancient pulpit, also decorated and colored by the Indians, the confessional built into the adobe wall, the floor of burnt brick laid in alternate rows of squares and oblongs, all remain as they were when first completed with such loving care by the padres and their charges. The monastery with its beautiful low-arched corridor,

Cortesi Adobe, San Luis Obispo

which extends from the side, is unique in the fact that its arches are of different sizes, the two central ones being larger than the others and elliptical in form, balanced by four smaller, semicircular arches set off by one still smaller on each side. A major part of the restoration of this mission establishment has been completed, and further work is now in progress.

At the south end of the town of San Miguel is a striking two-story adobe built in the 1850's by Petronillo Ríos. Called the Caledonia adobe, it served as a hotel and stage station. It is now owned by the County of San Luis Obispo and there are plans for its restoration.

The Asistencia of Santa Margarita

The Asistencia of Santa Margarita *(SRL 364)*, belonging to Mission San Luís Obispo, was an outpost, or chapel and storehouse, located north of the mission and across steep Cuesta Pass. It was built of stone on a knoll near Santa Margarita Creek, where many Indians lived whom the padres hoped to enroll as converts.

A visitor to this place in 1831, while the building was still intact, was Alfred Robinson, who wrote: "We reached 'El Rancho de Santa Rita,' a place used for the cultivation of grain, where, on an eminence that overlooked the grounds, an extensive building was erected. It was divided into store rooms for different kinds of grain, and apartments for the accommodation of the mayordomo, servants, and wayfarers. At one end was a chapel, and snug lodging-rooms for the priest, who, I was informed, frequently came and passed some weeks at the place during the time of harvest; and the holy friars of the two missions occasionally met there to acknowledge to each other their sins."

Of special interest today are the massive stone doorway, several windows with arched tops in almost perfect condition, and the side and end walls which still stand. A ranch barn has been constructed with the nave as the main part of the building. Here hay is stored and is fed through the window openings to cattle and horses in the stalls and mangers beneath a shed that extends the whole length of the building. The barn and other red-roofed ranch buildings (see Rancho Santa Margarita, p. 387) can be seen to the right of the freeway a short distance north of the turnoff to the town of Santa Margarita.

Ranchos of San Miguel

In compliance with the decree of Governor José M. Echeandía of October 7, 1827, that the missionaries make a detailed report on the lands of their respective missions, Father Juan Cabot reported on November 26, 1827, for Misión San Miguel as follows:

"Towards the south the lands of Mission San Luís Obispo are recognized to extend to the Rancho de la Asunción, distant from here seven leagues.

"Toward the north, the Mission claims the land to the Rancho de San Bartolomé, or Pleyto, distant about seven leagues to the boundary of Mission San Antonio.

"From the Mission to the beach the land consists almost entirely of mountain ridges, devoid of permanent water. For this reason that region is not occupied until one reaches the coast where the Mission has a house of adobe. Here it may cultivate some clear land for planting grain in summertime but it is entirely dependent upon rain, since there is no irrigated land there. In the same district eight hundred cattle, some tame horses and breeding mares are kept at said Rancho, which is called San Simeón.

"In the direction toward the south, all the land is occupied, for the Mission there maintains all its sheep, besides the horses of the guards. It is there it has the Rancho de Santa Isabel, where there is a small vineyard. Other ranchos of the Mission in that direction are San Antonio, where barley is planted; Rancho del Paso de Robles, where the wheat is sown; and the Rancho de la Asunción. In these last two named ranchos there is an adobe building, roofed with tiles, for keeping the seed grain. However, all is dependent upon rain, because there is no means to irrigate the land, save at Asunción, where there is a little spring with sufficient water for a garden; and at Santa Isabel, which has a little more in summer."

Ranchos of Senator Hearst

The ranchos of Piedra Blanca, San Simeón, and Santa Rosa became the property of George W. Hearst. The three stretch along the Pacific from the mouth of San Carpóforo (Carpojo) Creek southeast to the mouth of Villa Creek and extend far back into the hills.

Rancho Piedra Blanca is the farthest north. It was granted, in 1840, to José de Jesús Pico, one of the 13 children of Don José Dolores Pico. He was a former soldier at Monterey and shortly after receiving this grant was administrator of San Miguel Mission. Although at one time he was arrested by Frémont and condemned to death, he was pardoned at the intercession of a band of women and children led by Doña Ramona Carrillo de Wilson, wife of Captain John Wilson. Pico afterward became a devoted friend of Frémont and assisted him in bringing about the treaty of Cahuenga. In 1848 and again in 1849 he made successful trips to the gold mines but later spent his time on his rancho.

Mariano Pacheco purchased a portion of Rancho Piedra Blanca from Pico, and until the 1870's his family lived in the adobe house overlooking the ocean and located about three miles north of the town of San Simeon. Don Mariano was buried in the vicinity. After the departure of the Pacheco family, the extensive two-story adobe was used by tenants until about 1906. Its foundations, marked by a few old cypress trees, are hidden in a tangle of weeds on a hill in what is now a cattle pasture.

The town of San Simeon, which lies on this rancho, was for many years the center of an extensive whaling industry. As early as 1864 Captain Joseph Clark, still active in the 1880's, had a fleet of five boats outfitted for whaling. Many years ago a fire wiped out a large part of the little town, but several old frame buildings still stand.

Sebastian's store *(SRL 726)*, built in the 1860's one-half mile to the west and moved to its present location in 1878, is the oldest store building along the northern coast of San Luis Obispo County. The store and the adjacent post office are still in business. There is also a warehouse built in 1878 by the Hearst interests and bearing the date of its construction. A little farther from the wharf are red-tiled, stucco residences built in more recent times by William Randolph Hearst for his employees.

Up the road back of the town is the large frame ranch house of Senator George Hearst, built soon after he purchased Rancho Piedra Blanca in 1865. It is still the headquarters for the Hearst cattle ranch. This building can be seen from the bus that transports tourists through the private ranch property to Hearst–San Simeon State Historical Monument *(SRL 640)* on a commanding height overlooking San Simeon Bay.

Here, from 1919 to 1947, William Randolph Hearst, newspaper magnate and son of Senator George W. and Phoebe Apperson Hearst, created La Cuesta Encantada (The Enchanted Hill), at a cost of millions of dollars. Together with his architect, Julia Morgan, he planned the Spanish Renaissance buildings where he lived and operated his vast empire, entertaining famous guests from far and near, including Calvin Coolidge, Winston Churchill, George Bernard Shaw, and a multitude of motion picture personalities. The main residence, La Casa Grande, has four floors with scores of rooms and twin towers housing carillon bells. The structure was never finished. There are also three guest cottages, each a mansion in itself with from 10 to 18 rooms. Casa del Mar faces the Pacific, Casa del Monte the ridges of the Santa Lucia Range, and Casa del Sol the setting sun. All the buildings and the grounds are filled with art objects collected by Hearst all over the world. The warehouses at San Simeon contain treasures destined for the castle but still in the packing crates in which they were shipped from European palaces and monasteries. Hearst transplanted exotic trees to his hilltop hideaway and even established a private zoo. Some of the animals are still living on the ranch. There are both an indoor and an outdoor pool. Hearst died in 1951 at the age of 88, and in 1958 the Hearst Corporation presented the castle and about 125 acres of land surrounding it to the State of California to be opened to the public as a memorial to William Randolph Hearst and his mother, Phoebe Apperson Hearst.

Southeast of Rancho Piedra Blanca lies Rancho San Simeón, through which flows San Simeon Creek. This was a grant of one square league made to José Ramón Estrada, son of José Mariano Estrada, and patented to José Miguel Gómez in 1865. The San Simeón adobe, gone long ago, was on San Simeon Creek back from the beach about three-quarters of a mile.

The farthest south of the three is Rancho Santa Rosa, a three-league grant made to Julián Estrada, son of José Ramón Estrada, and patented to him in 1865. The Estrada adobe stood on the road north of Swallow Rock at an elevation of 130 feet. Nothing now remains to indicate the site. The town of Cambria, first called Rosaville, was located on the property. It originated during the copper excitement of 1863 and was aided in its growth by the quicksilver prospecting of 1871 and by the activities of lumbermen.

When the last-named rancho was purchased by Senator Hearst, Pancho Estrada, son of Don Julián, an expert horseman from early chilhood, entered the employ of the new owner and continued in the service of that family until his death, at the age of 83, on July 26, 1936. Don Pancho, as he was generally called, had great pride in the sleek horses under his care. He was a colorful figure, when, clad in Spanish vaquero costume, on fiesta days he headed the gay procession.

Rancho Moro y Cayucos

Cayuco is a nautical term applied to a small fishing boat, which is like a canoe and often made of skins. A point on the coast of California that was early used as a port was called by that name because the schooners, pausing offshore from the mouth of a small stream, had commerce with the land by means of these small boats. The creek, the little settlement that grew up near its mouth, and eventually the land nearby were all known by the name.

In 1842, Rancho Moro y Cayucos was granted to Martin Olivera, from Rancho Sausal in Monterey County, and to Vicente Feliz, former mayordomo of another rancho. It was later owned by James McKinley, a Scottish sailor, who married Carmen Amesti, daughter of José Amesti of Rancho Corralitos. McKinley sold it in smaller tracts for dairy farms.

In 1867 this coastal region was served by a weekly stage running from San Luis Obispo to San Simeon. In this year James Cass came to the vicinity of Cayucos Landing and lived first in the hills just back of the settlement, but soon he built a large house that still stands on Ocean Avenue at C Street near Cayucos Creek in the town of Cayucos. Because of his well-directed efforts the settlement began to increase. He built a wharf in 1870 and soon afterward a store and warehouse. In 1875 the broad streets of the town were laid out, and in the early 1880's a stage bringing passengers from San Miguel and way stations made connections with a weekly boat at Cayucos.

For many years considerable shipping was done from here, but finally a storm destroyed a large part of the pier and motor transportation eliminated the need of steamer calls. Only a small pleasure wharf is now on the site of the wharf built by Captain Cass.

Rancho San Bernardo

Vicente Cané (Canet), a Spanish sailor, settled in Alta California before 1828. On February 11, 1840, he received a grant of one square league of land lying between San Bernardo and Morro creeks, both of which empty into Morro Bay. The following year Don Vicente was *juez* at Misión San Luís Obispo. His rancho home was built about that time on a hill above San Bernardo Creek two miles east of Morro Rock. An idealized picture of the old adobe in which it is described as a "castle" or a "great mansion," whereas it was in reality only a story-and-a-half house, is here given, because it conveys something of the spirit of that time.

To this country Don Vicente came, in those days of romance, to seek "a place of great beauty where he might build his castle, gather about him his friends, his flocks and herds, and live the ideal life of a Spanish gentleman of the new world. He had chanced to hear of the famous Morro Rock from a sea-faring friend and hither he came and was fascinated by what he beheld.

"The great red cone rising majestically from the limpid blue of the sea, . . . the long sandbar that was a barrier to the rough waters of the ocean protecting the bay, the golden sunshine, the balmy breezes, and near at hand all sorts of wild game, . . . no farther would Don [Vicente] Canet seek, for here was Elysia.

"He sought the skilled labor of the Indians from the two great missions of San Luís de Tolosa and San Miguel the Arcángel. Some made adobe bricks for the walls of the castle while others hewed out the great oak timbers and bore them to the site of the castle. On a gently sloping knoll, beside the San Lusita [Luisito], with the mountains rising behind it, the great mansion was erected. . . .

"The Don spent over $40,000 for labor and materials for the castle. It was plastered with crushed gypsum from the nearby hills and the flooring was brought around the Horn in sailing vessels. The wings contained sleeping rooms and servants' quarters. In one wing was a chapel with a raised altar. Here in great grandeur lived Don [Vicente] Canet. Many a fiesta, many a bear and bull-fight, many a wild horse race broke the monotony of life, if monotony could ever be in a land so fair and favored. . . .

"It is said that long after master and horse were dust, his steed could be heard champing and neighing in the courtyard on moonlight nights and then madly galloping down to the bay. Those watching saw a misty form enter a phantom skiff and row away towards the rock."

Today this interesting and well-preserved house may be seen from the Morro Bay–San Luis Obispo highway as it stands to the left and above the

Canet Adobe, near Morro Bay

road, two miles east of Morro Bay just beyond the junction of San Bernardo Creek Road. Tar paper has replaced the tiles of the original roof. The front door is flanked by deep-set windows, which are protected by vertical iron bars. At the rear of the house is a patio, open on one side. An adobe house built by a son of the grantee faces the patio and forms one of its walls. In the patio are the remains of an old grapevine, and a few of the old cypress and eucalyptus trees are still in evidence on the property.

One and one-quarter miles beyond the Canet adobe toward San Luis Obispo, Canet Road leads half a mile to the old family cemetery.

Lands of Captain John Wilson

John Wilson, Scottish shipmaster and captain of the *Ayacucho,* who had engaged in trading for years on the coast, settled in California and married Ramona Carrillo de Pacheco, owner of Rancho Suey, a widow with two sons, one of whom, Romualdo, afterward held many high offices in the state and became acting governor in 1875. About 1839 Captain Wilson and James Scott, another native of Scotland, had entered into a business partnership, which continued until 1847.

Rancho Cañada del Chorro, on the southwest side of the Santa Lucia Range, consisting of 3,167 acres, was granted to them. James Scott died in 1851 and Captain Wilson in 1860, so the patent to it was issued to Wilson's heirs in 1861.

The Cañada de los Osos, so named by Portolá's men in 1769 because of the bears they killed here for food, was a part of Rancho Cañada de los Osos y Peche y Islay. This rancho was granted to Captain Wilson and James Scott, after having been previously granted to Francisco Padillo, a convict who came from Mexico in 1825; and Victor Linares, a soldier at San Diego in 1826, who came to San Luis Obispo before 1839. This all became the property of Captain Wilson.

Between Rancho El Chorro and Rancho Cañada de los Osos, an Indian named Romualdo cultivated a bit of level land at the base of Cerro Romualdo. This tract, consisting of 117 acres, was purchased by Captain Wilson and called Huerta (vegetable garden) de Romualdo.

Captain Wilson built an adobe house in the Cañada de los Osos and lived there from 1845 until his death. His widow continued to live there. Her eldest son, who had now gained an enviable position in governmental affairs, resided with her. The property afterward passed to her daughter. The house still stands eight miles west of San Luis Obispo via Los Osos Road. It serves as a barn on a ranch to the east of Turri Road at a point half a mile north of Los Osos Road. The dormer windows are still in evidence.

Rancho San Miguelito

Rancho San Miguelito lay along the shore of San Luis Obispo Bay with a further shoreline extending northwest along the ocean almost to Pecho Creek. On this rancho an outpost of Mission San Luís Obispo was maintained for a time, and along the valley of the San Luis Obispo River the padres tended fields of corn and beans. The outpost stood near the present town of Avila Beach.

Miguel Ávila, born in Santa Barbara and educated in San Francisco, was a soldier and copyist at Monterey, and in 1824 he was a corporal of the guard at Misión San Luís Obispo. One day at the mission Padre Martínez harshly reproved him in the presence of a group of Indians for talking with an Indian at the ranchería. Both padre and corporal apparently became angry. The padre called the corporal a perjurer and a traitor; and the soldier, trying to persuade the father to go with him and settle the matter quietly, touched his robe. This gave rise to curses and threat of excommunication. The corporal called the soldiers, and the padre rang the bell to call all his assistants and neophytes. "The two forces faced each other in battle array, armed on one side with guns and lances, and on the other with book, holy water, and cross. Martínez began to read and Ávila seized the book, thinking thus to escape damnation; but the padre went on, finished the rite in bad Latin from memory, and retired in triumph to the church." The matter, later sent to the comandante, was compromised and the excommunication of the corporal annulled.

In 1826, two years after the trouble with the padre, Miguel Ávila married María Inocenta, daughter of Dolores Pico, who was then in charge of Rancho Nacional. He lived in Monterey with his increasing family.

In 1839, 1842, and 1846, Don Miguel obtained the grant of San Miguelito, and in 1845 he obtained the use of another part of the mission lands, Rancho Laguna, patented to Bishop J. S. Alemany in 1859. In 1849, Don Miguel was alcalde at San Luis Obispo. In his later years he became interested in the preservation of documents, and the large collection, which he kept in his house, was lost when that building was destroyed by fire. His original house on the rancho was located near Avila, a town later named in his honor and now called Avila Beach. It is gone, but at least one other adobe built on his property still stands, the well-preserved home erected by David Castro, a son-in-law. It is located on the Moorefield apricot ranch to the west of the frontage road of Highway 101 at a point three-quarters of a mile north of the Avila Beach turnoff. The date 1860 is inscribed over the doorway.

The Ranchos of Francis Ziba Branch

Francis Ziba Branch, a native of New York, arrived in California with the Wolfskill party in 1831. For a few years he made his home at Santa Barbara, where he kept a store and boarding-house, leaving occasionally to hunt otter. In 1835 he married Manuela, daughter of Zefarino Carlón, a soldier of the Santa Barbara Company. In 1837 Branch received a grant of over 16,000 acres of land lying to the north of Santa Barbara and named it Rancho Santa Manuela.

When Branch moved to his rancho, which was situated in the Arroyo Grande Valley, Misión San Luís Obispo about 13 miles to the north was almost the only community in the entire region that was inhabited by white men. The valley that lay in front of his home was an impenetrable swamp—a thicket of willow and cottonwood trees where wildcats, lions, and grizzly bears lived. His stock was often attacked by wild animals and by the Tulare Indians from the east. Edwin Bryant, in *What I Saw in California,* describes the old Branch adobe and the usual life of that district. In contrast with the rough life of the wilds, domestic life furnished comforts and luxuries unexpected at that time on the Pacific Coast.

Five years after Francis Ziba Branch received his rancho, his father-in-law, Don Zefarino, obtained an adjoining grant of one square league named the Arroyo Grande but frequently called the Ranchita. It lay along the headwaters of the Arroyo Grande, and it was later patented to the son-in-law.

At the lower end of the Arroyo Grande Valley was Rancho Pismo, two leagues granted to José Ortega in 1840. This was purchased by Isaac Sparks, who resold it, half to Branch and half to John M. Price. To further add to his possessions, Branch bought a part of Rancho Bolsa de Chamisal adjoining the Pismo on the south and a tract of land, Rancho Huerhuero, lying several miles to the north of his earlier holdings in the vicinity of the present town of Creston.

The town of Arroyo Grande lies in the Arroyo Grande Valley on the boundary line between Ranchos Santa Manuela and Pismo. Near the town, at the mouth of Corralitos Canyon, long stood the remains of an old adobe believed by some to have been erected by Mission San Luís Obispo as one of the buildings of an asistencia. It is known that agricultural operations were carried on by the mission fathers on the rich bottom lands of the Arroyo Grande as early as 1780.

The adobe erected by Branch on Rancho Santa Manuela was for many years one of the most noted in the county. The unmarked site is located off the Huasna road about three and one-half miles east of Arroyo Grande, not far from the new Branch School. Nearby, old palms and cypresses indicate the site of the frame house in which Branch's son Fred lived. It has been destroyed by fire. Another adobe built by the Branch family stands at the left of the Huasna road, half a mile beyond the junction of the road leading to the new Branch School and the old homesites, and about four and one-half miles east of Arroyo Grande. This adobe has been much disguised as a modern stucco residence with Spanish-style arches. Still another Branch adobe stands on a knoll to the left of the road leading to the county park. It is half a mile beyond the junction of this road and the back road to San Luis Obispo, and about five and one-half miles northeast of Arroyo Grande.

John M. Price, who held the half of the Pismo grant not purchased by Francis Ziba Branch, built an adobe home on the land. It still stands but is unoccupied. An unusual feature of it is the three distinct gables. Price also built an adobe schoolhouse nearby; it is fast falling into ruin. These buildings, together with Price's last home, a frame structure, stand across the railroad tracks to the right of the Edna road half a mile north

William G. Dana Adobe, Nipomo

of the junction of this road and Bello Street in Pismo Beach. The town of Pismo Beach lies on the coast about in the center of the shoreline of the grant, i.e., halfway between the two ends of the grant.

In this area is the little settlement of Halcyon, which began as one of California's utopian colonies. Dr. William H. Dower and Mrs. Francia A. LaDue opened a sanatorium here in 1904. Out of this grew the cooperative, theosophical, quasi-socialistic colony of the Temple Home Association. Not far from the present site of Halcyon the old Victorian mansion in which the sanatorium was first located still stands. It is at Highway 1 and 25th Street, at the east end of the town of Oceano.

Rancho Nipomo

One of the most famous old ranchos of California was the vast domain of almost 38,000 acres which constituted Rancho Nipomo (an Indian word said to mean "foot of the mountain"), for many years the first stopping place on El Camino Real south of Mission San Luís Obispo. Nearly all of the early books on California, as well as government reports and orders, frequently mentioned Captain Dana, the owner of this rancho, his pleasant home at Nipomo, and his lavish hospitality. The venerable casa, which stands beneath huge eucalyptus trees on an elevation commanding an extensive view, is a conspicuous landmark, a monument to the historic past of the county—second only to the old missions. In ranchero days, when the great landholders of Alta California were the lords of the country, Rancho Nipomo was the headquarters for the region, and Casa de Dana was the stopping place for all travelers. Lieutenant Colonel John C. Frémont, Edwin Bryant, author of *What I Saw in California,* and General Henry W. Halleck were among the distinguished visitors who were entertained at the Casa de Dana.

William Goodwin Dana, a cousin of Richard Henry Dana, Jr., the author of *Two Years before the Mast,* was born in Boston on May 5, 1797, and there he received his education. When 18 years of age, he went to Canton, China, and later to India in the service of an uncle, a Boston merchant. Returning to Boston after three years, he soon reembarked, possibly on the *Waverley,* as we find him captain of that vessel a few years later. In this capacity he engaged for several years in trade

between China, the Sandwich (Hawaiian) Islands, California, and Boston.

In 1825 Captain Dana established his business in Santa Barbara, where he soon settled permanently. He became quite a prominent citizen, holding a number of important offices at different times. In 1828 he married María Josefa Carrillo, daughter of Carlos Antonio Carrillo, a resident of Santa Barbara and for a short time provisional governor of California in 1835, and about this time Dana applied for Rancho Nipomo. The grant, however, was not confirmed until April 6, 1837. In 1839 the Captain moved onto his rancho and built the large adobe house of 13 rooms that still stands and that was, until 1901–2, the home of one of Captain Dana's sons, Federico Dana. The adobe, now owned by the San Luis Obispo County Historical Society which plans to restore it, is located south of the town of Nipomo on Oakglen Avenue near Story Avenue.

Another of the Captain's sons, Juan Francisco Dana, died in the 1930's at the age of 98. As a child in 1846, he had been nicknamed the "blond ranchero" by John C. Frémont. Juan Francisco built an adobe house in Nipomo that has now been destroyed by fire. The ruins are at the east end of Dana Street.

Frémont, in December 1846 on his way from Monterey to Los Angeles, camped on Rancho Nipomo with his battalion of 430 hungry and footsore soldiers, soaked to the skin by the rain through which they had tramped on the long march from the north. The campsite was located in an oak grove at a point known as The Summit, not far from Casa de Dana. It is northwest of Nipomo on old Highway 101 that goes through the town.

Rancho El Paso de los Robles

Rancho El Paso de los Robles received its name from the many large white oaks that dotted the valley, and the name has survived in the modern town and the famous resort located there. Well known to the Indians, the hot springs on this rancho were also familiar to the Franciscan friars, who, possibly as early as 1797, placed a rude wall of logs about the edge of the main spring, forming a pool of water. Alfred Robinson, who visited San Miguel in 1830, says that Father Juan Cabot "had erected a small house over the spot for the purpose of shelter and con-

Estrella Adobe Church, near Paso Robles

venience for bathing, and it was resorted to by many persons." Even the grizzly bears of the region are said to have sought the warm waters of the spring. The following story from an old history is told of one such visitor: "There was formerly a large cottonwood tree growing on the bank of the spring, with a limb extending low over the water. A huge grizzly was in the habit of making nocturnal visits to the spring, plunge into the pool, and, with his fore paws grasping the limb, swing himself up and down in the water."

At first an outpost of Mission San Miguel, Rancho El Paso de los Robles was granted to Pedro Narváez on May 12, 1844, and later confirmed to Petronillo Ríos. It was purchased in 1857 by Daniel D. and James H. Blackburn and Lazare Godchaux, and improvements were begun at once. James Blackburn built a frame house near the old adobe, said to have been erected by the mission fathers, and used the adobe for servants' quarters. Both stood six and one-half miles south of Paso Robles near the entrance to the Crescent Dairy.

Drury James, a brother-in-law of James and Daniel Blackburn, purchased the hot springs tract along the west bank of the river where now the town of Paso Robles is situated and built the first substantial house on the site—a duplicate of the James Blackburn house south of town. The site of the original hot springs and the first bathhouse built for it is the northeast corner of Tenth and Spring streets, where a service station now stands, and across the street from the Paso Robles Hotel property.

An early Protestant church in the region was built of adobe through the cooperation of church members of several denominations, in 1877–78. This structure (*SRL 542*), restored by boys from the nearby Youth Authority school, stands beside the cemetery about five miles northeast of Paso Robles on the Estrella Plain.

Ranchos Atascadero and Asunción

Rancho Atascadero, granted to Trifon García on May 6, 1842, and Rancho Asunción, granted to Pedro Estrada on June 18, 1845, both of which lie between Ranchos Paso de Robles and Santa Margarita, became parts of the large Murphy estate, with headquarters at Santa Margarita. An adobe, demolished years ago, stood on Rancho Atascadero within the present town of Atascadero.

The adobe house in which Pedro Estrada lived on Rancho Asunción is now a fragmentary ruin about two miles out of Atascadero on Traffic Way, a section of old El Camino Real that was left out in the construction of Highway 101. Possibly it is a part of one of the large houses mentioned by Alfred Robinson in his tour of 1830. He wrote: "We afterwards stopped at the sheep farm belonging to the Mission of San Miguel where there were two large houses and a number of straw huts. Gardens were attached to them, in which a variety of vegetables were cultivated by the Indians who were there as keepers of eight or ten thousand sheep."

A spring with a plentiful supply of water, now called the Estrada Spring, is on the hillside above this adobe ruin. The quantity and quality of the water have not varied within the memory of man.

Rancho Santa Margarita

After secularization, Rancho Santa Margarita passed from the control of Mission San Luís Obispo and was granted to Joaquín Estrada, brother of Pedro. Comprising more than 17,000 acres, the rancho extended seven or eight miles along the rich bottom lands of the Salinas River Valley on which the mission fathers had raised beans, corn, and other vegetables. Estrada devoted his attention to the raising of vast herds of long-horned Mexican cattle, his estate becoming famed as the queen of cattle ranches.

After giving up the ownership of this place, Don Joaquín moved with his family to the place now known as Estrada Gardens on the east side of Highway 101 two and one-half miles north of Mission San Luís Obispo. Here he planted fruit and ornamental trees and had a small vineyard. At his death he was buried on the hill above the house. His adobe home still stands. The tiles of the roof rise above the frame additions that have been built adjoining the original structure. A frame barn and other outbuildings are nearby, while at the foot of a slope at the rear may be seen the darkened trunks of ancient grapevines and a picnic pavilion for summer gatherings. An inconspicuous gateway carries in faded letters across the top the words "Estrada Gardens."

Descendants of Joaquín Estrada and his brother Pedro still live around Santa Margarita.

Many tales of gay fiestas and extensive hospitality are told of the early days at Rancho Santa Margarita, and it is said that at one time the feasting was prolonged for 30 days. The rodeos here were festivals celebrated by people of leisure from all parts of the country, and during such times a great camp was formed, with every day a picnic and every night a round of revelry.

In 1860 Martin Murphy, Jr., who lived at Rancho Pastoria de las Borregas (Santa Clara County), came into possession of Rancho Santa Margarita, which, together with Ranchos Atascadero and Asunción and others that he also owned, made up a magnificent landed estate totaling 70,000 acres. Martin Murphy's son Patrick took charge of the entire domain, making Santa Margarita his home and business headquarters. As late as the 1880's, thousands of head of beef cattle were pastured upon this vast territory.

Three wood-covered adobe buildings, aside from the stone ruins of the old Santa Margarita Asistencia, remain today. The two-story residence, which faced that large building, stood in front of a row of low-roofed rooms used for preparing and serving food and also as quarters for employees. These two parts are now connected by a wooden structure which makes of the whole a roomy and comfortable country home. The tiles on the roof became loose and were replaced by shingles during the Murphy ownership. The reception rooms, entered from the long, broad veranda, are large, with high ceilings and thick walls, and outside there are old trees and ornamental shrubs and vines.

Standing some 200 or 300 feet from the front of the main residence and a little to the left is another adobe building, now called the hacienda. It consists of perhaps two rooms and was formerly used as a post office and store in stagecoach days. There is, besides, a still smaller adobe structure, of uncertain former use. All of these buildings are within a few hundred yards of the ruins of the old asistencia, over which a large barn has been built.

The property passed from Patrick Murphy to the Reis estate, which now holds it. It is north of Santa Margarita and east of, and visible from, the freeway.

Miscellaneous Ranchos

Other grants of land in the county made by the Mexican government and recognized by the United States were the following:

Rancho Huasna, containing five square leagues, was granted to the hunter and trapper Isaac Sparks in 1843. On this rancho an old adobe house stands in excellent condition about 12 miles east of Arroyo Grande. It is on private property two miles north of the Huasna road at a point three-quarters of a mile west of Huasna School crossroads.

Rancho Corral de Piedra, seven leagues, was granted in 1841 and 1846 to José María Villavicencio. An adobe built about 1846, near the town of Edna, was demolished about 1937. Rancho Corral de Piedra was one of the tracts purchased by the Steele brothers for the great dairy industry which, already established along the coast in Marin and San Mateo counties, spread to this county in the late 1860's.

Rancho Bolsa de Chamisal, lying on the coast near the southwest corner of the county, was granted to Francisco Quijada in 1837, was later owned by Lewis T. Burton, and was sold by him for a part of the Steele dairy lands.

Potrero de San Luís Obispo was granted to María Concepción Boronda. In 1878 her father, José Cantua Boronda, was living on the rancho with her.

Rancho San Luisito, west of Rancho El Chorro, was granted by Governor Alvarado to Guadalupe Cantua in 1841. The wife of Guadalupe was Carmen Castro.

Rancho San Gerónimo, consisting of two leagues lying on the coast northwest of Cayucos, was granted to Rafael Villavicencio in 1842. On it he had an adobe house, 120 feet long.

Rancho Santa Ysabel is a tract lying across the Salinas River from Rancho Paso de Robles. It consisted of four leagues and was granted to Francisco Arce in 1844. He was at one time employed to collect debts due to the missions.

Grants of land lying partially across the boundary lines of the county were the Cholame, stretching a little way over into Monterey County, and Ranchos Guadalupe, Suey, Punta de la Laguna, Cuyama No. 1, and Cuyama No. 2, extending into Santa Barbara County. The Cholame land figures prominently in early history as a stopping place for early travelers. Across it ran a road leading to San Luis Obispo and a branch road leading to the Visalia region. It consisted of six leagues granted to Mauricio Gonzales by Governor Micheltorena on February 5, 1844. It was named after the Cholam tribe of Indians, who lived in that area.

SOURCES

Angel, Myron. "Carrisa Plains," *Report of State Mineralogist*, State Office, Sacramento, 1890.
—— *History of San Luis Obispo County*. Thompson & West, Oakland, 1883.
Bolton, Herbert Eugene. *Anza's California Expeditions*. 5 vols. University of California Press, Berkeley, 1930.
—— *Fray Juan Crespí, Missionary Explorer on the Pacific Coast, 1769–1774*. University of California Press, Berkeley, 1927.
Bryant, Edwin. *What I Saw in California*. D. Appleton & Co., Philadelphia, 1849.
The California Missions, a Pictorial History. By the editorial staff of Sunset Books. Lane Book Co., Menlo Park, 1964.
Coy, Owen C. *Pictorial History of California*. University of California Extension Division, Berkeley, 1925.
Dana, Juan Francisco. "Ten Decades on a California Rancho," as told to John Edwin Hogg, *Touring Topics*, XXIII, No. 11 (November 1931), 16–19.
Darling, Velva G. "Cave Landing, A San Luis Obispo County Scenic Spot," *Touring Topics*, March 1926.
(Dart, Louisiana Clayton). *Parade of Our Golden Years*. San Luis Obispo County Historical Society, San Luis Obispo, 1963.
Elder, David Paul. *The Old Spanish Missions of California*. Paul Elder & Co., San Francisco, 1913.
Engelhardt, Zephyrin. *San Miguel Arcángel, the Mission on the Highway*. Mission Santa Barbara, Santa Barbara, 1929.
Hine, Robert V. *California's Utopian Colonies*. Huntington Library, San Marino, 1953.
Jackson, Helen Hunt. *Ramona*. Little, Brown, Boston, 1919.
Lewis, Oscar. *Fabulous San Simeon*. California Historical Society, San Francisco, 1958.
Older, Mrs. Fremont. *California Missions and Their Romances*. Coward-McCann, New York, 1938.
(Robinson, Alfred). *Life in California*. Published anonymously. (H. G. Collins, Paternoster Row, London, 1845).
Robinson, W. W. *The Story of San Luis Obispo County*. Title Insurance and Trust Co., Los Angeles, 1957.

San Mateo County

SAN MATEO COUNTY (San Mateo is Spanish for St. Matthew) was organized in 1856 from the southern portion of San Francisco County. The county seat, located through fraudulent election at Belmont in May 1856, was changed within a year to Redwood City, at which place it has remained, although the question of its removal came up in 1861 and at other times.

In 1868, by an act of the state legislature, the southern boundary, which had been a line running due west from the source of the south branch of San Francisquito Creek and reaching the coast at San Gregorio, became an irregular line running southwest to the coast below Point Año Nuevo. This change transferred a large tract, including Pescadero, from Santa Cruz County to San Mateo County.

Indian Mounds

Indian villages were widely scattered along the shores of both ocean and bay. Near Point Año Nuevo, the most southerly corner of the county, are acres of dunes, where the shifting sands have revealed from time to time such evidences of Indian occupation as are usually found in kitchen middens: broken shells, arrow points, bones of wild animals that were used for food, and occasional human skeletons that were buried near tribal dwellings. Farther north on the coast at Half Moon Bay are several mounds, the largest of which lies just inside Pillar Point in a marsh and extending below its level.

Perhaps the largest mounds in the county were in the vicinity of South San Francisco and Brisbane on the shore of San Francisco Bay, but here, as elsewhere, most of the material was taken away years ago for road surfacing, fertilizer, and other purposes. The last remnants of an unusually large mound, still occupied by Indian huts in the early historical period and now quite needlessly destroyed by irresponsible amateur diggers, can be seen beside a large spring about half a mile north of the Butler Avenue overpass, northwest of the Bayshore Freeway.

At and near San Mateo Point, one mile northeast of downtown San Mateo on the edge of the bay, were mounds composed largely of the shells of the succulent native oyster used extensively by the Indians for food. On and near the banks of San Mateo Creek, once a favorite haunt of native tribes, have been found many indications of early human habitation. In excavating for house foundations on Baywood Avenue west of Highway 82, as many as six skeletons were taken out of one small area. The ground in this vicinity is largely impregnated with broken shell. Across the highway where the creek, for a little distance, is held within bounds by concrete walls, larger shell mounds were found. The creek first passes south of Mills Memorial Hospital, separating it from the Public Library and the San Mateo Civic Center. At the corner of San Mateo Drive and Baldwin Avenue it is completely lost to sight as it turns sharply around the base of the mound upon which the Civic Center is located and flows beneath the pavement down one edge of Baldwin Avenue. Large oaks have grown upon this mound since the Indians abandoned it. About two feet of surface shell, in which a few relics such as mortars were found, were removed before the erection of school buildings on the Civic Center site. It was probably from this village that the helpful visitors, mentioned by Anza, came to his camp on San Mateo Creek in March 1776.

Farther down the creek is another mound site, now leveled and crossed by Cypress Avenue between Eldorado and Grant streets. To the north of the mouth of the creek were other mounds near the bayshore; one was located at the end of Monte Diablo Avenue between the bay and the Bayshore Freeway. West of the freeway between Poplar and Peninsular avenues and North Humboldt and North Delaware streets, is the site of the largest mound in or near the city of San Mateo. The dimensions of this heap through the base were 150 by 225 feet, and the height may have been as much as 15 feet. It was made up largely of oyster shells; the material was screened and put to various uses. The high school building and football field are now on this site.

In Redwood City the part of Main Street that runs between El Camino Real and the railroad track, formerly Mound Street, traverses the site of another Indian village. A small triangular park now marks the site.

La Punta de Año Nuevo

Sebastián Vizcaíno set sail from Mexico on May 5, 1602, to survey the California coasts for a good harbor to be used by the Spanish galleons on

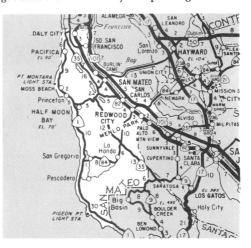

their trips to and from the Philippines. He found a harbor that pleased him at Monterey and remained there at anchor for a few days. When he resumed the voyage on January 3, 1603, the first conspicuous point he sighted was a low headland to which the name La Punta de Año Nuevo (New Year's Point) was given—the name that the extreme southwestern point of San Mateo County still bears. It was the point that mariners following Vizcaíno described as the northwestern extremity of Monterey Bay.

The Mexican grant of land made in this vicinity in 1842 perpetuated the name, and there is an improbable tradition that at the time the grant was made it was possible at low tide to walk from the mainland out to the point, a feat certainly impossible now on account of the shallow strait that makes an island of the extreme tip of land. This island is frequented by numerous sea lions. The United States Light Service long maintained a station here, but it is now abandoned. The point and beach are to be developed as a state park.

The Portolá Trail

On Monday, October 23, 1769, Gaspar de Portolá and the members of his party, including Father Crespí and Ensign Miguel Costansó, diarists of the expedition, having rested over Sunday in the Cañada de la Salud, which is now Waddell Creek in Santa Cruz County, resumed their march in search of the elusive bay of Monterey. Traveling two leagues that day, they entered the region now included in San Mateo County, passed La Punta de Año Nuevo without being sure of its identity, and camped for the night at an Indian village they called "La Casa Grande," for an unusually large house in its center. This site was identified by Bolton as Gazos Creek (SRL 23), but new evidence seems to point to Whitehouse Creek as the location. Here they thought they heard rumors of a port and a ship to the north, and were confirmed in their decision to continue.

During the following days they pursued their journey north, following the present Cloverdale Road inland to the site of Pescadero on Pescadero Creek, then over the hills near the shore to camp on San Gregorio Creek (SRL 26) at the present townsite of San Gregorio. They remained there for two days for the benefit of tired and sick soldiers. Father Crespí was impressed by the surroundings of the two Indian settlements, and proposed the place for a mission site. A historical marker on the coast highway, close to where the Indians' permanent village was situated, memorializes the explorers' stop.

On October 27 they halted on the south bank of Purissima Creek (SRL 22), and the next night they pitched camp (SRL 21) near the town of Half Moon Bay. Pillar Point, probably first seen by the navigator Francisco de Gali in 1585, could be discerned from this place, lying to the north-northwest. Here a halt was made over Sunday, October 29, as Portolá himself was ill. On October 30 they stopped on the bank of Martini's Creek (SRL 25), just north of Montara Beach, having had to bridge some of the creeks on the way. Here the route was blocked by Pedro Mountain, and Sergeant Ortega was sent to break a trail over the barrier.

Next morning the party ascended the mountain and looked down upon the Gulf of the Farallones. Some of the leaders identified this as the Bay of San Francisco of the ancient navigators, for Point Reyes was visible 40 miles to the north-northwest. A base camp (SRL 24) was established on October 31 on the south side of Pedro Valley near a lagoon at its mouth. From this point Sergeant Ortega made an extended exploring trip, discovering not the long-sought bay of Monterey, but the inner or modern bay of San Francisco instead. A hunting party, which left camp on November 2 and returned at nightfall with news of an inland sea, was the first to report the discovery of the bay, as Ortega did not return until the night of November 3. He had been drawn inland by a report from the Indians of "a port and a ship therein" only two days distant from their camp. A historical marker on the highway calls attention to the Pedro Valley camp and the discovery of San Francisco Bay (SRL 394).

On November 4, once more lured forward by the Indian report, Portolá and his men crossed Sweeney Ridge just south of the radar station behind San Bruno, paused beyond the summit to view the great arm of the sea drawing down far to the southeast on their right and disappearing on their left behind San Bruno Mountain, and then went down to camp by a pond now covered by the waters of San Andreas Lake (SRL 27), where a historical marker now stands on Skyline Boulevard. The trail followed on November 5 is today mostly covered by the Crystal Springs Lakes; camp (SRL 94) was made near a lake later called the Laguna de Raymundo or Laguna Grande, now included in the upper reservoir west of Ralston Avenue. Here the mountains on the right were covered with oak, redwood, and madrone trees. The party saw many herds of deer on the valley floor. This section is today the San Francisco Game Refuge, where numerous deer may often be seen grazing.

On November 6 the party turned east over the low hills along the Redwood City–Woodside city limits, and again established a base camp (SRL 2), one league from the bay on San Francisquito Creek in Menlo Park, on the opposite bank from the huge old redwood known as the "Palo Alto." From this point Ortega explored to the south and then up the east side of the bay, possibly as far as San Lorenzo. On November 10, he returned with the discouraging news that hostile Indians and another great arm of the sea barred further progress. After conference with the other members of the party, Portolá decided to discontinue the search for the harbor of Monterey.

Retracing their steps, the little company returned to the unrecognized Monterey Bay over the route by which they had come, camping on November 11 north of Woodside (SRL 92) near the Phleger Estate, on the 12th again at San Andreas Lake, and on the 13th at Pedro Valley. From there they proceeded down the coast, stopping to relieve their hunger with shellfish at Martini's Creek and with fowl at the "Plain of Wild Geese" at Half Moon Bay. Camping at Tunitas Creek (SRL 375), Butano Creek, and New Year's Creek, they entered Santa Cruz County once more on November 20. On November 27 they were back at the harbor of Monterey, which they again failed to recognize conclusively.

Rivera's Trail in 1774

The Spanish Viceroy in Mexico, Don Antonio María Bucareli, wanting to establish a mission at the port of San Francisco, ordered Don Fernando de Rivera y Moncada, who had been a member of the first expedition led by Governor Gaspar de Portolá, which had discovered that port, to go there to look for a suitable site.

Setting out from Monterey by Pedro Fages' inland route on November 23, 1774, the party of 20 reached San Francisquito Creek at the southern boundary line of San Mateo County on November 28. Accompanying Captain Rivera on this journey was Fray Francisco Palou, who, like the Captain, kept a journal. Their camping place at the creek seemed to them suitable for a mission, since it met the requirements of wood, water, and native people to be Christianized. Therefore a cross made of two beams was erected to mark the spot for future consideration.

On the next day's march northward, they turned into the hills between present Redwood City and San Carlos, where they found friendly Indians whom Fray Palou, in his religious zeal, embraced and to whom he made gifts of beads, hoping to hold their friendship until the time for gathering them into the fold of the mission. As the day wore on, more and more natives joined the travelers, pressing them to enter their villages, which were numerous along the route both in the hills and near the shore of the bay.

On November 30, the day of the feast of St. Andrew, Rivera and his party came to a pleasant valley (where Portolá had camped) which since that day has borne the name they gave—San Andrés or Andreas. On that day, too, friendly Indians enjoyed the company and the food of these strange white men, and again Fray Palou intimated that he would return and would bring seeds for planting so that they could grow similar food for themselves.

For the next few days they explored in the territory now included in northern San Mateo County and San Francisco, being the first white men to see the views from San Bruno Mountain and Mount Davidson. Then, deciding not to retrace their steps but to follow down the coast as the Portolá expedition had done, they reached Pedro Valley, crossed Pedro Mountain, and on December 6 camped at Purissima Creek south of Half Moon Bay. Spending a day at an Indian village there, they continued south to Butano Creek on December 8. They crossed the present border line of Santa Cruz County on December 10 and returned to Monterey on the 12th. Rivera and Palou recommended the establishment of Mission San Francisco on what later became known as San Francisquito Creek, but Father Serra decided instead in favor of the northern end of the peninsula, though the explorers had thought the place unsatisfactory.

Anza's Trail in 1776

Juan Bautista de Anza, on his way from Monterey to the port of San Francisco with a party of 13, including Lieutenant Don José Joaquín Moraga and Fray Pedro Font, entered what is now San Mateo County by crossing San Francisquito Creek on Tuesday, March 26, 1776. An Indian village of about 20 huts was near the creek, and on the north bank stood the cross erected by Father Palou when he had passed the place with Captain Rivera two years before. Font's diary gives the information that along this arroyo were various trees: laurel, ash, and a beautiful cypress called redwood.

After making gifts of beads to the women in this village, they proceeded through a plain of oaks, and at present North Fair Oaks they were met by a group of shouting natives whose long-haired chief was recognized by Corporal Robles as being one of a group whom his companions of a former journey had called the "Shouters." Approaching the place where Redwood City now stands, they came to another village, where they saw a large heap of mussel shells. During the day's march, they passed four Indian villages. The last one was located on San Mateo Creek shortly before they made their camp (SRL 48) for the night—in the present city of Burlingame, perhaps at Barroilhet Avenue—on one of the arroyos bordered with scented trees which they called laurel.

Arising early the next morning, they were on their way before seven o'clock, after Mass had been said by Father Font. This day, March 27, the line of travel led past Millbrae, San Bruno, and Daly City, toward the port of San Francisco. Two days later half of the party with the camp equipment returned to await the commander at San Mateo Creek. Anza, accompanied by his chaplain and five soldiers, spent the day exploring the hills for timber for the new settlements. In the course of the afternoon, Corporal Robles shot an immense bear which appeared out of the woods near the Crystal Springs Lakes. The skin of this animal was preserved as a gift for the viceroy.

On reaching camp at the site of the city of San Mateo, they found most of the men from the Indian village congregated there—"a poor-looking lot" but inclined to be helpful. After a heavy rain during the night, they set out in the morning in a southeasterly direction. When San Francisquito Creek was reached, Father Font set the graphometer 36 varas from the foot of the tallest redwood tree there and found its height something over 50 varas, a vara being a measure of approximately 33 inches. The Indians of the vicinity watched this proceeding in quiet wonder. The tree measured has long been assumed to have been the famous "Palo Alto" beside the Southern Pacific Railroad. It may, however, have been another redwood farther downstream.

From this point the party passed on into Santa Clara County. Within a short time the route thus established was again traveled, this time by Anza's great company of settlers which, bound for San Francisco from Mexico, had rested for a time in Monterey while their leader went ahead. The colonists camped at San Mateo for three days, June 24–26, 1776. A historical marker on Arroyo Court, just north of Third Avenue and west of El Camino Real, commemorates the campsite (SRL 47).

El Camino, the San José Road

Although the Bayshore Freeway has replaced it as the route of high-speed transportation, El Camino Real, as the old road leading south from San Francisco, still has a life and story of its own, distinct from the histories of the ranches, estates, and grown-together cities that sprang up along it. As Alexander von Humboldt remarked in 1810, the San Francisco settlements, the northernmost outpost of Spain's Pacific empire, stood at the terminus of one of the world's great post-routes: from Guatemala through New Spain, thence across the Sea of Cortés, and up the length of both Californias to the end of the civilized world.

When Mission San Francisco was founded in 1776, the trail from the south had already been established by Anza's exploration in the spring of that year. The present San Jose Avenue is part of this original route. Mission Street is so called because it is part of the road built across the sand hills between downtown San Francisco and the mission in 1850 and extended southward by San Francisco County in 1851. The original San José road also remained open in the same period because it was a boundary between land grants. Its common Spanish designation as "camino real" was retained on title papers and property maps.

At the top of the hill in the Mission Street Gap, now the center of Daly City, Mission Street and San Jose Avenue come together, and the original trail to the Spanish presidio branched off to the northwest. South from this point the Spanish trail and the partly planked stage road of the early 1850's ran considerably uphill and east of present El Camino, which was approximately the route of the slowly diverging trail to San Pedro and the coast, as far as Colma. Farther on, at the present South San Francisco city limits, present El Camino was relocated for two miles in 1914-15. Mission Road across the tracks represents the old route; on it in 1851 was built the Twelve Mile House, and the name is still borne by a roadhouse there, near the corner of Grand Avenue. Through San Bruno and Millbrae the Spanish trail was still in use in the middle 1850's; it ran generally a few hundred feet east of the later road, skirting the edge of the bay marsh past the Buriburi, Ojitos, Martínez, and Sánchez ranches.

At the Salinas just south of present Broadway in Burlingame, the road in Spanish times crossed a narrow neck of land between a natural salt-pan and a lake and knoll (on present California Drive), and thence went over a grassy plain to present El Camino in a northward extension of its line south of Peninsular Avenue. From this point to San Mateo Creek, where a toll bridge was built at the present crossing in 1851, El Camino still follows its original route, with a shallow bend around the site of the adobe San Mateo outpost of Mission San Francisco.

At San Mateo the traveler left the summer fogs and entered a country of oak groves and natural clearings, spread between the hills and the sloughs. Somewhere in this corridor stretching to present San Carlos, Captain George Vancouver with his officers and an escort of seven Spanish soldiers stopped for a picnic on November 20, 1792, on their way to Santa Clara. The great British navigator, the first foreign visitor to San Francisco, was impressed with the scene, particularly "a very pleasant and enchanting lawn, situated amidst a grove of trees at the foot of a small hill, by which flowed a very fine stream of excellent water. This delightful pasture was nearly in-closed on every side, and afforded sufficient space for resting ourselves and baiting our cavalry. The bank which overhung the murmuring brook was well adapted for taking the refreshment which our provident friends had supplied," as well as some English grog brought from the ship.

Leaving the steep south bank of San Mateo Creek, the road as traveled before the late spring of 1853 bore rapidly to the right of the present route, running nearly as far west as the present Alameda de las Pulgas in order to avoid the adobe soil north of Laurel Creek. South of present Hillsdale was a narrow pass and gap between hills and marsh at Belmont, then called the Portezuelo de las Pulgas, and the Spanish trail ran very near Old County Road. This road was bypassed when present El Camino was built west of the tracks in 1917-18, through Belmont and San Carlos.

At San Carlos the wide oak plain begins. To Vancouver in 1792 it was "a country I little expected to find in these regions. For about twenty miles it could only be compared to a park, which had originally been closely planted with the true old English oak; [with] the stately lords of the forest in complete possession of the soil, which was covered with luxuriant herbage, and beautifully diversified with pleasing eminences and valleys; which, with the range of lofty rugged mountains that bounded the prospect, required only to be adorned with the neat habitations of an industrious people, to produce a scene not inferior to the most studied effect of taste in the disposal of grounds." In the White Oaks district the well-defined Spanish trail turned to the west, keeping in the edge of the trees, and crossed Cordilleras or Finger Creek (Arroyo de los Cadillos) into Redwood City just east of Stanford Lane, where the broken bank of the old crossing still shows.

Turning sharply to the right to avoid the low-lying adobe lands, the original route—called the stage road in a deed of 1851—went by the foot of Eagle Hill at Jefferson Avenue, thence to the Indian village near Union Cemetery, and diagonally across El Camino and the tracks south of Five Points to Semicircular Road and Fifth Avenue in North Fair Oaks, the site of Steinberger's Woodlawn roadhouse, which was built early in 1852 and stood for many years.

From this point south the original Spanish highway is now called Middlefield Road. For the first half-mile the slight curve of the ancient trail is followed exactly by the modern street, but from Marsh Road through Menlo Park to the county line at San Francisquito Creek, the route was straightened by Steinberger's Middle Field Fence, the original trail having wandered slightly to the west in many places. At the 30-foot-high north bank of the creek, on property of the Lane Publishing Company, may still be seen vestiges of the slanting road dug for stagecoaches about 1850, and a piece of wire cable embedded in the heart of an oak that was once used as a stanchion for pulling vehicles up. The first bridge was built here in 1851, but it collapsed shortly after 1854 and was not replaced for nearly 50 years.

Although Middlefield Road was considered the main highway in Spanish times, this crossing could be used only by horsemen and pedestrians. In 1784, we learn from a letter of Father Palou, high water still stopped communication between San Francisco and San José, but by the time of Vancouver's visit in 1792 horsemen could get through by an alternate route. By 1803 there was cart traffic, which followed a well-marked detour crossing San Francisquito Creek farther downstream. This route left Middlefield Road in North Fair Oaks and ran down toward the bay to the Indian mound at Ninth and Fair Oaks avenues and thence to Marsh Road. From that point the *camino carretero* is still in use as present Bay Road, winding gently with the invisible contour of the land through two and a half miles of oaks and laurels. Just short of University Avenue in East Palo Alto the Spanish road bent away to the right, crossed an old channel of the San Francisquito, zigzagged through and around the mosquito-ridden willow swamps on both sides of the *paso de carretas* just below the Bayshore Freeway crossing, and rejoined the main bridle trail at the Mesa rancho in Palo Alto.

The still-existing portions of the Spanish highway were painfully developed over many years by those who plodded in the footsteps of the explorers, altering the route a little here and there by an intimate knowledge of the obstacles and quality of the land. The portions of El Camino laid down later, on the other hand, did not reflect such care and understanding, and as a result they provided great difficulties to travelers for many years. The route ran over poor soil, and the original bridges, fencing, and grading were little more than token. The road was laid out by a committee of the San Francisco Board of Supervisors in the early 1850's. Some degree of planning was involved as far as present Belmont, but from that point the survey was simply continued due southeast until it hit a tidal slough; then the line was slightly deflected for a distance of two miles, until the Palo Alto tree on the San Francisquito came in view. The committee had its surveyor take a bearing on the tree, and, as is still clear to anyone driving south in Atherton and Menlo Park, the job was done. In view of the projected railroad, which was not built until 1863, the highway was deflected to the west of the tree, where it still runs.

Old Land Grants

The northern boundary line of the county runs through the Mexican grant of Rancho Laguna de la Merced, only a small portion of which extends from San Francisco County south into San Mateo County. South of this, on the ocean side of the peninsula, are the lands of eight ranchos, each having one boundary line at the low-tide mark on the beach. The southernmost rancho reaches to the border of the adjoining county of Santa Cruz.

Rancho San Pedro

One of Father Francisco Palou's last plans for Mission San Francisco, before he retired from California in 1784, was the transferral of crop-raising operations to a fertile valley on the ocean shore 15 miles to the southwest, called by him the Cañada de las Almejas, in memory of the shellfish feast held by the Portolá expedition in 1769. The chief of Prúrstak, the largest Indian village, had been baptized in 1783, and a great harvest of souls was to be expected from the coast farther to the

south. Accordingly, in 1786, Fathers Cambón and Noriega dedicated a chapel in the valley to Saints Peter and Paul, and work was pushed forward on a quadrangle of buildings with an entrance looking east up the valley. Half or more of the mission's 800-odd neophytes were moved to the new establishment, and for some years most of the new converts from the peninsula and down the coast were baptized—and buried—at the chapel. After the early 1790's, apparently because of a pestilence, the settlement declined, but as late as 1828 the place, then called simply San Pedro, was occupied by over two dozen Indians as a mission crop and cattle ranch.

In 1834 Don Francisco de Haro, military *comandante* of San Francisco, petitioned the Mexican government for a grant of San Francisco Mission lands, and the following year he specifically requested San Pedro, including a sketch map that showed the old building as "ruins." One of De Haro's company presented a similar petition the same year, but none of these petitions was granted. In 1836 De Haro's successor in command, Francisco Sánchez, copied his predecessor's map and petition, and in 1839 he was finally given a formal grant of the two leagues of land.

Don Francisco, son of José Antonio Sánchez who owned Rancho Buriburi, was a native of San Francisco and a highly respected citizen. As a member of the San Francisco Company, he attained the rank of captain and finally that of acting commander. In 1846, on the occupation of San Francisco by American forces, he moved down to his ranch, to the large two-story balconied adobe *(SRL 391)* that now stands refurbished as a county historical monument in Pedro Valley, a mile east of the coast highway via Linda Mar Boulevard.

In December 1846, annoyed by the depredations of Americans, Sánchez headed the short-lived revolt in which Alcalde Bartlett of San Francisco was captured and held hostage, which revolt ended in surrender after the battle of Santa Clara. Sánchez, who was married to Teodora Higuera and had four children, Luisa, Luís, Dolores, and Pedro, lived largely at Mission Dolores in later years, until his death in 1862, by which time his country adobe had fallen somewhat into decay. There can be little doubt that the building occupies part of the northern or chapel side of the old mission quadrangle, which stood close under the hill on the same alignment. The courtyard on the south side of the building has kept the same dimensions found in the old annual mission reports. After the County of San Mateo acquired the property in 1947, bulldozing turned up strong and deep foundations stretching east along the road in the line of the house walls, which have the width of the original chapel. The cemetery, however, in which nearly 150 Indian neophytes were laid to rest, has never been found.

Rancho San Pedro, patented in 1858 for 8,926 acres, occupied very nearly the same bounds as the Indians' district of Aramai and as the present city of Pacifica, incorporated in 1957, which includes Sharp Park, Rockaway Beach, Pedro Valley, and other communities. At Pedro Valley, though it is now filled with tract houses, small buildings dating from the late 1850's and early

1860's can still be seen in the side canyons, witnesses to a century of large-scale irrigated truck gardening.

Rancho El Corral de Tierra

This rancho, extending from the south face of Pedro Mountain to Pilarcitos Creek, was first known as El Pilar or Los Pilares, from the rocks off Pillar Point, and was occupied by the horse and ox ranches of Mission San Francisco as early as the 1790's. It very nearly became the location of the town of Branciforte, established instead at Santa Cruz in 1797.

Rancho Corral de Tierra contained one and three-quarters leagues granted in two parts by Governors Manuel Jimeno and Manuel Micheltorena. The northern and larger part was given on October 16, 1839, to Francisco Guerrero Palomares, whose widow, Josefa Haro de Guerrero Denniston, filed her claim in 1852 and received the patent for the land in 1866. The ranch home, known as the Guerrero adobe, stood on a hillside near a creek about one mile northeast of the present town of Princeton and was in fair condition until the earthquake of 1906. It contained four rooms on the ground floor, with an attic above. This adobe, with a porch across its entire front, faced south on a garden of flowers and vegetables northeast of the present highway.

Princeton was formerly known as Old Landing. Produce from the country thereabouts was shipped by schooner to San Francisco.

A wharf called Amesport Landing was erected in 1867 by Ames, Byrnes, and Harlow. It was located near the mouth of Arroyo de en Medio, a small stream dividing the property of the two owners of Rancho Corral de Tierra. Warehouses used for the shipping of grain from this fertile region were built just south of the mouth of the creek.

J. P. Ames, the leader in the activity, was a native of England who had lived east of the Mississippi for some time before starting west as a member of Stevenson's Regiment. The men of this regiment had been chosen for qualities that would serve them well in a pioneer settlement after military duties should be ended. Ames was honorably discharged at Monterey in 1848 and, coming to this vicinity in 1856, became county treasurer in 1862. He was appointed by Governor Booth to settle the Yosemite claims and was a member of the state legislature in 1876–77.

Amesport Landing was afterward acquired by the Pacific Mail Steamship Company, which disposed in 1917 of the site of the old warehouses to the owner of a small hotel erected there. The settlement is now called Miramar.

The southern end of Rancho Corral de Tierra, granted to Tiburcio Vásquez on October 5, 1839, extended south from Arroyo de en Medio to Arroyo de los Pilarcitos, the latter name also used for the rancho. His claim was filed with the Land Commission in 1853, but the patent was not issued until 1873. The Vásquez adobe home of five rooms was built on the north bank of Pilarcitos Creek a little west of the Main Street bridge now at the northern edge of Half Moon Bay. A small flower garden was near the house. The family of

Don Tiburcio consisted of his wife, Alvira Hernández, and ten children. The youngest son, Pablo Vásquez, engaged in business in Spanishtown, now Half Moon Bay. He built a two-story wooden structure, still standing on the west side of Main Street just north of the bridge, in which he operated the Pilarcitos Livery Stable.

Above the gateway of a well-enclosed cemetery on the San Mateo highway a few hundred yards north of this bridge may be read "Pilarcitos Cemetery 1820–1923." Many of the graves within are of old Spanish settlers of Spanishtown. Here once stood the chapel of Nuestra Señora del Pilar, built by Tiburcio Vásquez in 1853.

The bridge, built of reinforced concrete in 1901, replaced an earlier bridge built of "preserved wood," which was considered at the time of its erection in 1866 to be the finest wagon bridge in the country. It was part of the San Mateo and Half Moon Bay Turnpike, and a tollgate stood two miles up Pilarcitos Canyon. The present road running from Crystal Springs Lakes to Half Moon Bay crosses the summit in approximately the same place as did the old turnpike. Descending the mountain at the head of the canyon, the road has been realigned to eliminate the former steep grades. The roadbed of the lower stretch remains in about the same place as in former years.

Rancho Miramontes

This rancho, known formally as San Benito, was granted to Candelario Miramontes by Governor Alvarado in 1841. When the first members of the Miramontes family, the sons Vicente and Rodolfo, took up residence there in the early or middle 1840's, grizzly bears and other predatory animals native to the country had not been subdued and proved destructive to the roaming herds of cattle. The Candelario Miramontes house was built on the south bank of Pilarcitos Creek east of present Main Street. A one-story adobe with an attic, immaculate in its exterior coat of white, it had a large reception room, two large bedrooms, and a kitchen. A porch extended in front, where doves fluttered in and out, and a woodshed was at the rear. The door leading to the attic storeroom was in the ceiling of the reception room, and access to it was by a removable ladder. Winter stores of beans, corn, and squash were kept there. The rosebush in front was so large that a child could hide beneath it. The daughter Carmelita, who married Francisco Gonzales, a ranchero's son from Santa Cruz and Pescadero, lived in this adobe after her marriage, and all of her children were born there. The site of this adobe is on the first street on the east side of Main Street south of the Pilarcitos Creek bridge.

The two families Vásquez and Miramontes were company and protection for each other. Around these houses the settlement called Spanishtown grew up. The adobe homes were landmarks for many years. One of the early American settlers was Henry Bidwell, nephew of John Bidwell, who ran a blacksmith shop and other businesses and was the first postmaster. The town was platted in 1863 in the southwest angle formed by the confluence of Arroyo León and Pilarcitos Creek and continued to be called San Benito or Spanishtown for 40 years or more, although the post office was called Half Moon Bay—the name of the town today.

Among the very first American settlers was James Johnston, who, arriving in 1853, purchased a half-league of land from the southern part of the Miramontes grant. Cut lumber was brought in boats to this part of the coast and floated ashore, and on a small rise, east of the southern intersection of Main Street and the present highway, Johnston erected the finest building in many miles—at a cost, it was said, of well over $10,000. There the large house still stands, weatherbeaten and alone, staring out across its commanding view from empty windows, awaiting an uncertain fate. In the canyons back up Johnston Lane, otherwise known as Higgins Road, which turns east at this point, are more modest farmhouses built by ranchers of the late 1850's and early 1860's.

The grant of Rancho Miramontes contained one and one-half square leagues lying between Pilarcitos Creek and Purissima Creek, as described in the petition filed by Don Candelario in 1852, but the patent issued in 1882 was for only one league and fixed the southern boundary at Cañada Verde Creek. The half-league between this creek and Purissima Creek was disputed between Miramontes and José Antonio Alviso, grantee of Rancho Cañada Verde y Arroyo de la Purísima. A Mexican court in the 1840's ruled against Miramontes, and the United States courts, though without knowledge of this decision, went on to deny the land to both parties.

Rancho Cañada Verde y Arroyo de la Purísima

This grant was made provisionally by Governor Alvarado on March 25, 1838, to José María Alviso (Alvizu), a military officer in San José in 1837, who had formerly held important posts in San Francisco and who was in command of troops with Arce in 1846. Alviso transferred his claim to his brother José Antonio Alviso, and the final grant was issued to the latter by Prefect José Castro on June 10, 1839. This property was surveyed in 1860, and United States patent was issued to José Antonio Alviso in 1864 for 8,906 acres lying between Purissima and Tunitas creeks. Alviso had built his adobe, however, about 1845 on the north bank of Purissima Creek, in the disputed section.

The once flourishing, but no longer extant, town of Purissima stood on the hill above the north bank of Purissima Creek. It was a lively place in the 1860's, with Richard Dougherty's good hotel (burned in the 1870's) as its center. Repair shops for wagons and farm machinery were maintained there, and the post office was served by the stage running from San Mateo to Santa Cruz. Before 1860 one of the first schools on the west side of the mountains was established on land donated by a large landowner for the purpose. In 1866 the Purissima district had 115 pupils, and in that year it was divided into school districts. The original schoolhouse, built of handsawed lumber, stood until 1875, when an imposing two-story building took its place. This large structure was later torn down, and from its material a smaller one, now a residence, was constructed.

Schoolhouse as Seen from Cemetery, Purissima

In 1868 Henry Dobbel, of Alameda, purchased 907 acres of land in the immediate vicinity of Purissima and erected the finest house in the settlement. In 1878, it is reported, he planted all of his land to potatoes, a venture that proved unfortunate because of the potato blight. His home, long a landmark, no longer stands, but the eucalyptus trees that he planted, now tall and dark around the site, remain. In the cemetery opposite the former school several members of the Dobbel family are buried. These landmarks, and a plaque placed by E Clampus Vitus, a social organization of historians, stand about four miles south of Half Moon Bay on Verde Road, a quarter of a mile east of its northern intersection with the coast highway.

Just before crossing Tunitas Creek by the long bridge at the southern border of this rancho, one encounters the road from Kings Mountain, which leads on as a private road toward the beach and the site of Tunitas Glen, the terminal of the defunct Ocean Shore Railroad from San Francisco. Plans had been made by a group of San Francisco men to connect that city and Santa Cruz by trains running through this scenic and productive coastal region, but the trains never ran beyond this point. A stage service completed the journey. The railroad was discontinued in 1920, and the supports of an unfinished bridge remain in the deep gulch of Tunitas Creek just south of Tunitas Glen.

An elaborate chute and extensive warehouses on the coast near this point antedated the railroad by several years. Occupying the spot known as Gordon's Landing, north of Tunitas and one mile south of Martin's Beach, the chute was constructed in 1873 by Horace Templeton and Alexander Gordon. Produce from the farms of the region was lowered to boats on the water below by a movable apron. It long remained a landmark of this coast area.

A flurry of excitement about oil deposits found in the canyons of the two creeks bordering this rancho ran through the countryside in 1888. Developments were carried on by C. M. Cook, who obtained a lease to properties on Tunitas and Purissima creeks, but the yield of oil amounted to very little.

Rancho San Gregorio

Rancho San Gregorio, consisting of four square leagues, was granted April 16, 1839, by Governor

Alvarado to Antonino Buelna, and the grant was approved by the Departmental Assembly in 1840. The northern line of this rancho was Tunitas Creek, from the mouth of which it extended south to the mouth of Pomponio Creek, a region that included the whole of the lower San Gregorio Creek watershed. At the time of receiving the grant of this rancho, Don Antonino was in command of an expedition against Indians and foreigners in the San Joaquín.

Don Antonino died in 1846. In 1849 Salvador Castro, one-time member of the San José Council, bought one square league of the grant lying toward the sources of San Gregorio Creek. In 1853 a petition on behalf of Concepción Buelna, Don Antonino's widow, "now married to Chino Rodríguez," was filed with the Land Commission. A patent was issued to her in 1861 for 13,344 acres. Also in 1853, however, the property had been sold by Rodríguez to Francisco Casanueva, a Chilean businessman, who conveyed it in parcels to speculators and settlers. The survey map, made in 1860 for the issuance of the patent, shows a fence belonging to Hugh Hamilton, the first American settler. His large frame house, now torn down, long stood on the north bank of San Gregorio Creek and was visible from the junction of the La Honda and the (old) Half Moon Bay roads in San Gregorio.

The settlement of San Gregorio is an old one. The original part of it lay just south of the bridge at the base of the hill. Here at one time were a number of shacks inhabited by Chinese, who were employed to cut brush on the hillsides. Here, too, was one of the old-time "wash-houses," where they did the laundry work for lumbermen and others. Eventually these shacks floated off toward the sea during a period of heavy rains and high water. In 1870, with the completion of the La Honda road, the Palmer or San Gregorio House, a saloon, and a store were built in a line on top of the hill along the west side of the highway (now officially renamed Stage Road), just above the creek. Refurbished and maintained by descendants of early owners, two of these buildings are still serving passersby, although the highway was rerouted nearer the beach in 1940–41. The San Gregorio House was at one time a popular vacation resort for families who lived on the other side of the mountains, and names of distinguished visitors appeared in its register. Horses were kept for hire; the sands of the beach where children

could play were not far distant; both salt- and fresh-water fishing were good; and great quantities of quail and deer afforded sport for the hunter.

Eastward up the valley, the road to La Honda passes many ranch buildings of various dates and styles—none, however, that seems to date back to the first homesteaders of the 1850's, unless it is the old Quentin ranch, a little building with cypress trees three-quarters of a mile from the town.

Pomponio Creek is named for Chief Pomponio, renegade from a mission, who was captured by Mexican authorities at Monterey in 1824. His mountain hideout had been at the headwaters of Pomponio Creek, a short stretch of which formed the southern line of Buelna's Rancho San Gregorio.

Rancho El Pescadero, or San Antonio

Rancho El Pescadero ("the fishery"), or San Antonio, was granted in 1833 by Governor José Figueroa to Juan José Gonzales, mayordomo of Santa Cruz Mission, and was patented to his descendants by the United States government in June 1866. It consisted of 3,282 acres in the vicinity of the town of Pescadero on Pescadero Creek.

By 1842 Gonzales was living in a small adobe on the north bank of the creek one block east of the bridge over that stream at the north end of town. The Bartlett V. Weeks family, natives of Maine who came to California in 1859 via Nicaragua, purchased in 1860 the 157-acre tract upon which this adobe stood. No vestige of it now remains; its site is at the south end of Goulson Street, formerly Pescadero Street, which was the original Spanish trail to the crossing of the creek.

The first American to take up permanent residence in this area was Alexander Moore, who after traveling across the plains by covered wagon reached California in 1847 with his father, Eli, and other members of the family. They camped for the night of November 15 on the plaza by the Santa Cruz Mission. The father remained around Santa Cruz until his death in 1859. Alexander went to the mines on the Tuolumne River for six months. In 1853, attracted to the Pescadero region by the fertile soil, evidenced by the rank growth of native grasses, he erected a large L-shaped house north of Pescadero Creek, using lumber hauled by ox team from Santa Cruz. This house still stands about a mile east of Pescadero on the right-hand side of Pescadero Road, at a bend a short distance beyond the intersection of North Road. Alexander's wife, Adeline Spainhower, was active in caring for the sick. Since no practicing physician was available nearer than San Mateo or Santa Cruz, and the fee for coming that distance was from $50 to $500, Mrs. Moore went long distances on horseback to relieve suffering.

Alexander and Adeline Moore had a family of six children: Eli, Joseph, William, Ida, David, and Walter; and for their benefit their father employed a teacher and started the first school in the area.

When the property was divided after the parents died, the portion on which the family house

Alexander Moore House, Pescadero

stood was given to Ida, the only daughter, then married to Charles Steele, a son of the owner of the ranch lying to the southeast. To Ida also went a large old clock, brought across the plains in the top of a covered wagon. Other portions of the land went to the sons, and to William went the muzzle-loading gun that had done duty on the long overland journey.

Two miles north of town, on the old highway, Thomas W. Moore founded the Willowside Farm. The drive leading between gum trees to the house is now part of the public road.

Rancho Bútano

Rancho Bútano, consisting of one square league lying along the Pacific Ocean between Butano Creek and the Arroyo de los Frijoles, was given to Ramona Sánchez on February 19, 1838, and was confirmed by Governor Micheltorena six years later. Manuel Rodríguez received the United States patent for it in 1866.

This rancho was afterward purchased by Clark & Coburn of San Francisco. Loren Coburn, a native of Vermont, arrived by steamer in San Francisco in 1851 and, after mining for a while on the American River, returned to San Francisco and engaged in business there for many years. He moved to this region in 1872 and spent the later years of his life in land development.

On the coast south of the mouth of Butano Creek is Pebble Beach, a deposit of varicolored, water-worn pebbles. They lie several feet deep over an area of approximately two acres; agate, chalcedony, jasper, moonstones, and sardonyx are found among them. On this beach Loren Coburn erected a large red-roofed three-story hotel in the 1890's, expecting to have it filled by people who, attracted to the resort, could reach it easily by means of the railroad then being planned to run south from San Francisco. He spent money lavishly on its construction, and the town of Pescadero nearby profited by the pay checks of the imported workmen. In 1906 the disaster of the earthquake and fire in San Francisco definitely ended further construction of the Ocean Shore Railroad, when the promoters' funds went elsewhere. The hotel was permanently closed, but stood until taken apart in the 1930's. The Coburn family residence, white-painted, with the emblem of the rising sun in a gable-end, stood unoccupied facing the main street in Pescadero for many years until it was destroyed by fire.

East of Rancho Bútano is the Butano Forest, lying along the two main branches of Butano Creek. Efforts in the middle 1950's to preserve this area with its superb trees from lumbering succeeded in saving only the drainage of the Little Butano, a minor branch issuing from the hills upon Cloverdale Road south of the main stream. The Butano State Park, which is now being prepared for public use, contains within its 2,100 acres the last small stand of virgin timber in this part of the mountains, as well as much that was logged selectively.

Rancho Punta de Año Nuevo

On April 15, 1839, one square league of land lying between Arroyo de los Frijoles (Bean Hollow) and Arroyo de las Garzas (Gazos Creek) was granted by Governor Alvarado to José Cornelio Bernal. The grant was given final approval by the Departmental Assembly in 1840, and between 1846 and 1849 was sold to Don Sebastián Rodríguez. The later history of this grant, known as Rincón de la Ballena, is typical of the occasional strange vicissitudes of land titles in early American times. Claim for the tract was brought before the Board of Land Commissioners in 1852, rejected by them in 1854, and finally rejected by the U.S. District Court in 1863, on the grounds of uncertainty of boundaries, conflicting testimony about occupation and use, and failure to produce the title deed. One strange result was that the adjacent Bútano and Punta de Año Nuevo grants were so surveyed as to overlap each other in the disputed area of the "lost" rancho.

Rancho Punta de Año Nuevo, as granted May 27, 1842, by Governor Alvarado to Simeón Castro (already the owner of two ranches in Monterey County), covered a vast tract of 17,753 acres in the extreme southwestern part of San Mateo County and stretched from the disputed lands at Butano Creek to south of Point Año Nuevo. In 1857, after the death of Don Simeón, his widow, María Antonia Pico, and his family received the United States patent for the property. However, in 1866, the part of this ranch that lay to the north between Butano Creek and Arroyo de los Frijoles was patented to Manuel Rodríguez as Rancho Bútano.

In 1851 Rancho Punta de Año Nuevo was sold to Isaac Graham of Santa Cruz, who leased parts of it. In 1852 the wooden ranch house built by Eugenio Antonio Soto, Simeón Castro's agent, on Whitehouse Creek, burned down, and Graham's tenant, one Van Houten, replaced it with a white-painted dwelling, large for the time and place, the pre-cut frame parts of which had been shipped around the Horn from the East. A two-story building with interior walls plastered, the "White House" still stands just east of the coast highway at Whitehouse Creek, about four miles north of the county line. For several years it had the distinction of being the finest dwelling in the region. The story is told that, before the tall gum trees grew up to hide it from the view of passing boats, mariners reckoned the distance to San Francisco by sighting this lone white house. About 1890 the house was moved 100 feet to permit the erection of a larger house for later owners. This newer house was destroyed by fire about 1961, and its burnt ruins still mark the original site of the White House.

The greater part of the original rancho of Simeón Castro came in 1862 into the hands of Loren Coburn, who the same year leased it to a group of men who carried on an extensive dairying business. In this group were Horace Gushee, Charles H. Willson, and three members of the Steele family: Rensselaer E., Isaac C., and Edgar W. The Steeles were natives of Delaware County, New York, who arrived in California in 1854–57. They located first north of San Francisco Bay, where they made butter and cheese of the highest quality and shipped it to San Francisco. After moving to Rancho Punta de Año Nuevo, they continued the same line of work. A brother of Isaac C. and E. W., and cousin of Rensselaer, was General Frederick Steele of the Union Army in the Civil War. As a donation to the Sanitary Fund (the forerunner of the Red Cross of today), the Steeles made a 3,850-pound cheese for display at the Mechanics' Fair at San Francisco. After the fair ended, slices of the cheese were sent to President Lincoln, General Grant, and General Steele, and the remainder was sold for one dollar a pound. The total amount realized by January 11, 1864, and sent to the Sanitary Fund was $2,820.

Isaac Steele was keenly interested in the furthering of business enterprise. He helped to establish the Grangers Bank in San Francisco and was a director of the Grangers' Business Association.

E. W. Steele built the Cloverdale Dairy, still standing, though badly weatherbeaten, two and a half miles east of the coast highway via Gazos Creek Road and Cloverdale Road. He later turned this property over to Horace Gushee and moved to San Luis Obispo County. In 1869, at the termination of their lease, the Steeles purchased just over 7,000 acres south of Gazos Creek. Shortly afterward I.C. and Rensselaer divided the two largest dairies, the adjoining Cascade and Green Oaks ranches, at which the fine old houses still stand, close to the coast highway. Cascade Creek is a mile and a half south of the White House, and Greenoaks Creek a mile farther south. The old houses are guarded by rows of Monterey cypress of immense size, which were planted to break the force of the wind off the ocean. General Steele died at San Mateo while on his way to visit his family's ranch; he was buried in the family cemetery at the Cascade Ranch. Both I.C. and Rensselaer continued to reside on this rancho for the remainder of their lives and left the property to their children. Much of the original land purchased by the Steeles remains in the possession of their descendants. Another early settlement is the W. F. Ramsay Ranch on Gazos Creek, a mile and a half north of the White House. It is now owned by Frank F. Latta, the well-known California historian.

Along the shoreline of this rancho are certain spots of interest. The old lumber wharf at Point Año Nuevo attracted a small settlement around a fresh-water spring near the beach. Horace Steele erected there a small frame building as a dwelling and a place for the sale of food and drink. After business at the wharf came to an end, this building was moved about a quarter of a mile to the Steele ranch on New Year's Creek.

Pigeon Point, where a lighthouse, still standing and in operation, was established in 1872, received the name because the clipper ship *Carrier Pigeon* was wrecked there on May 6, 1853. A chute for the loading of lumber was located there, and timber products were shipped from this place from 1853 until about 1920. A Portuguese company had a whaling station there from about 1862 to the 1890's. Other names have been applied to Pigeon Point. During the Spanish period, Herrera called it "Cabo de Fortunas" (Cape of Adventure), and another name, "Rincón de la Ballena" (Whale Point or Headland) was given to the rejected land grant in the area.

A point less noticeable than either Point Año Nuevo or Pigeon Point lies between them and is called Franklin Point, from the wreck of the schooner *Sir John Franklin*. On the top of a wind-swept sand dune on this beach lay for nearly a century, until stolen by a vandal, a fallen marble tombstone, inscribed "To the memory of Edward B. Church of Baltimore, Maryland, and ten other seamen lost on the ship, Sir John Franklin, January 17, 1865."

Rancho Feliz

Three of the old land grants later recognized by the United States government lay entirely in the interior of this county with no border on tidewater: Ranchos Feliz, Cañada de Raimundo, and Cañada del Corte de Madera.

The northernmost rancho of this group, Rancho Feliz, was granted April 30, 1844, by Governor Manuel Micheltorena to Domingo Feliz (Felis, Felix), to whom 4,448 acres were confirmed by United States patent in 1873. Don Domingo built a house situated, according to a grant-map of 1856, on the southern edge of his property west of a slough. Near it passed the road leading from San Mateo to the coast, converging near the location of his house with the one leading from Belmont to the coast. The Skyline Boulevard coincides with the old San Mateo road where it crosses between Upper and Lower Crystal Springs Lakes on an earthen causeway.

In this Rancho Feliz lie the upper lakes of the San Andreas Valley, which were made by damming the sloughs and lagoons to form reservoirs for the San Francisco water system. Lower Crystal Springs Lake now covers the site of the settlement of Crystal Springs, which included the hotel mentioned in one of the pivotal scenes in Bret Harte's *A First Family of the Tasajara*, and also the San Felix Station, of which M. Carey was proprietor in 1877, when the San Mateo–Half Moon Bay stages stopped there with passengers, mail, and freight. Byrnes's Store, a little farther on up the hill, was another stage stop. Its site is now marked by two tall cypress trees. The store was established in 1857.

In the vicinity of Crystal Springs an experimental planting of wine grapes was made very early in the 1850's by Colonel Agoston Haraszthy, who set out a half-dozen varieties imported from Europe. Colonel Haraszthy, a nobleman from Hungary, whose name is mentioned whenever the story of California's wine industry is told, was a naturalized American citizen before he came to the West Coast and, in the early years of California's statehood, a member of the Assembly. After a sufficient test of his 25-acre vineyard had proved that the fruit would not ripen properly in this location, he sold his property and removed the vines to Sonoma County, where soil and climate were fitted to grape culture and where he established the Buena Vista Vineyard.

Rancho Cañada de Raimundo

Rancho Cañada de Raimundo (Raymundo) was granted August 4, 1840, by Governor Alvarado to John Copinger, "a man of ability and learning," once a British naval officer and later, in Cali-

Charles Brown Adobe, near Woodside

fornia, a lieutenant in charge of the artillery company that had brought about the success of Alvarado's revolution and put the governor in power. The rancho lay to the northeast of the Sierra Morena and was bounded on the north by Rancho Feliz, on the south (at Arroyo Alambique) by Rancho Corte de Madera, and on the northeast by a line long in dispute with Rancho de las Pulgas.

John Copinger died in 1847, and in 1859 this property, 12,545 acres, was patented to his widow, María Luisa (daughter of Rafael Soto), who in 1851 had married Captain John Greer, and to his daughter, Manuela Copinger, who afterward married José Antonio Miramontes and lived in a large house that long stood near present Woodside and Miramontes roads.

The original Copinger residence was built in what is now the southwestern angle of the Y formed by Woodside Road and Kings Mountain Road, west and slightly south of Woodside. The adobe, erected in 1841, was destroyed by the earthquake of 1906, but an old wooden building, said to be a storehouse built by the Greers in 1854, remains standing under a large oak tree. With dormers, gables, and porches added, it is now a comfortable family dwelling.

The Mountain Home Ranch, on Portola Road just southeast of the junction with La Honda Road (Highway 84), is a part of Rancho Cañada de Raimundo sold by John Copinger to Charles Brown, a native of Baltimore who had deserted a whaling vessel in San Francisco in 1833. Brown lived at Sonoma and around San José before coming to this region. He built an adobe house here, probably about 1838, and a sawmill in 1849 near Alambique Creek, southwest of the house. A historical marker indicates the location of the sawmill (*SRL 478*), San Mateo County's first, and visible on the ranch below is the tile roof of the small square adobe. A thoroughfare not far from Searsville Lake takes its name, Mountain Home Road, from this ranch. The property has changed ownership several times, and has been subdivided, and now a number of luxurious homes stand within the confines of the Charles Brown holdings.

At the time of the American occupation in 1846, there had been a settlement at Woodside for some ten years or more. As early as 1832, William Smith, an Englishman, came here to saw lumber for barter and sale. He became so skillful

with the saw that he was known as "Bill the Sawyer." A few years later another settler arrived at Woodside, James Pease, who had deserted from a British ship anchored at Yerba Buena. Pease and Smith became partners. Other sawyers followed, amounting in all to a total of one or two dozen.

By 1849–50 sawmills were erected in the redwoods. Lumber was supplied to the incoming settlers of Santa Clara Valley and also shipped to San Francisco. Today the lumber camps of Woodside and Searsville are scarcely a memory. Dim roads into the hills, a few blackened stumps where thick green groves of young redwoods have partly covered the scars of former years, and stories of the vanished town at Searsville Lake—these are all that remain.

The old Woodside Store (*SRL 93*), the first store opened between San Francisco and Santa Clara, is the one surviving landmark of pioneer days in Woodside. The present structure was built in 1854 by M. A. Parkhurst and Dr. R. O. Tripp ("Doc" Tripp), a dentist, who had arrived as early as 1849 and engaged in cutting shingles. In 1851 they gave up the lumber business for merchandising. Until his death in 1909 Tripp kept his store at Tripp and Kings Mountain roads, one and one-half miles west of the present town of Woodside. There were once 15 sawmills within a radius of five miles of the store, where more than 1,000 lumberjacks found their mail, food supplies, and liquid refreshments. Nearby long stood the old "Temperance Hall," built in 1858 on an elevation above the road; its weather-beaten clapboards gave little evidence that it was once the social gathering place for young and old. The Woodside Store is now owned by the County of San Mateo and is open to the public as a museum.

The commercial part of Woodside moved gradually from the Tripp store to the vicinity known in the old days as "Whiskey Hill," because the three saloons there dominated the settlement. The only other structures were a blacksmith shop and two hotels. Roads in four directions from this present Woodside lead to large country estates. The settlement of Greersburg, named in honor of the Greer family, who owned Rancho Cañada de Raimundo on which these several settlements are located, is included in the modern Woodside.

Bear Gulch Creek comes down the mountain

Woodside Store

and flows under a bridge on the road running from the base of the La Honda grade to Woodside. The gulch was so named in the 1850's because of the encounter between "Grizzly" Ryder and one of the numerous grizzly bears that infested the region at that period.

Ryder, who was a lumberman, was returning one evening in 1850 from an unsuccessful day's tramp in the Portola Valley looking for his strayed oxen. He was attacked by a mother bear as he rose from drinking at a pool in the stream. Having no weapon other than a knife, he suffered a severe mauling; but, after he had made a pretense of being dead, the bear left him in a fainting condition with one ear torn off. Found in a short time by searchers, he was carried back over the trail to the adobe on the Mountain Home Ranch, where he had called earlier in the evening. His bleeding wounds were closed by a sailor, who used a sail needle and some string; there followed treatment with poultices of native herbs gathered and steeped by an Indian woman. These primitive methods proved efficacious, for he recovered after some weeks. The pool where the attack occurred is near the modern barns of the "Why Worry Farm" on the La Honda road near Woodside.

Searsville Lake, at the junction of Portola and Sand Hill roads, covers a part of the site of the old town of Searsville (SRL 474). John H. Sears, who came from New York state via Cape Horn in 1849, built in this vicinity, early in 1854, a house later used as a hotel and known as the "Sears House." A town grew up about this house, because the location was a convenient stopping place for drivers of mule and ox teams hauling lumber from the mills east of the La Honda ridge for loading on schooners at the Embarcadero at Redwood City.

The little settlement was the scene of considerable activity on Sundays, when ox-pulling, horse racing, and cockfighting were popular amusements. A hotel built by August Eikerenkotter stood on what is now the crossroads at the entrance to the Searsville Lake grounds. This hotel was pulled down in the early 1890's when the building of the dam forming the lake necessitated realignment of the roads. At the same time a large pine tree, used for years as a target for men whiling away their time on the porch of the hotel, was cut down. It was so full of leaden slugs that saws could not be used in working it up into firewood.

The Searsville schoolhouse, abandoned after the spring term of 1893, stood on the hill between the end of Sand Hill Road and the present lake. The lake now supplies irrigation water for the Stanford University campus and provides, as well, a place for swimming and boating.

At about the time of the excitement over the Comstock Lode in Nevada, a trace of silver was found in this vicinity. In 1875 John Murray, a resident of Searsville who owned land on the west edge of the ridge to the east of the settlement, sold his mineral rights to a group of six men from Redwood City. A tunnel was driven into the hill a short distance south of the Searsville

dam, but the occurrence of the ore was too erratic for profitable development. This old tunnel is now below the level of the lake.

About one-half mile northeast of Searsville on Sand Hill Road at the bridge across San Francisquito Creek, there stood for many years a broad and tall wooden barn built originally for the stabling of oxen used in lumber hauling. No vestige of the structure remains.

One of the tragic developments attendant upon the confused situation of boundary lines between some of the grants of land was the hardship inflicted upon the purchaser of a tract on the north bank of San Francisquito Creek while California was still under the Mexican government. Dennis Martin, who came to the state in 1844 with the Murphy-Townsend-Stevens party (the first emigrant party to bring wagons across the Sierra) and who heroically retraced his track into the mountains in the following year to rescue Moses Schallenberger, who had stayed behind to guard a stock of valuable merchandise, settled on San Francisquito Creek and became one of the first and most extensive lumbermen in the Woodside area. He purchased land then supposed to be in the lower part of Rancho Cañada de Raimundo, the deed for the tract from Juan Copinger to him being signed in the Pueblo de San José de Guadalupe on March 15, 1846.

Martin erected his house near the creek, built barns and corrals for his horses and cattle, planted a large fruit orchard, and fenced a goodly portion of his domain. He also purchased a piece of the neighboring Rancho Corte de Madera, making his holdings in all 1,250 acres. He built two mills, called the Upper and Lower, on Dennis Martin Creek in the timber region of his property and eight more houses for his workmen.

Since there was no church nearer than Mission Dolores to the north and Mission Santa Clara to the south and since he was a man of deep religious conviction, he built a place of worship near his home for his family, his employees, and his scattered neighbors. In this simple frame structure he placed costly candlesticks, a crucifix, and draping. The churchyard was enclosed by a fence, and another enclosure, a little farther up the hill, became the cemetery. Archbishop Alemany, who officiated at the dedication service in 1856, named the church St. Denis in honor of the donor's patron saint.

The question of the boundary line between the Las Pulgas and the Cañada de Raimundo ranchos came to the fore, and a petition for its settlement was filed by heirs and claimants. The United States courts decided that the line of Las Pulgas extended along San Francisquito Creek and included the Dennis Martin property. Since his land had been purchased from the owner of the adjoining Cañada de Raimundo, the decision had the effect of dispossessing him, and in 1864 he was obliged to give over his improvements, including a young orchard then bearing fruit. At his death in San Francisco on June 16, 1890, his body was brought back to the place and interred near the graves of other members of his family.

The site of the Dennis Martin house and the

church lies about one-half mile off Sand Hill Road toward San Francisquito Creek, on property now occupied by the Stanford Linear Accelerator. A historical monument with bronze plaque has been placed on the south side of the road, a little over a mile northeast of the Whiskey Hill Road junction.

When the Las Pulgas grant was broken up and sold to various owners and when Leland Stanford acquired a part of what had been the Martin property, it was his wish that the graves remain undisturbed. But the buildings were long ago removed, and many of the bodies in the enclosure were transferred to newer cemeteries. The last remains were reinterred in Holy Cross Cemetery at Menlo Park on February 12, 1953. They were buried in a common grave and marked by the headstone of Edward Lynch, who died in 1858 (one of only two broken stones that remained), which was repaired and appropriately inscribed on the reverse.

In 1961 a new Roman Catholic parish was established in the area and given the historic name of St. Denis.

Northwest of Woodside, Cañada Road, located by John Greer in 1862, runs along the compromise boundary line between the Pulgas and Cañada de Raimundo ranchos as surveyed in the early 1850's and upheld by the courts despite great litigation. On a map of Rancho Cañada de Raimundo made in 1856, several houses are shown, and a tavern is indicated near the Whipple Mill–Embarcadero road. The part of the Whipple road used today (Edgewood Road, Cordilleras Road, Upland Road, Whipple Avenue) extends from Cañada Road to Redwood City, but in former years it continued southwestward from Cañada Road.

The site of one of the several wineries that have from time to time operated in San Mateo County is on the Cañada de Raimundo tract. The brick building, later used as a sheep shelter, stood on a hillside southwest of Cañada Road until 1936, when it was removed. This structure had been erected by C. Scalmanini, who in 1882 owned over 1,000 acres here and whose name is given in the *Winegrowers Register* of 1889 as the owner of 82 acres of grapes from which he made three kinds of wine: Zinfandel, Burgundy, and Malvoisie.

Rancho Cañada del Corte de Madera

This rancho, which lay above the confluence of Los Trancos and San Francisquito creeks, covered a large tract between these streams. Portola Road runs across it, and Searsville, Coon, and Felt lakes, which are named for men who held property near them, are within the boundaries of the old rancho.

Governor Figueroa gave one square league of land there to Domingo Peralta and Máximo Martínez in 1833. Peralta, who had also part of Rancho San Ramón and a share of his father's great San Antonio rancho across the bay, kept his part of the Corte de Madera grant for only a short time and divided it on May 19, 1834, between his co-grantee, Martínez, and Cipriano Thurn. In

1879 a part of El Corte de Madera was patented to Thurn and Horace W. Carpentier. This part contained 3,566 acres.

More land appears to have been granted to Martínez in 1836 and about 1839, and Governor Micheltorena made a grant to him on May 1, 1844. The whole tract of 22,980 acres, of which a part extended across Los Trancos Creek, was confirmed in his name on September 10, 1855. The United States patent was given him on July 14, 1858.

Máximo Martínez had been a soldier in the San Francisco Company from 1819 to 1827 and at the time of receiving the first grant was *regidor* at San José, where the parents of his co-grantee, Peralta, were living. The wife of Don Máximo was Damiana Padilla; and in 1841, when his age was given as 51, their family consisted of seven children. The Martínez home place was on present Alpine Road opposite the end of Los Trancos Road, where a garage now stands.

As the children grew up, they established homes of their own on the land. The son Nicolás lived in an adobe that stood where the Ormondale Ranch home was later built. The adobe had been erected by Ignacio Miramontez, eldest son-in-law of Máximo Martínez. Nicolás and his family lived in it until after the death of his wife. He sold the place to Nicholas Larco in 1868 and moved with his young children to Half Moon Bay. Grandchildren of Don Máximo and Doña Damiana became scattered. One branch of the family long treasured the sword carried by Máximo when he was a Mexican soldier.

Nicholas Larco lost his very large tract through nonpaying ventures in silkworm growing and silver mining. Another owner was a man named Barroilhet. Since the early 1890's, when it was purchased by W. O. B. MacDonough, the place became noted for the fine stock raised there. Ormonde, winner of the English Derby in 1886, was purchased for this ranch, which was then named Ormondale. This animal had been unbeaten during his racing career in England and when sold by his English owners commanded the highest price given for a horse up to that date. After his death some years later, his bones, it is said, were given to the British Museum.

The Martínez adobe continued to be used as a family residence until 1901. It was composed of three rooms with a tile roof. A kitchen and a bedroom of frame construction gave additional space. The plan of incorporating the adobe rooms in a new house had to be abandoned for some reason, and the old structure was entirely demolished. A luxurious stucco home was erected by the owners of Ormondale Ranch on the commanding position of the earlier building. It was built in a style commemorative of mission days, with courts, pools, and spacious terraces. Now this house, with the remaining old trees, has also perished, this time to make way for the Westridge subdivision.

Within the old Corte de Madera grant on the ridge southeast of Searsville Lake is a mining property, called the Hermit Mine, on which were dug about the year 1875 two vertical shafts, one of 75 feet, the other of 200 feet. With them is identified Domenico Grosso, the hermit.

Grosso came to San Francisco about 1869 from Genoa, Italy. Little is known of his early life, but he told friends that he had served under the great Italian patriot Garibaldi. After living in San Francisco for a time and being unfortunate in financial ventures there, he came to this vicinity and entered the employment of Nicholas Larco, first as cook and later as ranch foreman. While there employed, he discovered silver on the Dennis Martin ranch southeast of Searsville and persuaded Larco to buy the mineral rights from Martin. After Larco became insolvent through his ventures in ranching, mining, and mulberry-tree growing for the culture of silkworms, the mineral rights came to Grosso. With the lumber from miners' bunkhouses, he constructed a home for himself in a canyon nearby.

He built a cabin, a barn, and a shop; he planted grapevines, roses, and fruit trees; he made hillside terraces and an ornamental pool for trout into which the waters of a spring trickled over an arrangement of serpentine rocks. This home he called the "Palace Hotel" and seemed pleased with occasional visitors, whom he honored by hoisting the American and the Italian flags and by bringing out wine and small bread cakes, while chatting in a friendly way. Sometimes he mentioned the name of "Julia," but in such a vague way that who Julia was and where he had known her were not divulged.

At length the deep shaft, called the Portola shaft, in which he had so much confidence, became filled with water, and he could do nothing with it. Since his death after years of proud isolation, some 20 or more "prospects" that had apparently been dug by him have been found. Although he had one or two rich specimens of ore to show, neither he nor anyone else has realized any profit from these mines other than the experience gained there by Stanford University mining students, who have at times been permitted to work in them. The area is now in Stanford's Jasper Ridge biological preserve.

The name Corte de Madera means "timber choppings," and in fact the redwoods in this area had been exploited from a very early date by the Pueblo of San José and Mission Santa Clara. In the 1830's a new draying road (arrastradero) was opened to get lumber to the southern markets. Following a trail made by wild cattle through the hills to the southeast, it crossed Los Trancos Creek at the present Arastradero Road bridge. In 1868 a section of the never-completed Menlo Park and Santa Cruz Turnpike, presently Alpine Road, was opened, and at the intersection of this road and Arastradero Road Fernando Valenzuela built a store. The old wooden building still stands as a wayside saloon and has for several generations been a favorite haunt of Stanford University students.

The name Portola Valley is a local shortening and re-pronunciation of the impressive term "Portolá–Crespí Valley" which a landowner and newspaper editor bestowed on the area from Crystal Springs to Searsville in 1886. The settlement of Portola grew up on land purchased in 1883 by Andrew S. Hallidie, inventor of San Francisco's cable cars. Here he later experimented with altered approach by building an aerial tramway suspended from an overhead cable from bottom to top of the mountainside on his property.

Rancho Cañada de Guadalupe, la Visitación y Rodeo Viejo

Of all the old land grants in the county, those bordering on San Francisco Bay have become most widely known and most thickly settled, because there ran El Camino Real of Spanish days and there today run the great highways that lead southward from San Francisco.

The northernmost of these ranchos was Rancho Cañada de Guadalupe, la Visitación y Rodeo Viejo consisting of two square leagues given in 1841 by Governor Alvarado to Jacob P. Leese. The grantee appears frequently in the early history of California because he engaged in commercial ventures in Monterey and San Francisco and because he married Rosalía, sister of General Mariano Vallejo. Leese's ranch house was in the sheltered and oak-covered corner of the hill now occupied by the small city of Brisbane, near Alvarado Street just west of Visitacion Avenue.

When in 1856 San Mateo County was formed by the division of San Francisco County, the dividing line ran through this rancho, placing most of its area in the new county.

Rancho Buriburi

Rancho Buriburi was granted to José Antonio Sánchez by the provincial government on November 5, 1835. Although the petition for patent was based on the grant of 1835, Sánchez had tentatively received it as early as 1827. The petition for confirmation was made in 1852 by the heirs of José Antonio Sánchez, and patent was given to José de la Cruz Sánchez and others of the family, in 1872, for 14,639 acres extending from the salt marshes on the bay to the Spring Valley lakes and from the Colma cemeteries to the middle of Burlingame.

Before this land was given to Don José Antonio Sánchez, it was used as a government cattle ranch. In 1797 Governor Borica had sent 265 head of cattle to it to provide meat for the Presidio of San Francisco. Some idea of the place just before Don José Antonio settled upon it may be found in the journal of Captain William Frederick Beechey of the British Navy, whose ship, the Blossom, anchored briefly in San Francisco Bay on his long voyage (1825–28). Since he was unable to obtain in San Francisco certain supplies necessary to continue the expedition, the captain dispatched his surgeon, purser, and interpreter to Monterey for them.

These men set out with horses and proper escort, and "about noon they reached a small cottage named Buri Buri, about twelve miles from San Francisco, being unused to traveling, especially upon Californian saddles, which are by no means constructed for comfort, they determined to rest, until the baggage that they had left in the rear should overtake them. The house in which they lodged was a small miserable cottage full of holes, which, however, afforded them some repose and some new milk. Its inhabitants had been engaged in tanning, in which process they used a liquid extracted from oak bark, contained in a hide suspended by the corners. They had also collected in great quantities a very useful root called in that country *amoles,* which seems to answer all the purposes of soap."

Immediately upon the formal grant of the enlarged Buriburi tract in 1835, the Sánchez family built two identical adobe dwelling houses, standing end to end upon a small knoll at the edge of the marsh where the main road then ran. The buildings were on a site that had been occupied for a few years by Ignacio Martínez. They stood at a slight angle to the present El Camino, their southern end touching its east edge at a point between 550 and 600 feet south of Millbrae Avenue in Millbrae. They stood until 1871.

When the survey of this rancho was made in 1864, a preliminary to the granting of the patent, several houses were found along the road that skirted the salt marshes. Near Laguna San Bruno on the north line of the rancho, the map of this survey shows the Corral de Madera, where stables were maintained by the stage company. Along the road southward were houses of Manuel Sánchez, Wilson, a grocery store, a Spanish house at the embarcadero, "charcoal Shanties," Frenchman's, San Bruno House, and two designated as "Irish house." The house of José Sánchez is shown a little to the west of the road. And on an earlier map in 1857 the house of Chino Sánchez is indicated on the southeast corner of the rancho between a small lagoon and the shore of the bay.

On Rancho Buriburi are now located the towns of South San Francisco, San Bruno, Millbrae, and a part of Burlingame. Millbrae received its name because of the home there of Darius Ogden Mills, a native of New York and a man of influence in both the East and the West, who in 1860 became the owner of the 1,100-acre headquarters tract of this rancho. In 1866 he erected on the west side of the road a large, three-storied, towered wooden mansion which he named Millbrae. In 1872, by employing a large group of Chinese as laborers to drain the marshland, Mills reclaimed many acres which he used as pasturage for his fine dairy herd. He, with other fanciers of fine stock on the Peninsula, had imported by way of Boston 11 Alderney cows from the Alderney Islands. In his later years he made his home in New York and spent only summers at Millbrae. After his death, his daughter, then the widow of Whitelaw Reid, former United States Ambassador to the Court of St. James, erected the Mills Memorial Hospital in San Mateo as a tribute to her father.

During World War II the old Mills mansion was used as a Merchant Marine convalescent home. The Millbrae Dairy operated until after the war. In the 1950's, however, the entire estate was leveled by bulldozers for apartments and a shopping center. Even the fine old shrubs and trees and the rolling terrain were razed. The mansion and grounds were located about where the block of apartments west of Ogden Drive now stand, and the entrance way is represented by Murchison Drive. The dairy stood between the highway and the railroad tracks, just south of the Millbrae station.

Rancho San Mateo

Rancho San Mateo was given in 1846 by Governor Pío Pico to his secretary, Cayetano Arenas, as a reward for military service. The two leagues (confirmed for 6,438 acres) was taken from an old rancho of Mission Dolores and was the last parcel of land to be granted in San Mateo County by the Mexican government. It lay along San Francisco Bay between Rancho Buriburi on the north and San Mateo Creek on the south and was bounded on the west by Rancho Feliz along the course of the San Andrés Creek, which is now covered by Crystal Springs Lakes.

In November 1827, when some of the officers of the British ship *Blossom* passed through this region on their way to Monterey, they were impressed by its strong resemblance to "a nobleman's park; herds of cattle and horses were grazing upon the rich pasture, and numerous fallow deer, startled at the approach of strangers, bounded off to seek protection among the hills. The resemblance, however, could not be traced farther. Instead of a noble mansion in character with so fine a country, the party arrived at a miserable hut dwelling before the door of which a number of half naked Indians were basking in the sun." The litter scattered about the building "sadly disgraced the park-like scenery. This spot is named San Matheo, and belongs to the mission."

What the British sailors saw was the San Mateo outpost *(SRL 393)* of Mission San Francisco de Asís. There were two large, long adobe structures, located end to end on the north bank of San Mateo Creek, with one end in what is now the intersection of Baywood Avenue and El Camino Real. The ruined state of the outpost is mentioned in *Eldorado* by Bayard Taylor, who saw it in 1849. One building survived well into the American period. The earthquake of 1868 completely wrecked the walls, and in 1870 all that remained of them was leveled to the ground. Some of the tiles from the roof were preserved and, with tile from Mission San Antonio (Monterey County), may be seen on the roof of the railroad station at Burlingame. Today there is only a small plaque at the site of the old adobe opposite the Mills Memorial Hospital.

In 1848 this rancho passed into the hands of William Davis Merry Howard, for which it was said he paid $25,000. On the map of the rancho made in 1857, following the death of Howard in 1856 and preliminary to the confirmation of the tract to the executors, a bridge is shown where El Camino Real crossed San Mateo Creek. The present-day bridge is probably on the same site. The Howard house was also shown a little way upstream.

W. D. M. Howard, a native of Boston, had first come to California as cabin boy of a hide-drogher and had afterward with Henry Mellus purchased the abandoned office buildings of the Hudson's Bay Company in San Francisco, where they carried on mercantile pursuits. Wishing to have property in whatever city might prove to be the metropolis of the new state, Howard bought large tracts of land in the towns of San Francisco, Sacramento, and Vallejo. Because of his renown in philanthropic and commercial activities, Howard Street in San Francisco was named in his honor, and a memorial to him stands in St. Matthew's Episcopal Church in the city of San Mateo, situated in one corner of his vast holdings.

That part of the city of San Mateo north of San Mateo Creek and the towns of Hillsborough and Burlingame lie within the confines of Rancho San Mateo. Anson Burlingame was one of the purchasers of a part of the Howard property. He was then U.S. Minister to China and was influential in having the doors of the Chinese Empire opened to foreign commerce, and it is in his honor that the town of Burlingame was named.

An early settler in what is now the city of San Mateo was John S. Cooper, a native of Suffolk, England, who had deserted as steward from a British man-of-war in 1833. In 1851 he made a brush booth around a large oak tree on his ranch on San Mateo Creek beside El Camino Real. There he lived with his wife, a native woman, and their children while he built a better home. His wife died two years later, leaving him with a family of small children.

The city itself had its beginning in Nicholas De Peyster's roadhouse. He started his business in 1849 in the old mission adobe, but in 1850–51 he moved across the creek and built a tall wooden structure, later called the San Mateo House. It stood until 1964, serving as a nurses' residence for the adjacent Mills Memorial Hospital, and was torn down for a municipal parking lot.

In 1863, after the railroad had been built down the Peninsula from San Francisco, a town was platted by C. B. Polhemus, and the San Mateo station became the northern terminus of the San Mateo, Pescadero, and Santa Cruz Stage Company lines owned by Taft and Garretson, who ran tri-weekly stages to the southern terminus at Santa Cruz. Outlying places thus afforded communication with the railroad were Crystal Springs, San Felix, Byrnes's Store, Eureka Gardens, Spanishtown, Purissima, Lobitos, San Gregorio, Pescadero, Pigeon Point, Seaside, Davenport, and Santa Cruz—the last three lying south of the present county line.

The town was eventually hedged around on three sides by large properties: that of W. D. M. Howard, who had purchased Rancho San Mateo on the north; that of Frederick Macondray, one of the first great merchants of San Francisco, who chose in 1854 for a country home land just south of San Mateo Creek; and that of Alvinza Hayward, retired mine operator and financier, on the southeast. The Macondray home was purchased by John Parrott, a man originally from Virginia, who was United States consul at Mazatlán during the year 1845–46 and who remained identified with shipping and financial interests along the Pacific Coast until 1859. The home that he developed there was called Baywood, and in it he lived the last 30 years of his life, an influential citizen whose counsel was widely sought. This property remained in the hands of the Parrott

family until 1927, after which it was made into a residential subdivision called Baywood. The site of the original house is west of El Camino Real on the south side of San Mateo Creek, atop the first small rise.

The property of Alvinza Hayward is a residential section south of San Mateo. His home, afterward used as a hotel, stood near the tall palms on what is now called Hayward Avenue. The stable, which stood between present Rosewood Drive and South B Street, near Ninth Avenue, had rosewood and mahogany stalls for the carefully groomed horses, which were their owner's pride. In this vicinity Hayward had a large enclosed area for deer; both the stables and the deer park were show places where visitors were welcome. Nothing is left of the park except some of the magnificent oaks under which the animals browsed. Hayward established as a private enterprise a system of waterworks whereby the town of San Mateo was supplied with pure spring water before the date of its incorporation. The name of the station for the residential district into which the Hayward property has been portioned, formerly called Leslie, is now Hayward Park.

The first services that led to the eventual establishment of St. Matthew's Episcopal Church were conducted by the Rev. G. A. Easton of San Francisco, who spent the spring and summer of 1864 in the town. They were held in the newly completed reception room of Miss Buckmaster's San Mateo Young Ladies Institute, afterward a school called Laurel Hall. In the autumn of 1864 the Rev. A. L. Brewer was sent out from Detroit, Michigan, under the auspices of the Episcopal Board of Domestic Missions; and in February 1865 he conducted services in the public school.

In July of the same year the family of George H. Howard donated a lot of two acres from their rancho and headed the list of subscriptions for a building with a substantial contribution. In October the church was organized; and on the 12th of that month the cornerstone was laid on the north side of San Mateo Creek and east of the county road where the present building still stands. The church was constructed of stone taken from a quarry on the Crystal Springs Road on the Howard property. It was rebuilt after the 1906 earthquake, but a small portion of the original building, including the memorial to W. D. M. Howard, remains in place.

Rancho de las Pulgas

The name Argüello stands for much that is best in the annals of the Spanish era in Alta California, and the history of Rancho de las Pulgas is traced through children and grandchildren of this pioneer family.

Don José Darío Argüello, one of the finest characters of that early period, arrived at San Gabriel with his bride in 1781 after having traveled overland from Mexico as ensign in the company that Rivera had formed for the Santa Barbara presidio, which was soon to be established. He remained at San Gabriel for a few months, and there his first child was born and baptized, before the company moved on to its destination.

In June 1787 he was promoted to the position of lieutenant in the San Francisco Company, where he served as *comandante* until March 1791 and again for a ten-year period beginning in 1796. He was holding a like position at Santa Barbara in 1814, when, at the death of Governor Arrillaga, he was made acting governor of Alta California. He continued to live at Santa Barbara during the year that he held the two offices simultaneously. Receiving a commission as governor of Baja California in October 1815, he traveled overland to that place with his wife and some of his children. He never returned to Alta California, although he wanted to. During his 34 years of residence in the northern territory, he had filled positions of trust continuously and was held in high esteem. His gentle wife, Ignacia Moraga, niece of Lieutenant José Joaquín Moraga—first *comandante* of San Francisco—made both arduous overland journeys with him in those days when riding a horse or traveling in a creaking carreta were the only alternatives to walking. Their daughter Concepción, awaiting word from her long-unheard-from lover, Rezanov, was one of the children who accompanied the parents to Baja California, where she stayed for a time before returning to Alta California to spend the rest of her life.

The nine children of Don José Darío and Doña Ignacia Argüello were all born in California, and all received a careful home education. The eldest son, José Ignacio Máximo, was sent to Mexico to be trained for the priesthood and in later years came back to California to officiate on special occasions. Francisco Rafael, Toribio de Jesús, Ana Paula (who married a man named Obregon in Guadalajara), and Gertrudis Rudesinda were four of whom little is known. Gervasio, of some military importance, married Encarnación Bernal during the year that his father was acting governor of Santa Barbara and spent his last years in Mexico.

Best known is the faithful María de la Concepción Marcela, whose romance with the Russian Rezanov has been immortalized by the pen of Bret Harte and others. Santiago, one year younger than his sister Concepción and a cadet at the San Francisco Presidio when Rezanov made the acquaintance of the family, married Pilar, daughter of Francisco Ortega of Santa Barbara, when he was very young and became the father of 22 children. He became grantee of several tracts of land, held many important military positions, and left an honorable record in all parts of the state when he died in 1862 at his Tijuana rancho (San Diego County) at the age of 71. The most prominent among the children of Don José Darío was Luís Antonio Argüello, one of the older ones, born in San Francisco in 1784. Having been elected acting governor of California in 1822, a position he held until 1825, he had the distinction of being the first native-born governor of the territory. He was frequently involved in controversies and, although he was concerned with the welfare of his country, he did not win universal approval as his father had.

Two tracts of land appear to have been granted to Don José Darío Argüello before the year

1800. One, called "El Pilar," was given "in consideration of his large family." Of this, little is known: according to Hittell, it was an indefinite tract on the coast between Point San Pedro and Point Año Nuevo, and the grant was never confirmed. The other, known at that time as "Cachanígtac" but afterward known as "Las Pulgas" (the fleas), contained about 12 square leagues and was situated on San Francisco Bay between San Mateo Creek on the north and San Francisquito Creek on the south. The western boundary line of this tract was the cause of much litigation.

The history of Rancho de las Pulgas was brought to light after a petition for settlement of title was filed on January 21, 1852, by the claimants, Doña María de la Soledad Ortega de Argüello (widow of Don Luís Antonio), and her two sons, José Ramón and Luís Antonio, and a third party, Simón Monserrate Mezes, a young Spanish lawyer who had been given a part of the land in return for his services in defending the title against squatters. A transcript of the ensuing court proceedings before the Land Commission was filed on July 26, 1854, and this document states that from an "early period in the settlement of Alta California the Argüello family held this property by a lawful and sufficient title. That as far back as 1795 Don José Darío Argüello ... was the owner of said tract of land at that time called Rancho 'Cachinetac' by a title or license derived from Don Diego Borica, then governor and by virtue of his said office authorized and empowered to grant lands, which said Rancho soon after obtained the name of Las Pulgas, and which by name and as the property and inheritance of said family it has since been known. That for many years Alta California was disturbed by political commotions and that from the comparatively small value of lands but little attention was paid to the preservation of title, that the said José Darío Argüello being long since dead the history of their early title is only in traditions and the memory of the old inhabitants in the county. That in 1820 or 1821, Don Pablo Vicente de Solá ... made a new title to said Rancho or tract of land to Don Luís Argüello, a son of the said Don José Darío Argüello, and that said Luís Argüello died about 1830 leaving his widow the petitioner Doña Soledad and the following named children, to wit:— Francisco, a child by a former marriage and who died without issue in 1832 and was never married; María Concepción, María Josefa, and the petitioners José Ramón and Luís Antonio, all children of his second wife Doña Soledad. That said María died in 1845 unmarried and without issue, and that said Doña Josefa is married to Don Eulogio de Celís and that her interest in said property has passed to the claimants by purchase."

The question of the Pulgas ranch house and its location has long puzzled historians. The best interpretation of available evidence is that it was a crude building of palisade construction, rather than adobe, with a thatched roof, and that it stood in a little bend of Pulgas Creek on the south edge of present San Carlos Avenue in San Carlos. Captain Alfred Robinson, who visited the rancho on one of his journeys down the Peninsula before 1840, wrote: "El Rancho de Las Pulgas was the next place of any importance in our route, and is situated a little retired from the road at the foot of a small rising ground. It is the property of Donna Soledad Ortega, widow of Don Luís Argüello, formerly governor of California. I found her a beautiful woman, and the mother of three or four fine children. She was very ladylike in her manner and treated us with the utmost courtesy. After dinner we bade her adieu and proceeded on our way."

This rancho consisted of very rich and accessible land, and there was much misunderstanding in regard to ownership. The western boundary "back to the sierra or range of mountains," long in dispute, was finally settled; and a patent was issued for 35,240 acres in 1856. Doña Soledad and her two sons and S. M. Mezes were then able to dispose of their respective parts as they saw fit. The widow received one-half; the son José Ramón, one-fourth; the son Luís Antonio, one-tenth; and S. M. Mezes, three-twentieths. About this time Mezes appears to have built a low frame house at present Cedar Street and Magnolia Avenue in San Carlos, a location formerly thought to have been that of the original ranch headquarters.

Since the 1850's the vast grant has been cut into uncounted portions of varying sizes, and the land that comprised this old rancho is now well populated. El Camino Real, on whose borders the towns of San Mateo, Belmont, San`Carlos, Redwood City, Atherton, and Menlo Park have clustered, runs from San Mateo Creek on the northern border of the grant to San Francisquito Creek on the southern boundary. The close proximity of the towns makes the road for the entire distance like a city street. To carry the congested traffic the parallel Bayshore Freeway was constructed, and now the towns have stretched some of their streets over to the freeway and beyond.

A railroad bridge and the Dumbarton Toll Bridge span the bay a short distance above the lower end of the rancho. South of these bridges, in the very southeastern corner of the grant, the now almost forgotten town of Ravenswood was platted. The John Beal Steinberger property at this point was purchased in 1853 by I. C. Woods, Rufus Rowe, D. H. Haskell, John K. Hackett, and C. D. Judah, who laid out the town. A long wharf (at the end of present Bay Road) was built to deep water to facilitate the shipping of lumber that was hauled from the mills in the mountains, lots were sold, a few houses were erected, and a store was opened by William Paul. Hope was later entertained by the promoters of the town that the Central Pacific Railroad Company would choose this spot for the end of a bridge across the bay. But when that plan did not materialize, the town was abandoned, and the temporary structures that had been erected soon disappeared.

Lester Phillip Cooley, a Vermont man who had come overland to California and had at first spent some time in the mining regions, later purchased property contiguous to Ravenswood for a ranch and in the 1870's constructed a home for his family from lumber brought around the Horn. Near the house long stood a sandstone monument, one of many erected by the United States Coast Survey. This monument was six feet high and 31 inches square at the base, tapering to 22 inches at the top. It was inscribed: "East end of the Pulgas base. Alexander Dallas Bache, U.S. Coast Survey. Measured in July and August, 1853." A similar marker for the west end still stands on the Sequoia Hospital grounds, six miles due west, and just west of the Alameda de las Pulgas.

The site of the old Ravenswood wharf was for many years known as Cooley's Landing. Not far away is a large pit, now made into a park just north of Bay Road, where clay was taken for the Hunter, Shackelford and Company brick-making plant established there in 1874. Its products were shipped to San Francisco and San Jose. The bricks for the original Palace Hotel in San Francisco were made here.

In 1873 Clark's Landing at the mouth of San Francisquito Creek, the extreme southeastern point of the rancho, was established and five years later was operating under lease to W. C. Wilson, who there erected a large and commodious warehouse.

The Ravenswood area is now known as East Palo Alto.

Belmont and San Carlos

The first permanent settler at present Belmont was Charles Aubrey Angelo, a native of England who in 1850 opened a stage station called the Angelo House on a spot now 1,200 feet south of Ralston Avenue between the railroad tracks and Old County Road. The town that grew up, which became the first county seat of San Mateo County in 1856, centered exclusively about the present Ralston Avenue–Old County Road intersection in its early years. At the northeast corner was the Belmont Hotel, begun by John T. Ellet in 1853. The main building no longer stands, but an annex, built by a later owner probably before 1877, remains—a very large, many-windowed building with three-pitched roof at 951 Old County Road. Adam Castor's small building, housing a store, blacksmith shop, and restaurant, was built on the southwest corner in 1857. It was later replaced by a larger hotel, which, much remodeled, still stands. On the southeast corner was Castor's residence. About 1880 Matthew J. O'Neill and Walter A. Emmett started a store on the northwest corner; it is still standing and in use. On the east side of Old County Road four-tenths of a mile north of Ralston Avenue is the large and well-appointed ranch house and residence built in 1857 or 1858 by N. C. Lassen. It has now been converted into a restaurant.

Back of the town lies the Cañada del Diablo, chosen by S. M. Mezes, one of the patentees of the Pulgas rancho, for his home. There, too, lived Leonetto Cipriani, Italian patriot, in a small villa set on the hillside. Count Cipriani's villa was the beginning of the mansion built there by William C. Ralston after his purchase of an acreage in this location in the early 1860's. With discriminating taste, Ralston made his large estate a place of unusual charm, where he entertained people of world-wide distinction .during the 1860's and 1870's.

William Chapman Ralston, a native of Ohio, who had already gained valuable experience in the shipping world before his arrival in San Francisco on September 1, 1854, became a powerful Western financier. He maintained both a city home and a country home, and upon the latter he spent lavishly. From the modest villa of Count Cipriani he evolved a residence of faultless architecture and furnishings. Here were great glass doors, crystal chandeliers, parquetry floors, and everything else of corresponding elegance and taste. Assisted by his wife, the home-loving and gracious Elizabeth Fry, he became the perfect host, giving delightful weekend parties, banquets, and balls. From his stone-built, mahogany-stalled stables, he was able to provide mounts for a score of guests.

For the illumination of his country seat he erected costly gas works that benefited also the town of Belmont; for his own use, primarily, he built a wharf on the bayshore but generously shared it with the public.

After his tragic death by drowning in August 1875, the marvelously developed estate was taken over by his former business associate, William Sharon, of Comstock Lode fame. Sharon built a great dam and reservoir in the hills to provide irrigation for the plantings that have now grown to parklike proportions. Rows of pines and other trees placed for windbreaks are now proving their value.

Following its occupancy by Senator Sharon, the house at Belmont was used for a private school kept by the widow of Alpheus Bull, a business associate of both Ralston and Sharon. Later, the house was turned into a hospital by Dr. Gardiner.

In 1923 the place was taken over by the Sisters of Notre Dame, who removed to it their convent and college established in San Jose in 1851. As a memento of their pioneer efforts, they brought to this new location, section by section, the simple wooden structure in which their labors had begun, and re-erected it within the spacious new grounds. It was later moved to the novitiate at Saratoga and was finally torn down.

The Ralston mansion is now Berchmans Hall, named in honor of one of the founding Sisters. The Cipriani villa is identifiable as one wing of the house. All that remains of the former magnificence of buildings and grounds is guarded and appreciated.

Although San Carlos was the site of the original Pulgas Ranch, the town dates only from 1887 and its name from the beginning of the following year; it is said to be called after the first ship to enter San Francisco Bay (1775), the *San Carlos*, which in turn had been named as a patriotic compliment to Carlos III of Spain. In 1886 S. M. Mezes and others laid out the road called Alameda de las Pulgas, thereby preserving the original name of the area. The principal landmark of San Carlos is the former railroad station, built in an ornamental style of sandstone blocks and somewhat resembling the Stanford University architecture of the same period and material.

Timothy Guy Phelps, or T. G. Phelps, as his

Ralston Mansion, Belmont

name usually appears, was born in New York, arrived in San Francisco in 1849, and went at once to the mines in Tuolumne County. He later purchased 3,500 acres of land around San Carlos. His large white-painted frame home stood until the 1930's on the east side of Old County Road, just north of Holly Street, where some large old Monterey pines of his planting are still conspicuous. He was elected to the state legislature in 1856 on the first Republican ticket in California, and there introduced a bill to correct mistakes made in the organization of San Mateo County the previous year. This bill was passed and became a law on April 18, 1857. He served as representative in Congress from 1861 to 1863, ably maintaining the cause of ranch owners in their struggle for rightful title to land. Phelps became president of the Southern Pacific Railroad. In 1887 he sold the land for the original subdivision of the present city, which was at first supposed to be named for him.

Embarcadero de las Pulgas, Redwood City

A little creek, running through Rancho de las Pulgas where Redwood City, the county seat, now stands and emptying into a slough or arm of the bay, formed a natural shipping point or embarcadero.

Lumbering became an important industry wherever the redwoods grew, and there were many of these trees in the mountains within a few miles of this place. In 1850 the shipment of lumber from the Woodside and Searsville mills began, and the Embarcadero became a busy wharf. Ships were built there, and a number of schooners were launched that year. Wagon making and blacksmithing were important adjuncts to the business of hauling the product of the mills to the Embarcadero and were early established there. This was the nucleus around which the present Redwood City developed. Redwood Creek flows under the city today, and Redwood Slough is filled in. On the spot where the vessels were launched in the 1850's, a bronze tablet was placed in 1926 by the history and civics classes of the Sequoia Union High School to commemorate the pioneer industry which created Redwood City. The marker is located on a store building at the southwest corner of Broadway and Jefferson Avenue.

William Carey Jones, who had come to the West Coast in 1849 as a special government agent to investigate the condition of land titles in California, acquired over 2,000 acres near Redwood City from the Pulgas Ranch. It extended from Five Points to Whipple Avenue and from El Camino Real to the brow of the hill. This property was put up for sheriff's sale on January 2, 1858, when it was purchased by Horace Hawes, a native of New York who had been appointed consul for the Society and other South Sea islands by President Polk in 1847. By an unanticipated routing of the vessel on which he took passage, he arrived in San Francisco, where a few years later he became prefect. He resided in San Francisco and at Redwood Farm, his country home in the foothills near Redwood City, until his death in 1870. He was a staunch supporter of the Union side during the Civil War. Western Redwood City is now on this land. If the original plans of the owner had been carried through, a seat of learning called "Mount Eagle University" would have been located in this area.

The first Protestant church in the county was organized in Redwood City in 1862. Land was purchased at the present corner of Middlefield Road and Jefferson Avenue for a building for the First Congregational Church, which had been meeting in the courthouse for some months. The second Protestant church was the St. Peter's Episcopal. Its members held their first meetings in the schoolhouse, then in the courthouse, and afterward in a small building of their own.

Nothing remains of the earliest period of Redwood City's existence, unless it is an interesting little house with a high porch, at 1018 Main Street, just south of Middlefield Road, which may have been built by George Heller in 1857.

Captain Morgan and the Oyster Industry

On the tidelands of the bay from San Bruno Point southward as far as San Francisquito Creek, native oysters had flourished for centuries. After the building of the transcontinental railroad in 1869, Eastern oysters were imported and planted along the bayshore off San Mateo County. Several companies engaged in this pursuit, most of them being finally consolidated into the Morgan Oyster Company. This company owned several houses built by ship joiners on piles above the water. Like cottages in a garden enclosed by a picket fence, these oyster houses stood within a water area surrounded by partially submerged wickets that ensured the safety of the bivalves growing in their salty beds.

John Stillwell Morgan, a frugal, industrious man and a native of New York, was made captain of the schooner *Telegraph* then (1846) plying the sea in the oyster business. Sailing in 1849 for California in the bark *Magdella*, he arrived in San Francisco and thoroughly prospected the bay for oysters without success. He then went to the mines and afterward to Oregon, where he again engaged in the oyster business.

The Morgan Oyster Company was formed in 1887 when Morgan took in four partners. The new company began by transplanting the bivalves from Shoalwaters Bay, Washington Territory, to the vicinity of Mission Creek, south of San Francisco.

The business did not come up to expectations. In the course of time, the oyster industry ceased, and the Morgan holdings were purchased by the Pacific Portland Cement Company, which now dredges the bay for shells which it uses in making cement. The first office building of this company on the wharf at Redwood City was one of the old oyster houses that was moved from the piles on which it was originally built south of Dumbarton Bridge. The last of the Morgan oyster houses in use for its original purpose stood two miles out in the tidewater opposite Millbrae and Burlingame. This station was established in 1874, and its location was one of the most valuable. Until 1940 it remained a landmark visible from the Bayshore Highway just south of the airport.

The house in which the Captain lived while directing his company was located at the junction of Steinberger and Corkscrew creeks. Legislators, met by the Captain in his launch at San Francisco or Oakland, were once taken for a tour of the bay and afterward entertained by him in the spacious dining room of his house before being returned to their respective duties, which included the making of suitable laws to cover industrial ownership of tidewaters. His house is said to have been moved from its piles in the water and relocated at the corner of Chestnut and Spring streets in Redwood City.

The San Mateo Bridge, now being reconstructed, was built entirely from shell material dredged from the spot. It was the longest highway bridge in the world (12 miles, seven over water) at the time of its opening in 1929.

Menlo Park and Atherton

The adjoining areas of Menlo Park and Atherton lie near the southern part of the county along El Camino Real. Their common boundaries are so irregular that it is difficult to distinguish the territory of the earlier-named Menlo Park from its newer neighbor.

Dennis J. Oliver and his brother-in-law, D. C. McGlynn, became owners of a 1,700-acre tract on the Pulgas rancho and erected in the 1850's, at present Middle Avenue and El Camino Real, a gate with a wooden arch across its top. The arch bore the inscription "Menlo Park," in memory of the "most beautiful spot in the world"—their former home in Menlough, County Galway, Ireland. This gate became weatherworn, but it was preserved while Camp Fremont, used for the concentration of troops during World War I, was in the area. It stood until July 7, 1922, when it was destroyed in an automobile accident.

Upon the building of the San Francisco–San Jose Railroad down the Peninsula in 1863, a station called Menlo Park was placed a short distance from this old gate. The old station still stands, although converted to other uses. Men successful in statesmanship, finance, and industry chose this locality for the luxurious country homes which they built on ample estates at convenient driving distances from the railroad station. A town of small houses, hotels, and stores grew up near the station, and in 1873 the first church in the town was organized by a group of Presbyterian residents. In the following year a house of worship was erected upon land donated for that purpose, and in it Protestant families of the town and the surrounding countryside attended services. This frame structure was located on Santa Cruz Avenue a little west of El Camino Real. The Roman Catholic Church of the Nativity, built in the same period, still stands on Oak Grove Avenue east of El Camino. On March 23, 1874, the town was incorporated, but the incorporation was allowed to lapse and was not renewed until November 15, 1927.

Not far from the station a fine residence was built by Milton S. Latham, a man from Ohio who had arrived in California in 1850 and had purchased land from John T. Doyle on December 18, 1871. He eventually bought several other small tracts adjoining his original purchase. He was elected governor of the state nine years after his arrival, only to renounce that honor to fill the unexpired term of United States Senator David C. Broderick, who had been slain in a duel that took place within the county. Latham entertained extensively in this country home. The house, with its stately pillars, costly interior, and elaborate fountains placed in well-landscaped grounds among large native oaks, became the property of Mary Hopkins, the widow of Mark Hopkins, one of the pioneers of the state who had arrived from New York in 1849 and one of the "Big Four" who put through the building of the Central Pacific Railroad. After her remarriage in 1888, the great house passed to their adopted son, Timothy, who followed in the footsteps of Mark Hopkins by becoming treasurer of the Central Pacific Railroad Company. The mansion was badly wrecked in the earthquake of 1906, but its damaged form stood for decades at the end of a once well-kept drive far back in the grounds entered at the keeper's gate on Ravenswood Avenue. The gatehouse still stands at 439 Ravenswood. The estate is now occupied, in part, by the Menlo Park Civic Center, the Stanford Research Institute, and Stanford Village housing units.

Across Ravenswood Avenue from the Hopkins estate stands the fine old home maintained with so much pride during the life of its owner, Edgar Mills, whose brother D. O. Mills lived at Millbrae

at that same period. The house passed from the ownership of the family years ago and has had various occupants since that time. It now houses a restaurant on Noel Drive.

Besides the wealthy residents who came to the region of Menlo Park for rest and recreation on their large estates there were permanent residents who worked there. One such family was established by John and Margaret Murray, who came around the Horn from New York in 1854. They purchased various lands within the confines of the present county. From Menlo Park they shipped milk to San Francisco by stage, and there twin sons were born to them. In later years Margaret divided 28 acres of land which she held on San Francisquito Creek among her four children. A son, John Jarvis, was given the part nearest the creek and on it erected a house and barn about the year 1885. To this son also fell the possession of a copper kettle brought around the Horn by his parents, and to his son James eventually passed both the land and the kettle. In 1930 the land was acquired by the Allied Arts Guild of California, and at the place where the old kettle was once treasured for its sentimental value many objects are now exhibited for their artistic value. The old barn of the Murrays has been utilized as a part of this attractive and philanthropic venture at Arbor Road and Creek Drive.

Atherton, incorporated in 1923, extends in its longest direction from Bay Road between Ringwood Avenue and Marsh Road, across Middlefield Road, the railroad, and El Camino Real, and to a little distance west of the Alameda de las Pulgas. Within this area are many stately modern homes and the sites of older ones no longer standing.

Faxon Dean Atherton, originally from Massachusetts, first visited California in 1836 while a resident of Chile and a member of a firm engaged in the hide-and-tallow trade. On September 29, 1860, he acquired a tract of over 400 acres, formerly occupied by James King of William, and built a country mansion among the native oaks growing there. He named his estate "Valparaiso Park," from the city of Valparaiso in South America where his wife had been born and where he had spent his early manhood. Life in this house is depicted by the daughter-in-law, Gertrude Atherton, in her *Adventures of a Novelist,* written of the period when the country was sparsely settled and quiet afternoons on a comfortable veranda had few interruptions.

After the Atherton family was gone, the place was used as a school for boys kept by Ira G. Hoyt, a former state superintendent of public instruction, and during the occupancy of this school the mansion was destroyed by fire. The location, near the intersection of Elena and Isabella avenues (names of two of the Atherton daughters), is now owned by the Menlo Circus Club, which was organized primarily for the purpose of raising funds for the Stanford Home for Convalescent Children. Valparaiso Avenue, not far distant, carries the name of the old house, and the name of the former Fair Oaks station where a post office was established in 1867 has been superseded by the name Atherton.

A 480-acre tract, adjoining that of Faxon D. Atherton, was purchased by Thomas H. Selby, a pioneer industrialist of the West Coast. Selby was born in New York City, landed in San Francisco in 1849, and originated the Selby Silver and Lead Smelting Works, where a vast quantity of the bullion from the mines of the state was handled. The home that he established there was a "model of rural attractiveness and high cultivation" and was his favorite resort after office hours in San Francisco. The house has since been destroyed by fire, but Selby Lane, a road running along two sides of the old estate, identifies the place where he specialized in the raising of grains and fine fruits. The smelting firm that he organized still carries his name in San Francisco and elsewhere.

John T. Doyle, a "scholar of rare culture and refinement" and one of the foremost lawyers of his day, in 1856 purchased land in the vicinity from Horace P. Jones and gradually added to the acreage until he owned a large tract. One of his accomplishments for the welfare of the new state was the final disentangling of the affairs of the missions at the request of Archbishop Alemany. In the course of his duties he often traveled the ill-kept roads between the missions, always receiving a welcome from the resident fathers. The highways, little more than trails then, were all but obscured by the rank-growing mustard; and yet his approach was always noted by a lookout so that when he reached the door a room with all possible comforts, even luxuries, was ready for his immediate occupancy.

General William Tecumseh Sherman was one of the honored and frequent visitors at the Doyle home, a palatial frame house. The ample veranda was shaded by a wisteria vine of huge proportions. The library built to contain Doyle's valuable books was a large and friendly room. Although the old house no longer stands, the tall palms of the drive leading to its site still border Toyon Road off Ringwood Avenue.

Not far from the Doyle house was the Joseph A. Donohoe residence on Middlefield Road, now the location of Menlo-Atherton High School. The Frank Fielding Moulton house, which grew from its original size of five rooms to 18 rooms before the family built a residence elsewhere in the Atherton region, stood about three miles from El Camino Real beyond Selby Lane Extension.

Another man who had one of the early houses in the Menlo-Atherton vicinity was Charles N. Felton, who entertained there extensively. Originally a New York man, he became sub-treasurer at San Francisco and also served from March 1891 to March 1893 as United States Senator. He built his house in 1870 and lived in it until his death in 1913. The mansion is no longer standing, but the property, near Encinal Avenue and the Southern Pacific Railroad tracks, is now a residential subdivision called "Felton Gables."

James Clair Flood, who arrived in San Francisco in 1849 on the boat Elizabeth Ellen and became one of the "Bonanza Kings" of the Comstock Lode days, bought a tract of land along Middlefield Road in 1876 and two years later began the erection of "a great white mansion" upon it. The house was called Linden Towers and was placed well back from the road and surrounded by lawn and fine trees. After Flood's death in Heidelberg during a world tour, the place passed by will to his daughter, who gave it to the University of California. After this institution found the property to be non-income-producing, it was sold to the son, James L. Flood, who purchased neighboring land as well and enclosed the estate by placing a brick wall along the entire frontage on Middlefield Road. The death of this son occurred in 1926. The brick wall still stands, but Linden Towers was torn down after the public auction of its contents in 1934. The attractive old gatehouse stood into the 1950's.

Until 1956 the oldest building in the Menlo Park–Atherton area was a unique structure that stood near the corner of Ringwood and Colby avenues, probably the only surviving example in California of an early Spanish type of construction, the *encajonada* or "boxed-house." The walls were made of rammed earth columns tamped down inside a movable frame, in this case a lattice of redwood laths, rather than the usual wattle covering. It was probably built in the Mexican period to house herdsmen of the Rancho de las Pulgas. There is evidence that it was constructed before 1846; its redwood laths, therefore, must have been hand-sawed in the sawpits of Woodside.

After standing over a century, the strange adobe found itself face to face with bulldozers clearing the land for a subdivision. The owner, John Wickett, a man with more than a passing interest in California history, could not bring himself to destroy it, and local authorities would not permit him to move the "substandard structure" to another site in the same area. He therefore had it raised on jacks and transported many miles over a winding mountain road to property he owned near the Skyline Boulevard, where it stands today, unscathed by the trip—no mean accomplishment, when it is remembered that what was moved were unframed, unsupported, foundationless walls held together only by their own compaction. The adobe stands at the edge of the summit directly across Skyline Boulevard from the Skeggs Point observation area. There, from an elevation of 2,350 feet and an airline distance of nine miles, it overlooks its original location on the flat.

La Honda

John H. Sears moved from Searsville in the winter of 1861–62 and settled 17 miles from Redwood City in the mountains. The place eventually acquired the name La Honda, from the creek, Arroyo Hondo ("deep"), so named for its deep and redwood-filled canyon. About 1877 Sears began the construction of a store, and in 1878 he became low bidder to build the present winding Old La Honda Road, first road through the isolated region. A county road was first surveyed in 1870 but was not completed. Sears and

Gatehouse, Flood Estate, Atherton

"Bandit-built Store," La Honda

others then organized the Searsville and La Honda Turnpike Company and made a new survey, which the county agreed to take over.

The Sears store *(SRL 343)* was often called the "Bandit-built Store," because the owner employed in its construction two newcomers to the vicinity who, after their departure, were believed to have been the Younger brothers, Jim and Bob, outlaws from the Midwest, where the pair were jailed soon after they left California. The old store, with its pillared porch, stood at the northwest corner of La Honda and Sears Ranch roads until it was torn down early in 1960. The frame residence built by Sears has been destroyed by fire, but his farm of perhaps 300 acres still extends back of the town along Sears Ranch Road. La Honda has long been the center of a popular camping and summer resort area.

The Broderick-Terry Duel

An aftermath of the bitter political campaign of 1859 in California was a duel that reverberated throughout the nation because of the prominence of the participants and the death of one; both men were pioneers of 1849 and members of the same political party, although they had espoused opposite factions.

David C. Broderick, born in Ireland in 1820, had lived in New York as a boy and had come from there to California, where he became a power in the Democratic party. He was acting lieutenant-governor in 1851 and became United States Senator in 1857.

David S. Terry, born in Kentucky in 1823, had seen military service in Texas and Mexico before coming to the Coast in 1849. He became Chief Justice of the California Supreme Court and was active in politics, first as a Whig, afterward as a leader in the American or Know-Nothing party; and in the campaign of 1859 he allied himself with the Chivalry faction of the Democratic party. Incensed by certain statements made by Senator Broderick of the Tammany faction in his campaign speeches, Terry challenged him to a duel, in which Senator Broderick was fatally wounded.

The site of the famous Broderick-Terry duel *(SRL 19)* was definitely located and marked in 1917 by the Landmarks Committee of the Native Sons of the Golden West as being just south of the San Francisco–San Mateo county line, near Lake Merced. Two granite shafts were later erected on the spot where the two principals

stood. On one appears the name Broderick in carved letters, and on the other, Terry. On the eminence nearby, where spectators witnessed the duel, there is a bronze tablet upon a foundation of granite, stating the historic facts of the event. The words are as follows: "U. S. Senator, David C. Broderick, and Chief Justice of the Supreme Court, David S. Terry, met here in the early morning of September 13, 1859, Senator Broderick receiving a mortal wound. This was the last of the great duels fought in California. With the exception of the Burr-Hamilton affair, no duel has taken place in the history of the United States where the principals were as well known or occupied as high official positions."

This event did not end Terry's stormy career. After the termination of the Civil War, in which he had been made a brigadier general in the Confederate Army, he returned to California and settled in Stockton, casting his influence with the "Sand-lotters" or Workingman's party. His fiery temper embroiled him in many an altercation, and he was finally shot to death in the railway station at Lathrop by United States Marshal David Neagle, bodyguard of United States Supreme Court Justice Stephen J. Field, whom he had threatened.

SOURCES

Atherton, F. D. *The California Diary . . . 1836–1839*, ed. Doyce B. Nunis, Jr. Special Publication 29, California Historical Society, San Francisco, 1964.
Atherton, Gertrude. *Adventures of a Novelist*. Liveright, Inc., New York, 1932.
Bancroft, Hubert Howe. "Pioneer Register" in *History of California*, Vols. II–VI. History Co., San Francisco, 1886.
Beechey, Frederick William. *Narrative of a Voyage to the Pacific and Beering's Strait, in the years 1825, 26, 27, 28*. 2 vols. Henry Colburn and Richard Bentley, London, 1831.
Bolton, Herbert Eugene. *Anza's California Expeditions*. 5 vols. University of California Press, Berkeley, 1930.
––– *Fray Juan Crespi, Missionary Explorer on the Pacific Coast, 1769–1774*. University of California Press, Berkeley, 1927.
Bonestell, Cutler L. *A Woodside Reminiscence as told by Grizzly Ryder*. Privately printed, San Francisco, 1920.
Bowman, J. N., and G. W. Hendry. "Spanish and Mexican Houses in the Nine Bay Counties." Ms., Bancroft Library, University of California, Berkeley; State Library, Sacramento, 1942.
Bromfield, D. Gordon. *The San Mateo We Knew*. Privately printed, Santa Barbara, 1957.
Bromfield, Davenport. Official Map of San Mateo County, California, 1894. (Reproduced, San Mateo County Historical Association, San Mateo, [1964].)
Brown, Alan K. "Rivera at San Francisco, A Journal of Exploration, 1774," *California Historical Society Quarterly*, XLI (December 1962), 325–41.
––– *Saw Pits in the Spanish Red Woods*. San Mateo County Historical Association, San Mateo, 1966.
––– Unpublished research. Notes at San Mateo County Historical Association.
Capron, E. S. *History of California, from Its Discovery to the Present Time*. J. P. Jewett & Co., Boston, 1854.
Carter, Charles Franklin. "Duhaut-Cilly's Account of California in the Years 1827–28," *California Historical Society Quarterly*, VIII (1929).
Cloud, Roy W. *History of San Mateo County, California*. 2 vols. The S. J. Clarke Publishing Co., Chicago, 1928.
Costansó, Miguel. *Diary of the Portolá Expedition, 1769–1770*, ed. Frederick J. Teggart. Publications of the Academy of Pacific Coast History, University of California, Berkeley, 1911.
Davidson, George. "Voyages of Discovery and Exploration on the Northwest Coast of America from 1539 to 1603," *United States Coast and Geodetic Survey, 1886*, Washington, D.C., 1887.

Dawson, Nicholas. *Narrative of Nicholas "Cheyenne" Dawson (Overland to California in '41 and '49, and Texas in '51)*, with an introduction by Charles L. Camp. Grabhorn Press, San Francisco, 1933.

Dougal, William H. *Off for California; the Letters, Log and Sketches of William H. Dougal, Gold Rush Artist*, ed. F. M. Stanger. Biobooks, Oakland, 1949.

Edwards, Philip Leget. *Diary of: The Great Cattle Drive from California to Oregon in 1837*. Grabhorn Press, San Francisco, 1932.

Evans, Colonel Albert S. *A la California, Sketches of Life in the Golden State*. A. L. Bancroft Co., San Francisco, 1873.

Farnham, Eliza W. *California, In-doors and Out*. New York, 1856.

Guinn, Professor J. M. *History of the State of California and Biographical Record of Coast Counties*. Chapman Publishing Co., Chicago, 1904.

Harte, Bret. "A Blue Grass Penelope," in *In the Carquinez Woods and Other Tales*. Houghton Mifflin, Boston, 1912.

——— *A First Family of the Tasajara*. Argonaut Edition. P. F. Collier & Son, New York, 1891.

History of San Mateo County, California. B. F. Alley, San Francisco, 1883.

History of San Mateo County. Illustrated. Moore and De-Pue, Publishers (no address), 1878.

[Hoffmann, Charles]. *Map of the Region Adjacent to San Francisco Bay*, 1867.

Hubbard, Elbert. *A Little Journey to San Mateo County*. Roycroft Shop, East Aurora, N.Y., 1915.

[Huntley, Sir Henry Vere]. *California: Its Gold and Its Inhabitants*. London, 1856.

Langsdorff, Georg Heinrich Freiherr von. *Bemerkungen auf einer Reise um die Welt in den Jahren 1803 bis 1807*. Im Verlag bey Friedrich Witmars, Frankfurt/Main, 1812.

Leonard, Zenas. *Narrative of the Adventures of Zenas Leonard, Written by Himself*, ed. Milo Milton Quaife. Lakeside Press, Chicago, 1934.

Lyman, Chester S. *Around the Horn to the Sandwich Islands and California*, ed. F. J. Teggart. Yale University Press, New Haven, Conn., 1924.

Millard, Bailey. *History of the San Francisco Bay Region*. 3 vols. American Historical Society, Inc., Chicago, San Francisco, 1924.

Miller, Guy C. Notes and Collections, Palo Alto, 1901–53.

Nelson, N. C. "Shellmounds of the San Francisco Bay Region," *University of California Publications in American Archaeology and Ethnology*, VII, No. 4 (1909).

Neuman, J. V. Unpublished research, map, 1907–18, by the Surveyor, San Mateo County.

Palou, Fray Francisco. *Historical Memoirs of New California*, ed. H. E. Bolton. University of California Press, Berkeley, 1926.

Repass, Merle M. "The Hermit Mine." Thesis, Stanford University, 1923.

[Robinson, Captain Alfred.] *Life in California*. [H. G. Collins, Paternoster Row, London, 1845.]

Stanger, Frank Merriman. *History of San Mateo County*. San Mateo, 1938.

——— " 'The Hospice' or 'Mission San Mateo,' " *California Historical Society Quarterly*, XXIII (September 1944), 247–58.

——— *La Peninsula, Journal of the San Mateo County Historical Association*, 1941–65.

——— *Peninsula Community Book*. San Mateo, 1938.

——— *South from San Francisco; San Mateo County, California, Its History and Heritage*. San Mateo County Historical Association, San Mateo, 1963.

Steele, Catherine Baumgarten. "The Steele Brothers, Pioneers in California's Great Dairy Industry," *California Historical Society Quarterly*, XX (September 1941), 259–73.

——— Unpublished research and documents.

Wait (Colburn), Frona Eunice. *Wines and Vines of California*. The Bancroft Co., San Francisco, 1889.

Watts, W. L. "San Mateo County," *Report of the State Mineralogist*, October 1890. State Printing Office, Sacramento, 1890.

Weymouth, Alice Jenkins. *The Palo Alto Tree*. Stanford University Press, Stanford, 1930.

Wheeler, Alfred. *Wheeler's Topographic Map of San Francisco County . . .*, 1855.

Wilkes, Charles. *Narrative of the United States Exploring Expedition . . .*, Vol. V. Philadelphia, 1845.

——— Ms. journal, National Archives, Washington, D.C.

Wyatt, Roscoe D. *Days of the Dons*. San Mateo County Title Co., Redwood City, 1949.

——— *Historic Names and Places in San Mateo County*. San Mateo County Title Co., Redwood City, 1947.

Santa Barbara County

SANTA BARBARA COUNTY took its name from Santa Barbara Channel, so called by Vizcaíno in honor of St. Barbara. This was one of the original 27 counties of the state, and the city of Santa Barbara has been the county seat from the beginning.

Painted Cave

On the top of the mountain east of San Marcos Pass, about 13 miles northwest of Santa Barbara, is a group of Indian pictographs, known as the Painted Cave. The cave, which is on private property, may be reached by a narrow road which branches off to the right of the San Marcos Pass Road (Highway 154) at a point six miles northwest of Freeway 101. The cave is on the left and above the road. Conventionalized pictures of the sun, human figures, trees, snakelike creatures, and circular designs and crosses, done in red, white, yellow, and black, cover the interior of the cavern. The origin and meaning of these crudely executed designs have not been determined. The cave is protected from defacement and injury by an iron gate.

Burton Mound

Burton Mound (*SRL 306*), located within circular Burton Drive between Natoma Avenue and Mason Street, is today merely a gentle rise in the ground surrounded by city streets and dwellings. The history of the site, however, extends back into antiquity. Excavations made in 1923 by the Museum of the American Indian, Heye Foundation, of New York City, under the supervision of John P. Harrington with David Banks Rogers in charge of the field work, revealed the fact that three distinct Indian cultures have lived on the site.

Covering the entire surface of the knoll, the village had spread to the fringes of the surrounding marsh. Over the entire area of about 550 × 425 feet evidences of long occupancy were traced. The residential section had been centered about a "strong spring of sweet water" upon the eastern slope of the rise. David Banks Rogers describes the site and the artifacts thus: "A great cemetery extended southwestward from near the crest to well into the marsh. Other burial plots, smaller but highly congested with graves, existed upon the northern and western slopes. Upon the crest of the mound had probably been arranged all of the ceremonial enclosures. . . .

"A pride in artistic accomplishment appears to have been a passion with these people," as is proved by the unusual beauty and perfection of the numerous relics unearthed. The more recent deposits showed evidence of the contact with white invaders and the loss of the old culture. In place of the "perfectly wrought sandstone bowls . . . great pestles, as true of contour as though turned in a lathe, and striking ollas . . . globular in form and narrow-necked," there were found "buttons from Spanish uniforms, glass beads from Venice, and all too frequently old-fashioned wine and rum bottles." The investigation also showed evidence of a more primitive people having occupied a part of the same site for a longer period of time.

The old Puerto de Santa Bárbara, or early landing place for the mission and presidio, was located at the foot of the present Chapala Street west of the mouth of Mission Creek and due east of and comprising the Burton Mound. During mission days this land was owned by Mission Santa Barbara and was called El Rancho de la Playa ("The Ranch of the Beach"). After secularization it became the property of the Mexican government, which granted it to James (Santiago) Burke, who, in turn, sold it to Joseph Chapman, the young New Englander who had escaped from Bouchard's pirate ship in 1818. Chapman, it is

said, erected a small adobe house on the mound, later conveying the land to Benjamin Foxen.

According to tradition, the massive adobe that for over 70 years stood on the mound and was long the most conspicuous landmark on the Santa Barbara waterfront was erected by Thomas Robins. For about ten years during the 1840's it was the home of Captain George C. Nidever, who, it is said, planted trees and gardens and added two outbuildings to the adobe house. Nidever, in 1851, sold the place to Augustus F. Hinchman, Santa Barbara attorney and prominent citizen. In 1860 it was acquired by Lewis T. Burton, who made the old house his home until his death in 1879. Burton had come to California with the Wolfskill party in 1831. He became a wealthy merchant and ranchero and in 1839 married María Antonia Carrillo, daughter of Carlos Carrillo. At the time of Burton's death the tract came into the possession of the Seaside Hotel Association, and plans to erect a hotel on the site were at once formulated. However, it was not until 20 years later that such a plan was realized. In 1901–2, under the direction of Milo M. Potter, the Potter Hotel was erected, and beautiful landscape gardens soon covered the old historic Indian mound. The property again changed hands when, in 1913, it was taken over by the Ambassador Hotel Corporation. The hotel burned in 1921 and the site was released for archaeological investigations. The place is now built up with apartment houses. A plaque has been placed in Ambassador Park.

Carpinteria

One-quarter of a mile southwest of the historical monument on U.S. Highway 101 at Carpinteria, on the east bank of Carpinteria Creek, is the site of an Indian shell mound, now subdivided and built up with homes. This was the location of the Chumash village of Mishopshnow (SRL 535), discovered by the Cabrillo expedition in 1542. One-half mile east of the mouth of the creek were asphalt pits, now excavated. The tar

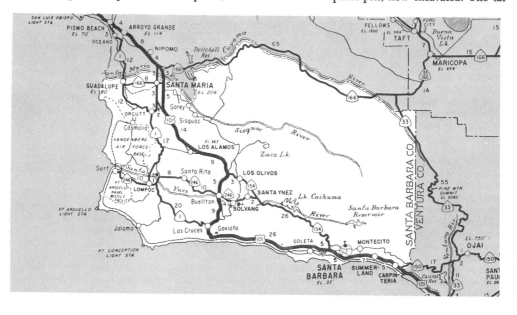

exuding from the banks along the shore was used by the natives for caulking boats, baskets, and vessels for carrying liquid. The story of the naming of the village is told by Father Crespí, diarist of the Portolá expedition of 1769:

"Not very far from the town we saw some springs of asphaltum. These Indians have many canoes, and at that time were constructing one, for which reason the soldiers named this town Carpintería ('carpenter shop') but I baptized it with the name of San Roque."

Excavations have revealed the presence not only of primitive peoples over long periods of time, but also of prehistoric animals similar to those taken from the famous La Brea Pits in Los Angeles.

In the early days of Santa Barbara County, wharves were built at this asphalt deposit and the material was taken out for shipment to San Francisco and other towns in California.

Cabrillo's Grave

Somewhere on the lonely island of San Miguel, which lies just off the coast of Santa Barbara in the Santa Barbara Channel, is the unmarked grave of Juan Rodríguez Cabrillo, discoverer of Alta California. There, in 1542, Cabrillo's ships, the San Salvador and the Victoria, lay anchored for eight days in a port at San Miguel awaiting the abatement of the autumn storms which delayed their passage north. During this time Cabrillo suffered a fall, breaking his arm near the shoulder.

In spite of his injury and in the face of many other misfortunes, he continued his voyage, going as far as the Northwest Cape near Fort Ross. Forced back by storms at that point, Cabrillo returned to Cuyler's Harbor on San Miguel. There, on January 3, 1543, he died from illness caused by the injury to his arm incurred several months before.

Sebastián Vizcaíno, 60 years later, entered the Channel on December 4, 1602, the feast day of St. Barbara, whose name was accordingly bestowed upon it by Padre Asunción.

A bronze tablet mounted on a granite boulder was placed in honor of Cabrillo by the Santa Barbara Chapter, D.A.R., in 1919, in the palm garden along the waterfront on East Cabrillo Boulevard between Santa Barbara and Punta Gorda streets.

Point Concepción

Point Concepción, which marks a change in the direction of the coastline, was first discovered by Juan Rodríguez Cabrillo on October 18, 1542, and many other early explorers and mariners sighted it by. Bolton says that, sailing up the coast from San Diego, the ships had anchored on October 14 off Carpintería, a mile west of Sand Point, on the 15th five miles west of Point Goleta off Naples, on the 16th off Cañada del Refugio, and on the 17th off Gaviota Pass. Cabrillo had difficulty in rounding Point Concepción because of storms, and for eight days he was forced to anchor his ships at San Miguel Island before finally attempting the passage. After several days of buf-

feting by the storms, he was driven back to anchorage off Gaviota Pass, where he remained three days, taking on wood and water. On November 6 he was finally able to round Point Concepción.

The Point Conception Light Station was established by the United States government in 1855, and the old lighthouse is still in use.

Point Argüello

Point Argüello, a rocky headland 20 miles southwest of Lompoc, forms, with Point Conception, the corners of California where the coastline turns from an approximate north and south direction to a line running east and west. Its historic interest is largely associated with the many ships that have been wrecked there.

The first of these was probably the U.S.S. Edith, wrecked in 1849. The story told is that the sailors aboard the Edith, being anxious to join the gold rush, deliberately ran the ship on the beach, where it was broken up by the waves. Some of the crew and passengers stayed for a short time at Rancho Nipomo (in San Luis Obispo County), where the hospitable ranchero, Captain William G. Dana, gave them horses and money so they could continue to the mines. Afterward the ship was salvaged by Dana and the materials were used on the rancho. The smokestack on the forge in the blacksmith shop was part of the wreckage put to good use by this thrifty Bostonian.

The most famous disaster occurring near Point Argüello took place on September 8, 1923, when seven United States destroyers southward bound in an evening fog piled on the rocks three miles north with a loss of some 22 men. Since then, the toll taken by the point from the procession of ships that constantly pass that way has included the passenger steamer Harvard, which went aground about one and one-half miles north of Point Argüello on May 30, 1931; the freighter Iowan in 1941; and the Greek freighter Ionnes Kulkundous on July 11, 1949. Remains of some of these vessels may still be seen just offshore. In 1941, in their fourth attack on coastal shipping, Japanese submarines attempted to torpedo the Standard Oil tanker H. M. Storey two miles offshore. The ship escaped unharmed. The old lighthouse at Point Argüello has been torn down and replaced with a fully automatic beacon and an electronic device known as Loran.

Along the coast some distance east of Points Argüello and Conception, and just a few miles west of Goleta, is the Ellwood Oil Field. On the evening of February 23, 1942, the Japanese submarine I-17, under Commander Kozo Nishino, came to the surface and, a little more than a mile offshore, shelled the oil field for 20 minutes. The damage was minor and there were no casualties. One oil well was hit and a pier was partially destroyed. Two large gasoline storage tanks, the primary target of the Japanese, were missed. The Tokyo press, however, reported that Santa Barbara had been devastated. Lumber from the damaged pier was subsequently sold as salvage and has been incorporated into "The Timbers," a nearby restaurant.

The Trail of Gaspar de Portolá

On the southwest corner of the grounds of Santa Barbara's courthouse is a boulder placed by the Santa Barbara Chapter, D.A.R., and set with a bronze tablet bearing the inscription: "In honor of Governor de Portolá, his officers and soldiers, and Fray Juan Crespí (diarist), the first white men to march through the wilderness of California. Arrived at Santa Barbara, August 18, 1769, and camped in this vicinity two days."

The land expedition from Mission San Diego to Monterey Bay, under direct command of Gaspar de Portolá, left San Diego on July 14, 1769. Traveling up the coast, the party had blazed a trail which was later the route followed approximately by El Camino Real ("the Royal Road"), along which the California mission chain was established.

On August 16 Portolá and his men made camp at an Indian village near what is now known as Rincón Point, on Rincón Creek, and the following day they reached another village where they found the natives building a canoe. From this incident, the place was called La Carpintería, a name retained by the present-day town near the site.

On August 18, Portolá reached a very large native town, where downtown Santa Barbara now stands. There he pitched camp. Proceeding up the coast along the Santa Barbara Channel, the party passed many Indian villages. The natives of this region were fishermen with large, well-made canoes, in which they plied between the mainland and the channel islands.

In the days following, the party passed up the coast, camping successively on the west side of the present city, at Goleta, Naples in Dos Pueblos Canyon, Tajiguas Creek, Gaviota, Santa Anita Creek, Cojo Ranch, Jalama Beach, Wild Horse Canyon under Point Argüello, Cañada Honda, and, on August 30, the mouth of the Santa Inés River at Surf. The next day camp was made near San Antonio Creek on the present Vandenberg Air Force Base, and on September 1 the party followed the route of the present state highway to Guadalupe Lake, beyond which lay the boundaries of what is now San Luis Obispo County.

The Anza Trail

Juan Bautista de Anza in 1774 followed a well-trodden path from San Gabriel to Monterey, broken first by Gaspar de Portolá and followed later a half-dozen times by Pedro Fages and also by Father Junípero Serra on his way to Mexico in 1772. On his hurried trip in the spring of 1774, Anza made only three camps in Santa Barbara County: west of Goleta, April 12; east of Rocky Point, April 13; and on the south bank of the Santa Inés River near its mouth, April 14. On April 15 Anza rode all the way from the Santa Inés River to Mission San Luís Obispo, a distance of over 50 miles. On his return from Monterey, he camped on the north bank of the Santa Inés River, April 26. On the 27th he met Father Serra on his way back from the City of Mexico. At the friar's urging, Anza recounted the story of his overland journey, and camped with him that night somewhere east of Point Concepción and west of Naples. On the 28th Anza continued, camping that night at Dos Pueblos (Naples).

The San Francisco colonists led by Anza in 1776 made camp at the following sites: Rincón Creek, west of Rincón Point, February 24; near Carpintería Landing, at an Indian village called by Father Font San Buenaventura, February 25; northeast of Mescal Island near the village of Mescaltitán which was west of Goleta, February 26; El Cojo Canyon, east of Point Concepción, February 27; near Surf, at the mouth of the Santa Inés River, February 28; and near the mouth of San Antonio Creek, February 29.

A tablet in honor of Anza has also been placed in the courthouse grounds at Santa Barbara.

An Ancient Sycamore Tree

The aged sycamore tree that stands on the corner of Milpas and Quinientos streets, Santa Barbara, was used as a bearing for sailing vessels as early as 1800. Travelers by land also passed by the great tree, which was visible for miles on land and sea. Portolá and his band of explorers, Serra and the other mission fathers, as they traveled up and down the coast founding missions, may, long ago, have been guided by the giant tree or have rested under its sheltering branches. It has been marked with a bronze tablet placed by the Santa Barbara Chapter, D.A.R.

Today, however, the old sycamore is outclassed as a landmark by the huge Moreton Bay fig tree at Chapala and Montecito streets, planted in 1877.

The Santa Barbara Presidio

Santa Barbara, the last of the four presidios founded by the Spanish government in Alta California, was established on April 21, 1782, by Governor Felipe de Neve and Lieutenant José Francisco Ortega and his 50 soldiers, accompanied by Fray Junípero Serra, who dedicated the site. Like the other presidios—San Diego, Monterey, and San Francisco—it was, for a time, under military rule but eventually acquired its own civil government.

The outlines of the old Santa Barbara Presidio (SRL 636) have been practically obliterated by the development of the modern city of Santa Barbara, but may still be roughly traced by the present De la Guerra, Carrillo, Anacapa, and Garden streets. The comandante's house, destroyed in the earthquake of 1925, formerly stood near the intersection of the present Santa Barbara and Cañon Perdido streets. Where the lines of the old presidio crossed these streets, the Native Sons of the Golden West have placed bronze markers in the sidewalks. El Cuartel, one of the small buildings in which the soldiers of the presidio were stationed, still stands at 122 East Cañon Perdido Street, between Santa Barbara and Anacapa streets. It is the oldest building in Santa Barbara and is now used by the Boy Scouts. Across the street at 121, the Caneda adobe is the second oldest and the only other structure remaining from the presidio. The southeast boundary of the presidio site has been marked by a boulder and tablet placed by the Santa Barbara Chapter, D.A.R.

The site of the Arrellanes adobe, also destroyed in the earthquake of 1925, was at 800 Santa Barbara Street at the corner of De la Guerra Street, at a point about 50 feet from the east corner of the old presidio walls. Said to have been erected as early as 1795, it was probably the first house of any importance to be built outside the presidio enclosure.

The site of the old presidio church, an adobe structure 24 × 60 feet, completed in 1797, was almost on the building line on the west side of Santa Barbara Street. Directly north, what was formerly Santa Barbara's first graveyard, the burial ground of the soldiers and early settlers until 1818, is now intersected by Carrillo Street.

Cañon Perdido Street, which cuts through the old site of the presidio, derives its name from an incident that occurred in the early spring of 1848. The American brig *Elizabeth* was wrecked on the coast near Santa Barbara, and one of its cannons became buried in the sand. An American official presumed that the gun had been stolen and caused the citizens of Santa Barbara to be fined $500. A cannon, allegedly the same one, is on display in the museum of the Santa Barbara Historical Society, but the most evident reminder of this bit of history is the street of the "lost cannon."

Mission Santa Barbara

Mission Santa Barbara *(SRL 309)* was not founded until four years after the establishment of the presidio. Father Serra had selected the site, and after his death in 1784, the work of building the mission was carried on by his successor, Father Fermín Francisco de Lasuén, who performed the ceremonies of consecration on December 16, 1786, although, according to Engelhardt, the feast day of St. Barbara, December 4, has always been "regarded and reported as the day of founding."

The building of the first temporary chapel and adjoining dwellings and storehouses was begun the following year. Gradually, the establishment grew in size and prosperity until, in 1807, there were over 1,700 neophytes living in the Indian village of 250 adobe huts that surrounded the mission.

In 1789 a new church of adobe roofed with tile replaced the temporary structure. In 1793 this church was replaced by a larger one, which was finished in 1794. This, in turn, was superseded by a more magnificent structure, the earthquake of 1812 having damaged the former building. The new structure, built on the same site, was dedicated on September 10, 1820. This building, with the marks of storm and earthquake upon it, has been maintained in keeping with its ancient aspect. The massive walls, six feet thick, the stone steps and tile floors, two of the six chapels built in the solid walls, which are of double thickness at these points, all make it the most solidly built of any of the missions. The temblor of 1925, however, necessitated almost rebuilding the church, and Father Augustine Hobrecht was tireless in seeing that the minutest detail was restored as before, only reinforcing the structure by modern methods so that the building might withstand future shocks. Further restoration was found to

Mission Santa Barbara

be necessary, and the towers and façade were rebuilt in 1953.

In the beautiful old cemetery, enclosed by high adobe walls and shaded by lovely trees and shrubs, are the graves of 4,000 Indians and 500 white people. One grave is said to be that of Juana María, an Indian woman reputed to have lived alone for 18 years on San Nicolás Island off the Santa Barbara Channel. Juana María was found and brought to Santa Barbara by Captain George Nidever in 1853. She died in 1854 and it is thought she was buried in the mission garden, although no record of the burial has been found in the mission archives nor is there any document bearing testimony of her baptism and the bestowal of the Christian name, Juana María, after her rescue. However, Captain Nidever's veracity and the high regard in which he was held in Santa Barbara, where he lived for over 50 years, lends sufficient weight to the story, to which he was the chief witness, to give it credence. A bronze tablet was placed at the grave by the Santa Barbara Chapter, D.A.R., in 1928.

Before the church stands a stone fountain of simple, harmonious design, and near it is a long stone trough, once used by the Indian women for laundry purposes. These units were constructed in 1808. About 500 feet north of the mission church, in what is now Mission Historical Park of the city of Santa Barbara, is a square stone reservoir, constructed in 1806, part of the irrigation system to collect water for the mission orchards and gardens. This reservoir, still in perfect condition, forms part of the water system of the city of Santa Barbara. Across Pedregoso Creek, about a mile and a half north of the mission in what is now called Mission Canyon, a dam was constructed in 1807. Now much silted up, it may be seen in the Santa Barbara Botanic Garden. Portions of the aqueduct may also be found there and at various points in the canyon. A bronze tablet has been placed just above the dam by La Cumbre Chapter, D.A.R.

Below the reservoir are ruins of the pottery kiln built in 1808, where utensils, adobe bricks, and tiles were made by the neophytes under the fathers' supervision. Northeast of the reservoir is the filter, or settling tank, where the water was purified for domestic use. Fairly well preserved, this interesting relic is decidedly picturesque, resembling an ornamental vault or tomb. East of the reservoir and above it are the ruins of a gristmill (1827) with its own reservoir, irregularly hexagonal in shape. The water system has been marked in Mission Historical Park by the State of California. (See Engelhardt, *Santa Barbara Mission*, p. 85, for a diagram of the mission irrigation system.)

Mission Santa Barbara has never suffered from the neglect and decay of the other missions after secularization. In 1842 the bishop's residence was changed from San Diego to Santa Barbara, and, in 1853, a petition to Rome resulted in making the mission a hospice, the beginning of an apostolic college for the education of Franciscan students for the priesthood, which is still maintained. This was the influence that saved Santa Barbara from neglect. Since its founding, it has been used continuously for religious observances. It is the only one of all the missions that has remained in the hands of the Franciscan Fathers since its founding, and is one of four now under their administration. For its historical and architectural importance to the United States, Mission Santa Barbara has been registered as a National Historic Landmark by the Department of the Interior.

The red-tiled corridors and domed belfries of Mission Santa Barbara stand on high ground west of the city, facing the sea, shedding "an air of Spanish languor, of perpetual siesta, over the pleasant city." Helen Hunt Jackson writes, "It is an inalienable benediction on the whole city."

Cieneguitas

In *Prehistoric Man of the Santa Barbara Coast*, David Banks Rogers gives the following description:

"About four miles west of the business center of the city, and nearly in front of St. Vincent's ... [School], the highway crosses an inconspicuous ravine in which thick undergrowth and small trees form an almost impenetrable jungle as far south as Modoc Road. Throughout this tangled growth meander spring-fed rivulets that in places expand into treacherous bogs, a characteristic that early gave to the locality the name that still endures, Cieneguitas, 'the swamps.' ...

"The first mention of Cieneguitas that we have found in the annals is when, on the morning of August 20th, 1769, Captain Gaspar de Portolá, at the head of his little army of sixty-five leather-jacketed soldiers, and two Franciscan monks,

Ruins at Original Site of La Purísima, Lompoc

emerged from Arroyo Burro, where they had camped the night before, and were met by a reception committee from the extensive village that clustered about the slough.

"At the time of the founding of the Mission, for some unknown reason, this village alone, of the many in the vicinity, was permitted to retain its organization. Early in 1803, the friars even went so far as to erect a substantial adobe chapel for the use of the villagers. This was located immediately to the west of the cienega, about midway between the present Modoc Road and the Coast Highway.

"About this same time, several substantial, single-roomed adobe residential huts, with tile roofs, were erected for the natives....

"All of the structures erected under the guidance of the fathers were especially sturdy. As late as 1886, a large part of the chapel was still in place."

Misión La Purísima Concepción

The first site of Misión La Purísima Concepción is one-half mile south of the center of the town of Lompoc. Father Fermín Francisco de Lasuén founded the mission on December 8, 1787, the Feast of the Immaculate Conception of Mary. A temporary building was begun in March 1788, but this was soon replaced by an adobe structure roofed with tile, which was finished in 1802. This building was totally destroyed by the earthquake of 1812, but fragmentary ruins can be seen to this day—the only instance among California's missions of physical evidence at a site other than the present one. The ruins are on both sides of the south end of F Street. On one side there are bits of wall and a historical marker; on the other, a mound of adobe is used as the backdrop for a garden at a private residence. The great gash made by the earthquake may still be seen on the hillside above the ruins.

A new church, about four miles northeast of the first site, was promptly erected by Father Mariano Payéras, who did effective work in both the old and the new locations. His death in 1823 was a great loss to the mission. The Indian uprising that spread from Mission Santa Inés in 1824 struck heavily at La Purísima, which was captured and held for several weeks. Soldiers from Monterey finally dispersed the Indians.

At one time La Purísima was very prosperous, but the neglect that followed secularization and confiscation and the inroads of the elements caused its steady disintegration. Finally it became a crumbling ruin, its roof gone, its walls fallen and half choked in wild mustard and elder bushes. Only the stately row of white pillars, in Grecian beauty, testified to past glory and charm. Such was its state when, in the mid-1930's, it was restored and rebuilt by the Civilian Conservation Corps and the National Park Service. Subsequently it became La Purísima Mission State Historic Park (*SRL 340*). It is one of two missions owned by the state, the other being San Francisco Solano at Sonoma.

La Purísima, in its lovely rural setting, far from the noise and activity of modern civilization, is

Interior, Mission Santa Inés

the only one of California's 21 missions to be restored as a complete mission establishment. The state property consists of almost 1,000 acres, an area large enough to take in the water system in Purísima Valley. A self-guiding round-trip hike of one mile enables the visitor to gain a complete picture of mission life at its height. Archaeological investigation continues to the present.

Besides the main buildings—church, shops and quarters, and padres' residence—restoration has included numerous outbuildings, gardens, soap factory, tannery, and reservoirs. A visit to Mission La Purísima Concepción is an educational experience unparalleled in California.

Misión Santa Inés

Mission Santa Inés *(SRL 305)* was founded in order to reach the Indians living east of the coast. Father Estévan Tápis made a survey of the country in 1798, and from his report a site for the proposed mission was chosen in the beautiful valley of Calahuasá, 45 miles northwest of Santa Barbara via Gaviota Pass. Thirteen Indian rancherías in the vicinity, with an estimated population of over 1,100, gave promise of many converts.

After the death of Father Lasuén in 1803, Father Tápis succeeded him as Padre Presidente, and in 1804 he founded the new church at Santa Inés. A simple chapel was erected at first, to be replaced, after the earthquake of 1812, by a building of brick and adobe, roofed and floored with tile. This structure, completed in 1817, still stands in the open fields with its background of rugged, purple mountains.

The Indian uprising of 1824 started at Mission Santa Inés, the occasion for discontent being the harsh treatment by the soldiers. The Indians revolted, burned a large number of the mission buildings, leaving the church unharmed, and escaped to La Purísima, where they were finally overcome by soldiers from Monterey.

After the secularization of the missions in the 1830's, Pope Gregory XVI took steps to establish California as a diocese with its own bishop. In 1840 one of the Franciscan friars, Francisco García Diego y Moreno, was appointed and consecrated Bishop of Both Californias, his territory including Baja California as well as the present state of California. Bishop Diego established the first seminary for the training of priests in California at Mission Santa Inés in 1844. The seminaries of the several Roman Catholic dioceses of California can all trace their beginnings to Santa Inés.

Santa Inés suffered in material wealth from the effects of secularization, as did nearly all of the missions. It was in a sad state of ruin until early in the twentieth century, when it was restored, retaining much of the old charm: Indian frescoes and hand-carved doors, harmonious arcades and flower-filled patio, and a beautiful campanile, its plain wall pierced, as at Mission San Gabriel, by niches for the ancient bells which ring for prayer.

Mission Santa Inés is located in the town of Solvang, a community of Danish people who hold the mission in high regard. It is three and one-half miles east of Buellton on Highway 246. It is now administered by the Capuchin Fathers, a branch of the Franciscan order.

Near the mission are the stone ruins of an old gristmill, built by Joseph Chapman in 1820 and marked by the California Centennials Commission on September 9, 1950.

Santa Barbara's Adobe Heritage

Santa Barbara ranks with Monterey as a city of beautiful old adobe homes. Through the efforts of the Santa Barbara Historical Society, under the leadership of W. Edwin Gledhill, steps have been taken by the city of Santa Barbara to ensure the permanent preservation of these striking evidences of its heritage. After an act was passed in Sacramento in 1959 enabling cities to take such steps, Santa Barbara enacted "El Pueblo Viejo" ordinance in 1960, setting aside 16 blocks bounded by State, Figueroa, Laguna, and Ortega streets, as a historic area. Within these boundaries no building of historical or architectural value is to be destroyed or altered, and no new construction is to be undertaken that does not conform to the style of architecture of the old adobes. This pioneer legislation may well serve as a model for similar protective zoning in other parts of California.

Casa de la Guerra (SRL 307), which, after the mission, is perhaps the most interesting remaining landmark of old Spanish days in Santa Barbara, was built by José Antonio Julián de la Guerra y Noriega, with the aid of Indian labor, during the years 1819–26. One of the adobe bricks in the front corridor of the old house still bears the date 1826 plainly marked on it.

Don José Antonio, a native of Spain, came from Mexico to California as a lieutenant in 1806. There he married María Antonia Juliana Carrillo, and in 1815 was made comandante of the Presidio of Santa Barbara, an office he held until 1842. De la Guerra was a man of more than ordinary character and ability, exercising a strong political and moral influence on the history of Alta California in his day. His home was the center of social life in Santa Barbara and a stopping place for many distinguished visitors. Among others, Richard Henry Dana, author of *Two Years Before the Mast,* visited the adobe mansion in 1834 and again in 1859. In his book he describes the wedding of his host's daughter and gives a pleasing picture of the gaieties, the beautiful women, and the courtly gentlemen.

The patios, shaded corridors, and rambling rooms of the De la Guerra adobe, at 11–19 East De la Guerra Street, are now occupied by studios and shops in old Spanish style. It has become the nucleus of an art colony, as well as the motif of the later Santa Barbara that grew up since the earthquake of 1925. An architectural renaissance, imbued with the breath of old Spain, has made of Santa Barbara a vivid, colorful, distinctive city in which unity and harmony of style form an artistic ensemble. And the heart of it all is the old De la Guerra house, typifying the cameo-sharp outlines of California-Spanish architecture and the romantic and historic charm of the past from which it survives.

El Paseo, the Street in Spain, designed by James Osborne Craig and built in 1923, centers about this old adobe and the two adjacent Gaspar Oreña adobes (1849 and 1858). There, during Santa Barbara's annual "Old Spanish Days" fiesta, the cool shops and corridors are thronged with costumed revelers, many of them descendants of the courtly Spanish dons and doñas who came to California in the eighteenth and nineteenth centuries. Across from the adobes is De la Guerra Plaza, center of Santa Barbara's city government, in which a state historical marker has been placed.

The Carrillo adobe (SRL 721), at 11 East Carrillo Street one-half block east of State Street, was built about 1825 by Daniel Hill, carpenter, mason, and "general factotum," a native of Massachusetts who came to California in 1823 and married Rafaela Ortega. In 1833 in this house was born the first child of American parents in Santa Barbara, Isobel, daughter of Thomas Oliver Larkin, first American consul in California, and Rachel (Hobson) Holmes Larkin. It became the home of Captain John Wilson and Doña Ramona Carrillo de Wilson, and, later, of Guillermo Carrillo. The building was purchased in 1928 by Major Max C. Fleischmann, and later it was given to the Santa Barbara Foundation to be preserved as one of the historic buildings of Santa Barbara.

On the north side of Carrillo Street just east of the Carrillo adobe is the site of the Casa de Aguirre, perhaps the most famous of all the old Spanish homes in its day. It was built by Don José Antonio Aguirre, and to it he brought his bride, Francisca Estudillo, in 1842. The house of 19 rooms was built in the form of a quadrangle, enclosing a paved court or patio. Around the patio a *corredor,* shaded by a roof supported on hand-carved posts, gave sheltered access to the house or served as an outdoor living room. An owner of ships, a man of "fine presence, affable in manner and well-liked by all . . . and a wealthy trader"—as Bancroft characterizes him—"Don Antonio was an excellent type of the old-time Spanish merchant, keeping aloof for the most part from smuggling and politics, though often employed by the government." The old house was torn down in 1880.

The Covarrubias adobe (SRL 308), located at 715 Santa Barbara Street between De la Guerra and Ortega streets, was built in 1817 by Domingo Carrillo, whose daughter María married José María Covarrubias in 1838. This house is a fine example of California architecture, and within its hospitable walls many gay social gatherings have taken place. Owing to the fact that the sunshine was permitted to enter the rooms through skylights, the building is in a remarkable state of preservation. Adjacent to this adobe is the so-called "Historic Adobe." It is supposed to have been built about 1836 near the present corner of State and Carrillo streets for Concepción Pico de Carrillo, sister of Governor Pío Pico. In 1903 it was taken down brick by brick and reconstructed at Carrillo and Anacapa streets. In 1922 it was again moved and rebuilt in the same fashion at its present location by John R. Southworth. In 1938 the Covarrubias and "Historic" adobes were acquired by Los Rancheros Visitadores, an equestrian organization. They are now the property of the Santa Barbara Historical Society, which has built its museum, of adobe in authentic style, on the adjoining land at Santa Barbara and De la Guerra streets.

Other adobes in downtown Santa Barbara include the Rafael Gonzales (about 1825) at 835 Laguna Street, the Birabent (late 1850's) at 820 Santa Barbara Street, the Santiago de la Guerra (reputedly built about 1812 but now much altered) at 110 East De la Guerra Street, the Bruno Orella (of which very little remains within a modern building) at 1029 State Street, and the Meridian at the rear of 114 East De la Guerra Street. The charming little Buenaventura Pico adobe, built before 1850, is dwarfed by the towering modern buildings that surround it. It is hidden behind the old Dr. Knox home at 916 Anacapa Street. The Miranda adobe, built about 1840, and the old guardhouse have been incorporated into a restaurant at De la Guerra Street and Presidio Avenue. The Cordero adobes stand at 304 East Carrillo Street and 906 Garden Street (behind a store). There are also the William Dover adobe at 725 Yanonali Street, the two-story Botiller at 1023 Bath Street, the Frank Kirk at 421 East Figueroa Street, and the Carlos Cota at the northwest corner of East Cañon Perdido and Laguna streets.

Amid all these historic adobes are buildings of later date that nevertheless contribute to the aesthetic interest of the city. The Lobero Theater, at 33 East Cañon Perdido Street, stands on the site of the old adobe theater (*SRL 361*) opened by José Lobero in 1872. The original structure was torn down in the 1920's. The culmination of Santa Barbara's architectural renaissance is the county courthouse, designed by William Mooser and dedicated on August 14, 1929. It is one of the most beautiful adaptations of Spanish-California architecture in the entire state and one of the notable public buildings of America.

At the corner of State and De la Guerra streets a bronze tablet was placed by the Native Sons of the Golden West on August 15, 1929, in commemoration of the first raising of the American flag in Santa Barbara by Lieutenant Colonel John C. Frémont on December 27, 1846. Lieutenant Theodore Talbot and his small band of rangers, who had occupied the town in July 1846, participated in the ceremonies. The house over which the flag was raised and in which Frémont had his headquarters at the time was the residence of Captain Alpheus B. Thompson, later known as the St. Charles Hotel. It no longer stands. Thompson came to California from New England in 1825 as supercargo on the ship *Washington*. He married Francisca Carrillo.

In addition to "El Pueblo Viejo," the Santa Barbara Historical Society has created an architectural-historical area centering around the Trussell-Winchester adobe (*SRL 559*) at 412 West Montecito Street. Captain Horatio Gates Trussell, a native of Maine, built it in 1854, shortly after his arrival in California. Into it he incorporated timbers from the *S. S. Winfield Scott*, wrecked in 1853 on Anacapa Island. The adobe was later acquired by the Winchester and Hastings families. It is an important example of the transition from adobe to frame construction in the early American period. To this location have been moved two old Victorian houses that would otherwise have been destroyed in the name of progress. The Judge Charles Fernald mansion, built in the early 1860's, formerly stood at 422 Santa Barbara Street. The Hunt-Stambach house was originally built in the 1870's at Victoria Street and Mora Villa Avenue.

Montecito, Santa Barbara's neighbor to the east, is a community of beautiful mansions. Here, too, are relics of adobe days. The Pedro Masini house, oldest two-story adobe in the Santa Barbara area, was reputedly built in 1820. It stands at the junction of Sheffield Drive, Ortega Hill Road, and North Jameson Lane, just north of Freeway 101. The Hosmer adobe is at 461 San Ysidro Road. The same road leads to the San Ysidro Guest Ranch, at 900 San Ysidro Lane, where one room of the old Casa San Ysidro still stands.

West of Santa Barbara is Goleta, location of the University of California at Santa Barbara. Here stands an adobe built in the 1840's by Daniel Hill, who also built the Carrillo adobe in the city. Enlarged and modernized by James G. Williams early in the twentieth century, it is covered with wooden siding and not easily recognizable as an adobe. It continues to serve as a private residence and is located at 35 La Patera Lane, north of Hollister Avenue.

El Refugio

About 20 miles west of the city of Santa Barbara, the Cañada del Refugio once marked the eastern boundary of the great Rancho Nuestra Señora del Refugio, which ran westward along the sea for 25 miles to the Cañada del Cojo. Here in the Cañada del Refugio the Ortega family lived for many years. José Francisco de Ortega, who had accompanied Portolá on his expedition to Monterey in 1769 and had assisted in the founding of the Presidio of Santa Barbara in 1782, was rewarded for his services by being given permission to occupy this land in 1794. After his death, it was granted to his son, José María Ortega.

The coast of El Refugio is closely linked with romance, for here on the beach Don José had his embarcadero, where he engaged in genteel smuggling, and here the pirate Hippolyte de Bouchard landed in 1818 and sacked and burned the adobe casa that stood at the canyon's entrance facing the sea and El Camino Real. Here, too, the Yankee lad, Joseph John Chapman, had deserted from the pirate ship. He later married into the Ortega family and proved to be a very useful citizen.

Don José built his second adobe about three miles back in the Cañada del Refugio. It and the old vineyard, one of the most famous in California, have disappeared. The road that winds through the canyon and up the mountain leads down into the valley of Santa Inés by way of Refugio Pass. Here the padres often passed on their way from Mission Santa Barbara to Mission Santa Inés beyond the mountains.

West of El Refugio two Ortega adobes still

Ortega Adobe, Arroyo Hondo near Gaviota

stand, one of them completely rebuilt, the other much as it was originally and still owned by the Ortega family. At a point two and one-half miles west of Cañada del Refugio and Refugio Beach State Park, a private road turns north from Highway 101 and leads two miles along Tajiguas Creek to one of California's most beautiful adobe homes. It was originally built perhaps as early as 1800 and enlarged and improved in 1879. It fell into ruin, and in 1924 it was taken down and rebuilt by Kirk B. Johnson, according to the designs of architect George Washington Smith. It has since passed out of Johnson's hands and has undergone further renovation.

The adobe presently owned by Vicente Ortega was built by Pedro and José Ortega about 1850. It may be glimpsed from the westbound lanes only of Highway 101 at a point a little over two miles west of the Tajiguas turnoff, or less than four and one-half miles east of Gaviota. The adobe is situated deep in the ravine of Arroyo Hondo. Before the railroad and the highway bridged the ravine, the old stage road passed the door of the adobe and wound up the canyon wall. A closer look would reveal that the adobe has seven rooms, besides frame additions, and that it retains the integrity of its original construction, but it is the view from above that merits it a place of honor among California landmarks. Cullimore describes it as "a rare gem, in a perfect setting."

North of Gaviota, Highway 101 crosses Gaviota Pass *(SRL 248)*. Soldiers from Santa Barbara waited in ambush here on Christmas Day, 1846, to prevent John C. Frémont and his battalion from taking the city. Frémont, however, was advised of the plot and accomplished his objective by using San Marcos Pass instead.

The San Marcos Pass

San Marcos Pass, about 15 miles northwest of Santa Barbara, was one of the passes over which the early explorers and mission fathers crossed from the coast to the inland valleys. Gaviota Pass, the most northerly of the passes, is 28 miles farther up the coast from Santa Barbara.

In 1846, on his way from Monterey to reinforce Commodore Stockton in Los Angeles during the period of American occupation, John C. Frémont eluded the Californian soldiers who were waiting for him in ambush in Gaviota Pass, by taking the route over the San Marcos grade instead. The lat-

ter route was known to very few and presented many difficulties. Guided by Benjamin Foxen, the Americans succeeded in reaching the top after swinging the artillery across the intervening chasms on ropes, an all-day struggle. From the summit, Foxen's eldest son, William, led the men down the mountain and into Santa Barbara.

Beside the old trail, 17 miles from Santa Barbara and about 12 miles northwest of the coast highway, U. S. 101, a boulder has been placed by the Santa Barbara Chapter, D.A.R., on which is a bronze tablet bearing the legend: "In honor of Lieutenant-Colonel John C. Frémont, his soldiers and guide, W. B. Foxen, who marched over the San Marcos Pass, December 25, 1846, and took peaceable possession of Santa Barbara, while the Californians waited for them in ambush in Gaviota Pass."

Foxen Canyon

Located in Foxen Canyon about 15 miles northwest of Los Olivos and 25 miles southeast of Santa Maria is the site of the old Foxen home, of which traces are still visible. Rancho Tinaquaic, on which it was located, comprised two leagues of land and was occupied by Victor Linares by May 1837. In 1837 and 1842, this rancho was granted to William Benjamin Foxen, an Englishman who had settled in California in 1828. He was baptized a Catholic as William Domingo Foxen, married Eduarda Osuna, and became a citizen of Alta California. The Californians often referred to him as Don Julián.

Here in December 1846, John C. Frémont arrived with his army of 700 men on their way to Santa Barbara and Los Angeles. According to Juan Francisco Dana, son of William G. Dana, in a 1931 account of the story, Frémont had been told by William G. Dana at Rancho Nipomo (San Luis Obispo County), where he had camped on December 18, that the Californians were waiting for him in ambush at Gaviota Pass, the main passage through the mountains, a narrow defile between towering walls of granite from which huge boulders could be rolled down upon a passing enemy. Frémont was advised to seek the services of Foxen, a man familiar with the country to the southwest where an alternate and more difficult pass might be crossed. (According to other accounts, it was Foxen himself who warned Frémont of the ambush.)

Proceeding to Rancho Tinaquaic, Frémont camped on December 20 in the woods near the Foxen home. There, according to Dana's account, he solicited the aid of Foxen, who, though "torn between loyalty to the Californians and the tie of English blood which bound him to the invaders," granted the request and led the little army over San Marcos Pass and into Santa Barbara unharmed. As a consequence of this deed Foxen, for some time afterward, suffered at the hands of his neighbors, who, on more than one occasion, set fire to his rancho buildings.

Benjamin Foxen died in the 1870's and lies buried under a marble column in the family cemetery at the head of Foxen Canyon, four miles southeast of Sisquoc via Foxen Canyon Road. Nearby stands the memorial chapel built in 1876 by his daughter Ramona Wickenden. It is located high on a hill and can be seen gleaming white for miles around.

From the chapel and cemetery it is less than two miles southeast on Foxen Canyon Road to the Frederick Wickenden adobe. Wickenden married Ramona Foxen in 1860 and two years later built the central portion of the structure of adobe, making frame additions through the years. The house, now designated as headquarters of Rancho Tinaquaic, served also as store, post office, and stage station. Wickenden died in 1918 at the age of 93. Another mile and a half along the road brings one to the approximate site of Frémont's camp on the old Foxen ranch, which has been marked by the Pioneers Section of the Minerva Literary Club of Santa Maria. Less than two miles southeast of this marker, on the right side of the road, is an adobe mound, all that remains of Benjamin Foxen's home. It has also been marked.

Other Landmarks of
Northern Santa Barbara County

On the south side of the Santa Inés River at Buellton, just west of Highway 101, is the adobe built in 1853 by Dr. Ramón de la Cuesta. It has 13 rooms and remains much in its original condition. De la Cuesta came to California in 1849 and two years later purchased Rancho La Vega, some 8,000 acres. The old adobe is a private residence.

East of Buellton is the Danish town of Solvang, home of Mission Santa Inés. The old mission stood practically alone until the founding of the settlement in 1911. Solvang, which means "sunny field," grew and prospered around Atterdag College, built in 1914. Many Danish farmers were attracted by the climate and soil fertility of the Santa Inés Valley.

North of Solvang is Ballard, a former stagecoach stop. Two old adobes are standing at Grand and Santa Barbara avenues. From early times a stage station had been maintained at Los Olivos, a town that really came into existence as a station on the narrow-gauge Pacific Coast Railroad in 1887. Mattei's Tavern, an old stage stop, is still standing here.

West of Buellton was Rancho Santa Rosa, a grant of some 17,000 acres made to Francisco Cota in 1839. The old ranch house, built of adobe on a knoll overlooking the property, is still standing, restored to something of its original grandeur. In 1868 the rancho was bought by Joseph W. Cooper and in the 1890's it was leased to Leon Carteri, who had married a daughter of Benjamin Foxen. Shortly thereafter the Cooper family returned to live in the old house but left it vacant in 1912. Subsequently it fell into a state of dilapidation and seemed doomed to crumble into ruin. Plans to make it a county park in 1938 did not materialize. Fortunately, however, it has since been renovated and once again serves as a private residence. It is located on Mail Road near Santos Road, less than a mile south of Highway 246 at a point six miles west of Buellton.

The Lompoc Oil Field lies in the Purísima Hills north of the old mission and the city of Lompoc. Here is a historic well, Hill 4 (*SRL 582*). It is the first oil well in which a water shut-off was attained by pumping cement through the tubing and back of the casing. The development of the modern cementing technique, of which this well was the forerunner, has increased the productive life of thousands of oil wells and made available millions of barrels of oil that might otherwise have remained in subterranean storage. Hill 4, spudded in 1905 and completed the following year, was drilled to a total depth of 2,507 feet by the Union Oil Company of California. It produced for over 45 years.

Rancho Jesús María, over 40,000 acres, was granted to Lucas Antonio and José A. Olivera on April 8, 1837. The old adobe ranch house is somewhat altered and is now used as a guest house by the military at Vandenberg Air Force Base, a missile-testing center that was once Camp Cooke, an army base. The area on which the adobe stands was at one time owned by E. G. Marshall of Casmalia. About four miles northwest of the Vandenberg main gate on the Lompoc-Casmalia road, and not far from the San Antonio Creek Road junction, a turnoff to the left is marked "Marshallia Ranch." From this point it is about one mile to the adobe. Vandenberg Air Force Base also includes Point Sal, an important shipping point for Santa Maria Valley grain in the 1890's. Only a little cemetery and a few old trees remain here from earlier days.

The first settlement in Santa Maria Valley was known as La Graciosa and was located a short distance southwest of Orcutt. Near Orcutt there is also an interesting pioneer cemetery. It is on Bradley Road, off Clark Avenue, about two and one-half miles southeast of town. Six miles northwest of Orcutt, at the right side of Highway 1, the old Elizalde adobe still serves as a private home on the Righetti Ranch.

The town of Guadalupe in the northwestern corner of Santa Barbara County was named for the old Mexican rancho on which it is located. Rancho Guadalupe, of 43,681 acres, was granted on March 21, 1840, to Diego Olivera, described by Bancroft as a man who "clung to his old Spanish ways, dress and ideas to the last," and to Teodoro Arrellanes, a man of "genial temper and gentlemanly manners, locally a kind of ranchero prince." The first adobes were erected at Guadalupe by Arrellanes in 1840. The large one-story adobe, picturesque and rambling, that still stands on 10th Street near Guadalupe Avenue (Highway 1) was built by the Arrellanes family about 1849. Nearby stood a two-story adobe erected in 1868 by John B. Ward, who married Concepción Estudillo, daughter of José Joaquín Estudillo of Rancho San Leandro (Alameda County); unfortunately this adobe has been torn down. The two adobes were at one time the property of the Druids, a fraternal order.

Santa Maria Valley, about 35 miles long and from three to ten miles wide, is known as the "Valley of the Gardens" because of its extensive agricultural development. The city of Santa Maria, first called Grangeville and then Central City, was founded in 1874.

Southeast of Santa Maria, across many miles of

Dr. Shaw Adobe, near Los Alamos

hills on which cattle still graze, is Los Alamos. Until 1876 the main stage line between Santa Barbara and San Luis Obispo ran through Foxen Canyon, and a station was maintained at the Foxen Ranch. After that year it went through Los Alamos Valley instead, and a station was established at Los Alamos. Near this old town a few adobes from Mexican days still stand. Rancho Los Alamos was a grant of 48,803 acres made to José Antonio de la Guerra y Carrillo by Governor Alvarado on March 9, 1839. De la Guerra was a son of José Antonio de la Guerra y Noriega of Santa Barbara. Subsequently the rancho was acquired by Gaspar Oreña, brother-in-law of the younger De la Guerra. The De la Guerra-Oreña adobe, now owned by the De Koch family, descendants of Oreña, is beautifully preserved. It is located three and one-half miles west of Los Alamos just off the road leading to Vandenberg Air Force Base. Part of Rancho Los Alamos eventually came into the hands of Edward L. Doheny, the oil magnate.

Adjoining Rancho Los Alamos was Rancho Laguna, the present main street of Los Alamos being the dividing line between these two old grants. On Rancho Laguna is an adobe built by Dr. James B. Shaw, who laid out the town of Los Alamos. It is located behind a frame house on Price Ranch Road, a mile and a half from town. This road branches from the frontage road on the northeast side of the freeway.

North of Los Alamos and southeast of Santa Maria is another area in which a few old adobe relics may be found. Near the junction of the Sisquoc and Cuyama rivers stands the beautiful Juan Pacífico Ontiveros adobe, built about 1830. It had fallen into a state of ruin but was carefully restored by Captain and Mrs. G. Allan Hancock. Half a mile north of the settlement of Garey is Santa Maria Mesa Road. At a point one mile east on this road, a private road turns north and leads one mile to the old adobe.

One mile southeast of Garey on the left side of the road is the Ruiz adobe, disguised as a green wooden house. Another mile and a quarter brings one to the community of Sisquoc. From this point it is one and three-quarters miles via Foxen Canyon Road to the Juan Flores adobe, now owned by Raymond Ontiveros Goodchild. One-half mile further southeast is the adobe built

by Juan Pedro Olivera and now owned by Grace Ontiveros. A short distance beyond this adobe Foxen Canyon Road intersects Tepusquet Canyon Road. Two and one-half miles north on the latter road is the Florentino Ontiveros adobe of Rancho Tepusquet, far off to the left of the road.

In the northeastern corner of Santa Barbara County are the two Ranchos Cuyama, both of which extend into San Luis Obispo County. They are located in the remote Cuyama Valley, which is currently experiencing an oil boom. One was granted to José María Rojo on April 24, 1843, and consisted of 22,193 acres; the other was granted to Cesario Lataillade on June 9, 1846, and encompassed some 48,827 acres. Both were patented to Lataillade's widow, María Antonia de la Guerra y Lataillade, who married Gaspar Oreña.

Much of Santa Barbara County is rugged mountainous area included in Los Padres National Forest and penetrated by few roads. As early as 1925 Robert E. Easton led the efforts to establish a sanctuary in the upper Sisquoc region for the vanishing California condor.

SOURCES

Bolton, Herbert Eugene. *Anza's California Expeditions.* 5 vols. University of California Press, Berkeley, 1930.
—— *Fray Juan Crespí, Missionary Explorer on the Pacific Coast, 1769–1774.* University of California Press, Berkeley, 1927.
Bryant, Edwin. *What I Saw in California.* D. Appleton & Co., New York, 1848, 1849.
The California Missions, a Pictorial History. By the editorial staff of Sunset Books. Lane Book Co., Menlo Park, 1964.
Carlson, Vada F. *This Is Our Valley.* Compiled by the Santa Maria Valley Historical Society. Ethel May Dorsey, editor in chief. Westernlore Press, Los Angeles, 1959.
Cullimore, Clarence. *Santa Barbara Adobes.* Santa Barbara Book Publishing Co., Santa Barbara, 1948.
Dana, Juan Francisco, as told to John Edwin Hogg. "Ten Decades on a California Rancho," *Touring Topics,* XXIII, No. 11 (November 1931), 16–19, 44.
Elder, David Paul. *The Old Spanish Missions of California.* Paul Elder & Co., San Francisco, 1913.
Engelhardt, Zephyrin. *Santa Barbara Mission.* The James H. Barry Co., San Francisco, 1923.
Hardacre, Emma. "Eighteen Years Alone," *Scribner's Magazine,* XX, 657 (September 1880).
Harrington, John P. "Exploration of the Burton Mound at Santa Barbara, California," *Forty-fourth Annual Report of the Bureau of American Ethnology,* pp. 30–168. Government Printing Office, Washington, D.C., 1928.
Hawley, Walter A. *Early Days in Santa Barbara.* Privately published, Santa Barbara, 1920.
Hill, Laurance L. *Santa Barbara, Tierra Adorada.* Security First National Bank of Los Angeles, Los Angeles, 1930.
Jackson, Helen Hunt. *Glimpses of California and the Missions.* Little, Brown, Boston, 1903.
Krec, Ted. "Enemy Off Ellwood," *Westways,* XLVIII, No. 2 (February 1956), 6–7.
Older, Mrs. Fremont. *California Missions and Their Romances.* Coward-McCann, New York, 1938.
Rogers, David Banks. *Prehistoric Man of the Santa Barbara Coast.* Santa Barbara Museum of Natural History, Santa Barbara, 1929.
Southworth, John R. *Santa Barbara and Montecito, Past and Present.* Oreña Studios, Santa Barbara, 1920.
Storke, Mrs. Yda Addis. *Memorial and Biographical History of the Counties of Santa Barbara, San Luis Obispo, and Ventura, California.* The Lewis Publishing Co., Chicago, 1891.
Tompkins, Walter A. "California's Unknown Soldier," *Westways,* XLVII, No. 11 (November 1955), 26–27.

Santa Clara County

SANTA CLARA COUNTY (named after Mission Santa Clara, which was established in that region in 1777) was one of the original 27 counties. San Jose has been the county seat from the beginning, and was California's first state capital. Many pre-state records written in Spanish are filed in the courthouse.

Indian Mounds

Indians in considerable numbers dwelt in the region of Santa Clara County when the first white explorers came this way. Portolá's party reported in 1769 "many and large villages" of generous and affable natives at the lower end of San Francisco Bay. Anza, in 1776, saw three large rancherías with many residents on the Guadalupe River and another about two miles to the north, possibly near the lower end of Moffett Field, where Chief Íñigo later had his ranch.

Even after homes had been established by the Spanish, some of the old Indian villages were occupied at times, for the wife of Don Secundino Robles said that three groups of natives were within a short distance of their house, which had been built between the present South Palo Alto and Castro Station on the Southern Pacific Railroad. One of these was undoubtedly the place known as the Castro Indian Mound. It lay near Castro Station and was, until its destruction, the largest mound in the lower bay region. Spreading out to a width of 290 feet, it had a length of 450 feet and a height of ten feet or more. Excavations were made in this mound in past years by scientists from the University of California at Berkeley and from Stanford University, both of which have museum specimens from the place.

The skeletons found there were from two to four feet below the surface of the ground and lay facing in differing directions, showing no particular system of burial. Certain peculiarities were noted in the skulls.

The main artifacts discovered were mortars, pestles, bone strigils, awls, needles, chains of small beads, and an occasional bowl of a soapstone pipe evidently obtained through barter. The few obsidian implements found must also have been brought in. The height of the mound was reduced by means of scrapers, and much of the soil was completely leveled and included within a subdivision. This "kitchen midden," unlike those farther north along the bayshore, showed a scarcity of certain ordinary species of shell and a preponderance of a small species less satisfactory for food but common in the entire bay area. The almost exclusive appearance of this small species

of shell throughout the depth of the mound seems to prove that the salt marsh along the bay has been an effective barrier to more desirable species of edible shellfish from the time of the earliest habitation of the mound.

Today at various places where excavations, or even mere cultivation of field crops, is carried on, artifacts and human remains are sometimes unearthed. Such was the case just south of Los Altos, where mortars and pestles were found. Skeletons have been discovered along the banks of Coyote Creek, and it is surmised by ethnologists and antiquarians that careful search would reveal the sites of old Indian encampments on many of the lesser streams.

On the northeast side of Middlefield Road south of Marion Avenue in Palo Alto, is the site of an Indian village. Many oaks formerly grew on the spot. This place is now built up with homes.

On the former Adams School grounds five miles west of Gilroy may be seen stationary mortars in large flat boulders. Arrowheads and stone implements have been plowed up in several fields in the vicinity.

Old Trails of Santa Clara

In 1769, Gaspar de Portolá was sent by José de Gálvez, visitador general to New Spain, to take possession of and fortify the ports of San Diego and Monterey in Alta California. Portolá failed to find Monterey on this expedition but discovered instead the Bay of San Francisco.

Leaving their camp on San Pedro Creek on November 4, Portolá's party passed down into the Santa Clara Valley, by way of what are now the Crystal Springs Lakes and Woodside, to the northwest bank of San Francisquito Creek at

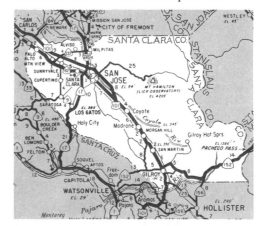

Menlo Park. Fray Crespí, chronicler of the expedition, says:

"We pitched camp in a plain some six leagues long, grown with good oaks and live oaks, and with much other timber in the neighborhood. This plain has two good arroyos with a good flow of water, and at the southern end of the estuary there is a good river, with plenty of water, which passes through the plain mentioned, well wooded on its banks [Guadalupe River]. . . . This entire port is surrounded by many and large villages of barbarous heathen who are very affable, mild, and docile, and very generous."

The site of the camp under a tall redwood is generally placed across the creek from the lone redwood tree that stands beside the Southern Pacific Railroad at Palo Alto. Beneath this tree is a boulder on which is a bronze tablet carrying the following inscription:

"Under this giant redwood, The Palo Alto, November 6–11, 1769, camped Portolá and his men on the expedition that discovered San Francisco Bay. This was the assembling point for their reconnoitering parties. Here in 1774, Padre Palou erected a cross to mark the site of a proposed mission. The celebrated Pedro Font topographical map, of 1776, contained the drawing of the original double-trunked tree, making The Palo Alto the first official living California landmark. Placed by the Historic Landmarks Committee, N.S.G.W., November 7, 1926."

This tree was long a landmark for the Indians and later for the Spanish explorers and the missionaries and soldiers traveling up and down the peninsula between San Francisco and the missions of Santa Clara and San José. The Spaniards called it the *palo alto* ("high tree"), and the name passed on to the modern city that grew up beside it, the college town of Stanford University.

From this central camp at the tall redwood, José Francisco de Ortega went up the eastern shore of the bay, and it is thought that he explored as far as Alameda Creek, near Niles, or farther. On their return journey to Monterey, Portolá's party retraced its former trail through San Mateo, Santa Cruz, and Monterey counties.

Pedro Fages was the first white man to go inland from Monterey Bay to San Francisco Bay. His first expedition was made in 1770. In 1772 he made a second trip which was recorded by Fray Juan Crespí, diarist of both the Portolá and Fages expeditions. Fages left Monterey on March 20, 1772, and, passing over the Salinas River and through the valley which bears its name, he climbed the Gabilán Mountains, dropping down into the valley on the other side, where, in 1797, Mission San Juan Bautista was to be established by Father Lasuén.

From there, continuing north, he entered the Santa Clara Valley north of Hudner (a Southern Pacific flag stop in San Benito County), passed Tesquisquita Slough and San Felipe Lake, traveled the broad valley which he named San Bernardino de Sena, and, on March 22, pitched camp on Llagas Creek a little north of Gilroy.

The next day the party followed along the west side of the Santa Clara Valley and climbed the low hills that extend eastward into the valley near San Martin. Camp that night was made near Coyote Creek, on the shores of a lake named San Benvenuto (erroneously called Benito) by Crespí. On March 25 the party passed along the edge of the eastern foothills and camped at San Lorenzo Creek in Alameda County.

After discovering the Sacramento Valley, Fages reentered the Santa Clara Valley by way of Mission Pass, continuing around the head of San Francisco Bay to a point near Milpitas. "Retracing their old course, on April 3, camp was made at the spur of hills near San Martin. Near there is the watershed between Coyote Creek and Pájaro River, hence 'the hills which separate the valley of the arroyo of the live oaks of the bay from that of San Bernardino' (Gilroy)." On April 4 the camp was pitched near the site of San Juan Bautista.

Juan Bautista de Anza, in 1775–76, made his second expedition from Sonora, Mexico, to San Francisco. After stopping a few days at Monterey, he proceeded northward on March 23, 1776, by way of the Salinas River and the Gabilán Mountains to the San Bernardino Valley, the southern end of what is now the Santa Clara Valley. There he camped at Llagas Creek. On March 24 he passed through the low hills to the Coyote River, and entered the Llano de los Robles del Puerto de San Francisco ("Plain of the Oaks of the Port of San Francisco"), now called the Santa Clara Valley. The party kept to the western side of the valley along the foothills, camping on the Arroyo de San Joseph Cupertino on March 25, from where they had a broad view of San Francisco Bay.

When, on March 26, the little band reached the tall redwood tree on the banks of San Francisquito Creek, they found the cross that Palou had placed there on November 28, 1774, just five years after Portolá first passed that way. From this point, Anza proceeded up the peninsula, where he explored and located the sites for the Presidio and Mission of San Francisco.

Over this old trail up the Santa Clara Valley, marked out by Pedro Fages, the mission fathers came later. El Camino Real, it was called, the "Royal Road" between the missions to the south, at Santa Clara, San Juan Bautista, and Monterey, and Mission San Francisco de Asís, at the northern end of the peninsula.

Mission Santa Clara de Asís

The founding of Mission Santa Clara de Asís took place on January 12, 1777, with Father Tomás de la Peña from Mission San Francisco de Asís officiating, and José Joaquín Moraga and his soldiers from the Presidio of San Francisco present at the ceremonies. The site chosen for the new mission was on the banks of Río Guadalupe, the chief camping and fishing grounds of the Indians of the region. They called it So-co-ís-ta-ka, meaning "at (the) laurel." Thámien was another name by which the area was known. Here the mission cross was planted on the bank of a stream, on a spot later forming a part of the Laurelwood Farm. The exact location of the original mission *(SRL 250)* has been determined to be the west bank of now-dry Mission Creek, some 1,350 feet south of the confluence of this creek and the Guadalupe River. A bronze plaque has been placed at Kifer Road and De la Cruz Boulevard to indicate this first site. Twice within the next two years, the river, swollen by the winter rains, flooded the church, and in 1779 the fathers moved a short distance south. This second location is now marked by a beautiful cross in a well-kept city park at the northeast corner of Martin Avenue and De la Cruz Boulevard.

One of the mission's very first works had been a bridge of tree trunks and earth laid across the Guadalupe River, about three-tenths of a mile below the present Bayshore Freeway crossing, possibly at the very point where Anza's party had attempted to cross on a fallen tree. The "Old Spanish Bridge" was later improved. Near its site, a cross may be seen in the field to the north of the freeway east of the Trimble Road overcrossing. This marker was placed many years ago before it was discovered through the research of Father Arthur D. Spearman, S.J., that the mission had had two sites near the Guadalupe. It refers to these two sites, consequently, as "Probable Location A" and "Probable Location B" of the first Mission Santa Clara.

The second site of the mission was used until 1784, but it was of only temporary nature, and in the meantime another location on higher ground was selected at what is now the southwest corner of Franklin Street and Campbell Avenue, near the Santa Clara station on the Southern Pacific Railroad. The building erected on this spot is said to have been one of the most elaborate and beautiful of all the mission structures in California. It was begun by Father José Antonio Murguía on November 19, 1781, and was dedicated by Father Junípero Serra on May 15, 1784. The Indians called the site Gerguensun (perhaps better transliterated as "Juquensen"), or "the Valley of the Oaks." The cornerstone of the third Mission Santa Clara was unearthed during construction in 1911, and a cross was placed at the street corner to mark the spot.

The earthquakes of 1812 and 1818, however, caused serious damage to the buildings at the third site, and the fathers were obliged to move again. This they did in 1819, to a point on the east side of the present campus drive (Alviso Street) of the University of Santa Clara, opposite the south half of the Jesuit residence. The mission remained here until the completion of the church at the fifth and last site *(SRL 338)*, a stone's throw away, where the university chapel now stands. The fifth church was begun in 1822 and dedicated on August 11, 1825.

After the secularization of the California missions in 1836, the lands of Mission Santa Clara were confiscated and the buildings became sadly neglected. In 1850, however, the Rt. Rev. Joseph S. Alemany, O.P., bishop of the new Diocese of Monterey, invited the Society of Jesus to Santa Clara to restore the church and to build up a college. Accordingly, on March 19, 1851, Santa Clara College was established in the old mission buildings by Rev. John Nobili, S.J., who adapted what was left of the old adobe buildings to the requirements of a school. Some of them were used as classrooms, while others became dormitories. Changes necessitated by the growth of the school finally altered the mission buildings until little of the original remained. By 1855 frame structures had replaced many of the former adobes. The 1825 adobe church, used as students' chapel and parish church, was encased in wood and given two towers quite out of keeping with mission architecture.

In 1855 the state granted a university charter to the college, but it was 57 years before it attained real university rank. On April 29, 1912, Santa Clara College became the University of Santa Clara, and since that date many fine new buildings have been built by the Jesuits around the site of the old mission. On October 25, 1926, the 1825 church was destroyed by fire. In its place a concrete structure was built in 1928–29, as nearly as possible like the adobe church dedicated on the same site by the Franciscans. Part of the altar end of the adobe church was saved after the fire and incorporated into the replica. The bricks may be seen through glass in the sacristy. Many relics, dating from the beginning of the mission's history, were rescued and preserved. Part of the 1777 cross from the first site is encased in the cross in front of the present church. To the right of the church is a gate leading into the old "Campo Santo" or cemetery. In the garden at the rear of the mission one adobe building and an adobe wall from the original cloisters built in 1822 still stand, shaded by aged olive trees planted by the padres.

El Pueblo San José de Guadalupe

Because the Spanish government found difficulty in supplying provisions for the religious and military establishments in Alta California, Governor Felipe de Neve, during his journey in 1777, under orders of Viceroy Antonio María Bucareli, selected certain locations for the placing of agricultural settlements. One of those chosen was near the newly established Mission Santa Clara in what has since become, under proper cultivation, the fertile Santa Clara Valley.

Here the first of these contemplated pueblo towns was established, the governor appointing in that same year Lieutenant José Joaquín Moraga to found a settlement on the Guadalupe River two and one-quarter miles from the Santa Clara Mission. He was to take with him nine soldiers of "known" skill in agriculture, two settlers, and three laborers.

On November 29, 1777, the new town was founded on the margin of the small river from which it derived its name, El Pueblo San José de Guadalupe. It was about one and one-half miles from the center of the present city of San Jose. The traditional site *(SRL 433)* is marked in the Jefferson School grounds on Hobson Street, adjoining the grounds of the old Hotel Vendome, now torn down.

The floods of March 1778 inundated the marshy land on which this first settlement had been started during the previous dry season and washed away the nearly completed dam built for irrigation purposes. In July a new dam was constructed farther upstream, and the handful of *pobladores,* or first settlers, moved to higher ground. This move caused a change in land titles, and Don José Moraga, who had directed the first settlement, was instructed in 1782 by Governor Pedro Fages to untangle the land lines, to make the allotments uniform and regular, and to designate the common lands and the vacant lands. The first houses, hastily constructed, were gradually replaced by more permanent adobe ones made from the local soil by admixture of a certain amount of cut grass and weeds and dried in brick form.

San José de Guadalupe was visited by Captain George Vancouver in 1792, when the beauty and fertility of the valley in which it was situated won his enthusiastic praise. He was especially impressed by its broad, oak-studded fields.

The site on the Guadalupe River proved unsatisfactory for a town because of the yearly winter floods. Consequently the town was moved to higher levels, and the center of the new location laid near what is now the corner of Market and San Fernando streets. The traditional date for the transfer of the pueblo to this site is 1797, but it may have been several years earlier.

In 1803 the mission fathers built a small adobe church on the new plaza. It was improved in 1835 and was later encased in brick, but was finally destroyed by fire. In 1877 the present stone structure, known as St. Joseph's Church, was completed. It stands on the site of the old adobe chapel. The park enclosed by South Market Street is a part of what was San José's second plaza.

San Jose, founded in 1777, is California's oldest civil settlement. For over a century and a half the seat of municipal government was maintained at the second site of the pueblo, on or around the plaza. Now a new Civic Center has been constructed—on the Guadalupe River, practically within sight of the original pueblo location of 1777. History repeats itself!

El Embarcadero de Santa Clara (Alviso)

Just as Mission San José had its embarcadero on the east shore of San Francisco Bay during the Spanish and Mexican periods, so Mission Santa Clara also had its embarcadero, or landing place. It was at the head of the navigable slough that extends south from San Francisco Bay and is known today as the Alviso Slough. In early mission days it was called the Embarcadero de Santa Clara de Asís, and played a very important part in the life of the settlers at Mission Santa Clara and the pueblo of San José.

Yankee ship captains, from 1835 to 1850, opened up an extensive trade with the dons who owned the vast ranchos bordering on San Francisco Bay. Every rancho had its embarcadero. Among them, the Embarcadero de Santa Clara was one of the foremost. Richard Henry Dana, Jr., in *Two Years Before the Mast,* says:

"The Mission of Dolores, near the anchorage, has no trade at all; but those of San José, Santa Clara, and others situated on the large creeks or rivers which run into the bay, . . . do a greater business in hides than any in California. Large boats, or launches, manned by Indians . . . are attached to the missions, and sent down to the vessels with hides, to bring away goods in return."

Ygnacio Alviso settled at the Embarcadero de Santa Clara in 1840. He had been granted, in 1838, Rancho Rincón de los Esteros. Alviso was mayordomo at the mission and was engaged in construction work there at about the time the building was moved to its last site. About this time the name of the old embarcadero was changed to Alviso.

The development of the quicksilver mines at New Almaden, in 1845 and for many years after, played a large part in Alviso's shipping industry. Then came the discovery of gold at Coloma in 1848. Trade increased so substantially that a steamer was run from San Francisco to Alviso, and the first warehouse was built there in 1849–50. It was during this period that the state capital was located at San Jose. It is rather astonishing to note that during those years the fare one way on that old steamer was $35 per passenger as far as Alviso and $10 from there on the stage to San Jose by way of Santa Clara and the Alameda.

From 1850 to 1861, Alviso enjoyed its greatest period of development. In 1865 the railroads began to divert trade from the embarcaderos on the bay, and Alviso, like many similar pioneer ports, became practically deserted. There was a slight revival of activity in 1876, when a branch railroad was built through the town.

The old brick Wade warehouse is one of the few landmarks remaining from busier days. Alviso still has aspirations, but it is chiefly as the scene of Spanish embarcadero days that the seeker of historic spots finds it interesting.

The Alameda

The tree-lined avenue known as the Alameda was first planted by the padres for the benefit of wayfarers between Mission Santa Clara and the Pueblo de San José. The planting of the trees was begun in 1799 by Father Magín Catalá, who employed 200 Indians to transplant common black willows from the river bank and to water and protect the young grove until the trees should be large enough to withstand the presence of roving herds of cattle that pastured in this unfenced territory. Bordering one side of this grove was a three-mile ditch, or *acequia,* detouring water from the Guadalupe to irrigate the mission garden and other land. Three rows of willows grew there in the early days, and they served as shade from the hot summer sun and as protection from the wild cattle that resented the presence of pedestrians.

Captain Alfred Robinson, who visited this locality on several occasions before 1841, says of this road: "It is frequented generally on the Sabbath or feast days when all the town repair to the church at Santa Clara. On a Sunday may be seen hundreds of persons of both sexes, gaily attired in silks and satins, mounted on their finest horses, and proceeding leisurely up the road. No carriages are used, and, of course, the scene is divested of all the pomp and splendor which accompanies church-going in the larger places of the republic, yet in one respect it excells them all, that is, in the display of female beauty. No part of Mexico can show so large a share of bright eyes, fine teeth, fair proportions, and beautiful complexions."

For nearly three-quarters of a century the grove remained undespoiled. As the region was opened up and traffic grew heavier over this highway, it became evident that a more solid roadbed would be necessary. Although it was the most important and the best road in the region, winter rains made travel difficult. In the winter of 1852 it became impassable, and all traffic was compelled to use a route to the west, making the journey from the mission to the town much longer. In 1856 Crandall Brothers established an omnibus line to carry passengers along the Alameda, but the roadbed was still far from satisfactory. In order to secure maintenance, a franchise to collect tolls was granted to the Alameda Turnpike Company in 1862 in return for making and maintaining a good road. When this franchise terminated in 1868, a railroad with horse-drawn cars began operations. Two years later, the means of locomotion was changed to steam and the line was extended some miles at the southern end.

When electrification of the line came in 1887, public opinion finally consented to the destruction of the center line of trees. One of the county papers on November 24, 1887, announced: "The last of the beautiful grove of trees which has stood for a century in the Alameda, San Jose's lovely drive, has been cut down to make room for the electric road to Santa Clara." Tradition has it that three willows on the east side of the Alameda that survived until 1960–61 were of the original 1799 planting.

On this section of El Camino Real that has seen the heyday of all modes of travel, automobiles now predominate. The well-paved United States Highway 101, originally stretching from the southern to the northern boundary of the state, long utilized the three miles of the old Alameda. Now it has been rerouted via the Bayshore Freeway, and the Alameda has become part of State Highway 82.

Adobes in San Jose

Many buildings in the pueblo were constructed of adobe, and travelers writing of them as late as 1850, when a few frame houses were being built among them, had little to say in their favor. One by one they were replaced by better structures.

In later years, when California's remaining adobes began to be regarded as historical landmarks, care was not exercised for the preservation of those in San Jose, as has been done in Monterey and Santa Barbara. Now San Jose has only two.

A part of one of those early dwellings stands at

Luís María Peralta Adobe, San Jose

the rear of a small cottage at 184 West St. John Street. This was the residence of Luís María Peralta, *comisionado* of the pueblo for the years immediately following 1807 and later grantee of the huge Rancho San Antonio in the East Bay. It was probably built about 1804, before Peralta acquired it, and is the oldest building in San Jose. Bowman claims it as the second oldest extant adobe in the nine Bay Area counties, bowing only to Mission Dolores in San Francisco. In the days of the pueblo the Peralta adobe stood at the extreme northern end of the plaza. Don Luís chose to live here rather than on his land grant, which he gave to his four sons, and here he died on August 25, 1851, at the age of 92, leaving the adobe along with 14 acres to his maiden daughters Josefa and Guadalupe. The main part of the adobe was torn down in 1918. The two rooms that remain are enclosed in walls about 18 by 40 feet and are used as storerooms. The building is partially covered with boards and has a tin roof. In 1949 a concrete structure was built so close to it that the adobe, standing out of line with the edge of the lot, lost part of a wall to accommodate the new building. The City Council of San Jose voted on September 20, 1965, to negotiate for the purchase of the Peralta adobe for restoration and preservation—a project long overdue and certainly merited by one of the most historic landmarks in California.

Until May 1965 a tiny adobe stood at 155 Park Avenue that may have been built even before the Peralta house. Only two adobe walls remained, incorporated into the rear portion, the kitchen, of a frame cottage. It was commonly called the De Quevedo adobe, from the name of the family that owned it for a century, descendants of the first non-Indian born in San Jose. They acquired it, however, only in the 1860's, and its history before that time, including the date of construction, is as yet undiscovered. It was removed as part of an urban redevelopment project, but 150 square feet of adobe bricks were saved and stored. There are plans to reconstruct it at the historic center now being built in Kelley Park on Senter Road. The 16-acre project at the southern end of the park was authorized by the City Council on September 21, 1964, and ground was broken on December 6, 1965. The center will consist of a "pioneer town" composed of historical buildings moved from various parts of Santa Clara County, and will be similar to those already in existence in Kern and Tulare counties. Target date for the opening of the center is 1969.

Another adobe relic stood for many years at the rear of what was 243 South Market Street, and on a direct line with the De Quevedo adobe. This little building, the history and age of which are also uncertain, was occupied in the late 1830's by José Feliz. The well-preserved structure was bull-dozed into oblivion in the 1950's, when a parking lot was constructed behind the Civic Auditorium. The De Quevedo and Feliz adobes stood on the west side of the plaza near its southern end, just two of the many adobes that lined both sides when San Jose was a pueblo.

Although the Peralta adobe is all that remains of El Pueblo San José de Guadalupe, there stands another adobe in San Jose, the ranch house of Rancho Los Coches, at 770 Lincoln Avenue. It will be treated in the section on that rancho.

Adobes in Santa Clara

At 1067 The Alameda, on Highway 82 between Franklin and Benton streets, is a one-story adobe building (SRL 249) that was part of José Peña's house, and may have been constructed as early as the 1790's as an Indian dwelling of the third Mission Santa Clara. It is being preserved by the Santa Clara Women's Club and is used by this group as a clubhouse. It stands well back from the street in a garden of pear and apricot trees and flowering shrubs.

In the grounds of the University of Santa Clara may be seen an adobe remnant of the old mission, a building now used for meetings and an adjoining wall.

At 373 Jefferson Street stands a modest family residence of one and one-half stories called the Fernández adobe. A narrow porch runs along the north side; at the rear is a wooden stairway leading to the one room upstairs, or attic. A large olive tree shades the front corner of the building.

Off Scott Boulevard, at a point east of the scene of the Battle of Santa Clara and north of El Camino Real, stood a large frame house that was beautifully kept in the days of the early American settlers. It was then the residence of John Grandon Bray. At the rear of this house was a low, oblong building, one adobe room of which was built perhaps in the middle 1850's. All four rooms were used during Bray's ownership, one for storing fruit and nuts, one for keeping cured meats, one as a milk room, and the fourth as quarters for the Chinese cook. Concrete later paved the stretch of a few feet between the two buildings, an area formerly laid over with red bricks that became uneven through use. These buildings were razed in 1952, when the Scott Lane School was constructed on the site.

The Courthouse

The former courthouse standing on First Street opposite St. James Square in San Jose, and its successor at Market and St. James Streets, were preceded by buildings of lesser dignity in various parts of the city. These buildings served as places for the administration of justice and the care of records.

The first tribunal of the region, the *juzgado,* was built in 1783 within the original Pueblo de San José. After removal of the pueblo to higher ground, a second *juzgado* was erected about 1798 in what is now the center of Market Street at the intersection of Post Street. That second adobe structure, before it was torn down in 1850 and the bricks removed for use elsewhere, saw the growth of the Spanish and Mexican pueblo into an American town. It was a low building with sloping tiled roof, and in front of it Thomas Fallon hoisted the United States flag on July 13, 1846. (Fallon later became mayor of San Jose. His home, built about 1859, still stands at 175 West St. John Street.)

Before the admission of California to statehood on September 9, 1850, the first county court had been organized. It convened in March 1850 in the adobe building on the west side of South First Street opposite the passageway then known as Archer Alley (now Fountain Alley). This remained the site of the hall of justice until the latter part of 1851, when it was moved into the "Bella Union" building on the north side of West Santa Clara Street. It remained there less than a year, when it was moved to the former capitol or "State House," which was purchased by the county from the city. From there it was forced to move again by a fire which destroyed the building in the spring of 1853. A temporary location was found in Lightstone's adobe building on the west side of Lightstone Alley.

For the next seven years, 1853 to 1860, the seat of justice was at the southeast corner of Second and San Fernando streets. The next move was to the San Jose city hall on the west side of North Market Street, where it remained until 1862. In that year it was changed to the two-story building just erected for the purpose by Martin Murphy. This structure is the only one of the number thus far named that is still standing. Located at the northeast corner of Post and South Market streets, it is one of San Jose's oldest extant business buildings and is worthy of preservation.

From this place, the courthouse went on January 1, 1868, to North First Street opposite St. James Square. This fine domed building had been carefully constructed in 1866–67, and it stood until the fire of May 18, 1931, ruined the interior and left only the staunchly built outer walls intact. A little over a year later the new courthouse was ready for occupancy on the same site and within the exterior walls of the burned building. The dome, however, was not replaced; instead, a third story was added to the original two. Dedication of the rebuilt courthouse took place on September 17, 1932. Now this, too, has been superseded, and Santa Clara County has a new courthouse at North Market and St. James streets, the former location of a separate hall of justice built in 1905. The hall of records, also a separate building, has likewise been torn down, and the fate of the 1868 courthouse is uncertain.

The Monterey Road

South from Santa Clara and San Jose stretches the route that was for long the main highway of the state, the *camino real* (or "kingsroad," as highways were once called in England also). Much of the road was located by the cautious footsteps of the first Spanish expeditions, but soon mission administrators and pueblo settlers introduced convenient deviations; in the 1850's county roadmen straightened, graded and fenced, and in the 1860's they relocated whole sections alongside the new railroad, causing old stagecoach stops to be abandoned and new ones to be built at the train stops where towns would arise. The advancing age of the automobile has brought wide pavement and a few detours and cutoffs, and now plans are drawn for a totally new route which will avoid the congestion of history along the old.

In Spanish times the highway to the capital at Monterey ran out of the south end of the plaza between the double row of mud houses that was San José. To avoid the pueblo's reservoir (a pond 800 feet in length, lying just south of Duane Street and east of Almaden Avenue), the road skirted the Canoas marshes on the right and continued south through the low bare hills called Las Lágrimas, approximately in the line of present South First Street, to the place, now Edenvale, where Tennant's Seven Mile House was built in the early 1850's. Thence the earliest route ran somewhat to the right of the present road, until the hills at Coyote were reached. Here travelers could go up over the Portezuelo and down to the Laguna Seca (named Laguna de San Benvenuto by Crespí in 1772), or around to the left, where a point of rocks forced traffic to take to the bed of Coyote Creek at the Alvírez field. Some of the difficulties of the latter route were overcome by work on the stage road about 1856, and railroad construction in the late 1860's established the highway's final location as well. The railroad's Coyote Station is near the site of the original Alvírez adobe, and the Laguna House (alias Twelve Mile House) had catered to travelers at this point as early as 1853, perhaps earlier. This picturesque two-story building, constructed of redwood from the Santa Cruz Mountains, gave service for well over a century, until it burned to the ground, with the ancient elms that sheltered it and the priceless antiques housed in it, on January 16, 1963. It stood on the east side of the highway, where the cattle-shipping office (built after 1869 and now the Coyote post office) and the old stage barn remain.

On southward the original trail ran through the oak-scattered valley, a half-mile, on the average, to the west of the later highway and railroad, but the way was straightened somewhat in the middle 1850's, the old road and the stage road coming together again at the Hernández adobe in the mouth of Hernández Valley on the north side of Morgan Hill. Along this stretch, at ill-measured intervals, sprang up Madrone Station (Eighteen Mile House) and the Fourteen and Fif-

Twelve Mile House, Coyote

teen Mile Houses. The last-named (Perry Station) was a typical two-story building with a large saloon, standing opposite large warehouses belonging to the Murphy ranchos. Later used as a ranch house, it was torn down and replaced after the 1906 earthquake. Two enormous plume-shaped eucalyptus trees, one of which remains, long marked the place.

Continuing past the Oreja del Oso ("Bear's Ear") or Murphy's Peak, and through the later town of Morgan Hill, the road to Monterey reached the slight bend where Tennant's later Twenty-One Mile House (*SRL 259*) long stood. The connection of the so-called "Vásquez Tree," still standing here, with the bandit Tiburcio Vásquez is nebulous, but it is known that in the 1860's the Brewer party camped at or near this point under old oak trees on their journey both up and down the state. William Brewer writes of it as a place where they had sweet sleep and pleasant memories. Here what was originally a branch road bore left along the present highway to cross the Llagas Creek at the end of the hills; instead of bending right again along the later railroad and highway, it continued diagonally across the valley to Old Gilroy, past the ranches of Martin Murphy and his sons. The original road ran straight ahead to a gap in the low Llagas Hills a mile and a half west of San Martin. Here the pathfinder Pedro Fages camped in late 1770 and again in 1772, and Captains Rivera and Anza camped in following years.

Until the construction of the railroad, which began service in 1869, the highway ran west of its present location, past the foot of a low oak-crowned knoll just north of Gilroy. As early as 1804 this "Lomita de la Linares" was "at the margin of the *camino Real*." According to the story told by her descendants, a Señora Linares was left to rest on the hill when the first settlers bound for the Pueblo of San José broke their journey for some elk-hunting. James Houck's settlement of 1850 at present Gilroy was on the old road, which continued south in nearly its present alignment to the Carneadero crossing. A bridge was ordered to be built here in 1816. Beyond, the highway skirted the point of a hill where a large American ranch was established in 1850, and followed the old highway away from and back to the present freeway as far as the wooden railway trestle and the overpass.

Here was the Rancho de la Brea, possession of which was long disputed between Mission San Juan Bautista and Mariano Castro. In 1803, to establish its title, the mission put a sheep ranch here, with buildings and corrals of pounded earth. The old road used by the early expeditions had run to the southeast along the east side of the Flint Hills, turning west only at the present Brook Hollow Ranch just north of Hollister. In order to shorten the distance to the sheep ranch, and to the timber in the mountains back of it which the mission needed for building its new church, the labor of many Indians was used to build the present road, filling marshes and ravines and bridging gulches and the Pajaro River, until an Indian could run the distance from San Juan in less than three-quarters of an hour. The Pajaro, however, was at this time a rapid and turbulent stream draining the large lakes of the upper Santa Clara Valley; the bridge was soon washed away, and the crossing shortly got the name of Mal Paso. The provincial government attempted to built another bridge in 1816, with what success is not known. Not until 50 years later was the river at last permanently spanned.

The San Francisco Road

The first road north from San José led to Santa Clara Mission, and beyond that point it followed the trail opened by Juan Bautista de Anza on March 30, 1776. Beginning in the plaza between the church and the royal granary, the road ran close among the adobes, emerging on the west side of a pond at the intersection of present Santa Clara and Market streets. The pueblo's main *acequia* ran parallel at some distance to the left, and a branch of it was crossed at present St. James Street. Between present Market and First at Julian Street the highway to the San José Mission and the Contra Costa forked off to the right, over a plain strewn with the bleached bones of slaughtered cattle, until it reached an immense sycamore grove near the Coyote Creek and became one with the present Old Oakland Road. At the road fork also began the *suertes,* or farming lots, of the residents of the pueblo; as late as 1850 most of the properties bore the names of the founding settlers to whom they had first been distributed. The first lot on the right was inhabited by the family of Plácido Californio, one of the first Lower Californian Indians brought north by the Franciscans, who retired from Santa Clara Mission and settled in the pueblo in 1796.

The road to San Francisco continued through the *suertes,* which were bordered by willow hedges and little alleys stretching to the river bank, and went on past the area called the Pueblo Viejo, where the town had first been founded. As it reached the open country, the road bore more and more to the west of present North First Street, finally reaching the Guadalupe River at or near the place where Anza's men had opened a ford. At this point, near the original site of Mission Santa Clara, the river was crossed, at first by the bridge built by the missionaries. In 1797,

when the crossing began to be used by travelers between the new San José Mission and the third Santa Clara as well as between the Pueblo San José and San Francisco, the civil-military authorities erected a more satisfactory bridge. In its later state, this consisted of two tree trunks supporting a roadbed of five-foot squared timbers topped with planks, the whole suspended above bank level by a heavy chain anchored from four tall sycamores. The "Old Spanish Bridge" remained a landmark until the 1880's, and a piece of the chain (said to have come from a Portuguese ship) is preserved in the museum at the University of Santa Clara. A map of 1852 seems to show the bridge as a double span.

From the Guadalupe River northwest, the original trail became a boundary between ranchos, and for this reason the present Bayshore Freeway still follows the same general line. At present Moffett Field, beyond the Indian settlement of Posolmi, the trail swung first to the right of the freeway, then inland to the left. In records of 1836–53 this route is called the old or summer road, the lowlands near the bay being nearly impassable in winter. Nonetheless the first American squatters found the northern end of the trail useful; they fenced and improved it, and it is now the longer portion of Charleston Road in Palo Alto.

After Mission Santa Clara was moved to near its present site, a better if slightly longer road was opened. This road began at the plaza in front of the church door and swung around to the north and west roughly in the line of present El Camino Real or a little northeast of it. Near the west side of the present city of Santa Clara the road passed to the north of the main ranchería or village inhabited by the mission Indians after secularization. In 1839 the alcalde or headman of this village was a Tulare Indian who could not speak Spanish.

Where present El Camino Real runs due west along a section line to Lawrence Expressway and Fremont Avenue, the main highway in use before the 1850's swung slowly to the right across what was known as the Bajío, an open area grown with mustard and intersected with sloughs, where the Battle of Santa Clara was fought in 1847. Where present Lawrence Expressway overpasses the railroad (site of Lawrence Station, and the Lawrence post office from 1887 to 1935) was the easternmost point of the Roblar, a great forest of white oaks and live oaks extending down the west side of the valley between the low adobe lands and the chaparral nearer the hills. In the 1830's and 1840's travelers coming from the north caught sight here of the mission church, glistening white with its bell tower beside it, far off across the fields.

Northward the main trail lay for several miles in the edge of the woods, east of the present railroad. The oaks in this section succumbed first to charcoal burners, then to the insatiable wood-burning locomotives and the needs of mechanized large-scale wheat farming, and finally to fruit orchards. The only trees left are the clumps surrounding the older farmhouses. In present

Mountain View the oak woods and the road formed a semicircle extending three-fourths of a mile east of the railroad, around the alluvial fan of Stevens Creek, which was fringed with willow swamps. This portion of the Posolmi claim was subdivided in 1847 and sold to a number of Americans and Englishmen who moved in and "kept shack." One of the shacks, located at what would now be the southwest side of Sherland Avenue halfway between Tyrella Avenue and Whisman Road, was shortly enlarged to cater to travelers and became the Fremont House, a well-known stopping place that gave its name to the township before the lower road was abandoned. After swinging west again to the mission's Corral de Pastoria near present Alma Street just south of Rengstorff Avenue, and the Castro and Robles ranch houses near the Palo Alto city limits, the Spanish road bore off to the right across Adobe Creek and the black-adobe flats to the Mesa ranch just east of David Starr Jordan Junior High School, and thence continued past the Palo Alto city hall to the Middlefield Road crossing of San Francisquito Creek.

In present Sunnyvale and Mountain View, El Camino Real follows still another route used in Spanish times, which was called the *deshecha* or cutoff road. The Americans knew it as the Upper San Francisco Road because it left the main or lower route southeast of present Lawrence Expressway (at what was for years afterward called San Francisco Avenue, but is now Warburton Avenue west of Pomeroy Avenue), and for several miles skirted the *chamisales* (greasewood chaparral) that extended down from Saratoga and Los Altos. On the east side of the road just south of the present Stevens Creek crossing was an Indian settlement, "called Sojorpi in the mother-tongue," with a large field of melons; the original section of the present Mountain View–Alviso highway was the Indians' trail from Sojorpi to Posolmi. The melons were marketed by Mexican land owners in the 1840's and by Americans in the 1850's. North of this point the upper road swung away from present El Camino Real to join the main lower route near the Castro ranch.

In 1849 John W. Whisman settled under an enormous bay tree near the lower road, between present Villa Street and the railroad opposite Palo Alto Avenue, and in the summer of that year he began the first stage service between San Francisco and San Jose—using a wagon drawn by mules. The torrential rains of the winter of 1849–50 rendered the road impassable, and since his business was at a standstill he sold out to Hall & Crandall and moved a short distance away, into the present Whisman district. The new proprietors, who had been engaged in staging in Mexico, at once turned the Whisman farm into a base of operations for their Concord stage-coaches and large herd of spirited horses, and began using the upper road as less liable to flooding. In December 1850 the county made the upper route the official one, and about that time Beeson's blacksmith shop was built on it, in present Sunnyvale an eighth of a mile south of Hollenbeck Avenue. Soon there was fierce competition between stage lines, and creek crossings were improved and better routes sought. To avoid the adobe flats, the upper road was extended to the old Arastradero crossing of Adobe Creek and present El Camino Way in Palo Alto. Shortly afterward the present route of El Camino Real was in use as far as Palo Alto Senior High School, and in 1852 the San Francisquito was bridged at the present crossing. In the same year the county proposed to shorten the whole route by making it run straight for miles across the adobe lands near the bay. This attempt pleased no one, and by petition of the settlers the "stage road," now El Camino Real, was made the official highway on condition that the local residents would keep it open and in repair. Slight relocations in the 1860's gave the present alignment on the west side of downtown Mountain View and the Old San Francisco Road–Wolfe Road jog (bypassed since 1929) in Sunnyvale.

Rancho Los Tularcitos

Rancho Los Tularcitos lay in the northern part of Santa Clara County near the lower end of San Francisco Bay. It extended south from the confluence of Calera and Penitencia creeks along the latter stream to Calaveras Road in the town of Milpitas, and east to include the mountains at the heads of Calera Creek and the Arroyo de los Coches. The southeastern point was marked by a live oak tree, which also denoted the northeastern point of the outlying lands of the Pueblo de San José.

This rancho was granted by Pablo Vicente de Solá, the last of the Spanish governors of Alta California, to José Higuera on October 4, 1821. The grant was renewed by the Mexican governor, Juan B. Alvarado, on February 18, 1839; and patent for 4,394 acres was issued by the United States government to the heirs on July 8, 1870. This land was afterward purchased by Henry Curtner, a native of Vermont, and some of it remains in the possession of his family.

One of the old adobes built on Rancho Tularcitos by José Higuera may still be seen on the banks of Calera Creek a few hundred yards from the old Curtner (now Weller) house. The adobe, originally and presently of one story, was constructed about 1828. About 150 feet farther south along the stream stood a later adobe, but it has been destroyed by fire and the bricks have eroded away into a heap of mud.

The older and larger of the two adobes was marked in 1928 by the Landmarks Committee of the Native Sons of the Golden West. It was long protected by a two-story wooden superstructure erected in the 1860's by a Frenchman named Clemente Columbet, who owned that part of the rancho before Curtner purchased it from him. This shell, much warped by earthquakes, threatened to collapse the entire building and was taken down about 1950, exposing the original one-story adobe, which has been restored.

Near the stream there may be seen a part of the ancient cactus hedge that enclosed the house and gardens over 100 years ago. There, also, is an ancient fig tree, gnarled with age but still prolific.

José Higuera Adobe, near Milpitas
(top) 1949, (center) 1951, (bottom) 1961

Near the Higuera house, old fig, pear, and olive trees still bear fruit.

The Curtner house itself is built on the site of an Indian temescal ("sweat house"). Stone implements, bowls and pestles, and hundreds of melted stones used in the sweathouse ceremonies, as well as several Indian skeletons, have been found during the process of building and garden making. Beads and arrowheads have also been found in neighboring hills and canyons.

This rancho had its part in the stirring times of 1846, for, on the day after Christmas of that year, Francisco Sánchez halted his troops near the house of Don José Higuera for two days before moving on toward San José. Sánchez had with him six American prisoners, one of them Lieutenant Washington A. Bartlett, then acting alcalde of San Francisco. He had captured all six near the Sixteen Mile House south of San Fran-

cisco, while they were on a foraging expedition for meat for the United States forces.

Of all the merrymakings at the Higuera home with its large family, the one longest remembered in the countryside was the marriage feast of the granddaughter Margarita. She was very beautiful; and when she became the wife of Nicolás Chavarria, the fiesta continued for three days and was attended by friends from far and near.

Valentín, the father of Margarita, sold his portion of land to Clemente Columbet and received $3,000 for it. Columbet, who had a hotel in San José in 1849, attempted to conduct a country hostelry in this old adobe. He divided the upstairs into several bedrooms and arranged a huge reception room on the ground floor. He ran a stage to connect with other conveyances at Alviso and Milpitas. But a short trial convinced him that the resort would yield no profit, and he therefore closed its doors.

The old adobe is about one mile east of the old San Jose–Oakland highway on a private extension of Rancho Higuera Road, which proceeds from the end of Diel Drive, a street in the subdivision on the east side of the highway one and three-quarters miles north of the center of Milpitas.

Rancho Rinconada de los Gatos

Rancho Rinconada de los Gatos, consisting of one and one-half square leagues, was granted by Governor Alvarado on May 21, 1840, to Sebastián Peralta and José Hernández, who reputedly had made application for it as early as 1824. The Arroyo San Tomás Aquino formed its western boundary and separated it from Rancho Quito. Rancho Rinconada extended a little way south of the town of Los Gatos into the broad lower end of the canyon; thence by various turns to north, northwest, and east the boundary line reached the spot called Austin Corners (Austin Way), which is a corner of the western part of the rancho.

The location of the rancho at the mouth of a canyon in the Santa Cruz Mountains is described by John C. Frémont in his *Memoirs* as being a valley "openly wooded with groves of oak, free from underbrush, and after the spring rains covered with grass. On the west it is protected from the chilling influence of the northwest winds by the Cuesta de los Gatos [Wildcat Ridge], which separates it from the coast."

It is said that a fight took place there in 1831 between the Indians of the region and soldiers from Santa Clara Mission. Several legends, too, are connected with the naming of the place, all having to do with the number of large native cats. These seem to have been both plentiful and fierce, as these legends tell of several encounters with them. The ridge was known by the name Los Gatos as early as 1831, and the rancho and the modern city of Los Gatos adopted the name from the ridge.

Sebastián Peralta, a former *regidor* (alderman) at San José, had led certain expeditions against troublesome Indians during his term of office. His adobe house on this grant is no longer standing, but its site is about 100 yards from Roberts Road near the bridge across Los Gatos Creek. It was a long one-story building with a sloping roof extending over an ell at one end.

About one and one-half miles by airline from this Peralta home was the adobe house of the other grantee, José Hernández, of which a part still stands incorporated into the country home of the present owner. The entrance to this residence on an elevation near a bend in the Arroyo de San Tomás Aquino is one-half mile from Austin Corners at 14610 Quito Road. It was a structure of two stories with small, square, deep-recessed windows both upstairs and down. Surrounding it is a pergola upon which are old-fashioned banksia and other kinds of roses that are still flourishing on their huge old trunks. Additions to the old house to fit it for comfortable, modern living have been carried out with great care in order to retain the original character of the place. A commemorative bronze tablet was affixed to the outer wall of the old part by the Colonial Dames of America in 1927.

New Almaden

Since ancient times the Indians of the Santa Clara Valley visited the hill of red earth (cinnabar) above the poplar-lined stream which the Spaniards later called the Arroyo de los Alamitos ("the Little River of the Poplar Trees"). The red earth made excellent pigment which the Indians used for adornment.

As early as 1824 the Spanish settlers of the valley knew about the red hill and its strange pigments. In that year an attempt was made by the Robles brothers, Secundino and Teodoro, and by Don Antonio Suñol, a member of the San José Council, to find silver or gold in the deposit; and in time the excavation was called "La Mina Santa Clara."

In the year 1842 Governor Alvarado made grants of land in this vicinity to two men; on August 1 he gave Rancho San Vicente to José de los Reyes Berryessa (Berrellesa, Berreyesa), and on June 16, Rancho Cañada de los Capitancillos to Justo Larios. Three years later actual interest arose in the mineral deposits contained in these lands.

Andrés Castillero had made several trips between Mexico and Alta California in the decade previous to 1845, the year in which he was shown a sample of ore from La Mina Santa Clara. His presence in the north at this time as a deputy of the Mexican government was occasioned by a plan for moving troops from Mexico to aid in the control of foreigners, who were invading California in considerable numbers. By some chance, upon this visit, he was told of this earlier identified but forgotten ore.

On November 22, 1845, Andrés Castillero filed with Alcalde Pedro Chaboya (Chabolla) in San José a document in which he claimed discovery of "silver with a ley of gold" on the rancho of José Reyes Berryessa. In conformity with the mining ordinances he asked that notices of his discovery and of his intention for its development be affixed in public places. After making certain crude tests he filed a second document in the following month reporting the discovery of "liquid quicksilver" in the deposit, and shortly thereafter went back to Mexico.

Soon there began the long-drawn-out litigation over the ownership of the mine—a litigation finally injected into affairs at Washington. The New Almaden Company, Barron, Forbes and Company of Mexico, and the Quicksilver Mining Company of New York were all involved.

In 1846, Barron, Forbes and Company of Tepic, Mexico, owned the controlling interest in the project, and after the discovery of gold at Coloma in 1848, there was a tremendous increase in the demand for quicksilver, used in the reduction of gold ore. New Almaden (SRL 339), named for the great Almaden mine in Spain, became the most famous and one of the most productive quicksilver mines in the world, and at one time there was a thriving town centered about it. In 1863 the mine and all the improvements were sold to the Quicksilver Mining Company of New York for $1,750,000.

Through the years the mine has been worked intermittently, but now it is again in regular production. Shafts and flumes are visible on the steep hillside topped by tall brick chimneys, like the ruins of an ancient castle. The upper Arroyo de los Alamitos is choked with "tailings," from which a little quicksilver is still taken.

A small plateau beyond the St. George Shaft, one of the many shafts that are still evident, was called Bull Run, and here were held the outdoor games and holiday festivities.

The mine office of the 1850's, a part-adobe structure with cupola, stood into the 1960's near the road that leads from the hacienda to the site of the old settlements on the hill. By following the curving road (permission is needed for its use) and "rounding Cape Horn," one reaches English town. An old wooden schoolhouse stands here, as does part of the old brick store. Still farther up is the Chilean camp, and to the left is Spanish town. The whole place is dotted with mine shafts. A brick powder magazine is another landmark.

Three cemeteries were used at New Almaden, two of them in the vicinity of Spanish town, where the graves were marked by wooden slabs with epitaphs in Spanish. These isolated burial places have been desecrated by vandals, and most of the markers are gone. The third, and oldest, cemetery is near Alamitos Creek, back of the hacienda. Here the graves are marked with slabs of stone.

The only part of the New Almaden complex ordinarily accessible to the public is the hacienda. The picturesque settlement has remained little changed over the years. Its main street follows the bank of the stream, where poplars still grow undisturbed. At the head of the long row of tiny, low-roofed frame, brick, and adobe houses with their tidy gardens, stands a great mansion, the "Casa Grande," home of the mine superintendent in times past. It is thought that it was erected on the site of the adobe built there by the Spanish in 1827.

This was truly one of the grandest mansions in all California in its day, being strongly built with walls almost two feet thick and with magnificent fireplaces, hand-carved and inlaid, material for which was brought around the Horn. It contains 20 rooms today and has wide balconies running completely around the lower story.

The little town awoke to new life in 1927, when it was restored as a weekend and summer resort. Happily, much of the picturesque aspect of the place has been preserved and the romance of old California still gathers about its quaint domiciles and its old adobe store.

For its importance to the nation and the world, New Almaden has been registered and marked as a National Historic Landmark by the Department of the Interior. An interesting museum is maintained in one of the old adobes at the hacienda.

The men to whom the grants of these lands were given by Governor Alvarado in 1842 are of some interest. José Reyes Berryessa, who received Rancho San Vicente, in which the mine works (hacienda) were established and where the mouth of the tunnel was dug, was the son of Nicolás and Gertrudis Peralta de Berryessa, who were among the earliest settlers in San Francisco. Don José had served his time in the militia of San Francisco and was a teacher there during the latter part of this military period. His wife was María Z. Bernal, a daughter of the owner of the neighboring Rancho Santa Teresa. In 1846, less than four years after receiving his land, Don José, then well on in years, was killed at the embarcadero of Mission San Rafael in Marin County. Patent to this rancho, consisting of 4,438 acres, was given to the widow on June 24, 1868.

Justo Larios, grantee of Rancho Capitancillos, on which was the peak of the New Almaden mine hill, was the son of José M. Larios, and was 34 years of age when he received his grant in 1842. He was a militia artilleryman and a soapmaker and was one of those unfortunate ranchers whose horses were appropriated by Frémont's men. His wife was Cecilia, daughter of Joaquín Castro. After giving possession of his rancho to the quicksilver interests, he went to the Mother Lode region, where he made a small fortune in the gold mines in 1849-50. He soon lost much of his wealth, however, and spent his later years in Gilroy. A part of his land through which Los Capitancillos Creek flows was patented as Rancho Capitancillos (3,360 acres) to Charles Fossat on February 3, 1865. A lesser part, Cañada de los Capitancillos, containing 1,110 acres, was patented to the Guadalupe Mining Company on September 20, 1871. This company developed the Guadalupe mine two miles beyond the New Almaden; while it has not had the spectacular career of the latter, the Guadalupe has been a heavy producer. Some of the old buildings, including a brick store and a wooden church, still stand at Guadalupe camp on Hicks Road.

The Almaden Vineyards (SRL 505), first planted by Charles LeFranc in 1852, are located at 13270 Kooser Road. The present winery and home were built in 1876.

Rancho Quito

In the fertile country between the town of Saratoga and State Highway 82 lies Rancho Quito, or "Tito" as it was sometimes called, granted by Governor Alvarado in 1841 to José Noriega and José Zenon Fernández. It is well watered: both Saratoga and Calabasas creeks flow through it, and along its eastern boundary flows the Arroyo San Tomás Aquino.

Both of the grantees were Híjar colonists who reached California under the spell of enthusiasm kindled by José María Padrés and his associate José María Híjar. Noriega came as supercargo on the vessel bringing this group, and Fernández was one of the six teachers in the party; both lived in San José after their arrival, and both became members of the council in that pueblo. Don José Fernández taught for a time at Santa Clara. In 1839 he was secretary of the ayuntamiento (municipal government), and in 1840-41, at the time of receiving this grant, he was secretary of the junta (council). He continued to hold important offices up to the time of his death three years later. Both owners transferred the property to Manuel Alviso, under date of July 8, 1844. Noriega continued to live in the vicinity. The land, comprising 13,310 acres, was patented on May 14, 1866, to Alviso jointly with the heirs of Fernández —the widow, Petra Enriques de Fernández, and her children, Manuel Loreto, Francisco Máximo, and Dionesa.

Manuel Alviso sold his interest in Rancho Quito on March 9, 1859, to José Ramón Argüello, Octavius F. Cipriani, and S. M. Mezes for "a valuable and considerable consideration." Two deeds bearing the signatures of him and his wife, Doña María Luisa Peralta de Alviso, were executed.

Don José Ramón Argüello, one of the purchasers of Alviso's land, was the grandson of Don José Darío Argüello and son of Don Luís. After the death of Don Luís, the family had continued to reside on the Rancho de las Pulgas in their house at San Carlos, but after José Ramón became the owner of this property, the widowed mother came to live with him. She died in 1874, and he in 1876. Their place there was about eight miles from San Jose, at the junction of Saratoga Avenue and Quito Road, and was called the Quito Farm. He planted olive trees, a fruit orchard, and a small vineyard, which passed in 1882 into the possession of Edward E. Goodrich, who further developed the property by building a winery, an oil mill, and houses for his employees.

The city of Saratoga lies at the southwest corner of Rancho Quito on Saratoga Creek. The old settlement of Gubserville (SRL 447) was on the road from Santa Clara that stretches through this rancho. This little settlement, remembered by few today, was the first place on this stage route out of Santa Clara at which the driver paused to leave mail. The post office existed here from 1882 to 1899, and Frank Gubser was postmaster as well as saloonkeeper. Gubser's "Half-Way House" stood on the northwest side of Saratoga

Avenue about opposite Los Felice Drive. The area is built up with homes and apartments today, but until the 1950's the bleak, old house of W. Forbes, whose blacksmith shop was near Gubser's establishment, remained as a local landmark at 11845 Saratoga Avenue. Nearby, at Payne and Saratoga avenues, is Moreland School (SRL 489), which, at the time it was marked by the State of California in 1953, was the educational center of the oldest known rural school district in the state. It began as a subscription school in 1851, meeting in private homes. The first public school building, formerly the home of Zechariah Moreland, was obtained the following year, and in 1853 the school was organized as Santa Clara Township School District No. 2. It was renamed in Moreland's honor in 1862. None of the older buildings remains.

Before the boundary lines of Rancho Quito were definitely known, several industrious families made homes in the region east of Cupertino on land then supposed to be public land. When it was suspected that this area might belong to the old grant, the farmers banded together and engaged an attorney to represent them. The court decided against the rights of these men, and many of them gave up their homes and moved away. Those who elected to remain were allowed a term of five years in which to make payments ranging from $20 to $30 an acre; at the end of this period they became the owners of their chosen locations.

Robert Glendenning was one of the group that remained. From their native Scotland, he and his wife arrived in San Francisco via Australia in 1850. In 1851 they took up 160 acres northeast of Cupertino, living at first in a tent with a board shed as a storage place where food and other goods that might prove tempting to wild animals or roving Indians would be safe. The family prospered, built a good home, purchased adjoining land, and was an asset to the community. Descendants of Robert Glendenning have remained on the property to the present time. Their home, built in 1871, is on a private road leading south from 19160 Homestead Road.

Rancho San Antonio and Los Altos

South of Los Altos on a hill overlooking a wide terrain long stood the crumbling ruins of an adobe building, called by many a fort but which was the home erected there by Prado Mesa, owner of Rancho San Antonio, who died about 1845.

Juan Prado Mesa, a soldier in the San Francisco Company from 1828 and a corporal in the Santa Clara Escolta (guard) beginning in 1832, was promoted to sergeant and acting alférez in 1837. Later in the same year he was made full alférez in charge of the San Francisco garrison. In 1841 he is mentioned by the Englishman Sir George Simpson as "Captain" Prado with a corporal's guard in the square huts that then made up the Presidio of San Francisco, back from a dismantled fort "fast crumbling into the undermining tide beneath."

Don Prado married into the Higuera family (according to a grandson, the name of Mesa's wife was Miciali Higuera) and had seven children:

Agustín, Antonio, Concepción, Mejín, Francisco, Ramón, and Nicandro. According to J. N. Bowman, the adobe house was built in 1844, although local tradition places the date earlier. On March 24, 1839, Mesa had received a grant from Governor Alvarado. Rancho San Antonio was an oblong strip of land stretching from San Antonio (Adobe) Creek to Cupertino (Stevens) Creek, and was divided near its center by Permanente Creek.

The square construction of the house and its corrals gave rise to the tradition of its having been a fort—a conclusion perhaps warranted by the fact that any house in those days was built to withstand attacks of unfriendly natives. Don Prado also owned a lot in San Francisco, as did Juana Briones de Miranda, whose Rancho Purísima Concepción was separated from Rancho San Antonio by San Antonio Creek and two of whose daughters, Manuela and Refugia, married Don Prado's sons Agustín and Ramón.

William A. Dana purchased the southern part of this rancho at executor's sale. He filed claim in 1853 for 3,542 acres of it lying along Permanente Creek and received patent for it on December 19, 1857. Several other claimants to certain parts of the rancho appeared: James W. Weeks, H. C. Curtis, William W. White, Mary S. Bennett, and Henry F. Dana. Patent, however, was given August 6, 1866, to Encarnación Mesa and other heirs for the remaining 4,440 acres.

The town of Los Altos with its surrounding country homes is on this Rancho San Antonio. The site of the original adobe house of Don Juan Prado Mesa is on a hill on the southeast side of El Monte Avenue near Summerhill Avenue.

Rancho La Purísima Concepción

Rancho La Purísima Concepción was granted June 30, 1840, to a former Santa Clara Mission Indian, José Gorgonio, by Governor Alvarado. He and José Ramón, another Indian, occupied the land for some years before it was formally granted; their home was on a hill on the west side of Adobe Creek near present Fremont Avenue. A large number of Gorgonio's relatives also lived on the grant. Gorgonio and Ramón continued to reside there until the grant was sold to Juana Briones de Miranda in 1844, which date the deed bears. José Gorgonio was literate, but José Ramón signed by making his mark. The deed was recorded in the courthouse November 6, 1850.

According to family tradition, the elder Briones, the parents of Juana, came with Father Magín Catalá, the much beloved Franciscan friar, to Monterey and on to Santa Clara Mission, when he was sent there in 1794. The children in the family were Guadalupe, who married Ramón de Miramontes of Half Moon Bay; María la Luce, who died unmarried at an advanced age; Juana, born at Carmel or Monterey, who married Apolinario Miranda; another daughter, who married into the Martínez family and lived in the town of Martinez; and one son, Gregorio, who became a doctor and lived in Bolinas.

The home of the pioneer Briones family was apparently broken up before all of the children were grown, as Juana lived with her elder sister

Guadalupe and moved with her to Mission Dolores. In San Francisco Juana married Apolinario Miranda, a soldier who was there from 1819 to 1836 and grantee of Rancho Ojo de Agua de Figueroa. In 1843 he was sent before the subprefect for not living harmoniously with his wife.

Juana had a house, built of adobe, in the North Beach region of San Francisco. She frequently went out on cases where she acted as doctor, nurse, or midwife, not only in San Francisco but also after moving to her rancho in Santa Clara County.

A three-day trip by oxcart brought her and her seven children to Rancho La Purísima Concepción, a rather hilly tract of land in which rise several small streams that unite to form a creek. Adobe Creek, sometimes known as Yeguas or San Antonio, carries the drainage waters to San Francisco Bay. The adobe house in which they lived is still standing on the top of a hill not far from the junction of West Fremont Avenue and Arastradero Road. This property was duly confirmed to her in 1856, the final patent being given August 15, 1871.

When the Briones de Miranda family lived on this hill, a shopping trip to San Francisco required a full week, three days going and three days returning and one day for the necessary errands in the city. The carreta, drawn by a team of oxen and piled with hides to be sold, got an early morning start and, jolting over the uneven road, reached the first night's destination at the Argüello rancho. The next day, a fresh team of oxen was supplied for the second lap of the journey, which ended at the Sánchez rancho. There another exchange of oxen took place and Mission Dolores was reached the third night. On the fourth day the travelers greeted old friends and took the hides to Davis or to Leidesdorff, the two most successful merchant-shipowners of the time, exchanging them for needed supplies. The return journey saw all the oxen returned to their home corrals, and the travelers reached home with their own animals on the night of the seventh day.

After the children were married and gone, with the exception of José de Jesús and José Dolores, who were never married, Juana continued to reside there, and each year, as long as she lived, the family gathered at the home place for a barbecue festivity, lasting for several days. The family reunion included Presentación and her English husband, Robert T. Ridley; Tomás and his wife, Bjorques; Narcisa and her husband, Jesús García; Refugia and her husband, Ramón Mesa, son of Prado Mesa of the neighboring Rancho San Antonio; and Manuela and her husband, Agustín, also a son of Prado Mesa. All of the grandchildren came too, as well as Juana's sister Guadalupe from Half Moon Bay with her musical family, which within its own circle formed a whole brass band and added much to the gaiety of the occasion.

Small tracts of this rancho nearest the original home were apportioned to the children, but the greater acreage early passed into the possession of collateral relatives and outsiders. The daughter Manuela continued to live at her mother's place for some time after her marriage, and her elder children were born in this adobe before she moved to a house located where Alta Mesa Cemetery is now (between Arastradero Road and Adobe Creek). In 1873 she moved to the neighboring town itself so that her children might attend the Mayfield School (a smaller schoolhouse than the present one located on the same site). Manuela lived for a year in a rented house on what was then Washington Street, now changed to Page Mill Road, and the next year she built a frame house on Sheridan Avenue.

Another daughter also lived in Mayfield (now South Palo Alto), and finally the mother Juana, crippled by rheumatism, left the adobe on the hill and moved to a little house in town near the two daughters, where she was cared for until her death on December 3, 1889, at an advanced age. The house in which she spent her last years was at the corner of Birch Street and Page Mill Road.

María la Luce survived her sister by two months. The family burials are at Holy Cross Cemetery in Menlo Park and at Mission Dolores in San Francisco. The daughter Manuela died in 1901, and her house, containing several family documents, was afterward destroyed by fire.

The Juana Briones de Miranda adobe (SRL 524) has since known other owners. Dr. Charles Palmer Nott, a botanist at Stanford University, purchased the place in 1900 and made many improvements to both the house and the grounds. The adobe, originally long and narrow and found falling into decay, was preserved by being covered with boards. As Dr. Nott's family grew in number, he added rooms, first two frame ells to the adobe so that an attractive court was formed around the old well. In this protected spot he and his wife planned pathways and cared for little flower borders. Later a stairway was built, leading through the former dining room, and a second story was added. The place kept its original charm and became more comfortable. Ornamental shrubs and vines, planted on the hillside by this owner, are now thriving. A later owner (1925) was Dr. George Lee Eaton of San Francisco. Since his death the property has remained in his family. The adobe stands on Old Trace Road east of West Fremont Avenue near its junction with Arastradero Road. Old Trace Road was originally a trail over which redwood logs were hauled from the hills to the bay for shipping. The residential city of Los Altos Hills is now situated on Rancho La Purísima Concepción.

Rancho Santa Teresa

Rancho Santa Teresa originally consisted of 9,647 acres granted to Joaquín Bernal, a native of Mexico. The land he chose lies in the Santa Clara Valley immediately south of San Jose and bounded on the east by Coyote Creek. On the other sides were the following ranchos: Cañada de San Felipe y las Animas on the east, Laguna Seca on the south, and San Juan Bautista and San Vicente on the west. In July 1834, when he petitioned Governor Figueroa for the property, he had lived on the place since about 1826, had built adobe houses, and had large flocks and herds. The grant was made to him within the month. He had petitioned for one league but described an area over twice as large. The legal description held, and the United States eventually confirmed title to his son, Agustín Bernal.

A large framed picture on the wall of a modern house on the ranch shows the place as it may have appeared in the year 1835: a spacious and well-built two-story adobe house with a balcony across the front, a tile-topped adobe wall enclosing perhaps an acre of ground into which the back of the house projects, a fenced kitchen garden at one side, a pool in a roofless enclosure, a sturdily built fence with heavy gate surrounding an arena for the "bull and grizzly" fights to which settlers from the whole countryside came on days of celebration, and on the hillside some 150 yards away the Santa Teresa Spring. This picture and family portraits of Don Joaquín and the gracious Josefa Sánchez, his wife, preserve the true feeling of early Spanish life as it existed in this hacienda eight miles south of San Jose.

Don Joaquín and his wife both died at an advanced age. Their home was on the site of the present frame house in which the fourth generation was born. The never failing spring supplies water, which flows through lead pipes as it did for the adobes over a century ago. A statue of Santa Teresa, brought from Rome by Father Seraphina, was presented to Jesusita, wife of Ygnacio Bernal, grandson of the original grantee. Pedro Bernal, Jesusita's son, placed the statue of the patron saint in a glass-enclosed niche on a boulder beside the Santa Teresa Spring.

Near the spring, on slightly lower ground, is the stonework of an old vat where a French saddle maker, Changara, was allowed to tan hides from some of the cattle slaughtered on the place. He was given a small adobe for living quarters and there made saddles much in demand by the horsemen of the period. When an extra supply accumulated, he journeyed up and down the state to dispose of them. On his return it was his custom, according to legend, to bury the proceeds nearby. On one of his journeys he was murdered, probably for the money he carried. Diligent search was instituted for the old cache in the ground near his vat, but as far as is known no treasure has ever been found there.

On this rancho was signed the Treaty of Santa Teresa, on November 29, 1844. Governor Manuel Micheltorena, who was opposed by Juan Bautista Alvarado and José Castro, agreed by its terms to send his army of *cholos*, an unpopular band of ex-convicts, out of California within three months. As a matter of fact he did not do so, and the "battle" of Cahuenga Pass, near Los Angeles, took place the following February. It resulted in Micheltorena's finally being unseated as governor.

Relics of Indian and Spanish life were found from time to time by workers in field and orchard. Among the articles treasured by the family are an earring of onyx, perhaps once worn by an Indian princess; mortars and pestles used by the Indians to grind food; two huge, hard millstones that ground flour for the Spanish; and a sweet-toned bell worn by the herd mare in a past generation. Some of the rancho is still held by descendants of the original grantee and is used for orchards; several hundred acres, however, are now a county park. The area is reached by Cottle Road.

Rancho El Potrero de Santa Clara

One of the very earliest boundary markers in California was placed somewhere between Mission Santa Clara and the Pueblo de San José to fix the extent of the mission pastures. In 1797 serious question of its exact position arose, and on July 29 a parley was held between Don Alberto de Córdoba, engineer extraordinary and envoy of the governor, and three founders of the pueblo, Manuel Gonzales, Tiburcio Vásquez (apparently the grandfather of the bandit of the same name), and Ignacio Archuleta. Don Alberto questioned each of the three separately, and all three pointed out the same spot as the one designated when the line was originally laid out by José Joaquín Moraga. But the fathers of the mission were not convinced. As it was of vital importance to know just where the mission lands ended and the pueblo lands began, most of the civil and religious authorities took part in the controversy before it was finally settled, with the Guadalupe River as the dividing line.

The Potrero (pasture lands) de Santa Clara was enclosed by a willow hedge and running ditch very early in mission history, at least at its northwestern end, before the Alameda was built around its southern end. This ditch and the other earliest irrigation ditches were fed from the Posa de Santa Clara, a natural pond excavated into a large shallow well, which had a perennial flow. This source is recognizably described in the very earliest mission reports, and its location has been identified as the middle of the block bounded by Mission Street, Park Avenue, and the Alameda. Beyond the Posa, the Alameda crossed the very extensive Ciénega de Santa Clara.

After the secularization of the missions, this land reverted to the Mexican government, and in 1844 Governor Manuel Micheltorena granted Rancho El Potrero de Santa Clara, consisting supposedly of one square league, to James Alexander Forbes, a native of Scotland, who had arrived in Alta California in 1830 or 1831. Against Forbes, this rancho was claimed, with some documentary support and a great deal of natural right, by a number of former mission Indians.

Forbes had been naturalized as a Mexican citizen ten years previous to receiving this rancho, and in 1834 had married Ana María, daughter of Juan Crisóstomo Galindo, claimant of mission lands near Milpitas. According to some authorities, El Potrero de Santa Clara was given as a marriage dower to the bride. In 1842 James Alexander Forbes, well educated and speaking Spanish with a Scottish accent, was appointed British vice-consul and assumed the office in October of the following year. He attended to his duties for some years, although he did not change his residence to Monterey, the capital. After holding his rancho a few years, he sold it in 1847 to Commodore Stockton, to whom 1,939 acres were twice confirmed: in 1853 by the Land Commission, and in 1855 by the District Court. Survey had shown the ranch to be considerably less than a league. It was known for a long time as the Stockton Ranch.

Commodore Robert Field Stockton, U.S.N., born in 1795, was one of the earliest notable Americans connected with the history of California. He served in the War of 1812, was sent West in command of a squadron in 1845, with Frémont conquered California in 1846–47, was made military governor of California by proclamation at Los Angeles on August 17, 1846, and organized the government in the newly acquired land. He appointed Colonel John C. Frémont to take the governorship in January 1847 before he started home on June 20, 1847, across the Rockies with his small and heterogeneous collection of men.

The rancho which he purchased from James Alexander Forbes lay in the angle formed by the Alameda and the Guadalupe River. Three business ventures in California are credited to Commodore Stockton: a nursery for the propagation of fruit trees, a residential subdivision called Alameda Gardens, and the importation of houses from the East around the Horn. All of these projects arose from the one idea of the establishment of pleasant living conditions for families in this new part of the United States. Although he had returned to California in 1848, the carrying out of his ideas must have been delegated to responsible agents, as he himself was in Washington, D.C., serving as United States Senator from his native state of New Jersey for the term of 1851–53. He had resigned from the United States Navy in 1850.

Nursery stock, consisting of apples, pears, plums, peaches, nectarines, and strawberry plants, was ordered from Hovey's Nursery in Massachusetts in 1852. When the stock arrived, two men, Fox and Egan, came in charge of it, as well as James F. Kennedy, a salesman. The nursery was well established by 1853. It is said that in this shipment came the first strawberry plants to be received in the Santa Clara Valley, where they are now so abundant. Stockton also imported bees from Italy—one queen bee and seven other bees as a start.

For the Alameda Gardens subdivision, Stockton ordered houses to be made in New England ready to be erected in California after being shipped around the Horn. Misfortune befell the first shipment, but, undaunted, he ordered another though smaller lot. Eventually the ten houses of the second shipment came and were put up. One of these, a two-story-and-attic structure with a cupola on the top, stood until 1947 at the end of Spring Street just beyond Newhall Street, a location now within the San Jose Municipal Airport. Called the "White House," it was occupied by James F. Kennedy, a native of Pennsylvania, who came from the East in 1852 to manage the

large rancho property for Stockton, bringing his family with him. He lived in it prior to 1853, for family tradition gives the birth of his daughter Clara there on January 1, 1853. During his occupancy a pergola extended along one side of the house and out to the stables, which stood at some distance from the house. An iron fence ran completely around the property. The house had a balcony on three sides of its first and second stories and a similar one completely around the cupola, within which appeared to be a fair-sized room with sufficient doors and windows to make a comfortable place for observation of the landscape in all directions. Kennedy, who served as adjutant general for California during the Civil War, later purchased a large ranch near Los Gatos. It is thought that the old residence of Judge Hester, now moved to 968 Emory Street, is one of the houses of the Stockton shipment. Other than this, they have all disappeared.

The border line of this rancho facing on the Alameda is entirely built up. Originally these buildings were all private homes, but lately business houses are creeping in along the "willow way" of early mission days. Among the hospitable homes of a former day still standing is that of James Henry, the man who built the first overhead electric trolley line connecting San Jose and Santa Clara. This elegant and ornamented mansion, built in the 1880's, stands at the northwest corner of University Avenue and the Alameda.

Rancho Los Coches

By the treaty between Mexico and the United States which was signed at the cessation of hostilities for the possession of California, all bona fide titles to land existing prior to that date were recognized by the conquering Americans. Claims to the ownership of land were immediately forthcoming, and it became an urgent matter to settle those claims in order that life in the newly acquired territory might proceed lawfully. The appointment on March 3, 1851, of a Federal Land Commission was secured by the first senators sent to Washington from the new state, John C. Frémont and William M. Gwin. This commission proceeded to San Francisco, where it sat for the hearing of the cases brought before it.

The first case decided for property in Santa Clara County was that of Rancho Los Coches (called "The Pigs" because it had been the mission's swine range), consisting of one-half square league lying southwest of the Alameda. The boundary began on the Alameda at the Ciénega de Santa Clara and extended westward to the Roblar del Torotal, thence southeast along this forest to the Arroyo de los Gatos, thence to the Guadalupe River. This rancho had been given by Governor Micheltorena on March 12, 1844, to Roberto, a Christianized Indian of Mission Santa Clara who had been living on the land with his wife and children before that date. The question in this case was concerned with the legality of a grant to an Indian and further with his right to dispose of the property. This question being decided in the affirmative by the commission, a claim, based on Roberto's ownership, was filed in 1852 by Antonio Suñol, Paula Suñol de Sansevain, and Henry M. Naglee, and the patent to the rancho was given on December 31, 1857, to the claimants.

Antonio María Suñol, a Spaniard in the French naval service, had lived in California since 1818, when he had deserted from the *Bordelais* in Monterey harbor. He settled in San José, where he kept a shop, and about 1824 he married María Dolores Bernal. He was postmaster from 1826 to 1829, *sindico* (receiver) from 1839 to 1840, and subprefect from 1841 to 1844. During his ranch activities, he sold cattle to Captain Sutter on credit and had difficulty in obtaining payment. Duflot du Mofras, as he journeyed through the state in 1841, found him to be sympathetic to France. Several children were born to Don Antonio and Doña María Dolores, one of the daughters, Paula, who married Pierre Sansevain, being named as one of the three patentees of this rancho.

In 1847 Suñol bought Rancho Los Coches from Roberto, the Indian grantee, and with it Roberto's adobe home. The Indian had built a low one-room adobe about 1839 and joined to it a much larger building in 1840 or 1841. He lived here until Suñol bought the property, and Suñol, in turn, made it his residence until 1853, when he sold the adobe and a small parcel of land surrounding it to Stephen Splivalo, an Italian sea captain. In 1854 Splivalo added a frame second story. This beautiful home still stands—Roberto's two adobes and Splivalo's addition—at 770 Lincoln Avenue, toward the Willow Glen section of San Jose. A porch across its front supports an upper balustrade. At the rear of the building are fig trees of the Black Mission variety. One of these trees is especially large, although from its trunk many large branches have been cut. A part of the tree lies across a trellis. It bears a never-failing crop of figs. A proposed crosstown freeway has been realigned to spare this historic and well-preserved adobe.

Henry Morris Naglee, a distinguished officer in the Civil War and one of the three joint patentees of Rancho Los Coches, long held a portion of it in his name. Naglee Park, which extended from 11th Street to Coyote Creek in the city of San Jose, was once his property (although not on Los Coches), and here on a 140-acre tract stood his residence, reached by a driveway one and one-half miles long. Now remodeled as an apartment house, the building stands at the northwest corner of San Fernando and 14th streets. The redwood trees and the stately palms remaining from his planting, which line some of the streets in this vicinity, give some idea of the extent and beauty of the grounds laid out around his home in 1865.

Rancho Las Animas

The first census of San José, taken in 1778, lists José Mariano Castro, 13 years of age, eldest son of Joaquín Castro and his wife, María Botiller, both of whom came to California in 1776 with the Anza colonists. This boy, grown to manhood and married to Josefa Romero, journeyed back to Mexico in 1801 and obtained the grant of Rancho La Brea. The document, directly from the Spanish Viceroy Marquinas, was dated August 17, 1802. Together with an addition to it granted in 1810 by Viceroy Lizano y Beaumont, it was the only rancho in the present state granted directly by a viceroy, in the studied opinion of Theodore Hittell. In later years some difficulty regarding the title was encountered, but in August 1835 the matter was adjusted by the regranting of it under the name of Rancho Las Animas by the Mexican governor, José Figueroa, to the widow of Don José Mariano, Doña Josefa.

In some way this rancho passed into the possession of José María Sánchez. The 26,519 acres patented to his heirs in 1873 extend from the border line of San Benito County near Sawyer Station northwest across U.S. Highway 101 south of Gilroy (incorporated in 1868) to Mount Madonna County Park in the Santa Cruz Mountains. On this rancho, the Carnadero Creek flows for miles through a series of rolling hills, after it leaves the higher region in the vicinity of Mount Madonna. Wonderful pasture lands are on these hills, and here around Miller's Station was the celebrated Bloomfield Farm of Henry Miller, the German boy who climbed to success through his ability to grow and market cattle and sheep.

Heinrich Alfred Kreiser was the name of this young German in his native land, but in his journey from New York via Havana he had used a ticket purchased from a chance acquaintance named Henry Miller. On March 30, 1858, eight years after he had reached California, he changed his name by legal procedure to Henry Miller. In that year he made the acquaintance of and formed a partnership with Charles Lux—a partnership that lasted until the death of Lux 25 years later. As time passed, the firm of Miller and Lux became familiar throughout the West. Henry Miller seemed to succeed in all that he undertook; his ability to foresee the outcome of his plans was remarkable. The lands and herds of this firm stretched well over the state; in several counties large feeding grounds and fields for cultivation were acquired. More than a dozen of the old ranchos were owned in whole or in part by them, and the number of their employees was legion. When their animals were driven to market in San Francisco, no matter how long the journey, feeding and resting places on their own property were always convenient.

The Bloomfield Ranch is easily recognizable by three large concrete silos, built in relatively modern times, along Highway 101 three and one-half miles south of Gilroy. It is said that one of the dwellings on the ranch, visible from the highway, is part of the old ranch house.

On Mount Madonna, which has an elevation of 1,897 feet in the mountains on the northwest part of this rancho, Henry Miller built an elaborate country home overlooking the broad valley below. There he entertained his friends. After his death in 1916, the house, which was purchased for erection elsewhere, was removed piece by piece, and the fountains, terraces, and choice trees and shrubs that graced the grounds were left untended. The ruins of the estate may be seen in Mount Madonna County Park.

Rancho San Francisco de las Llagas

The name Las Llagas de Nuestro Padre San Francisco (Stigmata of Our Father St. Francis), bestowed on March 22, 1772, by Don Pedro Fages on his stopping place beside a stream north of San Martin, has clung to the place ever since. It was a convenient and suitable campsite for the parties of explorers and colonists who trod the same path later. Anza spent the night there in March 1776, and the colonists of his party under the leadership of Lieutenant José Joaquín Moraga rested there for a day, about June 23, in the summer of the same year, as they proceeded from Monterey to the Port of San Francisco. The expedition consisted of Fray Francisco Palou, Fray Pedro Benito Cambón, the leather-jacketed soldiers, the colonists and their families equipped with utensils and provisions, as well as the herdsmen and muleteers driving plodding livestock for use in the permanent settlement. As they traveled along the dusty trail, they had seen herds of large animals which, when captured, proved to be elk with wide-spread horns and which they found most palatable for food. They had seen, as well, on this broad plain herds of antelope that sped away before them, frightened by this strange cavalcade.

The rancho granted by Governor José Figueroa to Carlos Castro on February 3, 1834, lay in this region and covered a long stretch of Llagas Creek. Don Carlos was probably Carlos Antonio, who as a child of three years had come with his parents to California with the Anza party in 1776. He had held important official positions at Santa Cruz and San José before receiving this rancho, to which he retired in his sixties in 1836. He is described by Bancroft as an eccentric host whose hospitality was shown by affecting the abuse of his guests. The northern line of the tract is at Tennant Station on the railroad which passes through the level lands of the central part of the grant.

The property, however, soon passed out of Castro's hands, for in the 1840's it is mentioned as belonging to Bernard and Daniel Murphy, and it was patented to James and Martin Murphy on March 19, 1868. It was bordered on the north by the land of Martin Murphy, Sr., who built a chapel in about the center of this rancho and called it San Martín in honor of his patron saint. This was considerably east of the present town of San Martin, which grew up along the railroad. Church Avenue is a reminder of the old chapel, of which nothing remains, and on the ranch at New Avenue and San Martin Avenue there is an old house, now used for storage, said to have been the residence of Daniel Murphy and presumably prefabricated in the 1850's on the East Coast, as was the home of his brother, Martin, Jr., at Sunnyvale. Highway 101 passes through the later settlement of San Martin, between Gilroy and Morgan Hill, bisecting the area originally contained in the 22,283-acre Rancho San Francisco de las Llagas.

Rancho La Laguna Seca

J. C. Frémont in his *Memoirs* says: "By the middle of February [1846] we were all re-united in the Valley of San Jose, about 13 miles south of the village of that name on the main road leading to Monterey which was about 60 miles distant.... The Place which I had selected for rest and re-fitting was a vacant rancho called the Laguna, belonging to Mr. Fisher. I remained here until February, in the most delightful spring season of a most delightful climate. The time was occupied in purchasing horses, obtaining supplies, and thoroughly re-fitting the party."

The rancho of four square leagues had been granted on July 22, 1834, by Governor José Figueroa to Juan Alvírez, former alcalde of San José (1812–13), and was confirmed to Liberata Ceseña Bull and other heirs of William Fisher, to whom it was also patented in 1865.

William Fisher was a sea captain from Boston, who came to California and purchased this rancho in 1845. The Fisher family had not yet arrived at their new home at the time of Frémont's February visit. In addition to managing the rancho, Captain Fisher conducted in San José a mercantile business which he sold on account of ill health in 1849, one year before his death, to Josiah Belden.

Rancho Laguna Seca, averaging four miles in width, begins about a mile north of Coyote and extends southward to include Madrone, now within the northern city limits of Morgan Hill. Coyote Creek flows through this grant, entering it from the hilly region near the southeast corner and flowing westward past Coyote Station. The Southern Pacific Railroad runs from north to south through the grant near the middle. Miller and Lux, holders of vast tracts of land, later purchased the southern part of this rancho adjoining Rancho Cañada de San Felipe y las Animas, and it became a part of the chain of ranches owned by this firm.

Rancho San Ysidro

John Gilroy, the first non-Hispanic foreign settler in California, arrived, ill of scurvy, at Monterey in 1814 on the *Isaac Todd*, which he there deserted. Of Scottish parentage, his rightful name was John Cameron, but he assumed his mother's maiden name of Gilroy to avoid being found and returned to the ship. In the September after his arrival he was baptized at Mission San Carlos as Juan Bautista María Gilroy. In 1821 he was married at Mission San Juan Bautista to María Clara de la Asunción, daughter of Ygnacio Ortega, the owner of Rancho San Ysidro.

Rancho San Ysidro seems to have been the home of Don Ygnacio for many years previous to this time. Bancroft says that this rancho, one of the finest in the district, was granted in 1810 to Ygnacio, son of Captain José F. Ortega, who probably came with his father from Mexico between 1769 and 1773. Don Ygnacio, whose wife was Gertrudis Arce, was a *"soldado distinguido"* of the San Diego Company in 1792.

Governor Figueroa granted this rancho in 1833 to the heirs of Don Ygnacio, following his death. It was divided approximately equally among Ysabel Ortega (the wife of Julián Cantua), Quentín, and Clara (the wife of John Gilroy). Ysabel received the third called Rancho La Polka, in the hills east of San Martin and northeast of Gilroy, consisting of 4,166 acres. Quentín Ortega's share was 4,438 acres, the Rancho San Ysidro (Ortega); and Clara's, 4,460 acres, the Rancho San Ysidro (Gilroy). The line dividing Quentín's property from Gilroy's ran along the old road from Gilroy to Pacheco Pass and, according to notes of the 1850 survey of the property, crossed "the former site of an oven between two adobe houses." The houses of these two younger men were about 50 yards apart, that of John lying in the sharp angle of the Y formed by the present Pacheco Pass Road and the Frazier Lake Road, and that of Quentín, his brother-in-law, on the opposite side of the latter road. On the site of Gilroy's three-room adobe, a blacksmith shop was later placed. Across Pacheco Pass Road from there is a place called the "old soap-factory site." Quentín's adobe, probably the home of his father before him, was larger and was a landmark for years. Its arches of hewn logs stood long after the adobe house itself was gone. Cultivation of the fields that cover the site has now removed every trace. W. T. Sherman relates in his *Memoirs* that, on a certain occasion, he and his men camped by a stream near three or four adobe huts known as Gilroy's Ranch.

John Gilroy, a man of fine physique and pleasant manners, though possessed of little education, had much natural ability and became influential in his locality. When he became a naturalized Mexican citizen in 1833, he produced certificates to show that he was a soapmaker and a millwright of good character, with a wife and four children, and had also some livestock on Rancho San Ysidro. Two millstones long remained on the property. As the years passed, he lost his Scottish thrift, lost all his property, and toward the end of his life became dependent on charity. He died in 1869, aged 73 years. The little settlement of San Ysidro, over which he was alcalde for a time, stretched along the Pacheco Pass Road. It is now known as Old Gilroy, and old settlers living there used to point out sites of many adobes that have fallen.

While John Gilroy was still living, the first American to locate permanently in the vicinity came upon the scene. This was Julius Martin, who, born in North Carolina in 1804, had come overland from his former home in Missouri with his wife and daughters and arrived at San Ysidro on December 26, 1843. For a part of the overland journey this family had been with a larger group, most of whom proceeded to Oregon. Near Fort Laramie they had met Joseph Reddeford Walker, who, returning to California as leader of the smaller group, brought them across Walker Pass. During the ensuing years Walker was a frequent

visitor at the Martin home, where he was always welcome, no matter how long he stayed.

Julius Martin settled in San Ysidro, where he constructed a small horsepower mill with a capacity of 20 bushels a day. He became a captain of the American Scouts under Frémont and saw the Bear Flag raised in Sonoma. When Charles Bennett, Sutter's messenger, paused in San Ysidro on his way to report the discovery of gold at government headquarters at Monterey, his story so intrigued the settlers that most of them left for the diggings. Julius Martin was among the number who went, and after he returned in 1850 he was able to pay cash for 1,220 acres of Rancho San Ysidro, which he purchased from John Gilroy. The deed, signed by John Gilroy and his wife, was dated January 8, 1852. This property Martin held until his death in 1891. Although blind for the last 30 years of his life, he was able to come out victorious in litigation which threatened to deprive him of his land. He was a man of good education and had an excellent memory. To his reminiscences, told to interviewers during his last years, are due many of the details of the early history not only of the immediate vicinity but also of other parts of the state. He built three houses on this property, one of which still stands in the eastern limits of the town of Gilroy at 610 I.O.O.F. Avenue, formerly Martin's Lane, at the end of the road half a mile east of the highway through town. Most of the city of Gilroy, however, lies on Rancho Las Animas.

About five miles east of Gilroy on the old road to Gilroy Hot Springs is an adobe, the history and age of which are uncertain. It now forms part of the Peabody residence, located on the right-hand side of Leavesley Road, half a mile beyond its junction with Crews Road.

Rancho Milpitas

The right to the lands of Rancho Milpitas (*milpa,* "maize field") was claimed by two men: Nicolás Berryessa, who considered it his by a decree issued by Alcalde Pedro Chaboya on May 6, 1834; and José María Alviso, to whom it was granted by Governor José Castro on September 23 and October 2, 1835.

These men were both sons of Spanish pioneers in Alta California, both soldiers of the military company in San Francisco, where they served together eight years, from 1819 to 1827. Both were leading men in the Pueblo de San José, Alviso being alcalde in 1836, at which time Berryessa was *regidor,* and both were residing in San José in 1841.

Berryessa was married to Gracia Padilla, and Alviso's wife was Juana, whose father was José de Jesús Galindo, a man who lived to the reputed age of 106 years and died in Milpitas in 1877.

Beginning at the time of the Bear Flag activities, Nicolás Berryessa's years were full of misfortune: his cattle were plundered by Frémont's battalion; his brother, José de los Reyes, was killed by Frémont's men; squatters settled on his land; and, as the last straw, his claim for Rancho Milpitas was rejected by the Land Commission when it finally reported on October 16, 1855. He died insane in 1863. His name Berryessa, however, is carried by a creek which flows through a part of the contested property, by the school and the settlement on adjoining pueblo lands, and by the road that leads from this settlement toward San Jose. It was in the town of Berryessa that Sierra Nevada Smith, a covered-wagon baby of 1853, lived. Born in Utah, she came here and in her later years lived in a house located on the spot where a Methodist church was burned in the 1860's.

On March 3, 1856, the year following the rejection of Berryessa's claim, the Land Commission decreed the confirmation of Alviso's claim, and on June 30, 1871, a patent for 4,457 acres was issued to him.

José María Alviso was the son of Ygnacio Alviso, a juvenile member of the Anza expedition. In 1841 he was living in San José with his wife and six children. His home on this rancho stood about two miles from the town of Milpitas and east of the old Oakland–San Jose highway, on Piedmont Road near the corner of Calaveras Road. The only remaining building of the original group of four adobes comprising the hacienda was built probably in the middle 1830's. The second story of this adobe above the upper veranda is covered by weatherboarding to afford adequate protection to the original material. The house, painted white with green trimming, stands in a colorful flower garden in the midst of fruitful orchards. It is occupied, and the remnant of the old rancho on which it stands is still farmed.

Near the western boundary of Rancho Milpitas, running parallel to the main direction of Penitencia Creek, are the railroad tracks and the Old Oakland Road, both of which pass through the town of Milpitas. The town was originally called Penitencia by the Spanish, but after the American settlers became more numerous it was changed. The area was once a part of the outlying land of the Pueblo de San José, and along this creek were the gardens where corn, peppers, and squashes were grown by residents of the pueblo. In these gardens were held the harvest-time merrymakings. The creek itself came by the name Penitencia because, according to tradition, at the place where it curves around a bank, once stood a house of penitence, a small adobe building where priests from the missions came at stated intervals to hear confessions. The structure was about 20 feet square. It was demolished about 1900.

Rancho Rincón de los Esteros

Rancho Rincón de los Esteros, lying between Penitencia Creek and the Guadalupe River and crossed lengthwise by Coyote Creek, was granted February 10, 1838, by Governor Alvarado to Ygnacio Alviso. He was one of the three children who accompanied their Spanish mother on the overland journey of the Anza colonists from Mexico to San Francisco. He was born in Sonora in 1772, both of his parents being Spanish. When he became 18, he enlisted as a soldier in the San Francisco Company, where he served for 29 years and retired in 1819 as sergeant on half pay.

At the age of 24 he married Margarita Bernal

in San Francisco. From 1840 to 1843 he was administrator of the Santa Clara Mission properties. He died in 1848, leaving eight children: Agustín, José Antonio, Gabriel, Anastasio, José María (grantee of Rancho Milpitas), Domingo, Concepción, and Dolores.

After the death of Don Ygnacio the rancho was divided into three parts. The 2,308 acres lying between Penitencia Creek and Coyote Creek were confirmed to Ellen E. White on December 28, 1857, and were patented to her in 1862. The lower part of her land, near the slough into which both streams flowed, was inundated much of the time. She and her husband, Charles E., whom she survived, were owners of several other pieces of land in this and other counties.

A second part of Rancho Rincón de los Esteros, which contained 1,845 acres, was confirmed to Francisco Berryessa on the same day that Ellen E. White received confirmation of her part. The Berryessa land reached from Coyote Creek to the town of Alviso, for which tract the heirs received a patent in 1873.

The tract of 2,200 acres retained by the Alviso family lay south of the other two and extended from the Guadalupe River across Coyote Creek to Penitencia Creek. It was confirmed to Rafael Alviso and other heirs on December 24, 1857, and was patented to them on July 29, 1872.

Rancho Ulistac

Rancho Ulistac lay between the Guadalupe River and Saratoga Creek, beginning at their confluence near Alviso, and contained about one-half square league granted by Governor Pío Pico on May 19, 1845, to three Indians, Marcelo, Cristoval, and Pío. (There may have been only two grantees, one of them being named Marcelo Pío.) On March 2, 1857, this was confirmed to the claimant Jacob D. Hoppe, to whose heirs a patent for 2,217 acres was given on October 12, 1868.

Jacob D. Hoppe, a native of Maryland and later a resident of Kentucky and Missouri, reached California in 1846 at the age of 33. A year after his arrival on the West Coast, he became interested in the establishment of a weekly newspaper. The printing materials that he had were afterward turned over to the proprietors of the *Alta California*. He lived in San Jose, except for a visit to the mines lasting a few months, and was San Jose's first American postmaster and a delegate to the Constitutional Convention before finally becoming one of the unfortunate victims of the steamer *Jenny Lind* explosion in San Francisco Bay on April 11, 1853.

Through the entire length of Rancho Ulistac ran the old narrow-gauge railroad from Alviso to San Jose, and paralleling the railroad was the old stage road between the two places.

About midway between the ends of this ranch, William Hannibal and his son-in-law, Edward Burrell, who both came overland from the East with their families in 1854, purchased 132 acres of land, which stretched from this road to the Guadalupe River and which they named Bay Tree Farm. In the central part of their tract was a house which Hannibal chose for his home; the daughter and her husband owned the lands on either side of it, on one of which they built an adobe house. On this grant was also the Laurelwood Farm belonging to Peter Donahue, and the Riverside Farm, adjoining it, belonging to W. W. Montague, for whom Montague Road, separating it from the James Lick property, is named.

James Lick, a native of Pennsylvania, was a piano maker by trade. Having accumulated $30,000 in South America, he came to San Francisco on January 7, 1848, and bought up, at low prices, a large amount of land there and elsewhere. Later this property increased greatly in value until it was worth millions.

In 1855 Lick built a four-stone, water-powered flour mill on the west bank of the Guadalupe River just north of the present Montague Road, at a cost of $380,000. The interior was finished in mahogany. The property is now the plant of the Commercial Solvents Corporation, which has preserved Lick's beautiful mansion and gardens, and a round, brick warehouse from the mill. Nearby is the town of Agnew and the Agnews State Hospital.

Lick began giving away his vast wealth in 1873, the year that he donated his mill to the Thomas Paine Memorial Association of Boston. He died on October 1, 1876, at the age of 80, leaving to a board of trustees a large part of the work of distributing his fortune. The amount of $700,000 was allocated to the establishment of Lick Observatory. The site, on the summit of Mount Hamilton, about 15 miles east of San Jose, was granted by act of Congress in 1876, and, with additional grants, the reservation now totals 3,133 acres. The observatory, provided with some of the best astronomical apparatus in the world, was first opened to the public by the University of California on June 1, 1888. Lick lies buried under a supporting pillar of one of the huge telescopes.

Mount Hamilton, 4,209 feet above sea level, was named in honor of the Rev. Laurentine Hamilton, a pioneer missionary preacher in San Jose, and also superintendent of schools. With William H. Brewer and Josiah D. Whitney, Hamilton was one of the first white men to climb the mountain, on August 26, 1861.

Rancho Posolmi

On the bay side of the Bayshore Freeway between Moffett Field and the junction of the freeway with the Mountain View–Alviso road, there used to be seen a picket fence enclosing a small plot of ground in which the original grantee of Rancho Posolmi lay buried. The neglected fence in the middle of the pasture land was finally knocked down by cattle, and later cultivation of field crops on the site has obliterated all surface trace of the spot.

From an early period a band of Indians had occupied this region near the lower end of San Francisco Bay, and on February 15, 1844, Governor Micheltorena gave to their chieftain, Lópe Iñigo, a formal grant of a tract shown on old maps as the Yñigo Reservation. It consisted of 1,697 acres of level land, about square in outline, partially a salt marsh before its subsequent reclamation for farming purposes. The apex of one right angle of this square jutted into Rancho

James Lick Mansion, Agnew

Pastoria de las Borregas at the junction of the Mountain View–Alviso road with the Bayshore Freeway. The United States patent to this land was given to Chief Iñigo and two others on January 18, 1881.

Before the date of the patent, the land had been sold, and the homes of five white men had been established within its confines: D. Frink, J. Bailey, E. Jenkins, W. Gallimore, and Robert Walkinshaw. Walkinshaw, a native of Scotland and long a resident of Mexico, arrived in California in 1847 as supercargo on the *William* and assumed charge of the New Almaden mines. He built his home not near the mines but on Rancho Posolmi, where he owned the largest of the five tracts and, in addition, had purchased an adjoining piece of land stretching to the Guadalupe Slough. His house, which stood within half a mile of the junction of the Alviso road with the Bayshore Freeway, was an elaborate frame structure of U-shape, and here he entertained lavishly, living the life of a British country squire and riding to hounds with his daughters. He returned to Scotland in 1858 and died there in the following year. The greater part of his land was purchased by an American pioneer, Henry Curtner, the owner of much property in Santa Clara and Alameda counties.

At first known simply as "the air base," Moffett Field was dedicated on April 12, 1933, construction having begun in 1931. It was to be a base for Navy dirigibles. The dedication ceremony was clouded with sadness, for just eight days earlier the great dirigible *Akron*, which was to have been based here, had crashed in the East, at a loss of 73 lives, including that of Rear Admiral William A. Moffett, for whom the field was later to be named. Hopes brightened, however, when the sister ship, the *Macon*, arrived at Moffett Field on October 15, 1933. But it, too, crashed—on February 12, 1935, off Point Sur—and the Navy soon abandoned its dirigible program. Moffett Field has since been witness to historic advances in all aspects of aviation.

Rancho Pastoria de las Borregas

Rancho Pastoria de las Borregas, also called Rancho Refugio, adjoined Rancho Rincón de San Franciscquito on the northwest, Ranchos San Antonio and La Purísima Concepción on the west and southwest, and extended in the direction of San Francisco Bay around two sides of the land given to the Indian Lópe Iñigo—a tract along the Bayshore Freeway south of Moffett Field.

On March 3, 1852, Martin Murphy, Jr., filed a claim with the Land Commission for a part of this area founded on a grant made January 15, 1842, by Governor Alvarado to Francisco Estrada, and in the same year Mariano Castro, father-in-law of the original grantee, also filed claim to a part of it. Confirmation of the rights of these two men are dated October 17, 1856, and November 23, 1859, respectively, and were followed by patents to Murphy on September 15, 1865, for 4,894 acres, and to Castro on September 17, 1881, for 4,172 acres. Permanente Creek was to be the dividing line between the two holdings.

Francisco Estrada had married Inéz, daughter of Don Mariano Castro, who had assisted the young couple to acquire the land. When both of the young people died, leaving no children, Don Mariano became claimant for the property, part of which he sold to Martin Murphy, Jr.

Don Mariano was the only child of Ignacio Castro and his wife Barbara Pacheco. After this rancho came into his hands, he and his wife, Trinidad Peralta, lived for a time upon it in an adobe house the site of which was on the northwest corner of Rengstorff Avenue and Alma Street near Castro Station. When right of way was given for the building of the railroad across his property, an agreement was made whereby a flag stop would be maintained near the house. A small shelter was built, and residents of this area are still able to board the passing trains. The adobe house and all its surrounding garden are gone. Across Rengstorff Avenue from the site is a subdivision on land that formerly belonged to the Castros. While it was still in their possession, the family awoke one morning to see a rough board shanty standing in what is now the subdivision. So noiselessly had neighbors erected and moved into it that no one had been awakened by their activities. This was an incident of the "squatter" period, when land titles were uncertain and only recourse to expensive litigation, lasting sometimes for years, proved the rightful owner.

Villa Francisca, the stucco house of Crisanto Castro, son of Don Mariano, stood on the opposite side of the railroad track on Crisanto Avenue east of Rengstorff Avenue near the flag station of Castro. It was built in 1911 on the site of the former frame house in which the children of Crisanto were born, and was surrounded by the eucalyptus trees and shrubs of the older house, some of which remain. It was built after the death of the wife, Francisca Armijo, a daughter of the grantee of the Armijo rancho in Solano County. Don Crisanto lived in the new structure about one year before he too died, in 1912, leaving the house with a few acres to his descendants. The house was demolished in 1961 after a fire, and a Mountain View city park now occupies the site.

Martin Murphy, Jr., eldest son of Martin, Sr., purchased the part of Rancho Pastoria de las Borregas lying south of Permanente Creek. He had made the trek from Ireland via Canada and Missouri, sometimes following and sometimes accompanying his father. The son had married in Canada and remained there for some time after his father departed for the United States. Finally taking his family and his goods on a devious course by boat on the lakes and rivers between Quebec, Canada, and St. Joseph, Missouri, he joined his father in Missouri.

Arriving in California with his father's party in 1844, he first settled on the Cosumnes River, whence in 1850 he came to Rancho Pastoria de las Borregas. The house of Martin Murphy, Jr., was framed on the East Coast, brought around the Horn about 1851, and occupied continuously for over a century by members of the same family. It was of two stories, with the stairs leading to the upper floor in the hall that ran through the center of the house from front to back, with doors opening into the garden at both ends. When the house was put in place, the travel up and down the peninsula passed on its bay side; passenger boats, plying between Alviso and San Francisco, could be seen from the door, and El Camino Real passed between the house and the bay. With the coming of the railroad the activities of travel changed to the opposite side of the dwelling, but now the main highway between San Francisco and San Jose once again passes on the bay side.

The ample white house of about 30 rooms stood in attractive grounds in which immense fig trees grown from mission cuttings still flourish. Within the house were family portraits, done in oil by various artists, of several generations of fine men and gracious women. Some of these are now in the historical museum in San Jose. To this house came the priests from Mission Santa Clara to celebrate Mass at regular intervals. A room with an altar and a consecrated altar stone was set aside for the purpose, and here marriage and baptismal ceremonies took place as well. Mary Bulger, whom Martin Murphy, Jr., had married in Canada, kept one of the rooms in the house always ready for the comfort of the archbishop, should he stop for a night's rest on his way between churches.

At the time of their golden wedding, Mr. and Mrs. Murphy issued a general invitation to their acquaintances to attend, with a request that no gifts be offered. A large platform was erected in an oak grove near the railroad, and special trains were engaged by the host for the transportation of the guests. Many came in their own carriages or on horseback. Thousands voiced their congratulations on that day, July 18, 1881. The material used for the great platform was afterward donated by Murphy to the priests, who constructed from it the first chapel erected in Mountain View.

The mantle of his kindly and capable father, Martin, Sr., fell upon Martin Murphy, Jr. Among the achievements in which he had a vital part was the establishment of Santa Clara College, from which his sons were graduated, and the Convent of Notre Dame, where his daughters obtained their education. He lived three years after the golden wedding, his wife long outliving him.

The Murphy house is no more. In the early

1950's the Murphy family sold what remained of the estate to the City of Sunnyvale for a park. The old home was registered as a State Historical Landmark and marked with a huge boulder bearing a bronze plaque. It seemed for a time as if Sunnyvale's only historically important building would be preserved for posterity. But despite valiant efforts of interested citizens and the formation of the Sunnyvale Historical Society, the beautiful old mansion, so carefully prefabricated and painstakingly assembled, was bulldozed into a pile of rubble in four hours on September 27, 1961. It is one of the most tragic losses in the annals of California landmarks. The site *(SRL 644)* is at 252 North Sunnyvale Avenue, between California and Arques.

Rancho Rincón de San Francisquito

The person most closely identified with Rancho Rincón de San Francisquito, or Rancho Santa Rita, was the tall, blue-eyed Castilian, Secundino Robles, long remembered by old-timers who had seen him genially conversing at his home near El Camino Real or capably driving a span of spirited horses over the country roadways. The rancho on which he lived had once been a part of the outlying land of Mission Santa Clara.

In 1824 José Peña, artilleryman at San Francisco and a teacher at that place in 1822, built a wood house on the south side of Lagunita, now on the Stanford University campus. Primitive domestic rosebushes now grow wild there. Later he went to Mexico but returned in the late 1830's to claim the land, sending his son, Narciso Antonio Peña, later justice of the peace in this area,

to occupy it by building an adobe near the old mission horse corral, where Secundino Robles later built. In 1841, at the age of 64, while teaching at Santa Clara, José Peña received a formal grant of the land from Governor Alvarado. The rancho, supposedly two square leagues, was formerly part of the mission cattle range and lay between San Francisquito and San Antonio (Adobe) creeks.

Secundino Robles, born in Santa Cruz in 1811 (or 1813?), and married in 1835 at Mission Santa Clara by Father Picos to María Antonia García, also a native of Santa Cruz, was mayordomo at the mission in 1841, and was commander of some of Francisco Sánchez' troops in 1846, when he was taken prisoner and distinguished himself by breaking his sword in two before surrendering it to his captors. Some years before his marriage he had discovered the location of an outcrop of cinnabar on Alamitos Creek—the secret source of the red paint so long prized by the Indians for the decoration of their bodies. Afterward, when the cinnabar deposit proved to be rich in quicksilver, he and his brother Teodoro received a payment of $13,000 in cash, besides a certain interest in the company that was formed for the development of the mine at New Almaden.

The brothers traded their interest in the mine to José Peña for his rancho and the buildings upon it, "orchard, corrals, and all property he may have on said land." The deed was drawn up in the presence of the *juez de paz,* Ygnacio Alviso, on September 10, 1847. Secundino took immediate possession with his wife and four children and set about enlarging the small Peña adobe. He gave

Martin Murphy, Jr., House, Sunnyvale

the contract for the carpentering to a Mexican named Meña and that for adobe work to Jesús Ramos, paying the two together, it is said, the $13,000 cash received from the mining company. Jesús Ramos continued for some years in the employ of Don Secundino, living in Mayfield with his family.

On the flat roof of the enlarged adobe a dancing floor open to the sky was laid. The hospitality of the family was unbounded, and the Robles adobe became widely known as a stage station between San Francisco and San Jose. Twenty-five children were born to Secundino and his wife María Antonia after they took up residence in this house, making 29 in all. As the family increased and more space became necessary, a shingle roof was put over the dancing floor and the upstairs was divided into three rooms similar to the three on the lower floor. From the middle and larger room on each floor, doors opened front and back to the verandas, six and a quarter feet wide, extending the full length of the house. The kitchen of the establishment was separate from the main building, except that a small wooden stairway ran at the rear of the house from the kitchen to the balcony.

Three attractions drew visitors to this place: the liquid refreshments so genially dispensed by the host, the bear and bull fights held in the arena in front of the house, and the game conveniently near—bear, mountain lion, and deer in the forested hills, and quail, ducks, geese, and snipe in the lowlands nearby. It became a rendezvous of hunters.

Not satisfied with the entertainments which he had at his own door, Don Secundino was an ardent patron of the traveling circus. On one occasion, finding himself short of funds, he borrowed $75 so that he might attend a circus at San Jose, for which sum he gave 50.6 acres of his fertile soil in repayment. In later years he sat more quietly at home in the shade of his grape arbor and conversed with visitors. His death occurred on January 10, 1890, his wife outliving him by several years.

The house, long unoccupied, stood near what is now the northwest corner of Alma Street and San Antonio Avenue. The three lower rooms had redwood ceilings; in the main room, which was a little over 17 feet square, a middle beam across the ceiling was painted with bacchanalian scenes. The walls, 29 inches thick, were composed of four-inch clay-and-gravel blocks and a one-inch layer of adobe. Sand-finish plaster covered the interior, white plaster laid upon a half-inch coating of clay and straw, the exterior. The separate kitchen was 15 × 33 feet, inside measurement, with a brick chimney at the west corner.

The steeply pitched roof of the main building had a middle height of six feet. A truck gardener purchased the 20 acres of land on which the adobe was standing shortly before the earthquake of April 18, 1906, when the structure collapsed. The shingle roof was salvaged by being supported on strong posts, while the underlying debris was removed and spread about on the adjacent garden patch. A barn was built under the old roof

on the identical adobe site, but it has now also disappeared.

The rancho, when confirmed by the United States to Teodoro E. and Secundino Robles, contained 4,418 acres of the larger tract that was asked for originally by José Peña, and for that number of acres the brothers received patent on February 19, 1868. Jeremiah Clarke of San Francisco purchased a part of it from María Rosalía Robles, former wife of José Teodoro, giving "all her right, title, and interest" on June 8, 1859; and gradually, from that time on, the vast property dwindled. The Encino Farm, bordering on San Antonio (Adobe) Creek, was the portion of one of Secundino's daughters.

Jeremiah Clarke held a considerable piece of land in the vicinity; he had a boat landing on Mayfield Slough and built a private road from it to Mayfield. He built a two-story house, a barn, and a granary on Matadero Creek east of Middlefield Road, and this house was his headquarters on his frequent trips from San Francisco. The road has been obliterated and the buildings are now gone. He sold his farm to the Spokane Land Company, which graded new roads and planned an extensive settlement. A hammer factory built and equipped during that period still stands on Matadero Creek at 2995 Middlefield Road. The old wooden building, from which the original machinery has long since been removed, is located back from the street behind newer structures. Colorado Avenue and Louis Road are on this old tract.

Rancho Ojo de Agua de la Coche

An epic of the Western movement might be written using as a theme the Martin Murphy family.

Martin Murphy, Sr., nearing the age of 60 years, arrived in 1844 in California with his sons and daughters and several grandchildren, having come across the plains from Missouri. At a point on the Missouri River the Murphy and Stevens parties had joined forces for mutual protection and aid; in the long westward journey Captain Elisha Stevens was co-leader with Martin Murphy.

Martin Murphy was born in 1785 in Ireland, where he married and where his elder children were born. Disliking future prospects in his native land, he took his family (with the exception of his eldest son and daughter, who joined him later) and moved in 1820 to Frampton, Canada, where he settled and remained 20 years.

At the end of this period another move was made, this time to a pioneer part of the United States west of the Mississippi River near St. Joseph. The new location proved unsatisfactory, because of the lack of religious and educational opportunities and because of the prevalence of malaria, to which his wife, Mary Foley, and three of his grandchildren succumbed. Again he took up his family and moved on; this time his destination was chosen because of the influence of a priest who had visited California and who described it enthusiastically. Selling all his land, he put the proceeds into provisions, wagons, oxen, and equipment for the long trek to the Far West in 1844.

With the young men of the party on horseback accompanying the wagons drawn by oxen and containing the family and all their household goods, the long journey was finally ended in safety around Sacramento. Here most of the men in the group enlisted at once under Sutter's leadership to go to the aid of Governor Micheltorena in putting down the Alvarado-Castro insurrection of 1845. When this episode was ended, the immigrants were free to settle where they chose, and the party disbanded. Martin Murphy, Jr., bought land nearby on the Cosumnes River, where he lived until the gold rush of 1849 enabled him to sell his land and livestock at a considerable profit, when he again followed his father.

The father, Martin, Sr., had settled in Santa Clara County near the present town of Morgan Hill. Purchasing Rancho Ojo de Agua de la Coche, which had been granted by Governor Figueroa to Juan María Hernández on August 4, 1835, he built an adobe residence between the town of Morgan Hill and Murphy's Peak, a hill that rises to the west of the town. This house, now crumbled to dust, in which Martin Murphy lived with his motherless unmarried children, stood near the road leading from San José to Monterey, then the most traveled road in the state. Here even the most humble wayfarer found welcome with Murphy, who was assisted by his daughters Ellen and Johanna. From here, the sons Bernard, John M., and Daniel later left to make their own way, and the daughters were married to men of importance and influence in the new country. Murphy was the pattern of industry, intelligence, and piety for his children.

Martin Murphy, Sr., died in 1865, in his eightieth year, just south of San Jose at the home of his daughter Margaret and her husband, Thomas Kell. Kell was an Englishman who came overland to California and arrived in 1846. He built his redwood house in 1848, and it still stands, probably the oldest frame house in Santa Clara County. It is located on the east side of (old) Almaden Road just south of Curtner Avenue. The fine old house is still in fair condition, although vacant and abandoned. It is worthy of preservation, and, since there are plans for development of the site, it may be moved to the historical center in Kelley Park on Senter Road. Thomas Kell died in 1878 and his wife in 1881.

Martin J. C. Murphy, a grandson of Martin Murphy, Sr., received in 1860 the United States patent to the Rancho Ojo de Agua de la Coche, containing 8,927 acres. This tract is hilly in its western portion along Llagas Creek, and hills rise again in its eastern boundary, but the main central part is rolling. The peak rising just west of the town of Morgan Hill was for long called, among other names, Murphy's Peak or Twentyone Mile Peak. U. S. Highway 101 and the Southern Pacific Railroad pass through the town, which was named for Hiram Morgan Hill, who married Martin Murphy's granddaughter Diana, daughter of Daniel Murphy. Hill's home, built in the 1880's or 1890's, still stands at 350 North Monterey Street. After his death in 1913, Diana married Sir George Rhodes and lived until 1937.

Rancho Uvas

Uvas, the Spanish word for "grapes," was the name given to the tract of land bordering on Uvas Creek and adjoining the rancho of Martin Murphy, Sr., to the southwest. Today a road winds along the edge of the stream where, colorful in the autumn season, the vines grow, descended from those that long ago gave to the rancho its name.

This piece of land was granted by Governor Alvarado to Lorenzo Pineda in 1842. No clue to the identity of Pineda is found, but the claimant for the property ten years later in 1852 was Bernard (Bryan) Murphy, who had lived with his father Martin Murphy, Sr., on the adjoining rancho to the east and who had married Catherine O'Toole. In 1853, the year following the filing of his claim to this land, Bernard was killed by an explosion on the steamer *Jenny Lind* in San Francisco Bay. In company with other notable men of that period, he was making the trip from Alviso to San Francisco. He left one son, Martin J. C., who received patent to the rancho in 1860; he also died at an early age, and the property passed to his mother, who later married James Dunne.

Rancho Rinconada del Arroyo de San Francisquito

Don Rafael Soto, born in the Pueblo de San José, was the son of Ignacio Soto, a member of the Anza expedition. He went about 1827 with his daughter María Luisa to live on Rancho Corte de Madera before he petitioned for the grant of Rancho Rinconada del Arroyo de San Francisquito, of which he took possession in 1835. He had received a small piece of land in a bend (rinconada) of San Francisquito Creek on loan from Santa Clara Mission after its secularization —the place that had been the headquarters of the mission's large sheep ranch. Later Soto moved to the north side of the creek, on land belonging to the Rancho de las Pulgas, and consequently was denied the grant for which he petitioned.

Don Rafael had discovered the navigability of San Francisquito Creek up to the point at which he established an embarcadero for the loading and unloading of boats. The way between the embarcadero and El Camino Real, some three miles away, was not a properly defined road until some time later. Much heavy traffic made tracks and ruts in the soil for a space perhaps a mile in width, each driver choosing the route that looked safest and best. For a long time it passed along the north bank of the creek. Finally, in 1874, the present route, called Embarcadero Road, was opened by county survey.

The children of Don Rafael and Doña María Antonia were John M., who married Concepción Mesa, a daughter of Don Prado Mesa of Rancho San Antonio; Francisco, who never married; María Luisa, who married first John Copinger and after his death John Greer; Jesús, who married first Gerónimo, a brother of Prado Mesa, and afterward Robal Caba; Dolores, who married a man named Altamirano; José, who married Luisa Buelna, an orphan who with her brother John had been reared by María Luisa; and Patricio, who never married. (Bancroft gives also Juan Cris., José Cruz, and Celia.)

After the death of Don Rafael, Doña María Antonia married into the Mesa family and received the grant of Rancho Rinconada del Arroyo de San Francisquito on February 16, 1841, from Governor Juan B. Alvarado. This property consisted of 2,230 acres lying adjacent to the south side of San Francisquito Creek from its mouth to the Palo Alto tree (a landmark that still stands beside the railroad bridge in the town of Palo Alto). The house in which the Mesas and the large Soto family lived stood for years a block and a half northeast of present Middlefield Road on Oregon Avenue, near an Indian shell mound.

In 1850 John Greer, an Irish sea captain, arrived at the ranch and leased a portion of it. He soon married Señora Mesa's daughter María Luisa, the widow of John Copinger, and they moved to Rancho Cañada de Raymundo in San Mateo County. In 1865 Greer built a large house on what was then Embarcadero Road and is now 353 Churchill Avenue in Palo Alto, planning to move to it with his family. Before completion it was found by litigation that the site chosen for it was not on his property and that it must be moved about one-half mile. However, for one season two of his young sons lived in it, then a bare shell with roof and walls, while they attended the Mayfield School. When it was moved across the newly completed railroad track, only two trains were running daily between San Francisco and San Jose, and the work of rolling the house over the rails was done between the passing of the morning train and the return of the train in the evening. Another difficulty to be overcome in moving the house was the lack of roads, necessitating the clearing of wide passageways through the dense chaparral that grew as high as a man's head almost the entire distance.

After being put into place on its new site, the house was properly completed by the addition of interior walls and fireplaces, which made it a comfortable and beautiful home of that period. It was of wood, painted white, a plain house but very solid and impressive, with its narrow end facing the street. In later years its condition deteriorated and an upstairs portion was damaged by fire. Long the home of Lucas Greer, one of the five children of John and María Luisa, it was razed about 1952 for the construction of the Town and Country Village shopping center on Embarcadero Road opposite the Palo Alto Senior High School.

Other early owners of parts of this rancho besides Greer were Dr. W. A. Newell, J. W. Boulware, J. Pitman, Jules Mercier, J. P. Rowe, J. Hastings, and H. W. Seale. The last-named acquired by far the largest part, and his once elegant house stood until 1937 on Webster Street near Oregon Avenue in Palo Alto.

The heirs of María Antonia Soto Mesa received the patent for the rancho in 1872. The daughter Dolores had previously received 120 acres and had lived in a house on this tract on what is now Newell Road near its intersection with Hamilton Avenue.

Rancho San Francisquito

Rancho San Francisquito, a tract of land lying on the southeast side of San Francisquito Creek and extending upstream from the railroad bridge, was granted by Governor Alvarado to Antonino Buelna, who had been active in the revolt that had put Alvarado in power. Permission to live on this land had been given Buelna in 1837, and the formal papers were signed May 1, 1839, when he was in command of expeditions against foreigners and Indians.

Don Antonino built an adobe house on the southeast bank of San Francisquito Creek near the most northerly point of the present Stanford Golf Course, where the old eucalyptus drive ends at the creek edge. In time this house received the name of "El Paso del Arroyo" ("the crossing of the creek"), for this ford was used for many years. It was also called the "doubling-up station," because ox teams, hauling logs and the lumber from mills on the mountainside, could at this point take on a double load for the easy grade in the valley.

Buelna, who had married Concepción Valencia, lived only seven years after receiving this grant, and two years later his widow married Francisco Rodríguez, a widower from Monterey, whose seven children opposed the marriage. The eldest son, Jesús, however, built himself a house only a few yards from his stepmother's door, between her adobe and the creek, and lived a close neighbor on the property for ten years.

It was not long before newcomers saw the desirability of owning property on Rancho San Francisquito, and in the early 1850's they began to take possession of choice portions, hoping that the United States government would not confirm the Mexican title and that the land would be thrown open for settlement by the public. Research in the county archives done by Roy P. Ballard shows that Thomas ("Sandy") Wilson settled at the Buelna adobe; a Frenchman named Julian settled in front of the present site of the Stanford Museum; William Little took up his holdings near the site upon which Leland Stanford later erected his mansion, now the site of the Stanford Convalescent Home; Thomas Bevins took the site that is now the Stanford University cactus gardens; and Jerry Eastin had his home where Xasmin House, home of the president of the university for many years, was built. Eastin farmed some of the land and had a blacksmith shop on the only road at that time running through the grant, afterward the Mayfield-Searsville road and later Eucalyptus Avenue.

On February 28, 1853, Doña Concepción filed a claim for a part of the land contained in the adjoining Rancho Corte de Madera, but this claim was not allowed by the courts.

On April 4, 1853, two deeds were executed, both conveying property to Francisco Casanueva, a San Francisco lawyer and ex-consul from Chile; one of these deeds was signed by Francisco Rodríguez *et al.*, Jesús Rodríguez, and Manuel Valencia; the other, by Manuel Valencia *et ux.*, F. Rodríguez, and J. Rodríguez. Rodríguez, after killing a man belonging to one of the local Spanish families by stabbing him in the back one night on the Sand Hill Road, fled the country and stayed away until danger of prosecution had passed. The rancho was divided. Thomas Wilson, who had moved into the Buelna-Rodríguez adobe and used the Jesús Rodríguez adobe for a stable, sold the two buildings and the land on which they stood when he enlisted for the Civil War in 1861. The purchaser, John W. Locker, took possession. In the flood of 1862 his stable was carried away, much of the good top soil from the sloping garden between the house and the creek was washed downstream, and three tall redwoods were undermined a little way down the creek.

In 1863 George Gordon, a wealthy businessman of San Francisco, chose this rancho for a country home, buying out some of the squatters and purchasing at a low price in 1865 the whole rancho from one of the heirs of the original grantee. The title to the 1,471 acres contained in it was cleared to the widow, María Concepción Valencia de Rodríguez, and other heirs by a confirmation and by the subsequent patent issued by the United States on June 8, 1868. Gordon laid out Eucalyptus Avenue and other drives, erected a house, and built stables for his driving horses. He died in San Francisco in 1869.

Leland Stanford purchased this property from the executors of the estate and used the Gordon house as a nucleus for his larger and finer residence. He greatly enlarged his holdings by the purchase of adjoining lands.

Buelna's adobe stood in fairly good condition until the 1890's but then collapsed, leaving broken walls that gradually melted into the ground. The site is now under Willow Road, adjacent to the Stanford campus, but old fruit trees still stand opposite the apartment building at 1850 Willow Road.

Rancho Cañada de Pala

Beginning just south of Alum Rock Canyon and extending upward to the present highway to Lick Observatory, the mountainous Rancho Cañada de Pala takes in 15,714 acres, granted in 1839 to José de Jesús Bernal by Governor Alvarado. About seven miles along Mount Hamilton Road from its junction with Alum Rock Avenue, a small adobe, the history of which is uncertain, stands on the Tiernan Ranch to the left of the road, not far from the junction with Quinby Road. The old adobe, partially wood-covered, is just north of the former Hall's Valley schoolhouse, now in use as a residence.

Scattering Ranchos

Other Mexican grants of land lying wholly within the confines of Santa Clara County also received confirmation by the United States government. They included Pala, Yerba Buena (or Socayre), Los Huecos, La Polka, Juristac, Cañada de San Felipe y las Animas, and Embarcadero de Santa Clara.

The Battle of Santa Clara

The American flag was first raised in California at Monterey on July 7, 1846, by Commodore John D. Sloat, thus signalizing the fact that California had passed from the hands of Mexico to the United States. This action was followed by the raising of the flag in other parts of California by American settlers, and on July 13 it was first raised at San José by Captain Thomas Fallon. The scene of this first flag raising was on the site of what is now the northwest corner of Market and Post streets.

The period of the American occupation was the most turbulent that California has known. During that time, dissatisfied Mexican leaders in both northern and southern California attempted to stem the tide of American conquest, but the so-called battles that took place were, in reality, mere skirmishes, with few casualties.

On January 2, 1847, one such skirmish, known as the Battle of Santa Clara, was fought about two and one-half miles west of the Santa Clara Mission at a place now bounded on the south by El Camino Real, on the west by Lawrence Expressway, on the north by Kifer Road, and on the east by Scott Boulevard. The American leaders were Captains Joseph Aram, Charles M. Weber, and John W. Murphy. The Mexican leader was Francisco Sánchez. The casualties for the one day of fighting were four Mexicans killed and four wounded and two Americans wounded. The battle was followed by an armistice of five days, during which time the Mexicans retreated to the Santa Cruz Mountains and a small reinforcement of federal soldiers from San Francisco came to the aid of the Americans. On January 8, Sánchez and his men surrendered.

This episode was of little more than local importance, it being the last encounter in Santa Clara County. The main theater of war was transferred to southern California, and on February 2, 1848, the Treaty of Guadalupe-Hidalgo was signed, ending all hostilities. Within a few weeks, soldiers of both sides were again fraternizing in friendly business and social relations.

The site of the Armistice Oak (*SRL 260*), under which, according to tradition, the Battle of Santa Clara or "Battle of the Mustard Stalks" ended, has been marked on the south side of El Camino Real just east of Lawrence Expressway.

California's First State Capital

San Jose was the first state capital of California after the adoption of the first state constitution on November 13, 1849. The first legislature convened there on December 15, nine months before the United States Congress passed the act that admitted California into the Union. Although serious work was accomplished at San Jose, it has gone down in history as the "Legislature of a Thousand Drinks," because of the freely imbibing Senator Thomas Jefferson Green and his advocacy of adjournment to the local saloon. The capital was removed from San Jose to Vallejo, by act of the second legislature on February 14, 1851, and the removal took effect on May 1.

The building that served as the first state capitol was a little two-story structure, adobe below and frame above, that stood on a site *(SRL 461)* directly across South Market Street from the spot now marked by a granite boulder and bronze plate on the east side of the old plaza. This tablet, placed by the Native Sons of the Golden West on May 19, 1923, bears an image of the old adobe capitol, which was destroyed by fire on April 29, 1853.

On December 15, 1949, during California's centennial celebrations, a replica of the State House was dedicated on the plaza, across from the site of the original. This building was later removed to the Santa Clara County Fairgrounds on Tully Road, where it is used as a historical museum. Plans are under way for a new museum and historical center in Kelley Park on Senter Road. To this location it is proposed to move historically important buildings that would otherwise be destroyed.

Unfortunately, the home of California's first American civil governor, Peter Hardeman Burnett, has not been preserved. It stood for years at 441 North First Street, but was originally erected at Alviso by Burnett during his governorship in 1850. Four years later he rebuilt it at the San Jose site, but it was torn down in the 1950's.

Mrs. Isbell's School and
The Santa Clara Female Seminary

The first American school in California was held in the crumbling buildings of Mission Santa Clara in the spring of 1847 by Mrs. Olive Mann Isbell. She and her husband, Dr. James C. Isbell, had just arrived from Ohio with other members of an overland immigrant party. While the men were called to do military duty, the women and children were left at the mission. Partly to relieve the mothers of the constant care of their little ones, Mrs. Isbell began to give rudimentary instruction to the children with the slender means at her command—no books, no paper, no pencils, no chalk. It was afterward related by one of the pupils that letters of the alphabet were drawn on the back of the hand with charcoal and thus made visual to the beginners. When the men returned from their short period of military service and the reunited families went their separate ways, this unique school ended. However, Mrs. Isbell taught for many years in other parts of the state.

A few years later a boarding school for girls was started near the mission as a result of a resolution passed by the Baptist Association of Churches at their first annual session held in June 1851: "... our obligation to the cause of Christ, and to the interest of our adopted state, demands that we, as Baptists, commence, at once and earnestly, united effort for the advancement of education in California."

The board of trustees that was appointed purchased from John C. Braley a building on what is now the corner of Santa Clara and Lafayette streets. The structure had been built by Henry J. Appleton and was described in a sale made to W. G. Bowden on September 4, 1850, as a "house to which is attached a brick building." John C. Braley had purchased this property, then called the Pacific Hotel, at a sheriff's sale on October 11, 1851, and resold it to the trustees.

The first principal of this, the Santa Clara Female Seminary, was Mary Julia Harwood Hamilton, a graduate of a young ladies' seminary in Troy, New York. Her husband, Hiram Hamilton, a graduate of the University of Michigan, came to California in 1850 leaving his bride of a few months to follow after he had established himself. She came west with her brother, David Harwood, early in 1851 by the Nicaragua route and accepted the seminary position on her arrival. A report on education given to the Baptist Association of Churches at their annual session of 1853 mentions that "during the year a flourishing school has been in progress at Santa Clara under the able management of Mr. and Mrs. Hamilton, aided by suitable assistants. The location of this school is delightful. The buildings are chiefly of brick, and capable of accommodating about twenty-five boarding and seventy day scholars. . . . This school is deservedly popular, and has already received such an amount of patronage that more room is necessary for the accommodation of its pupils."

Later a department for boys or young men was added, collegiate studies being taught by Hiram Hamilton. The school was maintained by the Baptist denomination for several years. The property was finally sold by the trustees on September 12, 1863, to Jane A. French, and in 1890 the building was torn down by later owners.

The College of Notre Dame

The story of the College of Notre Dame dates back in California to 1851, and can be traced for long years before that through Oregon and the eastern part of the United States to Europe.

Sister Mary Catherine and Sister Loyola had labored in Oregon for a few years before they journeyed to San Francisco to meet four sister missionaries en route by sea from Cincinnati. While awaiting the delayed arrival of the vessel, the two sisters from Oregon were entreated to remain in California, where the educational needs of children of Catholic parents were urgent. After due consideration, the sisters decided to stay and they chose a spot outside the Pueblo de San José near a pretty road—now Santa Clara Street—on which a partially completed adobe stood amid a field of luxuriant wild mustard. The lot was 37 by 50 Spanish varas in size and lay along the *acequia,* or irrigation ditch, from which water could be pumped.

A shed, immediately added to the unfinished adobe house, was soon supplemented by a very small two-story frame building. The upstairs of this latter building, reached by means of a rough ladder, served as sleeping quarters for the sisters. The downstairs room was used for the school. In 1855 the College of Notre Dame was chartered as an institution of higher learning. As the years passed, other buildings of a more substantial type were added, until by 1888 the sisters had a group of well-planned and attractive buildings located on land that, by further purchase, extended from West Santa Clara Street back to San Augustine (now West St. John) and from Notre Dame Street across to Santa Teresa. The town of San Jose at length crowded its way to the door and passed on toward the old Mission Santa Clara, yet life went on as formerly within the seclusion of these walls. Eventually, however, it was decided to remove from what had become the geographical center of San Jose to a spot some 25 miles farther up the peninsula.

The change was made in 1923. Because of the part it had played in the establishment of the college, the little two-story frame building that had seen all the development of Notre Dame during the years was carefully moved, bit by bit, and re-erected amid the stately structures of the new site at Belmont. Later, the pioneer building was moved again, this time to the headquarters of the California Province of the Sisters of Notre Dame de Namur on Bohlman Road in Saratoga. Unfortunately, it stood here only a few years before it was razed during expansion of the provincial house.

Two brick buildings of the College of Notre Dame remained in San Jose until the 1960's. One, located at 189 West Santa Clara Street and erected about 1876, was razed in September 1963. The Science Hall was under construction at the time of the great earthquake of April 18, 1906. It was tested, proved to be sound, and was carried to completion. The stately building, with its columned portico, was a familiar landmark for 60 years, being occupied in its later days by the Rosicrucian Press. In February 1966 it was demolished to permit the extension of Almaden Avenue to the north.

The University of the Pacific

The University of the Pacific, founded under Methodist auspices and now located at Stockton, is the oldest incorporated educational institution in California, having received its charter on July 10, 1851, under the name California Wesleyan University. Its inception was largely due to the energy and devotion of the Rev. Isaac Owen, lovingly called by his followers "Father Owen." It was first located in Santa Clara.

In 1870 the college, then called the University of the Pacific, was moved to College Park, about halfway between Santa Clara and San Jose, and now within the city limits of San Jose. In 1921 the name was changed to the College of the Pacific, and in 1924 the entire establishment was moved to Stockton. The site on the old College Park campus is now occupied by Bellarmine College Preparatory, operated by the Jesuits and originally the high school department of the University of Santa Clara.

Of all the numerous Protestant colleges started in northern California in pioneer days, the University of the Pacific, as it is once again called since 1961, is the only one of first rank that has survived. It is today a firmly established, growing institution.

San Jose State College

The first normal school to be established in California was the San Jose Normal School, now San Jose State College (*SRL 417*). It was started in San Francisco in 1857 as a private enterprise, Minns' Evening Normal School, taking its name from the first principal, George W. Minns. By act of the legislature on May 2, 1862, it was made a public normal school. In 1870, after a hard contest over the location, the school was permanently located at San Jose. The normal school was changed to a teachers' college in 1921, when all the normal schools in the state underwent the same change. In 1935 the legislature changed the name of the college to San Jose State College.

The main structure on Washington Square has been rebuilt three times—once in 1880, because of fire; again in 1906, because of earthquake; and the third building program, currently under way, to replace outmoded and inadequate structures. Fortunately, the picturesque campanile has been retained.

San Jose's Chinatown

Many Chinese were attracted to San Jose in the early days. Merchants of that nationality had their places of business in the vicinity of Market and San Fernando streets from the early 1850's to May 4, 1887, when that part of the town was swept by fire.

After this date attempts were made by two different groups to locate a new Chinatown in the northern part of the city. John Heinlen and Mitchell Phillips were the respective sponsors of the two factions, the former choosing a location at Fifth and Jackson streets (which came to be known as Heinlenville), and the latter favoring the vicinity of Taylor Street on the Guadalupe River, where a Chinese theater and other buildings were subsequently destroyed by fire.

Both Chinese and Japanese now have their shops and eating places in the vicinity of Heinlenville, where miscellaneous structures line the streets. A two-story brick structure, unmistakably Oriental in appearance, stood off Taylor Street facing Cleveland Avenue until 1948. It was a Chinese temple, or joss house, built under the direction of Yee Fook and first used at the time of the Chinese New Year celebration in 1887. Large pieces of elegant wood carving, superimposed on a background of mother of pearl, gave an air of magnificence to the place, one of California's few landmarks of this type, which regrettably has been torn down.

Milpitas

The first building in the town of Milpitas was erected by Frederick Creighton in 1855. A post office was established the following year, and he was made the postmaster.

Closely associated with the origin and growth of the town was Joseph Rush Weller, a native of New Jersey. He had grown to maturity in New York and had come to California on the ship *Columbus* from Panama, arriving in San Francisco on August 7, 1850. After a trip to the mines in El Dorado County, he took up residence in the vicinity of Milpitas in 1851. In May 1853 he purchased 400 acres of Rancho Los Tularcitos lying along Penitencia Creek and devoted his attention to the raising of hay, grain, fine cattle, and thoroughbred horses. In order to aid in the clearing of titles to land in which he was interested, he became proficient in the Spanish language, and afterward enlarged his property holdings.

In 1855 Judge Weller organized the Milpitas School District; he was one of the trustees of the school for 24 years. He was an associate judge of Santa Clara County and was elected a member of the Constitutional Convention of 1878. His property, lying at the extreme southern corner of Rancho Los Tularcitos, became a part of the growing town of Milpitas in the northwestern corner of the adjoining Rancho Milpitas. The town had originally been called Penitencia, but because of its usual mispronunciation by incoming settlers, Judge Weller promulgated the idea of changing it to Milpitas, already the name of the rancho, the school district, and the post office. The first Presbyterian church in this vicinity, of which he was one of the organizers, was built on land owned by Judge Weller. He continued to live in the town for the rest of his life, and some of his descendants still live in the area. Milpitas remained a small and unimportant town until the Ford Motor Company plant was constructed nearby in 1955.

Campbell

William Campbell, a native of Kentucky and a veteran of the War of 1812, arrived in Santa Clara County with his family in 1846, having traveled on the first part of the overland journey with the Donner party. The following year he assisted in the surveys of the towns of San Jose and Santa Clara, and in 1847–48 he built a sawmill, about three miles above present Saratoga near Long Bridge, on the creek long called by his name.

His elder son, David, went to another county to live, but Benjamin, a boy of 20 when the family arrived in California, purchased land some miles northeast of his father's mill, on which he raised wheat until 1885. In that year he subdivided the tract and sold lots for the town of Campbell.

This town, long the center of fruit-raising activities, has grown out from the junction of Campbell Avenue and the Santa Clara–Los Gatos road (Winchester Boulevard), and is now a sizable city. The deeds for lots sold by Benjamin Campbell contained a proviso that the land should be forfeit to the original owner should liquor be sold thereon. James Henry Campbell, Benjamin's son, lived in the town where he was born until his death in 1935.

On Winchester Boulevard north of Campbell is the 160-room mansion built from the 1880's to 1922 by Sarah L. Winchester. Widow of the heir to the fortune of the Winchester Repeating Arms Company, she was an architectural hobbyist and, it is said, a spiritualist with a compulsion to enlarge her home to avoid death. She frequently changed her mind about additions, resulting in stairways that lead nowhere and doors that open onto blank walls. The place has been open to the public for years as a commercial enterprise, and is commonly called the Winchester Mystery House.

Los Gatos

Situated on the Arroyo de los Gatos after it flows from the canyon into the broader open space at the foot of the mountains is the town of Los Gatos. It had its beginning in the flour mill (*SRL 458*) built on the creek by James Alexander Forbes in the early 1850's.

The mill had three stories of stone procured in the canyon nearby, and a fourth story of wood. A dam was built about a mile upstream, and water was carried from it through a wooden flume to run the millstones. In May 1855 Forbes bought 3,000 acres of Rancho Rinconada de los Gatos, and in November of that year he mortgaged it. His enterprises were not financial successes, and on December 10, 1856, he was declared insolvent by the court. In 1857 the mill property passed from his hands; other owners made a greater success. At one time a frame woolen mill was erected beside the stone flour mill, but that later burned down. When fruit-raising became the principal industry of the Santa Clara Valley, the mill fell into disuse. In 1916 the Pacific Gas and Electric Company, which had previously purchased the land on which the old stone mill stood, tore down most of the structure because of its unsafe condition. A two-story portion of the building, however, was retained and used for years as an electric substation. It still stands beside the freeway and is accessible from Church Street.

The road from San Jose into the Santa Cruz Mountains passed for many years close to the old stone mill, even as the freeway does today, but on the opposite side of the mill. Fine houses of early American settlers, among them that of the McMurtry family, were built across the road from the mill. After passing between these houses and the mill, the road wound upstream to a fording place and then downstream on the other side for some distance to find a suitable place to start the ascent into the pass over the summit.

Beginning in 1848, sawmills were operated in the canyons above the present town, and at that period the trail through the pass was used for hauling timber products. Later, these primitive roads were improved and a toll gate was placed at the southern end of town. The toll house, built about 1857, still stands at 142 South Santa Cruz Avenue, at the corner of Wood Road. After a stage line was established, the Ten Mile House Station was located across the street at the present southeast corner of Santa Cruz Avenue and Main Street. It was first kept by Henry Cobb and later by John Weldon Lyndon, a man from Vermont, who had purchased 100 acres of land in the vicinity. The successor of the Ten Mile House was the Los Gatos Hotel, which was moved across the street to the southwest corner in 1877 to give place to a station for the railroad built at that time. The hotel was destroyed by fire and replaced in 1898 by the Lyndon Hotel, a picturesque building that stood until about 1960. The old railroad station is also gone, but the Victorian residence and carriage house of John Lyndon, built in 1888, still stand at 55 Broadway.

Forbes's mill gave the first employment to men in this vicinity, and the place was then called simply Forbes Mill. As the settlement grew, it became Forbestown, and finally Los Gatos.

Lexington and Alma

The Lexington area above Los Gatos is inundated by the waters of Los Gatos Creek, backed up behind Lexington Dam, constructed in the early 1950's. The site gives no hint of the busy life of which it used to be a part when it was one of the most active centers of commerce in the county. Situated two miles above Forbes Mill, it early had a toll gate, which was later superseded by the one put up at Los Gatos.

In 1867 there were eight sawmills in the vicinity; here also were lumber dealers, a redwood-pipe factory, a wheelwright, grocers, blacksmiths, and the Santa Clara Petroleum Company. The Pioneer Stage Line, operated by Ward and Colegrove, served this section before 1875. This stage left the New York Exchange at San Jose daily at a quarter past ten upon the arrival of the morning train from San Francisco. It stopped at Los Gatos, Lexington, and way stations as it rumbled through "the finest mountain scenery and [over] the best mountain road in the state," on its way to Santa Cruz. Mrs. S. A. Paddock was proprietress of the Lexington House at the Lexington station. She advertised "a good stable in connection with the house in which stock will be cared for. The stage between San Jose and Santa Cruz stops here for dinner, and all stages stop for passengers."

The development of the Lexington area had begun as early as 1848, when Isaac Branham and Julian Hanks built a sawmill on Los Gatos Creek, the first operating sawmill in Santa Clara County even though construction of William Campbell's mill on Arroyo Quito (Saratoga Creek) had begun a month earlier. Branham and Hanks soon sold their mill to Zacariah "Buffalo" Jones, and the neighborhood became known as Jones Mill. The old Jones Hill road from Los Gatos still winds through the property of the Jesuit novitiate and over St. Joseph's Hill to the site of Lexington.

Alma originated in 1862 as the Forest House, a roadside hotel opened by Lysander Collins. When Lexington began to decline, its post office, established in 1861, was moved to the Forest House in 1873 and given the name Alma. The final demise of Lexington came in 1880 when James G. Fair's South Pacific Coast Railroad was opened and a station established at Alma. The railroad, later owned by Southern Pacific, operated until March 4, 1940.

When construction of the Lexington Dam began, the old hotel and stage barn still stood at Lexington. At Alma, a mile farther up the canyon, George Osmer's store and the former Southern Pacific depot remained. A small dam stood at the site of the Jones mill. The site of Forest

Southern Pacific Depot, Alma

House was occupied by the Alma fire station. All these places are now under water. The Alma post office was discontinued on August 31, 1952.

Alma College, in the mountains above the lake, is the college of theology of the Society of Jesus (Jesuits). It was established in 1934 on an estate first developed in the late 1880's by Captain Stillman H. (Harry) Knowles, a San Francisco vigilante of 1856. In 1894 the property was acquired by James L. Flood, son of the "bonanza king" James C. Flood, and in 1906 by Dr. Harry L. Tevis, whose heirs sold it to the Jesuits. Yehudi Menuhin, the famed violinist and one-time child prodigy, spent his boyhood at Alma, where he still maintains a home.

Burrell and Wrights

Rancho Soquel Augmentación, situated mainly in Santa Cruz County, extended over the line into Santa Clara County along the mountain ridge. In this vicinity was the settlement of Burrell.

Lyman John Burrell owned a large tract of this land and attempted stock raising in the early 1850's. Cougars and grizzly bears so infested the region that he finally gave up his hogs and goats and raised only long-horned cattle that could better protect themselves. Situated in this remote mountain region, he received his mail and supplies by the laborious and slow process of mule train from Santa Clara. He built a road along the ridge, which was purchased by the San Jose Turnpike Company when it built the San Jose–Soquel Road.

The original residence of Lyman J. Burrell no longer stands, but another house in which he lived remains, in dilapidated condition, at the western edge of the settlement of Burrell on the north side of Summit Road at the corner of Morrill Road. He sold the two-story structure to A. E. Sears, but it was later repurchased by the Burrell family. Across Summit Road, on a little elevation, is the larger house built about 1902 by descendants of Lyman J. Burrell. Farther east, also on the south side of the road, is the former Burrell School, astride the Santa Clara–Santa Cruz county line. This and other old schools in the mountain region are no longer used, having been consolidated into the Loma Prieta Joint Union School, just west of Burrell.

In 1870 James Richard Wright, a retired minister, and his wife, Sarah Vincent Wright, related by marriage to the Burrells, whose old neighbors they had been in Ohio, came to the region and settled on 48 acres of land which they purchased from Burrell. Their residence, rebuilt after a fire in the 1890's, stood for many years, as did the Wrights Presbyterian Church named for them, located on Loma Prieta Avenue at the corner of Summit Road in Burrell.

When in building the stretch of narrow-gauge railroad from Los Gatos to Santa Cruz in the late 1870's a point was reached on Los Gatos Creek at an elevation of 2,000 feet, the route turned sharply from the creek, and a tunnel a mile and one-eighth in length was made, passing under the ridge at the county line and emerging at Laurel in Santa Cruz County. The headquarters for the excavation were at the northern end of the tunnel, where a riotous camp housed the laborers. Here O. B. Castle, foreman of the more than 2,000 Chinese employed for the digging, built his famous saloon called "The Tunnel."

After the work was completed on May 15, 1880, and trains began to run over the line, the station at this place was called Wrights, after John Vincent Wright, son of the pioneer James Richard Wright, who kept the Arbor Villa Hotel established at Burrell. This station became a shipping center for all the vineyards and orchards of the Loma Prieta region, a popular year-round resort, and a picnic place to which special trains were run on holidays. Summer homes were built in the vicinity, one of which was "Monte Paraiso," owned by the poetess Josephine Clifford McCracken. This placed burned in 1899. Other literary people were attracted to the area, among them Jack London, Ambrose Bierce, and George Sterling. A building still standing in Burrell at 24170 Loma Prieta Avenue, above the site of the old Presbyterian church, was the "Bohemia," kept by Z. A. Cotton and his wife and freely patronized by these writers. It is recognizable by its two ornamented gables, although the tower has been removed.

The railroad was constructed in its several parts by several companies under as many names. In 1887 the lines were consolidated under the Southern Pacific Company, and after 1909 they were run on broad-gauge tracks. At the time the railroad was discontinued in 1940, Wrights was only a flag-stop station. Its post office, established in 1879, was closed in 1938. The site of Wrights is now owned by the San Jose Water Works, and all the buildings have been torn down. The entrance to the old tunnel can still be found, and the railroad bed is visible in several places. Wrights is located in the canyon of Los Gatos Creek, one and three-quarters miles northwest of Burrell via Morrill and Wrights Station roads.

Patchin

The old Los Gatos–Santa Cruz highway, before reaching the summit of the Santa Cruz Mountains, runs through the area once served by the Patchin post office. This is close to the place where Charles Henry "Mountain Charley" McKiernan, first permanent white settler in the Santa Cruz Mountains, took up residence in 1850.

The first mail delivered to this region was carried by a stage that ran to the summit over the Mountain Charley Road, later eliminated from the main line of travel by a realignment beyond the old Fowler's Summit. Mountain Charley Road still exists in both Santa Clara and Santa Cruz counties—an authentic bit of old stage road that will reward the traveler with beautiful scenery and a sense of history.

The spot called Patchin (SRL 448)—if, indeed, the name can be applied to any one point—is at the junction of Mountain Charley Road and the old Santa Cruz highway. About 1876 Josiah S. Fowler, son of the pioneer Jacob, built a one-story house in which the mail was cared for. This old post office stood north of the junction on the west side of the old highway, until it was destroyed by fire in the 1950's. Across the highway was the stage barn, torn down in 1949. The materials from this building went into the construction of a residence just below the highway and the site. The Patchin post office was established in 1872 and is said to have been named for George M. Patchen, a famous race horse of that period. Postal records indicate, however, that the name was always spelled "Patchin," lending some credibility, perhaps, to the oft-told story that it was named by a postal official who observed an old mountaineer "patchin' his trousers" in front of his shack. The post office was located at various places up and down the road through the years, until it finally ended in 1925 at the Edgemont resort.

Up the grade from the old Fowler's Summit is the now-dry Schultheis Lagoon, lying between Summit Road and the old Santa Cruz highway at their junction. Above this lagoon is the house of John Martin Schultheis and his wife, Susan Byerly, who took up a homestead there in 1852. Their house, believed to be the oldest building still standing in the Santa Cruz Mountains, was built by Schultheis himself, who was a skilled German cabinetmaker. The timbers wrought by him are now covered by factory-made lumber. The little old house stands at the rear of a later and larger house at 22849 Summit Road.

In 1899 an Episcopal church was built opposite this lagoon as a Patchin branch of the church in Los Gatos. Services were held at this house of worship for several years by visiting clergymen, but the brown building in the forest disappeared

Schultheis House, near Patchin

in the 1940's or earlier. A few hundred feet south of the church stood the Summit Opera House, built by a stock company headed by Volney Averill, a Union soldier who married Alice Schultheis, and Charles Aitken in the latter part of the nineteenth century. It was used for social activities, but was torn down some years ago and its materials used in the construction of a building at Laurel, across the line in Santa Cruz County.

Summit Road, from Schultheis Lagoon to Burrell, is a part of the old San Jose–Soquel road of the San Jose Turnpike Company. Beyond Burrell, the Soquel road turns south, while the Summit Road proceeds east and southeast along the county line to Mount Madonna.

In 1927 the Patchin post office was reestablished under a new name at Holy City, about a mile north of Fowler's Summit on the old Santa Cruz–Los Gatos highway, and in the same year another post office was established at the new subdivision of Redwood Estates, near "Mountain Charley" McKiernan's old homesite. Holy City was founded in 1918 by William E. "Father" Riker and became one of California's most unusual towns. Riker, perennial candidate for governor of the state, was the leader of a small white-supremacist religious cult. The members followed him to the chosen location and built their colony on 180 acres in one of the most beautiful sections of the Santa Cruz Mountains. The hodgepodge of wooden buildings plastered with garish signs quickly became a tourist attraction, located as it was on the main highway between the San Francisco Bay area and the beach resorts of Santa Cruz. Ultimately, Riker and his followers operated a printing shop, a mineral water concern, and a radio station, as well as store, service station, restaurant, and the "headquarters for the world's perfect government." After the highway was rerouted, Holy City began to decline, and gradually the dilapidated buildings were torn down. Little remains of the original settlement, and only a handful of colonists reside there, most of them members from the beginning. Riker himself, at the age of 93, still lived at Holy City in 1966. In that year, to the surprise of his followers and others, he joined the Roman Catholic Church.

Loma Prieta and Austrian Gulch

The long mountain that forms many miles of the skyline on the Los Gatos–Santa Cruz highway used to be called Mount Bache. The name was given in honor of Alexander Dallas Bache, superintendent of the United States Coast and Geodetic Survey from 1853 until his death in 1867. Bache, a grandson of Benjamin Franklin, organized and became the first president of Girard College before his connection with the survey. In the early 1850's he directed much work on the Pacific Coast. On some of the early maps, his name was mistakenly applied to a lesser peak in the same range, but all confusion between the peaks was eliminated by renaming both, the lesser one Mount Umunhum, a word of Indian derivation, and the greater peak Loma Prieta, a Spanish term meaning "dark hill."

Austrian Gulch, on the slope of Mount Umunhum, drains into Los Gatos Creek. It derives its name from the fact that after the Franco-Prussian War a group of Austro-Germans who became naturalized American citizens settled there in the 1870's. They took up public land and planted orchards and vineyards.

This industrious and thrifty colony, led by John Utschig, lived comfortably and happily until a terrific cloudburst swept away their possessions in 1889. The foundations of their immense winery were loosened so much that it collapsed and poured its contents—thousands of gallons of red wine—into Los Gatos Creek, which was thereby colored far below the town of Los Gatos. This disaster was the beginning of the end of the colony; some remained to rebuild their homes and replant their ruined vineyards, some returned to their native land, while others sought homes elsewhere in California. A forest fire in 1923 consumed many of the wooden buildings then standing. The area lies beyond the site of Wrights Station and is now controlled by the San Jose Water Works, which built Austrian Dam near the junction of Austrian Gulch and Los Gatos Creek.

About the time of the Austrian Gulch settlement another group of Europeans were gathering on Loma Prieta between Hall's Bridge and the summit. This group was composed mainly of artists, musicians, and professional people, and was largely of German origin. Among the group were E. E. Meyer of Denmark and his German wife, Marie Detje. He purchased 1,672 acres of land from Lyman J. Burrell, a part of Rancho Soquel Augmentación of Martina Castro. Meyer improved and sold the greater part of it, but on the 500 acres he retained, his son Emil founded the Mare Vista vineyard and winery.

Saratoga

William Campbell and his sons, David and Benjamin, began construction of a sawmill on Arroyo Quito late in 1847. Before the mill was finished, word reached them of the discovery of gold in the foothills of the Sierra Nevada. They rushed to the mines, and when they returned to complete their mill, they found that one was already in operation on Arroyo de Los Gatos, even though it had been begun a month later than their own. The Campbell mill was thus the second operating sawmill in Santa Clara County. It was located at or near Long Bridge, about three miles west of Saratoga at the junction of Highway 9 and Sanborn Road. The creek was called Campbell Creek until the early 1950's, when the name was officially changed to Saratoga Creek.

In 1850–51 Martin McCarty, another lumberman, built a toll road up the canyon to what had become known as Campbell's Redwoods. At the lower end of the road, a little settlement began to grow, known at first simply as Toll Gate. In 1855 a post office was established under the name of McCartysville. McCarty's toll gate crossed the present Big Basin Way (formerly Lumber Street) near the corner of Third Street, at a point indicated approximately by the house at 14477 Big Basin Way.

Meanwhile, in 1854, William Haun and John Whisman had established a gristmill called Redwood Mills. It was later purchased by Charles Maclay, who added a tannery and changed the name to Bank Mills. The McCartysville post office was renamed Bank Mills in 1863, but in 1865 it became Saratoga *(SRL 435),* because, like Saratoga, New York, it was in close proximity to valuable and popular medicinal springs.

Pacific Congress Springs, a short distance west of Saratoga on Highway 9, was one of the earliest and most fashionable recreational resorts in California. The mineral springs were discovered in the early 1850's by Jerd Caldwell. Wealthy men, including D. O. Mills and Alvinza Hayward, became interested in making it a more or less private vacation place for their families, but in November 1865 these men formed a corporation, and the original Congress Hall was opened to the public on June 16, 1866. The building stood about five minutes' walk from the springs. The management owned about 720 acres of wooded hillside, and as the popularity of the place increased, other buildings, including houses for hot and cold baths, were added for the accommodation of visitors. In 1872 Lewis A. Sage and his father, Lewis R., took over the establishment. The mineral water was proclaimed "a refreshing beverage and invigorating tonic." The resort was closed in 1942, and all the buildings are gone.

Saratoga reached the climax of its industrial development about 1870. In 1868 King, Meyer and Company established a mill for the manufacture of rough, brown wrapping paper. Two years later the Somervilles began making heavy pasteboard. One authority of the period stated that their mill "was the first of this kind on the coast." But Saratoga was never to realize its ambition to be a manufacturing center. Charles Maclay failed financially, and the gristmill and tannery were closed. Later he became one of the first developers of the San Fernando Valley in Los Angeles County. The pasteboard mill, finally owned by Brown Brothers, outgrew its plant and was moved to Corralitos in Santa Cruz County. The paper mill burned in 1883.

Saratoga continued as a hub of the lumbering industry and also pioneered in fruit raising, drying, and packing. The orchards of the area have now yielded in great measure to residential subdivisions, but for over 40 years, beginning in 1900, the annual Blossom Festival brought fame and visitors to the community.

Although the home of the town's founder, Martin McCarty, was torn down in the 1950's, there are at least two other homes still standing that were built in the 1850's. The former William Haun residence is at 14530 Big Basin Way, and the old McWilliams house is set back from the street at 14407. The beautiful home of Charles and Alexander Maclay, built in the 1860's, stands on Saratoga Creek on the right side of Highway 9 just west of town. The Marsh house, once located at 14567 Big Basin Way, was built about the same time. It has been moved to avoid demolition and will be relocated in Wildwood Park to serve as the museum of the Saratoga Historical Foundation. The home of Erwin T. King, one of the founders of the paper mill, was built in 1876 and still stands at 14605 Big Basin Way. Two old stone business buildings, built about 1870 but now remodeled, stand on Big Basin Way at the foot of Third Street. The former Brewer store, a wooden structure of the same period, is located at 14265 Saratoga Avenue. The old Methodist church, built in 1895, is now an antique shop at 20490 Saratoga–Los Gatos Road. In Madronia Cemetery, at Oak and Sixth streets, are buried A. T. Dowd, discoverer of the Calaveras Big Trees; Riley Moutrey, one of the heroic rescuers of the Donner party; and Mrs. Mary Ann Brown.

The widow of John Brown, famous abolitionist of Harper's Ferry, came to California in 1864, five years after her husband's execution. She and her family settled at Red Bluff, where the home built for her with money given by the townspeople is still standing. In 1870 the Browns moved to Humboldt County, and 11 years later to Saratoga. Mrs. Brown's home from 1881 to 1883 was on the side of the mountain three miles above town, overlooking a wide sweep of the Santa Clara Valley. The building no longer stands, but the site is on the property of the Stuart Camp of the Boy Scouts. It is reached by Bohlman Road, a continuation of Oak Street, a steep and winding mountain road bordered on either side by a tangle of wildflowers and native shrubs. In 1883, before moving to San Francisco, Mrs. Brown sold the mountain farm and lived a short time in the house still standing at 13915 Saratoga Avenue. Mary Ann Brown died in San Francisco on February 29, 1884, but her remains were returned to Saratoga for funeral services and burial.

Senator James Duval Phelan, philanthropist, brilliant statesman, and liberal patron of the arts, named his Saratoga country place Villa Montalvo in honor of the early Spanish author Ordóñez de Montalvo, in whose *Las Sergas de Esplandián* the name California appears for the first time. The house, built about 1910 on an estate of 175 acres, is situated in the foothills of the Santa Cruz Mountains in a region of great natural beauty with an extensive view over valley and mountains. In the 19-room mansion, which surrounds three sides of a colorful court, the owner placed priceless works of art gathered from many lands during a long period of years: paint-

Maclay Home, Saratoga

ings, wood carvings, rugs, hangings—the fruits of old looms. Here this native son of San Francisco entertained his many friends in the social, political, commercial, and artistic circles in which he moved.

At the death of Senator Phelan, on August 7, 1930, the place with all its precious furnishings was left by will to the San Francisco Art Association. It is now administered as an art gallery and cultural center by the Villa Montalvo Association. The gates at the beginning of a long driveway to the mansion are located beside the Saratoga–Los Gatos highway just southeast of the business section of Saratoga.

In the mountains northwest of Saratoga, off Pierce Road, is the picturesque sandstone winery of Paul Masson *(SRL 733)*, producer of fine wines and champagnes for many years.

Stevens Creek

Stevens Creek, or Arroyo de San Joseph Cupertino *(SRL 800)*, rising to the west of Black Mountain near the border line of Santa Clara County, flows southeast toward the bay, receiving in its course many small tributaries. Its upper reaches lie in lands wholly outside the confines of the early Spanish and Mexican grants; its history, therefore, with the exception of one important event, falls entirely within the American period.

The name Arroyo de San Joseph Cupertino was given by the Juan Bautista de Anza party to the creek on which they camped on March 25, 1776. The name Cupertino Creek was afterward used to refer to what is now called Stevens Creek, and this creek has traditionally been accepted as the site of Anza's camp, particularly that part of the creek near McClellan Road. Some historians, however, have wondered if the campsite may rather have been on Saratoga Creek at Saratoga.

The stream bears the name of Captain Elisha Stevens, of the Murphy-Townsend-Stevens overland party, who early took up government land on its banks opposite Rancho San Antonio. Captain Stevens built a house among the oak trees in a bend of the stream, where it is shown on an early map. The place was later acquired by one McCauley, who had there, before 1871, a vineyard, an orchard, and a five-acre blackberry patch. He maintained a summer resort, and to accommodate more visitors, he enlarged the house built by Captain Stevens.

The property, consisting of 69 acres, after passing through the hands of a Mr. Knowlton and N. Hays, was purchased by Garrett J. Byrne in 1879. Annie McCloud Byrne, wife of the purchaser, renamed the place Glenbrook Farm in memory of a place that she knew in her native Ireland. The Byrne family found the house much enlarged from its original size. It was then a long, narrow structure of two stories with the kitchen in the end nearest the creek. It stood until 1906, when it was so badly wracked by the earthquake that it had to be torn down. The Byrne family lived in tents until a smaller residence, a one-story, white-painted cottage, no longer standing, was constructed upon the same site from material salvaged from the demolished building. The name Glenbrook Farm did not succeed in supplanting the earlier one of Blackberry Farm.

Along Stevens Creek Boulevard, where Monte Vista is now, a tract of 100 acres was owned by William Hall, who with Samuel Williams had what is said to have been the first large planting of grapevines in the county. John T. Doyle, a well-known attorney of the 1860's, purchased Williams' half, lying along Stevens Creek, and built a winery on one side of the stream and a dwelling house on the other. The site of the wooden three-story winery is approached over a road flanked by old palm trees, now Palm Avenue off Foothill Boulevard. Pipes for conveying the pressed juice were laid from this building to the cement storage house, later called the Monte Vista Winery, across the creek, where the wine was ripened. Sand used for making the cement for this storage place was secured from the bed of the creek below. The Doyle family, whose main residence was near Menlo Park, built the house on their Stevens Creek property in 1873. In 1882 it became the location of the first Cupertino post office. The Doyle house and cement winery, or storage house, stand at 22044 McClellan Road, at the first bend of the road.

In 1892 a post office called West Side was established at the present Cupertino crossroads. The old Cupertino post office was discontinued in 1894, and the name of the West Side office was changed to Cupertino in 1900.

The oldest house in the vicinity of Stevens Creek is one now remodeled beyond recognition at 22221 McClellan Road. It was built by W. T. McClellan, who owned a few hundred acres adjoining Blackberry Farm.

Blackberry Farm lies along the creek and Byrne Avenue between McClellan Road and Stevens Creek Boulevard. The home of Nathan Hall across the boulevard from Blackberry Farm was torn down in the early 1930's, but an unusually fine old oak that stood beside it remains. The original tank house is also on the property, at 22021 Stevens Creek Boulevard. Hall too planted a vineyard in early days.

To provide a place of rest and recuperation for the Jesuit Fathers at Santa Clara, a villa was developed in the region of Stevens Creek. The location, ten miles away from the college and reached by horse and carriage, was sufficiently remote to ensure them a complete change from the daily routine of school work. Several small shrines were placed on the slope of the hill and on the plateau above. The chapel of St. Joseph of Cupertino was a frame building erected in 1873 as a place of worship for residents of the surrounding country. It stood for many years after a Catholic church had been built in the town of Cupertino. The vineyard on the hillside provided wine for sacramental purposes from the earliest days, but it has now become choked with weeds and brush. The winery, a plain, unpainted building erected in 1875, still stands near the site of the chapel. The location of Villa María is off Stevens Canyon Road at the entrance to the quarry of the Santa Clara Sand and Gravel Company.

A dozen or more houses built in the early 1880's

in the vicinity of Cupertino were homes of retired captains who had roved the seas in sailing vessels. With their families aboard, as was then the custom, these men had met many times in foreign ports. As they retired to live on land, one by one they purchased 40-acre plots. This region was favored by a number of the families for permanent homes.

The house of Captain John Parshley Crossley stands at the end of a straight lane off McClellan Road at No. 21440. A native of Connecticut, Captain Crossley had been mate on nearly a score of sailing vessels and during the Civil War was in the transport service that carried the first cargo of mules for General McClellan's army at Fortress Monroe. His eldest son, who had attained the rank of first mate on his father's vessel, was lost when the boat was becalmed north of Formosa; no trace was ever found of the little fishing boat on which he had set out from the larger boat in the still waters. The house has been renovated and is in excellent condition. In front are olive trees, and the whole is now surrounded by an orchard.

Almost opposite the entrance to the Crossley place is the one-story house of Captain Joseph Cluley Merithew, at 21439 McClellan Road, which he purchased in 1887 and occupied the following year. After his last trip, which was on the *John Bright* to the Sandwich Islands, he planted his whole tract to grapes, and when they came into bearing he made annually 6,000 gallons of wine. The typical New England cottage and its picturesque old barn have been allowed to fall into a state of dilapidation.

Captain Aaron H. Wood of the *Sovereign of the Seas*, a native of Rhode Island, whose elder brother had been in San Francisco since 1847, purchased land on the west side of Stelling Road between McClellan Road and Stevens Creek Boulevard and erected a house there in 1885. It was destroyed by fire, but a few old trees remained to mark the site, which is now part of the future campus of De Anza College, now under construction. Nearby is the cement Beaulieu Winery, built in the 1880's, with its house and formal garden, also on the college property.

Captains Ross and Blake and the latter's son-in-law, Captain Porter, each bought a 40-acre tract and settled near the corner of Homestead Road and the Sunnyvale–Saratoga highway. Captain Harriman, from Maine, and Captain Gibson lived not far away. The social gatherings of the group were enlivened by tales of far lands.

"The Frenchman," Peter Coutts

An almost legendary character is the "Frenchman" of Frenchman's Lake and Frenchman's Tower on the property now owned by Stanford University. Peter Coutts was the name borne by this gentleman during his residence in California, but Paulin Caperon is the real name left behind him in his native country and the name by which he was again known after his return to France.

A man of wealth and social position before the Franco-Prussian War, editor and publisher of *La Liberté*, in which his editorials during that troubled time involved him politically, he fled with other notables to Switzerland, where he lived for a time under the name of a cousin, Peter Coutts. From Switzerland, using the passport issued in the name of this cousin, he brought his family to the United States and about 1874 came west to California, where he settled on the Matadero Ranch in the vicinity of Mayfield.

He purchased land from Delevan Hoag and from William Paul and established a home and a stock farm west of El Camino Real bordering on the street now known as Stanford Avenue not far from the railroad station of Mayfield (now California Avenue station). The family residence, still standing off Escondido Road and modeled somewhat after the Petit Trianon of Versailles, was an L-shaped building of one story. The interior walls were of redwood covered with a French chintz bearing designs in pastel shades on a ground of soft gray; the parlor, extending the full width of one end of the ell, and the other family rooms were paneled with folds of the chintz. All these rooms opened on a hall running the full length of the wing. The shorter part of the ell contained the dining room and kitchen.

Outside the house this kindly man, past middle age but with the quick, elastic step of youth, had many interests. Close by were the young shade and fruit trees, as well as the vineyard that he had planted. His dovecots housed many pigeons. A race track, where his immaculately groomed horses were shown, was laid out between his house and El Camino Real, where afterward the Stanford Airport was located. Some distance to the rear of the house were buildings that stabled his thoroughbred horses and his sleek imported Ayrshire cattle that carried off many a trophy at the Sacramento State Fair. In convenient proximity to all was the plain, substantial brick structure erected to accommodate his fine library on its upper floor, the lower part serving as the managerial office of the estate.

It is supposed that his intention was to build ultimately a stately home, perhaps a castle, on a hill nearby, where he planted cypress trees and below which he developed a miniature lake by impounding the water from a spring found there. In this shrubbery-rimmed lake outlined by a wall of cut stone were fern-fringed little islands connected by picturesque arched bridges built of brick. One of these bridges has thus far escaped demolition and stands strangely alone above a tangle of weeds east of Frenchman's Road between Foothill Road and Gerona Road at the edge of the Stanford campus. A few trees and some of the rock work of a park surrounding the lake are still evident.

In his efforts to find an adequate supply of water for his future requirements, Monsieur Coutts started several tunnels into the hills near the lake and elsewhere, each of which was abandoned as the quest proved futile. A round red brick tower near the bank of Matadero Creek on Page Mill Road yet stands awaiting the tank that was to have contained some portion of a hoped-for water supply. This tower is about 200 yards from an abandoned tunnel dug perhaps 150 feet into a bushy hillside.

All of these activities on the part of the man who is now so little known gave rise to various wild rumors as to who he was, why he was there, and what he was doing. He and his children, a boy and a girl, his companions in frequent walks over the countryside, became friendly with many children in the sparsely settled area. Although his own children were instructed at home by their governess, Eugenie Clogenson, he displayed much interest in the Mayfield public school and gave prizes for various simple athletic endeavors.

All the political difficulties coupled with the aftermath of the Franco-Prussian War being removed, Peter Coutts took his family back to Europe in 1880, going first to Brussels and later to Paris, where he had a splendid town house. He built a magnificent castle, Chateau du Martelet, at Évian les Bains. His death occurred in 1890 and he was buried at Bordeaux.

The Matadero Ranch, or the Ayrshire Farm as it was sometimes called, was purchased by Governor Leland Stanford through agents in London and turned over to the use of the Leland Stanford Junior University along with other property. In 1891 Dr. David Starr Jordan, the young president of the new university, occupied the Coutts cottage for a few months, giving it the name of "Escondite" (hiding place). Since that time it has housed other living groups connected with the university and has undergone some remodeling. It serves now as the administration building for the university's housing project for married students. The original driveways have been changed, and the barns and all the buildings with the exception of the cottage and the two-story brick library and office have been removed. For a time the library building, at 860 Escondido Road across from the cottage, was used as a primary school for faculty children and later as a laboratory by the Psychology Department of the university. In more recent years it served as a faculty residence, and now it is used by the Art and Architecture Department.

Stanford University

Antonino Buelna, a resident of the Pueblo de San José, obtained permission in 1837 to occupy Rancho San Francisquito, comprising 1,471 acres, the smallest of the seven ranchos lying between the present towns of Mountain View and San Mateo. At its northeastern corner stood the tall redwood tree, the Palo Alto. Adjoining Buelna's holdings on the east was Rancho Rinconada del Arroyo de San Francisquito, granted to María Antonia Mesa, the widow of Rafael Soto, in 1841. Rancho San Francisquito is now a part of the Stanford University property, while Rancho Rinconada del Arroyo de San Francisquito is occupied, in part, by the city of Palo Alto.

After the American occupation in 1846, there was a period of great uncertainty as to land titles in California. Squatters settled on many of the Mexican ranchos, and it is safe to say that the land on Rancho San Francisquito alone, owned in 1852 by one man, had been claimed or owned by at least 20 persons between the years 1851 and 1862. The ranch was continually being divided, redivided, and sold.

During this period outsiders obtained permission from the ranchers to clear the land of its timber, and large charcoal ovens sprang up among the beautiful groves of oak and madroña which covered the entire estate. The few cherished trees which remain on the campus today give but a faint idea of the groves that once stood there. The charcoal obtained from the slaughter of these great trees was sacked and taken to the mouth of San Francisquito Creek, where it was loaded on barges and shipped to the port of San Francisco.

This period of disintegration ended in 1863, when George Gordon, a San Francisco businessman, chose the old rancho as his summer home. He did not purchase it all at once, but finally acquired the last of it from one of Buelna's heirs in 1865. The house he built near San Francisquito Creek later became the nucleus of the Stanford residence, and Eucalyptus Avenue was one of the several fine drives that he laid out.

Gordon died in 1869, and in 1870 the estate was purchased by Leland Stanford. He enlarged and remodeled the Gordon home, which later became the Stanford Convalescent Home at 520 Willow Road. It was torn down in 1965 for expansion of the hospital facility.

The old Rancho San Francisquito is thus the heart of what became known as the Palo Alto Farm, famous for the breeding and training of pedigreed race horses. The old stockyards and barns are now surrounded by the green links of the Stanford University golf course. Here, also, is the horse cemetery, including the grave of Palo Alto, the most famous of Stanford's horses, marked by the statue of a racer. This area is referred to as the birthplace of motion pictures, because of an experiment conducted in 1878–79 by Stanford and Eadweard Muybridge, a noted photographer. According to the plaque on the site, "men and animals in motion" were photographed in "consecutive instantaneous exposures . . . provided by a battery of 24 cameras fitted with electro-shutters." It was here demonstrated that a horse, while running rapidly, can have all four feet off the ground at the same time. The old Stanford winery, built in 1883, stands on Welch Road near the Palo Alto–Stanford Medical Center. It has now been converted to house restaurants, offices, and shops.

Leland Stanford, a native of New York, came to California in 1852 at the height of the gold fever. Stanford, however, did not seek gold but with his three brothers at once entered into extensive mercantile operations in Sacramento and the mining regions. He amassed a fortune in the eight years following. During the Civil War he was made governor of California and in that office he materially aided the Union cause. Declining a renomination, he threw all his energies into the building of the first transcontinental railroad, and was one of the "Big Four" (the others being Hopkins, Crocker, and Huntington) who built and owned the Central Pacific Railroad, later

Southern Pacific. He was United States Senator from 1885 until his death in 1893.

Stanford and his wife had an only child, Leland Stanford, Jr. On March 13, 1884, this son, then 16, died in Florence, Italy. On November 11, 1886, the Stanfords founded the university that was to be not only a memorial to their child but a gift of love to all the children of California. To provide an adequate campus, Senator Stanford purchased adjoining tracts: the Matadero Ranch lying to the southeast, Coon Farm lying between San Francisquito and Los Trancos creeks, and Felt Farm (also called Rancho de los Trancos) lying along Los Trancos Creek. The cornerstone of this memorial university was laid on May 14, 1887, and in October 1891 its doors were opened to students.

Stanford University has embodied in its architecture much of the picturesque atmosphere of Spanish California. The university buildings are grouped about a quadrangle, after the style of the early mission establishments. These buildings, with their graceful arcades and leafy courts, their red-tiled roofs contrasting with the soft cream of sandstone walls, make a memorable picture in the midst of the rich arboretums and richer hills which enfold the whole. And in the center of the south side of the Inner Quad is the Memorial Church, with its exquisite stained-glass windows and sweet-toned organ, Mrs. Stanford's memorial to her husband.

In the soft euphonious names one hears about the campus walks and drives, there comes again an echo of Spanish days: Roble (the White Oak) and Encina (the Live Oak), Madroño, and Toyon, the various dormitories and boarding houses named for native trees and shrubs; Alvarado Row, Lasuén and Salvatierra streets, named for Spanish leaders in Alta California; Escondite Cottage, Cedro Cottage, Lagunita, San Juan Hill, and Embarcadero Road. Many of these old Castilian names were chosen by Dr. David Starr Jordan, Stanford University's first president and a great scholar.

Stanford University's most famous graduate was Herbert Hoover, president of the United States from 1929 to 1933. He received the news of his election at his home on campus, at 623 Mirada Avenue on the crown of San Juan Hill. The 21-room house was built shortly after World War I and was largely designed by his wife, Lou Henry Hoover. After her death in 1944, it became the home of the president of the university. The Hoover Library with its 280-foot tower houses an extensive collection of documents on war, peace, and revolution, assembled by Hoover after World War I. Herbert Hoover graduated from Stanford in the class of 1895. He died in New York City on October 20, 1964, at the age of 90.

Mayfield, College Terrace, and Palo Alto

Mayfield and College Terrace are the two oldest parts of the city of Palo Alto. At about 429 California Avenue in Mayfield, now South Palo Alto, James Otterson constructed a public house called "Uncle Jim's Cabin." It was completed in 1853, and there he and his family gave a hearty welcome to travelers for many years. In 1855 a post office was established and the mail, delivered by stage, was dropped at "Uncle Jim's," where his stepdaughter, Sarah Ann Smith, became its custodian. At first, the bag was merely deposited upon the counter of the hostelry, and persons expecting mail looked through it for their own letters. Also in 1855, a school, a butcher shop, a store, and a bakery were added to the little settlement.

In 1856, William Paul, a Scottish bachelor who had kept a store across San Francisquito Creek, moved to Mayfield, bought out the store started the previous year by one Fuller, and combined the two stocks of goods. Paul bought a piece of farmland on Rancho Rincón de San Francisquito from Secundino Robles, where afterward the Stanford Flying Field was located.

The town of Mayfield was laid out on March 20, 1867. Its streets running northeast and southwest were named for distinguished Americans: Lincoln, Sherman, Grant, and Sheridan. Washington's name was also used, but that street is now a continuation of Page Mill Road and is known under that name.

South of the settlement of Mayfield, Elisha O. Crosby purchased land from Secundino Robles, obtaining the first tract in 1853. He called his place Mayfield Farm, and it was later sold to Judge Wallis, who erected a large house upon it. The property was sold by Judge Wallis to Edward Barron, who established his residence there in 1878. Barron was a retired stock dealer and mine operator, who took pleasure in continuing the improvement of the house and grounds. The old home burned down in 1936. The place has since been known as Barron Park, a residential and commercial development.

Another man whose name clings to the vicinity of Mayfield was William Page, who married the postmaster, Sarah Ann Smith. He was a native of New York, who first came to California in 1850 at the age of 18 and, being quickly successful in mining, returned to the East. Feeling the attraction of the West again in 1852, he went once more to the goldfields but was not successful a second time. After cutting timber for a sawmill in San Mateo County, he turned eventually to the establishment of his lumberyard in Mayfield. The Page Mill Road ran between this yard and the mills up in the mountains.

College Terrace, between Mayfield and the grounds of Stanford University, is located on a tract of 120 acres formerly owned by two men, Frederick William Weisshaar and Peter Spacher. Weisshaar, a native of Saxe-Weimar, and Spacher, a native of Alsace-Lorraine, became friends in San Francisco. When they purchased this piece of land belonging to Rancho Rincón de San Francisquito, they drew lots to determine their respective portions. Dividing it into two equal parts is the street now called College Avenue. Spacher drew the part nearest the campus and erected his house where now is the little square called Berkeley Park. Both men settled down to farming their acres. The Weisshaar house was erected on the site adjoining that upon which St. Aloysius Catholic Church now stands. This house was sold and later removed.

The town of Palo Alto was a grain field when Stanford University was opened in 1891. It promptly became a flag stop on the railway, and from that beginning it has grown to be the residential city of today. The house at 913 Emerson Street is the "birthplace" of electronics. Here Dr. Lee de Forest, inventor of the oscillating vacuum tube, conducted his early experiments in 1912.

Notable Writers

The county has a few unpretentious memorials to famous writers who once lived and wrote within its borders.

At 432 South Eighth Street, San Jose, back from the street, is the Edwin Markham Cottage (SRL 416), the house where Markham lived (1869–89) and wrote the first draft of his most famous poem, "The Man with the Hoe." After a boyhood spent in Solano County, Markham entered the normal school at San Jose, now San Jose State College, from which he was graduated. He taught his first school at Evergreen. The one-story schoolhouse in which he taught has given place to a larger one, but a redwood tree has been planted nearby in his honor.

The home of Henry Meade Bland was at Linda Vista, east of San Jose, on the rim of the Mount Hamilton hills. He was born in Solano County in 1863, and was educated in various schools throughout the state as he moved about with his clergyman father, Henry James Bland. He became professor of creative English in the San Jose State Teachers College, a position he held for 30 years. By act of the state legislature on March 21, 1929, Bland was made poet laureate of California. He died in April 1931.

Los Gatos has Royce Street, named in honor of Josiah Royce, historian, philosopher, psychologist, who spent a part of his early years on that street in the house of his mother, Sarah Eleanor Royce. The parents of Josiah Royce came overland to California in 1849, and the diary kept by his mother at that time, and now published, is an intimate narrative of the journey.

Near Redwood Retreat, ten miles west of Gilroy in the Mount Madonna region, is a log cabin built by the novelist Frank Norris a short time before his death in 1902. He and his wife established themselves there near the forest cabin of their friend, the widow of Robert Louis Stevenson. Here he planned to write The Wolf, which was to complete the trilogy begun by The Octopus and The Pit. His death at the age of 32 intervened before the manuscript was finished. A semicircular seat, built of stones brought from the stream nearby, is a memorial erected near the cabin by friends of the novelist. The Frank Norris cabin has been declared eligible for registration as a National Historic Landmark by the Department of the Interior. It is located on a private road and is reached from Gilroy by a route including the Hecker Pass highway, Watsonville Road, Redwood Retreat Road, and Sanders Road. The cabin is about three-quarters of a mile from the site of the old Redwood Retreat Hotel.

Other Landmarks

The French prune, for which the Santa Clara Valley became famous, was introduced into California at San Jose in the winter of 1856–57 by Louis Pellier, aided by his brothers Pierre and Jean. A native of France, Louis Pellier came to California in 1849, and in October 1850 opened a nursery called City Gardens (SRL 434). The site is at the northwest corner of North San Pedro Street and Chaboya Alley, an old lane between West St. John and West St. James streets.

John Townsend, said to have been the first graduate American doctor of medicine to settle in California, arrived in the present state in 1844 with the overland party led by Martin Murphy, Sr., and Captain Elisha Stevens, with which his name is also often associated. In 1848 he was prominent in public affairs in San Francisco, where Townsend Street is named for him. The following year he moved to the San Jose area, where he died of cholera in 1850. His ranch was located on the present Schallenberger Road.

The great financier A. P. Giannini was born in San Jose on May 6, 1870. The site of the old Swiss Hotel where he was born is marked at 79 North Market Street, a tablet having been placed by the San Jose Historic Landmarks Commission on November 12, 1965. In 1904 he founded the Bank of Italy, now Bank of America, in San Francisco, and in 1910 opened the first out-of-town branch at San Jose, at the corner of Santa Clara and Lightstone streets. Giannini died in San Mateo in 1949.

Henry W. Coe State Park is being developed in the mountains 14 miles east of Morgan Hill via Dunne Avenue. The area of almost 13,000 acres includes old buildings of the 1860's from the Coe Ranch and the Madrone Springs resort.

At First and San Fernando streets in San Jose is a plaque commemorating the site of the first broadcasting station in the world, established by Dr. Charles Herrold in 1909. It later became known as KQW, and is now KCBS, with headquarters in San Francisco.

Montgomery Hill (SRL 813), on Yerba Buena Road near San Felipe Road in Evergreen, is where Professor John J. Montgomery of Santa Clara College conducted many of his glider experiments. He made the world's first successful flight in heavier-than-air craft near San Diego in 1883. Montgomery was killed in a glider crash at the Evergreen site in 1911.

SOURCES

Abeloe, William N. "Lexington and Alma, Santa Clara County, California," The Pony Express, XIX, No. 8 (January 1953), 12.
――― "The Man Behind the Map," The Owl, a publication of the University of Santa Clara, XXIX, No. 11 (November 1952), 8–9, 14.
Arbuckle, Clyde, and Roscoe D. Wyatt. Historic Names, Persons and Places in Santa Clara County. Privately printed, San Jose, 1948.

Bolton, Herbert Eugene. *Anza's California Expeditions.* 5 vols. University of California Press, Berkeley, 1930.

—— *Fray Juan Crespí, Missionary Explorer on the Pacific Coast, 1769–1774.* University of California Press, Berkeley, 1927.

Bowman, Jacob N. "The Bridges of Provincial California," *El Palacio* (quarterly journal of the Museum of New Mexico), LXVIII, No. 4 (Winter, 1961), 223–30.

—— and G. W. Hendry. "Spanish and Mexican Houses in the Nine Bay Counties." Ms., Bancroft Library, University of California, Berkeley; State Library, Sacramento, 1942.

Brown, Alan K. Unpublished research on the Monterey Road and the San Francisco Road.

The California Missions, a Pictorial History. By the editorial staff of Sunset Books. Lane Book Co., Menlo Park, 1964.

Clark, George T. *Leland Stanford, War Governor of California, Railroad Builder, and Founder of Stanford University.* Stanford University Press, Stanford, 1931.

Colburn, Eunice Walton. *Wines and Vines of California.* The Bancroft Co., San Francisco, 1889.

Cunningham, Florence R. "Our First Hundred Years," *Saratoga Observer,* March 3–December 1, 1948.

Dana, Richard Henry, Jr. *Two Years Before the Mast, a Personal Narrative of Life at Sea,* ed. John Haskell Kemble. 2 vols. Ward Ritchie Press, Los Angeles, 1964.

Elder, David Paul. *The Old Spanish Missions of California.* Paul Elder & Co., San Francisco, 1913.

Eldredge, Zoeth Skinner. *The Beginnings of San Francisco, from the Expedition of Anza to the City Charter of April 15, 1850.* 2 vols. Privately printed, San Francisco, 1912.

Elliott, O. L., and O. V. Eaton. *Stanford University and Thereabouts.* C. A. Murdock, San Francisco, 1896.

Foote, H. S., ed. *Pen Pictures from the Garden of the World.* Lewis Publishing Co., Chicago, 1888.

Fox, Theron, ed. *After Harper's Ferry. John Brown's Widow—Her Family and the Saratoga Years.* Saratoga Historical Foundation, Saratoga, 1964.

Frémont, John C. *Memoirs of My Life, Including in the Narrative Five Journeys of Western Exploration.* Belford, Clarke & Co., Chicago, 1887.

Gifford, E. W. "Composition of California Shellmounds,"

University of California Publications in American Archaeology and Ethnology, XII, No. 1 (1916), 1–29.

Hall, Frederick. *History of San Jose and Surroundings with Biographical Sketches of Early Settlers.* Illustrated with map and engravings on stone. A. L. Bancroft & Co., San Francisco, 1871.

Hine, Robert V. *California's Utopian Colonies.* Huntington Library, San Marino, 1953.

Houghton, Dick. "SP's Picnic Line," *Trains,* VIII, No. 9 (July 1948), 46–51.

Kroeber, A. L. "California Place Names of Indian Origin," *University of California Publications in American Archaeology and Ethnology,* XII, No. 2 (1916–17), 21–29.

Older, Mrs. Fremont. *California Missions and Their Romances.* Coward-McCann, New York, 1938.

Pallette, Dr. E. M. "Peter Coutts," *Stanford Illustrated Review,* December 1925.

Preliminary Inventory of Historical Landmarks in Santa Clara County. County of Santa Clara Planning Department, San Jose, 1962.

(Robinson, Alfred). *Life in California.* (H. G. Collins, Paternoster Row, London, 1845).

Sanchez, Nellie Van de Grift. *Spanish and Indian Place Names of California.* A. M. Robertson, San Francisco, 1922.

Sawyer, Eugene T. *History of Santa Clara County.* Historic Record Co., Los Angeles, 1922.

Sheehan, E. M. "Famous Vineyards of California," *California Journal of Development,* XXIII, No. 12 (December 1933), 11, 42.

Spearman, Arthur Dunning, S.J. *The Five Franciscan Churches of Mission Santa Clara, 1777–1825.* National Press, Palo Alto, 1963.

Stuart, Reginald R., ed. "The Burrell Letters," *California Historical Society Quarterly,* XXVIII, No. 4, 297–322; XXIX, No. 1, 39–59, and No. 2, 173–79.

University of Santa Clara, Diamond Jubilee Volume, 1851–1926.

Winther, Oscar Osburn. "The Story of San José, 1777–1869, California's First Pueblo," *California Historical Society Quarterly,* Vol. XIV, 1935.

Young, John V. "Ghost Towns of the Santa Cruz Mountains," *San Jose Mercury Herald,* 1934.

Santa Cruz County

SANTA CRUZ COUNTY (named after Misión Santa Cruz, "holy cross") was one of the original 27 counties, created on February 18, 1850. It was first called Branciforte County, but the name was changed to Santa Cruz in March 1850. The northwestern part of its original area, including the town of Pescadero, was annexed to San Mateo County in 1868. The county seat is at Santa Cruz, where pre-statehood documents are housed in the Hall of Records.

The Portolá Trail

Leaving the region of Monterey County and proceeding northward, Gaspar de Portolá and his men crossed the Pajaro River on October 8, 1769, unaware that they were leaving behind them the bay for which they sought. A bronze plate on a monument at the Watsonville end of the Pajaro River bridge commemorates the fact that Portolá passed that way and named the river. Camp was

made near Watsonville on October 9, and from this point the party traveled northward up Corralitos Creek, camping for several days at Corralitos Lagoon, and again just east of Aptos. Finally, on October 16, they crossed Soquel Creek about three miles from the coast, their route having been very close to the present highway from Watsonville to Soquel.

It was before reaching Soquel on October 10 that the party first saw the famous "big trees," which were later named *palos colorados* because of the color of the wood. This is the first recorded mention of the coast redwoods, or *Sequoia sempervirens,* to be distinguished from their giant cousins of the High Sierra, known as *Sequoia gigantea.*

On October 17 the party camped on the west bank of a large river which they called the San Lorenzo, the name it still bears. Here they again saw many redwoods and "roses of Castile" but,

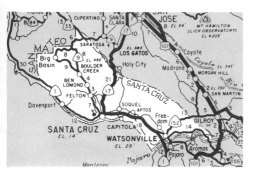

much to the disappointment of Father Crespí, no Indians. The city of Santa Cruz is now located at this place.

From October 17 to the end of the month, the expedition traversed the route now covered by State Highway 1, along the coast of Santa Cruz and San Mateo counties. This route, for a few miles northwest of Santa Cruz, lies across the ancient sea beaches now raised to form fertile benches on which vegetable crops are grown. The region is well known to scientists because of the plainly pictured story of geologic changes shown by the series of sea terraces between the hills and the present tide line.

On Wednesday, October 18, as recorded in Father Crespí's diary, the party stopped at an arroyo which the soldiers called La Puente, because a bridge of poles and earth had to be made before the men and animals could cross. This stream is now called Coja Creek. The next day they crossed seven gulches, some of which were very difficult. (One, especially, had very steep sides, and Father Crespí wrote that the mule on which the *olla,* or cooking pot, was loaded fell to the bottom of the bank.)

On Thursday, October 19, they stopped at what is now known as Scott Creek, where they found vestiges of an Indian village; then proceeding north up the coast, they arrived on October 20 "at the mouth of a very deep stream that flowed out from between very high hills of the mountain chain. This place, which was named the Arroyo or Cañada de la Salud ... was open toward the north-northeast and extended inland for about a league in that direction." Here they encamped for three nights.

On Sunday, October 22, Father Crespí wrote: "the day dawned, overcast and gloomy; the men were wet and wearied for want of sleep, as they had no tents, and it was necessary to let them rest.... What excited our wonder on this occasion was that all the sick, for whom we feared the wetting might prove exceedingly harmful, suddenly found their pains very much relieved. This was the reason for giving the canyon the name of La Salud." La Salud (Spanish for "health") is now known as Waddell Creek, and still becomes, after heavy rains, the "very deep stream" that these weary travelers found. At this place, the engineer of Portolá's party, Don Miguel Costansó, recorded that Punta de Año Nuevo, which was to be left behind on the next day's journey, had

approximately the same latitude as did Cañada de la Salud, where they had been encamped for three days.

Mission Santa Cruz

The Viceroy Condé de Revilla Gigedo and Father Matías de Noriega decided in 1789 to establish a mission on the spot called Santa Cruz between those missions already established at San Carlos and Santa Clara. Two years after this decision was made, Father Fermín Francisco de Lasuén consecrated a site at the lower end of the San Lorenzo Valley. Here, on St. Augustine's Day, August 28, 1791, in the presence of many Indians of all ages, he said Mass and raised a cross.

The following month Fathers Alonzo Salazar and Baldomero López, accompanied by Hermenegildo Sal, commanding officer of the San Francisco Presidio, and his military escort, arrived at the prospective site. Christian Indians brought along from Santa Clara were set to work at once cutting wood for the construction of a brush shelter for the fathers, probably resembling an enramada such as may be seen in Mexico today.

At eight o'clock on Sunday morning, September 25, 1791, the formal ceremony for the founding of Misión la Exaltación de la Santa Cruz was celebrated. The program consisted of the Mass said by one of the padres, the act of taking possession in the name of His Majesty King Carlos IV of Spain by Ensign Sal, and the firing of the guns in salute. The fathers had brought with them as a nucleus for the mission a painting of Our Lady of Sorrows and an image of Our Father Saint Francis. From the neighboring missions of Carmel, Santa Clara, and San Francisco came donations of horses, cows, oxen, mules, sheep, and two bushels of barley for seed. At the end of the first three months 87 Indians had been baptized. It is thought that the first church was constructed about where North Pacific Avenue and River Street now intersect, with the southern end of the spacious plaza at the present juncture of Pacific Avenue and Mission and Water streets. Soon the establishment was found to be too near the river, and in the move to higher ground only the garden was left on the lower level.

The first stone of the new Mission Santa Cruz was laid February 27, 1793, and the completed structure was dedicated in the spring of 1794, with Commander Sal and Father Tomás de la Peña of Mission Santa Clara present. The church, built on the mesa above the river, was 112½ feet long, 29 feet wide, and 25½ feet high, with walls five feet thick. The lower part of the walls was made of native rock and the upper part of adobe. The vaulted roof, at first covered with thatch, was later recovered with tile.

Other buildings, erected as needed, formed an open square that is now outlined by the modern streets High, Emmet, Mission, and Sylvar. The mission church and the priests' quarters were on what is now High Street. On the present Sylvar Street were storehouses and rooms for looms. Back from Emmet Street, along the thoroughfare now known as School Street, were the women's quarters; and on the other side of School Street was the adobe building, still standing and known as the Neary-Hopcroft house, which was then the mission guard headquarters. This, the oldest building in the city of Santa Cruz, consists of two sections joined by a five-foot party wall. It seems always to have stood alone, detached from other buildings, and may possibly have been a part of the first mission establishment of 1791–93. The name Rodríguez became associated with it after the secularization of the mission; this was the family of José Antonio Rodríguez, Branciforte *inválido* of 1798. The Neary family acquired one section by purchase in the 1860's. The adobe has the distinction of having been occupied continuously since its completion; thus it is in very good condition for its age. Descendants of the Rodríguez and Neary families long resided there. The old garden at the rear located on the bluff above Mission Street is full of quaint charm. In 1959 the Neary-Hopcroft adobe became Santa Cruz Mission State Historical Monument.

Another adobe of that period, no longer standing, extended from the Neary-Hopcroft adobe to Emmet Street. After the influx of Americans, it was used by William Blackburn, an overland pioneer from Virginia in 1845 and later judge, as the Eagle Hotel and Store; but in 1862 it was taken over by the Sisters of Charity, who founded there the Holy Cross School. This site is now occupied by the kindergarten and grammar school, while a high school has been established diagonally across the plaza.

All went well at the mission for more than 20 years; then came trouble with the Branciforte pueblo; and, in addition to this annoyance, in 1818 the pirate Hippolyte de Bouchard, flying the insurgent flag of Buenos Aires, threatened an attack, which, fortunately, never materialized because of a storm at sea. However, in the effort to save mission properties in this emergency, much damage was done to the church and its furnishings by misdirected zeal.

The mission was secularized by Governor Figueroa in 1834. In 1840 an earthquake weakened the walls; and on January 9, 1857, another tremor caused the final destruction, for a month later at three o'clock in the morning the southwestern corner fell with a loud crash. In 1858 a frame church was built, which stood until 1889, when the present brick one was erected upon a portion of the site of the old mission (*SRL 342*). In 1891, a hundred years after the founding of the mission, a memorial arch of granite was erected in front of this brick church. The bell that rings out from the church was recast from the old bells salvaged from the earthquake-ruined mission.

In 1931 a concrete replica of the original mission was built on Emmet Street facing the upper plaza. It is identical in proportions to the first structure, but is about half the size, and is approximately 75 yards from the original site. In this replica are housed many objects that were in the original mission, notably a chandelier now altered for electricity and hung near the entrance. A statue of Our Lady of Sorrows occupies a niche in the front part of the little church, while in a room off the outer corridor are preserved richly ornamented vestments.

Mora Street is on the site of the old mission orchard. Two trees now standing, a walnut and a pear, are said to be of the original planting.

Villa de Branciforte

Three pueblos were established in California by the Spanish: San José, Los Angeles, and Branciforte. The last, named in honor of the Marquis de Branciforte, viceroy of Mexico, was established in 1797 under the direction of Governor Diego de Borica and was located across the San Lorenzo River from Mission Santa Cruz. Governor Borica showed his practical mind when he chose this place: good building material was close at hand, there was a plentiful supply of fish in the waters of the bay, and the facilities for shipping could easily be developed to handle the future produce of the pueblo. His recommendations were likewise sensible: "An adobe house to be built for each settler so that the prevalent state of things at San José and Los Angeles, where the settlers still live in tule huts, being unable to build better buildings without neglecting their fields, may be avoided; the houses not to cost over $200." Each colonist was to receive from the government a musket, a plow, a few necessary animals, and a subsidy of 116 pesos on a plan of easy repayment. The observance of religious duties was to be enforced. He called for farmers, mechanics, artisans, and sailors as settlers. Gabriel Moraga was taken from his position as *comisionado* of San José and placed in charge of the new pueblo. The original document, dated May 26, 1797, ordered Sergeant Moraga to proceed with this work and was signed by Governor Borica. It is preserved in the Hall of Records in Santa Cruz.

On May 12, 1797, the schooner *Concepción* arrived in Monterey Bay with colonists from Guadalajara, but no houses were ready for them. Don Alberto Cordoba, lieutenant of engineers in the Spanish Army who had visited there the previous year, arrived in August with instructions to follow a plan that had been drawn up in Mexico. He began a canal for irrigation, erected a few temporary houses, and sent estimates for further work to the governor and the viceroy, before the work was suspended in October.

Among the passengers on the *Concepción* were three men who became alcaldes. José Vicente Mojica, who brought a wife and five children, was alcalde in 1802; José Antonio Robles, who married first Rosalía Merlopes and at her death her sister, Gertrudis, and reared several children, held a number of offices before becoming alcalde in 1842; and Agustín Narvaez, 19 when he arrived, stayed at Branciforte only a few years but was alcalde in San José in 1821. Among the disabled soldiers sent there in 1798 were José Joaquín Castro and José Antonio Rodríguez, both of whom played an important part in the affairs of their time and whose descendants are now widely scattered throughout the state.

In 1799 Gabriel Moraga was succeeded by Ignacio Vallejo as *comisionado*, and the pueblo continued under the military jurisdiction of Monterey, except for two years under the civil jurisdiction of San José, until the time of its dissolution.

After the American occupation and the coming of American pioneers, Branciforte became a township of pleasantly located homes; by a special election in 1907 it became part of the city of Santa Cruz. The mile-long race track, laid out in 1797 by Cordoba, is now Branciforte Avenue, and the intersection of this avenue with Water Street is the center of the old Villa de Branciforte (*SRL 469*), which occupied a rectangle one-half mile wide from east to west and one mile long from north to south. A bull-and-bear-fight arena was located on the flats near the Soquel Avenue bridge, between the San Lorenzo River and Branciforte Creek. As late as July 13, 1867, four bulls "from the Gabilan and Taurian mountains" fought here, lances, firecrackers, and red flags adding to the excitement. "Admission and seats—$1.00. Standing room on the sunny side—50 cents."

The City of Santa Cruz

A period of disintegration followed the Mexican order to secularize the missions, but before the gold rush several industries had developed in the town of Santa Cruz, which had grown up around the plaza of the mission.

Thomas Fallon, who had arrived in Branciforte in 1845 and who had raised the flag of the United States in San José in 1846, put up a building on the plaza. This had an outside stairway and did double duty as a residence and saddlery shop. The county later purchased this property for use as the County Courthouse, paying Fallon $3,500. The portrait of Fallon now hangs with those of other pioneers on the walls of the Pioneer Society building in San Francisco.

William Blackburn, a Virginia cabinetmaker who came overland to California with the Swasey-Todd company in 1845, worked as a lumberman in the Santa Cruz Mountains before joining the California Battalion Artillery, Company A, as a second lieutenant. He was alcalde of Santa Cruz from 1847 to 1849 and became county judge in 1850, at which time the decisions of his court became famous for their originality. His orchards were one of the chief attractions of Santa Cruz during his life. His home grounds, extending from Chestnut Avenue to Walnut Avenue and to the Neary Lagoon, covered the present site of the Southern Pacific Railroad yards. The old Blackburn house still stands at 101 Cedar Street, at the head of Sycamore Street.

Richard C. Kirby, born in England in 1817, left a whaling boat in Oregon in 1845 and came by land to California in 1846, to become associated with Paul Sweet in a tannery business on the San Agustín rancho shortly after his arrival. In the fall of 1850 he put up a small establishment for tanning leather in Squabble Hollow, now Glen Canyon. He bought other property later and built a yard with a capacity output of 1,500 skins a month. Kirby leather soon became famous. He tanned not only hides from local

ranches but also those shipped from South America. In 1852 he married Georgiana Bruce, who had been a member of the Brook Farm Colony near Boston in the 1840's and had come to California to establish a school. Born in England, she had come to America as a governess and had taught for a time in the South, where she became an ardent abolitionist. Here she met Mrs. Eliza Farnham, writer and lecturer, who caused Miss Bruce to come to California when she came. Mrs. Kirby has left a vivid picture of life in Santa Cruz in the 1850's in the pages of her journal. She was much interested in the beautification of her home and surroundings and for this purpose imported rare shrubs and trees. The Kirby home, a frame house, stood at 321 Mission Street, above Green Street.

Adna A. Hecox, a native of Michigan, who came across the plains with his wife and three children in 1846, preached the first Protestant sermon in Santa Cruz in May 1847 and assisted in the movement toward the establishment of the Methodist Church. James Dunleavy, also a Protestant preacher, and Elihu Anthony, who had been a circuit-riding pastor for a few years in Indiana, assisted him in forming a branch of the Sons of Temperance, a society very strong in the East at that time. The Sons of Temperance Hall, built on Mission Street in 1860, was afterward moved to Bulkhead Street, where it was used by the Salvation Army until its demolition in 1935. Aside from his religious activities, Hecox took part in other phases of pioneer life. Shortly after his arrival he erected a sawmill for Michael Lodge at Soquel. He was alcalde for Santa Cruz and continued in other important offices until he became custodian of the Lighthouse at its establishment in 1869, a post that he held until his death in 1883.

Elihu Anthony, a native of New York who came with a company of 100 wagons across the plains, arrived in Santa Cruz in 1847 at the age of 28 with his wife, the former Sarah A. Van Ande, and infant daughter. The following year he established a foundry below the bluff, fronting on what is now the Post Office Plaza. There he made the first cast-iron plows produced in California. Immediately after the discovery of gold, he made 90 light-weight iron picks, which he sent to the gold fields by Thomas Fallon, who went by ox team with his family. Each pick weighed three pounds and sold for three ounces of gold, until a load of picks from Oregon brought the price down to two ounces. Anthony was the second postmaster in Santa Cruz, succeeding Alexander McLean. Anthony's wife was a woman of ability, who found a large field for charitable work in the pioneer settlement. Their 20-room house on School Street, damaged by fire, was razed in 1935.

The city of Santa Cruz was granted a charter by the state legislature in 1866 and was incorporated in 1876. Passing through the city's streets, one is impressed by the number of old houses that give evidence of a background of historical significance; their generous size and decorated eaves and gables set them apart from the modern buildings. Unfortunately, many of the finest old homes have been razed in the name of progress. One of the earliest frame houses in the town stood at 314 Vine Street for many years. It was made of lumber brought around Cape Horn by Hiram Daniel Scott, purchaser of the San Agustín rancho, for whom Scotts Valley is named. A house once located at 223 Church Street was associated with the name of Bret Harte, who spent a few weeks' vacation there. This house was built by John Pinkham in 1856 and was purchased by Joseph Boston, who remodeled it in 1862. Almost opposite the Bret Harte cottage on Church Street stood the home of Frederick A. Hihn, a pioneer to whom the business interests of the town—and indeed of the whole county—owe much. He built this house in 1873, and it was one of the finest and best of the period. It was afterwards used as the City Hall. When new civic buildings were ready for occupancy in October 1937, it was razed. Some of the fine old trees and shrubbery were donated to the Golden Gate International Exposition on Treasure Island in 1939. The Alzina residence, its external appearance little altered since the 1850's, when it was constructed of lumber from the mills near Pescadero, stands at 109 Sylvar Street. One adobe outside the vicinity of the mission is still standing, the Lorenzana, or Winchester, house, at the southwest corner of North Branciforte and Goss avenues. It can be recognized as adobe from the deeply set windows. The date of erection is unknown.

Rancho San Andrés

Three grants, given to members of the Castro family in 1833, stretched along the shore of Monterey Bay from the mouth of Soquel Creek almost to the mouth of the Pajaro River and extended well inland. The southernmost of these ranchos had been occupied for possibly ten years by José Joaquín Castro, a pensioned soldier. As a boy, he came to California in Juan Bautista de Anza's party. He held several minor positions in the pueblo of Branciforte and was alcalde in 1831. His wife, María Antonia Amador, died in 1827, having given birth to 11 children, and he then married Rosario Briones. His Rancho San Andrés, consisting of two square leagues, was confirmed to his eldest son, Guadalupe, in 1854, and a United States patent was given Guadalupe "et al." in 1876.

The first house of Don José Joaquín on the rancho was located not far from the beach, but when he erected his large adobe house he chose a site on a hill above Larkin Valley overlooking in the distance a great sweep of the Pajaro Valley. The house stands today, a large two-story adobe with an upper and a lower veranda stretching the whole length of the front. A simple stairway at one end of the veranda connects the two floors, and the doorways both upstairs and downstairs lead to the interior. At the back of the house is a narrower porch with posts extending to the roof of the house.

A ballroom, 25 by 50 feet, located on the upper floor, has windows opening out to front and rear

José Joaquín Castro Adobe, near Watsonville

views of the broad expanse of the family domains that spread over hill and valley to north, east, south, and west.

This house, at 184 Old Adobe Road, is one of the few pretentious ones remaining from the times of the earliest settlers. Neglected for many years and often mistaken for an old barn, it deteriorated to the point that it appeared doomed to crumble into ruin beyond repair. Happily, in the 1950's, it was purchased and beautifully restored. The narrow road over which this dignified adobe is reached climbs a hill from the crossroads of Larkin Valley Road and Buena Vista Drive, a few miles northwest of Watsonville.

In the coastal part of the old rancho, west of Watsonville, was Camp McQuaide, an active army camp during World War II. Its site and some of its buildings are now occupied by the Monterey Bay Academy of the Seventh-Day Adventists.

Rancho Aptos

Rancho Aptos, of one square league, was granted in November 1833 by Governor José Figueroa to Rafael Castro, an industrious and prosperous ranchero who had held a few minor official positions. The southeast line of this grant adjoined the larger Rancho San Andrés belonging to his father, José Joaquín Castro, and extended north along the bay to the Sanjón de Borregas, "ditch of the lambs," a small stream across which runs the road from Santa Cruz toward Watsonville.

He built a home, of which nothing remains today, on a bluff a little south of the present town of Aptos. In the early 1870's he donated property for the erection of a Catholic chapel, the Church of Our Lady of Mount Carmel, at the present corner of Seacliff Beach State Park Drive and the old Santa Cruz–Watsonville highway (Soquel Drive). It was a quaint structure built by five pioneers, four of whom had crossed the continent in covered wagons. In time it was surrounded by picturesque cypress trees; but storms, earthquakes, and vandals caused its ruin, and it was condemned in 1925, dismantled and removed in 1930. The sweet-toned silver bell, given to the church by Don Rafael, was stolen and never recovered; but the one that replaced it, purchased by donations from residents, is preserved at the Santa Cruz Mission. A statue of Our Lady of Mount Carmel, a gift of the Rev. J. Adam, who had secured it from Spain, escaped disaster and is now in Saint Joseph's Catholic Church at Capitola. In the 1960's a new church was constructed on the Aptos property.

In a niche in the tall marble monument that marks his grave in the cemetery near the church is a miniature bust of Don Rafael. He died in 1878. In the family plot his wife, Soledad Cota, and other members of his family are buried. In the outlying part of this churchyard but still within the confines of the old cypress hedge lie the bones of many Indians removed from an early Indian burying ground not far away when the property was taken over by Claus Spreckels. The Indian burying ground had been called The Island and lay just below the junction of Aptos and Valencia creeks. It is now called Treasure Island, although no longer surrounded by water.

Ranchos Soquel and Soquel Augmentación

Martina, a daughter of José Joaquín Castro, obtained the grant Rancho Soquel, 1,668 acres, from Governor Figueroa in November 1833. To her was given also the larger grant, Rancho Soquel Augmentación, of 32,702 acres, on which lies the greater part of the Soquel watershed, containing vast forests of redwood, live oak, and madroña. It stretched to the mountaintops at the county boundary line and over to Loma Prieta. Both of these grants were confirmed and patented to her in March 1860.

She was married three times: first to a Spaniard, Simón Cota, who died, leaving her with two daughters; second to Michael Lodge, a sailor from Dublin; and third to a Frenchman, Louis Depeaux. After her marriage to Lodge she received the grants of land, and on a point of high ground near a ravine and springs of pure water, just off the road from Monterey to Santa Cruz, they lived in an adobe house.

This structure had a 50-foot frontage divided into three rooms, each with a depth of 30 feet. The larger, middle room with fireplace and board floor was the general living and reception room; its rough beams were covered with horsehide tanned with the hair on. Here the mother and her seven daughters entertained their friends with gay dancing parties. The house and garden were surrounded by a fence of redwood pickets driven into the ground. There was an ox-power flour mill. The millstones are now mounted in Pringle Grove, the property of the Soquel Pioneer Club, off north Main Street. The site of the adobe is found by turning east from Capitola Avenue on Hill Street and proceeding until the road ends at a ravine. Here a home stands on one side of the road, and on the other is the now empty small field where the Lodge adobe once stood.

Little is known of Doña Martina's life with her third husband. She died in 1890. In 1850 she divided her property, giving one-ninth to each of her eight children and keeping one-ninth for herself. In 1856 her share, which had passed into the hands of the Catholic Church, was purchased by August Noble, who built the Noble house, which stands at 308 Hill Street, about 200 feet from the site of Martina's adobe, one mile southeast of Soquel. Martina's adobe stood in good condition and was still in a fair state of preservation when torn down in 1925.

Rancho de los Corralitos

In the eastern part of the county lies Rancho Corralitos, which was granted in 1823, 1841, and 1844 to José Amesti, a native of Spain who came to California on the *Panther* in 1822 and became a prominent citizen and merchant in the land of his adoption. He married Prudencia, daughter of Ignacio Vallejo, in 1824. The 15,000 acres contained in this property were patented to his heirs in 1861 by the United States. The exact location of the adobe on this rancho is not evident today, but is supposed to be in the vicinity of the Amesti schoolhouse.

The town of Corralitos in the northern part of the rancho was a place of bustling activity in the pioneer days of the 1860's. It was surrounded by forests in which sawmills were moved from place to place as each location became "sawed out"; today it is a quiet settlement amid orchards and gardens. As early as 1865 several families living there had the luxury of water in their homes, running through pipes made by boring a hole lengthwise through redwood logs.

The first sawmill in this region was in Brown's Valley near García's bridge three and a half miles above Corralitos and was owned and operated from 1865 to 1867 by Brown and Williamson. The same company later built Gamecock Mill farther up the canyon. The narrow, rough logging roads, when abandoned by their original users, were improved for general travel by the settlers "working out" their taxes by filling chuck holes, hauling gravel, and widening the track.

In 1855 Benjamin Hames bought a site just above the present town, where the city of Watsonville filter plant is now located, and built a flour mill to which settlers as far away as Salinas hauled grain to be ground. The water from a dam in Eureka Canyon was brought through redwood flumes to operate the mill. When Hames lost the property through a mortgage, it was purchased by an employee, Robert Orton, who afterward served several times as sheriff of Santa Cruz County. In 1877 the site and buildings were bought by Peter and James Brown for a paper mill, where sun-dried strawboard was made from straw grown on Pajaro Valley ranches. For a few years the binding boards used in making textbooks for the schools throughout the state were manufactured there.

The first school serving the settlement was built among oak trees one and a half miles south of the town on the road leading to Watsonville and was called Oak Grove. The oaks are now gone, but a redwood grove on the opposite side of the road identifies the spot. The school was next moved one mile nearer to town, and the third schoolhouse was built in the town itself.

The present school is about a mile south of Corralitos.

Rancho Salsipuedes

The Salsipuedes grant of 31,201 acres was made to Francisco de Haro on November 4, 1834, and regranted to Manuel Jimeno on February 1, 1840. The final grant was for a total of eight leagues. These lands extended on the south from the Pajaro River north to the mountains at the county line, and a small part, in the vicinity of Bodfish Canyon, lay in Santa Clara County.

Don Manuel, who came to California from Mexico in 1830, was a man of great influence and was much respected in civil affairs. His wife, said to have been as vivacious as he was witty, was Agustías, daughter of José de la Guerra y Noriega. He was secretary of state for several years under governors Alvarado and Micheltorena. He sent two of his sons, Antonio and Porfirio, East in the company of William T. Sherman to be educated. After many years in poor health he died in Mexico, in December 1853, leaving 11 children. The site of his now almost forgotten adobe is on the Chittenden Pass road, which runs for many miles through this rancho.

Other men interested in public affairs later became owners of this land. William F. White, who had come from Pennsylvania with his young wife in 1849, acquired land from Don Manuel five miles east of Watsonville, and in 1853 he built the first substantial, American-owned house in the Pajaro Valley. The outside lumber, shipped from Maine, was of exceptionally high quality. He installed a pump, which was a great curiosity. Visiting Californians were much interested in manipulating the handle and seeing the water flow from the spout. One Sunday a month the family residence was used as a place of worship, the officiating priest coming from Mission San Juan Bautista.

White was a bank commissioner, appointed by Governor Irwin, and was a member of the Constitutional Convention of 1878 before becoming a candidate for governor on the Workingman's ticket in 1879. Associated with him in the purchase of this rancho were three other influential men: William Tecumseh Sherman, of Civil War fame; Secretary Montgomery, of President Lincoln's cabinet; and E. D. Baker, a lawyer.

A United States patent for this land was issued to James Blair *et al.* March 2, 1861.

Rancho Bolsa del Pájaro and Watsonville

Rancho Bolsa del Pájaro, consisting of two separate grants that stretch along both sides of the Pajaro River northeast of its mouth, which are probably "acre for acre the richest land on earth," was granted by Governor Alvarado on September 30, 1837, to Sebastián Rodríguez, who also claimed the Rincón de la Ballena in present San Mateo County, a claim that was rejected by United States authorities.

Don Sebastián, a sergeant of the Monterey Company and *comisionado* of Santa Cruz in 1831, married María Perfecta Pacheco. When he died in 1855, he left a large family. His will, signed at Monterey on April 26, 1854, gave the names of his parents as Antonio and Vicenta León de Rodríguez and named his wife and two sons, Pedro and José, as executors. Before the estate was settled, numerous squatters built small houses on the property and caused much trouble.

According to the treaty of the United States with Mexico, at the time of the American occupation, all titles to former grants were to be respected. But it took years of search on the part of the Land Commission to confirm the titles and to issue patents to the rightful owners. The litigation concerning Rancho Bolsa del Pájaro was finally ended when a patent was issued to the heirs in 1860 for one of the grants.

D. S. Gregory and Judge John H. Watson, the latter a native of Georgia, obtained the other grant before the death of Don Sebastián and laid out the town of Watsonville in 1852. W. L. Thrift, one of its first settlers, put up a tent that served as a hotel. When a post office was established the following year, he became the first postmaster in the town.

The principal crop raised in the vicinity was potatoes. An apple orchard was planted in 1853 by Jesse D. Carr, and a second one was planted by William F. White the next year. The success of these first plantings encouraged others to set out trees, and Watsonville has for many years been famed for its apple industry.

An interesting adobe house stands at 514 Blackburn Street between East Third Street and Center Avenue. It was originally constructed by Jesús Vallejo on his Rancho Bolsa de San Cayetano on the San Juan road in Monterey County. When the news of the imminent destruction of the building following 1906 earthquake damage came to the attention of Dr. Saxton T. Pope, he purchased it and had the material hauled four miles to Watsonville and re-erected on his own property. The original house had two stories, but in the restoration the material was fashioned into a one-story, three-room dwelling. The original oak doors are in place, and the lintel over the front door bears the carved words "Jesús Vallejo 1820." This is now inside the house, because of remodeling. In front of the adobe stands a small sundial bearing the date 1908 on its base.

Rancho Arroyo del Rodeo

Rancho Arroyo del Rodeo, mentioned sometimes in old records as "Los Coyotes," was granted by Governor Figueroa to Francisco Rodríguez, the early California poet, on July 28, 1834. It consisted of one-quarter of a square league lying on the shore of Monterey Bay between the Arroyo Soquel and the Arroyo del Rodeo. The highway from Watsonville to Santa Cruz, passing near the town of Soquel, crosses the entire width of the grant.

The surveyor's map of 1858 shows a dam and a flour mill on the creek above the town and a wharf on the bay to the west of the mouth of the stream. The mill was built and operated by John Hames and John Daubenbiss in 1847. John Hames was a member of the Santa Cruz Council in 1848 and in San José three years earlier had signed the "Call to Foreigners." John Daubenbiss, a native of Bavaria, served in Frémont's Battalion.

The flour mill then became a sawmill, from which timbers were sent by schooner to San Francisco in 1849 to build the "Long Wharf." In 1879 the site was purchased by Edward and Frank O'Neill, who ran a paper mill there for 25 years. After 1904 the spot was used intermittently. A tannery is said to have occupied the site at one period. The mill, which was razed in 1934, stood one-half mile north of the town of Soquel, at the side of a bypassed stretch of the old Soquel–San Jose road that has been given the name of Paper Mill Road.

This spot has still another claim to a passing thought, for here Lieutenant Frémont camped with his men on March 1, 1846.

The lands of this rancho were patented to Hames and Daubenbiss on May 3, 1882. Its name was derived from the fact that the cattle roundups or rodeos of the herds of the Rodríguez and Castro families took place in a natural amphitheater a half-mile south of the present Soquel Avenue bridge across Rodeo Creek, now covered by a huge freeway fill. This area was once the John S. Mattison ranch.

The town of Soquel is located on both sides of Soquel Creek. Among old buildings in the town is the picturesque Congregational Church erected in 1870, the congregation having been organized in 1868.

Rancho San Agustín and Scotts Valley

Rancho San Agustín, the northern tip of which is at Glenwood, was granted in 1841 to Juan José Crisóstomo Majors, the name that Joseph L. Majors, a native of Tennessee, had assumed when he became a Mexican citizen in 1838. He received a United States patent for his land, in his original name, in 1866.

When he was in Los Angeles in 1834, Majors had signed with other foreigners a protest against being obliged to do military service for the Mexican government. However, four years later he became a naturalized citizen of Mexico and married María de los Angeles Castro. He was one of the men arrested with Captain Isaac Graham as an undesirable foreigner, but, probably owing to his Spanish connections, was released before the captives were taken to Mexico. Also in 1841 he received a grant of the Zayante rancho.

Hiram Daniel Scott came into Monterey Bay in 1846 as second mate on the *C. Whiting*, and in 1852 he purchased Rancho San Agustín. The father, also named Hiram, followed the son West and took the ranch over. This area is now known as Scotts Valley.

Rancho Carbonera

Rancho Carbonera, bordering the San Lorenzo River north of Santa Cruz, was granted by Governor Alvarado to José Guillermo Bocle in 1838. It was patented to him in 1873.

Bocle was a man of many aliases—Boc, Buckle, Thompson, and Mead being a few. He and his brother Samuel, who had come to California in 1823, according to his own statement, and was naturalized in 1841, both took the name of Thompson after the American occupation. Guillermo, or William, was an English sailor who came to California in 1823, married María Antonia Castro, and became the father of a large family. At his death, unable to sign his own name, he left "to those now living with me" 15,000 acres of land along with horses, cattle, and money. Thompson's Flat, a section of his old holdings, on which is now located the Pasatiempo Golf Course, includes the campsite of John C. Frémont, then lieutenant in the topographical engineering corps of the United States Army, and his 60 men on February 25–28, 1846.

Paradise Masonic Park is also within the boundaries of this rancho. Here in 1855 was a sawmill. James Waters, a carpenter from Maryland who was in charge of this mill, later erected many buildings in the counties of Santa Cruz and Monterey and rose to a position of importance in the Pajaro Valley. Here in 1860 a paper mill was established with a reputed peak daily output of a ton of coarse brown paper. It survived two years, until the flume was carried away by high water, and the superintendent, Henry Van Valkenburg, died.

In 1865 the California Powder Works were constructed with an entrance about where the gates to Paradise Park now stand. A 1,300-foot tunnel through the mountain brought water from the San Lorenzo River to operate the grinding mills, the output of which was used for blasting in the construction of the Central Pacific Railroad. This plant continued operation until 1916, when it was absorbed by the DuPont Company, and work was discontinued at this place. The tunnel and some of the foundations remain, and the locality is still known as Powder Mill Flat. It is here that smokeless powder was first produced.

Santa Cruz County is the only county in the state to have as many as three covered bridges still intact. One of these, built in 1872, stands within Paradise Park and is in daily use by its residents. Except for metal nuts and bolts, it was constructed entirely of local wood. Built by the San Francisco Bridge Company to serve the California Powder Works, it is the only covered span in the West to be equipped with fire hoses at both ends. Other distinctive features are the diamond windows in its siding and the center doorway leading to an observation platform overlooking the San Lorenzo River. The 180-foot-long structure is about three miles northwest of Santa Cruz, off the highway to Boulder Creek.

Rancho Zayante and Felton

Rancho Zayante was granted in 1834 to Joaquín Buelna, who had previously held the post of alcalde at Branciforte; but it was regranted in 1841 to Joseph L. Majors, who immediately sold it to Isaac Graham, to whom it was patented in 1870, although he had died in 1863. A survey of this boundary was made in 1867. One stake on the west line was placed between Felton and Ben

Covered Bridge, near Felton

Lomond in the big curve of the San Lorenzo River near Brackney Road.

Graham, a thorough frontiersman, had come from Hardin County, Kentucky, in 1833. Three years after his arrival he assisted Juan B. Alvarado in expelling Governor Gutiérrez, with the understanding that the country thereafter should be free from Mexican domination. However, shortly after Alvarado came into power, Graham and his associates were arrested as dangerous foreigners and placed in confinement on a boat in Monterey harbor. A few of the group were released before Don José Castro sailed with the prisoners for Mexico, and all were released by the Mexican authorities after their arrival. It was reported that Isaac Graham received $36,000 as indemnity for the outrage done him and that a part of this sum was used in the purchase of the rancho. Within a year after he came into possession of the land, he built on the west bank of the Zayante Creek opposite Bean Creek the first power sawmill in California. This was in 1842, about two months before the one at Bodega Bay was installed.

Both Mount Hermon and Felton in the southern part of this rancho are near the junction of Zayante Creek and the San Lorenzo River. Between these two settlements is another covered bridge *(SRL 583)*, built across the San Lorenzo River. No bridge was built across the river near Felton until about 1879. In 1868 the San Lorenzo road from Santa Cruz was cut through as far as Felton, and the settlers there tried to get a bridge in place of the ford, which they had used in good

weather. To promote the undertaking, a "Bridge Benefit Ball" was given in Santa Cruz, a festivity at which the women appeared in calico dresses. Finally, after a petition was sent to the supervisors in 1876 and another in 1878, a bridge was built, consisting of a wooden truss tied together with steel bars, and a notice for horse vehicles was posted: "$5.00 fine for crossing faster than a walk." It was replaced in 1892 by the covered bridge now standing. This bridge, the tallest covered span in the nation, was built of local redwood and is 186 feet long. It was replaced by a concrete bridge nearby in 1938 and became the first example in the West of preserving a bypassed covered bridge. In the spirit of the "Bridge Benefit Ball," an annual pancake breakfast, to raise funds for its preservation and restoration, is held on the bridge, which is no longer open to vehicular traffic.

The county's third remaining covered bridge once crossed Branciforte Creek on the Glen Canyon Road after it leaves Santa Cruz via Market Street. Only 83 feet long, it was built in 1892 and used until 1939, when it was moved half a block into De Laveaga Park for preservation. Though not in use, it still graces the same creek and looks so much a part of the surroundings that one would think it had been there from the beginning. It is said to be the most photographed of all covered bridges, having been featured in several motion pictures and television productions. Its location is about two miles northeast of Santa Cruz. Another covered span, within the city of Santa Cruz itself, crossed the San Lorenzo River at Soquel Avenue from 1874 until its destruction in 1921.

Felton was named for Senator Charles N. Felton, attorney for one of the owners of Rancho Zayante. About 1878 Mr. and Mrs. George Day ran the first hotel in Felton, the Big Tree House. Supplies for the hotel had to be brought across the river. When the river was in flood, a horse had to swim, carrying the rider and food. But usually sufficient supplies to last over the wet season were obtained in advance. In addition to his hotel, Day conducted a livery stable and ran a stage line. George U. Collins, brother of Mrs. Day, a lumberman from Maine, who was then operating a shingle mill on Bean Creek, built a road from Felton to the Big Trees, placing a toll house at the point where the Toll House Resort now is.

Rancho Refugio

This rancho was situated on the shore of Monterey Bay southwest of Rancho de la Cañada del Rincón. Its northwestern boundary was Laguna de Pala, now called Laguna Creek. The smaller creeks, Coja, Baldwin, and Meder, flow from the hills through this tract into the bay. The old coast road, successively used by the Portolá expedition, vaqueros, lumber wagons, and stagecoaches, extended the full length of the rancho, as does State Highway 1 over the same route today.

In 1839 this land was apparently granted to María de los Angeles Castro and her sisters, one of whom was the wife of José Antonio Bolcoff, to whom it was definitely granted by Governor Alvarado on April 7, 1841. It was later claimed by his sons, Francisco and Juan, as executors of the estate.

José Antonio Bolcoff was one of the earliest foreign settlers in Spanish California. A native of Kamchatka, he deserted a Russian sailing vessel when it visited Monterey Bay in 1815, settled in Santa Cruz, and in 1822 married Candida, one of the daughters of José Joaquín Castro, and reared a family of 11 children. After being naturalized as a Mexican citizen, he became alcalde at three different times and held that office at the time the American flag was raised over California.

Following the order of secularization, he was put in charge of the buildings and properties of Mission Santa Cruz, and assumed those duties in July 1839. For the regulation of the little group of people over which he had control, he immediately promulgated 22 statutes. These laws, intended for a few Spanish families and about 70 Indians, dealt with precautions to be taken against fires spreading to grass and timber, the responsibility of each resident for keeping the street in front of his house clean, prohibition of the sale of liquor after eight o'clock, and an eight-o'clock curfew, the hour being later changed to ten.

On receiving the grant of Rancho Refugio, he built an adobe residence, part of which is still standing at the Wilder Ranch on Meder Creek, about four miles west of Santa Cruz on the coast road. The original tiles remain on one end of the long, low building now used as a storeroom, the other end of which fell years ago. Excavation for the foundation of the Wilder family home, a frame house now standing between the historic adobe and the road, uncovered the base of the old fireplace, and in the earth about it were found old utensils—knives, spoons, and crockery.

This land passed from the Bolcoff heirs to Moses Meder, one of the Mormons brought by Sam Brannan on the ship *Brooklyn*, landing in San Francisco in 1846. The place has now (1965) been in the possession of the Delos Wilder family for five generations, and the old adobe is respected by them. One of the frame ranch houses standing within a few yards of the adobe and the later Wilder residence was built during the early pioneer days and shows on its roof the original hand-split and hand-planed shingles.

Rancho Arroyo de la Laguna

Adjoining Rancho Refugio on the northwest at the Arroyo de la Laguna, now Laguna Creek, and extending along the coast as far as San Vicente Creek was Rancho Arroyo de la Laguna, granted February 20, 1840, by Governor Alvarado to Gil Sánchez, a tithe collector at Branciforte.

James Williams, a lumberman and blacksmith, who with a brother Isaac came overland to California with the Chiles-Walker party, settled near Santa Cruz. Another brother, Squire, a former member of Frémont's Battalion, died in the Yuba mines in 1848. In 1852 James and the heirs of Squire filed claim for the lands of this grant, and it was patented to them on February 21, 1881. On the edge of this rancho, at the mouth of San Vicente Creek, is the site of Williams Landing, where in the 1850's lumber from the hills was loaded on schooners.

Two men from Switzerland who later developed small farms on this tract were Respini and Moretti; they lived at the place later called the Yellowbank Dairy in a valley near the mouth of Respini Creek, sometimes called Yellowbank Creek. The dairy is no longer in existence.

Rancho Agua Puerca y las Trancas

This square league of land, given by Governor Micheltorena October 31, 1843, to Ramón Rodríguez and Francisco Alviso, extends along the coast from the mouth of the Arroyo Agua Puerca at the old Davenport Landing on the east to the Cañada de las Trancas on the west. Scott Creek, flowing almost the entire length of the rancho, enters it from the hills at its northeast corner and near the southwest corner pours its waters into the Pacific or, as early geographers recorded it, into the Bay of Monterey.

Near the confluence of Big Creek, Little Creek, and Scott Creek is a country settlement, formerly the stage station Laurel Grove, now called Swanton after one of the men who built a power house, now gone, farther up Big Creek.

The rancho was purchased by James Archibald. He employed Ambrogio Gianone, who came from Switzerland via the dairies of Marin County in 1869, and the Gianone name since that time has been closely identified with this locality. The ranch headquarters at that date were on Archibald Creek, where now an old barn and other farm buildings stand beside the Swanton Road, one and a quarter miles north of its junction with Highway 1. Across the road is a small, substantial "rock" house, which young Gianone built soon after his arrival. Set into the hillside, it was erected for the making of Swiss cheese. It ceased to be used for that purpose some years ago, but it stands as firm as ever, a storehouse for other things.

After being employed by James Archibald for some years, Ambrogio Gianone rented a tract of land at the northwestern end of the rancho, to which he took his wife. There most of his family were born. Later he moved back to the house on

Gianone Rock House, near Swanton

Archibald Creek, but at the end of another ten years he purchased the land he had formerly rented at the northwestern end of the property, making his home for the rest of his life at the top of Gianone Hill.

A small piece of nine acres at this far end of the grant on the Arroyo de las Trancas had earlier been purchased by David Post, who operated there a small hotel and stage station. Post also had the Sea Side post office, and nearby was the first schoolhouse in the Seaside district. Afterward the schoolhouse was moved to the top of Gianone Hill, where now stand three cypress trees west of the two Gianone houses in which descendants of Ambrogio Gianone live. The school for the Seaside district was later held in a neat little house at the foot of the same hill toward Swanton. This building still stands but is no longer in use. It is one and a half miles northwest of Swanton. The top of Gianone Hill is a mile farther.

On the shoreline of Rancho Agua Puerca is a local landmark, a spot called "China Ladder," on the cliffs about one and a half miles southeast of the Cañada de las Trancas. On the top of the bluff was a shack in which lived several Chinese, who obtained abalone from the rocks below and dried them for the Chinese trade. From the bluff they followed a trail, then down a rope, and finally a ladder to reach the beach.

Other Mexican Grants

Stretching back from the coast between San Vicente and Molino creeks is Rancho San Vicente, granted in 1846 to Blas A. Escamilla and patented to him in 1870 (although Bancroft states that it was previously granted to Antonio Rodríguez in 1839). On this tract was the Agua Puerca School, which, although it changed location several times for the convenience of families with children of school age, always retained the name Agua Puerca, because its earliest site was near the creek of that name.

In the northwestern part of the city of Santa Cruz a grant of less than 200 acres was given in 1844 to Nicolás Dodero, an Italian sailor, who left the *María Ester* at San Francisco in 1827 and spent most of his life in San José and Branciforte. This rancho, Tres Ojos de Agua, was patented to him in 1866. The name ("three eyes of water") refers to the springs near High Street in the Escalona Heights district, whence a stream flows down through the town. In this area Joseph L. Majors built a grist mill that remained a landmark for many years. In 1870 J. F. Cunningham, a prominent lumberman, built a house near Spring Street, which was later occupied by the Honorable William T. Jeter while he was lieutenant-governor of the state. This old and well-built house has now been wrecked and its material used elsewhere.

Rancho Arroyoita, on which once stood the adobe home of Sacramenta, wife of Martín Castro, was a gift to her in 1860 from her mother Concepción, widow of Alejandro Rodríguez, whose father José Antonio Rodríguez had come to Branciforte as an *inválido* in 1798. This rancho was a part of the larger Rancho Encinalitos left by Alejandro at his death in 1852 to his widow. So far as can be ascertained, no grant had been made of this land, but it was patented to Concepción by the United States in 1867. Sacramenta Castro's adobe was located about one mile east of Santa Cruz on Paul Sweet Road, about one-quarter mile north of the Santa Cruz–Watsonville highway. It was built on a side hill and was surrounded by old Monterey cypress and fruit trees. It had a large wooden addition of two stories and a frame upper story over the adobe kitchen. In 1887 the Pérez family, direct descendants of the original owner, repurchased the property and made their home in the old adobe until it was razed in 1956, when the property was purchased by the Odd Fellows Cemetery Association and became a part of Oakwood Memorial Park.

Other grants in the county received United States recognition in the form of patents. Cañada del Rincón del Río de San Lorenzo de Santa Cruz was granted to Pedro (Pierre) Sansevain in 1846 and patented to him in 1858 (he erected a sawmill and there, on Gold Creek, some gold has been found). Laguna de las Calabazas was granted in 1833 to Felipe Hernández and patented to his heirs in 1868. Las Aromitas y Agua Caliente is located partly in San Benito County. Aguajito, a small tract within the present city limits of Santa Cruz, was patented to M. Villagrana. Two grants were claimed by T. W. Russell, the Mesa de Ojo de Agua and the Potrero y Rincón de San Pedro de Regalado, both of which were long under consideration by the authorities for patents.

Schooner Landings

Early map makers show Punta de Año Nuevo, now sometimes called by its English equivalent, New Year's Point, at the northern extremity of Monterey Bay. La Pérouse, voyaging along the coast in September 1786, described the bay as being open eight leagues across the entrance from Punta de Año Nuevo to Cypress Point and extending from this imaginary line "eastward to where the land is sandy and low."

Santa Cruz County lies along the northeastern shore of this bay. With few wagon roads and no railroads in the pioneer days, and with the products of its kilns, tanneries, and mills too great for local needs, the active residents of this region depended upon water transportation for a wider market. Inlets at the mouths of streams were used as landing places for schooners, and loading was sometimes done through the surf before wharves were built.

The southernmost landing was that of Pajaro at the mouth of the Pajaro River; next came Miller's Landing, on the beach of the land purchased from Rancho San Andrés by Captain C. F. Miller. As early as 1849 the landing at the mouth of Soquel Creek was in use, and Porter's Landing, either there or nearby, is mentioned in early annals. The present town of Capitola, developed by Frederick A. Hihn in 1869 as a summer resort, is in the vicinity of Soquel Landing.

A wharf was built in 1849 near the mouth of the San Lorenzo River at Santa Cruz by Elihu

Anthony. It was purchased two years later by Isaac E. Davis and Albion P. Jordan, who maintained a fleet of small schooners to haul lime to San Francisco and who, in 1855, had the $150,000 schooner *Santa Cruz* built in the East and brought around the Horn. Davis and Jordan had the largest industry in the town of Santa Cruz in the 1850's. Both Forty-niners from New England, they had been engineers on a Sacramento River steamboat before coming to this region. Their original kiln was at the upper end of Bay Street; later they moved farther north to the Rincón rancho. The names of these two American pioneers were given to two streets, Davis (now part of Escalona Drive) and Jordan, which intersect north of Mission Street.

In the shale on the beach, about one-half mile northwest of Meder Creek, are a number of mooring irons used by schooners that once called there for the produce of the Cowell Lime Company. The brick-built kilns, now unused, are located about three miles up Meder Canyon back of the Wilder Ranch, and from the kilns ox teams hauled the burned lime to this natural wharf.

Williams Landing was at the mouth of San Vicente Creek. Lime from the kilns in the vicinity was shipped from there, and in 1851 W. W. Waddell shipped lumber from the mill he had established there, the first of four mills that he eventually operated within the county.

Davenport Landing, farther northwest, at the mouth of the Arroyo del Agua Puerca, was the site of extensive whaling operations. La Pérouse, in 1786, wrote while in Monterey Bay, "It is impossible to conceive the number of whales by which we are surrounded." Captain John P. Davenport, an old whaling master, who 55 years later was residing on the shore of the bay, also observed the number of whales. According to Hittell, he devised a scheme whereby he could go out from shore in a whaling boat, capture a whale, and tow it to land, where the blubber could be removed and prepared in great pots, instead of completing the whole operation at sea. While directing this work, which began in the 1850's, Captain Davenport lived in a frame house on the west side of the arroyo overlooking the 450-foot wharf, which he had built. His men lived in cabins or in the hotel which stood a little way up the arroyo and served as headquarters for the lumber and lime men of the countryside.

Despite the action of wind and wave, the captain's wharf outlasted a newer one built by the Reese Lime Works near their storehouse on the opposite side of the arroyo. Captain Davenport spent his later years in the town of Santa Cruz.

Two schooners were once built at the mouth of this little creek, both of them constructed for the purpose of transporting split redwood material from lumber camps to San Francisco. One of them was wrecked on returning from its maiden voyage in a storm which drove it past its destination and beached it several miles to the south.

The hotel that housed the workers in those early industries and the few small houses of the time have all disappeared, along with the old wharves, giving way to a one-room country school, now abandoned, and a few scattered homes just west of State Highway 1. Old Davenport shows no trace of its former shipping or other activities, but a new Davenport, about one mile south on the hillside above San Vicente Creek, has grown up around a busy cement plant, to which runs a 12-mile branch of the Southern Pacific Railroad, connecting with main lines at Santa Cruz. In 1934 the cement company built a 2,400-foot pier for use in conveying its product through tunnel and pipe to specially constructed ocean steamers.

The landing farthest north and west in the county was between Punta de Año Nuevo and the mouth of Waddell Creek. Through the change of county line made in 1868, this spot is now in San Mateo County. But at the time of its operation it was a part of Santa Cruz County, and pickets, posts, and sawn lumber from the forests in the canyons for miles around were shipped from there. This wharf was erected by W. W. Waddell for the purpose of transporting the lumber from his mill on the creek that still bears his name.

Waddell Creek, Cañada de la Salud

Waddell Creek, the perennial coast stream that rises in Big Basin Redwoods State Park, is fed by water trickling down from springs on the mountain slopes bordering its banks and continues to flow from its upper reaches to its lagoon on the Pacific. The valley through which this stream flows, narrow in most places but widening out into grassy meadows in others, has a history paralleling, in miniature, that of the state.

Little is known of the earliest human inhabitants of this canyon. But the discovery, as late as 1920, of broken arrowheads and chips of flint on a knoll on the west side of the creek bank about a quarter of a mile back from the lagoon, and the unearthing, in 1916, of a large and perfectly made obsidian spearhead in the clearing out of a spring on the mountainside about 500 feet west of this knoll, prove that at least a few primitive Indians used this place as a camping ground.

The name Cañada de la Salud, or "Canyon of Health," was given to the valley in 1769, when the Portolá expedition rested there from Friday, October 20, to the following Monday during that first land journey up the coast from San Diego to San Francisco Bay. Father Crespí, who was an important member of the party, first gave the name of La Cañada de San Luís Baltran to the campsite; but as the men who had been so ill that the rites for the dying had been administered "suddenly felt their pains very much relieved" and were able to proceed on Monday, the permanent name recorded in the diaries was La Cañada, or Arroyo, de la Salud. The place is easily identified because the engineer of the party, Don Miguel Costansó, appended a note to his diary stating that Punta de Año Nuevo, which had been discovered and named by the Vizcaíno sea expedition of 1602–3, was in approximately the same latitude as their camping place.

A second visit of early Spanish explorers to this place occurred about five years later, when, "at nine o'clock in the morning" of December 10, 1774, three men paused on the beach to offer a prayer of thanksgiving for that miracle of health restored to their compatriots of the former expedition. These three men were Father Palou, Captain Rivera, and a soldier. The latter two had been there with Portolá in 1769 and were now returning from a tour of the San Francisco Bay region.

After the establishment of the mission at Santa Cruz, the mission herds roamed the coast up to a point where they mingled with the cattle from the mission at San Francisco, according to Duhaut-Cilly, who voyaged along the coast in 1827. The land of this valley, however, was never included in any Spanish or Mexican grant but lay between Rancho Agua Puerca y las Trancas and Rancho Punta de Año Nuevo.

After the advent of the American with his utilitarian ideas, the wooded sides of the canyon resounded with the blows of the woodsman's axe and the buzz of his saw. At this time the place became known and recorded on maps as "Big Gulch." There William W. Waddell, who had been born in 1818 in Kentucky and had arrived in California in 1851, established his fourth and last sawmill in 1862 (others were at Williams Landing, at Rincón, and at Branciforte). To transport lumber to the wharf built between the mouth of the creek and Punta de Año Nuevo, he constructed a five-mile horse tramway in as straight a line as possible, following the course of the stream, and built 12 bridges across the meandering channel.

The mill was located on high ground between, and at the confluence of, the east and west forks of the creek known from that time to the present as Waddell Creek. Many men were employed; the mess house, the bunkhouse, the cottages of the men with families, Waddell's own house, and the hothouse where he raised choice flowers were all located near the mill.

After Waddell died in 1875 of an injury inflicted by a grizzly bear, lumbering and woodcutting in the valley gradually ceased. The wharf was finally destroyed by a storm. At the mill the huge boilers were left in place and are still there, although they are now hedged round by second-growth redwoods. In the vicinity were found fire-scarred tires of the oxcarts used in logging; a heavy, square timber, once part of a manger for oxen; and heaps of stones on the flats that were once fireplaces in the simple cabins. Along the downward course of the stream, fern-covered piles in alder groves are all that remain of the bridges over the stream bed, now long abandoned as the creek has changed course.

Descendants of families that made up part of the Waddell Mill payroll have been able to give some idea of the activities in the valley during the lumbering period and afterward. The frame houses have disappeared, although some of those in the lower and broader part of the canyon, more substantial than the temporary houses near the mill site, endured for many years and were occupied by men who cultivated small farms. Horatio S. Soper was one of the teamsters on the tramline. He brought the horse-drawn cars of lumber from the mill down the canyon as far as his house, where another man relieved him and took the train down to the wharf. The Soper farm had a comfortable house, a large barn, a fruit orchard, a granary, and a blacksmith shop. The family remained in the valley for a number of years, occupying first a house on the east side of Waddell Creek and later one on the opposite side but farther upstream. There were five children in the family, whose early education was directed by a resident teacher. Later, however, the children attended the Seaside School near the Sea Side post office at the David Post place up the hill toward Santa Cruz.

Another family in the valley was that of Bryan Bolton, who first lived near the beach on the east side of the creek and later moved to the house from which the Soper family had moved. Several families lived up near the mill, among them the Pinkham family, who later kept the hotel at Davenport Landing.

A well on the west side of the creek just back of the sheltering point of the cliff long marked the site of the old "Precinct House"; how it came by that name is not known. The house was at one time occupied by the William Barrett family, who kept a store with a small stock of merchandise. The well has been filled; the old houses are gone; but many trees of the old orchards survive and still bear pears and apples on their neglected, lofty branches.

The lower part of the valley was owned at one time by the Ocean Shore Land and Investment Company. When it abandoned the prospect of building the Ocean Shore Railway from San Francisco to Santa Cruz, it sold the property in 1914 to Theodore J. Hoover, who had previously purchased the upper part of the valley. His family still owns the valley and is much interested in the conservation of natural resources. Permission has been granted to Stanford University, the University of California, and the State Fish and Game Commission to make scientific studies of the flora and fauna of the area, including the life history of the trout and salmon that annually seek Waddell Creek in the spawning season.

Mountain Charley

Charles Henry McKiernan, formerly an Irish quartermaster in the British Army, arrived in San Francisco during the Gold Rush and went directly to the mines. In 1850, coming with his wages as a miner into the Santa Cruz Mountains, he followed a rough trail through the Los Gatos region, to a place near the Laguna del Sargento where earlier the Indians and Spanish had camped from time to time. Using whipsawed lumber from the redwood trees, which grew thickly around him, he built a house near a spring and with redwood pickets enclosed corrals for the livestock. Grizzly bears, mountain lions, coyotes, and eagles took a heavy toll of the calves and lambs. However, he became so adept with his muzzle-loading blunderbuss that he won fame as a bear hunter. An attack by a wounded mother bear nearly cost him his life, and he ever after wore in his skull a silver plate made by a Santa Cruz physician from two Mexican silver dollars.

McKiernan was for two years the only resident of this region, and he was known to the later arrivals as "Mountain Charley." He made many trails and roads through his property; one of them was a cut-off down the old Indian trail near his home through the Moody Gulch territory to Los Gatos Creek. When the Santa Clara Turnpike was organized, he became a stockholder, and one of his roads became part of the route from Los Gatos to Santa Cruz. Leaving Los Gatos, this stage road curved to the west above the later site of Alma and climbed to the summit. A relic of it, designated by a sign reading "Mt. Charley Road" and now practically unused except by the few local residents, may be followed from Summit Road south to a junction on the Glenwood Highway (old Santa Cruz highway) at a point two and one-half miles southwest of Glenwood. Narrow and winding, the road is little changed since stagecoach days and provides an interesting glimpse into the past. It passes, at one mile, McKiernan's log house, which stands at some distance from the site of his original home, twists and turns high above Glenwood, which may be seen below, and finally, before entering the Glenwood Highway, goes by the Station Ranch, site of the old "changing station." Mountain Charley's original home was built at the highest point on the ridge, about where the southwest corner of the community of Redwood Estates joins the Summit Road. The site was long indicated by a road sign.

Mountain Charley, after settling down as stockman and stage owner, did not forget his experience as a miner but carried on investigations of the mineral possibilities of his property. His mineral claim was filed for record at the Courthouse in Santa Cruz on December 1, 1864, but apparently this venture, shared by five other men, was unproductive. McKiernan moved to San Jose in 1884 so that his children might be closer to schools. He died there in 1892, and his home at 225 West St. John Street was razed in 1951.

As a memorial to this pioneer, a redwood tree, one of the largest of its kind, has been named the "Mountain Charley Big Tree." It stands 300 feet back from the road and is one-half mile north of Glenwood.

Stage Lines out of Santa Cruz

After the close of Mexican rule in California, the former methods of travel—on foot, on horseback, and in bumping, creaking carts—became inadequate, and various kinds of omnibuses and stages were put into use as soon as roads connected the pivotal points.

A stage line was established between Santa Cruz and San Jose, via San Juan, in 1854. Passengers for San Francisco stopped overnight in San Jose and in the winter season proceeded by boat from Alviso the next morning. In summer it was possible to continue the journey on another stage line.

A driver on this line between Santa Cruz and San Juan was "Cock-eyed Charley," written on

Grave of Charley Parkhurst, Watsonville

the Great Register in 1867 as Charley Darkey Parkhurst, aged 55, a farmer and a native of New Hampshire. Charley was a typical stage driver, who took his nip at roadhouses, carried the United States mail, swore at his horses, and voted as a good citizen. After giving up public driving, he retired to a ranch near the Twelve-Mile House out of Santa Cruz and began stock raising on a small scale. Not until his death in 1879 was it learned that Charley was a woman. Her grave is in the Watsonville Cemetery on the west side of Freedom Boulevard.

Another old stage road to San Jose left Santa Cruz by fording the San Lorenzo River, where the Water Street bridge now is. From there it turned up the Graham Grade, used by Isaac Graham in hauling lumber to the wharf on the Santa Cruz beach, and turned again to pass over what is now the Pasatiempo Golf Course and on to the first stop, the ranch of Abraham Hendricks in Scotts Valley, where two horses were added for the long pull ahead. From this station the road led up to Mountain Charley's station on Mountain Charley Road at the summit and thence over the county line and down to San Jose. Mountain Charley was owner and operator of this line until he sold it, in 1874, to George Colegrove— the capable and spectacular driver of the yellow-bodied Concord coach which for a number of years swayed on its leather springs over the narrow mountain roads. This route had been put through in 1857, and Charles C. Martin gave the right of way across his land in the forest north of Rancho San Agustín, now Scotts Valley. He established a stage stop on Mountain Charley Road at the present Station Ranch, which is still in the Martin family.

By 1858 a road over the mountains from Soquel, now called the "Old San Jose Road," had been completed through the efforts of Frederick A. Hihn, a native of Germany and a public-spirited resident of Santa Cruz since 1851. A stage immediately put on between Santa Cruz and San Jose used this route, which today joins the old Los Gatos–Santa Cruz highway beyond Burrell at the site of Schultheis Lagoon in Santa Clara County. One of the old stations on this route was at the point where Terrace Grove Road now joins the Soquel road, high up in the mountains. A resort was maintained there for many years. At one time the place was called

"Bonny Blink," perhaps because of the broad extent of the view over the mountains to the Pacific Ocean on the west and to Monterey Bay on the south. Terrace Grove Road, a private road, joins the Soquel road at a point two and one-quarter miles southwest of the junction of the Soquel road and Summit Road at Burrell. Less than half a mile north of the Terrace Grove junction was another popular resort, the Hotel de Redwood, known in its later years as Redwood Lodge. De Redwood was the name of a post office from 1879 to 1882. Redwood Lodge stood beside the Soquel road until 1953, when it was destroyed by fire. A stone chimney marks the site.

Above the old Soquel–San Jose road in this same area is the small community of Skyland, with a picturesque old Presbyterian church, built in 1887, standing with its detached bell tower under spreading oaks. This place had its own post office from 1884 to 1886, and from 1893 to 1910, and even boasted a small newspaper at one time. The economy was based on the vineyards and fruit orchards in the vicinity, and also on the lumbering activities in the surrounding forests, most of which were owned by Frederick A. Hihn, who at one time paid one-tenth of all Santa Cruz County's taxes. A few old ranch homes still stand in the area.

In an old directory of 1875 appears an advertisement of a stage line of which Charles G. Sykes was proprietor: "A new stage line Santa Clara to Santa Cruz, via Saratoga, Congress Springs, Ocean View, San Francisco Saw-Mills, San Lorenzo Flume and Transportation Company Mills, Boulder Creek, and Felton. This delightful route ... for fourteen miles follows the San Lorenzo V-Flume and passes one paper mill, ten saw mills, one fuse factory, three lime kilns, and the California Powder Company's works. It also passes Boulder, Bear, Newell, Love, Fall, and Sayante [sic] creeks whose waters are well stocked with mountain trout, the forests abounding with game of all kinds." The stage left the Cameron House in Santa Clara on Mondays, Wednesdays, and Fridays at seven in the morning and, returning, left Santa Cruz on the alternate mornings at seven, making connections with the Alviso boat. The one-way fare was $2.50.

In 1872 a horse-drawn stage was driven by "Billy" Bias up the coast from Santa Cruz to San Gregorio. Turning inland here, the stage followed a road winding over the mountains to Redwood City, via La Honda, similar to the present route. The stations from Santa Cruz were Hall's Natural Bridge, Williams Landing, Davenport Landing, Berry Falls, Laurel Grove (now Swanton), Seaside (the old Post place on the bluff at the mouth of Las Trancas Creek); then, across the county line, Pigeon Point, and Pescadero.

This route was a hazardous one, not only because of narrow and poorly built mountain roads but also because of the precipitous cliffs at Waddell Beach, which had to be passed by driving over the sand at low tide. A road has since been cut in the face of the cliff at this point; but even yet, in wet weather, slides of crumbling rock sometimes block the road. Nathan P. Ingalls, a native of New Hampshire, who had driven a four-yoke cow team across the Plains in 1853, succeeded Bias as owner and driver on this line. On July 1, 1874, he took the mail contract, in addition to others, from Santa Cruz to San Mateo and drove the route as far as Pescadero once a day for over 12 years, a distance of 37 miles. A veteran stage driver, he had previously put on the first stage from Napa to Clear Lake and had driven a stage for Wooly and Taft from San Mateo to Pescadero for three years before taking the Santa Cruz route. It was his boast that he had never been held up in his life. After being county supervisor in 1890, he again became interested in stage lines, this time in Monterey County.

Glenwood

Charles Christopher Martin, born in Nova Scotia, came around Cape Horn from Maine in the late 1840's. Arriving in California, he worked for a time as a teamster in the lumbering area of Lexington (Santa Clara County), and in 1851 he began homesteading land adjoining that of Mountain Charley McKiernan. He operated a toll-gate and stage station on Mountain Charley Road at a point now called the "Station Ranch" and still owned by his descendants.

In the 1860's, while engaged in lumbering, Martin built a home in a quiet, sheltered valley below the stage route. There he and his wife, Hannah Carver Martin, raised their six children. By 1873 he had built and opened a store. The place was at first called Martinville but soon became known as Glenwood (SRL 449). The post office was established in 1880 and Martin became first postmaster.

That same year, 1880, saw the passage of the first train over the completed narrow-gauge South Pacific Coast Railroad of the James G. Fair interests. By 1877 it had been built from Alameda, along the eastern side of San Francisco Bay, to San Jose and Los Gatos. Then came the task of tunneling through the Santa Cruz Mountains to join the previously built Felton–Santa Cruz line. Two of the tunnels were over a mile long, and one of these emerged at Glenwood. Southern Pacific took over the line in 1887, and it was converted to broad gauge early in the twentieth century.

Glenwood Resort Hotel

Many resorts were developing in the mountains, and they became even more popular now that there was rail service from the Bay Area. The railroad that passed through Glenwood became known as the "Picnic Line." Charles Martin himself built a hotel in the 1890's that became a social center for San Francisco millionaires. Perhaps the biggest boost to the local economy came when the main automobile road to Santa Cruz was constructed through the settlement in 1916. Martin had made a number of surveys of possible routes for this highway, and when it was surfaced with concrete in 1919 he was asked to put his name and footprints in the new surface. (These are still visible on the east side of the road.) Not long after, the old pioneer died at the age of 90.

But Glenwood's prosperity as a tourist stop on a main highway was to be short-lived. In 1934 the highway was realigned, and Glenwood was left off the beaten track. The store, which had been remodeled and to which had been added a gasoline station, was closed the same year, and it was razed in 1949. Another crushing blow was dealt when the Southern Pacific discontinued its Los Gatos–Santa Cruz service and pulled up the tracks. The line had been failing for several years, and final abandonment was caused by storm damage during the severe winter of 1939–40. The last train passed through Glenwood on March 4, 1940. The entrance to the old tunnel can be seen below the road at the north end of town. Rails are still in place from Santa Cruz through Felton to Olympia.

In the spring of 1948 many of the location scenes of what was to be Jeanette MacDonald's last motion picture, "The Sun Comes Up," were filmed in Glenwood by Metro-Goldwyn-Mayer. The town's last post office, finally discontinued in 1954, was built of lumber from one of the movie sets. Last postmaster was Margaret Koch, great-granddaughter of Charles C. Martin.

A few historic buildings still stand at Glenwood, notably the Martin home of the 1860's, a charming New England cottage located next to the old hotel, at the southern edge of the town and to the east of the road. This property was used for some years as a Catholic summer camp. Part of Martin's old winery on Bean Creek also remains.

The Glenwood railroad tunnel emerged at the little settlement of Laurel, and from there the trains almost immediately plunged into another mile-long tunnel to Wrights in Santa Clara County. Laurel was a busy place in the 1890's, when it was headquarters of the Frederick A. Hihn timber holdings, but now little remains to hint of its past. The Laurel post office existed from 1882 to 1953.

Boulder Creek

One of the early post offices in the county was Boulder Creek, situated at the point where Boulder Creek from the northwest and Bear Creek from the east flow into the San Lorenzo River, a lumber center for many years. An older settlement, called Lorenzo in the 1870's, is now within its limits.

The timber from the site of the town had been cut out by James F. Cunningham, a man who had come West after considerable military service in the East and had taken up government land on the San Lorenzo River and who, after the early 1870's, was identified with the lumber interests in the county. J. W. Peery was another mill proprietor. He had the Silver Lumber Mills and in connection with them operated a tannery. Peery's Toll Road ran up the San Lorenzo River and across to Saratoga. The Bear Creek Toll Road also ran across the mountains to Lexington. Completed in 1875, it never even paid the wages of a tollkeeper, and was finally sold to the county in 1891.

The lumber produced in the vicinity of Boulder Creek was sent over the V-flume built by the San Lorenzo Flume and Transportation Company. This V-flume originally extended from a point about five miles north of Boulder Creek to a point in the lower end of Felton. The "Flume House" stood at its upper end; and, although the structure has been removed, the spot is marked by the very large eucalyptus trees that were planted about it as saplings. From Felton the lumber was shipped to the wharf at Santa Cruz over a narrow-gauge railroad. The "dump" at the end of the flume was at about the point where the Felton Bowl now stands in the lower end of the town and extended some 300 or 400 feet.

A branch of the San Lorenzo, coming in near the Flume House, is called Feeder Creek because it was used as a feeder to the flume to augment the San Lorenzo water supply. The flume was never an entire success—some said because there was not enough fall in the valley and others because the fall was too great for the volume of water. In 1884 that part of the flume south of Boulder Creek was replaced by a branch of the South Pacific Coast Railroad.

Around Boulder Creek during timber cutting, over 50 saw and shingle mills operated within a radius of seven miles. Because of the size of this operation, the Southern Pacific changed the railroad line to standard gauge in 1907. But in 1934, when the timber was exhausted and the mills were closed, the last train was run and the rails between Boulder Creek and Felton were removed. Boulder Creek is now a quiet town surrounded by secluded summer homes.

Three country newspapers have been published at Boulder Creek. The first one was aptly named *The Boulder Creek Hatchet;* the second was *The Mountain Echo;* and the last, becoming defunct in 1924, was *The Valley Echo.*

Ben Lomond

Ben Lomond Mountain was named by Thomas Burns, a native of Scotland. The town that grew up in the 1880's on the river at the base of the mountain took on the name. James J. Pierce, of Santa Clara, owned much timberland there and operated a mill at a site between Mill Street and the river. He laid out the town, and two bridges, still located on the highway passing through the town, are built on the site of two early ones that he gave to the county in exchange for bringing the main road through his new townsite.

At the confluence of Love Creek and the San Lorenzo River stood a waterpower sawmill first operated by Vardamon Bennett, a native of Georgia, who brought his large family to California in 1834. This mill was later owned by Harry Love, a former captain of spies appointed by General Zachary Taylor during the Mexican War. In 1853, when the California state legislature raised a special force to run down the bandit Joaquín Murieta, Harry Love was made its captain. Love and his rangers overtook and shot the outlaw at a place then in Tulare County, now included in Fresno County; and in the following year the captain was rewarded for his services on that occasion by a state appropriation of $5,000. With this money he began logging in the mountains, and, by marrying the widow of Vardamon Bennett, he came into possession of the mill. To get the logs to the mill, he built a road since known as the "Harry Love grade," and the creek where the mill stood is Love Creek, over which one of the bridges on the main street of Ben Lomond extends. His flowing hair and the costume that he affected gave him the sobriquet "The Black Knight of Zayante," Zayante being the name of the Mexican grant in this region.

The Loganberry

John H. Logan, a young lawyer, moved to Santa Cruz from San Jose in 1867 and later became superior judge. He made his home on a hill in town, where he took great interest in his garden. In 1890 he sent samples of an accidental hybrid to a firm in Salem, Oregon. The berry proved to be something quite new and fine, and it was given the name of Loganberry in honor of the discoverer. The plant, supposedly a cross between the Auginbaugh (a sport from the native blackberry) and the Red Antwerp raspberry, is now widely distributed. The mammoth blackberry was also the result of one of Judge Logan's horticultural experiments. The hill where he lived has been named Logan Heights.

"The Ruins"

Supposed by the credulous who first saw them to be chimneys protruding from a fallen castle or from a buried prehistoric village, a small group of natural curiosities locally known as "The Ruins" has elicited comment by certain writers.

Geologists who have visited the spot, some few miles northeast of Santa Cruz in Scotts Valley, give a scientific explanation of this outcropping. The six columns, each four or five feet high, are harder portions of the rocks of the Santa Margarita formation and are "the result of the weathering away of the soft sandstone surrounding locally hardened portions along joint cracks." They are on private property on Bean Creek north of Mount Hermon.

Redwoods, *Sequoia sempervirens*

The many coast redwoods throughout the Santa Cruz foothills and mountains have made the region famous. Because it was in this county that these trees were first glimpsed by white men (by the Portolá expedition, in October 1769, probably on Corralitos Creek), it is fitting that here the first state park was set aside for their preservation.

Although the lumbering industry early endangered the ancient trees of the whole section, the passing years have witnessed a cessation of that threat; although thousands of acres of them were cut, a good number remain, and even the cut-over lands are now sending up a growth of strong young trees encircling the old stumps. The movement for making a state park was started in time to preserve for the public hundreds of acres of virgin timber as well as a vast cut-over territory that is now in luxuriant second growth.

The Big Basin Redwoods State Park, formerly called the California State Redwood Park, situated in the northwestern part of the county in the heart of the "Big Basin" in the Waddell drainage area 23 miles from Santa Cruz, contains over 10,000 acres. In addition to the redwoods, hundreds of which doubtless antedate the discovery of America by Columbus, the park contains magnificent stands of oak, madroño, Tumion, toyon, and Ceanothus on ridges between fern-bordered streams.

Apparently the first person to mention the desirability and necessity of acquiring redwood forests for posterity was Ralph Smith, who, in editorials in the *Redwood City Times and Gazette*, awakened general interest before his untimely death in 1887. Next came Captain Ferdinand Lee Clark and Andrew P. Hill. The latter, then living in San Jose, made many trips to photograph the trees in the Big Basin section and was tireless in his efforts to bring them before the public and to force legislative action.

On May 1, 1900, a group of interested persons was called together in the library of Stanford University, and a committee was appointed to visit and report upon this almost inaccessible region. On the last evening of their inspection visit, May 18, 1900, sitting on the west bank of Sempervirens Creek, they organized the Sempervirens Club, the main object of which was the acquisition and preservation of the surrounding forest.

The idea of state parks was new. Editors of newspapers in the two counties most interested united in giving publicity to the project. Among these papers were the *Boulder Creek Mountain Echo*, the *Santa Cruz Surf*, the *Santa Cruz Sentinel,* and the *San Jose Mercury*.

In 1901 the state legislature passed an enabling act whereby 3,800 acres were purchased by the state in the next year for a quarter of a million dollars, and the following men were subsequently appointed by Governor Gage to be commissioners: Father Robert E. Kenna, S.J., president of Santa Clara University; Professor William Russell Dudley, botanist of Stanford University;

A. W. Foster, regent of the State University and president of the Northwestern Railway; and William H. Mills, land agent of the Southern Pacific Railway Company. The governor of the state was ex officio chairman.

Governor's Camp, now the center of all control and of all activities within the park, came by its name logically because of certain notable early visitors. At about the time of the purchase of the first land in the park, Governor Henry T. Gage accompanied a party of investigation to the tract. To provide accommodation for this group, a five-room cabin and a cook house were built, the lumber for which had to be packed in by mule. In the following year, the newly elected governor, George Pardee, and his family spent some weeks at the cabin. During the course of this visit Governor West of Utah was a guest. Since the visits of these three distinguished men, the name Governor's Camp has clung to the place.

Near the crossroads in Governor's Camp is a memorial fountain placed by the Sempervirens Club in 1923 to honor the memory of A. P. Hill, who had put forth more individual effort than anyone else in securing the park for the people of the state.

Another group of redwoods 20 miles south of the Big Basin Park is the Henry Cowell Redwoods State Park, formerly Santa Cruz Big Trees County Park. Once privately owned, and known as the "Welch Grove" until 1931, it has a station on the Southern Pacific Railroad called "Big Trees." It became a state park in 1954. The largest tree in this group is the "Giant," 306 feet high. Another much visited tree there is the "General Frémont," in the hollow trunk of which John C. Frémont, then lieutenant, is said to have spent a few rainy days during a march through this region with his men in 1846. In later years, after attaining the rank of general, he visited the grove with his wife and daughter; but, unwilling to verify the story of his having occupied the tree, he passed it over with the remark, "It is a good story; let it stand."

World War II's Strangest Naval Battle

On the afternoon of December 20, 1941, off the California coast in view of the Santa Cruz Mountains, an incident took place that has been called "World War II's strangest naval battle." The opponents were the Japanese submarine *I-23*, under Commander Genichi Shibata, and the Richfield Oil Company tanker *Agwiworld*, commanded by Captain Frederico B. Goncalves, bound for San Francisco from Los Angeles Harbor with a full cargo of oil. When the submarine surfaced and began to shell the unarmed tanker, Captain Goncalves, in a moment of audacity, headed his ship toward the Japanese vessel with the intention of ramming it. The submarine withdrew, but by this time the *Agwiworld's* master realized the futility of counterattack and headed full speed for Santa Cruz. The *I-23* pursued and continued firing, but the tanker, by following a zigzag course and heading directly into a heavy wind and a rough sea, escaped being hit. Meanwhile, the sailors of the *Agwiworld* replied to the shots by hurling potatoes at the pride of the Japanese navy! The submarine, her low deck awash in the turbulent seas, finally abandoned the attack, and the oil tanker reached Santa Cruz in safety.

The *I-23*, strangely, made no attempt to torpedo the helpless *Agwiworld*. On the same day, several hundred miles to the north, another Japanese submarine successfully torpedoed the tanker *Emidio*, at a loss of five lives.

SOURCES

Adams, Kramer A. *Covered Bridges of the West*. Howell-North, Berkeley, 1963.
Arbuckle, Clyde, and Roscoe D. Wyatt. *Historic Names, Persons and Places in Santa Clara County*. Privately printed, San Jose, 1948.
Atkinson, Fred W. *100 Years in the Pajaro Valley*. Register and Pajaronian Press, Watsonville.
Bancroft, H. H. *History of California*. 7 vols. History Co., San Francisco, 1886.
Bolton, Herbert Eugene. *Fray Juan Crespí, Missionary Explorer on the Pacific Coast, 1769–1774*. University of California Press, Berkeley, 1927.
Bolton, Herbert Eugene, ed. *Historical Memoirs of New California, by Fray Francisco Palou*. Trans. from ms. in archives of Mexico. 4 vols. University of California Press, Berkeley, 1926.
The California Missions, a Pictorial History, by the editorial staff of Sunset Books. Lane Book Co., Menlo Park, 1964.
Chapman, Charles E. *A History of California: The Spanish Period*. Macmillan, New York, 1921.
Clyman, James. *Diary of James Clyman, 1844–5–6*. Ms. in Huntington Library, San Marino.
County Records. Ms. files in Recorder's Office, Santa Cruz.
Delcigsegus, Rebecca, and Lucretia Mylar. "Early Days in Corralitos and Soquel," *Evening Free Lance*, Hollister.
Elder, David Paul. *The Old Spanish Missions of California*. Paul Elder & Co., San Francisco, 1913.
Fages, Pedro. *Diary from Monterey to San Francisco in 1770*. Academy of Pacific Coast Publications, II, No. 3, University of California Press, Berkeley, 1911.
Farnham, J. T. *The Early Days of California*. John E. Potter, Philadelphia, 1862.
Harrison, E. S. *History of Santa Cruz County*. Pacific Press Publishing Co., San Francisco, 1892.
Hill, Frank, and Florence W. Hill. *The Acquisition of California Redwood Park*. Florence W. Hill, San Jose, 1927.
Hittell, Theodore H. *History of California*. 4 vols. Pacific Press Publishing House and Occidental Publishing Co., San Francisco, 1885.
Houghton, Dick. "SP's Picnic Line," *Trains*, VIII, No. 9 (July 1948), 46–51.
Hunt, Rockwell D., and Nellie Van de Grift Sanchez. *A Short History of California*. Crowell, New York, 1929.
Koch, Margaret. *Santa Cruz, Exciting Early History of an Era*. Heritage Days Committee of the Greater Santa Cruz Chamber of Commerce, Santa Cruz.
La Pérouse, Jean François Galaup de. *A Voyage Round the World in the Years 1785, 1786, 1787, 1788*. Ed. M. L. A. Milet-Mureau. 3 vols. Printed for J. Johnson, St. Paul's Churchyard, London, 1798.
MacMullen, Jerry. "World War II's Strangest Naval Battle," *Westways*, XLVII, No. 6 (June 1955), 10–11.
Martin, Ed. "Situation of the Pajaro Valley," *Sketch of the General History of Santa Cruz County*. Wallace W. Elliott, San Francisco, 1879.
Older, Mrs. Fremont. *California Missions and Their Romances*. Coward-McCann, New York, 1938.
Patten, Phyllis. "History of Neary-Hopcroft Adobe and City Related," *Santa Cruz Sentinel*, July 21, 1957.
Paulson, L. L., compiler. *Handbook and Directory of Santa Clara, San Benito, Santa Cruz, Monterey, and San Mateo Counties*. L. L. Parker, Francis and Valentine Commercial Steam Presses, 517 Clay St., San Francisco, 1875.
Rodgers, W. S. *Reminiscences*. Files of *Santa Cruz Sentinel*, 1933–35.

Rowland, Leon. *Annals of Santa Cruz.* Privately printed, Santa Cruz, 1947.

—— Local history articles, in files of *Santa Cruz News,* 1931–35.

—— *Villa de Branciforte, the Village That Vanished.* Privately printed, Santa Cruz, 1941.

Taylor, A. A. "Short History of Aptos," *Santa Cruz Surf,* 1896.

Taylor, Arthur A., compiler. *California Redwood Park.* State Printing Office, Sacramento, 1912.

Teggart, Frederick, ed. *The Portolá Expedition of 1769–1770, Diary of Miguel Costansó,* Publications of the

Academy of Pacific Coast History, II, No. 4, University of California Press, Berkeley, 1911.

Torchiana, H. A. Van Coenen. *Story of the Mission Santa Cruz.* Paul Elder & Co., San Francisco, 1933.

Watkins, Major Roland C. *History of Monterey and Santa Cruz Counties.* S. J. Clarke Publishing Co., Chicago, 1925.

Willey, S. H. "A Sketch of the General History of Santa Cruz County," *Illustrations of Santa Cruz County.* Wallace W. Elliott & Co., San Francisco, 1879.

Young, John V. "Ghost Towns of the Santa Cruz Mountains," *San Jose Mercury Herald,* April 22, June 10, December 2, 1934.

Shasta County

SHASTA COUNTY was one of the original 27 counties, and at first included within its boundaries all of the territory that later became Modoc and Lassen counties, as well as parts of the present Siskiyou, Plumas, and Tehama counties. (Shasta is apparently a corruption of the name of a tribe of Indians living in the vicinity of Mount Shasta.) The county seat was placed first at Reading's Ranch, but was transferred to Shasta in 1851, and, finally, on May 19, 1888, was moved to Redding, named in honor of B. B. Redding, for many years land agent for the Central Pacific Railroad Company.

Lassen Volcanic National Park

Lassen Peak (10,453 feet), the only active volcano on the North American continent outside of Alaska, was called Monte San José by the padres who accompanied Luís Argüello on an exploring expedition in 1821 to seek for mission sites. Early maps of California, however, give it as Mount St. Joseph. It was later named Lassen Buttes after Peter Lassen, the noted pioneer of Tehama County, and finally Lassen Peak. The Maidu Indians called it "La Lapham Yerman y'aidum," meaning "the long, high mountain that was broken." On May 30, 1914, after having been quiescent for more than 200 years, Lassen Peak began a series of about 300 eruptions. Since 1915 the old volcano has been relatively quiet, although quantities of smoke, at decreasing intervals, have issued from its crater.

Lassen Peak and Cinder Cone were set aside as national monuments on May 6, 1907. On August 9, 1916, the region was designated the Lassen Volcanic National Park, and in January 1929 it was enlarged to its present area of 163 square miles.

The park contains other interesting volcanic cones, such as Prospect Peak and Harkness Peak, as well as numerous fumaroles, hot springs, mud pots, and boiling lakes, since the entire region is of volcanic origin. Lying at the southern end of the Cascades where they join the Sierra Nevada, the park presents a magnificent skyline. Within the area are outstanding scenic features—multicolored lava crags of varied and fantastic forms rising to a height of over 8,500 feet above sea level, impressive canyons, and primeval forests.

Among the most beautiful of the individual wonders included in the park is Lake Tartarus, or Boiling Springs Lake, which lies "jade-green and ominous" amid the encircling forest. Clouds of steam arising from its surface at dawn and dusk add to the enchantment of the scene. Lake Tartarus is part of a group of volcanic phenomena south of Lassen Peak, which includes the Devils Kitchen, Willow Creek Geyser, Bumpas Hell, and many other mud pots and hot springs. Through the northern gateway to the park one may visit the Hat Creek and Lost Creek areas, which were devastated by the 1914 eruptions of Lassen Peak, as well as scenic Manzanita and Reflection lakes, Chaos Crags, and the Loomis Museum.

Old Trails

A number of old trails crossed the Upper Sacramento Valley in the vicinity of Redding. The earliest to be blazed, known as the Trinity Trail, was made by Jedediah Strong Smith in the spring of 1828. Smith's route led across what are now Trinity and Humboldt counties and on up the coast through the Del Norte region into southern Oregon. Learning of the new pathway from Smith, a party of Hudson's Bay Company trappers, led by Alexander Roderick McLeod, almost immediately set out for California, with John Turner, a former member of Smith's expedition, acting as guide. McLeod probably reached the Upper Sacramento Valley by this trail, and for a number of years trappers no doubt continued to follow it into California.

The Trinity River was discovered and named in 1845 by Pierson B. Reading, who was trapping in the Trinity country at that time. In 1848 he found the first gold in the region. Somewhere between Kennett (an old copper-mining town now inundated by Shasta Lake) and Castle Crags,

Reading's earliest trail into the Trinity country crossed over the stretch of steep mountains separating the Sacramento and Shasta valleys known as the "Devil's Backbone." On his way back he crossed the same mountains at a point between Castella and Delta. In 1848 he took a new route, this time over the mountains that lie at the head of the Middle Fork of Cottonwood Creek, and on his return he blazed the trail later known as the Shasta–Weaverville Road, followed by thousands of miners in 1849 and the 1850's. Supplies for the mines of the Trinity, Scott, and Salmon rivers, brought in by way of the town of Shasta, were taken over this trail by muleback. "Between Shasta, the head of 'Whoa navigation,' and the vast mining region to the north, more than 2,000 pack mules were constantly plying." In 1861 the main section of the trail—that west from Shasta to Weaverville—was widened into a wagon road by Charles Camden. The Redding–Eureka highway today follows roughly this early thoroughfare.

In 1859 a through stage road to Oregon was opened up, which ran from Shasta to Yreka by way of French Gulch, Carrville (Trinity County), Callahan (Siskiyou County), and Fort Jones. Today this route is no longer a main artery of travel, but during the 1860's it was the principal wagon road to the north. At the junction of this road and the Shasta–Weaverville Road formerly stood the Tower House, a landmark famous in the early days.

When Levi H. Tower and Charles Camden arrived at this spot in November 1850, they found a log cabin, occupied by a man named Schneider. Here Tower built the Tower House Hotel with lumber hewn from the surrounding forests and split by hand. For many years after it was abandoned, remains of the old hostelry still stood near the highway. It was described as "a gaunt framework of huge timbers from which the siding has long since been stripped. Upon those timbers appear the marks of adzes used in hewing them from tree trunks, and they are held together by hand-made nails." The residence of Charles Camden, erected some time later near the old hotel, still serves as the summer home of a descendant. In its beautiful mountain setting, Tower House with its lands was the showplace of the county in early days, and it is still a magnificent estate.

The second oldest trail through the Upper Sacramento Valley may have been the east branch of the California–Oregon Trail, although no absolute proof of this has yet been found. It seems likely that McLeod took this route on his way out of the valley in 1828. It is known that he was forced to cache his furs at the approach of winter and that on his return the following spring he found them spoiled, a circumstance that led to his discharge from the Hudson's Bay Company. At the headwaters of the North Fork of the McCloud River on Bartle's Ranch in Siskiyou County, a wooden trough and some guns were uncovered in 1874. At the time it was believed that these were the remains of McLeod's cache. In any event this early trail was followed by explorers and trappers before 1829, for in Ogden's diary of that year "Pitt's River" is mentioned. In 1841 Pitt's Lake (now Goose Lake) and Pitt's River (since known as the Pit River) were quite accurately mapped by Charles Wilkes, whose source of information had been the Hudson's Bay Company, which indicates that its trappers had explored the region through which the trail passed.

The east branch of the California–Oregon Trail, after leaving the Sacramento Valley, crossed a ruggedly mountainous country before passing out of the state between Tule and Clear lakes in the north. In crossing this difficult region, early travelers developed variations of the road.

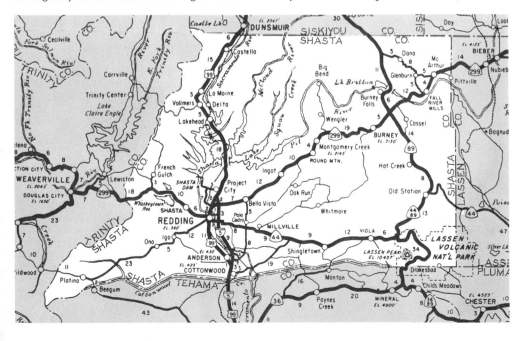

One such was taken by Frémont and his men in the spring of 1846. In the latter part of April they had passed up the east bank of the Sacramento River as far as its confluence with Cottonwood Creek, opposite which they turned east and then northeast across what is now Shasta County. In Lassen County, some distance east of Fall River, Frémont's party forded the Pit River. Crossing the mountains to Big Valley (called by Frémont "Round Valley"), they spent the night of April 30 at its upper end. From there the party journeyed north over the route followed later by emigrants from Oregon.

In the fall of 1848 the first wagon train into California from Oregon followed the Applegate Road as far as Clear Lake (Modoc County). There the emigrants turned south over the trail used by Frémont, connecting with Lassen's Trail ten miles north of Lookout (Modoc County). The lure of gold brought many Oregonians into California in 1849 and the early 1850's. From Big Valley, most of the Argonauts bound for Shasta and the Trinity mines climbed the mountains to the west and crossed the Pit River west of Fall River Mills. Leaving the Pit at this point, they went south for some distance and then turned west through Burney Valley and thence southwest to Shasta, the trading center of the Trinity region. In 1856 a road to Yreka was built by way of the Pit River crossing, and shortly thereafter the California Stage Company inaugurated a daily schedule from Sacramento to Yreka, the first through stage service to that point. Because of Indian massacres in Fall River Valley and attacks on the stage, this line was discontinued in January 1857 for a short time.

It is not known who first blazed the west branch of the California–Oregon Trail, which followed up the Sacramento River Canyon and around the west side of Mount Shasta, but it is certain that Hudson's Bay Company trappers used it annually from 1832 to 1845. Ewing Young, the trapper, making his way into Oregon to settle in 1834, followed this route, being the first to travel the entire length of the Oregon Trail from San Bernardino in southern California to the Methodist mission in northern Oregon. In 1837 the demand for cattle in the Willamette Valley led to Young's second expedition over the Oregon Trail, when he accomplished the arduous task of driving 700 head of cattle and 40 horses over the Devil's Backbone. Young's party included P. L. Edwards, the diarist of the company, and 20 others, among whom were settlers bound for Oregon.

In 1841 a contingent of the Wilkes Exploring Expedition, consisting of about 18 persons under the command of Lieutenant George F. Emmons, came down the Oregon Trail across the Siskiyou Mountains and through what are now Siskiyou and Shasta counties to New Helvetia and Yerba Buena. A number of Oregonians had joined the party, making a total of 39 persons and about 76 animals. On his map Wilkes designated that part of the Sacramento River above its confluence with the Pit River as "Destruction River," a name that may have been given originally by

Hudson's Bay Company trappers to the McLeod (now spelled "McCloud") River, on the banks of which McLeod met disaster in the winter of 1829. That part of the Pit River in Shasta County was called the Sacramento.

The largest early expedition to use the west branch of the California–Oregon Trail was led by Joseph Gale, who in May 1843, in company with 42 settlers bound for Oregon, drove 250 head of cattle, 650 horses, and 3,000 sheep northward over this difficult path. On May 30 of the same year Lansford W. Hastings started for California with a party of discontented Oregonians. At the Rogue River they met Joseph Gale, who persuaded about two-thirds of the party to return to the Willamette Valley. With the remaining emigrants Hastings continued to California over the route just traveled by Gale. In 1845 James Clyman, with 35 men, one woman, and three children, also passed over this trail on the way south.

All of these parties had to cross the Devil's Backbone, and over these lofty, barren mountains they struggled slowly and painfully. The Wilkes party, while traversing these precipitous slopes, which Clyman described as "almost too steep for brush to grow . . . and in many places too narrow for a rabbit to walk over," lost their way but were guided to safety by the Indian wife of one of the company.

Late in 1848 gold seekers from the north began using the Oregon Trail; and after the Siskiyou region was opened up in 1850, miners poured over it from the south. Because of the mountainous character of the route, it remained a pack trail until 1860, when a wagon road was constructed from Upper Soda Springs to Yreka. Today Interstate Highway 5 and the Shasta Route of the Southern Pacific Railroad follow the old California–Oregon Trail quite closely—many of the railroad stations are on the exact line of the trail—making this the oldest continuously used road in northern California.

Where the California–Oregon stage road (SRL 58) crossed the present highway two miles north of Anderson, a marker has been placed by the McCloud Parlor of the Native Sons of the Golden West of Redding. On the banks of the Sacramento River opposite this point was an early steamboat landing. This place, designated on a map of 1862 as "Reading," was the most northern point on the Sacramento to be reached by river boats.

On the summit of Bass Hill (SRL 148), 14 miles north of Redding, a remnant of the stage road crosses the highway and descends to the Pit River. A marker was placed there in 1931 in memory of Williamson Lyncoya Smith, division stage agent of the California and Oregon Stage Company, and of the pioneer stage drivers along this road. A similar marker was placed at Shasta. Both monuments were the gift of Mae Helene Bacon Boggs of San Francisco, a niece of W. L. Smith. Mrs. Boggs died on August 1, 1963, at the age of 100.

The McCloud River north of its junction with the Pit (now within Shasta Lake) was the site of a

Wintun Indian settlement, and the home of the last Wintun chief, Consalulu. About two miles above the mouth of the McCloud River, fossil remains of at least 25 distinct species, including the mastodon, elephant, giant sloth, large extinct lion, and cave bear, were taken from the Potter Creek Cave. In the same area was a place known as Joaquin Miller's Pass, where the poet is said to have forded the McCloud River on muleback.

On the park highway in the Lassen Volcanic National Park, a few hundred yards northwest of the checking station at Manzanita Lake, is a monument marking the Nobles Pass Road (SRL 11), followed by the pioneers of 1852. A large lava rock about five feet high, bearing a bronze plaque, stands at the junction of the two park highways, one going down Lost Creek and Hat Creek to Burney, and the other turning west to Viola, Shingletown, and Redding. The latter was the route used by early emigrants who came over Nobles' Pass. It was at this point that they caught their first glimpse of the Sacramento Valley. The summit of Nobles' Pass is about three miles to the northeast.

Rancho Buena Ventura

The Reading adobe (SRL 10) once stood just south of Ball's Ferry on the west bank of the Sacramento River near its confluence with Cottonwood Creek. The original rancho consisted of a strip of land three miles wide extending for 19 miles along the west bank of the Sacramento River from the mouth of Cottonwood Creek at the head of Bloody Island in the south to Salt Creek in the north. Later the towns of Anderson and Redding were established on the rancho.

Pierson Barton Reading, a native of New Jersey, came West with the Chiles-Walker party in 1843. He and 12 other men, among whom was Joseph B. Chiles, separated from the main party at Fort Hall, coming into California by an uncharted trail, now known as the Yellowstone Cut-Off. Passing through what is now Shasta County, Reading and his companions arrived at Sutter's Fort on November 10, 1843.

A comparison of Reading's descriptions of the trail followed by the Chiles party in 1843 with the geographical features in northern California indicates quite clearly the route traveled. Leaving Big Valley (in Lassen County) on October 25, the band of 13 men followed the course of the Pit River through the mountains, camping on the stream 18 miles to the southwest. The next day they continued over mountainous country above the Pit River Canyon. "In some places," Reading writes, "the descent from the top of the bank to the water must have been 1,200 feet, the stream pitching over rocks and ledges, forming beautiful cascades, one of which had an abrupt fall of about 150 feet." This was, without doubt, Burney Falls, in the McArthur Memorial Park, whose actual drop is 128 feet.

Successive halts were made by Reading and his companions: at Goose Valley on October 28, at the head of Hatchet Creek on the 29th, and on Cow Creek on the 31st. On the first day of November they traveled 16 miles down Cow Creek,

again pitching their tents on its banks. The next day, camp was made on Battle Creek, a part of the present boundary line between Shasta and Tehama counties, and the day after, upon traveling eight miles, they passed through Iron Canyon, where they found the course of the stream "very crooked." Camp was made at the end of the day in the valley east of Red Bluff, whence the journey was continued to Sutter's Fort.

Here Reading worked for a time in Captain Sutter's employ. In December 1844, through Sutter's friendship and influence, Reading obtained a grant of 26,000 acres from Governor Micheltorena, the most northerly grant in California, which he took over in August 1845. A house was built for Reading's overseer on Rancho Buena Ventura, as Reading called his new estate, and the land was stocked with cattle. This first house was burned by the Indians the following spring.

Reading participated in the Bear Flag Revolt at Sonoma in June 1846, and on July 5 or 6 he enlisted in Frémont's Battalion, serving first as lieutenant of artillery and then as paymaster with the rank of major, which office he held until May 31, 1847. In June he returned to his rancho and erected a permanent adobe house, which stood for many years, seven miles east of Cottonwood via Balls Ferry Road and Adobe Lane.

Ranch life, however, did not claim all of Reading's attention this early. In February 1848 he was among the first to visit the scene of Marshall's momentous discovery of gold at Coloma. An examination of the soil satisfied the Major that gold must be present on his own rancho, and he returned at once to investigate. In March he and his Indians washed out the first gold to be found in Shasta County, at the mouth of Clear Creek Canyon on a spot later known as Reading's Bar. In July of the same year he found gold on the Trinity River. In 1849 he again mined on the Trinity, and during the summer located diggings on the site of the present town of Shasta, known for a time as Reading's Springs.

When Shasta County was established in 1850, Reading's Ranch was designated as the county seat. But with the organization of the Court of Sessions at the Major's adobe on February 10, 1851, the county seat was ordered removed to Shasta. "In the lonely stillness of the night" the court packed up the county records and carried them on horseback 25 miles to the new location, perhaps "the most quiet county-seat removal on record in California." No one rejoiced more heartily over the change than Major Reading.

In 1852 Reading was appointed United States Special Indian Agent, and for several years, without remuneration, he carried on work among the Indians, with splendid results. His kindliness was one of Reading's outstanding characteristics.

Going to Washington in 1855 to settle his land grant title, Reading met Miss Fannie Wallace Washington, whom he brought with him to California as his bride. With her coming the adobe on Rancho Buena Ventura was enlarged, and became noted for its unfailing hospitality. About the great fireplace many celebrities gathered—Bidwell, Frémont, Sutter, Lassen, and Joaquin

Miller, among others. Here at his home on May 29, 1868, Pierson B. Reading died. A simple granite slab bearing a bronze memorial plate marks his grave, on Adobe Lane a quarter of a mile from the site of the historic adobe, on a slight eminence overlooking the Sacramento River and the valley beyond. The old house, built with thick walls and high windows for protection from Indian arrows, has now eroded away to a shapeless mound. The site has been given by the Shasta Historical Society to the County of Shasta in the hope of an ultimate restoration.

Burney's Grave

The grave of Samuel Burney, a Scotsman, who was the first settler in Burney Valley, is close beside the Redding–Alturas highway one-half mile east of Burney. Numerous place names in the vicinity perpetuate the memory of this pioneer—the mountain, the valley, the falls, and the town all bear his name. Burney Falls, one of the most beautiful natural phenomena in California, is the chief attraction in the McArthur Memorial Park, a tract of 160 acres deeded to the state on May 11, 1920, by Frank McArthur as a memorial to his father and mother.

Burney came to the valley early in 1857 and built a log cabin, barn, and corral a mile north of the present town of Burney. Although friendly with the Indians and speaking their language, he met death at their hands in March 1859.

Shasta

"Shasta, through which a stream of golden treasure once flowed, now lies in ruins. Six miles west of Redding, its crumbling [brick] structures flank the highway in serried rows. Roofs have long since caved in, and paneless windows stare vacuously into the grass-grown street." The old courthouse, seat of county government between 1861 and 1888, had moldered away until only its brick walls and iron-bound jail cells remained. It was given by the Native Sons of the Golden West (McCloud Parlor No. 149 of Redding) to the State of California, and has now been restored and is a state historical museum. The local court of justice is also held there. The courthouse bears a plaque placed by the California Centennials Commission. The Litsch store, built in 1894, and the old post office also have been acquired by the

Interior of Old Jail, Shasta,
before Restoration

state for museum purposes. The ruins of the other brick buildings in Shasta *(SRL 77)* are included in the Shasta State Historical Monument.

The town was called Reading's Springs by the first settlers who arrived in June 1849, but the name was changed to Shasta on June 8, 1850. By that time the place had become the center of wagon transportation, from which all supplies for the outlying mines were sent on pack mules. "Measured by standards of the '50's and '60's, Shasta was indeed no mean city. She was a gateway to a large hinterland, rich in gold, that lay to the west in Trinity County." As many as 100 freight teams have been known to stop in Shasta on a single night. Its strategic position soon made it the commercial shipping center of northern California, and its merchants did a thriving wholesale and retail business. It was not uncommon for the mercantile house of Bull, Baker and Company, whose brick store, erected in 1853, still stands in ruins on Main Street, to sell a consignment of goods to be taken by pack mules as far north as southern Oregon. The story is told of a member of this firm who early one morning before he had breakfasted sold a bill of goods valued at over $3,000.

The site of the first log house in Shasta, built by Milton McGee in October 1849, is near the intersection of Main and High streets. The log house was torn down in 1856. The St. Charles Hotel and the Trinity House, the first frame buildings in town, have also disappeared. Erected in the spring of 1850, they were destroyed in 1853 by the conflagration that swept Shasta's entire business section. Both stood on Main Street, the Trinity House being on the west side of Main above and adjoining High Street.

On Shurtleff Hill stands the fine old Shurtleff residence erected in the summer of 1851 by Dr. Benjamin Shurtleff, pioneer physician and Shasta's first and only alcalde. This house was used for a time by the Masons, after the fire of 1853 had destroyed their original building. This Masonic lodge was the first to be established in the state, its charter having been brought to California by Peter Lassen in 1848. The lodge was first organized at Benton City on Lassen's Ranch (Tehama County), but on May 9, 1851, it was moved to Shasta. The present hall, which has been in use since 1853, is owned and carefully preserved by Western Star Lodge, No. 2.

At the eastern edge of town a marker indicates directions to the foundation of a Catholic church that was never built *(SRL 483)*. Father Raphael Rinaldi, an Italian priest who arrived in the Shasta diggings in 1855, was dissatisfied with the small church in which the Catholics of the camp worshiped, and determined to build a magnificent basilica-like edifice of cut stone, modeled on the Renaissance architecture of his homeland. The cornerstone was laid in 1857 by Archbishop Joseph Sadoc Alemany, O.P., of San Francisco, but the church never rose above its foundation, which remains today, a mute testimony to the grand dream of a pioneer missionary.

A short distance northwest of town, near the highway to Eureka, is the grave of a baby boy

(SRL 377), all that remains of a pioneer Jewish cemetery. The headstone was discovered in 1923 by engineers planning the highway. When it was found that the grave, with a little iron fence surrounding it, was directly in the line of the proposed highway, the officials altered the route. This road has since been abandoned in favor of a higher routing. The stone, which also bears an inscription in Hebrew, reads: "Charles, son of George and Helena Brownstein, Red Bluff. Born April 16, 1864. Died December 14, 1864."

On June 17, 1950, during the Shasta Centennial Celebration, the California Centennials Commission dedicated an official state plaque on Shasta Dam, several miles north of the old town. The ceremony was followed by the formal dedication of the dam by the federal government. The tablet is inscribed: "If you seek their monument, look about you. To pioneer mothers and fathers of California—whose urge to envision what lay beyond the far horizon and whose courage to overcome hardship opened the unknown West, converting wilderness into empire."

Shasta Mining Camps

Reading's Bar *(SRL 32),* where Major Reading in 1848 discovered the first gold in Shasta County, and where he washed out as much as 52 ounces daily with the aid of friendly Indians, is now only a memory. On a flat adjoining the bar a camp grew up which was known at first as Clear Creek Diggings and later as Horse Town. By October 1849, 300 or 400 miners had congregated at Clear Creek Diggings, and considerable gold was taken out, although most of the miners did little more than prospect.

One of these prospectors, who had arrived in camp with one pack horse, settled there permanently and later built a hotel. As a result, so the story goes, the name of the place was changed to "One-Horse Town" in 1851. It did not remain a "one-horse" town, however, for before many years it boasted 1,000 inhabitants and had two hotels, stores, shops, a Catholic church, a newspaper *(The Northern Argus,* established in 1857), and 14 saloons.

The marked site of Reading's Bar and Horse Town is at the Clear Creek bridge seven miles west of Highway 99 on Clear Creek Road, which intersects the highway at a point four miles south of Redding and less than a mile north of Clear Creek itself. Horse Town was destroyed by fire in 1868, and the site has since been thoroughly dredged out.

Reading's discovery of gold at this place is also commemorated by a native boulder bearing a bronze tablet placed by the California Highway Commission on a now-bypassed stretch of Highway 99 at the end of the Clear Creek bridge *(SRL 78).*

In the vicinity of Horse Town were other early mining camps: Centerville to the north, Muletown to the northwest, and Piety Hill, Igo, and Ono to the west. Of the several stories told of the naming of Igo and Ono, the following is perhaps the most colorful. A Mr. McPherson, one of the first miners to build a substantial house there,

Masonic Hall, Shasta

had a small son who, whenever his father set out for the mines, would put on his own hat and say, "I go"; and always his father would answer, "Oh, no." When the appellation "Igo" became affixed to the place, a neighboring camp about six miles away became known as "Ono." A more credible account of the origin of Ono is that it was named by a pioneer preacher, Rev. William Kidder, for the Biblical "plains of Ono."

Whiskeytown *(SRL 131),* on the Eureka highway between Shasta and Weaverville, was settled in 1849. It was a lively place, as its name might imply, where money was plentiful and freely spent. The U.S. Post Office Department refused to allow the name Whiskeytown as a postal designation until 1952. Prior to that, the post office had been called Blair, later Stella, and finally Schilling. The old hotel and a stone ruin remained at Whiskeytown until the early 1960's, when they were removed for construction of Whiskeytown Dam, which has now inundated the site and caused the relocation of the town to higher ground. Whiskeytown Dam was dedicated by President John F. Kennedy on September 28, 1963, on his last trip to California and less than two months before his assassination.

At French Gulch *(SRL 166),* originally called Morrowville, the diggings were very rich. In their avid search for gold, some of the miners even tore down their cabins to follow the leads extending under them. This once wild camp is today a peaceful community. Still standing are several old stone buildings which give the place something of the atmosphere of the gold days.

Last Remnant of Whiskeytown,
Now under Water

In October and November, 1849, hundreds of gold seekers, many of them Missourians, camped at the mouth of Middle Creek. From this camp, which was nearly equal in size to Reading's Springs, groups of prospectors went out to all the creeks, gulches, and ravines in the surrounding country. One such company camped at or near Churn Creek, so named because a hole carved in the rocks by a waterfall in the stream resembled an old-fashioned churn. Upon being attacked by Indians, the miners returned to the Middle Creek camp, bringing exaggerated reports of the rich diggings they had found. A larger company was soon organized for the purpose of making a permanent camp on the east side of the Sacramento River and of thoroughly prospecting the new site. In spite of trouble with the Indians, a prosperous mining camp, which was called Churntown because of its proximity to Churn Creek, grew up there. Nothing remains of Churntown today.

In 1849 or 1850 gold was discovered on what is now known as the Vollmer Ranch, about 30 miles north of Redding on Interstate Highway 5. At first little mining was carried on because of the hostility of the Indians. By 1855, however, a thriving camp had grown up, about where the settlement of Delta is located today, with 200 or 300 miners working the stream for its gold. During its heyday, Dog Creek, or Dogtown (as it was first called), was the largest and richest camp on the Upper Sacramento, and was the gathering place for miners from the diggings of the entire region. Today no evidence exists to indicate the former importance of this historic spot.

Five miles north of Dog Creek was Portuguese Flat, a mining camp of the early 1850's made up largely of Portuguese. This place, with its rich diggings, gained the reputation of being one of the roughest camps in the county. The site is just north of Pollard's Gulch on the old highway.

Southern's Station

Simeon Fisher Southern arrived in Shasta in 1855, where at first he operated the Eagle Hotel, and later the St. Charles. In the autumn of 1856, he went to French Gulch, where he ran the Empire Hotel for two years. Then, with J. S. Cameron, he became proprietor of the Dog Creek House at the mining camp of Dog Creek on the Oregon Trail. The following year Southern located 45 miles north of Redding, at the site later known as Southern's, where he erected a cabin of shakes and hand-hewn logs. This developed into a busy trading post for miners from Hazel Creek and the Upper Sacramento River. When stage coaches replaced pack-mule trains on the Oregon Trail in 1871, Southern's became an important station on the old road. Gradually the place took on the aspect of a summer resort, as the fame of the surrounding region spread. In 1882 a two-story extension was added to the original cabin. Eventually the old cabin was torn down and the two-story addition was considerably enlarged to care for the increasing number of summer visitors.

After the death of Southern in 1892, changes crept in. With the sale of the property to lumber interests in 1902, the surrounding forests were cut and the old hotel disappeared, to be replaced by a modern service station and auto camp. The spot on which the hotel stood *(SRL 33)* is marked by a few old apple trees, planted in the 1860's, and by a native boulder bearing a bronze tablet on which is an engraving of the original Southern cabin and its two-story addition. The site is on the old highway half a mile south of the Sims Road junction, which is about seven miles south of Castella on the west side of the freeway. The names of many famous people appear on the old hotel register (still treasured by the family), among them President Rutherford B. Hayes, Generals William Tecumseh Sherman and Philip Henry Sheridan, Robert Ingersoll, Mrs. Jay Gould, George Jay Gould, and the "Big Four"— Huntington, Hopkins, Stanford, and Crocker.

The American Ranch

Elias Anderson, one of Shasta County's first settlers, purchased the American Ranch in 1856, and on his land grew up the nucleus of what is now the town of Anderson. The ranch also was an early stopping place for teamsters and travelers on the California–Oregon Road, and from it a trail branched off to the Trinity mines. The first buildings of the old stage station, the site of which is near the highway across the creek from central Anderson, were of adobe.

Bell's Bridge

Five miles south of Redding off Highway 99, a few hundred yards above the Clear Creek bridge, is the old Bell hostelry, built by J. J. Bell, who settled on the Oregon Road in May. 1851. During the gold rush the place teemed with activity, and thousands of men and animals found refreshment there on their way to the Shasta, Trinity, and Siskiyou gold fields. Fabulous prices were paid for food and lodging, and with the proceeds Bell was able to make lavish improvements on his ranch. He also operated a toll bridge *(SRL 519)* across Clear Creek at this point. The tavern now serves as a hay barn. The marker commemorating Bell's bridge has been placed just off Clear Creek Road on the frontage road of Highway 99, at a point 2,200 feet north of the actual site of the bridge.

The Dersch Homestead

Northeast of the small city of Anderson stood the Dersch homestead (*SRL 120*). The main portion of the original house, built by George Dersch in the early 1860's, remained until destroyed by fire on July 12, 1934. In 1850 a Mr. Baker had set up a tent hotel there, making the place an emigrant station on the Nobles Pass Road. George Dersch used Indian labor from rancherías then flourishing at Jelly's Ferry (Tehama County), Cottonwood, Reading's adobe, and Millville. Roving Indians raided the ranch in 1863, driving off the cattle, stealing the household provisions, and leaving the family destitute. In 1866 a second raid was made, in which Mrs. Dersch was killed. The soldiers at Fort Reading were appealed to but with no results. This led to an uprising of the settlers, resulting in the extermination of most of the Indians in the surrounding rancherías.

The old house stood on the northeast side of Dersch Road at the Bear Creek bridge. A replica of the original house has been built. It is located seven and eight-tenths miles east of the junction of Dersch and Airport roads.

Fort Reading

Fort Reading (*SRL 379*), named in honor of Major Pierson B. Reading, was established in May 1852 on Cow Creek on the Nobles Pass Road at a site six miles northeast of the present town of Anderson on Dersch Road. It was abandoned in 1867 as part of the demobilization of the army, after the close of the Civil War. Nothing remains of the old fort itself, but the site, now in a cultivated field on the Hawes Ranch, has been marked. The last building, a barn built in 1852, was razed in 1964. The location is three and four-tenths miles east of the junction of Dersch and Airport roads.

Millville

Fourteen miles east of Redding on the road to Lassen Park is Millville, a thriving place with a distinctive atmosphere of pioneer days. It was settled in 1853 by S. E. and N. T. Stroud, who built the first house there on the banks of Clover Creek. The first gristmill in Shasta County was built in Millville in 1856, by D. D. Harrell and Russell Furman, who named the place Bunscombe Mills, in honor of Harrell's birthplace in North Carolina. Eventually the name was changed to Millville.

Fort Crook

On July 1, 1857, a fort was established by Lieutenant George Crook on Fall River at the upper end of Fall River Valley to serve as a buffer against Indian attacks on the early settlers. The post consisted of 20 small log buildings placed in the form of an oblong. With the abandonment of Fort Crook in 1869 and the transfer of the soldiers to Fort Bidwell, the buildings were used for a time as a school, but were later sold and moved to Burgettville (now Glenburn). The site of the fort (*SRL 355*) is now in a cultivated field on private property about ten miles northwest of Fall River Mills on the road through Glenburn. A marker was placed by the state in 1934.

Lockhart's Fort

The first settlers in Fall River Valley were two men named Bowles and Rogers, who came there from Yreka in 1855. They brought heavy mill machinery with them by ox team and at once set to work cutting trees—many of which still lie where they fell. In the autumn other settlers joined them, among whom were the Lockhart brothers, who located on the site of Fall River Mills. Bowles, Rogers, and William Lockhart spent the winter at this place but were killed by Indians early the following spring. When Sam Lockhart returned to the valley, he was saved from a similar fate only by the timely arrival of a company of men from Yreka. The remains of "Lockhart's Fort," in which he made a gallant five-day fight for life, may be seen today on the hill near Fall River Mills. Shortly after his arrival, Sam Lockhart established a ferry (*SRL 555*) where the California–Oregon stage road crossed the Pit River just below the mouth of Fall River. There, also, in the autumn of 1859 he built a bridge across the Pit River, only to have it washed away in the flood of 1862.

The first school in Fall River Valley (*SRL 759*) was built in 1868 at a spot that is now three and one-half miles east of McArthur on the south side of Highway 299. It was a simple log building, 20 × 30 feet, without floor or windows. About two years later the first sawmill in the valley was set up at Dana, and lumber from this mill was used to floor the school and to construct desks.

Castle Crags

Sharply outlined against a blue sky, the lofty gray turrets of Castle Crags afford a striking contrast to the dark green of the pine-covered mountains that surround them. This superb group rises more than 6,600 feet above sea level and includes among its towers the Cathedral Spires, Castle Dome, and Battle Rock. Hidden high up in the recesses of Castle Crags lies Castle Lake, discovered by Crook and his men while in pursuit of Indians.

Below this castled pile, at first known as Castle Rocks, lay historic Lower Soda Springs (called Castle Crag with the advent of the railroad in

Bell Hotel, Clear Creek

1886) in a green meadow east of the river at the confluence of Soda Creek and the Sacramento. It was long the favorite camping ground of the Shastas and other mountain Indian tribes. It is known that Lansford W. Hastings and 16 companions, who had started from Rogue River, Oregon, in May 1843, camped at the springs. An old fort of huge pine logs, known as Hastings' Barracks and said to have been built by him, once stood at the base of the hill on the north side of the little valley opposite the soda springs.

It is said that Hastings was so pleased with the magnificent location of Lower Soda Springs that he applied for a grant of land that should include both Castle Rocks and its snow-covered neighbor to the north, then known as Shasta Butte and now as Mount Shasta. The grant never materialized, since Hastings would not become a Mexican citizen.

The first permanent settler in the region of Lower Soda Springs was Joe Doblondy, or "Mountain Joe," frontiersman and guide for Frémont. It is not known just when Mountain Joe came to this spot. On the Lower Soda Springs Ranch he tilled the soil, built houses, kept a sort of hotel, guided travelers up the Oregon Trail past Mount Shasta, and fought the Indians. He was also the friend of Joaquin Miller, who in 1854 ran away from school in Oregon and came to live with Mountain Joe under the shadow of the Crags. "He was my ideal, my hero," wrote the poet in later years, and it was from Mountain Joe's seemingly inexhaustible store of tales (first heard in Oregon), as well as from the majesty of the surroundings in which he lived, that Miller gained the inspiration for much of his finest poetry.

The first mining on Soda Creek was carried on in the early 1850's by Bill Fox, who had escaped from the Yreka jail and hid in this isolated spot. He took out a large amount of gold, but was discovered and had to leave the country. Mountain Joe's tales of the fabulous Lost Cabin Mine and other supposedly rich diggings lured a large number of miners to Soda Creek and the Upper Sacramento River in the spring of 1855. The little valley was soon "a white sea of tents. Every bar on the Sacramento was the scene of excitement.... The rivers ran dark and sullen with sand and slime. The fish turned on their sides and died," or hid under the muddy clouds that obscured the deepest pools.

But the tales of wealth told by Mountain Joe proved unfounded, and the army of angry, disgusted miners soon left the region. The results of their short sojourn, however, were not so easily removed. The fish and game on which the Indians depended had been killed or driven out, and the desire for vengeance stirred the warriors to action. One morning while Mountain Joe was absent, a band of Indians, descending from Castle Rocks, plundered and burned the settlement at Lower Soda Springs. On his return, Mountain Joe and Joaquin Miller traced the flight of the marauders up the Rocks by the flour they had spilled. With recruits from the neighboring settlements of Portuguese Flat and Dog Creek,

Mountain Joe soon gathered together a company to punish the Indians. Judge R. P. Gibson, who had married the daughter of the chief of the Shastas, persuaded this tribe to join with the white settlers against the Pits and the other hostile tribes.

The Battle of the Crags, graphically described by Joaquin Miller, youthful participant in the fight, took place on Battle Rock *(SRL 116)*, the most prominent of all the spires and domes of the group. Directly under the highest crag in the northwest corner of the great castle, the settlers, led by Gibson and his Shasta allies, fought face to face with the Indians. Many on both sides were killed or wounded, and among the latter was young Miller, who afterward told how he was carried down the mountainside in a large buckskin bag tied to the back of a wrinkled old Indian woman. Camp was made on the riverbanks below the site of the later Soda Springs Hotel, and there Joaquin was cared for by Mountain Joe until he recovered from his wounds. The Battle of the Crags was one of that long series of conflicts between the Indians and the white settlers of northeastern California which culminated in the Modoc War.

After passing through several hands, Lower Soda Springs came into the possession of G. W. Bailey on May 14, 1858. In order to reach his newly acquired property, he and his family were obliged to cross the river on a packer's log bridge. Bailey ranched and operated a wayside inn and summer resort at this spot until about 1887, when he sold the place to Leland Stanford for a summer home. For a short time it was called Stanford, but the name was soon changed to Castle Crag.

In 1892 the Pacific Improvement Company built the Castle Crag Tavern, the largest summer hotel ever erected in Shasta County. Its first manager was George Schoenwald, who was later manager of Hotel Del Monte at Monterey. The Castle Crag Tavern became famous, and people from all parts of the world visited it; but it was destroyed by fire in the early part of 1900 and was never rebuilt. A number of log cabins were erected in its stead and the place was operated as a summer camp until 1930, when it passed into private hands and was closed to the public—the first time in 86 years. It is now known as the Berry Estate. The site of the world-renowned Castle Crag Tavern is three miles south of Dunsmuir on a good dirt road one and a half miles from Interstate Highway 5.

SOURCES

Boggs, Mae Helene Bacon. *My Playhouse was a Concord Coach.* Howell-North Press, Oakland, 1942.
Camp, Charles L. "James Clyman, His Diaries and Reminiscences," *California Historical Society Quarterly,* IV, No. 2, to VI, No. 1 (June 1925–March 1927).
Cox, Isaac. *The Annals of Trinity County.* Commercial Book and Job Steam Printing Establishment, San Francisco, 1858.
Edgar, William F. "Historical Notes of Old Land Marks in California," *Annual Publications of the Historical Society of Southern California,* II (1893), 25–26.
Edwards, Philip Leget. *The Diary of Philip Leget Edwards.* The Grabhorn Press, San Francisco, 1932.

Frank, B. F., and H. W. Chappell. *History and Business Directory of Shasta County.* Redding Independent, Redding, 1881.

Hanna, Phil Townsend. "Where Vulcan Works in California," *Touring Topics,* XX, No. 7 (July 1928), 22–25, 46–47.

Hastings, Lansford Warren. *The Emigrants' Guide to California.* A facsimile of the edition of 1845 with introduction and notes by Charles H. Carey. Princeton University Press, Princeton, N.J., 1932.

Johnston, Philip. "Gold Trails of the Trinity," *Touring Topics,* XXIV, No. 11 (November 1932), 10–17, 38.

Jones, David Rhys. "Pre-Pioneer Pathfinders, California–Oregon Trail, 1826–1846," *Motor Land,* XXIX (August–November 1931).

McGowan, Joseph A. *History of the Sacramento Valley.* 3 vols. Lewis Historical Publishing Co., New York, 1961.

Miller, Joaquin (Cincinnatus Heine). "The Battle of Castle Crags," *Leslie's Monthly,* March 1893.

—— *Life Amongst the Modocs.* Richard Bentley & Son, London, 1873.

Ogden, Peter Skene. "Journals of Snake Expeditions, 1827–28 and 1828–29," with editorial notes by T. C. Elliott, *Quarterly of the Oregon Historical Society,* XI (December 1910), 355–97.

Reading, Pierson Barton. "Journal of Pierson Barton Reading," *Quarterly of the Society of California Pioneers,* VII, No. 3 (September 1930).

Shurtleff, Dr. Benjamin. "Shasta," *Overland Monthly,* XXXVI, No. 212 (August 1900), 153–58.

Southern, May H. "The Trails of '49," *Courier–Free Press,* Redding, August 1930.

Wilkes, Charles. *Narrative of the United States Exploring Expedition during the Years 1838, 1839, 1840, 1841, 1842.* 5 vols. and an atlas. Lea & Blanchard, Philadelphia, 1845.

Williams, Howel. "Geology of the Lassen Volcanic National Park, California," *University of California Publications. Bulletin of the Department of Geological Sciences,* XXI, No. 8 (December 1932), 195–385.

Sierra County

SIERRA COUNTY was organized from a part of Yuba County in 1852, and Downieville was made the county seat. The name Sierra Nevada ("snow-covered, saw-toothed mountains") is applied to the mountain range that extends from Tehachapi Pass on the south to Lassen Peak on the north.

Goodyear's Bar

Superb mountain peaks look down upon the old river camp at Goodyear's Bar—Saddle Back, Monte Cristo, Fir Cap, Grizzly Peak, and others—while beneath it lie the shining, jade-green reaches of the North Fork of the Yuba River, joined at this point by the tumbling, ice-cold waters of Goodyear Creek. The small triangular flat on which a horde of miners once lived and worked has today not more than a few dozen inhabitants, with only a scattering of houses which stand almost upon the abandoned diggings. The old two-story-and-attic frame hotel is the town's principal landmark.

Goodyear's Bar, settled in the summer of 1849 by Andrew and Miles Goodyear and two companions, was one of the first mining camps on the North Fork of the Yuba. By 1852 the place had become the center for a number of lively camps up and down the river as well as on the neighboring ridges. Nearby were the Ranse Doddler and Hoodoo bars, with St. Joe's Bar two miles below and Woodville, at first known as Cutthroat Bar, farther up the river. On the steep slope above St. Joe's Bar was Nigger Slide.

The diggings in the vicinity yielded rich returns. At Kennedy Ranch, located at the upper end of Goodyear's Bar, Pete Yore's men "cleaned up" $2,000 in gold dust from a single wheelbarrow load of earth, a find that was kept secret from the other miners until a considerable harvest had been gathered.

Goodyear's Bar prospered through the 1850's, but it declined in the early 1860's, with the gradual exhaustion of ore deposits along the river. Decline was further hastened by the devastating fire that swept through the town in 1864. The old river diggings will never again yield great wealth, but the summer vacationist is today discovering that the region offers a more lasting treasure in the joys of mountain life.

There was a Chinatown at Goodyear's Bar of considerable size. The gold in its diggings could be obtained only by long hours of patient and laborious toil.

Downieville

Downieville, in one of the highest and most rugged regions in the state, is set like a toy village in a magnificent wooded amphitheater surrounded by lofty, pine-clad mountains. Perhaps no county seat in California has a setting more picturesque or a history more dramatic. At its door the Downie River, also called the North Fork of the North Fork of the Yuba River, flows into the larger stream, a part of that "network of forks and tributaries which reach through deep canyons upwards into the higher altitudes of the Sierra."

Penetrating this aerie, William Downie (usually called "Major" Downie), a Scotsman, for whom the town was later named, arrived at "The Forks" in November 1849. With him were ten Negro sailors, an Indian, an Irish boy named Michael Deverney, and Jim Crow, a Kanaka, who later became quite a notorious character in the North Yuba River country and for whom Jim

Crow Canyon was named. Erecting a few log cabins, the Major and his men wintered at the flat just above the present townsite. Some of the men spent their time digging into the rocky crevices under the snow, taking out $100 to $200 in gold each day.

There was a rush of miners into the area the following spring, accompanied by rich strikes on all the neighboring bars and flats. "The Forks" soon became the center of a wide circle of camps reaching up and down both rivers and their tributaries, and before long the name of the place was changed to Downieville. By 1851 the population of the town had increased to more than 5,000.

Stories told of the miners and their life on the Yuba indicate the phenomenal richness of the placers. On Durgan Flat, where the courthouse now stands, Frank Anderson and three companions in 11 days took out ore valued at $12,900 from a claim only 60 feet square. One day's yield was valued at $4,300, while the total yield during the first six months that the location was worked brought over $80,000. Jersey Flat, just above the present town, at the spot where Downie and his party first made temporary camp, was a close second to Durgan Flat in production. According to the Major, Jim Crow killed a salmon weighing 14 pounds here, and after the fish had been cooked for supper gold was found at the bottom of the kettle. At Zumwalt Flat each man averaged five ounces a day for three and one-half hours' labor, while at Tin Cup Diggings, opposite Zumwalt Flat, three men who worked there in 1850 were said to have made it a rule to fill a tin cup with gold before quitting work at night, which they had no trouble doing.

But the miners were not satisfied, and in order to get out the gold that still lay in the bedrock of the river, they flumed the entire Yuba between Downieville and Goodyear's Bar out of its channel. When the winter floods came, however, their means of harnessing the tremendous forces of the mountains was swept away like so much straw.

Other diggings in the canyon country brought vast wealth. At Gold Bluff, two miles above Downieville, in the fall of 1850 a nugget of pure gold was taken out which weighed 25 pounds, the largest ever found on the North Yuba. The black slate of this area continued to produce thousands of dollars up to the time of World War I, when mining activities were discontinued. Below Slug Canyon, so called because of the coarse lump or slug gold found there, the Steamboat Company on Steamboat Bar took out an average of $5,000

a day for several weeks during 1851. At the head of this canyon and about three miles south of Downieville is the City of Six Quartz Mine, a famous producer in the early days. Another famous mine, Monte Cristo, is located on the south slope of Monte Cristo, 1,000 feet above Goodyear Creek and three miles northwest of Downieville. It was opened in 1854, and at one time the adjoining camp had a population as large as that of Downieville.

To Downieville, the center of this wild region, which swarmed with all types of men, came the young Congregational minister, Rev. William C. Pond, and his wife in 1855, at a time when gambling saloons with their shining bars and roulette wheels did a thriving nightly business; when lumbering freight wagons, or "mountain schooners," and long lines of picturesque pack mules, marshaled into town by their no less picturesque Mexican drivers, afforded the only means of travel; and when sugar sold for $4 a pound and boots and shoes for from $25 to $150 a pair.

Pond preached his first sermon in a structure called the "Downieville Amphitheater" on "Piety Flat." Within a few months after his arrival a church was erected, but before services could be held in the new building it was destroyed by fire. The embers were barely cool when a miner reached the minister's home from his mountain cabin four miles away with the offer "A hundred dollars, Mr. Pond, for another church." A substantial basement structure of brick and stone was built at once, and in it Pond preached until 1865. In that year, however, with the marked decline of mining activity in the region, services in the Downieville church were discontinued, the building was sold, and Pond went to Petaluma to carry on his work.

Pond's influence, like that of most of the other pioneer ministers of California, reached far beyond the home parish. "Sometimes in unoccupied theaters, sometimes in the dining rooms of the hotels or of miners' boarding houses, sometimes in miners' cabins" in outlying districts, he imparted his message. Regular services were held also at the two out-stations of Goodyear's Bar and Monte Cristo. In addition, Pond served as county superintendent of schools for three terms.

Downieville remains much as it was in the early gold days. Along the crooked main street, which is still lined by boardwalks, stand the same buildings, now old and quaint looking. Along the riverbanks and up the mountainsides the old-fashioned houses, set amid aged locust and fruit trees, line the shady streets and alleyways, making

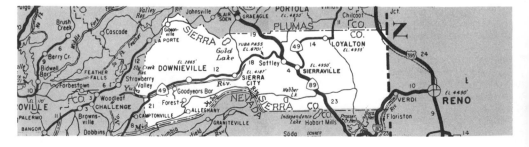

the residential part of Downieville one of the town's most charming features.

One of the first buildings in Downieville, thought to have been erected in 1852, a stone structure with heavy iron doors and shuttered windows, was restored and presented to the town for use as a museum by the heirs of J. M. B. Meroux, a pioneer. The Native Daughters and Native Sons of the Golden West of Downieville dedicated it to the pioneers of Sierra County on July 3, 1932. The walls of this building are made entirely of flat rocks laid horizontally, a very early type of construction. The nucleus of the museum is a collection of valuable relics gathered by former Sheriff George C. Bynon.

Costa's (now James's) grocery store is another stone structure that has stood since 1852, as is the Craycroft Building. The frame Masonic Hall dates from the same year. The Catholic and Methodist Episcopal churches, both built in the 1850's, have been marked by official state plaques, although neither has been assigned a registration number.

Across the river from the business section stands the courthouse, a modern structure. Here there are two old cannon, an arrastra wheel which was used by the pioneers to grind the gold-impregnated quartz, and at the rear of the building the desolate old gallows. Nearby are the diggings —huge piles of granite boulders marking the rich river claims where miners in 1850 and 1851 averaged $100 to $200 daily. Here the Chinese came after others had ceased to consider the location worth while. Lifting the heavy stones one by one, they cleared out the bed of the North Yuba, leaving mammoth heaps as evidence of their Herculean labors. The historic old courthouse that stood here for nearly a century was destroyed by fire in 1947. Another fire the same year claimed the town's principal landmark, the old St. Charles Hotel on the main street.

Upon the site of the present steel bridge over Downie River, where the first structure formerly stood, was enacted the closing scene of a pathetic tragedy in 1851, when Juanita, a Mexican dance-hall girl, was hanged for the murder of Jack Cannon, an Australian, who had attempted to force himself into her room. Contemporary opinion did not condone this action of the miners' court, and much criticism was aroused in the United States and abroad.

Sierra City

Following the line of the old stage road from Downieville, a modern highway sweeps up the tortuous canyon of the North Fork of the Yuba River. Above green alpine meadows and old apple orchards, where an occasional farmhouse or miner's cabin may still be seen, the road leads past the little old settlement of Loganville, 11 miles from Downieville, to Sierra City, two miles farther, nestled at the base of the majestic Sierra Buttes, which tower almost a mile above.

These jagged granite peaks look down upon a region of great scenic grandeur and filled with mining lore, for in the feverish gold-rush days of 1849 and the early 1850's camps sprang up

St. Charles Hotel, Downieville

throughout the entire section. The tributary streams of the North Fork were panned to the very base of the Buttes, and even the almost perpendicular sides of the granite pile were climbed in the search for gold.

In the spring of 1850 P. A. Haven and Joseph Zumwalt located on the site of Sierra City, in a region then thickly populated with Indians. In the same year a Mr. Murphy discovered the Sierra Buttes quartz ledge. Here a mine was located which proved to be one of the state's big producers. By 1852 tunnels penetrated the craggy Sierra Buttes in all directions, and the miners were using as many as 20 arrastras, run by mules, to pulverize the rock. During that winter a heavy blanket of snow and avalanches from the steep mountain above crushed every house in the mining camp. In the face of this disaster it was not until 1858 that a permanent settlement was established on the townsite.

Another rich quartz deposit of the Sierra Buttes was opened up at the Monumental Quartz Mine, where on August 18, 1860, an immense gold nugget, weighing 1,596 troy ounces and valued at $25,500, was taken out, the second largest to be found in California.

Among the interesting historic structures still standing in Sierra City is the Busch Building on Main Street erected in 1871. The lower two stories of brick survived a fire about 1948 which destroyed the third story of wood. The building was begun during the Fourth of July celebration and the ceremonies were conducted by the E Clampus Vitus, which had been organized in Sierra City in 1857. The letters "ECV" still mark the doorway in the old building through which the "Clampers" passed. The society, under the title of E Clampus Vitus Redivivus, was reorganized in the early 1930's by a few members of the California Historical Society interested in preserving the lore of gold-rush days. The Busch Building at one time housed the Wells Fargo Express office, as a sign still proclaims. Other early landmarks include the Catholic church and the Masonic Hall.

Sierra City, fortunately, has never been devastated by fire, as most early mining camps were, owing to the proximity of numerous streams which come tumbling down the mountainside. These watercourses have been harnessed to furnish power not only for the mills at the mines,

NORTHWESTERN SIERRA COUNTY

as in the old days, but to generate electricity and to supply other needs of the town.

In Sierra Valley, across Yuba Pass and 23 miles east of Sierra City, is the old town of Sierraville, a supply center rather than a mining camp. Here the old Globe Hotel, now outfitted as a motel, and the Monte Carlo Saloon remain from earlier days.

Forest City

Forest City, 14 miles south of Downieville via Goodyear's Bar, was one of the liveliest camps in Sierra County during the middle 1850's. According to Fariss and Smith, the first white men to come to the site were a company of sailors, who found gold there in the summer of 1852. They named their camp Brownsville after one of their party. Hittell, however, cites as the probable discoverer Michael Savage, who came there in 1853.

When "the place began to look like a town," after the establishment of the first store or trading post, it was sometimes called by the Indian name "Yomana," said to designate the high bluff just above the town, which was a sacred hill or holy ground. It was also called "Forks of Oregon Creek." Hittell concludes that the present name of Forest City is derived not from the magnificent forest of conifers surrounding it, as is generally supposed, "but from Mrs. Forest Mooney, the newspaper correspondent." Mrs. Mooney, the wife of Captain Mooney, was a woman with a bent for newspaper writing. Her first name was Forest, and she invariably signed her journalistic effusions "Forest City."

Having worked out the streams, bars, and banks about Forest City, the miners began to tunnel into the mountain to the south. The name of one of these tunnels, the Alleghany, was given to a flourishing camp on the opposite side of the mountain, where pay dirt was struck in 1855. The town of Alleghany increased in importance so rapidly the following year that the entire population of Forest City flocked to the new camp, leaving the older place an empty shell. When a

rich strike was made in the Bald Mountain district in 1870, Forest City awoke from its Rip Van Winkle sleep, only to relapse after a few years into the quiet hamlet of today. A few empty stores still stand along the main street, and a little Catholic church crowns the hill above. Steep-roofed houses clinging to the mountain on either side of the canyon, reached only over narrow, precipitous roads, give the place a picturesquely alpine air.

Alleghany

Alleghany may be reached by a variety of routes, all of them winding mountain roads with sections that are narrow, steep, and rough. From Downieville on the north, one would proceed by way of Goodyear's Bar and Forest City, a trip of 19 miles in all. From Camptonville on the west, the road along Gold Ridge joins the route from Downieville at the site of Mountain House, between Goodyear's Bar and Forest City. From Freeman's Crossing at the Nevada–Yuba county line, the main road to Alleghany, partly paved in contrast to the others, is about 19 miles in length. From North Columbia, 18 miles to the southwest, a road leads to Alleghany by way of Foote's Crossing on the Middle Fork of the Yuba River. Alleghany may also be reached from the east over the Henness Pass route.

Of all these roads, the most interesting, and most recently built, is the Foote's Crossing approach. A portion of the route, on the Nevada County side above the Middle Fork, has been described as "America's most spectacular mile of mountain road." Others have said, "Few roads in Switzerland are more spectacular," or "It is one road for which every driver has a wholesome respect!" The road is perfectly safe for the driver who is willing to take it slowly and carefully. It is one-way in most places but there are frequent turnouts. This picturesque thoroughfare was built by A. D. Foote as a toll road about the time the automobile was coming into general use. The road is a marvel of engineering skill. Cut into the face of a stupendous precipice high above the deep gorge of the Middle Fork, it takes a narrow, threadlike course along the almost perpendicular cliffs reaching hundreds of feet above and below. A bend in the tortuous defile now and then reveals the nature of this awesome roadway and the daring and skill of its builder. The rock walls, above and below, are of the type known as dry masonry, and are "so perfectly matched and carefully laid that, after decades of winter storms, soaking water, and swelling ice, they remain in perfect condition." In places the canyon walls are so nearly perpendicular that huge iron bars had to be anchored far into the solid rock underneath the roadbed. At the bottom of the canyon is the Foote's Crossing Bridge, where a roadhouse once stood. Beyond, the great gorge of the Middle Fork converges with that of Kanaka Creek to make one immense canyon.

Kanaka Creek was discovered in May 1850 by one of several parties of Hawaiian prospectors sent out by a certain Captain Ross, the reputed son of King Kamehameha. A general rush of miners followed. Kanaka Creek proved to be extraordinarily rich in the precious mineral and some very large nuggets were taken out.

Up the north side of Kanaka Creek Canyon to Alleghany, new vistas of scenic grandeur successively unfold. Evidences of one-time mining activities are visible on every hand: masses of green serpentine rock, polished and of great beauty; old "glory holes," reminding one of vanished hopes; deserted mines visible far up the wooded ravines. Nearer Alleghany the country becomes increasingly rocky, and one can glimpse a few mines of this world-famous district: the Madden, Rainbow, Oriental, Spoohn Gold, and others, the smaller ones having produced $1,500 to $2,000 each year and the larger ones millions. According to authentic record, one chunk of ore found in this region weighed 163 pounds and brought $27,000 from the mint, and from one pocket as much as $80,000 was taken. Some of these rich deposits have been lost through faulty surveys or the sudden caving-in of a tunnel and have never been relocated, as happened in the case of the old Red Star Mine, from which as much as $80,000 was taken from one chute in 1912. Hope of recovering such leads is continually reviving, and the fascination of the quest lures the modern treasure hunter as it did the Argonauts of old.

Alleghany is still essentially a "gold camp"— one of the few left in California—where most of the several hundred citizens are directly or indirectly connected with the gold-mining industry. Clinging like a cluster of cliff swallows' nests to the side of the mountain, the houses of the town are built on a series of terraces connected by streets. The lowest of these narrow benches is about 100 feet above Kanaka Creek, while the uppermost shelf is about 600 feet higher. In pioneer days, when the town was snowbound for weeks at a time, the people of Alleghany communicated with the citizens of Forest City on the opposite side of the mountain by means of the long tunnel that early miners had driven through in their search for gold.

Alleghany stands on the ancient channel of one of the numerous tributaries of the Blue Gravel or Blue Lead, which extended from near the northern boundary line of Sierra County in a southeasterly direction to the southern line of Placer County at Forest Hill. Here, as elsewhere, much of the old channel was covered by lava flows, which the miners had to penetrate in order to reach the rich deposits of gold in the underlying gravel. By tunneling and drifting, and, in some places, by means of hydraulic mining, they took immense fortunes from these ancient accumulations during the 1850's and 1860's and extending even into the 1890's.

Just below Alleghany the famous Original Sixteen-to-One Mine, so called to distinguish it from the Sixteen-to-One above Washington in Nevada County, was located in 1896 by Thomas J. Bradbury. Year after year Bradbury lived at Alleghany and worked his claim on a small scale. Then in 1907 the rich Tightner Mine was discovered nearby. In 1916 it was found that this location and the Original Sixteen-to-One were tapping the same vein, its apex in the backyard of the old Bradbury home. This discovery led to the consolidation of the Tightner and the Twenty-One, another adjacent property, with the Sixteen-to-One as the Original Sixteen-to-One Company. The combined claim has produced thousands of dollars for its owners and continues to be worked. The high cost of operation and the low price of gold threaten, however, to force its closing and the resultant demise of Alleghany as a mining center, a pattern that has occurred throughout the Mother Lode country.

Following the line of the ancient Blue Lead river channel across Kanaka Creek Canyon, one finds auriferous gravel deposits on the opposite slopes at Chips Flat, and again at what was once the mining camp of Minnesota Flat on the other side of the ridge. An outcropping of blue gravel at the latter location was discovered in July 1852 by an old English sailor, known to his fellows as "Chips," because he had previously been employed as ship's carpenter. Later "Chips" located even richer diggings on the northern slope of the same ridge, at Chips Flat.

The old scenic road from Camptonville (Yuba County) to Downieville along the backbone of Gold Ridge overlooked the heavily timbered canyons of Oregon Creek to the south and the North Yuba River to the north. A fairly good dirt road, over which Alleghany may be reached, follows the same course today, passing the sites of several historic stopping places along the way. A little over three miles east of Camptonville, across the Sierra County line, long stood the old Sleighville House, a two-story hotel. The original structure, built in 1849 by Peter Yore, was added to from time to time as the needs of the family increased. Not far from the site of the old hostelry lies the burial ground of the Yore family. Dense evergreen forests enclose the place on all sides, and in winter the entire landscape is heavily mantled with snow. At this point, in early days, it was necessary to transfer goods from wagons to sleighs during the winter months, and from this circumstance the house took its name.

The next historic point on the Gold Ridge route, about five miles beyond Sleighville House, is the site of Nigger Tent, around which centers many a thrilling tale. On this spot in 1849 a Negro put up a tent to serve as a wayside station on the pack trail to Downieville. Later, according to J. D. Borthwick, he replaced the tent with a cabin, on the site of which a subsequent owner erected a substantial frame hotel. In spite of changes, the original name of Nigger Tent stuck to the locality. Several miles beyond, where the road forks, is the site of the Mountain House, where a magnificent panorama of wooded mountains and deeply chiseled canyons may be seen. From here one road goes south to Forest City, while the other leads north to Goodyear's Bar and Downieville. The Mountain House was burned many years ago.

The main road to Alleghany begins at Highway 49, in the area of Freeman's Crossing on the Nevada–Yuba county line between North San Juan and Camptonville. The road crosses Oregon Creek over the famous old covered bridge built about 1862 and, a few miles beyond, enters Sierra County. At a point about six miles beyond the bridge a road leads north two miles to what remains of Pike City, a few old cabins and foundations. About four miles beyond the Pike turnoff a handsome monument stands beside the main road at the site of the Plum Valley House *(SRL 695)*, built in 1854 by John Bope. Deriving its name from the wild plums that grow in this area, it was a toll station on the Henness Pass Road *(SRL 421)* between Marysville and Virginia City, Nevada. This route had been in use as an emigrant trail as early as 1849. A dirt Forest Service road still follows its course across Henness Pass (6,806 feet) to join State Highway 89 nine miles southeast of Sierraville.

Gold beyond the Mountains

Towering thousands of feet above the towns of the North Yuba River canyon "a huge mass of mountains crowned with castellated peaks and knife-like crests forms an effective barrier to direct travel" into the old mining districts of northwestern Sierra County. In order to reach this section by automobile one must turn north above Sierra City and follow a circuitous route by way of Gold Lake, Mohawk, and Johnsville to Gibsonville, or one must retrace to Bullard's Bar in Yuba County and from there proceed northward via Challenge and Strawberry Valley, through La Porte in Plumas County, and thence to Gibsonville on the road to Quincy.

This remote section of Sierra County was first

Rear of Old Store, Port Wine

prospected in the spring of 1850, when gold was found along the ridge between the North Fork of the Yuba River and the South Fork of the Feather River by an old sea captain named Sears, whose name was later given to the ridge.

Returning to the Yuba, Sears prepared to lead a company of prospectors to the scene of his discovery. But the news that Sears had "struck it rich" spread, and before proceeding very far his party found that they were being followed by a group under the leadership of a man named Gibson. When ordered to turn back, Gibson's men refused, saying that the mountains of California were as free to them as to any man, and that if there was gold beyond those mountains they were going to get their share. A compromise was at length reached and the two parties proceeded to Sears' Ridge, where operations were begun at a place afterward known as Sears' Diggings.

Before long a number of other locations were staked out in the vicinity, some of which proved to be richer than the original strike. Gibson, who was an especially enterprising prospector, discovered very rich deposits on an adjoining ridge overlooking Little Slate Creek, a site later developed into the large and thriving camp of Gibsonville, which even as late as 1870 was still a busy place. But with the passing years Gibsonville, in wind-swept isolation, has grown more deserted. The few remaining wooden houses straggle up and down the crazy street like wizened dwarfs, bleached almost to the whiteness of skeletons by the weather.

The enterprising Gibson struck another rich deposit at a place that became known as Secret Ravine because he had kept the location a secret from his comrades, who charged him with playing them false. The resultant dissension among Gibson's followers and growing dissatisfaction among Sears's men caused a scattering of the two groups, resulting in new discoveries in all directions. Many new camps were established, among them Howland Flat (or Table Rock), Pine Grove, Potosi, St. Louis, Queen City, Poker Flat, Craig's Flat, Deadwood, Chandlerville, Port Wine, Scales, Poverty Hill, Brandy City, Hepsidam, Whiskey Diggings (or Newark), McMahon's, Morristown, and Eureka City at the source of Goodyear Creek.

At La Porte a good dirt road turns southeast across the Sierra County line and runs four miles to Queen City, marked by a few old cabins. At this point a road running northeast and southwest is intersected. The branch to the northeast goes to Howland Flat via St. Louis. St. Louis, staked out on the site of Sears' Diggings in the fall of 1852 by a party of Missourians, enjoyed a brief period of prosperity until it was swept by fire in 1857. Later, during the 1860's, a short-lived hydraulic boom revived the place. Howland Flat, where the post office (1857–1922) was always called Table Rock, is situated on the north side of Table Rock at an elevation of 6,000 feet. It reached such prominence in 1869 as a result of hydraulic operations that it was classed as one of the populous camps of the Sierra. A fair number of the old houses remain. From here a trail leads three miles to Poker Flat on Canyon Creek. The road continues from Howland Flat to join the Johnsville road east of Gibsonville.

The road southwest from Queen City goes to Port Wine, Poverty Hill, and Scales. Less than a mile from Queen City the traveler is surprised to see a magnificent old stone building, a strange sight in this wilderness. This former store, with its iron doors, plus an old cemetery and the weird piles of long-forgotten diggings are all that remain of Port Wine, named by prospectors who found a cask of port wine hidden in a nearby canyon. The road continues past the turnoff to Poverty Hill to the little community of Scales with its neat white homes. From here the motorist can follow the road west into Yuba County, joining the main road to La Porte about two and a half miles northeast of Strawberry Valley.

Brandy City, though part of the same mining area, is reached by turning north from State Highway 49 at the Indian Valley outpost, 13 miles west of Downieville. Here is mounted the old Brandy City cannon. The last part of the Brandy City road is poor, and all that could be found at the site in the summer of 1956 was the old cemetery, a number of fallen cabins, and one standing building that apparently was the post office.

Old Town of Scales

SOURCES

Borthwick, J. D. *Three Years in California.* William Blackwood & Sons, Edinburgh, 1857.
California Mining Journal, featuring Nevada and Sierra County mines. I, No. 1 (August 1931).
Coy, Owen Cochran. *Gold Days,* of the series *California,* ed. John Russell McCarthy. Powell Publishing Co., Los Angeles, 1929.

Downie, Major William. *Hunting for Gold.* The California Publishing Co., San Francisco, 1893.
Fariss and Smith. *Illustrated History of Plumas, Lassen, and Sierra Counties.* San Francisco, 1882.
Geologic Guidebook along Highway 49—Sierran Gold Belt, the Mother Lode Country. State of California, Division of Mines, San Francisco, 1948.
Gold Rush Country. Lane Publishing Co., Menlo Park, 1957.
Hanson, George Emmanuel. *The Early History of Yuba River Valley.* Master's thesis, University of California, August 1924.
Hittell, Theodore H. *History of California.* 4 vols. N. J. Stone & Co., San Francisco, 1898.
Johnston, Philip. "Relics of the Gold-Rush among the Northern Diggin's," *Touring Topics,* XXIV, No. 1 (January 1932), 10–25, 45–46.
Pond, William C. *Gospel Pioneering in California.* Privately printed, Oberlin, Ohio, 1921.
Weston, Otheto. *Mother Lode Album.* Stanford University Press, Stanford, 1948.
Wolff, J. L. *Yuba River Canyon Country.* Ms., 1932.

Siskiyou County

SISKIYOU COUNTY (from an Indian name of undetermined meaning) was created in 1852 from the northern part of Shasta County and a part of Klamath County. Yreka has always been the county seat. After Klamath County was dissolved in 1874, Siskiyou County received still more of its territory.

Mount Shasta

"Lonely as God, and white as a winter moon, Mount Shasta starts up sudden and solitary from the heart of the great black forests of Northern California." Thus did the indelible picture of this majestic peak imprint itself upon the mind and heart of Joaquin Miller, who spent several years of his youth within the radius of its influence. The beautiful Indian legend of how the Great Spirit "made this mountain first of all" was told him by the simple people among whom

he lived, and in that story was incorporated the tradition long held by the Shasta Indians that "before the white man came they could see the fire ascending from the mountain by night and the smoke by day, every time they chose to look in that direction."

"Shasta," wrote John Muir, "is a fire-mountain, an old volcano gradually accumulated and built up into the blue deep of the sky by successive eruptions of ashes and molten lava." Periods of quiescence intervened between eruptions. Then the glacial winter came on, "a down-crawling mantle of ice upon a fountain of smouldering fire, crushing and grinding its brown, flinty lavas, and thus degrading and remodeling the entire mountain." The summit was a mass of ruins, considerably lowered, and the sides deeply grooved and fluted. Beneath the snowy surface the fires still glowed, but the glaciers still flowed on, "sculpturing the mountain with stern, resistless energy."

Five of these glaciers—Hotlum, Bolam, Whitney, Wintun, and Konwakiton—still scour the sides of the great mountain, principally on the north and east slopes above the 10,000-foot level. Hundreds of streams are fed by these ice rivers, which "have a habit of disappearing as you follow down their courses. The porous slopes are ever ready to absorb moisture and to allow it to flow underground unimpeded until, at the lower slopes, it gushes forth in mighty springs that give birth, full-fledged, to the McCloud and Sacramento rivers and other important streams." Big Spring, one source of the Sacramento River, gushes from the mountainside in an ice-cold flood just one mile north of Mount Shasta City.

John Muir, in one of his rare word pictures, describes the fountainhead of the McCloud. "Think of a spring giving rise to a river," he wrote, "a spring fifty yards wide at the mouth, issuing from the base of a lava bluff with wild songs—not gloomily from a dark cavey mouth, but from a world of ferns and mosses gold and green."

The Mud Creek area, four miles northeast of McCloud, was devastated in August 1924 by a vast flow of mud washed down by the melting snows of the Konwakiton Glacier. Water and sediment spread out from the creek bed over the country, killing a vast extent of timber and leaving a desolate waste.

Shasta's snowy summit dominates the landscape for a hundred miles and is visible for almost twice that distance. The first recorded mention of it, as "Shatasla," was in 1814, in the journal of Alexander Henry. It is possible that Spanish explorers in 1817 observed it from a distance when Fray Narciso Durán, accompanied by Luís Argüello,

led an expedition from San Francisco by boat up the Sacramento River, reaching as far north as the mouth of the Feather. Durán made this entry in his journal on May 20: "At about ten leagues to the northwest of this place we saw the very high hill called by soldiers that went near its slope 'Jesús María.' It is entirely covered with snow." There is considerable doubt, however, that the mountain which these early explorers saw was Mount Shasta.

Peter Skene Ogden, a Hudson's Bay Company trapper, wintered on the streams east and north of the mountain in 1826–27, and on February 14, 1827, he wrote in his journal: "There is a mountain equal in height to Mount Hood or Vancouver I have named Mt. Sastise." In reference to the stream he wrote: "I have named this river Sastise River."

Shasta is undoubtedly a word of Indian origin, although both derivation and meaning are uncertain. Ogden says that he derived "these names from the tribes of Indians" living there, and according to Powers, Shas-ti-ka was the tribal name of the natives in this region. Alleged Russian or French origins for the name (*tchastal*, "white," and *chaste*, "pure") are now generally discredited.

English and American explorers during the early part of the nineteenth century viewed the great mountain and placed it on their maps under variant spellings. Lieutenant Emmons, of the Wilkes Exploring Expedition, who saw it on October 3, 1841, mentioned it in his report and on accompanying maps as "Mount Shaste"; Frémont, who five years later saw it while on his third expedition, referred to it in his subsequent report as "Shastl" and on his map of 1848 as "Tsashtl"; Lieutenant Robert S. Williamson, of the United States Topographical Engineers, in his report of

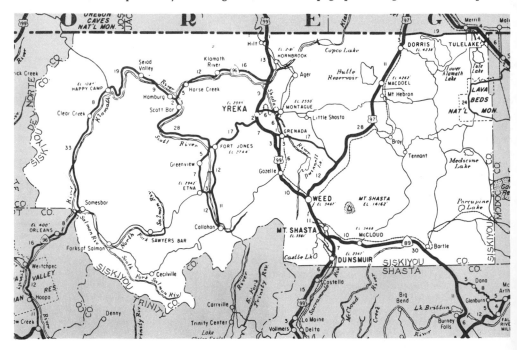

the expedition which surveyed for a railroad route from Oregon to the Sacramento Valley in 1851 and 1855, designated the mountain as "Shasta Butte," butte being a name freely used by American trappers in the West.

The first recorded ascent of Mounta Shasta appears to have been that made by Captain E. D. Pearce (Pierce) in August or September of 1854. Shortly after, Pearce led a party of 13 prominent citizens from Yreka, Humbug, and Scott valleys to the summit. Other ascents followed. Israel S. Diehl, of Yreka, climbed to the top alone on October 11, 1855. He was followed by Anton Roman, a German, in April 1856. Joaquin Miller, who ascended the mountain several times, climbed it for the last time in 1858 when a boy of 17. It was his book, *Life Amongst the Modocs*, written in London in 1873, which made Mount Shasta known to the world.

In the summer of 1859 N. C. Mayhew and two companions spent the night at the hot spring just below the top crest, an experience duplicated in 1870 by Clarence King and three companions while engaged in the Survey of the Fortieth Parallel, and by John Muir and Jerome Fay on April 30, 1875. The previous November John Muir had observed the stormy grandeur of its summit at close range.

The first scientific ascent of the mountain was made in September 1862 by Josiah Dwight Whitney, of the Whitney State Geological Survey, William H. Brewer, his chief assistant, and Chester Averill, but it was not until 1870 that its glaciers were discovered by Clarence King. Captain A. F. Rodgers, of the United States Coast and Geodetic Survey, in 1875 began a series of observations from the summit. In October of that year he erected a steel monument, some 14 feet high and capped by a nickel reflector, on the highest point. This monument stood for many years. In the summer of 1877 John Muir visited Mount Shasta's forests and wild gardens with Sir Joseph Hooker, the great English botanist, and Professor Asa Gray, America's foremost botanist at that time. B. A. Colonna, of the Coast and Geodetic Survey, spent nine successive days and nights on the summit of Mount Shasta in July and August of 1878. At the end of that period he succeeded in exchanging heliograph flashes with observers posted on Mount St. Helena, 192 miles to the south.

The latest figure for the height of Mount Shasta as given by the United States Coast and Geodetic Survey is 14,162 feet. Geographically, according to some authorities, Mount Shasta is "a connecting link between three mountain masses," although a part of none of them—"the Sierra Nevada, a hundred miles to the southeast; the Cascade Range, whose southern terminus is but fifty miles to the northeast; and the diversified ridges of the Klamath Mountains, just westward across Strawberry Valley." Other writers include Shasta in the Cascade Range. The Mount Shasta Recreation Area, including 29,620 acres of forest, river, and mountain vacation lands, was set aside by the national government in 1926 for the use and enjoyment of the general public.

Through the efforts of M. Hall McAllister, a stone lodge, known as the Shasta Alpine Lodge, was erected in 1922 nine miles from Mount Shasta City at Horse Camp (7,992 feet) under the auspices of the Sierra Club. Two San Franciscans made the first winter stay at the lodge when they climbed the mountain on February 22, 1924. The lodge affords a shelter to storm-bound mountaineers throughout the year, and during the summer months a record is kept by the attendant of all those making the ascent, so that rescue parties may be sent out to search for any who fail to return within a reasonable time.

The Modoc Lava Beds

For the archaeologist and the student of early Western history, as well as for the lover of unique natural formations, the Modoc Lava Beds in the Lava Beds National Monument (proclaimed by President Coolidge in 1925) hold a distinct fascination. The old Indian name for the region is said to have meant "The land of burned-out fires," and its labyrinthine caves, seemingly bottomless fumaroles, and extinct craters testify to the fitness of that designation. This vast mesa-like formation is broken here and there by buttes or cinder cones several hundred feet high, but the harsh outlines of these volcanic masses are relieved by the contrast of blossoming plants and shrubs, clumps of pine or juniper, and the softening beauty of varicolored rock.

The center of the region is 60 miles due east of Yreka. The entire section is traversed by a good automobile road, along which one may visit the numerous caves—the prehistoric camping ground of a forgotten people, and the last refuge of the Indian in the West. This was the "castle" of the Modocs, their "stone house, into which no white man could come so long as they cared to defend it." Walls and entrances to many of the rooms in this gigantic castle are still decorated with aboriginal pictographs done in red, yellow, and black.

In and out among the gray and twisted rocks the road leads by Indian Well, where moccasined feet, in centuries long past, wore a trail which still entices the adventurous down through a worn-out crater into the vast interior of a dark cavern. An ancient Indian sign painted on the rocks near the entrance directs the way to two pools of crystal-clear ice water which seem never to diminish, even during the driest seasons, and from which present-day tourists from a public campground nearby obtain water.

Near Indian Well are Labyrinth Cave, Skull Cave, Symbol Cave, and Symbol Bridge. Labyrinth Cave is a series of subterranean cells connected by a maze of tunnels running in all directions, the main gallery being almost two miles in length, with a part of the distance navigable only in a crouching position. Skull Cave, the largest cavern in the region yet explored, has three stories at its lower end. A river of ice covers the floor of the lower chamber and in it are imbedded bones of now extinct animals and even scattered human bones. From the numerous skulls of Rocky Mountain sheep, prong-horned antelope, and other animals found there the place derived its name. On the rocks and about one of the entrances to Symbol Cave, Indian pictographs appear as clear and unfaded as the day they were placed there by the artists or medicine men of a vanished race.

Beyond Symbol Bridge and Antelope Well, with its abundant, clear, sweet water, is Bearpaw Cave, a series of rock and ice chambers connected by underground corridors. One of the chambers contains a river of ice that lasts throughout the year, while at the opposite end of the abyss another immense cavity holds an unfailing water supply. Sentinel Cave, Crystal Cave, Chocolate Bridge, Painted Cave, Jove's Thunderbolt, and "The Chimneys" (large vents projecting 20 feet or more above the ground and extending straight down into the earth to a depth so great that a rock dropped from the top is never heard to strike bottom) are among the natural phenomena most accessible to the tourist. The Catacombs Cavern, the most beautiful of the entire group, resembles an ancient cathedral. The roof is "buttressed by massive columns, the walls and ceilings frescoed by a delicate coral-like formation traced in a thousand fanciful designs." About 150 caves in this interesting group have been discovered and have been explored more or less thoroughly.

To the south of the Lava Beds is Glass Mountain (7,622 feet), a gigantic mass of jet-black obsidian glass which glistens and sparkles in the sunlight. At its western base lies Medicine Lake, its deep-blue waters well stocked with fish and its wide, sandy beaches bordered by dense stands of lodgepole pine. A public camp, maintained by the Forest Service, is located on the lakeshore. To the northeast rises Mount Hoffmann (7,913 feet), while to the southwest are Little Mount Hoffmann and Little Glass Mountain.

North of the Lava Beds is the Tule Lake National Wildlife Refuge, and to the northwest and extending into Oregon is the Lower Klamath National Wildlife Refuge, which has been declared a National Historic Landmark. Established in 1908, it was one of the first major waterfowl reserves in the United States.

Sheep Rock and Pluto's Cave

At the foot of Shasta Pass 20 miles north of Sisson's Station (now Mount Shasta City), the first wagon road from the Sacramento Valley to Yreka led over a low divide from the eastern slopes of the mountain into Shasta Valley. There the bold and craggy summit of Sheep Rock rises 2,000 feet above the gray sagebrush and sand of the valley and 5,714 feet above the level of the sea. The rock's several square miles of comparatively level surface, dotted with bunch grass, long afforded one of the chief winter pastures of the wild mountain sheep that came down from the lofty ridges of Mount Shasta to the warm lava crags and plateaus of Sheep Rock, where the snow never lies deep. Cattlemen and sheepmen still follow the ruts of the old stage road at Sheep Rock.

A marker has been placed on Highway 97 about 15 miles northeast of Weed at a point 600 feet south of the crossing of the old emigrant trail *(SRL 517)*. The marker stands at the intersection of the old Military Pass Road from Fort Crook (Shasta County).

John Muir draws a graphic word picture of the leaping or "diving" habits of the Shasta flocks that once made Sheep Rock their winter rendezvous. The facts were related by a stock raiser who lived at the foot of the rock, and who had observed the movements of the sheep each winter. On one occasion hunters had pursued the little band to a narrow bench or lava headland 150 feet and more above the floor of the valley and very nearly perpendicular. There the hunters had expected to trap the entire flock, only to find themselves eluded by the wily animals, which "made the frightful descent without evincing any extraordinary concern, hugging the rock closely, and controlling the velocity of their half-falling, half-leaping movements by striking at short intervals and holding back with their cushioned, rubber feet upon small ledges and roughened inclines until near the bottom, when they 'sailed off' into the free air and lighted on their feet, but with their bodies so nearly in a vertical position that they appeared to be diving."

Near Sheep Rock in a north–northwesterly direction from the foot of the pass is Pluto's Cave, "a long cavern sloping to the northward, nearly a mile in length, thirty or forty feet wide, and fifty or more in height, regular in form and direction like a railroad tunnel, and probably formed by the flowing away of a current of lava after the hardening of the surface." The place is not easily found, its several "mouths," caused by the falling in of portions of the roof, all being on a level with the surface of the ground. At one of these entrances, "where the light and shelter is good," says Muir, "I found many of the heads and horns of wild sheep, and the remains of campfires, no doubt those of Indian hunters who in stormy weather had camped there and feasted after the fatigues of the chase. A wild picture that must have formed on a dark night—the glow of the fire, the circle of crouching savages around it seen through the smoke, the dead game, and the weird darkness and half-darkness of the walls of the cavern, a picture of cave-dwellers at home in the stone age!" William H. Brewer visited Pluto's Cave on October 10, 1863, shortly after its discovery.

Muir, who loved and explored Mount Shasta from summit to base, wrote with characteristic enthusiasm: "Far better than climbing the mountain is going around its warm fertile base, enjoying its bounties like a bee circling around a bank of flowers. The distance is about a hundred miles, [and] a good level road may be found all the way round, by Shasta Valley, Sheep Rock, Elk Flat, Huckleberry Valley, Squaw Valley, following for a considerable portion of the way the old Emigrant Road, which lies along the east disk of the mountain, and is deeply worn by the wagons of the early gold-seekers." Portions of this old road are still used by the Forest Service and it is possible during the summer months to circle Mount Shasta by automobile, a distance of 65 miles from

Weed or Mount Shasta City. The road takes one through aspen thickets and forests of Shasta fir, across glacial washes, and to points where superb views may be had, all within a few miles of the snow belt.

Marble Mountain

The Marble Mountain Wilderness Area in the Klamath National Forest is a region of magnificent mountains and forests covering 237,527 acres. In it lies Marble Mountain, from which the area derives its name.

Lying between the Klamath River and its tributary, Scott River, the Marble Mountain Range culminates in a castellated peak, 7,396 feet in elevation. Composed of limestone, a large proportion of which is marble of high commercial value, the rugged grandeur and the "monumental purity" of this massive upheaval long inspired the traditions and superstitions of the Indians, who knew the great peak as the "White Mountain."

Owing to its striking appearance, Marble Mountain served as a landmark for early pioneers, and the old Kelsey Trail, lying almost directly at its base, was one of the first paths ever blazed across these mountains into Scott Valley. Travelers over this rugged old trail almost invariably checked their mules to gaze upward with wonder and amazement at the beetling cliffs and towering domes of Marble Mountain rising above them. This route, at best a rough and dangerous one for man and beast, was long ago abandoned for more accessible passes through the mountains.

The California–Oregon Trail

Lying halfway between San Francisco Bay and the Columbia River, the Siskiyou region, first crossed by pre-pioneer trappers and settlers, was soon marked by a well-defined route of travel. This trail was the principal thoroughfare during the gold period (1850–60), and down to the present the tide of trade and commerce has continued to flow over it. In general it has been called the California–Oregon Trail, but it should be noted that this term has been applied to several routes to and from Oregon through northern California. The first in time was the coast route, through Del Norte County, blazed by Jedediah Strong Smith and followed for a time by Hudson's Bay Company trappers. In 1830 Peter Skene Ogden opened up a route by way of Klamath Lake, and in his footsteps came Michel La Framboise, the leader of trapping expeditions from the north during the years from 1830 to 1845. The central route leading up the Sacramento River Canyon was first crossed in its entire length by Ewing Young in 1834. During the 1850's, when gold mining was the chief industry of the Siskiyou region, two variations of the latter route developed, one of which led around the eastern base of Mount Shasta while the other crossed over Trinity and Scott mountains into Scott Valley and thence to Yreka.

Early in 1827, Ogden and his party of Hudson's Bay Company trappers wintered on the streams to the east and north of Mount Shasta. From his journal, written on poorly cured slabs of beaver skins, we learn that Ogden and his men left the headwaters of the Des Chutes River in the latter part of November 1826. Guided by the indomitable Thomas McKay, who, the year before, had accompanied Finnan McDonald over the same route, the party crossed the divide into the country of the "Clammitte" (Klamath), a route followed by hundreds of trappers in the interval between 1826 and 1845.

What is apparently the first recorded crossing of the Siskiyou Mountains is found in Ogden's journal for March 13 and 22, 1827. On the 13th Ogden wrote:

"We left the Sasty Forks in our rear taking W.N.W. 8 miles encamped by a lofty range of mountains," and on March 22 "reached a fine large river having crossed the mtns," probably the Siskiyou divide, the stream no doubt being the Rogue River.

Ewing Young in 1834, on his way to settle in Oregon, was the first to follow the California–Oregon Trail around the western base of Mount Shasta. A scarcity of cattle in the Willamette Valley led Young to return to the San Francisco Bay region in 1837. With a drove of 700 Spanish longhorns and about 20 other men started for Oregon. On reaching Shasta Valley Young found that they had succeeded in driving 680 of the animals over the rugged mountains of the Sacramento River Canyon. Again in 1843 the enterprising Joseph Gale, with a much larger herd of livestock, made the same difficult climb.

The old trail and the difficulties experienced by the many early travelers who passed over it are described in the journals of Philip L. Edwards, diarist of the Young party of 1837; in the George Emmons report of the Wilkes Expedition in 1841; in the account by Lansford W. Hastings of his trip in 1843; and in the diary of James Clyman, depicting vividly a journey in 1845. By 1840 California began to attract settlers, and every year of that decade saw an increasing number of emigrants passing over the California–Oregon Trail from the Willamette Valley to the Sacramento Valley, the climax being reached during the years of the gold rush, 1848–49 and the early 1850's.

Lieutenant Emmons and his men camped on September 28, 1841, at the foot of the Boundary Range (the Siskiyou Mountains) within sight of that unique landmark known as Pilot Rock, "a singular, isolated rock, which stands like a tower on the top of the ridge, rising above the surrounding forest with a bare and apparently unbroken surface.... From its top an extensive country is overlooked, and as soon as the party came in sight of it a dense column of smoke arose, which was thought to be a signal made by the Klamet Indians, to the Shaste tribe, of the approach of our party." Charles Wilkes, commander of the entire expedition, named this Emmons' Peak, in honor of the officer in charge of the California contingent of the expedition, but the name Pilot Rock has since been applied to it. Located in southern Oregon, it is visible for many miles on both sides of the mountains.

Fear of the Indians characterized the Wilkes

Expedition through the Siskiyous, causing the party to avoid all contact with the natives and thus frustrating one of the main objects of the trip, that of making scientific observations of the Indians in their natural habitat. Ascending the Siskiyou Mountains on September 29, the party was in constant fear of these so-called "Rogues." To the travelers the whole mountainside seemed "admirably adapted for an ambuscade." However, little difficulty was encountered except from fires set by the hostiles. At the summit the men had their first glorious view of the "Klamet Valley," and of "Mount Shaste, a high, snowy peak, of a sugar-loaf form, which rose through the distant haze."

Descending the southern slope of the Siskiyous, the expedition pitched their tents on "Otter Creek [now Camp Creek] within a mile of the Klamet River," and on October 1 they camped on the Shasta River, somewhere near the site of the present town of Montague. There they found the Indians spearing salmon, which were plentiful. Near the present Gazelle, not far from Sheep Rock, large herds of antelope, as well as longhorned mountain sheep, were seen the next day. At midday the party left the Shasta Valley and encamped on a stream near the site of the present town of Edgewood (formerly Butteville). This place was the camping ground of a tribe of Indians, which Emmons observed closely and which he pronounced "a fine-looking race," extremely skillful in the manufacture and use of the bow and arrow. Continuing their journey on October 3, the travelers "entered the forest on the slopes of the Shaste Range.... After passing this ridge, they soon met the head waters of the Sacramento, flowing to the southward, and their camp was pitched on the banks of another stream, that came from the Shaste Peak." This was in Strawberry Valley.

Little escaped the observation of James Clyman when he climbed the Siskiyous and made his way down the Sacramento River Canyon in 1845. His diary is full of vivid descriptions revealing the rugged character of the old trail. Like other early travelers he was constantly on guard against Indian attacks. Climbing the "Siskiew mountain" on June 23, the party neared the summit, where there was "a bad thicket to pass whare nearly all the parties passing this Trail have been attacted." The Clyman company, however, met with no misadventure and soon came in sight of the vast wilderness lying to the south, "wild and awfully sublime." On June 24, the "Clamet" (Klamath) River was crossed, a few hundred feet east of the present bridge near the site of the now extinct lumbering camp of Klamathon (1890–1900) near the mouth of Willow Creek. Following up Willow Creek on June 25, the emigrants passed over Little Shasta River, where they made camp. The unique volcanic character of Shasta Valley, with its "round conicle peaks of rock standing out in an uneven plain," appeared as striking to James Clyman as it does to the present-day tourist who looks upon its strange beauty for the first time. They traversed the valley the next day, and, after

crossing the Shasta River, set up camp on a site near the present town of Edgewood. From this point Clyman describes Pilot Rock, plainly visible across the Oregon border to the north. They resumed the line of march on June 28, and "the course of the trail lay through the valley west of Black Butte," later known as Wagon Valley. To the east of the pass rose the snowy peaks of Mount Shasta, while on the west stood Mount Eddy, the whole region then magnificently timbered.

This old trail, broken by explorers and trappers and followed by early emigrants in the 1840's, became a well-defined pack trail in the 1850's, thronged by gold seekers in their mad rush to the mines. Pack trains transported supplies during the years of the gold rush. In 1860 a stage road from Yreka to Upper Soda Springs and from there down the Sacramento River Canyon was completed by Stone and Company, but with the coming of the winter rains floods carried away all the bridges, restricting stage travel to that section of the road between Yreka and Upper Soda Springs. From that point southward, transportation was continued by pack train to the Pit River, where stages again took up the journey. Not until 1870 did stage travel become permanently established down the entire length of the Sacramento River Canyon.

The first wagon party to cross the Siskiyou Mountains into California was led by Lindsey Applegate in June 1849. After climbing the mountains with their six wagons, the little party crossed Shasta Valley to what became known as Wagon Valley. The feelings of remoteness and the anxiety about the Indians caused the emigrants to abandon their project and to return to Oregon, leaving four of the cumbersome wagons to rot in the wilderness. Governor Joseph Lane of Oregon Territory, en route to the California goldfields in 1850, also abandoned a wagon in this locality. The iron from these vehicles was salvaged and sold during World War I.

The first wagon team (1854) and the first transportation by stage and freight team (the California Stage Company, 1856) from the Sacramento Valley crossed the Pit River at Fall River Mills. Continuing northwest, the road passed around the eastern base of Mount Shasta, down through Sheep Rock Pass into Shasta Valley, and then again northwest to Yreka. From there it continued northeast, crossing the Shasta River about five miles northwest of Montague. The Klamath River was ferried just north of its junction with Willow Creek, where the road became identical with the older trail followed by trappers on their way over the Siskiyou Mountains. That part of the road which passed east of Mount Shasta was used for about a year, when Indian troubles caused traffic to be transferred to the Yreka–Callahan–Shasta route, which became known as the California–Oregon Stage Road and was operated until the advent of the railroad in 1887–88.

Henry Slicer had already opened a stage line to Callahan's in 1854. After abandoning the route around the eastern base of Mount Shasta, the

California Stage Company bought out Greathouse and Slicer and began, at great expense, to complete the road to the town of Shasta (in early days sometimes called Shasta City). This road was pushed over Trinity Mountain in 1857, and in 1859 Scott Mountain was also crossed. Meanwhile the Oregon Stage Company had completed its turnpike over the Siskiyous. It connected with the California Stage Line at Yreka in 1860, and a through route was thus staged for the first time from Portland, Oregon, to Sacramento, California. It was over this route that the first telegraph line from California to Oregon was constructed.

Two and one-half miles southeast of Callahan's on the road to Carrville and Trinity Center, a former stage station still stands at the foot of Scott Mountain.

After 1870 the route from Yreka to the Klamath River went by way of the Anderson Grade, crossing the Shasta River about four miles north of Yreka. On this road the Ten Mile House, a stage station of the 1870's, still stands. Ascending the mountain over a high-line grade, the road descended to the Klamath River about six miles south of Cottonwood (Henley), where the river was ferried. The old trappers' trail over the Siskiyous continued to be used from this point on. The magnificent Pioneer Bridge on Highway 99 was erected over the Shasta River three miles north of Yreka in 1931 and dedicated to the memory of the early-day stage drivers who traveled this road.

Stopping Places on the California–Oregon Trail

Along the old California–Oregon Trail many historic spots—strategic stopping places for a long succession of travelers—invite the interest of the present-day tourist. They were, at first, mere campsites (in some cases on or in close proximity to the ancient rancherías of the Indians) where the trailblazers and their immediate successors—the trappers and explorers of the 1830's and 1840's—stopped on their way through the wilderness. The sites have been identified by means of diaries and journals kept by a few of these earliest travelers. Before long, the faint trails of the pathfinders were being widened by the feet of pre-pioneer settlers seeking new homes in Oregon or California, and they, too, have left records of favored campsites on streams or by springs of clear mountain water or in green meadows.

With the discovery of gold in California, the procession down the Oregon Trail became a flood of humanity bound for the numerous El Doradoes that California had opened. Hotels or inns were built on the early campgrounds, and proved popular stopping places for gold seekers and settlers. With the coming of the first wagons a road was constructed, and soon the picturesque mule trains were superseded by freighters and stagecoaches. Then the wayside inns became stage stations, with towns growing up about them. When the Southern Pacific Railroad was constructed from Redding into Oregon in 1886–87, its route was practically identical with that of the California–Oregon Trail and portions of the early stage road. Many of the railroad stations are on the exact line of the first trail, or very close to it.

As one traveled north, the first station on the Oregon Trail passing through Siskiyou County was at Upper Soda Springs, a mile below Shasta Springs, where summer tourists today enjoy the mountain scenery, the piney air, and the pure water. Once a camp of Hudson's Bay Company trappers, the soda springs with their health-giving waters were doubtless also a rendezvous of the Indians. During the years 1860–70, Upper Soda Springs was the terminus for the stage line run from Yreka by Stone and Company. From that time until the building of the railroad it continued to be a stopping place on the through stage line to Oregon. The old stage station no longer stands. It was located in the bend of the Sacramento River just north of Dunsmuir.

The next camp on the old trail, which here ran about half a mile west of the present Highway 99, was located in Strawberry Valley, where a settlement grew up in the early 1850's. A post office was established in 1870 under the name of Berryvale. For 12 years J. H. Sisson was postmaster and hotelkeeper. When the railroad came through in 1887, the station, one mile east of Berryvale, was named Sisson's, and the town that soon grew up on the new site was called Sisson, a name it bore until 1924, when it was changed to Mount Shasta.

Sisson's Hotel at Berryvale was a favorite summer resort and outfitting point for early-day mountain climbers. From there, trails radiated in all directions: Mount Shasta, with its glaciers and panoramas of northern California, southern Oregon, and western Nevada; Black Butte, an odd cinder cone that sits like a dwarf in the shadow of Mount Shasta's glowing height; Mount Eddy, with its lovely Shasta lilies and gemlike Castle Lake; and the simple "flowery fringes" and wooded streams of Strawberry Valley.

The route of the old stage road that passed before Sisson's door was identical with that of the present road that goes by the State Fish Hatchery west of town. Sisson's Hotel, built about 1865 and destroyed by fire in 1916, stood almost at the top of the low hill just before one enters the hatchery gate. Across the road is the site of the Strawberry Valley stage station (SRL 396). On the same side of the road as this site is a small white house with a red roof. This was the old post office and store kept by Mrs. S. J. Fellows, who followed J. H. Sisson as postmaster of Berryvale.

About 15 miles north of Berryvale the old trail passed the site of Butteville (now Edgewood), a camping ground mentioned in most of the early journals. There in 1851 William and Jackson Brown built a log cabin, and in 1856 W. Starr opened a store. Starr was succeeded by Joseph Foreman and John Lennox in 1859, and in 1860 by Joseph Cavanaugh, a genial Irishman. Cavanaugh's hotel became a popular stage station on the California–Oregon Road, and he was still operating his establishment there in the 1880's.

Leaving Butteville, travelers on the California–Oregon Trail next stopped where the settlement of Edson's (called Gazelle since 1870) later grew up. There a Mr. Brady started a station very early, and in 1853 the place was purchased by E. B. and J. R. Edson, who conducted it as a station on the stage road for many years. The Edson farm, with its beautiful home, was a very prosperous place in the 1880's.

From Edson's the trail proceeded straight north across Shasta Valley, forded the Shasta River near the site of Montague, where there was an important campsite, and continued to Willow Creek. After 1850 the trail, which had developed into a stage road, made a detour to Yreka, turning northwest eight miles north of Edson's. From Yreka this road went northeast, crossing the Shasta River five miles northwest of Montague and rejoining the old trail before it reached Willow Creek.

Near where Willow Creek runs into the Klamath River from the south, the next stopping place on the old emigrant trail was not far from the site of the later settlement of Klamathon (still a flag station on the railroad). Proceeding downstream three miles to Cottonwood Creek, which runs into the Klamath from the north, the trail followed up Cottonwood Creek Canyon and crossed the summit of the Siskiyous about where the present railroad passes over. The last camp before reaching Oregon was made in the canyon of Cottonwood Creek just before the trail began climbing over the mountain.

In 1870 the stage road into Oregon was rerouted over the so-called Anderson Grade. Cottonwood (later Henley) was the place where stage coaches and freighters en route from Yreka to Oregon changed horses from 1860 to 1887, when the completion of the railroad ended stage operations.

Trails of the Northern El Dorado

The first Argonauts from Oregon passed through Siskiyou County without stopping to prospect its streams, and no mining was done there until the summer of 1850. As early as June of that year gold seekers penetrated the wild and rugged Salmon Mountains. Crossing the ridge from the North Fork of the Trinity River, they came upon the South Fork of the Salmon River, down which they followed to the mouth of the North Fork, where rich diggings were found. The camp established at this point came to be known as the Forks of the Salmon, and during the summer several hundred men gathered there. From this central point they spread out up the North Fork of the Salmon River and over the divide into the Scott River Valley.

Meanwhile, a party of miners had traveled the length of the Klamath River from its mouth to the Shasta River, panning for gold at every bar. "It was this group of miners," says David Rhys Jones, "that established the course of the Klamath River below the junction of the Shasta. From that time on, the river that had been variously known as the Clamitte, the Klamet, Indian Scalp River, and Smith River, has borne the name by which it was known near its source." Again, Jones says that "prior to 1850 all maps delineating the Klamath River represented its source and upper course correctly—as it had been observed by trappers. The course of the river below Shasta River was unexplored, but the mouth of a large stream in southern Oregon had been crossed by Jedediah S. Smith in 1828. This was the mouth of the Rogue. So the Hudson's Bay Company map presented to Wilkes, and published as part of his travel records, shows the Klamath River turning back into Oregon through the Siskiyous, below the Shasta, and emptying into the ocean at the mouth of the Rogue."

When winter approached, the miners on the Klamath left for the settlements of the Sacramento Valley, following a southerly course and passing the future sites of Yreka and Greenhorn, where gold was discovered on the creek. A few miles to the east they came upon the Oregon Trail, where they found a fresh wagon track. Camping that night near the site of Edson's, they reached Wagon Valley the following day. There they found the abandoned wagon that Governor Joseph Lane had recently transported across the Siskiyou Mountains. Later they overtook Lane himself, bound for the goldfields.

In San Francisco two years before, while on his way to organize the Oregon territory, Lane had resisted the gold fever, but in the summer of 1850 it hit him. With the goldfields on the Sierra Nevada as an objective, he crossed the border into California. At this time the Lane party did a little incidental prospecting on the Klamath River and on the Shasta River at Joe Lane's Bar near the mouth of Yreka Creek. The following year Governor Lane came to Siskiyou County at the head of a large company of men bound for Scott Bar, where they did considerable mining.

Scott Valley was first explored in 1850 by a group of miners led by John Scott, who had crossed the Salmon Mountains from the North Fork of the Salmon River. These men panned for gold at a point on Scott River named for their leader, Scott Bar. Indians soon drove them from this location. Returning to the Salmon River and crossing the mountains to the Trinity River, they spread the news of their discovery of gold at Scott Bar. Many parties started at once for the new location and the place was soon overcrowded with miners. As a result, prospecting parties spread over the entire region, and many new diggings, the scene of thriving camps in 1851, were uncovered.

One such find was the chance discovery of gold on the site later occupied by Yreka. This location attracted little attention at the time, for a rich bonanza was found at Ingall's Gulch on Greenhorn Creek soon afterward. Its discoverers came to Scott Bar for provisions, where they organized as secretly as possible and returned to Ingall's Gulch. They were followed, however, and while they lay asleep their claims were occupied by others. This was the beginning of mining on Greenhorn Creek, in January 1851.

Salmon River Camps

The first mining camp up the Salmon River from its mouth is Somes' Bar. Today a country store there serves a small scattered population. Continuing up the river, one finds it difficult to imagine that in the early 1850's every bar, creek, and gulch along the river's course teemed with miners.

Forks of Salmon had a population of several hundred in the summer of 1850, although fewer than 50 spent the winter of 1850–51 there. Before winter had passed, the report of rich diggings attracted miners from all directions, many rushing to the spot without supplies. As a result, when late snows blocked the trails in March, thousands all up and down the Salmon River and its branches were on the verge of starvation. Forks of Salmon still exists as a small settlement.

Sawyer's Bar, on the North Fork of the Salmon River, is today a town of 75 people. Most of the wooden buildings, over a century old, along its picturesque, winding main street were destroyed by fire on July 16, 1963, and August 12, 1966. The area is a center of forest fires nearly every summer, but, until these recent fires, the town itself was spared. Fortunately, the outstanding landmark at the edge of town was saved from the flames. This is St. Joseph's Catholic Church, built in the 1850's of whipsawed lumber. The story of St. Joseph's is the story of Father Florian Schwenninger, O.S.B., the "Padre of Paradise Flat." A Benedictine monk from the Austrian Tyrol, he came to California as a missionary and served the people of Sawyer's Bar and many other Siskiyou County mining towns for over ten years. He was schoolteacher, musician, and artist, as well as pastor, counselor, and friend. He even carved the wooden grave markers in the cemetery. Worn out by his labors and travels over the tortuous roads and trails of the mining country, he moved to Marysville in 1866 and there engaged in lighter work until his death two years later. The oil painting of The Crucifixion that Father Florian brought so carefully from Austria still hangs over the altar in St. Joseph's Church, which has been restored and is used for services one Sunday a month. Paradise Flat, the little piece of ground on which it stands, has never been mined and is thought to contain a small fortune in gold.

Four miles west of Sawyer's Bar on the Little North Fork of the Salmon River is one of California's covered bridges. Although it looks as if it might have been there since gold rush days, the 82-foot bridge, now bypassed by the road to Forks of Salmon, was actually built in 1924. It is being preserved by the U. S. Forest Service and Siskiyou County. South of Sawyer's Bar are a number of quartz mines, chief among them being the Black Bear Mine seven or eight miles to the southwest. Material for the mill for this mine was carried over the mountains on muleback or dragged in on sleds by oxen.

Cecilville, a tiny hamlet, is located on the South Fork of the Salmon River in a remote section of the county. It was reached only by trail

Old Town of Sawyer's Bar in 1954

until 1926, when a road was constructed from Sawyer's Bar, passing near the old Black Bear Mine.

For many years the only means of communication between the Salmon River region and Yreka during the winter season was over the snow-covered Jackson Creek Pass 6,000 feet high. Until late in June, mail and supplies had to be brought in on the backs of mules shod with snowshoes. In 1926 a new road was built up the Salmon River by way of Somes' Bar. In summer this rugged region attracts vacationers to its wooded mountains and clear trout streams.

Scott Valley

Scott Valley, named after John Scott, the discoverer of gold at Scott Bar, is still the beautiful, "rich bottom, with fertile ranches, surrounded with high and very steep mountains, rough and rugged, and furrowed into very deep canyons," described by William H. Brewer, who visited the region in the autumn of 1863. Formerly famed for its rich gold production, the valley is now devoted to agriculture.

According to Brewer, Scott Bar was once quite an important town. "Placers, rich and abundant, called together a busy and thriving population. ...But the placers are mostly worked out, the population has started after new mines and fresh excitements, over half the houses are empty, four-fifths of the population gone, business has decayed, and the town is dilapidated. We stopped at a rather large hotel, now desolate—its few boarders look lonely in it. ...

"The mines are not all exhausted, the deeper bars still pay. Deep excavations are dug below the river bed, large water wheels, turned by the swift current, pump the water out of these claims, and some are paying well.... The big wheels creaked dolefully all night long, and seemed to bewail the decline of the decaying town."

The Scott Bar of 1850 was located a few hundred yards above and on the opposite bank of Scott River from the Scott Bar of 1851 and succeeding years. The old trail of the 1850's zigzagged for three miles through the precipitous canyon that lay between Scott Bar and the mouth of the Scott River, the canyon proper being, in many places, at least 3,000 feet deep. In the early

1850's this great gorge was teeming with life. Among the bustling camps of the region were French Bar (one of the largest), Johnson's Bar, Poorman's Bar, Lytle's Bar, Slapjack Bar, Michigan Bar, and Junction Bar. Governor Lane worked Lane's Gulch on Whitney Hill near Scott Bar in 1851.

Some of the old buildings in the vicinity of Scott Bar are still intact. The Quartz Hill Mine has yielded millions, and continued to operate into the twentieth century.

Etna Mills (now Etna), originally known as Rough and Ready Mills, grew up around the flour mill established there in 1856 in competition with a neighboring concern known as the Etna Mills, erected in 1854. There was considerable rivalry between the two communities, but the newer place finally won out as a town, when in 1863 the post office was shifted from Etna Mills to the more successful Rough and Ready. Since there was another Rough and Ready post office in Nevada County, the name of its rival, Etna Mills, was bestowed upon it. The present abbreviated title was legalized by the legislature in 1874, but the name of the post office was not shortened until 1924.

Etna, now a town of about 600 inhabitants, lies in the midst of a rich agricultural district shut in by the heavily forested Salmon Mountains on the west and the Scott Mountains on the south and east.

Callahan's Ranch

Callahan's Ranch (or Callahan), near the junction of the East and South forks of the Scott River, was the first stopping place after crossing Scott Mountain from the south. Here in the autumn of 1851 M. B. Callahan opened a public house and store. Soon after Callahan sold out in 1855, the place became the terminus of Greathouse and Slicer's stage line from Yreka, which used the two Concord coaches that Henry Slicer had brought over the Siskiyou Mountains from Oregon in 1854, the first in Siskiyou County. At Callahan's, passengers were transferred to mules for the difficult journey over Scott Mountain to the Trinity River and over the Trinity Mountains to French Gulch and the town of Shasta.

Callahan's old station is still on the map. Its main street is reminiscent of early mining and stagecoach days, although some of the old buildings are deserted. The Callahan Ranch Hotel, built in 1854, is one of the most picturesque old stage stops left in California. The entire township contains fewer than 300 persons.

Fort Jones

The town of Wheelock (named after its founder) was started in 1851 as a hotel and stage station on the road from Yreka to Callahan's and Shasta. As the settlement grew, it was variously known as Wheelock, Scottsburg, and Ottitiewa (the name of a group of Shasta Indians). In 1860 the present name of Fort Jones was adopted from the United States Army camp that had once existed one mile to the south (on the present road to the Scott River Valley Airport). This old military outpost (SRL 317), established by Major Edward H. Fitzgerald of the First United States Dragoons on October 16, 1852, served as protection against the Indians during the 1850's. The first log houses were later replaced by frame buildings, which in turn were sold and moved when the post was abandoned in June 1858.

West of Fort Jones, Oro Fino, on Oro Fino Creek, and Mugginsville, in Quartz Valley, were booming gold camps in the 1850's, but by 1880 Oro Fino, where an old brick building remains, had become depopulated. Mugginsville was the center of quartz mining in the region in the 1850's and 1860's. Here an eight-stamp mill was erected in 1852, and a sawmill and a gristmill on Shackleford Creek were added in 1854. The place polled 300 votes in 1860. Oro Fino and Mugginsville are a few miles northwest of the later town of Greenview.

Deadwood

Northeast of Fort Jones, at the junction of Deadwood and Cherry creeks, the town of Deadwood once thrived. It was there that young Joaquin Miller wrote his first poem, in honor of the marriage of Deadwood's cook to a woman in Yreka. Miller recited the poem at the reception given the bride and groom on their return to Deadwood.

In 1854–55 Deadwood ranked second to Yreka in importance, and Brewer says that it was still "a busy little mining town in 1863." The site of Deadwood is marked. It may be reached by a narrow, winding mountain road, but nothing is left of it today.

One of Deadwood's neighbors in mining days was Hardscrabble, a little settlement in Hi You Gulch, while on Indian Creek was the town of Indian Creek and on McAdams' Creek was Hooperville, both prosperous camps in the 1850's.

Klamath River Camps

Among the more thriving gold bars of the Klamath River during the 1850's (Mead's, Hamburg, China, Walker, Masonic, and Fort Goff), Hamburg Bar, located a few miles below the mouth of Scott River, was the most important. Above the mouth of the river, on the Klamath, were Oak and Virginia bars. All along the river picturesque water wheels were to be seen. A few dip wheels still operate on the Klamath, most of

Callahan Ranch Hotel

them being used to raise water for irrigation. Today State Highway 96, very narrow in parts, gives access to the Klamath and its old towns.

Brewer, in October 1863, wrote: "We passed what was once the town of Hamburg, two years ago a bustling village—a large cluster of miners' cabins, three hotels, three stores, two billiard saloons, and all the other accompaniments of a mining town—now all is gone. The placers were worked out, the cabins became deserted, and the floods of two years ago finished its history by carrying off all the houses, or nearly all—a camp of Klamath Indians on the river bank is the only population at present! . . . Just below were some Indian graves. A little enclosure of sticks surrounded them. Each grave is a conical mound, and lying on them, or hanging on poles over them, are the worldly goods of the deceased—the baskets in which they gathered their acorns, their clothing and moccasins, arms and implements, strings of beads, and other ornaments—decaying along with their owners.

"In contrast with this was a sadder sight—a cluster of graves of the miners who had died while the town remained. Boards had once been set up at their graves, but most had rotted off and fallen—the rest will soon follow. Bushes have grown over the graves, and soon they, as well as the old town, will be forgotten. . . . Alas, how many a sad history is hidden in the neglected and forgotten graves that are scattered among the wild mountains that face the Pacific!

"The population has not entirely left this portion of the river, however. Here and there may be seen a white man, and industrious Chinamen patiently ply with rockers for the yellow dust."

From time to time mining resumed at Hamburg Bar, but today it is a quiet hamlet of only a few dozen inhabitants.

About midway between Scott Bar and Happy Camp, Seiad (Sciad) Creek runs into the Klamath River from the northeast. Brewer, on his way down the river, visited the spot, describing it as "a fertile little flat of about a hundred acres, the best ranch perhaps in the entire county of Siskiyou. It is known as the Sciad Ranch. We crossed the river by a ferry to it. . . . It is a delightful spot —it seems an oasis in a desert. Here lives a thriving New York farmer . . . named Reeves, and he is making money faster than if he were mining for gold. He treated us very kindly indeed and we luxuriated on delicious apples, pears, and plums. His table groaned under the weight of well-cooked food, in pleasing contrast with the miserable taverns of the last few days. . . . He came here in 1854, and says that the first year he raised twenty thousand pounds of potatoes per acre, which he sold for *fifteen cents per pound!*"

Brewer and his party left the Seiad Ranch on October 26, traveling for "thirty miles over a good but rough trail." For 18 miles down the Klamath River they enjoyed "the most picturesque views to be imagined, the mountains rising three or four thousand feet on both sides from the swift river." The travelers passed many deserted cabins and houses before reaching Happy Camp, one of the oldest settlements in Siskiyou County and in 1863 already on the decline. Today Happy Camp is much as it was in the early days, with a few modern houses scattered among the old buildings that date from mining days.

At Elk Creek, one and a half miles below Happy Camp, some 300 men worked the stream in 1856, making from $10 to $20 a day, while north of Happy Camp between 400 and 500 miners panned for gold in Indian Creek and its branches. Twelve miles up the creek was the little settlement of Indiantown, already "falling into piteous dilapidation" when Brewer, in 1863, stopped at the "miserable hole" which once served as a hotel.

The Klamath River country experienced a revival of mining activity in 1931. New options were taken and fresh capital invested. It is estimated that between 300 and 400 placer claims were being operated along the Klamath that year.

Pick-i-a-wish Camp, on the Klamath River, just below the old mining town of Happy Camp, is the scene of a yearly Indian festival. Here, in the light of the August moon, Indians from the surrounding settlements and ranches gather and, with beating of drums, dance the Deerskin Dance, the Brush Dance, and the Coyote Dance. Many legends still cling about these Indian settlements and are told by their old men and women.

Cottonwood

The little town of Cottonwood, located on Cottonwood Creek just north of Hornbrook on the old Oregon Road, was the center of trade for a number of rich mining locations during the 1850's. The flats and gulches nearby presented a strange medley of names: Stone, Dan Davies', Dutch, Rich, Printer's, Rocky, Carruck, and Milk Cañon gulches, and Todhunter, Buffalo, Milk Ranch, and Turnip Patch flats, with John Hatch Hill, Brass Wire Channel, and Ranchería Creek added to the colorful array.

"Cottonwood," said Brewer in October 1863, "is a little mining town, once busy and hustling, now mostly 'played out,' two-thirds of its houses empty, its business dull, the whole place looking as if stricken with a curse." Cottonwood was established as a post office in 1856 under the name of Henley. In 1881 it still had a hotel, a store, a saloon, and a blacksmith shop, but today only one or two old landmarks and the cemetery remain.

Yreka

In Yreka, with its streets lined with old-fashioned houses, an atmosphere of adventure lingers, heightened by the tales told of stagecoaches, Indians, and fabulous gold nuggets, and by the many traces of mining in the hills nearby. Among the old buildings still standing in good condition is the Odd Fellows Hall, at Oregon and Miner streets, a two-story brick structure erected in 1859. Although it has been somewhat remodeled, the upper story of the front portion remains in its original state. The former Arcade Saloon at 219 West Miner Street and the meat market at 319 are other old-timers. The first log house, built about 1853, stands on North Street between North Gold Street and North West Street.

At the southern end of Yreka is the Siskiyou County Museum, housed in a replica of the old Callahan Ranch Hotel at Callahan.

In March 1851 a gold strike was made at Yreka Flats, an event that brought 2,000 men to the spot in less than six weeks. This discovery was made by Abraham Thompson in a ravine later known as Black Gulch. The camp that grew up was called Thompson's Dry Diggings and was located on a knoll near a spring at the intersection of the present Yama and Discovery streets in Yreka.

Meanwhile, miners' cabins were built for three miles along Yreka Creek from Greenhorn to Hawkinsville, and business soon moved away from the Flats and nearer to the creek. A town, at first called Shasta Butte City, was laid out on the present site of Yreka in May 1851. In order to avoid confusion with the older Shasta City (in Shasta County) the name was changed to Yreka (I-e-ka, the Indian word for Mount Shasta) when the county was organized in 1852. That name was retained by the legislature when the place was made the county seat of Siskiyou County.

Among the stirring episodes that enlivened the early history of Yreka, the Greenhorn War of 1855 was perhaps the most exciting. This was a contest over water rights waged by two mining factions, the Yreka Flats Ditch Association and the miners on Lower Greenhorn Creek. The latter precipitated the war when they cut the Yreka Flats Ditch because it was diverting water from their claims on the creek. The matter was taken before the local court, which supported the Yreka faction and enjoined against further cutting of the ditch. The injunction was disobeyed and the guilty party arrested. This was the signal for the Greenhorn miners to act. In a body they marched to the Yreka jail and got the prisoner released after an encounter with the law. Nevertheless, the decision of the court stood, and the Yreka Flats Association continued to use the water brought from Greenhorn Creek.

Many mining camps formerly existed near Yreka. Two miles to the north was Hawkinsville, where a number of very early camps were concentrated, one of them being Frogtown, the chief center of trade in 1851. Others were Long Gulch, Rich Gulch, Canal Gulch, and Rocky Gulch. The present brick Catholic church at Hawkinsville was remodeled from a structure originally built in 1858. To the south of Yreka was Greenhorn, a settlement of miners' cabins, while up Greenhorn Creek was Wheeler's Store.

The name Greenhorn is typical of the unique nomenclature that grew out of the rough life of the Argonauts. A company of miners had dug a ditch some distance back from the creek, but finding their claims unprofitable they had abandoned the location. A new arrival, at once dubbed a "greenhorn" by his more experienced companions, asked where he could find a good place to work. Thinking to enjoy a joke at his expense, the miners directed the young fellow to the hill they had just vacated. The "greenhorn," setting to work on the abandoned ditch, was rewarded by a rich strike. He kept his find a secret, and since no one dreamed of his success the joke grew bigger every day. When the jokers finally learned that the "greenhorn" had been quietly working the richest ground along the creek, there was a rush for claims on the new lead. To perpetuate the joke, so the story goes, the creek was baptized "Greenhorn," a name it still bears. Similar stories have been told in other sections of the mining regions in California to explain the origin of this name.

Vast piles of rock and gravel which fill the canyons and gullies with debris in the hills to the south of Yreka give evidence of early mining operations. These relics, like the graves of a forgotten race of giants, will long disfigure the landscape with their gaunt, gray sterility, covering spots once made beautiful with the delicate hues of wildflowers, the pale blue of juniper berries, and the autumn flame of the Oregon grape.

Klamath Peggy

The story of Klamath Peggy forms a romantic episode in Yreka's history. Peggy's people, the Klamaths, were on the warpath against the encroaching whites, but trying to avoid bloodshed, this Indian woman traveled 20 miles over rough mountains to warn the white men. When the Klamath warriors approached the town along the devious trails of the brush-covered hills, they found it strongly guarded by sentries and were forced to retreat.

For years after this event, Klamath Peggy, fearing to associate with her kinsmen, lived among the people of Yreka, who never forgot the service she had rendered. When the remnants of her tribe were finally placed on the reservation four miles to the south of town, Peggy was pensioned and cared for until her death at the advanced age of 105 years. Then all Yreka paid tribute to her memory. The humble grave of Klamath Peggy at the old Indian Reservation on Greenhorn's slopes memorializes her deed.

Humbug City

Ten miles northwest of Yreka, Humbug City once flourished on Humbug Creek, where gold was discovered in May 1851. The story goes that a company of men on their way to mine on the creek were met by a returning group who said it was all a humbug. Undaunted, the first group continued to the stream, where they set to work with pan and rocker. Their diligence was rewarded, and with a wry twist they called it Humbug Creek. News of the find spread quickly, and before long the stream was thronged with miners and dotted with camps.

Two miles above Humbug City was Freetown, while on the North Fork of the Humbug was Riderville, a large camp in 1859. For a time it was known as Plugtown, after old Dr. Nichols, who wore a plug hat. Two miles below the Forks was Mowry's Flat, known as Frenchtown in 1864, when a number of Frenchmen were mining there. A saloon was doing business at Frenchtown as late as 1881.

Joaquin Miller, who as a youth lived among the Indians of the Siskiyous, often joined the miners in their search for gold along the various streams. He draws a rather gloomy picture of the Humbug mining region: "It lay west of the city [Yreka], a day's ride down in a deep, densely timbered cañon, out of sight of Mount Shasta, out of sight of everything—even the sun; save here and there where a landslide had ploughed up the forest, or the miners had mown down the great evergreens about their cabins, or town sites in the camp."

It was a rough place, and wild—as wild as the mountains that hemmed it in. "A sort of Hades, a savage Eden, with many Adams walking up and down, and plucking of every tree, nothing forbidden here; for here, so far as it would seem, are neither laws of God or man." The Forks, where "three little streams joined hands, and went down from there to the Klamat together," was the common center of the region. Miller's cabin stood on the steep bank of the main stream, not far from the river. He was particularly impressed by the "Howlin' Wilderness," the principal saloon in the town. It was an immense log cabin with a huge fireplace, "where crackled and roared, day and night, a pine-log fire," the memory of which spelled enchantment to the poet for years after. The "Howlin' Wilderness" was the scene, too, of many a fight, "in this fierce little mining camp of the Forks," and the saying, "We will have a man for breakfast tomorrow," was a common one.

The Modoc War

"In the land of great lakes, high mountains, and long shadowy mornings and evenings, may be found the 'Sacred Lands' of Modoc tradition, where it is claimed can be seen the identical sacred stone ('I-sees Jo-kol-e-kas') whereon the Son of God gave His red children His last advice. In this strange land, and among its strange people," the opening scenes in the tragic drama of the Modoc War were enacted. It was here on Lost River (in southern Oregon) that the first engagement of the war took place on November 30, 1872, climaxing a long series of troubles between the Indians and the whites, which had begun in 1834 when a member of Ewing Young's party shot two Indian boys.

Alfred B. Meacham, Superintendent of Indian Affairs for the State of Oregon during the years 1869–72, and chairman of the Peace Commission in 1873, describes the circumstances and events of the war as he himself witnessed them, presenting "'the other side of the Modoc story,' with the hope that a better understanding between white and red men may be had, and that justice to both may be promoted."

"The 16th of Jan., 1873," writes Meacham, "found the Modocs in the Lava-beds, numbering one hundred and sixty-nine souls. Who shall be able to paint the anxiety, the fears, the hopes, the long councils, the great 'Ka-okes' (medicine dances), which were in reality religious meetings, in which every phase of the situation was discussed by these despised people." The same day

found General Wheaton "with two hundred men encamped on the high bluff, overlooking the Lava-beds from the north, four miles distant from the Modoc camp. The remainder numbering two hundred men . . . encamped about equal distance south of the Modocs." The full fighting force of the Modocs numbered 53 men, but the lava beds, with their secret dens and unknown crevices, formed an almost impregnable fortress for the little band. Day after day shells were rained upon them without effect, while the white soldiers suffered heavy losses.

Repeated attempts made by the leaders of both sides to make peace were frustrated by unfortunate events and misunderstanding. Finally, on April 11, 1873, in spite of repeated warnings of treachery given by Wi-ne-ma, Indian wife of Frank Riddle, the four unarmed peace commissioners, General Edward R. S. Canby, the Rev. Eleazer Thomas, A. B. Meacham, and L. S. Dyar, with Wi-ne-ma and Riddle as interpreters, met Captain Jack and his men at the Peace Tent, "which stood out all alone upon the rocky plain" not far from the Modoc stronghold. Canby and Thomas were killed, and Meacham, saved from a similar fate by Wi-ne-ma, was severely wounded. Dyar and Riddle escaped, as did Wi-ne-ma, after risking her life to save the others.

During the last engagement in the lava beds, when *one thousand white* soldiers and *seventy-two* Indian allies opened the battle upon fifty-three Modocs," only one Modoc warrior was killed during the three days' conflict. "The hospital at the army camp was full of wounded soldiers," and as "the sun went behind Van Bremen's Mountain" more than one salute was fired in honor of the dead. It was during this time that Wi-ne-ma "became a Florence Nightingale in the army hospital . . . bathing the burning brows, and administering nourishment prepared by her own hands. The soldiers were assured of her fidelity, and with united voice declared her to be a ministering angel. When the wounded were brought in from the battlefield, Wi-ne-ma was always among the first to reach the side of the stretcher."

Captain Jack held his position in the lava beds until April 18, when the Modocs finally abandoned their stronghold. After the Battle of Dry Lake, on May 10, the band broke up. Captain Jack, betrayed by members of his own tribe, was captured in Langell's Valley, Oregon, on June 1, and with his subsequent trial and execution on October 3, 1873, the closing act in that tragic drama of the last Indian war in the Far West came to an end.

For many years the spot where General Canby was killed was marked by a large wooden cross placed there by soldiers of his regiment. The Native Daughters of the Golden West and other patriotic organizations have restored Canby's Cross (SRL 110) and have erected near the spot a monument of native rock surmounted by the figure of a grizzly bear. In later years a pension was bestowed upon Wi-ne-ma by the federal government for distinguished services, and a public school on Lost River, where, in an earlier encounter, in December 1869, she had averted

Canby's Cross, Lava Beds National Monument

bloodshed and brought about a better understanding between Captain Jack and the Americans, was named for her.

Captain Jack's stronghold *(SRL 9),* three miles east of Canby's Cross at the southern end of Tule Lake, remains almost unchanged. Rude rock forts, used by soldiers and Indians alike, are now overgrown with sage and bitterbrush, and bleached bones of horses, fragments of leather, and empty cartridge shells were picked up for years at the scene of conflict. The Forest Service has marked a number of sites on the battlefield. Nine-tenths of a mile west of Canby's Cross is Guillem's Graveyard *(SRL 13),* where almost 100 men were buried in one spot. The bodies were removed to the National Cemetery in Washington, D. C., in the early 1890's, but the rock wall surrounding the old cemetery may still be distinguished. It is on the west side of the main road, just past a junction. Hospital Rock was a fortified position maintained by the white troops for the care of their sick and wounded soldiers. Captain Jack's Cave, where the Indian leader had his headquarters, and other interesting sites have also been marked. All these landmarks are in the Lava Beds National Monument.

SOURCES

Adams, Kramer A. *Covered Bridges of the West.* Howell-North, Berkeley, 1963.

Badè, Frederic William. *The Life and Letters of John Muir.* 2 vols. Houghton Mifflin, Boston, 1924.

Bland, T. A. *Life of Alfred B. Meacham, Together with His Lecture: "The Tragedy of the Lava Beds."* T. A. & M. C. Bland, Washington, D.C., 1883.

Brown, William S. "The Land of Burned Out Fires," *Touring Topics,* XIX, No. 8 (August 1927), 14–17, 38–39.

Clyman, James. "James Clyman, His Diaries and Reminiscences," ed. Charles L. Camp, *California Historical Society Quarterly,* IV, No. 2 (June 1925), to VI, No. 1 (March 1927).

Edwards, Philip L. *The Diary of Philip Leget Edwards.* The Grabhorn Press, San Francisco, 1932.

Farquhar, Francis P., ed. *Up and Down California in*

1860–64. The Journal of William H. Brewer. University of California Press, Berkeley, 1949.

Frémont, John Charles. *Geographical Memoir upon Upper California in Illustration of His Map of Oregon and California.* Government Printing Office, Washington, D.C., 1848.

Hall, Ansel F. "Mount Shasta," *Sierra Club Bulletin,* XII, No. 3 (1926), 252–67.

Hastings, Lansford W. *The Emigrants' Guide to California.* A facsimile of the edition of 1845 with introduction and notes by Charles H. Carey. Princeton University Press, Princeton, N.J., 1932.

Jones, David Rhys. "Early History of the Klamath." Ms., 1930.

—— "Pre-pioneer Pathfinders, California–Oregon Trail, 1826–1846," *Motor Land,* XXIX (August–November, 1931).

McGowan, Joseph A. *History of the Sacramento Valley.* 3 vols. Lewis Historical Publishing Co., New York, 1961.

Maloney, Alice B. "Shasta Was Shatasla in 1814," *California Historical Society Quarterly,* XXIV, No. 3 (September 1945).

Meacham, Hon. A. B. *Wigwam and Warpath; or The Royal Chief in Chains.* John P. Dale & Co., Boston, 1875.

—— *Wi-ne-ma (The Woman Chief) and Her People.* American Publishing Co., Hartford, Conn., 1876.

Miller, Joaquin. *Life Amongst the Modocs: Unwritten History.* Richard Bentley & Son, London, 1873.

Muir, John. *Mountains of California.* 2 vols. Houghton Mifflin, Boston, 1917.

—— *Steep Trails . . .* Houghton Mifflin, Boston, 1918.

Ogden, Peter Skene. "The Peter Skene Ogden Journals of the Snake Expedition, 1827–28; 1828–29," with editorial notes by T. C. Elliott, *Oregon Historical Society Quarterly,* XI (1910), 355–97.

Riddle, Jeff C. *The Indian History of the Modoc War and the Causes That Led to It.* Marnell & Co., San Francisco, 1914.

Show, S. B. "Primitive Areas in the National Forests of California," *Sierra Club Bulletin,* XVIII, No. 1 (February 1933), 24–30.

Walsh, Henry L., S.J. *Hallowed Were the Gold Dust Trails.* University of Santa Clara Press, Santa Clara, 1946.

Wells, Harry L. *History of Siskiyou County, California.* Stewart & Co., Oakland, 1881.

Wilkes, Charles. *Narrative of the United States Exploring Expedition during the Years 1838, 1839, 1840, 1841, 1842.* 5 vols. and an atlas. Lea & Blanchard, Philadelphia, 1845.

Williamson, Robert S. *Pacific Railroad Reports,* VI, Part I. Government Printing Office, Washington, D.C., 1855.

Captain Jack's Cave,
Lava Beds National Monument

Solano County

SOLANO COUNTY (named in honor of an Indian chief) was one of the original 27 counties. The first county seat was at Benicia, but in 1858 it was removed to Fairfield.

Solano, Chief of the Suisuns

The last of the missions established in California by the Franciscan friars was at Sonoma about 1823 and was called San Francisco Solano after St. Francis Solano, an illustrious Franciscan missionary to the New World who died in Peru in 1610. Padre Altimira, founder of the mission, bestowed this name in baptism upon Sem Yeto, who was an exceptionally intelligent Indian and chief over most of the rancherías between Petaluma Creek and the Sacramento River. The chief accepted the title and the new faith and prevented his people from making ashes of Mission San Francisco Solano.

When General Mariano Guadalupe Vallejo was made *comandante* of Sonoma, he, too, won Chief Solano's friendship, the outgrowth of General Vallejo's victory over the Soscol Indians, of whom Sem Yeto was chief. This occurred in 1835 at a place later known as Thompson's Gardens, on Soscol Creek north of the city of Vallejo.

Another tribe over which Sem Yeto was chief was the Suisun ("west winds"), which occupied the valley east of the Soscol (corrupted to Suscol) Hills, with a ranchería at present Rockville. When a county was formed in this area, General Vallejo requested that it be named Solano County in honor of his friend.

On the county library grounds at the southwest corner of Texas Street and Union Avenue in Fairfield, just opposite the Courthouse, stands a bronze statue of heroic size of the proud chief, the work of sculptor William Gordon Huff. This monument was originally erected in 1934 with funds appropriated by the people of the State of California on a hill in Suisun Valley near the legendary burial spot of Chief Solano. The site

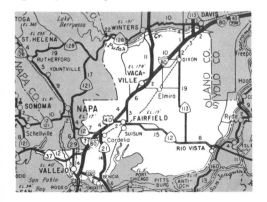

was donated by the Improved Order of Redmen of the Reservation of California. In 1939 the statue was moved to Fairfield to protect it from vandalism.

General Vallejo wrote the following tribute to Francisco Solano, Chief of the Suisun Indians and friend of the white man: "To the bravery and in particular to the diplomacy of that great chieftain of the Suisun Indians civilization is indebted for the conquest of the territory which today comprises the counties of Solano, Napa, Sonoma, and Lake."

Rancho Suisun

Five Mexican grants in this county were recognized by the United States government and patented to the legal claimants after due process of law. The first was Rancho Suisun, given to Francisco Solano. In his petition, dated January 16, 1837, Solano described himself as the "principal chief of the unconverted Indians and born captain of the Suisun" and asked for four square leagues. Said lands belonged "to him by hereditary right from his ancestors," and he wished "to revalidate his right." The grant was temporarily made to him and approved by Pío Pico in 1845, when he became governor for the second time.

This land was afterward purchased by M. G. Vallejo, and still later was acquired, also by purchase, by Archibald A. Ritchie, who received United States patent for 17,754 acres in January 1857. Fairfield, the county seat, is located on the border of this grant. It was established by Captain R. H. Waterman, a joint owner with Ritchie.

Rancho Tolenas

"José Francisco Armijo, by birth a Mexican, having four sons natives of the same country without any lands to cultivate," petitioned for the Tolenas, or Armijo, grant in November 1839. The following spring Governor Alvarado gave him three square leagues of land with the proviso that he should not in any manner molest the Indians already located there. Armijo died in 1850, and the title to 13,315 acres was acquired by his son Antonio Armijo, who received patent for them in 1868.

Five miles northwest of Fairfield once stood the five-room adobe built on this rancho. The walls fell about 1900, and the destruction was completed by herds of cattle pasturing on the land. The name of Armijo, however, is borne by the local high school in Fairfield.

Rancho Los Putos

The Los Putos grant was given to two Spaniards, Juan Manuel Vaca (Baca) and Juan Felipe Peña (Armijo), both of whom had come from

New Mexico with their families and settled there
in 1842. In the names of immigrants arriving in
Pueblo Los Angeles in November 1841 with the
Rowland-Workman party appear "J. Manuel
Vaca and families." Family tradition says that
they then followed the Camino Real of the Missions north to Sonoma, where General Vallejo
housed the women and children. The men journeyed on to occupy their chosen lands and to
build homes. By June 6, 1842, they petitioned
Comandante Vallejo for ten square leagues of
stock lands, vaguely described and called Lihuaytos. This was accorded to "Manuel Baca and the
families which he brings."

Then, on January 27, 1843, Governor Micheltorena officially granted Juan Manuel Vaca and
Juan Felipe Armijo the rancho of Lihuaytos,
again vaguely described and encompassing far
more than the allotted ten leagues. It overlapped
the prior Wolfskill or Río de los Putos grant,
and a heated controversy developed which was
finally compromised by Micheltorena in Wolfskill's favor. A correcting grant was given August
30, 1845, by Governor Pío Pico to the same
grantees. The name Los Putos was used and the
description was still vague, except for a mention
of Wolfskill's boundary. Los Putos was not surveyed until just prior to the United States patent
given on June 4, 1858, which enclosed 44,384
acres. The zigzag boundaries indicate that engineer Dewitt C. Cage found it difficult to reduce
the excess area to ten square leagues. The names
of the grantees were shown in the patent correctly for the first time as Juan Manuel Vaca and
Juan Felipe Peña. By 1879 much of this grant
had been sold to others.

The settlers' adobe homes were built about
two miles southwest of the present town of Vacaville in the lower end of Vaca Valley and its
lateral Lagoon Valley. Vaca's *casa* stood about
one-third mile north of Peña's but was damaged
by the earthquake of 1892, razed, and replaced
by a frame structure then owned by Portia Hill.
The Peña adobe *(SRL 534)*, closer to Lake Laguna
and still standing beside Interstate Highway 80,
was continuously occupied by descendants of the
Peña family until 1918. Its restoration was begun
in 1963 through the initial efforts of the Solano
County Historical Society. The adobe structure,
50 × 18 feet, was found in good condition, since
it had been sheathed in frame about 1870–80.
Replacement bricks have been made with native
adobe from the shores of Lake Laguna, sun-
baked on the site. Indications are that the hand-
split shake roof now installed is probably the
fifth one. The first roof was of tule thatch obtained from the lake. Some of the old fig, olive,
locust, and elm trees surround the *casa*, but the
Castilian rose bushes and the mission grapevines
are gone.

Ulatis Creek, which flows through this rancho,
was named for the "Ooloolatis" tribe of Indians,
who occupied the area and left many artifacts.
These Indians were wiped out by the smallpox
epidemic of 1837–39, although the life of Francisco Solano, chief of the neighboring Suisuns,
was saved by vaccination.

Rancho Río de los Putos

The Río de los Putos grant, traditionally
claimed at an earlier date by Francisco Guerrero,
was made to William Wolfskill in 1842; and
17,754 acres were patented to him in December
1858, part of which was in Yolo County and part
in Solano County.

John Reed Wolfskill, the first American settler
in Solano County, arrived in California in 1838
and lived in the southern part of the state for a
few years with his brother William, a trapper,
who had reached California a few years earlier.
In 1842 John drove 96 head of cattle north, past
the home of his brother's trapper friend, George
C. Yount, to a point near the bank of Putah
Creek, where he erected a wattle hut. This stream
flows through the property and now forms, in
the vicinity, the dividing line between Yolo and
Solano counties. An adobe that he constructed on
the south bank about three miles west of present
Winters was used as a storehouse and blacksmith
shop for many years, and when it was finally
pulled down, the earth in its walls was used to
strengthen the banks of the encroaching creek.

John was joined there in 1852 by his brother
Sarchel, and together they built and occupied a
log house only a few feet away from the adobe
built earlier. This log cabin also has been removed. A frame house of more modern style, in
which Sarchel spent his adult life with his family,
was erected near its site. This two-story house
stood until it was destroyed by fire in 1958 and
was long occupied by his descendants. Now the
property has passed into other hands.

Two other brothers, Milton and Mathus, joined
John and Sarchel on this vast tract of land, and
all four made homes along the fertile banks of the
Río de los Putos. John erected a house one and
a half miles southeast of Sarchel's and farther
from the creek, using the smooth, white, native
stone, a volcanic tufa. A true horticulturist, he
planted many acres of nuts and seeds on the rancho. From this planting came black walnuts,
pecans, pomegranates, apricots, oranges, figs, and
olives—the beginning of Solano County's orchards. The stone house fell in the earthquake
of 1892 and was replaced the following year by
a 17-room frame home, which stood, as the former one did, at the end of a long driveway lined
with magnificent olive trees. Emblazoned on this
later house was the number 96, the Wolfskill cattle brand, a reference to the cattle John had
driven north in 1842. This house, in which John
Reed Wolfskill lived until his death in his nineties in 1897, burned in 1948.

Over a hundred acres of this property, owned
by John Wolfskill and after him by his daughter
and then by his grandchildren, was willed to the
University of California at Davis for an agricultural experiment station, with the provision that
the old olive plantings be retained. The spot
(SRL 804) is two miles southwest of Winters, off
Putah Creek Road. It is easily identifiable by the
avenue of gnarled olive trees leading to two university buildings erected on the site of John Wolfskill's stone house.

The Mathus Wolfskill adobe was on the south side of Putah Creek, one-half mile east of Winters and 200 yards east of the bridge. The Milton Wolfskill house was seven miles west of Winters, outside the confirmed rancho grant. Both these adobes are gone.

Rancho Los Ulpinos

The Los Ulpinos, or Bidwell, grant contained 17,726 acres in the eastern part of the county along the western bank of the Sacramento River. John (Juan) Bidwell, who had become a naturalized Mexican citizen, petitioned for this tract in April 1844, and it was granted to him in November of the same year by Governor Manuel Micheltorena "for his own benefit and that of his family." The further provision was appended that he "may fence it, but he shall have no power to sell it," a precaution taken to prevent the land from falling into alien hands. He immediately built an adobe house and placed workmen on the land but did not himself reside there. After the Mexican government lost claim to all land in California, Bidwell sold parts of the grant to several persons, until the boundary lines were in a state of chaos. In 1855 these properties were all defined amicably when the entire rancho was divided into 20 equal tracts made by measurements along the river front extending back one league. The tracts were sold in front of the Courthouse door in Benicia on December 3, 1855, and the proceeds were allocated to the various claimants. The land was finally patented to Bidwell by the United States in August 1866, thus making all the titles valid.

Unpatented Land Grants

Troublesome litigation followed the making of the Soscol and the Sobrante grants. The former, containing 11 square leagues, was claimed by General M. G. Vallejo as having been given to him by Governor Micheltorena in 1843 in consideration of his services as an officer and of the large sums of money that he had furnished to the Mexican government. His title to this vast acreage, extending northward from the Straits of Carquinez, was declared invalid by the United States courts, but purchases made under it were allowed when further small payments were made. The greater parts of the cities of Vallejo and Benicia, as well as the community of Cordelia and the area called Green Valley, lie within its borders.

The Sobrante grant of fifty square leagues was claimed by Juan and José Luco, brothers, by reason of their having purchased it from a Mexican vaquero, who had received it from the Mexican government. This land also became part of the public domain after the claim was rejected by the courts. Most of the Montezuma Hills and the communities of Denverton, Birds Landing, and Collinsville are within its borders.

Montezuma House

Lansford W. Hastings, a lawyer from Ohio, who reached California by way of Oregon in 1843 in command of the immigrant party that bore his name, was active in the early settlement of the state. He traveled extensively in his effort to attract new residents, returning to the East in 1844, when he published *The Emigrant's Guide*. Coming back to California, he became agent for the Mormons and selected a site for the location of one of their colonies on the north side of the Sacramento River near its junction with the San Joaquin. There he laid out a town and built an adobe for himself in 1846. This building was called "Montezuma House," and Bayard Taylor, in *Eldorado* thus makes mention of it (1849): "'City of Montezuma,' a solitary house on a sort of headland, projecting into Suisun Bay, and fronting the rival three-house city, New York of-the-Pacific." (The latter is now Pittsburg, Contra Costa County.) Hastings had hoped to obtain a large grant of land from the Mexican government, but the American flag was raised over California on July 7, 1846, and the Mormons lost interest in the site. During his stay, Hastings established a ferry across to the Contra Costa side. After leaving Montezuma, he became attorney for the northern district of California and was a member of the Constitutional Convention, where his geographical knowledge was useful in fixing boundaries.

This one-story-and-attic adobe built by Hastings stands one and one-quarter miles east of Collinsville at the end of Stratton Lane and is well preserved inside its redwood casing. Numerous machines for fabricating and stamping coins were found in the house after the builder left it; they were probably intended for the use of the Mormons. Two families have since occupied the house. L. P. Marshall came from the East in 1852 with a herd of cattle and, hearing of the house from Dr. Semple of Benicia, took possession of it with his two sons, John and Charles Knox. The S. O. Stratton family entered it after the Marshalls and lived in it from 1908 until 1963. The land is now owned by the Pacific Gas and Electric Company, which hopes to perpetuate this second oldest intact adobe in Solano County, the oldest being the Peña adobe near Vacaville.

Collinsville

Formerly a picturesque salmon fishing village built on piles at the edge of the Sacramento River, Collinsville was named for C. J. Collins, who settled in the area in 1856. After the re-

Hastings Adobe, near Collinsville

jection of the Luco claim, and under the influence of promoter S. C. Bradshaw, he filed a map of the City of Collinsville in 1862. It covered a grandiose 2,390 acres, which Bradshaw purchased and renamed Newport, the post office receiving its new name in 1867. Many of the lots were under water at high tide and sales soon lagged, even at five dollars a lot. After a sheriff's sale in 1869, the town was again called Collinsville. F. E. Booth & Co. erected a salmon cannery there about 1873 and employed many Italian fishermen, who lived in homes built on stilts to allow free circulation of flood tides beneath them. But the salmon decreased, and there were fires, and in 1963 there were only six inhabited houses in the city on stilts which once bore the sobriquet "Little Venice."

Benicia

Benicia is situated on the north side of Carquinez Straits between San Pablo and Suisun bays. Once the rival of San Francisco and a pioneer military, religious, and educational center, Benicia's early history adds a romantic chapter to the story of California.

The town was laid out in 1847 by Dr. Robert Semple, who had taken part in the Bear Flag Revolt of 1846 at Sonoma, in which General Vallejo was captured. Dr. Semple, impressed with beautiful Carquinez Straits as the possible site for a city, made a bargain with his prisoner (whose estate covered much of the present Solano, Sonoma, and Napa counties) for a part of his Soscol grant, the land now occupied by the city of Benicia. The site was deeded to Dr. Semple and Thomas O. Larkin after General Vallejo had been released from prison at Sutter's Fort, and in 1847 the city was surveyed to cover 2,100 acres.

The name first selected for the new town was Francisca, in honor of the wife of General Vallejo. For a time, Francisca's enthusiasts expected it to become the metropolis of San Francisco Bay, but the rivalry became so keen between it and the older town of Yerba Buena across the Bay that, when the latter changed its name to San Francisco, Francisca felt it necessary to adopt Benicia, one of Mrs. Vallejo's other names.

Dr. Semple established the first ferry across the Straits in 1847. It proved to be a very lucrative operation, especially during the gold rush. There was continuous ferry service between Benicia and Martinez (laid out in 1849) for 115 years, until the highway bridge was completed in 1962.

Many noted men and women connected with the early history of California are associated with this place: General Mariano Guadalupe Vallejo, donor of the land; Dr. Robert Semple, founder of the city and president of the State Constitutional Convention at Monterey in 1849; General Persifer F. Smith, commanding officer of the Pacific Division of the United States Army after California became a state; General Bennett Riley, who located the Benicia Arsenal; Thomas O. Larkin, the first and only American consul in California during the Mexican period; Concepción Argüello, the heroine of tales by Bret Harte, Richard White, and Gertrude Atherton.

In addition, in the early history of the first city in Solano County are found educators, jurists, and religious leaders of prominence, such as Professor C. J. Flatt, who established the Collegiate Institute; Miss Mary Atkins, the first principal of the Benicia Seminary; the Rev. C. T. Mills, her successor and the founder afterwards of Mills College at Oakland; Judge Serranus Clinton Hastings, founder of Hastings Law College in 1878, who settled at Benicia in 1849 and was immediately appointed chief justice of the Supreme Court of California; Judge Joseph McKenna, who came there in 1855 and later became associate justice of the Supreme Court of the United States; the Rev. J. L. Breck, founder of two diocesan schools of the Episcopal Church in Benicia; and Bishop Wingfield, of the Sacramento Episcopal Diocese, who had his bishopric in Benicia from 1876 to 1898.

On the west side of First Street between C and D was the adobe built in 1847 and rented then to Captain E. H. Von Pfister. The Captain was keeping a store in the building in May 1848, when a man by the name of Charles Bennett stopped by. He was on his way to Monterey to have tests made on some gold nuggets picked up by James Marshall at Coloma on the American River on January 24, 1848. Bennett told the story of Marshall's discovery, showed the nuggets, and thus helped to precipitate the rush to the gold fields. Although the old adobe store no longer stands, its site has been marked, and in the alley west of this site may still be seen an unkept wood-covered adobe that was probably a storehouse used by the Captain.

One of the first hotels in northern California was built in 1847 for Major Stephen Cooper. The bricks may have been made by William Tustin, who, with his wife and child, was the first white settler in Benicia. In this building the first wedding ceremony in Benicia was read, when Miss Frances Cooper, daughter of Major Cooper, became the wife of Dr. Semple. The ceremony was performed by the former governor of Missouri, L. W. Boggs, then alcalde of Sonoma. The original adobe building was run as a hotel by Major Cooper and was known as the California House until 1854, when it was sold to John Rueger and turned into a brewery. Remodeled, it stood until 1945, when it was destroyed by fire. It was located on the south side of West H Street near First, a site now occupied by a tavern called "The Brewery," which contains interesting murals of Benicia's pioneer days.

Also destroyed by fire in 1945 was the old frame Solano Hotel, built in 1851, located at the northwest corner of First and E streets. For many years it was the leading hotel in the area. Many social functions were held there and famous names appeared on its register.

Perhaps the most interesting old hotel still standing is the Washington House, a frame structure erected in the 1850's at 333 First Street. Remodeled in 1897, it exchanged its lurid past for the status of first-class hotel and restaurant. With the advent of prohibition, however, it became a speakeasy, and a Chinese lottery operated there until 1946. Now it is an art gallery and antique shop.

Dr. W. F. Peabody established a hospital in Benicia in 1849 and "secured a large and paying patronage from returning miners." He served on the Benicia Seminary Board in 1852 while mayor of the city, in which he resided until 1864. The hospital has been completely rebuilt into a residence at 245 West H Street. Some of the original timbers were retained.

The first Masonic Hall built in California (SRL 174) was formally dedicated December 27, 1850, at Benicia. The two-story frame building is located at 106 West J Street. The lower floor was used as the county courthouse until 1852, when the famous capitol building was finished. The Masons sold the hall about 1888 for community use but reacquired it in 1950. Many of California's prominent pioneers received their degrees in this building, including George Yount, noted early settler of Napa Valley. Still in use, it is one of the three places in California where any Masonic lodge may hold meetings to confer degrees.

The first Pony Express relay rider from St. Joseph, Missouri, William Hamilton, reached Benicia April 23, 1860, and was ferried across the Straits. A bronze marker commemorating the event is set at the southeast corner of First and A streets. At the same location are the unused 1879 tracks of the transcontinental railroad where it crossed the Straits by the steamboats *Port Costa* and *Solano*. The latter transported 48 cars and a locomotive in one trip and served until 1929, when the Southern Pacific Railroad bridge was completed.

Twenty feet from the Pony Express marker is the Jack London plaque. The youthful writer frequented the Benicia waterfront while gathering firsthand material for his *Tales of the Fish Patrol* and *John Barleycorn*. The old Jorgenson saloon, now the Lido, stands 100 feet north of the plaque.

First Protestant Church in California

On the site of what is now the Benicia City Park, the first Protestant church in California (SRL 175) was established on April 15, 1849, by Rev. Sylvester Woodbridge, a missionary sent to California by the Presbyterian Church of New York. Until 1854, it was the only Protestant church in Benicia, and its pastor, Mr. Woodbridge, exerted considerable influence in the community, not only as a preacher, but also as a teacher, farmer and keeper of the town records. He likewise established the first school in Benicia, which was one of the first in California. However, because of controversy over the question of leaving the Union during the Civil War, the church declined; it was abandoned in 1871, and Woodbridge moved to San Francisco. The site is marked on the north side of West K Street.

The Benicia Arsenal and Barracks

The Benicia Barracks (SRL 177), one of the first United States military posts in the state, was established on April 30, 1849, by Lieutenant Colonel Silas Casey, in command of Companies C and G of the Second United States Infantry. The first buildings were erected that year, and the United States Army headquarters were established there, as Benicia promised to become the central military post of the region. It was strategically located on the Carquinez Straits, into which both the Sacramento and the San Joaquin rivers empty, and thus stood at the gateway to the interior of California and the mining regions. However, San Francisco, instead of Benicia, became the metropolis of San Francisco Bay and the port of entry to central California; consequently, the Benicia military post was superseded in importance by the Presidio at the Golden Gate. In 1908 the Barracks was placed under the control of the Benicia Arsenal. A marker at the eastern end of Hillcrest Avenue indicates the site of the Barracks.

In August 1851 the Army began the very necessary task of setting up an ordnance supply depot, the first in California. A small wooden powder magazine was erected, soon to be followed by others of brick, frame, and stone. Benicia Arsenal (SRL 176) was officially designated as such in April 1852. The oldest stone magazine, built in 1857 at a cost of $35,000, has walls four and one-half feet thick, with a vaulted ceiling and modified Corinthian pillars, constructed by French artisans recruited by the United States government. The beautiful interior makes it hard for one to realize that the building was intended for such a prosaic purpose as the storage of gunpowder. This and other structures of hand-hewn sandstone blocks from the surrounding hills are among the finest examples of the stonecutter's art in the state. Some of the others, still standing in excellent condition, are the first hospital, built in 1856, which served as the Post Chapel during World War II; the famous clock-tower building of 1859; and two fine stone warehouses built in 1853 and 1854 and afterwards converted into camel barns.

The 1859 sandstone clock-tower building with fortress-like walls pierced by gun ports overlooks the Straits. It was originally a three-story building with two towers, but was damaged by an explosion and fire in 1912 and reduced to two stories, except for the single massive tower housing the clock.

The camel barns made of stone, with the high

Original Three-Story Clock-Tower Building, Benicia Arsenal

arched entrances, were used to stable the United States Army camels brought from the Near East in 1856–57 for the transportation of military supplies across the desert wastes of our Southwest. The experiment proved to be a failure, and the animals were ordered driven to Benicia Arsenal, where they were sold at public auction to a single bidder in February 1864. Between the barns stands a small sandstone guardhouse of the same period, most recently used as a radio station.

Many troops were stationed at the Arsenal from time to time, including, as young lieutenants, William Tecumseh Sherman and Ulysses S. Grant. Its facilities were continuously used for ammunition storage and ordnance repair, even after the last of the troops moved out. Through the years more buildings were erected, reflecting the architectural modes of different eras, until the Arsenal grounds contained structures from virtually every period of the state's history. World War II brought an increase of the Arsenal's size from 345 acres to 2,192 acres. For the storage of high explosives, 109 igloo-type concrete bunkers were concealed by burrowing into the rolling hills. As the bombing hazard increased, most of these explosives were removed inland to Utah, but the Arsenal served well as a depot for shipments over the Pacific.

For more than a century the Arsenal and its magnificent buildings were closed to the general public, but in 1961 the Army began deactivation of the post, which was completed on March 31, 1964. The property is to be converted to industrial use, but efforts are being made to secure the preservation of the old stone buildings and other historic structures.

Other landmarks at the Arsenal include the cemetery, with burials as early as 1849 and as recent as eight German prisoners-of-war from World War II; the headquarters building of 1870; the guardhouse of 1872; three shop buildings erected in 1876, 1884, and 1887; permanent barracks of 1872; and the commanding officer's mansion built in 1860, once a center of gala social life. One of the commanding officers was Colonel James W. Benet, father of poets Stephen Vincent Benet and William Rose Benet.

The main entrance to the Arsenal is at the eastern end of M Street.

Port Landmarks

Benicia was of great importance as a port of entry for many years. It had the advantage of deep water at the shore, where seagoing vessels could discharge their cargos directly on the land. Captain John Walsh, having led a seafaring life, settled there in 1849 and became collector of the port. His house was one of three almost identical ones brought around the Horn in 1849. The other two were set up in San Francisco and Sonoma. Walsh spent much time in building and ornamenting it and in dispensing its hospitality to his many friends in the Army and Navy. This two-story house is still standing in fair condition and occupied at 235 East L Street.

Diagonally west near the southeast corner of First and East L streets is the site of the rambling frame home of Lansing Bond Mizner, a stepnephew of Dr. Semple and a partner of William McDaniel in the founding of Vacaville in 1850, as well as ambassador to five Central American countries. His six sons were said to be "three-quarters Irish and one-quarter devil" by the victims of their pranks, which continued through adult life. The old house was razed about 1914, and the site is now occupied by city buildings, but Benicia remembers those boys.

The Pacific Mail Steamship Company established headquarters in Benicia in 1850, and the expansion of its business demanded the enlargement of its wharf in 1853. Foundries and machine shops were built, and the company enjoyed prosperity. Here the great seagoing ships of the period were repaired and coaled.

The *California*, first steamer of the line to make the journey around the Horn from New York, arrived in San Francisco on February 28, 1849, crowded with passengers owing to the great influx of gold seekers at Panama. Coal for refueling for the return journey had to be brought to California by boat; and, since the first shipload had not arrived, the steamer was forced to wait. Refueled, the *California*, with Captain Forbes in command, made an excursion to Benicia with a party of invited guests in April before returning to New York in May. After the establishment of the docks, all the great boats of this company, the *California*, the *Oregon*, and the *Panama*, berthed in Benicia between regular trips until the removal of the company headquarters to San Francisco.

The competition of the overland railway, completed in 1869, was felt keenly by the Pacific Mail Steamship Company. As a result, in 1881 its docks and buildings were taken over by the Benicia Agricultural Works. Three of the original large brick buildings, now used by the Yuba Construction Company, are standing at the end of East H Street between Sixth and Seventh.

The last 290 freighters (as of 1965), known as the Mothball Fleet, moored since World War II in Suisun Bay, can be seen three miles northeast of Benicia from the highway leading to Cordelia.

The Old State Capitol Building

The most noteworthy and prominent structure of the pioneer days in Benicia is the third State Capitol building (*SRL 153*), located on the northwest corner of First and G streets. The pretentious two-story brick building built in 1852 at a cost of $24,800 was ostensibly intended for the City Hall but was promptly offered for the use of the state. The offer was accepted and Benicia became the third capital of the State of California, after San Jose and Vallejo. It held the honor from February 4, 1853, to February 25, 1854, three days after which the "capital on wheels" made its final journey to Sacramento.

The stately building was designed to resemble a Greek temple. This simple design was the fashion of the time in capitol structures; the domed edifices came later, with the erection of the national capitol during Civil War days. Two fluted columns are set flush with the entrance way instead of projecting. Salmon-colored brick walls, plastered on the interior, support the iron-covered roof. Two angular staircases connect the Senate chamber on the lower floor with the Assembly room on the second story. The entrance door is a massive structure.

After the loss of the state capital to Sacramento, the building was used as the county courthouse until 1858, when Fairfield captured that honor. Other uses over the years have been a judges' court, school, library, theater, church, and police station, as well as city hall. It was marked by the State Society of the D.A.R. in 1924.

In 1949 it was deeded to the state. Restored to its pristine glory in 1956–57 at a cost of $230,000, it is now a State Historical Monument and is open to the public daily.

The Benicia Seminary

Because of its many early educational institutions, Benicia has been called the "Athens of California." Among these schools were the Young Ladies' Seminary, St. Augustine's for Boys, St. Mary's for Girls, Benicia Collegiate Institute (the pioneer law school), and St. Catherine's Academy of the Dominican Sisters.

The Benicia Seminary was one of the first Protestant girls' schools in California, being established in 1852. Several denominations were interested in it, and Rev. Sylvester Woodbridge and Rev. Samuel Willey were two of its most notable promoters. The Governor of Vermont was also interested and sent out the first teachers on its faculty.

One of the most notable of the seminary's teachers was Miss Mary Atkins, and it was she who gave the school fame and success. She became its principal in 1854, and in 1855 she became the owner. She attracted students not only from Sacramento and San Francisco but even from the mining camps of Gold Hill, Volcano, and Hangtown. Miss Atkins was a strict disciplinarian whose catalogues advised fond parents against "over indulgence in spending money; and the boxes of indigestion that come in form of sweetmeats, cakes, pies and sugar plums; and fine clothes that are entirely out of place." In 1865, because of ill health, she sold the seminary to Rev. Cyrus T. Mills and his wife. Mr. and Mrs. Mills conducted the school at Benicia until 1871, when they moved to Oakland and established Mills College.

A board of prominent businessmen of Benicia undertook to continue a school in the old Benicia Seminary. Rev. C. H. Pope, pastor of the Congregational Church, became the principal. After three years, Pope left California, and a Miss Snell became principal. In 1878, Miss Mary Atkins, then Mrs. Lynch, bought her old school back again and conducted it until her death in 1882.

The old Benicia Seminary was finally closed in 1886, but it served its day well. It may, indeed, be called the "Mother of Seminaries," for not only did the famous Mills College of Oakland

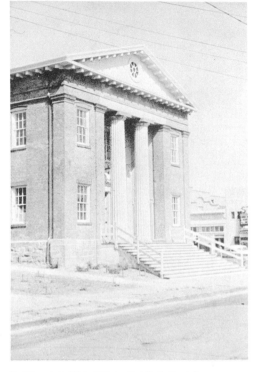

California's Third State Capitol, Benicia

come out of it, but many members of its faculty went out to teach elsewhere in the state, and, in several instances, to found other seminaries. Some of Miss Atkins' pupils also became prominent teachers in public and private schools in California.

The seminary site *(SRL 795)* is on the north side of I Street west of First. It is indicated by a small marker, but, for reasons of space, the state bronze plaque and monument were placed in the Benicia City Park facing L Street.

St. Augustine College

When Dr. Robert Semple founded Benicia in 1847, he set aside certain grounds for a college. On these grounds Rev. C. M. Blake established a nondenominational boys' school in 1852. This school lasted two years, when it was sold to C. J. Flatt, who reopened it in 1857. Under his management it flourished until 1867, when it became the Episcopalian College of St. Augustine, under the management of Rev. J. L. Breck, leader of a missionary company from the East. Dr. Breck was never able to carry out his plans for developing the college, and it later became a military school, still under Episcopalian auspices.

The campus covered 52 acres and was adjacent to the entire block occupied in 1870 by its sister school St. Mary's College of the Pacific. Gertrude Horn (Atherton) was a pupil at St. Mary's, which was closed in 1885. St. Augustine College continued until 1889.

Bishop Wingfield of the Sacramento Diocese

supervised both schools for a time and had his residence on the campus from 1876 to 1898. The Bishop's house, today a private residence at 36 Wingfield Way, is the only building left on either campus. The Bishop now has his headquarters at Sacramento, and the campus has been subdivided and sold for homes.

St. Paul's Episcopal Church, in downtown Benicia, is a picturesque and significant landmark of early days. It is unique in having a ceiling like an inverted ship's hull, designed by Captain Julian McAllister, Commander of the Benicia Arsenal. The church was consecrated January 11, 1860, with Captain McAllister as lay reader until October of that year, when the Rev. James Cameron arrived. Within three years the church was enlarged and a bell tower added. Mr. Cameron presented a fine organ, which was used for 86 years. Maintained and improved, the church stands in excellent condition today at First and East J streets.

Saint Dominic's Church and Priory

The block bounded by Fourth, Fifth, East I, and East J streets has been almost from the beginning of the town the center of Catholic parish activity in Benicia; here, on the corner of Fourth and East I streets, the first Catholic church was built in 1852. It was an octagonal frame building without pillars and had a seating capacity of 200. The present stone and concrete Church of Saint Dominic, on the north side of East I Street between Fourth and Fifth, was solemnly blessed on March 17, 1890, shortly before the demolition of the early one.

Before the first of these edifices was built, Mass was celebrated in a building termed "The Hall," which stood on the corner of East I and Sixth streets midway between the Arsenal and the Pacific Mail docks. This building was owned by Judge James Barry, who had come to Benicia in 1850 and who frequently entertained the priests and the Bishop in his home. In still earlier years, devout Catholic families drove by oxcart to the Sonoma Mission for Mass.

Saint Dominic's parish was formally established on March 16, 1854, when the Very Reverend Francis Sadoc Vilarrasa, O.P., arrived from Monterey with his whole religious community and accepted the care of the parish in the name of the Order of Preachers. Father Vilarrasa and the Most Reverend Joseph Sadoc Alemany, O.P., had arrived in San Francisco in December 1850. The latter, who became the first Archbishop of San Francisco in 1853, gave to the former for the use of the Order the church already built in Benicia. Near the church was built in 1854 the first residence for the community. This was used until the erection in 1887 of a new priory on Fifth Street facing East I Street.

The work most dear to Father Vilarrasa on his arrival in California was the establishing of a convent and a novitiate for the education of Dominican priests. These he had established in Monterey, but had moved them to Benicia when he came in 1854. The Dominican priory existed until 1935, when it was changed to a vicariate.

By this change very valuable old books brought from Spain in early years and protected within these walls were made available to interested historians.

St. Catherine's Convent

The Dominican Sisters arrived in California in 1850. They settled first at Monterey, where, in the spring of 1851, they established the first convent school in California. However, the old adobe building in which they were located was in bad condition, and since the population in Monterey was diminishing and that around San Francisco Bay was rapidly increasing, the Sisters decided to move to Benicia, which was a more central point.

St. Catherine's Convent was established in Benicia in 1854, and was operated as a convent and school until June 1959. Many of the young ladies of pioneer days, including Luisa and María Vallejo, received their education at this convent, and many orphan children were given shelter and schooling there. In 1889 the Sisters moved to what is now the Dominican College of San Rafael but continued to operate St. Catherine's at Benicia.

The first school building used by the Sisters was rented from Dr. Semple. Their success was so marked that Judge S. C. Hastings donated Solano Square for a permanent site. The expansive buildings, begun in 1859 and remodeled about 1912, stood until March 1966, when they were razed. They occupied a prominent position on the north side of L Street opposite its junction with First.

Bret Harte, Richard White, and Gertrude Atherton have given to the literary world versions of one of the saddest romances of early California history, the story of Concepción Argüello and her Russian lover, the gallant Count Rezanov. Its opening chapter took place at the Presidio in San Francisco, but it is the beautiful aftermath of this tale that has become immortal. For years, Concepción waited for her lover. Not a rumor of his fate reached her until several years had passed, and not for 36 years was the manner of his death made known to her.

She refused all suitors, and at length joined the Third Order of St. Francis, giving her life to teaching the poor and caring for the sick. Up and down the state, from San Francisco to Santa Barbara and from Santa Barbara to Baja California, this gray-robed sister of mercy traveled on her errands of love.

When the Dominican Sisters founded their convent school in Monterey in 1851, Concepción became their first native-born novice, and when the convent was moved in 1854, she came to Benicia with Mother Superior Mary Goemaere, O.P. Concepción died at the Convent of St. Catherine on December 23, 1857, at age 66. Her simple tombstone in St. Dominic's Cemetery on Hillcrest Avenue at the northeastern outskirts of town reads "Sister Mary Dominica Argüello." It is near the entrance, in the second row of stones of the section reserved for Sisters' graves.

Her kindliness and her charities, as well as the

beauty and pathos of her romance, made her famous, so that she was venerated by all in her own time, and has since become "the most cherished figure in the romance of Alta California history."

Forty years on wall and bastion swept the hollow
    idle breeze,
Since the Russian eagle fluttered from the
    California seas;
Forty years on wall and bastion wrought its slow
    but sure decay,
And St. George's cross was lifted in the port of
    Monterey;
And the citadel was lighted, and the hall was
    gayly drest,
All to honor Sir George Simpson, famous traveler
    and guest.
Far and near the people gathered to the costly
    banquet set,
And exchanged congratulations with the English
    baronet;
Till, the formal speeches ended, and amidst the
    laugh and wine,
Some one spoke of Concha's lover—heedless of
    the warning sign.
Quickly then cried Sir George Simpson: "Speak
    no ill of him, I pray!
"He is dead. He died, poor fellow, forty years
    ago this day—
"Died while speeding home to Russia, falling
    from a fractious horse.
"Left a sweetheart, too, they tell me. Married, I
    suppose, of course!
"Lives she yet?" A deathlike silence fell on
    banquet, guests, and hall,
And a trembling figure rising fixed the awe-struck
    gaze of all.
Two black eyes in darkened orbits gleamed
    beneath the nun's white hood;
Black serge hid the wasted figure, bowed and
    stricken where it stood.
"Lives she yet?" Sir George repeated. All were
    hushed as Concha drew
Closer yet her nun's attire. "Señor, pardon, she
    died, too!"

BRET HARTE

Cordelia

The town of Cordelia, next to Benicia the oldest in the county, was named in honor of the wife of Captain Waterman, founder of Fairfield. Situated at the lower end of Green Valley on the route from Benicia to Sacramento, it was a stopping place for stages, and a hotel for the accommodation of travelers was operated there in 1855 by John Charles Pitman, a native of Bristol, England. A post office was established there in 1854, but moved to Rockville in 1858. The Cordelia post office was reestablished in 1869 and operated until 1943.

Stone quarried near Cordelia was taken by barges through the Cordelia Slough and across the Bay to San Francisco, where it was used in building and in paving the streets. The shipping point was called Bridgeport; and when in 1868 the California Pacific Railroad was routed through it, the community of Cordelia was moved a short distance south to the newer site. The Pitman House was succeeded by the Cordelia Hotel, which years later became a family residence and survived until it burned in 1937. The Thompson Bar in Cordelia is said to be one of the oldest in the county. The settlement lies just south of Interstate Highway 80.

Just north of Cordelia on the other side of the freeway stretches Green Valley, an area long famous for its cherry orchards but now rapidly developing into a residential community. Five old landmarks remain. About three and one-half miles north along Green Valley Road, and set back some distance to the west of the road, is the imposing stone residence started in 1860 by Granville P. Swift, Bear Flagger and builder of Temelec Hall near Sonoma. He deeded the property to his sister, Mary Swift Jones, on November 14, 1868; and her husband, Frederick S. Jones, completed the building. Jones later found that the house was not on the property deeded and he purchased the adjacent 137.5 acres in 1873 to perfect the title to the house. Carefully maintained, it was sold for headquarters of the Green Valley Country Club after 80 years in the family. About one and one-fourth miles south of the country club entrance, and directly on the west side of the road, is the two-story white frame home of F. S. Jones, a grandson of the 1868 cherry pioneer. Into this residence is incorporated a portion of the oldest building in Green Valley, the 1847 Stilts adobe. Another three-fourths of a

Dingley Flour Mill, Green Valley

mile south the Charles Ramsay house is visible on the west side of the road. The two-and-a-half-story stone building, called the Nightingale Place, retains its original appearance and is a private home. In the northerly end of Green Valley, beyond the country club entrance, two stone outbuildings of the 1860's still stand. The first seen, to the west of Green Valley Road on the creek, is the two-story Dingley flour mill, now reroofed and used as a fruit-packing shed. A little over a mile farther northeast, on a private road in the Kolbert property, is the two-story winery built by John Votypka, who came from Austria in 1856, now also used for fruit packing. All the historic Green Valley structures are on private property and unmarked.

Rockville

A settlement on the old stage road between Benicia and Sacramento was Rockville, site of an Indian encampment and burying ground of the Suisun tribe before the Spanish came to the region. The tribe was virtually wiped out by smallpox in 1837–39, but their chief Solano, who lived there at times, was saved, for the Spaniards had brought vaccine as well as smallpox. An Indian, Jesús Molino, had the only house in the vicinity when, in the fall of 1847, Captain E. H. Von Pfister passed through the place and found about a hundred acres of ground under cultivation, with peas, wheat, and other crops being raised. The tools used on the farm are described as being very primitive; the plow was the "crooked branch of a tree armed with a pointed iron socket." The town grew to the extent of having a few little stores where necessities could be purchased, a blacksmith shop, a post office, hotel, stage station, and church. It has dwindled considerably, but remains as a crossroads about two miles north of Interstate Highway 80 on Suisun Valley Road. Through this area runs the approximate northern boundary line of the unconfirmed Soscol grant.

The most interesting feature of this vicinity is the number of solid buildings constructed of local stone between 1856 and 1865, the most notable one being the church, described below. A short distance north of the church on the same side of Suisun Valley Road stands the J. M. Baldwin stone barn, built in 1865, with its solid stone floor and its white horse's head over the arched carriage entrance. The former Baldwin home a few yards away is a frame house surrounded by trees and shrubs. It is, however, not the original Baldwin home. This is now the Robbins property.

About one-half mile south of Rockville is a stone house on a rise at the west side of the road. This was the home of Samuel Martin, who came from Pennsylvania with his family in 1849 and located there in 1850. He brought herds of cattle, driven across the plains and the mountains by men on horseback. His family with their personal belongings traveled in covered wagons drawn by wooden-yoked oxen with their clanging chains. Samuel Martin became the owner of 450 acres, and his house was built in 1861 on the site of the Indian ranchería where Chief Solano once dwelt. In the large, deeply imbedded boulders on the wooded knoll at the rear of the residence are mortar holes worn smooth by the grinding of acorns and seeds by the Indian families whose home had been there from some remote and unrecorded time. The old Indian burying ground is in a field on the east side of the road opposite the house. Near the roadside a buckeye tree keeps vigil over the spot where, reputedly, the body of Chief Solano was laid to rest. During their first years on the place, the Martin family harvested the wild oats for their cattle and gradually established fruit raising also as a means of livelihood. The ranch is still owned and operated by this family, who had the house remodeled in the 1920's by descendants of the original stone masons. The second story still shows the old date stone 1861.

Hidden among orchards about one mile southeast of Rockville and on the opposite side of Suisun Creek is the unaltered stone home of Nathan Barbour, which bears the date 1859. Barbour was a son-in-law of Landy Alford, who gave the land for the Rockville church. These pioneers declined to follow the route taken by the Donner party and arrived by the Oregon route safely in 1847, making their home at first in Benicia. The Barbour house is situated on private property to the west of Russell Road and just north of Interstate Highway 80, from which it is visible over the treetops. Nothing remains of the 1865 stone Abernathie home, which was gutted by fire and finally dismantled in 1945, the building blocks being used for a patio and swimming pool. Some three miles of old stone fences erected by the first settlers for restraining cattle can be seen along the road over the hill west of Rockville to Green Valley.

The Rockville Stone Chapel

By 1852 Suisun Valley Creek, where baptism by total immersion was possible, had become an accepted spot for summer camp meetings. The settlers gathered from afar with their tents and cook stoves and even the family milk cow, prepared to spend a week. Circuit riders preached at the meetings and services lasted into the night, with the aid of lanterns hung in the oak trees. At two such camp meetings, in 1854 and 1855, $5,000 was raised to build a permanent structure, the Rockville Stone Chapel. Landy and Sarah Alford gave five acres for the site of the church and a cemetery. Stone was quarried from the adjacent hills and the church was erected by volunteer labor, led by stone masons Joel Price and George Whitely. The cornerstone was laid October 3, 1856, by the Rev. Sylvester Woodbridge of Benicia, aided by the Masonic order. Christmas services were held in the church that year, although it was not formally dedicated until February 1857 by the Revs. Morris Evans and Orcenith Fisher. The latter became known as the "Son of Thunder" because his voice was not trained to speak within stone walls.

Many pioneers were Southerners and deeply conscious of the split in the Methodist Episcopal

Church caused by the question of slavery. One Sunday in 1863 the predominating Northerners sang the "Battle Cry of Freedom." The Southerners promptly installed a stone plaque, still visible, reading "M. E. Church South 1856," and the Northerners began to worship elsewhere.

Tragically, the first white burial in the cemetery was the Alfords' three-year-old daughter, in December 1856. An unusual stone cairn with deeply carved letters on the top marks her grave. Among other pioneer graves is that of Granville P. Swift, a Bear Flag party member, who met his death in a fall from a horse while prospecting in the Suisun hills. The cemetery was subsequently expanded by donations of land from Lewis Pierce and J. M. and Caroline Baldwin.

Regular services were held in the chapel (*SRL 779*), just north of the Rockville crossroads, until 1895 and occasional services until 1919. The building gradually deteriorated except for the stone walls, which had withstood the 1906 earthquake. In 1929 the reunited Methodist Episcopal Church deeded it to the Rockville Public Cemetery District on condition that it be restored as a pioneer monument. This was accomplished in 1940. It is best described in the words of Mrs. Walter Scarlett as "a sturdy rock-walled church among great brooding trees that spread green arms around it and raise still heads above it as though in wordless prayer."

Suisun

In October 1850 Dr. John Baker and Curtis Wilson sailed up the Suisun Slough to Suisun Island, a bit of hard upland rising from the marsh, and landed at the present site of the city of Suisun, where they discovered a herd of elk among the tules. In this same year Captain Josiah Wing began to run various watercraft to the island; in 1852 he erected a warehouse on this "embarcadero" (the name by which the place was then known), and his schooner, the *Ann Sophia*, transported the produce of the valley, beginning an industry that assumed vast proportions as the country became more populous. In 1854 the Captain and John Owen, who later became a merchant in the place, laid out the town of Suisun west of the wharf and just below the southern boundary line of the Suisun grant. In 1857 the first church was built under the auspices of the "old school" Presbyterians, the land and building being donated by the people of the vicinity. In 1858 Captain Wing built a residence for himself in the town; and in 1868, the year of the coming of the railroad, Suisun was incorporated as a city.

The old plaza is formed by the broadening of Main Street between Solano and Morgan streets. On a town map of 1877, the post office, a flouring-mill, and the Roberts Hotel are shown as three of the buildings on the plaza. This hotel was replaced in 1888 by the Arlington Hotel, which stood at the northwest corner of Main and Solano streets until 1959. The oldest surviving house, reputed to have been built in 1856, was once owned by Samuel Brecht and is located at 259 Line Street. Years ago a plank walk nearly a mile

Rockville Stone Chapel

long spanned the marsh between Suisun and Fairfield. Today, after draining and filling work, the pavement is continuous between the two towns, and transcontinental trains have a station on the dividing line that serves both towns. Benjamin F. Rush, a State Senator for 24 years, claimed Suisun as his home.

Tolenas Springs, an early Indian spa, is located in the hills about one and one-half miles west of the freeway and five miles north of Suisun. It is on private property, and access is barred by a padlocked gate. The medicinal water was bottled and was very popular until about 1905. The Indians called the area "Land of Healing Waters." Tolenas Springs has a deposit of clear, textured white onyx crossed by light yellow veins. The polished onyx was used in the 1880's for ornamental clocks. Today the onyx ledge is a quarry for crushed white rock used on dwelling roofs and in garden patios.

The Suisun marsh was a famous duck-hunting area for San Francisco sportsmen. It was made available by the completion of the Northern Railroad through the swamplands in 1879. Stations named Jacksnipe, Teal, Cygnus, and Goodyear gave access to such gun clubs as Gray Goose, Sheldrake, Red Rooster, Teal, Family, Ibis, Sunrise, Roos Bros., and Goodyear.

California's Second State Capital

Just west of the former intersection of York and Sacramento streets in the city of Vallejo, and on the south side of what was York Street, the second capitol of the State of California (*SRL 574*) was located in 1852. The first state capital was at San Jose, and it had been moved to Vallejo because of the magnificent offers made to the state legislature by General Mariano G. Vallejo. Out of his vast estate, Vallejo had generously granted land on which to build the city of Vallejo and had also promised to erect a capitol building, lodgings, and social institutions, such as schools, churches, and asylums. The legislature, out of compliment to the General, named the new town Vallejo, although he himself had suggested "Eureka."

A frame capitol building was erected in the new town by the end of 1850, and on January 5, 1852, the legislature met. But it was dissatisfied with the poor housing facilities, and, as Vallejo found himself unable to fulfill his promises of accessory buildings, the legislature moved out precipitately on January 12, and went to Sacramento. A devastating flood in Sacramento caused them to adjourn on May 4, 1852, to meet again in Vallejo, January 3, 1853. On February 4 this "Peripatetic Government," or "Capital on Wheels," as it has been variously designated, was carried to the neighboring town of Benicia, where it remained until February 25, 1854, when Sacramento finally won the fight for the state capital.

The buildings that comprised the town of Vallejo in 1850 were situated between Sonoma Street on the east, Branciforte Street on the west, Virginia Street on the north, and Pennsylvania Street on the south.

A Methodist Episcopal church was organized there in 1855. It was the outcome of a Sunday school that Mrs. David G. Farragut, wife of the first commandant of the Mare Island Navy Yard, and others had been conducting for some months. In 1856 General John B. Frisbie donated a site for the edifice, giving a deed to five gentlemen, one of them being Commander (later Admiral) Farragut—"In trust for the Methodist Episcopal Church in the town of Vallejo." Upon this lot and largely through the exertion of Farragut, a small rough structure was built, which served for a time the double purpose of chapel and schoolhouse—the first record of a publicly supported school in Vallejo. When this was burned, it was replaced by another, which was later sold. The site is at 420 Virginia Street. General Frisbie likewise contributed the land upon which the Ascension Episcopal Church (1867) stands, and was a benefactor in other civic projects.

Vallejo became the terminus of the California Pacific Railroad in 1865–66, with the line running to Sacramento; by 1870 another terminus was established in Marysville. The same Vallejo terminus now serves the Southern Pacific Railroad. Vallejo was the site of one of California's earliest orphanages, built by the Good Templars of California and Nevada in 1869 and operated until the early 1920's. The site of the large home and school is on the hilltop near the present intersection of La Crescenda and Rincon Way. Vallejo was the leading shipping point for wheat exports in the United States in 1869–70. The elevators were located where the Sperry Division of General Mills, Inc., now operates—at the railroad terminus in south Vallejo.

Mare Island

The United States Naval Shipyard (SRL 751) is located on Mare Island, just across the Napa River from Vallejo. The island was granted to one Castro by Governor Alvarado. Castro sold it to John B. Frisbie, son-in-law of General Vallejo, and a man named Simmons, and in 1851 Frisbie and Simmons sold it to W. H. Aspinwall and G. W. P. Bissell.

The island was first named "Isla Plana" in 1775 by Juan Manuel de Ayala of the San Carlos. The legend of its present name is connected with General Vallejo. One day a barge transporting horses and cattle across the Carquinez Straits was caught in a sudden squall. The frightened animals stampeded, capsizing the frail craft. Some of them were lost, but one white mare, much prized by the General's wife, swam to a neighboring island, where she was rescued a few days later. General Vallejo was so glad to have the horse back again that he named the island "La Isla de la Yegua" (Mare Island).

In 1851 the Congress authorized a floating drydock for the West Coast; in 1852 a Naval Commission headed by Commodore John D. Sloat was sent to the San Francisco Bay area to investigate and recommend a site for a navy yard and depot. Mare Island was selected and purchased by the federal government for $83,401. The first commandant arrived on September 16, 1854, and immediately began construction of a shipyard. This young officer was Commander David G. Farragut, U.S.N., who was later to become the hero of the battles of Vicksburg and Mobile Bay in the Civil War and to be named the Navy's first full admiral.

Mare Island covers some 2,700 acres of ground. In addition to the shipyard, it has an ammunition depot, a marine barracks, the Navy's West Coast radio transmitting station, a nuclear power school, and a naval missile school (which occupies the former buildings of the naval hospital). The naval shipyard has built over 500 craft for the Navy, including the battleship California. It built the first warship on the coast (Saginaw, 1859), converted the Navy's coal burner to oil (Cheyenne, 1908), built the first flight deck on any ship in the world (cruiser Pennsylvania, 1911), and built the hull of the world's first aircraft carrier (Langley). Mare Island had the first radio station in the Pacific. The Navy's oldest chapel, St. Peter's, dedicated in 1901, stands here. Mare Island's cemetery was established in 1856 and contains 900 graves, including those of sailors of eight nationalities and the daughter of Francis Scott Key, author of our national anthem.

Mare Island's gun park includes the two guns from the Union ship Kearsarge, which sank the Confederate blockade runner Alabama off Cherbourg, France, in 1864; the two forward guns of Farragut's flagship Hartford, which helped to silence the forts at the entrance of Mobile Bay; and the figurehead of the frigate Independence, built in 1812 and station ship at Mare Island from 1855 to 1913.

Mare Island is the only shipyard on the West Coast, private or public, equipped at this time to build nuclear-powered submarines. It has built both fast attack and Polaris-firing A-submarines since 1955. An earthen causeway now connects Mare Island with the mainland. The vehicle entrance is from the south side of the Sears Point road just west of Mare Island Straits. Visitors may apply to the Public Information Officer for permission to enter the grounds.

Vacaville

On August 21, 1850, Don Manuel Vaca deeded nine square miles of Rancho Los Putos to William McDaniel, who paid the sum of $3,000 in cash and agreed to lay out a townsite on one of the square miles, to name it Vacaville, and to give to the former owner certain town lots. This agreement was fulfilled by McDaniel and his partner, L. B. Mizner, and the plat of Vacaville was filed for record in 1851. The streets were given Spanish names, which were not retained by the American settlers. The earliest occupation of the settlers here was cutting the rank growth of wild oats and transporting the hay to landings on the Sacramento River.

A private school called Ulatis Academy was started in Vacaville in 1855 by a Professor Anderson from San Francisco. The academy was succeeded about 1861 by the Pacific Methodist College under the auspices of the Methodist Episcopal Church, South, with the Rev. J. C. Steward as its first president. The poet Edwin Markham was one of the students. The college was moved to Santa Rosa in October 1871 and was succeeded by the California College. The site of the college grounds, as shown on a map of 1877, was the plaza between Ulatis Creek and Callen Street. A high school was afterwards built, but now the plaza is a city park, with only a grammar school on the eastern portion. The one surviving college building, thought to have been a girls' dormitory, is a brick dwelling south of Ulatis Creek, at 712 East Main Street.

Fruit growing replaced the cattle ranchos, and in 1869 this caused the Vaca Valley and Clear Lake Railroad spur to be built to Elmira, formerly called Vaca Station. A one-horsepower "locomotive" was first installed on a treadmill on a small flatcar. A down-grade led to Elmira, and unfortunately acceleration proved faster than the "locomotive"—Mr. Stevenson's buggy horse. The horse fell, brakes were applied, and the return to Vacaville was attempted. Again, the pull of gravity proved stronger than the "locomotive" and an engine had to be substituted.

Vacaville grew; fires destroyed the wooden buildings; brick structures were erected on Main Street, only to be shaken down by the earthquake of 1892. None of the pioneer business buildings survive today.

The famous "Nut Tree" wayside place, now within the city limits, was started by a black walnut planted in 1860 by Josiah Allison, a pioneer of 1854. Sally Fox, his small niece, had picked up the nut in Arizona while crossing the Great American Desert. A huge tree grew beside the Western Wagon Road, now Interstate Highway 80, and became shelter for a fruit stand. The tree is gone, but from this meager beginning Allison's descendants have developed the nationally known "Nut Tree" restaurant and recreation center.

Silveyville

Silveyville, on the old route between Napa and Sacramento, was a halfway house established by Elijah S. Silvey, who made two trips from Missouri to California, accompanied by his wife and two children, before settling permanently here. Coming first in 1849, he remained in the West for two years. On his second arrival in 1852, he built a house for his family and a corral for the herd of 100 milk cows he had brought. His house

became a country hotel, and the corral accommodated horses of the stagecoaches and freight wagons. It became his custom to place a red lantern aloft at night to guide travelers to and from the gold regions. A trading center called Silveyville developed there, only to be moved bodily five miles east to the new California Pacific Railroad in 1868. Thomas Dickson donated ten acres on the exact line of the railway for a station, and at that spot a town grew up, taking the name of its benefactor but misspelling it Dixon. Silveyville gradually disappeared. The townsite is now a farm. Some of the frame buildings were moved intact, while the bricks of the merchandise store were hauled to the new town and employed in constructing the Capitol Hotel, which stood until 1920. The old Methodist Episcopal church was moved in the spring of 1870 to Dixon, where services are still held at its present location on the corner of North Jefferson and West B streets.

Fairfield

The location of the county seat at Benicia caused dissatisfaction because it was on the very edge of the county—a serious defect in those days of slow locomotion, when residents of outlying sections had business to transact. The agitation for a change became acute in 1857. As a result, R. H. Waterman, an old sea captain, once warden of the Port of San Francisco, who in 1848 had purchased with Archibald A. Ritchie four leagues of the Suisun grant, made a gift of a block of land and money to place the county buildings upon it. On September 2, 1858, a vote of the people chose Fairfield to replace Benicia, and Captain Waterman's offer was accepted. The plat of the town was filed for record on May 15, 1859. The name Fairfield, after Captain Waterman's birthplace in Connecticut, was given to the place. An effort in 1873 to move the county seat to Vallejo met with failure.

The home in which Captain Waterman lived is one mile north of Fairfield off Mankas Corner Road. The carefully built two-story frame house, standing at the end of a long drive between eucalyptus trees planted by him, is in excellent condition; the marble fireplaces, high ceilings, and curved staircase are in as good condition as if the owner only yesterday had stepped out of the place. The bronze ship's bell is carefully preserved. Seven fine old fig trees planted by him grow near the house, which was built in 1853. A cupola that he called his "pilot house" has been removed. The present owner is E. C. Allan.

The huge Travis Air Force Base, home of most of the transpacific military air traffic, is located four miles northeast of Fairfield. It is named in honor of Brigadier General Robert F. Travis, who was killed there in an airplane accident on August 5, 1950.

Rio Vista

In the fall of 1857 a town called "Brazos del Río" (Arms of the River) was laid out by Colonel N. H. Davis on his land at the upper end of the Ulpinos grant near the junction of Cache Slough and the Sacramento River. The wharf constructed by Colonel Davis in 1858 was sold the following year to the Steam Navigation Company, which doubled the size of the wharf to accommodate large steamers.

The name of the settlement was changed to Rio Vista, but on January 9, 1862, heavy rains swept the town away. The inhabitants began to look for a better location, and negotiations were entered into with Joseph Bruning for a location in the upper edge of the Montezuma Hills, in the northeast corner of his ranch. The new town plat was surveyed and recorded; part of the site was on the Bruning property and part on the adjoining ranch of T. J. McWorthy. The main street of the New Rio Vista now runs between these two old farms, but the "New," as used in the recorded plat, has been dropped in favor of simple Rio Vista.

Saint Gertrude's Academy was founded and erected in Rio Vista by Joseph Bruning in 1876 and was placed under the direction of the Sisters of Mercy. It was a boarding school for young ladies and a day academy for girls and small boys, and was named in honor of the patron saint of Elizabeth Gertrude Bruning, wife of the donor. Located on an eminence in the western part of the town, it remained a popular and useful school until 1928. The site, at the head of California Street, is now a subdivision. Saint Joseph's Academy, built about the same time as Saint Gertrude's, was on the corner of Front Street and St. Gertrude's Avenue. Nothing remains of it. The Catholic church built in 1862 at the northwest corner of California and Fourth streets is still in use. The oldest residence, built in 1862, is still occupied as such and is located at 198 Logan Street.

Rio Vista, on the edge of the rich asparagus lands of the delta, sits on the largest gas field in northern California. Since the discovery well in 1936, more than 100 producing wells have been drilled. These may be recognized by the "Christmas trees" (machinery) above them.

Landings

Solano County, bordered on the south and east by the Sacramento River, Suisun and San Pablo bays, and the Straits of Carquinez, began at an early date to make use of water transportation for freight and passengers. Embarcaderos were placed in many inland sloughs and landings along the river. Maine Prairie, at the head of navigation on the Maine Prairie Slough (Cache Slough, circa 1877), shipped much of the wild oat hay and wheat from northern Solano County, even before Captain J. C. Merithew settled there, in 1859. Fifty thousand tons were said to be transported in one season. The settlement grew until a flood in January 1862 swept it away. A new town called Alton was erected on higher ground about a quarter of a mile distant. On recession of the flood waters, some of the inhabitants rebuilt at the original site. The Maine Prairie post office had been established late in 1861, and Captain Merithew was named postmaster the following year. With the advent of railroads, the prosperity of these communities decreased and the last

buildings burned about 1925. The embarcadero was on Maine Prairie Slough south of the intersection of Bartlett Road and Bunker Station Road.

Newton Landing, just north of Rio Vista, and Toland Landing, five miles south of that city, were both on the Sacramento River. Near Toland Landing stood the "Twin Houses," the home of Robert E. Beasley, one of the purchasers of the tracts sold from Rancho Ulpinos in 1855. Beasley had settled on the southern end of this grant in 1851 and established a ferry from the mainland, near Toland Landing, across to Sherman Island, using a flatboat and chains. Like many another pioneer, he had ordered a house to be sent to him around the Horn. When the house arrived in 1851, he was surprised to see that it had been framed a double house. This he erected about two hundred yards above the Landing and occupied for some years. Toland Landing was named for Dr. Hugh Hugar Toland, founder of what became the University of California Medical School in San Francisco. He gradually acquired 11,800 acres of the Los Ulpinos grant, but did not reside on it. The ranch was operated for him by W. B. Pressley and E. C. Dozier, who, after Dr. Toland's death, rented and eventually purchased part of it. Descendants of Dozier and Pressley own Toland Landing today. It is accessible only by a three-mile, narrow road through their ranch, known as Toland Lane, and only a few burned piles remain at the site of the embarcadero.

The town of Denverton grew out of Nurse's Landing. Dr. Stephen K. Nurse, in 1849 a partner of L. B. Mizner in a four-mule stage line from Benicia to Sacramento, purchased property in 1853 on the slough afterward called by his name. There he built a house, and the next year he followed it with a store building and a wharf. The place, originally called Nurse's Landing, was established as a post office and given the name Denverton in 1858, honoring J. W. Denver, member of Congress from the district, who was locally popular at the time, because he had stood out firmly against a bill to confirm all existing land grants under ten leagues in extent. Dr. Nurse was made postmaster, and held the position for 19 years. In 1875 he constructed a telegraph line from Denverton to Suisun, which in 1876 was merged into the Montezuma Telegraph Company, of which he was president. None of the original buildings stand at Denverton, which still exists as a tiny hamlet just off Highway 12 and is indicated by a road sign.

Birds Landing, south of Denverton and on Montezuma Slough northwest of Collinsville, was originally a shipping point for John Bird, a native of New York, who had arrived in California in 1859. He purchased 1,000 acres of land in 1865 and started a storage and commission business. The building of the wharf about 1869 afforded an easy means of shipment of hay and wheat, which were the main products of the surrounding farms. Only a few piles remain of the wharf today. A post office was established in 1876 at a crossroads about half a mile northeast of the embarcadero and was given the same name. Birds Landing is now a favorite haunt for bass fishermen.

From Dillon's Point at the east end of the Carquinez Strait, Patrick W. Dillon, farmer and stonecutter from Ireland, shipped stone which he quarried from his own ground. Having arrived in Benicia in 1851, he soon started the pioneer stone business in San Francisco, furnishing some of the stone for the old St. Mary's Cathedral.

On the slough northwest of Collinsville were Mein's and Dutton's landings. At Mein's Landing, one mile due west of the Birds Landing crossroads, the house built about 1880 by Captain Mein is still standing, used as headquarters for a private duck club. Dutton's Landing, about two miles northwest of Collinsville, was the site of a former ferry. It can now be reached only by the Grizzly Island Road, across that island. Lord Landing and Goodyear Landing on Goodyear Slough northeast of Benicia were also early landings within the county limits.

Binghamton Hall

In Maine Prairie Township a military company called the "Maine Prairie Rifles" was organized in 1863 during the Civil War period. The company headquarters were at Binghamton, about four miles west of Maine Prairie, where a brick, fireproof armory was erected. After the necessity for using the place as an armory had passed, an upper story was added to the structure for use as a public hall, the main floor being used for a store. Later the whole building was purchased for a public school, which was conducted upstairs above the store. Long idle, it was finally razed in July 1950 and the brick salvaged. The unmarked site is seven miles south of Dixon on the east side of the Dixon–Rio Vista Road.

SOURCES

Bowman, J. N., and G. W. Hendry. "Spanish and Mexican Houses in the Nine Bay Counties." Ms., Bancroft Library, Berkeley; State Library, Sacramento, 1942.

Chapman, Charles E. *A History of California: The Spanish Period.* Macmillan, New York, 1921.

Cleland, Robert Glass. *From Wilderness to Empire. A History of California,* ed. Glenn S. Dumke. Knopf, New York, 1959.

Coy, Owen C. *Pictorial History of California.* University of California Extension Division, Berkeley, 1925.

Crystal, Helen Dormody. "The Beginnings of Vacaville." M.A. thesis, University of California, 1933.

Dykes, William. *Historical Benicia.* Folder published at Benicia.

Fowler, Harlan D. *Camels to California.* Stanford University Press, Stanford, 1950.

Gregory, Tom. *History of Solano and Napa Counties, California.* Historic Record Company, Los Angeles, 1912.

Guinn, J. M. *History of the State of California.* Chapman Publishing Co., Chicago, 1904.

Harte, Bret. "Concepción de Argüello," *Complete Poetical Works.* Household Ed., Houghton Mifflin, Boston, 1912.

Historical Atlas of Solano County. Thompson & West, San Francisco, 1878.

History of Solano County. Wood, Alley & Co., San Francisco, 1879.

Hunt, Marguerite, and Lawrence Gunn. *History of Solano County and Napa County.* 2 vols. S. J. Clarke Publishing Co., Chicago, 1926.

Hyatt, T. Hart. *Handbook of Grape Culture.* H. H. Bancroft and Co., San Francisco, 1867.

Kemble, John Haskell. "The Genesis of the Pacific Mail Steamship Company in California," *Historical Society Quarterly,* XIII, Nos. 3 and 4.

McGowan, Joseph A. *History of the Sacramento Valley.* 3 vols. Lewis Historical Publishing Co., New York, 1961.

Rensch, Hero Eugene. "Educational Activities of the Protestant Churches in California, 1849–1860." M.A. thesis in history, Stanford University, 1929.

Sanchez, Nellie Van de Grift. "Solano, Noted California Indian," *Motor Land,* XXXIII, No. 2 (February 1933), 8, 17.

Taylor, Bayard. *Eldorado, or Adventures in the Path of Empire.* 7th ed. Putnam, New York, 1855.

Young, Wood. *Vaca-Peña Los Putos Rancho and the Peña Adobe.* Wheeler Printing and Publishing, Vallejo, 1965.

Sonoma County

SONOMA COUNTY was one of the original 27 counties. (Sonoma is of Indian origin and is said to have been the name of an Indian chief who was baptized by the mission fathers in 1824.) The county seat was located at the town of Sonoma from 1850 to 1854. Since 1854 it has been at Santa Rosa.

Discovery and Naming of Bodega Bay

On October 3, 1775, Juan Francisco de la Bodega y Cuadra, Spanish explorer, in the little schooner *Sonora* discovered the bay that bears his name. Bodega's voyage was a part of Spain's plan of approach to California from the sea and was

very successfully accomplished, his careful observations and acts of possession being of great benefit to succeeding explorers and colonizers.

On October 20, 1793, Archibald Menzies, a naturalist of the expedition led by Captain George Vancouver, landed on the northwestern shore of Bodega Bay near an island (probably Bodega Rock), which the party named Gibson Island, in the hope of collecting botanical specimens. Partly because the ground had been burned over recently by the Indians and partly because of the season of the year he found few plants; and, to his disappointment, these few were similar to those that he had already found at Mon-

terey and San Francisco. The party, which encountered a small group of peaceful Indians, did,
however, find something of interest—a cross
formed of a "piece of stave of a cask fastened to
a pole by rope yarn."

Coming of the Russians

In 1741, Admiral Vitus Bering discovered the
sea and the strait that bear his name. On this
voyage he also discovered Alaska, whose waters
were alive with fur seal. Other expeditions followed in 1765.

These activities on the part of the Russians undoubtedly had some influence in rousing Spain
to the danger of losing California, and led to a
speedier occupation of San Diego and Monterey.
Subsequently, they led also to the founding of
missions, military posts, and pueblos north of San
Francisco Bay.

The Russians eventually came down from the
north and settled in California. By the close of
the eighteenth century, the Russian-American
Fur Company had established itself on the Aleu-
tian Islands and on the coast of Alaska. These
colonies were rich in furs but lacked immediate
trade connections by which they could obtain
food and other necessary supplies. Russia began
to look southward to California, with its warm
climate and fertile soil, from which she might
supply her starving northern colonists with food.

In 1806 the Czar's chamberlain, Count Nikolai
Rezanov, went to Sitka on official business. He
found the colonists starving and stricken with
scurvy and fever. Temporary relief was obtained
from an American ship, but something more permanent was needed. Accordingly, Rezanov sailed
south to seek negotiations with the Spanish officials of San Francisco, well knowing that trade
with foreigners was forbidden.

The advent of the Russians into California is
closely associated with the names of two women:
in the opening chapter of the story, that of the
lovely Spanish girl, Concepción Argüello, and, at
the close, that of the Russian princess, Helena de
Gagarin.

The story of Concepción and her love for the
Russian Count Rezanov is told in connection with
the San Francisco Presidio, where the romance
began, and with Benicia, where Concepción spent
the closing years of her life in the Convent of St.
Catherine.

Undoubtedly, Nikolai Rezanov had political
ambitions for Russia when he visited California
in 1806. Doubtless, too, his courtship of Concepción Argüello, though not unmixed with diplomacy, was sincere. Certainly, its result was very
propitious for his enterprise. That his ultimate
purpose was to establish a Russian colony in
northern California is quite clearly shown in the
account of the expedition by Langsdorff, his
friend and companion.

Rezanov's untimely death on the steppes of
Russia prevented him from carrying out this plan
himself. His purpose, however, was fulfilled a
few years later by another Russian, Ivan A. Kuskov, an agent of the Russian-American Fur Company.

Founding of Bodega Bay, Kuskov,
and Fort Ross

Rezanov had taken careful observations all
along the coast on his return voyage to Alaska
in 1806, and his report was most favorable. In
1809, Kuskov came down from Sitka prepared to
make temporary settlements. One was made at
Bodega Bay and another in the Salmon Creek
Valley six miles inland. Wheat was sown and
harvested, and in August, with the precious store
of food and 2,000 otter skins, Kuskov returned to
Alaska.

In 1811, Kuskov came again as governor of the
Russian settlements to be established in California. Although he went through no ceremony of
taking possession of the land for Russia, he made
permanent settlements at Kuskov, in Salmon
Creek Valley, and, in 1812, at Fort Ross, 12 miles

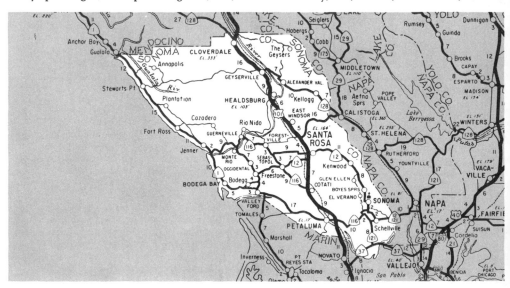

north of the mouth of the Russian River on a high bluff overlooking the sea.

These settlements, especially the one at Fort Ross, were fortified and the Russian flag raised over them. Title to the territory for a considerable distance had been secured from the Indians who inhabited the region.

Today nothing remains to mark the site of the settlement in Salmon Creek Valley. This location, where Stephen Smith later settled, is about a mile northwest of Bodega.

Fort Ross

The Russian settlements flourished, and the one at Fort Ross, which had been dedicated in 1812, became the center of activities. Not only did the settlers gather rich fur harvests on land and sea, but they became a prosperous agricultural community, supplying food to the Alaskan colonies as well as to their own people. During the years 1810–22, they also carried on a considerable trade with their Spanish neighbors, who were eager to secure the finely made manufactured articles which the Russians had to exchange for food supplies. This trade was carried on in spite of the fact that it was still officially forbidden. The Californians made opportunities for it, and almost no friction arose between the two peoples.

However, fear of the Russian advance in northern California undoubtedly led the Spanish authorities to explore and settle the regions north of San Francisco Bay in what are now Solano, Sonoma, and Marin counties.

In December 1823 the Monroe Doctrine was promulgated by the United States. Monroe was not only thinking of the newly liberated colonies in South America when he issued this famous document; he was also considering the growing menace of the Russian Empire in Alaska and on the whole Pacific Coast, especially in Alta California.

"The challenge of Fort Ross, with its cannon, its high palisades, its farms and herds of cattle— all tangible evidences of a permanent plan of colonization—was met by Monroe" in his message. It brought a definite end to any Russian program of acquiring California.

In 1824, Russia agreed to limit all future settlements to Alaska, but for nearly 20 years longer the colony at Ross remained independent of Mexican control. By 1840, however, the sea otter had been almost exterminated, and the Russian-American Fur Company could no longer maintain the American colonies. The political aspect had also ceased to be of moment, and, by 1839, Russian officials had sent orders for the withdrawal of all colonists from California. The entire property was sold in 1841 to Johann August Sutter of New Helvetia (Sacramento) and the colonists returned to Alaska.

The original inhabitants of Fort Ross consisted of about 100 Russians and 80 Aleuts, the maximum population never exceeding 400. The settlement stood on a bluff above a little cove in the sea. The land sloped gently upward to the base of a range of hills covered with pine, fir, cedar,

and laurel. The whole setting was exceedingly picturesque in a wild rugged way.

The fort itself was enclosed by a palisade built of heavy redwood timbers and mounted with cannon. Two blockhouses, one octagonal and the other heptagonal, surmounting the corners of the palisade, faced the sea on the southwest and the land on the northeast corners. Within the enclosure were nine buildings, among them the commander's quarters and chapel. Outside were 50 buildings, besides blacksmith, carpenter, and cooper shops and a large stable for 200 milk cows. At the landing place on the beach below was the boathouse, and there seagoing vessels were built.

Fort Ross State Historical Monument (SRL 5) has been owned by the state since 1906 and is partially restored. The quaint Russian Orthodox chapel with its hexagonal tower and round cupola, all built of redwood, remains, also the commander's house and the bastions, and the grounds are enclosed by the reconstructed stockade. Restoration of other buildings is contemplated. A tablet was placed on the chapel by the Native Sons of the Golden West in 1928. Fort Ross has merited to be registered as a National Historic Landmark by the United States Department of the Interior.

Founding of Misión San Francisco Solano

In 1823, Governor Argüello became anxious to check the Russian advance into the interior north of San Francisco Bay, a region that Gabriel Moraga had already explored during the years 1812–14 and earlier. The Governor advised Father José Altimira, a young priest newly stationed at San Francisco, to transfer the Missions of San Francisco de Asís and San Rafael Arcángel to Sonoma without delay. The Sonoma site was chosen because of its proximity to the Russians and because its climate was more favorable for the Indian neophytes than that of the former missions. Without waiting for the final authorization by the proper church authorities, Father Altimira, young and zealous, set out at once to choose the site for the new mission, the foundations for which were laid perhaps as early as 1823.

Such a radical and unauthorized step occasioned much dissatisfaction among the fathers. A compromise was finally arranged, however, by which neither San Francisco de Asís nor San Ra-

Commander's House, Fort Ross

fael Arcángel was to be suppressed and the foundation of the new mission was to be recognized. It was called Misión San Francisco Solano *(SRL 3)*, in honor of St. Francis Solano, an illustrious Franciscan missionary to the New World who died in Peru in 1610, and was thus distinguished from Misión San Francisco de Asís at San Francisco, named in honor of St. Francis of Assisi.

This, the last and most northerly of the 21 California missions, was a plain, low building with an overhanging roof covering the corridors of the wing. After the secularization in 1834, the mission chapel was rebuilt by Don Mariano Guadalupe Vallejo, who was appointed *comisionado*. The mission then became the parish church, until it was sold in 1881 to Solomon Schocken by Archbishop Alemany and subsequently was used for secular purposes. In 1903 a public fund was raised and the old mission was deeded to the State of California. Today it is a State Historical Monument. It stands diagonally across from the northeast corner of the old Sonoma plaza. The padres' house, built about 1825, is the oldest structure remaining in Sonoma today. The present adobe church dates from about 1840, the earlier church having stood east of the padres' quarters.

Founding of the Pueblo of Sonoma

In 1833 Governor Figueroa, one of the greatest figures in the history of Alta California, proceeded to occupy and settle Marin and Sonoma counties. The primary object was to force the Russians out of California. Other governors had attempted to do this, but Figueroa was the first to be successful.

The man who was chiefly responsible for this success was Mariano Guadalupe Vallejo, then military commander and director of colonization on the northern frontier. In the summer of 1833 he made an official tour of the Russian settlements, where he made his mission clearly known to the Russian governor.

Spanish settlements were attempted at Petaluma, Santa Rosa, and Fulton, but the hostility of the Indians caused their abandonment. Sonoma Valley was then chosen as the place of settlement, and in 1835 the Pueblo de Sonoma was founded by General Vallejo at Mission San Francisco Solano.

The Sonoma Plaza

General Vallejo himself laid out the new pueblo around a square or plaza, which was used as a drilling ground from 1835 to 1846 for the soldiers who defended the pueblo. On the northeast corner of the plaza stood the mission church and next to it the padres' house. Adjoining the padres' house on the right was a larger adobe, in which Vallejo is said to have lived temporarily. This has long since disappeared. To the left of the church stood the barracks, a two-story building with a balcony. This house *(SRL 316)*, which is still standing, was built about 1837 by General Vallejo for his Mexican soldiers and was occupied by United States officers and soldiers from 1846

to 1848. It became a State Historical Monument in 1958.

Next to the barracks, a large two-story adobe mansion was erected soon after the founding of Sonoma. Here General Vallejo lived during the eventful years preceding California's annexation to the United States. The Vallejo adobe had a balcony extending across the front, and on the southwest corner there was a tall square tower. This tower served as a citadel from which there was an open view of the country in all directions. The mansion known as the Casa Grande, where 11 of General Vallejo's children were born, and the *torreon* (tower) were destroyed by fire on April 13, 1867. The long, low adobe in the rear, used as the Vallejo kitchen and servants' quarters, survived the fire, and is now owned, with the site of Casa Grande, by the State of California.

Other adobes were gradually built around the open plaza. A few of these remain today, some of them encased in wood but still retaining the picturesque Spanish balconies. One of these is the Fitch House, erected by Jacob P. Leese, a brother-in-law of General Vallejo. After the conquest it was used as the headquarters of General Persifer F. Smith. It is located at 487 First Street West near the corner of Napa Street.

The first home in Sonoma of Don Salvador Vallejo, the General's brother, was directly west of the Casa Grande, separated from it by a castellated wall. It was finished in time for him to bring there in September 1840 his bride, María de la Luz Carrillo, sister of the General's wife. The building is in good condition today and serves as the Swiss Hotel *(SRL 496)*. It stands at 18 West Spain Street.

Another picturesque remnant of early days is the Blue Wing Inn *(SRL 17)*, at 133 East Spain Street, opposite the mission. This was a rendezvous for the Argonauts of '49 and is said to have been frequented by Joaquín Murieta, the notorious Mexican bandit of the 1850's.

At 415–417 First Street West, opposite the northwest corner of the plaza, stands a large two-story structure *(SRL 501)*, with a balcony extending across the front, now housing the Hotel El Dorado and other businesses. It was built as a one-story adobe by Don Salvador Vallejo in the early 1840's and in 1848–49 was considered one of the finest hotels in California. Later a second story of wood was added, and it became the home of the Sonoma Academy, later Cumberland College, a Presbyterian co-educational boarding school from 1858 to 1864. In the 1880's it was the home and winery of Camille Aguillon.

Opposite the southwest corner of the plaza, at Napa Street and First Street West, long stood the Union Hotel and Union Hall *(SRL 627)*. The original hotel at this site was a one-story adobe and the adjoining hall was a one-story frame building. These were later replaced by a two-story stone hotel and a two-story frame hall with rooms upstairs for hotel guests. In 1955 the Bank of America acquired the property, and the following year the structures were razed. The bank now stands on the site of the hall and the hotel site is used as the parking lot.

The Sonoma plaza has been designated as a National Historic Landmark.

Sonoma can boast a few other old adobe buildings standing at some distance from the plaza. Among these are the John G. Ray house, built about 1847 at 205 East Spain Street, and the so-called Nash adobe (SRL 667) at 579 First Street East, built about 1847 by H. A. Green. Here John H. Nash, Sonoma alcalde, was arrested in July 1847 by Lieutenant William Tecumseh Sherman for refusing to relinquish his post to Lilburn W. Boggs.

In Sonoma's Mountain Cemetery is the grave of the only veteran of the American Revolutionary War to be buried in California. Captain William Smith, who joined the Virginia Navy as a boy of 11 in 1779, died in Sonoma in 1846. His grave was marked by the California State Society, Daughters of the American Revolution, on February 22, 1965.

The Naming of Mount St. Helena

The web of romance which the years have woven about majestic St. Helena has been traced by Honoria Tuomey. "We have, handed down to us in the Sonoma region," she said, "stories to the effect that pioneer representatives of each of the three races of white men that, in turn, settled here, gave a name to the striking elevation that rises into the blue to twice the height of the mother range running northwest and southeast as far as the eye can see. The startling, almost incredible part is, that the name Helena was bestowed at each christening, and that neither party knew if that or any other name had already been given."

The earliest of these tales is that of a Spanish friar who, seeking a mission site in the north, saw the great mountain rising above the wilderness. "After a few moments of fixed observation, there flashed to his mind a recollection of a tomb in an old abbey . . . of Rheims, and he pointed to the distant mountain and exclaimed: 'Behold St. Helena on her bier! It is her effigy, even to the pall.'" Many subsequent visitors have affirmed that the great mountain, with its six symmetrical peaks and graceful, flowing lines, does resemble the form of a woman "asleep in eternal repose."

In 1841 there came to Fort Ross a beautiful young bride of royal blood, Princess Helena de Gagarin, niece of the Czar of Russia and the bride of Count Alexander Rotcheff, governor-general of Siberia and of the Russian colonies on the shores of the North Pacific.

Princess Helena was an enterprising and romantic young woman. Having read the fascinating descriptions of California by Kotzebue, the Russian navigator, she was fired with a great desire to see the interior of California for herself. Accordingly, she planned the expedition, since become famous, which included the ascent and christening of Mount St. Helena in the Mayacama Mountains 15 miles northeast of the present town of Santa Rosa.

Traveling by way of age-old Indian trails across the head of the Estero Americano and the Llano de las Petalumas through the hill passes to the south, they proceeded northward over the old trail between Petaluma and Santa Rosa.

The mountain was ascended on June 20, after a difficult climb of 5,000 feet. At the summit, Princess Helena, enthralled by the magnificent view, had the Russian flag raised over the spot, and a memorial plate was placed, while she christened the mountain in honor of the patron saint of Helena, Empress of Russia.

In May 1853 the tablet placed on Mount St. Helena by the Princess was discovered by Dr. T. A. Hylton of Petaluma. It was later placed in the museum of the Society of California Pioneers in San Francisco but was destroyed in the fire of 1906. Dr. Hylton had made a facsimile of the tablet, and from this bit of paper, yellowed by time, a replica of the original plate was made years later. At the centenary of the founding of Fort Ross, in 1912, this tablet was placed on the summit of Mount St. Helena in honor of the first white people to climb it.

Mount St. Helena is the converging point of three counties, Sonoma, Lake, and Napa. On one of the northwest spurs of the mountain, seven airline miles northeast of Geyserville, are the Geysers, while on its southern slope, partly in Napa County and partly in Sonoma, lies the Petrified Forest—indications of the mountain's volcanic origin.

The closing episode in the fascinating story of the triple christening of the great mountain is associated with the coming of the Americans. "Hardly had the Russian colonists abandoned their settlements in the Bodega and Fort Ross regions . . . than, for the third time, Mount Saint Helena was confirmed in her name. It was a Yankee . . . that performed the service . . . none other than Captain Stephen Smith, noted pioneer ship-captain and trader in the days of the Dons, the first owner, by virtue of a Mexican grant, of the lion's share of the territory that the Russians had occupied during their stay in California . . .

"There was little of the romantic in Stephen Smith, tough, sturdy old master of men and of the sea. He had a sailing vessel down at yonder landing that had come to him from Russian ownership. On the bows was borne its name, 'Saint Helena' . . . and he proceeded to bestow it on the mountain that seemed an outpost between the wide interior of the continent and his far Pacific home."

The Bear Flag Revolt

In the spring of 1846 many American settlers in the Sacramento Valley and neighboring valleys believed that there was danger of their being driven from the country by General José Castro, commander of the Mexican Army. Encouraged by Captain John C. Frémont of the United States forces, a group of 33 men surprised General Vallejo at Sonoma and took possession of his fortified stronghold on June 14, 1846. In spite of the fact that Vallejo had always been favorable to the United States, he and his brother, Don Salvador, and Victor Prudon (Prudhomme) were taken prisoners of war and carried to Sutter's Fort, where they were kept for two months.

William B. Ide was left in command of the rebel forces at Sonoma. Since the action of the insurgents did not represent the United States government, the Stars and Stripes could not be raised in place of the Mexican flag. A new flag was therefore created for the purpose which was called the Bear Flag of the "California Republic." It was made with a white field and a border of red on the lower part. A bear and a star were its emblems. On July 9, 1846, the Bear Flag was lowered and the Stars and Stripes raised by Lieutenant Joseph Warren Revere, the grandson of Paul Revere.

The Bear Flag Monument (SRL 7), in the form of a bronze statue representing a young pioneer clutching the staff of the Bear Flag, which floats above him, was placed on the old Sonoma plaza by the State of California and dedicated June 14, 1915. A bas-relief on the face of the pedestal shows the raising of the Bear Flag in 1846.

One of the Bear Flaggers later settled about four miles southwest of Sonoma. In 1858 Captain Granville Perry Swift constructed Temelec Hall (SRL 237), the magnificent stone mansion that still stands, using forced Indian labor. Its cost was estimated at $250,000, the most expensive home in the county at the time. It contains about 20 large rooms and nine fireplaces, all with marble mantels. Long a private home, Temelec Hall is now the community center of a retirement subdivision off Arnold Drive.

Petrified Forest

Surrounded by groves of living oak, fir, and redwood, the famous Petrified Forest lies across a small valley from the western base of Mount St. Helena at an elevation of 1,000 feet. The petrified trees comprising the group are mainly redwood, silicified and opalized. They lie "in two tiers in a parallelogram a mile in extent from east to west and about a quarter of a mile from north to south." The trees, measuring from three and a half to 12 feet in diameter and as much as 126 feet in length, were buried millions of years ago by lava from the great crater five miles to the north. The fact that the trees are all lying with their tops pointing away from Mount St. Helena seems to indicate that lava streams from the great cone caused their downfall and their ultimate preservation in forms of stone.

The forest was discovered in the 1850's, but excavation was not begun until 1871, when Charles Evans, "Petrified Charlie," a prospector, homesteaded the land. Much of the brush, volcanic ashes, and deposits of silica which had pressed upon the trees for ages was removed by Charlie Evans, who enclosed the ground and charged a small fee to visitors. After his death in 1878 the place was given over to agriculture until 1914. On October 1 of that year it was acquired by a new owner, who carried on extensive developments. Under her management the place has become a goal for lovers of natural phenomena.

In all the specimens found in this ancient "stone forest," the transmutation from wood to stone has been so perfect that texture and fiber are completely preserved, making it easy for scientists to determine species. Many of the trees are of great size, and, though broken, retain the relative positions of the pieces. The largest tree in the group was uncovered in 1919 at a depth of 90 feet. It lies intact and is one of the most perfect specimens known. In 1930 Professor Erlingdorf of Princeton University found 12 varieties of prehistoric fossilized leaves on the property, which he pronounced a valuable discovery in the scientific world.

The Petrified Forest can be reached by leaving Freeway 101 at the Russell Avenue exit north of Santa Rosa, driving one and one-half miles north on Business Route 101 to Mark West Springs Road, then 12 miles northeast via this road and its continuations, Porter Creek Road and Petrified Forest Road. The forest lies five miles west of Calistoga (Napa County).

En route from Santa Rosa are the Mark West Springs, mineral hot springs discovered in 1857 by William Travis. The place became one of the popular spas of the nineteenth century and is one of the few still operating as a resort.

The Geysers

Long before the coming of the white man, the Indians had brought their sick to the healing waters of the many mineral springs in the vicinity of the Geysers. To the red man the region was the last creation of the Great Spirit, a place sacred to his medicine man, who worked miracles through the wonders of its medicinal waters.

In April 1847 William B. Elliott, pioneer hunter and trapper, came suddenly upon the Geysers while tracking a wounded bear. Returning to Sonoma, he told his friends that he had found the gates to the Inferno.

The variety and beauty of the region, its hissing fumaroles or volcanic vents from which shoot immense jets of steam a hundred feet or more into the air, and many other natural wonders may well call forth awe, if not superstition. Some of the most notable features are known as "The Devil's Grist Mill," "Steamboat Geyser," "The Witches' Cauldron," and "The Mountain of Fire."

Since 1854, when 20 people registered at the inn, visitors in increasing numbers have come to see this attraction. During 1875 as many as 3,500 passed that way. The first stage road, which went only to the foot of the mountain, had then been extended to the Geysers themselves and since 1869 had been a toll road. The first wheeled vehicle to go into the place was a double team and buggy driven by R. C. Flournoy on May 15, 1861. The old hotel, built in 1856–58 from lumber sawed on the spot, is still a landmark in the region. On its register are the names of many famous people: U. S. Grant, William McKinley, Theodore Roosevelt, Mark Twain, Horace Greeley, Garibaldi, William Jennings Bryan, and J. Pierpont Morgan.

The Geysers, which are now being used as a

source of thermopower by the Pacific Gas and Electric Company, are located 18 miles east of Cloverdale and 25 miles northeast of Healdsburg on a good modern road. They may be reached from the Redwood Highway from Cloverdale, Geyserville, or Lytton.

Rancho Arroyo de San Antonio
Rancho Roblar de Miseria

After the issuance on August 17, 1833, of the government decree to secularize the missions and to give their lands to private individuals, inducements were held out to Mexican citizens to migrate to California. A colony under the charge of Don José M. Híjar arrived in Alta California in 1834, and one of the number was Antonio Ortega, a Mexican officer, who came with the express purpose of obtaining a grant of land. Proceeding northward, he arrived at Sonoma Mission and was at once appointed administrator by General Vallejo at a salary of $500 a year. This appointment was approved by Governor Figueroa.

Ortega later married Francisca, daughter of Juan Miranda, and applied for permission to settle upon Rancho Arroyo de San Antonio, consisting of three square leagues about eight miles from the town of Sonoma. The permission granted, he at once built a log house and corral and stocked the place with cattle and horses which he purchased from Vallejo. The cultivation of a portion of the land was begun; 50 or more acres were planted to corn, pumpkins, and many other kinds of vegetables. His family and that of his father-in-law moved to the rancho and lived as one family, the father-in-law being placed in charge of its operation.

Difficulty regarding the title seems to have arisen out of a series of mishaps. The first of these was that when Ortega was ready to file his map of the property the Departmental Assembly (the body to which it must be presented) was not in session. The papers were said to have been left in the keeping of Governor Alvarado. Some years later, in 1843, Ortega took some of his stock to Oregon and did not return for three years. Upon his return he found that his father-in-law was claiming a part of his rancho, and litigation ensued.

Consequently, on February 17, 1852, and on February 7, 1853, rival claims were filed, one based on Miranda's claim and the other on Ortega's. The two attorneys became convinced that Miranda's claim was not a just one and accordingly abandoned it. On June 26, 1855, the Land Commission confirmed the Ortega claim. The matter was afterward reopened by T. B. Valentine, one of the attorneys, who claimed that the land had actually been granted to Miranda in October 1844, while Ortega was absent in Oregon. The matter was finally compromised. Of the area, 13,316 acres were sold as public land.

Rancho Roblar de Miseria seems to have been granted in 1845 to a young Mexican captain, Juan Padilla, who, the next year, took part in the Bear Flag Revolt, and shortly afterward moved to the southern part of the state. A group of eight men, one of whom was Daniel Wright, filed claim for this tract of four square leagues on February 24, 1852, and it was patented to them January 18, 1858.

The city of Petaluma, whose land titles in certain areas were long clouded by the Rancho San Antonio controversy, lies not only on a part of that grant but also on parts of Rancho Roblar de Miseria and Rancho Petaluma.

A few miles northwest of Petaluma, on Stony Point Road at Roblar Road, stands the Washoe House, once an important stage stop, and today one of the diminishing number of typical roadhouses to be found along the old routes of California. It was built about 1859. Farther to the west are Two Rock, a community that has all but disappeared, with the two large boulders that gave it its name still prominent landmarks on the hillside; and Bloomfield, a collection of photogenic old homes and business buildings.

Mariano G. Vallejo and His Lands

The dominant figure in provincial affairs north of Monterey in the 1830's and 1840's was Mariano Vallejo, who was chosen one of the eight California members of the Constitutional Convention held in Monterey in September 1849.

Mariano Guadalupe Vallejo, born on July 4, 1807, was the son of Ignacio Vallejo and his wife, María Antonia Lugo, who lived in Monterey County. In the school at Monterey, where he was educated, he had as schoolmates Juan B. Alvarado and José Castro. A military career being his choice, he entered the Monterey Company in 1823 as a cadet and was promoted to *alférez* in San Francisco in 1827. In 1830 he was elected to the *diputación*, in 1832 he was married to Francisca Benicia, daughter of Joaquín Carrillo, and in 1834 he was elected *disputador suplente* to congress.

José Figueroa, governor of Alta California from 1833 to 1835, chose him *comisionado* to secularize Mission San Francisco Solano and to found the town of Sonoma. In compensation for his services, the Governor gave him large tracts of land north of the bay and on July 5, 1835, a plot of ground in Pueblo de Sonoma. On this plot, extending 150 varas along the plaza with a depth of 130 varas and lying across the way from the mission, General Vallejo built a house which he made his home. This "Casa Grande" with its tower was destroyed by fire in 1867, but the servants' quarters still stand. Adjoining the site are the old barracks, facing Spain Street along the north side of the plaza, as did the Casa Grande. From the veranda that stretches in front of the barracks may be seen the marker placed on the site of the raising of the Bear Flag, the mission, and the old Blue Wing Hotel.

Vallejo was the outstanding native Californian of his day; his position came to him because of his ability and experience. Advanced to the rank of colonel on November 29, 1836, he assumed the position of commander general, took the oath of allegiance to the new government, and issued a patriotic proclamation on that occasion. From this time his efforts and money were expended to an even greater extent than before to serve his country. He induced the Mexican government to unite the military and civil commands in one officer and turned over his command to Governor Micheltorena in 1842.

Rancho Soscol, a tremendous area in Solano County, was granted to him for supplies furnished the government. His ranch home, however, was in Sonoma County on Rancho Petaluma, ten leagues, which had been granted to him October 22, 1843, by Governor Micheltorena. Another five leagues were granted on June 22, 1844. The United States patent was issued under Ulysses S. Grant in 1874.

On Rancho Petaluma, which he may have occupied for several years before the formal granting, the farseeing General Vallejo carried out a plan of agriculture that benefited not only himself but also the Indians who labored for him. In the foothills of the Sonoma Mountains, he built between 1834 and 1844 a large adobe house, which still stands above the open fields of Petaluma Valley. It was larger and built on a grander scale than any other adobe in northern California. Its three façades, the main one 200 feet long, are shaded by broad balconies, while the spacious patio, open on the fourth side, overlooks the valley below. The walls, three feet thick, are made of adobe bricks, and the framework is constructed of beams hewn from solid trees and bound together with rawhide thongs as strong as iron. Not a single nail is in evidence anywhere. Stout iron grills, solid shutters, and wickets provided double protection in the event of attack.

This was the center of the ranch activities: there apprentices were taught the ways of thrifty living; from this headquarters, the cattle ranges, the planting of the vast fields, and the harvesting of crops were managed; while close to the hacienda meat curing, herb drying, basket making, blanket weaving. and other more sedentary operations were carried on. Looking through the long verandas as they remain today, one can easily picture groups of dusky workers young and old. The railings of the balconies seem a fitting place for daylight inspection of finished weaving, while under the protecting roof of the inner three-sided patio may have been stored piles of colorful squash and pumpkins beneath the festoons of peppers so essential to Spanish cookery.

The Petaluma adobe *(SRL 18)*, four miles east

M. G. Vallejo Adobe, near Petaluma

of the city of Petaluma, became a State Historical Monument in February 1951. In 1857, after clearing his title to the Petaluma Rancho, Vallejo had sold the adobe for $25,000 to William H. Whiteside, who, in turn, sold it for $30,000 to William D. Bliss. His heirs presented the long-deserted but still picturesque building to the Petaluma Parlor of the Native Sons of the Golden West, which retained it for some years, finally deeding it to the State of California in 1951. The Division of Beaches and Parks has carried out an extensive program of restoration, with magnificent results. Many authorities consider this building the finest example in California of an adobe constructed during the Mexican period.

General Vallejo purchased a part of Rancho Agua Caliente, which had been given to Lazaro Piña in 1840 by Governor Alvarado. It stretched along Sonoma Creek beyond the outer line of the lands of Pueblo de Sonoma. Thaddeus M. Leavenworth, who had come to California as chaplain with Stevenson's Regiment of New York Volunteers, became the owner of that part of the grant lying closest to Sonoma.

Adjoining the property of Leavenworth, the General built a frame mansion *(SRL 4)* in 1850. He called it Lachryma Montis or "Mountain Tears," because of the large hot and cold springs in the hillside nearby. He lived there many years before his death in 1890, and his burial place is on an eminence north of Sonoma quite near Lachryma Montis. In the immediate vicinity of the residence is a building called the Swiss Chalet. Its exterior is of wood and brick, the lumber having been brought around the Horn in 1849–50. The State Park Commission purchased on July 7, 1933, both Lachryma Montis and the Swiss Chalet with the surrounding 17 acres. After its purchase, the family mansion was found to require renovation, in the course of which the adobe bricks used as filling between the exterior and interior walls were removed and the wooden timbers were treated for preservation against termites. The Vallejo Home State Historical Monument is reached by driving north on Third Street West, Sonoma. A museum is maintained in the Swiss Chalet.

The house built by the original grantee, Lazaro Piña, of Rancho Agua Caliente stood on the piece of ground associated with Captain Joseph Hooker. It was constructed of adobe bricks with wood finishing. Its first owner, Piña, was drafted into the Mexican War and lost his life in the Battle of Cerro Gordo, leaving a wife and children. Hooker, who attained his rank of captain in that war, applied for and received 550 acres. He was afterward made a general in the Civil War and finally returned to the East to live. This house, built by Piña, was long known as the "Fighting Joe" Hooker barn. It stood about four miles northwest of Sonoma, on the Serres ranch at 16060 Sonoma Highway, until its destruction by fire some years ago. The remains have eroded away to a heap of adobe rubble. An old cabin in which Hooker lived stands nearby. It was prefabricated in Norway and shipped to California about 1850. The exterior siding is now covered with asphalt paper, simulating brick.

Two old adobes still stand on Rancho Agua Caliente. They are the Justi home and winery-stable, built in the late 1840's and early 1850's, about three miles southeast of Kenwood on Dunbar Road. The adobe construction of the old barn is apparent, but, in the case of the long, low house, it is well hidden behind woodworking. At one time the Glen Ellen post office was located here.

In the same area, at 13255 Sonoma Highway, is Glen Oaks, a beautiful old stone mansion built in 1860.

Rancho Cabeza de Santa Rosa
Rancho Llano de Santa Rosa

Several tracts of land in Sonoma County were granted to relatives of General Vallejo's wife, Francisca Benicia Carrillo. These tracts included Rancho Cabeza de Santa Rosa, given to her widowed mother in 1837; Rancho Sotoyome, to Henry Fitch, a brother-in-law; Rancho Los Guilicos, to John Wilson, another brother-in-law; and Rancho Llano de Santa Rosa, to Joaquín Carrillo, a brother.

Both Fitch and his mother-in-law were residents of San Diego. Fitch continued to live in the south. Señora María Ignacia López de Carrillo moved to her Rancho Cabeza de Santa Rosa with her unmarried children and continued to reside there during the remainder of her life. The city of Santa Rosa, now the county seat, is situated upon a part of her grant.

Her residence was located on the south side of Santa Rosa Creek. Of the original buildings only one remains, another having washed away in the mid-1940's. The existing structure is near the corner of Hartley Drive and Franquette Avenue, just north of Montgomery Drive, in eastern Santa Rosa. It is now owned by the Roman Catholic Diocese of Santa Rosa and is being restored. There is a strong local tradition that the Carrillo adobes were originally built as an outpost of the mission at Sonoma, but records of the Franciscan Order offer no substantiation of this claim. In his later years Salvador Vallejo confessed that he had mentioned the "Mission of Santa Rosa" in jest to Duflot de Mofras, a visitor to California in the early 1840's. Evidently the Frenchman took him seriously, for he included the "Mission" in the voluminous account of his travels, published upon his return to Paris. This, perhaps, explains the origin of the legend surrounding the Carrillo adobes. The name of Santa Rosa Creek was supposedly bestowed by Father Juan Amorós of San Rafael when he baptized an Indian girl there in honor of St. Rose of Lima in the late 1820's. A monument along the highway on the north side of Santa Rosa Creek, roughly opposite the Carrillo adobe, commemorates this event, but the baptism is recorded neither at San Rafael nor at Sonoma. It is known that a chapel was maintained at the Carrillo home, but this was common practice in rancho days. In any event, whatever its ecclesiastical connections, the Carrillo adobe may safely be said to be the first dwelling erected in the vicinity of Santa Rosa.

In 1853, the son Julio Carrillo filed claim for a part of his mother's property, two square leagues lying between Rancho San Miguel and Santa Rosa Creek, and he built his house near the stream on a site that is now Second Street in Santa Rosa. In the early days of the settlement, he gave land for a plaza where the courthouse now stands.

After the death of the mother, Juana de Jesús Carrillo became the wife of David Mallagh and continued to live in the family home. When the merchandise firm of Mallagh and MacDonald was formed in 1851, a part of this house was used as a store. The first Santa Rosa post office was later located here. Another sister, Felicidad, became the second wife of Victor Castro. Both of these daughters inherited portions of their mother's land which lay across Santa Rosa Creek from the portion belonging to their brother Julio.

Beaver House, now within the city of Santa Rosa, was built in 1854 on land bought from Julio Carrillo by Henry Beaver. Constructed of red brick made by Beaver himself on the property, the house suffered damage in the earthquake of 1868. H. W. McGee, the owner at that time, sold the remaining land for subdivision, and the house was rehabilitated for use as an auxiliary to Pacific Methodist College, then under construction. Serving as a student residence until the turn of the century, Beaver House then again became a private residence, as it is today. It is located at 610 Beaver Street.

One of Santa Rosa's landmarks is the First Baptist Church, constructed in 1873 of lumber from a single redwood tree felled near Guerneville. It stood on B Street between Fifth and Sixth, but has now been moved to the 400 block of Ellis Street near Juilliard Park.

The eldest son of the Carrillo family, who was named Joaquín after his father, received the grant of Llano de Santa Rosa from Governor Micheltorena in 1844. This tract of three square leagues adjoined his mother's property and lies due west of Santa Rosa. The tract previously had been granted to Marcus West, who had allowed his right to lapse; upon petition, it was regranted to Joaquín Carrillo, who at once built a small house and afterward erected a large and comfortable one. This adobe, long ago torn down, faced the east on what is now Petaluma Avenue in Sebastopol. This street was once part of the old Spanish Trail and later was used by the stage lines.

Rancho Sotoyome

Henry Delano Fitch, a dashing young sea captain from Massachusetts, met Señorita Josefa Carrillo upon his arrival in San Diego in 1826. Three years later, plans were made for their marriage, but certain legal technicalities arose whereby the marriage was postponed. The fact that the young captain was a foreigner was the main obstacle, but, since the parents gave consent, the date for the ceremony was set for April 15, 1829. At the last moment the friar who had planned to officiate weakened and decided that he could not do so. Sympathizing relatives and friends made it possible for the young people to elope on the captain's boat the next day, and, as the story goes, the marriage took place in Valparaiso on July 3. (According to a document in the Bancroft Library at Berkeley, the wedding in Valparaiso occurred on January 18, 1831.)

Difficulties beset the pair on their return to California. Finally, as penance, Captain Fitch was asked to give a "bell of at least fifty pounds in weight for the church at Los Angeles," which he did. Thereafter he lived in San Diego, where he kept a store.

In 1841 Captain Fitch received a grant of three square leagues of land lying in Sonoma County, where his wife's sister and her husband, Mariano G. Vallejo, lived. Eight more leagues were added to the tract in 1844. Instead of residing on the property, Captain Fitch traveled north, inspected it, made arrangements for its upkeep, and returned to his merchandising business in the south. He sent an acquaintance, Cyrus Alexander, to live there and offered to give him, as remuneration, two leagues of land. Alexander, a trapper and trader, who had reached San Diego in 1833, agreed. Alexander Valley, northeast of Healdsburg, is named for him, and a portion of one of his adobe houses, built in 1845–46, still stands there. It is located on a private ranch (8644 Highway 128) about a quarter of a mile east of Highway 128 at a point about half a mile southeast of the old (former) Alexander School.

Before Captain Fitch died in 1849, he had built a one-story adobe on his property. Later his widow and children occupied it. This stood south of Healdsburg on the bank of the Russian River north of Bailache Avenue until a fire in 1913. The remains were destroyed in the 1920's.

Rancho El Molino

In 1836 a tract of land along the Russian River was granted to Juan Bautista Roger Cooper, one of the most prominent English-speaking pioneers of California. His home, after he gave up a seafaring life, was at Monterey, where he met and married Encarnación Vallejo.

When Mariano G. Vallejo, Captain Cooper's brother-in-law and military commander and director of colonization on the northern frontier, returned to Monterey after an official visit to Bodega and Fort Ross, he told Cooper of the productive region that he had seen. That region, lying between the Estero Americano and the Russian River, was then inhabited by only a few Russians and Indians. Vallejo encouraged Cooper to make a tour of inspection. This Cooper did and obtained a grant of four leagues along the Russian River in exchange for two tracts previously held by him on the American River.

On his new grant he erected a sawmill and called the tract Rancho El Molino. He also built a house of redwood lumber and stocked the land with cattle. In the journal kept by Philip L. Edwards of the Ewing Young journey from Oregon to California to purchase cattle, Edwards mentions a visit to Cooper's mill in 1837. At that time

Young left at Rancho El Molino eight white men and three Indians belonging to his expedition.

Since the question of Russian encroachment on Mexican territory was troubling Vallejo during those years, in order to discourage the invasion he planned to establish settlers on land that might otherwise be occupied by representatives of that nationality. At Vallejo's request for persons of the proper qualifications for such a duty, Captain Cooper suggested the names of three men, McIntosh, Dawson, and Black, whom he had known as sailors. All three were granted tracts of land between the Estero Americano and the Russian River.

Rancho Estero Americano

Rancho Estero Americano lay to the east of the Rancho Bodega of Stephen Smith, both ranchos having the Estero Americano for a southern boundary. Consisting of two square leagues, it was granted in 1839 to Edward Manuel McIntosh, a naturalized Scottish sailor. McIntosh engaged in 1833 in otter hunting with Job Dye and afterward became an agent of the Hudson's Bay Company. He, James Dawson, and James Black were originally sent to the western Sonoma County region by Vallejo to discourage the advance of the Russian settlements. In partnership with James Dawson, who established in 1834 a sawmill on Salmon Creek, he built a frame house in which the two lived together. This companionship lasted until 1839, when the grant of land was made to McIntosh alone. Offended by this turn of affairs, Dawson sawed the house in two and moved his half by ox team some distance to the east, where he later obtained a grant of land for himself. McIntosh afterward became alcalde at San Rafael and sold his land to Jasper O'Farrell, who was the claimant for it in 1852.

Rancho Cañada de Pogolimi

Along the Estero Americano lies Rancho Cañada de Pogolimi granted in 1844 by Governor Micheltorena to James Dawson, the Irish sailor who had turned lumberman for a time with Edward Manuel McIntosh on the adjoining tract of land. After his quarrel with McIntosh, which resulted in his moving his half of the house which they had owned jointly, he established himself on Rancho Cañada de Pogolimi and the next year married at Sonoma and brought to his home a young girl, María Antonia Caseres, eldest daughter of Francisco Caseres (or Caceres), at one time the only Spanish resident of Yerba Buena. Dawson's death occurred within a few years, and his widow, who later married Frederick Blume, continued to reside on the property. The half house was razed in the 1930's.

Rancho Cañada de Jonive

Jasper O'Farrell, who had received the grant of Rancho Nicasio in Marin County as remuneration for services in surveying land grants, exchanged that piece of property for the Cañada de Jonive, which was held by James Black. In 1849 O'Farrell married Mary McChristian and brought her to live on the Jonive rancho, which they renamed the Annaly Ranch. (The spelling of the township name was corrupted to Analy.) Their home was an adobe dwelling erected at the foot of Jonive Hill near Freestone by the former owner. It was built about 1848 of adobe and wood. Later turned into a store, it fell in 1906.

This rancho lay to the east of the Estero Americano and originally contained two and one-half square leagues. Patent for it was issued to Jasper O'Farrell, the man who laid out the streets of San Francisco, in 1858.

Rancho Bodega

Rancho Bodega, consisting of eight square leagues on the coast between Estero Americano and the Russian River, was granted to Stephen Smith by Governor Micheltorena on September 12, 1844. When the land was confirmed in 1859 and patented to the heirs of the grantee, the more than 35,000 acres claimed were accepted by the court as being "the same land described in the grant to Stephen Smith (now deceased)."

Smith, a native of Maryland who visited California in 1841, came from Peru, where he had spent a little time. On this visit, he made plans to return to California after a trip East and to set up a sawmill. This he did. The mill machinery was brought from Baltimore and set up in the redwood region east of Bodega Head. Although confident that the country would eventually belong to the United States, he obtained Mexican citizenship in order to become a landowner. Within two years after receiving the grant of Rancho Bodega, he had the pleasure of raising the United States flag over his property. The eastern boundary line of his rancho lay a little way to the east of his mill, which was placed to the north of Salmon Creek. His house was erected near to Salmon Creek and north of the Estero Americano, the boundary between Ranchos Bodega and Blucher. To both of these tracts he laid claim, and both were awarded to his descendants on that claim.

After the death of Stephen Smith in 1855, his widow married another southern gentleman, Tyler Curtis, in 1856. Squatters caused trouble, resulting in what is called the "Bodega War"; and Curtis was forced to sell land including the part known as the Homestead Tract. Upon it is the site of the settlement by the Russians in 1811. Captain Smith's adobe mansion, built in 1851, stood on the site of this outpost. The house was oblong in shape with a row of five dormer windows opening from the upper story on the balcony at the front.

The Curtis family moved to San Francisco in 1872. In the 1890's a fire burned the inflammable part of the old dwelling, leaving only the adobe walls standing, and even these have now disappeared. The adobe stood about a mile northwest of Bodega. In the little town itself is St. Tercsa's Catholic Church built about 1860, a much-photographed white-painted frame building high on a hill.

Adjoining Rancho Bodega on the north was Rancho Muniz, of 17,760 acres, bounded on the west by the Pacific Ocean. It was granted in 1845 to Manuel Torres, a brother of the wife of Stephen Smith.

Rancho Mallacomes, or Maristal y Plan de Agua Caliente

This rancho, lying in the upper part of Knight's Valley, consisted of 17,742 acres granted October 14, 1843, to José de los Santos Berryessa (Berrellesa, Berreyesa) by Governor Micheltorena. The grantee, a son of José Reyes Berryessa of Rancho San Vicente (in Santa Clara County), was a soldier at Sonoma from 1840 to 1842 and alcalde there in 1846.

Knight's Valley, in which this grant lay, received its name from Thomas P. Knight, a native of Maine, who came to California in 1845. After he reached the Sierra on his overland journey, an explosion of a keg of powder under his wagon destroyed all of his possessions, including a stock of goods which he had expected to sell. He took part in the Bear Flag Revolt and then went to the mines before settling down to be a farmer in Napa and Sonoma counties.

Knight lived in the two-story adobe built by Berryessa and made additions to it. A part of the house still stands in Knight's Valley west of Mount St. Helena. The ground level is constructed of stone. It is about seven and one-half miles northwest of Calistoga on Highway 128, on the east side of the highway three-tenths of a mile south of the intersection of Franz Valley Road.

Among many other settlers on this rancho were Calvin Holmes, Rockwell, Woodshire, Martin F. Cook, and Rufus Ingalls.

Rancho Los Guilicos

John Wilson, who reached California in 1837 and married Ramona Carrillo, was the grantee of Rancho Los Guilicos, containing 18,833 acres and given by Governor Alvarado. It was patented in the name of William Hood in 1866. Afterward it was owned jointly by Mrs. Wilson and William Hood, who had purchased a part of it. Hood's old home (SRL 692), built of fired brick in 1858, still stands, now within the grounds of the Los Guilicos State School for Girls, some nine miles east of Santa Rosa off Highway 12. It is open annually on the first Sunday of May at the "open house" held by the school.

This rancho lies between Santa Rosa and

Berryessa-Knight Adobe, Knight's Valley

Sonoma, the town of Glen Ellen being on its southern tip. The former Southern Pacific stations of Kenwood and Melita are on this old grant.

A vineyard was planted in 1858, and a winery was built in 1861 on this property. The winery, a three-story stone structure, is on the bank of Los Guilicos Creek. On the opposite side of the stream is the wine cellar and distillery.

Rancho Tzabaco

The name of this grant is an Indian word, the name of either the locality or the Indians that inhabited it.

Rancho Tzabaco was granted in 1843 to José German Piña, son of Lazaro Piña of Rancho Agua Caliente. In the central part of this land rises the dividing ridge between the Russian River, which runs across the end of the rancho, and Dry Creek Valley, which is also within the grant boundary. In this valley are two old adobes built by the grantee in 1841 and 1844, which sit back among trees on the west side of Dry Creek Road about half a mile south of the intersection of Canyon Road, west of Geyserville.

Rancho San Miguel

Rancho San Miguel, containing 6,663 acres granted to Marcus West in the years 1840 and 1844, was claimed in 1852 by his widow, Guadalupe Vásquez de West, and their three children. A creek running through its northern part is called Mark West Creek. On the bank of this stream, West had a store. His large adobe house near the bridge on the old Santa Rosa–Healdsburg road not far from the store was destroyed long ago. The family burying ground was in the rolling hills to the east of the store and the road. The Northwestern Pacific Railroad and the state highway running northwest of Santa Rosa pass through this grant.

Miscellaneous Grants

Among the other grants of land made by the Mexican government and later recognized by the United States, certain ones may be specified.

Rancho German, which extended along the Pacific Ocean in the extreme northwestern part of the county, originally contained 17,580 acres granted by Governor Pico to Ernesto Rufus and was claimed jointly by a group of six men in 1852.

Rancho Rincón de Muscalón lay on both sides of the Russian River and contained 8,766 acres. It was granted in 1846 to Francisco Berryessa by Governor Pío Pico and patented to Johnson Horrell and others in 1866.

Rancho Caslamayomi, or Laguna de los Gentiles, near the Russian River but separated from it by rough and broken chaparral hills, was granted to Eugenio Montenegro in 1844 by Governor Micheltorena and contained eight leagues.

Rancho Cotati, granted to Juan Castañeda in 1844, was patented to Thomas Page in 1858. The rancho contained 17,238 acres and lay to the south of Santa Rosa. The Northwestern Pacific Railway passed through it from northeast to southwest, and the station of Cotati is in the southwestern quarter of the rancho.

Two border-line ranchos, the Blucher and the Laguna de San Antonio, extended over the county line into Marin County. Rancho Huichica, which consisted of 18,704 acres lying southeast of Sonoma, was patented to J. P. Leese in 1859. It was situated partly in Napa County.

The Vineyard of Colonel Haraszthy

Sonoma County ranks second to Napa County in the productiveness of vineyards and wineries, but it was here that the first wine grapes from European countries were successfully grown. Colonel Agoston Haraszthy, a Hungarian nobleman, father of wine making in California, attempted first to ripen grapes from his imported stock at Crystal Springs in San Mateo County in 1852, but met with slight success in that locality. Looking for a proper soil and climate for the purpose, he moved to the protected Sonoma Valley, where already one variety of wine had been made from the ordinary mission grape by General Vallejo.

In 1856 Colonel Haraszthy purchased a piece of land east of the town of Sonoma that became known as the Buena Vista Vineyard and immediately placed his son Attila in charge. By 1858 he had planted 85,556 vines, in addition to thousands of cuttings which he had started in his nursery. Many of these vines were of choice foreign varieties. In 1857 he had dug a tunnel into the hillside, using Chinese labor, and stored five thousand gallons of wine as an initial vintage. This tunnel was followed by another in 1858 and a third in 1862. In that year the first stone cellar was built of rock excavated from the tunnels. Another and larger cellar, also with three tunnels, was begun in 1864. In 1862 Haraszthy's winery was the first in the world to use California redwood for wine tanks. It is now standard storage for wines in many areas. The old cellars (SRL 392) are still in evidence about two miles northeast of Sonoma via Napa Street and Old Winery Road. During the year of 1858, at the urgent request of the State Agricultural Society, Colonel Haraszthy wrote an article describing minutely the planting and practical management of a vineyard and the subsequent making of the fruit into mature wine. From that time on, "a tidal wave of inquiry swept over the quiet valley of Sonoma, strangers came and went, the Pony Express and the United States Mail were laden with letters, papers, pamphlets, cuttings, and vines. Not only had the little town of Sonoma become the head center of the distribution of viticultural knowledge, but it suddenly became the supplying grape-vine nursery of foreign vines for the whole state. It was from here that the Zinfandel was distributed to the four parts of the state prior to 1859, so likewise . . . the Flame Tokay, the Black Morocco, the Muscat of Alexandria . . . the Seedless Sultana . . . and numerous others."

In 1861, Governor Downey appointed a committee to report upon the ways and means of improving viticulture in the state. One member of the committee was Colonel Haraszthy, who went to Europe and brought home cuttings of every attainable variety. In 1868, Colonel Haraszthy went to Nicaragua. On July 6, 1869, he mysteriously disappeared, and it was supposed that he met death while crossing a river.

His son, Arpad Haraszthy, went to Europe in 1857 to attend school for five years. After having spent two of the five years in the study of wine making, particularly champagne, and in visiting vineyards and wineries, he returned to California. He immediately put into practice the art he had learned, but years of experimental work were necessary before he was satisfied with the champagne made under Western conditions. Arpad became the first president of the California Viticultural Commission.

Another interesting winery at Sonoma is that of Samuele Sebastiani *(SRL 739)* on Fourth Street East near Spain Street. Early in the twentieth century he purchased the original vineyard of Misión San Francisco Solano, first planted in 1825. It was here that General Vallejo, after the secularization of the mission, produced many prize-winning wines. The Sebastiani family continues the tradition.

Just north of Santa Rosa, to the east of Business 101 near its northern junction with Freeway 101, the Fountain Grove Winery stands as a memorial to one of several Utopian colonies that flourished in Sonoma County in the late nineteenth century. Thomas Lake Harris, spiritualist leader of the Brotherhood of New Life, moved some of his followers here from the East in the late 1870's. Ultimately he acquired 1,500 acres of land, much of which was planted to vineyards. Thus about 30 colonists, most of them living in a community house, supported themselves for several years, until difficulties, including rumors of scandalous activities, caused the downfall of the project. After the dispersal of the colonists, Harris' disciple, Kanaye Nagasawa, remained at Fountain Grove, of which he became sole owner in the 1920's, and managed the winery until his death in 1934. The community house burned early in the twentieth century, but the other buildings remain, including the winery, Harris' beautiful mansion, and some interesting round barns.

The Asti Colony

The Italian Swiss Agricultural Colony *(SRL 621)* was organized in 1881 under the leadership of Andrea Sbarboro. It consisted of a membership of 100, who paid monthly the sum of one dollar for each share of stock that they owned. The committee appointed to choose a location selected the Truett Ranch, a tract of 1,500 acres bordering on the Russian River. The tract was a succession of rolling hills with red soil on which grew oak trees. Higher hills beyond thickly covered with forests of fir, oak, madroño, and pine made this a sheltered basin.

Similar in appearance to the famed wine district of Mount Ferat in northern Italy, it was put to a like use in the planting of vineyards. A substantial winery 150 by 52 feet was constructed of concrete in 1887. Adjoining it was a cooper shop where trained men from Germany put together large casks and puncheons, while the outside work of the vineyards was done entirely by Italians. As the colony prospered, the acreage was increased and larger equipment was needed. To celebrate the completion of a wine vat with a capacity of 500,000 gallons built for blending purposes, a dance was given at which 50 couples and a ten-piece band were accommodated on its floor.

The quaint little church of Our Lady of Mount Carmel, built in the shape of half a wine barrel, remains as a landmark, although it has been replaced by a newer church.

Asti, the station for this colony, is on the Northwestern Pacific Railway four miles south of Cloverdale.

Home of Jack London

On a wooded hillside overlooking the "Valley of the Moon" is the ranch that was once the home of Jack London, author of *The Call of the Wild, John Barleycorn, The Sea Wolf,* and other tales of adventure. Jack London chose for his home a spot pre-eminently picturesque, both in its setting of wooded mountains and orchard-covered hills and valleys, and in its romantic environment, rich in history and legend.

Here the writer lived from 1905 until his death in 1916 at the age of 40. His widow, Charmian, continued to live on the property, and in 1919 she built the "House of Happy Walls" of native fieldstone as a memorial to her husband. Through his writings, London made the name "Valley of the Moon" world-famous, although the Sonoma Valley is known to have been called "Valle de la Luna" as early as 1841.

In 1959 Irving Shepard, nephew of Jack London, gave 40 acres of the ranch to the State of California. This includes Charmian's home, now a museum of Jack London manuscripts and belongings, and the author's grave, marked by a red lava boulder and close to the graves of two pioneer children that were on the ranch when London bought it. By far the most interesting landmark, however, is the ruined "Wolf House," which was to have been the Londons' home and was nearly completed when it burned September 22, 1913. Built of native volcanic stone, the house with its archways and chimneys is a photographer's paradise. Although "Wolf House" is within the State Park boundaries, the house in which Jack London actually lived stands on the neighboring Shepard ranch.

Jack London Historical State Park *(SRL 743)* is a short distance northwest of Glen Ellen. It has also been registered by the Department of the Interior as a National Historic Landmark.

Church of Our Lady of Mount Carmel, Asti

Jack London's "Wolf House," near Glen Ellen

The Burbank Experimental Farm

Luther Burbank, whose name first was brought prominently before the public by the appearance of the Burbank potato, was born in Massachusetts in 1849. Having been a student of nature from his earliest years and desiring a mild climate in which to work, he purchased four acres of land at the edge of the town of Santa Rosa in 1878.

On this tract he grew specimens from many parts of the world and carried on extensive research in plant life. He developed a marked improvement in certain vegetables, fruits, and flowers and, by hybridization, produced drastic changes in size, form, and color.

As time went on, more space was needed; and on December 5, 1885, he purchased 18 acres just outside the city limits of Sebastopol, where he established the Burbank Experimental Farm and where by planting large fields he was able to carry on even more extensive experiments than before. He became known as the "plant wizard," and the results of his labors have obtained places in orchards and gardens. Dying in his late seventies, he left behind him an enviable record of accomplishment. He lies buried under a tree in his Santa Rosa garden.

The Luther Burbank home and gardens (*SRL 234*) in Santa Rosa are at the corner of Tupper Street and Santa Rosa Avenue. They have also been registered as a National Historic Landmark.

SOURCES

Bowman, J. N., and G. W. Hendry. "Spanish and Mexican Houses in the Nine Bay Counties." Ms., Bancroft Library, Berkeley; State Library, Sacramento, 1942.

The California Missions, a Pictorial History. By the editorial staff of Sunset Books. Lane Book Co., Menlo Park, 1964.

[Cassiday, Sam.] *An Illustrated History of Sonoma County, California.* Lewis Publishing Co., Chicago, 1889.

Cleland, Robert Glass. *From Wilderness to Empire. A History of California,* ed. Glenn S. Dumke. Knopf, New York, 1959.

Hansen, Harvey J., and Jeanne Thurlow Miller. *Wild Oats in Eden.* Santa Rosa, 1962.

Hine, Robert V. *California's Utopian Colonies.* Huntington Library, San Marino, 1953.

Ide, William Brown. *Who Conquered California?* S. Ide, Claremont, N.H., 1882.

Munro-Fraser, J. P. *History of Sonoma County.* Alley, Bowen & Co., San Francisco, 1880.

Older, Mrs. Fremont. *California Missions and Their Romances.* Coward-McCann, New York, 1938.

Peixotto, Ernest Clifford. *Romantic California.* Scribner, New York, 1910.

Rogers, Fred B. *Bear Flag Lieutenant.* California Historical Society, San Francisco, 1951.

Trussel, Margaret Edith. "Settlement of the Bodega Bay Region." M.A. thesis in geography, University of California, n.d.

Tuomey, Honoria. *History of Sonoma County, California.* 2 vols. S. J. Clarke Publishing Co., San Francisco, 1926.

Tuomey, Honoria, and Luisa Vallejo Emparan. "Historic Mount St. Helena," *California Historical Society Quarterly,* III (1924), 171–77.

——— *History of the Mission, Presidio, and Pueblo of Sonoma.* Press-Democrat, Santa Rosa, 1923.

Warren, Herbert Otis. "So This Is Where They Lived," *Sunset Magazine,* LX, No. 2 (August 1928), 40–43, 60.

Stanislaus County

STANISLAUS COUNTY was named for a Christianized Indian chief who was baptized by the padres under the Spanish name Estanislao, for one of the two Polish saints, Stanislaus Kostka or Stanislaus of Cracow. The county was organized in 1854 from a part of Tuolumne County, and the first county seat was placed at Adamsville. Within a few months the seat of justice was moved to Empire City; in December 1855 it was transferred to La Grange; in 1862 to Knight's Ferry; and in 1872 it was finally located at Modesto. This town was first called Ralston, after an official of the Central Pacific Railroad. Being a very modest man, Ralston objected to the honor, and so the name was changed to Modesto, Spanish for "modest."

The Stanislaus

The first white man to look upon the waters of the Stanislaus, one of the most important of the wild and picturesque streams of the Sierra, was Gabriel Moraga, who discovered and named it in 1806 while on one of his several exploring expeditions through the river country of the north in search of mission sites. He explored it again on that remarkable expedition of 1808, when he crossed for the second time all the Sierra rivers as far north as the Upper Sacramento, and discovered the territory of at least ten additional counties. In 1810 he again ranged the country watered by the Stanislaus, in an unsuccessful attempt to capture runaway Indians.

John C. Frémont, who ferried the river on March 30, 1844, and camped on the Stanislaus side, described its scenery thus: "Issuing from the woods, we rode about sixteen miles over open prairie partly covered with bunch grass, the timber reappearing on the rolling hills of the River Stanislaus, in the usual belt of evergreen oaks. The level valley was about forty feet below the upland, and the stream seventy yards broad, with the usual fertile bottom land which was covered with green grass among large oaks. We encamped on one of these bottoms, in a grove of the large white oaks previously mentioned."

The Old West Side

Recently occupied Indian campsites existed on the arroyos along the west side of the San Joaquin Valley when the first white men came to the region. Remains of some of these ancient villages were long in evidence, the most noteworthy being located on Arroyo de las Garzas, about six miles from the edge of the valley, and on arroyos de Orestimba, del Puerto and del Hospital.

El Camino Viejo, the old refuge road of the Spanish and Mexican periods which followed along the west side of the San Joaquin Valley, crossed creeks many of which are known today by their early Spanish names. Among those in Stanislaus County are Arroyo de las Garzas ("the herons"), Arroyo de Orestimba ("the meeting place," so called because the padres, when gathering the first Indians in the region, made an agree-

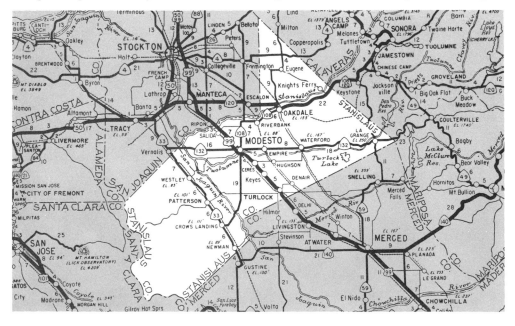

ment with the remaining natives to meet them there again the following year), Arroyo Salado Grande ("big salty creek," where the pioneer known as "Salty" Smith settled in 1855), Arroyo del Puerto ("the gate," so named because of the natural cut in the hills west of Patterson through which the creek flows during the rainy season), and Arroyo del Hospital (named from the experience of a party of Spaniards who, overcome by sickness, rested beside this stream and were healed).

Spanish settlement on the west side seems to have had an early beginning, for at least one Spaniard, a deserter from the Spanish cavalry, settled on Arroyo de las Garzas as early as 1820. A battle took place in the vicinity that year, when a detachment of Spanish cavalry came to get both the fugitive soldier and some runaway mission Indians. American pioneers in 1852 found the half-breed son of this former cavalryman living in an adobe on Arroyo de las Garzas just across the line in Merced County several miles west of the present town of Gustine. Jesse Hill (one of the owners of Hill's Ferry on the San Joaquin River) settled on the spot in 1854, and built a house from lumber brought around the Horn and hauled to Las Garzas by ox team. The site was later occupied by one of the Simon Newman Company sheep camps.

Above the sycamore grove on Arroyo de Orestimba stood the ranch house of Rancho Orestimba y las Garzas, granted to Sebastián Nuñez on February 22, 1844.

Hill's Ferry

A ferry across the San Joaquin River at the site later known as Hill's Ferry was first operated in the autumn of 1849, when a man named Thompson carried emigrants from Mexico who were traveling to the mines via Pacheco Pass across the river at this point. Jesse Hill and John de Hart later purchased the ferry from Thompson. After De Hart's death, Hill became the sole owner, until in 1865 the ferry passed into the hands of C. G. Hubner.

By this date the town of Hill's Ferry had achieved some importance as a shipping point for grain. During the high-water season, from April to July, boats customarily came up the river this far to exchange their cargoes for grain and other farm produce. But during the balance of the year the isolation of the town was quite complete. There was no telegraph service, and the mails had to be brought in by stage from Banta, a day's journey away. Nevertheless, during its heyday, Hill's Ferry was a lively place. Its very isolation infused into it a decidely "Wild West" spirit. Horse thieves and outlaws found it a convenient crossing place en route to mountain hideouts. The place became noted for its tough characters, and there was much gambling, drinking, and shooting.

In 1886–87, at the time the west-side railroad was being constructed, Simon Newman, who was the chief merchant at Hill's Ferry, donated some land to the railroad. When the town of Newman was laid out on this land in 1887, the people of Hill's Ferry and those living at Dutch Corners, two miles away, were induced to move to the new town. With this change Hill's Ferry literally ceased to exist, since most of the houses were soon carted away to other locations. The site of Hill's Ferry is on the west bank of the San Joaquin River about five miles northeast of Newman. The weather-beaten two-story hotel that long marked the site has disappeared.

Knight's Ferry

Knight's Ferry (SRL 347), an old mining town and trading post on the Stanislaus River 40 miles southeast of Stockton, was founded in the spring of 1849 by William Knight, scout and fur trader, who was reputed to have been educated as a physician. He came to California originally with the Workman-Rowland party in 1841. The following year he brought his family from New Mexico, and in 1843 they settled at Knight's Landing in Yolo County.

The first ferry to be established on the Stanislaus River was the one at Knight's Ferry, on the old Sonora Road from Stockton to the southern mines. As early as 1850 thousands of miners passed this way, when ferry receipts could scarcely have been less than $500 a day. The importance and prosperity of Knight's Ferry were further enhanced by the fact that the river bars and banks, hills and gulches, were rich in gold for miles in all directions. Above the ferry was Two Mile Bar, and below it was Keeler's Flat, where Keeler's Ferry, in the shadow of what is now called Lover's Leap, was started later in 1849.

After the death of William Knight on November 9, 1849, John and Lewis Dent came into possession of the ferry, but in 1854 it was superseded by a bridge built on the site of the present structure. During the same year the Dents and D. M. Locke erected a gristmill and a sawmill on the riverbank some 300 yards above the ferry. In 1856 a town was laid out on the north bank of the river. This was referred to by some as Dentville, but the name was always officially Knight's Ferry. The place continued to grow and prosper, and from 1862 to 1872 it was the county seat of Stanislaus County.

Knight's Ferry is still one of the most picturesque of the old river towns. The approach from the settlement of Buena Vista on the south is over an old-time covered bridge, made entirely of

Covered Bridge, Knight's Ferry

wood, which crosses the river just above the mill. This bridge was built in 1864 to replace the earlier structure erected in 1854, which was swung so close to the water that it was swept away by the flood of 1862. Along with the bridge went the gristmill nearby and its flour. The story is told of the rescue of sacks of flour from a gully where the high water had deposited them, outwardly coated with a thick paste of flour and water but with the grist inside perfectly dry and clean and fit for human consumption. The present ruined mill was erected after the flood of 1862 by David Tulloch. Not far away is a stone wall, the beginning of a woolen mill that was never completed.

Farther down the street is the site of a once populous Chinatown. Continuing down the narrow thoroughfare, past the iron jail, one comes at length to the site of the former courthouse, erected in 1858 as the Fisher Hotel. The building was destroyed by fire in the 1890's. Opposite the courthouse site a beautiful monument of native rock, dedicated by the Major Hugh Moss Chapter, D.A.R., Modesto, commemorates the early history of Knight's Ferry. On the right at the end of the main street are a former bank and the Masonic Hall.

On the hill above the town is the Dent house, built in the early 1850's and still well preserved. It was here that Ulysses S. Grant, whose wife was Julia Dent, visited his brothers-in-law in 1854.

About two miles southeast of Knight's Ferry on the old road to La Grange are the headquarters of the Willms Ranch (SRL 415). John R. Willms, a German-born '49er, and his partner, John H. Kappelmann, began to acquire land here in 1852 and eventually had 3,600 acres. Kappelmann died in 1881, and Willms carried on alone until, at his death in 1910, the ranch totaled 8,600 acres. The present ranch house, built in 1892, replaced an earlier one destroyed by fire. Members of the Willms family still own the ranch and live on it.

La Grange

La Grange (SRL 414) was first known as French Bar, French miners having come to that region to prospect as early as 1852. Later the settlement was moved higher up on the bank of the Tuolumne River away from the original bar. By 1855 La Grange had become a thriving center of trade, since the bulk of the population in the county had moved up into the mining regions. The county seat was transferred from Empire City to La Grange in December 1855, and there it remained until 1862, when another contest took it to Knight's Ferry by a majority of only 29 votes.

At the height of its prosperity, La Grange had from 4,000 to 5,000 inhabitants and was served daily by three or more stage lines. With the early development of agriculture on the rich bottom lands along the river, a flour mill was erected by John Talbot and Company half a mile below Branch's Ferry. The mill was washed away by the high waters of 1856. During the 1870's extensive hydraulic operations were carried on in the vicinity, when ditches were built at a cost of $5 million to convey water to the diggings. The La Grange

Old Bank, Knight's Ferry

Dam was built in 1891–93, and today it is part of the system of Stanislaus County reservoirs which supplies the Modesto and Turlock irrigation districts.

The tiny town of La Grange has a strikingly picturesque setting on the Tuolumne River. For several miles along its banks, thousands of rock mounds and pyramids stand as monuments to the Herculean efforts of early miners to harvest the golden treasure from the river's bed. Within the town may be seen two old stores, built of stone with heavy iron doors, which are reminiscent of the gold-rush days. Part of the old adobe post office has been incorporated into a barn. St. Louis' Catholic Church and the Odd Fellows Hall are other landmarks.

A ferry was operated at La Grange, first by Nathan McFarland and later by Anthony B. McMillan, from the early 1850's until about 1880, when a bridge was built across the Tuolumne at this point. Two miles below the town, where the present bridge spans the river, is the site of Branch's Ferry, which was put into operation in 1851 by George C. Branch. After Branch sold the ferry in 1862, successive owners operated it until it finally came into the possession of a Mr. Basso, who long resided on the site of the ferry landing at the north end of the present bridge.

Adamsville and Empire City

When Adamsville, which was founded in 1849, was made the first county seat of Stanislaus County in 1854, there were so few buildings in the place that the initial session of court was held out of doors, under a large tree. Before many months the county government was moved to Empire City and Adamsville had lost its one claim to distinction. The town no longer exists, but its site is on the south bank of the Tuolumne River.

Empire City (SRL 418) was originally situated on the Tuolumne River 20 miles from its mouth. It was laid out on the south side of the river by John G. Marvin, a lawyer from Boston, who later became the first state superintendent of schools in California.

Because it was at the head of navigation, Empire City, in 1851, was made the Army supply station for outlying forts, including Fort Miller and Fort Tejón. Floods nearly destroyed the place in 1852, but it was rebuilt and became the county seat in 1854, after a hard political fight, only to have the seat of justice moved to La Grange little more than a year later. Today the cemetery is all that remains of the first Empire City, which had lost its importance some time before the later Empire City was laid out as a trade center for a growing farm community. The pioneer burial ground has been incorporated into Lakewood Memorial Park, about one mile south of the present town of Empire on Highway J-7. A monument has been erected to the memory of the citizens of old Empire City, which lay about half a mile west of the cemetery.

Aspinwall, which was located on the south bank of the Tuolumne River several miles above Empire City, was another early town of which no trace remains today.

Tuolumne River Ferries

There were a number of ferries up and down the Tuolumne which served as crossings to the Mariposa mines in the 1850's. Dickenson's Ferry, located below the present Roberts' Bridge and about eight miles east of Waterford, was established in the early 1850's by Gallant Duncan Dickenson, and developed into one of the most important stopping places on the old Fort Miller Road. Dickenson, who came overland with his family from Missouri in 1846, was an active, energetic man who engaged in many pioneer enterprises. Shortly after his arrival in California he became a member of Aram's garrison at Santa Clara, and in 1847 he won the distinction of building at Monterey the first brick house in California. The year 1848 saw him mining for gold at Dickenson's Gulch in Tuolumne County. From there he went to Stockton, where he built and operated a hotel and served as Prefect of the San Joaquin District in 1849–50.

In 1862 John W. Roberts, who had come from Boston in 1849, purchased the properties at Dickenson's Ferry, which now became known as Roberts' Ferry. When the original Dickenson Hotel was destroyed by fire on February 22, 1865, Roberts immediately replaced it with a two-story brick structure, the lower story of which still stands near the river.

At Horr's Ranch, near Dickenson's Ferry, an attempt was made in the 1860's by Dr. B. D. Horr to found the town of Horrsville. A little pioneer cemetery located near the present highway a half-mile north of the river and a half-mile west of Roberts' Bridge gives the approximate site of the town.

Among other early ferries on the Tuolumne was Salter and Morley's Ferry. Calvin Salter and his partner, I. D. Morley, took up ranch land two miles east of Dickenson's Ferry and four miles below Branch's Ferry. There they established a ferry, stage station, and post office. Salter's farm was on the river near the ford, while Morley's land occupied the site on which the Turlock Owens Reservoir now stands.

Near Waterford, Baker's Ferry was established about 1878. Five miles to the northeast was Bill Martin's hotel and stage station, a busy place on the Mariposa Road in the 1850's and 1860's.

Tuolumne City

Among the several towns founded with great expectations along the Tuolumne River was Tuolumne City, located about three miles from the mouth of the river. Paxson McDowell, its promoter, dreamed of great wealth when he established the town in the spring of 1850. Lots were staked out on a plot of 160 acres and were sold at high prices. Unfortunately, when summer came it was found that the river was too low for navigation, and the place soon became deserted.

In the middle 1860's Tuolumne City was revived as the center of a small farming community, and navigation on the river during high water was resumed. All was life and activity in the little river settlement until 1871, when the inhabitants moved en masse to Modesto. A few of the older houses in Modesto once stood in Tuolumne City, and some of its institutions—the *Modesto Bee,* among others—originated there.

The site of the old ferry at Tuolumne City is still evident on the bank near the present bridge over which Shiloh Road crosses the river. The city extended for a half-mile along the river from this point. For years bricks were plowed up in the fields once covered by Tuolumne City.

A rival of this town existed for a time in Paradise, laid out in 1867 by John Mitchell on his ranch in Paradise Valley five miles east of Tuolumne City. A flour mill, a warehouse, and a number of stores were erected. During the several years of prosperity which Paradise experienced, regular weekly and tri-weekly boat service from Stockton was maintained. But with the founding of Modesto, Paradise also came to an end. The brick warehouse stood for many years on Paradise Road about four miles west of downtown Modesto. Across the river from Paradise, Westport Landing was established in 1868.

A. J. Grayson, in 1850, established a ferry on the San Joaquin River eight miles above the mouth of the Tuolumne, and a settlement known as Grayson grew up there. After 1852 the place was practically deserted for several years, although the ferry was still operated. In 1868, after the development of grain farming in the region, the place was surveyed and a town was laid out by J. W. Van Benschotten, who had purchased the ferry. A brisk up-river trade caused the place to flourish until the building of the west-side railroad in the middle 1880's. A tiny settlement still exists at Grayson, about two miles northeast of Westley.

Langworth and Burneyville

The present towns of Oakdale and Riverbank, which date from the 1870's, are the successors of Langworth and Burneyville, respectively, which had been established before the coming of the railroad. Langworth, plotted as a town in 1860 by Henry Langworthy, was located on the Mariposa Road on the hill above the ferry owned by Major James Burney, a former sheriff of Mariposa County and a member of the Yosemite Battalion under Major Savage in 1851. Major Burney was a gallant host, famed for his hospitality. The

Walker's Ford Hotel, near Riverbank

ferry and hotel were later purchased by a Mr. Walker, and Burney moved to the site of Burneyville on the south bank of the Stanislaus River near the present bridge at the north edge of Riverbank.

At Walker's Ford the old frame hotel still stands among the peach orchards on the rich bottom lands just south of the river about a mile north of Highway 108 via Walker Road and its private extension, and three miles northeast of Riverbank. Burneyville, where Major Burney established his second ferry, has been absorbed by the growing town of Riverbank. Near the bridge that crosses the river about where the old ferry once plied stands a historical marker erected by E Clampus Vitus. A few hundred feet up the river is the site of Burney's home.

SOURCES

Adams, Kramer A. *Covered Bridges of the West.* Howell-North, Berkeley, 1963.
Branch, L. C. *History of Stanislaus County, California.* Elliott & Moore, San Francisco, 1881.
Elias, Solomon Philip. *Stories of Stanislaus. A Collection of Stories on the History and Achievements of Stanislaus County.* Privately printed, Modesto, 1924.
Frémont, John C. *Memoirs of My Life, Including in the Narrative Five Journeys of Western Exploration.* Belford, Clarke & Co., Chicago, 1887.
Geologic Guidebook along Highway 49 — Sierran Gold Belt, the Mother Lode Country. State of California, Division of Mines, San Francisco, 1948.
Gold Rush Country. Lane Publishing Co., Menlo Park, 1957.
Latta, F. F. "San Joaquin Primeval—Archaeology," *Tulare Daily Times,* 1931.
——— "San Joaquin Primeval — Spanish," *Tulare Daily Times,* 1932.
——— "San Joaquin Primeval—Yokuts Indians," *Tulare Daily Times,* 1931.
McMillan, Mrs. Minerva Josephine (Browder). "Sketches of an Early Pioneer, Anthony Bolan McMillan, of Stanislaus County, California." Ms., 1932.
Sanchez, Nellie Van de Grift. *Spanish and Indian Place Names of California.* A. M. Robertson, San Francisco, 1922.
Tinkham, George H. *History of Stanislaus County, California.* Historic Record Company, Los Angeles, 1921.
Weston, Otheto. *Mother Lode Album.* Stanford University Press, Stanford, 1948.

Sutter County

SUTTER COUNTY (named in honor of General John A. Sutter) was one of the original 27 counties. During the first two years of its existence the county seat was claimed by four towns in succession: Oro, Nicolaus, Auburn, and Vernon. Auburn was later included in Placer County. The county seat was finally located at Yuba City, where it has remained.

Spanish Expeditions

Gabriel Moraga, in 1808, traversed, for a second time, the river country of the great interior valleys, searching for suitable mission sites. Proceeding farther north than he had gone on the expedition of 1806, he camped on the lower Feather River on October 9, "remarking its width and overflow plain. To this," according to Chapman, "they gave the name 'Sacramento,' employing it also, henceforth, for the great river which it in fact joins farther down. In this connection it may be remarked that at the point where the Sacramento and Feather come together it is the latter which makes a straight course north and south with the lower Sacramento, whereas the upper Sacramento flows in at that point from the west.

"Moraga crossed the Feather River, presumably below Nicolaus, and went north-northwest seven leagues to 'a mountain range, in the middle of the valley'—the Marysville Buttes. Turning west he came to the upper Sacramento." It is probable that the Sacramento River was named prior to 1808.

Interest in the great river country lagged for several years, but in 1817 the founding of missions in the interior was again urged by Padre Presidente Mariano Payéras. As a result, in May of that year, a voyage was made by boat up the Sacramento, probably as far north as the mouth of the Feather River, or within sight of the Sutter Buttes, sometimes miscalled the Marysville Buttes. This expedition was commanded by Father Narciso Durán, accompanied by Luís Argüello and Father Ramón Abella.

The Sutter Buttes

The Sutter Buttes, a unique and picturesque series of volcanic hills rising like a miniature

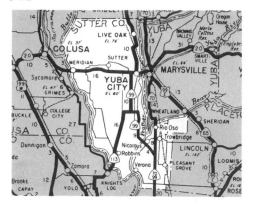

mountain range from the vast, level floor of the valley in northern Sutter County, bear within their rugged declivities the same marks and fossils found in the Coast Range. In the spring their slopes blossom with many wildflowers and shrubs. First discovered by the Spaniards, the Buttes were again seen by Jedediah S. Smith in 1828, and by a Hudson's Bay Company trapper, Michel La Framboise, and others who followed after him. In the various documents relating to Sutter's Grant, these peaks were designated simply as *"los tres picos,"* and John C. Frémont, who camped there from May 30 to June 8, 1846, spoke of them as "the three Buttes." A monument in Frémont's honor was placed three miles northwest of Sutter City in the South Pass of the Buttes on the old stage road to Colusa, by the Bi-county Federation of Women's Clubs of Sutter and Yuba counties in 1923.

Hock Farm

One of General John A. Sutter's several ranchos was Hock Farm *(SRL 346),* a corruption of the German word *hoch* or "upper." An Indian village nearby was called after the farm. On this rancho, which was located on the west side of the Feather River about eight miles below Yuba City, Sutter kept agents to look after his cattle from 1841 until 1850. An adobe house was erected on the estate in the winter of 1841–42, followed by other structures from time to time. Hock Farm, referred to as Upper Farm as late as 1845, became Sutter's principal stock ranch, the animals ranging freely over the entire countryside between the Feather and Sacramento rivers and south of the Buttes.

By 1850 gold-seekers had despoiled Sutter of the greater part of his lands at New Helvetia. It was at this time that he retired to a plot of ground at Hock Farm which he had reserved for his home. There he erected a mansion one and a half miles above the site of the adobe house. The grounds were laid out to beautiful gardens, an orchard, and a vineyard, and there Sutter kept open house to the many travelers and friends who called to pay their respects. Following the flood of 1862, debris from the mines gradually buried the best part of the gardens and orchard at Hock Farm. In 1868 Sutter left the land he so loved, and found a home among the Moravians at Lititz,

Pennsylvania, where he lies buried. He died in Washington, D.C., on June 18, 1880.

The old adobe, as well as the later mansion, has disappeared. For many years the remnant of the garden and orchard was used as a picnic grounds. Today the site is marked by one wall of the old iron fort, which stands on the Garden Highway eight miles south of Yuba City. A tablet on it reads: "This memorial is constructed of the original iron from the fort of Hock Farm, established in 1841 by John Augustus Sutter, being the first white settlement in Sutter County. The fort and farm buildings were located on the banks of the Feather River opposite this point. Erected by Sutter and Yuba Bi-county Federation of Women's Clubs, 1927."

Nicolaus

Nicolaus, the ranch and trading post of Nicolaus Allgeier, was established on the road between New Helvetia and Hock Farm because of the need for ferry transportation at this point on the Feather River. Allgeier, a native of Germany and for a time a Hudson's Bay Company trapper, was employed by Sutter to help build the adobe at Hock Farm. In compensation for this work, as well as for anticipated services as ferryman, Allgeier was given a plot of land one mile square, at the crossing. Here he put up a rude hut of mud-covered tules, and in 1843 he constructed a primitive ferry, which he manned with Indians.

The ferry at Nicolaus was one of many places in California to come into the hands of land speculators. The arrival of a United States government barque in 1849, with supplies for Camp Far West, was the signal for a broadside issued by its promoters, in August 1850, to the effect that Nicolaus was "the head of navigation," and that it was "the only port of entry that has ever been established north of Sacramento—the only town north of that city that has ever had a full-rigged seagoing vessel lying at her landing." Its advantages were already "too manifest," they said, "to be any longer denied and doubted. Furthermore, the close proximity of the town to the rich placers on the Feather and Yuba rivers, Deer, Dry, and Bear creeks, and the Forks of the American ensures its continuance as a depot for the supplies for all the northern mines."

Allgeier, who had put up an adobe house at his landing place in 1847, built a two-story adobe hotel there in 1849. During the following year, as a result of advertising, over 300 lots were sold, and three hotels, a dozen stores, and over 100 dwellings were erected. For a time the little river town showed such business activity that it presented a more flourishing appearance than Marysville, 20 miles to the north.

Realization that Nicolaus was not at the head of navigation fell heavily upon that hopeful metropolis in the winter of 1849–50. Boats could usually reach Marysville, but when the river was low they were compelled to unload at Vernon, nine miles below Nicolaus. By 1853 many of the houses had been torn down and carted away, and the town was almost deserted. Until the building of the railroad, however, the place served as a ship-

Old Home, Nicolaus

ping point and center of trade for surrounding ranches.

Nicolaus was the second county seat of Sutter County, from 1850 to 1851, but during the years 1851–52 it lost that honor, first to Auburn and then to Vernon, after Auburn had become county seat of the newly created Placer County. The seat of justice was reestablished at Nicolaus in 1852, but in 1854 it was transferred to Yuba City for a few months. Returned again to Nicolaus for a period of two years, it was permanently established at Yuba City after 1856. Nicolaus still exists as a small center for farms located in southeastern Sutter County. There are a few of the old residences left as landmarks, including a substantial two-story house with lower story of brick and upper of wood.

Samuel Brannan on May 11, 1849, bought from Sutter two square miles of land on the Feather River opposite Nicolaus. There he built a story-and-a-half dwelling of lumber brought around the Horn. In this house, with its beautiful winding stairway, its eight rooms, each with a fireplace, and its surrounding gardens, Brannan gave royal entertainment to many gay river-boat parties made up of friends and celebrities from San Francisco. The "White House," as it was often called, was later moved from its original site on the riverbank to the present Garden Highway, but it no longer stands.

Oro

"A noble city of broad streets, imposing buildings, and splendid public squares—on paper— but in fact a tract of land fronting on the south bank of Bear Creek." Such was Oro, "mushroom" neighbor of Nicolaus, on the Feather River just below the mouth of the Bear. Thomas Jefferson Green had purchased the tract from Sutter, and as State Senator he caused his "paper city" to be declared by legislative act the county seat of Sutter County when the county was formed in 1850.

In order to win over his rivals at Auburn, Nicolaus, Vernon, and Yuba City, each better fitted for the position than Oro, Green exercised to its full extent the power of a shrewd, energetic, and imposing presence, a persuasive tongue, and a good-natured, bluff-mannered personality. The outcome was that "the active, talkative, merry-mannered" Senator won the day.

Since there was not a house in town for any purpose, much less for the holding of court, a zinc structure 20 × 20 feet was put up, "without glass or shutters for the windows, or doors for the entrances. Not a tree, or bush, or shrub grew near enough to give its shade to the building." Under a brilliant May sun the first court met in the "zinc house," but "law and equity, lawyers and litigants, jurors and witnesses, with a spontaneity of action that would astonish nothing but a salamander, rushed out of and fled that building, never again to return."

Barham's Crossing, on the river road to Marysville, was established at the site of Oro in the early 1850's.

Vernon

Vernon, another of those short-lived "mushroom" cities existing along the Sacramento and Feather rivers in 1849 and 1850, enjoyed the brief illusion that it was the head of navigation and the entrepôt to the mining regions. Buffum, a contemporary writer, says:

"Vernon is situated on the east bank of the Feather River at the point of its confluence with the Sacramento, one of the most eligible positions for a town in the whole northern region of California. The banks of the river are high and not subject to overflow, and this point is said to be at the head of ship navigation on the Sacramento. ... From the town of Vernon good and well-traveled roads diverge to the rich mineral regions of the North and Middle Forks, Bear Creek, Yuba, and Feather rivers, rendering the distance much less than by any other route. The town is growing rapidly, and promises to become a great depot for the trade of the above-mentioned mines."

John A. Sutter in April 1849 sold a strip of land along the Sacramento and Feather rivers three miles in length and one mile back. The group of men who purchased this tract laid out a town one mile square at the junction of the rivers, "while the two miles above were designed for the country residences and elegant villas that would be the necessary accompaniments of a city such as this was designed to be."

The winter of 1849 was such a dry one that the Feather River was not navigable. Vessels were compelled to unload at Vernon, and hopes were aroused that the place would become the head of navigation. During the summer of 1849 a number of wholesale stores were erected. The prospect of a glorious future seemed bright indeed, and lots were sold rapidly at a high figure. One hotel was built entirely of mahogany from a shipment bought in Chile. Originally intended for New York, this expensive wood had been brought to California because the ship's captain desired to reach the gold fields.

The heavy rains of 1849–50 caused the rivers to rise so that it was possible for ships to go as far as Marysville. This was a deadly blow to Vernon, as well as to most of the infant cities along the river. Erstwhile enthusiastic speculators transferred their affections to other towns farther up the river. But Vernon did not expire without a struggle. E. O. Crosby, a property owner who was a member of the state senate, succeeded in having the county seat transferred from Auburn to Vernon in 1851. The position was lost the next year, however, and in 1853 the hotel ceased to be a public house and the post office was removed. No vestige of Vernon remains today. Only its name is preserved in Vernon Township. A settlement called Verona was later established on the site.

Yuba City

Samuel Brannan, Pierson B. Reading, and Henry Cheever laid out Yuba City in July 1849 on the site of the Indian village found at this spot by the first white men in the region. Where the round earthen huts of the Indians once clustered on the riverbank at the foot of what is now Second Street, the levee and terraced lots of the white man now stand, and no vestige of the old mound is visible.

Until the year 1938, at 229 B Street, Yuba City's giant walnut tree lifted a massive spread of 108 feet and extended to a height of 99.6 feet, the huge trunk measuring 15.5 feet in circumference at four feet above the ground. The little Lyman house and garden beneath it were completely in the dense shade of the great tree planted there over 60 years earlier. The variety (*paradox*) was a cross between the English walnut and the California black walnut.

Camp Bethel

The site of Camp Bethel, one of the largest of the old religious camp meetings in northern California, is just east of the Buttes, two miles north of Sutter City. The land was leased to the North and South Methodist churches for 99 years without cost, the donor, Gilbert Smith of East Butte, stipulating that the land revert automatically to him whenever the churches ceased to hold religious services in the grove. Rev. George Baker, pastor in charge of the Butte circuit in 1862, helped to raise a subscription fund with which to erect a board pavilion about 100 feet square and furnished with seats. In this pavilion, situated in the midst of the beautiful oaks which then dotted the broad wooded plains at the foot of the Buttes, the Methodist camp meetings were held for three weeks each year. Families from all over the state lived in the grove in small wooden cabins, doing their own cooking or boarding with Mrs. Smith, whose husband dispensed candies and soft drinks.

Gradually, during the 1870's, the meetings

dwindled in attendance, and early in the 1880's were discontinued altogether, the land reverting to Smith. The site later became the Lang Ranch. Most of the oaks and the dense groves of native shrubs once carpeted with wildflowers have given way to cultivated fields and orchard lands.

The Bland Ranch

About a mile south of the site of Camp Bethel once stood the house in which Henry Meade Bland, California's second poet laureate, spent much of his boyhood. His father, Henry James Bland, was a pastor on the Butte circuit at various times, beginning in 1868, and in 1872 he purchased the Massou Ranch of 160 acres about two miles directly south of Camp Bethel and two miles northeast of Sutter City. In the midst of changing pastorates, the Blands returned often to the beloved ranch, sometimes living there for a year or two at a time.

While in this neighborhood, Henry Meade Bland attended the Union School, a little unpainted clapboard building located in a thick grove of oaks near the camp, a site later occupied by the Lang house. The second school which he attended in this district, and the one in which he first made his acquaintance with Tennyson, was on what later became the Howard place, about halfway to the Bland homesite.

At "Saint's Rest," as his father called the Sutter ranch, the homely duties of the farm mingled pleasantly with long hours of delight in the woods and fields and hills about his home and nurtured those impulses which the poet later expressed in lyric verse.

SOURCES

Bland, Henry Meade. "Autobiographical Notes." Ms., 1929.
Buffum, E. Gould. *Six Months in the Gold Mines.* Lea & Blanchard, Philadelphia, 1850.
Chapman, Charles E. *A History of California: The Spanish Period.* Macmillan, New York, 1921.
Coy, Owen Cochran. *Gold Days,* of the series *California,* ed. John Russell McCarthy. Powell Publishing Co., Los Angeles, 1929.
Delay, Peter J. *History of Yuba and Sutter Counties, California.* Historic Record Co., Los Angeles, 1924.
Maas, Willard. "The Poet of the Pioneers," *Overland Monthly,* LXXXV, No. 10 (October 1927), 299–300.
McGowan, Joseph A. *History of the Sacramento Valley.* 3 vols. Lewis Historical Publishing Co., New York, 1961.
Schoonover, T. J. *The Life and Times of General John A. Sutter.* Bullock-Carpenter Printing Co., Sacramento, 1907.
Wells, Harry L. *History of Sutter County.* Thompson & West, Oakland, 1879.

Tehama County

TEHAMA, a word of undetermined meaning, was derived from the name of an Indian tribe. Nellie Van de Grift Sanchez says that "two definitions have been offered: 'high water,' in reference to the overflowing of the Sacramento River, and 'low land,'" but that this may be an attempt to make the name fit the circumstances. "All that can be positively stated is that the word is of Indian origin." Tehama County was organized in 1856 from parts of Colusa, Butte, and Shasta counties, and the county seat was located at the town of Tehama. In 1857 the seat of government was changed to Red Bluff, where it has remained to the present.

First Trails

The first recorded expedition into Tehama County was that of the Spanish explorer Luís Argüello, who in 1821 probably pushed as far north as Cottonwood Creek. Then came the American Jedediah Strong Smith in 1828, and in his footsteps came a stream of hunters and traders from the south. Hudson's Bay Company trappers from the north followed much the same general course during the years 1830–45. This old Sacramento Valley route, known at first as the California-Oregon Trail and later as the California-Oregon Road, was soon beaten into a well-defined path by trappers and explorers, among them Ewing Young, Lieutenant Emmons of the Wilkes Expedition, and Joseph Gale. Sometimes proceeding all the way down the western side of the river, and at other times crossing over to the east side somewhere between Red Bluff and Tehama (a variation used most frequently by the gold seekers of 1849 and the 1850's), many travelers have used this historic road through the years —pack-mule trains, horsemen and footmen, herds of cattle and sheep, slow and cumbersome ox teams and covered wagons, stagecoaches and freighters, and finally automobiles, trucks, and buses.

In 1843 John Bidwell, accompanied by Peter Lassen and John Burheim, chased a band of horse thieves over this trail, pursuing them as far north as Red Bluff, where they overtook them and recovered the property. It was on this trip that Lassen selected the land that was later granted to him by the Mexican government.

Returning to this region the following year, Bidwell brought with him five other men who were destined to become the first settlers in the upper Sacramento Valley. Of them, Pierson B. Reading settled in what is now Shasta County, while Job Francis Dye, William George Chard, Robert Hasty Thomes, and Albert G. Toomes followed Lassen as the earliest white settlers in Tehama County. Each of them located on Mexican grants chosen on this trip with Bidwell in 1844.

An incident of this early reconnoitering tour illustrates the charm which the vast unspoiled regions of the Great Valley held for those who first looked upon it. Going up the east side of the river, the Bidwell party crossed to the west side north of where Red Bluff now is. Continuing north perhaps as far as the site of Redding, they returned along the west side of the stream all the way. On reaching a beautiful grove of oaks south of Elder Creek, the company halted.

"Boys," said Thomes, looking up at a magnificent tree, "the land that will grow an oak like this is good enough for me. Here is where I stay." Thomes was the first of the group to go back and settle on the land of his choice.

It was on this trip, also, that Bidwell mapped

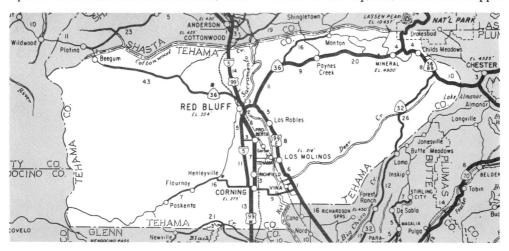

the valley, giving those names to its streams which they still bear.

Bloody Island

Samuel J. Hensley, who had accompanied Reading to California in 1843, while rafting logs on the Sacramento River in the northern part of Tehama County early in 1844, had an encounter with some Indians on the island that lies in the river just below the mouth of Cottonwood Creek. It is said that Hensley named the place "Bloody Island" because of this experience. During his stay in the region, Hensley noted the fine land north of Cottonwood Creek (in what is now Shasta County), and later recommended it to Reading as suitable for a ranch. It was this land which the latter obtained as a grant in 1844.

Lassen's Ranch

Through the influence of General Sutter, Rancho Bosquejo ("the Wooded Place"), comprising 26,000 acres of excellent farming land, was granted in 1843 to Peter Lassen, a pioneer blacksmith who was a native of Denmark and who had come overland to Oregon in 1839. He set sail for California on an English ship and landed at Fort Ross. From there he went to Pueblo de San José, where he spent the winter of 1839–40. After ranching at Santa Cruz in 1841, he was at Sutter's Fort in 1842–43. In December 1843 (according to some accounts) Lassen started for Rancho Bosquejo, but he did not reach his destination until the following February, because high water forced him to camp at the Sutter Buttes. Other authorities place these events one year later, in 1844–45. Surrounded by hundreds of Indians, Lassen established a trading post near the mouth of Deer Creek on the east side of the Sacramento River. There is no trace left of the buildings today, but the site is near Vina, 18 miles south of the present city of Red Bluff on Route 99.

In 1847 Lassen laid out a town on his ranch, calling it Benton City in honor of Senator Thomas H. Benton of Missouri. That same year he returned to Missouri to induce settlers to come to his ranch in California, and to obtain a charter for a Masonic lodge which he wished to establish in the new town. This charter, granted on May 10, 1848, antedates, by six months, any other charter granted for a Masonic lodge in California.

In the summer of the same year Lassen returned to his ranch with a party of settlers, the first to come into California over the famous Lassen Trail and the first to come with the intention of settling in the upper Sacramento Valley. The party's destination was Benton City, the town which Lassen had already laid out. But the discovery of gold, in the spring of 1848, disrupted the entire plan and caused the dissolution of the proposed settlement. On May 9, 1851, the Masonic chapter was moved from Benton City to Shasta, in Shasta County. Benton City no longer exists, but the Masons of Shasta and Tehama counties have erected a monument on the site. It stands on the east side of Highway 99 just north of Deer Creek.

In 1848 Lassen gave to Daniel Sill, a trapper,

one league of land on which the latter built an adobe and on which the town of Danville was later projected but never settled. Lassen, in 1852, conveyed his remaining lands to Henry Gerke, a German, who settled there in 1869. In 1881 Senator Leland Stanford (later founder of Stanford University) purchased from Gerke 9,000 acres of the original Lassen Grant. Subsequently Stanford purchased additional lands, all of which were included in the famous Vina Ranch of 55,000 acres, which the Senator conveyed to Stanford University by the Founding Grant, November 11, 1885. The name was derived from the fact that here Senator Stanford planted a vast vineyard, one of the largest in the world. After the ranch became the property of the University, plans for developing the vineyard were abandoned. On July 2, 1955, 580 acres of the Lassen Grant, including the headquarters buildings of the original Stanford-Vina Ranch, were purchased by Our Lady of the New Clairvaux Trappist Monastery. Visitors are welcome at the monastery.

Frémont at Lassen's Ranch

Frémont, coming up from New Helvetia in March 1846 on his way to Oregon, spent a month at Lassen's Ranch, from which he made a local exploring trip through what is now Tehama County. Arriving at the ranch on March 30, he noted that Lassen had a vineyard, that he was experimenting with cotton, and that his wheat crop was large.

On April 5 Frémont and his men set out up the valley, encamping that night "on a little creek on the Sacramento, where an emigrant from 'the states' was establishing himself and was already building a house." This was probably Albert Toomes on his Rancho de los Molinos. On April 6 the expedition crossed the river in canoes to another farm on the right bank, no doubt that of Toomes's friend and partner, Robert Thomes. There Frémont made camp on "a creek wooded principally with large oaks," the same oaks, perhaps, that had won the admiration of Thomes in 1844.

During the next few days the party crossed Red Bank Creek and Cottonwood Creek (later the boundary line between Tehama and Shasta counties), and on April 9 they crossed the Sacramento River to the east side, camping on Cow Creek in what is now Shasta County. Two days later they were back at Lassen's Ranch, where they remained until April 24, when the march to Oregon was resumed. A month later, on May 24, when returning from Oregon to participate in the stirring events of the American occupation, Frémont again stopped at Lassen's Ranch.

First Settlers

Robert Hasty Thomes, a native of Maine, came to California with the Bidwell-Bartleson party in 1841. For a time he was engaged as a carpenter and builder in San Francisco and Monterey in partnership with Albert Toomes, as is evidenced by the frequent appearance of the firm name of Thomes and Toomes in Larkin's books and other records.

In the winter of 1844, Thomes received the

Mexican land grant of Rancho de los Saucos ("elder trees"), located south of Elder Creek in what is now Tehama County. Although he stocked the place in 1845, he did not settle there permanently until 1846 or 1847, when he built an adobe house on his property. This house was burned in 1858. In the late 1860's or early 1870's Thomes erected the brick house which stood until 1943, when it was destroyed by fire, on what was long known as the Finnell Ranch, later as the El Camino Colony, and now as the Elder Creek Ranch. A hotel, known as the Tehama House, was erected on the site of the old adobe.

Robert Thomes was a man of character and influence in his community. He died in 1878 and lies buried under the largest and most ornamental monument in the Tehama Cemetery, a monument composed of granite from the quarries of Penryn, Placer County.

William George Chard, a native of New York, came to California from New Mexico in 1832. He was at Los Angeles until 1836 and at Santa Cruz from 1837 to 1841. During the years 1843–45 he was in partnership with Josiah Belden in a store and boardinghouse at Monterey. In 1844 Chard obtained a grant of land on the north side of Elder Creek (in Tehama County), naming it Rancho de las Flores ("the flowers"). In this same year Josiah Belden obtained Rancho de la Barranca Colorada north of Chard's grant. Chard took his cattle to Rancho de las Flores in 1845 and in 1846 erected a log cabin on the Sacramento River at a site four miles north of the present Tehama, but he did not go to his rancho to live until the following year, as he was employed at the New Almaden Mine (in Santa Clara County) from 1845 to 1847. The log house at Rancho de las Flores came to be known as the Sacramento House, and was a popular stopping place on the road to the northern mines.

Across the river from Chard's rancho, Job Francis Dye built an adobe in 1847 on Rancho de los Berrendos ("the antelopes"). Dye, a Kentucky trapper who came from New Mexico with Ewing Young in 1831–32, for a time engaged in hunting sea otter along the coast. Later he ran a store and distillery at Santa Cruz, where he also had a ranch. Until the 1880's, Dye's adobe stood on the west bank of Antelope Creek on what later became known as the Cone Ranch. It was located on a spot not far from where the Cone Methodist Church now stands. This old adobe was long distinguished by the hospitality of its owner, who kept open house and entertained in true Southern manner the many guests who gathered there.

Albert G. Toomes, a native of Missouri who came to California with the Workman-Rowland party in 1841, was given the grant of Rancho Río de los Molinos ("river of the mills") in 1844. Toomes visited his rancho in 1845 and again in 1847, to stock it with cattle, and in 1846 he erected an adobe on the east side of the river not far from the site of the old Ellis flour mill near where the settlement of Los Molinos later grew up. That Toomes did not go to live permanently on the estate until 1849 is evident from the fact that the firm of Thomes and Toomes is mentioned in records at Monterey until the end of 1848.

William C. Moon, who also came to California with the Rowland-Workman party in 1841, settled on the west side of the Sacramento River opposite the mouth of Deer Creek as early as 1845, and ran a ferry at this point during the gold rush. The ferry was located about where the present Squaw Hill Bridge crosses the Sacramento River on the road from Vina to Corning. Moon lived on his ranch until his death in 1878.

Henry L. Ford, a captain in Frémont's Battalion, also settled on the Sacramento opposite Deer Creek in 1848. John Myers, thought to have been the first settler on the site of Red Bluff, is reputed to have built a hotel within the present limits of that city during the fall or winter of 1849.

The Lassen Trail

Lassen's Ranch was the end of the famous Lassen Trail across the Sierra Nevada, the first northern emigrant route into California from the East. The earliest emigrant party to come over this trail started from Missouri in the spring of 1848 under the leadership of Peter Lassen, reaching his ranch in California in the fall of the same year. A considerable number of emigrants undertook to shorten their journey overland in 1849–50 by using this same route. While it never became popular, since it proved to be a long cut-off, steep, precipitous, and infested with hostile Indians, it did serve to introduce many emigrants to northern California, thus quickening an early interest in that part of the state.

Lassen's Trail came into California from northwestern Nevada through Surprise Valley and over the Fandango Pass. It continued in a southeast direction, following Pit River part of the way and on to Big Meadows, now covered by the waters of Lake Almanor. The historic trail entered Tehama County over Deer Creek Pass to Deer Creek Meadows before following the ridge between Mill Creek and Deer Creek over the once precipitous "Narrows," now less risky since it has been widened for logging trucks. Other historic spots along the way include Bruff's Camp high in the forest belt, and Steep Hollow and Emigrant Springs in the rocky foothill slopes, before the trail emerges into the Sacramento Valley near Toomes Creek, at a point near the railroad two miles below Los Molinos and some four miles above Vina.

The William Ide Adobe

William B. Ide, a native of Rutland, Massachusetts, came with his family from New Hampshire to what is now Tehama County in 1845. He built a log cabin on the R. H. Thomes ranch and spent the winter there. In the spring of 1846 he moved to the Belden ranch, where he put up another log house in Ide's Bottom south of what was later Red Bluff. In 1847 Ide purchased, from Belden, Rancho de la Barranca Colorada ("Ranch of the Red Bluff"), so called because of an adjacent cliff on the river, 50 feet high, composed of sand and gravel of a reddish hue.

Ide was the commandant of the Bear Flag Revolt in 1846. After 1850 he resided much of the time at Monroeville, Colusa County, where he

William B. Ide Adobe, near Red Bluff,
before Restoration

eventually held virtually all the county offices
and where he died in 1852. The spot is now in
Glenn County.

One and one-half miles northeast of Red Bluff
on the west bank of the Sacramento River stands
an adobe house built in the late 1840's or early
1850's. For years it has been known as the Ide
adobe *(SRL 12)*, presumably built by William B.
Ide. Careful research, however, fails to prove conclusively that Ide built the house or owned the
land on which it stands, or that he established
the ferry that crossed the river at that point. The
Adobe Ferry, as it was known, operated for more
than three decades, being abandoned in the autumn of 1876 when the first bridge was opened.
The restored adobe is the main feature of the
four-acre William B. Ide Adobe State Historical
Monument, dedicated on May 1, 1960. Whether
or not Ide built the adobe, it seems proper that
this historical site be set aside in memory of a
man who helped to shape decisively, though
briefly, the destiny of the state.

Tehama

Robert Thomes's adobe was built on a spot
later covered by Tehama, the first town in the
county. It has been authentically established,
however, that before Thomes settled on the site
he had given to his friend Albert Toomes a small
tract of land where Tehama now stands, thus
making Toomes the founder of the town. In 1849
Tehama (then known as Hall's Ranch), located
on the west side of the Sacramento River 12 miles
south of Red Bluff, was an important center of
trade and freighting on the Oregon Road as well
as the principal ferry crossing between Marysville
and Shasta. Other ferries were soon established
at Moon's Ranch, Ide's adobe, and Red Bluff.
When the *Orient* landed at Red Bluff in 1850,
Tehama at once lost its prestige as a river town.
As a stage center, however, it held its own for a
number of years.

The first stage line from Colusa to Shasta was
opened up by Baxter and Monroe in 1851. An
opposition line from Marysville, via Hamilton,
Neal's Ranch, and Bidwell's Ranch, in Butte
County, was started by Hall and Crandall in 1852.
The two lines converged in Tehama, creating a
prosperous activity which continued until the
coming of the railroad.

Tehama, with its old buildings and tree-lined

streets, is today a quiet settlement. The courthouse *(SRL 183)*, built while the town was the
county seat of the newly created Tehama County,
is used as a lodge room for the Masons.

Across the river the town of Sesma once flourished. A Mr. Payne, in 1851, erected a sawmill on
Mill Creek above the town, and in the 1870's the
Sierra Lumber Company built a mill in the
neighborhood but later abandoned the site when
the railroad was extended to Red Bluff. A part
of the cobblestone foundations of the old Ellis
Flour Mill, begun near Sesma by a Dr. Crosby in
the autumn of 1854, is still visible near the Te-
hama-Vina road. This mill, later purchased by
M. C. Ellis, was twice destroyed by fire prior to
1880, and both times it was rebuilt by Ellis. The
stone foundations of another flour mill, built a
year or so later on the Dye Ranch, may still be
seen on the banks of Antelope Creek a few miles
east of Red Bluff (on the Henry Edwards Ranch).

The Nomi Lackee Indian Reservation

The Nomi Lackee Indian Reservation *(SRL 357)*
was established in 1854 by the United States government to provide a home for displaced Indians
as white men settled the land. Grain was the
major crop raised on the more than 25,000 acres
of land that comprised the reservation. From 300
to 2,500 Indians lived there until 1866, when
they were moved to Round Valley in Mendocino
County where Covelo is today.

Colonel B. F. Washington, great-grandson of
Lawrence Washington, brother of George Washington, came overland to California from Virginia
in 1849, finally settling in Tehama County. He
acquired title to a considerable tract of land near
the Nomi Lackee Indian Reservation. His home,
located by a spring, was known for many years
as Washington's Gardens, but it has long since
disappeared.

A. J. Henley, one of several agents of the Indian
Reservation, also acquired land nearby. Hence,
the name Henleyville was and still is used for the
small community to the east.

A monument with a descriptive plaque marks
the location of the Nomi Lackee Indian Reservation four miles north of Flournoy on Osborn
Road.

The "Stone House" and the "Brick House"

The Wilson home, better known as the "Stone
House," still stands in excellent condition on the

Courthouse, Tehama

south side of Thomes Creek about five miles northwest of Corning on Davis Road. The two-story cobblestone structure was erected and completed in 1859 by Henry Clay Wilson, later State Senator and a leader in local and state politics. The once easily visible home is now half hidden among the trees and shrubs that surround it.

The old "Brick House," also known as the Jelly house, was built in 1856 by Andrew Jelly in the community that still bears his name, northeast of Red Bluff. He came to California in 1848 and gained title to his land by buying script which soldiers of the Mexican War had received instead of pay for military service. The script entitled the holder to 160 acres of frontier land. Jelly was a brickmason by trade. He built the house large enough to take care of his family and to accommodate travelers. The brick was made and burned from the clay soil on the ranch. At one time a post office was established and maintained there. The house is in excellent condition, having been remodeled several times in keeping with the changing modes of life.

Home of John Brown's Widow

In 1864, near the close of the Civil War, the widow of John Brown, the famous abolitionist of Harper's Ferry, came to Red Bluff with her children. So great was the admiration for John Brown in that section of the country that a considerable sum of money was raised for the purpose of providing his widow and children with a home. The house (SRL 117) was built at what is now 135 Main Street, and there Mrs. Brown lived until the summer of 1870, when she and her three daughters moved to Humboldt County. The house, somewhat remodeled, is still standing and occupied as a private dwelling.

Tuscan Springs

The spring-fed area known as Tuscan Springs is located near the head of Little Salt Creek, approximately nine miles east of Red Bluff. They were named after the similar sulphur-type springs of Tuscany, Italy, by their first owner, Dr. John A. Veatch, who purchased the property in 1854. Two years later, in present Lake County, he discovered the first borax ever found in California, but the quantities were insufficient for lasting commercial development.

Various owners developed Tuscan Springs as a health resort, the most extensive and widely known work being done by Ed Walbridge during the years from 1892 to 1912. He built a two-story hotel to accommodate 125 guests, ran a daily stagecoach from Red Bluff, and established a post office. His first hotel burned to the ground in 1899 and was replaced with a three-story hotel. Walbridge established the first commercial motor transportation in the county between Red Bluff and his Tuscan Springs resort, and from the spring waters he developed and sold bottled mineral salts for medicinal purposes. In 1912 Walbridge's hotel was again razed by fire. He was unable to finance the rebuilding at that time, and the springs fell into disuse, until today little remains of the once world-famous health resort except a few of the medicinal springs.

Lyman Springs and Lyonsville

When lumbering operations were developed in the pine belt of the northern Sierra Nevada, a major problem in the early days was transporting the lumber to shipping points in the valley. To solve this problem C. F. Ellsworth designed and constructed the first V-flume in the state. His original Empire Flume was built in the early 1870's and was referred to in the beginning as "Ellsworth's Folly." It was over 40 miles in length, extending from Lyman Springs in the mountains east of Red Bluff to Sesma, the closest point to the railroad on the east side of the Sacramento River, a site near present-day Los Molinos. His high-trestle flume followed the course of the Belle Mill Road, past Finley Lake, down the steep, rugged Grecian Bend, across the Mud Springs Plains, and entered the valley near the Antelope Flouring Mills. In 1881 the route was shortened by extending it to the east bank of the Sacramento River across from Red Bluff instead of continuing across the valley to Sesma.

Near Lyman Springs the small settlement of Lyonsville became the home for the loggers and millworkers and their families. It was so named for Darwin B. Lyon, a division superintendent of the Sierra Flume and Lumber Company. The homes that once dotted the Lyonsville landscape are no longer there, many of them having been removed for use on nearby ranches and in the valley.

The V-flume, which occasionally transported people as well as lumber, was discontinued in the winter of 1913–14, after an unusually strong windstorm wrecked great sections of it. Now logging operations have been resumed to some extent at Lyman Springs by the Diamond National Corporation.

SOURCES

Anderson, R. A. Fighting the Mill Creeks. Chico Record Press, Chico, 1909.
Bruff, J. Goldsborough. Gold Rush: The Journals, Drawings and Other Papers of J. Goldsborough Bruff, April 2, 1849–July 20, 1851, ed. Georgia Willis Read and Ruth Gaines. New York, 1944.
Dornin, May. "The Emigrant Trails into California," M.A. thesis in history, University of California, 1921.
Frémont, John C. Memoirs of My Life. Including in the Narrative Five Journeys of Western Exploration. Belford, Clarke & Co., Chicago, 1887.
Geiger, V., and W. Bryarly. Trail to California, ed. David M. Potter. Yale University Press, New Haven, 1945.
Gudde, Erwin G. California Place Names . . . The Original Etymology of Current Geographical Names. University of California Press, Berkeley, 1962.
Hisken, Clara Hough. Tehama, Little City of the Big Trees. Exposition Press, New York, 1948.
Hust, Stephen G. This Is My Own, My Native Land. Independent Press, Yuba City, 1956.
Hutchinson, W. H. California Heritage, A History of Northern California Lumbering. A Diamond National Corporation booklet, n.d.
——— One Man's West. Hurst and Yount, Chico, 1948.
Ide, William Brown. Biographical Sketch. Edited and printed by Simeon Ide, Claremont, N.H., 1880.
Kroeber, Theodora. Ishi in Two Worlds, A Biography of the Last Wild Indian in North America. University of California Press, Berkeley, 1963.
Lewis, E. J. Tehama County, California, With Historical Reminiscences. Elliott & Moore, San Francisco, 1880.
McCoy, L. L. "Story of Early Days in Tehama County," River Rambler, June 28, 1926.

McGowan, Joseph A. *History of the Sacramento Valley.* 3 vols. Lewis Historical Publishing Co., New York, 1961.

McNamar, Myrtle. *'Way Back When.* Privately printed, 1952. Tehama County Free Library.

Moak, Sim. *The Last of the Mill Creeks and Early Life in Northern California.* Chico, 1923. Tehama County Free Library.

Nielsen, Valentina. "Geographical Features of Tehama County," *Wagon Wheels,* February 1956. Colusi County Historical Society, Colusa.

Paden, Irene D. *Prairie Schooner Detours.* Macmillan, New York, 1949.

Rogers, Fred B. *William Brown Ide, Bear Flagger.* J. Howell, San Francisco, 1962.

Sanchez, Nellie Van de Grift. *Spanish and Indian Place Names of California.* A. M. Robertson, San Francisco, 1922.

Schoenfeld, Golda. "Some Landmarks and History of Tehama County, California." Ms. read before Antelope Women's Club, December 1, 1922. Tehama County Free Library.

Sherman, Edwin A. *Fifty Years of Masonry in California.* 2 vols. George Spaulding & Co., San Francisco, 1898.

Swartzlow, Ruby Johnson. *Lassen, His Life and Legacy.* Loomis Museum Association, Mineral, 1964.

—— *Peter Lassen, Northern California's Trail-Blazer.* California Historical Society. Lawton Kennedy, San Francisco, 1939.

Sweeney, J. D. *History and Geography of Tehama County for Use in the Public Schools.* Red Bluff, 1930. Tehama County Free Library.

Woodson, Warren N. *The Trail of the Trail Blazers.* Rotary Club, Corning, 1935. Tehama County Free Library.

Trinity County

TRINITY COUNTY, one of the original 27 counties, derived its name from Trinidad Bay, which was discovered and named by Captain Bruno Heceta on Trinity Sunday in the year 1775. Weaverville has always been the county seat.

Trinity National Forest and Trinity Alps Wilderness Area

Although gold mining brought the pioneer population to Trinity County, the chief importance of this county is now as a recreational and lumbering center. "The major part of the land area of Trinity County is within the Trinity National Forest." This forest, covering approximately 77 percent of the area of the county, comprises 1,780,960 acres of timberland, in which Douglas fir predominates, with sugar pine and yellow pine second. Within the National Forest lies the Trinity Alps Wilderness Area, 136,000 acres, which is being preserved as nearly as possible in its original state. "Here is real wilderness, only the borders of which can be reached by saddle horse."

Noteworthy in the National Forest are the Stewart's Fork region, a mecca for huntsmen, and the headwaters of Canyon Creek, accessible only by horse, in which is located Thompson Peak, the highest peak in the Trinity Mountains. Ideal hunting is afforded by the forests, and the mountain streams and lakes abound in fish.

This region, with the charm of its primitive state so well preserved, is not the inaccessible territory that it once was. A fine state highway runs across the county. Every post office can be reached in an automobile over roads extending from Weaverville, within half a day's travel. The Forest Service has constructed good trails through many of the forests, and jeep roads lure the motorist into the back country.

Early Explorations

Jedediah Strong Smith and his party were among the first white men to explore Trinity County. In early April 1828 Smith came up the eastern side of the "Buenaventura" (the present Sacramento River) to the vicinity of Red Bluff. There he found "the rocky hills coming in so close to the river as to make it impossible to travel." After scouting parties had been sent north and northwest, it was decided that the most practicable route was to the northwest. He crossed the Sacramento River on April 11, 1828, and, traveling in very rough country, passed over the divide into the present Trinity Forest on April 17. So far Smith's route seems to have followed approximately that of the present Red Bluff–Eureka highway.

The next day Smith's party followed down one of the tributaries of the South Fork of the Trinity River (probably the Hay Fork). On April 21 they reached "a small valley on the river which turned in its course nearly North and . . . received a branch from the South." Smith states in his diary that he named the river he had been following Smith's River, and many of the early maps so designate the rivers later known as the Trinity River and the Klamath River below the junction. Later the name was transferred to the present Smith River in Del Norte County.

On April 24 he had to cross to the west bank because the mountain came so close to the river that it was impossible to proceed. There he found the traveling rough; the ground was so rocky that the horses' feet were being mangled. Climbing the high ridge to the west of the river, the party crossed over into Humboldt County. Jedediah Smith had opened up the coast route to Oregon on the first journey ever made by a white man

from California into Oregon. This route was followed in later years, at least in part, by trappers
of the Hudson's Bay Company from Oregon.
Ewing Young, noted trapper, made his first passage to the north this way in 1832.

The Old Trinity Trail

The modern highway that crosses the mountains of Shasta and Trinity counties between Redding and Weaverville follows, approximately, the
old Trinity Trail opened up by early trappers
and gold seekers. Trappers of the Hudson's Bay
Company may have used this route to some extent in the 1830's and 1840's. The first trails were
Indian trails, and the first white men to travel
this country used these paths. The first definite
knowledge (with the exception of Smith's recorded journey) comes from Major P. B. Reading,
who says that in 1848 he had crossed the mountains "where the travel passed ... from Shasta to
Weaver." Reading had previously visited the area
for the purpose of trapping as early as 1845.

The Forty-niners also used the Trinity Trail
on their way to the Trinity goldfields, and the
need for safe transportation of gold in the early
1850's led to the establishment of express offices
and what were known as Pony Express lines. Over
these trails mail and bullion from Trinity County
were carried on horseback. The mail route for
Trinity County led from Red Bluff in Tehama
County to Weaverville, 50 miles northwest in
Trinity County. These trails were for pack trains
of horses and mules only. Such slow and laborious
means of transportation delayed the development
of the county and the coming of families.

The Buckhorn or Grass Valley Creek Toll Road

The route of the old Trinity Trail was followed
until the first wagon road in the county was
built. This Buckhorn–Grass Valley Creek Toll
Road, connecting Weaverville, Shasta, and Redding, was begun in 1857 and completed in 1858.
The entrance of the first stagecoach into Weaverville was a gala occasion. In a contemporary account it is stated that "William Lawrence handled the ribbons, when the first stage was wildly
greeted in Weaverville. Trinity County citizens
went out in buggies and on horseback, led by the
German brass band, to greet and escort it into
town."

The credit for the construction of this road is
given to William Lowden of Lowden's Ranch, located on Grass Valley Creek. Lowden, a deputy
United States surveyor, was a relay Pony Express
rider in the celebrated ride made in January
1854, when two express companies, Adams and
Wells Fargo, raced the President's message from
San Francisco to Portland, Oregon. Lowden was
then a young man of 24, and it is said that he
rode his relay of 60 miles from Tehama to Shasta
in two hours and 37 minutes. While another rider
took the bags and dashed on to Yreka, Lowden
continued west 40 miles farther to Weaverville.
In his ride from Tehama to Shasta it is reported
that he changed horses 19 times, touching the
ground only once.

During the early 1860's, what is known as the

Lewiston Turnpike Road, a variation of the
Shasta–Weaverville Road, was constructed from
near the Tower House in Shasta County to Lewiston in Trinity County. This, as well as the Grass
Valley Creek Road, was originally a private toll
road.

The Hyampon Trail

An important pioneer line of travel called the
Hyampon Trail passed through the settlement
of Hyampon (Hyampom). It started at Hydesville
in Humboldt County in the center of an agricultural region. A wagon road came from Humboldt
Bay as far as Hydesville. From Hydesville the
road became a trail which ran east through Car-
lotta and Yager. Beyond Yager the trail passed
by the Redwood House and Fort Baker and over
Coyote Flat. Crossing Mad River and climbing
Hohn Ridge, it reached Pilot Creek, where it
turned northeast over South Fork Mountain to
Hyampon. Here the trail branched, one branch
going to Big Bar and the other up the Hay Fork
to the Sacramento Valley.

The Hyampon Trail was always a pack trail.
The country was rough and the way often steep
and dangerous. Parts of it are still used by ranchers to bring in winter supplies. In 1922 a road
was completed between Hyampon Valley and
Hayfork.

The Oregon Road

Although a road had been built over Trinity
Mountain, Scott Mountain had still to be crossed
by mule pack. In 1859, however, this obstacle to
travel was overcome, when Scott Mountain Road

was built at an expense of $25,000 from Shasta and French Gulch in Shasta County over Trinity Mountain into Trinity County. From there it went through Trinity Center and Carrville, after which it climbed over Scott Mountain into Siskiyou County to Yreka. This road became the main artery for interstate commerce between California and Oregon, until the railroad up the Sacramento Canyon was built in the 1880's. In spite of the heavy snowfall, this road was kept open all winter. Oxen housed at the summit were driven back and forth over the road after a snowstorm in order to tramp down the loose snow. Because of difficulties, the stage to Jacksonville had been run only in the summertime up to the fall of 1859. That year the Oregon Company spent $10,000 in improving the road over the Siskiyous, and in 1860 a daily line of stages was established between Sacramento and Portland. When the railroad was built, this road did not pay as a toll road and was taken over by the county.

The First Discovery of Gold

In 1858 Major Pierson B. Reading described his discovery of gold at Reading's Bar in the summer of 1848: "In the month of July 1848, I crossed the mountains of the Coast Range at the head of Middle Cottonwood Creek, struck the Trinity at what is now called Reading's Bar; prospected for two days, and found the bars rich in gold; returned to my home on Cottonwood, and in ten days fitted out an expedition for mining purposes; and crossed the mountains where the travel passed about two years ago from Shasta to Weaver.

"My party consisted of three white men, one Delaware, one Chinook, and about sixty Indians from the Sacramento Valley. With this force I worked the bar bearing my name. I had with me one hundred and twenty head of cattle with an abundant supply of other provisions. After about six weeks work, parties came in from Oregon, who at once protested against my Indian labor. I then left the stream and returned to my home where I have since remained in the enjoyment of the tranquil life of a farmer."

The identity of the parties from Oregon who caused Reading to abandon his mining operations is not known. But Reading's Bar, on which the Major and his Indians worked, is located on Trinity River at the mouth of Reading's Creek immediately below the Douglas City bridge.

River and Creek Mining

The man reputed to be the first settler in Trinity County was a Frenchman named Gross. Crossing Trinity Mountain from Oregon in the spring of 1849 before the snow had melted, he found a quantity of gold at a place called Rich Gulch. From there he went to Evans' Bar on the Trinity River, where he is said to have built the first cabin in that part of the country.

"During 1850 a large number of gold seekers came into the country, some crossing the mountains to the east of the Trinity River from Shasta County, others coming up the Klamath and Trinity Rivers, after coming up the coast from San Francisco by vessel and making a difficult and dangerous landing at Trinidad Bay. By the end of 1851 all the gold bearing sections of the county had been explored and prospected, and in the spring of 1852 there were occupants of every bar along the Trinity River from Salyer to Carrville, and every tributary stream leading into the Trinity River within the county had been traversed and prospected. The mountains lying to the west of Trinity River had been crossed, and the agricultural lands in Hayfork and Hyampon valleys were at that period being located and improved."

The early mining was done on the river bars and along the creeks. On the Trinity River below Lowden's Ranch at the mouth of Grass Valley Creek were numerous river-bar camps; Ingrams, Union, Ferry, Douglas, Trinity, and Texas bars were all active before 1856. The placers at the mouth of Weaver Creek, which flows into Trinity River at Douglas City a few miles below Lowden's Ranch, were among the richest in the country. Down the river, southwest of Douglas City, was the Kanaka Bar. Farther down were Reading's Bar and Cape Horn Bar, where German and Danish miners erected neat houses. Opposite Cape Horn Bar was Turner's Bar, from which six Germans and Danes took $32,000 in one year. One-half mile below Turner's was Buckeye Bar, with a water dip-wheel 42 feet in diameter. Steiner's Flat, four miles below Douglas City, is one of the few places worked intermittently from 1850 to the present day.

Eight miles down-river from Steiner's Flat is the site of the Arkansas Dam across Trinity River, about four miles above Junction City. "Some sixty miners made the first attempt to construct this dam during the summer and fall of 1850. The dam was completed, and the water turned from the bed of the river into a canal, and some work in the bed of the river was proving the gravels of high value, when the first rain of the season came and washed away the dam by the rise in the waters of the river that resulted. The dam was again constructed in the following year, to be once more destroyed by the rise in the river at the first rainfall, and it was not until some three years later that a log dam placed across the river successfully withstood the waters passing through it in the late fall and winter months."

Near Junction City were Hocker's Ranch, Ferry Bar, and Red Hill. In 1851 Joseph McGillivray, a Scotsman of wonderful resource, persistence, and native ability, came to Cooper's Bar, five miles down the river from Junction City, and began to develop it into a home, ranch, orchard, and garden spot. He employed William Berber, a trained horticulturist from New York. All of the leading varieties of fruit trees, flowering shrubs, and other plants were introduced, and before long he was supplying the whole county. McGillivray's Ranch became famous as a beauty spot. Now it is a waste of heaped-up dredge tailings.

At Junction City was located the sawmill of Seeley and Dowles. In later years a grave was discovered on Slattery Creek near Junction City.

The fallen headboard had the following inscription: "Col. H. Seeley, September 2, 1852, aged 54 years." The grave was fenced and at one time had been well cared for.

Canon City, located above Junction City on Canon Creek, was one of the first mining camps, originally known as Jackass Bar. It became one of the largest gold-producing settlements in the county. The last trading post there closed its door in 1885.

At the mouth of the North Fork of Trinity River was formerly an important town and trading post called North Fork, now renamed Helena. Here Herbert Hoover worked for a time as a young mining engineer. Until 1926 this was the end of the road; from here the traveler had to ride a trail. In that year the state highway was opened all the way down the Trinity River.

Big Bar, eight miles below Helena, was an important mining center in the 1850's. Weaver and Company, who mined there in 1850, spent $10,000 diverting water from Little Weaver Creek and took out $100,000 in gold.

The canyon of the Trinity River between North Fork and Big Bar was once the scene of much mining activity in the bed of the river. Chinese miners were the last to "clean up" there. Manzanita Flat, worked for many years, had a twentieth-century revival with the use of the water of Manzanita Creek.

Cox's Bar was quite famous in the early days, but nothing remains to show for the extensive mining done there except moss-covered tailing piles and scarred banks. Mosses have been taken from the rock there and burned, the ashes yielding fine "flour" gold. At Big Flat, near Cox's Bar, was a large settlement—450 people in 1856.

The largest gold nugget ever found in Trinity County, valued at $1,800, was discovered on Digger Creek by Georg Van Matre. Minersville, near the mouth of Stewart's Fork, was a center of rich pocket mines. In 1880 the noted Brown Bear Quartz Mines were discovered on Deadwood Creek; they have produced more than a million dollars' worth of ore. Crow's Bar, of 80 acres, was mined by water brought from Rush Creek through a ditch eight miles long, built at a cost of $20,000.

Since the 1850's much gold has been taken from the banks and bed of the Trinity River and its tributaries, but none of them has been worked completely. During the depression of the 1930's, a large number of men worked along the bars with appliances such as were used by the early miners, the pan, the rocker, the sluice. Many earned enough to live on.

La Grange Mine

In Oregon Gulch, four miles northwest of Weaverville, is what was for years one of the most important hydraulic mines in California, the La Grange Mine (SRL 778), opened in 1851. It was being operated in 1890 by the Trinity Gold and Mining Company, which had bought up claims totaling 432 acres.

Water for washing the gravel in this tremendous deposit was first obtained through ditches from Weaver Creek. As this supply proved inadequate, a water right on the East Fork of Stewart's Fork 30 miles away was acquired. The mine had an ideal dumping ground. The tailings were run into a narrow valley owned by the company and from this valley drained directly into the Trinity River. Since this stream is not navigable and the surrounding country is not farmland, little damage resulted from this disposal of mine waste.

For many years the La Grange Mine was known as the largest operating hydraulic mine in the world, but it has been closed since World War I. A vast quantity of low-grade gravel is left, but the cost of reopening the works would be considerable because of the necessity of driving tunnels and cuts.

Bridge Gulch Massacre of 1852

When the first settlers came to Trinity County, depredations from Indians were a constant source of annoyance. A number of expeditions were organized to drive them out. In 1852 the killing of a man named Anderson aroused high feeling among the white settlers. Anderson had gone alone to the range to bring in some of his cattle, when he was attacked and killed by the Indians, who drove off the cattle. When Anderson failed to return to Weaverville and his riderless mule appeared at the corral, a searching party was formed, who found his arrow-pierced body. A portion of the party set out after the Indians, while the remainder went back to Weaverville to spread the alarm. Soon afterward 70 men were ready to start, and, joining the advance party whose position was relayed by messengers sent back to Weaverville, they again picked up the Indians' trail. After tracking them to their camp at Bridge Gulch in Hayfork Valley, the whites surrounded the camp and, in an attack from four sides, massacred 153 Indians. Only two little Indian girls, who were overlooked, survived. These children were brought back to town and reared by white families. One of them was Ellen Clifford —long a resident of Weaverville. At a later date Indian Bob of Douglas City claimed that he was a boy of nine at the time of the massacre and had hidden behind a log until the whites had left the scene. There is no one to verify or discredit his story.

The natural bridge where the massacre took place is located on Hayfork Creek, about nine miles above the town of Hayfork and a mile from the Leach Ranch–Wildwood road. Carved from limestone by the action of the water, it has a span of 150 feet and is 30 feet high. The highway to Hayfork makes this point easily accessible.

Weaverville

The old mining town of Weaverville, named in 1850 for John Weaver, a gold prospector who arrived in the vicinity in 1849, is located in what was one of the wildest and most inaccessible regions of California. Now it is easily reached by the state highway from Redding. It was the center of great mining activity in the days of '49, and in 1850 it became the county seat of Trinity County. Many old buildings, some with iron shutters and

Spiral Staircase,
Native Sons' Building, Weaverville

winding outside stairways leading to upper balconies, give charm and romance to the narrow streets of Weaverville today. It is probably one of the best preserved of all the old towns, and for many years was far from the beaten path.

Like many other towns of the county, it has suffered heavily from loss by fire. The first fire, in March 1853, destroyed 35 of the 41 buildings in the town, but immediately the inhabitants started reconstruction, this time replacing the wooden and canvas buildings wherever possible with brick ones. On the site of the present County Library was the first brick structure, formerly used as a blacksmith shop for many years. During the summer of 1853, the first courthouse and jail were built; and the Masonic Lodge, chartered in the summer of 1852, was for a time housed on the second floor of the courthouse building.

Early in the winter of 1853 fire once more swept the town, but again the citizens began rebuilding immediately. More brick buildings were constructed in 1855, some of red-burnt brick and some of adobe, and by 1858 there were 25 brick buildings on Main Street. Some of these were two-story structures, and nearly all were equipped with the iron doors and shutters which many believe were necessary for the protection of the gold stored within but which were in reality for protection against fire.

In 1963 there were 16 of the old brick buildings, erected between 1855 and 1859, still standing and in use in Weaverville. One of these is the courthouse, built in 1856 as a saloon, store, and office

building. It was purchased by Trinity County in 1865 and has been used continuously as a courthouse ever since. Three buildings, including the halls of the Native Sons of the Golden West and the International Order of Odd Fellows, have outside spiral staircases from the sidewalks to the overhanging balconies of the second floors. These iron staircases were handmade by the town blacksmith. When the buildings were erected, they had the distinction of having two owners, one for the lower floor and one for the upper. Since space was at a premium and all the buildings were wall to wall, the only solution was an outside front stairway. The old wooden sidewalks are deemed a fire hazard and are being replaced as rapidly as wear and tear make it necessary.

The Chinese population of Weaverville in those early days numbered at one time about 2,000, and Chinatown was a busy two blocks on both sides of the street—stores, laundries, gambling houses, and other places of business. After the toll taken by repeated fires and the changes wrought by time, there are now remaining only a few adobe houses, one tong house, and the famous Joss House. The present Joss House (*SRL 709*), situated back from the street on a knoll across the bridge over Weaver Creek, was built in 1874 to replace the one that burned. The carefully preserved building is now Weaverville Joss House State Historical Monument and is open to the public. It is still a place of worship. Burning incense and carved figures give a decided Oriental atmosphere to the place. The furnishings, for the most part, are those saved from the fires and are the very ones brought from China in 1854. In a small room there is a sort of frieze near the ceiling, on which are the names of hundreds of Chinese who once constituted a part of Weaverville's Chinatown.

The Chinese Tong War of 1854 occupies quite a place in the town's history. About 600 Chinese took part in the battle on a flat near Five Cent Gulch, about a mile east of town on the East Weaver Road that leads toward Trinity Alps. The site of the battle has since been mined, so that little of the 1854 contours remains. However, in the collections of the J. J. Jackson Memorial Museum, which is in the basement of the courthouse, there are sword, pike, and spear relics of this war between the tongs.

Among other possessions of the town is one of the early fire engines brought to California. This, one of three originally brought to San Francisco, came around the Horn in 1858. Weaverville acquired it about 1905, and it was in use there for a time.

Historic Townsites and Stopping Places

Aside from the historic landmarks preserved in the town of Weaverville, there are very few early structures in Trinity County that have come down to the present day. There are two brick buildings at Helena, constructed in 1859; the public schoolhouse, built near Junction City in the early 1860's, still stands, and a few old residences are intact.

In the 1850's and 1860's, settlements equipped

with homes, store, sawmill, blacksmith shop, and meat market flourished at Carrville, Trinity Center, Minersville, Lewiston, Douglas City, Indian Creek, Hayfork, Evans' Bar, Junction City, Canon City, North Fork, Logan Gulch, Big Bar, Cox Bar, Burnt Ranch, and Campbell Ranch. "Much of the travel in those days was over trails on foot, requiring frequent stopping places, and making them remunerative places of business." The Trinity House, long since vanished, was a famous inn on the north bank of Trinity River below the old Lowden Bridge. The present bridge is one mile above the site.

Carrville, formerly the ranch of Curry and Noyes, became one of the best-known pleasure resorts in northern California. James E. Carr was the founder of the family that owned the place. It is one mile below the mouth of Coffee Creek.

Fitch's Ferry, or Feeney's Crossing, is not now as important as it was in 1858. It is seven miles below the junction of the East Fork of Trinity River. A toll bridge was located there for many years, but it burned and was never rebuilt. The Bonanza King Quartz Mine, lying on the mountain east of Trinity River, is one of the valuable mines of the county. There has been much gold dredging along the river here and below.

Trinity Center was a lively and populous place in the early 1850's and for over a century was the center of one of the principal mining sections of Trinity County. The water ditches built in 1853 leading from Swift Creek were still in use a hundred years later. The old Chadbourne Ranch was a substantial one in 1858. The district was settled in 1851, and by 1853 it had become a famous mining center. Trinity Center and the old

camp of Minersville have been inundated by the Trinity Dam project, but a new town of Trinity Center has been built on the shore of the reservoir, named Lake Clair Engle, in honor of a United States Senator who died in 1964.

Two miles below the mouth of Coffee Creek was the Buckeye Ranch. It and nearby Meyer's Ranch are also now under water.

Lewiston is one of the oldest settlements and the site of the first ferry for pack horses between Shasta and Weaverville. The route was from the Tower House to the summit of Trinity Mountain, thence down Deadwood Creek to Lewiston, and along Trinity River until it turned north up Weaver Creek to Weaverville. Lewiston was always a trade center, on various roads. A toll bridge, located at this place, was owned by Olney Phillips for many years. Today Lewiston is the gateway to Trinity Dam, completed in 1962.

Rush Creek was formerly actively mined. At the mouth of the creek was Dutch John's Trading Post, later Jacob Paulsen's. This was a well-known spot.

Logan Gulch, midway down the canyon from Helena to Big Flat, was a leading trade center in the 1850's. Rich returns were obtained from the bed of the river.

Burnt Ranch, or McWhorter's, was one of the oldest settlements of Trinity County. It was occupied first in 1853. Destroyed by Indians, the charred remains of the house caused the place to be named Burnt Ranch. In this section of the county are Salyer, Fountain's, Hawkins' Bar, Daily's, and New River. It is one of the choice fruit-raising regions of the state. The New River area is very mountainous. During the early days

Old Town of Helena

an average of 400 to 500 miners worked there. Lake City was the main settlement, but it was destroyed by Indians in 1865 and never rebuilt. In the 1880's New River was the scene of a large quartz-mining boom. Heavy milling machinery was packed in by mules, and gold worth millions of dollars was taken out.

Hayfork is an important agricultural and mining area. There, in the pioneer period, Bayles's saw- and flour-mill supplied nearly all the flour used in Trinity County. Hyampon (Hyampom) is another agricultural section. The ranches there were taken up in the early 1850's.

Southern Trinity County was quite isolated until the turn of the century. State Highway 36 now goes through this country, and man-made Ruth Lake and other attractions are causing it to become a desirable recreation area.

SOURCES

Bartlett, James W. *Trinity County, California—Summary of Its History from May, 1845, to September, 1926.* News Publishing Co., Sacramento.
Boggs, Mae Helene Bacon. "Early Stage Days Recalled," in *Daily Siskiyou News*, Yreka, August 22, 1931.
Buck, Franklin A. *A Yankee Trader in the Gold Rush.* Compiled by Katherine A. White. Houghton Mifflin, Boston, 1930.
Carr, John. *Pioneer Days in California.* Times Publishing Co., Eureka, 1891.
Cox, Isaac. *The Annals of Trinity County.* Commercial Book and Job Steam Printing Establishment, San Francisco, 1858.
Dale, Harrison Clifford. *The Ashley-Smith Explorations and the Discovery of a Central Route to the Pacific, 1822–1829, with Original Journals.* The Arthur H. Clark Co., Cleveland, 1918.
Dornin, May. "The Emigrant Trails into California." Master's thesis in history, University of California, Berkeley, 1921.
Haley, Charles Scott. *Gold Placers of California.* California State Mining Bureau Bulletin, No. 92, State Printing Office, Sacramento, 1923.
McGowan, Joseph A. *History of the Sacramento Valley.* 3 vols. Lewis Historical Publishing Co., New York, 1961.
Miller, William P. "Trinity County," *Report of State Mineralogist.* State Office, Sacramento, 1890.
Reading, Pierson Barton. "Journal of Pierson Barton Reading," *Quarterly of the Society of California Pioneers.* VII, No. 3 (September 1930).
Sullivan, Maurice S. *The Travels of Jedediah Smith, a Documentary Outline, Including a Journal of the Great American Pathfinder.* The Fine Arts Press, Santa Ana, 1934.
Wilbur, Margaret Eyer, trans. "A Frenchman in the Gold Rush," translated from the *Journal of Ernest de Massey,* in *California Historical Society Quarterly,* V, Nos. 1–4 (1926); VI, No. 1 (1927).

Tulare County

TULARE COUNTY was created in 1852 from the southern part of Mariposa County and the northern part of Los Angeles County. (Tulare is Spanish for "a place of tules, or rushes.") The first county seat was at Wood's Cabin, afterward known as Woodsville, but in 1853 it was moved to Visalia, where it has remained.

Sequoia National Forest and Park

Sequoia National Forest and Sequoia National Park (in which is the General Sherman Tree, the largest of all the sequoias) comprise the most extensive as well as the most remarkable group of trees in the entire Sierra Big Tree belt, numbering 53 individual groves in all. Within this vast assemblage some of the most magnificent of the Sierra groves are to be found, a few of the most notable being Little Boulder Grove; the General Grant Grove section of Kings Canyon National Park, containing the General Grant or the Nation's Christmas Tree, one of the three largest of the Big Trees; the Muir Grove; Giant Forest, generally considered to be the largest and finest of all the Sierra Big Tree forests, where scores of separate groves merge, one into another; Redwood Canyon, another magnificent stand of over 3,000 trees; Redwood Meadow; Atwell; Garfield; Dillon Wood; and Mountain Home or Balch Park.

Giant Forest, in what is now Sequoia National Park, was discovered by Hale Tharp, a stockman, who in the summer of 1856 had located in the Three Rivers district at what became known as the Tharp Ranch, now inundated by Lake Kaweah, about two and one-half miles below the present town of Three Rivers. Friendly Indians told Tharp of the existence of a neighboring forest of "big trees," and in the summer of 1858, wanting to see for himself and needing summer pasture for his cattle, he made his first trip into the Giant Forest, accompanied by two Indians.

A huge hollow sequoia log still lying at Tharp's old camp in Log Meadow testifies to this first visit of the white man to the great forest. On this log Tharp carved his name and the year, 1858, on the day he arrived. The inscription has now been obliterated by vandals. In this log Tharp built a unique home, where he spent many summers. It was fitted with a door, a window, and a stone fireplace, and contained one large room 56.5 feet long. The tree itself is 24 feet in diameter at the base and is estimated to have been 311 feet high when it fell. It is now carefully preserved by the National Park Service and is reached by a paved path extending six-tenths of a mile from the Crescent Meadow parking area.

Tharp was the first white man not only to dis-

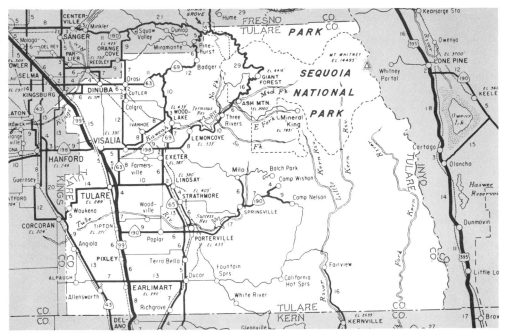

cover the Sequoia National Park region but also to live in the park, and his discovery led to further search and discovery of other important groves—Kings River, Tule River, and Deer Creek. By the summer of 1862 all of the groves in the state had been made known.

A movement for the protection of the groves of giant sequoias in the mountains of Tulare County for purposes of permanent drainage, lumber supply, recreation, and scenic beauty was begun in 1878. A long, hard fight followed with the private interests which were seeking to buy up the Big Trees for commercial purposes. The leader in this fight was Colonel George W. Stewart, who, as publisher and editor of the *Visalia Delta* in 1890, was also the chief promoter of the campaign for the creation of the Sequoia and General Grant National Parks. The latter is now part of Kings Canyon National Park.

Because of his unselfish and persistent work in pushing the cause of the giant trees, George Stewart has been justly acclaimed the "Father of the Sequoia National Park." A mountain in the Great Western Divide, rising almost 13,000 feet above sea level and about 5,000 feet above the Big Trees of the park, has been named in his honor, Mount George Stewart.

The John Muir Trail

For years a ridge trail from Yosemite to the headwaters of the Kern River had been the dream of many lovers of the High Sierra. In 1914, on the annual trip of the Sierra Club, Meyer Lissner suggested that the state legislature be requested to appropriate money to build such a trail. While plans were being made, John Muir, for many years leader and president of the club, passed away. "In seeking a fitting memorial to the man who had done so much to explore and

make known to the world the wonders and beauty of the High Sierra, it seemed but fitting that a trail to be constructed near the crest of his 'range of light' should bear his name."

The first appropriation of $10,000 was approved by Governor Hiram Johnson in 1915, and another $10,000 was made available in 1917. No further appropriations were secured until 1925, and work on the trail was then resumed.

"In its course the trail passes Thousand Island Lake and the Devil's Post Pile National Monument, rounds the flanks of the loftiest and most famous mountain peaks, from Mt. Ritter and Banner Peak on the north to the Evolution Group, Mt. Goddard, the Palisades and Mt. Tyndall on the south, zigzags up a succession of the highest and most impregnable divides, and affords approach to the Tehipite Valley, Kings River Canyon, and the Canyon of the Kern. It is the gateway to the best fishing, the most ambitious mountaineering, the sublimest and most diversified scenery that the High Sierra has to offer."

Tharp's Cabin in Giant Sequoia Log,
Sequoia National Park

Walter L. Huber described the trail thus: "The southern terminus of the trail is Mount Whitney, the highest point in the United States, exclusive of Alaska. Along the route are 148 peaks rising to elevations of more than thirteen thousand feet, including twelve of the fourteen summits in California which attain elevations of more than fourteen thousand feet. The crest of the Sierra is more than thirteen thousand feet in elevation for eight and a half miles continuously adjacent to Mt. Whitney. Even these cold statistics give an inkling of the grandeur of the region which this trail has made accessible, but not *too* accessible; for here is, I am glad to say, one of the most extensive areas in any of our Western states yet remaining practically free from automobile invasion."

Huber added that with the John Muir Trail should be mentioned the High Sierra Trail, constructed by the National Park Service in the Sequoia National Park from the Giant Forest to Mount Whitney. This trail opened some of the finest mountain scenery on the American continent and, with the John Muir Trail, made a complete loop through one of the most scenic areas of the High Sierra.

Another trail to Mount Whitney begins at Mineral King, an old mining center outside Sequoia National Park but reached by a road through the park.

Indian Mounds

As in other areas of California, the inroads of progress have virtually obliterated the sites of early Indian habitation in Tulare County.

The largest of a group of very remarkable mounds, once surrounded at flood time by the waters of Tulare Lake, was situated 15 miles due west of Tulare on what is known as the old Jacobs Ranch. This mound, about 150 yards long and six feet above the surrounding country, was composed of a solid mass of the common softshell clams of Tulare Lake, which were found in layers "as clean and as closely packed as if they had been washed and stacked by hand." Wagon loads of these thin, white shells were gradually hauled away for chicken feed.

Locally known as the Paige Mound, one of the largest rancherías ever reported in that section of the San Joaquin Valley was located along an old channel of Cameron Creek about two miles east of the settlement of Paige, southwest of Tulare. Many years ago an irrigation ditch was cut along the top of this mound, disclosing ancient burials and many Indian artifacts. Gradually over a period of years the mound was leveled.

Several miles from the eastern shore of Tulare Lake there was a long island or series of islands which remained unknown to American settlers for many years on account of the dense screen of tule swamps which stretched for miles along the lakeshore in both directions. These islands always escaped the winter floods. Said to have been discovered in 1853 by a cattleman, the land was acquired soon afterward by Judge J. J. Atwell, of Visalia, who used it as pasture for hogs. Atwell's Island, as it came to be known, formed at least

two islands during the highest water, the one to the west being called Skull Island because the remains of Indian houses and skeletons uncovered by wave action were found there by the first white settlers to visit it. The present town of Alpaugh is located on what was once Atwell's Island, and a little to the south and west of town many artifacts and remains of Indian villages have been found along old stream beds.

The Derby Expedition, which entered the San Joaquin Valley in April 1850, a few weeks after the Wood Massacre on the Kaweah River, reported that there were two large rancherías at Outside, Cameron, and Deep creeks; and that the 200 inhabitants of these villages had treated them with great hospitality. The Broder family, which settled on Cameron Creek in the early 1850's, also found several hundred Indians living in huts on what came to be known as Broder's Mound and along the ridge to the southwest. Various epidemics, however, soon reduced this number to not more than 20. The Broders built their first house in this region about 200 yards from the old mound, but later a more pretentious dwelling was erected on the mound itself. This house became a refuge for neighboring white settlers during the flood of 1862, when the mound was the only dry land for miles around. The Broder Mound property finally came into the hands of a Visalia bank in 1927, when, owing to a series of delays in leveling and building operations, local archaeologists working under the supervision of F. F. Latta succeeded in making one of the most extensive studies of ancient Indian culture in the San Joaquin Valley. Perhaps "the most remarkable example of Yokuts burial customs ever unearthed" was found at this site, yielding more than 800 specimens within an area of not over 45 × 60 feet. Three distinct cultures were uncovered, including that of what was probably the first migration into the valley, as well as that of the later Indians found at the site by the first white settlers.

The Sweet Mound, located on the west bank of Elk Bayou, four and a half miles south of Waukena, was the site of one of the most extensive permanent rancherías on the east shore of Tulare Lake. This mound was found by two boys on the property of Adolph Sweet on Thanksgiving Day, 1928, and was subsequently excavated by local archaeologists. Early American settlers testified that this site was occupied by Indians as late as 1860. The burials and house sites unearthed at the Sweet Mound appeared to be extremely ancient, showing no signs of contact with later Indian cultures or with the whites.

Many ancient rock writings made by the Indians of prehistoric times may be seen along the western slope of the eastern foothills throughout Tulare County. The most remarkable of these are located north and slightly east of Visalia at Woodlake, Dillon's Point, and Kaweah Caves.

The Old Spanish Trail Through Visalia

Gabriel Moraga, in 1806, went into the river country on the western side of the Great Valley to search for mission sites. On his return trip he ascended Kings River a short distance, crossing what is now Tulare County seven miles east of Visalia at Venice Hills, known as Kaweah Hills to local Indians and early pioneers.

Another party (possibly under the leadership of Juan Ortega) accompanied by Father Juan Cabot, chronicler of the expedition, went into the tulares in 1814, also in search of mission sites. In 1815, Juan Ortega and Father Cabot led an expedition from Mission San Miguel to hunt for runaway Indians. Proceeding up Kings River, the party crossed over to Kaweah River in Tulare County and from there went on to the area of Venice Hills.

These expeditions reported favorably on the region near the present town of Visalia. They considered it especially suitable for mission sites, and in the biennial report for the years 1815–16 Padre Presidente Mariano Payéras renewed his recommendation to found a mission and presidio in the valley, and the district about Visalia was urged as the most suitable location. Two sites were recommended, one at Telumne, probably within the city limits of the present Visalia, and the other at Venice Hills, where the river was forded. The proposal was repeated two years later.

One other Spanish expedition crossed the Visalia Trail when, in 1819, Lieutenant José María Estudillo went into the valley in an attempt to subdue uprisings among the Indians. Estudillo was emphatic in his report that a presidio would be necessary in connection with any mission established in that country, where the Indians were both numerous and unfriendly.

American Pathfinders

The first American to travel the Tulare Trail was Jedediah S. Smith, in 1826 and 1827. Skirting the Sierra foothills along the eastern side of the valley, he probably followed much the same route as that taken later by the Stockton–Los Angeles Stage Road, and now followed approximately by a modern highway through the towns of Porterville, Lindsay, Exeter, Woodlake, and others to the north. Smith was followed, in 1834, by Joseph Walker, who led the Bonneville hunters out of California over the Sierra by way of the pass that now bears his name, which forms an outlet from the South Fork of Kern River to the eastern side of the divide.

John C. Frémont, in 1844, followed the old Tulare Trail out of California. In the winter of 1845–46, a second expedition under Frémont reached Walker's Lake in Nevada. There the company divided, Frémont himself crossing the mountains with a few men to Sutter's Fort, while the main body, under the leadership of Joseph Walker, went through Walker Pass and down the Kern River, where they camped for three weeks early in 1846. Frémont, who had hurried south to meet his men, and who had understood the Kings River to be the appointed meeting place, waited for several weeks before returning to Sutter's Fort. During this time he ascended the Kings River along the right bank to its junction with the North Fork, up which he climbed to an altitude of 10,000 feet. Walker with the main body, after waiting in vain at the Kern River camp for Frémont's arrival, pushed on northward through Tulare County, finally rejoining Frémont near Mission San José.

On these expeditions, Smith, Walker, and Frémont traveled the Tulare Trail. Others soon followed in their footsteps—explorers, hunters, settlers, and gold seekers. A tablet placed beside the road just west of Lindsay in 1928 by the Alta Mira Chapter, D.A.R., commemorates the opening of the valley route by these resolute pioneers.

Woodsville

Under the leadership of John Wood, a party that was said to have come from the Mariposa mines settled on the southern bank of the Kaweah River either in December 1849 or early in 1850. A substantial log cabin was erected a short distance south of the Kaweah River delta, seven miles east of the site of the present town of Visalia.

Wood and his party had been established only a few months when a group of Kaweah Indians arrived and, because of earlier mistreatment at the hands of the Wood party, demanded that they leave the region within ten days. The white men were slow in making preparations to leave, delaying beyond the allotted time; all but three of them were massacred.

Another settlement had been made at the same time, about half a mile distant, by Loomis St. Johns, for whom the St. Johns River was named. Although it was near the Wood cabin, the Indians left the St. Johns settlement unmolested. Also about the same time two brothers, A. A. and C. R. Wingfield, claimed squatter's rights on land along the Kaweah River from the Wood cabin south.

When Tulare County was created in April 1852, the legislature provided that the seat of justice be placed at the cabin on the south side of Kaweah Creek, near the bridge built by Dr. Thomas Payne, and that it be called Woodsville (Woodville).

The first election board, a party under the command of Major James D. Savage, opened its polls on July 10 under the tree that stood farthest out in the open, now known as the "Election Tree" or "Charter Oak." The old "Election Tree" (*SRL 410*) stands today on a quiet country road near the quarry seven miles east of Visalia, and is the property of Tulare County. The county seat remained under the "Election Tree" for some time, although the Wood cabin, half a mile to the south, had been designated as the legal location. In 1854, after the county seat had been transferred to Visalia, Abraham Hilliard and his family moved into the Wood cabin.

Visalia

In 1852 a group of settlers led by Nathaniel Vise located a few miles to the southwest of the Wood cabin, at a place then known as Buena Vista. They erected in November a log fort on the north bank of Mill Creek for protection against the Indians. Gradually a town grew up around it and was given the name Visalia, probably by Vise himself, who was related to the Nathaniel Vise for whom Visalia, Kentucky, was named. Fort Visalia stood in the area now bounded by Garden, Bridge, Race, and Oak streets.

The county seat was moved from Woodsville to the new and growing settlement in 1853. The first house outside the fort stockade was built the same year by Samuel C. Brown. This log residence, later enlarged and remodeled, was long a Visalia landmark at the southwest corner of Court and Oak streets. The town's first store was erected in 1854 across Mill Creek from Fort Visalia by Nathan Baker. It stood at the southeast corner of Garden and Main streets until 1905, when it was destroyed by fire. Although it was not incorporated until February 27, 1874, Visalia was for many years the most important town between Stockton and Los Angeles.

About five miles south of Visalia on Mooney Boulevard (State Highway 63) is Mooney Grove County Park, 100 acres of virgin oak timber purchased from the Hugh Mooney heirs in August 1909 and preserved as a remnant of the valley oaks that formerly covered much of the Kaweah River delta. In the park is the Tulare County Museum with its "Pioneer Village," a collection of old and historically important buildings from various parts of the county that have been moved and reconstructed there for posterity. In this way preservation has been assured for these links with the past that would otherwise inevitably have been destroyed in the name of progress. Among them are an 1854 log cabin, the Cramer residence and post office (built perhaps as early as 1863) from the vanished settlement of the same name in the North Tule River valley, and the Surprise School (1908). One of the most interesting relics is the ornate Gothic façade saved from the Masonic and Odd Fellows Hall in Visalia. This structure, built in 1873 at the northeast corner of Center and Church streets, was torn down in 1963.

Stone Corral

Possibly the oldest existing structure in Tulare County built by white men is the 50-foot-square stone corral on the southeast corner of Stokes Mountain, east of Cutler and northeast of Seville. It was constructed of large rocks in 1853 by James Smith as a hog pen. Near here, on the night of June 11, 1893, occurred the fight between a sheriff's posse and the notorious outlaws Sontag and Evans. Sontag was killed, and his companion was wounded and captured the next day.

Tule River Indian Reservation

In 1857, after the war between the Tule River Indians and the white men had ended, a reservation was established near the present city of Porterville. To it were brought Indians from several tribal groups of a widespread area. The reservation was placed near the rancherías of the Koyeti and Yaudanchi (Yaulanchi) tribes. Both were branches of the Yokuts Indians who occupied the San Joaquin Valley. The first Tule River

Indian Reservation (SRL 388) was located on both sides of the Old Springville Highway, where, for about a quarter of a mile, it runs south to join the later highway at the Alta Vista School— about two miles east of Porterville. The location did not prove satisfactory, and in 1873 the reservation was moved ten miles southeast to its present location.

The Stockton–Los Angeles Stage Road

The old Stockton–Los Angeles Stage Road crossed the Kaweah River delta at a place long known as Four Creeks, that portion of the delta lying south of the Venice Hills. Stages and freight teams used this road, which went from Los Angeles north to Fort Miller and the mines.

The route was divided into the Upper and Lower Detours, as they were called. These detours paralleled each other as they passed along the base of the hills a few miles apart, and the southern junction of the two was near the base of the Venice Hills and a little to the southwest, near where the Southern Pacific Railroad now crosses the St. Johns River. The Lower Detour came in from the west, while the Upper Detour passed to the east of Twin Buttes and skirted the western side of the Venice Hills. Uniting at the junction on the St. Johns, the road then passed the "Election Tree" at Woodsville and followed the base of the Venice Hills about a quarter of a mile before crossing the St. Johns River. For a half-mile it continued south and then turned to the southwest for a quarter of a mile, crossing the Kaweah River a half-mile south of the "Election Tree."

Butterfield Stage Stations

During dry weather the northbound Butterfield Overland Stages, during the years 1858–61, turned off from the old Stockton–Los Angeles route east of Visalia (where one of the main stage stations was located at what is now the southeast corner of Main and Court streets) and crossed the country to the Kings River Station (Whitmore's Ferry). When the river was too high to be crossed at Whitmore's, a route along the base of the hills was followed to Smith's Ferry near present Reedley in Fresno County.

Proceeding southeast from Visalia, one passed the following stations: the "Pike" Lawless Ranch, one mile south of the present Outside Creek Bridge; the Tule River Station, later Porterville; and Fountain Springs.

At the Tule River Station (SRL 473), Peter Goodhue erected the first building, a shake house with a fireplace at each end and a porch on the south side. The site of this old overland station is at the foot of Scenic Hill at the north city limits of Porterville.

In 1859 a young man named Porter Putnam arrived at the Lawless Ranch, where he obtained a job caring for the stage horses. Soon afterward he went to the Tule River Station. Putnam was an enterprising young man, with an affable, hospitable nature. He bought out Goodhue and developed the station into a popular stopping place and hotel, and the place came to be known as Porter's Station. The town which grew up around it was called Portersville, later Porterville. After the coming of the railroad in the late 1880's, Porterville increased in prosperity until today it is a city of over 8,000 inhabitants. It is located in the heart of the "thermal belt," where high-grade oranges are produced.

A monument stands at the small crossroads community of Fountain Springs to commemorate the early stage station *(SRL 648)* that stood one and one-half miles to the northwest at the junction of the Stockton–Los Angeles Road and the road to the Kern River gold mines. The actual site is on private range land half a mile from the road.

Another marker has been placed just west of Lindsay on a portion of the old Butterfield stage route *(SRL 471)*. At this point Highway 65 follows the course of the venerable road. The marker is adjacent to the one placed in 1928 on the Frémont Trail.

Tailholt, a Ghost of the White River

The present hamlet of White River, for many years and in some localities still known as Tailholt *(SRL 413)*, was at one time a mining camp almost as well known as Angel's, Columbia, or Sonora. Not more than a dozen people make it their home today.

It was first established about 1856, during the Kern River gold rush. Placer gold was discovered on a small tributary stream in Coarse Gold Gulch about two miles east of the present town, and the original settlement called Dogtown grew up. When the first road into Linns Valley was built, old Dogtown was left one and one-half miles to the east. A new settlement, for a short time also known as Dogtown, was established at the present site. An interesting happening gave it the curious name of Tailholt. The story, as told by F. F. Latta, is as follows:

" 'Yank' Booth, the old stage driver, while en route to Visalia, stopped at Tailholt to change horses. He had with him a society lady who was returning from the Kern River Mines after having visited her husband, a mine operator at that place. This lady seriously offended the dignity of Yank by effectively 'high hatting' him. She further aroused the ire of Yank by carrying with her in the stage a pet poodle.

"As the horses were being changed at Dogtown, a large cat crossed the street ahead of them, leaving the restaurant of Mother Cummings and proceeding to the hotel of Levi Mitchell. The dog spied the cat and attempted to jump from a small window at the side of the stagecoach. The lady made one wild grab at the dog and succeeded in catching it by the tail as it was leaving the stage. Yelping at the top of its voice, the dog hung suspended from the window, and the lady screamed for help. Yank took in the situation at a glance and went ahead changing horses. Mother Cummings came to the rescue. While lifting the dog through the window she remarked, 'Well, ma'am, a tail-holt is better than no holt

at all.' When Yank reached Visalia he told the postmaster and keeper of the stage station that the name of the new place on White River was Tailholt."

Two old cemeteries at Tailholt are especially interesting. One, situated on the crest of a hill to the north of the river, was reserved for respectable people, while to the other, located on "Boot Hill," south of the river, were relegated the renegades—desperate characters who died with their boots on. Five persons were buried on Boot Hill, four of them having been participants in gun battles in old Tailholt. Three of these outlaws were named Dan, while the fourth, Jack Gordon, was a member of the notorious Mason-Henry gang, wiped out at the close of the Civil War.

Traver, a Ghost City

"White irregular patches of alkali ... reaching ... far out among the dingy salt grass" cover the once productive and thickly settled tracts of land on which were located Traver, Vina, Scaironi, and Kitchener. Traver, once the center of the region, had a population of about 1,000 in 1887. Modest homes, each with its cultivated plot of ground, adjoined the flourishing city with its warehouses, lumber yards, agricultural implement factories and mills, stores, hotels, churches, a post office, express office, and railroad depot, as well as saloons, gambling dens, and the inevitable Chinatown, which occupied two city blocks. Traver in its heyday was a typical example of the "wild and woolly" Western town. Of this once flourishing farm community, a bit still remains, while scattered over the bleak fields are occasional broken windmills and dilapidated barns, all that remains of a hundred or more farmsteads.

The story of Traver's brief period of prosperity, followed by a rapid decline, has often been repeated in mining towns, but Traver is one of the few such examples in California's agricultural history. In 1882 P. Y. Baker, a civil engineer, conceived the idea of a large irrigation project which would furnish water to some 130,000 acres of land on the south side of and adjoining Kings River in both Tulare and Fresno counties. His plan met with favor when presented to a few investors, and options on about 30,000

Remains of the Town of Traver

acres of this land were secured on June 7 of the same year.

A portion of the tract was covered by the "76 Ranch," located on the Kings River bottom lands in Fresno County and owned by Senator Thomas Fowler, who turned his estate over to the newly formed company, becoming one of the original stockholders. The name of this ranch was given to the new corporation, "The 76 Land and Water Company."

Eventually, an immense irrigation canal was built through this territory. A portion of the tract, comprising 2,000 acres, lay along the Southern Pacific Railroad near the northwest corner of Tulare County a short distance southeast of where the railroad crossed Kings River. Part of this was set aside for a townsite and the remainder subdivided and sold as colony lots.

The new town reached phenomenal prosperity in a very short time and continued to enjoy this state until October 30, 1887, when the first of five destructive fires all but wiped it out. By this time, too, the alkali in the soil had begun to affect the crops noticeably. In spite of all efforts to counteract this blight, before long practically every tree, shrub, and plant on many of the colony lots had been killed. Utter desolation gradually ensued. This decline was further hastened after 1888 by the development of the new towns of Dinuba and Reedley in the heart of the fertile "76 country" and on the branch railroad line to Porterville.

But the blasted hopes that formed the common experience of the members of this colony formed a lasting bond among them. For many years, annually on or near April 8, a gay crowd assembled at the old townsite to celebrate the founding of Traver and to continue the custom of earlier days when thousands of visitors from all parts of the San Joaquin Valley gathered there to participate in the festivities.

The Kaweah Cooperative Commonwealth

Tulare County was the home, from 1886 to 1892, of a socialist utopian colony, the Kaweah Cooperative Commonwealth. Under the leadership of Burnette G. Haskell and James J. Martin, several dozen people established themselves on the banks of the Kaweah River "for the purpose of demonstrating the advantages of cooperation in social and industrial life." The population of the colony at its peak reached about 300, but for long periods it averaged only 50 to 75. One of the objectives of the colonists was to support themselves by cutting timber in what is now Sequoia National Park, and they did succeed in building a sawmill and an 18-mile lumber road. It is debatable whether they would ever have cut the magnificent sequoias in Giant Forest, for they recognized their value to scientists and tourists. What is known today as the General Sherman Tree was called by the colonists "the Karl Marx."

The dissolution of the colony was due to internal troubles as well as to external pressure—from the large timber interests, the press, and the federal government, which established Sequoia National Park on September 25, 1890, and a few days later declared the adjacent lands a national forest. The colonists were never able to secure title to their land and soon disbanded, but many of them remained as residents of Tulare County. The road from Kaweah to Old Colony Mill, painstakingly built by hand in 1886–90, was completed to Giant Forest by the government in 1903. It was the only road into the forest until the Generals Highway was opened in 1931. Today, the old road is maintained as a fire road. Another tangible reminder of the hopes of the colonists is the Kaweah post office (SRL 389), about three miles north of Three Rivers.

SOURCES

Farquhar, Francis P. "Spanish Discovery of the Sierra Nevada," Sierra Club Bulletin, XIII, No. 1 (February 1928), 54–61.
——— "The Topographical Reports of Lieutenant George H. Derby," with Introduction and Notes by Francis P. Farquhar, California Historical Society Quarterly, XI, Nos. 2–4 (June–December 1932).
Fry, Walter, and John R. White. Big Trees. Stanford University Press, Stanford, 1930.
Gifford, E. W., and W. Egbert Schenck. "Archaeology of the Southern San Joaquin Valley, California," University of California Publications in American Archaeology and Ethnology, XXIII, No. 1 (1926), 1–122.
Hine, Robert V. California's Utopian Colonies. Huntington Library, San Marino, 1953.
Huber, Walter L. "The John Muir Trail," Sierra Club Bulletin, XV, No. 1 (February 1930), 37–46.
Latta, F. F. "San Joaquin Primeval—Archaeology," Tulare Daily Times, 1931, 1932.
——— "San Joaquin Primeval—Uncle Jeff's Story," Tulare Daily Times, 1929.
Los Tulares. Quarterly bulletin of the Tulare County Historical Society, Visalia.
McCubbin, J. C. Papers on the History of the San Joaquin Valley, California. Collected and edited by Raymund F. Wood, 1960. Fresno State College Library.
Mitchell, Annie R. Jim Savage and the Tulareño Indians. Westernlore Press, Los Angeles, 1957.
——— Land of the Tules. Visalia, 1949.
Rider, Fremont, ed. Rider's California, A Guide-Book for Travellers. Macmillan, New York, 1925.
Robinson, W. W. The Story of Tulare County and Visalia. Title Insurance and Trust Co., Los Angeles, 1955.
Small, Kathleen. History of Tulare County. S. J. Clarke Publishing Co., Chicago, 1926.
Smith, Wallace. Garden of the Sun. Lymanhouse, Los Angeles, 1939.
Stewart, George W. Big Trees of the Giant Forest. A. M. Robertson, San Francisco, 1930.
——— "The Yokut Indians of the Kaweah Region," Sierra Club Bulletin, XII, No. 4 (1927), 385–400.
Thompson, Thomas H. Historical Atlas Map of Tulare County. Privately published, Tulare, 1872.

Tuolumne County

TUOLUMNE COUNTY was one of the original 27 counties, and Sonora has been the county seat from the beginning.

Prehistoric Landmarks

Table Mountain, mentioned again and again by Bret Harte in his tales, is a conspicuous feature of the Tuolumne County landscape. For many miles its "rocky entablature and splintered capitals" dominate river gorge or spreading valley. A particularly fine view of its long, level top is obtained while crossing Rawhide Flat on the road from Tuttletown to Jamestown. The topography in the Miocene period consisted of an andesite lava flow that filled the hollows. Table Mountain is a part of this huge mass of lava, a quarter of a mile wide on the average and 40 miles long, that filled one of the ancient stream beds. Ages of erosion have cut away the banks that hemmed in this ancient river, leaving the hard andesite mountain standing out in bold relief. Deep beneath this once molten mass have been found bones of extinct animals, traces of an early flora, and implements of stone. Water-worn pebbles, gravel, and smoothly polished gold nuggets have been taken from the ancient river channel by miners, who tunneled great distances into the heart of the mountain until it was honeycombed with subterranean passageways. And, even yet, Table Mountain, once the maker of vast fortunes, holds millions of dollars in gold within its seemingly inexhaustible treasure house.

Southeast of Dardanelle, a resort on the Sonora–Mono Highway, is the largest and oldest known specimen of the western juniper, called the Bennett Juniper for Clarence Bennett, who discovered it in 1932. Several thousand years old, it is over 40 feet in circumference and about 85 feet tall. The ancient tree is reached by a seven-mile trail from Dardanelle or a 12-mile dirt road via Niagara Creek and Eagle Meadow.

There are two groups of *Sequoia gigantea* in Tuolumne County, the South Grove of the Calaveras Big Trees and the Tuolumne Grove. The South Grove, seven miles southeast of the North Grove of the Calaveras Big Trees in Calaveras County (both of which are in the Calaveras Big Trees State Park) is reached only by trail. It is a magnificent stand of 974 giant trees, all over 12 feet in diameter. Among them is the Louis Agassiz, one of the largest of all the Big Trees. The Tuolumne Grove on the western boundary of Yosemite National Park on the Big Oak Flat Road contains only a small number of trees.

In Pate Valley, a wooded flat in the Grand Canyon of the Tuolumne River below Muir Gorge, there are hundreds of Indian picture-writings, the first of them discovered by Harnden and McKibbie while exploring the river in 1907. These pictographs, colored with red ocher, are painted on the face of a high cliff on Piute Creek a little way from its junction with the Tuolumne River. Near the middle of the precipice there is a small cave, partly natural and partly hollowed out by human hands, in which other pictographs may be seen.

The Gabriel Moraga Expedition

Gabriel Moraga in 1806 named both the Tuolumne and Stanislaus rivers. Chapman says that "the Indian village of Tualamne, visited by them, is perhaps the origin of the modern name in Tuolumne River and County, although it was located on the Stanislaus." A diary kept by Padre

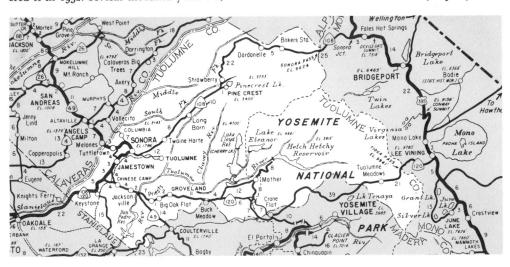

Pedro Muñoz contains these lines, which indicate the origin of the name:

"On the morning of this day the expedition went toward the east, along the banks of the river, and having traveled about six leagues, we came upon a village called Tautamne. This village is situated on some steep precipices, inaccessible on account of their rough rocks. The Indians live in their *sótanos* (cellars or caves)."

Tuolumne, according to Bancroft, is a corruption of the Indian word *talmalamne,* meaning "a group of stone huts or caves." Although Kroeber thinks this interpretation is unlikely, since the California Indians did not build stone houses and lived in caves only in mountain regions, the extract from the diary of Padre Muñoz is worthy of consideration. Kroeber also says that "the word Tawalimni, which perhaps was really Tawalamni or Tawalumni, would easily give rise, in either English or Spanish, to Tuolumne," and that it was the name of a tribe of Indians, "possibly Miwok, but more probably Yokuts," living in the vicinity of the lower Tuolumne and Stanislaus rivers as far up as Knight's Ferry. The river, meadows, canyon, and county now bear the name.

Sonora Pass

In the early days of California's development, the Sierra Nevada stood as an almost insurmountable barrier between the western American plains and the Pacific slope. The jagged crest on the eastern edge of Tuolumne County, which is also the eastern boundary line of parts of both Stanislaus National Forest and Yosemite National Park, was one of the most impassable stretches in the entire range. The great difficulty was not in the ascent of the eastern side, nor yet in passing the summit, but was rather in the western descent, which, though spoken of figuratively as a slope, is in reality a series of granite domes, lakes, and canyons with almost perpendicular walls.

Sonora Pass, in the northeastern corner of Tuolumne County near its conjunction with Alpine and Mono counties, rises to an elevation of 9,624 feet. Wagons hauling supplies to the mines east of the Sierra have used this pass since 1864. It was also the route of the early passenger stage on its weekly journey from Sonora to Bodie. The Sonora–Mono Highway of today, as it winds through scenic Stanislaus Forest, over the crest, and on down to Bridgeport, 110 miles from Sonora, follows the old road approximately. Portions of the former roadbed can be seen clearly from the present highway at several points. Historical signs have been placed near the summit and along the route to call attention to points of interest. Fourteen miles northeast of Sonora a monument has been erected commemorating the Sonora–Mono Road *(SRL 422).*

In 1841 the Bidwell-Bartleson party, the first overland group of American settlers to enter California by crossing the Sierra Nevada, used a pass located ten miles south of the present Sonora Pass. By the time the party had begun the western descent, the last ox had been consumed and the travelers had begun to eat crow and wildcat. In the attempt to add to their provisions, young

Bidwell left the party to hunt, planning to cut across country and rejoin them later. When night overtook him he found himself in a grove of large trees. In the darkness he had particular difficulty in getting around a fallen tree, the butt of which seemed to extend some 20 or more feet into the air. In after years he visited the North Grove of the Calaveras Big Trees and found what he believed was the same spot. However, since the route of the party followed down the south side of the Stanislaus, rather than the north side, it is quite likely that Bidwell discovered the South Grove rather than the North Grove.

The emigrant trails to the west of Sonora Pass were not easy to follow, and various parties became entangled in the vast labyrinth of canyons, mountains, and rivers through which it was necessary to travel. In the early 1850's a party of goldseekers were caught in a heavy snowstorm on the eastern slope of the mountains. As a result, they were forced to abandon their wagons, but finally succeeded in crossing the pass and finding a comparatively sheltered spot on the western side. From this place a few members of the party proceeded as far as the Jarboe ranch, about where the town of Tuolumne now is, and from there assistance was sent back to the men in camp. It is from this episode that Relief Valley gets its name.

Among the first wagon trains to cross Sonora Pass were the Duckwall party and the Washington Trahern party, named after a Cherokee Indian who was leader of the outfit. The former, consisting of W. J. Duckwall, his wife, six children, and three other men, found themselves marooned on one of the granite domes southwest of Sonora Pass, but managed to extricate themselves by hitching one pair of oxen to the front of a wagon and three pair to the rear and letting the vehicles down the precipitous granite wall. The Duckwalls arrived at Upper Relief Valley on September 27, 1853. The Washington Trahern party, who had lost most of their wagons in crossing the summit, reached the valley a day later. No road has ever been built over this stretch of the old emigrant trail, and the country has remained primitive and isolated.

From Strawberry or Pinecrest to Burst Rock (also known as Birth Rock because in the natural chamber formed by the great boulder a baby girl was born to an emigrant mother) a trail follows the old emigrant road marked by trees on which blazes made by the pioneers are still visible. Near Emigrant Lake there is a blazed tree upon which has been carved the epitaph of a traveler who perished at that spot in October 1853. For many years parts of ox wagons abandoned by the snowbound emigrants were to be found at Upper Relief Valley.

Virginia Pass and Conness Pass

Long before the white man came, the passes of the High Sierra were used by the Indians to reach the deer and acorns that abounded on the western side and the pine nuts on the eastern slopes or to get the choice larvae that are found at Mono Lake at certain seasons.

Two of the lesser known passes that cross the

eastern border of Tuolumne County and are reached only by trail are the Virginia and the Conness, both of which lead from Yosemite National Park into the Hoover Primitive Area on the western side of Mono National Forest. The United States Forest Service has set aside here certain typical forest and mountain sections to be preserved in their primitive state and to be known as Primitive Areas. The Hoover Primitive Area contains 30 square miles at the headwaters of Green and Lee Vining creeks, and within it are Tioga, Conness, Excelsior, and Dunderberg peaks, as well as several glacial lakes. Two of these lakes, lying close together not far from the summit, are the Hoover Lakes, so named in honor of Theodore J. Hoover, mining engineer, who explored and mapped this region in the summers of 1904 and 1905 while in charge of the Standard Consolidated Mines at Bodie. Conness Peak was named in 1863 for John Conness, later United States Senator, in appreciation of his efforts in promoting the bill that organized the California Geological Survey. Dominating the landscape, it lifts its majestic summit 12,565 feet above the sea.

Tioga Pass

Of the several Sierra passes on the eastern border of Tuolumne County, the Tioga Pass is one of the most used at the present time. Over this pass the Tioga Road crosses the summit at an elevation of 9,941 feet. The pass is dominated on the southeast by Mount Dana, 13,050 feet elevation, named in 1863 by the Whitney Survey in honor of James Dwight Dana, professor of geology at Yale University from 1850 to 1894.

Mining carried on in the Tioga district by the Great Sierra Consolidated Silver Mining Company, incorporated in 1881, necessitated a road from Sonora to the summit. The Tioga Road, or the "Great Sierra Wagon Road," which was completed in 1883 at a cost of $61,000, was built in part over the Mono Trail, but from the point where the latter turned south toward Mono Pass, the Tioga Road was continued eastward to Tioga Pass. When the mines in this rugged eastern part of Yosemite National Park were closed in July 1884, the road also was abandoned. A few of the buildings at the mines are to be found in a fair state of preservation even today.

The Tioga Road was donated to the United States Department of the Interior in 1915 and is now one of the most scenic in California. Passing south of the Hetch Hetchy Valley through the Yosemite National Park via Tuolumne Meadows and Lake Tenaya, it bisects the park from east to west. At the first ranger station west of the pass is a bronze plaque, which bears the following legend: "This tablet commemorates the successful labors of Stephen T. Mather, Director of the National Park Service, in securing for the people the Tioga Pass Road. Dedicated to the enduring memory of a faithful public servant by the members of the Brooklyn Daily Eagle National Park Development Tour, July 20, 1924." The last stretch of the original Tioga Road in use, extending 21 miles west of Lake Tenaya, was reconstructed in 1956–60.

The Grand Canyon of the Tuolumne

One of America's most spectacular scenic canyons is the Grand Canyon of the Tuolumne, lying wholly within Tuolumne County 15 miles due north of Yosemite Valley. Within a distance of 20 miles the Tuolumne River descends this majestic gorge from the level of Tuolumne Meadows to Hetch Hetchy Valley, a drop of almost 5,000 feet, the greater part of which occurs within the two miles immediately west of the California Falls. John Muir, in one of his matchless word-pictures, describes the marvelous beauty of the canyon's superb, cascading river: "It is the cascades of sloping falls of the main river that are the crowning glory of the Canyon.... For miles the river is one wild, exulting, onrushing mass of snowy purple bloom, spreading over glacial waves of granite without any definite channel, gliding in magnificent silver plumes, dashing and foaming through huge bowlder-dams, leaping high in the air in wheel-like whirls ... doubling, glinting, singing in exuberance of mountain energy."

Tuolumne Meadows, one of the most beautiful of the numerous alpine meadows found in the Sierra, lies at the junction of the Dana and Lyell forks of the Tuolumne River about 15 miles northeast of Yosemite Valley. It is surrounded on all sides by the highest peaks of the Sierra Nevada, and many intriguing trails wind up from it into the very heart of the range. Conness, Dana, Mammoth, and Lyell peaks stand guard at the north and east. Cathedral Range, with its unique and picturesque Cathedral Peak, protects the southern boundary of the meadow. Out of the floor of the valley itself rises Lembert Dome; while at the lower end, at the entrance to the Tuolumne Grand Canyon, towers beautiful Fairview Dome.

Hetch Hetchy (originally spelled Hatchatchie), a deep valley at the lower end of Tuolumne Canyon, was discovered by Joseph Screech, in 1850, while hunting game. The valley was then occupied by Indians. John Muir is authority for the

WESTERN TUOLUMNE COUNTY

statement that the name is a Miwok Indian word for a certain grass with edible seed that grew in the vicinity. The valley was visited in 1863 by Professor J. D. Whitney and in 1871 by John Muir, who called it the "Tuolumne Yosemite." Muir explored the valley later, in 1875, with Galen Clark. The city of San Francisco, through Congressional Act in 1913, acquired rights in the Tuolumne River for a project to supply water for city use. The dam was completed and the reservoir was filled in 1923. The height of the dam was increased in 1938.

River Camps

Activity on the bars of the Tuolumne and Stanislaus rivers began early in 1849. Hawkins' Bar, below Jacksonville, was the site of the first river diggings on the Tuolumne. From a population of 15 in April 1849, it increased to one of 700 by September. Extensive plans for damming and diverting the river were made but had to be abandoned because of an unexpected rise in the flow of the water. By 1852 Hawkins' Bar was practically deserted.

The history of Swett's Bar, where mining was begun in November 1849, is typical. A company of 70 men cut a race to divert the stream, but here, too, the sudden rise of water caused the project to be abandoned—temporarily. In August 1850 the work was resumed, and after 59 days of hard labor the dam was completed—only to be washed away that very evening. The process was repeated a third time, with the same result. The season being then too far advanced to resume the undertaking, the work was laid aside for the year. In August 1851 the camp, although reduced to 27 men, completed a dam after a few weeks' effort, and for some time thereafter an ounce of gold per man was taken out each day.

During 1850 the river camps along the Tuolumne were among the largest in the county, thousands of miners being engaged in attempts to divert the river in order to mine its bed. Few of the camps, however, enjoyed any great prosperity, and all of them, Hawkins', Swett's, Stevens', Payne's, Hart's, Morgan's, Roger's, Signorita, York, and Texas bars, have completely disappeared. Not a vestige of former days remains to show where the cabins of miners once stood. Not even the bars themselves remain as they were, for the river has changed its course several times since the 1850's.

Along that part of the old channel now covered by the Don Pedro Reservoir lay the bars of Don Pedro, Indian, and Red Mountain. From one claim at Don Pedro's Bar, gold valued at $100,000 was taken out before 1889, the cost of operation being only $5,000. At the time of Lincoln's election in 1860, as many as 1,500 votes were cast at Don Pedro's Bar. Indian Bar, the scene of active mining in the 1850's, continued to exist until the building of the Don Pedro Dam.

Moccasin, once a thriving camp at the mouth of Moccasin Creek, is now the site of the Moccasin Creek Power House, a unit in the Hetch Hetchy water system.

Woods' Crossing

The first discovery of gold in Tuolumne County was made in August 1848 at Woods' Crossing on Woods' Creek by a party of men led by James Woods. James Savage, J. H. Rider, and Charles Bassett were members of the party. The richness of the field proved remarkable, and for a time gold in the amount of $200 to $300 a day per man was taken out with pick and knife alone. Surface mining remained very good for a number of years, and a thriving camp grew up on the spot. It is said that more gold was taken from this creek than from any other stream of its size in California. Almost equally famous were two of its branches, Sullivan's Creek and Curtis Creek.

At Woods' Crossing, on Highway 49 one mile southwest of Jamestown, a small monument of gold-bearing quartz has been erected by the Tuolumne County Chamber of Commerce commemorating the finding of gold there. The spot at which the discovery was made is located 500 feet southeast of this marker where the old road crosses Woods' Creek.

Sonora

Very soon after the discovery of gold at Woods' Crossing, settlements were made at Jamestown and at Sonora, farther up on Woods' Creek. Located in a famous gold region of California, Sonora is one of the most picturesque and beautiful of all the old mining towns on the Mother Lode. Changing conditions have brought innovations that have somewhat marred its charm and individuality, but much of interest still remains. The trees that once interlaced their branches above Washington Street, the main thoroughfare of the town, have been removed, and the street has been widened and paved to care for the traffic that pours through it. Along Washington Street the heavy iron shutters of early days have been replaced by plate-glass windows, which display relics of the mining era and recently found gold nuggets, as well as up-to-date merchandise. On Saturday evenings in summer the street is like a plaza on fiesta day. A walk along this same route in the daytime reveals narrow side streets, along which may be seen old stone buildings "with iron shutters, regular fortresses, the walls thick enough to stand a siege." Entering these little side passageways is like going into an Old World village. Old trees, old houses, old gardens, old stone walls covered with ivy that must have been planted in the very earliest years, lure the pedestrian.

Sonorian Camp, as it was first known, was located by a party of Mexicans who pushed up Woods' Creek beyond Woods' Crossing and were the sole occupants of this region for several months. In the spring of 1849 the first white settlers arrived, a group of 19 men, 12 of whom were Americans. A little later they held a miners' meeting, at which R. S. Ham was elected alcalde. The "inborn quality for creating order" displayed by these and other Americans held in check the degenerate characters that came later. In July 1849 fully 1,500 foreigners, largely Mexicans and

Chileans, poured into the camps of Tuolumne County, and by autumn there were 5,000 people in Sonora. The narrow streets were constantly thronged and on Sundays were almost impassable. A tax on foreigners, which incited a bloodless war in June 1850, brought an exodus which cut the population almost in half.

In spite of frequent fires from which Sonora has suffered, some buildings reminiscent of the 1850's still remain in and about the town. On Washington Street south of the center of town stands the Gunn House, oldest residence in Sonora. Dr. Lewis C. Gunn, who had arrived in Jamestown in 1849, built the house and in 1851 brought his wife and family of young children from the East to live there. At that time the house, a two-story adobe, had a balcony across the entire front of the second story. The parlor at the left of the front entrance on the ground floor was used as a printing office and the county recorder's office, Dr. Gunn having been elected recorder in 1850. From this office was issued the *Sonora Herald*, the first number of which came out on July 4, 1850. After the Gunn family moved to San Francisco in 1861, the house was converted into a hospital, and in 1899 it was remodeled as a private residence. Only the middle part of the present structure comprises the original Gunn adobe. The house has been remodeled as a motor hotel and is an outstanding example of a building in keeping with the historic theme.

St. James Episcopal Church *(SRL 139)*, built in 1860, is one of the most attractive small churches in the Mother Lode or anywhere in California. The Higgins home, located on Washington Street just north of the Episcopal church, is built of lumber brought around the Horn. The house is a classic of the architecture of the 1850's. Other early-day residences still standing include the Vanderhoff, Burden, and Sugg homes. The Wells Fargo Building, which bears a bronze plaque, is located at the northeast corner of Washington and Linoberg streets. The Odd Fellows Hall on Washington Street is another old structure. The City Hotel was built of adobe in 1852, but has been extensively remodeled. A modern building, but an outstanding example of period architecture, is the Mother Lode Bank.

On a hill at the edge of town beyond the grammar school building is the Masonic cemetery, in which the graves of many early residents lie shadowed by oak and cypress trees. Here stands the monument of gold-bearing quartz erected by Tuolumne Lodge No. 8, F.&A.M., of Sonora, the Sonora Welfare Club, and the Tuolumne County Chamber of Commerce in honor of Jacob Richard Stoker, 1820–96. The inscription reads in part: "His heart was finer metal than any gold his shovel ever brought to light." Dick Stoker was a Mexican War veteran, who came to California in 1849. He was intimately associated with Mark Twain and the Gillis brothers on Jackass Hill in the 1860's, and was a member of Tuolumne Lodge No. 8. With a reputation for being just and fair, Dick settled many miners' disputes and served his community faithfully.

The Big Bonanza Mine in the heart of Sonora is the greatest pocket mine ever discovered. It is located on Piety Hill less than 100 yards from the St. James Episcopal Church and within a short distance of four other churches. It was first worked in 1851 by Chileans, who took out a large amount of surface gold. In the 1870's it was purchased for a pittance by three partners, who worked it for years and then one day broke into a body of almost solid gold. The next day they shipped gold valued at $160,000 to the San Francisco Mint. Within a week $500,000 worth was taken out and another half-million was mined before the property was again sold.

Among other mines in this vicinity were the San Giuseppe, located about a quarter of a mile northwest of the center of Sonora, and the Golden Gate, known all over the world for the pureness of its gold. It has been estimated that gold valued at $40 million has been mined within a radius of two miles of Sonora.

Jamestown

Jamestown *(SRL 431)*, frequently called "Jimtown," lies in the shadow of Table Mountain about four miles southwest of Sonora on the Mother Lode Highway. Colonel George F. James, a lawyer from San Francisco, located at this point on Woods' Creek in 1848. James fell into disfavor, and after his departure the inhabitants changed the name of the settlement to American Camp. The old name, however, had more appeal to the miners and was revived.

St. James Masonic Hall, Jamestown

Rawhide Quartz Mine, which had a production record of over $6 million up to 1909. At one time this mine, owned by Captain William Nevills, was considered one of the greatest gold mines in the world. There has been much pocket mining in the vicinity of Rawhide.

Jeffersonville, a thriving town in the 1850's and a stage stop between Rawhide and Tuttletown, was the scene of extensive tunnel mining under Table Mountain. Nothing remains to mark the site of the town but a small tree-shaded graveyard on top of a hill. West of Jeffersonville is the site of French Flat, now overgrown with chaparral. The Humbug Mine, on the east slope of the mountain a little way from the road leading from Jamestown to Rawhide, was the richest of all the tunnel mines, with a total yield of more than $4 million. Nuggets the size of hen's eggs were found there.

Columbia

Columbia (SRL 123), one of the most typical of the Argonaut towns still existing in the Mother Lode, was a city of several thousand persons, one of the largest mining camps in California. From an area of 640 acres on the outskirts of the town, more gold was recovered from gravel than in any equal area in the Western Hemisphere. Most of the topsoil here, averaging from 20 to 60 feet in depth, was removed by hand cart, leaving a vast expanse of fantastic, ghostlike rocks. "Truly a page from the past . . . few if any towns like Columbia remain in California. . . . Constructed of enduring brick and stone it has escaped the ravages of fire that have laid waste so many of the most picturesque of the old mining towns."

The rush for gold at Columbia had few parallels. On March 27, 1850, Dr. Thaddeus Hildreth, his brother George, and some other miners made camp for the night under an oak tree in the vicinity of what is now Columbia. The tree stood near the site of the bridge later built at the foot of Main Street. Rain during the night obliged the men to remain the next morning in order to dry their blankets. While there, one of the party, John Walker, found "color" in Columbia Gulch or a small adjoining gulch. Finding a promising prospect, the party remained and located at this point.

For a time the place was called Hildreth's Diggings, but was soon named Columbia. Almost from the first the camp was troubled by a lack of water. The winter of 1850–51 provided little rain to remedy the situation. In June 1851 the Tuolumne County Water Company was organized at Columbia. Its attempt to build a ditch to Five Mile Creek was at first frustrated, however, by the fact that there was insufficient water-power to operate its sawmill. Heavy steam equipment had to be hauled in, and by late November the mill was in operation. The ditch was completed by the following spring. In the meantime merchants were coming in to supply the needs of the 200 men working on the ditch. About the first of September 1851 a citizens' committee was appointed to lay out the streets and lots, and subsequently the town was platted on its present

Modern pavements cannot wholly mar the quaint charm of Jamestown's main street, with its balconied brick stores and hotels. The building formerly occupied by the St. James Masonic Lodge has been partly remodeled and the original stone has been covered with stucco, but the thickness of the walls is evident at the entrance door. It is located on the west side of Main Street two doors north of the picturesque Emporium. The Methodist Episcopal church was built in 1852 and is still in use.

The Sonora Road, which passes through this region, was alight with campfires in 1849, and travelers needed no other guidance than the embers, which marked the route of those who had gone ahead. Later, roadhouses sprang up as thickly and as rapidly as do gas stations today. Cloudman's, Keystone, and Crimea House were three of these old stage stations. Crimea House has been destroyed by fire, but the old stone corral across the way remains just as it was in pioneer days. It is two miles southeast of Highway 120 via Highway J-59. On the Otis Rosasco Ranch, just north of Yosemite Junction, is another stone corral, said to have been built by an industrious Chinese ranch laborer in his spare time.

At Montezuma (SRL 122), three miles south of Jamestown off the Mother Lode Highway, mining operations were begun in the summer and fall of 1852. Deep and extensive mines in this neighborhood produced exceptionally pure gold. Two stage lines passed through this settlement: the line from Stockton to Sonora, and Dr. Clarke's line from Sonora and Columbia to Don Pedro's, La Grange, and other points. The old Fox Building at Montezuma has been rebuilt and is now used as a private dwelling. Remains of a cemetery are near the corral.

Yorktown, Curtisville, Sullivan's Creek, Green Springs, Campo Seco, and Hardtack were other camps in the vicinity of Jamestown.

At Quartz Mountain, south of Jamestown and east of the Mother Lode Highway, is the famous App Mine, which produced $6,500,000 in gold up to the year 1909. The mine was closed down a few years after this date, and in 1927 the town of Quartz was destroyed by fire. John App and others became interested in property on this mountain as early as 1856, when they located the quartz claim on the west side. App married Leanna Donner, one of the six Donner girls orphaned by the Donner Pass tragedy. Mrs. App, who reached the age of 95, lived for 78 years in Tuolumne County. After the death of her husband, whom she survived many years, she continued to make her home on the old App homestead near Quartz, until her death in 1930.

South of Quartz is Stent, formerly known as Poverty Hill, where an old cemetery is about all that remains of pioneer days. To the southeast stood Algerine, once a notoriously wild mining camp, which boasted two streets lined with business houses. Today only a few cellars show the sites of the old stores.

Climbing Table Mountain west of Jamestown one comes to Rawhide, the location of the famous site. It was incorporated in May 1854, only to be almost destroyed by fire in July of the same year. The reconstructed buildings were substantial and more nearly fireproof. In the summer of that year another ditch company, the Columbia and Stanislaus Water Company, was formed, but eventually it was absorbed by the older company. Ultimately, after years of supplying the county with water for mining and irrigation, the Tuolumne County Water Company and its successors were absorbed by the Pacific Gas and Electric Company, which continues to furnish power and electricity for the entire county.

Families had begun to settle at Columbia as early as the fall of 1851, and soon gardens were planted and ranches cultivated in the vicinity. From January 1858 to January 1860 Columbia was illuminated by gas made from pitch, the lamps being set on cedar posts. Churches and public buildings were illuminated free. The gasworks were located on the east side of Gold Street, midway between Washington and State streets, about opposite the end of Fulton Street. After two years this fuel was found to be unsatisfactory.

Marble from the Columbia Quarry is of even grain and is remarkable for its elasticity. In color it ranges from white to gray and is either banded or rose-mottled. The sidewalks laid around the Palace Hotel in San Francisco in 1878 were made of this marble.

The town was often spoken of as "Columbia, the Gem of the Southern Mines," because of the great extent and rich character of its placer deposits. With the decline of mining, its population diminished to a few hundred, but it never became a real ghost town. Columbia's post office has operated continuously from September 15, 1852. Through the years its sturdy old brick buildings weathered the vicissitudes of age and neglect. As the centennial of the gold rush approached, the Mother Lode country began to attract the earnest attention of historians, and Columbia was adjudged the best preserved of the old camps and the most worthy of restoration as a memorial to the pioneers and a piece of "living history" for the enjoyment and education of future generations. Thus the picturesque old town was purchased by the State of California and in 1945 became Columbia State Historic Park. It has since been registered as a National Historic Landmark.

In July 1949 the William Cavalier Museum was dedicated and the park officially opened. There remain along the tree-shaded streets of Columbia 27 brick buildings and a stone jail, which were built between 1854 and the end of 1860. Several of these have already been restored, and a number of buildings, including the Masonic Hall, have been reconstructed to replace historic structures that had been razed or destroyed by fire. Ultimately each building will bear a sign giving a brief résumé of its history—its date of construction, owner, and the type of business once carried on within. Some buildings, of course, will always be in use for the necessary business of the townspeople, but others are to serve as museums with interiors furnished as of about 1860. It is esti-

mated that the planned restoration project will not be completed until well into the 1970's.

The little engine house contains one of the oldest pieces of fire-extinguishing apparatus in the state, the hand pumper "Papeete," polished and painted to look as it did when it arrived in Columbia in December 1859. It was originally destined for shipment to the Sandwich Islands. The adjoining two-story building contained the office where the *Columbia Gazette* was printed. At the "Gold Dust Exchange" and bank of D. O. Mills and Company, home-made candies have replaced the golden treasure that once poured over its counters. The post office is located in an old grocery store building on Jackson Street and displays the earliest set of boxes to be used in Columbia, built locally in 1861. Among the oldest buildings in town are the Franklin & Wolf and Brainard buildings, adjacent and having a common wall. The Stage Drivers' Retreat and the Pioneer Saloon (Aberdeen's) are just two of the numerous establishments where miners gathered to slake their thirst and pass the time. The beautiful old Fallon Hotel stands at the edge of town, and next to it is a replica of Eagle Cotage [sic], the original of which was put up as a boarding-house in the very earliest days of the diggings and later became Owen Fallon's first hotel. A stone monument on the west side of Broadway about opposite the restored Masonic Hall bears a bronze tablet recounting major events in Columbia's history.

The brick Columbia School on the hill was opened for its first term by John Graham on

Old Printing Office, Columbia

March 18, 1861, using the furnishings from the old school. On September 9 of that year school opened with new desks and seats all in place. The first election for school trustees was held there on April 14, 1862. Restoration of the brick schoolhouse was effected through the efforts of the California Teachers' Association in collecting pennies from schoolchildren throughout the state. On a hill beyond the school is the cemetery of Columbia Lodge No. 28, F.&A.M., which has been restored by the Grand Lodge, which also rebuilt the meeting hall in the town itself.

Todd & Co.'s Express maintained an office at Columbia at least as early as 1852, the year in which William Daegener took charge, at a location unknown to historians. By September 1853 Todd had sold out to Wells, Fargo & Co., and within the next few months the office was moved to the American Hotel. This was at the site of the present brick Wells Fargo Building, which Daegener built in 1858. Now thoroughly renovated and restored, it is perhaps the most picturesque of all Columbia's buildings; certainly it is one of the most photographed buildings in the Mother Lode. Wells Fargo operated there until 1914.

At Columbia there are several residences that were built between 1854 and 1860. Some have been remodeled beyond recognition, but a few maintain the beauty of their original construction. One of these, directly across the street from the restored post office, was built as a combination store and residence by Louis Braquihai in the spring of 1856.

Quaint St. Ann's Church, the mecca of artists as well as historians, crowns Kennebec Hill, overlooking the world's richest placer grounds, with the ghostlike rocks of the diggings encroaching to the very edge of the little cemetery. The church was erected in 1856 with funds donated for its construction by the miners. Father Daniel Slattery, leader in the work, was the first priest to officiate in the sacred edifice. The walls of this historic church were built of brick fired in a kiln which was located on the Sonora-Springfield road, while the timbers used in its construction were obtained from Saw Mill Flat about three miles southeast of Columbia. The belfry was added in 1857. The interior decorations and altar paintings are the work of James Fallon, son of a pioneer hotelkeeper. After having stood for half a

Old Town of Saw Mill Flat

century, the walls of the old church were considered to be unsafe and its doors were closed, but through the united efforts of the Native Sons of the Golden West and the Knights of Columbus the structure was repaired and was rededicated on June 15, 1906. It is now in regular use.

As might be expected, the history of such an old and important place as Columbia has been beclouded through the years with legends—colorful to the telling but with no basis in truth. One of these stories has it that Columbia came within two votes of being the capital of California; another, that the signatures on the petition for this honor were attached instead to a petition for gubernatorial pardon of a convicted murderer, thus depriving Columbia of the seat of government. Other fables glorify the town with a "boom days" population as high as 15,000 to 20,000. State Park historians have dedicated themselves to a realistic interpretation of Columbia's history as well as to an honest and careful restoration of its buildings.

Between Columbia and Vallecito was Parrott's Ferry *(SRL 438)* on the Stanislaus River. Thomas H. Parrott established it in 1860, and it operated until 1903, when the first bridge was built.

Gold Springs

In the sands of a large spring, which is still visible about a mile and a half northwest of Columbia, a Mr. Hatch and others discovered gold in the latter part of April 1850. This spring and another were the source of a stream which was used for mining operations employing some 300 miners. A camp boasting a two-story brick building, at least three food stores, several boarding houses, a soda works, and a number of mechanics' shops and hardware stores, with an area population of 500, had grown up at the springs by 1856. Its citizens were quiet, orderly, and enterprising. Several gardens and small ranches in the immediate vicinity supplied fresh fruits and vegetables to the miners at Columbia and Yankee Hill to the southeast, and to Red Dog, Dow's Flat, Heavy Tree Hill, Wayne's Bar, Simpson's Bar, Italian Bar, and Texas Bar to the north.

Saw Mill Flat

Saw Mill Flat *(SRL 424)*, so named because of the two sawmills erected there to supply mining timbers in the early 1850's, was situated on a fork of Woods' Creek, three miles southeast of Columbia and one and a half miles south of Yankee Hill. At first it was a great resort for Mexicans and Peruvians, and it is said that Joaquín Murieta, at the time a monte dealer, had headquarters there in 1852, before he began his career of murder and robbery.

Shaw's Flat

Shaw's Flat *(SRL 395)*, on the eastern edge of Table Mountain, was named by Mandeville Shaw, who planted an orchard there in 1849. A number of substantial cottages surrounded by gardens planted with fruit and ornamental trees give the place a homelike appearance today. Black walnut trees planted by Tarleton Caldwell flourish in the

Swerer's Store, Tuttletown, Before It Collapsed

place known as Caldwell's Gardens, now a home. The Mississippi House, well known in early days, still attracts the passerby. It was built in 1850 and served as a store, bar, and post office. Also preserved at Shaw's Flat is the old miners' bell, used to announce the convening of court and to summon the men to work. It may be seen at the school.

In 1855 miners sinking a shaft at Caldwell's Gardens discovered river gravel under the lava. At this point, the ancient stream was wide and flat and the lava coat consequently thin. Caldwell's claim is said to have yielded $250,000 in gold. Following this discovery, tunnels, some of great length, were made under Table Mountain and immense fortunes were taken out.

At the south end of Shaw's Flat once stood "Uncle Tom's Cabin." This "Uncle Tom" was a slave who purchased his freedom with gold that he took from the ground. In appreciation of his blessings he kept a pail of pure drinking water outside his door for the use of thirsty wayfarers who chanced to pass that way.

Brown's Flat and Squabbletown

Brown's Flat, located on Woods' Creek one mile north of Sonora, had its beginning in 1851. Extensive hill and surface diggings independent of the creek bed were worked in the vicinity. Among these mines were the Page, the Ford, and the Sugarman, the last-named producing crystallized gold of great beauty. After 1852 steam and horse power were used in draining the many claims. At Brown's Flat the Sonora-Milton stage was held up on several occasions, and on January 15, 1878, over $5,000 was obtained by highwaymen.

Squabbletown, a small camp farther north on Woods' Creek, has disappeared. Only the decaying remnants of old cabins show where the settlement once stood.

Tuttletown

Tuttletown (*SRL 124*), about six miles west of Sonora on the Mother Lode Highway, was named after Judge A. A. H. Tuttle, who built a log cabin there in 1848. The earliest dwellings consisted of tents and Mexican *ramadas*, or brush houses. It was a stopping place for packers carrying miners' supplies over the old Slum-gullion Road from Angels Camp to Sonora, and by 1849–50 it was a flourishing camp. Since that time its population has dwindled to a family or two. Here are the ruins of a little country store built of stone, known as Swerer's, where Mark Twain once traded. Nearby stood the Tuttletown Hotel, built in 1852 and destroyed by fire in 1950. On the outskirts of Tuttletown, opposite the Patterson Mine, are three old Spanish cork trees.

Jackass Hill

Jackass Hill, just west of Tuttletown, achieved much notoriety in 1851 and 1852. The diggings were rich in coarse gold and excitement was intense. Hundreds of men rushed to the scene, and many a lucky miner made his "pile" in a few hours. Some claims of 100 square feet yielded as high as $10,000, and one quartz pocket produced from $100 to $300 a day for three years. Numerous small pocket mines made rich yields of ore.

The hill received its name from the braying of the jackasses in the pack trains that paused overnight on their way to and from the mines. As

Replica of Mark Twain's Cabin, Jackass Hill

many as 200 of the animals are said to have been picketed on the hill at one time.

Mark Twain (Samuel Langhorne Clemens), the great American humorist, spent five months on Jackass Hill in 1864–65 as the guest of William R. Gillis. A replica of the cabin *(SRL 138)* stands on the hilltop about one mile from Tuttletown, built around the old stone fireplace, uninjured when flames destroyed the original cabin. Here, in imagination, one may see Dick Stoker, the "Dick Baker" of *Roughing It;* James Gillis, "The Sage of Jackass Hill"; and William Gillis seated with Mark Twain before a crackling wood fire on many a long winter evening.

The Landmarking Pilgrimage to the Bret Harte country, the Mark Twain Society, and other Mark Twain admirers joined at the Mark Twain Cabin on May 22, 1922, to take part in its dedication, thus making it a national event. The crowd was welcomed by Bill Gillis, Mark Twain's old-time friend. A tablet telling the story of Jackass Hill was placed near the cabin in 1929 by the Tuolumne County Chamber of Commerce.

Springfield

Springfield *(SRL 432)*, a camp southwest of Columbia near the head of Mormon Creek, received its name from the fine springs there, which afforded sufficient water for the placer-mining operations of several hundred men who worked the rich gold claims in the vicinity. The miners often uncovered Indian mortars and pestles, showing that Indians had camped at the springs.

The town, with its stores, shops, and hotels, was well laid out about a plaza. The erection of a Methodist church before that of a gambling house makes Springfield unique in the annals of mining towns. It was noted for the quiet orderliness and sobriety of its citizens, many of whom worked in the mines under Table Mountain nearby. Today the site of the town is indicated by an abandoned brick schoolhouse, which formerly served as a church.

Chinese Camp

Some ten miles southwest of Sonora is Chinese Camp *(SRL 423)*, which in 1856 had a population of 1,000 and boasted a church, several stores and hotels, a bank, an express office, and two fraternal orders, the Masonic Lodge and the Sons of Temperance. Mining there consisted principally of surface diggings on the hilltop and in the valley. Water was brought to the mines in the vicinity from Woods' Creek by means of a flume and ditch.

One of several stories told of the origin of this old place name is that the town was founded by a ship's captain who deserted his vessel in San Francisco Bay and brought his entire Chinese crew there to mine. A less dramatic version is that Chinese miners were employed there by English prospectors. A third story says that after gold became exhausted at Campo Salvado, the miners, working up over the hill, ultimately joined the Chinese on the other side and named the new location after them. It is estimated that at one time 5,000 Chinese worked there, but none remain today. One may still see at Chinese Camp old stone and brick buildings with heavy iron doors typical of the early gold days. These, interspersed with a few small modern homes, make up the present town. The ruins of the Wells Fargo building *(SRL 140)* are in evidence, but its iron doors are in the Wells Fargo Museum in San Francisco. On a hill at the edge of Chinese Camp is picturesque little St. Francis Xavier Catholic Church, built in 1855 and restored in 1949.

Chinese Camp was the rallying place of the second big tong war in California. Two Mile Bar on the Stanislaus River was the scene of the incident that led to this war. Twelve members of the Sam-Yap Tong were working near six members of the Yan-Wo Tong when a huge stone rolled from one property to the other. Words and blows ensued. Calls went out for assistance. American blacksmiths in neighboring camps were engaged to make crude weapons—pikes, daggers, and tridents—and a few firearms were supplied from San Francisco. On September 26, 1856, 900 members of the Yan-Wo Tong went forth from Chinese Camp to meet 1,200 members of the opposing tong near Crimea House. The battle took place amid the beating of gongs and the reverberations of random shots from inexperienced marksmen. The casualties were four killed and four wounded. American officers of the law finally arrested 250 of the combatants. The State Historical Museum at Sutter's Fort, Sacramento, has specimens of these locally manufactured weapons.

An old fort built by Chinese miners in 1856 may be seen near Shawmut, a mining town about two miles from Chinese Camp. At one time Shaw-

Church (later Schoolhouse), Springfield

mut boasted the longest payroll and the deepest mine shaft in the county.

Jacksonville

Jacksonville *(SRL 419)*, on the Tuolumne River, was established by Colonel Alden Jackson in June 1849, and by the summer of 1851 it ranked second only to Sonora. At Jacksonville was planted the first orchard in that part of the state, known as Smart's Garden, and for many years a sparse scattering of the old apple trees remained. Mining through the orchard brought about its final destruction. In the early 1850's Jacksonville was the scene of extensive river operations, including the building of great dams and wing dams at high cost of labor and materials. Today the tiny hamlet is but a shadow of the once prosperous mining town. Fire and the vicissitudes of time have removed most of its early landmarks, and upon completion of the new Don Pedro Dam, Jacksonville will be inundated.

Priest's Hotel and Big Oak Flat

Priest's Hotel (named after its original owner) was on the main road to Yosemite Valley in the late 1850's and 1860's. A wagon road over this route was not completed to the floor of the valley until July 17, 1874. The winding road up Priest's Grade today is one of the most picturesque in the Sierra. The original Priest's Hotel was destroyed by fire, and a later building occupies the site. From a hill in the rear a panorama of seven counties may be viewed.

About a mile from the hotel stood a famous landmark during mining days, the big oak *(Quercus lobata)* from which Big Oak Flat *(SRL 406)* derived its name. This huge tree, 11 feet in diameter, was gradually killed by miners digging about its roots for gold. It was eventually felled and the stump was burned, but three small pieces have been preserved in a monument which stands on the site.

James Savage, with a retinue of Indian laborers in 1850, was the first man to mine Big Oak Flat, originally called Savage Diggings. In the vicinity, the Lumsden, Big Oak Flat, Longfellow, Cosmopolite, and Mississippi mines were notable producers. A large stone building, the Odd Fellows Hall, still stands at Big Oak Flat.

First and Second Garrote

Groveland *(SRL 446)*, formerly known as Garrote or First Garrote, on the Big Oak Flat Road, is still a thriving community. On its main street stands a memento of the past, the old stone Tannehill store, and at the opposite end of the block is the Masonic Hall, an old two-story adobe. About two miles above Groveland, near the edge of the Stanislaus National Forest, is Second Garrote *(SRL 460)*, a tiny mountain hamlet. Here at the edge of the road is a huge, misshapen, old dead tree, known as the Hangman's Tree. A monument nearby bears a tablet telling the story of its violent past. Across the road and enclosed by a fence is a two-story frame house, formerly the home of Chaffee and Chamberlain, alleged to have been the originals of one of Bret Harte's

stories. Mines in the vicinity of Second Garrote were the Kanaka, the Big Betsy, and the Mexican. The Big Oak Flat Road continues on through Buck Meadows, called Big Gap in the early days.

Tuolumne

Tuolumne, just west of the border of the Stanislaus National Forest, is a lumber center and the terminus of the Sierra Railway. It is less than a mile from the old mining camp of Carter's, first known as Summersville *(SRL 407)*, named in honor of Mrs. Elizabeth Summers, wife of an early settler. Six miles east of Tuolumne and within the borders of the Stanislaus National Forest is located one of the largest canyon oaks in the state, measuring ten feet in diameter. Some years ago the county expended a large sum of money for its preservation.

The Buchanan Mine ten miles south of Tuolumne has yielded over $2 million.

The East Belt Mines

Mining activity in the East Belt began early in the 1850's. The Soulsby Quartz Mine at Soulsbyville was discovered by Benjamin Soulsby in 1856 and worked by Cornish miners. Its total production up to 1909 was over $7 million. Other mines in the vicinity were the Black Oak, the Live Oak, the Golden Treasure, and the Platt and Gilson. Soulsbyville *(SRL 420)* has always been a place of well-kept homes, pretty gardens, and law-abiding people.

Over the lava ridge just east of Soulsbyville was Cherokee *(SRL 445)*, near neighbor to Arastraville. The Confidence Mine at Confidence, 13 miles northeast of Sonora on the Sonora–Mono State Highway leading to Sonora Pass, was discovered in 1853 and was one of several good producers in this vicinity. This group of claims included the Independence, the Little Jessie, the Mary Ellen, and the Plowboy. The Excelsior Mine at Sugar Pine produced $420,000 worth of gold before the quartz vein was lost. Many attempts to relocate the vein have failed.

SOURCES

Beasley, Thomas Dykes. *A Tramp through the Bret Harte Country*. Paul Elder & Co., San Francisco, 1914.
Bidwell, General John. "Echoes of the Past," *Chico Advertiser*, Chico.
Chapman, Charles E. *A History of California: The Spanish Period*. Macmillan, New York, 1921.
Cleland, Robert Glass. *Pathfinders*, Vol. I of the series *California*, ed. John Russell McCarthy. Powell Publishing Co., Los Angeles, 1929.
Conlin, Thomas. "The Story of Columbia," *Pacific Underwriter and Banker*, Jubilee Edition, XXXIX, No. 18, September 25, 1925.
Eastman, Barbara. Ms. notes in Bancroft Library, University of California, Berkeley.
Farquhar, Francis P. *Place Names of the High Sierra*. Sierra Club, San Francisco, 1926.
Geologic Guidebook along Highway 49—Sierran Gold Belt, the Mother Lode Country. State of California, Division of Mines, San Francisco, 1948.
Gillis, William R. *Gold Rush Days with Mark Twain*. Albert & Charles Boni, New York, 1930.
——— *Memories of Mark Twain and Steve Gillis*. Privately published, Sonora, 1924.
Gold Rush Country. Lane Publishing Co., Menlo Park, 1957.
Gunn, Lewis C., and Elizabeth Le Breton. *Records of a*

California Family, ed. Anna Lee Marston. Privately printed, San Diego, 1928.

Heckendorn and Wilson. *Miners' and Business Men's Directory.* Clipper Office, Columbia, 1856.

Hittell, John S. *The Resources of California.* 5th ed. A. Roman & Co., San Francisco, 1869.

Holmes, Roberta Evelyn. *The Southern Mines of California. Early Development of the Sonora Mining Region.* The Grabhorn Press, San Francisco, 1931.

Johnston, Philip. "Legends and Landmarks of '49 along the Mother Lode," *Touring Topics,* XXIII, No. 2 (February 1931), 12–27, 52–53.

Kroeber, Alfred Louis. "California Place Names of Indian Origin," *University of California Publications in American Archaeology and Ethnology,* XII, No. 2 (1916–17).

Lang, H. O. *History of Tuolumne County.* B. F. Alley, San Francisco, 1882.

Muir, John. "Hetch Hetchy Valley," *Overland Monthly,* XI, No. 1 (July 1873), 42–43.

Paden, Irene D., and Margaret E. Schlichtmann. *The Big Oak Flat Road.* Lawton Kennedy, San Francisco, 1955.

Peterson, H. C. "Footprints of California Argonauts," *Oakland Tribune,* April 26, 1931.

—— "Forty-Nine Tour," *Oakland Tribune,* March 14, 1922.

Reports of the State Mineralogist. State Printing Office, Sacramento, 1880–96.

Sanchez, Nellie Van de Grift. *Spanish and Indian Place Names of California.* A. M. Robertson, San Francisco, 1922.

Shinn, H. C. *Mining Camps. A Study in American Frontier Government.* Scribner, New York, 1885.

Stewart, George R., Jr. *Bret Harte, Argonaut and Exile.* Houghton Mifflin, Boston, 1931.

"Tuolumne County, California," *The Union Democrat.* J. A. Van Harlingen Co., Sonora, 1909.

Weston, Otheto. *Mother Lode Album.* Stanford University Press, Stanford, 1948.

Woods, Daniel B. *Sixteen Months at the Gold Diggings.* Sampson Low, London; Harper, New York, 1852.

Yard, Robert Sterling. *The National Parks Portfolio.* 6th ed., rev. by Isabelle F. Story. U.S. Government Printing Office, Washington, D.C., 1931.

Ventura County

VENTURA COUNTY was organized as a county in 1872, and Ventura was made the county seat. (Ventura is a corruption of San Buenaventura, so called after Mission San Buenaventura; the name was derived from the saint whose title, Bonaventure, meaning "good fortune," is said to have been bestowed after he was healed by Saint Francis.) The city is still officially known as San Buenaventura, although the post office has been designated Ventura since 1889. The present courthouse, completed in 1913, is beautifully situated overlooking the heart of the city. In front of it stands a statue of Father Serra, founder of the mission.

Cabrillo's Landing Place

In ancient times there were numerous Indian villages along the shore of what is now Ventura County. When Cabrillo, the discoverer of California, sailed up the coast in 1542, it is thought by some historians that he came ashore on October 10 at a place where there was a large Indian village, doubtless the one to which Cabrillo gave the name El Pueblo de las Canoas ("the Town of the Canoes"), because he was so impressed by the large, finely built boats that these tribes used. The boats carried from 15 to 20 persons, were built of boards crudely hewn by hand, and were calked with asphalt from the neighboring hills. Their boats, homes, implements, and utensils, as well as their mode of life, exhibited a skill in workmanship and a superiority of culture that placed a distinguishing mark upon the Chumash Indians of Ventura and Santa Barbara counties and of the Channel Islands. Among all the Indians of California, they were perhaps the most advanced. Being also the most friendly, as well as exceedingly numerous, they proved a rich harvest for the zealous Franciscans who followed Cabrillo some 200 years later.

Relics of this superior civilization have been found throughout the region and are preserved

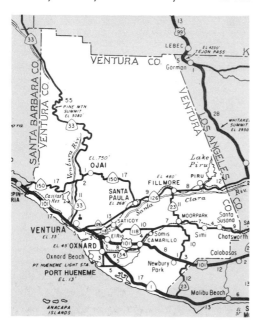

in the Ventura County Pioneer Museum located at 77 North California Street in Ventura. Water baskets lined and covered with native asphalt, skillfully wrought bowls and mortars, and finely shaped arrowheads are among the many interesting treasures displayed. There is a crude hand-hewn board, found in an Indian cave in the Wheeler Springs region. It seems to have served as a fleshing board, for its sharp edge is evidence that it was used to scrape the meat side of hides in the process of tanning.

The ancient village at which Cabrillo landed may have been the one located on the seashore at the foot of what are now Figueroa and Palm streets, Ventura. In the 1870's, a kitchen midden was still visible very near the sea, on Figueroa Street, on the lot now occupied by the Associated Oil Company's fire-extinguishing tanks. There is, however, some difference of opinion among historians as to the location of Pueblo de las Canoas. Henry R. Wagner, eminent historian and geographer, believed that the site was Mugu Lagoon, southeast of Oxnard. It was formerly held by some that Rincón Point was the probable location, but this view is no longer accepted. Most authorities currently favor the Ventura location.

Cabrillo remained at the Pueblo de las Canoas until October 13, when he sailed "six or seven leagues, passing along the shores of two large islands," anchoring off Rincón Point.

The Trail of Portolá

Leaving the campsite near Castaic in Los Angeles County on August 10, 1769, Captain Gaspar de Portolá and his men continued down the verdant valley which was later called the Santa Clara, after a village that Fray Juan Crespí had named, halting for the night on the banks of an arroyo in the vicinity of Rancho Camulos very near the county line. On the three succeeding days the tents were pitched near the Indian villages in the neighborhood of Fillmore, Santa Paula, and Saticoy, where the friendly natives gave the strangers gifts of seeds, acorns, and baskets of pine nuts in exchange for beads. Monuments have been erected at Piru's Warring Park (SRL 624) and the eastern edge of Santa Paula (SRL 727) in commemoration of Portolá's visit. On August 14 the party stopped near the site of Mission San Buenaventura, where a large ranchería was located. Father Crespí, who named the village La Asunción de Nuestra Señora, expressed the hope "that such a fine site, where nothing is lacking, will become a good mission." The next night found the travelers at another native town where, the father wrote, the villagers "disturbed us and kept us awake playing all night on some doleful pipes or whistles." The name bestowed upon this place by the soldiers has persisted in Pitas ("whistles") Point. On August 16, Rincón Point was rounded and camp was made at a native fishing village on Rincón Creek.

When Portolá's men twice again traversed this county in the first half of 1770, their route was the shorter one along the present highway via Conejo Grade and Calabasas.

The Anza Trail

Juan Bautista de Anza, on April 10, 1774, traveling north on his notable overland journey from Sonora to San Francisco, camped near Triunfo (a former post office at the junction of El Camino Real and the road to Lake Sherwood) in Russell Valley west of Calabasas. "Passing among many docile heathens," the party continued their march the next day, halting for the night near San Buenaventura on the San Buenaventura River. Returning from the north a little later, Anza camped on April 29 east of Camarillo at the foot of Conejo Grade, this being his only stop in Ventura County on that trip. In 1776 Anza passed this way again as leader of the first overland emigrant train to California. Retracing his former route, he made only one halt in Ventura County. This was near El Rio, on February 23, 1776.

Mission San Buenaventura

In the midst of these populous native villages with their friendly people, halfway between San Diego on the south and Monterey on the north, Father Junípero Serra at length planted the ninth of the missions and named it San Buenaventura. It was the last one to be dedicated by the zealous founder of the California mission chain, for his death occurred just two years later, on August 28, 1784.

From the very beginning of his work in California the Padre Presidente had contemplated the founding of this halfway station in the fruitful valley of San Buenaventura. However, the Indian uprisings at San Diego and, more especially, the difficulties between the mission fathers and the civil authorities, had long delayed the fulfillment of his wish. It was 13 years after the founding of San Diego de Alcalá, the first of the missions, before Mission San Buenaventura was finally established on March 31, 1782. In the vicinity of the Indian village locally known as Mitz-Kana-Kan, Father Serra erected the first crude enramada for the celebration of the first Mass.

It was the custom, when a mission was dedicated, to erect a cross, not only as an emblem of faith but as a beacon to guide travelers to the mission. Along the coast a site was usually chosen which was visible both by land and by sea. At Ventura, the place selected was a lofty hill called La Loma de la Cruz ("the Hill of the Cross"), which rises immediately back of the mission church in the present city of Ventura.

For nearly 50 years Serra's cross (SRL 113) stood upon the hilltop above the mission. At last, however, wind and rain so weakened it that it fell. The old central timber was replaced by a new one, but the original scroll and crosspiece were retained. Thus it stood for another half-century, when in 1875 it was again blown down. After that, for 38 years, the hillside was without a cross. The scroll of the original cross, however, was saved and is now preserved in the Pioneer Museum. In 1913 a new cross was raised on the original hilltop site. It was made of Jeffrey pine from Santa Paula Canyon, where, it is thought, the mission fathers obtained timber for the original cross. In 1933 the present cross was placed. La Loma de la Cruz is now a city park.

Very soon after the erection of the first enramada, or chapel, the first mission church was built. According to Captain George Vancouver, this was destroyed by fire. Church records indicate that if such was the case, the disaster occurred between December 9, 1791, and June 21, 1792. "Thereupon," said Engelhardt, "buildings of a superior quality were erected" in the summer of 1792. The church built at this time, he added, "could not have been more than a temporary structure."

The present mission church was begun as early as 1793 but was not completed until 1809. While it was in course of construction, a temporary chapel, called the Chapel of Santa Gertrudis, was erected for the Indian community, at the entrance to Casitas Pass, about seven miles north of the mission. This chapel was used intermittently for many years, even as late as 1868. After the earthquakes of 1812 and 1857, it was doubtless used for divine worship while the church was being restored.

Most of the Indians of the community soon settled about the Chapel of Santa Gertrudis, and the great numbers of their little willow-thatched houses gave the name Casitas ("Little Houses") to the entire region. The settlement was located at the present junction of the Ojai road and the road leading through Foster Park in Casitas Pass. The chapel was near what is now the gateway to Foster Park, on the property of the Canet Company. Nothing remains to indicate the thriving villages which once stood in the vicinity.

About a quarter of a mile from the mission church (near the southwest corner of the present Palm and Meta streets), near the ancient village of the Indians, stood the little chapel of San Miguel Arcángel. For many years, processions chanting the litanies and the rosary wended their way periodically from the church to the chapel, to the great delight of the Indians. The earthquake of 1812 damaged the building, and by 1816 it had become unserviceable and another was built on more solid ground. In 1832 it was reported that "the chapel of San Miguel, the pride of Fr. Señan, could not be saved, the floods having destroyed it entirely." The crumbling walls were still standing as late as 1873, the last vestige of the ruins being removed in the late 1870's.

Even before the dedication of the present mission structure on September 10, 1809, the mission garden had become famous. In the autumn of 1793, Vancouver, on his second visit to California, wrote in his journal about the gardens of San Buenaventura, describing them as "far exceeding anything" he had seen elsewhere in California. At a later date, Richard Henry Dana spoke of them as "the finest in the whole country." Today, nothing remains of this wonderful garden save the trunk of one palm tree.

It is said that the palms were planted by the padres when the garden was first laid out on a tract of 17 acres on what is now the south side of Main Street. A bend in the street indicates the location of the old wall which surrounded the orchard. The historic palms have suffered much through the years from windstorms. One was blown down in 1876. For many years the Native Daughters of the Golden West cared for the last two, building a wall about them and bracing them with wire cables. One of these fell about 1940. The one remaining, which lost its top to a storm in 1961, stands on Colombo Street a half block south of Main. Beneath it is a tiny structure built from adobe bricks salvaged from the mission quadrangle when it was razed in the 1880's. The little park is city property.

The boundaries of the old walled garden began on what is now Main Street and extended westward to just beyond the southwest corner of Ventura Avenue and Main Street, thence south to a bit beyond Meta Street, thence eastward to a point that would be in line with the east line of Colombo Street, making the southeast corner of Colombo and Main streets the point of beginning.

The present mission structure *(SRL 310)* was built not within this walled garden but directly opposite, on what is now the north side of Main Street. During the height of its prosperity it was considered one of the richest of the missions, being especially famous for its horticulture. After the secularization of the missions, it suffered with the others. From 1840 to 1850 it was without a resident pastor, a priest from Santa Barbara coming down to hold occasional services. It was roofless for many years after the earthquake of 1857, and while in this condition it was abandoned. For how long is not known, but we do know that the Chapel of Santa Gertrudis was being used in its stead in 1868. In 1895 the present mission structure was described by J. Torrey as a "well-preserved building, its walls still bearing traces of the rude frescoing affected by the builders of that time."

In 1957 the interior of the church was restored, as nearly as possible, to its original condition, undoing the work of an earlier regrettable "restoration," which had obliterated much of its ancient charm. Ceiling and flooring were torn out to reveal the original beams and floor tiles. The crudely beautiful Indian frescoes, which had been covered up by ornate scroll work, unfortunately could not be saved, but a small section of them, which had escaped modernization, may be seen in the baptistry, where the original baptismal font is still in use. Many relics are on display in the mission museum, including part of the old wooden pulpit, carved and painted by the Indians, which had been torn out of the church in the earlier restoration, and the original confessionals, likewise showing Indian handiwork. Old records in Father Serra's handwriting and a pair of unusual wooden bells, probably used during the last three days of Holy Week and the only ones known in the California mission chain, are also to be seen there.

The water system built by the padres to irrigate their gardens and orchard was complete and well constructed in every way. The pic-

turesque old settling tank and receiving reservoir
(*SRL 114*), which distributed water to the mission
establishment and to the homes of the Spanish
families in the vicinity, still stands intact. The
"horse's head," or spout, carved from sandstone
by the Indians, is broken, but the massive walls
of the tank itself look as if they would last forever. It was used as the early calaboose or jail of
the town of Ventura. It is now city property and
may be seen from the steps going down the hill
from the western end of Poli Street. A similar
small reservoir building stands behind the mission church.

The great water ditch or stone aqueduct, which
was also a part of the padres' water system and
which was seven miles in length, was demolished
by the floods and landslides of 1866–67. The
massive ruins may still be seen near the mouth
of the Cañada Larga, eloquent testimonials of the
wonderful workmanship of the mission fathers
and their Indian helpers. The remnants are
about one-fourth mile east of the Ojai road on
Cañada Larga Road.

The Mission Town

Standing on a slight elevation at the foot of
La Loma de la Cruz, the mission church dominated the tiny town which grew out from it westward to the San Buenaventura River. Two irregular bridle paths formed the streets of the
little settlement and along these the adobe homes
were built, sometimes flat-roofed and covered
with brea, again more picturesquely tiled, and,
occasionally, shingled. Information on the locations of these adobes and the names of their
builders has been handed down to us through
two descendants of the old families, Luís Are-
llanes and E. C. Ortega, and is preserved in manuscript form in the Pioneer Museum in Ventura.
Only one of these old adobe homes remains in
part today, the Ortega house.

Seventy years before the Ortega house was built
on the east bank of the San Buenaventura River,
an adobe home had been erected on the Rancho
Sespe near the site of Fillmore, 28 miles east of
Ventura. The unknown builders of this homestead were murdered by a band of Mojave Indians, leaving the house deserted and forgotten
until 1857, when it was remembered by Miguel
Emigdio Ortega, who needed its sturdy timbers
for his new home. Four arduous days were taken
for the journey, a bodyguard of mounted horsemen accompanying the expedition as a protection
against the Indians. The house was dismantled
and the coveted timbers were hauled back to
Ventura, where they were incorporated in the
new house. In 1897, E. C. Ortega, son of the
original builder, had occasion to repair the old
home. The center beam, brought from the Sespe
house 40 years before, was found to be in perfect
condition and so solid that a 20-penny spike
could not penetrate it more than a quarter of
an inch.

In the flood of 1866–67, the swollen waters of
the San Buenaventura swept away half of the
Ortega adobe and a portion of the orchard of
pear, peach, and fig trees. The remaining portion

of the house is still in good condition and has
been added to slightly at the eastern front end.
It is owned by the city and stands at 215 West
Main Street.

What remained of the Valdez adobe was razed
about 1958. It originally belonged to the Valdez
family and fronted on the present Main Street.
Later, for many years, it belonged to an Italian
called Pedro Constancia. Constancia conducted a
stage station on his place, the stage office being
in the Santa Clara Hotel from 1870 on. This
hotel, much remodeled, is now called Poinsettia
Hotel and is on the south side of Main Street
directly opposite the site of the Valdez house.

In the beginning all of the lands about San
Buenaventura belonged to the mission. After
secularization of the missions, grants were made,
and the people to whom the land was given began
establishing homes and building their adobe
casas throughout the county. These tracts, however, were very large, over 4,000 acres being included in the smaller ones. Consequently, the
country homes scattered over the entire area
were few, not more than a dozen all told. Of
these, only a handful remain.

On what was formerly the Lower Ojai Rancho
stands the López adobe, called the "Barracks"
because it once defended the lower Ojai Valley
from the Matílija Indians. Extensively renovated
but preserving a flavor of earlier days, it is beautifully situated on the McCaleb ranch just to the
left of the highway about two and one-half miles
northwest of Ojai. About nine miles north of
Ventura, and just east of the Ojai highway on
Old Creek Road, stands the Santa Ana Rancho
adobe house of Don José de Arnaz.

Frémont's Camp

Don José de Arnaz was mayordomo of San
Buenaventura at the time of General Frémont's
arrival at the mission in 1846. Frémont, on his
way south to the reconquest of Los Angeles,
wished to gain possession of Mission San Buenaventura for the United States. In order to obtain
the knowledge that would enable him to carry
out his plan, he arrested Arnaz and tried to get
the desired information from him. Arnaz, however, claimed that he was unable to give this information and was finally released.

Until the publication in 1928 of the memoirs
of Don José de Arnaz, the site of General Fré-

Arnaz Adobe, Rancho Santa Ana

mont's camp while at Ventura was unknown or forgotten. Arnaz writes that he "established his camp on the west side of the mission orchard." The boundary of the orchard was what is now the western boundary of the property at the southwest corner of Ventura Avenue and Main Street. This places the site of the camp about opposite the Cabrillo Hotel near Garden Street, in the vicinity of the city jail.

Arnaz's town house was on what is now West Main Street, midway between South Ventura Avenue and the river. In the late 1850's he moved to his Santa Ana Rancho and his old home in town became the American Hotel.

An old sycamore tree *(SRL 756)*, passed by Frémont on his journey to Los Angeles, stands on the highway between Santa Paula and Fillmore and has been marked. It served as a "community center" for the area. In this vicinity the highway passes through the prosperous Rancho Sespe, modern counterpart of the Mexican grant of the same name.

Rancho San Miguel

Perhaps the best preserved of the historic adobes in the vicinity of Ventura is the Olivas house *(SRL 115)*, which stands near the Santa Clara River about one and one-half miles south of East Main Street on a private road extending from Callens Road and Transport Street.

Don Raymundo Olivas, the original owner, was born in Los Angeles in 1801. In 1821 he came to the vicinity of Ventura. Twenty years later, on July 6, 1841, he received the grant of 4,693 acres which constituted Rancho San Miguel. The western half of this rancho, which formed the eastern boundary line of the present city of Ventura, was purchased later by Dixie Thompson for $1,000 cash.

The Olivas adobe was a long two-story building with balcony and veranda overlooking a walled garden below and wide fields and marshlands beyond. There was a large family of 21 children, and many were the gay assemblages held in the great *casa*, for the Olivases were famous for their fine entertainment and generous hospitality.

Romance and adventure still cling about the old house, and its ancient adobe walls could tell fascinating stories, such as the time that Olivas was surprised and robbed by bandits. Wild ducks still come by hundreds to feed in the neighboring swamplands. The house has been restored, but the simple rural aspect of the place has been preserved. It was owned for a number of years by the Max C. Fleischmann Foundation, which donated it in 1963 to the City of San Buenaventura for eventual development as a State Historical Monument.

Rancho Camulos

About 30 miles east of Ventura, on the road to Los Angeles by way of Santa Paula and Newhall, is one of the most famous adobes in California. Located on Rancho Camulos, it was, until the mid-1920's, the home of the Del Valle family and famous as the setting for part of the novel *Ramona*, written by Helen Hunt Jackson.

Rancho Camulos *(SRL 553)* was originally a part of Rancho San Francisco, granted to Antonio del Valle in 1833 and 1839. Gradually, Don Antonio purchased 2,000 acres of the Rancho Temescal, and on this he built his home in the early 1860's.

Travelers between Missions San Buenaventura and San Fernando never failed to stop at Rancho Camulos. The hospitality of the Del Valles was famous from Spanish days well down into our own time.

The Camulos adobe is probably the best preserved and most typical of all of California's old rancho houses. From Rancho Camulos, Helen Hunt Jackson drew largely for her remarkable pictures of Spanish life in early California. There she heard the stories out of which gradually grew her composite heroine, and there she saw the scenes that wove themselves into the opening threads of her tale. Ramona, as her creator fashioned her, was inspired, not by one real person, but by two or three, and the result was a creature of fiction and romance woven on the loom of actual life. For the stories, Mrs. Jackson was largely indebted to Señora del Valle, the widowed mistress of Camulos at the time of the author's visit there in 1881.

Second in interest only to the adobe house itself is the charming Del Valle family chapel, a separate wooden building. Here for many years Mass was offered regularly, attended by the family, employees, and Indians living in the vicinity. Mounted outside the chapel is an old Russian bell the family had acquired. Through the years Rancho Camulos has remained unchanged in most of its aspects. It was long a literary and historical shrine. The present owner, who purchased it from the Del Valles, cherishes and maintains the relics of long ago, while at the same time operating it as a modern ranch. Its gates are now closed to visitors, but a monument stands near the highway. Another plaque, commemorating the entire Rancho San Francisco, has been placed in Los Angeles County near the junction of Highways 126 and 5, about nine miles east of Camulos.

Piru, closest town to Camulos, was founded by David Cook in 1887, during the railroad, health, and real estate boom. It has as landmarks an old hotel and Cook's beautiful tree-hidden mansion, owned now for years by the Warring family, on a hill overlooking the town.

Rancho Simi

South of Camulos, but reached from Ventura by still another highway providing an enjoyable alternate route to Los Angeles, is the Simi Valley, location of old Spanish Rancho Simi, first grant in present Ventura County. Including the valley and surrounding hills to an extent of 113,009 acres (by a later United States survey) and projecting into present Los Angeles County, the huge ranch, one of California's largest, was granted in 1795 and 1821 to Patricio, Miguel, and Francisco Javier Pico, whose interests were sold soon thereafter to José de la Guerra y Noriega of Santa Barbara, who also acquired part of adjoining El Conejo Rancho.

De la Guerra's adobe house on Rancho Simi, built probably in the 1820's, still stands and forms the rear portion of the Strathearn home at 17333 Tierra Rejada Road in Simi. During renovation work charred timbers were uncovered, relics of Indian attempts to burn the house. The ruins of a later adobe, guarded by tall palm trees, may be seen to the west of Tapo Road, several miles north of Santa Susana. The towns of Simi and Santa Susana are children of the real estate boom of the late nineteenth and early twentieth centuries, and are currently expanding rapidly under pressure of the subdivision movement westward from the Los Angeles metropolitan area.

Rincón Point

About 12 miles west of Ventura, close to the sea, rise the jagged cliffs of Rincón Point, battleground of the ancient tribes of the Chumash Indians. It is chiefly noted for its connection with the Battle of San Buenaventura, fought between rival factions of Californians on March 27–28, 1838, and for the dramatic poem "The Fight of the Paso del Mar" (Spanish for "The Pass of the Sea"), written by Bayard Taylor.

The rival factions concerned in the Battle of San Buenaventura were led by Juan Bautista Alvarado in the north and by Andrés and Pío Pico in the south. It was a common saying among the Californians that the general who held Rincón Point could withstand any adversary with ease. Alvarado, with General Castro in command, hastened, therefore, to take the point before his opponents, under Carlos Antonio Carrillo, could do so. Castro arrived at Rincón Point to find that Carrillo did not have even a sentinel there, and so he marched down to San Buenaventura, taking it by surprise. Only a few shots were fired. Alvarado lost one man and Carrillo none, but Rincón Point became famous.

When Bayard Taylor wrote "The Fight of the Paso del Mar" in 1840, he had never seen the place of which he wrote. In 1849 he visited California for the first time, and early in January 1850 he saw Rincón Point. In his book *Eldorado*, written after this visit, he said:

"We touched at Santa Barbara on the third morning out . . . we ran astray in the channel between the Island of Santa Rosa and the mainland, making the coast about twenty-five miles south of the town. I did not regret this as it gave me an opportunity of seeing the point where the Coast Mountains come down to the sea, forming a narrow pass. . . . It is generally known as the Rincón, or Corner. . . . I had made it the scene of an imaginary incident, giving the name of Paso del Mar—The Pass of the Sea—to the spot. I was delighted to find so near a correspondence between its crags of black rock, its breakers and reaches of spray-wet sand, and the previous picture in my imagination."

Taylor evidently was geographically confused in the writing of this poem, for it seems that the story it immortalizes was a Point Loma folktale connected with the days of hide droghing at La Playa, when old San Diego was the shipping point for the great ranchos of the Southwest. The story, as related in full by A. M. Loop in *The Silver Gate* (January 1900), an early San Diego magazine, seems to have been substantiated by old residents of San Diego. But although the tragic climax of this tale was in reality set at Point Loma, Taylor himself, by his reminiscence in *Eldorado*, made it also a legend of Ventura's Rincón.

Other Historic Spots

The town of Camarillo, usually associated with the nearby State Hospital and St. John's Seminary (location of the Edward L. Doheny Memorial Library), was named for Juan Camarillo, who purchased Rancho Calleguas from the heirs of the grantee, José Pedro Ruiz. Extensive rodeos, great social affairs, were held here in cattle days, but the present town did not come into existence until about the turn of the century.

About eight miles east of Camarillo, in the growing town of Newbury Park, is an attractive reminder of stagecoach days. The white two-story frame inn *(SRL 659)*, built in 1876 by James Hammel, served as a stage stop until the coming of the railroad. It has since been used as a school, community center, restaurant, gift shop, and private residence. In 1966 the old building was moved to a site off Ventu Park Road, about half a mile south of its original location on Newbury Road. The area was once a part of Rancho El Conejo.

Ojai was first called Nordhoff, after Charles Nordhoff, whose book *California for Health, Pleasure and Residence* was a prime factor in the influx of population to southern California in the 1870's. The post office, established in 1874, had its name changed to Ojai (a Chumash word interpreted variously as "moon" and "the nest") in 1917, but "Nordhoff" is still to be seen on the schools and a few of the stores. The pioneer resort town, with its picturesque mission-style business buildings, is situated in the spectacularly beautiful Ojai Valley and on the old Mexican rancho of the same name.

Union Oil Co. Building, Santa Paula

Oil is today one of Ventura County's principal industries, and fittingly the California Oil Museum is located here, in a building at Tenth and Main Streets in Santa Paula. Interesting exhibits of early-day oil machinery may be seen in this well-kept structure, in which the Union Oil Company was organized in 1890 by Lyman Stewart and Wallace L. Hardison, oil men from Pennsylvania, who consolidated their California interests with those of Thomas R. Bard, who became first president of the corporation. Although Bard had drilled the first well in the present county as early as 1865, Ventura County did not achieve real prominence in the oil industry until the 1920's, when spectacular discoveries were made near the city of Ventura.

Bard's name is remembered in the little settlement of Bardsdale, just across the Santa Clara River from Fillmore. He was also associated with the development of the Simi Valley and with Port Hueneme, once, according to Robinson, "the biggest California shipping point south of San Francisco" and, during World War II, the harbor through which was shipped "the major portion of all the supplies for our Armed Forces in the Pacific." It is the location of the Naval Construction Battalion Center, "Home of the Seabees"; the Naval Air Missile Test Center is at nearby Point Mugu. These facilities and Oxnard Air Force Base (near Camarillo) have influenced the growth of the city of Oxnard, which now exceeds Ventura in population. Oxnard was founded in 1898, home of a large beet sugar factory no longer in existence. In the vicinity are El Rio, once called New Jerusalem, and Montalvo, named for the early Spanish author who first used the word "California."

Northern Ventura County is a ruggedly beautiful area included in Los Padres National Forest and penetrated by few roads. The Sespe Wildlife Area north of Fillmore and Piru is dedicated to the preservation of the California condor. The county also includes two of the Channel Islands —Anacapa and San Nicolás.

SOURCES

Arnaz, José. "Memoirs of a Merchant—Being the recollections of life and customs in pastoral California by José Arnaz, trader and ranchero," translated and edited by Nellie Van de Grift Sanchez, in *Touring Topics*, XX (September, October, 1928).
Bolton, Herbert E. *Anza's California Expeditions*, 5 vols. University of California Press, Berkeley, 1930.
——— *Fray Juan Crespí, Missionary Explorer on the Pacific Coast, 1769–1774*. University of California Press, Berkeley, 1927.
——— "Spanish Explorations in the Southwest, 1542–1706," in *Original Narratives of Early American History*, Vol. XVII. Scribner, New York, 1916.
The California Missions, a Pictorial History. Lane Book Co., Menlo Park, 1964.
Davidson, Winifred. *Where California Began*. McIntyre Publishing Co., San Diego, 1929.
Engelhardt, Zephyrin. *San Buenaventura, the Mission by the Sea*. Mission Santa Barbara, Santa Barbara, 1930.
Harrington, Robert E. *Early Days in Simi Valley*. Privately published, Simi, 1961.
Jackson, Helen Hunt. *Ramona*. Little, Brown, Boston, 1900.
James, George Wharton. *Through Ramona's Country*. Little, Brown, Boston, 1909.
Loop, A. M. "The Fight of the Paso del Mar," *The Silver Gate*, II, No. 1 (January 1900), ed. James A. Jasper, San Diego.
Older, Mrs. Fremont. *California Missions and Their Romances*. Coward-McCann, Inc., New York, 1938.
Ortega, E. C. *Old Ortega Adobe, History by a Scion of the Ortega Family*, in a letter dated February 14, 1925, a copy of which is in the Pioneer Museum, Ventura.
Robinson, W. W. *The Story of Ventura County*. Title Insurance and Trust Co., Los Angeles, 1956.
Rogers, David Banks. *Prehistoric Man of the Santa Barbara Coast*. Santa Barbara Museum of Natural History, Santa Barbara, 1929.
Sheridan, E. M. "Historic Spots of Ventura County." Ms., Pioneer Museum, Ventura, 1930.
Taylor, Bayard. *Eldorado, or Adventures in the Path of Empire*. Putnam, New York, 1850 and 1864.

Yolo County

YOLO COUNTY was one of the original 27 counties. (Yolo, or Yo-doy, was the name of a tribe of Indians, and is said to mean "a place abounding with rushes.") Fremont was the first county seat, from 1850 to 1851, when the honor was bestowed upon Washington, now Broderick. In 1857 another move was made, this time to Cacheville, but after four years, in 1861, Washington again became the county seat. In 1862, Woodland was finally chosen as the permanent seat of justice.

The Trail of the Fur Hunter

In the marshlands west of the Río de Jesús María, now the Upper Sacramento River, lived the Yo-doy, a tribal branch of the Suisun Indians. To the south lay fertile, unbroken plains where game abounded. These plains were bounded on the north and south by Cache and Putah creeks, while on the east flowed the great river, and on the west lay a range of hills.

For hundreds of years, Indian hunters had roamed this region undisturbed, but in the year 1821 the first known white man crossed its trails. This was Luís Argüello, in command of the last expedition of the Spanish government into the river country of the Great Valley in search of mission sites. The party crossed what are now Solano and Yolo counties before reaching the

Sacramento River at a point in the present Colusa County in the vicinity of Grimes.

In 1828 the American explorer Jedediah Strong
Smith is thought to have hunted and trapped on
the streams of Yolo County, followed by the
great army of Hudson's Bay Company trappers,
who found this a rich field. They cached their
furs along the river and smaller streams, one of
which became known as Cache Creek. One of
their camps, known to early settlers as French
Camp, was situated in a grove of oaks on the
north bank of Cache Creek one mile east of the
present town of Yolo, formerly Cacheville.

In the spring and summer of 1830 another
band of hunters, under Ewing Young, trapped
along the San Joaquin and Sacramento rivers
and remained for a time on Cache Creek. Two
years later, on his way to Oregon, Young again
passed through Yolo County territory, camping
near the mouth of Cache Creek. Following up
Capay Valley past Clear Lake, the party reached
the coast some 75 miles north of Fort Ross, where
they continued north as far as the Umpqua River
in Oregon.

Joseph Gale, who had come to California with
Ewing Young in 1831, had a cattle rendezvous on
Cache Creek in 1843. The need for more livestock
in the Willamette Valley, Oregon, was the in-
centive to a daring project begun by Gale in
1841. Undaunted by the difficulties of getting the
cattle to Oregon, he set to work to construct an
ocean-going vessel which he proposed to take to
California and there exchange for livestock.
Through the intervention of Charles Wilkes, the
Hudson's Bay Company equipped the vessel, and
Gale, after passing a seaman's examination, was
granted a seaman's license. The schooner, *Star of
Oregon*, was launched on May 19, 1841, and
toward the end of August 1842 Gale and his
crew started down the Columbia River to California. At San Francisco, José Y. Limantour, a
Frenchman, purchased the vessel in exchange for
350 cows.

Needing more men for the vast stock-driving
venture over the mountains as well as for the
Oregon settlement project, Gale waited until the
spring of 1843 before starting north. Circulars
had been sent out describing the advantages of
the Willamette Valley for settlement, and by
the middle of May, 42 men, among them Jacob
P. Leese, had gathered at Cache Creek. From a
tall cottonwood tree trimmed into the form of a
flagstaff the Stars and Stripes floated for several
weeks that spring. The expedition finally started
northward on May 14, driving 1,250 head of cattle, 600 horses and mules, and 3,000 sheep, most
of which were safely guided over the northern
mountain barrier after a journey of 75 days.

Along the banks of historic Cache Creek the
earliest settlements in the region of Yolo County
were made: the Quesesosi Grant or Gordon's
Ranch, Knight's Landing, Rancho Río de Jesús
María, Rancho Cañada de Capay, and Hutton's
Ranch or Travelers' Home, later known as Cacheville. The stream flowing out of Clear Lake in the
mountains of Lake County furnishes a natural
water supply for the irrigation today of thousands

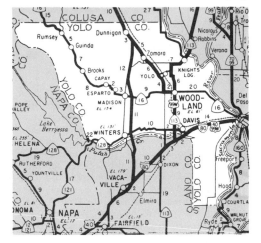

of acres of orchard and farmlands on the rich
plains of Yolo County.

Gordon's Ranch

William Gordon, a native of Ohio, came to
California with the Workman-Rowland party in
1841, and in 1842 he became the first white settler
in what is now Yolo County. Gordon had spent
some time in New Mexico, where he became a
Mexican citizen and married a Mexican woman.
On reaching California he obtained a grant of
two square leagues of land on the left bank of
Cache Creek about three miles above the Stephens
bridge and ten miles west of the present city of
Woodland. "Uncle Billy" Gordon had been a
trapper and hunter, "rough, uneducated, honest,
and hospitable." His place on Cache Creek was a
"general rendezvous for settlers and hunters"
from 1843 to 1846. James Clyman, in his diary for
July 12, 1845, notes that at the time of his visit
Gordon was the only permanent settler on Cache
Creek. Gordon moved to Cobb Valley in Lake
County in 1866 and lived there until his death in
1876.

On this estate, known as Rancho Quesesosi, or
Gordon's Ranch, the first wheat in Yolo County
was grown, and there, in 1847, in a primitive
building one mile from the Gordon home, the
first school was started with an enrollment of
eight pupils.

Knight's Landing

William Knight, a native of Indiana, who was
said to have been educated as a physician, also
came to California with the Workman-Rowland
party in 1841. In 1843 he settled at a natural
landing place on the Sacramento River later
known as Knight's Landing. In 1846 he received
a grant to this land, but the title was never confirmed.

Knight's first home on the river rancho was
made of tules and willow poles fastened with
rawhide and plastered with mud. It was built in
1843 on an ancient Indian mound, called by the
natives the Yo-doy mound. Since this site was
at the junction of the lower Sycamore Slough
with the Sacramento River, it proved suitable

for a ferry, which was established by Knight soon after his arrival, and the place became an important landing and shipping point on the Sacramento. Knight died on November 9, 1849, at Knight's Ferry in Stanislaus County. Because of a lack of business foresight, his entire estate was lost to the heirs.

An attempt to start a town at Knight's was made in 1849 under the name of Baltimore, but it never materialized because of disagreements over the sale of lots. In 1853, however, Charles F. Reed laid out another townsite and the place was officially named Knight's Landing. That same year, J. W. Snowball, Knight's son-in-law, and J. J. Perkins opened a general store on the Indian mound, and Captain J. H. Updegraff established a hotel business in the Yolo House. In 1860 this was superseded as the hotel by a brick structure, when the Yolo House became a private residence.

Knight's Landing, which is located about 12 miles north of Woodland, retained the early river-town atmosphere in the older portion of the settlement so perfectly that about 1929 it was chosen by film directors as the locale for the making of Mississippi River scenes in *Showboat*. The modern town which has grown up away from the river seems detached and remote from the days when the river, then the only highway, was a scene of lively traffic.

Rancho Río de Jesús María

The third grant made in Yolo County territory was given to Thomas M. Hardy, a Canadian, in 1843, and consisted of 26,637 acres along Cache Creek east of Gordon's Ranch, reaching as far as the Sacramento River. It was called Rancho Río de Jesús María, an early name given to the Upper Sacramento River. Hardy built a tule shack on the west bank of the Sacramento near the mouth of the Feather River, but he spent very little time there, having enlisted in military service under the Mexican government.

After Hardy's death by drowning in Suisun Bay in 1848 or 1849, his property was sold by the public administrator. Among those who purchased portions of the original rancho was James M. Harbin, who had come to this part of California in 1847. On Harbin's land the town of Fremont was afterward laid out. In 1857 Harbin moved to Lake County, where he settled at the springs that bear his name.

Rancho Cañada de Capay

Rancho Cañada de Capay was located on Cache Creek and was granted to Francisco Berryessa and his brothers, Santiago and Demesio, in 1843. (Kroeber says that Capay is from the Indian word *kapai*, meaning "stream.") Their great holdings were later taken over by incoming Americans, one of whom was George Dickson Stephens. In 1850 Stephens camped on Cache Creek on what he supposed was government land, but he afterward learned that it was a part of the Berryessa grant. With his brother, John D., he acquired the property that same year and erected an adobe dwelling. This house, around which a larger frame structure was built as the needs of the

Stephens Adobe, Rancho Cañada de Capay

family grew, is the only adobe standing in Yolo County today. The building is well preserved and is still occupied by Stephens' descendants. It stands half a mile south of Highway 16 midway between Madison and Esparto.

The first irrigation ditch in Yolo County was constructed by James Moore in 1856. It headed on Cache Creek about eight miles above the site of Woodland and within the bounds of Gordon's Ranch. Almost simultaneously with the building of the Moore canal, another dam and ditch were begun by David Quincy Adams in 1857. The Adams canal, which was completed in 1870, was laid out by Adams on Rancho Cañada de Capay, 4,693 acres of which he had purchased with money made in the mines of the Mother Lode during the years from 1849 to 1852. Adams built his canal for the purpose of irrigating 150 acres of alfalfa and 40 acres of gardens cared for by Chinese. This alfalfa, probably the first to be grown in California, was raised from seed obtained by Adams from Chile, and nearly all of the alfalfa grown in northern California today is known as Chilean alfalfa. The Adams Dam, which was located on Cache Creek about two miles west and a little north of Capay, no longer exists, but the prior water rights on Cache Creek obtained by David Adams are now owned by the Winters Ditch Company. The old Adams ranch home, two miles north of Esparto, stood until 1932.

Historic Capay Valley is famous for the redbud and almond blossoms to be seen in the spring.

Washington

In December 1844 Rancho Nueva Flandria, consisting of three square leagues of land bordering on the west bank of the Sacramento River, was granted to John Schwartz (Juan de Swat), an eccentric Dutch emigrant who had come to California with the Bidwell-Bartleson party in 1841.

In the spring of 1846 Schwartz sold 600 acres of his rancho to James McDowell, who had come overland with his wife and daughter in 1845. McDowell built a cabin in the northwest corner of his ranch opposite the site of the present city of Sacramento, where he took his family to live. He died in 1849, and in 1850 his widow had a townsite laid out on the land. This was the beginning of the little town of Washington, now known as Broderick.

When the town of Fremont began to decline in 1851, Washington became the center of commerce as well as of judicial and political activity in Yolo County. From 1851 to 1857 it was the county seat, and again from 1861 to 1862.

Washington was the site of the first Pacific Coast salmon cannery, established in the spring of 1864 on the west side of the Sacramento River opposite the foot of Sacramento's K Street. William and George Hume and Andrew Hapgood, fishermen from Maine, began with crude equipment in a converted cabin and scow, performing every operation by hand. During the first year, at least half the cans burst at the seams in cooking, but the partners managed to produce 2,000 cases of a dozen cans each, selling them at five dollars a case. As the business became more successful, other salmon canneries sprang up. By 1882, the peak year, there were 20 canneries along the Sacramento River and San Francisco Bay producing 200,000 cases of salmon a year. Decline set in when the number of salmon entering the Sacramento River was sharply reduced, a consequence of the silting of the river by hydraulic mining in the Sierra. In recognition of the fact that the multi-million-dollar salmon canning industry of the Pacific Coast is a direct outgrowth of this pioneer effort, the Department of the Interior has registered the site of Hapgood, Hume and Company as a National Historic Landmark, and on April 28, 1964, a plaque was placed in Broderick just up river from Tower Bridge.

For several years most of the traffic from the northern and western sections of Yolo County passed through Washington. So great was its early promise that the citizens for a time had hopes of its becoming a great city. Later, with the transfer of growth and activity from Washington to Sacramento across the river, and with the coming of the railroad, which decreased its importance as a center of navigation, Washington's boom days were ended.

Fremont

On the west shore of the Sacramento River one-half mile below the mouth of the Feather River, within the boundaries of the Harbin Ranch, Jonas Spect, a native of Pennsylvania, who had come overland to Oregon in 1847 and from there to San Francisco on the *Henry* early in 1848, established the town of Fremont in March 1849. Spect erected a temporary store of tules, willow poles, and canvas, and with the help of the Indians established a ferry across the Sacramento River. A sand bar at this point made an excellent ford across the Feather River; this seemed to be the head of navigation for both streams.

With miners, teamsters, and packers constantly passing through on their way to the mining regions, Fremont grew by leaps and bounds, and at the height of its prosperity claimed a population of 3,000. But its promise was short-lived. In the winter of 1849 heavy storms washed away the sand bars and the Feather River became navigable as far as Marysville. Commerce on both rivers passed Fremont by, and it was soon superseded in importance by Washington.

The loyal citizens of Fremont did not give up their town at once, and by means of desperate lobbying succeeded in making it the first county seat in 1850. In July of 1851, however, popular vote took the seat of government to Washington, and Fremont, its last hope gone, gradually disappeared. Some of its buildings were moved to Knight's Landing, some to Marysville, and others out upon newly established ranches in the vicinity. Soon empty lots were all that remained of the little river metropolis. Today the old Fremont site makes an excellent place for a day's outing for the citizens of Knight's Landing and Woodland.

Spect, who became a member of the first state senate, lived at Fremont until 1856, when he moved to Vernon, in Sutter County.

Cacheville

In September 1849 Thomas Cochran camped on the north bank of Cache Creek about ten miles west of Fremont, on the site of the present town of Yolo, and put up a rude hotel for the accommodation of travelers along the west side of the Sacramento River. The place grew and became known as Cochran's Crossing. In 1853 James A. Hutton arrived and erected a large, commodious structure which he opened to the public. The hospitality of Hutton and his family became so well known that the name of the place was changed to Hutton's Ranch, or Travelers' Home. The old Hutton house is still standing at 325 Main Street. In 1857 the place became the county seat of Yolo County and was rechristened Cacheville. The post office had been established under the name of Yolo in 1853.

Located in a rich farming region, Cacheville (Yolo) grew rapidly for a few years, but was outstripped by the more promising Yolo City, later known as Woodland, a few miles to the south. The Pacific Methodist (South) College was established at Cacheville in 1859 but was moved to Vacaville in 1861 and to Santa Rosa in 1871. The old Methodist church, built in 1867, is still standing.

Woodland

The fine groves of oak trees just south of Cache Creek, where the city of Woodland now stands, were centrally located in the midst of an extensive and fertile region, which later became one of the principal agricultural belts of the county. The first settlers in this region were James McClure, James McClure, Jr., and Henry Wyckoff, who came in 1853. The McClures started a blacksmith shop, and, nearby, Wyckoff opened a small store on what is now Court Street. That was the beginning of Yolo City, which continued to grow in importance until 1861, when a post office was established there under the name of Woodland.

A pioneer experiment in agriculture was begun there as early as 1856 by the diversion of water from Cache Creek, and by 1862 Woodland had become an important agricultural center. In that year the people voted to make it the county seat in place of Washington. Today, a series of canals augments the natural outlet of Cache Creek, and about 100,000 acres of land are under irrigation. In the midst of this prosperous rural section Woodland has become a thriving city.

Woodland was also a center of pioneer cultural

Opera House, Woodland

development. Schools were established in the late 1850's, and in 1860 Hesperian College was located there by the Christian Church. Typical of the many small denominational colleges founded throughout northern California during the 1860's and the 1870's, Hesperian College performed a worthy pioneer work in higher education for over 35 years. Modern high schools and universities began to take the place of the small colleges in the latter part of the nineteenth century, and, in 1896, the trustees of Hesperian College deeded land and buildings to the new union high school district of Woodland. The college stood on Bush Street between First and College streets.

Woodland retains a number of interesting brick business buildings from earlier days. Among these are the Woodland Opera House, opened in 1891 to replace an earlier building, on the west side of Second Street north of Main, and the Julian Hotel, built in 1893, at the northeast corner of Second and Main streets.

Davisville

Where the little town of Davisville grew up in the late 1860's and where the University of California at Davis now draws thousands of students annually, Jerome C. Davis settled in the early 1850's while the entire district was not yet broken up. The State Agricultural Report of 1856 says that Davis had 8,000 acres of land, 1,000 of which were enclosed, and that he was irrigating a portion of the ranch by pumping water from Putah Creek with a steam engine. Even that early he had a large peach orchard and several thousand

bearing grapevines, and 400 acres of wheat and barley, as well as many horses, cattle, and sheep. By 1858 he had 21 miles of fences. In 1864 his ranch totaled approximately 13,000 acres, more than 8,000 of which were fenced.

William Dresbach leased the old Davis home in 1867 and made it into a hotel, which he called the Yolo House. As a settlement began to grow up, Dresbach named it Davisville. With the advent of the railroad the place became a thriving grain shipping point. In 1868, however, when a branch of the Central Pacific Railroad was extended northward to Marysville, Davisville began to decline as a trade center. Its decline was further hastened when the Vaca Valley Railroad was constructed to Madison in 1875.

The rich farming lands that surrounded Davisville continued to be developed, however, and in 1905 the University Farm was established by an act of the state legislature. The bill had been prepared and submitted by Peter J. Shields in 1900. The first buildings were erected there in 1907, the same year that the name of the Davisville post office was shortened to the present Davis. The first courses for adult farmers were given in the autumn of 1908, and the following January the farm school for young men and boys was opened. In 1922 it was officially organized as a branch of the College of Agriculture of the University of California at Berkeley. Even this early there began a gradual shift in the educational mission of the school. More and more courses not directly related to agriculture were offered, and finally, in 1951, these were combined into the College of Letters and Science. In 1959 Davis was authorized as a general campus of the University of California, and a graduate division was established in 1961.

SOURCES

Bryant, Edwin. *What I Saw in California.* D. Appleton & Co., New York, 1848, 1849.
Buffum, E. Gould. *Six Months in the Gold Mines.* Lea & Blanchard, Philadelphia, 1850.
Clyman, James. "James Clyman, His Diaries and Reminiscences," ed. Charles L. Camp. *California Historical Society Quarterly,* V, No. 2 (June 1926), 109–38.
Gilbert, Frank T. *The Illustrated Atlas and History of Yolo County, California.* De Pue & Co., San Francisco, 1879.
Gregory, Tom. *History of Yolo County, California, with Biographical Sketches.* Historic Record Co., Los Angeles, 1913.
Hill, Joseph J. "Ewing Young in the Fur Trade of the Far Southwest, 1822–1834." *Oregon Historical Society Quarterly,* XXIV, No. 1 (March 1923), 1–35.
History of Yolo County, California, Its Resources and Its People. William O. Russell, ed. Nelle S. Coil, historian, Woodland, 1940.
Jones, David Rhys. "Pre-Pioneer Pathfinders, California–Oregon Trail, 1826–1846." *Motor Land,* XXIX, Nos. 4–5 (October–November, 1931).
Kroeber, Alfred Louis. "California Place Names of Indian Origin," *University of California Publications in American Archaeology and Ethnology,* XII, No. 2 (1916–17).
McGowan, Joseph A. *History of the Sacramento Valley.* 3 vols. Lewis Historical Publishing Co., New York, 1961.
Ware, E. B. *History of the Disciples of Christ in California.* F. W. Cooke, Healdsburg, 1916.
Western Shore Gazetteer and Commercial Directory for the State of California . . . Yolo County. C. P. Sprague & H. W. Atwell, Woodland, 1870.

Yuba County

YUBA COUNTY was one of the original 27 counties. (Yuba is said by some authorities to have been the name of a tribe of Maidu Indians, the Yu-ba, who lived on the banks of the Feather River.) Marysville has been the only county seat.

Yuba Trails

Before the arrival of the white man in the territory of what is now Yuba County, its dim trails were trodden only by wild animals and by the Maidu Indians of the tribe of Yu-ba. Frémont, in his *Memoirs*, describes their villages as he saw them in 1846:

"We traveled across the valley plain, and in about sixteen miles reached Feather River, at twenty miles from its junction with the Sacramento, near the mouth of the Yuba, so called from a village of Indians who live on it. The Indians aided us across the river with canoes and small rafts. Extending along the bank in front of the village was a range of wicker cribs, about twelve feet high, partly filled with what is there the Indians' staff of life, acorns. A collection of huts, shaped like bee-hives, with naked Indians sunning themselves on the tops, and these acorn cribs, are the prominent objects in an Indian village." Powers, in his *Tribes of California*, also ascribes the name Yuba to this Indian tribe.

Perhaps the first white man to cross the plains and streams of Yuba County was Gabriel Moraga, who traversed this region in 1808, probably proceeding as far north as the present Nevada County. Some say that the name Yuba is a corruption of the Spanish word *uba*, or *uva*, meaning "grapes," and was given to the river by this expedition on account of the wild grapes which grew luxuriantly along its banks.

Hudson's Bay Company trappers occasionally crossed the region during the years 1830–41, on hunting and trapping expeditions, and in the 1840's a branch of the old California emigrant trail crossed the High Sierra through Donner Pass and followed down the mountains to Johnson's Rancho, an outpost of civilization at that time, located on the Bear River about three miles east of where Wheatland now stands.

Marysville

A large portion of what is now Yuba County became a part of the princely domain of Captain John A. Sutter after 1841, but, since the lands included on his map covered a much larger area than the Mexican laws allowed, he resorted to the practice of subletting parts of his estate to other settlers. Some of these farms were in what are now Sutter and Placer counties, while others lay within the present boundaries of Yuba County.

The land on which the town of Marysville was later founded was located on that part of Sutter's Ranch which was leased in the fall of 1842 to Theodore Cordua, a Prussian, for a period of 19 years. Cordua made it a stock ranch and in 1842–43 built an adobe dwelling house, with a trading room and outbuildings, at what is now the foot of D Street in Marysville.

Cordua, "a fat, jolly, whist-loving man, popular with everybody," called his settlement "New Mecklenburg," after his native land, but his neighbors called it Cordua's Ranch. It stood on the California–Oregon Trail through the Sacramento Valley, and by 1846 travel over this route from Oregon had become so extensive that Cordua's adobe became an important way station and trading post for hunters, emigrants, and, later, miners. The old adobe with its thick walls, seemingly built to withstand a siege, was destroyed by fire in 1851.

There was an Indian village on Cordua's Ranch at the point where the railroad now crosses the Yuba River. Cordua made friends with these Indians and they worked the ranch and herded sheep for him.

In 1844, Cordua obtained a grant of seven leagues of land from the Mexican government north of the Yuba River in what is now Yuba County, but not included in his former lease from Sutter.

Charles Covillaud, a native of France and a former employee of Cordua, purchased a half-share in the ranch at New Mecklenburg in 1848, and in January 1849, the other half was sold to

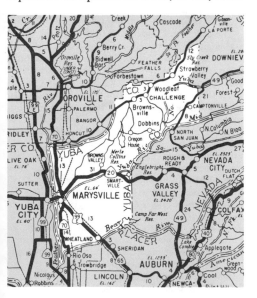

two brothers-in-law of Covillaud's wife, Michael C. Nye, who married Mrs. Harriet Murphy Pike, a survivor of the Donner party tragedy, and William Foster, also a member of the Donner party and husband of Sarah Murphy. For a time it was known as Nye's Ranch. Nye and Foster sold out to Covillaud in September 1849, and in October Covillaud in turn sold all but one-fourth to José Manuel Ramírez, John Sampson, and Theodore Sicard. Discovery of gold at Coloma in 1848 had brought a period of great development to the region, and a town was laid out in January 1850. Covillaud's wife, formerly Mary Murphy, another member of the Donner party, received the honor of having the new town named for her, Marysville.

Marysville became the actual head of navigation on the Feather River and a center of trade for the northern mines. Its location gave it a decided superiority over all other candidates for such a position on the river, above and below. The distance to the mines, north and east, was not great, and cargoes from the river boats could be transported readily by pack-mule trains to the outlying goldfields. These proved to be rich producers, and as a result Marysville experienced a phenomenal growth from the start.

Freight and passenger boats landed at a point adjoining the old plaza, on Front between D and E streets. Today the river, held in leash by stone levees, actually flows above the city streets, but in the early days the plaza looked down upon the stream and its rich bottom lands, which were originally covered with groves of cottonwood,

Old Courthouse, Marysville

willow, and sycamore, but which soon became dotted with the homes and orchards and vineyards of early settlers. Hydraulic mining, however, changed the face of the entire countryside, burying homes and settlements beneath acres of debris, raising the bed of the river 70 feet or more, and necessitating the construction of miles of levees. On the tailings today grow thrifty peach orchards, and new farmhouses have replaced the old ones.

A Chinese temple, one of the oldest in the state and the only one in the nation erected to the water god Bok Kai, still stands on Front Street near E, but no longer does it watch the passing of ships upon the river as it did in the stirring days of the 1850's. The roof of this sturdy old brick shrine is now about on a level with the dike, which keeps the river from washing the whole structure down to the sea. It is still used by worshipers.

Among Marysville's many interesting old houses is the José M. Ramírez residence at 220 Fifth Street between B and C. Of elaborate construction, with marble basement and Gothic windows, it is known locally as "The Castle." It later became the home of W. T. Ellis, father of the Marysville levee system. Beautiful Ellis Lake in downtown Marysville is named for him.

The brick house at 630 D Street, said to have been built by Stephen J. Field, young New York lawyer and son of a Connecticut minister, who came to Marysville in 1849, still serves as a private dwelling. Field worked with John A. Sutter, Charles J. Covillaud, José M. Ramírez, Theodore Cordua, Theodore Sicard, John Sampson, and others in laying out the town of Marysville and organizing the county. He purchased 200 lots within the prospective city and named the first streets after his associates, Covillaud, Ramírez, Sicard, and Sampson. Later he became the first alcalde of the town, a state legislator, and a Justice of the California Supreme Court. In 1863, during Lincoln's administration, Field was appointed a Justice of the United States Supreme Court, a position he held until 1897.

The old Aaron home at 704 D Street was willed to the City of Marysville and opened as the Mary Aaron Memorial Museum in 1960. It was built about 1856 by Warren Miller and had been in the Aaron family since 1868.

Up to the early 1960's, a large number of historic buildings in the business district, interestingly designed and sturdily constructed of brick or stone in the 1850's and 1860's, made Marysville one of the most fascinating towns dating from the early American period in California. Since then, however, most of these have fallen victim, one by one, to the wrecker's ball and the bulldozer in the process of urban redevelopment. The former City Hall, built in 1854, and the firehouse of 1857 were razed in 1961. Many business buildings fell in 1964, including the structure in which the large Macy's department store chain was founded. In the same year the former Yuba County Courthouse, its three towers looming castle-like above solid brick walls, was replaced by a modern bank building.

The courthouse was built in 1855–56 at Sixth and D streets.

Of Marysville's earliest churches, only St. Joseph's Catholic Church, built in 1855 at Seventh and C streets, remains. From 1861 to 1868 it served as headquarters for Bishop Eugene O'Connell of the Vicariate Apostolic of Marysville, which later became the Diocese of Grass Valley and finally the Diocese of Sacramento. The Episcopal church at Fifth and E streets, constructed of brick in Norman Gothic style, was torn down in 1940. The old brick Presbyterian church, constructed in 1860 at Fifth and D streets, met a similar fate in 1950.

Among the graves of pioneers in the Marysville Cemetery is that of Mary Murphy Covillaud and that of Father Florian Schwenninger, a Tyrolean-born Benedictine monk, who labored heroically in the churches of the mining camps during the gold rush. Particularly known for his work at Sawyer's Bar in Siskiyou County, he spent his last years, 1866–68, at St. Joseph's Church in Marysville.

Nearby Beale Air Force Base was established as Camp Beale in 1942. It was named for Edward Fitzgerald Beale, a prominent figure in California history.

Johnson's Rancho

Pablo Gutiérrez, an employee of Captain Sutter, received a grant of five leagues of land on the north side of Bear River in 1844. Here he built an adobe house at a point later called Johnson's Crossing, about three miles east of present Wheatland.

Gutiérrez was killed late in 1844, and his grant and cattle were sold at auction by Captain Sutter, magistrate of the region. The land was purchased for $150 by William Johnson and Sebastian Kayser, Johnson taking the eastern half and Kayser the western half. Just below the crossing they built an adobe house.

This place came to be known as Johnson's Rancho (*SRL 493*), on which Wheatland was later located, and was the first settlement reached by the Argonauts who crossed the Sierra over that branch of the California Trail which went through Donner Pass and down the ridge north of Bear River into Yuba County. Here many footsore emigrants rested and obtained supplies. Among them were the seven members of the Donner party who succeeded in getting over the mountains in the winter of 1846–47, finally reaching Johnson's Rancho, where they sought aid for those imprisoned at snowbound Donner Lake.

Johnson was the first husband of Mary Murphy of the Donner party, who later married Charles Covillaud.

Camp Far West

Camp Far West was established up river from Johnson's Rancho by the United States government in 1849 for the protection of American settlers in the Yuba region. Two companies of soldiers were stationed there under command of Captain Hannibal Day, but the post was abandoned in 1852.

No trace of the old log fort, barracks, and officers' quarters remains today, but the site, about four miles east of Wheatland, has been marked by the Native Sons of the Golden West.

Gold Bars on the Yuba

The first prospectors in the Sierra worked along the rivers and especially on the sand bars, which were rich in gold. Like other gold-bearing streams, the Yuba River above Marysville was dotted thickly with river-bar towns by 1850, a camp to every one or two miles. According to some authorities Jonas Spect was the first to find gold in the county. His discovery was made on June 2, 1848, at a place later known as Rose's Bar, located 18 miles east of Marysville. Almost simultaneously with Spect's discovery at Rose's Bar, Michael Nye and William Foster found pay gravel on Dry Creek near its junction with the Yuba.

In the fall of 1848 John Rose and William J. Reynolds opened a store at Rose's Bar, so called because Rose did the purchasing of goods at Sacramento. The partners also supplied the miners with fresh beef and other farm products brought from their ranch south of Marysville. In the spring of 1849 Rose's Bar was so overcrowded with miners that at a meeting called for the purpose it was decided to limit claims to 100 feet square per man. By 1850, 2,000 men were at work on this bar alone.

The floods of 1850 drove the miners away from the sand bars to higher ground, where more gold was uncovered. Gatesville, or Sucker Flat (virtually an extension of Rose's Bar away from the river), grew up at this time and had developed into a town of some importance by the time the bars along the river became depleted of their gold. Squaw Creek, another rich locality, enjoyed its brief heyday in common with such neighboring camps as Cordua, Sawmill, Lander's, and Kennebec bars. Opposite Lander's Bar near the mouth of Deer Creek was Malay Camp, worked by miners from the Malay Peninsula.

The richest of all the Yuba River bars was Parks' Bar, located two or three miles west of Rose's Bar. To this location came David Parks with his wife and children on September 8, 1848. Since a man with a family was very unusual in the earliest camps, the place was named in his honor. Parks' Bar, which had become a populous camp by 1849, reached the height of its prosperity in 1852, when it rivaled Marysville for a time. When gold along the river bars became worked out, in 1855, decline set in, and Parks', as well as its neighbors, Barton's and Union bars, was soon depopulated.

Near Parks' Bar was Sicard's Bar, where Theodore Sicard was the first to find "color." The name Sicard Flat was given to the town that grew up about a mile back from the river and is still perpetuated in the Sicard Flat School District with its handful of scattered ranch houses. Other bars still farther up the river were the National, Negro, Missouri No. 1, and Horse bars.

The first mining camp of importance above Marysville was Swiss Bar, opposite Sand Flat, nine miles up the river. Little mining was done there before 1850, and the place was never the equal of Long Bar, a little farther up the river. Long Bar, in addition to being the longest bar on the Yuba, also boasted the longest period of success. It was occupied as early as October 1848, and the first organized body of miners to come to California from the outside stopped there in November. By 1851 a ferry boat was plying between Long Bar and Kennebec Bar a few miles below. A post office called Dry Creek was established in 1854, but the name was changed to Long Bar in 1858, and the office was discontinued in 1864. Above Long Bar was Chimney Hill, and at the mouth of Dry Creek was Owsley's Bar, named after a Dr. Owsley, who mined there in early days.

Hydraulic mining, after 1857, slowly destroyed the old river bars and their camps along the Yuba. They became buried cities, lying no less than 70 feet beneath the debris washed down from the titanic diggings in the Sierra. The once famous Rose's and Parks' bars, like all their neighbors, were simply obliterated. Today the names of a few of the more important remain as school districts or townships, such as Foster's Bar Township, Rose Bar Township, Parks' Bar Township, and Long Bar Township.

Gold still lies in the bed of the Yuba River, and in later years extensive dredging activities took out vast sums from the old tailings. In 1905 the Yuba Consolidated Goldfields began operations nine miles east of Marysville, with a capital of $12,500,000. The towns of Marigold and Hammonton, the latter named after Wendell P. Hammon, moving spirit of the company, grew up, direct descendants of the mining camps of the 1850's. During the depression of the 1930's the field was taken over by men, otherwise unemployed, who were learning to wield pan and rocker in approved pioneer style. On Parks' Bar alone, from 50 to 100 people were mining by these primitive methods in the summer of 1932.

"Speculative Cities"

Population increased so rapidly in the fall of 1849 and in 1850 that land speculators saw possibilities of accumulating wealth by laying out cities on paper. Few mining camps had been established in the mountains before the winter of 1850, but there were a large number of flourishing towns in the foothills, settlements entirely dependent on the continuance of profitable gold diggings. In the valley, even where there was no gold, prospective cities of vaunted magnificence were laid out. Interested promoters, "with a flourish of oratorical and newspaper trumpets," proclaimed the advantages of their respective cities, both as places of residence and as centers of business and trade. Particularly did those places tributary to the mines witness "a high degree of the spirit of venture and speculation that was so noticeable in the mining camps."

Delano says of these pioneer real estate booms: "There seemed to be a speculative mania spreading over the land, and scores of new towns were heard of which were never known, only the puffs of newspapers, the stakes which marked the size of lots, and the nicely drawn plot of the surveyor." Delano spoke from experience, for he took part in some of the speculation, buying lots in Marysville and losing half of his earnings in the operation. In an effort to recoup his losses he and a friend laid out a town on the Feather River 20 miles north of Marysville, but they were unable to attract population to their town.

Yuba County boasted about eight of these "speculative cities": Marysville, Eliza, Linda, Oakland, El Dorado, Plumas City, Featherton, and Kearney (Kearny). Of all these aspiring towns, Marysville was the only one to survive and to become a thriving city. Nevertheless, at first there were sufficient doubts and misgivings as to the future of Marysville to cause some capitalists to put their money into other less fortunate ventures.

Eliza, some three miles below Marysville, proved to be one of the will-o'-the-wisps followed for a time by early speculators. Several stores and houses were built there in the spring of 1850, but by summer it was evident that the place could not rival Marysville, and Eliza soon ceased to exist.

Linda, on the south bank of the Yuba River above Marysville, lasted a little longer than Eliza, its allotted span being about two years. Arrival of the little steamer *Linda* at the site was the occasion for the establishment of the town, but the hope that Linda would become the head of navigation and a rival of Marysville was never realized. The site is now buried more than 30 feet beneath the tailings washed down from the hydraulic mines in the hills, and the only reminder of this would-be city is the modern Marysville suburb called Linda.

Of the other "speculative cities" in Yuba County, none of which existed for very long, Plumas City was situated at the mouth of Reed's Creek; El Dorado City, just across from Sutter's Hock Farm; Kearney (named in honor of General Stephen W. Kearny), on Bear River on Johnson's Rancho; Featherton, on the Feather River at the mouth of Honcut Creek; and Oakland, between Featherton and Marysville.

Smartsville

The first building at Smartsville (*SRL 321*) was a hotel built in the spring of 1856 by a Mr. Smart. The Catholic church, first organized at Rose's Bar by Father Peter Magagnotto, C.P., in 1852, was erected at Smartsville in 1861. This edifice was burned in 1870, but another took its place the following year, and still stands at Main and O'Brien streets. As the present-day traveler approaches the town, the most conspicuous feature of the landscape is still its church, which stands like a faithful guardian among the handful of old homes half-hidden among trees. The old frame Masonic Temple on O'Brien Street, moved to Smartsville from Rose's Bar, is still in use. The post office designation, strangely, has always been Smartville.

Remains of the rich mines developed at Smartsville in the late 1850's, as well as scars of the hydraulic operations of the 1860's and 1870's, may still be seen in the surrounding hills. By 1878 the Excelsior Company at Smartsville had washed eight million cubic yards of detritus into the Yuba River, while ten times that amount remained in the company's claims when hydraulic activities ceased in 1883.

To the north of Smartsville is a great gash in the hillside, the site of the once populous mining camp of Sucker Flat.

The Empire Ranch Station

In the early 1850's, the period of stagecoach and "six-in-hand," before the advent of railroads, the California Stage Company carried passengers from one end of the state to the other. One of the many stations used by this company was maintained on the Empire Ranch near the town of Smartsville, where meals were served and horses changed. The old Empire Ranch Station stood for over a century. It was one of the last remaining stations used by the California Stage Company. Now only a pile of debris marks the site, on the road to Beale Air Force Base just south of Smartsville and a stone's throw from Highway 20. The barn, built in 1852 with rough hand-hewn timbers held together by wooden pegs, still stands across the road from the site of the station. Halfway up the hill, hidden among the oaks on the right side of the road, is a neglected graveyard. Beyond this graveyard on the opposite side is another cemetery that has seen more recent use.

In 1849 a Mr. Berry and his wife built a log cabin on the site of the later Empire Ranch Station, and by 1851 this location had become the rallying point of miners for miles around. Thomas Mooney and Michael Riley bought the place that year and established a trading post and hotel there. Sunday was a gala day at the Empire Ranch, when hundreds of miners gathered in a convivial mood for sports and other pleasures.

Mooney Flat, nearby in Nevada County, was named for Thomas Mooney. Other early-day inns in the vicinity were the Union House on the county line east of Empire Ranch, and Round Tent and Cabbage Patch on the Sacramento–Grass Valley road by way of Spenceville. At Round Tent a circular tent was set up in 1851 by a Mr. Baker, and the name was retained when a more substantial structure was erected later.

Empire Ranch Stage Station, near Smartsville

Timbuctoo

Timbuctoo (*SRL 320*), also a neighbor of Smartsville, has only one of its original buildings left—the old Wells Fargo Express Office. Solidly built of locally manufactured brick, it retains the heavy iron doors and shutters which once protected its precious contents from fire and robbery. Several million dollars' worth of gold dust passed through its doors in the gold days. On the building is a placard, painted in 1859 and still legible, which indicates that the place served as a general merchandise store as well as an agency for Wells Fargo and Company. A bronze marker on the building reads:

"Old Wells Fargo Office & Stewart Bros. Store (1855). Restored and dedicated to the memory of the pioneer men and women of Timbuctoo, May 10, 1928, by Marysville Parlour No. 6, N.S.G.W. Presented by Wells Fargo Bank and Union Trust Co., San Francisco." The building has since suffered heavy damage from vandalism. The stone foundations of other buildings long since destroyed by fire, aged fig and locust trees, and an old well may be seen near the road—reminders of the vanished hopes of Timbuctoo.

The first mining in this region was done as early as 1850 in the ravines nearby, one of which was named Timbuctoo after a Negro from Africa who was one of the first miners in the locality. The town of Timbuctoo was started in 1855. During the period when hydraulic mining flourished, it was the largest town in the eastern part of Yuba County, with a total population of 1,200 at the height of its prosperity. It contained a church and a theater, as well as the usual saloons, stores, and hotels. The old building that marks the site of the town is northwest of Smartsville and just north of Highway 20, from which it is visible and accessible.

Gold Camps on Honcut Creek

Honcut Creek and its tributaries, crowded with gold-seekers during the 1850's and 1860's, are today deserted except for a few ranches and country stores. One of the many camps there was Natchez, on the Natchez branch of the Honcut, so named because of its fancied resemblance to Natchez, Mississippi. A "Major" Brown came to the locality alone in 1850, carrying with him a store of blankets and trinkets with which to win the favor of the Indians. He found the diggings in the vicinity to be very rich. These he guarded jealously, and with the aid of his Indians very soon accumulated a considerable fortune.

The story goes that a prospector from below arrived on the scene. The stranger asked Brown how far his claim extended. In reply "the Major took up his rifle and pointing it upstream calmly remarked: 'Up this way as far as she will carry a bullet,' and pointing down stream, 'down this way about the same distance.' The stranger, although he thought it was a pretty large claim, concluded not to express his opinion." It was not long, however, before "Major" Brown was surrounded by miners claiming equality with himself, and by 1851 the camp of Natchez had sprung

Wells Fargo Express Office & Stewart Bros. Store, Timbuctoo

up, reaching the height of its prosperity in 1852 and 1853. For a few years mining lagged in the district, but a revival of activities took place in 1858. This proved short-lived, and after 1860 steady decline set in.

Some of the ravines mined in the vicinity of Natchez were Brown's, Steward's, Grub, Slug, Jackass, Jennie, Hovey, and Dicksburg.

James H. Hanson came to the site of Hansonville, now Rackerby, on Hansonville Creek 28 miles northeast of Marysville in 1851, and within a year a town of about 1,000 miners, with eight hotels and seven stores, had grown up. Scarcely a trace of the old town remains today.

Brown's Valley

On the old road to Downieville, 13 miles northeast of Marysville and one mile north of Highway 20, is Brown's Valley. An early settler named Brown, who came to this spot in 1850, discovered gold near a huge boulder adjoining the temporary camp he had set up. After taking out over $12,000 in quartz, Brown "was satisfied to retire." Not long after his discovery four Frenchmen developed the famous Jefferson Mine in the vicinity; other rich discoveries, among them the Flag, the Donnebrouge (Donnebroge), the Pennsylvania, and the Sweet Vengeance mines, followed rapidly. One of the first stamp mills to be erected in California was put up at the Sweet Vengeance Mine by a French company, which purchased the mine from Spaniards who had been milling the ore by means of an arrastra on Little Creek.

Ruins of some of the old mills still rise above the shafts of once prosperous mines, and within the town a stone store is another vivid reminder of the past. It is difficult to realize that the present hamlet once possessed five hotels, 24 saloons, and numerous stores. The Central Hotel remained standing into the 1950's. Just north of Brown's Valley was Prairie Diggings, no trace of which is left today. Mining began there in 1854, the rich surface diggings of the locality attracting many who later became residents of the City of Marysville.

Along the old Marysville–Downieville road the sites of many taverns and stage stations are passed. Eight miles from Marysville was Adriance's Ranch, on the north bank of the Yuba River just west of Swiss Bar. North of Brown's Valley, in rapid succession, are the sites of the Galena House (14 miles from Marysville), the Empire House, the Peoria House, the Sixteen Mile House, the Yuba County House, the Stanfield House, the Abbott House, the Martin House, the Phillips' House, and several others, including the Zinc House, Bowers' Place, and the Comstock Place. The Peoria House was conducted by Captain Thomas Phillips. The name is retained in the Peoria Cemetery, on Peoria Road about five miles north of Brown's Valley, in which some members of the Phillips family lie buried. The present community of Stanfield Hill, about nine miles northeast of Brown's Valley, stands on the site of the house opened up in 1852 by a man named Stanfield. The Abbott House was erected by John M. Abbott in the early 1850's at the

Central Hotel, Brown's Valley

Dry Creek crossing, and was at first known as Oak Grove House. Abbott was one of the first growers of fruit in this section.

The Oregon House

Where the branch turnpike to La Porte turned north from the Downieville Trail, 24 miles northeast of Marysville, the Oregon House was erected in 1852. It became one of the most popular of the several hostelries along that trail, and many a traveler in search of gold found rest and entertainment awaiting him within its hospitable doors. In January 1853, on the anniversary of the Battle of New Orleans, a grand party was given in the Oregon House, the first in that section of the Sierra foothills. There were 250 tickets sold and 18 ladies present, a good showing for those days. The original Oregon House was destroyed by fire many years ago, but the name is preserved in a country post office.

The Downieville Trail continued east from the Oregon House and thence northeast to Camptonville by way of Indiana Ranch and Foster's Bar, while the branch turnpike went north through Frenchtown, at one time the center of trade for surrounding mines and lumber mills. Only a few grass-grown ruins mark the place where the buildings of Frenchtown, among them two hotels, formerly stood.

North of Frenchtown on the west side of Dry Creek is the site of the Jefferson House, erected in 1852 by James Evans. This building disappeared many years ago.

Indiana Ranch and Greenville

The Downieville Trail and, later, the first wagon road from the Oregon House to Camptonville went by way of Foster's Bar, passing through Indiana Ranch and the town of Greenville. Beyond the Oregon House several stopping places broke the loneliness of the old trail, among them the California House and the Keystone House, the latter a large hotel with a racetrack attached. Indiana Ranch was at one time a thriving town. It was first settled in 1851 by the Page brothers from Indiana, Peter Labadie, and John Tolles, and the settlement was called Indiana Creek or Tolles' New Diggins. Tolles and Labadie kept the first hotels in the place. After 1860 mining declined in the vicinity, and although rich pockets have been found from time to time, not one of them has proved lasting.

One and one-half miles northeast of Indiana Ranch stood the Maple Springs House, erected in 1852, and afterward sold to Peter Labadie, when it became known also as Labadie's. The Maple Springs House continued to serve as a hotel until 1860, when travel became diverted over a different route by the building of the Atchison and Rice Turnpike. Bennett's Ranch was an early settlement on the flat just below Labadie's. Additional public houses were soon established on the new road: Eich's, the New York Star, Oldfield's, and the Fountain House. The last place, opened up in 1860 by Robert Johnston, ceased to be a public house in 1878.

Greenville, now a quiet mountain community northwest of Bullards Bar Dam on Oregon Hill Road, was originally known as Oregon Hill. Gold was first found there in 1850, but the place did not become prosperous until a ditch was constructed to bring water to the diggings. The company responsible for the building of this ditch was composed of nine members, and in order to let everyone know that it was no "one-horse" affair that they were putting in, they named it the Nine-Horse Ditch.

Halfway between Greenville and Foster's Bar was Stroud's, or the Milk Ranch, a popular stopping place in the 1850's, especially noted for its balls and gay hospitality.

Brownsville and Northeastern Yuba County

Brownsville, located on what was known in early days as the Central Turnpike to La Porte, was named after I. E. Brown, who erected a sawmill in the vicinity in 1851. For a decade or more a number of sawmills and lumbering camps, as well as mining camps, existed in the surrounding country. Among these were the Sharon Valley Mills, two miles northeast, completed in 1853 by L. T. Crane; the Challenge Mills, a mile farther northeast, erected in 1856; and the Washington (1851–63) and Page (1852–60) mills, located on Dry Creek, south of Challenge.

Brownsville was a "temperance town" and in 1878 became something of an educational center with the establishment there of the Knoxdale Institute by Martin Knox and his wife, with Professor E. K. Hill acting as principal. Knox, in partnership with P. E. Weeks, had purchased Brown's mill in 1852 and conducted the business until 1857. In 1855 they built a large hotel. This was subsequently burned but was replaced by another structure in 1866.

South of the Challenge Mills on the branch turnpike was the New York House, established by the same men who owned the New York Ranch north of Brownsville on the road to Forbestown. North and northeast from Challenge Mills to La Porte a number of stage stations were passed, all important stopping places on the way to the gold mines of northwestern Sierra County and Plumas County.

Woodville, now Woodleaf, just south of the present Butte County line, was formerly known as Barker's Ranch, or the Barker House, first settled in 1850 by Charles Barker. James Wood bought the place in 1858 and erected the beautiful two-story brick hotel, long known as the Woodville House, which still stands by the road.

Leaving Woodleaf behind, the motorist of today passes the site of Oroliva, a mile to the northeast in Butte County. Going through Clipper Mills one again enters Yuba County, passing the site of Barton's House before reaching Strawberry Valley, known to the Indians as "Pomingo." The origin of the present name of Strawberry Valley is uncertain. Some contend that the presence of numerous beds of wild strawberries gave rise to the name, while others say that it was the combination of the names of two early settlers, Straw and Berry. Both are explanations heard also in other localities where this name is found.

Once in the midst of a large mining area, the Strawberry Valley district included the rich diggings on Deadwood Creek, Kentucky Gulch, Rich Gulch, and Whiskey Gulch. The town of Strawberry Valley became a lively center of trade for the surrounding mines, and in the late 1850's its main street was lined with stores, shops, saloons, and dwellings, the leading hostelry being the Columbus Hotel, still standing with its old well. The buildings on one side of this street were originally in Butte County while those on the opposite side were located in Yuba County, but in 1860 the legislature moved the county line a short distance north. All that is left of the town today is now in Yuba County.

Proceeding up the ridge from Strawberry Val-

Woodville House, Woodleaf

ley, the early-day traveler passed in turn the Seneca House, the Union Hotel, Eagleville, and the North Star House.

Dobbins' Ranch

Located in the lovely foothill valley of Dobbins' Creek, Dobbins' Ranch was first settled in 1849 by William M. and Mark D. Dobbins. By 1850 it had become the terminus of the stage-carried express business of Langton's Pioneer Express. From that point the express had to be transported over the mountains to Downieville on muleback. Turnpikes ultimately took the place of the narrow pack trails, and in 1860 Atchison and Rice, with others, constructed a road to Downieville by way of Dobbins' Ranch, Bullard's Bar, and Camptonville, a course followed today by a good county road.

Dobbins' Ranch exchanged hands several times from 1855 to 1862, when it came into the possession of Joseph Merriam. The pioneer store which still stands in Dobbins, as it is called today, was opened in 1867 by William Slingsby and Dan Gattens, who formed a partnership, maintaining a pack train on the Downieville Trail continuously for a number of years, furnishing the surrounding country with supplies, and taking an active part in community affairs.

High on the ridge halfway between Dobbins' Ranch and Bullard's Bar there stood for many years the Mountain Cottage House, built at the Five Mile Ranch by Colonel Prentice, government Indian Agent in charge of the 4,000 or 5,000 Yuba Indians.

Three miles southwest of Dobbins is the site of the Kentucky Ranch. Continuing west is the site of the next stopping place on the old stage road, the Golden Ball, two miles south of the Oregon House, which was on the Downieville Trail. Where the road crossed Dry Creek was the Virginia Ranch, two miles south of the Abbott House, also on the Downieville Trail. The Virginia Ranch was settled in 1850 by J. A. Paxton, who built a hotel there and kept a trading post. After Peter Rice bought the place in 1859, it ceased to be a public house.

The Gold Bars of the North Yuba River

The early miners of northeastern Yuba County had a wild and rugged country to contend with. Carl I. Wheat, in a note to the De Long Journals, describes this section as follows: "The map of Northeastern Yuba County gives no hint of the wildly broken nature of the terrain. The general contour of the ridges suggests an old plateau, slightly tilted to the west, greatly cut away by erosion during recent geologic times. The Yuba River and its many branches have cut deeply into this old plateau, its gorges being from five hundred to over a thousand feet in depth. Oregon Creek canyon just south of Camptonville falls away on a grand scale. The 'bars' were located along the rivers, with mountains towering up on both sides. The other towns and 'diggins' were generally located on or near the tops of the highest ridges, where the miners discovered the rich, gold-bearing gravels left by the rivers of earlier geologic ages. To one familiar with this broken terrain, De Long's active journeyings to and fro, on foot and on muleback, take on a new significance. It is a heavily wooded country, and to become lost was, and is, very easy, if one were to leave the beaten paths. . . .

"The very names of many of the populous mining camps of these wild ridges have been lost, and in other localities only a lone cabin or an ancient apple tree remains to recall the teeming life of the early 'fifties,' for the pines have grown up even over the burying places of the dead, and Nature has hastened to take back her own."

This region, now in solitude, was once alive with hard-working miners. It is said that in 1849 and the early 1850's miners along the Yuba River could send a message by word of mouth all the way from Downieville to Marysville, so numerous were the camps along the river's course.

The most famous of the bars along the North Yuba River were Foster's Bar and Bullard's Bar. Early in 1849 William M. Foster, a survivor of the Donner party tragedy, mined on the west bank of the river between the mouths of Willow and Mill creeks, where he erected a store. The place soon became so crowded with gold seekers that it was necessary to limit claims to 30 feet in width along the riverbank, although a claim could extend up the hill as far as desired. Foster's Bar cast 1,500 votes in 1850 and was known as the roughest and toughest spot on the Yuba. The principal hotel, spoken of in the De Long Journals as "that Hell of bedbugs," was the El Dorado. Not even the site of Foster's Bar can be seen today, for it is covered by water backed up by the dam at Bullard's Bar to a depth of more than 100 feet.

Bullard's Bar, three-quarters of a mile below Foster's Bar, was named after one of its pioneer miners, a Dr. Bullard, who had been shipwrecked off the coast of California while on his way from Brooklyn, New York, to the Sandwich Islands. As early as 1850 a bridge was built at Bullard's Bar, but it was washed away by the next winter's rains. Each succeeding bridge suffered a similar fate until 1858, when George Mix built a substantial structure at a cost of $7,000 which stood until carried away by the great flood of 1862. Subsequently a bridge was erected a short distance up the river, which was later purchased by John Ramm, of Ramm's Ranch. In 1875 this bridge likewise was washed away. Ramm soon built another at a cost of $15,000, which he continued to operate as a toll bridge until it was purchased by the county shortly before the beginning of the twentieth century.

Bullard's Bar and its bridges are no more. In their place is the immense Bullards Bar Dam, which impounds 12,000 acre-feet of water to operate generators in a powerhouse at the base of the structure.

Among the numerous camps below Bullard's Bar were the following: Kanaka Bar, first worked by Hawaiians; Winslow Bar, an important place in the 1850's, named after Captain Winslow, who brought the first shipload of Chinese to California and worked them there; English Bar, which proved unprofitable to the Englishmen who mined it but brought $90,000 in gold to a man named Wilkins, who purchased the ground in 1851; Clingman's Point; Negro Bar; Missouri Bar; Condemned Bar; and Frenchman's Bar.

Even more numerous were the camps above Bullard's Bar. Between Bullard's Bar and Foster's Bar on the opposite side of the river was a small location called Ferry Bar, probably named after the crude ferry used on the river at this point before bridges were built at Foster's and Bullard's bars. Above Foster's Bar was Stoney Bar, where 500 men were working in 1850 and where the principal hotel housed 250 men. Opposite Stoney was Atchison's Bar. The following bars were located up the river on the right bank: Long Bar No. 2, two miles above Foster's; Oregon Bar, two miles farther on; French Bar; Pittsburg Bar; Scott's Bar, at the mouth of Scott's Bar Creek; Rock Island Bar; Missouri Bar No. 2, first mined by men from Pike County, Missouri; Willow Bar; New York Bar; Mississippi Bar; Alabama Bar; Slate Range Bar; Cut Eye Foster's Bar near the Yuba-Sierra county line; and Cherokee Bar. A road crossed the river at Cherokee Bar over Wood's Bridge, later known as the Cherokee Bridge. Today the state highway from Nevada City to Downieville crosses the North Yuba near this spot.

On the left bank of the Yuba above Atchison's and Stoney bars were Texas Bar, opposite Long Bar No. 2; Elbow Bar, south of Missouri Bar No. 2; Sucker Bar, opposite Willow Bar; Fraser's and Wambo (Wambaugh's) bars, east of the mouth of Deadwood Creek; and Finley's Bar, south of Slate Range Bar.

"Today there remains no vestige of human habitation on most of these bars, and the lower portions of them are covered many feet deep with the detritus of later hydraulic washing."

Camptonville

Camptonville's present buildings date from after the gold rush, the town having been completely destroyed by fire several times, but its citizens have wisely retained the simple New England type of architecture which influenced the earlier builders. The schoolhouse on the hill and the dozen or more white cottages surrounded by trees and old-fashioned flowers lend a delightful early American atmosphere to this mountain hamlet, unspoiled by the modern highway, which fortunately has passed it a little to the west.

As one enters the present settlement from the highway, attention is arrested by a stone monument surmounted by the model of a waterwheel and bearing an inscription that reads:

"On this spot in 1878, Lester Allen Pelton invented the Pelton water wheel. Erected in 1929 by Gravel Range Lodge, Free & Accepted Masons."

A hotel was built on the site of Camptonville as early as 1850, when it was on the main road from Marysville and Nevada City to Downieville, and pack-mule trains stopped there daily on their way to the higher mountains. The toll road via Foster's Bar was completed to Camptonville in

1854, and the California Stage Company began running stages that far the following year. The first great boom, however, came to the town in 1852, when gold was discovered on Gold Ridge to the east. Among the new arrivals at that time was Robert Campton, a blacksmith, for whom the town was named. By 1866 Camptonville numbered 1,500 residents and was the center for hydraulic operations which produced $500,000 annually. A plank road a mile long formed the main street of the town. This was lined by more than 30 stores, numerous hotels and boarding-houses, as well as the ubiquitous saloons. Most of this ground was soon washed out by the activities of giant hydraulic monitors.

Rich strikes other than that of Gold Ridge soon caused a number of settlements to spring up throughout the region. Two miles north of Camptonville a group of men from Galena, Illinois, found gold in 1852, and the camp that grew up there was known as Galena Hill. The place boasted a large hotel, two stores, and two saloons in 1856, with more than 100 miners working the placers in the neighborhood. The site is on Weeds Point Road west of Highway 49.

Young's Hill, three miles northwest, also had its beginnings in 1852, when William Young and his brother settled there. By 1856 it was a thriving center of trade, with hotels, stores, saloons, blacksmith shops, and even a theater flanking its main street. This camp is mentioned frequently in the De Long diary, Charles E. De Long, the writer, having made it his home for some time.

Ramm's Ranch to the southwest was located early by John Ramm, who saw the value of the perpetual spring which existed on the spot and which he used to advantage later in his grape culture. Early settlers in the region had found there an important ranchería of the Yuba Indians.

The first iron rails used in the Yuba mines, to convey dirt to sluice boxes, furnished the name of Railroad Hill, settled in 1852 some four miles north of Camptonville. Its neighbor, Depot Hill, was a center of hydraulic mining during the 1860's and 1870's.

Oak Valley, a small camp located on the headwaters of Oak Valley Creek six miles northeast of Camptonville, had 100 miners in 1855. Three miles west of Oak Valley was Dadd's Gulch, where gold was discovered in 1851 by a man named Parsons. Weed's Point, between Oak Valley and Galena Hill on Horse Valley Creek, was first mined in 1853. Some three miles northwest of Oak Valley was Slate Range, a small but active mining community situated 1,500 feet above Slate Range Bar on the North Yuba River. The trail up from Slate Range Bar to Deadwood and La Porte was a back-breaking climb, and for this reason the wild declivity was called Hell's Hill.

On Oregon Creek, 1,000 feet below Camptonville and accessible only by trail, was Celestial Valley, where numerous Chinese mined in very early days. On a high ridge east of the Oregon Creek canyon, visible for miles in all directions, was Indian Springs, a station on the road from Camptonville to Pike City. There is one old covered bridge in Yuba County, at the mouth of Oregon Creek, five miles southwest of Camptonville and just off Highway 49. It is a stone's throw from the Nevada County line, and its story is told in that chapter.

Camptonville Road

Camptonville, on the main road to Downieville and the center of trade for northeastern Yuba County, was located at the junction of a number of roads. The earliest trail from Marysville crossed the North Fork of the Yuba River at Foster's Bar, continuing eastward from there by way of Willow Creek and Garden Valley, where the Atchison brothers had a ranch and kept a hotel. In 1854 they built a wagon road over this route as far as Camptonville. Another trail from Marysville crossed the North Yuba at Bullard's Bar, where George Mix kept the toll bridge. Mix also built the approach roads from the ridges to Bullard's Bar. By 1860 the Bullard's Bar route had superseded the one by way of Foster's Bar.

Two important hotels were located on this road —the Junction House, two miles southwest of Camptonville, and the Wisconsin House, two miles farther south. The Junction House, also known as Bogardus' Ranch, later became the James Ranch. At this point a branch of the Grass Valley–Forest City road via Emory's Crossing joined the Bullard's Bar road. At the Wisconsin House the road from Nevada City by way of North San Juan, Freeman's Crossing, and Oregon Creek likewise joined the Bullard's Bar road. The present state highway to Downieville follows the old route up the slopes above Oregon Creek to Camptonville. Beyond Camptonville it continues to the North Yuba River and Downieville by a new route, whereas the old road turned eastward at Camptonville and followed up Gold Ridge.

The Wheatland Riot

East of Wheatland was the Durst Ranch, scene of one of California's most famous riots. A Dr. Durst had planted the first hops in the Wheatland area as early as 1874, but at first demand for them was limited. In 1913, however, there was need for a large number of pickers. The ranch advertised, and on August 1, as many as 2,800 men, women, and children showed up. Pay was very low, the company store gouged the workers for food and supplies, and, as was not unusual in California's labor camps at that time, sanitary and housing conditions were woefully insufficient. There were, for example, only eight or nine crude toilets for these thousands of people.

On August 2, a protest meeting was called by the Industrial Workers of the World, called "Wobblies" by their enemies, and a strike was organized. The local I.W.W. leaders were Blackie Ford and Herman Suhr. On Sunday, August 3, at the close of another meeting, a sheriff's posse attempted to stop the unrest and a deputy fired a warning shot. The result was a full-scale riot by the hop pickers, ending with four dead and from four to 12 wounded. District Attorney E. T. Manwell and a deputy sheriff, as well as two workers, lost their lives. Ford and Suhr were convicted of murder and sentenced to life imprisonment.

SOURCES

Amy's Marysville Directory for the Year 1858. Daily News Print, Marysville, 1858.

Borthwick, J. D. *Three Years in California*. William Blackwood & Sons, Edinburgh, 1857.

Buffum, E. Gould. *Six Months in the Gold Mines*. Lea & Blanchard, Philadelphia, 1850.

Burnett, Peter H. *Recollections and Opinions of an Old Pioneer*. D. Appleton & Co., New York, 1880.

Colville's Marysville Directory for the Year 1855, Together with a Historical Sketch of Marysville. Monson & Valentine, San Francisco, 1855.

Coy, Owen Cochran. *Gold Days*, of the series *California*, ed. John Russell McCarthy. Powell Publishing Co., Los Angeles, 1929.

Delano, A. *Life on the Plains and among the Diggings*. Miller, Orton & Mulligan, Buffalo, 1854.

Delay, Peter J. *History of Yuba and Sutter Counties*. Historic Record Co., Los Angeles, 1924.

Field, Stephen J. *Personal Reminiscences of Early Days in California, with Other Sketches*. Privately printed, 1893.

Frémont, John C. *Memoirs of My Life, Including in the Narrative Five Journeys of Western Exploration*. Belford, Clarke & Co., Chicago, 1887.

Gold Rush Country. Lane Publishing Co., Menlo Park, 1957.

Hanson, George E. "The Early History of Yuba River Valley." Master's thesis in history, University of California, Berkeley, 1924.

Hittell, John S. *The Resources of California*. San Francisco, 1863.

McGowan, Joseph A. *History of the Sacramento Valley*. 3 vols. Lewis Historical Publishing Co., New York, 1961.

Sanchez, Nellie Van de Grift. *Spanish and Indian Place Names of California*. A. M. Robertson, San Francisco, 1922.

Walsh, Henry L., S.J. *Hallowed Were the Gold Dust Trails*. University of Santa Clara Press, Santa Clara, 1946.

Wells, Harry L., and William H. Chamberlain. *History of Yuba County, California*. Thompson & West, Oakland, 1879.

Weston, Otheto. *Mother Lode Album*. Stanford University Press, Stanford, 1948.

Wheat, Carl I. " 'California's Bantam Cock'—The Journals of Charles E. De Long, 1854–1863," edited with an introduction by Carl I. Wheat, in *California Historical Society Quarterly*, VIII, IX, X (September 1929–December 1931).

Index